AF771416

St. Anthony's™

PPS 2000 Alert

for St. Anthony's hospital subscribers

Inside this issue...

Additional copies: $50

IAD, IAS, ICD, OUT, CFR

Despite the Y2K Focus HCFA Has Released the Proposed Rules

The Health Care Financing Administration (HCFA) issued its proposed rules on changes to the hospital inpatient prospective payment system (PPS) and the fiscal year (FY) 2000 rates (*Federal Register*, May 7, 1999). The changes that will be published in the final rule—expected by August 1, 1999—become effective on October 1, 1999.

Highlights of both the diagnosis-related group (DRG) and payment issues are summarized in this special report in two sections: DRG and Code Changes, and Payment Issues.

As usual, the proposed rule establishes amounts and factors for determining the fiscal 2000 prospective payment rates for operating and capital-related costs. This year's proposed update to the standardized amount is 0.9 percent for inpatient operating costs. This is based on the currently forecasted market basket increase of 2.7 percent for hospitals included in and excluded from the PPS minus 1.8 percentage points. The proposed federal rate for capital PPS is $374.31, a decrease of 1 percent over the fiscal 1999 rate.

DRG and Coding Proposals

No Revisions to the ICD-9-CM Codes FY 2000

HCFA is not implementing any revisions to the ICD-9-CM codes for FY 2000 in order to ensure that all of the Medicare computer systems are ready to function on January 1, 2000. Changes to the ICD-9-CM codes on October 1, 1999, would endanger the functioning of the Medicare computer systems and, specifically, might compromise the ability to process hospital bills. Please see page 4 for details concerning your St. Anthony subscription (ICD-9-CM code book).

HCFA Proposes Reclassification and Recalibration for the DRG System

Despite the fact that there will be no revisions to the ICD-9-CM codes, HCFA is proposing reclassification of existing codes into different DRGs and recalibration of the DRG weights for discharges occurring on or after October 1, 1999.

HCFA is proposing to make the following changes in the DRG categories:

- Include diagnosis codes V29.2 and V29.3 in the list of allowable secondary diagnosis under DRG 391.
- Revise the title for DRG 425 to "Acute Adjustment Reaction and Psychosocial Dysfunction."

- Reclassify codes in category 948 with a fifth digit of zero from DRGs 506-509 to DRGs 510-511.
- Revise the surgical hierarchy for the Pre-Major Diagnostic Category (Pre-MDC) DRGs and MDC 3 (Diseases and Disorders of the Ear, Nose, Mouth, and Throat).
- Make no changes to the Complications and Comorbidities (CC) List.
- Reclassify a few procedure codes currently assigned to DRGs 468, 476, and 477.
- Recalibrate the DRG relative weights as required by the Social Security Act.

HCFA is seeking comments and suggestions for many of the issues proposed for the inpatient PPS for FY 2000. Written comments will be considered if received no later than 5 p.m. on July 6, 1999. An original and three copies should be mailed to:

Health Care Financing Administration
Department of Health and Human Services
Attention: HCFA-1053-P
P.O. Box 7517
Baltimore, MD 21207

HCFA does not accept facsimile transmission. ▲

DRG Changes

Additional Secondary Diagnosis Codes Assigned to DRG 391

Currently, when diagnosis codes for newborn observation for a suspected respiratory condition, V29.2, and newborn observation for other genetic problem, V29.3, are assigned as the only secondary diagnosis, the cases group to DRG 390 (Neonate with Other Significant Problems).

Category V29 is assigned when the condition is suspected but not found. The presence of diagnosis code from category V29 should not preclude a newborn from being classified as normal. Therefore, HCFA is proposing to include V29.2 and V29.3 in the list of secondary diagnosis codes for DRG 391 (Normal Newborn).

Title Revision Proposed for DRG 391

The title of DRG 425, "Acute Adjustment Reaction and Disturbances of Psychosocial Dysfunction" reflects a redundancy with the terms "disturbances" and "dysfunction." HCFA is proposing that the title of DRG 425 be revised to read "Acute Adjustment Reaction and Psychosocial Dysfunction."

Further Adjustments to MDC 22

In the FY 1999 final PPS rule that was effective October 1, 1998 (63 FR 40957), HCFA implemented an extensive redesign of the DRGs for burn cases. The redesigned DRGs more appropriately capture the variation in resource use associated with different classes of burn patients. Factors such as whether there is an extensive burn, a full-thickness burn, or an inhalation injury, as well as other factors such as skin graft, trauma, or presence of a CC now define the DRGs within MDC 22. DRGs 504 and 505 are assigned to cases with extensive third-degree burns in which the burns cover at least 20 percent of body surface area combined with a third-degree burn covering at least 10 percent of body surface area. DRGs 506-509 are assigned to all other cases with third-degree burns. Finally, DRGs 510 and 511 are assigned to cases with nonextensive burns.

Category 948 with a fifth digit of "0" is currently included in the list of principal or secondary diagnosis for DRGs 506-509. Since category 948 with a fifth digit of zero may be assigned to cases in which there is no third-degree burn, HCFA proposes to reassign 948.x0 to DRGs 510-511. According to coding guidelines, coders should code the site of the burn first using codes from categories 940-947 when the site is known. Codes from categories 940-947 will also capture the degree of the burn. Codes from category 948 may be used as a principal diagnosis only when the site of the burn is unspecified. Further, category 948 is used as an additional code to provide information on the percentage of total body that is burned and to show the percentage of burn with third-degree burn. (*AHA Coding Clinic for ICD-9-CM*, 4Q, '94, 22-28.) For those rare cases where the site is not provided, but it is known that 10 percent or more of the body has a third-degree burn, hospitals may report this information through the use of category 948 with a fifth digit of "1"through "9." All of these cases will be classified as full-thickness burns in DRGs 506-509.

DRG Changes

Surgical Hierarchy for the Pre-MDC and MDC 3 Revised

On occasion there are some inpatient stays that involve multiple surgical procedures, each of which, occurring by itself, could result in assignment of the case to a different DRG with in the MDC to which the principal diagnosis is assigned. It is necessary to have a decision rule by which these cases are assigned to the highest DRG, since patients can be assigned to only one DRG for each inpatient stay. The surgical hierarchy performs this function by arranging the surgical DRGs in a manner that allows for the assignment of a patient with multiple procedures related to the principal diagnosis to a surgical DRG that best reflects the resources used in the care of that patient.

HCFA is proposing the following revisions to the surgical hierarchy of the Pre-MDC and MDC 3.

- Pre-MDC: DRG 495 (Lung Transplant) will be reordered above DRG 481 (Bone Marrow Transplant)
- MDC 3: DRGs 57 and 58 (Tonsil and Adenoid Procedure Except Tonsillectomy and/or Adenoidectomy Only) will be reordered above DRG 52 (Cleft Lip and Palate Repair).

Refinements to the CC List

There are no proposed changes to the standard list of diagnoses that when present as a secondary condition would be considered substantial complications and comorbidities (CC) that would affect DRG assignment. This list of CC is then used to develop the CC Exclusion List, a list of invalid combinations of principal diagnoses and CC conditions.

Review Results of the Procedure Codes in DRGs 468, 476, and 477

Each year cases assigned to the DRGs intended to capture atypical cases (DRGs 468, 476, and 477) are reviewed in order to determine whether it would be appropriate to reclassify procedures to other DRGs. Several procedures were identified in DRG 468 that HCFA proposes to move to surgical DRGs. No changes are proposed for DRG 477.

DRG 468 is intended to capture cases where an extensive operating room (OR) procedure is unrelated to the principal diagnosis.

As a result of the review, three codes are to be moved from DRG 468 and assigned to DRGs 7 and 8 (Peripheral and Cranial Nerve and Other Nervous System Procedures) in MDC 1. Those procedures are as follows:

- 38.7, interruption of the vena cava, which is appropriately performed for neurological conditions, such as
  cerebral embolism with infarction
- 83.92, insertion or replacement of skeletal muscle stimulator, which is appropriately performed for neurological conditions, such as quadriplegia or monoplegia. Both implantation of a muscle stimulator (83.92) and the associated tendon transfer (82.56) may be performed on quadriplegic patients to achieve hand-grasping ability. When the two procedures are performed during the same admission the case groups to DRGs 7 and 8. If the muscle stimulator implantation is performed subsequent to the tendon transfer, the second admission would group to DRG 486 under current code assignment. It is more appropriate to include both 82.56 and 83.92 under DRGs 7 and 8 to capture these cases.

Also HCFA proposes to move code 39.50, angioplasty or artherectomy of noncoronary vessel, from DRG 468 to DRGs 76 and 77 (MDC 1) (Other Respiratory System OR Procedures). Procedure 39.50 is appropriately performed for patients who develop pulmonary embolism. Therefore, adding procedure 39.50 to DRGs 76-77 increases clinical coherence.

Finally, procedure 86.06, insertion of totally implantable infusion pump, would be moved from DRG 468 to DRG 120 (MDC 5) (Other Circulatory System OR Procedures). Procedure 86.06 may be performed on patients with circulatory condition such as phlebitis and thrombophlebitis of the deep veins of the extremities.

HCFA did not identify any necessary changes to procedures listed under DRG 477.

Based on the review there will be no reassignment of procedure codes from DRG 468 to DRG 476 or 477; from DRG 476 to DRG 468 or 477; or from DRG 477 to DRG 468 or 476.

Recalibration of DRG Weights

The weights were recalibrated based upon current charge information available from FY 1998 MedPAR file using the same methodology as in the past years. The DRG weights published in the *Federal Register*, July 31,1998, as part of the final rule were compared with those listed in the May 7, 1999, proposed rules for fiscal 2000.

25 Most Common DRGs

The following DRGs were determined to represent those most frequently assigned according to the fiscal year 1997 MedPAR file. Those in bold indicate increased relative weights for FY 2000. Fourteen of the top 25 DRGs will have an increase in relative weights in FY 2000. Two new additions to the top 25 DRGs are 462 (Rehabilitation) and 475 (Respiratory System Diagnosis with Ventilator Support).

DRG	Description
014	**Specific cerebrovascular disorders except TIA**
015	**Transient ischemic attack and precerebral occlusions**
079	**Respiratory infections and inflammations, age >17 with CC**
088	Chronic obstructive pulmonary disease
089	**Simple pneumonia and pleurisy, age >17 with CC**
106	Coronary bypass with cardiac catheterization
112	Percutaneous cardiovascular procedures
121	Circulatory disorders with AMI and CV complications discharged alive
124	**Circulatory disorders except AMI, with cardiac catheterization and complex diagnosis**
127	**Heart failure and shock**
132	**Atherosclerosis with CC**
138	Cardiac arrhythmia and conduction disorders with CC
143	**Chest pain**
148	**Major small and large bowel procedures with CC**
174	**Gastrointestinal hemorrhage with CC**
182	**Esophagitis, gastroenteritis and miscellaneous digestive disorders, age >17 with CC**
209	Major joint and limb reattachment procedures of lower extremity
210	Hip and femur procedures except major joint, age >17 with CC
296	**Nutritional and miscellaneous metabolic disorders, age >17 with CC**
320	Kidney and urinary tract infections age >17 with CC
416	**Septicemia, age >17**
430	Psychoses
462	Rehabilitation
475	Respiratory system diagnosis with ventilator support
478	**Other vascular procedures with CC**

Free One-Year Extension to Your Subscription

HCFA has announced that there will be no ICD-9-CM coding changes for FY 2000. We know that you have come to depend on St. Anthony's valuable update service, which provides you with all the latest coding changes, AHA *Coding Clinic* references, Medicare Code Edits, and DRG alerts. These important features ensure accurate coding and appropriate reimbursement. **As you are a valued customer, we are extending your subscription to the updatable ICD-9-CM code books for 12 months at no cost.**

FREE UPDATES

We are providing a listing of the AHA *Coding Clinic* references for the second, third, and fourth quarters of 1998, as well as the first and second quarter of 1999 in this issue of the *PPS Alert*. During your 12-month extension period, we have scheduled the following two FREE newsletters:

- January 2000 Newsletter. A newsletter listing the second and third quarter 1999 AHA *Coding Clinic* references, DRG alerts, and any Medicare Code Edit (MCE) changes.

- July 2000 *PPS Alert*. The *PPS Alert* newsletter will contain advanced notice of FY 2001 ICD-9-CM coding changes and proposed reclassification and recalibration to the DRG payment system.

SPECIAL OFFER

If you would prefer actual pages for your binder that reflect the AHA Coding Clinic references, the DRG alerts, and the Medicare code edits changes, we have a special offer. You may purchase, as a package, both the October 1999 and January 2000 pages reflecting the above mentioned changes. You will still be entitled to the FREE January 2000 newsletter and the July 2000 *PPS Alert*. Please call our Customer Service Department at (800) 632-0123 to place your order.

- *Professional ICD-9-CM Special Edition Update—1999-2000* for the *Updatable ICD-9-CM* Code Book (blue binder) order code #3016 $59.95

- *Premier ICD-9-CM Special Edition Update—1999-2000* for the *Illustrated ICD-9-CM* Code Book (includes NEW definitions and illustrations) (green binder) order code #3015 $69.95

If you have purchased your St. Anthony ICD-9-CM code book through a distributor, please contact your distributor directly for more information concerning your subscription.

AHA Coding Clinic References

The following *AHA Coding Clinic* references are provided in order to keep you informed of the latest official coding advice. Coding advice referenced is effective as follows: 2Q, '98 with discharges July 1, 1998; 3Q, '98 with discharges September 1, 1998; 4Q,'98 with discharges October 1, 1998; 1Q,'99 with discharges February 15, 1999; and 2Q, '99 with discharges June 1, 1999.

Second, Third, and Fourth Quarter 1998 *AHA Coding Clinic* References

Disease Tabular

Code	Reference
038.11	4Q, '98, 42
041.11	4Q, '98, 42, 54
078.5	3Q, '98, 4
112.4	2Q, '98, 7
250	2Q, '98, 15
251.8	2Q, '98, 15
273.8	2Q, '98, 11
282.62	2Q, '98, 8
337.3	4Q, '98, 37
342.9	4Q, '98, 87
344.00	4Q, '98, 38
344.09	4Q, '98, 39
349.2	2Q, '98, 18
357.0	2Q, '98, 12
357.4	2Q, '98, 15
357.8	2Q, '98, 12
365.23	2Q, '98, 16
365.89	2Q, '98, 16
410	3Q, '98, 15
411.1	4Q, '98, 86
412	3Q, '98, 15
424.0	3Q, '98, 11
428.0	3Q, '98, 5
434.9	4Q, '98, 87
438	4Q, '98, 39, 88
438.53	4Q, '98, 39
438.89	4Q, '98, 39
480.9	3Q, '98, 5
481	2Q, '98, 7
482.83	2Q, '98, 5
482.9	2Q, '98, 6
486	3Q, '98, 7
486	2Q, '98, 4, 5
513.0	2Q, '98, 7
514	2Q, '98, 6
518.81	4Q, '98, 41
519.01	4Q, '98, 41
536.4	4Q, '98, 42
536.41	4Q, '98, 42
536.49	4Q, '98, 42
560.0	4Q, '98, 82
560.39	4Q, '98, 38
564.81	4Q, '98, 45
567.2	2Q, '98, 19
569.62	4Q, '98, 44
569.69	3Q, '98, 16
573.3	3Q, '98, 3, 4
577.0	2Q, '98, 19
585	3Q, '98, 6, 7
585	4Q, '98, 55
585	2Q, '98, 20
586	3Q, '98, 6
591	2Q, '98, 9
592.1	2Q, '98, 9
593.3	2Q, '98, 9
646.8	3Q, '98, 16
648.3	2Q, '98, 13
648.4	2Q, '98, 13
648.6	3Q, '98, 11
658.1	4Q, '98, 77
659.7	4Q, '98, 48
674.8	3Q, '98, 16
682.2	4Q, '98, 42
718.4	4Q, '98, 40
733.00	2Q, '98, 12
733.15	2Q, '98, 12
751.2	2Q, '98, 16
756.0	3Q, '98, 9
759.89	3Q, '98, 8
763.8	4Q, '98, 46
763.82	4Q, '98, 46
770.8	2Q, '98, 10
780.39	4Q, '98, 39
780.71	4Q, '98, 48
784.3	4Q, '98, 87
786.03	4Q, '98, 50
786.04	4Q, '98, 50
786.05	4Q, '98, 50
786.06	4Q, '98, 50
786.07	4Q, '98, 50
786.09	2Q, '98, 10
813.81	2Q, '98, 19
907.2	4Q, '98, 38
965.6	4Q, '98, 50
965.61	4Q, '98, 50
995.86	4Q, '98, 51
996.4	2Q, '98, 19
996.54	2Q, '98, 14
996.55	4Q, '98, 52
996.56	4Q, '98, 54
996.68	4Q, '98, 54
996.69	4Q, '98, 53
996.8	3Q, '98, 3, 4
996.81	3Q, '98, 6, 7
996.82	3Q, '98, 3, 4
996.83	3Q, '98, 5
996.84	3Q, '98, 5
998.59	3Q, '98, 3
998.89	2Q, '98, 16
V02.51	4Q, '98, 56
V06.1	3Q, '98, 13
V10	4Q, '98, 69
V10.3	4Q, '98, 65
V12.49	4Q, '98, 59
V12.59	4Q, '98, 88
V13.6	4Q, '98, 63
V23.8	4Q, '98, 56, 63
V23.81	4Q, '98, 58
V27.0	4Q, '98, 77
V29.3	4Q, '98, 59, 68
V30	4Q, '98, 46, 59
V42	3Q, '98, 3, 4
V42.8	4Q, '98, 64
V43.1	4Q, '98, 65
V45.6	4Q, '98, 65
V45.7	4Q, '98, 65
V49.6	4Q, '98, 42
V49.7	4Q, '98, 42
V53.0	4Q, '98, 66
V56	4Q, '98, 66
V56.0	2Q, '98, 20
V56.0	3Q, '98, 6
V56.1	2Q, '98, 20
V56.2	4Q, '98, 55
V56.8	4Q, '98, 55
V58.62	4Q, '98, 59
V58.89	4Q, '98, 59
V64.4	4Q, '98, 68
V67	4Q, '98, 69
V76.1	4Q, '98, 67

Procedure Tabular

Code	Reference	Code	Reference	Code	Reference
01.18	3Q, '98, 12	38.95	3Q, '98, 13	83.14	3Q, '98, 8
01.59	3Q, '98, 12	39.49	2Q, '98, 17	84.3	2Q, '98, 15
02.06	3Q, '98, 9	39.50	2Q, '98, 17	85.53	2Q, '98, 14
03.6	2Q, '98, 18	39.95	2Q, '98, 20	85.93	2Q, '98, 14
03.91	2Q, '98, 18	42.23	3Q, '98, 11	85.94	2Q, '98, 14
03.92	2Q, '98, 18	44.66	3Q, '98, 10	86.67	4Q, '98, 76, 79
04.01	2Q, '98, 20	46.80	4Q, '98, 82	86.89	2Q, '98, 20
04.03	2Q, '98, 20	48.32	2Q, '98, 18	88.01	2Q, '98, 13
12.79	2Q, '98, 16	49.79	2Q, '98, 16	88.72	3Q, '98, 11
20.92	2Q, '98, 20	51.23	3Q, '98, 10	92.3	4Q, '98, 79
35.52	3Q, '98, 11	54.25	2Q, '98, 19	93.90	3Q, '98, 14
36.01	4Q, '98, 74, 85	54.91	3Q, '98, 12	96.29	4Q, '98, 82
36.04	4Q, '98, 85	63.73	2Q, '98, 13	97.29	3Q, '98, 12
36.3	4Q, '98, 73	73.59	4Q, '98, 76	99.10	4Q, '98, 83
36.32	4Q, '98, 74	75.37	4Q, '98, 76	99.20	4Q, '98, 85
37.23	3Q, '98, 11	77.45	2Q, '98, 12	99.21	4Q, '98, 76
37.67	4Q, '98, 75	78.05	2Q, '98, 12	99.28	2Q, '98, 10
38.02	2Q, '98, 23	79.35	2Q, '98, 12	99.29	4Q, '98, 83; 2Q, '98, 17, 18, 23, 24
38.93	2Q, '98, 24	82.56	4Q, '98, 40		

First and Second Quarter 1999 *AHA Coding Clinic* References

Disease Tabular

Code	Reference	Code	Reference	Code	Reference
042	1Q, '99, 14	441.4	1Q, '99, 15, 16, 17	821.01	1Q, '99, 5
170.4	2Q, '99, 9	442.2	1Q, '99, 16, 17	850.1	1Q, '99, 10
171.0	2Q, '99, 6	442.3	1Q, '99, 16	854	1Q, '99, 10
197.0	2Q, '99, 9	528.0	2Q, '99, 9	959.01	1Q, '99, 10
202.1	2Q, '99, 7	576.1	2Q, '99, 13	996.01	2Q, '99, 11
202.2	2Q, '99, 7	576.2	2Q, '99,13	996.2	2Q, '99, 4
278.00	1Q, '99, 5, 6	576.8	2Q, '99, 14	996.4	2Q, '99, 10
288.0	2Q, '99, 9	595.0	2Q, '99, 15	996.59	2Q, '99, 13
294.1	1Q, '99, 14	599.0	2Q, '99, 15	997.4	2Q, '99, 14
331.4	1Q, '99, 9	668.8	2Q, '99, 9	V08	2Q, '99, 8
344.89	2Q, '99, 4	724.4	2Q, '99, 3	V15.81	2Q, '99, 17
349.0	2Q, '99, 9	742.4	1Q, '99, 9	V16.0	1Q, '99, 4
379.29	1Q, '99, 11	746.89	1Q, '99, 11	V53.09	2Q, '99, 3, 4
414.11	1Q, '99, 17	747.10	1Q, '99, 11	V58.69	2Q, '99, 17
421.0	1Q, '99, 12	748.3	1Q, '99, 14	V67.51	1Q, '99, 5, 6
427.31	2Q, '99, 17	780.39	2Q, '99, 17	V76.49	1Q, '99, 4
428.0	1Q, '99, 11	786.05	1Q, '99, 6		

Procedure Tabular

Code	Reference	Code	Reference	Code	Reference
01.59	1Q, '99, 9	38.29	1Q, '99, 7	86.06	2Q, '99, 4
03.91	1Q, '99, 8	38.4	2Q, '99, 5, 6	86.22	1Q, '99, 8
03.97	2Q, '99, 4	39.52	1Q, '99, 15, 16, 17	88.42	1Q, '99, 17
14.79	1Q, '99, 11	40.29	1Q, '99, 6	88.41	1Q, '99, 7
32.5	1Q, '99, 6	40.41	2Q, '99, 6	88.72	1Q, '99, 6
33.23	1Q, '99, 6	48.49	2Q, '99, 13	88.76	2Q, '99, 14
34.04	1Q, '99, 10	51.10	2Q, '99, 13	88.77	1Q, '99, 12, 13
34.04	2Q, '99, 12	54.91	2Q, '99, 14	93.59	1Q, '99, 12, 13
36.01	1Q, '99, 17	54.99	1Q, '99, 4	97.05	2Q, '99, 13
36.06	1Q, '99, 17	77.6	1Q, '99, 8	97.41	1Q, '99, 10
37.26	1Q, '99, 3	78.5	2Q, '99, 11	99.23	1Q, '99, 7
37.75	2Q, '99, 11	82.56	2Q, '99, 10	99.25	1Q, '99, 4
37.94	1Q, '99, 3	83.45	1Q, '99, 8	99.28	2Q, '99, 8
37.98	1Q, '99, 3	83.5	2Q, '99, 11	99.88	2Q, '99, 7
38.1	2Q, '99, 5	83.92	2Q, '99, 10		

Medicare Code Edits Update

The following Medicare code edits (MCEs) are provided in order to keep you informed of the latest changes concerning the edits Medicare uses to detect and report errors in the coding of claims data. The code edits referenced below represent only the new edits that are effective with discharges on or after October 1, 1998. This listing supplements the edits already indicated by color, symbol, or footnote in your code book.

Medicare Code Edit 1 Invalid Diagnosis or Procedure Code

The following codes have been added for fiscal 1999-2000 to the invalid diagnosis and procedure code lists.

Diagnosis Codes		Procedure Codes
482.4	V02.5	36.3
519.0	V13.6	92.3
564.8	V16.5	
763.8	V18.6	
780.7	V23.8	
965.6	V44.5	

Medicare Code Edit 2 E-Code as Principal Diagnosis

This edit is not addressed in our code book.

Medicare Code Edit 3 Duplicate of Principal Diagnosis

This edit is not addressed in our code book.

Medicare Code Edit 4 Age Conflict

The following diagnosis codes were added for fiscal 1999-2000 list of diagnoses consistent with certain age categories.

Newborn	Pediatric	Maternity	Adult
Patient age of 0	Patient age 0 to 17	Patient ages 12 to 55	Patient age over 14 years
763.81	None	None	659.70
763.82			659.71
763.83			659.73
763.89			

Medicare Code Edit 5 Sex Conflict

Inconsistencies between a patient's sex and any diagnosis or procedure are detected with the sex conflict edit. The following codes were added for fiscal 1999-2000 to the list of diagnoses allowed only for males or only for females.

Male Only		Female Only	
Diagnosis	Procedure	Diagnosis	Procedure
V10.48	None	659.70	None
V13.61		659.71	
V26.52		659.73	
V76.44		V23.81	
V76.45		V23.82	
		V23.83	
		V23.84	
		V23.89	
		V26.51	

Medicare Code Edit 6 Manifestation Not Allowed As Principal Diagnosis

For fiscal 1999-2000 no changes were made to the list of codes that describe the manifestation of an underlying disease and should not be used as a principal diagnosis.

Medicare Code Edit 7 Nonspecific Principal Diagnosis

The following codes were added for fiscal 1999-2000 to the list of codes identified as non-specific. A more specific diagnosis code should be used for an inpatient principal diagnosis designation.

Diagnosis Codes			
519.00	536.40	763.83	780.79

Medicare Code Edit 8 Questionable Admission–Principal Diagnosis Only

For fiscal 1999-2000 no changes were made to the list of codes that describe conditions that are usually not sufficient justification for admission to an acute care hospital.

Medicare Code Edit 9 Unacceptable Principal Diagnosis

The following codes were added for fiscal 1999-2000 to the list of codes identified as unacceptable principal diagnosis for patients admitted to an acute care facility.

Diagnosis Codes				
V02.51	V13.69	V23.82	V29.3	V56.2
V02.52	V16.51	V23.83	V43.83	V58.62
V02.59	V16.59	V23.84	V44.50	V23.83
V10.48	V18.61	V23.89	V44.51	V76.44
V13.61	V18.69	V26.51	V44.52	V76.45
V13.69	V23.81	V26.52	V44.59	

Medicare Code Edit 11 Non-Covered Procedure

No changes were made for fiscal 1999-2000 to the list of codes identified as non-covered procedures for which Medicare will not provide reimbursement.

Medicare Code Edit 12 Open Biopsy and Non-Open biopsy Procedure

No changes were made for fiscal 1999-2000 to the list of codes identified as open and non-open biopsy procedures for which affects DRG assignment.

Medicare Code Edit 13 Medicare as Secondary Payer (MSP) Alert

This Medicare code edit identifies certain trauma codes for claims that may be covered by automobile insurance, no-fault insurance, workmen's compensation or other liability insurance. For these claims Medicare may be considered the secondary payer. No changes were made for fiscal 1999-2000 to this list of codes.

Diagnoses Defined as Complication or Comorbidities (CC)

The following codes were added to the list of Complications and Comorbidities for fiscal 1999-2000.

Diagnosis Codes				
482.40	519.00	536.41	786.04	V23.81
482.41	519.01	536.42	995.86	V23.82
482.49	519.02	536.49	996.55	V23.83
518.83	519.09	569.62	996.56	V23.84
518.84	536.40	786.03	996.68	V23.89

Diagnoses Codes Considered "Major Complication" for DRG 121

The following codes were added to the list of diagnosis codes that are considered "major complications" causing a DRG assignment to change from DRG 122 to DRG 121.

Diagnosis Codes			
482.41	482.49	518.83	518.84

Diagnoses Codes Considered "Complex Diagnosis" for DRG 124

The following codes were added to the list of diagnosis codes that are considered "complex diagnoses" causing a DRG assignment to change from DRG 125 to DRG 124.

Procedure Codes Considered Valid Operating Room Procedures or Non-Operating Room Procedure

The following codes were added to the list of diagnosis codes that were considered operating room and non-operating room procedure codes that affect DRG assignment.

Valid OR Procedures		Non-Operating Room Procedures	
36.31	37.67	92.30	92.33
36.32	86.67	92.31	92.39
36.39		92.32	

Proposed Changes and Updates to the Prospective Payment System for Operating Costs

Standardized Amounts Proposed for Fiscal 2000

The proposed rule establishes amounts and factors for determining the fiscal year (FY) 2000 prospective payment rates for operating costs, and capital-related costs. Except for sole community hospitals, Medicare-dependent, small rural hospitals, and hospitals located in Puerto Rico, each hospital's payment per discharge is based on 100 percent of the federal national rate.

The proposed standardized amounts are based on the per discharge averages of adjusted hospital costs from a base period, or for Puerto Rico, adjusted target amounts from a base period. Factors used to determine the prospective payment rate for inpatient operating costs also include adjustments to the standardized amounts such as

- calculating the large urban and other area average standardized amounts
- updating the average standardized amount
- adjusting the average standardized amount for geographic reclassifications and outlier thresholds.

Two average standardized amounts are calculated: one for hospitals in large urban areas and one for hospitals in other areas. Payment for discharges from hospitals in large urban areas is based on the large urban standardized amount. Payment for discharges from hospitals in other urban and rural areas is based on the other standardized amount. For FY 2000, 61 areas have been defined as large urban areas. (*Federal Register,* May 7, 1999. See table 4A beginning on page 24793.)

Also, the average standardized amount per discharge is determined for hospitals in urban and other areas in Puerto Rico. Hospitals in Puerto Rico are paid a blend of 50 percent of the applicable Puerto Rico standardized amount and 50 percent of the national standardized amount.

Hospital Operating Market Basket and Proposed Update Factor

As defined in the proposed rules, market basket pertains to the hospital input price index and is used to develop the inflation component update factors for operating costs. Percentage changes in the market basket reflect the average change in the price of goods and services hospitals purchase to render inpatient services. It answers the question of "how much it would cost at another time to purchase the same mix of goods and services that were purchased in the base period."

The percentage change in the market basket reflects the average change in the price of goods and services purchased by hospitals to furnish inpatient care. As usual, the standardized amounts are adjusted to remove the affect of geographic reclassification and to ensure budget neutrality. The proposed update factor for the standardized amounts for FY 2000 reflects the market basket percentage increase of 2.7 percent minus 1.8 percentage points. Therefore, the proposed standardized amounts reflect an update factor of 0.9 percent for hospitals located in large urban and other areas.

The proposed 0.9 percent update factor presented in the *Federal Register* is mandated by current law for all prospective payment system (PPS) hospitals. However, HCFA also has recommended to Congress that the update factor for FY 2000 be frozen at current rates. (See *Federal Register,* appendix C.)

Cost Outlier Threshold

For cost outliers, HCFA proposes a fixed loss cost outlier threshold equal to the diagnosis-related group (DRG) payment plus $14,575 and to maintain the marginal cost factor at 80 percent. This threshold will result in outlier payments of 5.1 percent of operating DRG payments and 6.0 percent of capital payments based on the federal rate.

The proposed outlier adjustment factors applied to the operating standardized amounts are 0.948934 for national and 0.969184 for Puerto Rico.

Changes to Fiscal 2000: Payments per Case for Operating PPS

Geographic Location	# of Hospitals	Average FY 1999 Payments per Case	Average FY 2000 Payments per Case	% Change
All hospitals	4,875	$6,770	$6,730	-0.6
Urban	2,712	$7,346	$7,285	-0.8
Large urban areas	1,552	$7,879	$7,787	-1.2
Other urban areas	1,160	$6,623	$6,604	-0.3
Rural areas	2,162	$4,505	$4,546	0.9

(Source: *Federal Register*, May 7, 1999, Table II "Impact Analysis of Changes for FY 2000 Operating Prospective Payment System," page 24837)

$ Payment Issues

Hospital Wage Index

In determining prospective payments to hospitals, the secretary of the Department of Health and Human Services directed HCFA to adjust the standardized amounts for differences in the hospital wage levels for an individual area as compared to the national wage level. This is done annually by defining hospital labor market areas using the metropolitan statistical areas (MSAs), primary MSAs (PMSAs), and New England County metropolitan statistical areas (NECMAs) issued by the Office of Management and Budget; updating the wage index; and adjusting the wage index to take into account changes caused by hospital reclassifications.

The wage data used to calculate the wage index are updated annually. The FY 2000 proposed wage index update, effective for hospital discharges on or after October 1, 1999, is based on Medicare cost reports filed beginning with FY 1996 using the following cost data categories:

- salaries and hours from short-term, acute care hospitals
- home office costs and hours
- certain contract labor costs and hours
- wage-related costs.

The proposed wage index for FY 2000 continues to exclude the direct and overhead salaries and hours for services not paid through the inpatient PPS such as skilled nursing facility, home health, and other subprovider services that are not paid on a prospective payment basis. A separate specific wage index has been calculated for Puerto Rico based solely on its own data to be applied to the Puerto Rico standardized amounts in FY 2000.

Hospital Reclassification Changes

The Medicare Geographic Classification Review Board (MGCRB) considers applications for geographic reclassification for purposes of PPS payment. Hospitals in certain rural counties, adjacent to one or more MSAs, may be reclassified to one of the adjacent MSAs if certain standards are met.

At the time the proposed wage index values were determined, the MGCRB had completed its review of applications for reclassification. The proposed FY 2000 wage index values include 441 hospitals that were redesignated for purposes of the wage index. This number may change for the final rule. Some applications are still under review by the MGCRB. Also, hospitals that determine that the redesignations will affect them adversely may withdraw their applications for reclassification by June 21, 1999. HCFA will incorporate any additions or withdrawals into the wage index values published in the final rule.

Modification to the Hospital Wage Index Calculation

The hospital wage index should reflect the wage costs associated with the areas of the hospital included under the inpatient PPS. Since the costs of teaching physicians, residents and certified registered nurse anesthetists (CRNAs) are reimbursed separately from the PPS, HCFA is proposing to phase out these costs from the wage index calculation over a five-year period. Therefore, the proposed fiscal 2000 wage index is based on a blend of 80 percent of an average hourly wage including the physician Part A wage costs that are teaching-related, residents costs and Part A CRNA costs, and 20 percent of an average hourly wage excluding these costs. The percentages would be adjusted by 20 percent each year until FY 2004 when all of these costs would be eliminated from the wage index calculation.

Source of Wage Index Data

To develop the wage index for FY 2000, HCFA included FY 1996 data filed electronically by 5,035 hospitals to the Hospital Cost Report Information System (HCRIS) by February 1999. The HCRIS is used to process and compile cost report data. In carrying out this function, fiscal intermediaries (FIs) work with hospitals to identify and resolve data elements that do not pass the requirements of this system.

FIs were expected to complete their review and verify any questionable items by April 5, 1999, and transmit the revised data to the HCRIS at that time. The data will be included in the wage index calculation for the final rules.

The proposed wage index values for discharges after October 1, 1999, can be found in tables 4A-4C and 4F in the *Federal Register* addendum to the proposed rule. Hospitals that are redesignated should use the wage index values listed in table 4C.

Table 3C in the addendum contains each hospital's adjusted average hourly wage used to construct the proposed wage index value. In addition, final wage data public use files were to be released on May 7, 1999. Hospitals should review both values to verify their correctness. If a data entry or tabulation error is identified, hospitals must initiate a correction request to the FI by June 7, 1999. The final wage index with corrections will be published by July 30, 1999, and will go into effect on October 1, 1999.

$ Payment Issues

Other Proposed Changes Affecting the PPS for Inpatient Operating Costs and Graduate Medical Education Costs

Rural Referral Centers

Rural referral centers (RRCs) receive special treatment under the Medicare PPS. Specifically they receive special treatment under the disproportionate share hospital payment adjustment and the criteria for geographic reclassification. Therefore, to be classified as an RRC, a rural hospital must meet specific criteria.

One criterion requires that the rural hospital have 275 or more beds available for use. If the rural hospital does not meet the bed size requirement, then it may qualify as an RRC if it meets two other mandatory criteria (case-mix index [CMI] and the number of discharges), and at least one of three optional criteria (medical staff, source of inpatients, or volume of referrals). Also, a hospital retains its status as an RRC by undergoing a review every three years or by meeting the criteria in effect for the current year.

CMI criterion: A hospital's CMI must be equal to the lower of the median CMI for urban hospitals in its census region, excluding hospitals with approved teaching programs or the median CMI for all urban hospitals nationally.

For FY 2000, to qualify for initial rural referral status or to meet the triennial review standards, a hospital's case-mix value for FY 1998 must have been at least 1.3438 or the median CMI value for urban hospitals (excluding teaching). The median CMI regional values are indicated in the following table that will be updated when the final rule comes out. (See box 1.) See also table 3C in section IV of the addendum to the proposed rule for each hospital's FY 1998 CMI value.

Box 1

Region	CMI Value
New England (CT, ME, MA, NH, RI, VT)	1.2480
Middle Atlantic (PA, NJ, NY)	1.2504
South Atlantic (DE, DC, FL, GA, MD, NC, SC, VA, WV)	1.3269
East North Central (IL, IN, MI, OH, WI)	1.2593
East South Central (AL, KY, MS, TN)	1.2772
West North Central (IA, KS, MN, MO, NE, ND, SD)	1.1871
West South Central (AR, LA, OK, TX)	1.3003
Mountain (AZ, CO, ID, MT, NV, NM, UT, WY)	1.3280
Pacific (AK, CA, HI, OR, WA)	1.3277

Discharge Criterion: The standard for the number of discharges for cost reporting periods beginning in FY 1998 must be at least 5,000 per year or the median number of discharges for urban hospitals in the census region. For osteopathic hospitals the number of discharges is 3,000.

The following table reflects the median number of discharges by census region (see box 2).

Box 2

Region	Number of Discharges
New England (CT, ME, MA, NH, RI, VT)	6,672
Middle Atlantic (PA, NJ, NY)	8,635
South Atlantic (DE, DC, FL, GA, MD, NC, SC, VA, WV)	7,753
East North Central (IL, IN, MI, OH, WI)	7,390
East South Central (AL, KY,MS, TN)	6,741
West North Central (IA, KS, MN, MO, NE, ND, SD)	5,662
West South Central (AR, LA, OK, TX)	5,344
Mountain (AZ, CO, ID, MT, NV, NM, UT, WY)	7,993
Pacific (AK, CA, HI, OR, WA)	5,993

Graduate Medical Education to Hospitals and Nonhospital Providers

Currently Medicare pays hospitals for the direct costs of graduate medical education (GME) based on the number of residents trained by the hospital. In these proposed rules, HCFA clarifies and proposes to change certain GME policies related to the accrediting of geriatric programs, the definition of "all or substantially all" of the education costs, adjustments to the caps using the actual number of residents participating in the new program, and other issues. See pages 24733 through 24736 for details concerning the proposals related to payment for direct costs of GME.

Prospective Payment System for Capital-Related Costs

Hospital inpatient capital-related costs are paid based on a blend of the capital PPS federal rate and the hospital-specific historical costs throughout the 10-year transition period that ends in FY 2001. Beginning in FY 2001 at the conclusion of the transition period for capital PPS, capital payments will be based solely on the federal rate for most hospitals.

With the changes being proposed for FY 2000, the federal rate is $374.31, a decrease of 1.00 percent from the FY 1999 federal rate.

HCFA uses a number of factors to establish the federal rate each year. For FY 2000 the following factors are proposed:

- update factor of 0.9940 that incorporates changes in CMI, intensity, errors in the previous capital input price index amounts
- outlier adjustment factor of 0.9397
- an exceptions payment adjustment factor of 0.9752
- a budget neutrality factor for geographic adjustments and DRG weights of 0.9986.

The combined effect of these adjustments is to decrease the federal rate by 1.0 percent from the previous year.

The proposed special rate for Puerto Rico in fiscal 2000 is $174.15.

Published by **St. Anthony Publishing, Inc.**
Mail: St. Anthony Publishing, 11410 Isaac Newton Sq., Reston, VA 21090
Telephone: (800) 632-0123 **Fax:** (703) 904-3900
Publisher: David Schultz
Technical Editors: Carol Endahl, Anita C. Hart, ART, CCS, CCS-P
Editorial Director: Elizabeth Boudrie

Changes to Fiscal 2000: Total Capital Payments per Case

Geographic Location	# of Hospitals	Average FY 1999 Payments per Case	Average FY 2000 Payments per Case	% Change
All hospitals	4,834	$632	$645	1.9
Large urban areas	1,531	$731	$742	1.5
Other urban areas	1,146	$622	$636	2.3
Rural areas	2,157	$426	$438	2.8

(Source: *Federal Register*, May 7, 1999, Table V "Comparison of Total Payments per Case," page 24843)

Capital Input Price Index

The Capital Input Price Index (CIPI) is used to calculate the price increase for prospective payment hospital capital-related expenses including depreciation, capital-related interest expenses, insurance, and taxes. The forecast for the CIPI for fiscal 2000 is a 0.5 percent increase.

Proposed Changes to Payment Rates for Blood Clotting Factors

The add-on payment for the costs of administering blood clotting factor to Medicare beneficiaries with hemophilia and who are hospital inpatients was reinstated effective October 1, 1997. For fiscal 2000, HCFA proposes to establish a price per unit of clotting factor based on the average wholesale price (AWP) of several products that are available on the market, discounted by 15 percent. In addition, HCFA proposes to add HCPCS codes J7191 (clotting factor, porcine) to the list of clotting factors that are paid under this benefit.

Based on the above information, the following blood clotting factors and per unit prices go into effect for Medicare discharges beginning on or after October 1, 1999, through September 30, 2000:

HCPCS Code	Description	Per Unit Price
J7190	Factor VIII (antihemophilic factor, human)	0.79
J7191	Factor VIII (antihemophilic factor, porcine)	1.87
J7192	Factor VIII (antihemophilic factor, recombinant)	1.03
J7194	Factor IX (complex)	0.45
J7196	Other hemophilia clotting factors (for example, antiinhibitors)	1.43
Q0160	Factor IX (antihemophilic factor, purified, nonrecombinant)	0.97
Q0161	Factor IX (antihemophilic factor, purified, recombinant)	1.00

Payment is made for blood clotting factor only if there is an ICD-9-CM diagnosis code for hemophilia reported on the Medicare claim. ▲

St. Anthony's

ICD•9•CM

Code Book for Hospitals

1999–2000

October 1999 •CCS

St. Anthony's 2000 Publications

The Ultimate ICD-9-CM Code Books

1999-2000 Premier ICD-9-CM Code Book, Volumes 1, 2 & 3

Our *Premier ICD-9-CM Code Book* is the most comprehensive code book on the market. We've taken input from both professional coders and our technical experts to develop the ultimate ICD-9-CM code book.

- **EXCLUSIVE—Color Coding System.** Alerts coders to coding and reimbursement issues.
- **EXCLUSIVE—Compliance Symbol.** Yield sign added to higher-paying DRGs, targeted by the government, that require documentation to support that DRG selection.
- **EXCLUSIVE—Pharmacological Listings.** Allow you to link treatments with disease processes.
- **Illustrations and Definitions.** Over 160 color illustrations and nearly 2,000 definitions give you an in-depth understanding of anatomy and disease processes.
- **AHA *Coding Clinic* References.** Listed next to codes to quickly find official guidelines.
- **Fourth and Fifth Digit Symbols.** Alerts you if additional digits are necessary for coding to the highest level of specificity.
- **Age and Sex Edits.** Verify code selection.
- **CC Exclusions.** Listed right with the code. Know at a glance whether the diagnosis is considered as a complication and comorbidity in DRG assignment.

$89.95 Item No. 2999

ALSO AVAILABLE:

Premier ICD-9-CM Code Book, Updatable, Volumes 1, 2 & 3

In addition to the features listed to the left, the updatable binder includes:

- **Updates.** With the update service, you'll receive a full-text update with FY 2001 code changes as well as the latest AHA *Coding Clinic* References, errata changes, new illustrations and definitions, and our exclusive *PPS Alert,* which includes advance notice of any code changes and proposed DRG changes.
- **FREE—*Clinical Coder.*** Helps you interpret information contained in medical records. A $75.95 value.

$179.95
Item No. 2581

Up to 5 CEUs from AAPC

ORDER TOLL FREE 1-800-632-0123

The Industry Standard in Code Books

1999-2000 PROFESSIONAL ICD-9-CM CODE BOOK, VOLUMES 1, 2 & 3

This code book provides official ICD-9-CM codes for hospital health information management and utilization review staff along with others who perform inpatient coding. With St. Anthony's technical expertise and exclusive color coding system, you will code confidently every time.

- **EXCLUSIVE—Color Coding System.** Alerts coders to coding and reimbursement issues.
- **EXCLUSIVE—Compliance Symbol.** Yield sign added to higher-paying DRGs, targeted by the government, require documentation to support that DRG selection.
- **AHA *Coding Clinic* References.** Listed next to codes to quickly find official guidelines.
- **Fourth and Fifth Digit Symbols.** Alerts you if additional digits are necessary for coding to the highest level of specificity.
- **Age and Sex Edits.** Verify code selection.
- **CC Exclusions.** Listed right with the code. Know at a glance whether the diagnosis is considered as a complication and comorbidity in DRG assignment.

$69.95

Item No. 3009

ALSO AVAILABLE:

PROFESSIONAL ICD-9-CM CODE BOOK, UPDATABLE, VOLUMES 1, 2 & 3

In addition to the features listed to the left, the updatable binder includes:

- **Updates.** With the update service, you'll receive a full-text update with FY 2001 code changes as well as the latest AHA *Coding Clinic* References, errata changes, and our exclusive *PPS Alert,* which includes advance notice of any code changes and proposed DRG changes.
- **FREE—*Clinical Coder.*** Helps you interpret information contained in medical records. A $75.95 value.

$139.95

Item No. 3007

Up to 5 CEUs from AAPC

ORDER TOLL FREE 1-800-632-0123

A

B

C

D

Don't Risk Filing With Obsolete CPT Codes

Hundreds of CPT code changes will soon be in effect. Make sure you have a current CPT Code Book in your office—or risk rejected claims, delayed payments, and even charges of fraud and abuse!

Ordering your CPTs from us TODAY will help you avoid the rush. Don't risk being put on waiting lists by other publishers.

We offer you a wide range of CPT formats for your convenience:

(A) CPT PROFESSIONAL BINDER VERSION—with color keys, illustrations, and medical terminology. The ultimate in coding ease and speed!

$74.95 Item No. 2516

(B) CPT PROFESSIONAL SPIRALBOUND VERSION—with color keys, illustrations, and medical terminology.

$66.95 Item No. 2515

(C) CPT STANDARD SPIRALBOUND—with tabs.

$51.95 Item No. 2518

(D) CPT STANDARD SOFTBOUND—with tabs.

$47.95 Item No. 2517

2000 CPT MINIBOOKS

You can now order AMA Minibooks individually for just **$29.95** each. Eight specialties to choose from.

DERMATOLOGY, PLASTIC & RECONSTRUCTIVE SURGERY
Item No. 3267

GENERAL SURGERY
Item No. 3264

GYNECOLOGY, OBSTETRICS & UROLOGY
Item No. 3261

HEAD & NECK SURGERY, ORAL & MAXILLOFACIAL SURGERY, OPHTHALMOLOGY & OTORHINOLARYNGOLOGY
Item No. 3265

MEDICAL SPECIALTIES
Item No. 3266

NEUROLOGICAL & ORTHOPAEDIC SURGERY
Item No. 3262

PATHOLOGY & LABORATORY MEDICINE
Item No. 3260

RADIOLOGY
Item No. 3263

ORDER TOLL FREE 1-800-632-0123

St. Anthony's 2000 Publications

Most Comprehensive HCPCS Book Available

2000 Premier HCPCS Level II Code Book

Our HCPCS book offers an easy-to-use format to guide you confidently through current modifiers, code changes, additions, and deletions. *Premier HCPCS Level II Code Book* provides codes for services, supplies, drugs, and procedures required by Medicare and some private payers.

- **NEW—Payers Appendix.** Lets you know which payers accept HCPCS Level II Codes so you can file claims with confidence.
- **NEW—Expanded Introduction.** Extensive introduction and new clinical scenarios to help train personnel.
- **EXCLUSIVE—ASC Icons.** Identify codes that can be billed separately when provided in an ASC setting.
- **EXCLUSIVE—HCPCS Fees.** Supplies an appendix of Medicare and private payer fee data for HCPCS Level II codes.
- **FREE—2000 J Code Fast Finder.** Lists over 300 commonly used drug codes. A $24.95 value.
- **Deleted Codes History.** Tabular maintains a two-year history on all deleted codes.
- **Medicare Carriers Manual and Coverage Issues Manual.** Know which drugs and DME Medicare does not cover.

$79.95

Item No. 3065

Most Widely Used DRG Guide From the Nation's DRG Expert

2000 DRG Guidebook

With *DRG Guidebook*, you will be able to make sure that every case is accurately assigned the most appropriate DRG. Have the latest DRG information at your fingertips.

- **NEW—Surgical Hierarchy Table.** Quickly shows DRG hierarchy to help assign the DRG that accurately reflects the resource utilization for multiple surgery cases.
- **NEW—Deleted DRG Conversion Table.** Easily track the reclassification of diagnosis and procedure codes to the new DRG.
- **EXCLUSIVE—Main Term Code Search.** Find codes quickly with our customized code descriptions that list main conditions or operative terms first.
- **EXCLUSIVE—Links to *The DRG Companion*.** References *The DRG Companion* to help find additional information when deciding the most appropriate DRG assignment.
- **Indexes ICD-9-CM.** Numerically and alphabetically indexed diagnoses and procedures for fast look up.
- **HCFA Rate Structure.** Updated to provide current relative weight, geometric length of stay, and average length of stay for each DRG.

$79.95

Item No. 4094

ORDER TOLL FREE 1-800-632-0123

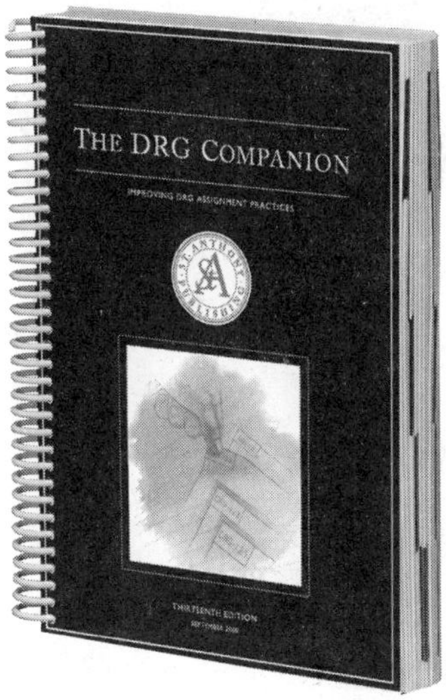

Audit Your DRG Assignments for Compliance

2000 DRG COMPLIANCE AUDITOR

This book helps you understand all of the coding and documentation requirements for the 22 DRG pairs targeted by OIG for potential fraud and abuse. For every ICD-9-CM code in each DRG pair, the *DRG Compliance Auditor* contains physician documentation issues, ICD-9-CM coding guidelines, and AHA *Coding Clinic* for ICD-9-CM coding advice.

- **EXCLUSIVE—One of a Kind.** No other book on the market serves as a companion to *DRG Guidebook* and *The DRG Companion.*
- **Instructional Tips.** Avoid potential fraud and abuse charges through a DRG selection process based on physician documentation.
- **Internal Audits.** Reviewing procedures helps correct coding problems and verify DRG assignments before submitting claims.

$69.95

Item No. 2512

Receive Proper Reimbursement While Staying in Compliance

2000 THE DRG COMPANION (FORMERLY DRG OPTIMIZER)

The DRG Companion is the only guide that shows you the major factors in clinical documentation that justify moving a patient to a higher-paying DRG.

- **NEW—DRG Decision Trees.** Easily select DRGs through flow chart-type decision trees.
- **EXCLUSIVE—One of a Kind.** *The DRG Companion* is the only book of its kind in the industry, and it was written to complement St. Anthony's *DRG Guidebook.*
- **Optimal Reimbursement.** Shows major factors that can move a patient from a lower-paying DRG to a higher paying one.
- **Documentation.** Identifies which documents need to be reviewed and what to look for in order to improve DRG assignment practices.
- **CC Conditions.** Lists commonly missed CC conditions to serve as a reminder to check medical records for overlooked information.

$139.95

Item No. 4093

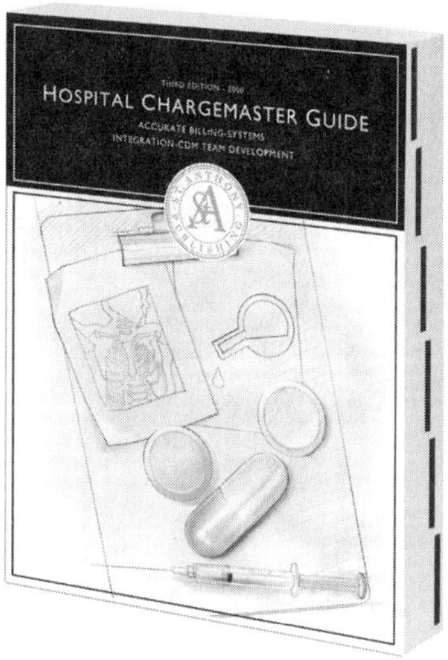

Avoid Fraud Risk—Keep Your Chargemaster Clean, Current, and Accurate!

2000 HOSPITAL CHARGEMASTER GUIDE

This "consultant in a book" provides step-by-step guidance for implementing and maintaining an accurate hospital chargemaster from a coding, billing, and reimbursement prospective.

- **Easy-to-Follow Instructions.** Makes educating and training department heads easier.
- **Know Who Should Be on Your Chargemaster Team—and Why.** Improves accuracy and compliance throughout the departments.
- **Department-Specific Medicare Compliance Fraud Alerts.** Keeps you aware of issues the OIG considers fraud.
- **Relevant CPT/HCPCS Codes.** Fast reference.
- **Coding Instructions.** Easy-to-understand language from the latest Medicare guidelines help eliminate coding errors.

PLUS—Diskette of standardized procedure descriptions listed by department and in CPT/HCPCS code order. Allows you to customize description codes between departments—eliminating confusion, billing errors, and delayed claims.

$199.95 Item No. 4246

Every Official Medicare Document Relating to Billing Compliance

Updated, Organized, Indexed, and Tabbed

MEDICARE BILLING COMPLIANCE REFERENCE MANUAL

Don't wait until that letter arrives from your Fiscal Intermediary or the OIG ... *Medicare Billing Compliance Reference Manual* ensures that your facility is in compliance with every Medicare billing and coding compliance rule.

This powerful resource puts dozens of key source documents from HCFA, the Federal Register, and the Code of Federal Regulations at you finger tips.

- **NEW—Includes Archive of Federal Register Notices on CD-ROM.** Easily store, retrieve, and access past Federal Register notices.
- **Tabbed and Fully Indexed.** Easily locate official Medicare documents.
- **Official Source Documents.** Allow you to conduct internal audits to determine where your facility is vulnerable.
- **Updates.** Give you the latest official billing compliance regulations as they change.
- **Fax Alerts.** You know immediately when Medicare delivers rulings that will affect your facility.

$349.95

Item No. 2455

ORDER TOLL FREE 1-800-632-0123

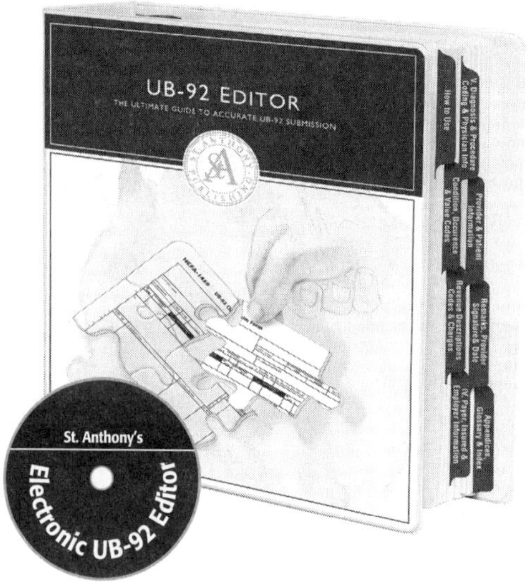

UB-92 Billing Perfection

UB-92 Editor

UB-92 billing and coding requirements are constantly changing. Staying current is essential to ensure fast and accurate payment for all submitted claims.

- **EXCLUSIVE—Step-by-Step Instructions to Filling Out UB-92 Form.** Guides you through all 86 data elements, ensuring proper claim submission.
- **EXCLUSIVE—Links HCPCS and CPT Codes to Applicable Revenue Codes.** Prevents the most common reason for claim rejections.
- **NEW—HCPCS Coding and 15-Minute Increment Reporting.** Requirements for home health services.
- **NEW—Clarified Billing Guidelines.** For skilled nursing facility patients.
- **FREE—Quarterly Updates (a $219 value).** Keep you up-to-date with changes and eliminate billing with outdated information.
- **Billing and Coding Tips for Specific Form Locators.** Help increase efficiency and accuracy ensuring timely payment.
- **FREE—CD-ROM with Hypertext Links.** Easily locate revenue code and field locators.

5 CEUs from AAPC

$239.95

Item No. 4787 (call for multi-user pricing)

Will You Be Prepared When the New E/M Guidelines Are Released?

Evaluation and Management Coding and Documentation Guide

HCFA has advised doctors to use the 1995 or 1997 E/M guidelines until they can come to a consensus with the AMA over several elements in the 1997 guidelines. So, we have added the 1995 guidelines, plus our exclusive cross-walk to the 1997 guidelines. The cross-walk will help you prepare for future documentation requirements by showing you how the two sets of guidelines differ and what additional information needs to go into the medical record.

- **EXCLUSIVE—Self-Audit Forms and Actual Audit Scenarios.** Help ensure documentation supports the level of E/M service coded to reduce claims denial.
- **NEW—Real-Life Clinical Case Studies—Updated for 2000.** Illustrates how to apply the guidelines in everyday situations. Use them to train your staff.
- **FREE—Handy *E/M Fast Finder*.** A portable reference for practitioners organized by place of service to make compliance part of daily activity.
- **FREE—Updates for 1 Full Year** ($99.95 Value). When new guidelines are released, you will be updated automatically.

5 CEUs from AAPC

$129.95

Item No. 3022

ORDER TOLL FREE 1-800-632-0123

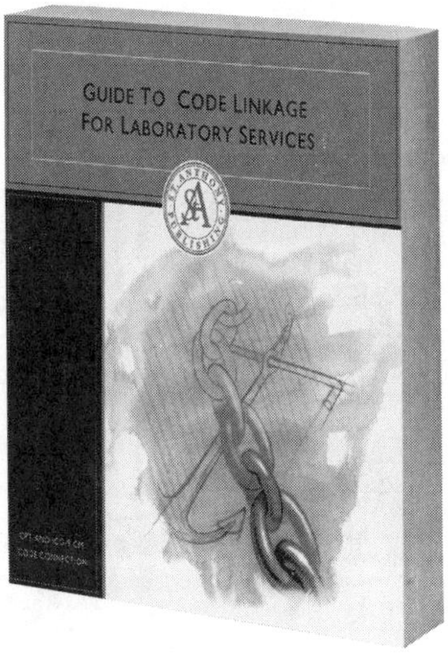

Confirm Medical Necessity for Laboratory Procedures

2000 GUIDE TO CODE LINKAGE FOR LABORATORY SERVICES

Laboratories have been on the government's "hit list" for billing compliance, with medical necessity being the biggest culprit. Confirm medical necessity and double-check coding of laboratory procedures to prevent claim delays and denials.

- **"Link" CPT and ICD-9-CM Codes.** Simply look up the CPT code and get the corresponding ICD-9-CM code to verify medical necessity.
- **Instructions.** Submit accurate claim information the first time, thereby improving cash flow.
- **Symbols.** Coders are alerted to important coding rules, such as unspecified codes and manifestation codes, to ensure appropriate claim submission.
- **Encyclopedia-Style Page Headings.** Easily and quickly locate CPT codes.
- **Medicare Clinical Diagnostic Lab Schedule.** Compare your lab tests to national averages.

5 CEUs from AAPC

$199.95

Item No. 3068

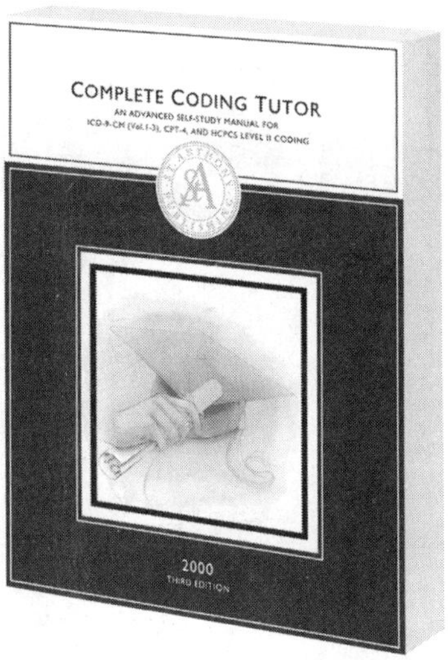

Learn to Code Diagnoses and Procedures for All 3 Coding Systems

2000 COMPLETE CODING TUTOR

To code accurately you must understand all three coding systems. This self-study manual helps coders develop an in-depth understanding of complex coding conventions, terminology, and rules for ICD-9-CM, CPT-4, and HCPCS Level II coding systems.

- **EXCLUSIVE—Provides Detailed Descriptions of Each Major Disease Category, Including Coding Tips and Official Coding Guidelines.** Learn to code from the diagnosis—not a "cheat sheet" or superbill.
- **NEW—Extensive Index.** Locate the information you need to teach a specific coding section or to confirm answers to coding questions.
- **Organizes CPT Coding Information by Procedure Section—Just Like the CPT Book.** Helps you build on previous knowledge of CPT coding.
- **Explains HCPCS Level II, Including Basic Coding Steps, Use of Modifiers, and Guidelines For Coding Durable Medical Equipment.** Helps you avoid claims denials caused by incorrect or missing information.

8 CEUs from AAPC

$99.95

Item No. 3072

ST. ANTHONY'S 2000 PUBLICATIONS

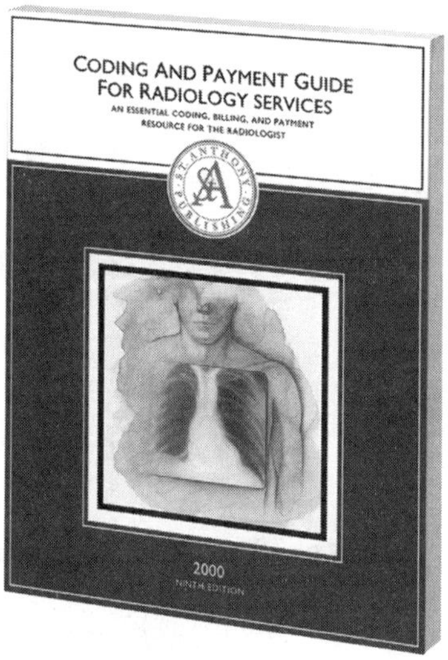

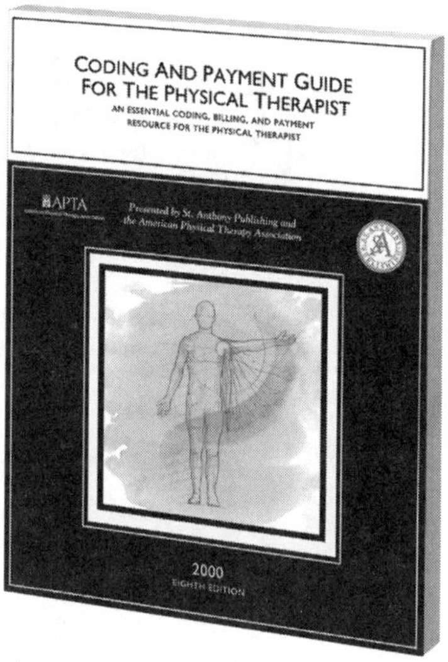

A Vital Resource for the Radiologist

2000 CODING AND PAYMENT GUIDE FOR RADIOLOGY SERVICES

This unique, comprehensive resource focuses exclusively on radiology reimbursement, with information and advice to manage medical necessity, coverage, and coding issues.

- **EXCLUSIVE—ICD-9-CM Color-Coding and Symbol.** Helps you choose the most accurate application of ICD-9-CM codes.
- **Describes Reimbursement Methodologies.** Verify accuracy of payments received.
- **Provides National Coverage Policies.** Helps keep your facility in compliance.
- **Organizes CPT, ICD-9-CM, and HCPCS Level II Codes.** Allows for fast and easy coding of your claims.
- **Links ICD-9-CM Codes to Related CPT Procedures.** Substantiate medical necessity.
- **Includes Index Guides to Interventional, Revenue, and Radiology Code Revisions.** Quick references for coding and chargemaster review.

$199.95

Item No. 3923

An Essential Coding, Billing, and Payment Resource for the Physical Therapist

2000 CODING AND PAYMENT GUIDE FOR THE PHYSICAL THERAPIST

This best selling, comprehensive reference focuses exclusively on physical therapy coding, documentation, and reimbursement from A to Z. Developed in conjunction with the American Physical Therapy Association, this unique resource is designed to meet the specific needs of the physical therapy practice.

- **EXCLUSIVE—ICD-9-CM Color-Coding and Symbols.** Help you choose the most accurate application of ICD-9-CM codes.
- **Organizes CPT, ICD-9-CM, and HCPCS Level II Codes.** Allows for fast and easy coding of your claims.
- **Medical Documentation.** Outlines how to maintain complete documentation to demonstrate compliance to third-party payers.
- **Provides Definitions and Guidelines.** Helps you understand diagnostic conditions and procedures.
- **Includes Workers' Compensation Information, Medical Review Criteria, and Sample Documentation Forms.** Helps you demonstrate proper compliance.

$169.95

ORDER TOLL FREE 1-800-632-0123

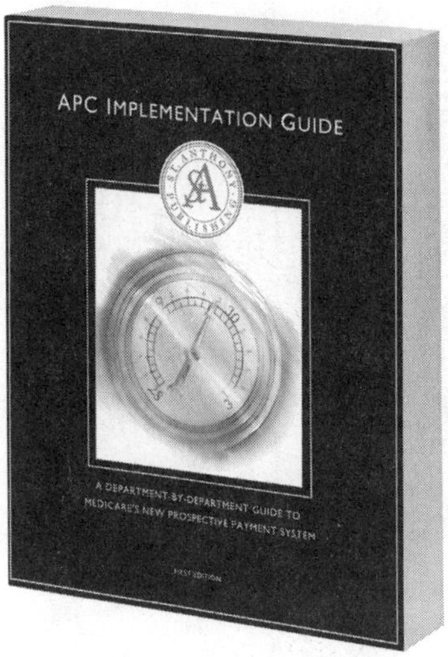

Prepare Now For The Biggest Change Ever In Medicare Outpatient Payment

APC REFERENCE MANUAL

This manual makes clear the complex and lengthy regulations proposed for APCs. You'll understand how the new payment system will work, determine the financial impact of new payment rules, and educate coding and billing staff.

- **EXCLUSIVE—Case Studies.** Illustrates the APC payment structure and highlights new packaging, bundling, and discounting rules.
- **Sample Payment Simulations.** Predict how APCs affect payments using claims data for ambulatory surgery, emergency room visits, psychiatric care, cast room, and observation stay services.
- **Expert-Level Analysis of APCs.** Understand APC components and implications through detailed discussion of topics such as:

✓ Bundling and discounting of services
✓ Medical visit grouping logic
✓ Outpatient payment window
✓ Ancillary services under APCs
✓ Ungroupable codes under APCs
✓ Use of hospital outpatient modifiers
✓ Payment calculations for facility services and beneficiary copayments
✓ APC included and excluded services
✓ UB-92 billing requirements and more!

$279.95 Item No. 3055

Step-By-Step APC Implementation For Every Department In Your Facility

APC IMPLEMENTATION GUIDE

APC Implementation Guide gives you a reliable, time-saving blueprint for successful APC implementation—and prompt, accurate payment for every covered service you perform. With this manual you will be able to identify and analyze the impact of APCs on each department.

- **Organized by Department.** Allow each department head to identify a course of action for training and educating staff.
- **EXCLUSIVE—APC Reimbursement Worksheets.** Analyze, on a case-by-case basis, the financial impact of APCs on your facility.
- **Easy-to-Follow Forms and Strategies.** Help you to establish an APC task force and ensure a successful transition to APCs.
- **Identifies "Key" Indicators.** Pinpoint how successful your facility will perform under APCs.

$329.95
Item No. 4008

A Clinical Coding and Reimbursement Reference

GUIDE TO APC AND ASC GROUPS

For Hospitals and ASCs

This best-selling *Guide* will help hospital outpatient departments and freestanding ambulatory surgery centers make informed decisions—improving the accuracy of outpatient reimbursement for procedures on Medicare's ASC list.

- **NEW—Code Alert Symbols.** Notify you that a CPT code has been added, revised, or deleted.
- **NEW—Proposed APC Group Numbers, Relative Values, Payment Rates, and Status Indicators.** Allow you to compare APC reimbursement to ASC reimbursement.
- **APC Implementation Chapter for Freestanding ASCs.** Outlines major registration, coding, billing, claims processing, and payment reconciliation issues.
- **EXCLUSIVE—ASC Alternate CPT Code Choices.** Identifies related CPT codes on the ASC list that, if appropriate, can move payment to a higher weighted ASC group.
- **Appendices and Forms.** Bring together valuable resources to calculate payments, monitor reimbursements, determine your facility's specific labor adjusted ASC payment rates and the HCFA Wage Index.

$199.95 Item No. 3051

Locate and Understand Crucial Guidelines Quickly

SKILLED NURSING FACILITY PROSPECTIVE PAYMENT SYSTEM REFERENCE MANUAL

This time-saving, all-in-one reference manual compiles the essential rules, regulations, and significant documents issued by HCFA concerning PPS, consolidated billing, and other billing and coding requirements for skilled nursing facilities.

- **Authoritative Directions.** Official instructions for reporting RUGs group codes, HIPP rate codes, modifiers and assessment indicators, billing for rehabilitation services, and more.
- **Federal Register Notices.** Final rules for implementing SNF prospective payment, consolidated billing, automating MDS, and other key rules.
- **Clinical Requirements.** Understand the Medicare MDS, RAPS, RUGS III, and focused medical review criteria.

$279.95

Item No. 4711

ORDER TOLL FREE 1-800-632-0123

Step-by-Step Solutions to Comply with Revised Home Health COPs

HOME HEALTH CONDITIONS OF PARTICIPATION IMPLEMENTATION GUIDE

This *Guide* gives you clear, concise guidance and ready-to-use professional tools to help your agency comply with the revised Medicare Home Health Conditions of Participation. Written by experts in the field, this comprehensive manual provides expert implementation guidelines and strategies to measure and improve patient outcomes and the effectiveness of home health services.

- **EXCLUSIVE—All-in-One Reproducible Assessment Forms.** Incorporates OASIS-B1, Medicare Secondary Payer, and 485 Data Elements—you'll be able to use one form for all your patient assessment tasks.
- **EXCLUSIVE—Pre-Written Model Policies and Implementation Instructions.** Ready-to-adapt policies for record security, competency testing, clinical pathways, infection control, teaching pathways, and more—save you hours of time.
- **FREE—Updates.** Keep you on top of all changes, ensuring that you meet all requirements.
- **PLUS—Resources on Disk.** Help you create custom reports, forms, job descriptions, occurrence/complaint reporting, and more to simplify the accreditation process.

$199.95

Item No. 2569

Color Coding for Home Health, Nursing Facilities and Hospices

1999-2000 ICD-9-CM CODE BOOK FOR HOME HEALTH SERVICES, NURSING FACILITIES, & HOSPICES

Accurate coding is essential to proper coding and reimbursement. This is the only ICD-9-CM code book on the market with color coding specifically for home health agencies, skilled nursing facilities, and hospices.

- **EXCLUSIVE—Code of Federal Regulations.** Special section describes how RUG-III categories were developed to enhance comprehension of the new SNF Prospective Payment System.
- **EXCLUSIVE—Reference Section.** Addresses qualifications for coverage of Medicare home health services coverage.
- **Color Coding for Hospice Care.** Identifies acceptable non-cancer diagnoses for admission to hospice care.
- **Check Fifth-Digit Symbols.** Alerts you when a fifth digit is needed.
- **Age and Sex Edits.** Verify code selection.
- **AHA *Coding Clinic* References.** Listed next to codes to quickly find official guidelines.

$119.95

Item No. 4222

ORDER TOLL FREE 1-800-632-0123

Determine Reimbursement and Set Fees for Your Services

2000 RELATIVE VALUES FOR PHYSICIANS

When establishing fees and determining productivity, be assured the relative values you are using are accurate and widely used in the industry. *Relative Values for Physicians* is one of the most well established and respected relative value scales in existence. Establish, defend, and negotiate fees for medical and surgical procedures with the same relative values used by insurance companies. Relative values are provided for all procedures, not just those utilized by Medicare.

- **Data Developed by Physicians.** Procedure values based on extensive physician surveys. Services are valued by those performing procedures, not by an arbitrary committee.
- **Assure Complete Reimbursement.** All CPT codes are valued, not just those codes used by Medicare.
- **Anesthesia Values.** Determine anesthesia charges and payment.
- **Valued Professional and Technical Components.** Determine charges and reimbursement based on the components your organization performs.
- **Eliminate Subjective Charge Data.** All relative values are based on the time and skill necessary to perform a procedure, not on subjective charge data.

$239.95 Item No. 4250

$599.95 Diskette Item No. 4251

Calculate Fair, Defensible Fees for Every Physician Service

ST. ANTHONY'S 2000 RBRVS

St. Anthony's RBRVS gives you all the procedures valued by HCFA's Physician Fee Schedule, as well as the relative values for those codes not valued by HCFA ("gap" codes). This is a must-have tool for reimbursement disputes, contract negotiations, and determining accurate fees for Medicare or private payers.

- **Determine Medicare Reimbursement.** Provides you with the same relative values for Medicare services as found in the Federal Register.
- **Provides Global Periods.** Be aware of the required follow-up days under the Medicare Physician Fee Schedule.
- **Know How Each Procedure is Valued.** Work, practice expense, and malpractice expense components are provided for each procedure so you can evaluate and analyze the costs and effort associated with a service.
- **Non-Medicare Codes Valued by Proprietary Methodology.** Codes not valued by HCFA are valued by the same organization that created the original RBRVS methodology, Cambridge Health Economics Group (CHEG).

$189.95 Item No. 4255

$599.95 Diskette Item No. 4253

ORDER TOLL FREE 1-800-632-0123

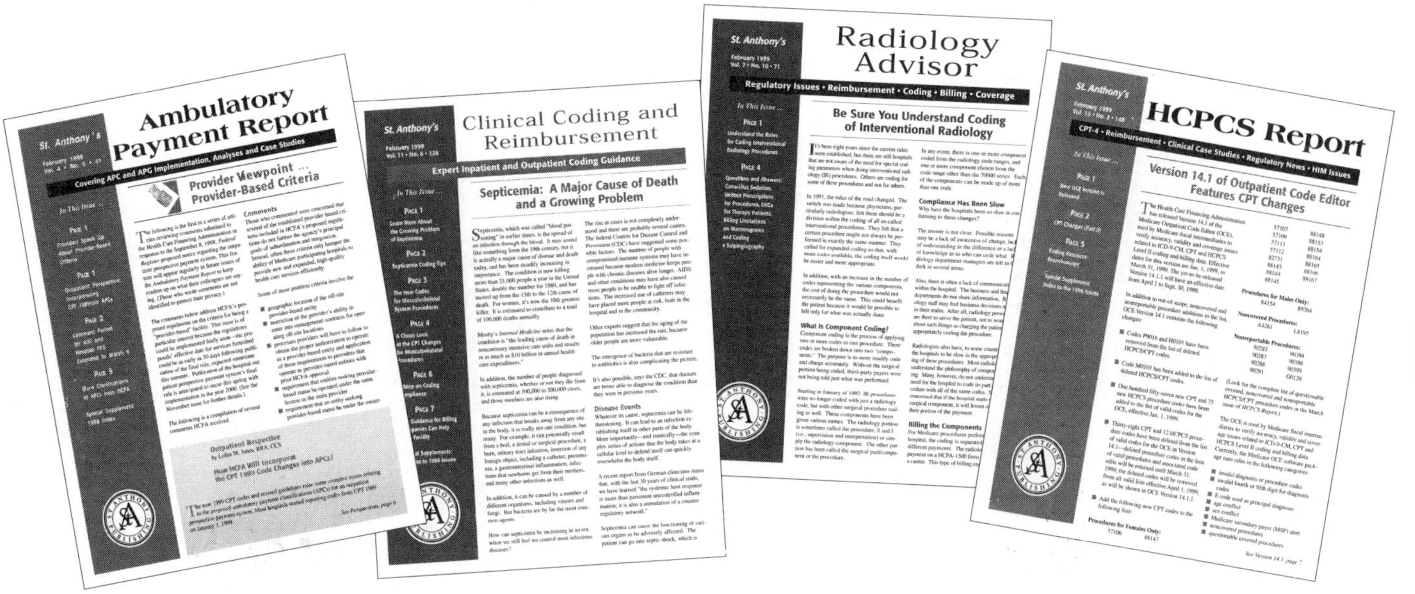

Ambulatory Payment Report

Ambulatory Payment Report, written by the leading experts on APCs and APGs, brings you revenue enhancement strategies and expert level analysis in a concise, but thorough, eight-page monthly format.

- Learn how APCs will work and how they differ from APGs
- Assess the potential financial impact of APCs on your organization
- Understand and implement new billing and coding guidelines

$249 Item No. 2428

Clinical Coding and Reimbursement

This eight-page must-have monthly newsletter provides expert ICD-9-CM, CPT, and HCPCS Level II coding advice for your inpatient and outpatient services.

- Provides in-depth clinical analysis of diseases and procedures. Helps you choose the right code the first time.
- Reviews ongoing changes to the ICD-9-CM, CPT, and HCPCS Level II coding systems and reimbursement methodologies. Keeps you up-to-date and ensures the appropriate reimbursement to which you are entitled.
- Actual case studies and a Question and Answer column offer solutions to your difficult coding scenarios.

Up to 10 CEUs from AAPC

$159.95 Item No. 4031

Radiology Advisor

This monthly resource is designed for hospital radiology departments, freestanding radiology facilities, and radiologists to properly code, document, and bill for their services.

- Choose the correct code. Explanation of how to choose the correct ICD-9-CM, CPT, and HCPCS Level II codes (Medicare and other third-party payers).
- Billing. Covers hospital as well as physician billing.
- In-depth analysis. Expert advice on how to avoid common radiology coding and billing problems.
- Chargemaster and superbill updates. Keep current on these billing essentials to safeguard against lost revenue and ensure billing compliance.
- Authoritative information. Stay in compliance with official guidelines and receive the appropriate reimbursement for your provider's services.
- Review ongoing changes to the reimbursement systems. Saves you time and expense of resubmitting claims due to denials and rejection for claim errors.
- Question and Answer column. Solutions to problems that specifically affect radiology.

Up to 10 CEUs from AAPC

$199.95 Item No. 4114

HCPCS Report

Provides clinical, coding, and reimbursement guidelines for documenting, interpreting, and assigning CPT surgery codes for hospital or freestanding ambulatory surgery centers. This monthly eight-page newsletter helps coding professionals to achieve optimal data quality, coding accuracy, and reimbursement under ASC payment methodology or APCs.

$269 Item No. 4063

Financial and Operating Indicators for the Nation's Hospitals

2000 Almanac of Hospital Financial & Operating Indicators

Review more than 90 financial ratios and operating indicators to help you assess your competitive position and establish appropriate financial targets backed by audited hospital financial statements from more than 3,000 U.S. hospitals.

- **Regional Benchmarks of Facility Costs and Revenue.** Ensure your organization is financially competitive.
- **150 Financial Indicators.** Gives a clear and concise picture of the hospital being evaluated.
- **Regional Medians.** Compare and contrast your facility to others in your region of operation.
- **Data from Over 3,400 Hospitals.** Assures a comprehensive and statistically valid sample of facilities.
- **33 Financial Indicators.** Evaluate and analyze a peer organizations' cost and profit.
- **Analyzes Trends, Costs, and Operations.** Data on the hospital industry over the last year provides necessary information to make rational and informed decisions.

$349.95 Item No. 9604

$1,199.95 CD-ROM Item No. 9699

Financial Insights into Outpatient Procedures

2000 Outpatient Procedures Resource Book

The *Outpatient Procedures Resource Book* provides unique and useful insights into the financial and operating performance of 56 key outpatient procedures. This information proves invaluable to senior and financial managers throughout the health care industry.

- **Regional Utilization of Outpatient Services.** Provides a look at the most frequently performed procedures in a given area.
- **Be Financially Competitive.** Analyze facility profit/loss scenarios with data on average costs and charges per procedures.
- **56 Outpatient Procedures.** Compare and contrast the most common procedural settings and costs.
- **ASC Payment Rates.** A tool to see what the payment will be for ASC procedures.
- **Departmental Cost.** Know specific costs by department.
- **Benchmarks.** Three separate benchmarks to evaluate costs based on low, medium, or high managed care penetration.

$299.95 Item No. 9605

$599.95 CD-ROM Item No. 9700

ORDER TOLL FREE 1-800-632-0123

Who Are the Top Performing Hospitals in Terms of Quality, Cost, and Financial Stability?

2000 The Performance Review

Performance Review 2000—A Guide to U.S. Hospitals has the answers. The latest publication by the Center for Healthcare Industry Performance Studies (CHIPS) reviews cost, quality, and financial stability indicators over a three-year period. This resource provides hospital characteristics and performance indicators for more than 3,000 U.S. facilities. It is the perfect off-the-shelf reference for hospital executives, healthcare consultants, and industry analysts.

- **Data From Over 3,000 U.S Hospitals.** Evaluate peer organizations' performance from around the country.
- **Become More Efficient and Competitive.** Evaluate your hospital's costs, debt, overhead percentage, and more.
- **Benchmark Quality of Care.** Compare quality ratings of other hospitals.
- **Costs and Financial Stability Indicators.** Identify areas in which performance can be improved.
- **Scoring of Hospitals in Your Area.** Objectively evaluate what hospitals to contract with.

$399.95 Item No. 3202

$599.95 CD-ROM Item No. 3203

Learn What Makes A Successful Capitation Agreement

Capitation Reference Manual

Now you can benefit from existing capitation agreements and discover the specific language, provisions, and terms that make them work! This comprehensive manual provides contract strategies from health plans, networks, and providers.

- **NEW—Overview of Capitation Today.** Capitation evolves monthly. Learn the latest trends.
- **NEW—Sample Contracts and Case Studies.** See what other providers are doing and find out what worked for them and what didn't.
- **NEW—National Capitation Data.** Get the latest in Reden and Anders-certified utilization data to help negotiate your fees. Also includes utilization and PMPM Rates to prepare yourself for negotiation.
- **NEW—Three-Month Trial to *Health Care Risk Contracting Report*.** Trial subscription to St. Anthony Publishing's popular capitation newsletter helps you know what's going on month-to-month.
- **FREE—Capitation Diskette.** Contracts and data you can manipulate before and during negotiations.
- **FREE—Receive Updates for 1 Full Year.** Updated twice a year to keep you up-to-date with the dynamic capitation environment.

$398.95 Item No. 3031

3 Easy Ways to Order

Mail this form with payment and/or purchase order to:
St. Anthony Publishing
PO Box 96561
Washington, DC 20090

Call toll-free
(800) 632-0123 and mention the source code on this order form

FAX this order form with credit card information and purchase order to
(703) 707-5700

Publication Order and Fax Form

FOBA

Customer No.__________________ Purchase Order No.____________________
(Attach copy of Purchase Order)

Company____

Address ____
(no P.O. Boxes, please)

City__________________________________ State______ Zip______________

Phone (______)_______________________ Fax (______)__________________
(in case we have questions about your order)

No. of Beds ____

Contact Name ____

Title______________________________ E-mail ________________________

Item #	Qty	Item Description	Price	Total
2999	1	Premier ICD-9-CM Code Book	$89.95	$89.95

Sub Total	
OH and VA residents please add applicable sales tax	
Shipping & handling (1-10 units) *(11 plus units, foreign and Canadian orders, please call for shipping costs)*	*8.95*
Total enclosed	

Payment Options:

❍ Check enclosed. (Make payable to St. Anthony Publishing) Check #__________ ❍ Bill me. ($5 fee)

❍ Charge my: ❍ MasterCard ❍ VISA ❍ AMEX ❍ Discover

Card # | | | | | | | | | | | | | | | | | Exp. Date: | | | (MM YR)

Signature ____

100% Money Back Guarantee!

If our merchandise ever fails to meet your expectations, please contact our Customer Service Department at (800) 632-0123 for an immediate response. We will resolve any concern without hesitation.

3 Easy Ways to Order

Mail this form with payment and/or purchase order to:
St. Anthony Publishing
PO Box 96561
Washington, DC 20090

Call toll-free
(800) 632-0123 and
mention the source code
on this order form

FAX this order form with credit card information and purchase order to
(703) 707-5700

Publication Order and Fax Form

FOBA

Customer No.________________ Purchase Order No.________________
(Attach copy of Purchase Order)

Company________________________________

Address ________________________________
(no P.O. Boxes, please)

City________________________ State_____ Zip____________

Phone (_____)________________ Fax (_____)________________
(in case we have questions about your order)

No. of Beds ________________________________

Contact Name ________________________________

Title________________________ E-mail ________________

Item #	Qty	Item Description	Price	Total
2999	1	Premier ICD-9-CM Code Book	$89.95	$89.95

Sub Total	
OH and VA residents please add applicable sales tax	
Shipping & handling (1-10 units) *(11 plus units, foreign and Canadian orders, please call for shipping costs)*	*8.95*
Total enclosed	

Payment Options:

❍ Check enclosed. (Make payable to St. Anthony Publishing) Check #__________ ❍ Bill me. ($5 fee)

❍ Charge my: ❍ MasterCard ❍ VISA ❍ AMEX ❍ Discover

Card # | | | | | | | | | | | | | | | | | Exp. Date: | | | (MM YR)

Signature ________________________________

100% Money Back Guarantee!

If our merchandise ever fails to meet your expectations, please contact our Customer Service Department at (800) 632-0123 for an immediate response. We will resolve any concern without hesitation.

St. Anthony's
Softbound
ICD-9-CM Code Book

St. Anthony...
Leading the way

August 1999

Dear St. Anthony Subscriber:

HCFA has announced that there will be no ICD-9-CM code changes for the year 2000 and that current code sets will be effective through September 30, 2000. The codes in your 1999-2000 edition of the Professional ICD-9-CM Code Book are effective October 1, 1998 through September 30, 2000.

Features:

- fiscal 1999–2000 ICD-9-CM codes
- a CC exclusion list with each affected code
- the *most current* Official Coding Guidelines
- the *addition of* ✓5th in the disease tabular
- AHA *Coding Clinic for ICD-9-CM* references
- *new* DRG compliance symbol to prevent inappropriate coding or upcoding

You can code confidently, knowing you're using the most current ICD-9-CM coding information available. Because St. Anthony understands the pressures you face every day—to optimize payments and consistently maintain a high level of data quality—we are constantly improving our products to give you the very best coding manuals on the market today.

Code changes are identified by brackets in the margin. The date (month and year) at the bottom of the page indicates when the change was made on that particular page.

We appreciate your choosing St. Anthony to meet your coding needs. If you have any questions or comments concerning your code book or any other St. Anthony product, please don't hesitate to call our customer service department. The call is free: (800) 632-0123.

Cordially,

David Schultz

David Schultz
Publisher

CCS 10.99

St. Anthony Publishing
11410 Isaac Newton Square
Reston, VA 20190
(703) 904-3900
Fax: (703) 707-5700

ST. ANTHONY HOSPITAL PRODUCTS ORDER FORM

16739

1. SHIP TO: SHIP BOOKS TO ADDRESS BELOW

NAME ______ TITLE ______

FACILITY ______

ADDRESS ______ TELEPHONE ______

CITY ______ STATE ______ ZIP ______ FAX ______

2. ORDER INFORMATION

Quantity	Product	Code	Price	Total
	ICD-9-CM CODE BOOKS			
______	Softbound, Illustrated ICD-9-CM Code Book—2000 Edition	SIAS-00	$ 89.95	$ ______
______	Illustrated, Updatable ICD-9-CM Code Book With Full-Text Refill in October	IAD	$ 179.00	$ ______
______	Softbound, Color Coded ICD-9-CM Code Book—2000 Edition	CCS-00	$ 69.95	$ ______
______	Color Coded, Updatable ICD-9-CM Code Book With Full-Text Refill in October	ICD	$ 139.00	$ ______
______	Color Coded Updatable ICD-9-CM Code Book for Outpatient Services With Full-Text Refill in October	OUT	$ 159.00	$ ______
	DRG, APC and ASC RESOURCES			
______	DRG Guidebook—2000 Edition	DRG-00	$ 69.95	$ ______
______	DRG Optimizer—2000 Edition	OPT-00	$ 139.00	$ ______
______	Guide to APC and ASC Groups	ASC	$ 199.00	$ ______
______	Ambulatory Payment Guidebook	APG-99	$ 79.00	$ ______
	NEWSLETTERS			
______	Clinical Coding for Reimbursement [ ] 1 yr (12 issues) $169 [ ] 2 yr $304 [ ] 3 yr $406	CFR		$ ______
______	HCPCS Report [ ] 1 yr (12 issues) $269 [ ] 2 yr $484 [ ] 3 yr $645	HCP		$ ______
______	Ambulatory Payment Report [ ] 1 yr (12 issues) $249 [ ] 2 yr $448 [ ] 3 yr $596	APN		$ ______

3. PAYMENT METHOD

[ ] Bill me (add $5.00 Invoicing fee)

[ ] Check Enclosed [ ] Invoice P.O.#

Make Checks payable to: St. Anthony Publishing
Mail to: P.O. Box 96561 • Washington, D.C. 20090

[ ] Credit Card:

[ ] Visa [ ] MasterCard [ ] Amex [ ] Discover

ACCT # ______ EXP DATE ______

SIGNATURE ______

OH and VA Residents Add Sales Tax $ ______

Invoicing fee $ ______

S & H $ 8.95

TOTAL $ ______

For fastest service call toll free (800) 632-0123 and mention priority code 16739, or fax (703) 707-5700

100% Money Back Guarantee

If for any reason you are not completely satisfied, return your purchase within 30 days for an exchange or full refund.

Professional

ICD·9·CM CODE BOOK

Volumes 1,2,3

Edited by:
Anita C. Hart
Sheila R. Parvis

St Anthony Publishing™

Effective Oct. 1, 1998 – Sept. 30, 2000
ICD

USE OF OFFICIAL SOURCES

St. Anthony's ICD-9-CM Code Book contains the official U.S. Department of Health and Human Services, Ninth Revision, Sixth Edition ICD-9-CM codes, effective for the current year.

The color coding, footnotes and symbols, which identify coding and reimbursement issues, have been derived from official federal government sources, including the Medicare code editor (MCE).

The American Hospital Association (AHA) *Coding Clinic for ICD-9-CM* references are used with permission of the AHA.

DISCLAIMER

All the codes, indices and other material in *St. Anthony's ICD-9-CM Code Book* are compiled from official ICD-9-CM codes and instructions as well as the Medicare regulations and manuals issued or authorized by the Health Care Financing Administration. The code book is designed to provide accurate and authoritative information in regard to the subject covered, and every reasonable effort has been made to ensure the accuracy of the information within these pages. However, the ultimate responsibility for correct coding lies with the provider of services.

St. Anthony Publishing, its employees, agents and staff make no representation, warranty or guarantee that this compilation of codes and narratives is error-free or that the use of this code book will prevent differences of opinion or disputes with Medicare or other third-party payers as to the codes that are accepted or the amounts that will be paid to providers of services, and will bear no responsibility or liability for the results or consequences of the use of this code book.

Second Printing—August 1999

Please address all editorial correspondence to:
Technical Editor—ICD
St. Anthony Publishing
11410 Isaac Newton Square
Reston, VA 20190

Printed in the United States of America.
CCS ISBN 1-56329-656-X

THE EDITORS

Anita C. Hart, BA, ART, CCS, CCS-P

Technical Consultant, Product Manager
St. Anthony Publishing
Reston, VA

Ms. Hart's experience includes eleven years conducting and publishing research in clinical medicine and human genetics for Yale University, Massachusetts General Hospital, and Massachusetts Institute of Technology. Her research conclusions have been published in several peer-reviewed journals. In addition, Ms. Hart has supervised medical records management, health information management, coding and reimbursement, and worker's compensation issues as the office manager for a physical therapy rehabilitation clinic. Ms. Hart is an expert in physician and facility coding, reimbursement systems, and compliance issues. Ms. Hart is also the author of the Complete Coding Tutor, an advanced self-study guide for ICD-9-CM, CPT, and HCPCS Level II coding, as well as, technical editor for numerous other publications for hospital and physician practices.

Sheila R. Parvis, CCS

Technical Consultant
St. Anthony Publishing
Reston, VA

Ms. Parvis has over 21 years experience in reimbursement with specific emphasis in ICD-9-CM coding. Her previous experience has been in acute care facilities as a coding specialist, medical records technician, concurrent coder/reviewer and tumor registrar. In addition, she has worked in a multi-specialty billing agency as a coding specialist. She has provided education on basic and advanced ICD-9-CM coding, physician documentation as well as, coding and billing compliance. Since her employment with St. Anthony she has developed numerous publications specific to hospital and physician coding, reimbursement, billing reference and compliance plan implementation.

The following also contributed to this book

- **Catherine A. Hopkins, *technical consultant***
- **Stacy McNew, *desktop publishing specialist***

PREFACE

Since the federal government implemented diagnosis-related groups (DRGs) on Oct. 1, 1983, medical record professionals and others have had to refer to many sources for ICD-9-CM codes and coding and reimbursement principles.

St. Anthony's ICD-9-CM Code Book has been designed with the hospital coder in mind. All three volumes of the most recent official government version of ICD-9-CM have been combined into one book.

In addition, the code book compiles as much information from the many coding resources as possible into one convenient reference without sacrificing readability and ease of locating codes.

St. Anthony's technical experts have drawn upon their extensive hands-on experience to enhance the government's book with valuable features essential to correct coding and reimbursement. Without these enhancements, health information management departments would spend hours locating the information required to code each record accurately. Because of the code book's thoroughness, accuracy, timeliness and ease of use, medical record departments nationwide have turned to it for their coding needs.

As you review the content, you'll find the following:

- ICD-9-CM official guidelines for coding and reporting, published by the U.S. Department of Health and Human Services and approved by the cooperating parties (American Hospital Association, American Health Information Management Association, Health Care Financing Administration and National Center for Health Statistics)

- all the official ICD-9-CM codes, indices, notes, footnotes and symbols

- St. Anthony color coding, symbols and footnotes that alert coders to coding and reimbursement issues. The majority of the Medicare code edits, such as non-operating-room procedures that affect DRG assignment and circumstances under which Medicare is a secondary payer (MSP), are identified.

- the complication and comorbidity (CC) exclusion list, integrated beneath the applicable codes to make it easier to determine complications and comorbidities excluded with a particular principal diagnosis

- the American Hospital Association's (AHA) *Coding Clinic for ICD-9-CM* references, integrated beneath the applicable codes to provide easy reference to official coding advice as designated by the four cooperating parties (AHA, AHIMA, HCFA and NCHS)

- tabs for quick, easy location of terms and codes in the indices and tabular lists.

In response to requests from our subscribers, St. Anthony added many of the above enhancements to the code book with the 1992 edition. We encourage you to review "How to Use *St. Anthony's ICD-9-CM Code Book*" in this section to discover the features that assist in assigning and reporting correct codes, ensuring appropriate reimbursement. We are proud to offer you the revised and improved edition of *St. Anthony's ICD-9-CM Code Book*.

IMPORTANT INFORMATION ABOUT YOUR SUBSCRIPTION

Updates

If you have *St. Anthony's Updatable ICD-9-CM Code Book,* your subscription includes an updating service throughout the year to keep the code book current and accurate. Whenever HCFA issues changes or corrections to the ICD-9-CM codes, St. Anthony will issue an update to the book.

If you have *St. Anthony's Softbound ICD-9-CM Code Book*, you must purchase a new book each year to stay up-to-date.

What to Do If You Have Questions

If you are not receiving your updates or have any questions about your subscription, call our customer service department toll free at (800) 632-0123.

If you have comments on the content of the code book, please address them in writing to:

Technical Editor—ICD
St. Anthony Publishing
11410 Isaac Newton Square
Reston, VA 20190
Fax no. (703) 707-5700

Additional Copies

If you would like additional subscriptions to the code book, use the convenient order card in the book, or contact St. Anthony's order department toll free at (800) 632-0123.

HOW TO USE *ST. ANTHONY'S ICD-9-CM CODE BOOK*

St. Anthony's ICD-9-CM Code Book is based upon the official version of the International Classification of Diseases, Ninth Revision, Clinical Modification, Sixth Edition, issued by the U.S. Department of Health and Human Services. Annual code changes are implemented by the government and are effective Oct. 1 and valid through Sept. 30 of the following year.

This book is totally compatible with its parent system, ICD-9, thus meeting the need for comparability of morbidity and mortality statistics at the international level.

St. Anthony's ICD-9-CM Code Book is consistent with the content of the government's version of ICD-9-CM. However, to accommodate the coder's approach to coding, the alphabetic index has been placed before the tabular list in both the disease and procedure classifications. This allows the user to locate the correct codes in a logical, natural manner by locating the term in the index, then confirming the accuracy of the code in the tabular list.

Steps to Correct Coding

1. Look up the main term in the alphabetic index and scan the subterm entries as appropriate. Do not code from the alphabetic index without verifying the accuracy of the code in the tabular list.

2. Locate the code in the numerically arranged tabular list.

3. Observe the punctuation, footnotes, cross-references, color-coded prompts and other conventions described on pages ix–xi.

4. To determine the appropriateness of the code selection, read all instructional material:

   - "includes" and "excludes" notes
   - "see," "see also" and "see category" cross-references
   - "use additional code" and "code first underlying disease" instructions
   - "code also" and "*omit code*" notes
   - fourth- and fifth-digit requirements
   - CC exclusions.

5. Consult St. Anthony's color coding and reimbursement prompts, including the Medicare as secondary payer and nonspecific OR procedure colors. Also note the check fifth digit, age and sex symbols. Refer to the color/symbol key in the front of the book and the legend for symbols and list of footnotes beginning on page xii.

6. Consult the official ICD-9-CM guidelines for coding and reporting, and refer to the AHA's *Coding Clinic for ICD-9-CM* for coding guidelines governing the use of specific codes.

7. Confirm and transcribe the correct code.

Organization

In *St. Anthony's ICD-9-CM Code Book,* Volumes 1, 2 and 3 are identified by tabs. The indices appear before the tabular lists in both the disease and procedure classifications.

Disease Classification: Alphabetic Index to Diseases

The Alphabetic Index to Diseases contains diagnosis terms for illnesses, injuries and reasons for encounters with health care professionals.

Disease Classification: Tabular List of Diseases

The Tabular List of Diseases numerically arranges the ICD-9-CM codes and descriptors.

The tabular list includes two supplementary classifications:

- V Codes: Supplementary Classification of Factors Influencing Health Status and Contact with Health Services (V01–V82)

- E Codes: Supplementary Classification of External Causes of Injury and Poisoning (E800–E999)

Following the supplementary classifications are five appendices:

Appendix A:	Morphology of Neoplasms
Appendix B:	Glossary of Mental Disorders
Appendix C:	Classification of Drugs by American Hospital Formulary Service List Number and their ICD-9-CM Equivalents
Appendix D:	Classification of Industrial Accidents According to Agency
Appendix E:	List of Three-Digit Categories

These appendices are included as a reference to provide further information about the patient's circumstances, help further define a diagnostic statement, maintain a tumor registry and aid in classifying new drugs.

Procedure Classification: Alphabetic Index to Procedures

The Alphabetic Index to Procedures lists common surgical procedural terminology.

Procedure Classification: Tabular List of Procedures

The Tabular List of Procedures numerically arranges the procedure codes and their descriptors.

ICD-9-CM FOOTNOTES, SYMBOLS, INSTRUCTIONAL NOTES AND CONVENTIONS

St. Anthony's ICD-9-CM Code Book preserves all the footnotes, symbols, instructional notes and conventions found in the government's official code book. Accurate coding depends upon understanding the meaning of these elements.

The following appear in both the disease and procedure tabular lists, unless otherwise noted.

Official Government Symbols

□	The lozenge printed in the left margin preceding the disease code denotes a four-digit code or description unique to ICD-9-CM. The contents of these codes in ICD-9-CM are not the same as those in ICD-9. This symbol is used only in the Tabular List of Diseases.
§	The section mark preceding a code denotes a footnote on the page. This symbol is used only in the tabular lists of the disease and procedure classifications.

ICD-9-CM Conventions Used in the Tabular Lists

In addition to the symbols and footnotes above, the ICD-9-CM disease and procedure tabular lists share certain abbreviations, punctuation, symbols and other conventions. *St. Anthony's ICD-9-CM Code Book* preserves these conventions. Proper use of the conventions will lead to efficient and accurate coding.

Abbreviations

NEC	Not elsewhere classified This abbreviation is used when the ICD-9-CM Code Book does not provide a code specific for the patient's condition.
NOS	Not otherwise specified This abbreviation is the equivalent of "unspecified" and is used only when the coder lacks the information necessary to code to a more specific four-digit subcategory.

Punctuation

[ ]	Brackets enclose synonyms, alternative terminology or explanatory phrases: **482.2** **Pneumonia due to Hemophilus influenzae [H. influenzae]**
( )	Parentheses enclose supplementary words, called nonessential modifiers, that may be present in the narrative of a disease or procedure without affecting the code to which it is assigned: **198.4** **Other parts of nervous system** Meninges (cerebral) (spinal)
:	Colons are used in the tabular list after an incomplete term that needs one or more of the modifiers that follow in order to make it assignable to a given category: **021.1** **Enteric tularemia** Tularemia: cryptogenic intestinal typhoidal

Punctuation — *continued*

}	Braces enclose a series of terms, each of which is modified by the statement appearing to the right of the brace: **560.2 Volvulus** Knotting Strangulation Torsion Twist } of intestine, bowel, or colon

Other Conventions

Boldface	Boldface type is used for all codes and titles in the tabular lists.
Italicized	Italicized type is used for all exclusion notes and to identify codes that should not be used for describing the principal diagnosis.

Instructional Notes

Includes:

This note further defines or clarifies the content of the chapter, subchapter, category, subcategory or subclassification:

> **461 Acute sinusitis**
>
> Includes: abscess, empyema, infection, inflammation, suppuration } acute, of sinus (accessory)(nasal)

Excludes:

Terms following the word "excludes" are not classified to the code under which it is found. The note also may indicate that another code more fully describes a diagnosis or procedure. Excludes notes are italicized and boxed:

> **461 Acute sinusitis**
>
> Includes: abscess, empyema, infection, inflammation, suppuration } acute, of sinus (accessory)(nasal)
>
> *Excludes: chronic or unspecified sinusitis (473.0-473.9)*

Use additional code:

This instruction signals the coder that an additional code should be used if the information is available to provide a more complete picture of that diagnosis or procedure:

> **330 Cerebral degenerations usually manifest in childhood**
>
> Use additional code to identify associated mental retardation

Code first underlying disease:
This note appears only in the Tabular List of Diseases. This instruction is used in those categories not intended for primary tabulation of disease. These codes, called manifestation codes, *may never* be used alone or indicated as the principal diagnosis (i.e., sequenced first). They must *always* be preceded by another code.

The code and its descriptor appear in italics in the tabular list. St. Anthony has identified the manifestation codes with the color orange as another signal to report the code correctly. (See page xv for color coding.) The instruction "code first underlying disease" is usually followed by the code or codes for the most common underlying disease (etiology). Report the code for the etiology or origin of the disease, and then report the italicized manifestation code in the next position:

> ***590.81*** ***Pyelitis or pyelonephritis in diseases classified elsewhere***
>
> *Code first underlying disease as:*
> tuberculosis (016.0)

Omit code:
"Omit code" is used to instruct the coder that no code is to be assigned. When this instruction is found in the Alphabetic Index to Diseases the medical term should not be coded as a diagnosis.

> **Metaplasia**
> cervix—*omit code*

When used in volume 3, "*omit code*" is meant to indicate procedures that do not merit separate code assignments such as minor procedures performed in conjunction with more extensive procedures or procedures that represent an operative approach.

> **Arthrotomy** 80.10
> as operative approach—*omit code*

ST. ANTHONY ADDITIONS TO THE OFFICIAL ICD-9-CM

Coding Guidelines

These guidelines were developed and approved for coding and reporting by the four cooperating parties, American Hospital Association, American Health Information Management Association, Health Care Financing Administration and the National Center for Health Statistics. The guidelines are printed in their entirety in the front of this book directly preceding the Alphabetic Index to Diseases.

St. Anthony's AHA *Coding Clinic* References

The four cooperating parties, the American Hospital Association (AHA), the American Health Information Management Association (AHIMA), the Health Care Financing Administration (HCFA) and the National Center for Health Statistics (NCHS), have designated the AHA's *Coding Clinic* as the official publication for coding guidelines. The AHA *Coding Clinic for ICD-9-CM* references in *St. Anthony's ICD-9-CM Code Book* are identified by the notation ➡ **AHA Coding Clinic:**, followed by the issue, year and page number.

In the example below, AHA *Coding Clinic for ICD-9-CM*, third quarter 1991, page 15, contains a discussion on code assignment for vitreous hemorrhage:

> **379.23 Vitreous hemorrhage**
>
> ➡ **AHA Coding Clinic:** 3Q, '91, 15

The table below explains the abbreviations in the *Coding Clinic* references:

J-F	January/February
M-A	March/April
M-J	May/June
J-A	July/August
S-O	September/October
N-D	November/December
1Q	First quarter
2Q	Second quarter
3Q	Third quarter
4Q	Fourth quarter

CC Exclusion List

A unique feature of *St. Anthony's ICD-9-CM Code Book* is the integration of the government's complication and comorbidity (CC) exclusion list with each affected code.

The government's CC exclusion list indicates secondary diagnosis codes that are excluded as CC conditions with certain principal diagnoses. This exclusion occurs because the cited conditions are inherent to the disease process of the principal diagnosis.

Below each code that is considered as complications and comorbidities (CC) diagnosis, St. Anthony has indicated the codes or code ranges of principal diagnosis with which the CC code cannot be used.

In the example below, code 254.1 is normally a CC condition. However, the CC exclusion (➡ **CC Excl:**) notation indicates that if a code from the listed code ranges is assigned as the principal diagnosis, the secondary diagnosis of 254.1 will not be recognized as a CC condition.

> **254.1** **Abscess of thymus**
>
> ➡ **CC Excl:** 254.0-254.1, 254.8-254.9, 259.8-259.9

Medicare Code Edits

Fiscal intermediaries use the Medicare code editor (MCE) to check the coding accuracy on claims. The Medicare code edits are listed below:

1. Invalid diagnosis or procedure code
2. E code as principal diagnosis
3. Duplicate of principal diagnosis (PDx) (as applied to a secondary diagnosis)

* 4. Age conflict
* 5. Sex conflict
* 6. Manifestation code as principal diagnosis
* 7. Nonspecific principal diagnosis
* 8. Questionable admission
*9. Unacceptable principal diagnosis
*10. Nonspecific OR procedure
*11. Noncovered procedure
*12. Open biopsy check
*13. Medicare as secondary payer (MSP alert)
*14. Bilateral procedure
15. Invalid age
16. Invalid sex
17. Invalid discharge status

Starred edits are identified by colors, symbols or footnotes as described below.

St. Anthony Footnotes

All St. Anthony footnotes are identified by a numeric superscript that appears to the upper left of the code:

> [4] **493.0** **Extrinsic asthma**

Footnote 4 indicates "CC Coding = 1." This means that when the fifth digit 1 (with status asthmaticus) is assigned to complete the code, the code is a CC condition. If the fifth digit 0 is assigned (without status asthmaticus), the code is not considered a CC condition.

The following list identifies the meaning of each footnote number and the classification in which the footnote appears:

Disease Tabular

1 CC Coding = 0	6 CC Coding = 4–9	11 CC Coding = 1–4
2 CC Coding = 0–2	7 CC Coding = 9	12 CC Coding = 1–8
3 CC Coding = 0–4	8 Nonspecific PDx = 0	13 CC Coding = 2 or 4
4 CC Coding = 1	9 Nonspecific PDx = 9	14 CC Coding = 0–5
5 CC Coding= 4	10 CC Coding = 0 or 2	15 CC Coding = 1–3

16 These V codes may be used as principal diagnosis on Medicare patients.

17 Rehabilitation codes acceptable as a principal diagnosis when accompanied by a secondary diagnosis reflecting the condition treated.

18 These codes, with the fourth digit of 0 or 1, may be used as a principal diagnosis for Medicare patients.

19 This V code, with the fourth digit of 1 or 2, is unacceptable as a principal diagnosis.

20 These V codes are acceptable as principal diagnosis when accompanied by a diagnosis of personal history of malignancy. These codes group to DRG 465.

20a Questionable admission = 0-1.

Procedure Tabular

21 Open biopsy.

22 Closed biopsy.

23 Valid OR procedure code if accompanied by one of the following codes: 37.80, 37.81, 37.82, 37.85, 37.86, 37.87.

24 Valid OR procedure code if accompanied by one of the following codes: 37.80, 37.83.

25 Valid OR procedure code if accompanied by one of the following codes: 37.80, 37.85, 37.86, 37.87.

26 Valid OR procedure code if accompanied by any one of the following codes: 37.80, 37.81, 37.82, 37.83, 37.85, 37.86, 37.87.

27 Valid OR procedure code if accompanied by any other pacemaker procedure except 37.72, 37.74.

28 Valid OR procedure code if accompanied by any other pacemaker procedure except 37.70, 37.71, 37.73, 37.74.

29 Nonspecific OR procedure = 0.

30 Noncovered procedure only if none of the following codes are present as either a principal or secondary diagnosis: 200.00-202.08, 202.80-202.98, 204.01, 205.01, 206.01, 207.01, 208.01.

31 Noncovered procedure only if none of the following codes are present as either a principal or secondary diagnosis: 204.00-208.91, 279.12, 279.2, 284.0-284.9

St. Anthony Symbols and Notations

[	The bracket to the left of a code or narrative signals a change. The date, in the lower outside corner of the page (e.g., October 1998), identifies when the change became effective. This symbol appears in both the indices and tabular lists.

Note: If a sequential group of codes includes both changes and deletions, only the corner brackets (⌐ or ∟) appear.

To alert the coder to the importance of accurate code assignment, St. Anthony has added a ✓5th symbol in the Alphabetic Index to Diseases to subcategory codes requiring a fifth digit to complete the code.

✓5th	Abdominalgia 789.0 ✓5th periodic 277.3

To alert the coder to the importance of accurate code assignment, St. Anthony has added a ✓5th symbol in the Tabular List of Diseases to subcategory codes requiring a fifth digit to complete the code.

✓5th	✓5th **789.0 Abdominal pain**

➡ **CC Excl:**	This indicates a complication/comorbidity exclusion reference. This reference appears only in the Tabular List of Diseases.
➡ **AHA Coding Clinic:**	This indicates an AHA *Coding Clinic for ICD-9-CM* reference. This reference appears in both the disease and procedure tabular lists.
YIELD **DRG**	This symbol indicates the diagnosis-related group (DRG) payment associated with the ICD-9-CM code. The condition must be thoroughly documented in the medical record to prevent inappropriate coding or upcoding.
✔ **St. Anthony's Clinical Coder:**	This indicates a reference to *St. Anthony's Clinical Coder.* The *Clinical Coder* is a cross-reference tool for abnormal EKGs, laboratory values, and possible pathogens. It also assists with the identification of commonly missed CC conditions, major complications and complex diagnoses, and includes a quick alphabetic reference for commonly prescribed drugs.

The age symbols address MCE 4 and are used to detect inconsistencies between the patient's age and diagnosis. They appear to the right of the code description in the Tabular List of Diseases:

A: 0	Newborn diagnosis only
A: 0-17	Pediatric diagnosis only
A: 12-55	Maternity diagnosis only
A: 15-124	Adult diagnosis only

In the example that follows, the age reference indicates the code can be assigned only for pediatric patients, age 0-17, as indicated by the MCE:

259.1 **Precocious sexual development and puberty, not elsewhere classified** **A: 0-17**
Sexual precocity:
NOS
constitutional
cryptogenic
idiopathic

The sex symbols address Medicare code editor (MCE) sex edits and are used to detect inconsistencies between the patient's sex and diagnosis or procedure.

♂	**Male diagnosis /procedure only** This symbol appears to the right of the code description. This reference appears in the disease and procedure tabular lists.
♀	**Female diagnosis /procedure only** This symbol appears to the right of the code description. This reference appears in the disease and procedure tabular lists.

In the example below, the sex notation indicates that the codes for this category can be assigned only for a male diagnosis, as indicated by the MCE.

222	**Benign neoplasm of male genital organs**	♂

Color Coding

For a quick reference to the color codes and their meaning, refer to the color/symbol key on the inside front cover of the book.

To alert the coder to important reimbursement issues affected by the code assignment, St. Anthony has added color bars over the code description, and in one instance (the color gray) over the code itself. The colors represent Medicare code edits as well as other reimbursement issues.

Color coding appears in both tabular lists. Some codes carry more than one color. Please note that the same color may appear in the disease and procedure tabular lists, but with different meanings.

For example, the color gray identifies a CC condition in the disease tabular list but a valid OR procedure in the procedure tabular list. Red signals "noncovered operating room procedure" in the procedure tabular list, or "inappropriate/unacceptable principal diagnosis" or "questionable admission" in the disease tabular list. Be sure to know the tabular list to which you are referring when consulting the color/symbol key.

Example:
Locate the following subcategory code in the disease tabular list:

800.0	**Closed without mention of intracranial injury**

Note that the subcategory code itself, 800.0, is shaded in gray. Gray in the disease tabular list alerts the coder to a CC condition.

The description for subcategory code 800.0 is shaded lavender, which, in the disease tabular list, signals a trauma diagnosis that may indicate Medicare as secondary payer.

Example:
Locate the following code in the procedure tabular list:

81.51	**Total hip replacement**

In the procedure tabular list, the gray over the code represents a valid OR procedure that may trigger a change in the DRG assignment. The lavender over the code description represents a unilateral procedure, which may have optimization potential as a bilateral procedure.

OFFICIAL ICD-9-CM GUIDELINES FOR CODING AND REPORTING

The Public Health Service and the Health Care Financing Administration of the U.S. Department of Health and Human Services present the following guidelines for coding and reporting using the International Classification of Diseases, 9th Revision, Clinical Modification (ICD-9-CM). These guidelines should be used as a companion document to the official versions of the ICD-9-CM.

These guidelines for coding and reporting have been developed and approved by the cooperating parties for ICD-9-CM: American Hospital Association, American Health Information Management Association, Health Care Financing Administration and the National Center for Health Statistics. These guidelines previously appeared in the Coding Clinic for ICD-9-CM, published by the American Hospital Association.

These guidelines have been developed to assist the user in coding and reporting in situations where the ICD-9-CM manual does not provide direction. Coding and sequencing instructions in the three ICD-9-CM manuals take precedence over any guidelines.

These guidelines are not exhaustive. The cooperating parties are continuing to conduct review of these guidelines and develop new guidelines as needed. Users of the ICD-9-CM should be aware that only guidelines approved by the cooperating parties are official. Revision of these guidelines and new guidelines will be published by the U.S. Department of Health and Human Services when they are approved by the cooperating parties.

OUTPATIENT SERVICES (Hospital-Based and Physician Office)

TABLE OF CONTENTS

INPATIENT SERVICES

TABLE OF CONTENTS

Official Guidelines for Coding and Reporting Outpatient Services (Hospital-Based and Physician Office)

Introduction

These revised coding guidelines for outpatient diagnoses have been approved for use by hospitals/physicians in coding and reporting hospital-based outpatient services and physician office visits.

The terms encounter and visit are often used interchangeably in describing outpatient service contacts and, therefore, appear together in these guidelines without distinguishing one from the other.

Coding guidelines for outpatient and physician reporting of diagnoses will vary in a number of instances from those for inpatient diagnoses, recognizing that:

The Uniform Hospital Discharge Data Set (UHDDS) definition of principal diagnosis applies only to inpatients in acute, short-term, general hospitals.

Coding guidelines for inconclusive diagnoses (probable, suspected, rule out, etc.) were developed for inpatient reporting and do not apply to outpatients.

Diagnoses often are not established at the time of the initial encounter/visit. It may take two or more visits before the diagnosis is confirmed.

The most critical rule involves beginning the search for the correct code assignment through the Alphabetic Index. Never begin searching initially in the Tabular List as this will lead to coding errors.

BASIC CODING GUIDELINES FOR OUTPATIENT SERVICES

A. Code Range

The appropriate code or codes from 001.0 through V82.9 must be used to identify diagnoses, symptoms, conditions, problems, complaints, or other reason(s) for the encounter/visit.

B. Accurate Reporting

For accurate reporting of ICD-9-CM diagnosis codes, the documentation should describe the patient's condition, using terminology which includes specific diagnoses as well as symptoms, problems, or reasons for the encounter. There are ICD-9-CM codes to describe all of these.

C. Code Selection

The selection of codes 001.0 through 999.9 will frequently be used to describe the reason for the encounter. These codes are from the section of ICD-9-CM for the classification of diseases and injuries (e.g. infectious and parasitic diseases; neoplasms; symptoms, signs, and ill-defined conditions, etc.).

D. Symptoms, Signs and Ill-defined Conditions

Codes that describe symptoms and signs, as opposed to diagnoses, are acceptable for reporting purposes when an established diagnosis has not been diagnosed (confirmed) by the physician. Chapter 16 of ICD-9-CM, Symptoms, Signs, and Ill-defined conditions (codes 780.0 - 799.9) contain many, but not all codes for symptoms.

E. Circumstances other than Disease or Injury

ICD-9-CM provides codes to deal with encounters for circumstances other than a disease or injury. The Supplementary Classification of factors Influencing Health Status and Contact with Health Services (V01.0- V82.9) is provided to deal with occasions when circumstances other than a disease or injury are recorded as diagnosis or problems. The V codes should be used for encounters of this type. For example, the correct code for a cancer patient who is seen solely for radiotherapy is V58.0, radiotherapy session.

Example:
Discharge diagnosis: Open-angle glaucoma
Reason for visit code: 365.10

Discharge diagnosis: Follow-up examination after surgery
Reason for visit code: V67.0

F. Code Specificity

ICD-9-CM is composed of codes with either 3, 4, or 5 digits. Codes with 3 digits are included in ICD-9-CM as the heading of a category of codes that may be further subdivided by the use of fourth and/or fifth digits which provide greater specificity. A code is invalid if it has not been coded to the full number of digits required for that code.

- Assign three-digit codes only if there are no four-digit codes within that code category.
- Assign four-digit codes only if there is no fifth-digit subclassification for that subcategory.
- Assign the fifth-digit subclassification code for those subcategories where it exists.

Example:
Diagnosis: Acute tonsillitis
Correct code: 463

Diagnosis: Benign neoplasm of colon
Incorrect code: 211
Correct code: 211.3

G. Code Sequence

List first the ICD-9-CM code for the diagnosis, condition, problem, or other reason for encounter/visit shown in the medical record to be chiefly responsible for the services provided. List additional codes that describe any coexisting conditions.

H. Uncertain Diagnosis

Do not code diagnoses documented as "probable", "suspected," "questionable," "rule out," or working diagnosis. Rather, code the condition(s) to the highest degree of certainty for that encounter/visit, such as symptoms, signs, abnormal test results, or other reason for the visit.

Coders should be aware that this is contrary to the coding practices used by health information management departments for coding the diagnoses of hospital inpatients. For inpatient coding, all discharge diagnoses listed as "probable," "suspected," "questionable" or "rule out" would be coded as if the condition existed. Further, coding symptoms for inpatients is generally unacceptable, particularly when there is an established diagnosis. A requirement that conditions listed as "probable," "suspected," "questionable" or "rule out" be coded in the outpatient setting as if the condition existed would lead to significant over-reporting of conditions. Therefore codes for symptoms and signs are appropriate and acceptable for hospital outpatient reporting.

Example:
Reason for visit: Chest pain, code 786.50

Discharge diagnosis: Rule out angina, code 413.9

Correct code: 786.50

Comment: Do not code angina as if it were established; code the reason for the visit.

I. Chronic Disease

Chronic diseases treated on an ongoing basis may be coded and reported as many times as the patient receives treatment and care for the condition(s).

Example:

History of illness: Patient is seen for monthly lumbar epidural block with steroid injection.

Discharge diagnosis: Chronic low back pain, code 724.2

Comment: Report code 724.2, low back pain, for each visit during which the patient receives lumbar-block treatment, regardless of the number or frequency of visits.

J. Coexisting Conditions

Code all documented conditions that coexist at the time of the encounter/visit, and require or affect patient care treatment or management. Do not code conditions that were previously treated and no longer exist. However, history codes (V10- V19) may be used as secondary codes if the historical condition or family history has an impact on current care or influences treatment.

Coders are advised to exercise care in identifying (a) conditions presently existing, (b) conditions no longer existing, (c) residuals (late effects) of conditions no longer existing, and (d) certain postoperative status conditions that require consideration in managing patient care and that warrant coding. Some physicians add to the list of conditions currently being treated any previous surgery or conditions that no longer exist to provide easy reference of the patient's history for recapitulation in the ongoing care of the patient. These conditions should not be coded unless they require or affect patient care treatment or management.

Example:

Chief complaint: Uncontrolled diabetes mellitus, 250.02

Review of systems: Patient has congestive heart failure (428.0) and is curently on Lasix.

Medical history: Patient is status three months post right inguinal herniorrherapy for incarcerated inguinal hernia.

Comment: First code "uncontrolled diabetes mellitus" as the reason for the visit, followed by "congestive heart failure" as a coexisting condition. Do not code the incarcerated inguinal hernia; it was treated successfully.

Code sequence: 250.02, 428.0

K. Ancillary Diagnostic Services

For patients receiving diagnostic services only during an encounter/visit, sequence first the diagnosis, condition, problem, or other reason for encounter/visit shown in the medical record to be chiefly responsible for the outpatient services provided during the encounter/visit. Codes for other diagnoses (e.g., chronic conditions) may be sequenced as additional diagnoses.

Example:

Chief complaint: Hematuria, code 599.7

Laboratory studies: Intravenous pyelogram, code V72.5

History of illness: Patient was referred to hospital outpatient clinic for intravenous pyelogram only. Will provide patient's physician with the results.

Code sequence: 599.7

L. Ancillary Therapeutic Services

For patients receiving therapeutic services only during an encounter/visit, sequence first the diagnosis, condition, problem, or other reason for encounter/visit shown in the medical record to be chiefly responsible for the outpatient services provided during the encounter/visit. Codes for other diagnoses (e.g., chronic conditions) may be sequenced as additional diagnoses.

Example:

Chief complaint: Chronic renal failure, code 585

Procedure performed: Hemodialysis, code V56.0

History of illness: Patient is being seen for hemodialysis treatment.

Code sequence: 585

NOTE: The appropriate V code can be listed first for patients receiving the following (the diagnosis or problem for which the service is being performed should be listed second):

- chemotherapy
- radiation therapy
- rehabilitation.

Example:
Chief complaint: Trigone bladder cancer, code 188.0
Procedure performed: Chemotherapy infusion, code V58.1
History of illness: Patient is being seen for second course of five chemotherapy infusions.
Code sequence: V58.1, 188.0

N. Preoperative Evaluations

For patient's receiving preoperative evaluations only, sequence a code from category V72.8, Other specified examinations, to describe the pre-op consultations. Assign a code for the condition to describe the reason for the surgery as an additional diagnosis. Code also any findings related to the pre-op evaluation.

Example:
Chief complaint: Rhegmatogenous retinal detachment in left eye, code 361.00
Procedure performed: Preoperative cardiovascular examination, V72.81
History of illness: Patient is being seen for preoperative cardiovascular examination, due to history of myocardial infarction 1 year ago. Patient is scheduled for a repair of his retinal detachment next week.
Code sequence: V72.81, 361.00

O. Ambulatory Surgery

For ambulatory surgery, code the diagnosis for which the surgery was performed. If the postoperative diagnosis is known to be different from the preoperative diagnosis at the time the diagnosis is confirmed, select the postoperative diagnosis for coding, since it is the most definitive.

Example:
Preoperative diagnosis: Breast mass, code 611.72
Postoperative diagnosis: Fibrocystic breast disease, code 610.3
Comment: Code 610.3 as the reason for the visit because it is the postoperative diagnosis.

Official Guidelines for Coding and Reporting Inpatient Services

1. GENERAL INPATIENT CODING GUIDELINES

1.1. Use of Both Alphabetic Index and Tabular List

A. Use both the Alphabetic Index and the Tabular List when locating and assigning a code. Reliance on only the Alphabetic Index or the Tabular List leads to errors in code assignments and less specificity in code selection.

B. Locate each term in the Alphabetic Index and verify the code selected in the Tabular List. Read and be guided by instructional notations that appear in both the Alphabetic Index and the Tabular List.

1.2. Level of Specificity in Coding

Diagnostic and procedure codes are to be used at their highest level of specificity:

- Assign three-digit codes only if there are no four-digit codes within that code category.
- Assign four-digit codes only if there is no fifth-digit subclassification for that category.
- Assign the fifth-digit subclassification code for those categories where it exists.

1.3. Other (NEC) and Unspecified (NOS) Code Titles

Codes labeled "other specified" (NEC—not elsewhere classified) or "unspecified" (NOS—not otherwise specified) are used only when neither the diagnostic statement nor a thorough review of the medical record provides adequate information to permit assignment of a more specific code.

- Use the code assignment for "other" or NEC when the information at hand specifies a condition but no separate code for that condition is provided.
- Use "unspecified" (NOS) when the information at hand does not permit either a more specific or "other" code assignment.
- When the Alphabetic Index assigns a code to a category labeled "other (NEC)" or to a category labeled "unspecified (NOS)", refer to the Tabular List and review the titles and inclusion terms in the subdivisions under that particular three-digit category (or subdivision under the

four-digit code) to determine if the information at hand can be appropriately assigned to a more specific code.

1.4. Acute and Chronic Conditions

If the same condition is described as both acute (subacute) and chronic and separate subentries exist in the Alphabetic Index at the same indentation level, code both and sequence the acute (subacute) code first.

1.5. Combination Code

A single code used to classify two diagnoses or a diagnosis with an associated secondary process (manifestation) or an associated complication is called a combination code. Combination codes are identified by referring to subterm entries in the Alphabetic Index and by reading the inclusion and exclusion notes in the Tabular List.

Assign only the combination code when that code fully identifies the diagnostic conditions involved or when the Alphabetic Index so directs. Multiple coding should not be used when the classification provides a combination code that clearly identifies all of the elements documented in the diagnosis. When the combination code lacks necessary specificity in describing the manifestation or complication, an additional code may be used as a secondary code.

1.6. Multiple Coding of Diagnoses

Multiple coding is required for certain conditions not subject to the rules for combination codes.

Instruction for conditions that require multiple coding appear in the Alphabetic Index and the Tabular List.

A. Alphabetic Index: Codes for both etiology and manifestation of a disease appear following the subentry term, with the second code in brackets. Assign both codes in the same sequence in which they appear in the Alphabetic Index.

B. Tabular List: Instructional terms, such as "Code first...," "Use additional code for any...," and "Note...," indicate when to use more than one code.

- "Code first underlying disease" - Assign the codes for both the manifestation and underlying cause. The codes for manifestations cannot be used (designated) as principal diagnosis.
- "Use additional code, to identify manifestation, as ..." - Assign also the code that identifies the manifestation, such as, but not limited to, the examples listed. The codes for manifestations cannot be used (designated) as principal diagnosis.

C. Apply multiple coding instructions throughout the classification where appropriate, whether or not multiple coding directions appear in the Alphabetic Index or the Tabular List. Avoid indiscriminate multiple coding or irrelevant information, such as symptoms or signs characteristic of the diagnosis.

1.7. Late Effect

A late effect is the residual effect (condition produced) after the acute phase of an illness or injury has terminated. There is no time limit on when a late effect code can be used. The residual may be apparent early, such as in cerebrovascular accident cases, or it may occur months or years later, such as that due to a previous injury.

Coding of late effects requires two codes:

- The residual condition or nature of the late effect
- The cause of the late effect

The residual condition or nature of the late effect is sequenced first, followed by the cause of the late effect, except in those few instances where the code for late effect is followed by a manifestation code identified in the Tabular List and title or the late effect code has been expanded (at the fourth and fifth-digit levels) to include the manifestation(s).

The code for the acute phase of an illness or injury that led to the late effect is never used with a code for the cause of the late effect.

A. Late Effects of Cerebrovascular Disease

Category 438 is used to indicate conditions classifiable to categories 430-437 as the causes of late effects (neurologic deficits), themselves classified elsewhere. These "late effects" include neurologic deficits that persist after initial onset of conditions classifiable to 430-437. The neurologic deficits caused by cerebrovascular disease may be present from the onset or may arise at any time after the onset of the condition classifiable to 430–437.

- Codes from category 438 may be assigned on a health care record with codes from 430–437, if the patient has a current CVA and deficits from an old CVA.

- Assign code V12.59 (and not a code from category 438) as an additional code for history of cerebrovascular disease when no neurologic deficits are present.

1.8. Uncertain Diagnosis

If the diagnosis documented at the time of discharge is qualified as "probable", "suspected", "likely", "questionable", "possible", or "still to be ruled out", code the condition as if it existed or was established. The bases for this guidelines are the diagnostic workup, arrangements for further workup or observation, and initial therapeutic approach that correspond most closely with the established diagnosis.

1.9. Impending or Threatened Condition

Code any condition described at the time of discharge as "impending" or "threatened" as follows:

If it did occur, code as confirmed diagnosis.

If it did not occur, reference the Alphabetic Index to determine if the condition has a subentry term for "impending" or "threatened" and also reference main term entries for Impending and for Threatened.

- If the subterms are listed, assign the given code.
- If the subterms are not listed, code the existing forerunner condition(s) and not the condition described as impending or threatened.

2. SELECTION OF PRINCIPAL DIAGNOSIS

The circumstances of inpatient admission always govern the selection of principal diagnosis. The principal diagnosis is defined in the Uniform Hospital Discharge Data Set (UHDDS) as "that condition established after study to be chiefly responsible for occasioning the admission of the patient to the hospital for care".

In determining principal diagnosis the coding directives in the ICD-9-CM manuals, Volumes I, II, and III, take precedence over all other guidelines.

The importance of consistent, complete documentation in the medical record cannot be overemphasized. Without such documentation the application of all coding guidelines is a difficult, if not impossible, task.

2.1. Codes for symptoms, signs, and ill-defined conditions

Codes for symptoms, signs, and ill-defined conditions from Chapter 16 are not to be used as principal diagnosis when a related definitive diagnosis has been established.

2.2. Codes in brackets

Codes in brackets in the Alphabetic Index can never be sequenced as principal diagnosis. Coding directives require that the codes in brackets be sequenced in the order as they appear in the Alphabetic Index.

2.3. Acute and chronic conditions

If the same condition is described as both acute (subacute) and chronic and separate subentries exist in the Alphabetic Index at the same indentation level, code both and sequence the acute (subacute) code first.

2.4. Two or more interrelated conditions, each potentially meeting the definition for principal diagnosis

When there are two or more interrelated conditions (such as diseases in the same ICD-9-CM chapter or manifestations characteristically associated with a certain disease) potentially meeting the definition of principal diagnosis, either condition may be sequenced first, unless the circumstances of the admission, the therapy provided, the Tabular List, or the Alphabetic Index indicate otherwise.

2.5. Two or more diagnoses that equally meet the definition for principal diagnosis

In the unusual instance when two or more diagnoses equally meet the criteria for principal diagnosis as determined by the circumstances of admission, diagnostic workup and/or therapy provided, and the Alphabetic Index, Tabular List, or another coding guidelines does not provide sequencing direction, any one of the diagnoses may be sequenced first.

2.6. Two or more comparative or contrasting conditions

In those rare instances when two or more contrasting or comparative diagnoses are documented as "either/or" (or similar terminology), they are coded as if the diagnoses were confirmed and the diagnoses are sequenced according to the circumstances of the admission. If no further determination can be made as to which diagnosis should be principal, either diagnosis may be sequenced first.

2.7. A symptom(s) followed by contrasting/comparative diagnoses

When a symptom(s) is followed by contrasting/comparative diagnoses, the symptom code is sequenced first. All the contrasting/comparative diagnoses should be coded as suspected conditions.

2.8. Codes from the V71.0-V71.9 series, Observation and evaluation for suspected conditions

Codes from the V71.0-V71.9 series are assigned as principal diagnoses for encounters or admissions to evaluate the patient's condition when there is some evidence to suggest the existence of an abnormal condition or following an accident or other incident that ordinarily results in a health problem, and where no supporting evidence for the suspected condition is found and no treatment is currently required. The fact that the patient may be scheduled for continuing observation in the office/clinic setting following discharge does not limit the use of this category.

2.9. Original treatment plan not carried out

Sequence as the principal diagnosis the condition which after study occasioned the admission to the hospital, even though treatment may not have been carried out due to unforeseen circumstances.

2.10. Residual condition or nature of late effect

The residual condition or nature of the late effect is sequenced first, followed by the late effect code for the cause of the residual condition, except in a few instances where the Alphabetic Index or Tabular List directs otherwise.

2.11. Multiple burns

Sequence first the code that reflects the highest degree of burn when more than one burn is present. (See also Burns guideline 8.3)

2.12. Multiple injuries

When multiple injuries exist, the code for the most severe injury as determined by the attending physician is sequenced first.

2.13. Neoplasms

A. If the treatment is directed at the malignancy, designate the malignancy as the principal diagnosis, except when the purpose of the encounter or hospital admission is for radiotherapy session(s), V58.0, or for chemotherapy session(s), V58.1, in which instance the malignancy is coded and sequenced second.

B. When a patient is admitted for the purpose of radiotherapy or chemotherapy and develops complications such as uncontrolled nausea and vomiting or dehydration, the principal diagnosis is Encounter for radiotherapy, V58.0, or Encounter for chemotherapy, V58.1.

C. When an episode of inpatient care involves surgical removal of a primary site or secondary site malignancy followed by adjunct chemotherapy or radiotherapy, code the malignancy as the principal diagnosis, using codes in the 140-198 series or where appropriate in the 200-203 series.

D. When the reason for admission is to determine the extent of the malignancy, or for a procedure such as paracentesis or thoracentesis, the primary malignancy or appropriate metastatic site is designated as the principal diagnosis, even though chemotherapy or radiotherapy is administered.

E. When the primary malignancy has been previously excised or eradicated from its site and there is not adjunct treatment directed to that site and no evidence of any remaining malignancy at the primary site, use the appropriate code from the V10 series to indicate the former site of primary malignancy. Any mention of extension, invasion, or metastasis to a nearby structure or organ or to a distant site is coded as a secondary malignant neoplasm to that site and may be the principal diagnosis in the absence of the primary site.

F. When a patient is admitted because of a primary neoplasm with metastasis and treatment is directed toward the secondary site only, the secondary neoplasm is designated as the principal diagnosis even though the primary malignancy is still present.

G. Symptoms, signs, and ill-defined conditions listed in Chapter 16 characteristic of, or associated with, an existing primary or secondary site malignancy cannot be used to replace the malignancy as principal diagnosis, regardless of the number of admissions or encounters for treatment and care of the neoplasm.

H. Coding and sequencing of complications associated with the malignant neoplasm or with the therapy thereof are subject to the following guidelines:

- When admission is for management of an anemia associated with the malignancy, and the treatment is only for anemia, the anemia is designated at the principal diagnosis and is followed by the appropriate code(s) for the malignancy.
- When the admission is for management of an anemia associated with chemotherapy or radiotherapy and the only treatment is for the anemia, the anemia is designated as the principal diagnosis followed by the appropriate code(s) for the malignancy.
- When the admission is for management of dehydration due to the malignancy or the therapy, or a combination of both, and only the dehydration is being treated (intravenous rehydration), the dehydration is designated as the principal diagnosis, followed by the code(s) for the malignancy.
- When the admission is for treatment of a complication resulting from a surgical procedure performed for the treatment of an intestinal malignancy, designate the complication as the principal diagnosis if treatment is directed at resolving the complication.

2.14. Poisoning

When coding a poisoning or reaction to the improper use of a medication (e.g., wrong dose, wrong substance, wrong route of administration) the poisoning code is sequenced first, followed by a code for the manifestation. If there is also a diagnosis of drug abuse or dependence to the substance, the abuse or dependence is coded as an additional code.

2.15. Complications of surgery and other medical care

When the admission is for treatment of a complication resulting from surgery or other medical care, the complication code is sequenced as the principal diagnosis. If the complication is classified to the 996-999 series, an additional code for the specific complication may be assigned.

2.16. Complication of pregnancy

When a patient is admitted because of a condition that is either a complication pregnancy or that is complicating the pregnancy, the code for the obstetric complication is the principal diagnosis. An additional code may be assigned as needed to provide specificity.

3. REPORTING OTHER (ADDITIONAL) DIAGNOSES

A joint effort between the attending physician and coder is essential to achieve complete and accurate documentation, code assignment, and reporting of diagnoses and procedures.

These guidelines have been developed and approved by the Cooperating Parties to assure both the physician and the coder in identifying those diagnoses that are to be reported in addition to the principal diagnosis. Hospitals may record other diagnoses as needed for internal data use.

The UHDDS definitions are used by acute care short-term hospitals to report inpatient data elements in a standardized manner. These data elements and their definitions can be found in the July 31, 1985, Federal Register (Vol. 50, No, 147), pp. 31038-40.

The UHDDS item #11-b defines Other Diagnoses as "all conditions that coexist at the time of admission, that develop subsequently, or that affect the treatment received and/or the length of stay. Diagnoses that relate to an earlier episode which have no bearing on the current hospital stay are to be excluded".

General Rule

For reporting purposes the definition for "other diagnoses" is interpreted as additional conditions that affect patient care in terms of requiring:

- clinical evaluation; or
- therapeutic treatment; or
- diagnostic procedures; or
- extended length of hospital stay; or
- increased nursing care and/or monitoring.

The following guidelines are to be applied in designating "other diagnoses" when neither the Alphabetic Index nor the Tabular List in ICD-9-CM provide direction.

The listing of the diagnoses on the attestation statement is the responsibility of the attending physician.

3.1. Previous conditions

If the physician has included a diagnosis in the final diagnostic statement, such as the discharge summary or the face sheet, it should ordinarily be coded. Some physicians include in the diagnostic statement resolved conditions or diagnoses and status-post procedures from previous admission that have no bearing on the current stay. Such conditions are not to be reported and are coded only if required by hospital policy.

However, history codes (V10-V19) may be used as secondary codes if the historical condition or family history has an impact on current care or influences treatment.

3.2. Diagnoses not listed in the final diagnostic statement

When the physician has documented what appears to be a current diagnosis in the body of the record, but has not included the diagnosis in the final diagnostic statement, the physician should be asked whether the diagnosis should be added.

3.3. Conditions that are an integral part of a disease process

Conditions that are integral to the disease process should not be assigned as additional codes.

3.4. Conditions that are not an integral part of a disease process

Additional conditions that may not be associated routinely with a disease process should be coded when present.

3.5. Abnormal findings

Abnormal findings (laboratory, x-ray, pathologic, and other diagnostic results) are not coded and reported unless the physician indicates their clinical significance. If the findings are outside the normal range and the physician has ordered other tests to evaluate the condition or prescribed treatment, it is appropriate to ask the physician whether the diagnosis should be added.

4. HYPERTENSION

4.1. Hypertension, Essential, or NOS

Assign hypertension (arterial) (essential) (primary) (systemic) (NOS) to category code 401 with the appropriate fourth digit to indicate malignant (.0), benign (.1), or unspecified (.9). Do not use either .0 malignant or .1 benign unless medical record documentation supports such a designation.

4.2. Hypertension with Heart Disease

Certain heart conditions (425.8, 428, 429.0-429.3, 429.8, 429.9) are assigned to a code from category 402 when a causal relationship is stated (due to hypertension) or implied (hypertensive). Use only the code from category 402.

The same heart conditions (425.8, 428, 429.0-429.3, 429.8, 429.9) with hypertension, but without a stated casual relationship, are coded separately. Sequence according to the circumstances of the admission.

4.3. Hypertensive Renal Disease with Chronic Renal Failure

Assign codes from category 403, Hypertensive renal disease, when conditions classified to categories 585-587 are present. Unlike hypertension with heart disease, ICD-9-CM presumes a cause-and-effect relationship and classifies renal failure with hypertension as hypertensive renal disease.

4.4. Hypertensive Heart and Renal Disease

Assign codes from combination category 404, Hypertensive heart and renal disease, when both hypertensive renal disease and hypertensive heart disease are stated in the diagnosis. Assume a relationship between the hypertension and the renal disease, whether or not the condition is so designated.

4.5. Hypertensive Cerebrovascular Disease.

First assign codes from 430-438, Cerebrovascular disease, then the appropriate hypertension code from categories 401-405.

4.6. Hypertensive Retinopathy

Two codes are necessary to identify the condition. First assign the code from subcategory 362.11, Hypertensive retinopathy, then the appropriate code from categories 401-405 to indicate the type of hypertension.

4.7. Hypertension, Secondary

Two codes are required: one to identify the underlying condition and one from category 405 to identify the hypertension. Sequencing of codes is determined by the reason for admission to the hospital.

4.8. Hypertension, Transient

Assign code 796.2, Elevated blood pressure reading without diagnosis of hypertension, unless patient has an established diagnosis of hypertension. Assign code 642.3x for transient hypertension of pregnancy.

4.9. Hypertension, Controlled

Assign appropriate code from categories 401-405. This diagnostic statement usually refers to an existing state of hypertension under control by therapy.

4.10. Hypertension, Uncontrolled

Uncontrolled hypertension may refer to untreated hypertension or hypertension not responding to current therapeutic regimen. In either case. assign the appropriate code from categories 401-405 to designate the stage and type of hypertension. Code to the type of hypertension.

4.11. Elevated Blood Pressure

For a statement of elevated blood pressure without further specificity, assign code 796.2, Elevated blood pressure reading without diagnosis of hypertension, rather than a code from category 401.

5. OBSTETRICS

Introduction

These guidelines have been developed and approved by the Cooperating Parties in conjunction with the Editorial Advisory Board of Coding Clinic and the American College of Obstetricians and Gynecologists, to assist the coder in coding and reporting obstetric cases. Where feasible, previously published advice has been incorporated. Some advice in these new guidelines may supersede previous advice. The guidelines are provided for reporting purposes. Health care facilities may record additional diagnoses as needed for internal data needs.

5.1. General Rules

A. Obstetric cases require codes from chapter 11, codes in the range 630-677, Complications of Pregnancy, Childbirth, and the Puerperium. Should the physician document that the pregnancy is incidental to the encounter then code V22.2 should be used in place of any chapter 11 codes. It is the physician's responsibility to state that the condition being treated is not affecting the pregnancy.

B. Chapter 11 codes have sequencing priority over codes from other chapters. Additional codes from other chapters may be used in conjunction with chapter 11 codes to further specify conditions.

C. Chapter 11 codes are to be used only on the maternal record, never on the record of the newborn.

D. An outcome of delivery code, V27.0-V27.9, should be included on every maternal record when a delivery has occurred. These codes are not to be used on subsequent records or on the newborn record.

5.2. Selection of Principal Diagnosis

A. The circumstances of the encounter govern the selection of the principal diagnosis.

B. In episodes when no delivery occurs the principal diagnosis should correspond to the principal complication of the pregnancy which necessitated the encounter. Should more than one complication exist, all of which are treated or monitored, any of the complications codes may be sequenced first.

C. When a delivery occurs the principal diagnosis should correspond to the main circumstances or complication of the delivery. In cases of cesarean deliveries, the principal diagnosis should correspond to the reason the cesarean was performed, unless the reason for admission was unrelated to the condition resulting in the cesarean delivery.

D. For routine prenatal visits when no complications are present codes V22.0, Supervision of normal first pregnancy, and V22.1, Supervision of other normal pregnancy, should be used as principal diagnoses. These codes should not be used in conjunction with chapter 11 codes.

E. For prenatal outpatient visits for patients with high-risk pregnancies, a code from category V23, Supervision of high-risk pregnancy, should be used as the principal diagnosis. Secondary chapter 11 codes may be used in conjunction with these codes if appropriate. A thorough review of any pertinent excludes note is necessary to be certain that these V codes are being used properly.

5.3. Chapter 11 Fifth-digits

A. Categories 640-648, 651-676 have required fifth-digits which indicate whether the encounter is antepartum, postpartum and whether a delivery has also occurred.

B. The fifth-digits which are appropriate for each code number are listed in brackets under each code. The fifth-digits on each code should all be consistent with each other. That is, should a delivery occur all of the fifth-digits should indicate the delivery.

5.4. Fetal Conditions Affecting the Management of the Mother.

Codes from category 655, Known or suspected fetal abnormality affecting management of the mother, and category 656, Other fetal and placental problems affecting the management of the mother, are assigned only when the fetal condition is actually responsible for modifying the management of the mother, i.e., by requiring diagnostic studies, additional observation, special care, or termination of pregnancy. The fact that the fetal condition exists does not justify assigning a code from this series to the mother's record.

5.5. Normal Delivery, 650

A. Code 650 is for use in cases when a woman is admitted for a full-term normal delivery and delivers a single, healthy infant without any complications antepartum, during the delivery, or postpartum during the delivery episode.

B. 650 may be used if the patient had a complications at some point during her pregnancy but the complication is not present at the time of the admission for delivery.

C. Code 650 is always a principal diagnosis. It is not to be used if any other code from chapter 11 is needed to describe a current complication of the antenatal, delivery, or perinatal period. Additional codes from other chapters may be used with code 650 if they are not related to or are in any way complicating the pregnancy.

D. V27.0, Single liveborn, is the only outcome of delivery code appropriate for use with 650.

5.6. Procedure Codes

A. In cases of cesarean delivery, the selection of the principal diagnosis should correspond to the reason the cesarean delivery was performed unless the reason for admission was unrelated to the condition resulting in the cesarean delivery.

B. A delivery procedure code should not be used for a woman who has delivered prior to admission to the hospital. Any postpartum repairs should be coded.

5.7. The Postpartum Period

A. The postpartum period begins immediately after delivery and continues for 6 weeks following delivery.

B. A postpartum complication is any complication occurring within the 6 week period.

C. Chapter 11 codes may also be used to describe pregnancy-related complications after the 6 week period should the physician document that a condition is pregnancy related.

D. Postpartum complications that occur during the same admission as the delivery are identified with a fifth digit of "2". Subsequent admissions for postpartum complications should identified with a fifth digit of "4".

E. When the mother delivers outside the hospital prior to admission and is admitted for routine postpartum care and no complications are noted, code V24.0, Postpartum care and examination immediately after delivery, should be assigned as the principal diagnosis.

5.8. Abortions

A. Fifth-digits are required for abortion categories 634-637. Fifth-digit 1, incomplete, indicates that all of the products of conception have not been expelled from the uterus. Fifth-digit 2, complete, indicates that all products of conception have been expelled from the uterus prior to the episode of care.

B. A code from categories 640-648 and 651-657 may be used as additional codes with an abortion code to indicate the complication leading to the abortion.

Fifth digit 3 is assigned with codes from these categories when used with an abortion code because the other fifth digits will not apply. Codes from the 660-669 series are not to be used for complications of abortion.

C. Code 639 is to be used for all complications following abortion. Code 639 cannot be assigned with codes from categories 634-638.

D. Abortion with Liveborn Fetus. When an attempted termination of pregnancy results in a liveborn fetus assign code 644.21, Early onset of delivery, with an appropriate code from category V27, Outcome of Delivery. The procedure code for the attempted termination of pregnancy should also be assigned.

E. Retained Products of Conception following an abortion. Subsequent admissions for retained products of conception following a spontaneous or legally induced abortion are assigned the appropriate code from category 634, Spontaneous abortion, or legally induced abortion, with a fifth digit of "1" (incomplete). This advice is appropriate even when the patient was discharged previously with a discharge diagnosis of complete abortion.

5.9. Code 677, Late effect of complication of pregnancy, childbirth, and the puerperium

A. Code 677, Late effect of complication of pregnancy, childbirth, and the puerperium is for use in those cases when an initial complication of a pregnancy develops a sequelae requiring care or treatment at a future date.

B. This code may be used at any time after the initial postpartum period.

C. This code, like all late effect codes, is to be sequenced following the code describing the sequelae of the complication.

6. NEWBORN GUIDELINES

Definition

The newborn period is defined as beginning at birth and lasting through the 28th day following birth.

The following guidelines are provided for reporting purposes. Hospitals may record other diagnoses as needed for internal data use.

General Rule

All clinically significant conditions noted on routine newborn examination should be coded. A condition is clinically significant if it requires:

- clinical evaluation; or
- therapeutic treatment; or
- diagnostic procedures; or
- extended length of hospital stay; or
- increased nursing care and/or monitoring; or
- has implications for future health care needs.

Note: The newborn guidelines listed above are the same as the general coding guidelines for "other diagnoses," except for the final bullet regarding implications for future health care needs. Whether or not a condition is clinically significant can only be determined by the physician.

6.1. Use of Codes V30-V39

When coding the birth of an infant, assign a code from categories V30-V39, according to the type of birth. A code from this series is assigned as a principal diagnosis, and assigned only once to a newborn at the time of birth.

6.2. Newborn Transfers

If the newborn is transferred to another institution, the V30 series is not used.

6.3. Use of Category V29

A. Assign a code from category V29, Observation and evaluation of newborns and infants for suspected conditions not found, to identify those instances when a healthy newborn is evaluated for a suspected condition that is determined after study not to be present. Do not use a code from category V29 when the patient has identified signs or symptoms of a suspected problem; in such cases, code the sign or symptom.

B. A V29 code is to be used as a secondary code after the V30, Outcome of delivery, code. It may also be assigned as a principal code for readmissions or encounters when the V30 code no longer applies. It is for use only for healthy newborns and infants for which no condition after study is found to be present.

6.4. Maternal Causes of Perinatal Morbidity

Codes from categories 760-763, Maternal causes of perinatal morbidity and mortality, are assigned only when the maternal condition has actually affected the fetus or newborn. The fact that the mother has an associated medical condition or experiences some complication of pregnancy, labor or delivery does not justify the routine assignment of codes from these categories to the newborn record.

6.5. Congenital Anomalies

Assign an appropriate code from categories 740-759, Congenital Anomalies, when a specific abnormality is diagnosed for an infant. Such abnormalities may occur as a set of symptoms or multiple malformations. A code should be assigned for each presenting manifestation of the syndrome if the syndrome is not specifically indexed in ICD-9-CM.

6.6. Coding of Other (Additional) Diagnoses

A. Assign codes for conditions that require treatment or further investigation, prolong the length of stay, or require resource utilization.

B. Assign codes for conditions that have been specified by the physician as having implications for future health care needs.

NOTE: This guideline should not be used for adult patients.

C. Assign a code for Newborn conditions originating in the perinatal period (categories 760-779), as well as complications arising during the current episode of care classified in other chapters, only if the diagnoses have been documented by the responsible physician at the time of transfer or discharge as having affected the fetus or newborn.

D. Insignificant conditions or signs or symptoms that resolve without treatment are not coded.

6.7. Prematurity and Fetal Growth Retardation

Codes from categories 764 and 765 should not be assigned based solely on recorded birthweight or estimated gestational age, but upon the attending physician's clinical assessment of maturity of the infant.

NOTE: Since physicians may utilize different criteria in determining prematurity, do not code the diagnosis of prematurity unless the physician documents this condition.

7. SEPTICEMIA AND SEPTIC SHOCK

When the diagnosis of septicemia with shock or the diagnosis of general sepsis with septic shock is documented, code and list the septicemia first and report the septic shock code as a secondary condition. The septicemia code assignment should identify the type of bacteria if it is known.

Sepsis and septic shock associated with abortion, ectopic pregnancy, and molar pregnancy are classified to category codes in Chapter 11 (630-639).

Negative or inconclusive blood cultures do not preclude a diagnosis of septicemia in patients with clinical evidence of the condition.

8. TRAUMA

8.1. Coding for Multiple Injuries

When coding multiple injuries such as fracture of tibia and fibula, assign separate codes for each injury unless a combination code is provided, in which case the combination code is assigned. Multiple injury codes are provided in ICD-9-CM, but should not be assigned unless information for a more specific code is not available.

A. The code for the most serious injury, as determined by the physician, is sequenced first.

B. Superficial injuries such as abrasions or contusions are not coded when associated with more severe injuries of the same site.

C. When a primary injury results in minor damage to peripheral nerves or blood vessels, the primary injury is sequenced first with additional code(s) from categories 950-957, Injury to nerves and spinal cord, and/or 900-904, Injury to blood vessels. When the primary injury is to the blood vessels or nerves, that injury should be sequenced first.

8.2. Coding for Multiple Fractures

The principle of multiple coding of injuries should be followed in coding multiple fractures. Multiple fractures of specified sites are coded individually by site in accordance with both the provisions within categories 800-829 and the level of detail furnished by medical record content. Combination categories for multiple fractures are provided for use when there is insufficient detail in the medical record (such as trauma cases transferred to another hospital), when the reporting form limits the number of codes that can be used in reporting pertinent clinical data, or when there is insufficient specificity at the fourth-digit or fifth-digit level. More specific guidelines are as follows:

A. Multiple fractures of same limb classifiable to the same three-digit or four-digit category are coded to that category.

B. Multiple unilateral or bilateral fractures of same bone(s) but classified to different fourth-digit subdivisions (bone part) within the same three-digit category are coded individually by site.

C. Multiple fracture categories 819 and 828 classify bilateral fractures of both upper limbs (819) and both lower limbs (828), but without any detail at the fourth-digit level other than open and closed type of fractures.

D. Multiple fractures are sequenced in accordance with the severity of the fracture and the physician should be asked to list the fracture diagnoses in the order of severity.

8.3. Current Burns and Encounters for Late Effects of Burns

Current burns (940-948) are classified by depth, extent and, if desired, by agent (E code).

By depth burns are classified as first degree (erythema), second degree (blistering), and third degree (full-thickness involvement).

A. All burns are coded with the highest degree of burn sequenced first.

B. Classify burns of the same local site (three-digit category level, (940-947) but of different degrees to the subcategory identifying the highest degree recorded in the diagnosis.

C. Non-healing burns are coded as acute burns. Necrosis of burned skin should be coded as a non-healed burn.

D. Assign code 958.3, Posttraumatic wound infection, not elsewhere classified, as an additional code for any documented infected burn site.

E. When coding multiple burns, assign separate codes for each burn site. Category 946 Burns of Multiple specified sites, should only be used if the location of the burns are not documented.

   Category 949, Burn, unspecified, is extremely vague and should rarely be used.

F. Assign codes from category 948, Burns classified according to extent of body surface involved, when the site of the burn is not specified or when there is a need for additional data. It is advisable to use category 948 as additional coding when needed to provide data for evaluating burn mortality, such as that needed by burn units. It is also advisable to use category 948 as an additional code for reporting purposes when there is mention of a third-degree burn involving 20 percent or more of the body surface. In assigning a code from category 948:

   - Four-digit codes are used to identify the percentage of total body surface involved in a burn (all degree).
   - Fifth-digits are assigned to identify the percentage of body surface involved in third-degree burn.
   - Fifth-digit zero (0) is assigned when less than 10 percent or when no body surface is involved in a third-degree burn.

   Category 948 is based on the classic "rule of nines" in estimating body surface involved: head and neck are assigned nine percent, each arm nine percent, each leg 18 percent, the anterior trunk 18 percent, posterior trunk 18 percent, and genitalia one percent. Physicians may change these percentage assignments where necessary to accommodate infants and children who have proportionately larger heads than adults and patients who have large buttocks, thighs, or abdomen that involve burns.

G. Encounters for the treatment of the late effects of burns (i.e., scars or joint contractures) should be coded to the residual condition (sequelae) followed by the appropriate late effect code (906.5-906.9). A late effect E code may also be used, if desired.

H. When appropriate, both a sequelae with a late effect code, and a current burn code may be assigned on the same record.

8.4. Debridement of Wound, Infection, or Burn

A. For coding purposes, excisional debridement, 86.22, is assigned only when the procedure is performed by a physician.

B. For coding purposes, nonexcisional debridement performed by the physician or nonphysician health care professional is assigned to 86.28. Any "excisional" type procedure performed by a nonphysician is assigned to 86.28.

9. ADVERSE EFFECTS AND POISONING

The properties of certain drugs, medicinal and biological substances or combinations of such substances, may cause toxic reactions. The occurrence of drug toxicity is classified in ICD-9-CM as follows:

9.1. Adverse Effect

When the drug was correctly prescribed and properly administered, code the reaction plus the appropriate code from the E930-E949 series.

Adverse effects of therapeutic substances correctly prescribed and properly administered (toxicity, synergistic reaction, side effect, and idiosyncratic reaction) may be due to (1) differences among patients, such as age, sex, disease, and genetic factors, and (2) drug-related factors, such as type of drug, route of administration, duration of therapy, dosage, and bioavailability.

Codes from the E930-E949 series must be used to identify the causative substance for an adverse effect of drug, medicinal and biological substances, correctly prescribed and properly administered. The effect, such as tachycardia, delirium, gastrointestinal hemorrhaging, vomiting, hypokalemia, hepatitis, renal failure, or respiratory failure, is coded and followed by the appropriate code from the E930-E949 series.

9.2. Poisoning

Poisoning when an error was made in drug prescription or in the administration of the drug by physician, nurse, patient, or other person, use the appropriate code from the 960-979 series. If an overdose of a drug was intentionally taken or administered and resulted in drug toxicity, it would be coded as a poisoning (960-979 series). If a nonprescribed drug or medicinal agent was taken in combination with a correctly prescribed and properly administered drug, any drug toxicity or other reaction resulting from the interaction of the two drugs would be classified as a poisoning.

10. HUMAN IMMUNODEFICIENCY VIRUS (HIV) INFECTIONS

10.1. Code only confirmed cases of HIV infection/illness.

This is an exception to guideline 1.8 which states "If the diagnosis documented at the time of discharge is qualified as 'probable,' 'suspected,' 'likely,' 'questionable,' 'possible,' or 'still to be ruled out,' code the condition as if it existed or was established..."

In this context, "confirmation" does not require documentation of positive serology or culture for HIV; the physician's diagnostic statement that the patient is HIV positive, or has an HIV-related illness is sufficient.

10.2. Selection of HIV code

042 Human Immunodeficiency Virus [HIV] Disease

Patients with an HIV-related illness should be coded to 042, Human Immunodeficiency Virus [HIV] Disease.

V08 Asymptomatic Human Immunodeficiency Virus [HIV] Infection

Patients with physician-documented asymptomatic HIV infections who have never had an HIV-related illness should be coded to V08, Asymptomatic Human Immunodeficiency Virus [HIV] Infection.

795.71 Nonspecific Serologic Evidence of Human Immunodeficiency Virus [HIV]

Code 795.71, Nonspecific serologic evidence of human immunodeficiency virus [HIV], should be used for patients (including infants) with inconclusive HIV test results.

10.3. Previously diagnosed HIV-related illness

Patients with any known prior diagnosis of an HIV-related illness should be coded to 042. Once a patient had developed an HIV-related illness, the patient should always be assigned code 042 on every subsequent admission. Patients previously diagnosed with any HIV illness (042) should never be assigned to 795.71 or V08.

10.4. Sequencing

The sequencing of diagnoses for patients with HIV-related illnesses follows guideline 2 for selection of principal diagnosis. That is, the circumstances of admission govern the selection of principal diagnosis, "that condition established after study to be chiefly responsible for occasioning the admission of the patient to the hospital for care."

Patients who are admitted for an HIV-related illness should be assigned a minimum of two codes: first assign code 042 to identify the HIV disease and then sequence additional codes to identify the other diagnoses. If a patient is admitted for an HIV-related condition, the principal diagnosis should be 042, followed by additional diagnosis codes for all reported HIV-related conditions.

If a patient with HIV disease is admitted for an unrelated condition (such as a traumatic injury), the code for the unrelated condition (e.g., the nature of injury code) should be the principal diagnosis. Other diagnoses would be 042 followed by additional diagnosis codes for all reported HIV-related conditions.

Whether the patient is newly diagnosed or has had previous admissions for HIV conditions (or has expired) is irrelevant to the sequencing decision.

10.5. HIV Infection in Pregnancy, Childbirth and the Puerperium

During pregnancy, childbirth or the puerperium, a patient admitted because of an HIV-related illness should receive a principal diagnosis of 647.6X, Other specified infectious and parasitic diseases in the mother classifiable elsewhere, but complicating the pregnancy, childbirth or the puerperium, followed by 042 and the code(s) for the HIV-related illness(es). This is an exception to the sequencing rule found in 10.4 above.

Patients with asymptomatic HIV infection status admitted during pregnancy, childbirth, or the puerperium should receive codes of 647.6X and V08.

10.6. Asymptomatic HIV Infection

V08 Asymptomatic human immunodeficiency virus [HIV] infection, is to be applied when the patient without any documentation of symptoms is listed as being "HIV positive," "known HIV," "HIV test positive," or similar terminology. Do not use this code if the term "AIDS" is used or if the patient is treated for any HIV-related illness or is described as having any condition(s) resulting from his/her HIV positive status; use 042 in these cases.

10.7. Inconclusive Laboratory Test for HIV

Patients with inconclusive HIV serology, but no definitive diagnosis or manifestations of the illness may be assigned code 795.71.Inconclusive serologic test for Human Immunodeficiency Virus [HIV]

10.8. Testing for HIV

If the patient is asymptomatic but wishes to know his/her HIV status, use code V73.89, Screening for other specified viral disease. Use code V69.8, Other problems related to lifestyle, as a secondary code if an asymptomatic patient is in a known high-risk group for HIV. Should a patient with signs or symptoms or illness, or a confirmed HIV related diagnosis be tested for HIV code the signs and symptoms or the diagnosis. An additional counseling code V65.44 may be used if counseling is provided during the encounter for the test.

When the patient returns to be informed of his/her HIV test results use code V65.44, HIV counseling, if the results of the test are negative. If the results are positive but the patient is asymptomatic use code V08, Asymptomatic HIV infection. If the results are positive and the patient is symptomatic use code 042, HIV infection, with codes for the HIV related symptoms or diagnosis. The HIV counseling code may also be used if counseling is provided for patients with positive test results.

11. GUIDELINES FOR CODING EXTERNAL CAUSES OF INJURIES, POISONINGS AND ADVERSE EFFECTS OF DRUGS (E Codes)

Introduction

These guidelines are provided for those who are currently collecting E codes in order that there will be standardization in the process. If your institution plans to begin collecting E codes, these guidelines are to be applied. The use of E codes are supplemental to the application of basic ICD-9-CM codes. E codes are never to be recorded as principal diagnosis (first listed in the outpatient setting) and are not required for reporting to the Health Care Financing Administration.

Injuries are a major cause of mortality, morbidity and disability. In the United States, the care of patients who suffer intentional and unintentional injuries and poisonings contributes significantly to the increase in medical care costs. External causes of injury and poisoning codes (E codes) are intended to provide data for injury research and evaluation of injury prevention strategies. E codes capture how the injury or poisoning happened (cause), the intent (unintentional or accidental; or intentional, such as suicide or assault), and the place where the event occurred. Some major categories of E codes include:

- transport accidents
- poisoning and adverse effects of drugs, medicinal substances and biologicals
- accidental falls
- accidents caused by fire and flames
- accidents due to natural and environmental factors
- late effects of accidents, assaults or self injury
- assaults or purposely inflicted injury
- suicide or self inflicted injury

These guidelines apply for the coding and collection of E code from records in hospitals, outpatient clinics, emergency departments, other ambulatory care settings and physician offices except when other specific guidelines apply. (See Reporting Diagnostic Guidelines for Hospital-based Outpatient Services/Reporting Requirements for Physician Billing.)

11.1. General E Code Coding Guidelines

A. An E code may be used with any code in the range of 001-V82.9 which indicates an injury, poisoning, or adverse effect due to an external cause.

B. Assign the appropriate E-code for all initial treatments of an injury, poisoning, or adverse effect of drugs.

C. Use a late effect E code for subsequent visits when a late effect of the initial injury or poisoning is being treated. There is no late effect E code for adverse effects of drugs.

D. Use the full range of E codes to completely describe the cause, the intent and the place of occurrence, if applicable, for all injuries, poisonings, and adverse effects of drugs.

E. Assign as many E codes as necessary to fully explain each cause. If only one E code can be recorded, assign the E code most related to the principal diagnosis.

F. The selection of the appropriate E code is guided by the Index to External Causes which is located after the alphabetical index to diseases and by Inclusion and Exclusion notes in the Tabular List.

G. An E code can never be a principal (first listed) diagnosis.

11.2. Place of Occurrence Guideline

Use an additional code from category E849 to indicate the Place of Occurrence for injuries and poisonings. The Place of Occurrence describes the place where the event occurred and not the patient's activity at the time of the event.

Do not use E849.9 if the place of occurrence is not stated.

11.3. Poisonings and Adverse Effects of Drugs, Medicinal and Biological Substances Guidelines

A. Do not code directly from the Table of Drugs and Chemicals. Always refer back to the Tabular List.

B. Use as many codes as necessary to describe completely all drugs, medicinal or biological substances.

C. If the same E code would describe the causative agent for more than one adverse reaction, assign the code only once.

D. If two or more drugs, medicinal or biological substances are reported, code each individually unless the combination code is listed in the Table of Drugs and Chemicals. In that case, assign the E code for the combination.

E. When a reaction results from the interaction of a drug(s) and alcohol, use poisoning codes and E codes for both.

F. If the reporting format limits the number of E codes that can be used in reporting clinical data, code the one most related to the principal diagnosis. Include at least one from each category (cause, intent, place) if possible.

- If there are different fourth digit codes in the same three digit category, use the code for "Other specified" of that category. If there is no "Other specified" code in that category, use the appropriate "Unspecified" code in that category.
- If the codes are in different three digit categories, assign the appropriate E code for other multiple drugs and medicinal substances.

11.4. Multiple Cause E Code Coding Guidelines

If two or more events cause separate injuries, an E code should be assigned for each cause. The first listed E code will be selected in the following order:

- E codes for child and adult abuse take priority over all other E code—see Child and Adult abuse guidelines
- E codes for cataclysmic events take priority over all other E codes except child and adult abuse
- E codes for transport accidents take priority over all other E codes except cataclysmic events and child and adult abuse

The first list E code should correspond to the cause of the most serious diagnosis due to an assault, accident, or self-harm, following the order of hierarchy listed above.

11.5. Child and Adult Abuse Guideline

A. When the cause of an injury or neglect is intentional child or adult abuse, the first listed E code should be assigned from categories E960-E968, Homicide and injury purposely inflicted by other persons, (except category E967). An E code from category E967, Child and adult battering and other maltreatment, should be added as an additional code to identify the perpetrator, if known.

B. In cases of neglect when the intent is determined to be accidental E code E904.0, Abandonment or neglect of infant and helpless person, should be the first listed E code.

11.6. Unknown or Suspected Intent Guideline

A. If the intent (accident, self-harm, assault) of the cause of an injury or poisoning is unknown or unspecified, code the intent as undetermined E980-E989.

B. If the intent (accident, self-harm, assault) of the cause of an injury or poisoning is questionable, probable or suspected, code the intent as undetermined E980-E989.

11.7. Undetermined Cause

When the intent of an injury or poisoning is known, but the cause is unknown, use codes: E928.9, Unspecified accident, E958.9, Suicide and self-inflicted injury by unspecified means, and E968.9, Assault by unspecified means.

These E codes should rarely be used as the documentation in the medical record, in both the inpatient and outpatient settings, should normally provide sufficient detail to determine the cause of the injury.

11.8. Late Effects of External Cause Guidelines

A. Late effect E codes exist for injuries and poisonings but not for adverse effects of drugs, misadventures and surgical complications.

B. A late effect E code (E929, E959, E969, E977, E989, or E999) should be used with any report of a late effect or sequela resulting from a previous injury or poisoning (905-909).

C. A late effect E code should never be used with a related current nature of injury code.

11.9. Misadventures and Complications of Care Guidelines

A. Assign a code in the range of E870-E876 if misadventures are stated by the physician.

B. Assign a code in the range of E878-E879 if the physician attributes an abnormal reaction or later complication to a surgical or medical procedure, but does not mention misadventure at the time of the procedure as the cause of the reaction.

NOTES

NOTES

NOTES

NOTES

NOTES

NOTES

NOTES

NOTES

A

- **AAV** (disease) (illness) (infection) — *see* Human immunodeficiency virus (disease) (illness) (infection)
- **Abactio** — *see* Abortion, induced
- **Abactus venter** — *see* Abortion, induced
- **Abarognosis** 781.9
- **Abasia** (-astasia) 307.9
  - atactica 781.3
  - choreic 781.3
  - hysterical 300.11
  - paroxysmal trepidant 781.3
  - spastic 781.3
  - trembling 781.3
  - trepidans 781.3
- **Abderhalden-Kaufmann-Lignac syndrome** (cystinosis) 270.0
- **Abdomen, abdominal** — *see also* condition
  - accordion 306.4
  - acute 789.0 [5th]
  - angina 557.1
  - burst 868.00
  - convulsive equivalent (*see also* Epilepsy) 345.5 [5th]
  - heart 746.87
  - muscle deficiency syndrome 756.79
  - obstipum 756.79
- **Abdominalgia** 789.0 [5th]
  - periodic 277.3
- **Abduction contracture, hip or other joint** — *see* Contraction, joint
- **Abercrombie's syndrome** (amyloid degeneration) 277.3
- **Aberrant** (congenital) — *see also* Malposition, congenital
  - adrenal gland 759.1
  - blood vessel NEC 747.60
    - arteriovenous NEC 747.60
    - cerebrovascular 747.81
    - gastrointestinal 747.61
    - lower limb 747.64
    - renal 747.62
    - spinal 747.82
    - upper limb 747.63
  - breast 757.6
  - endocrine gland NEC 759.2
  - gastrointestinal vessel (peripheral) 747.61
  - hepatic duct 751.69
  - lower limb vessel (peripheral) 747.64
  - pancreas 751.7
  - parathyroid gland 759.2
  - peripheral vascular vessel NEC 747.60
  - pituitary gland (pharyngeal) 759.2
  - renal blood vessel 747.62
  - sebaceous glands, mucous membrane, mouth 750.26
  - spinal vessel 747.82
  - spleen 759.0
  - testis (descent) 752.51
  - thymus gland 759.2
  - thyroid gland 759.2
  - upper limb vessel (peripheral) 747.63
- **Aberratio**
  - lactis 757.6
  - testis 752.51
- **Aberration** — *see also* Anomaly
  - chromosome — *see* Anomaly, chromosome(s)
  - distantial 368.9
  - mental (*see also* Disorder, mental, nonpsychotic) 300.9
- **Abetalipoproteinemia** 272.5
- **Abionarce** 780.79
- **Abiotrophy** 799.8
- **Ablatio**
  - placentae — *see* Placenta, ablatio
  - retinae (*see also* Detachment, retina) 361.9
- **Ablation**
  - pituitary (gland) (with hypofunction) 253.7
  - placenta — *see* Placenta, ablatio
  - uterus 621.8
- **Ablepharia, ablepharon, ablephary** 743.62
- **Ablepsia** — *see* Blindness
- **Ablepsy** — *see* Blindness
- **Ablutomania** 300.3
- **Abnormal, abnormality, abnormalities** — *see also* Anomaly
  - acid-base balance 276.4
    - fetus or newborn — *see* Distress, fetal
  - adaptation curve, dark 368.63
  - alveolar ridge 525.9
  - amnion 658.9 [5th]
    - affecting fetus or newborn 762.9
  - anatomical relationship NEC 759.9
  - apertures, congenital, diaphragm 756.6
  - auditory perception NEC 388.40
  - autosomes NEC 758.5
    - 13 758.1
    - 18 758.2
    - 21 or 22 758.0
    - D_1 758.1
    - E_3 758.2
    - G 758.0
  - ballistocardiogram 794.39
  - basal metabolic rate (BMR) 794.7
  - biosynthesis, testicular androgen 257.2
  - blood level (of)
    - cobalt 790.6
    - copper 790.6
    - iron 790.6
    - lithium 790.6
    - magnesium 790.6
    - mineral 790.6
    - zinc 790.6
  - blood pressure
    - elevated (without diagnosis of hypertension) 796.2
    - low (*see also* Hypotension) 458.9
      - reading (incidental) (isolated) (nonspecific) 796.3
  - bowel sounds 787.5
  - breathing behavior — *see* Respiration
  - caloric test 794.19
  - cervix (acquired) NEC 622.9
    - congenital 752.40
    - in pregnancy or childbirth 654.6 [5th]
      - causing obstructed labor 660.2 [5th]
        - affecting fetus or newborn 763.1
  - chemistry, blood NEC 790.6
  - chest sounds 786.7
  - chorion 658.9 [5th]
    - affecting fetus or newborn 762.9
  - chromosomal NEC 758.89
    - analysis, nonspecific result 795.2
    - autosomes (*see also* Abnormal, autosomes NEC) 758.5
    - fetal, (suspected) affecting management of pregnancy 655.1 [5th]
    - sex 758.81

Abnormal, abnormality, abnormalities — *see also* Anomaly — *continued*

  - clinical findings NEC 796.4
  - communication — *see* Fistula
  - configuration of pupils 379.49
  - coronary
    - artery 746.85
    - vein 746.9
  - cortisol-binding globulin 255.8
  - course, Eustachian tube 744.24
  - dentofacial NEC 524.9
    - functional 524.5
    - specified type NEC 524.8
  - development, developmental NEC 759.9
    - bone 756.9
    - central nervous system 742.9
  - direction, teeth 524.3
  - Dynia (*see also* Defect, coagulation) 286.9
  - Ebstein 746.2
  - echocardiogram 793.2
  - echoencephalogram 794.01
  - echogram NEC — *see* Findings, abnormal, structure
  - electrocardiogram (ECG) (EKG) 794.31
  - electroencephalogram (EEG) 794.02
  - electromyogram (EMG) 794.17
    - ocular 794.14
  - electro-oculogram (EOG) 794.12
  - electroretinogram (ERG) 794.11
  - erythrocytes 289.9
    - congenital, with perinatal jaundice 282.9 *[774.0]*
  - Eustachian valve 746.9
  - excitability under minor stress 301.9
  - fat distribution 782.9
  - feces 787.7
  - fetal heart rate — *see* Distress, fetal
  - fetus NEC
    - affecting management of pregnancy — *see* Pregnancy, management affected by, fetal
    - causing disproportion 653.7 [5th]
      - affecting fetus or newborn 763.1
      - causing obstructed labor 660.1 [5th]
        - affecting fetus or newborn 763.1
  - findings without manifest disease — *see* Findings, abnormal
  - fluid
    - amniotic 792.3
    - cerebrospinal 792.0
    - peritoneal 792.9
    - pleural 792.9
    - synovial 792.9
    - vaginal 792.9
  - forces of labor NEC 661.9 [5th]
    - affecting fetus or newborn 763.7
  - form, teeth 520.2
  - function studies
    - auditory 794.15
    - bladder 794.9
    - brain 794.00
    - cardiovascular 794.30
    - endocrine NEC 794.6
    - kidney 794.4
    - liver 794.8
    - nervous system
      - central 794.00
      - peripheral 794.19
    - oculomotor 794.14

Note — Use the following fifth-digit subclassification with categories 634–637:

0 unspecified
1 incomplete
2 complete

- **Abscess** (acute) (chronic) (infectional) (lymphangitic) (metastatic) (multiple) (pyogenic) (septic) (with lymphangitis) (*see also* Cellulitis) — *continued*
  - extraperitoneal — *see* Abscess, peritoneum
  - eye 360.00
  - eyelid 373.13
  - face (any part, except eye) 682.0
  - fallopian tube (*see also* Salpingo-oophoritis) 614.2
  - fascia 728.89
  - fauces 478.29
  - fecal 569.5
  - femoral (region) 682.6
  - filaria, filarial (*see also* Infestation, filarial) 125.9
  - finger (any) (intrathecal) (periosteal) (subcutaneous) (subcuticular) 681.00
  - fistulous NEC 682.9
  - flank 682.2
  - foot (except toe) 682.7
  - forearm 682.3
  - forehead 682.0
  - frontal (sinus) (chronic) (*see also* Sinusitis, frontal) 473.1
  - gallbladder (*see also* Cholecystitis, acute) 575.0
  - gastric 535.0 ✓5th
  - genital organ or tract NEC
    - female 616.9
      - with
        - abortion — *see* Abortion, by type, with sepsis
        - ectopic pregnancy (*see also* categories 633.0–633.9) 639.0
        - molar pregnancy (*see also* categories 630–632) 639.0
      - following
        - abortion 639.0
        - ectopic or molar pregnancy 639.0
      - puerperal, postpartum, childbirth 670
    - male 608.4
  - genitourinary system, tuberculous (*see also* Tuberculosis) 016.9 ✓5th
  - gingival 523.3
  - gland, glandular (lymph) (acute) NEC 683
  - glottis 478.79
  - gluteal (region) 682.5
  - gonorrheal NEC (*see also* Gonococcus) 098.0
  - groin 682.2
  - gum 523.3
  - hand (except finger or thumb) 682.4
  - head (except face) 682.8
  - heart 429.89
  - heel 682.7
  - helminthic (*see also* Infestation, by specific parasite) 128.9
  - hepatic 572.0
    - amebic (*see also* Abscess, liver, amebic) 006.3
    - duct 576.8
  - hip 682.6
    - tuberculous (active) (*see also* Tuberculosis) 015.1 ✓5th
  - ileocecal 540.1
  - ileostomy (bud) 569.61
  - iliac (region) 682.2
    - fossa 540.1
  - iliopsoas (tuberculous) (*see also* Tuberculosis) 015.0 ✓5th *[730.88]*
    - nontuberculous 728.89

- **Abscess** (acute) (chronic) (infectional) (lymphangitic) (metastatic) (multiple) (pyogenic) (septic) (with lymphangitis) (*see also* Cellulitis) — *continued*
  - infraclavicular (fossa) 682.3
  - inguinal (region) 682.2
    - lymph gland or node 683
  - intersphincteric (anus) 566
  - intestine, intestinal 569.5
    - rectal 566
  - intra-abdominal (*see also* Abscess, peritoneum) 567.2
    - postoperative 998.59
  - intracranial 324.0
    - late effect — *see* category 326
  - intramammary — *see* Abscess, breast
  - intramastoid (*see also* Mastoiditis, acute) 383.00
  - intraorbital 376.01
  - intraperitoneal — *see* Abscess, peritoneum
  - intraspinal 324.1
    - late effect — *see* category 326
  - intratonsillar 475
  - iris 364.3
  - ischiorectal 566
  - jaw (bone) (lower) (upper) 526.4
    - skin 682.0
  - joint (*see also* Arthritis, pyogenic) 711.0 ✓5th
    - vertebral (tuberculous) (*see also* Tuberculosis) 015.0 ✓5th *[730.88]*
      - nontuberculous 724.8
  - kidney 590.2
    - with
      - abortion — *see* Abortion, by type, with urinary tract infection
      - calculus 592.0
      - ectopic pregnancy (*see also* categories 633.0–633.9) 639.8
      - molar pregnancy (*see also* categories 630–632) 639.8
    - complicating pregnancy or puerperium 646.6 ✓5th
      - affecting fetus or newborn 760.1
    - following
      - abortion 639.8
      - ectopic or molar pregnancy 639.8
  - knee 682.6
    - joint 711.06
    - tuberculous (active) (*see also* Tuberculosis) 015.2 ✓5th
  - labium (majus) (minus) 616.4
    - complicating pregnancy, childbirth, or puerperium 646.6 ✓5th
  - lacrimal (passages) (sac) (*see also* Dacryocystitis) 375.30
    - caruncle 375.30
    - gland (*see also* Dacryoadenitis) 375.00
  - lacunar 597.0
  - larynx 478.79
  - lateral (alveolar) 522.5
    - with sinus 522.7
  - leg, except foot 682.6
  - lens 360.00
  - lid 373.13
  - lingual 529.0
    - tonsil 475
  - lip 528.5
  - Littre's gland 597.0

- **Abscess** (acute) (chronic) (infectional) (lymphangitic) (metastatic) (multiple) (pyogenic) (septic) (with lymphangitis) (*see also* Cellulitis) — *continued*
  - liver 572.0
    - amebic 006.3
      - with
        - brain abscess (and lung abscess) 006.5
        - lung abscess 006.4
    - due to Entamoeba histolytica 006.3
    - dysenteric (*see also* Abscess, liver, amebic) 006.3
    - pyogenic 572.0
    - tropical (*see also* Abscess, liver, amebic) 006.3
  - loin (region) 682.2
  - lumbar (tuberculous) (*see also* Tuberculosis) 015.0 ✓5th *[730.88]*
    - nontuberculous 682.2
  - lung (miliary) (putrid) 513.0
    - amebic (with liver abscess) 006.4
      - with brain abscess 006.5
  - lymph, lymphatic, gland or node (acute) 683
    - any site, except mesenteric 683
    - mesentery 289.2
  - lymphangitic, acute — *see* Cellulitis
  - malar 526.4
  - mammary gland — *see* Abscess, breast
  - marginal (anus) 566
  - mastoid (process) (*see also* Mastoiditis, acute) 383.00
    - subperiosteal 383.01
  - maxilla, maxillary 526.4
    - molar (tooth) 522.5
      - with sinus 522.7
    - premolar 522.5
    - sinus (chronic) (*see also* Sinusitis, maxillary) 473.0
  - mediastinum 513.1
  - meibomian gland 373.12
  - meninges (*see also* Meningitis) 320.9
  - mesentery, mesenteric — *see* Abscess, peritoneum
  - mesosalpinx (*see also* Salpingo-oophoritis) 614.2
  - milk 675.1 ✓5th
  - Monro's (psoriasis) 696.1
  - mons pubis 682.2
  - mouth (floor) 528.3
  - multiple sites NEC 682.9
  - mural 682.2
  - muscle 728.89
  - myocardium 422.92
  - nabothian (follicle) (*see also* Cervicitis) 616.0
  - nail (chronic) (with lymphangitis) 681.9
    - finger 681.02
    - toe 681.11
  - nasal (fossa) (septum) 478.1
    - sinus (chronic) (*see also* Sinusitis) 473.9
  - nasopharyngeal 478.29
  - nates 682.5
  - navel 682.2
    - newborn NEC 771.4
  - neck (region) 682.1
    - lymph gland or node 683
  - nephritic (*see also* Abscess, kidney) 590.2
  - nipple 611.0
    - puerperal, postpartum 675.0 ✓5th
  - nose (septum) 478.1
    - external 682.0

Note — Use the following fifth-digit subclassification with the following codes 305.0, 305.2-305.9:

0 unspecified
1 continuous
2 episodic
3 in remission

- **Activity decrease, functional** 780.9
- **Acute** — *see also* condition
  - abdomen NEC 789.0 ✓5th
  - gallbladder (*see also* Cholecystitis, acute) 575.0
- **Acyanoblepsia** 368.53
- **Acyanopsia** 368.53
- **Acystia** 753.8
- **Acystinervia** — *see* Neurogenic, bladder
- **Acystineuria** — *see* Neurogenic, bladder
- **Adactylia, adactyly** (congenital) 755.4
  - lower limb (complete) (intercalary) (partial) (terminal) (*see also* Deformity, reduction, lower limb) 755.39
    - meaning all digits (complete) (partial) 755.31
    - transverse (complete) (partial) 755.31
  - upper limb (complete) (intercalary) (partial) (terminal) (*see also* Deformity, reduction, upper limb) 755.29
    - meaning all digits (complete) (partial) 755.21
    - transverse (complete) (partial) 755.21
- **Adair-Dighton syndrome** (brittle bones and blue sclera, deafness) 756.51
- **Adamantinoblastoma** (M9310/0) — *see* Ameloblastoma
- **Adamantinoma** (M9310/0) — *see* Ameloblastoma
- **Adamantoblastoma** (M9310/0) — *see* Ameloblastoma
- **Adams-Stokes** (-Morgagni) disease or syndrome (syncope with heart block) 426.9
- **Adaptation reaction** (*see also* Reaction, adjustment) 309.9
- **Addiction** — *see also* Dependence
  - absinthe 304.6 ✓5th
  - alcoholic (ethyl) (methyl) (wood) 303.9 ✓5th
    - complicating pregnancy, childbirth, or puerperium 648.4 ✓5th
      - affecting fetus or newborn 760.71
    - suspected damage to fetus affecting management of pregnancy 655.4 ✓5th
  - drug (*see also* Dependence) 304.9 ✓5th
  - ethyl alcohol 303.9 ✓5th
  - heroin 304.0 ✓5th
  - hospital 301.51
  - methyl alcohol 303.9 ✓5th
  - methylated spirit 303.9 ✓5th
  - morphine (-like substances) 304.0 ✓5th
  - nicotine 305.1
  - opium 304.0 ✓5th
  - tobacco 305.1
  - wine 303.9 ✓5th
- **Addison's**
  - anemia (pernicious) 281.0
  - disease (bronze) (primary adrenal insufficiency) 255.4
    - tuberculous (*see also* Tuberculosis) 017.6 ✓5th
  - keloid (morphea) 701.0
  - melanoderma (adrenal cortical hypofunction) 255.4
- **Addison-Biermer anemia** (pernicious) 281.0
- **Addison-Gull disease** — *see* Xanthoma
- **Addisonian crisis or melanosis** (acute adrenocortical insufficiency) 255.4
- **Additional** — *see also* Accessory
  - chromosome(s) 758.5
    - 13–15 758.1
    - 16–18 758.2
    - 21 758.0
    - autosome(s) NEC 758.5
    - sex 758.81
- **Adduction contracture, hip or other joint** — *see* Contraction, joint
- **Adenasthenia gastrica** 536.0
- **Aden fever** 061
- **Adenitis** (*see also* Lymphadenitis) 289.3
  - acute, unspecified site 683
    - epidemic infectious 075
  - axillary 289.3
    - acute 683
    - chronic or subacute 289.1
  - Bartholin's gland 616.8
  - bulbourethral gland (*see also* Urethritis) 597.89
  - cervical 289.3
    - acute 683
    - chronic or subacute 289.1
  - chancroid (Ducrey's bacillus) 099.0
  - chronic (any lymph node, except mesenteric) 289.1
    - mesenteric 289.2
  - Cowper's gland (*see also* Urethritis) 597.89
  - epidemic, acute 075
  - gangrenous 683
  - gonorrheal NEC 098.89
  - groin 289.3
    - acute 683
    - chronic or subacute 289.1
  - infectious 075
  - inguinal (region) 289.3
    - acute 683
    - chronic or subacute 289.1
  - lymph gland or node, except mesenteric 289.3
    - acute 683
    - chronic or subacute 289.1
    - mesenteric (acute) (chronic) (nonspecific) (subacute) 289.2
  - mesenteric (acute) (chronic) (nonspecific) (subacute) 289.2
    - due to Pasteurella multocida (P. septica) 027.2
  - parotid gland (suppurative) 527.2
  - phlegmonous 683
  - salivary duct or gland (any) (recurring) (suppurative) 527.2
  - scrofulous (*see also* Tuberculosis) 017.2 ✓5th
  - septic 289.3
  - Skene's duct or gland (*see also* Urethritis) 597.89
  - strumous, tuberculous (*see also* Tuberculosis) 017.2 ✓5th
  - subacute, unspecified site 289.1
  - sublingual gland (suppurative) 527.2
  - submandibular gland (suppurative) 527.2
  - submaxillary gland (suppurative) 527.2
  - suppurative 683
  - tuberculous — *see* Tuberculosis, lymph gland
  - urethral gland (*see also* Urethritis) 597.89
  - venereal NEC 099.8
  - Wharton's duct (suppurative) 527.2
- **Adenoacanthoma** (M8570/3) — *see* Neoplasm, by site malignant
- **Adenoameloblastoma** (M9300/0) 213.1
  - upper jaw (bone) 213.0
- **Adenocarcinoma** (M8140/3) — *see also* Neoplasm, by site, malignant

> *Note — The list of adjectival modifiers below is not exhaustive. A description of adenocarcinoma that does not appear in this list should be coded in the same manner as carcinoma with that description. Thus, "mixed acidophil-basophil adenocarcinoma," should be coded in the same manner as "mixed acidophil-basophil carcinoma," which appears in the list under "Carcinoma." Except where otherwise indicated, the morphological varieties of adenocarcinoma in the list below should be coded by site as for "Neoplasm, malignant."*

  - with
    - apocrine metaplasia (M8573/3)
    - cartilaginous (and osseous) metaplasia (M8571/3)
    - osseous (and cartilaginous) metaplasia (M8571/3)
    - spindle cell metaplasia (M8572/3)
    - squamous metaplasia (M8570/3)
  - acidophil (M8280/3)
    - specified site — *see* Neoplasm, by site, malignant
    - unspecified site 194.3
  - acinar (M8550/3)
  - acinic cell (M8550/3)
  - adrenal cortical (M8370/3) 194.0
  - alveolar (M8251/3)
    - and
      - epidermoid carcinoma, mixed (M8560/3)
      - squamous cell carcinoma, mixed (M8560/3)
  - apocrine (M8401/3)
    - breast — *see* Neoplasm, breast, malignant
    - specified site NEC — *see* Neoplasm, skin, malignant
    - unspecified site 173.9
  - basophil (M8300/3)
    - specified site — *see* Neoplasm, by site, malignant
    - unspecified site 194.3
  - bile duct type (M8160/3)
    - liver 155.1
    - specified site NEC — *see* Neoplasm, by site, malignant
    - unspecified site 155.1
  - bronchiolar (M8250/3) — *see* Neoplasm, lung, malignant
  - ceruminous (M8420/3) 173.2
  - chromophobe (M8270/3)
    - specified site — *see* Neoplasm, by site, malignant
    - unspecified site 194.3
  - clear cell (mesonephroid type) (M8310/3)
  - colloid (M8480/3)
  - cylindroid type (M8200/3)
  - diffuse type (M8145/3)
    - specified site — *see* Neoplasm, by site, malignant
    - unspecified site 151.9
  - duct (infiltrating) (M8500/3)
    - with Paget's disease (M8541/3) — *see* Neoplasm, breast, malignant
    - specified site — *see* Neoplasm, by site, malignant
    - unspecified site 174.9

> *Note — Except where otherwise indicated, the morphological varieties of adenoma in the list below should be coded by site as for "Neoplasm, benign."*

Adhesion(s) adhesive (postinfectional) (postoperative) — *continued*
- cornea — *see* Opacity, cornea
- cystic duct 575.8
- diaphragm (*see also* Adhesions, peritoneum) 568.0
- due to foreign body — *see* Foreign body
- duodenum (*see also* Adhesions, peritoneum) 568.0
  - with obstruction 537.3
- ear, middle — *see* Adhesions, middle ear
- epididymis 608.89
- epidural — *see* Adhesions, meninges
- epiglottis 478.79
- Eustachian tube 381.89
- eyelid 374.46
  - postoperative 997.99
    - surgically created V45.69
- gallbladder (*see also* Disease, gallbladder) 575.8
- globe 360.89
- heart 423.1
  - rheumatic 398.99
- ileocecal (coil) (*see also* Adhesions, peritoneum) 568.0
- ileum (*see also* Adhesions, peritoneum) 568.0
- intestine (postoperative) (*see also* Adhesions, peritoneum) 568.0
  - with obstruction 560.81
    - with hernia — *see also* Hernia, by site, with obstruction
      - gangrenous — *see* Hernia, by site, with gangrene
- intra-abdominal (*see also* Adhesions, peritoneum) 568.0
- iris 364.70
  - to corneal graft 996.79
- joint (*see also* Ankylosis) 718.5 ✓5th
- kidney 593.89
- labium (majus) (minus), congenital 752.49
- liver 572.8
- lung 511.0
- mediastinum 519.3
- meninges 349.2
  - cerebral (any) 349.2
    - congenital 742.4
  - congenital 742.8
  - spinal (any) 349.2
    - congenital 742.59
  - tuberculous (cerebral) (spinal) (*see also* Tuberculosis, meninges) 013.0 ✓5th
- mesenteric (*see also* Adhesions, peritoneum) 568.0
- middle ear (fibrous) 385.10
  - drum head 385.19
    - to
      - incus 385.11
      - promontorium 385.13
      - stapes 385.12
  - specified NEC 385.19
- nasal (septum) (to turbinates) 478.1
- nerve NEC 355.9
  - spinal 355.9
    - root 724.9
      - cervical NEC 723.4
      - lumbar NEC 724.4
      - lumbosacral 724.4
      - thoracic 724.4
- ocular muscle 378.60
- omentum (*see also* Adhesions, peritoneum) 568.0
- organ or site, congenital NEC — *see* Anomaly, specified type NEC

Adhesion(s), adhesive (postinfectional) (postoperative) — *continued*
- ovary 614.6
  - congenital (to cecum, kidney, or omentum) 752.0
- parauterine 614.6
- parovarian 614.6
- pelvic (peritoneal)
  - female (postoperative) (postinfection) 614.6
  - male (postoperative) (postinfection) (*see also* Adhesions, peritoneum) 568.0
  - postpartal (old) 614.6
  - tuberculous (*see also* Tuberculosis) 016.9 ✓5th
- penis to scrotum (congenital) 752.69
- periappendiceal (*see also* Adhesions, peritoneum) 568.0
- pericardium (nonrheumatic) 423.1
  - rheumatic 393
  - tuberculous (*see also* Tuberculosis) 017.9 ✓5th *[420.0]*
- pericholecystic 575.8
- perigastric (*see also* Adhesions, peritoneum) 568.0
- periovarian 614.6
- periprostatic 602.8
- perirectal (*see also* Adhesions, peritoneum) 568.0
- perirenal 593.89
- peritoneum, peritoneal (fibrous) (postoperative) 568.0
  - with obstruction (intestinal) 560.81
    - with hernia — *see also* Hernia, by site, with obstruction
      - gangrenous — *see* Hernia, by site, with gangrene
    - duodenum 537.3
  - congenital 751.4
  - female (postoperative) (postinfective) 614.6
  - pelvic, female 614.6
  - pelvic, male 568.0
  - postpartal, pelvic 614.6
  - to uterus 614.6
- peritubal 614.6
- periureteral 593.89
- periuterine 621.5
- perivesical 596.8
- perivesicular (seminal vesicle) 608.89
- pleura, pleuritic 511.0
  - tuberculous (*see also* Tuberculosis, pleura) 012.0 ✓5th
- pleuropericardial 511.0
- postoperative (gastrointestinal tract) (*see also* Adhesions, peritoneum)
  - eyelid 997.99
    - surgically created V45.69
  - pelvic, female 614.6
  - pelvic, male 568.0
  - urethra 598.2
- postpartal, old 624.4
- preputial, prepuce 605
- pulmonary 511.0
- pylorus (*see also* Adhesions, peritoneum) 568.0
- Rosenmüller's fossa 478.29
- sciatic nerve 355.0
- seminal vesicle 608.89
- shoulder (joint) 726.0
- sigmoid flexure (*see also* Adhesions, peritoneum) 568.0
- spermatic cord (acquired) 608.89
  - congenital 752.8

Adhesion(s), adhesive (postinfectional) (postoperative) — *continued*
- spinal canal 349.2
  - nerve 355.9
    - root 724.9
      - cervical NEC 723.4
      - lumbar NEC 724.4
      - lumbosacral 724.4
      - thoracic 724.4
- stomach (*see also* Adhesions, peritoneum) 568.0
- subscapular 726.2
- tendonitis 726.90
  - shoulder 726.0
- testicle 608.89
- tongue (congenital) (to gum or roof of mouth) 750.12
  - acquired 529.8
- trachea 519.1
- tubo-ovarian 614.6
- tunica vaginalis 608.89
- ureter 593.89
- uterus 621.5
  - to abdominal wall 614.6
    - in pregnancy or childbirth 654.4 ✓5th
      - affecting fetus or newborn 763.89
- vagina (chronic) (postoperative) (postradiation) 623.2
- vaginitis (congenital) 752.49
- vesical 596.8
- vitreous 379.29

Adie (-Holmes) syndrome (tonic pupillary reaction) 379.46

Adiponecrosis neonatorum 778.1

Adiposa dolorosa 272.8

Adiposalgia 272.8

Adiposis 278.0 ✓5th
- cerebralis 253.8
- dolorosa 272.8
- tuberosa simplex 272.8

Adiposity 278.00
- heart (*see also* Degeneration, myocardial) 429.1
- localized 278.1

Adiposogenital dystrophy 253.8

Adjustment
- prosthesis or other device — *see* Fitting of
- reaction — *see* Reaction, adjustment

Administration, prophylactic
- antibiotics V07.39
- antitoxin, any V07.2
- antivenin V07.2
- chemotherapeutic agent NEC V07.39
- chemotherapy NEC V07.39
- diphtheria antitoxin V07.2
- fluoride V07.31
- gamma globulin V07.2
- immune sera (gamma globulin) V07.2
- passive immunization agent V07.2
- RhoGAM V07.2

Admission (encounter)
- as organ donor — *see* Donor
- by mistake V68.9
- for
  - adjustment (of)
    - artificial
      - arm (complete) (partial) V52.0
      - eye V52.2
      - leg (complete) (partial) V52.1

- **Agalactia** 676.4 5th
- **Agammaglobulinemia** 279.00
  - with lymphopenia 279.2
  - acquired (primary) (secondary) 279.06
  - Bruton's X-linked 279.04
  - infantile sex-linked (Bruton's) (congenital) 279.04
  - Swiss-type 279.2
- **Aganglionosis** (bowel) (colon) 751.3
- **Age** (old) (*see also* Senile) 797
- **Agenesis** — *see also* Absence, by site, congenital
  - acoustic nerve 742.8
  - adrenal (gland) 759.1
  - alimentary tract (complete) (partial) NEC 751.8
    - lower 751.2
    - upper 750.8
  - anus, anal (canal) 751.2
  - aorta 747.22
  - appendix 751.2
  - arm (complete) (partial) (*see also* Deformity, reduction, upper limb) 755.20
  - artery (peripheral) NEC (*see also* Anomaly, peripheral vascular system) 747.60
    - brain 747.81
    - coronary 746.85
    - pulmonary 747.3
    - umbilical 747.5
  - auditory (canal) (external) 744.01
  - auricle (ear) 744.01
  - bile, biliary duct or passage 751.61
  - bone NEC 756.9
  - brain 740.0
    - specified part 742.2
  - breast 757.6
  - bronchus 748.3
  - canaliculus lacrimalis 743.65
  - carpus NEC (*see also* Deformity, reduction, upper limb) 755.28
  - cartilage 756.9
  - cecum 751.2
  - cerebellum 742.2
  - cervix 752.49
  - chin 744.89
  - cilia 743.63
  - circulatory system, part NEC 747.89
  - clavicle 755.51
  - clitoris 752.49
  - coccyx 756.13
  - colon 751.2
  - corpus callosum 742.2
  - cricoid cartilage 748.3
  - diaphragm (with hernia) 756.6
  - digestive organ(s) or tract (complete) (partial) NEC 751.8
    - lower 751.2
    - upper 750.8
  - ductus arteriosus 747.89
  - duodenum 751.1
  - ear NEC 744.09
    - auricle 744.01
    - lobe 744.21
  - ejaculatory duct 752.8
  - endocrine (gland) NEC 759.2
  - epiglottis 748.3
  - esophagus 750.3
  - Eustachian tube 744.24
  - extrinsic muscle, eye 743.69
  - eye 743.00
    - adnexa 743.69
  - eyelid (fold) 743.62

- **Agenesis** — *see also* Absence, by site, congenital — *continued*
  - face
    - bones NEC 756.0
    - specified part NEC 744.89
  - fallopian tube 752.19
  - femur NEC (*see also* Absence, femur, congenital) 755.34
  - fibula NEC (*see also* Absence, fibula, congenital) 755.37
  - finger NEC (*see also* Absence, finger, congenital) 755.29
  - foot (complete) (*see also* Deformity, reduction, lower limb) 755.31
  - gallbladder 751.69
  - gastric 750.8
  - genitalia, genital (organ)
    - female 752.8
      - external 752.49
      - internal NEC 752.8
    - male 752.8
      - penis 752.69
  - glottis 748.3
  - gonadal 758.6
  - hair 757.4
  - hand (complete) (*see also* Deformity, reduction, upper limb) 755.21
  - heart 746.89
    - valve NEC 746.89
      - aortic 746.89
      - mitral 746.89
      - pulmonary 746.01
  - hepatic 751.69
  - humerus NEC (*see also* Absence, humerus, congenital) 755.24
  - hymen 752.49
  - ileum 751.1
  - incus 744.04
  - intestine (small) 751.1
    - large 751.2
  - iris (dilator fibers) 743.45
  - jaw 524.09
  - jejunum 751.1
  - kidney(s) (partial) (unilateral) 753.0
  - labium (majus) (minus) 752.49
  - labyrinth, membranous 744.05
  - lacrimal apparatus (congenital) 743.65
  - larynx 748.3
  - leg NEC (*see also* Deformity, reduction, lower limb) 755.30
  - lens 743.35
  - limb (complete) (partial) (*see also* Deformity, reduction) 755.4
    - lower NEC 755.30
    - upper 755.20
  - lip 750.26
  - liver 751.69
  - lung (bilateral) (fissures) (lobe) (unilateral) 748.5
  - mandible 524.09
  - maxilla 524.09
  - metacarpus NEC 755.28
  - metatarsus NEC 755.38
  - muscle (any) 756.81
  - musculoskeletal system NEC 756.9
  - nail(s) 757.5
  - neck, part 744.89
  - nerve 742.8
  - nervous system, part NEC 742.8
  - nipple 757.6
  - nose 748.1
  - nuclear 742.8

- **Agenesis** — *see also* Absence, by site, congenital — *continued*
  - organ
    - of Corti 744.05
    - or site not listed — *see* Anomaly, specified type NEC
  - osseous meatus (ear) 744.03
  - ovary 752.0
  - oviduct 752.19
  - pancreas 751.7
  - parathyroid (gland) 759.2
  - patella 755.64
  - pelvic girdle (complete) (partial) 755.69
  - penis 752.69
  - pericardium 746.89
  - perineal body 756.81
  - pituitary (gland) 759.2
  - prostate 752.8
  - pulmonary
    - artery 747.3
    - trunk 747.3
    - vein 747.49
  - punctum lacrimale 743.65
  - radioulnar NEC (*see also* Absence, forearm, congenital) 755.25
  - radius NEC (*see also* Absence, radius, congenital) 755.26
  - rectum 751.2
  - renal 753.0
  - respiratory organ NEC 748.9
  - rib 756.3
  - roof of orbit 742.0
  - round ligament 752.8
  - sacrum 756.13
  - salivary gland 750.21
  - scapula 755.59
  - scrotum 752.8
  - seminal duct or tract 752.8
  - septum
    - atrial 745.69
    - between aorta and pulmonary artery 745.0
    - ventricular 745.3
  - shoulder girdle (complete) (partial) 755.59
  - skull (bone) 756.0
    - with
      - anencephalus 740.0
      - encephalocele 742.0
      - hydrocephalus 742.3
        - with spina bifida (*see also* Spina bifida) 741.0 5th
      - microcephalus 742.1
  - spermatic cord 752.8
  - spinal cord 742.59
  - spine 756.13
    - lumbar 756.13
      - isthmus 756.11
      - pars articularis 756.11
  - spleen 759.0
  - sternum 756.3
  - stomach 750.7
  - tarsus NEC 755.38
  - tendon 756.81
  - testicular 752.8
  - testis 752.8
  - thymus (gland) 759.2
  - thyroid (gland) 243
    - cartilage 748.3
  - tibia NEC (*see also* Absence, tibia, congenital) 755.36
  - tibiofibular NEC 755.35
  - toe (complete) (partial) (*see also* Absence, toe, congenital) 755.39

Alpers' disease 330.8
Alpha-lipoproteinemia 272.4
Alpha thalassemia 282.4
Alphos 696.1
Alpine sickness 993.2
Alport's syndrome (hereditary hematuria-nephropathy-deafness) 759.89
Alteration (of), **altered**
- awareness 780.09
  - transient 780.02
- consciousness 780.09
  - persistent vegetative state 780.03
  - transient 780.02
- mental status 780.9

Alternaria (infection) 118
Alternating — *see* condition
Altitude, high (effects) — *see* Effect, adverse, high altitude
Aluminosis (of lung) 503
Alvarez syndrome (transient cerebral ischemia) 435.9
Alveolar capillary block syndrome 516.3
Alveolitis
- allergic (extrinsic) 495.9
  - due to organisms (fungal, thermophilic actinomycete, other) growing in ventilation (air conditioning systems) 495.7
  - specified type NEC 495.8
- due to
  - Aspergillus clavatus 495.4
  - Cryptostroma corticale 495.6
- fibrosing (chronic) (cryptogenic) (lung) 516.3
  - idiopathic 516.3
  - rheumatoid 714.81
- jaw 526.5
- sicca dolorosa 526.5

Alveolus, alveolar — *see* condition
Alymphocytosis (pure) 279.2
Alymphoplasia, thymic 279.2
Alzheimer's
- dementia (senile) 331.0 *[294.1]*
- disease or sclerosis 331.0
  - with dementia — *see* Alzheimer's, dementia

Amastia (*see also* Absence, breast) 611.8
Amaurosis (acquired) (congenital) (*see also* Blindness) 369.00
- fugax 362.34
- hysterical 300.11
- Leber's (congenital) 362.76
- tobacco 377.34
- uremic — *see* Uremia

Amaurotic familial idiocy (infantile) (juvenile) (late) 330.1
Ambisexual 752.7
Amblyopia (acquired) (congenital) (partial) 368.00
- color 368.59
  - acquired 368.55
- deprivation 368.02
- ex anopsia 368.00
- hysterical 300.11
- nocturnal 368.60
  - vitamin A deficiency 264.5
- refractive 368.03
- strabismic 368.01
- suppression 368.01
- tobacco 377.34
- toxic NEC 377.34
- uremic — *see* Uremia

Ameba, amebic (histolytica) — *see also* Amebiasis
- abscess 006.3
  - bladder 006.8
  - brain (with liver and lung abscess) 006.5
  - liver 006.3
    - with
      - brain abscess (and lung abscess) 006.5
      - lung abscess 006.4
  - lung (with liver abscess) 006.4
    - with brain abscess 006.5
  - seminal vesicle 006.8
  - spleen 006.8
- carrier (suspected of) V02.2
- meningoencephalitis
  - due to Naegleria (gruberi) 136.2
  - primary 136.2

Amebiasis NEC 006.9
- with
  - brain abscess (with liver or lung abscess) 006.5
  - liver abscess (without mention of brain or lung abscess) 006.3
  - lung abscess (with liver abscess) 006.4
    - with brain abscess 006.5
- acute 006.0
- bladder 006.8
- chronic 006.1
- cutaneous 006.6
- cutis 006.6
- due to organism other than Entamoeba histolytica 007.8
- hepatic (*see also* Abscess, liver, amebic) 006.3
- nondysenteric 006.2
- seminal vesicle 006.8
- specified
  - organism NEC 007.8
  - site NEC 006.8

Ameboma 006.8
Amelia 755.4
- lower limb 755.31
- upper limb 755.21

Ameloblastoma (M9310/0) 213.1
- jaw (bone) (lower) 213.1
  - upper 213.0
- long bones (M9261/3) — *see* Neoplasm, bone, malignant
- malignant (M9310/3) 170.1
  - jaw (bone) (lower) 170.1
    - upper 170.0
- mandible 213.1
- tibial (M9261/3) 170.7

Amelogenesis imperfecta 520.5
- nonhereditaria (segmentalis) 520.4

Amenorrhea (primary) (secondary) 626.0
- due to ovarian dysfunction 256.8
- hyperhormonal 256.8

Amentia (*see also* Retardation, mental) 319
- Meynert's (nonalcoholic) 294.0
  - alcoholic 291.1
- nevoid 759.6

American
- leishmaniasis 085.5
- mountain tick fever 066.1
- trypanosomiasis — *see* Trypanosomiasis, American

Ametropia (*see also* Disorder, accommodation) 367.9
Amianthosis 501
Amimia 784.69
Amino acid
- deficiency 270.9
  - anemia 281.4
- metabolic disorder (*see also* Disorder, amino acid) 270.9

Aminoaciduria 270.9
- imidazole 270.5

Amnesia (retrograde) 780.9
- auditory 784.69
  - developmental 315.31
  - secondary to organic lesion 784.69
- hysterical or dissociative type 300.12
- psychogenic 300.12
- transient global 437.7

Amnestic (confabulatory) **syndrome** 294.0
- alcohol-induced 291.1
- drug-induced 292.83
- posttraumatic 294.0

Amniocentesis screening (for) V28.2
- alpha-fetoprotein level, raised V28.1
- chromosomal anomalies V28.0

Amnion, amniotic — *see also* condition
- nodosum 658.8 ✓5th

Amnionitis (complicating pregnancy) 658.4 ✓5th
- affecting fetus or newborn 762.7

Amoral trends 301.7
Amotio retinae (*see also* Detachment, retina) 361.9
Ampulla
- lower esophagus 530.89
- phrenic 530.89

Amputation
- any part of fetus, to facilitate delivery 763.89
- cervix (supravaginal) (uteri) 622.8
  - in pregnancy or childbirth 654.6 ✓5th
    - affecting fetus or newborn 763.89
- clitoris — *see* Wound, open, clitoris
- congenital
  - lower limb 755.31
  - upper limb 755.21
- neuroma (traumatic) — *see also* Injury, nerve, by site
  - surgical complication (late) 997.61
- penis — *see* Amputation, traumatic, penis
- status (without complication) — *see* Absence, by site, acquired
- stump (surgical) (posttraumatic)
  - abnormal, painful, or with complication (late) 997.60
  - healed or old NEC — *see also* Absence, by site, acquired
    - lower V49.70
    - upper V49.60
- traumatic (complete) (partial)

> *Note — "Complicated" includes traumatic amputation with delayed healing, delayed treatment, foreign body, or major infection.*

  - arm 887.4
    - at or above elbow 887.2
      - complicated 887.3

Anemia — *continued*
- pyridoxine-responsive (hypochromic) 285.0
- pyruvate kinase (PK) deficiency 282.3
- refractoria sideroblastica 285.0
- refractory (primary) 284.9
  - with hemochromatosis 285.0
  - megaloblastic 281.3
  - sideroblastic 285.0
  - sideropenic 280.9
- Rietti-Greppi-Micheli (thalassemia minor) 282.4
- scorbutic 281.8
- secondary (to) 285.9
  - blood loss (chronic) 280.0
    - acute 285.1
  - hemorrhage 280.0
    - acute 285.1
  - inadequate dietary iron intake 280.1
- semiplastic 284.9
- septic 285.9
- sickle-cell (*see also* Disease, sickle-cell) 282.60
- sideroachrestic 285.0
- sideroblastic (acquired) (any type) (congenital) (drug-induced) (due to disease) (hereditary) (primary) (refractory) (secondary) (sex-linked hypochromic) (vitamin B_6 responsive) 285.0
- sideropenic (refractory) 280.9
  - due to blood loss (chronic) 280.0
    - acute 285.1
- simple chronic 281.9
- specified type NEC 285.8
- spherocytic (hereditary) (*see also* Spherocytosis) 282.0
- splenic 285.8
  - familial (Gaucher's) 272.7
- splenomegalic 285.8
- stomatocytosis 282.8
- syphilitic 095.8
- target cell (oval) 282.4
- thalassemia 282.4
- thrombocytopenic (*see also* Thrombocytopenia) 287.5
- toxic 284.8
- triosephosphate isomerase deficiency 282.3
- tropical, macrocytic 281.2
- tuberculous (*see also* Tuberculosis) 017.9 [5th]
- Vegan's 281.1
- vitamin
  - B_6-responsive 285.0
  - B_{12} deficiency (dietary) 281.1
    - pernicious 281.0
- von Jaksch's (pseudoleukemia infantum) 285.8
- Witts' (achlorhydric anemia) 280.9
- Zuelzer (-Ogden) (nutritional megaloblastic anemia) 281.2

Anencephalus, anencephaly 740.0
- fetal, affecting management of pregnancy 655.0 [5th]

Anergasia (*see also* Psychosis, organic) 294.9
- senile 290.0

Anesthesia, anesthetic 782.0
- complication or reaction NEC 995.2
  - due to
    - correct substance properly administered 995.2
    - overdose or wrong substance given 968.4
      - specified anesthetic — *see* Table of Drugs and Chemicals

Anesthesia, anesthetic — *continued*
- cornea 371.81
- death from
  - correct substance properly administered 995.4
  - during delivery 668.9 [5th]
  - overdose or wrong substance given 968.4
    - specified anesthetic — *see* Table of Drugs and Chemicals
- eye 371.81
- functional 300.11
- hyperesthetic, thalamic 348.8
- hysterical 300.11
- local skin lesion 782.0
- olfactory 781.1
- sexual (psychogenic) 302.72
- shock
  - due to
    - correct substance properly administered 995.4
    - overdose or wrong substance given 968.4
      - specified anesthetic — *see* Table of Drugs and Chemicals
- skin 782.0
- tactile 782.0
- testicular 608.9
- thermal 782.0

Anetoderma (maculosum) 701.3

Aneuploidy NEC 758.5

Aneurin deficiency 265.1

Aneurysm (anastomotic) (artery) (cirsoid) (diffuse) (false) (fusiform) (multiple) (ruptured) (saccular) (varicose) 442.9
- abdominal (aorta) 441.4
  - ruptured 441.3
  - syphilitic 093.0
- aorta, aortic (nonsyphilitic) 441.9
  - abdominal 441.4
    - dissecting 441.02
    - ruptured 441.3
    - syphilitic 093.0
  - arch 441.2
    - ruptured 441.1
  - arteriosclerotic NEC 441.9
    - ruptured 441.5
  - ascending 441.2
    - ruptured 441.1
  - congenital 747.29
  - descending 441.9
    - abdominal 441.4
      - ruptured 441.3
    - ruptured 441.5
    - thoracic 441.2
      - ruptured 441.1
  - dissecting 441.00
    - abdominal 441.02
    - thoracic 441.01
    - thoracoabdominal 441.03
  - due to coarctation (aorta) 747.10
  - ruptured 441.5
  - sinus, right 747.29
  - syphilitic 093.0

Aneurysm (anastomotic) (artery) (cirsoid) (diffuse) (false) (fusiform) (multiple) (ruptured) (saccular) (varicose) — *continued*
- aorta, aortic (nonsyphilitic) — *continued*
  - thoracoabdominal 441.7
    - ruptured 441.6
  - thorax, thoracic (arch) (nonsyphilitic) 441.2
    - dissecting 441.01
    - ruptured 441.1
    - syphilitic 093.0
  - transverse 441.2
    - ruptured 441.1
  - valve (heart) (*see also* Endocarditis, aortic) 424.1
- arteriosclerotic NEC 442.9
  - cerebral 437.3
    - ruptured (*see also* Hemorrhage, subarachnoid) 430
- arteriovenous (congenital) (peripheral) NEC (*see also* Anomaly, arteriovenous) 747.60
  - acquired NEC 447.0
    - brain 437.3
      - ruptured (*see also* Hemorrhage, subarachnoid) 430
    - coronary 414.11
    - pulmonary 417.0
  - brain (cerebral) 747.81
    - ruptured (*see also* Hemorrhage, subarachnoid) 430
  - coronary 746.85
  - pulmonary 747.3
  - retina 743.58
  - specified site NEC 747.89
    - acquired 447.0
  - traumatic (*see also* Injury, blood vessel, by site) 904.9
- basal — *see* Aneurysm, brain
- berry (congenital) (ruptured) (*see also* Hemorrhage, subarachnoid) 430
- brain 437.3
  - arteriosclerotic 437.3
    - ruptured (*see also* Hemorrhage, subarachnoid) 430
  - arteriovenous 747.81
    - acquired 437.3
      - ruptured (*see also* Hemorrhage, subarachnoid) 430
    - ruptured (*see also* Hemorrhage, subarachnoid) 430
  - berry (congenital) (ruptured) (*see also* Hemorrhage, subarachnoid) 430
  - congenital 747.81
    - ruptured (*see also* Hemorrhage, subarachnoid) 430
  - meninges 437.3
    - ruptured (*see also* Hemorrhage, subarachnoid) 430
  - miliary (congenital) (ruptured) (*see also* Hemorrhage, subarachnoid) 430
  - mycotic 421.0
    - ruptured (*see also* Hemorrhage, subarachnoid) 430
  - nonruptured 437.3
  - ruptured (*see also* Hemorrhage, subarachnoid) 430
    - syphilitic 094.87
  - syphilitic (hemorrhage) 094.87
  - traumatic — *see* Injury, intracranial
- cardiac (false) (*see also* Aneurysm, heart) 414.10

Aneurysm (anastomotic) (artery) (cirsoid) (diffuse) (false) (fusiform) (multiple) (ruptured) (saccular) (varicose) — *continued*
- carotid artery (common) (external) 442.81
  - internal (intracranial portion) 437.3
    - extracranial portion 442.81
    - ruptured into brain (*see also* Hemorrhage, subarachnoid) 430
  - syphilitic 093.89
    - intracranial 094.87
- cavernous sinus (*see also* Aneurysm, brain) 437.3
  - arteriovenous 747.81
    - ruptured (*see also* Hemorrhage, subarachnoid) 430
  - congenital 747.81
    - ruptured (*see also* Hemorrhage, subarachnoid) 430
- celiac 442.84
- central nervous system, syphilitic 094.89
- cerebral — *see* Aneurysm, brain
- chest — *see* Aneurysm, thorax
- circle of Willis (*see also* Aneurysm, brain) 437.3
  - congenital 747.81
    - ruptured (*see also* Hemorrhage, subarachnoid) 430
  - ruptured (*see also* Hemorrhage, subarachnoid) 430
- common iliac artery 442.2
- congenital (peripheral) NEC 747.60
  - brain 747.81
    - ruptured (*see also* Hemorrhage, subarachnoid) 430
  - cerebral — *see* Aneurysm, brain, congenital
  - coronary 746.85
  - gastrointestinal 747.61
  - lower limb 747.64
  - pulmonary 747.3
  - renal 747.62
  - retina 743.58
  - specified site NEC 747.89
  - spinal 747.82
  - upper limb 747.63
- conjunctiva 372.74
- conus arteriosus (*see also* Aneurysm, heart) 414.10
- coronary (arteriosclerotic) (artery) (vein) (*see also* Aneurysm, heart) 414.11
  - arteriovenous 746.85
  - congenital 746.85
  - syphilitic 093.89
- cylindrical 441.9
  - ruptured 441.5
  - syphilitic 093.9
- dissecting 442.9
  - aorta 441.00
    - abdominal 441.02
    - thoracic 441.01
    - thoracoabdominal 441.03
  - syphilitic 093.9
- ductus arteriosus 747.0
- embolic — *see* Embolism, artery
- endocardial, infective (any valve) 421.0
- femoral 442.3
- gastroduodenal 442.84
- gastroepiploic 442.84
- heart (chronic or with a stated duration of over 8 weeks) (infectional) (wall) 414.10
  - acute or with a stated duration of 8 weeks or less (*see also* Infarct, myocardium) 410.9 [5th]

Aneurysm (anastomotic) (artery) (cirsoid) (diffuse) (false) (fusiform) (multiple) (ruptured) (saccular) (varicose) — *continued*
- heart (chronic or with a stated duration of over 8 weeks) (infectional) (wall) — *continued*
  - congenital 746.89
  - valve — *see* Endocarditis
- hepatic 442.84
- iliac (common) 442.2
- infective (any valve) 421.0
- innominate (nonsyphilitic) 442.89
  - syphilitic 093.89
- interauricular septum (*see also* Aneurysm, heart) 414.10
- interventricular septum (*see also* Aneurysm, heart) 414.10
- intracranial — *see* Aneurysm, brain
- intrathoracic (nonsyphilitic) 441.2
  - ruptured 441.1
  - syphilitic 093.0
- jugular vein 453.8
- lower extremity 442.3
- lung (pulmonary artery) 417.1
- malignant 093.9
- mediastinal (nonsyphilitic) 442.89
  - syphilitic 093.89
- miliary (congenital) (ruptured) (*see also* Hemorrhage, subarachnoid) 430
- mitral (heart) (valve) 424.0
- mural (arteriovenous) (heart) (*see also* Aneurysm, heart) 414.10
- mycotic, any site 421.0
  - ruptured, brain (*see also* Hemorrhage, subarachnoid) 430
- myocardium (*see also* Aneurysm, heart) 414.10
- neck 442.81
- pancreaticoduodenal 442.84
- patent ductus arteriosus 747.0
- peripheral NEC 442.89
  - congenital NEC (*see also* Aneurysm, congenital) 747.60
- popliteal 442.3
- pulmonary 417.1
  - arteriovenous 747.3
    - acquired 417.0
  - syphilitic 093.89
  - valve (heart) (*see also* Endocarditis, pulmonary) 424.3
- racemose 442.9
  - congenital (peripheral) NEC 747.60
- radial 442.0
- Rasmussen's (*see also* Tuberculosis) 011.2 [5th]
- renal 442.1
- retinal (acquired) 362.17
  - congenital 743.58
  - diabetic 250.5 [5th] *[362.01]*
- sinus, aortic (of Valsalva) 747.29
- specified site NEC 442.89
- spinal (cord) 442.89
  - congenital 747.82
  - syphilitic (hemorrhage) 094.89
- spleen, splenic 442.83
- subclavian 442.82
  - syphilitic 093.89
- superior mesenteric 442.84
- syphilitic 093.9
  - aorta 093.0
  - central nervous system 094.89

Aneurysm (anastomotic) (artery) (cirsoid) (diffuse) (false) (fusiform) (multiple) (ruptured) (saccular) (varicose) — *continued*
- syphilitic — *continued*
  - congenital 090.5
  - spine, spinal 094.89
- thoracoabdominal 441.7
  - ruptured 441.6
- thorax, thoracic (arch) (nonsyphilitic) 441.2
  - dissecting 441.01
  - ruptured 441.1
  - syphilitic 093.0
- traumatic (complication) (early) — *see* Injury, blood vessel, by site
- tricuspid (heart) (valve) — *see* Endocarditis, tricuspid
- ulnar 442.0
- upper extremity 442.0
- valve, valvular — *see* Endocarditis
- venous 456.8
  - congenital NEC (*see also* Aneurysm, congenital) 747.60
- ventricle (arteriovenous) (*see also* Aneurysm, heart) 414.10
- visceral artery NEC 442.84

Angiectasis 459.89

Angiectopia 459.9

Angiitis 447.6
- allergic granulomatous 446.4
- hypersensitivity 446.20
  - Goodpasture's syndrome 446.21
  - specified NEC 446.29
- necrotizing 446.0
- Wegener's (necrotizing respiratory granulomatosis) 446.4

Angina (attack) (cardiac) (chest) (effort) (heart) (pectoris) (syndrome) (vasomotor) 413.9
- abdominal 557.1
- agranulocytic 288.0
- aphthous 074.0
- catarrhal 462
- crescendo 411.1
- croupous 464.4
- cruris 443.9
  - due to atherosclerosis NEC (*see also* Arteriosclerosis, extremities) 440.20
- decubitus 413.0
- diphtheritic (membranous) 032.0
- erysipelatous 034.0
- erythematous 462
- exudative, chronic 476.0
- faucium 478.29
- gangrenous 462
  - diphtheritic 032.0
- infectious 462
- initial 411.1
- intestinal 557.1
- ludovici 528.3
- Ludwig's 528.3
- malignant 462
  - diphtheritic 032.0
- membranous 464.4
  - diphtheritic 032.0
- mesenteric 557.1
- monocytic 075
- nocturnal 413.0
- phlegmonous 475
  - diphtheritic 032.0
- preinfarctional 411.1
- Prinzmetal's 413.1

Anomaly, anomalous (congenital) (unspecified type) — *continued*
- genitalia, genital organ(s) or system — *continued*
  - male (external and internal) — *continued*
    - hypospadias 752.61
    - micropenis 752.64
    - testis, undescended 752.51
      - retractile 752.52
  - specified type NEC 752.8
- genitourinary NEC 752.9
- Gerbode 745.4
- globe (eye) 743.9
- glottis 748.3
- granulation or granulocyte, genetic 288.2
  - constitutional 288.2
  - leukocyte 288.2
- gum 750.9
- gyri 742.9
- hair 757.9
  - specified type NEC 757.4
- hand 755.50
- hard tissue formation in pulp 522.3
- head (*see also* Anomaly, skull) 756.0
- heart 746.9
  - auricle 746.9
  - bands 746.9
  - fibroelastosis cordis 425.3
  - folds 746.9
  - malposition 746.87
  - maternal, affecting fetus or newborn 760.3
  - obstructive NEC 746.84
  - patent ductus arteriosus (Botalli) 747.0
  - septum 745.9
    - acquired 429.71
    - aortic 745.0
    - aorticopulmonary 745.0
    - atrial 745.5
    - auricular 745.5
    - between aorta and pulmonary artery 745.0
    - endocardial cushion type 745.60
      - specified type NEC 745.69
    - interatrial 745.5
    - interventricular 745.4
      - with pulmonary stenosis or atresia, dextraposition of aorta, and hypertrophy of right ventricle 745.2
      - acquired 429.71
    - specified type NEC 745.8
    - ventricular 745.4
      - with pulmonary stenosis or atresia, dextraposition of aorta, and hypertrophy of right ventricle 745.2
      - acquired 429.71
  - specified type NEC 746.89
  - tetralogy of Fallot 745.2
  - valve NEC 746.9
    - aortic 746.9
      - atresia 746.89
      - bicuspid valve 746.4
      - insufficiency 746.4
      - specified type NEC 746.89
      - stenosis 746.3
        - subaortic 746.81
        - supravalvular 747.22
    - mitral 746.9
      - atresia 746.89
      - insufficiency 746.6

Anomaly, anomalous (congenital) (unspecified type) — *continued*
- heart — *continued*
  - valve NEC — *continued*
    - mitral — *continued*
      - specified type NEC 746.89
      - stenosis 746.5
    - pulmonary 746.00
      - atresia 746.01
      - insufficiency 746.09
      - stenosis 746.02
        - infundibular 746.83
        - subvalvular 746.83
    - tricuspid 746.9
      - atresia 746.1
      - stenosis 746.1
  - ventricle 746.9
- heel 755.67
- Hegglin's 288.2
- hemianencephaly 740.0
- hemicephaly 740.0
- hemicrania 740.0
- hepatic duct 751.60
- hip (joint) 755.63
- hourglass
  - bladder 753.8
  - gallbladder 751.69
  - stomach 750.7
- humerus 755.50
- hymen 752.40
- hypersegmentation of neutrophils, hereditary 288.2
- hypophyseal 759.2
- ileocecal (coil) (valve) 751.5
- ileum (intestine) 751.5
- ilium 755.60
- integument 757.9
  - specified type NEC 757.8
- intervertebral cartilage or disc 756.10
- intestine (large) (small) 751.5
  - fixational type 751.4
- iris 743.9
  - specified type NEC 743.46
- ischium 755.60
- jaw NEC 524.9
  - closure 524.5
  - size (major) NEC 524.00
  - specified type NEC 524.8
- jaw-cranial base relationship 524.10
  - specified NEC 524.19
- jejunum 751.5
- joint 755.9
  - hip
    - dislocation (*see also* Dislocation, hip, congenital) 754.30
    - predislocation (*see also* Subluxation, congenital, hip) 754.32
    - preluxation (*see also* Subluxation, congenital, hip) 754.32
    - subluxation (*see also* Subluxation, congenital, hip) 754.32
  - lumbosacral 756.10
    - spondylolisthesis 756.12
    - spondylosis 756.11
  - multiple arthrogryposis 754.89
  - sacroiliac 755.69
- Jordan's 288.2
- kidney(s) (calyx) (pelvis) 753.9
  - vessel 747.62

Anomaly, anomalous (congenital) (unspecified type) — *continued*
- Klippel-Feil (brevicollis) 756.16
- knee (joint) 755.64
- labium (majus) (minus) 752.40
- labyrinth, membranous (causing impairment of hearing) 744.05
- lacrimal
  - apparatus, duct or passage 743.9
    - specified type NEC 743.65
  - gland 743.9
    - specified type NEC 743.64
- Langdon Down (mongolism) 758.0
- larynx, laryngeal (muscle) 748.3
  - web, webbed 748.2
- leg (lower) (upper) 755.60
  - reduction NEC (*see also* Deformity, reduction, lower limb) 755.30
- lens 743.9
  - shape 743.36
  - specified type NEC 743.39
- leukocytes, genetic 288.2
  - granulation (constitutional) 288.2
- lid (fold) 743.9
- ligament 756.9
  - broad 752.10
  - round 752.9
- limb, except reduction deformity 755.8
  - lower 755.60
    - reduction deformity (*see also* Deformity, reduction, lower limb) 755.30
    - specified type NEC 755.69
  - upper 755.50
    - reduction deformity (*see also* Deformity, reduction, upper limb) 755.20
    - specified type NEC 755.59
- lip 750.9
  - harelip (*see also* Cleft, lip) 749.10
  - specified type NEC 750.26
- liver (duct) 751.60
  - atresia 751.69
- lower extremity 755.60
  - vessel 747.64
- lumbosacral (joint) (region) 756.10
- lung (fissure) (lobe) NEC 748.60
  - agenesis 748.5
  - specified type NEC 748.69
- lymphatic system 759.9
- Madelung's (radius) 755.54
- mandible 524.9
  - size NEC 524.00
- maxilla 524.90
  - size NEC 524.00
- May (-Hegglin) 288.2
- meatus urinarius 753.9
  - specified type NEC 753.8
- meningeal bands or folds, constriction of 742.8
- meninges 742.9
  - brain 742.4
  - spinal 742.59
- meningocele (*see also* Spina bifida) 741.9 [5th]
  - acquired 349.2
- mesentery 751.9
- metacarpus 755.50
- metatarsus 755.67
- middle ear, except ossicles (causing impairment of hearing) 744.03
  - ossicles 744.04

- **Antenatal**
  - care, normal pregnancy V22.1
    - first V22.0
  - screening (for) V28.9
    - based on amniocentesis NEC V28.2
      - chromosomal anomalies V28.0
      - raised alphafetoprotein levels V28.1
    - chromosomal anomalies V28.0
    - fetal growth retardation using ultrasonics V28.4
    - isoimmunization V28.5
    - malformations using ultrasonics V28.3
    - raised alphafetoprotein levels in amniotic fluid V28.1
    - specified condition NEC V28.8
    - Streptococcus B V28.6
- **Antepartum** — *see* condition
- **Anterior** — *see also* condition
  - spinal artery compression syndrome 721.1
- **Antero-occlusion** 524.2
- **Anteversion**
  - cervix (*see also* Anteversion, uterus) 621.6
  - femur (neck), congenital 755.63
  - uterus, uterine (cervix) (postinfectional) (postpartal, old) 621.6
    - congenital 752.3
    - in pregnancy or childbirth 654.4 ✓5th
      - affecting fetus or newborn 763.89
      - causing obstructed labor 660.2 ✓5th
        - affecting fetus or newborn 763.1
- **Anthracosilicosis** (occupational) 500
- **Anthracosis** (lung) (occupational) 500
  - lingua 529.3
- **Anthrax** 022.9
  - with pneumonia 022.1 *[484.5]*
  - colitis 022.2
  - cutaneous 022.0
  - gastrointestinal 022.2
  - intestinal 022.2
  - pulmonary 022.1
  - respiratory 022.1
  - septicemia 022.3
  - specified manifestation NEC 022.8
- **Anthropoid pelvis** 755.69
  - with disproportion (fetopelvic) 653.2 ✓5th
    - affecting fetus or newborn 763.1
    - causing obstructed labor 660.1 ✓5th
      - affecting fetus or newborn 763.1
- **Anthropophobia** 300.29
- **Antibioma, breast** 611.0
- **Antibodies**
  - maternal (blood group) (*see also* Incompatibility) 656.2 ✓5th
    - anti-D, cord blood 656.1 ✓5th
      - fetus or newborn 773.0
- **Antibody deficiency syndrome**
  - agammaglobulinemic 279.00
  - congenital 279.04
  - hypogammaglobulinemic 279.00
- **Anticoagulant, circulating** (*see also* Circulating anticoagulants) 286.5
- **Antimongolism syndrome** 758.3
- **Antimonial cholera** 985.4
- **Antisocial personality** 301.7
- **Antithrombinemia** (*see also* Circulating anticoagulants) 286.5
- **Antithromboplastinemia** (*see also* Circulating anticoagulants) 286.5
- **Antithromboplastinogenemia** (*see also* Circulating anticoagulants) 286.5
- **Antitoxin complication or reaction** — *see* Complications, vaccination
- **Anton** (-Babinski) syndrome (hemiasomatognosia) 307.9
- **Antritis** (chronic) 473.0
  - acute 461.0
- **Antrum, antral** — *see* condition
- **Anuria** 788.5
  - with
    - abortion — *see* Abortion, by type, with renal failure
    - ectopic pregnancy (*see also* categories 633.0–633.9) 639.3
    - molar pregnancy (*see also* categories 630–632) 639.3
  - calculus (impacted) (recurrent) 592.9
    - kidney 592.0
    - ureter 592.1
  - congenital 753.3
  - due to a procedure 997.5
  - following
    - abortion 639.3
    - ectopic or molar pregnancy 639.3
  - newborn 753.3
  - postrenal 593.4
  - puerperal, postpartum, childbirth 669.3 ✓5th
  - specified as due to a procedure 997.5
  - sulfonamide
    - correct substance properly administered 788.5
    - overdose or wrong substance given or taken 961.0
  - traumatic (following crushing) 958.5
- **Anus, anal** — *see* condition
- **Anusitis** 569.49
- **Anxiety** (neurosis) (reaction) (state) 300.00
  - alcohol-induced 291.89
  - depression 300.4
  - drug-induced 292.89
  - due to or associated with physical condition 293.84
  - generalized 300.02
  - hysteria 300.20
  - in
    - acute stress reaction 308.0
    - transient adjustment reaction 309.24
  - panic type 300.01
  - separation, abnormal 309.21
  - syndrome (organic) (transient) 293.84
- **Aorta, aortic** — *see* condition
- **Aortectasia** 441.9
- **Aortitis** (nonsyphilitic) 447.6
  - arteriosclerotic 440.0
  - calcific 447.6
  - Döhle-Heller 093.1
  - luetic 093.1
  - rheumatic (*see also* Endocarditis, acute, rheumatic) 391.1
  - rheumatoid — *see* Arthritis, rheumatoid
  - specific 093.1
  - syphilitic 093.1
    - congenital 090.5
- **Apathetic thyroid storm** (*see also* Thyrotoxicosis) 242.9 ✓5th
- **Apepsia** 536.8
  - achlorhydric 536.0
  - psychogenic 306.4
- **Aperistalsis, esophagus** 530.0
- **Apert's syndrome** (acrocephalosyndactyly) 755.55
- **Apert-Gallais syndrome** (adrenogenital) 255.2
- **Apertognathia** 524.2
- **Aphagia** 787.2
  - psychogenic 307.1
- **Aphakia** (acquired) (bilateral) (postoperative) (unilateral) 379.31
  - congenital 743.35
- **Aphalangia** (congenital) 755.4
  - lower limb (complete) (intercalary) (partial) (terminal) 755.39
    - meaning all digits (complete) (partial) 755.31
    - transverse 755.31
  - upper limb (complete) (intercalary) (partial) (terminal) 755.29
    - meaning all digits (complete) (partial) 755.21
    - transverse 755.21
- **Aphasia** (amnestic) (ataxic) (auditory) (Broca's) (choreatic) (classic) (expressive) (global) (ideational) (ideokinetic) (ideomotor) (jargon) (motor) (nominal) (receptive) (semantic) (sensory) (syntactic) (verbal) (visual) (Wernicke's) 784.3
  - developmental 315.31
  - syphilis, tertiary 094.89
  - uremic — *see* Uremia
- **Aphemia** 784.3
  - uremic — *see* Uremia
- **Aphonia** 784.41
  - clericorum 784.49
  - hysterical 300.11
  - organic 784.41
  - psychogenic 306.1
- **Aphthae, aphthous** — *see also* condition
  - Bednar's 528.2
  - cachectic 529.0
  - epizootic 078.4
  - fever 078.4
  - oral 528.2
  - stomatitis 528.2
  - thrush 112.0
  - ulcer (oral) (recurrent) 528.2
    - genital organ(s) NEC
      - female 629.8
      - male 608.89
    - larynx 478.79
- **Apical** — *see* condition
- **Aplasia** — *see also* Agenesis
  - alveolar process (acquired) 525.8
    - congenital 750.26
  - aorta (congenital) 747.22
  - aortic valve (congenital) 746.89
  - axialis extracorticalis (congenital) 330.0
  - bone marrow (myeloid) 284.9
    - acquired (secondary) 284.8
    - congenital 284.0
    - idiopathic 284.9
  - brain 740.0
    - specified part 742.2
  - breast 757.6
  - bronchus 748.3
  - cementum 520.4
  - cerebellar 742.2
  - congenital pure red cell 284.0
  - corpus callosum 742.2
  - erythrocyte 284.8
    - congenital 284.0
  - extracortical axial 330.0
  - eye (congenital) 743.00
  - fovea centralis (congenital) 743.55
  - germinal (cell) 606.0
  - iris 743.45
  - labyrinth, membranous 744.05

Aplasia — *see also* Agenesis — *continued*
limb (congenital) 755.4
lower NEC 755.30
upper NEC 755.20
lung (bilateral) (congenital) (unilateral) 748.5
nervous system NEC 742.8
nuclear 742.8
ovary 752.0
Pelizaeus-Merzbacher 330.0
prostate (congenital) 752.8
red cell (pure) (with thymoma) 284.8
acquired (secondary) 284.8
congenital 284.0
hereditary 284.0
of infants 284.0
primary 284.0
round ligament (congenital) 752.8
salivary gland 750.21
skin (congenital) 757.39
spinal cord 742.59
spleen 759.0
testis (congenital) 752.8
thymic, with immunodeficiency 279.2
thyroid 243
uterus 752.3
ventral horn cell 742.59
Apleuria 756.3
Apnea, apneic (spells) 786.03
newborn, neonatorum 770.8
psychogenic 306.1
sleep NEC 780.57
with
hypersomnia 780.53
hyposomnia 780.51
insomnia 780.51
sleep disturbance NEC 780.57
Apneumatosis newborn 770.4
Apodia 755.31
Apophysitis (bone) (*see also* Osteochondrosis) 732.9
calcaneus 732.5
juvenile 732.6
Apoplectiform convulsions (*see also* Disease, cerebrovascular, acute) 436
Apoplexia, apoplexy, apoplectic (*see also* Disease, cerebrovascular, acute) 436
abdominal 569.89
adrenal 036.3
attack 436
basilar (*see also* Disease, cerebrovascular, acute) 436
brain (*see also* Disease, cerebrovascular, acute) 436
bulbar (*see also* Disease, cerebrovascular, acute) 436
capillary (*see also* Disease, cerebrovascular, acute) 436
cardiac (*see also* Infarct, myocardium) 410.9 [5th]
cerebral (*see also* Disease, cerebrovascular, acute) 436
chorea (*see also* Disease, cerebrovascular, acute) 436
congestive (*see also* Disease, cerebrovascular, acute) 436
newborn 767.4
embolic (*see also* Embolism, brain) 434.1 [5th]
fetus 767.0
fit (*see also* Disease, cerebrovascular, acute) 436

Apoplexia, apoplexy, apoplectic (*see also* Disease, cerebrovascular, acute) — *continued*
healed or old V12.59
heart (auricle) (ventricle) (*see also* Infarct, myocardium) 410.9 [5th]
heat 992.0
hemiplegia (*see also* Disease, cerebrovascular, acute) 436
hemorrhagic (stroke) (*see also* Hemorrhage, brain) 432.9
ingravescent (*see also* Disease, cerebrovascular, acute) 436
late effect — *see* Late effect(s) (of) cerebrovascular disease
lung — *see* Embolism, pulmonary
meninges, hemorrhagic (*see also* Hemorrhage, subarachnoid) 430
neonatorum 767.0
newborn 767.0
pancreatitis 577.0
placenta 641.2 [5th]
progressive (*see also* Disease, cerebrovascular, acute) 436
pulmonary (artery) (vein) — *see* Embolism, pulmonary
sanguineous (*see also* Disease, cerebrovascular, acute) 436
seizure (*see also* Disease, cerebrovascular, acute) 436
serous (*see also* Disease, cerebrovascular, acute) 436
spleen 289.59
stroke (*see also* Disease, cerebrovascular, acute) 436
thrombotic (*see also* Thrombosis, brain) 434.0 [5th]
uremic — *see* Uremia
uteroplacental 641.2 [5th]
Appendage
fallopian tube (cyst of Morgagni) 752.11
intestine (epiploic) 751.5
preauricular 744.1
testicular (organ of Morgagni) 752.8
Appendicitis 541
with
perforation, peritonitis (generalized), or rupture 540.0
with peritoneal abscess 540.1
peritoneal abscess 540.1
acute (catarrhal) (fulminating) (gangrenous) (inflammatory) (obstructive) (retrocecal) (suppurative) 540.9
with
perforation, peritonitis, or rupture 540.0
with peritoneal abscess 540.1
peritoneal abscess 540.1
amebic 006.8
chronic (recurrent) 542
exacerbation — *see* Appendicitis, acute
fulminating — *see* Appendicitis, acute
gangrenous — *see* Appendicitis, acute
healed (obliterative) 542
interval 542
neurogenic 542
obstructive 542
pneumococcal 541
recurrent 542
relapsing 542
retrocecal 541
subacute (adhesive) 542

Appendicitis — *continued*
subsiding 542
suppurative — *see* Appendicitis, acute
tuberculous (*see also* Tuberculosis) 014.8 [5th]
Appendiclausis 543.9
Appendicolithiasis 543.9
Appendicopathia oxyurica 127.4
Appendix, appendicular — *see also* condition
Morgagni (male) 752.8
fallopian tube 752.11
Appetite
depraved 307.52
excessive 783.6
psychogenic 307.51
lack or loss (*see also* Anorexia) 783.0
nonorganic origin 307.59
perverted 307.52
hysterical 300.11
Apprehension, apprehensiveness (abnormal) (state) 300.00
specified type NEC 300.09
Approximal wear 521.1
Apraxia (classic) (ideational) (ideokinetic) (ideomotor) (motor) 784.69
oculomotor, congenital 379.51
verbal 784.69
Aptyalism 527.7
Arabicum elephantiasis (*see also* Infestation, filarial) 125.9
Arachnidism 989.5
Arachnitis — *see* Meningitis
Arachnodactyly 759.82
Arachnoidism 989.5
Arachnoiditis (acute) (adhesive) (basic) (brain) (cerebrospinal) (chiasmal) (chronic) (spinal) (*see also* Meningitis) 322.9
meningococcal (chronic) 036.0
syphilitic 094.2
tuberculous (*see also* Tuberculosis, meninges) 013.0 [5th]
Araneism 989.5
Arboencephalitis, Australian 062.4
Arborization block (heart) 426.6
Arbor virus, arbovirus (infection) NEC 066.9
ARC 042
Arches — *see* condition
Arcuatus uterus 752.3
Arcus (cornea)
juvenilis 743.43
interfering with vision 743.42
senilis 371.41
Arc-welders' lung 503
Arc-welders' syndrome (photokeratitis) 370.24
Areflexia 796.1
Areola — *see* condition
Argentaffinoma (M8241/1) — *see also* Neoplasm, by site, uncertain behavior
benign (M8241/0) — *see* Neoplasm, by site, benign
malignant (M8241/3) — *see* Neoplasm, by site, malignant
syndrome 259.2
Argentinian hemorrhagic fever 078.7
Arginosuccinicaciduria 270.6
Argonz-Del Castillo syndrome (nonpuerperal galactorrhea and amenorrhea) 253.1

- **Arteriosclerosis, arteriosclerotic** (artery) (deformans) (diffuse) (disease) (endarteritis) (general) (obliterans) (obliterative) (occlusive) (senile) (with calcification) — *continued*
  - heart (disease) — *see also* Arteriosclerosis, coronary
    - valve 424.99
      - aortic 424.1
      - mitral 424.0
      - pulmonary 424.3
      - tricuspid 424.2
  - kidney (*see also* Hypertension, kidney) 403.90
  - labyrinth, labyrinthine 388.00
  - medial NEC (*see also* Arteriosclerosis, extremities) 440.20
  - mesentery (artery) 557.1
  - Mönckeberg's (*see also* Arteriosclerosis, extremities) 440.20
  - myocarditis 429.0
  - nephrosclerosis (*see also* Hypertension, kidney) 403.90
  - peripheral (of extremities) — *see* Arteriosclerosis, extremities
  - precerebral 433.9 [5th]
    - specified artery NEC 433.8 [5th]
  - pulmonary (idiopathic) 416.0
  - renal (*see also* Hypertension, kidney) 403.90
    - arterioles (*see also* Hypertension, kidney) 403.90
    - artery 440.1
  - retinal (vascular) 440.8 *[362.13]*
  - specified artery NEC 440.8
    - with gangrene 440.8 *[785.4]*
  - spinal (cord) 437.0
  - vertebral (artery) (*see also* Occlusion, artery, vertebral) 433.2 [5th]
- **Arteriospasm** 443.9
- **Arteriovenous** — *see* condition
- **Arteritis** 447.6
  - allergic (*see also* Angiitis, hypersensitivity) 446.20
  - aorta (nonsyphilitic) 447.6
    - syphilitic 093.1
  - aortic arch 446.7
  - brachiocephalica 446.7
  - brain 437.4
    - syphilitic 094.89
  - branchial 446.7
  - cerebral 437.4
    - late effect — *see* Late effect(s) (of) cerebrovascular disease
    - syphilitic 094.89
  - coronary (artery) — *see also* Arteriosclerosis, coronary
    - rheumatic 391.9
      - chronic 398.99
    - syphilitic 093.89
  - cranial (left) (right) 446.5
  - deformans — *see* Arteriosclerosis
  - giant cell 446.5
  - necrosing or necrotizing 446.0
  - nodosa 446.0
  - obliterans — *see also* Arteriosclerosis
    - subclaviocarotica 446.7
  - pulmonary 417.8
  - retina 362.18
  - rheumatic — *see* Fever, rheumatic
  - senile — *see* Arteriosclerosis
  - suppurative 447.2
- **Arteritis** — *continued*
  - syphilitic (general) 093.89
    - brain 094.89
    - coronary 093.89
    - spinal 094.89
  - temporal 446.5
  - young female, syndrome 446.7
- **Artery, arterial** — *see* condition
- **Arthralgia** (*see also* Pain, joint) 719.4 [5th]
  - allergic (*see also* Pain, joint) 719.4 [5th]
  - in caisson disease 993.3
  - psychogenic 307.89
  - rubella 056.71
  - Salmonella 003.23
  - temporomandibular joint 524.62
- **Arthritis, arthritic** (acute) (chronic) (subacute) 716.9 [5th]
  - meaning Osteoarthritis — *see* Osteoarthrosis

> *Note — Use the following fifth-digit subclassification with categories 711–712, 715–716:*
>
> *0 site unspecified*
> *1 shoulder region*
> *2 upper arm*
> *3 forearm*
> *4 hand*
> *5 pelvic region and thigh*
> *6 lower leg*
> *7 ankle and foot*
> *8 other specified sites*
> *9 multiple sites*

  - allergic 716.2 [5th]
  - ankylosing (crippling) (spine) 720.0 *[713.2]*
    - sites other than spine 716.9 [5th]
  - atrophic 714.0
    - spine 720.9
  - back (*see also* Arthritis, spine) 721.90
  - Bechterew's (ankylosing spondylitis) 720.0
  - blennorrhagic 098.50 *[711.6]* [5th]
  - cervical, cervicodorsal (*see also* Spondylosis, cervical) 721.0
  - Charcôt's 094.0 *[713.5]*
    - diabetic 250.6 [5th] *[713.5]*
    - syringomyelic 336.0 *[713.5]*
    - tabetic 094.0 *[713.5]*
  - chylous (*see also* Filariasis) 125.9 *[711.7]* [5th]
  - climacteric NEC 716.3 [5th]
  - coccyx 721.8
  - cricoarytenoid 478.79
  - crystal (-induced) — *see* Arthritis, due to crystals
  - deformans (*see also* Osteoarthrosis) 715.9 [5th]
    - spine 721.90
      - with myelopathy 721.91
  - degenerative (*see also* Osteoarthrosis) 715.9 [5th]
    - idiopathic 715.09
    - polyarticular 715.09
    - spine 721.90
      - with myelopathy 721.91
  - dermatoarthritis, lipoid 272.8 *[713.0]*
  - due to or associated with
    - acromegaly 253.0 *[713.0]*
    - actinomycosis 039.8 *[711.4]* [5th]
    - amyloidosis 277.3 *[713.7]*
    - bacterial disease NEC 040.89 *[711.4]* [5th]
- **Arthritis, arthritic** (acute) (chronic) (subacute) — *continued*
  - due to or associated with — *continued*
    - Behçet's syndrome 136.1 *[711.2]* [5th]
    - blastomycosis 116.0 *[711.6]* [5th]
    - brucellosis (*see also* Brucellosis) 023.9 *[711.4]* [5th]
    - caisson disease 993.3
    - coccidioidomycosis 114.3 *[711.6]* [5th]
    - coliform (Escherichia coli) 711.0 [5th]
    - colitis, ulcerative (*see also* Colitis, ulcerative) 556.9 *[713.1]*
    - cowpox 051.0 *[711.5]* [5th]
    - crystals — *see also* Gout
      - dicalcium phosphate 275.49 *[712.1]* [5th]
      - pyrophosphate 275.49 *[712.2]* [5th]
      - specified NEC 275.49 *[712.8]* [5th]
    - dermatoarthritis, lipoid 272.8 *[713.0]*
    - dermatological disorder NEC 709.9 *[713.3]*
    - diabetes 250.6 [5th] *[713.5]*
    - diphtheria 032.89 *[711.4]* [5th]
    - dracontiasis 125.7 *[711.7]* [5th]
    - dysentery 009.0 *[711.3]* [5th]
    - endocrine disorder NEC 259.9 *[713.0]*
    - enteritis NEC 009.1 *[711.3]* [5th]
      - infectious (*see also* Enteritis, infectious) 009.0 *[711.3]* [5th]
        - specified organism NEC 008.8 *[711.3]* [5th]
      - regional (*see also* Enteritis, regional) 555.9 *[713.1]*
      - specified organism NEC 008.8 *[711.3]* [5th]
    - epiphyseal slip, nontraumatic (old) 716.8 [5th]
    - erysipelas 035 *[711.4]* [5th]
    - erythema
      - epidemic 026.1
      - multiforme 695.1 *[713.3]*
      - nodosum 695.2 *[713.3]*
    - Escherichia coli 711.0 [5th]
    - filariasis NEC 125.9 *[711.7]* [5th]
    - gastrointestinal condition NEC 569.9 *[713.1]*
    - glanders 024 *[711.4]* [5th]
    - Gonococcus 098.50
    - gout 274.0
    - H. influenzae 711.0 [5th]
    - helminthiasis NEC 128.9 *[711.7]* [5th]
    - hematological disorder NEC 289.9 *[713.2]*
    - hemochromatosis 275.0 *[713.0]*
    - hemoglobinopathy NEC (*see also* Disease, hemoglobin) 282.7 *[713.2]*
    - hemophilia (*see also* Hemophilia) 286.0 *[713.2]*
    - Hemophilus influenzae (H. influenzae) 711.0 [5th]
    - Henoch (-Schönlein) purpura 287.0 *[713.6]*
    - histoplasmosis NEC (*see also* Histoplasmosis) 115.99 *[711.6]* [5th]
    - hyperparathyroidism 252.0 *[713.0]*
    - hypersensitivity reaction NEC 995.3 *[713.6]*
    - hypogammaglobulinemia (*see also* Hypogammaglobulinemia) 279.00 *[713.0]*
    - hypothyroidism NEC 244.9 *[713.0]*

> *Note — Use the following fifth digit subclassification with category 493:*
>
> *0 without mention of status asthmaticus*
>
> *1 with status asthmaticus*

B

Birthmark 757.32
Bisalbuminemia 273.8
Biskra button 085.1
Bite(s)
- with intact skin surface — *see* Contusion
- animal — *see* Wound, open, by site
  - intact skin surface — *see* Contusion
- centipede 989.5
- chigger 133.8
- fire ant 989.5
- flea — *see* Injury, superficial, by site
- human (open wound) — *see also* Wound, open, by site
  - intact skin surface — *see* Contusion
- insect
  - nonvenomous — *see* Injury, superficial, by site
  - venomous 989.5
- mad dog (death from) 071
- poisonous 989.5
- red bug 133.8
- reptile 989.5
  - nonvenomous — *see* Wound, open, by site
- snake 989.5
  - nonvenomous — *see* Wound, open, by site
- spider (venomous) 989.5
  - nonvenomous — *see* Injury, superficial, by site
- venomous 989.5

Biting
- cheek or lip 528.9
- nail 307.9

Black
- death 020.9
- eye NEC 921.0
- hairy tongue 529.3
- lung disease 500

Blackfan-Diamond anemia or syndrome (congenital hypoplastic anemia) 284.0
Blackhead 706.1
Blackout 780.2
Blackwater fever 084.8
Bladder — *see* condition
Blast
- blindness 921.3
- concussion — *see* Blast, injury
- injury 869.0
  - with open wound into cavity 869.1
  - abdomen or thorax — *see* Injury, internal, by site
  - brain (*see also* Concussion, brain) 850.9
    - with skull fracture — *see* Fracture, skull
  - ear (acoustic nerve trauma) 951.5
    - with perforation, tympanic membrane — *see* Wound, open, ear, drum
  - lung (*see also* Injury, internal, lung) 861.20
  - otitic (explosive) 388.11

Blastomycosis, blastomycotic (chronic) (cutaneous) (disseminated) (lung) (pulmonary) (systemic) 116.0
- Brazilian 116.1
- European 117.5
- keloidal 116.2
- North American 116.0
- primary pulmonary 116.0
- South American 116.1

Bleb(s) 709.8
- emphysematous (bullous) (diffuse) (lung) (ruptured) (solitary) 492.0
- filtering, eye (postglaucoma) (status) V45.69
  - with complication 997.99
  - postcataract extraction (complication) 997.99
- lung (ruptured) 492.0
  - congenital 770.5
- subpleural (emphysematous) 492.0

Bleeder (familial) (hereditary) (*see also* Defect, coagulation) 286.9
- nonfamilial 286.9

Bleeding (*see also* Hemorrhage) 459.0
- anal 569.3
- anovulatory 628.0
- atonic, following delivery 666.1 ✓5th
- capillary 448.9
- due to subinvolution 621.1
  - puerperal 666.2 ✓5th
- ear 388.69
- excessive, associated with menopausal onset 627.0
- familial (*see also* Defect, coagulation) 286.9
- following intercourse 626.7
- gastrointestinal 578.9
- gums 523.8
- hemorrhoids — *see* Hemorrhoids, bleeding
- intermenstrual
  - irregular 626.6
  - regular 626.5
- intraoperative 998.11
- irregular NEC 626.4
- menopausal 627.0
- mouth 528.9
- nipple 611.79
- nose 784.7
- ovulation 626.5
- postclimacteric 627.1
- postcoital 626.7
- postmenopausal 627.1
  - following induced menopause 627.4
- postoperative 998.11
- preclimacteric 627.0
- puberty 626.3
  - excessive, with onset of menstrual periods 626.3
- rectum, rectal 569.3
- tendencies (*see also* Defect, coagulation) 286.9
- throat 784.8
- umbilical stump 772.3
- umbilicus 789.9
- unrelated to menstrual cycle 626.6
- uterus, uterine 626.9
  - climacteric 627.0
  - dysfunctional 626.8
  - functional 626.8
  - unrelated to menstrual cycle 626.6
- vagina, vaginal 623.8
  - functional 626.8
- vicarious 625.8

Blennorrhagia, blennorrhagic — *see* Blennorrhea
Blennorrhea (acute) 098.0
- adultorum 098.40
- alveolaris 523.4
- chronic or duration of 2 months or over 098.2
- gonococcal (neonatorum) 098.40
- inclusion (neonatal) (newborn) 771.6
- neonatorum 098.40

Blepharelosis (*see also* Entropion) 374.00
Blepharitis (eyelid) 373.00
- angularis 373.01
- ciliaris 373.00
  - with ulcer 373.01
- marginal 373.00
  - with ulcer 373.01
- scrofulous (*see also* Tuberculosis) 017.3 ✓5th *[373.00]*
- squamous 373.02
- ulcerative 373.01

Blepharochalasis 374.34
- congenital 743.62

Blepharoclonus 333.81
Blepharoconjunctivitis (*see also* Conjunctivitis) 372.20
- angular 372.21
- contact 372.22

Blepharophimosis (eyelid) 374.46
- congenital 743.62

Blepharoplegia 374.89
Blepharoptosis 374.30
- congenital 743.61

Blepharopyorrhea 098.49
Blepharospasm 333.81
Blessig's cyst 362.62
Blighted ovum 631
Blind
- bronchus (congenital) 748.3
- eye — *see also* Blindness
  - hypertensive 360.42
  - hypotensive 360.41
- loop syndrome (postoperative) 579.2
- sac, fallopian tube (congenital) 752.19
- spot, enlarged 368.42
- tract or tube (congenital) NEC — *see* Atresia

Blindness (acquired) (congenital) (both eyes) 369.00
- blast 921.3
  - with nerve injury — *see* Injury, nerve, optic
- Bright's — *see* Uremia
- color (congenital) 368.59
  - acquired 368.55
  - blue 368.53
  - green 368.52
  - red 368.51
  - total 368.54
- concussion 950.9
- cortical 377.75
- day 368.60
  - acquired 368.62
  - congenital 368.61
  - hereditary 368.61
  - specified type NEC 368.69
- due to
  - injury NEC 950.9
  - refractive error — *see* Error, refractive
- eclipse (total) 363.31

Block — *continued*
- nodal 426.10
- optic nerve 377.49
- organ or site (congenital) NEC — *see* Atresia
- parietal 426.6
- peri-infarction 426.6
- portal (vein) 452
- sinoatrial 426.6
- sinoauricular 426.6
- spinal cord 336.9
- trifascicular 426.54
- tubal 628.2
- vein NEC 453.9

Blocq's disease or syndrome (astasia-abasia) 307.9

Blood
- constituents, abnormal NEC 790.6
- disease 289.9
  - specified NEC 289.8
- donor V59.01
  - other blood components V59.09
  - stem cells V59.02
  - whole blood V59.01
- dyscrasia 289.9
  - with
    - abortion — *see* Abortion, by type, with hemorrhage, delayed or excessive
    - ectopic pregnancy (*see also* categories 633.0–633.9) 639.1
    - molar pregnancy (*see also* categories 630–632) 639.1
  - fetus or newborn NEC 776.9
  - following
    - abortion 639.1
    - ectopic or molar pregnancy 639.1
  - puerperal, postpartum 666.3 [5th]
- flukes NEC (*see also* Infestation, Schistosoma) 120.9
- in
  - feces (*see also* Melena) 578.1
    - occult 792.1
  - urine (*see also* Hematuria) 599.7
- mole 631
- occult 792.1
- poisoning (*see also* Septicemia) 038.9
- pressure
  - decreased, due to shock following injury 958.4
  - fluctuating 796.4
  - high (*see also* Hypertension) 401.9
    - incidental reading (isolated) (nonspecific), without diagnosis of hypertension 796.2
  - low (*see also* Hypotension) 458.9
    - incidental reading (isolated) (nonspecific), without diagnosis of hypotension 796.3
- spitting (*see also* Hemoptysis) 786.3
- staining cornea 371.12
- transfusion
  - without reported diagnosis V58.2
  - donor V59.01
    - stem cells V59.02
  - reaction or complication — *see* Complications, transfusion
- tumor — *see* Hematoma
- vessel rupture — *see* Hemorrhage
- vomiting (*see also* Hematemesis) 578.0

Blood-forming organ disease 289.9

Bloodgood's disease 610.1

Bloodshot eye 379.93

Bloom (-Machacek) (-Torre) syndrome 757.39

Blotch, palpebral 372.55

Blount's disease (tibia vara) 732.4

Blount-Barber syndrome (tibia vara) 732.4

Blue
- baby 746.9
- bloater 491.20
  - with acute bronchitis or exacerbation 491.21
- diaper syndrome 270.0
- disease 746.9
- dome cyst 610.0
- drum syndrome 381.02
- sclera 743.47
  - with fragility of bone and deafness 756.51
- toe syndrome — *see* Atherosclerosis

Blueness (*see also* Cyanosis) 782.5

Blurring, visual 368.8

Blushing (abnormal) (excessive) 782.62

Boarder, hospital V65.0
- infant V65.0

Bockhart's impetigo (superficial folliculitis) 704.8

Bodechtel-Guttmann disease (subacute sclerosing panencephalitis) 046.2

Boder-Sedgwick syndrome (ataxia-telangiectasia) 334.8

Body, bodies
- Aschoff (*see also* Myocarditis, rheumatic) 398.0
- asteroid, vitreous 379.22
- choroid, colloid (degenerative) 362.57
  - hereditary 362.77
- cytoid (retina) 362.82
- drusen (retina) (*see also* Drusen) 362.57
  - optic disc 377.21
- fibrin, pleura 511.0
- foreign — *see* Foreign body
- Hassall-Henle 371.41
- loose
  - joint (*see also* Loose, body, joint) 718.1 [5th]
    - knee 717.6
  - knee 717.6
  - sheath, tendon 727.82
- Mallory's 034.1
- Mooser 081.0
- Negri 071
- rice (joint) (*see also* Loose, body, joint) 718.1 [5th]
  - knee 717.6
- rocking 307.3

Boeck's
- disease (sarcoidosis) 135
- lupoid (miliary) 135
- sarcoid 135

Boerhaave's syndrome (spontaneous esophageal rupture) 530.4

Boggy
- cervix 622.8
- uterus 621.8

Boil (*see also* Carbuncle) 680.9
- abdominal wall 680.2
- Aleppo 085.1
- ankle 680.6
- anus 680.5
- arm (any part, above wrist) 680.3
- auditory canal, external 680.0
- axilla 680.3
- back (any part) 680.2
- Baghdad 085.1
- breast 680.2
- buttock 680.5
- chest wall 680.2
- corpus cavernosum 607.2
- Delhi 085.1
- ear (any part) 680.0
- eyelid 373.13
- face (any part, except eye) 680.0
- finger (any) 680.4
- flank 680.2
- foot (any part) 680.7
- forearm 680.3
- Gafsa 085.1
- genital organ, male 608.4
- gluteal (region) 680.5
- groin 680.2
- hand (any part) 680.4
- head (any part, except face) 680.8
- heel 680.7
- hip 680.6
- knee 680.6
- labia 616.4
- lacrimal (*see also* Dacryocystitis) 375.30
  - gland (*see also* Dacryoadenitis) 375.00
  - passages (duct) (sac) (*see also* Dacryocystitis) 375.30
- leg, any part except foot 680.6
- multiple sites 680.9
- Natal 085.1
- neck 680.1
- nose (external) (septum) 680.0
- orbit, orbital 376.01
- partes posteriores 680.5
- pectoral region 680.2
- penis 607.2
- perineum 680.2
- pinna 680.0
- scalp (any part) 680.8
- scrotum 608.4
- seminal vesicle 608.0
- shoulder 680.3
- skin NEC 680.9
- specified site NEC 680.8
- spermatic cord 608.4
- temple (region) 680.0
- testis 608.4
- thigh 680.6
- thumb 680.4
- toe (any) 680.7
- tropical 085.1
- trunk 680.2
- tunica vaginalis 608.4
- umbilicus 680.2
- upper arm 680.3
- vas deferens 608.4
- vulva 616.4
- wrist 680.4

Bold hives (*see also* Urticaria) 708.9

Bolivian hemorrhagic fever 078.7

Bombé, iris 364.74

Bomford-Rhoads anemia (refractory) 284.9

Bone — *see* condition

Bonnevie-Ullrich syndrome 758.6

Bonnier's syndrome 386.19

Bonvale Dam fever 780.79

Bony block of joint 718.80
- ankle 718.87
- elbow 718.82
- foot 718.87
- hand 718.84

Bony block of joint — *continued*
- hip 718.85
- knee 718.86
- multiple sites 718.89
- pelvic region 718.85
- shoulder (region) 718.81
- specified site NEC 718.88
- wrist 718.83

Borderline
- intellectual functioning V62.89
- pelvis 653.1 5th
  - with obstruction during labor 660.1 5th
    - affecting fetus or newborn 763.1
- psychosis (*see also* Schizophrenia) 295.5 5th
  - of childhood (*see also* Psychosis, childhood) 299.8 5th
- schizophrenia (*see also* Schizophrenia) 295.5 5th

Borna disease 062.9

Bornholm disease (epidemic pleurodynia) 074.1

Borrelia vincentii (mouth) (pharynx) (tonsils) 101

Bostock's catarrh (*see also* Fever, hay) 477.9

Boston exanthem 048

Botalli, ductus (patent) (persistent) 747.0

Bothriocephalus latus infestation 123.4

Botulism 005.1

Bouba (*see also* Yaws) 102.9

Bouffée délirante 298.3

Bouillaud's disease or syndrome (rheumatic heart disease) 391.9

Bourneville's disease (tuberous sclerosis) 759.5

Boutonneuse fever 082.1

Boutonniere
- deformity (finger) 736.21
- hand (intrinsic) 736.21

Bouveret (-Hoffmann) disease or syndrome (paroxysmal tachycardia) 427.2

Bovine heart — *see* Hypertrophy, cardiac

Bowel — *see* condition

Bowen's
- dermatosis (precancerous) (M8081/2) — *see* Neoplasm, skin, in situ
- disease (M8081/2) — *see* Neoplasm, skin, in situ
- epithelioma (M8081/2) — *see* Neoplasm, skin, in situ
- type
  - epidermoid carcinoma in situ (M8081/2) — *see* Neoplasm, skin, in situ
  - intraepidermal squamous cell carcinoma (M8081/2) — *see* Neoplasm, skin, in situ

Bowing
- femur 736.89
  - congenital 754.42
- fibula 736.89
  - congenital 754.43
- forearm 736.09
  - away from midline (cubitus valgus) 736.01
  - toward midline (cubitus varus) 736.02
- leg(s), long bones, congenital 754.44
- radius 736.09
  - away from midline (cubitus valgus) 736.01
  - toward midline (cubitus varus) 736.02
- tibia 736.89
  - congenital 754.43

Bowleg(s) 736.42
- congenital 754.44
- rachitic 268.1

Boyd's dysentery 004.2

Brachial — *see* condition

Brachman-de Lange syndrome (Amsterdam dwarf, mental retardation, and brachycephaly) 759.89

Brachycardia 427.89

Brachycephaly 756.0

Brachymorphism and ectopia lentis 759.89

Bradley's disease (epidemic vomiting) 078.82

Bradycardia 427.89
- chronic (sinus) 427.81
- newborn 763.83
- nodal 427.89
- postoperative 997.1
- reflex 337.0
- sinoatrial 427.89
  - with paroxysmal tachyarrhythmia or tachycardia 427.81
  - chronic 427.81
- sinus 427.89
  - with paroxysmal tachyarrhythmia or tachycardia 427.81
  - chronic 427.81
  - persistent 427.81
  - severe 427.81
- tachycardia syndrome 427.81
- vagal 427.89

Bradypnea 786.09

Brailsford's disease 732.3
- radial head 732.3
- tarsal scaphoid 732.5

Brailsford-Morquio disease or syndrome (mucopolysaccharidosis IV) 277.5

Brain — *see also* condition
- death 348.8
- syndrome (acute) (chronic) (nonpsychotic) (organic) (with neurotic reaction) (with behavioral reaction) (*see also* Syndrome, brain) 310.9
  - with
    - presenile brain disease 290.10
    - psychosis, psychotic reaction (*see also* Psychosis, organic) 294.9
  - congenital (*see also* Retardation, mental) 319

Branched-chain amino-acid disease 270.3

Branchial — *see* condition

Brandt's syndrome (acrodermatitis enteropathica) 686.8

Brash (water) 787.1

Brass-founders' ague 985.8

Bravais-Jacksonian epilepsy (*see also* Epilepsy) 345.5 5th

Braxton Hicks contractions 644.1 5th

Braziers' disease 985.8

Brazilian
- blastomycosis 116.1
- leishmaniasis 085.5

Break
- cardiorenal — *see* Hypertension, cardiorenal
- retina (*see also* Defect, retina) 361.30

Breakbone fever 061

Breakdown
- device, implant, or graft — *see* Complications, mechanical
- nervous (*see also* Disorder, mental, nonpsychotic) 300.9
- perineum 674.2 5th

Breast — *see* condition

Breast feeding difficulties 676.8 5th

Breath
- foul 784.9
- holder, child 312.81
- holding spells 786.9
- shortness 786.05

Breathing
- asymmetrical 786.09
- bronchial 786.09
- exercises V57.0
- labored 786.09
- mouth 784.9
- periodic 786.09
- tic 307.20

Breathlessness 786.09

Breda's disease (*see also* Yaws) 102.9

Breech
- delivery, affecting fetus or newborn 763.0
- extraction, affecting fetus or newborn 763.0
- presentation (buttocks) (complete) (frank) 652.2 5th
  - with successful version 652.1 5th
  - before labor, affecting fetus or newborn 761.7
  - during labor, affecting fetus or newborn 763.0

Breisky's disease (kraurosis vulvae) 624.0

Brennemann's syndrome (acute mesenteric lymphadenitis) 289.2

Brenner's
- tumor (benign) (M9000/0) 220
  - borderline malignancy (M9000/1) 236.2
  - malignant (M9000/3) 183.0
  - proliferating (M9000/1) 236.2

Bretonneau's disease (diphtheritic malignant angina) 032.0

Breus' mole 631

Brevicollis 756.16

Bricklayers' itch 692.89

Brickmakers' anemia 126.9

Bridge
- myocardial 746.85

Bright's
- blindness — *see* Uremia
- disease (*see also* Nephritis) 583.9
  - arteriosclerotic (*see also* Hypertension, kidney) 403.90

Brill's disease (recrudescent typhus) 081.1
- flea-borne 081.0
- louse-borne 081.1

Brill-Symmers disease (follicular lymphoma) (M9690/3) 202.0 5th

Brill-Zinsser disease (recrudescent typhus) 081.1

Brinton's disease (linitis plastica) (M8142/3) 151.9

Brion-Kayser disease (*see also* Fever, paratyphoid) 002.9

Briquet's disorder or syndrome 300.81

Brissaud's
- infantilism (infantile myxedema) 244.9
- motor-verbal tic 307.23

Brissaud-Meige syndrome (infantile myxedema) 244.9

Bronchorrhea (chronic) (purulent) 491.0
 acute 466.0
Bronchospasm 519.1
 with
  asthma — *see* Asthma
  bronchiolitis, acute 466.19
   due to respiratory syncytial virus 466.11
  bronchitis — *see* Bronchitis
  chronic obstructive pulmonary disease (COPD) 496
  COPD 496
  emphysema — *see* Emphysema
   due to external agent — *see* Condition, respiratory, acute, due to
Bronchospirochetosis 104.8
Bronchostenosis 519.1
Bronchus — *see* condition
Bronze, bronzed
 diabetes 275.0
 disease (Addison's) (skin) 255.4
  tuberculous (*see also* Tuberculosis) 017.6 ✓5th
Brooke's disease or tumor (M8100/0) — *see* Neoplasm, skin, benign
Brown's tendon sheath syndrome 378.61
Brown enamel of teeth (hereditary) 520.5
Brown-Séquard's paralysis (syndrome) 344.89
Brow presentation complicating delivery 652.4 ✓5th
 causing obstructed labor 660.0 ✓5th
Brucella, brucellosis (infection) 023.9
 abortus 023.1
 canis 023.3
 dermatitis, skin 023.9
 melitensis 023.0
 mixed 023.8
 suis 023.2
Bruck's disease 733.99
Bruck-de Lange disease or syndrome (Amsterdam dwarf, mental retardation, and brachycephaly) 759.89
Brug's filariasis 125.1
Brugsch's syndrome (acropachyderma) 757.39
Bruhl's disease (splenic anemia with fever) 285.8
Bruise (skin surface intact) — *see also* Contusion
 with
  fracture — *see* Fracture, by site
  open wound — *see* Wound, open, by site
 internal organ (abdomen, chest, or pelvis) — *see* Injury, internal, by site
 umbilical cord 663.6 ✓5th
  affecting fetus or newborn 762.6
Bruit 785.9
 arterial (abdominal) (carotid) 785.9
 supraclavicular 785.9
Brushburn — *see* Injury, superficial, by site
Bruton's X-linked agammaglobulinemia 279.04
Bruxism 306.8
Bubbly lung syndrome 770.7
Bubo 289.3
 blennorrhagic 098.89
 chancroidal 099.0
 climatic 099.1
 due to Hemophilus ducreyi 099.0
 gonococcal 098.89
 indolent NEC 099.8

Bubo — *continued*
 inguinal NEC 099.8
  chancroidal 099.0
  climatic 099.1
  due to H. ducreyi 099.0
 scrofulous (*see also* Tuberculosis) 017.2 ✓5th
 soft chancre 099.0
 suppurating 683
 syphilitic 091.0
  congenital 090.0
 tropical 099.1
 venereal NEC 099.8
 virulent 099.0
Bubonic plague 020.0
Bubonocele — *see* Hernia, inguinal
Buccal — *see* condition
Buchanan's disease (juvenile osteochondrosis of iliac crest) 732.1
Buchem's syndrome (hyperostosis corticalis) 733.3
Buchman's disease (osteochondrosis, juvenile) 732.1
Bucket handle fracture (semilunar cartilage) (*see also* Tear, meniscus) 836.2
Budd-Chiari syndrome (hepatic vein thrombosis) 453.0
Budgerigar-fanciers' disease or lung 495.2
Büdinger-Ludloff-Läwen disease 717.89
Buerger's disease (thromboangiitis obliterans) 443.1
Bulbar — *see* condition
Bulbus cordis 745.9
 persistent (in left ventricle) 745.8
Bulging fontanels (congenital) 756.0
Bulimia 783.6
 nonorganic origin 307.51
Bulky uterus 621.2
Bulla(e) 709.8
 lung (emphysematous) (solitary) 492.0
Bullet wound — *see also* Wound, open, by site
 fracture — *see* Fracture, by site, open
 internal organ (abdomen, chest, or pelvis) — *see* Injury, internal, by site, with open wound
 intracranial — *see* Laceration, brain, with open wound
Bullis fever 082.8
Bullying (*see also* Disturbance, conduct) 312.0 ✓5th
Bundle
 branch block (complete) (false) (incomplete) 426.50
  bilateral 426.53
  left (*see also* Block, bundle branch, left) 426.3
   hemiblock 426.2
  right (*see also* Block, bundle branch, right) 426.4
 of His — *see* condition
 of Kent syndrome (anomalous atrioventricular excitation) 426.7
Bungpagga 040.81
Bunion 727.1
Bunionette 727.1
Bunyamwera fever 066.3

Buphthalmia, buphthalmos (congenital) 743.20
 associated with
  keratoglobus, congenital 743.22
  megalocornea 743.22
  ocular anomalies NEC 743.22
 isolated 743.21
 simple 743.21
Bürger-Grütz disease or syndrome (essential familial hyperlipemia) 272.3
Buried roots 525.3
Burke's syndrome 577.8
Burkitt's
 tumor (M9750/3) 200.2 ✓5th
 type malignant, lymphoma, lymphoblastic, or undifferentiated (M9750/3) 200.2 ✓5th
Burn (acid) (cathode ray) (caustic) (chemical) (electric heating appliance) (electricity) (fire) (flame) (hot liquid or object) (irradiation) (lime) (radiation) (steam) (thermal) (x-ray) 949.0

> *Note — Use the following fifth-digit subclassification with category 948 to indicate the percent of body surface with third degree burn:*
>
> *0 less than 10 percent or unspecified*
> *1 10–19 percent*
> *2 20–29 percent*
> *3 30–39 percent*
> *4 40–49 percent*
> *5 50–59 percent*
> *6 60–69 percent*
> *7 70–79 percent*
> *8 80–89 percent*
> *9 90 percent or more of body surface*

 with
  blisters — *see* Burn, by site, second degree
  erythema — *see* Burn, by site, first degree
  skin loss (epidermal) — *see also* Burn, by site, second degree
   full thickness — *see also* Burn, by site, third degree
    with necrosis of underlying tissues — *see* Burn, by site, third degree, deep
 first degree — *see* Burn, by site, first degree
 second degree — *see* Burn, by site, second degree
 third degree — *see also* Burn, by site, third degree
  deep — *see* Burn, by site, third degree, deep
 abdomen, abdominal (muscle) (wall) 942.03
  with
   trunk — *see* Burn, trunk, multiple sites
  first degree 942.13
  second degree 942.23
  third degree 942.33
   deep 942.43
    with loss of body part 942.53
 ankle 945.03
  with
   lower limb(s) — *see* Burn, leg, multiple sites
  first degree 945.13
  second degree 945.23
  third degree 945.33
   deep 945.43
    with loss of body part 945.53

- **Burn** (acid) (cathode ray) (caustic) (chemical) (electric heating appliance) (electricity) (fire) (flame) (hot liquid or object) (irradiation) (lime) (radiation) (steam) (thermal) (x-ray) — *continued*
  - anus — *see* Burn, trunk, specified site NEC
  - arm(s) 943.00
    - first degree 943.10
    - second degree 943.20
    - third degree 943.30
      - deep 943.40
        - with loss of body part 943.50
    - lower — *see* Burn, forearm(s)
    - multiple sites, except hand(s) or wrist(s) 943.09
      - first degree 943.19
      - second degree 943.29
      - third degree 943.39
        - deep 943.49
          - with loss of body part 943.59
    - upper 943.03
      - first degree 943.13
      - second degree 943.23
      - third degree 943.33
        - deep 943.43
          - with loss of body part 943.53
  - auditory canal (external) — *see* Burn, ear
  - auricle (ear) — *see* Burn, ear
  - axilla 943.04
    - with
      - upper limb(s) except hand(s) or wrist(s) — *see* Burn, arm(s), multiple sites
    - first degree 943.14
    - second degree 943.24
    - third degree 943.34
      - deep 943.44
        - with loss of body part 943.54
  - back 942.04
    - with
      - trunk — *see* Burn, trunk, multiple sites
    - first degree 942.14
    - second degree 942.24
    - third degree 942.34
      - deep 942.44
        - with loss of body part 942.54
  - biceps
    - brachii — *see* Burn, arm(s), upper
    - femoris — *see* Burn, thigh
  - breast(s) 942.01
    - with
      - trunk — *see* Burn, trunk, multiple sites
    - first degree 942.11
    - second degree 942.21
    - third degree 942.31
      - deep 942.41
        - with loss of body part 942.51
  - brow — *see* Burn, forehead
  - buttock(s) — *see* Burn, back
  - canthus (eye) 940.1
    - chemical 940.0
  - cervix (uteri) 947.4
  - cheek (cutaneous) 941.07
    - with
      - face or head — *see* Burn, head, multiple sites
    - first degree 941.17
    - second degree 941.27
    - third degree 941.37
      - deep 941.47
        - with loss of body part 941.57

- **Burn** (acid) (cathode ray) (caustic) (chemical) (electric heating appliance) (electricity) (fire) (flame) (hot liquid or object) (irradiation) (lime) (radiation) (steam) (thermal) (x-ray) — *continued*
  - chest wall (anterior) 942.02
    - with
      - trunk — *see* Burn, trunk, multiple sites
    - first degree 942.12
    - second degree 942.22
    - third degree 942.32
      - deep 942.42
        - with loss of body part 942.52
  - chin 941.04
    - with
      - face or head — *see* Burn, head, multiple sites
    - first degree 941.14
    - second degree 941.24
    - third degree 941.34
      - deep 941.44
        - with loss of body part 941.54
  - clitoris — *see* Burn, genitourinary organs, external
  - colon 947.3
  - conjunctiva (and cornea) 940.4
    - chemical
      - acid 940.3
      - alkaline 940.2
  - cornea (and conjunctiva) 940.4
    - chemical
      - acid 940.3
      - alkaline 940.2
  - costal region — *see* Burn, chest wall
  - due to ingested chemical agent — *see* Burn, internal organs
  - ear (auricle) (canal) (drum) (external) 941.01
    - with
      - face or head — *see* Burn, head, multiple sites
    - first degree 941.11
    - second degree 941.21
    - third degree 941.31
      - deep 941.41
        - with loss of a body part 941.51
  - elbow 943.02
    - with
      - hand(s) and wrist(s) — *see* Burn, multiple specified sites
      - upper limb(s) except hand(s) or wrist(s) — *see also* Burn, arm(s), multiple sites
    - first degree 943.12
    - second degree 943.22
    - third degree 943.32
      - deep 943.42
        - with loss of body part 943.52
  - electricity, electric current — *see* Burn, by site
  - entire body — *see* Burn, multiple, specified sites
  - epididymis — *see* Burn, genitourinary organs, external
  - epigastric region — *see* Burn, abdomen
  - epiglottis 947.1
  - esophagus 947.2

- **Burn** (acid) (cathode ray) (caustic) (chemical) (electric heating appliance) (electricity) (fire) (flame) (hot liquid or object) (irradiation) (lime) (radiation) (steam) (thermal) (x-ray) — *continued*
  - extent (percent of body surface)
    - less than 10 percent 948.0 ✓5th
    - 10–19 percent 948.1 ✓5th
    - 20–29 percent 948.2 ✓5th
    - 30–39 percent 948.3 ✓5th
    - 40–49 percent 948.4 ✓5th
    - 50–59 percent 948.5 ✓5th
    - 60–69 percent 948.6 ✓5th
    - 70–79 percent 948.7 ✓5th
    - 80–89 percent 948.8 ✓5th
    - 90 percent or more 948.9 ✓5th
  - extremity
    - lower — *see* Burn, leg
    - upper — *see* Burn, arm(s)
  - eye(s) (and adnexa) (only) 940.9
    - with
      - face, head, or neck 941.02
        - first degree 941.12
        - second degree 941.22
        - third degree 941.32
          - deep 941.42
            - with loss of body part 941.52
      - other sites (classifiable to more than one category in 940–945) — *see* Burn, multiple, specified sites
      - resulting rupture and destruction of eyeball 940.5
    - specified part — *see* Burn, by site
  - eyeball — *see also* Burn, eye
    - with resulting rupture and destruction of eyeball 940.5
  - eyelid(s) 940.1
    - chemical 940.0
  - face — *see* Burn, head
  - finger (nail) (subungual) 944.01
    - with
      - hand(s) — *see* Burn, hand(s), multiple sites
      - other sites — *see* Burn, multiple, specified sites
      - thumb 944.04
        - first degree 944.14
        - second degree 944.24
        - third degree 944.34
          - deep 944.44
            - with loss of body part 944.54
    - first degree 944.11
    - second degree 944.21
    - third degree 944.31
      - deep 944.41
        - with loss of body part 944.51
    - multiple (digits) 944.03
      - with thumb — *see* Burn, finger, with thumb
      - first degree 944.13
      - second degree 944.23
      - third degree 944.33
        - deep 944.43
          - with loss of body part 944.53
  - flank — *see* Burn, abdomen
  - foot 945.02
    - with
      - lower limb(s) — *see* Burn, leg, multiple sites
    - first degree 945.12
    - second degree 945.22
    - third degree 945.32
      - deep 945.42
        - with loss of body part 945.52

C

- **Cacergasia** 300.9
- **Cachexia** 799.4
  - cancerous (M8000/3) 199.1
  - cardiac — *see* Disease, heart
  - dehydration 276.5
    - with
      - hypernatremia 276.0
      - hyponatremia 276.1
  - due to malnutrition 261
  - exophthalmic 242.0 ✓5th
  - heart — *see* Disease, heart
  - hypophyseal 253.2
  - hypopituitary 253.2
  - lead 984.9
    - specified type of lead — *see* Table of Drugs and Chemicals
  - malaria 084.9
  - malignant (M8000/3) 199.1
  - marsh 084.9
  - nervous 300.5
  - old age 797
  - pachydermic — *see* Hypothyroidism
  - paludal 084.9
  - pituitary (postpartum) 253.2
  - renal (*see also* Disease, renal) 593.9
  - saturnine 984.9
    - specified type of lead — *see* Table of Drugs and Chemicals
  - senile 797
  - Simmonds' (pituitary cachexia) 253.2
  - splenica 289.59
  - strumipriva (*see also* Hypothyroidism) 244.9
  - tuberculous NEC (*see also* Tuberculosis) 011.9 ✓5th
- **Café au lait spots** 709.09
- **Caffey's disease or syndrome** (infantile cortical hyperostosis) 756.59
- **Caisson disease** 993.3
- **Caked breast** (puerperal, postpartum) 676.2 ✓5th
- **Cake kidney** 753.3
- **Calabar swelling** 125.2
- **Calcaneal spur** 726.73
- **Calcaneoapophysitis** 732.5
- **Calcaneonavicular bar** 755.67
- **Calcareous** — *see* condition
- **Calcicosis** (occupational) 502
- **Calciferol** (vitamin D) **deficiency** 268.9
  - with
    - osteomalacia 268.2
    - rickets (*see also* Rickets) 268.0
- **Calcification**
  - adrenal (capsule) (gland) 255.4
    - tuberculous (*see also* Tuberculosis) 017.6 ✓5th
  - aorta 440.0
  - artery (annular) — *see* Arteriosclerosis
  - auricle (ear) 380.89
  - bladder 596.8
    - due to S. hematobium 120.0
  - brain (cortex) — *see* Calcification, cerebral
  - bronchus 519.1
  - bursa 727.82
  - cardiac (*see also* Degeneration, myocardial) 429.1
  - cartilage (postinfectional) 733.99
  - cerebral (cortex) 348.8
    - artery 437.0
  - cervix (uteri) 622.8

Calcification — *continued*

  - choroid plexus 349.2
  - conjunctiva 372.54
  - corpora cavernosa (penis) 607.89
  - cortex (brain) — *see* Calcification, cerebral
  - dental pulp (nodular) 522.2
  - dentinal papilla 520.4
  - disc, intervertebral 722.90
    - cervical, cervicothoracic 722.91
    - lumbar, lumbosacral 722.93
    - thoracic, thoracolumbar 722.92
  - fallopian tube 620.8
  - falx cerebri — *see* Calcification, cerebral
  - fascia 728.89
  - gallbladder 575.8
  - general 275.40
  - heart (*see also* Degeneration, myocardial) 429.1
    - valve — *see* Endocarditis
  - intervertebral cartilage or disc (postinfectional) 722.90
    - cervical, cervicothoracic 722.91
    - lumbar, lumbosacral 722.93
    - thoracic, thoracolumbar 722.92
  - intracranial — *see* Calcification, cerebral
  - intraspinal ligament 728.89
  - joint 719.80
    - ankle 719.87
    - elbow 719.82
    - foot 719.87
    - hand 719.84
    - hip 719.85
    - knee 719.86
    - multiple sites 719.89
    - pelvic region 719.85
    - shoulder (region) 719.81
    - specified site NEC 719.88
    - wrist 719.83
  - kidney 593.89
    - tuberculous (*see also* Tuberculosis) 016.0 ✓5th
  - larynx (senile) 478.79
  - lens 366.8
  - ligament 728.89
    - intraspinal 728.89
    - knee (medial collateral) 717.89
  - lung 518.89
    - active 518.89
    - postinfectional 518.89
    - tuberculous (*see also* Tuberculosis, pulmonary) 011.9 ✓5th
  - lymph gland or node (postinfectional) 289.3
    - tuberculous (*see also* Tuberculosis, lymph gland) 017.2 ✓5th
  - massive (paraplegic) 728.10
  - medial (*see also* Arteriosclerosis, extremities) 440.20
  - meninges (cerebral) 349.2
  - metastatic 275.40
  - Mönckeberg's — *see* Arteriosclerosis
  - muscle 728.10
    - heterotopic, postoperative 728.13
  - myocardium, myocardial (*see also* Degeneration, myocardial) 429.1
  - ovary 620.8
  - pancreas 577.8
  - penis 607.89
  - periarticular 728.89
  - pericardium (*see also* Pericarditis) 423.8

Calcification — *continued*

  - pineal gland 259.8
  - pleura 511.0
    - postinfectional 518.89
    - tuberculous (*see also* Tuberculosis, pleura) 012.0 ✓5th
  - pulp (dental) (nodular) 522.2
  - renal 593.89
  - Rider's bone 733.99
  - sclera 379.16
  - semilunar cartilage 717.89
  - spleen 289.59
  - subcutaneous 709.3
  - suprarenal (capsule) (gland) 255.4
  - tendon (sheath) 727.82
    - with bursitis, synovitis or tenosynovitis 727.82
  - trachea 519.1
  - ureter 593.89
  - uterus 621.8
  - vitreous 379.29
- **Calcified** — *see also* Calcification
  - hematoma NEC 959.9
- **Calcinosis** (generalized) (interstitial) (tumoral) (universalis) 275.49
  - circumscripta 709.3
  - cutis 709.3
  - intervertebralis 275.49 *[722.90]*
  - Raynaud's phenomenonsclerodactylytelangiectasis (CRST) 710.1
- **Calcium**
  - blood
    - high (*see also* Hypercalcemia) 275.42
    - low (*see also* Hypocalcemia) 275.41
  - deposits — *see also* Calcification, by site
    - in bursa 727.82
    - in tendon (sheath) 727.82
      - with bursitis, synovitis or tenosynovitis 727.82
  - salts or soaps in vitreous 379.22
- **Calciuria** 791.9
- **Calculi** — *see* Calculus
- **Calculosis, intrahepatic** — *see* Choledocholithiasis
- **Calculus, calculi, calculous** 592.9
  - ampulla of Vater — *see* Choledocholithiasis
  - anuria (impacted) (recurrent) 592.0
  - appendix 543.9
  - bile duct (any) — *see* Choledocholithiasis
  - biliary — *see* Cholelithiasis
  - bilirubin, multiple — *see* Cholelithiasis
  - bladder (encysted) (impacted) (urinary) 594.1
    - diverticulum 594.0
  - bronchus 518.89
  - calyx (kidney) (renal) 592.0
    - congenital 753.3
  - cholesterol (pure) (solitary) — *see* Cholelithiasis
  - common duct (bile) — *see* Choledocholithiasis
  - conjunctiva 372.54
  - cystic 594.1
    - duct — *see* Cholelithiasis
  - dental 523.6
    - subgingival 523.6
    - supragingival 523.6
  - epididymis 608.89
  - gallbladder — *see also* Cholelithiasis
    - congenital 751.69

> *Note — Use the following fifth-digit subclassification with category 574:*
> *0 without mention of obstruction*
> *1 with obstruction*

> *Note — Use the following fifth-digit subclassification with category 574:*
> *0 without mention of obstruction*
> *1 with obstruction*

Complications — *continued*
transfusion (blood) (lymphocytes) (plasma) NEC — *continued*
embolism
air 999.1
thrombus 999.2
hemolysis NEC 999.8
bone marrow 996.85
hepatitis (serum) (type B) (within 8 months after administration) — *see* Hepatitis, viral
incompatibility reaction (ABO) (blood group) 999.6
Rh (factor) 999.7
infection 999.3
jaundice (serum) (within 8 months after administration) — *see* Hepatitis, viral
sepsis 999.3
shock or reaction NEC 999.8
bone marrow 996.85
subacute yellow atrophy of liver (within 8 months after administration) — *see* Hepatitis, viral
thromboembolism 999.2
transplant — *see also* Complications, due to (presence of) any device, implant, or graft classified to 996.0–996.5 NEC
bone marrow 996.85
organ (immune or nonimmune cause) (partial) (total) 996.80
bone marrow 996.85
heart 996.83
intestines 996.89
kidney 996.81
liver 996.82
lung 996.84
pancreas 996.86
specified NEC 996.89
trauma NEC (early) 958.8
ultrasound therapy NEC 999.9
umbilical cord
affecting fetus or newborn 762.6
complicating delivery 663.9 ✓5th
affecting fetus or newborn 762.6
specified type NEC 663.8 ✓5th
urethral catheter NEC 996.76
infection or inflammation 996.64
mechanical 996.31
urinary, postoperative NEC 997.5
vaccination 999.9
anaphylaxis NEC 999.4
cellulitis 999.3
encephalitis or encephalomyelitis 323.5
hepatitis (serum) (type B) (within 8 months after administration) — *see* Hepatitis, viral
infection (general) (local) NEC 999.3
jaundice (serum) (within 8 months after administration) — *see* Hepatitis, viral
meningitis 997.09 *[321.8]*
myelitis 323.5
protein sickness 999.5
reaction (allergic) 999.5
Herxheimer's 995.0
serum 999.5
sepsis 999.3
serum intoxication, sickness, rash, or other serum reaction NEC 999.5
shock (allergic) (anaphylactic) 999.4
subacute yellow atrophy of liver (within 8 months after administration) — *see* Hepatitis, viral
vaccinia (generalized) 999.0
localized 999.3

Complications — *continued*
vascular
device, implant, or graft NEC 996.74
infection or inflammation 996.62
mechanical NEC 996.1
cardiac (*see also* Complications, mechanical, by type) 996.00
following infusion, perfusion, or transfusion 999.2
postoperative NEC 997.2
ventilation therapy NEC 999.9
Compound presentation, complicating delivery 652.8 ✓5th
causing obstructed labor 660.0 ✓5th
Compressed air disease 993.3
Compression
with injury — *see* specific injury
arm NEC 354.9
artery 447.1
celiac, syndrome 447.4
brachial plexus 353.0
brain (stem) 348.4
due to
contusion, brain — *see* Contusion, brain
injury NEC — *see also* Hemorrhage, brain, traumatic
birth — *see* Birth, injury, brain
laceration, brain — *see* Laceration, brain
osteopathic 739.0
bronchus 519.1
by cicatrix — *see* Cicatrix
cardiac 423.9
cauda equina 344.60
with neurogenic bladder 344.61
celiac (artery) (axis) 447.4
cerebral — *see* Compression, brain
cervical plexus 353.2
cord (umbilical) — *see* Compression, umbilical cord
cranial nerve 352.9
second 377.49
third (partial) 378.51
total 378.52
fourth 378.53
fifth 350.8
sixth 378.54
seventh 351.8
divers' squeeze 993.3
duodenum (external) (*see also* Obstruction, duodenum) 537.3
during birth 767.9
esophagus 530.3
congenital, external 750.3
Eustachian tube 381.63
facies (congenital) 754.0
fracture — *see* Fracture, by site
heart — *see* Disease, heart
intestine (*see also* Obstruction, intestine) 560.9
with hernia — *see* Hernia, by site, with obstruction
laryngeal nerve, recurrent 478.79
leg NEC 355.8
lower extremity NEC 355.8
lumbosacral plexus 353.1
lung 518.89
lymphatic vessel 457.1
medulla — *see* Compression, brain
nerve NEC — *see also* Disorder, nerve
arm NEC 354.9
autonomic nervous system (*see also* Neuropathy, peripheral, autonomic) 337.9

Compression — *continued*
nerve NEC — *see also* Disorder, nerve — *continued*
axillary 353.0
cranial NEC 352.9
due to displacement of intervertebral disc 722.2
with myelopathy 722.70
cervical 722.0
with myelopathy 722.71
lumbar, lumbosacral 722.10
with myelopathy 722.73
thoracic, thoracolumbar 722.11
with myelopathy 722.72
iliohypogastric 355.79
ilioinguinal 355.79
leg NEC 355.8
lower extremity NEC 355.8
median (in carpal tunnel) 354.0
obturator 355.79
optic 377.49
plantar 355.6
posterior tibial (in tarsal tunnel) 355.5
root (by scar tissue) NEC 724.9
cervical NEC 723.4
lumbar NEC 724.4
lumbosacral 724.4
thoracic 724.4
saphenous 355.79
sciatic (acute) 355.0
sympathetic 337.9
traumatic — *see* Injury, nerve
ulnar 354.2
upper extremity NEC 354.9
peripheral — *see* Compression, nerve
spinal (cord) (old or nontraumatic) 336.9
by displacement of intervertebral disc — *see* Displacement, intervertebral disc
nerve
root NEC 724.9
postoperative 722.80
cervical region 722.81
lumbar region 722.83
thoracic region 722.82
traumatic — *see* Injury, nerve, spinal
traumatic — *see* Injury, nerve, spinal
spondylogenic 721.91
cervical 721.1
lumbar, lumbosacral 721.42
thoracic 721.41
traumatic — *see also* Injury, spinal, by site
with fracture, vertebra — *see* Fracture, vertebra, by site, with spinal cord injury
spondylogenic — *see* Compression, spinal cord, spondylogenic
subcostal nerve (syndrome) 354.8
sympathetic nerve NEC 337.9
syndrome 958.5
thorax 512.8
iatrogenic 512.1
postoperative 512.1
trachea 519.1
congenital 748.3
ulnar nerve (by scar tissue) 354.2
umbilical cord
affecting fetus or newborn 762.5
cord prolapsed 762.4
complicating delivery 663.2 ✓5th
cord around neck 663.1 ✓5th
cord prolapsed 663.0 ✓5th

Contraction, contracture, contracted — *continued*
- ocular muscle (*see also* Strabismus) 378.9
  - paralytic (*see also* Strabismus, paralytic) 378.50
- organ or site, congenital NEC — *see* Atresia
- outlet (pelvis) — *see* Contraction, pelvis
- palmar fascia 728.6
- paralytic
  - joint (*see also* Contraction, joint) 718.4 ✓5th
  - muscle 728.85
    - ocular (*see also* Strabismus, paralytic) 378.50
- pelvis (acquired) (general) 738.6
  - affecting fetus or newborn 763.1
  - complicating delivery 653.1 ✓5th
    - causing obstructed labor 660.1 ✓5th
    - generally contracted 653.1 ✓5th
      - causing obstructed labor 660.1 ✓5th
    - inlet 653.2 ✓5th
      - causing obstructed labor 660.1 ✓5th
    - midpelvic 653.8 ✓5th
      - causing obstructed labor 660.1 ✓5th
    - midplane 653.8 ✓5th
      - causing obstructed labor 660.1 ✓5th
    - outlet 653.3 ✓5th
      - causing obstructed labor 660.1 ✓5th
- plantar fascia 728.71
- premature
  - atrial 427.61
  - auricular 427.61
  - auriculoventricular 427.61
  - heart (junctional) (nodal) 427.60
  - supraventricular 427.61
  - ventricular 427.69
- prostate 602.8
- pylorus (*see also* Pylorospasm) 537.81
- rectosigmoid (*see also* Obstruction, intestine) 560.9
- rectum, rectal (sphincter) 564.89
  - psychogenic 306.4
- ring (Bandl's) 661.4 ✓5th
  - affecting fetus or newborn 763.7
- scar — *see* Cicatrix
- sigmoid (*see also* Obstruction, intestine) 560.9
- socket, eye 372.64
- spine (*see also* Curvature, spine) 737.9
- stomach 536.8
  - hourglass 536.8
    - congenital 750.7
    - psychogenic 306.4
  - psychogenic 306.4
- tendon (sheath) (*see also* Short, tendon) 727.81
- toe 735.8
- ureterovesical orifice (postinfectional) 593.3
- urethra 599.84
- uterus 621.8
  - abnormal 661.9 ✓5th
    - affecting fetus or newborn 763.7
  - clonic, hourglass or tetanic 661.4 ✓5th
    - affecting fetus or newborn 763.7
  - dyscoordinate 661.4 ✓5th
    - affecting fetus or newborn 763.7
  - hourglass 661.4 ✓5th
    - affecting fetus or newborn 763.7
  - hypotonic NEC 661.2 ✓5th
    - affecting fetus or newborn 763.7

Contraction, contracture, contracted — *continued*
- uterus — *continued*
  - incoordinate 661.4 ✓5th
    - affecting fetus or newborn 763.7
  - inefficient or poor 661.2 ✓5th
    - affecting fetus or newborn 763.7
  - irregular 661.2 ✓5th
    - affecting fetus or newborn 763.7
  - tetanic 661.4 ✓5th
    - affecting fetus or newborn 763.7
- vagina (outlet) 623.2
- vesical 596.8
  - neck or urethral orifice 596.0
- visual field, generalized 368.45
- Volkmann's (ischemic) 958.6

Contusion (skin surface intact) 924.9
- with
  - crush injury — *see* Crush
  - dislocation — *see* Dislocation, by site
  - fracture — *see* Fracture, by site
  - internal injury — *see also* Injury, internal, by site
    - heart — *see* Contusion, cardiac
    - kidney — *see* Contusion, kidney
    - liver — *see* Contusion, liver
    - lung — *see* Contusion, lung
    - spleen — *see* Contusion, spleen
  - intracranial injury — *see* Injury, intracranial
  - nerve injury — *see* Injury, nerve
  - open wound — *see* Wound, open, by site
- abdomen, abdominal (muscle) (wall) 922.2
  - organ(s) NEC 868.00
- adnexa, eye NEC 921.9
- ankle 924.21
  - with other parts of foot 924.20
- arm 923.9
  - lower (with elbow) 923.10
  - upper 923.03
    - with shoulder or axillary region 923.09
- auditory canal (external) (meatus) (and other part(s) of neck, scalp, or face, except eye) 920
- auricle, ear (and other part(s) of neck, scalp, or face except eye) 920
- axilla 923.02
  - with shoulder or upper arm 923.09
- back 922.31
- bone NEC 924.9

Contusion (skin surface intact) — *continued*
- brain (cerebral) (membrane) (with hemorrhage) 851.8 ✓5th

> *Note — Use the following fifth-digit subclassification with categories 851–854:*
>
> *0 unspecified state of consciousness*
> *1 with no loss of consciousness*
> *2 with brief [less than one hour] loss of consciousness*
> *3 with moderate [1–24 hours] loss of consciousness*
> *4 with prolonged [more than 24 hours] loss of consciousness and return to pre-existing conscious level*
> *5 with prolonged [more than 24 hours] loss of consciousness, without return to pre-existing conscious level*
>
> *Use fifth-digit 5 to designate when a patient is unconscious and dies before regaining consciousness, regardless of the duration of the loss of consciousness*
>
> *6 with loss of consciousness of unspecified duration*
> *9 with concussion, unspecified*

  - with
    - open intracranial wound 851.9 ✓5th
    - skull fracture — *see* Fracture, skull, by site
  - cerebellum 851.4 ✓5th
    - with open intracranial wound 851.5 ✓5th
  - cortex 851.0 ✓5th
    - with open intracranial wound 851.1 ✓5th
  - occipital lobe 851.4 ✓5th
    - with open intracranial wound 851.5 ✓5th
  - stem 851.4 ✓5th
    - with open intracranial wound 851.5 ✓5th
- breast 922.0
- brow (and other part(s) of neck, scalp, or face, except eye) 920
- buttock 922.32
- canthus 921.1
- cardiac 861.01
  - with open wound into thorax 861.11
- cauda equina (spine) 952.4
- cerebellum — *see* Contusion, brain, cerebellum
- cerebral — *see* Contusion, brain
- cheek(s) (and other part(s) of neck, scalp, or face, except eye) 920
- chest (wall) 922.1
- chin (and other part(s) of neck, scalp, or face, except eye) 920
- clitoris 922.4
- conjunctiva 921.1
- conus medullaris (spine) 952.4
- cornea 921.3
- corpus cavernosum 922.4
- cortex (brain) (cerebral) — *see* Contusion, brain, cortex
- costal region 922.1
- ear (and other part(s) of neck, scalp, or face except eye) 920
- elbow 923.11
  - with forearm 923.10
- epididymis 922.4
- epigastric region 922.2
- eye NEC 921.9
- eyeball 921.3
- eyelid(s) (and periocular area) 921.1

Note — In general, cysts are not neoplastic and are classified to the appropriate category for disease of the specified anatomical site. This generalization does not apply to certain types of cysts which are neoplastic in nature, for example, dermoid, nor does it apply to cysts of certain structures, for example, branchial cleft, which are classified as developmental anomalies.

The following listing includes some of the most frequently reported sites of cysts as well as qualifiers which indicate the type of cyst. The latter qualifiers usually are not repeated under the anatomical sites. Since the code assignment for a given site may vary depending upon the type of cyst, the coder should refer to the listings under the specified type of cyst before consideration is given to the site.

Cyst (mucus) (retention) (serous) (simple) — *continued*
  congenital NEC — *continued*
    thymus (gland) 759.2
    tongue 750.19
    ureterovesical orifice 753.4
    vulva 752.41
  conjunctiva 372.75
  cornea 371.23
  corpora quadrigemina 348.0
  corpus
    albicans (ovary) 620.2
    luteum (ruptured) 620.1
  Cowper's gland (benign) (infected) 599.89
  cranial meninges 348.0
  craniobuccal pouch 253.8
  craniopharyngeal pouch 253.8
  cystic duct (*see also* Disease, gallbladder) 575.8
  Cysticercus (any site) 123.1
  Dandy-Walker 742.3
    with spina bifida (*see also* Spina bifida) 741.0 5th
  dental 522.8
    developmental 526.0
    eruption 526.0
    lateral periodontal 526.0
    primordial (keratocyst) 526.0
    root 522.8
  dentigerous 526.0
    mandible 526.0
    maxilla 526.0
  dermoid (M9084/0) — *see also* Neoplasm, by site, benign
    with malignant transformation (M9084/3) 183.0
    implantation
      external area or site (skin) NEC 709.8
      iris 364.61
      skin 709.8
      vagina 623.8
      vulva 624.8
    mouth 528.4
    oral soft tissue 528.4
    sacrococcygeal 685.1
      with abscess 685.0
  developmental of ovary, ovarian 752.0
  dura (cerebral) 348.0
    spinal 349.2
  ear (external) 706.2
  echinococcal (*see also* Echinococcus) 122.9
  embryonal
    cervix uteri 752.41
    genitalia, female external 752.41
    uterus 752.3
    vagina 752.41
  endometrial 621.8
    ectopic 617.9
  endometrium (uterus) 621.8
    ectopic — *see* Endometriosis
  enteric 751.5
  enterogenous 751.5
  epidermal (inclusion) (*see also* Cyst, skin) 706.2
  epidermoid (inclusion) (*see also* Cyst, skin) 706.2
    mouth 528.4
    not of skin — *see* Cyst, by site
    oral soft tissue 528.4
  epididymis 608.89
  epiglottis 478.79
  epiphysis cerebri 259.8

Cyst (mucus) (retention) (serous) (simple) — *continued*
  epithelial (inclusion) (*see also* Cyst, skin) 706.2
  epoophoron 752.11
  eruption 526.0
  esophagus 530.89
  ethmoid sinus 478.1
  eye (retention) 379.8
    congenital 743.03
    posterior segment, congenital 743.54
  eyebrow 706.2
  eyelid (sebaceous) 374.84
    infected 373.13
    sweat glands or ducts 374.84
  falciform ligament (inflammatory) 573.8
  fallopian tube 620.8
  female genital organs NEC 629.8
  fimbrial (congenital) 752.11
  fissural (oral region) 526.1
  follicle (atretic) (graafian) (ovarian) 620.0
    nabothian (gland) 616.0
  follicular (atretic) (ovarian) 620.0
    dentigerous 526.0
  frontal sinus 478.1
  gallbladder or duct 575.8
  ganglion 727.43
  Gartner's duct 752.11
  gas, of mesentery 568.89
  gingiva 523.8
  gland of moll 374.84
  globulomaxillary 526.1
  graafian follicle 620.0
  granulosal lutein 620.2
  hemangiomatous (M9121/0) (*see also* Hemangioma) 228.00
  hydatid (*see also* Echinococcus) 122.9
    fallopian tube (Morgagni) 752.11
    liver NEC 122.8
    lung NEC 122.9
    Morgagni 752.8
      fallopian tube 752.11
    specified site NEC 122.9
  hymen 623.8
    embryonal 752.41
  hypopharynx 478.26
  hypophysis, hypophyseal (duct) (recurrent) 253.8
    cerebri 253.8
  implantation (dermoid)
    anterior chamber (eye) 364.61
    external area or site (skin) NEC 709.8
    iris 364.61
    vagina 623.8
    vulva 624.8
  incisor, incisive canal 526.1
  inclusion (epidermal) (epithelial) (epidermoid) (mucous) (squamous) (*see also* Cyst, skin) 706.2
    not of skin — *see* Neoplasm, by site, benign
  intestine (large) (small) 569.89
  intracranial — *see* Cyst, brain
  intraligamentous 728.89
    knee 717.89
  intrasellar 253.8
  iris (idiopathic) 364.60
    exudative 364.62
    implantation (surgical) (traumatic) 364.61
    miotic pupillary 364.55
    parasitic 360.13
  Iwanoff's 362.62

Cyst (mucus) (retention) (serous) (simple) — *continued*
  jaw (bone) (aneurysmal) (extravasation) (hemorrhagic) (traumatic) 526.2
    developmental (odontogenic) 526.0
    fissural 526.1
  keratin 706.2
  kidney (congenital) 753.10
    acquired 593.2
    calyceal (*see also* Hydronephrosis) 591
    multiple 753.19
    pyelogenic (*see also* Hydronephrosis) 591
    simple 593.2
    single 753.11
    solitary (not congenital) 593.2
  labium (majus) (minus) 624.8
    sebaceous 624.8
  lacrimal
    apparatus 375.43
    gland or sac 375.12
  larynx 478.79
  lens 379.39
    congenital 743.39
  lip (gland) 528.5
  liver 573.8
    congenital 751.62
    hydatid (*see also* Echinococcus) 122.8
      granulosis 122.0
      multilocularis 122.5
  lung 518.89
    congenital 748.4
    giant bullous 492.0
  lutein 620.1
  lymphangiomatous (M9173/0) 228.1
  lymphoepithelial
    mouth 528.4
    oral soft tissue 528.4
  macula 362.54
  malignant (M8000/3) — *see* Neoplasm, by site, malignant
  mammary gland (sweat gland) (*see also* Cyst, breast) 610.0
  mandible 526.2
    dentigerous 526.0
    radicular 522.8
  maxilla 526.2
    dentigerous 526.0
    radicular 522.8
  median
    anterior maxillary 526.1
    palatal 526.1
  mediastinum (congenital) 748.8
  meibomian (gland) (retention) 373.2
    infected 373.12
  membrane, brain 348.0
  meninges (cerebral) 348.0
    spinal 349.2
  meniscus knee 717.5
  mesentery, mesenteric (gas) 568.89
    chyle 457.8
    gas 568.89
  mesonephric duct 752.8
  mesothelial
    peritoneum 568.89
    pleura (peritoneal) 568.89
  milk 611.5
  miotic pupillary (iris) 364.55
  Morgagni (hydatid) 752.8
    fallopian tube 752.11
  mouth 528.4
  mullerian duct 752.8
  multilocular (ovary) (M8000/1) 239.5

D

> *Note — Use the following fifth-digit subclassification with categories 640–648, 651–676:*
>
> 0 *unspecified as to episode of care*
> 1 *delivered, with or without mention of antepartum condition*
> 2 *delivered, with mention of postpartum complication*
> 3 *antepartum condition or complication*
> 4 *postpartum condition or complication*

Dependence — *continued*
- DMT 304.5 5th
- Dolophine 304.0 5th
- DOM 304.2 5th
- Doriden 304.1 5th
- dormiral 304.1 5th
- Dormison 304.1 5th
- Dromoran 304.0 5th
- drug NEC 304.9 5th
  - analgesic NEC 304.6 5th
  - combination (excluding morphine or opioid type drug) NEC 304.8 5th
    - morphine or opioid type drug with any other drug 304.7 5th
  - complicating pregnancy, childbirth, or puerperium 648.3 5th
    - affecting fetus or newborn 779.5
  - hallucinogenic 304.5 5th
  - hypnotic NEC 304.1 5th
  - narcotic NEC 304.9 5th
  - psychostimulant NEC 304.4 5th
  - sedative 304.1 5th
  - soporific NEC 304.1 5th
  - specified type NEC 304.6 5th
  - suspected damage to fetus affecting management of pregnancy 655.5 5th
  - synthetic, with morphine-like effect 304.0 5th
  - tranquilizing 304.1 5th
- duboisine 304.6 5th
- ectylurea 304.1 5th
- Endocaine 304.6 5th
- Equanil 304.1 5th
- Eskabarb 304.1 5th
- ethchlorvynol 304.1 5th
- ether (ethyl) (liquid) (vapor) (vinyl) 304.6 5th
- ethidene 304.6 5th
- ethinamate 304.1 5th
- ethoheptazine 304.6 5th
- ethyl
  - alcohol 303.9 5th
  - bromide 304.6 5th
  - carbamate 304.6 5th
  - chloride 304.6 5th
  - morphine 304.0 5th
- ethylene (gas) 304.6 5th
  - dichloride 304.6 5th
- ethylidene chloride 304.6 5th
- etilfen 304.1 5th
- etorphine 304.0 5th
- etoval 304.1 5th
- eucodal 304.0 5th
- euneryl 304.1 5th
- Evipal 304.1 5th
- Evipan 304.1 5th
- fentanyl 304.0 5th
- ganja 304.3 5th
- gardenal 304.1 5th
- gardenpanyl 304.1 5th
- gelsemine 304.6 5th
- Gelsemium 304.6 5th
- Gemonil 304.1 5th
- glucochloral 304.1 5th
- glue (airplane) (sniffing) 304.6 5th
- glutethimide 304.1 5th
- hallucinogenics 304.5 5th
- hashish 304.3 5th
- headache powder NEC 304.6 5th
- Heavenly Blue 304.5 5th
- hedonal 304.1 5th

Dependence — *continued*
- hemp 304.3 5th
- heptabarbital 304.1 5th
- Heptalgin 304.0 5th
- heptobarbitone 304.1 5th
- heroin 304.0 5th
  - salt (any) 304.0 5th
- hexethal (sodium) 304.1 5th
- hexobarbital 304.1 5th
- Hycodan 304.0 5th
- hydrocodone 304.0 5th
- hydromorphinol 304.0 5th
- hydromorphinone 304.0 5th
- hydromorphone 304.0 5th
- hydroxycodeine 304.0 5th
- hypnotic NEC 304.1 5th
- Indian hemp 304.3 5th
- intranarcon 304.1 5th
- Kemithal 304.1 5th
- ketobemidone 304.0 5th
- khat 304.4 5th
- kif 304.3 5th
- Lactuca (virosa) extract 304.1 5th
- lactucarium 304.1 5th
- laudanum 304.0 5th
- Lebanese red 304.3 5th
- Leritine 304.0 5th
- lettuce opium 304.1 5th
- Levanil 304.1 5th
- Levo-Dromoran 304.0 5th
- levo-iso-methadone 304.0 5th
- levorphanol 304.0 5th
- Librium 304.1 5th
- Lomotil 304.6 5th
- Lotusate 304.1 5th
- LSD (-25) (and derivatives) 304.5 5th
- Luminal 304.1 5th
- lysergic acid 304.5 5th
  - amide 304.5 5th
- maconha 304.3 5th
- magic mushroom 304.5 5th
- marihuana 304.3 5th
- MDA (methylene dioxyamphetamine) 304.4 5th
- Mebaral 304.1 5th
- Medinal 304.1 5th
- Medomin 304.1 5th
- megahallucinogenics 304.5 5th
- meperidine 304.0 5th
- mephobarbital 304.1 5th
- meprobamate 304.1 5th
- mescaline 304.6 5th
- methadone 304.0 5th
- methamphetamine(s) 304.4 5th
- methaqualone 304.1 5th
- metharbital 304.1 5th
- methitural 304.1 5th
- methobarbitone 304.1 5th
- methohexital 304.1 5th
- methopholine 304.6 5th
- methyl
  - alcohol 303.9 5th
  - bromide 304.6 5th
  - morphine 304.0 5th
  - sulfonal 304.1 5th
- methylated spirit 303.9 5th
- methylbutinol 304.6 5th
- methyldihydromorphinone 304.0 5th

Dependence — *continued*
- methylene
  - chloride 304.6 5th
  - dichloride 304.6 5th
  - dioxyamphetamine (MDA) 304.4 5th
- methylparafynol 304.1 5th
- methylphenidate 304.4 5th
- methyprylone 304.1 5th
- metopon 304.0 5th
- Miltown 304.1 5th
- morning glory seeds 304.5 5th
- morphinan(s) 304.0 5th
- morphine (sulfate) (sulfite) (type) (drugs classifiable to 965.00–965.09) 304.0 5th
- morphine or opioid type drug (drugs classifiable to 965.00–965.09) with any other drug 304.7 5th
- morphinol(s) 304.0 5th
- morphinon 304.0 5th
- morpholinylethylmorphine 304.0 5th
- mylomide 304.1 5th
- myristicin 304.5 5th
- narcotic (drug) NEC 304.9 5th
- nealbarbital 304.1 5th
- nealbarbitone 304.1 5th
- Nembutal 304.1 5th
- Neonal 304.1 5th
- Neraval 304.1 5th
- Neravan 304.1 5th
- neurobarb 304.1 5th
- nicotine 305.1
- Nisentil 304.0 5th
- nitrous oxide 304.6 5th
- Noctec 304.1 5th
- Noludar 304.1 5th
- nonbarbiturate sedatives and tranquilizers with similar effect 304.1 5th
- noptil 304.1 5th
- normorphine 304.0 5th
- noscapine 304.0 5th
- Novocaine 304.6 5th
- Numorphan 304.0 5th
- nunol 304.1 5th
- Nupercaine 304.6 5th
- Oblivon 304.1 5th
- on
  - aspirator V46.0
  - hyperbaric chamber V46.8
  - iron lung V46.1
  - machine (enabling) V46.9
    - specified type NEC V46.8
  - Possum (patient-operated-selector-mechanism) V46.8
  - renal dialysis machine V45.1
  - respirator V46.1
- opiate 304.0 5th
- opioids 304.0 5th
- opioid type drug 304.0 5th
  - with any other drug 304.7 5th
- opium (alkaloids) (derivatives) (tincture) 304.0 5th
- ortal 304.1 5th
- Oxazepam 304.1 5th
- oxycodone 304.0 5th
- oxymorphone 304.0 5th
- Palfium 304.0 5th
- Panadol 304.6 5th
- pantopium 304.0 5th
- pantopon 304.0 5th
- papaverine 304.0 5th

- **Deviation** — *continued*
  - sexual — *continued*
    - satyriasis 302.89
    - specified type NEC 302.89
    - transvestic fetishism 302.3
    - transvestism 302.3
    - voyeurism 302.82
    - zoophilia (erotica) 302.1
  - teeth, midline 524.2
  - trachea 519.1
  - ureter (congenital) 753.4
- **Devic's disease** 341.0
- **Device**
  - cerebral ventricle (communicating) in situ V45.2
  - contraceptive — *see* Contraceptive, device
  - drainage, cerebrospinal fluid V45.2
- **Devil's**
  - grip 074.1
  - pinches (purpura simplex) 287.2
- **Devitalized tooth** 522.9
- **Devonshire colic** 984.9
  - specified type of lead — *see* Table of Drugs and Chemicals
- **Dextraposition, aorta** 747.21
  - with ventricular septal defect, pulmonary stenosis or atresia, and hypertrophy of right ventricle 745.2
  - in tetralogy of Fallot 745.2
- **Dextratransposition, aorta** 745.11
- **Dextrinosis, limit** (debrancher enzyme deficiency) 271.0
- **Dextrocardia** (corrected) (false) (isolated) (secondary) (true) 746.87
  - with
    - complete transposition of viscera 759.3
    - situs inversus 759.3
- **Dextroversion, kidney** (left) 753.3
- **Dhobie itch** 110.3
- **Diabetes, diabetic** (brittle) (congenital) (familial) (mellitus) (severe) (slight) (without complication) 250.0 5th

> *Note — Use the following fifth-digit subclassification with category 250:*
>
> 0 *type II [non-insulin dependent type] [NIDDM type] [adult-onset type] or unspecified type, not stated as uncontrolled*
>
> *Note — Fifth-digit 0 is for use for type II, adult-onset diabetic patients, even if the patient requires insulin*
>
> 1 *type I [insulin dependent type] [IDDM type] [juvenile type], not stated as uncontrolled*
>
> 2 *type II [non-insulin dependent type] [NIDDM type] [adult-onset type] or unspecified type, uncontrolled*
>
> *Note — Fifth-digit 2 is for use for type II, adult-onset diabetic patients, even if the patient requires insulin*
>
> 3 *type I [insulin dependent type] [IDDM type] [juvenile type], uncontrolled*

  - with
    - coma (with ketoacidosis) 250.3 5th
      - hyperosmolar (nonketotic) 250.2 5th
    - complication NEC 250.9 5th
      - specified NEC 250.8 5th
    - gangrene 250.7 5th *[785.4]*
    - hyperosmolarity 250.2 5th
    - ketosis, ketoacidosis 250.1 5th
    - osteomyelitis 250.8 5th *[731.8]*
    - specified manifestations NEC 250.8 5th

- **Diabetes, diabetic** (brittle) (congenital) (familial) (mellitus) (severe) (slight) (without complication) — *continued*
  - acetonemia 250.1 5th
  - acidosis 250.1 5th
  - amyotrophy 250.6 5th *[358.1]*
  - angiopathy, peripheral 250.7 5th *[443.81]*
  - asymptomatic 790.2
  - autonomic neuropathy (peripheral) 250.6 5th *[337.1]*
  - bone change 250.8 5th *[731.8]*
  - bronze, bronzed 275.0
  - cataract 250.5 5th *[366.41]*
  - chemical 790.2
    - complicating pregnancy, childbirth, or puerperium 648.8 5th
  - coma (with ketoacidosis) 250.3 5th
    - hyperglycemic 250.3 5th
    - hyperosmolar (nonketotic) 250.2 5th
    - hypoglycemic 250.3 5th
    - insulin 250.3 5th
  - complicating pregnancy, childbirth, or puerperium (maternal) 648.0 5th
    - affecting fetus or newborn 775.0
  - complication NEC 250.9 5th
    - specified NEC 250.8 5th
  - dorsal sclerosis 250.6 5th *[340]*
  - dwarfism-obesity syndrome 258.1
  - gangrene 250.7 5th *[785.4]*
  - gastroparesis 250.6 5th *[536.3]*
  - gestational 648.8 5th
    - complicating pregnancy, childbirth, or puerperium 648.8 5th
  - glaucoma 250.5 5th *[365.44]*
  - glomerulosclerosis (intercapillary) 250.4 5th *[581.81]*
  - glycogenosis, secondary 250.8 5th *[259.8]*
  - hemochromatosis 275.0
  - hyperosmolar coma 250.2 5th
  - hyperosmolarity 250.2 5th
  - hypertension-nephrosis syndrome 250.4 5th *[581.81]*
  - hypoglycemia 250.8 5th
  - hypoglycemic shock 250.8 5th
  - insipidus 253.5
    - nephrogenic 588.1
    - pituitary 253.5
    - vasopressin-resistant 588.1
  - intercapillary glomerulosclerosis 250.4 5th *[581.81]*
  - iritis 250.5 5th *[364.42]*
  - ketosis, ketoacidosis 250.1 5th
  - Kimmelstiel (-Wilson) disease or syndrome (intercapillary glomerulosclerosis) 250.4 5th *[581.81]*
  - Lancereaux's (diabetes mellitus with marked emaciation) 250.8 5th *[261]*
  - latent (chemical) 790.2
    - complicating pregnancy, childbirth, or puerperium 648.8 5th
  - lipoidosis 250.8 5th *[272.7]*
  - macular edema 250.5 5th *[362.01]*
  - maternal
    - with manifest disease in the infant 775.1
    - affecting fetus or newborn 775.0
  - microaneurysms, retinal 250.5 5th *[362.01]*
  - mononeuropathy 250.6 5th *[355.9]*
  - neonatal, transient 775.1
  - nephropathy 250.4 5th *[583.81]*
  - nephrosis (syndrome) 250.4 5th *[581.81]*
  - neuralgia 250.6 5th *[357.2]*
  - neuritis 250.6 5th *[357.2]*
  - neurogenic arthropathy 250.6 5th *[713.5]*

- **Diabetes, diabetic** (brittle) (congenital) (familial) (mellitus) (severe) (slight) (without complication) — *continued*
  - neuropathy 250.6 5th *[357.2]*
  - nonclinical 790.2
  - osteomyelitis 250.8 5th *[731.8]*
  - peripheral autonomic neuropathy 250.6 5th *[337.1]*
  - phosphate 275.3
  - polyneuropathy 250.6 5th *[357.2]*
  - renal (true) 271.4
  - retinal
    - edema 250.5 5th *[362.83]*
    - hemorrhage 250.5 5th *[362.01]*
    - microaneurysms 250.5 5th *[362.01]*
  - retinitis 250.5 5th *[362.01]*
  - retinopathy 250.5 5th *[362.01]*
    - background 250.5 5th *[362.01]*
    - proliferative 250.5 5th *[362.02]*
  - steroid induced
    - correct substance properly administered 251.8
    - overdose or wrong substance given or taken 962.0
  - stress 790.2
  - subclinical 790.2
  - subliminal 790.2
  - sugar 250.0 5th
  - ulcer (skin) 250.8 5th *[707.9]*
    - lower extremity 250.8 5th *[707.1]*
    - specified site NEC 250.8 5th *[707.8]*
  - xanthoma 250.8 5th *[272.2]*
- **Diacyclothrombopathia** 287.1
- **Diagnosis deferred** 799.9
- **Dialysis** (intermittent) (treatment)
  - anterior retinal (juvenile) (with detachment) 361.04
  - extracorporeal V56.0
  - peritoneal V56.8
  - renal V56.0
    - status only V45.1
  - specified type NEC V56.8
- **Diamond-Blackfan anemia or syndrome** (congenital hypoplastic anemia) 284.0
- **Diamond-Gardener syndrome** (autoerythrocyte sensitization) 287.2
- **Diaper rash** 691.0
- **Diaphoresis** (excessive) NEC 780.8
- **Diaphragm** — *see* condition
- **Diaphragmalgia** 786.52
- **Diaphragmitis** 519.4
- **Diaphyseal aclasis** 756.4
- **Diaphysitis** 733.99
- **Diarrhea, diarrheal** (acute) (autumn) (bilious) (bloody) (catarrhal) (choleraic) (chronic) (gravis) (green) (infantile) (lienteric) (noninfectious) (presumed noninfectious) (putrefactive) (secondary) (sporadic) (summer) (symptomatic) (thermic) 787.91
  - achlorhydric 536.0
  - allergic 558.9
  - amebic (*see also* Amebiasis) 006.9
    - with abscess — *see* Abscess, amebic
    - acute 006.0
    - chronic 006.1
    - nondysenteric 006.2
  - bacillary — *see* Dysentery, bacillary
  - bacterial NEC 008.5
  - balantidial 007.0
  - bile salt-induced 579.8
  - cachectic NEC 558.9

- **Disease, diseased** — *see also* Syndrome — *continued*
  - synovium 727.9
  - syphilitic — *see* Syphilis
  - systemic tissue mast cell (M9741/3) 202.6 [5th]
  - Taenzer's 757.4
  - Takayasu's (pulseless) 446.7
  - Talma's 728.85
  - Tangier (familial high-density lipoprotein deficiency) 272.5
  - Tarral-Besnier (pityriasis rubra pilaris) 696.4
  - Tay-Sachs 330.1
  - Taylor's 701.8
  - tear duct 375.69
  - teeth, tooth 525.9
    - hard tissues NEC 521.9
    - pulp NEC 522.9
  - tendon 727.9
    - inflammatory NEC 727.9
  - terminal vessel 443.9
  - testis 608.9
  - Thaysen-Gee (nontropical sprue) 579.0
  - Thomsen's 359.2
  - Thomson's (congenital poikiloderma) 757.33
  - Thornwaldt's, Tornwaldt's (pharyngeal bursitis) 478.29
  - throat 478.20
    - septic 034.0
  - thromboembolic (*see also* Embolism) 444.9
  - thymus (gland) 254.9
    - specified NEC 254.8
  - thyroid (gland) NEC 246.9
    - heart (*see also* Hyperthyroidism) 242.9 [5th] *[425.7]*
    - lardaceous 277.3
    - specified NEC 246.8
  - Tietze's 733.6
  - Tommaselli's
    - correct substance properly administered 599.7
    - overdose or wrong substance given or taken 961.4
  - tongue 529.9
  - tonsils, tonsillar (and adenoids) (chronic) 474.9
    - specified NEC 474.8
  - tooth, teeth 525.9
    - hard tissues NEC 521.9
    - pulp NEC 522.9
  - Tornwaldt's (pharyngeal bursitis) 478.29
  - Tourette's 307.23
  - trachea 519.1
  - tricuspid — *see* Endocarditis, tricuspid
  - triglyceride-storage, type I, II, III 272.7
  - triple vessel (coronary arteries) — *see* Arteriosclerosis, coronary
  - trisymptomatic, Gougerot's 709.1
  - trophoblastic (*see also* Hydatidiform mole) 630
    - previous, affecting management of pregnancy V23.1
  - tsutsugamushi (scrub typhus) 081.2
  - tube (fallopian), noninflammatory 620.9
    - specified NEC 620.8
  - tuberculous NEC (*see also* Tuberculosis) 011.9 [5th]
  - tubo-ovarian
    - inflammatory (*see also* Salpingo-oophoritis) 614.2
    - noninflammatory 620.9
      - specified NEC 620.8
  - tubotympanic, chronic (with anterior perforation of ear drum) 382.1
  - tympanum 385.9
  - Uhl's 746.84
  - umbilicus (newborn) NEC 779.8
  - Underwood's (sclerema neonatorum) 778.1
  - undiagnosed 799.9
  - Unna's (seborrheic dermatitis) 690.18
  - unstable hemoglobin hemolytic 282.7
  - Unverricht (-Lundborg) 333.2
  - Urbach-Oppenheim (necrobiosis lipoidica diabeticorum) 250.8 [5th] *[709.3]*
  - Urbach-Wiethe (lipoid proteinosis) 272.8
  - ureter 593.9
  - urethra 599.9
    - specified type NEC 599.84
  - urinary (tract) 599.9
    - bladder 596.9
      - specified NEC 596.8
    - maternal, affecting fetus or newborn 760.1
  - Usher-Senear (pemphigus erythematosus) 694.4
  - uterus (organic) 621.9
    - infective (*see also* Endometritis) 615.9
    - inflammatory (*see also* Endometritis) 615.9
    - noninflammatory 621.9
      - specified type NEC 621.8
  - uveal tract
    - anterior 364.9
    - posterior 363.9
  - vagabonds' 132.1
  - vagina, vaginal
    - inflammatory 616.9
      - specified NEC 616.8
    - noninflammatory 623.9
      - specified NEC 623.8
  - Valsuani's (progressive pernicious anemia, puerperal) 648.2 [5th]
    - complicating pregnancy or puerperium 648.2 [5th]
  - valve, valvular — *see* Endocarditis
  - van Bogaert-Nijssen (-Peiffer) 330.0
  - van Creveld-von Gierke (glycogenosis I) 271.0
  - van den Bergh's (enterogenous cyanosis) 289.7
  - van Neck's (juvenile osteochondrosis) 732.1
  - Vaquez (-Osler) (polycythemia vera) (M9950/1) 238.4
  - vascular 459.9
    - arteriosclerotic — *see* Arteriosclerosis
    - hypertensive — *see* Hypertension
    - obliterative 447.1
      - peripheral 443.9
    - occlusive 459.9
    - peripheral (occlusive) 443.9
      - in diabetes mellitus 250.7 [5th] *[443.81]*
      - specified type NEC 443.89
  - vas deferens 608.9
  - vasomotor 443.9
  - vasospastic 443.9
  - vein 459.9
  - venereal 099.9
    - chlamydial NEC 099.50
      - anus 099.52
      - bladder 099.53
      - cervix 099.53
      - epididymis 099.54
      - genitourinary NEC 099.55
        - lower 099.53
        - specific NEC 099.54
      - pelvic inflammatory disease 099.54
      - perihepatic 099.56
      - peritoneum 099.56
      - pharynx 099.51
      - rectum 099.52
      - specified site NEC 099.59
      - testis 099.54
      - vagina 099.53
      - vulva 099.53
    - fifth 099.1
    - sixth 099.1
    - complicating pregnancy, childbirth, or puerperium 647.2 [5th]
    - specified nature or type NEC 099.8
      - chlamydial — *see* Disease, venereal, chlamydial
  - Verneuil's (syphilitic bursitis) 095.7
  - Verse's (calcinosis intervertebralis) 275.49 *[722.90]*
  - vertebra, vertebral NEC 733.90
    - disc — *see* Disease, Intervertebral disc
  - vibration NEC 994.9
  - Vidal's (lichen simplex chronicus) 698.3
  - Vincent's (trench mouth) 101
  - Virchow's 733.99
  - virus (filterable) NEC 078.89
    - arbovirus NEC 066.9
    - arthropod-borne NEC 066.9
    - central nervous system NEC 049.9
      - specified type NEC 049.8
    - complicating pregnancy, childbirth, or puerperium 647.6 [5th]
    - contact (with) V01.7
    - exposure to V01.7
    - Marburg 078.89
    - maternal
      - with fetal damage affecting management of pregnancy 655.3 [5th]
    - nonarthropod-borne NEC 078.89
      - central nervous system NEC 049.9
        - specified NEC 049.8
  - vitreous 379.29
  - vocal cords NEC 478.5
  - Vogt's (Cecile) 333.7
  - Vogt-Spielmeyer 330.1
  - Volhard-Fahr (malignant nephrosclerosis) 403.00
  - Volkmann's
    - acquired 958.6
  - von Bechterew's (ankylosing spondylitis) 720.0
  - von Economo's (encephalitis lethargica) 049.8
  - von Eulenburg's (congenital paramyotonia) 359.2
  - von Gierke's (glycogenosis I) 271.0
  - von Graefe's 378.72
  - von Hippel's (retinocerebral angiomatosis) 759.6
  - von Hippel-Lindau (angiomatosis retinocerebellosa) 759.6
  - von Jaksch's (pseudoleukemia infantum) 285.8

> *Note — "Closed" includes simple, complete, partial, uncomplicated, and unspecified dislocation.*
>
> *"Open" includes dislocation specified as infected or compound and dislocation with foreign body.*
>
> *"Chronic", "habitual", "old", or "recurrent" dislocations should be coded as indicated under the entry "Dislocation, recurrent"; and "pathological" as indicated under the entry "Dislocation, pathological."*
>
> *For late effect of dislocation see Late, effect, dislocation*

E

Eagle-Barrett syndrome 756.71

Eales' disease (syndrome) 362.18

Ear — *see also* condition
- ache 388.70
  - otogenic 388.71
  - referred 388.72
- lop 744.29
- piercing V50.3
- swimmers' acute 380.12
- tank 380.12
- tropical 111.8 *[380.15]*
- wax 380.4

Earache 388.70
- otogenic 388.71
- referred 388.72

Eaton-Lambert syndrome (*see also* Neoplasm, by site, malignant) 199.1 *[358.1]*

Eberth's disease (typhoid fever) 002.0

Ebstein's
- anomaly or syndrome (downward displacement, tricuspid valve into right ventricle) 746.2
- disease (diabetes) 250.4 ✓5th *[581.81]*

Eccentro-osteochondrodysplasia 277.5

Ecchondroma (M9210/0)— *see* Neoplasm, bone, benign

Ecchondrosis (M9210/1) 238.0

Ecchordosis physaliphora 756.0

Ecchymosis (multiple) 459.89
- conjunctiva 372.72
- eye (traumatic) 921.0
- eyelids (traumatic) 921.1
- newborn 772.6
- spontaneous 782.7
- traumatic — *see* Contusion

Echinococciasis — *see* Echinococcus

Echinococcosis — *see* Echinococcus

Echinococcus (infection) 122.9
- granulosus 122.4
  - liver 122.0
  - lung 122.1
  - orbit 122.3 *[376.13]*
  - specified site NEC 122.3
  - thyroid 122.2
- liver NEC 122.8
  - granulosus 122.0
  - multilocularis 122.5
- lung NEC 122.9
  - granulosus 122.1
  - multilocularis 122.6
- multilocularis 122.7
  - liver 122.5
  - specified site NEC 122.6
- orbit 122.9 *[376.13]*
  - granulosus 122.3 *[376.13]*
  - multilocularis 122.6 *[376.13]*
- specified site NEC 122.9
  - granulosus 122.3
  - multilocularis 122.6 *[376.13]*
- thyroid NEC 122.9
  - granulosus 122.2
  - multilocularis 122.6

Echinorhynchiasis 127.7

Echinostomiasis 121.8

Echolalia 784.69

ECHO virus infection NEC 079.1

Eclampsia, eclamptic (coma) (convulsions) (delirium) 780.39
- female, child-bearing age NEC — *see* Eclampsia, pregnancy
- gravidarum — *see* Eclampsia, pregnancy
- male 780.39
- not associated with pregnancy or childbirth 780.39
- pregnancy, childbirth, or puerperium 642.6 ✓5th
  - with pre-existing hypertension 642.7 ✓5th
  - affecting fetus or newborn 760.0
- uremic 586

Eclipse blindness (total) 363.31

Economic circumstance affecting care V60.9
- specified type NEC V60.8

Economo's disease (encephalitis lethargica) 049.8

Ectasia, ectasis
- aorta (*see also* Aneurysm, aorta) 441.9
  - ruptured 441.5
- breast 610.4
- capillary 448.9
- cornea (marginal) (postinfectional) 371.71
- duct (mammary) 610.4
- kidney 593.89
- mammary duct (gland) 610.4
- papillary 448.9
- renal 593.89
- salivary gland (duct) 527.8
- scar, cornea 371.71
- sclera 379.11

Ecthyma 686.8
- contagiosum 051.2
- gangrenosum 686.09
- infectiosum 051.2

Ectocardia 746.87

Ectodermal dysplasia, congenital 757.31

Ectodermosis erosiva pluriorificialis 695.1

Ectopic, ectopia (congenital) 759.89
- abdominal viscera 751.8
  - due to defect in anterior abdominal wall 756.79
- ACTH syndrome 255.0
- adrenal gland 759.1
- anus 751.5
- auricular beats 427.61
- beats 427.60
- bladder 753.5
- bone and cartilage in lung 748.69
- brain 742.4
- breast tissue 757.6
- cardiac 746.87
- cerebral 742.4
- cordis 746.87
- endometrium 617.9
- gallbladder 751.69
- gastric mucosa 750.7
- gestation — *see* Pregnancy, ectopic
- heart 746.87
- hormone secretion NEC 259.3
- hyperparathyroidism 259.3
- kidney (crossed) (intrathoracic) (pelvis) 753.3
  - in pregnancy or childbirth 654.4 ✓5th
    - causing obstructed labor 660.2 ✓5th
- lens 743.37
- lentis 743.37

Ectopic, ectopia (congenital) — *continued*
- mole — *see* Pregnancy, ectopic
- organ or site NEC — *see* Malposition, congenital
- ovary 752.0
- pancreas, pancreatic tissue 751.7
- pregnancy — *see* Pregnancy, ectopic
- pupil 364.75
- renal 753.3
- sebaceous glands of mouth 750.26
- secretion
  - ACTH 255.0
  - adrenal hormone 259.3
  - adrenalin 259.3
  - adrenocorticotropin 255.0
  - antidiuretic hormone (ADH) 259.3
  - epinephrine 259.3
  - hormone NEC 259.3
  - norepinephrine 259.3
  - pituitary (posterior) 259.3
- spleen 759.0
- testis 752.51
- thyroid 759.2
- ureter 753.4
- ventricular beats 427.69
- vesicae 753.5

Ectrodactyly 755.4
- finger (*see also* Absence, finger, congenital) 755.29
- toe (*see also* Absence, toe, congenital) 755.39

Ectromelia 755.4
- lower limb 755.30
- upper limb 755.20

Ectropion 374.10
- anus 569.49
- cervix 622.0
  - with mention of cervicitis 616.0
- cicatricial 374.14
- congenital 743.62
- eyelid 374.10
  - cicatricial 374.14
  - congenital 743.62
  - mechanical 374.12
  - paralytic 374.12
  - senile 374.11
  - spastic 374.13
- iris (pigment epithelium) 364.54
- lip (congenital) 750.26
  - acquired 528.5
- mechanical 374.12
- paralytic 374.12
- rectum 569.49
- senile 374.11
- spastic 374.13
- urethra 599.84
- uvea 364.54

Eczema (acute) (allergic) (chronic) (erythematous) (fissum) (occupational) (rubrum) (squamous) 692.9
- asteatotic 706.8
- atopic 691.8
- contact NEC 692.9
- dermatitis NEC 692.9
- due to specified cause — *see* Dermatitis, due to
- dyshidrotic 705.81
- external ear 380.22
- flexural 691.8

Effect, adverse NEC — *continued*
- cobalt, radioactive (*see also* Effect, adverse, radioactive substance) 990
- cold (temperature) (weather) 991.9
  - chilblains 991.5
  - frostbite — *see* Frostbite
  - specified effect NEC 991.8
- drugs and medicinals NEC 995.2
  - correct substance properly administered 995.2
  - overdose or wrong substance given or taken 977.9
    - specified drug — *see* Table of Drugs and Chemicals
- electric current (shock) 994.8
  - burn — *see* Burn, by site
- electricity (electrocution) (shock) 994.8
  - burn — *see* Burn, by site
- exertion (excessive) 994.5
- exposure 994.9
  - exhaustion 994.4
- external cause NEC 994.9
- fallout (radioactive) NEC 990
- fluoroscopy NEC 990
- foodstuffs
  - allergic reaction (*see also* Allergy, food) 693.1
    - anaphylactic shock due to food NEC 995.60
  - noxious 988.9
    - specified type NEC (*see also* Poisoning, by name of noxious foodstuff) 988.8
- gases, fumes, or vapors — *see* Table of Drugs and Chemicals
- glue (airplane) sniffing 304.6 [5th]
- heat — *see* Heat
- high altitude NEC 993.2
  - anoxia 993.2
  - on
    - ears 993.0
    - sinuses 993.1
  - polycythemia 289.0
- hot weather — *see* Heat
- hunger 994.2
- immersion, foot 991.4
- immunization — *see* Complications, vaccination
- immunological agents — *see* Complications, vaccination
- implantation (removable) of isotope or radium NEC 990
- infrared (radiation) (rays) NEC 990
  - burn — *see* Burn, by site
  - dermatitis or eczema 692.82
- infusion — *see* Complications, infusion
- ingestion or injection of isotope (therapeutic) NEC 990
- irradiation NEC (*see also* Effect, adverse, radiation) 990
- isotope (radioactive) NEC 990
- lack of care (child) (infant) (newborn) 995.52
  - adult 995.84
- lightning 994.0
  - burn — *see* Burn, by site
- Lirugin — *see* Complications, vaccination
- medicinal substance, correct, properly administered (*see also* Effect, adverse, drugs) 995.2
- mesothorium NEC 990
- motion 994.6
- noise, inner ear 388.10

Effect, adverse NEC — *continued*
- overheated places — *see* Heat
- polonium NEC 990
- psychosocial, of work environment V62.1
- radiation (diagnostic) (fallout) (infrared) (natural source) (therapeutic) (tracer) (ultraviolet) (x-ray) NEC 990
  - with pulmonary manifestations
    - acute 508.0
    - chronic 508.1
  - dermatitis or eczema 692.82
    - due to sun NEC (*see also* Dermatitis, due to, sun) 692.70
  - fibrosis of lungs 508.1
  - maternal with suspected damage to fetus affecting management of pregnancy 655.6 [5th]
  - pneumonitis 508.0
- radioactive substance NEC 990
  - dermatitis or eczema 692.82
- radioactivity NEC 990
- radiotherapy NEC 990
  - dermatitis or eczema 692.82
- radium NEC 990
- reduced temperature 991.9
  - frostbite — *see* Frostbite
  - immersion, foot (hand) 991.4
  - specified effect NEC 991.8
- roentgenography NEC 990
- roentgenoscopy NEC 990
- roentgen rays NEC 990
- serum (prophylactic) (therapeutic) NEC 999.5
- specified NEC 995.89
  - external cause NEC 994.9
- strangulation 994.7
- submersion 994.1
- teletherapy NEC 990
- thirst 994.3
- transfusion — *see* Complications, transfusion
- ultraviolet (radiation) (rays) NEC 990
  - burn — *see also* Burn, by site
    - from sun 692.71
  - dermatitis or eczema 692.82
    - due to sun NEC (*see also* Dermatitis, due to, sun) 692.70
- uranium NEC 990
- vaccine (any)— *see* Complications, vaccination
- weightlessness 994.9
- whole blood — *see also* Complications, transfusion
  - overdose or wrong substance given (*see also* Table of Drugs and Chemicals) 964.7
- working environment V62.1
- x-rays NEC 990
  - dermatitis or eczema 692.82

Effect, remote
- of cancer — *see* condition

Effects, late — *see* Late, effect (of)

Effluvium, telogen 704.02

Effort
- intolerance 306.2
- syndrome (aviators) (psychogenic) 306.2

Effusion
- amniotic fluid (*see also* Rupture, membranes, premature) 658.1 [5th]
- brain (serous) 348.5
- bronchial (*see also* Bronchitis) 490
- cerebral 348.5
- cerebrospinal (*see also* Meningitis) 322.9
  - vessel 348.5
- chest — *see* Effusion, pleura

Effusion — *continued*
- intracranial 348.5
- joint 719.00
  - ankle 719.07
  - elbow 719.02
  - foot 719.07
  - hand 719.04
  - hip 719.05
  - knee 719.06
  - multiple sites 719.09
  - pelvic region 719.05
  - shoulder (region) 719.01
  - specified site NEC 719.08
  - wrist 719.03
- meninges (*see also* Meningitis) 322.9
- pericardium, pericardial (*see also* Pericarditis) 423.9
  - acute 420.90
- peritoneal (chronic) 568.82
- pleura, pleurisy, pleuritic, pleuropericardial 511.9
  - bacterial, nontuberculous 511.1
  - fetus or newborn 511.9
  - malignant 197.2
  - nontuberculous 511.9
    - bacterial 511.1
  - pneumococcal 511.1
  - staphylococcal 511.1
  - streptococcal 511.1
  - traumatic 862.29
    - with open wound 862.39
  - tuberculous (*see also* Tuberculosis, pleura) 012.0 [5th]
    - primary progressive 010.1 [5th]
- pulmonary — *see* Effusion, pleura
- spinal (*see also* Meningitis) 322.9
- thorax, thoracic — *see* Effusion, pleura

Eggshell nails 703.8
- congenital 757.5

Ego-dystonic
- homosexuality 302.0
- lesbianism 302.0

Egyptian splenomegaly 120.1

Ehlers-Danlos syndrome 756.83

Eichstedt's disease (pityriasis versicolor) 111.0

Eisenmenger's complex or syndrome (ventricular septal defect) 745.4

Ejaculation, semen
- painful 608.89
  - psychogenic 306.59
- premature 302.75

Ekbom syndrome (restless legs) 333.99

Ekman's syndrome (brittle bones and blue sclera) 756.51

Elastic skin 756.83
- acquired 701.8

Elastofibroma (M8820/0)— *see* Neoplasm, connective tissue, benign

Elastoidosis
- cutanea nodularis 701.8
- cutis cystica et comedonica 701.8

Elastoma 757.39
- juvenile 757.39
- Miescher's (elastosis perforans serpiginosa) 701.1

Elastomyofibrosis 425.3

Elastosis 701.8
- atrophicans 701.8
- perforans serpiginosa 701.1
- reactive perforating 701.1

- **Enterocele** (*see also* Hernia) 553.9
  - pelvis, pelvic (acquired) (congenital) 618.6
  - vagina, vaginal (acquired) (congenital) 618.6
- **Enterocolitis** — *see also* Enteritis
  - fetus or newborn 777.8
    - necrotizing 777.5
  - fulminant 557.0
  - granulomatous 555.2
  - hemorrhagic (acute) 557.0
    - chronic 557.1
  - necrotizing (acute) (membranous) 557.0
  - primary necrotizing 777.5
  - pseudomembranous 008.45
  - radiation 558.1
    - newborn 777.5
  - ulcerative 556.0
- **Enterocystoma** 751.5
- **Enterogastritis** — *see* Enteritis
- **Enterogenous cyanosis** 289.7
- **Enterolith, enterolithiasis** (impaction) 560.39
  - with hernia — *see also* Hernia, by site, with obstruction
    - gangrenous — *see* Hernia, by site, with gangrene
- **Enteropathy** 569.9
  - exudative (of Gordon) 579.8
  - gluten 579.0
  - hemorrhagic, terminal 557.0
  - protein-losing 579.8
- **Enteroperitonitis** (*see also* Peritonitis) 567.9
- **Enteroptosis** 569.89
- **Enterorrhagia** 578.9
- **Enterospasm** 564.1
  - psychogenic 306.4
- **Enterostenosis** (*see also* Obstruction, intestine) 560.9
- **Enterostomy status** V44.4
  - with complication 569.60
- **Enthesopathy** 726.90
  - ankle and tarsus 726.70
  - elbow region 726.30
    - specified NEC 726.39
  - hip 726.5
  - knee 726.60
  - peripheral NEC 726.8
  - shoulder region 726.10
    - adhesive 726.0
  - spinal 720.1
  - wrist and carpus 726.4
- **Entrance, air into vein** — *see* Embolism, air
- **Entrapment, nerve** — *see* Neuropathy, entrapment
- **Entropion** (eyelid) 374.00
  - cicatricial 374.04
  - congenital 743.62
  - late effect of trachoma (healed) 139.1
  - mechanical 374.02
  - paralytic 374.02
  - senile 374.01
  - spastic 374.03
- **Enucleation of eye** (current) (traumatic) 871.3
- **Enuresis** 788.30
  - habit disturbance 307.6
  - nocturnal 788.36
    - psychogenic 307.6
  - nonorganic origin 307.6
  - psychogenic 307.6
- **Enzymopathy** 277.9
- **Eosinopenia** 288.0
- **Eosinophilia** 288.3
  - allergic 288.3
  - hereditary 288.3
  - idiopathic 288.3
  - infiltrative 518.3
  - Loeffler's 518.3
  - myalgia syndrome 710.5
  - pulmonary (tropical) 518.3
  - secondary 288.3
  - tropical 518.3
- **Eosinophilic** — *see also* condition
  - fasciitis 728.89
  - granuloma (bone) 277.8
  - infiltration lung 518.3
- **Ependymitis** (acute) (cerebral) (chronic) (granular) (*see also* Meningitis) 322.9
- **Ependymoblastoma** (M9392/3)
  - specified site — *see* Neoplasm, by site, malignant
  - unspecified site 191.9
- **Ependymoma** (epithelial) (malignant) (M9391/3)
  - anaplastic type (M9392/3)
    - specified site — *see* Neoplasm, by site, malignant
    - unspecified site 191.9
  - benign (M9391/0)
    - specified site — *see* Neoplasm, by site, benign
    - unspecified site 225.0
  - myxopapillary (M9394/1) 237.5
  - papillary (M9393/1) 237.5
  - specified site — *see* Neoplasm, by site, malignant
  - unspecified site 191.9
- **Ependymopathy** 349.2
  - spinal cord 349.2
- **Ephelides, ephelis** 709.09
- **Ephemeral fever** (*see also* Pyrexia) 780.6
- **Epiblepharon** (congenital) 743.62
- **Epicanthus, epicanthic fold** (congenital) (eyelid) 743.63
- **Epicondylitis** (elbow) (lateral) 726.32
  - medial 726.31
- **Epicystitis** (*see also* Cystitis) 595.9
- **Epidemic** — *see* condition
- **Epidermidalization, cervix** — *see* condition
- **Epidermidization, cervix** — *see* condition
- **Epidermis, epidermal** — *see* condition
- **Epidermization, cervix** — *see* condition
- **Epidermodysplasia verruciformis** 078.19
- **Epidermoid**
  - cholesteatoma — *see* Cholesteatoma
  - inclusion (*see also* Cyst, skin) 706.2
- **Epidermolysis**
  - acuta (combustiformis) (toxica) 695.1
  - bullosa 757.39
  - necroticans combustiformis 695.1
    - due to drug
      - correct substance properly administered 695.1
      - overdose or wrong substance given or taken 977.9
        - specified drug — *see* Table of Drugs and Chemicals
- **Epidermophytid** — *see* Dermatophytosis
- **Epidermophytosis** (infected)— *see* Dermatophytosis
- **Epidermosis, ear** (middle) (*see also* Cholesteatoma) 385.30
- **Epididymis** — *see* condition
- **Epididymitis** (nonvenereal) 604.90
  - with abscess 604.0
  - acute 604.99
  - blennorrhagic (acute) 098.0
    - chronic or duration of 2 months or over 098.2
  - caseous (*see also* Tuberculosis) 016.4 ✓5th
  - chlamydial 099.54
  - diphtheritic 032.89 *[604.91]*
  - filarial 125.9 *[604.91]*
  - gonococcal (acute) 098.0
    - chronic or duration of 2 months or over 098.2
  - recurrent 604.99
  - residual 604.99
  - syphilitic 095.8 *[604.91]*
  - tuberculous (*see also* Tuberculosis) 016.4 ✓5th
- **Epididymo-orchitis** (*see also* Epididymitis) 604.90
  - with abscess 604.0
  - chlamydial 099.54
  - gonococcal (acute) 098.13
    - chronic or duration of 2 months or over 098.33
- **Epidural** — *see* condition
- **Epigastritis** (*see also* Gastritis) 535.5 ✓5th
- **Epigastrium, epigastric** — *see* condition
- **Epigastrocele** (*see also* Hernia, epigastric) 553.29
- **Epiglottiditis** (acute) 464.30
  - with obstruction 464.31
  - chronic 476.1
  - viral 464.30
    - with obstruction 464.31
- **Epiglottis** — *see* condition
- **Epiglottitis** (acute) 464.30
  - with obstruction 464.31
  - chronic 476.1
  - viral 464.30
    - with obstruction 464.31
- **Epignathus** 759.4
- **Epilepsia**
  - partialis continua (*see also* Epilepsy) 345.7 ✓5th
  - procursiva (*see also* Epilepsy) 345.8 ✓5th
- **Epilepsy, epileptic** (idiopathic) 345.9 ✓5th

> *Note — Use the following fifth-digit subclassifications with categories 345.0, 345.1, 345.4–345.9*
>
> *0 without mention of intractable epilepsy*
>
> *1 with intractable epilepsy*

  - abdominal 345.5 ✓5th
  - absence (attack) 345.0 ✓5th
  - akinetic 345.0 ✓5th
    - psychomotor 345.4 ✓5th
  - automatism 345.4 ✓5th
  - autonomic diencephalic 345.5 ✓5th
  - brain 345.9 ✓5th
  - Bravais-Jacksonian 345.5 ✓5th
  - cerebral 345.9 ✓5th
  - climacteric 345.9 ✓5th
  - clonic 345.1 ✓5th
  - clouded state 345.9 ✓5th
  - coma 345.3
  - communicating 345.4 ✓5th

Examination (general) (routine) (of) (for) — *continued*
- medical (for) (of) V70.9
  - administrative purpose NEC V70.3
  - admission to
    - old age home V70.3
    - prison V70.3
    - school V70.3
  - adoption V70.3
  - armed forces personnel V70.5
  - at health care facility V70.0
  - camp V70.3
  - child, routine V20.2
  - clinical research, normal comparison in V70.7
  - control subject in clinical research V70.7
  - defined subpopulation NEC V70.5
  - donor (potential) V70.8
  - driving license V70.3
  - general V70.9
    - routine V70.0
    - specified reason NEC V70.8
  - immigration V70.3
  - inhabitants of institutions V70.5
  - insurance certification V70.3
  - marriage V70.3
  - medicolegal reasons V70.4
  - naturalization V70.3
  - occupational V70.5
  - population survey V70.6
  - pre-employment V70.5
  - preschool children V70.5
    - for admission to school V70.3
  - prison V70.3
  - prisoners V70.5
    - for entrance into prison V70.3
  - prostitutes V70.5
  - refugees V70.5
  - school children V70.5
  - specified reason NEC V70.8
  - sport competition V70.3
  - students V70.5
- medicolegal reason V70.4
- pelvic (annual) (periodic) V72.3
- periodic (annual) (routine) V70.0
- postpartum
  - immediately after delivery V24.0
  - routine follow-up V24.2
- pregnancy (unconfirmed) (possible) V72.4
- prenatal V22.1
  - first pregnancy V22.0
  - high-risk pregnancy V23.9
    - specified problem NEC V23.8 [5th]
- preoperative V72.84
  - cardiovascular V72.81
  - respiratory V72.82
  - specified NEC V72.83
- psychiatric V70.2
  - follow-up not needing further care V67.3
  - requested by authority V70.1
- radiological NEC V72.5
- respiratory preoperative V72.82
- screening — *see* Screening
- sensitization V72.7
- skin V72.7
  - hypersensitivity V72.7
- special V72.9
- specified type or reason NEC V72.85
  - preoperative V72.83
    - specified NEC V72.83

Examination (general) (routine) (of) (for) — *continued*
- teeth V72.2
- victim or culprit following
  - alleged rape or seduction V71.5
  - inflicted injury NEC V71.6
- vision V72.0
- well baby V20.2

Exanthem, exanthema (*see also* Rash) 782.1
- Boston 048
- epidemic, with meningitis 048
- lichenoid psoriasiform 696.2
- subitum 057.8
- viral, virus NEC 057.9
  - specified type NEC 057.8

Excess, excessive, excessively
- alcohol level in blood 790.3
- carbohydrate tissue, localized 278.1
- carotene (dietary) 278.3
- cold 991.9
  - specified effect NEC 991.8
- convergence 378.84
- development, breast 611.1
- diaphoresis 780.8
- divergence 378.85
- drinking (alcohol) NEC (*see also* Abuse, drugs, nondependent) 305.0 [5th]
  - continual (*see also* Alcoholism) 303.9 [5th]
  - habitual (*see also* Alcoholism) 303.9 [5th]
- eating 783.6
- eyelid fold (congenital) 743.62
- fat 278.00
  - in heart (*see also* Degeneration, myocardial) 429.1
  - tissue, localized 278.1
- foreskin 605
- gas 787.3
- gastrin 251.5
- glucagon 251.4
- heat (*see also* Heat) 992.9
- large
  - colon 564.7
    - congenital 751.3
  - fetus or infant 766.0
    - with obstructed labor 660.1 [5th]
    - affecting management of pregnancy 656.6 [5th]
    - causing disproportion 653.5 [5th]
  - newborn (weight of 4500 grams or more) 766.0
  - organ or site, congenital NEC — *see* Anomaly, specified type NEC
- lid fold (congenital) 743.62
- long
  - colon 751.5
  - organ or site, congenital NEC — *see* Anomaly, specified type NEC
  - umbilical cord (entangled)
    - affecting fetus or newborn 762.5
    - in pregnancy or childbirth 663.3 [5th]
      - with compression 663.2 [5th]
- menstruation 626.2
- number of teeth 520.1
  - causing crowding 524.3
- nutrients (dietary) NEC 783.6
- potassium (K) 276.7
- salivation (*see also* Ptyalism) 527.7

Excess, excessive, excessively — *continued*
- secretion — *see also* Hypersecretion
  - milk 676.6 [5th]
  - sputum 786.4
  - sweat 780.8
- short
  - organ or site, congenital NEC — *see* Anomaly, specified type NEC
  - umbilical cord
    - affecting fetus or newborn 762.6
    - in pregnancy or childbirth 663.4 [5th]
- skin NEC 701.9
  - eyelid 743.62
    - acquired 374.30
- sodium (Na) 276.0
- sputum 786.4
- sweating 780.8
- tearing (ducts) (eye) (*see also* Epiphora) 375.20
- thirst 783.5
  - due to deprivation of water 994.3
- vitamin
  - A (dietary) 278.2
    - administered as drug (chronic) (prolonged excessive intake) 278.2
      - reaction to sudden overdose 963.5
  - D (dietary) 278.4
    - administered as drug (chronic) (prolonged excessive intake) 278.4
      - reaction to sudden overdose 963.5
- weight 278.00
  - gain 783.1
    - of pregnancy 646.1 [5th]
  - loss 783.2

Excitability, abnormal, under minor stress 309.29

Excitation
- catatonic (*see also* Schizophrenia) 295.2 [5th]
- psychogenic 298.1
- reactive (from emotional stress, psychological trauma) 298.1

Excitement
- manic (*see also* Psychosis, affective) 296.0 [5th]
  - recurrent episode 296.1 [5th]
  - single episode 296.0 [5th]
- mental, reactive (from emotional stress, psychological trauma) 298.1 [5th]
- state, reactive (from emotional stress, psychological trauma) 298.1 [5th]

Excluded pupils 364.76

Excoriation (traumatic) (*see also* Injury, superficial, by site) 919.8
- neurotic 698.4

Excyclophoria 378.44

Excyclotropia 378.33

Exencephalus, exencephaly 742.0

Exercise
- breathing V57.0
- remedial NEC V57.1
- therapeutic NEC V57.1

Exfoliation, teeth due to systemic causes 525.0

Exfoliative — *see also* condition
- dermatitis 695.89

Exhaustion, exhaustive (physical NEC) 780.79
- battle (*see also* Reaction, stress, acute) 308.9
- cardiac (*see also* Failure, heart) 428.9

Exhaustion, exhaustive (physical NEC) — *continued*
  delirium (*see also* Reaction, stress, acute) 308.9
  due to
    cold 991.8
    excessive exertion 994.5
    exposure 994.4
  fetus or newborn 779.8
  heart (*see also* Failure, heart) 428.9
  heat 992.5
    due to
      salt depletion 992.4
      water depletion 992.3
  manic (*see also* Psychosis, affective) 296.0 [5th]
    recurrent episode 296.1 [5th]
    single episode 296.0 [5th]
  maternal, complicating delivery 669.8 [5th]
    affecting fetus or newborn 763.89
  mental 300.5
  myocardium, myocardial (*see also* Failure, heart) 428.9
  nervous 300.5
  old age 797
  postinfectional NEC 780.79
  psychogenic 300.5
  psychosis (*see also* Reaction, stress, acute) 308.9
  senile 797
    dementia 290.0
Exhibitionism (sexual) 302.4
Exomphalos 756.79
Exophoria 378.42
  convergence, insufficiency 378.83
  divergence, excess 378.85
Exophthalmic
  cachexia 242.0 [5th]
  goiter 242.0 [5th]
  ophthalmoplegia 242.0 [5th] *[376.22]*
Exophthalmos 376.30
  congenital 743.66
  constant 376.31
  endocrine NEC 259.9 *[376.22]*
  hyperthyroidism 242.0 [5th] *[376.21]*
  intermittent NEC 376.34
  malignant 242.0 [5th] *[376.21]*
  pulsating 376.35
    endocrine NEC 259.9 *[376.22]*
  thyrotoxic 242.0 [5th] *[376.21]*
Exostosis 726.91
  cartilaginous (M9210/0)— *see* Neoplasm, bone, benign
  congenital 756.4
  ear canal, external 380.81
  gonococcal 098.89
  hip 726.5
  intracranial 733.3
  jaw (bone) 526.81
  luxurians 728.11
  multiple (cancellous) (congenital) (hereditary) 756.4
  nasal bones 726.91
  orbit, orbital 376.42
  osteocartilaginous (M9210/0)— *see* Neoplasm, bone, benign
  spine 721.8
    with spondylosis — *see* Spondylosis
  syphilitic 095.5
  wrist 726.4
Exotropia 378.10
  alternating 378.15
    with
      A pattern 378.16
      specified noncomitancy NEC 378.18
      V pattern 378.17
      X pattern 378.18
      Y pattern 378.18
    intermittent 378.24
  intermittent 378.20
    alternating 378.24
    monocular 378.23
  monocular 378.11
    with
      A pattern 378.12
      specified noncomitancy NEC 378.14
      V pattern 378.13
      X pattern 378.14
      Y pattern 378.14
    intermittent 378.23
Explanation of
  investigation finding V65.4 [5th]
  medication V65.4 [5th]
Exposure 994.9
  cold 991.9
    specified effect NEC 991.8
  effects of 994.9
  exhaustion due to 994.4
  to
    AIDS virus V01.7
    asbestos V15.84
    body fluids (hazardous) V15.85
    cholera V01.0
    communicable disease V01.9
      specified type NEC V01.8
    German measles V01.4
    gonorrhea V01.6
    hazardous body fluids V15.85
    HIV V01.7
    human immunodeficiency virus V01.7
    lead V15.86
    parasitic disease V01.8
    poliomyelitis V01.2
    potentially hazardous body fluids V15.85
    rabies V01.5
    rubella V01.4
    smallpox V01.3
    syphilis V01.6
    tuberculosis V01.1
    venereal disease V01.6
    viral disease NEC V01.7
Exsanguination, fetal 772.0
Exstrophy
  abdominal content 751.8
  bladder (urinary) 753.5
Extensive — *see* condition
Extra — *see also* Accessory
  rib 756.3
    cervical 756.2
Extraction
  with hook 763.89
  breech NEC 669.6 [5th]
    affecting fetus or newborn 763.0
  cataract postsurgical V45.61
  manual NEC 669.8 [5th]
    affecting fetus or newborn 763.89
Extrasystole 427.60
  atrial 427.61
  postoperative 997.1
  ventricular 427.69
Extrauterine gestation or pregnancy — *see* Pregnancy, ectopic
Extravasation
  blood 459.0
    lower extremity 459.0
  chyle into mesentery 457.8
  pelvicalyceal 593.4
  pyelosinus 593.4
  urine 788.8
    from ureter 788.8
Extremity — *see* condition
Extrophy — *see* Exstrophy
Extroversion
  bladder 753.5
  uterus 618.1
    complicating delivery 665.2 [5th]
      affecting fetus or newborn 763.89
    postpartal (old) 618.1
Extrusion
  breast implant (prosthetic) 996.54
  device, implant, or graft — *see* Complications, mechanical
  eye implant (ball) (globe) 996.59
  intervertebral disc — *see* Displacement, intervertebral disc
  lacrimal gland 375.43
  mesh (reinforcing) 996.59
  ocular lens implant 996.53
  prosthetic device NEC — *see* Complications, mechanical
  vitreous 379.26
Exudate, pleura — *see* Effusion, pleura
Exudates, retina 362.82
Exudative — *see* condition
Eye, eyeball, eyelid — *see* condition
Eyestrain 368.13
Eyeworm disease of Africa 125.2

F

Note — For foreign body with open wound or other injury, see Wound, open, or the type of injury specified.

Fracture (abduction) (adduction) (avulsion) (compression) (crush) (dislocation) (oblique) (separation) (closed) — *continued*
- metatarsus, metatarsal (bone(s)), of one foot (closed) 825.25
  - with tarsal bone(s) 825.29
    - open 825.39
  - open 825.35
- Monteggia's (closed) 813.03
  - open 813.13
- Moore's — *see* Fracture, radius, lower end
- multangular bone (closed)
  - larger 814.05
    - open 814.15
  - smaller 814.06
    - open 814.16
- multiple (closed) 829.0

> Note — *Multiple fractures of sites classifiable to the same three- or four-digit category are coded to that category, except for sites classifiable to 810–818 or 820–827 in different limbs.*
>
> *Multiple fractures of sites classifiable to different fourth-digit subdivisions within the same three-digit category should be dealt with according to coding rules.*
>
> *Multiple fractures of sites classifiable to different three-digit categories (identifiable from the listing under "Fracture"), and of sites classifiable to 810–818 or 820–827 in different limbs should be coded according to the following list, which should be referred to in the following priority order: skull or face bones, pelvis or vertebral column, legs, arms.*

  - arm (multiple bones in same arm except in hand alone) (sites classifiable to 810–817 with sites classifiable to a different three-digit category in 810–817 in same arm) (closed) 818.0
    - open 818.1
  - arms, both or arm(s) with rib(s) or sternum (sites classifiable to 810–818 with sites classifiable to same range of categories in other limb or to 807) (closed) 819.0
    - open 819.1
  - bones of trunk NEC (closed) 809.0
    - open 809.1
  - hand, metacarpal bone(s) with phalanx or phalanges of same hand (sites classifiable to 815 with sites classifiable to 816 in same hand) (closed) 817.0
    - open 817.1
  - leg (multiple bones in same leg) (sites classifiable to 820–826 with sites classifiable to a different three-digit category in that range in same leg) (closed) 827.0
    - open 827.1
  - legs, both or leg(s) with arm(s), rib(s), or sternum (sites classifiable to 820–827 with sites classifiable to same range of categories in other leg or to 807 or 810–819) (closed) 828.0
    - open 828.1
  - open 829.1
  - pelvis with other bones except skull or face bones (sites classifiable to 808 with sites classifiable to 805–807 or 810–829) (closed) 809.0
    - open 809.1

Fracture (abduction) (adduction) (avulsion) (compression) (crush) (dislocation) (oblique) (separation) (closed) — *continued*
- multiple (closed) — *continued*
  - skull, specified or unspecified bones, or face bone(s) with any other bone(s) (sites classifiable to 800–803 with sites classifiable to 805–829) (closed) 804.0 [5th]

> Note — *Use the following fifth-digit subclassification with categories 800, 801, 803, and 804:*
>
> *0 unspecified state of consciousness*
> *1 with no loss of consciousness*
> *2 with brief [less than one hour] loss of consciousness*
> *3 with moderate [1–24 hours] loss of consciousness*
> *4 with prolonged [more than 24 hours] loss of consciousness and return to pre-existing conscious level*
> *5 with prolonged [more than 24 hours] loss of consciousness, without return to pre-existing conscious level*
>
> *Use fifth-digit 5 to designate when a patient is unconscious and dies before regaining consciousness, regardless of the duration of the loss of consciousness*
>
> *6 with loss of consciousness of unspecified duration*
> *9 with concussion, unspecified*

    - with
      - contusion, cerebral 804.1 [5th]
      - epidural hemorrhage 804.2 [5th]
      - extradural hemorrhage 804.2 [5th]
      - hemorrhage (intracranial) NEC 804.3 [5th]
      - intracranial injury NEC 804.4 [5th]
      - laceration, cerebral 804.1 [5th]
      - subarachnoid hemorrhage 804.2 [5th]
      - subdural hemorrhage 804.2 [5th]
    - open 804.5 [5th]
      - with
        - contusion, cerebral 804.6 [5th]
        - epidural hemorrhage 804.7 [5th]
        - extradural hemorrhage 804.7 [5th]
        - hemorrhage (intracranial) NEC 804.8 [5th]
        - intracranial injury NEC 804.9 [5th]
        - laceration, cerebral 804.6 [5th]
        - subarachnoid hemorrhage 804.7 [5th]
        - subdural hemorrhage 804.7 [5th]
  - vertebral column with other bones, except skull or face bones (sites classifiable to 805 or 806 with sites classifiable to 807–808 or 810–829) (closed) 809.0
    - open 809.1
- nasal (bone(s)) (closed) 802.0
  - open 802.1
  - sinus — see Fracture, skull, base
- navicular
  - carpal (wrist) (closed) 814.01
    - open 814.11
  - tarsal (ankle) (closed) 825.22
    - open 825.32
- neck — *see* Fracture, vertebra, cervical
- neural arch — *see* Fracture, vertebra, by site
- nonunion 733.82
- nose, nasal, (bone) (septum) (closed) 802.0
  - open 802.1

Fracture (abduction) (adduction) (avulsion) (compression) (crush) (dislocation) (oblique) (separation) (closed) — *continued*
- occiput — *see* Fracture, skull, base
- odontoid process — *see* Fracture, vertebra, cervical
- olecranon (process) (ulna) (closed) 813.01
  - open 813.11
- open 829.1
- orbit, orbital (bone) (region) (closed) 802.8
  - floor (blow-out) 802.6
    - open 802.7
  - open 802.9
  - roof — *see* Fracture, skull, base
  - specified part NEC 802.8
    - open 802.9
- os
  - calcis (closed) 825.0
    - open 825.1
  - magnum (closed) 814.07
    - open 814.17
  - pubis (with visceral injury) (closed) 808.2
    - open 808.3
  - triquetrum (closed) 814.03
    - open 814.13
- osseous
  - auditory meatus — *see* Fracture, skull, base
  - labyrinth — *see* Fracture, skull, base
- ossicles, auditory (incus) (malleus) (stapes) — *see* Fracture, skull, base
- osteoporotic — *see* Fracture, pathologic
- palate (closed) 802.8
  - open 802.9
- paratrooper — *see* Fracture, tibia, lower end
- parietal bone — *see* Fracture, skull, vault
- parry — *see* Fracture, Monteggia's
- patella (closed) 822.0
  - open 822.1
- pathologic (cause unknown) 733.10
  - ankle 733.16
  - femur (neck) 733.14
    - specified NEC 733.15
  - fibula 733.16
  - hip 733.14
  - humerus 733.11
  - radius 733.12
  - specified site NEC 733.19
  - tibia 733.16
  - ulna 733.12
  - vertebrae (collapse) 733.13
  - wrist 733.12
- pedicle (of vertebral arch) — *see* Fracture, vertebra, by site
- pelvis, pelvic (bone(s)) (with visceral injury) (closed) 808.8
  - multiple (with disruption of pelvic circle) 808.43
    - open 808.53
  - open 808.9
  - rim (closed) 808.49
    - open 808.59
- peritrochanteric (closed) 820.20
  - open 820.30
- phalanx, phalanges, of one
  - foot (closed) 826.0
    - with bone(s) of same lower limb 827.0
      - open 827.1
    - open 826.1

G

Gangrene, gangrenous (anemia) (artery) (cellulitis) (dermatitis) (dry) (infective) (moist) (pemphigus) (septic) (skin) (stasis) (ulcer) — *continued*
- stomatitis 528.1
- symmetrical 443.0 *[785.4]*
- testis (infectional) (*see also* Orchitis) 604.99
  - noninfective 608.89
- throat 462
  - diphtheritic 032.0
- thyroid (gland) 246.8
- tonsillitis (acute) 463
- tooth (pulp) 522.1
- tuberculous NEC (*see also* Tuberculosis) 011.9 [5th]
- tunica vaginalis 608.4
  - noninfective 608.89
- umbilicus 785.4
- uterus (*see also* Endometritis) 615.9
- uvulitis 528.3
- vas deferens 608.4
  - noninfective 608.89
- vulva (*see also* Vulvitis) 616.10

Gannister disease (occupational) 502
- with tuberculosis — *see* Tuberculosis, pulmonary

Ganser's syndrome, hysterical 300.16

Gardner-Diamond syndrome (autoerythrocyte sensitization) 287.2

Gargoylism 277.5

Garré's
- disease (*see also* Osteomyelitis) 730.1 [5th]
- osteitis (sclerosing) (*see also* Osteomyelitis) 730.1 [5th]
- osteomyelitis (*see also* Osteomyelitis) 730.1 [5th]

Garrod's pads, knuckle 728.79

Gartner's duct
- cyst 752.11
- persistent 752.11

Gas
- asphyxia, asphyxiation, inhalation, poisoning, suffocation NEC 987.9
  - specified gas — *see* Table of Drugs and Chemicals
- bacillus gangrene or infection — *see* Gas, gangrene
- cyst, mesentery 568.89
- excessive 787.3
- gangrene 040.0
  - with
    - abortion — *see* Abortion, by type, with sepsis
    - ectopic pregnancy (*see also* categories 633.0–633.9) 639.0
    - molar pregnancy (*see also* categories 630–632) 639.0
  - following
    - abortion 639.0
    - ectopic or molar pregnancy 639.0
  - puerperal, postpartum, childbirth 670
- on stomach 787.3
- pains 787.3

Gastradenitis 535.0 [5th]

Gastralgia 536.8
- psychogenic 307.89

Gastrectasis, gastrectasia 536.1
- psychogenic 306.4

Gastric — *see* condition

Gastrinoma (M8153/1)
- malignant (M8153/3)
  - pancreas 157.4
  - specified site NEC — *see* Neoplasm, by site, malignant
  - unspecified site 157.4
- specified site — *see* Neoplasm, by site, uncertain behavior
- unspecified site 235.5

Gastritis 535.5 [5th]

> *Note — Use the following fifth-digit subclassification for category 535:*
>
> *0 without mention of hemorrhage*
>
> *1 with hemorrhage*

- acute 535.0 [5th]
- alcoholic 535.3 [5th]
- allergic 535.4 [5th]
- antral 535.4 [5th]
- atrophic 535.1 [5th]
- atrophic-hyperplastic 535.1 [5th]
- bile-induced 535.4 [5th]
- catarrhal 535.0 [5th]
- chronic (atrophic) 535.1 [5th]
- cirrhotic 535.4 [5th]
- corrosive (acute) 535.4 [5th]
- dietetic 535.4 [5th]
- due to diet deficiency 269.9 *[535.4]* [5th]
- eosinophilic 535.4 [5th]
- erosive 535.4 [5th]
- follicular 535.4 [5th]
  - chronic 535.1 [5th]
- giant hypertrophic 535.2 [5th]
- glandular 535.4 [5th]
  - chronic 535.1 [5th]
- hypertrophic (mucosa) 535.2 [5th]
  - chronic giant 211.1
- irritant 535.4 [5th]
- nervous 306.4
- phlegmonous 535.0 [5th]
- psychogenic 306.4
- sclerotic 535.4 [5th]
- spastic 536.8
- subacute 535.0 [5th]
- superficial 535.4 [5th]
- suppurative 535.0 [5th]
- toxic 535.4 [5th]
- tuberculous (*see also* Tuberculosis) 017.9 [5th]

Gastrocarcinoma (M8010/3) 151.9

Gastrocolic — *see* condition

Gastrocolitis — *see* Enteritis

Gastrodisciasis 121.8

Gastroduodenitis (*see also* Gastritis) 535.5 [5th]
- catarrhal 535.0 [5th]
- infectional 535.0 [5th]
- virus, viral 008.8
  - specified type NEC 008.69

Gastrodynia 536.8

Gastroenteritis (acute) (catarrhal) (congestive) (hemorrhagic) (noninfectious) (*see also* Enteritis) 558.9
- aertrycke infection 003.0
- allergic 558.9
- chronic 558.9
  - ulcerative (*see also* Colitis, ulcerative) 556.9
- dietetic 558.9

Gastroenteritis (acute) (catarrhal) (congestive) (hemorrhagic) (noninfectious) (*see also* Enteritis) — *continued*
- due to
  - food poisoning (*see also* Poisoning, food) 005.9
  - radiation 558.1
- epidemic 009.0
- functional 558.9
- infectious (*see also* Enteritis, due to, by organism) 009.0
  - presumed 009.1
- salmonella 003.0
- septic (*see also* Enteritis, due to, by organism) 009.0
- toxic 558.2
- tuberculous (*see also* Tuberculosis) 014.8 [5th]
- ulcerative (*see also* Colitis, ulcerative) 556.9
- viral NEC 008.8
  - specified type NEC 008.69
- zymotic 009.0

Gastroenterocolitis — *see* Enteritis

Gastroenteropathy, protein-losing 579.8

Gastroenteroptosis 569.89

Gastroesophageal laceration-hemorrhage syndrome 530.7

Gastroesophagitis 530.19

Gastrohepatitis (*see also* Gastritis) 535.5 [5th]

Gastrointestinal — *see* condition

Gastrojejunal — *see* condition

Gastrojejunitis (*see also* Gastritis) 535.5 [5th]

Gastrojejunocolic — *see* condition

Gastroliths 537.89

Gastromalacia 537.89

Gastroparalysis 536.3
- diabetic 250.6 [5th] *[536.3]*

Gastroparesis 536.3
- diabetic 250.6 [5th] *[536.3]*

Gastropathy, exudative 579.8

Gastroptosis 537.5

Gastrorrhagia 578.0

Gastrorrhea 536.8
- psychogenic 306.4

Gastroschisis (congenital) 756.79
- acquired 569.89

Gastrospasm (neurogenic) (reflex) 536.8
- neurotic 306.4
- psychogenic 306.4

Gastrostaxis 578.0

Gastrostenosis 537.89

Gastrostomy
- attention to V55.1
- complication 536.40
  - specified type 536.49
- infection 536.41
- malfunctioning 536.42
- status V44.1

Gastrosuccorrhea (continuous) (intermittent) 536.8
- neurotic 306.4
- psychogenic 306.4

Gaucher's
- disease (adult) (cerebroside lipidosis) (infantile) 272.7
- hepatomegaly 272.7
- splenomegaly (cerebroside lipidosis) 272.7

Gayet's disease (superior hemorrhagic polioencephalitis) 265.1

Gayet-Wernicke's syndrome (superior hemorrhagic polioencephalitis) 265.1

> *Note — Use the following fifth-digit subclassification with category 242:*
>
> *0 without mention of thyrotoxic crisis or storm*
>
> *1 with mention of thyrotoxic crisis or storm*

- **Grinding, teeth** 306.8
- **Grip**
  - Dabney's 074.1
  - devil's 074.1
- **Grippe, grippal** — *see also* Influenza
  - Balkan 083.0
  - intestinal 487.8
  - summer 074.8
- **Grippy cold** 487.1
- **Grisel's disease** 723.5
- **Groin** — *see* condition
- **Grooved**
  - nails (transverse) 703.8
  - tongue 529.5
    - congenital 750.13
- **Ground itch** 126.9
- **Growing pains, children** 781.9
- **Growth** (fungoid) (neoplastic) (new) (M8000/1) — *see also* Neoplasm, by site, unspecified nature
  - adenoid (vegetative) 474.12
    - benign (M8000/0) — *see* Neoplasm, by site, benign
  - fetal, poor 764.9 ✓5th
    - affecting management of pregnancy 656.5 ✓5th
  - malignant (M8000/3) — *see* Neoplasm, by site, malignant
  - rapid, childhood V21.0
  - secondary (M8000/6) — *see* Neoplasm, by site, malignant, secondary
- **Gruber's hernia** — *see* Hernia, Gruber's
- **Gruby's disease** (tinea tonsurans) 110.0
- **G-trisomy** 758.0
- **Guama fever** 066.3
- **Gubler** (-Millard) **paralysis or syndrome** 344.89
- **Guérin-Stern syndrome** (arthrogryposis multiplex congenita) 754.89
- **Guertin's disease** (electric chorea) 049.8
- **Guillain-Barré disease or syndrome** 357.0
- **Guinea worms** (infection) (infestation) 125.7
- **Guinon's disease** (motor-verbal tic) 307.23
- **Gull's disease** (thyroid atrophy with myxedema) 244.8
- **Gull and Sutton's disease** — *see* Hypertension, kidney
- **Gum** — *see* condition
- **Gumboil** 522.7
- **Gumma** (syphilitic) 095.9
  - artery 093.89
    - cerebral or spinal 094.89
  - bone 095.5
    - of yaws (late) 102.6
  - brain 094.89
  - cauda equina 094.89
  - central nervous system NEC 094.9
  - ciliary body 095.8 *[364.11]*
  - congenital 090.5
    - testis 090.5
  - eyelid 095.8 *[373.5]*
  - heart 093.89
  - intracranial 094.89
  - iris 095.8 *[364.11]*
  - kidney 095.4
  - larynx 095.8
  - leptomeninges 094.2
  - liver 095.3
  - meninges 094.2
  - myocardium 093.82
  - nasopharynx 095.8
  - neurosyphilitic 094.9
  - nose 095.8
  - orbit 095.8
  - palate (soft) 095.8
  - penis 095.8
  - pericardium 093.81
  - pharynx 095.8
  - pituitary 095.8
  - scrofulous (*see also* Tuberculosis) 017.0 ✓5th
  - skin 095.8

Gumma (syphilitic) — *continued*
  - specified site NEC 095.8
  - spinal cord 094.89
  - tongue 095.8
  - tonsil 095.8
  - trachea 095.8
  - tuberculous (*see also* Tuberculosis) 017.0 ✓5th
  - ulcerative due to yaws 102.4
  - ureter 095.8
  - yaws 102.4
    - bone 102.6
- **Gunn's syndrome** (jaw-winking syndrome) 742.8
- **Gunshot wound** — *see also* Wound, open, by site
  - fracture — *see* Fracture, by site, open
  - internal organs (abdomen, chest, or pelvis) — *see* Injury, internal, by site, with open wound
  - intracranial — *see* Laceration, brain, with open intracranial wound
- **Günther's disease or syndrome** (congenital erythropoietic porphyria) 277.1
- **Gustatory hallucination** 780.1
- **Gynandrism** 752.7
- **Gynandroblastoma** (M8632/1)
  - specified site — *see* Neoplasm, by site, uncertain behavior
  - unspecified site
    - female 236.2
    - male 236.4
- **Gynandromorphism** 752.7
- **Gynatresia** (congenital) 752.49
- **Gynecoid pelvis, male** 738.6
- **Gynecological examination** V72.3
  - for contraceptive maintenance V25.40
- **Gynecomastia** 611.1
- **Gynephobia** 300.29
- **Gyrate scalp** 757.39

H

Haas' disease (osteochondrosis head of humerus) 732.3
Habermann's disease (acute parapsoriasis varioliformis) 696.2
Habit, habituation
- chorea 307.22
- disturbance, child 307.9
- drug (*see also* Dependence) 304.9 [5th]
- laxative (*see also* Abuse, drugs, nondependent) 305.9 [5th]
- spasm 307.20
  - chronic 307.22
  - transient of childhood 307.21
- tic 307.20
  - chronic 307.22
  - transient of childhood 307.21
- use of
  - nonprescribed drugs (*see also* Abuse, drugs, nondependent) 305.9 [5th]
  - patent medicines (*see also* Abuse, drugs, nondependent) 305.9 [5th]
- vomiting 536.2

Hadfield-Clarke syndrome (pancreatic infantilism) 577.8
Haff disease 985.1
Hageman factor defect, deficiency, or disease (*see also* Defect, coagulation) 286.3
Haglund's disease (osteochondrosis os tibiale externum) 732.5
Haglund-Läwen-Fründ syndrome 717.89
Hagner's disease (hypertrophic pulmonary osteoarthropathy) 731.2
Hag teeth, tooth 524.3
Hailey-Hailey disease (benign familial chronic pemphigus) 757.39
Hair — *see also* condition
- plucking 307.9

Hairball in stomach 935.2
Hairy black tongue 529.3
Half vertebra 756.14
Halitosis 784.9
Hallermann-Streiff syndrome 756.0
Hallervorden-Spatz disease or syndrome 333.0
Hallopeau's
- acrodermatitis (continua) 696.1
- disease (lichen sclerosis et atrophicus) 701.0

Hallucination (auditory) (gustatory) (olfactory) (tactile) 780.1
- alcoholic 291.3
- drug-induced 292.12
- visual 368.16

Hallucinosis 298.9
- alcoholic (acute) 291.3
- drug-induced 292.12

Hallus — *see* Hallux
Hallux 735.9
- malleus (acquired) 735.3
- rigidus (acquired) 735.2
  - congenital 755.66
  - late effects of rickets 268.1
- valgus (acquired) 735.0
  - congenital 755.66
- varus (acquired) 735.1
  - congenital 755.66

Halo, visual 368.15
Hamartoblastoma 759.6
Hamartoma 759.6
- epithelial (gingival), odontogenic, central, or peripheral (M9321/0) 213.1
  - upper jaw (bone) 213.0
- vascular 757.32

Hamartosis, hamartoses NEC 759.6
Hamman's disease or syndrome (spontaneous mediastinal emphysema) 518.1
Hamman-Rich syndrome (diffuse interstitial pulmonary fibrosis) 516.3
Hammer toe (acquired) 735.4
- congenital 755.66
- late effects of rickets 268.1

Hand — *see* condition
Hand-Schüller-Christian disease or syndrome (chronic histiocytosis x) 277.8
Hand-foot syndrome 282.61
Hanging (asphyxia) (strangulation) (suffocation) 994.7
Hangnail (finger) (with lymphangitis) 681.02
Hangover (alcohol) (*see also* Abuse, drugs, nondependent) 305.0 [5th]
Hanot's cirrhosis or disease — *see* Cirrhosis, biliary
Hanot-Chauffard (-Troisier) syndrome (bronze diabetes) 275.0
Hansen's disease (leprosy) 030.9
- benign form 030.1
- malignant form 030.0

Harada's disease or syndrome 363.22
Hard chancre 091.0
Hardening
- artery — *see* Arteriosclerosis
- brain 348.8
- liver 571.8

Hare's syndrome (M8010/3) (carcinoma, pulmonary apex) 162.3
Harelip (*see also* Cleft, lip) 749.10
Harkavy's syndrome 446.0
Harlequin (fetus) 757.1
- color change syndrome 779.8

Harley's disease (intermittent hemoglobinuria) 283.2
Harris'
- lines 733.91
- syndrome (organic hyperinsulinism) 251.1

Hart's disease or syndrome (pellagra-cerebellar ataxia-renal aminoaciduria) 270.0
Hartmann's pouch (abnormal sacculation of gallbladder neck) 575.8
Hartnup disease (pellagra-cerebellar ataxia-renal aminoaciduria) 270.0
Harvester lung 495.0
Hashimoto's disease or struma (struma lymphomatosa) 245.2
Hassall-Henle bodies (corneal warts) 371.41
Haut mal (*see also* Epilepsy) 345.1 [5th]
Haverhill fever 026.1
Hawaiian wood rose dependence 304.5 [5th]
Hawkins' keloid 701.4
Hay
- asthma (*see also* Asthma) 493.0 [5th]
- fever (allergic) (with rhinitis) 477.9
  - with asthma (bronchial) (*see also* Asthma) 493.0 [5th]
  - allergic, due to grass, pollen, ragweed, or tree 477.0
  - conjunctivitis 372.05

Hay — *continued*
- fever (allergic) (with rhinitis) — *continued*
  - due to
    - dander 477.8
    - dust 477.8
    - fowl 477.8
    - pollen 477.0
    - specified allergen other than pollen 477.8

Hayem-Faber syndrome (achlorhydric anemia) 280.9
Hayem-Widal syndrome (acquired hemolytic jaundice) 283.9
Haygarth's nodosities 715.04
Hazard-Crile tumor (M8350/3) 193
Hb (abnormal)
- disease — *see* Disease, hemoglobin
- trait — *see* Trait

H disease 270.0
Head — *see also* condition
- banging 307.3

Headache 784.0
- allergic 346.2 [5th]
- cluster 346.2 [5th]
- due to
  - loss, spinal fluid 349.0
  - lumbar puncture 349.0
  - saddle block 349.0
- emotional 307.81
- histamine 346.2 [5th]
- lumbar puncture 349.0
- menopausal 627.2
- migraine 346.9 [5th]
- nonorganic origin 307.81
- postspinal 349.0
- psychogenic 307.81
- psychophysiologic 307.81
- sick 346.1 [5th]
- spinal fluid loss 349.0
- tension 307.81
- vascular 784.0
  - migraine type 346.9 [5th]
- vasomotor 346.9 [5th]

Health
- advice V65.4 [5th]
- audit V70.0
- checkup V70.0
- education V65.4 [5th]
- hazard (*see also* History of) V15.9
  - specified cause NEC V15.89
- instruction V65.4 [5th]
- services provided because (of)
  - boarding school residence V60.6
  - holiday relief for person providing home care V60.5
  - inadequate
    - housing V60.1
    - resources V60.2
  - lack of housing V60.0
  - no care available in home V60.4
  - person living alone V60.3
  - poverty V60.3
  - residence in institution V60.6
  - specified cause NEC V60.8
  - vacation relief for person providing home care V60.5

Healthy
- donor (*see also* Donor) V59.9

Hemorrhage, hemorrhagic (nontraumatic) — *continued*
pregnancy (concealed) 641.9 ✓5th
accidental 641.2 ✓5th
affecting fetus or newborn 762.1
affecting fetus or newborn 762.1
before 22 completed weeks' gestation 640.9 ✓5th
affecting fetus or newborn 762.1
due to
abruptio placenta 641.2 ✓5th
affecting fetus or newborn 762.1
afibrinogenemia or other coagulation defect (conditions classifiable to 286.0–286.9) 641.3 ✓5th
affecting fetus or newborn 762.1
coagulation defect 641.3 ✓5th
affecting fetus or newborn 762.1
hyperfibrinolysis 641.3 ✓5th
affecting fetus or newborn 762.1
hypofibrinogenemia 641.3 ✓5th
affecting fetus or newborn 762.1
leiomyoma, uterus 641.8 ✓5th
affecting fetus or newborn 762.1
low-lying placenta 641.1 ✓5th
affecting fetus or newborn 762.1
marginal sinus (rupture) 641.2 ✓5th
affecting fetus or newborn 762.1
placenta previa 641.1 ✓5th
affecting fetus or newborn 762.0
premature separation of placenta (normally implanted) 641.2 ✓5th
affecting fetus or newborn 762.1
threatened abortion 640.0 ✓5th
affecting fetus or newborn 762.1
trauma 641.8 ✓5th
affecting fetus or newborn 762.1
early (before 22 completed weeks' gestation) 640.9 ✓5th
affecting fetus or newborn 762.1
previous, affecting management of pregnancy or childbirth V23.4
unavoidable — *see* Hemorrhage, pregnancy, due to placenta previa
prepartum (mother) — *see* Hemorrhage, pregnancy
preretinal, cause unspecified 362.81
prostate 602.1
puerperal (*see also* Hemorrhage, postpartum) 666.1 ✓5th
pulmonary — *see also* Hemorrhage, lung
newborn (massive) 770.3
renal syndrome 446.21
purpura (primary) (*see also* Purpura, thrombocytopenic) 287.3
rectum (sphincter) 569.3
recurring, following initial hemorrhage at time of injury 958.2
renal 593.81
pulmonary syndrome 446.21
respiratory tract (*see also* Hemorrhage, lung) 786.3
retina, retinal (deep) (superficial) (vessels) 362.81
diabetic 250.5 ✓5th *[362.01]*
due to birth injury 772.8
retrobulbar 376.89
retroperitoneal 459.0
retroplacental (*see also* Placenta, separation) 641.2 ✓5th

Hemorrhage, hemorrhagic (nontraumatic) — *continued*
scalp 459.0
due to injury at birth 767.1
scrotum 608.83
secondary (nontraumatic) 459.0
following initial hemorrhage at time of injury 958.2
seminal vesicle 608.83
skin 782.7
newborn 772.6
spermatic cord 608.83
spinal (cord) 336.1
aneurysm (ruptured) 336.1
syphilitic 094.89
due to birth injury 767.4
fetus or newborn 767.4
spleen 289.59
spontaneous NEC 459.0
petechial 782.7
stomach 578.9
newborn 772.4
ulcer — *see* Ulcer, stomach, with hemorrhage
subaponeurotic, newborn 767.1
massive (birth injury) 767.1
subarachnoid (nontraumatic) 430
fetus or newborn (anoxic) (traumatic) 772.2
puerperal, postpartum, childbirth 674.0 ✓5th
traumatic — *see* Hemorrhage, brain, traumatic, subarachnoid
subconjunctival 372.72
due to birth injury 772.8
newborn 772.8
subcortical (*see also* Hemorrhage, brain) 431
subcutaneous 782.7
subdiaphragmatic 459.0
subdural (nontraumatic) 432.1
due to birth injury 767.0
fetus or newborn (anoxic) (hypoxic) (due to birth trauma) 767.0
puerperal, postpartum, childbirth 674.0 ✓5th
spinal 336.1
traumatic — *see* Hemorrhage, brain, traumatic, subdural
subhyaloid 362.81
subperiosteal 733.99
subretinal 362.81
subtentorial (*see also* Hemorrhage, subdural) 432.1
subungual 703.8
due to blood dyscrasia 287.8
suprarenal (capsule) (gland) 255.4
fetus or newborn 772.5
tentorium (traumatic) — *see also* Hemorrhage, brain, traumatic
fetus or newborn 767.0
nontraumatic — *see* Hemorrhage, subdural
testis 608.83
thigh 459.0
third stage 666.0 ✓5th
thorax — *see* Hemorrhage, lung
throat 784.8
thrombocythemia 238.7
thymus (gland) 254.8
thyroid (gland) 246.3
cyst 246.3
tongue 529.8

Hemorrhage, hemorrhagic (nontraumatic) — *continued*
tonsil 474.8
postoperative 998.11
tooth socket (postextraction) 998.11
trachea — *see* Hemorrhage, lung
traumatic — *see also* nature of injury
brain — *see* Hemorrhage, brain, traumatic
recurring or secondary (following initial hemorrhage at time of injury) 958.2
tuberculous NEC (*see also* Tuberculosis, pulmonary) 011.9 ✓5th
tunica vaginalis 608.83
ulcer — *see* Ulcer, by site, with hemorrhage
umbilicus, umbilical cord 772.0
after birth, newborn 772.3
complicating delivery 663.8 ✓5th
affecting fetus or newborn 772.0
slipped ligature 772.3
stump 772.3
unavoidable (due to placenta previa) 641.1 ✓5th
affecting fetus or newborn 762.0
upper extremity 459.0
urethra (idiopathic) 599.84
uterus, uterine (abnormal) 626.9
climacteric 627.0
complicating delivery — *see* Hemorrhage, complicating delivery
due to
intrauterine contraceptive device 996.76
perforating uterus 996.32
functional or dysfunctional 626.8
in pregnancy — *see* Hemorrhage, pregnancy
intermenstrual 626.6
irregular 626.6
regular 626.5
postmenopausal 627.1
postpartum (*see also* Hemorrhage, postpartum) 666.1 ✓5th
prepubertal 626.8
pubertal 626.3
puerperal (immediate) 666.1 ✓5th
vagina 623.8
vasa previa 663.5 ✓5th
affecting fetus or newborn 772.0
vas deferens 608.83
ventricular (*see also* Hemorrhage, brain) 431
vesical 596.8
viscera 459.0
newborn 772.8
vitreous (humor) (intraocular) 379.23
vocal cord 478.5
vulva 624.8

Hemorrhoids (anus) (rectum) (without complication) 455.6
bleeding, prolapsed, strangulated, or ulcerated NEC 455.8
external 455.5
internal 455.2
complicated NEC 455.8
complicating pregnancy and puerperium 671.8 ✓5th
external 455.3
with complication NEC 455.5
bleeding, prolapsed, strangulated, or ulcerated 455.5
thrombosed 455.4

History (personal) of — *continued*
malignant neoplasm (of) — *continued*
gastrointestinal tract V10.00
gum V10.02
hematopoietic NEC V10.79
hypopharynx V10.02
ileum V10.09
intrathoracic organs NEC V10.20
jejunum V10.09
kidney V10.52
large intestine V10.05
larynx V10.21
lip V10.02
liver V10.07
lung V10.11
lymphatic NEC V10.79
lymph glands or nodes NEC V10.79
male genital organ V10.45
specified site NEC V10.49
mediastinum V10.29
melanoma (of skin) V10.82
middle ear V10.22
mouth V10.02
specified part NEC V10.02
nasal cavities V10.22
nasopharynx V10.02
nervous system NEC V10.86
nose V10.22
oropharynx V10.02
ovary V10.43
pancreas V10.09
parathyroid V10.88
penis V10.49
pharynx V10.02
pineal V10.88
pituitary V10.88
placenta V10.44
pleura V10.29
prostate V10.46
rectosigmoid junction V10.06
rectum V10.06
respiratory organs NEC V10.20
salivary gland V10.02
skin V10.83
melanoma V10.82
small intestine NEC V10.09
soft tissue NEC V10.89
specified site NEC V10.89
stomach V10.04
testis V10.47
thymus V10.29
thyroid V10.87
tongue V10.01
trachea V10.12
ureter V10.59
urethra V10.59
urinary organ V10.50
uterine adnexa V10.44
uterus V10.42
vagina V10.44
vulva V10.44
manic-depressive psychosis V11.1
mental disorder V11.9
affective type V11.1
manic-depressive V11.1
neurosis V11.2
schizophrenia V11.0
specified type NEC V11.8
metabolic disorder V12.2
musculoskeletal disorder NEC V13.5
myocardial infarction 412

History (personal) of — *continued*
neglect (emotional) V15.42
nervous system disorder V12.40
specified type NEC V12.49
neurosis V11.2
noncompliance with medical treatment V15.81
nutritional deficiency V12.1
obstetric disorder V13.2
affecting management of current pregnancy V23.4
parasitic disease V12.00
specified NEC V12.09
perinatal problems V13.7
physical abuse V15.41
poisoning V15.6
poliomyelitis V12.02
polyps, colonic V12.72
poor obstetric V23.4
psychiatric disorder V11.9
affective type V11.1
manic-depressive V11.1
neurosis V11.2
schizophrenia V11.0
specified type NEC V11.8
psychological trauma V15.49
emotional abuse V15.42
neglect V15.42
physical abuse V15.41
rape V15.41
psychoneurosis V11.2
radiation therapy V15.3
rape V15.41
respiratory system disease V12.6
reticulosarcoma V10.71
schizophrenia V11.0
skin disease V13.3
smoking (tobacco) V15.82
subcutaneous tissue disease V13.3
surgery (major) to
great vessels V15.1
heart V15.1
major organs NEC V15.2
thrombophlebitis V12.52
thrombosis V12.51
tobacco use V15.82
trophoblastic disease V13.1
affecting management of pregnancy V23.1
tuberculosis V12.01
ulcer, peptic V12.71
urinary system disorder V13.00
calculi V13.01
specified NEC V13.09
HIV infection (disease) (illness) — *see* Human immunodeficiency virus (disease) (illness) (infection)
Hives (bold) (*see also* Urticaria) 708.9
Hoarseness 784.49
Hobnail liver — *see* Cirrhosis, portal
Hobo, hoboism V60.0
Hodgkin's
disease (M9650/3) 201.9 ✓5th
lymphocytic
depletion (M9653/3) 201.7 ✓5th
diffuse fibrosis (M9654/3) 201.7 ✓5th
reticular type (M9655/3) 201.7 ✓5th
predominance (M9651/3) 201.4 ✓5th
lymphocytic-histiocytic predominance (M9651/3) 201.4 ✓5th
mixed cellularity (M9652/3) 201.6 ✓5th
nodular sclerosis (M9656/3) 201.5 ✓5th
cellular phase (M9657/3) 201.5 ✓5th

Hodgkin's — *continued*
granuloma (M9661/3) 201.1 ✓5th
lymphogranulomatosis (M9650/3) 201.9 ✓5th
lymphoma (M9650/3) 201.9 ✓5th
lymphosarcoma (M9650/3) 201.9 ✓5th
paragranuloma (M9660/3) 201.0 ✓5th
sarcoma (M9662/3) 201.2 ✓5th
Hodgson's disease (aneurysmal dilatation of aorta) 441.9
ruptured 441.5
Hodi-potsy 111.0
Hoffa (-Kastert) disease or syndrome (liposynovitis prepatellaris) 272.8
Hoffmann's syndrome 244.9 *[359.5]*
Hoffmann-Bouveret syndrome (paroxysmal tachycardia) 427.2
Hole
macula 362.54
optic disc, crater-like 377.22
retina (macula) 362.54
round 361.31
with detachment 361.01
Holla disease (*see also* Spherocytosis) 282.0
Holländer-Simons syndrome (progressive lipodystrophy) 272.6
Hollow foot (congenital) 754.71
acquired 736.73
Holmes' syndrome (visual disorientation) 368.16
Holoprosencephaly 742.2
due to
trisomy 13 758.1
trisomy 18 758.2
Holthouse's hernia — *see* Hernia, inguinal
Homesickness 309.89
Homocystinemia 270.4
Homocystinuria 270.4
Homologous serum jaundice (prophylactic) (therapeutic) — *see* Hepatitis, viral
Homosexuality — *omit code*
ego-dystonic 302.0
pedophilic 302.2
problems with 302.0
Homozygous Hb-S disease 282.61
Honeycomb lung 518.89
congenital 748.4
Hong Kong ear 117.3
HOOD (hereditary osteo-onychodysplasia) 756.89
Hooded
clitoris 752.49
penis 752.69
Hookworm (anemia) (disease) (infestation) — *see* Ancylostomiasis
Hoppe-Goldflam syndrome 358.0
Hordeolum (external) (eyelid) 373.11
internal 373.12
Horn
cutaneous 702.8
cheek 702.8
eyelid 702.8
penis 702.8
iliac 756.89
nail 703.8
congenital 757.5
papillary 700
Horner's
syndrome (*see also* Neuropathy, peripheral, autonomic) 337.9
traumatic 954.0
teeth 520.4

Hyperreflexia 796.1
- bladder, autonomic 596.54
  - with cauda equina 344.61
- detrusor 344.61

Hypersalivation (*see also* Ptyalism) 527.7

Hypersarcosinemia 270.8

Hypersecretion
- ACTH 255.3
- androgens (ovarian) 256.1
- calcitonin 246.0
- corticoadrenal 255.3
- cortisol 255.0
- estrogen 256.0
- gastric 536.8
  - psychogenic 306.4
- gastrin 251.5
- glucagon 251.4
- hormone
  - ACTH 255.3
  - anterior pituitary 253.1
  - growth NEC 253.0
  - ovarian androgen 256.1
  - testicular 257.0
  - thyroid stimulating 242.8 [5th]
- insulin — *see* Hyperinsulinism
- lacrimal glands (*see also* Epiphora) 375.20
- medulloadrenal 255.6
- milk 676.6 [5th]
- ovarian androgens 256.1
- pituitary (anterior) 253.1
- salivary gland (any) 527.7
- testicular hormones 257.0
- thyrocalcitonin 246.0
- upper respiratory 478.9

Hypersegmentation, hereditary 288.2
- eosinophils 288.2
- neutrophil nuclei 288.2

Hypersensitive, hypersensitiveness, hypersensitivity — *see also* Allergy
- angiitis 446.20
  - specified NEC 446.29
- carotid sinus 337.0
- colon 564.1
  - psychogenic 306.4
- DNA (deoxyribonucleic acid) NEC 287.2
- drug (*see also* Allergy, drug) 995.2
- esophagus 530.89
- insect bites — *see* Injury, superficial, by site
- labyrinth 386.58
- pain (*see also* Disturbance, sensation) 782.0
- pneumonitis NEC 495.9
- reaction (*see also* Allergy) 995.3
  - upper respiratory tract NEC 478.8
- stomach (allergic) (nonallergic) 536.8
  - psychogenic 306.4

Hypersomatotropism (classic) 253.0

Hypersomnia 780.54
- with sleep apnea 780.53
- nonorganic origin 307.43
  - persistent (primary) 307.44
  - transient 307.43

Hypersplenia 289.4

Hypersplenism 289.4

Hypersteatosis 706.3

Hyperstimulation, ovarian 256.1

Hypersuprarenalism 255.3

Hypersusceptibility — *see* Allergy

Hyper-TBG-nemia 246.8

Hypertelorism 756.0
- orbit, orbital 376.41

	Malignant	Benign	Unspecified
Hypertension, hypertensive (arterial) (arteriolar) (crisis) (degeneration) (disease) (essential) (fluctuating) (idiopathic) (intermittent) (labile) (low renin) (orthostatic) (paroxysmal) (primary) (systemic) (uncontrolled) (vascular)	401.0	401.1	401.9
with			
— heart involvement (conditions classifiable to 425.8, 428, 429.0–429.3, 429.8, 429.9 due to hypertension) (*see also* Hypertension, heart)	402.00	402.10	402.90
—— with kidney involvement— *see* Hypertension, cardiorenal			
— renal involvement (*only* conditions classifiable to 585, 586, 587) *(excludes conditions classifiable to 584)* (*see also* Hypertension, kidney)	403.00	403.10	403.90
—— with heart involvement — *see* Hypertension, cardiorenal			
—— failure (and sclerosis) (*see also* Hypertension, kidney)	403.01	403.11	403.91
—— sclerosis without failure (*see also* Hypertension, kidney)	403.00	403.10	403.90
accelerated (*see also* Hypertension, by type, malignant)	401.0	—	—
antepartum — *see* Hypertension, complicating pregnancy, childbirth, or the puerperium			
cardiorenal (disease)	404.00	404.10	404.90
— with			
—— heart failure (congestive)	404.01	404.11	404.91
——— and renal failure	404.03	404.13	404.93
—— renal failure	404.02	404.12	404.92
——— and heart failure (congestive)	404.03	404.13	404.93
cardiovascular disease (arteriosclerotic) (sclerotic)	402.00	402.10	402.90
— with			
—— heart failure (congestive)	402.01	402.11	402.91
—— renal involvement (conditions classifiable to 403) (*see also* Hypertension, cardiorenal)	404.00	404.10	404.90
cardiovascular renal (disease) (sclerosis) (*see also* Hypertension, cardiorenal)	404.00	404.10	404.90
cerebrovascular disease NEC	437.2	437.2	437.2
complicating pregnancy, childbirth, or the puerperium	642.2 [5th]	642.0 [5th]	642.9 [5th]
— with			
—— albuminuria (and edema) (mild)	—	—	642.4 [5th]
——— severe	—	—	642.5 [5th]
—— edema (mild)	—	—	642.4 [5th]
——— severe	—	—	642.5 [5th]
—— heart disease	642.2 [5th]	642.2 [5th]	642.2 [5th]
——— and renal disease	642.2 [5th]	642.2 [5th]	642.2 [5th]
—— renal disease	642.2 [5th]	642.2 [5th]	642.2 [5th]
——— and heart disease	642.2 [5th]	642.2 [5th]	642.2 [5th]
— chronic	642.2 [5th]	642.0 [5th]	642.0 [5th]
—— with pre-eclampsia or eclampsia	642.7 [5th]	642.7 [5th]	642.7 [5th]
—— fetus or newborn	760.0	760.0	760.0
— essential	—	642.0 [5th]	642.0 [5th]
—— with pre-eclampsia or eclampsia	—	642.7 [5th]	642.7 [5th]
—— fetus or newborn	760.0	760.0	760.0
— fetus or newborn	760.0	760.0	760.0
— gestational	—	—	642.3 [5th]
— pre-existing	642.2 [5th]	642.0 [5th]	642.0 [5th]
—— with pre-eclampsia or eclampsia	642.7 [5th]	642.7 [5th]	642.7 [5th]
—— fetus or newborn	760.0	760.0	760.0
— secondary to renal disease	642.1 [5th]	642.1 [5th]	642.1 [5th]
—— with pre-eclampsia or eclampsia	642.7 [5th]	642.7 [5th]	642.7 [5th]
—— fetus or newborn	760.0	760.0	760.0
— transient	—	—	642.3 [5th]
due to			
— aldosteronism, primary	405.09	405.19	405.99
— brain tumor	405.09	405.19	405.99
— bulbar poliomyelitis	405.09	405.19	405.99
— calculus			
—— kidney	405.09	405.19	405.99
—— ureter	405.09	405.19	405.99
— coarctation, aorta	405.09	405.19	405.99
— Cushing's disease	405.09	405.19	405.99
— glomerulosclerosis (*see also* Hypertension, kidney)	403.00	403.10	403.90
— periarteritis nodosa	405.09	405.19	405.99
— pheochromocytoma	405.09	405.19	405.99
— polycystic kidney(s)	405.09	405.19	405.99
— polycythemia	405.09	405.19	405.99
— porphyria	405.09	405.19	405.99
— pyelonephritis	405.09	405.19	405.99

	Malignant	Benign	Unspecified
Hypertension, hypertensive (arterial) (arteriolar) (crisis) (degeneration) (disease) (essential) (fluctuating) (idiopathic) (intermittent) (labile) (low renin) (orthostatic) (paroxysmal) (primary) (systemic) (uncontrolled) (vascular) — *continued*			
due to — *continued*			
renal (artery)			
aneurysm	405.01	405.11	405.91
anomaly	405.01	405.11	405.91
embolism	405.01	405.11	405.91
fibromuscular hyperplasia	405.01	405.11	405.91
occlusion	405.01	405.11	405.91
stenosis	405.01	405.11	405.91
thrombosis	405.01	405.11	405.91
encephalopathy	437.2	437.2	437.2
gestational (transient) NEC	—	—	642.3 ✓5th
Goldblatt's	440.1	440.1	440.1
heart (disease) (conditions classifiable to 425.8, 428, 429.0–429.3, 429.8, 429.9 due to hypertension)	402.00	402.10	402.90
with			
heart failure	402.01	402.11	402.91
congestive	402.01	402.11	402.91
hypertensive kidney disease (conditions classifiable to 403) (*see also* Hypertension, cardiorenal)	404.00	404.10	404.90
renal sclerosis (*see also* Hypertension, cardiorenal)	404.00	404.10	404.90
intracranial, benign	—	348.2	—
intraocular	—	—	365.04
kidney	403.00	403.10	403.90
with			
heart involvement (conditions classifiable to 425.8, 428, 429.0–429.3, 429.8, 429.9 due to hypertension) (*see also* Hypertension, cardiorenal)	404.00	404.10	404.90
hypertensive heart (disease) (conditions classifiable to 402) (*see also* Hypertension, cardiorenal)	404.00	404.10	404.90
lesser circulation	—	—	416.0
necrotizing	401.0	—	—
ocular	—	—	365.04
portal (due to chronic liver disease)	—	—	572.3
postoperative	—	—	997.91
psychogenic	—	—	306.2
puerperal, postpartum — *see* Hypertension, complicating pregnancy, childbirth, or the puerperium			
pulmonary (artery) (idiopathic) (primary) (solitary)	—	—	416.0
with cor pulmonale (chronic)	—	—	416.8
acute	—	—	415.0
secondary	—	—	416.8
renal (disease) (*see also* Hypertension, kidney)	403.00	403.10	403.90
renovascular NEC	405.01	405.11	405.91
secondary NEC	405.09	405.19	405.99
due to			
aldosteronism, primary	405.09	405.19	405.99
brain tumor	405.09	405.19	405.99
bulbar poliomyelitis	405.09	405.19	405.99
calculus			
kidney	405.09	405.19	405.99
ureter	405.09	405.19	405.99
coarctation, aorta	405.09	405.19	405.99
Cushing's disease	405.09	405.19	405.99
glomerulosclerosis (*see also* Hypertension, kidney)	403.00	403.10	403.90
periarteritis nodosa	405.09	405.19	405.99
pheochromocytoma	405.09	405.19	405.99
polycystic kidney(s)	405.09	405.19	405.99
polycythemia	405.09	405.19	405.99
porphyria	405.09	405.19	405.99
pyelonephritis	405.09	405.19	405.99
renal (artery)			
aneurysm	405.01	405.11	405.91
anomaly	405.01	405.11	405.91
embolism	405.01	405.11	405.91
fibromuscular hyperplasia	405.01	405.11	405.91
occlusion	405.01	405.11	405.91
stenosis	405.01	405.11	405.91
thrombosis	405.01	405.11	405.91
transient	—	—	796.2
of pregnancy	—	—	642.3 ✓5th

Hyperthecosis, ovary 256.8
Hyperthermia (of unknown origin) (*see also* Pyrexia) 780.6
- malignant (due to anesthesia) 995.86
- newborn 778.4

Hyperthymergasia (*see also* Psychosis, affective) 296.0 ✓5th
- reactive (from emotional stress, psychological trauma) 298.1
- recurrent episode 296.1 ✓5th
- single episode 296.0 ✓5th

Hyperthymism 254.8
Hyperthyroid (recurrent) — *see* Hyperthyroidism
Hyperthyroidism (latent) (preadult) (recurrent) (without goiter) 242.9 ✓5th

> *Note — Use the following fifth-digit subclassification with category 242:*
> *0 without mention of thyrotoxic crisis or storm*
> *1 with mention of thyrotoxic crisis or storm*

- with
  - goiter (diffuse) 242.0 ✓5th
    - adenomatous 242.3 ✓5th
      - multinodular 242.2 ✓5th
      - uninodular 242.1 ✓5th
    - nodular 242.3 ✓5th
      - multinodular 242.2 ✓5th
      - uninodular 242.1 ✓5th
  - thyroid nodule 242.1 ✓5th
- complicating pregnancy, childbirth, or puerperium 648.1 ✓5th
- neonatal (transient) 775.3

Hypertonia — *see* Hypertonicity
Hypertonicity
- bladder 596.51
- fetus or newborn 779.8
- gastrointestinal (tract) 536.8
- infancy 779.8
  - due to electrolyte imbalance 779.8
- muscle 728.85
- stomach 536.8
  - psychogenic 306.4
- uterus, uterine (contractions) 661.4 ✓5th
  - affecting fetus or newborn 763.7

Hypertony — *see* Hypertonicity
Hypertransaminemia 790.4
Hypertrichosis 704.1
- congenital 757.4
- eyelid 374.54
- lanuginosa 757.4
  - acquired 704.1

Hypertriglyceridemia, essential 272.1

I

Iatrogenic syndrome of excess cortisol 255.0
Iceland disease (epidemic neuromyasthenia) 049.8
Ichthyosis (congenita) 757.1
  acquired 701.1
  fetalis gravior 757.1
  follicularis 757.1
  hystrix 757.39
  lamellar 757.1
  lingual 528.6
  palmaris and plantaris 757.39
  simplex 757.1
  vera 757.1
  vulgaris 757.1
Ichthyotoxism 988.0
  bacterial (*see also* Poisoning, food) 005.9
Icteroanemia, hemolytic (acquired) 283.9
  congenital (*see also* Spherocytosis) 282.0
Icterus (*see also* Jaundice) 782.4
  catarrhal — *see* Icterus, infectious
  conjunctiva 782.4
    newborn 774.6
  epidemic — *see* Icterus, infectious
  febrilis — *see* Icterus, infectious
  fetus or newborn — *see* Jaundice, fetus or newborn
  gravis (*see also* Necrosis, liver) 570
    complicating pregnancy 646.7 ✓5th
      affecting fetus or newborn 760.8
    fetus or newborn NEC 773.0
    obstetrical 646.7 ✓5th
      affecting fetus or newborn 760.8
  hematogenous (acquired) 283.9
  hemolytic (acquired) 283.9
    congenital (*see also* Spherocytosis) 282.0
  hemorrhagic (acute) 100.0
    leptospiral 100.0
    newborn 776.0
    spirochetal 100.0
  infectious 070.1
    with hepatic coma 070.0
    leptospiral 100.0
    spirochetal 100.0
  intermittens juvenilis 277.4
  malignant (*see also* Necrosis, liver) 570
  neonatorum (*see also* Jaundice, fetus or newborn) 774.6
  pernicious (*see also* Necrosis, liver) 570
  spirochetal 100.0
Ictus solaris, solis 992.0
Identity disorder 313.82
  dissociative 300.14
  gender role (child) 302.6
    adult 302.85
  psychosexual (child) 302.6
    adult 302.85
Idioglossia 307.9
Idiopathic — *see* condition
Idiosyncrasy (*see also* Allergy) 995.3
  drug, medicinal substance, and biological — *see* Allergy, drug
Idiot, idiocy (congenital) 318.2
  amaurotic (Bielschowsky) (-Jansky) (family) (infantile (late)) (juvenile (late)) (Vogt-Spielmeyer) 330.1
  microcephalic 742.1
  Mongolian 758.0
  oxycephalic 756.0
Id reaction (due to bacteria) 692.89
IgE asthma 493.0 ✓5th
Ileitis (chronic) (*see also* Enteritis) 558.9
  infectious 009.0
  noninfectious 558.9
  regional (ulcerative) 555.0
    with large intestine 555.2
  segmental 555.0
    with large intestine 555.2
  terminal (ulcerative) 555.0
    with large intestine 555.2
Ileocolitis (*see also* Enteritis) 558.9
  infectious 009.0
  regional 555.2
  ulcerative 556.1
Ileostomy status V44.2
  with complication 569.60
Ileotyphus 002.0
Ileum — *see* condition
Ileus (adynamic) (bowel) (colon) (inhibitory) (intestine) (neurogenic) (paralytic) 560.1
  arteriomesenteric duodenal 537.2
  due to gallstone (in intestine) 560.31
  duodenal, chronic 537.2
  following gastrointestinal surgery 997.4
  gallstone 560.31
  mechanical (*see also* Obstruction, intestine) 560.9
  meconium 777.1
    due to cystic fibrosis 277.01
  myxedema 564.89
  postoperative 997.4
  transitory, newborn 777.4
Iliac — *see* condition
Iliotibial band friction syndrome 728.89
Ill, louping 063.1
Illegitimacy V61.6
Illness — *see also* Disease
  factitious 300.19
    with
      combined physical and psychological symptoms 300.19
      physical symptoms 300.19
      psychological symptoms 300.16
    chronic (with physical symptoms) 301.51
  heart — *see* Disease, heart
  manic-depressive (*see also* Psychosis, affective) 296.80
  mental (*see also* Disorder, mental) 300.9
Imbalance 781.2
  autonomic (*see also* Neuropathy, peripheral, autonomic) 337.9
  electrolyte 276.9
    with
      abortion — *see* Abortion, by type, with metabolic disorder
      ectopic pregnancy (*see also* categories 633.0–633.9) 639.4
      hyperemesis gravidarum (before 22 completed weeks' gestation) 643.1 ✓5th
      molar pregnancy (*see also* categories 630–632) 639.4
    following
      abortion 639.4
      ectopic or molar pregnancy 639.4
    neonatal, transitory NEC 775.5
  endocrine 259.9
  eye muscle NEC 378.9
    heterophoria — *see* Heterophoria
  glomerulotubular NEC 593.89
  hormone 259.9
Imbalance — *continued*
  hysterical (*see also* Hysteria) 300.10
  labyrinth NEC 386.50
  posture 729.9
  sympathetic (*see also* Neuropathy, peripheral, autonomic) 337.9
Imbecile, imbecility 318.0
  moral 301.7
  old age 290.9
  senile 290.9
  specified IQ — *see* IQ
  unspecified IQ 318.0
Imbedding, intrauterine device 996.32
Imbibition, cholesterol (gallbladder) 575.6
Imerslund (-Gräsbeck) syndrome (anemia due to familial selective vitamin B_{12} malabsorption) 281.1
Iminoacidopathy 270.8
Iminoglycinuria, familial 270.8
Immature — *see also* Immaturity
  personality 301.89
Immaturity 765.1 ✓5th
  extreme 765.0 ✓5th
  fetus or infant light-for-dates — *see* Light-for-dates
  lung, fetus or newborn 770.4
  organ or site NEC — *see* Hypoplasia
  pulmonary, fetus or newborn 770.4
  reaction 301.89
  sexual (female) (male) 259.0
Immersion 994.1
  foot 991.4
  hand 991.4
Immobile, immobility
  intestine 564.89
  joint — *see* Ankylosis
  syndrome (paraplegic) 728.3
Immunization
  ABO
    affecting management of pregnancy 656.2 ✓5th
      fetus or newborn 773.1
  complication — *see* Complications, vaccination
  Rh factor
    affecting management of pregnancy 656.1 ✓5th
      fetus or newborn 773.0
    from transfusion 999.7
Immunodeficiency 279.3
  with
    adenosine-deaminase deficiency 279.2
    defect, predominant
      B-cell 279.00
      T-cell 279.10
    hyperimmunoglobulinemia 279.2
    lymphopenia, hereditary 279.2
    thrombocytopenia and eczema 279.12
    thymic
      aplasia 279.2
      dysplasia 279.2
  autosomal recessive, Swiss-type 279.2
  common variable 279.06
  severe combined (SCID) 279.2
  to Rh factor
    affecting management of pregnancy 656.1 ✓5th
      fetus or newborn 773.0
  X-linked, with increased IgM 279.05
Immunotherapy, prophylactic V07.2

Note — Use the following fifth-digit subclassification with category 410:
0 episode unspecified
1 initial episode
2 subsequent episode without recurrence

- **Infection, infected, infective** (opportunistic) — *continued*
  - branchial cyst 744.42
  - breast 611.0
    - puerperal, postpartum 675.2 ✓5th
      - with nipple 675.9 ✓5th
        - specified type NEC 675.8 ✓5th
      - nonpurulent 675.2 ✓5th
      - purulent 675.1 ✓5th
  - bronchus (*see also* Bronchitis) 490
    - fungus NEC 117.9
  - Brucella 023.9
    - abortus 023.1
    - canis 023.3
    - melitensis 023.0
    - mixed 023.8
    - suis 023.2
  - Brugia (Wuchereria) malayi 125.1
  - bursa — *see* Bursitis
  - buttocks (skin) 686.9
  - Candida (albicans) (tropicalis) (*see also* Candidiasis) 112.9
    - congenital 771.7
  - Candiru 136.8
  - Capillaria
    - hepatica 128.8
    - philippinensis 127.5
  - cartilage 733.99
  - cat liver fluke 121.0
  - cellulitis — *see* Cellulitis, by site
  - Cephalosporum falciforme 117.4
  - Cercomonas hominis (intestinal) 007.3
  - cerebrospinal (*see also* Meningitis) 322.9
    - late effect — *see* category 326
  - cervical gland 683
  - cervix (*see also* Cervicitis) 616.0
  - cesarean section wound 674.3 ✓5th
  - Chilomastix (intestinal) 007.8
  - Chlamydia 079.98
    - specified NEC 079.88
  - Cholera (*see also* Cholera) 001.9
  - chorionic plate 658.8 ✓5th
  - Cladosporium
    - bantianum 117.8
    - carrionii 117.2
    - mansoni 111.1
    - trichoides 117.8
    - wernecki 111.1
  - Clonorchis (sinensis) (liver) 121.1
  - Clostridium (haemolyticum) (novyi) NEC 041.84
    - botulinum 005.1
    - congenital 771.8
    - histolyticum (*see also* Gangrene, gas) 040.0
    - oedematiens (*see also* Gangrene, gas) 040.0
    - perfringens 041.83
      - due to food 005.2
    - septicum (*see also* Gangrene, gas) 040.0
    - sordellii (*see also* Gangrene, gas) 040.0
    - welchii (*see also* Gangrene, gas) 040.0
      - due to food 005.2
  - Coccidioides (immitis) (*see also* Coccidioidomycosis) 114.9
  - coccus NEC 041.89
  - colon (*see also* Enteritis, due to, by organism) 009.0
    - bacillus — *see* Infection, Escherichia coli
  - colostomy or enterostomy 569.61

- **Infection, infected, infective** (opportunistic) — *continued*
  - common duct 576.1
  - complicating pregnancy, childbirth, or puerperium NEC 647.9 ✓5th
    - affecting fetus or newborn 760.2
  - Condiobolus 117.7
  - congenital NEC 771.8
    - Candida albicans 771.7
    - chronic 771.2
    - clostridial 771.8
    - Cytomegalovirus 771.1
    - Escherichia coli 771.8
    - hepatitis, viral 771.2
    - Herpes simplex 771.2
    - listeriosis 771.2
    - malaria 771.2
    - poliomyelitis 771.2
    - rubella 771.0
    - Salmonella 771.8
    - streptococcal 771.8
    - toxoplasmosis 771.2
    - tuberculosis 771.2
    - urinary (tract) 771.8
    - vaccinia 771.2
  - corpus luteum (*see also* Salpingo-oophoritis) 614.2
  - Corynebacterium diphtheriae — *see* Diphtheria
  - Coxsackie (*see also* Coxsackie) 079.2
    - endocardium 074.22
    - heart NEC 074.20
    - in diseases classified elsewhere — *see* category 079
    - meninges 047.0
    - myocardium 074.23
    - pericardium 074.21
    - pharynx 074.0
    - specified disease NEC 074.8
    - unspecified nature or site 079.2
  - Cryptococcus neoformans 117.5
  - Cryptosporidia 007.4
  - Cunninghamella 117.7
  - cyst — *see* Cyst
  - Cysticercus cellulosae 123.1
  - cytomegalovirus 078.5
    - congenital 771.1
  - dental (pulpal origin) 522.4
  - deuteromycetes 117.4
  - Dicrocoelium dendriticum 121.8
  - Dipetalonema (perstans) 125.4
    - streptocerca 125.6
  - diphtherial — *see* Diphtheria
  - Diphyllobothrium (adult) (latum) (pacificum) 123.4
    - larval 123.5
  - Diplogonoporus (grandis) 123.8
  - Dipylidium (caninum) 123.8
  - Dirofilaria 125.6
  - dog tapeworm 123.8
  - Dracunculus medinensis 125.7
  - Dreschlera 118
    - hawaiiensis 117.8
  - Ducrey's bacillus (any site) 099.0
  - due to or resulting from
    - device, implant, or graft (any) (presence of) — *see* Complications, infection and inflammation, due to (presence of) any device, implant, or graft classified to 996.0-996.5 NEC
    - injection, inoculation, infusion, transfusion, or vaccination (prophylactic) (therapeutic) 999.3

- **Infection, infected, infective** (opportunistic) — *continued*
  - due to or resulting from — *continued*
    - injury NEC — *see* Wound, open, by site, complicated
    - surgery 998.59
  - duodenum 535.6 ✓5th
  - ear — *see also* Otitis
    - external (*see also* Otitis, externa) 380.10
    - inner (*see also* Labyrinthitis) 386.30
    - middle — *see* Otitis, media
  - Eaton's agent NEC 041.81
  - Eberthella typhosa 002.0
  - Ebola 065.8
  - echinococcosis 122.9
  - Echinococcus (*see also* Echinococcus) 122.9
  - Echinostoma 121.8
  - ECHO virus 079.1
    - in diseases classified elsewhere — *see* category 079
    - unspecified nature or site 079.1
  - Endamoeba — *see* Infection, ameba
  - endocardium (*see also* Endocarditis) 421.0
  - endocervix (*see also* Cervicitis) 616.0
  - Entamoeba — *see* Infection, ameba
  - enteric (*see also* Enteritis, due to, by organism) 009.0
  - Enterobacter aerogenes NEC 041.85
  - Enterobius vermicularis 127.4
  - Enterococcus NEC 041.04
  - enterovirus NEC 079.89
    - central nervous system NEC 048
    - enteritis 008.67
    - meningitis 047.9
  - Entomophthora 117.7
  - Epidermophyton — *see* Dermatophytosis
  - epidermophytosis — *see* Dermatophytosis
  - episiotomy 674.3 ✓5th
  - Epstein-Barr virus 075
  - erysipeloid 027.1
  - Erysipelothrix (insidiosa) (rhusiopathiae) 027.1
  - erythema infectiosum 057.0
  - Escherichia coli NEC 041.4
    - congenital 771.8
    - enteritis — *see* Enteritis, E. coli
    - generalized 038.42
    - intestinal — *see* Enteritis, E. coli
  - ethmoidal (chronic) (sinus) (*see also* Sinusitis, ethmoidal) 473.2
  - Eubacterium 041.84
  - Eustachian tube (ear) 381.50
    - acute 381.51
    - chronic 381.52
  - exanthema subitum 057.8
  - external auditory canal (meatus) (*see also* Otitis, externa) 380.10
  - eye NEC 360.00
  - eyelid 373.9
    - specified NEC 373.8
  - fallopian tube (*see also* Salpingo-oophoritis) 614.2
  - fascia 728.89
  - Fasciola
    - gigantica 121.3
    - hepatica 121.3
  - Fasciolopsis (buski) 121.4
  - fetus (intra-amniotic) — *see* Infection, congenital
  - filarial — *see* Infestation, filarial

Infection, infected, infective (opportunistic) — *continued*
- lung — *continued*
  - fungus NEC 117.9
  - spirochetal 104.8
  - virus — *see* Pneumonia, virus
- lymph gland (axillary) (cervical) (inguinal) 683
  - mesenteric 289.2
- lymphoid tissue, base of tongue or posterior pharynx, NEC 474.00
- madurella
  - grisea 117.4
  - mycetomii 117.4
- major
  - with
    - abortion — *see* Abortion, by type, with sepsis
    - ectopic pregnancy (*see also* categories 633.0-633.9) 639.0
    - molar pregnancy (*see also* categories 630-632) 639.0
  - following
    - abortion 639.0
    - ectopic or molar pregnancy 639.0
  - puerperal, postpartum, childbirth 670
- malarial — *see* Malaria
- Malassezia furfur 111.0
- Malleomyces
  - mallei 024
  - pseudomallei 025
- mammary gland 611.0
  - puerperal, postpartum 675.2 ✓5th
- Mansonella (ozzardi) 125.5
- mastoid (suppurative) — *see* Mastoiditis
- maxilla, maxillary 526.4
  - sinus (chronic) (*see also* Sinusitis, maxillary) 473.0
- mediastinum 519.2
- medina 125.7
- meibomian
  - cyst 373.12
  - gland 373.12
- melioidosis 025
- meninges (*see also* Meningitis) 320.9
- meningococcal (*see also* condition) 036.9
  - brain 036.1
  - cerebrospinal 036.0
  - endocardium 036.42
  - generalized 036.2
  - meninges 036.0
  - meningococcemia 036.2
  - specified site NEC 036.89
- mesenteric lymph nodes or glands NEC 289.2
- Metagonimus 121.5
- metatarsophalangeal 711.97
- microorganism resistant to drugs — *see* Resistance (to), drugs by microorganisms
- Microsporidia 136.8
- microsporum, microsporic — *see* Dermatophytosis
- mima polymorpha NEC 041.85
- mixed flora NEC 041.89
- Monilia (*see also* Candidiasis) 112.9
  - neonatal 771.7
- Monosporium apiospermum 117.6
- mouth (focus) NEC 528.9
  - parasitic 136.9
- Mucor 117.7
- muscle NEC 728.89
- mycelium NEC 117.9
- mycetoma
  - actinomycotic NEC (*see also* Actinomycosis) 039.9
  - mycotic NEC 117.4
- Mycobacterium, mycobacterial (*see also* Mycobacterium) 031.9
- mycoplasma NEC 041.81
- mycotic NEC 117.9
  - pathogenic to compromised host only 118
  - skin NEC 111.9
  - systemic 117.9
- myocardium NEC 422.90
- nail (chronic) (with lymphangitis) 681.9
  - finger 681.02
    - fungus 110.1
  - ingrowing 703.0
  - toe 681.11
    - fungus 110.1
- nasal sinus (chronic (*see also* Sinusitis) 473.9
- nasopharynx (chronic) 478.29
  - acute 460
- navel 686.9
  - newborn 771.4
- Neisserian — *see* Gonococcus
- Neotestudina rosatii 117.4
- newborn, generalized 771.8
- nipple 611.0
  - puerperal, postpartum 675.0 ✓5th
    - with breast 675.9 ✓5th
      - specified type NEC 675.8 ✓5th
- Nocardia — *see* Actinomycosis
- nose 478.1
- nostril 478.1
- obstetrical surgical wound 674.3 ✓5th
- Oesophagostomum (apiostomum) 127.7
- Oestrus ovis 134.0
- Oidium albicans (*see also* Candidiasis) 112.9
- Onchocerca (volvulus) 125.3
  - *eye 125.3 [360.13]*
  - *eyelid 125.3 [373.6]*
- operation wound 998.59
- Opisthorchis (felineus) (tenuicollis) (viverrini) 121.0
- orbit 376.00
  - chronic 376.10
- ovary (*see also* Salpingo-oophoritis) 614.2
- Oxyuris vermicularis 127.4
- pancreas 577.0
- Paracoccidioides brasiliensis 116.1
- Paragonimus (westermani) 121.2
- parainfluenza virus 079.89
- parameningococcus NEC 036.9
  - with meningitis 036.0
- parasitic NEC 136.9
- paratyphoid 002.9
  - Type A 002.1
  - Type B 002.2
  - Type C 002.3
- paraurethral ducts 597.89
- parotid gland 527.2
- Pasteurella NEC 027.2
  - multocida (cat-bite) (dog-bite) 027.2
  - pestis (*see also* Plague) 020.9
  - pseudotuberculosis 027.2
  - septica (cat-bite) (dog-bite) 027.2
  - tularensis (*see also* Tularemia) 021.9
- pelvic, female (*see also* Disease, pelvis, inflammatory) 614.9
- penis (glans) (retention) NEC 607.2
  - herpetic 054.13
- Peptococcus 041.84
- Peptostreptococcus 041.84
- periapical (pulpal origin) 522.4
- peridental 523.3
- perineal wound (obstetrical) 674.3 ✓5th
- periodontal 523.3
- periorbital 376.00
  - chronic 376.10
- perirectal 569.49
- perirenal (*see also* Infection, kidney) 590.9
- peritoneal (*see also* Peritonitis) 567.9
- periureteral 593.89
- periurethral 597.89
- Petriellidium boydii 117.6
- pharynx 478.29
  - Coxsackie virus 074.0
  - phlegmonous 462
  - posterior, lymphoid 474.00
- Phialophora
  - gougerotii 117.8
  - jeanselmei 117.8
  - verrucosa 117.2
- Piedraia hortai 111.3
- pinna, acute 380.11
- pinta 103.9
  - intermediate 103.1
  - late 103.2
  - mixed 103.3
  - primary 103.0
- pinworm 127.4
- pityrosporum furfur 111.0
- pleuropneumonia-like organisms NEC (PPLO) 041.81
- pneumococcal NEC 041.2
  - generalized (purulent) 038.2
- Pneumococcus NEC 041.2
- postoperative wound 998.59
- posttraumatic NEC 958.3
- postvaccinal 999.3
- prepuce NEC 607.1
- Proprionibacterium 041.84
- prostate (capsule) (*see also* Prostatitis) 601.9
- Proteus (mirabilis) (morganii) (vulgaris) NEC 041.6
  - enteritis 008.3
- protozoal NEC 136.8
  - intestinal NEC 007.9
- Pseudomonas NEC 041.7
  - mallei 024
  - pneumonia 482.1
  - pseudomallei 025
- psittacosis 073.9
- puerperal, postpartum (major) 670
  - minor 646.6 ✓5th
- pulmonary — *see* Infection, lung
- purulent — *see* Abscess
- putrid, generalized — *see* Septicemia
- pyemic — *see* Septicemia
- Pyrenochaeta romeroi 117.4
- Q fever 083.0

- **Infection, infected, infective** (opportunistic) *— continued*
  - thumb (skin) 686.9
    - abscess (with lymphangitis) 681.00
      - pulp 681.01
    - cellulitis (with lymphangitis) 681.00
    - nail 681.02
  - thyroglossal duct 529.8
  - toe (skin) 686.9
    - abscess (with lymphangitis) 681.10
    - cellulitis (with lymphangitis) 681.10
    - nail 681.11
      - fungus 110.1
  - tongue NEC 529.0
    - parasitic 112.0
  - tonsil (faucial) (lingual) (pharyngeal) 474.00
    - acute or subacute 463
    - and adenoid 474.02
    - tag 474.00
  - tooth, teeth 522.4
    - periapical (pulpal origin) 522.4
    - peridental 523.3
    - periodontal 523.3
    - pulp 522.0
    - socket 526.5
  - Torula histolytica 117.5
  - Toxocara (cani) (cati) (felis) 128.0
  - Toxoplasma gondii (*see also* Toxoplasmosis) 130.9
  - trachea, chronic 491.8
    - fungus 117.9
  - traumatic NEC 958.3
  - trematode NEC 121.9
  - trench fever 083.1
  - Treponema
    - denticola 041.84
    - macrodenticum 041.84
    - pallidum (*see also* Syphilis) 097.9
  - Trichinella (spiralis) 124
  - Trichomonas 131.9
    - bladder 131.09
    - cervix 131.09
    - hominis 007.3
    - intestine 007.3
    - prostate 131.03
    - specified site NEC 131.8
    - urethra 131.02
    - urogenitalis 131.00
    - vagina 131.01
    - vulva 131.01
  - Trichophyton, trichophytid *— see* Dermatophytosis
  - Trichosporon (beigelii) cutaneum 111.2
  - Trichostrongylus 127.6
  - Trichuris (trichiuria) 127.3
  - Trombicula (irritans) 133.8
  - Trypanosoma (*see also* Trypanosomiasis) 086.9
    - cruzi 086.2
  - tubal (*see also* Salpingo-oophoritis) 614.2
  - tuberculous NEC (*see also* Tuberculosis) 011.9 [5th]
  - tubo-ovarian (*see also* Salpingo-oophoritis) 614.2
  - tunica vaginalis 608.4
  - tympanic membrane *— see* Myringitis
  - typhoid (abortive) (ambulant) (bacillus) 002.0
  - typhus 081.9
    - flea-borne (endemic) 081.0
    - louse-borne (epidemic) 080
    - mite-borne 081.2
    - recrudescent 081.1
    - tick-borne 082.9
      - African 082.1
      - North Asian 082.2
  - umbilicus (septic) 686.9
    - newborn NEC 771.4
  - ureter 593.89
  - urethra (*see also* Urethritis) 597.80
  - urinary (tract) NEC 599.0
    - with
      - abortion *— see* Abortion, by type, with urinary tract infection
      - ectopic pregnancy (*see also* categories 633.0-633.9) 639.8
      - molar pregnancy (*see also* categories 630-632) 639.8
    - candidal 112.2
    - complicating pregnancy, childbirth, or puerperium 646.6 [5th]
      - affecting fetus or newborn 760.1
      - asymptomatic 646.5 [5th]
        - affecting fetus or newborn 760.1
    - diplococcal (acute) 098.0
      - chronic 098.2
    - due to Trichomonas (vaginalis) 131.00
    - following
      - abortion 639.8
      - ectopic or molar pregnancy 639.8
    - gonococcal (acute) 098.0
      - chronic or duration of 2 months or over 098.2
    - newborn 771.8
    - trichomonal 131.00
    - tuberculous (*see also* Tuberculosis) 016.3 [5th]
  - uterus, uterine (*see also* Endometritis) 615.9
  - utriculus masculinus NEC 597.89
  - vaccination 999.3
  - vagina (granulation tissue) (wall) (*see also* Vaginitis) 616.10
  - varicella 052.9
  - varicose veins *— see* Varicose, veins
  - variola 050.9
    - major 050.0
    - minor 050.1
  - vas deferens NEC 608.4
  - Veillonella 041.84
  - verumontanum 597.89
  - vesical (*see also* Cystitis) 595.9
  - Vibrio
    - cholerae 001.0
      - el Tor 001.1
    - parahaemolyticus (food poisoning) 005.4
    - vulnificus 041.85
  - Vincent's (gums) (mouth) (tonsil) 101
  - virus, viral 079.99
    - adenovirus
      - in diseases classified elsewhere *— see* category 079
      - unspecified nature or site 079.0
    - central nervous system NEC 049.9
      - enterovirus 048
        - meningitis 047.9
          - specified type NEC 047.8
      - slow virus 046.9
        - specified condition NEC 046.8
    - chest 519.8
    - conjunctivitis 077.99
      - specified type NEC 077.89
    - Coxsackie (*see also* Infection, Coxsackie) 079.2
    - Ebola 065.8
    - ECHO
      - in diseases classified elsewhere *— see* category 079
      - unspecified nature or site 079.1
    - encephalitis 049.9
      - arthropod-borne NEC 064
      - tick-borne 063.9
        - specified type NEC 063.8
    - enteritis NEC (*see also* Enteritis, viral) 008.8
    - exanthem NEC 057.9
    - Hantavirus 079.81
    - human papilloma 079.4
    - in diseases classified elsewhere *— see* category 079
    - intestine (*see also* Enteritis, viral) 008.8
    - Lung *— see* Pneumonia, viral
    - respiratory syncytial (RSV) 079.6
    - retrovirus 079.50
    - rhinovirus
      - in diseases classified elsewhere *— see* category 079
      - unspecified nature or site 079.3
    - salivary gland disease 078.5
    - slow 046.9
      - specified condition NEC 046.8
    - specified type NEC 079.89
      - in diseases classified elsewhere *— see* category 079
    - unspecified nature or site 079.99
    - warts NEC 078.10
  - vulva (*see also* Vulvitis) 616.10
  - whipworm 127.3
  - Whitmore's bacillus 025
  - wound (local) (posttraumatic) NEC 958.3
    - with
      - dislocation *— see* Dislocation, by site, open
      - fracture *— see* Fracture, by site, open
      - open wound *— see* Wound, open, by site, complicated
    - postoperative 998.59
    - surgical 998.59
  - Wuchereria 125.0
    - bancrofti 125.0
    - malayi 125.1
  - yaws *— see* Yaws
  - yeast (*see also* Candidiasis) 112.9
  - yellow fever (*see also* Fever, yellow) 060.9
  - Yersinia pestis (*see also* Plague) 020.9
  - Zeis' gland 373.12
  - zoonotic bacterial NEC 027.9
  - Zopfia senegalensis 117.4
- **Infective, infectious** *— see* condition
- **Inferiority complex** 301.9
  - constitutional psychopathic 301.9
- **Infertility**
  - female 628.9
    - associated with
      - adhesions, peritubal 614.6 *[628.2]*

- **Inflammation, inflamed, inflammatory** (with exudation) — *continued*
  - rectosigmoid — *see* Rectosigmoiditis
  - rectum (*see also* Proctitis) 569.49
  - respiratory, upper (*see also* Infection, respiratory, upper) 465.9
    - chronic, due to external agent — *see* Condition, respiratory, chronic, due to, external agent
    - due to
      - fumes or vapors (chemical) (inhalation) 506.2
    - radiation 508.1
  - retina (*see also* Retinitis) 363.20
  - retrocecal (*see also* Appendicitis) 541
  - retroperitoneal (*see also* Peritonitis) 567.9
  - salivary duct or gland (any) (suppurative) 527.2
  - scorbutic, alveoli, teeth 267
  - scrotum 608.4
  - sigmoid — *see* Enteritis
  - sinus (*see also* Sinusitis) 473.9
  - Skene's duct or gland (*see also* Urethritis) 597.89
  - skin 686.9
  - spermatic cord 608.4
  - sphenoidal (sinus) (*see also* Sinusitis, sphenoidal) 473.3
  - spinal
    - cord (*see also* Encephalitis) 323.9
      - late effect — *see* category 326
    - membrane — *see* Meningitis
    - nerve — *see* Disorder, nerve
  - spine (*see also* Spondylitis) 720.9
  - spleen (capsule) 289.59
  - stomach — *see* Gastritis
  - stricture, rectum 569.49
  - subcutaneous tissue NEC 686.9
  - suprarenal (gland) 255.8
  - synovial (fringe) (membrane) — *see* Bursitis
  - tendon (sheath) NEC 726.90
  - testis (*see also* Orchitis) 604.90
  - thigh 686.9
  - throat (*see also* Sore throat) 462
  - thymus (gland) 254.8
  - thyroid (gland) (*see also* Thyroiditis) 245.9
  - tongue 529.0
  - tonsil — *see* Tonsillitis
  - trachea — *see* Tracheitis
  - trochlear nerve 378.53
  - tubal (*see also* Salpingo-oophoritis) 614.2
  - tuberculous NEC (*see also* Tuberculosis) 011.9 [5th]
  - tubo-ovarian (*see also* Salpingo-oophoritis) 614.2
  - tunica vaginalis 608.4
  - tympanic membrane — *see* Myringitis
  - umbilicus, umbilical 686.9
    - newborn NEC 771.4
  - uterine ligament (*see also* Disease, pelvis, inflammatory) 614.4
    - acute 614.3
  - uterus (catarrhal) (*see also* Endometritis) 615.9
  - uveal tract (anterior) (*see also* Iridocyclitis) 364.3
    - posterior — *see* Chorioretinitis
    - sympathetic 360.11
  - vagina (*see also* Vaginitis) 616.10
  - vas deferens 608.4
  - vein (*see also* Phlebitis) 451.9
    - thrombotic 451.9
      - cerebral (*see also* Thrombosis, brain) 434.0 [5th]
      - leg 451.2
        - deep (vessels) NEC 451.19
        - superficial (vessels) 451.0
      - lower extremity 451.2
        - deep (vessels) NEC 451.19
        - superficial (vessels) 451.0
  - vocal cord 478.5
  - vulva (*see also* Vulvitis) 616.10
- **Inflation, lung imperfect** (newborn) 770.5
- **Influenza, influenzal** 487.1
  - with
    - bronchitis 487.1
    - bronchopneumonia 487.0
    - cold (any type) 487.1
    - digestive manifestations 487.8
    - hemoptysis 487.1
    - involvement of
      - gastrointestinal tract 487.8
      - nervous system 487.8
    - laryngitis 487.1
    - manifestations NEC 487.8
      - respiratory 487.1
        - pneumonia 487.0
    - pharyngitis 487.1
    - pneumonia (any form classifiable to 480-483, 485-486) 487.0
    - respiratory manifestations NEC 487.1
    - sinusitis 487.1
    - sore throat 487.1
    - tonsillitis 487.1
    - tracheitis 487.1
    - upper respiratory infection (acute) 487.1
  - abdominal 487.8
  - Asian 487.1
  - bronchial 487.1
  - bronchopneumonia 487.0
  - catarrhal 487.1
  - epidemic 487.1
  - gastric 487.8
  - intestinal 487.8
  - laryngitis 487.1
  - maternal affecting fetus or newborn 760.2
    - manifest influenza in infant 771.2
  - pharyngitis 487.1
  - pneumonia (any form) 487.0
  - respiratory (upper) 487.1
  - stomach 487.8
  - vaccination, prophylactic (against) V04.8
- **Influenza-like disease** 487.1
- **Infraction, Freiberg's** (metatarsal head) 732.5
- **Infusion complication, misadventure, or reaction** — *see* Complication, infusion
- **Ingestion**
  - chemical — *see* Table of drugs and chemicals
  - drug or medicinal substance
    - overdose or wrong substance given or taken 977.9
      - specified drug — *see* Table of drugs and chemicals
  - foreign body NEC (*see also* Foreign body) 938
- **Ingrowing**
  - hair 704.8
  - nail (finger) (toe) (infected) 703.0
- **Inguinal** — *see also* condition
  - testis 752.51
- **Inhalation**
  - carbon monoxide 986
  - flame
    - lung 947.1
    - mouth 947.0
  - food or foreign body (*see also* Asphyxia, food or foreign body) 933.1
  - gas, fumes, or vapor (noxious) 987.9
    - specified agent — *see* Table of drugs and chemicals
  - liquid or vomitus (*see also* Asphyxia, food or foreign body) 933.1
    - lower respiratory tract NEC 934.9
  - meconium (fetus or newborn) 770.1
  - mucus (*see also* Asphyxia, mucus) 933.1
  - oil (causing suffocation) (*see also* Asphyxia, food or foreign body) 933.1
  - pneumonia — *see* Pneumonia, aspiration
  - smoke 987.9
  - steam 987.9
  - stomach contents or secretions (*see also* Asphyxia, food or foreign body) 933.1
    - in labor and delivery 668.0 [5th]
- **Inhibition, inhibited**
  - academic as adjustment reaction 309.23
  - orgasm
    - female 302.73
    - male 302.74
  - sexual
    - desire 302.71
    - excitement 302.72
  - work as adjustment reaction 309.23
- **Inhibitor, systemic lupus erythematosus** (presence of) 286.5
- **Iniencephalus, iniencephaly** 740.2
- **Injected eye** 372.74
- **Injury** 959.9

> *Note — For abrasion, insect bite (nonvenomous), blister, or scratch, see Injury, superficial.*
>
> *For laceration, traumatic rupture, tear, or penetrating wound of internal organs, such as heart, lung, liver, kidney, pelvic organs, whether or not accompanied by open wound in the same region, see Injury, internal.*
>
> *For nerve injury, see Injury, nerve.*
>
> *For late effect of injuries classifiable to 850-854, 860-869, 900-919, 950-959, see Late, effect, injury, by type.*

  - abdomen, abdominal (viscera) — *see also* Injury, internal, abdomen
    - muscle or wall 959.1
  - acoustic, resulting in deafness 951.5
  - adenoid 959.09
  - adrenal (gland) — *see* Injury, internal, adrenal
  - alveolar (process) 959.09
  - ankle (and foot) (and knee) (and leg, except thigh) 959.7
  - anterior chamber, eye 921.3
  - anus 959.1
  - aorta (thoracic) 901.0
    - abdominal 902.0
  - appendix — *see* Injury, internal, appendix
  - arm, upper (and shoulder) 959.2

Note — Multiple internal injuries of sites classifiable to the same three- or four-digit category should be classified to that category.

Multiple injuries classifiable to different fourth-digit subdivisions of 861.- (heart and lung injuries) should be dealt with according to coding rules.

> *Note — Use the following fourth-digit subdivisions with categories 910-919:*
> *.0 Abrasion or friction burn without mention of infection*
> *.1 Abrasion or friction burn, infected*
> *.2 Blister without mention of infection*
> *.3 Blister, infected*
> *.4 Insect bite, nonvenomous, without mention of infection*
> *.5 Insect bite, nonvenomous, infected*
> *.6 Superficial foreign body (splinter) without major open wound and without mention of infection*
> *.7 Superficial foreign body (splinter) without major open wound, infected*
> *.8 Other and unspecified superficial injury without mention of infection*
> *.9 Other and unspecified superficial injury, infected*
> *For late effects of superficial injury, see category 906.2.*

- **Intussusception** (colon) (enteric) (intestine) (rectum) 560.0
  - appendix 543.9
  - congenital 751.5
  - fallopian tube 620.8
  - ileocecal 560.0
  - ileocolic 560.0
  - ureter (obstruction) 593.4
- **Invagination**
  - basilar 756.0
  - colon or intestine 560.0
- **Invalid** (since birth) 799.8
- **Invalidism** (chronic) 799.8
- **Inversion**
  - albumin-globulin (A-G) ratio 273.8
  - bladder 596.8
  - cecum (*see also* Intussusception) 560.0
  - cervix 622.8
  - nipple 611.79
    - congenital 757.6
    - puerperal, postpartum 676.3 [5th]
  - optic papilla 743.57
  - organ or site, congenital NEC — *see* Anomaly, specified type NEC
  - sleep rhythm 780.55
    - nonorganic origin 307.45
  - testis (congenital) 752.51
  - uterus (postinfectional) (postpartal, old) 621.7
    - chronic 621.7
    - complicating delivery 665.2 [5th]
      - affecting fetus or newborn 763.89
  - vagina — *see* Prolapse, vagina
- **Investigation**
  - allergens V72.7
  - clinical research V70.7
- **Inviability** — *see* Immaturity
- **Involuntary movement, abnormal** 781.0
- **Involution, involutional** — *see also* condition
  - breast, cystic or fibrocystic 610.1
  - depression (*see also* Psychosis, affective) 296.2 [5th]
    - recurrent episode 296.3 [5th]
    - single episode 296.2 [5th]
  - melancholia (*see also* Psychosis, affective) 296.2 [5th]
    - recurrent episode 296.3 [5th]
    - single episode 296.2 [5th]
  - ovary, senile 620.3
  - paranoid state (reaction) 297.2
  - paraphrenia (climacteric) (menopause) 297.2
  - psychosis 298.8
  - thymus failure 254.8
- **IQ**
  - under 20 318.2
  - 20-34 318.1
  - 35-49 318.0
  - 50-70 317
- **IRDS** 769
- **Irideremia** 743.45
- **Iridis rubeosis** 364.42
  - diabetic 250.5 [5th] *[364.42]*
- **Iridochoroiditis** (panuveitis) 360.12
- **Iridocyclitis** NEC 364.3
  - acute 364.00
    - primary 364.01
    - recurrent 364.02
  - chronic 364.10
    - in
      - lepromatous leprosy 030.0 *[364.11]*

- **Iridocyclitis** NEC — *continued*
  - chronic — *continued*
    - in — *continued*
      - sarcoidosis 135 *[364.11]*
      - tuberculosis (*see also* Tuberculosis) 017.3 [5th] *[364.11]*
  - due to allergy 364.04
  - endogenous 364.01
  - gonococcal 098.41
  - granulomatous 364.10
  - herpetic (simplex) 054.44
    - zoster 053.22
  - hypopyon 364.05
  - lens induced 364.23
  - nongranulomatous 364.00
  - primary 364.01
  - recurrent 364.02
  - rheumatic 364.10
  - secondary 364.04
    - infectious 364.03
    - noninfectious 364.04
  - subacute 364.00
    - primary 364.01
    - recurrent 364.02
  - sympathetic 360.11
  - syphilitic (secondary) 091.52
  - tuberculous (chronic) (*see also* Tuberculosis) 017.3 [5th] *[364.11]*
- **Iridocyclochoroiditis** (panuveitis) 360.12
- **Iridodialysis** 364.76
- **Iridodonesis** 364.8
- **Iridoplegia** (complete) (partial) (reflex) 379.49
- **Iridoschisis** 364.52
- **Iris** — *see* condition
- **Iritis** 364.3
  - acute 364.00
    - primary 364.01
    - recurrent 364.02
  - chronic 364.10
    - in
      - sarcoidosis 135 *[364.11]*
      - tuberculosis (*see also* Tuberculosis) 017.3 [5th] *[364.11]*
  - diabetic 250.5 [5th] *[364.42]*
  - due to
    - allergy 364.04
    - herpes simplex 054.44
    - leprosy 030.0 *[364.11]*
  - endogenous 364.01
  - gonococcal 098.41
  - gouty 274.89 *[364.11]*
  - granulomatous 364.10
  - hypopyon 364.05
  - lens induced 364.23
  - nongranulomatous 364.00
  - papulosa 095.8 *[364.11]*
  - primary 364.01
  - recurrent 364.02
  - rheumatic 364.10
  - secondary 364.04
    - infectious 364.03
    - noninfectious 364.04
  - subacute 364.00
    - primary 364.01
    - recurrent 364.02
  - sympathetic 360.11
  - syphilitic (secondary) 091.52
    - congenital 090.0 *[364.11]*
    - late 095.8 *[364.11]*

- **Iritis** — *continued*
  - tuberculous (*see also* Tuberculosis) 017.3 [5th] *[364.11]*
  - uratic 274.89 *[364.11]*
- **Iron**
  - deficiency anemia 280.9
  - metabolism disease 275.0
  - storage disease 275.0
- **Iron-miners' lung** 503
- **Irradiated enamel** (tooth, teeth) 521.8
- **Irradiation**
  - burn — *see* Burn, by site
  - effects, adverse 990
- **Irreducible, irreducibility** — *see* condition
- **Irregular, irregularity**
  - action, heart 427.9
  - alveolar process 525.8
  - bleeding NEC 626.4
  - breathing 786.09
  - colon 569.89
  - contour of cornea 743.41
    - acquired 371.70
  - dentin in pulp 522.3
  - eye movements NEC 379.59
  - menstruation (cause unknown) 626.4
  - periods 626.4
  - prostate 602.9
  - pupil 364.75
  - respiratory 786.09
  - septum (nasal) 470
  - shape, organ or site, congenital NEC — *see* Distortion
  - sleep-wake rhythm (non-24-hour) 780.55
    - nonorganic origin 307.45
  - vertebra 733.99
- **Irritability** (nervous) 799.2
  - bladder 596.8
    - neurogenic 596.54
      - with cauda equina syndrome 344.61
  - bowel (syndrome) 564.1
  - bronchial (*see also* Bronchitis) 490
  - cerebral, newborn 779.1
  - colon 564.1
    - psychogenic 306.4
  - duodenum 564.89
  - heart (psychogenic) 306.2
  - ileum 564.89
  - jejunum 564.89
  - myocardium 306.2
  - rectum 564.89
  - stomach 536.9
    - psychogenic 306.4
  - sympathetic (nervous system) (*see also* Neuropathy, peripheral, autonomic) 337.9
  - urethra 599.84
  - ventricular (heart) (psychogenic) 306.2
- **Irritable** — *see* Irritability
- **Irritation**
  - anus 569.49
  - axillary nerve 353.0
  - bladder 596.8
  - brachial plexus 353.0
  - brain (traumatic) (*see also* Injury, intracranial) 854.0 [5th]
    - nontraumatic — *see* Encephalitis
  - bronchial (*see also* Bronchitis) 490
  - cerebral (traumatic) (*see also* Injury, intracranial) 854.0 [5th]
    - nontraumatic — *see* Encephalitis

J

- **Jaccoud's nodular fibrositis, chronic** (Jaccoud's syndrome) 714.4
- **Jackson's**
  - membrane 751.4
  - paralysis or syndrome 344.89
  - veil 751.4
- **Jacksonian**
  - epilepsy (*see also* Epilepsy) 345.5 [5th]
  - seizures (focal) (*see also* Epilepsy) 345.5 [5th]
- **Jacob's ulcer** (M8090/3) — *see* Neoplasm, skin, malignant, by site
- **Jacquet's dermatitis** (diaper dermatitis) 691.0
- **Jadassohn's**
  - blue nevus (M8780/0) — *see* Neoplasm, skin, benign
  - disease (maculopapular erythroderma) 696.2
  - intraepidermal epithelioma (M8096/0) — *see* Neoplasm, skin, benign
- **Jadassohn-Lewandowski syndrome** (pachyonychia congenita) 757.5
- **Jadassohn-Pellizari's disease** (anetoderma) 701.3
- **Jadassohn-Tièche nevus** (M8780/0) — *see* Neoplasm, skin, benign
- **Jaffe-Lichtenstein** (-Uehlinger) syndrome 252.0
- **Jahnke's syndrome** (encephalocutaneous angiomatosis) 759.6
- **Jakob-Creutzfeldt disease or syndrome** 046.1
  - with dementia 046.1 *[294.1]*
- **Jaksch** (-Luzet) disease or syndrome (pseudoleukemia infantum) 285.8
- **Jamaican**
  - neuropathy 349.82
  - paraplegic tropical ataxic-spastic syndrome 349.82
- **Janet's disease** (psychasthenia) 300.89
- **Janiceps** 759.4
- **Jansky-Bielschowsky amaurotic familial idiocy** 330.1
- **Japanese**
  - B type encephalitis 062.0
  - river fever 081.2
  - seven-day fever 100.89
- **Jaundice** (yellow) 782.4
  - acholuric (familial) (splenomegalic) (*see also* Spherocytosis) 282.0
    - acquired 283.9
  - breast milk 774.39
  - catarrhal (acute) 070.1
    - with hepatic coma 070.0
    - chronic 571.9
    - epidemic — *see* Jaundice, epidemic
  - cholestatic (benign) 782.4
  - chronic idiopathic 277.4
  - epidemic (catarrhal) 070.1
    - with hepatic coma 070.0
    - leptospiral 100.0
    - spirochetal 100.0
  - febrile (acute) 070.1
    - with hepatic coma 070.0
    - leptospiral 100.0
    - spirochetal 100.0

- **Jaundice** (yellow) — *continued*
  - fetus or newborn 774.6
    - due to or associated with
      - ABO
        - antibodies 773.1
        - incompatibility, maternal/fetal 773.1
        - isoimmunization 773.1
      - absence or deficiency of enzyme system for bilirubin conjugation (congenital) 774.39
      - blood group incompatibility NEC 773.2
      - breast milk inhibitors to conjugation 774.39
        - associated with preterm delivery 774.2
      - bruising 774.1
      - Crigler-Najjar syndrome 277.4 *[774.31]*
      - delayed conjugation 774.30
        - associated with preterm delivery 774.2
        - development 774.39
      - drugs or toxins transmitted from mother 774.1
      - G-6-PD deficiency 282.2 *[774.0]*
      - galactosemia 271.1 *[774.5]*
      - Gilbert's syndrome 277.4 *[774.31]*
      - hepatocellular damage 774.4
      - hereditary hemolytic anemia (*see also* Anemia, hemolytic) 282.9 *[774.0]*
      - hypothyroidism, congenital 243 *[774.31]*
      - incompatibility, maternal/fetal NEC 773.2
      - infection 774.1
      - inspissated bile syndrome 774.4
      - isoimmunization NEC 773.2
      - mucoviscidosis 277.01 *[774.5]*
      - obliteration of bile duct, congenital 751.61 *[774.5]*
      - polycythemia 774.1
      - preterm delivery 774.2
      - red cell defect 282.9 *[774.0]*
      - Rh
        - antibodies 773.0
        - incompatibility, maternal/fetal 773.0
        - isoimmunization 773.0
      - spherocytosis (congenital) 282.0 *[774.0]*
      - swallowed maternal blood 774.1
    - physiological NEC 774.6
  - from injection, inoculation, infusion, or transfusion (blood) (plasma) (serum) (other substance) (onset within 8 months after administration) — *see* Hepatitis, viral
  - Gilbert's (familial nonhemolytic) 277.4
  - hematogenous 283.9
  - hemolytic (acquired) 283.9
    - congenital (*see also* Spherocytosis) 282.0
  - hemorrhagic (acute) 100.0
    - leptospiral 100.0
    - newborn 776.0
    - spirochetal 100.0
  - hepatocellular 573.8
  - homologous (serum) — *see* Hepatitis, viral
  - idiopathic, chronic 277.4
  - infectious (acute) (subacute) 070.1
    - with hepatic coma 070.0
    - leptospiral 100.0
    - spirochetal 100.0
  - leptospiral 100.0
  - malignant (*see also* Necrosis, liver) 570
  - newborn (physiological) (*see also* Jaundice, fetus or newborn) 774.6

- **Jaundice** (yellow) — *continued*
  - nonhemolytic, congenital familial (Gilbert's) 277.4
  - nuclear, newborn (*see also* Kernicterus of newborn) 774.7
  - obstructive NEC (*see also* Obstruction, biliary) 576.8
  - postimmunization — *see* Hepatitis, viral
  - posttransfusion — *see* Hepatitis, viral
  - regurgitation (*see also* Obstruction, biliary) 576.8
  - serum (homologous) (prophylactic) (therapeutic) — *see* Hepatitis, viral
  - spirochetal (hemorrhagic) 100.0
  - symptomatic 782.4
    - newborn 774.6
- **Jaw** — *see* condition
- **Jaw-blinking** 374.43
  - congenital 742.8
- **Jaw-winking phenomenon or syndrome** 742.8
- **Jealousy**
  - alcoholic 291.5
  - childhood 313.3
  - sibling 313.3
- **Jejunitis** (*see also* Enteritis) 558.9
- **Jejunostomy status** V44.4
- **Jejunum, jejunal** — *see* condition
- **Jensen's disease** 363.05
- **Jericho boil** 085.1
- **Jerks, myoclonic** 333.2
- **Jeune's disease or syndrome** (asphyxiating thoracic dystrophy) 756.4
- **Jigger disease** 134.1
- **Job's syndrome** (chronic granulomatous disease) 288.1
- **Jod-Basedow phenomenon** 242.8 [5th]
- **Johnson-Stevens disease** (erythema multiforme exudativum) 695.1
- **Joint** — *see also* condition
  - Charcôt's 094.0 *[713.5]*
  - false 733.82
  - flail — *see* Flail, joint
  - mice — *see* Loose, body, joint, by site
  - sinus to bone 730.9 [5th]
  - von Gies' 095.8
- **Jordan's anomaly or syndrome** 288.2
- **Josephs-Diamond-Blackfan anemia** (congenital hypoplastic) 284.0
- **Jumpers' knee** 727.2
- **Jungle yellow fever** 060.0
- **Jungling's disease** (sarcoidosis) 135
- **Junin virus hemorrhagic fever** 078.7
- **Juvenile** — *see also* condition
  - delinquent 312.9
    - group (*see also* Disturbance, conduct) 312.2 [5th]
    - neurotic 312.4

K

L

Note — Use the following fifth-digit subclassification with categories 851-854:

0 unspecified state of consciousness
1 with no loss of consciousness
2 with brief [less than one hour] loss of consciousness
3 with moderate [1-24 hours] loss of consciousness
4 with prolonged [more than 24 hours] loss of consciousness and return to pre-existing conscious level
5 with prolonged [more than 24 hours] loss of consciousness, without return to pre-existing conscious level

Use fifth-digit 5 to designate when a patient is unconscious and dies before regaining consciousness, regardless of the duration of the loss of consciousness

6 with loss of consciousness of unspecified duration
9 with concussion, unspecified

Lesion — *continued*
cranial nerve — *continued*
eleventh 352.4
twelfth 352.5
cystic — *see* Cyst
degenerative — *see* Degeneration
dermal (skin) 709.9
duodenum 537.89
with obstruction 537.3
eyelid 373.9
gasserian ganglion 350.8
gastric 537.89
gastroduodenal 537.89
gastrointestinal 569.89
glossopharyngeal nerve 352.2
heart (organic) — *see also* Disease, heart
vascular — *see* Disease, cardiovascular
helix (ear) 709.9
hyperchromic, due to pinta (carate) 103.1
hyperkeratotic (*see also* Hyperkeratosis) 701.1
hypoglossal nerve 352.5
hypopharynx 478.29
hypothalamic 253.9
ileocecal coil 569.89
ileum 569.89
iliohypogastric nerve 355.79
ilioinguinal nerve 355.79
in continuity — *see* Injury, nerve, by site
inflammatory — *see* Inflammation
intestine 569.89
intracerebral — *see* Lesion, brain
intrachiasmal (optic) (*see also* Lesion, chiasmal) 377.54
intracranial, space-occupying NEC 784.2
joint 719.90
ankle 719.97
elbow 719.92
foot 719.97
hand 719.94
hip 719.95
knee 719.96
multiple sites 719.99
pelvic region 719.95
sacroiliac (old) 724.6
shoulder (region) 719.91
specified site NEC 719.98
wrist 719.93
keratotic (*see also* Keratosis) 701.1
kidney (*see also* Disease, renal) 593.9
laryngeal nerve (recurrent) 352.3
leonine 030.0
lip 528.5
liver 573.8
lumbosacral
plexus 353.1
root (nerve) NEC 353.4
lung 518.89
coin 793.1
maxillary sinus 473.0
mitral — *see* Endocarditis, mitral
motor cortex 348.8
nerve (*see also* Disorder, nerve) 355.9
nervous system 349.9
congenital 742.9
nonallopathic NEC 739.9
in region (of)
abdomen 739.9
acromioclavicular 739.7
cervical, cervicothoracic 739.1
costochondral 739.8
costovertebral 739.8

Lesion — *continued*
nonallopathic NEC — *continued*
in region (of) — *continued*
extremity
lower 739.6
upper 739.7
head 739.0
hip 739.5
lower extremity 739.6
lumbar, lumbosacral 739.3
occipitocervical 739.0
pelvic 739.5
pubic 739.5
rib cage 739.8
sacral, sacrococcygeal, sacroiliac 739.4
sternochondral 739.8
sternoclavicular 739.7
thoracic, thoracolumbar 739.2
upper extremity 739.7
nose (internal) 478.1
obstructive — *see* Obstruction
obturator nerve 355.79
occlusive
artery — *see* Embolism, artery
organ or site NEC — *see* Disease, by site
osteolytic 733.90
paramacular, of retina 363.32
peptic 537.89
periodontal, due to traumatic occlusion 523.8
perirectal 569.49
peritoneum (granulomatous) 568.89
pigmented (skin) 709.00
pinta — *see* Pinta, lesions
polypoid — *see* Polyp
prechiasmal (optic) (*see also* Lesion, chiasmal) 377.54
primary — *see also* Syphilis, primary
carate 103.0
pinta 103.0
yaws 102.0
pulmonary 518.89
valve (*see also* Endocarditis, pulmonary) 424.3
pylorus 537.89
radiation NEC 990
radium NEC 990
rectosigmoid 569.89
retina, retinal — *see also* Retinopathy
vascular 362.17
retroperitoneal 568.89
romanus 720.1
sacroiliac (joint) 724.6
salivary gland 527.8
benign lymphoepithelial 527.8
saphenous nerve 355.79
secondary — *see* Syphilis, secondary
sigmoid 569.89
sinus (accessory) (nasal) (*see also* Sinusitis) 473.9
skin 709.9
suppurative 686.00
space-occupying, intracranial NEC 784.2
spinal cord 336.9
congenital 742.9
traumatic (complete) (incomplete) (transverse) — *see also* Injury, spinal, by site
with
broken
back — *see* Fracture, vertebra, by site, with spinal cord injury
neck — *see* Fracture, vertebra, cervical, with spinal cord injury

Lesion — *continued*
spinal cord — *continued*
traumatic (complete) (incomplete) (transverse) — *see also* Injury, spinal, by site — *continued*
with — *continued*
fracture, vertebra — *see* Fracture, vertebra, by site, with spinal cord injury
spleen 289.50
stomach 537.89
syphilitic — *see* Syphilis
tertiary — *see* Syphilis, tertiary
thoracic root (nerve) 353.3
tonsillar fossa 474.9
tooth, teeth 525.8
white spot 521.0
traumatic NEC (*see also* nature and site of injury) 959.9
tricuspid (valve) — *see* Endocarditis, tricuspid
trigeminal nerve 350.9
ulcerated or ulcerative — *see* Ulcer
uterus NEC 621.9
vagina 623.8
vagus nerve 352.3
valvular — *see* Endocarditis
vascular 459.9
affecting central nervous system (*see also* Lesion, cerebrovascular) 437.9
following trauma (*see also* Injury, blood vessel, by site) 904.9
retina 362.17
traumatic — *see* Injury, blood vessel, by site
umbilical cord 663.6 [5th]
affecting fetus or newborn 762.6
visual
cortex NEC (*see also* Disorder, visual, cortex) 377.73
pathway NEC (*see also* Disorder, visual, pathway) 377.63
warty — *see* Verruca
white spot, on teeth 521.0
x-ray NEC 990
Lethargic — *see* condition
Lethargy 780.79
Letterer-Siwe disease (acute histiocytosis X) (M9722/3) 202.5 [5th]
Leucinosis 270.3
Leucocoria 360.44
Leucosarcoma (M9850/3) 207.8 [5th]
Leukasmus 270.2
Leukemia, leukemic (congenital) (M9800/3) 208.9 [5th]

> *Note — Use the following fifth-digit subclassification for categories 203–208:*
> *0 without mention of remission*
> *1 with remission*

acute NEC (M9801/3) 208.0 [5th]
aleukemic NEC (M9804/3) 208.8 [5th]
granulocytic (M9864/3) 205.8 [5th]
basophilic (M9870/3) 205.1 [5th]
blast (cell) (M9801/3) 208.0 [5th]
blastic (M9801/3) 208.0 [5th]
granulocytic (M9861/3) 205.0 [5th]
chronic NEC (M9803/3) 208.1 [5th]
compound (M9810/3) 207.8 [5th]
eosinophilic (M9880/3) 205.1 [5th]
giant cell (M9910/3) 207.2 [5th]

- **Luxatio**
  - bulbi due to birth injury 767.8
  - coxae congenita (*see also* Dislocation, hip, congenital) 754.30
  - erecta — *see* Dislocation, shoulder
  - imperfecta — *see* Sprain, by site
  - perinealis — *see* Dislocation, hip
- **Luxation** — *see also* Dislocation, by site
  - eyeball 360.81
    - due to birth injury 767.8
    - lateral 376.36
  - genital organs (external) NEC — *see* Wound, open, genital organs
  - globe (eye) 360.81
    - lateral 376.36
  - lacrimal gland (postinfectional) 375.16
  - lens (old) (partial) 379.32
    - congenital 743.37
      - syphilitic 090.49 *[379.32]*
    - Marfan's disease 090.49
    - spontaneous 379.32
  - penis — *see* Wound, open, penis
  - scrotum — *see* Wound, open, scrotum
  - testis — *see* Wound, open, testis
- **L-xyloketosuria** 271.8
- **Lycanthropy** (*see also* Psychosis) 298.9
- **Lyell's disease or syndrome** (toxic epidermal necrolysis) 695.1
  - due to drug
    - correct substance properly administered 695.1
    - overdose or wrong substance given or taken 977.9
      - specified drug — *see* Table of Drugs and Chemicals
- **Lyme disease** 088.81
- **Lymph**
  - gland or node — *see* condition
  - scrotum (*see also* Infestation, filarial) 125.9
- **Lymphadenitis** 289.3
  - with
    - abortion — *see* Abortion, by type, with sepsis
    - ectopic pregnancy (*see also* categories 633.0-633.9) 639.0
    - molar pregnancy (*see also* categories 630-632) 639.0
  - acute 683
    - mesenteric 289.2
  - any site, except mesenteric 289.3
    - acute 683
    - chronic 289.1
    - mesenteric (acute) (chronic) (nonspecific) (subacute) 289.2
    - subacute 289.1
      - mesenteric 289.2
  - breast, puerperal, postpartum 675.2 [5th]
  - chancroidal (congenital) 099.0
  - chronic 289.1
    - mesenteric 289.2
  - dermatopathic 695.89
  - due to
    - anthracosis (occupational) 500
    - Brugia (Wuchereria) malayi 125.1
    - diphtheria (toxin) 032.89
    - lymphogranuloma venereum 099.1
    - Wuchereria bancrofti 125.0
  - following
    - abortion 639.0
    - ectopic or molar pregnancy 639.0
  - generalized 289.3
  - gonorrheal 098.89
  - granulomatous 289.1

- **Lymphadenitis** — *continued*
  - infectional 683
  - mesenteric (acute) (chronic) (nonspecific) (subacute) 289.2
    - due to Bacillus typhi 002.0
    - tuberculous (*see also* Tuberculosis) 014.8 [5th]
  - mycobacterial 031.8
  - purulent 683
  - pyogenic 683
  - regional 078.3
  - septic 683
  - streptococcal 683
  - subacute, unspecified site 289.1
  - suppurative 683
  - syphilitic (early) (secondary) 091.4
    - late 095.8
  - tuberculous — *see* Tuberculosis, lymph gland
  - venereal 099.1
- **Lymphadenoid goiter** 245.2
- **Lymphadenopathy** (general) 785.6
  - due to toxoplasmosis (acquired) 130.7
    - congenital (active) 771.2
- **Lymphadenopathy-associated virus** (disease) (illness) (infection) — *see* Human immunodeficiency virus (disease) (illness) (infection)
- **Lymphadenosis** 785.6
  - acute 075
- **Lymphangiectasis** 457.1
  - conjunctiva 372.8
  - postinfectional 457.1
  - scrotum 457.1
- **Lymphangiectatic elephantiasis, nonfilarial** 457.1
- **Lymphangioendothelioma** (M9170/0) 228.1
  - malignant (M9170/3) — *see* Neoplasm, connective tissue, malignant
- **Lymphangioma** (M9170/0) 228.1
  - capillary (M9171/0) 228.1
  - cavernous (M9172/0) 228.1
  - cystic (M9173/0) 228.1
  - malignant (M9170/3) — *see* Neoplasm, connective tissue, malignant
- **Lymphangiomyoma** (M9174/0) 228.1
- **Lymphangiomyomatosis** (M9174/1) — *see* Neoplasm, connective tissue, uncertain behavior
- **Lymphangiosarcoma** (M9170/3) — *see* Neoplasm, connective tissue, malignant
- **Lymphangitis** 457.2
  - with
    - abortion — *see* Abortion, by type, with sepsis
    - abscess — *see* Abscess, by site
    - cellulitis — *see* Abscess, by site
    - ectopic pregnancy (*see also* categories 633.0-633.9) 639.0
    - molar pregnancy (*see also* categories 630-632) 639.0
  - acute (with abscess or cellulitis) 682.9
    - specified site — *see* Abscess, by site
  - breast, puerperal, postpartum 675.2 [5th]
  - chancroidal 099.0
  - chronic (any site) 457.2
  - due to
    - Brugia (Wuchereria) malayi 125.1
    - Wuchereria bancrofti 125.0
  - following
    - abortion 639.0
    - ectopic or molar pregnancy 639.0
  - gangrenous 457.2

- **Lymphangitis** — *continued*
  - penis
    - acute 607.2
    - gonococcal (acute) 098.0
      - chronic or duration of 2 months or more 098.2
  - puerperal, postpartum, childbirth 670
  - strumous, tuberculous (*see also* Tuberculosis) 017.2 [5th]
  - subacute (any site) 457.2
  - tuberculous — *see* Tuberculosis, lymph gland
- **Lymphatic** (vessel) — *see* condition
- **Lymphatism** 254.8
  - scrofulous (*see also* Tuberculosis) 017.2 [5th]
- **Lymphectasia** 457.1
- **Lymphedema** (*see also* Elephantiasis) 457.1
  - acquired (chronic) 457.1
  - chronic hereditary 757.0
  - congenital 757.0
  - idiopathic hereditary 757.0
  - praecox 457.1
  - secondary 457.1
  - surgical NEC 997.99
    - postmastectomy (syndrome) 457.0
- **Lymph-hemangioma** (M9120/0) — *see* Hemangioma, by site
- **Lymphoblastic** — *see* condition
- **Lymphoblastoma** (diffuse) (M9630/3) 200.1 [5th]
  - giant follicular (M9690/3) 202.0 [5th]
  - macrofollicular (M9690/3) 202.0 [5th]
- **Lymphoblastosis, acute benign** 075
- **Lymphocele** 457.8
- **Lymphocythemia** 288.8
- **Lymphocytic** — *see also* condition
  - chorioencephalitis (acute) (serous) 049.0
  - choriomeningitis (acute) (serous) 049.0
- **Lymphocytoma** (diffuse) (malignant) (M9620/3) 200.1 [5th]
- **Lymphocytomatosis** (M9620/3) 200.1 [5th]
- **Lymphocytopenia** 288.8
- **Lymphocytosis** (symptomatic) 288.8
  - infectious (acute) 078.89
- **Lymphoepithelioma** (M8082/3) — *see* Neoplasm, by site, malignant
- **Lymphogranuloma** (malignant) (M9650/3) 201.9 [5th]
  - inguinale 099.1
  - venereal (any site) 099.1
    - with stricture of rectum 099.1
  - venereum 099.1
- **Lymphogranulomatosis** (malignant) (M9650/3) 201.9 [5th]
  - benign (Boeck's sarcoid) (Schaumann's) 135
  - Hodgkin's (M9650/3) 201.9 [5th]
- **Lymphoid** — *see* condition
- **Lympholeukoblastoma** (M9850/3) 207.8 [5th]
- **Lympholeukosarcoma** (M9850/3) 207.8 [5th]

M

Meningismus (infectional) (pneumococcal) 781.6
- due to serum or vaccine 997.09 *[321.8]*
- influenzal NEC 487.8

Meningitis (basal) (basic) (basilar) (brain) (cerebral) (cervical) (congestive) (diffuse) (hemorrhagic) (infantile) (membranous) (metastatic) (nonspecific) (pontine) (progressive) (simple) (spinal) (subacute) (sympathetica) (toxic) 322.9
- abacterial NEC (*see also* Meningitis, aseptic) 047.9
- actinomycotic 039.8 *[320.7]*
- adenoviral 049.1
- Aerobacter aerogenes 320.82
- anaerobes (cocci) (gram-negative) (gram-positive) (mixed) (NEC) 320.81
- arbovirus NEC 066.9 *[321.2]*
  - specified type NEC 066.8 *[321.2]*
- aseptic (acute) NEC 047.9
  - adenovirus 049.1
  - Coxsackie virus 047.0
  - due to
    - adenovirus 049.1
    - Coxsackie virus 047.0
    - ECHO virus 047.1
    - enterovirus 047.9
    - mumps 072.1
    - poliovirus (*see also* Poliomyelitis) 045.2 ✓5th *[321.2]*
  - ECHO virus 047.1
  - herpes (simplex) virus 054.72
    - zoster 053.0
  - leptospiral 100.81
  - lymphocytic choriomeningitis 049.0
  - noninfective 322.0
- Bacillus pyocyaneus 320.89
- bacterial NEC 320.9
  - anaerobic 320.81
  - gram-negative 320.82
    - anaerobic 320.81
- Bacteroides (fragilis) (oralis) (melaninogenicus) 320.81
- cancerous (M8000/6) 198.4
- candidal 112.83
- carcinomatous (M8010/6) 198.4
- caseous (*see also* Tuberculosis, meninges) 013.0 ✓5th
- cerebrospinal (acute) (chronic) (diplococcal) (endemic) (epidemic) (fulminant) (infectious) (malignant) (meningococcal) (sporadic) 036.0
  - carrier (suspected) of V02.59
- chronic NEC 322.2
- clear cerebrospinal fluid NEC 322.0
- Clostridium (haemolyticum) (novyi) NEC 320.81
- coccidioidomycosis 114.2
- Coxsackie virus 047.0
- cryptococcal 117.5 *[321.0]*
- diplococcal 036.0
  - gram-negative 036.0
  - gram-positive 320.1
- Diplococcus pneumoniae 320.1
- due to
  - actinomycosis 039.8 *[320.7]*
  - adenovirus 049.1
  - coccidiomycosis 114.2
  - enterovirus 047.9
    - specified NEC 047.8

Meningitis (basal) (basic) (basilar) (brain) (cerebral) (cervical) (congestive) (diffuse) (hemorrhagic) (infantile) (membranous) (metastatic) (nonspecific) (pontine) (progressive) (simple) (spinal) (subacute) (sympathetica) (toxic) — *continued*
- due to — *continued*
  - histoplasmosis (*see also* Histoplasmosis) 115.91
  - Listerosis 027.0 *[320.7]*
  - Lyme disease 088.81 *[320.7]*
  - moniliasis 112.83
  - mumps 072.1
  - neurosyphilis 094.2
  - nonbacterial organisms NEC 321.8
  - oidiomycosis 112.83
  - poliovirus (*see also* Poliomyelitis) 045.2 ✓5th *[321.2]*
  - preventive immunization, inoculation, or vaccination 997.09 *[321.8]*
  - sarcoidosis 135 *[321.4]*
  - sporotrichosis 117.1 *[321.1]*
  - syphilis 094.2
    - acute 091.81
    - congenital 090.42
    - secondary 091.81
  - trypanosomiasis (*see also* Trypanosomiasis) 086.9 *[321.3]*
  - whooping cough 033.9 *[320.7]*
- E. coli 320.82
- ECHO virus 047.1
- endothelial-leukocytic, benign, recurrent 047.9
- Enterobacter aerogenes 320.82
- enteroviral 047.9
  - specified type NEC 047.8
- enterovirus 047.9
  - specified NEC 047.8
- eosinophilic 322.1
- epidemic NEC 036.0
- Escherichia coli (E. coli) 320.82
- Eubacterium 320.81
- fibrinopurulent NEC 320.9
  - specified type NEC 320.89
- Friedländer (bacillus) 320.82
- fungal NEC 117.9 *[321.1]*
- Fusobacterium 320.81
- gonococcal 098.82
- gram-negative bacteria NEC 320.82
  - anaerobic 320.81
  - cocci 036.0
    - specified NEC 320.82
- gram-negative cocci NEC 036.0
  - specified NEC 320.82
- gram-positive cocci NEC 320.9
- H. influenzae 320.0
- herpes (simplex) virus 054.72
  - zoster 053.0
- infectious NEC 320.9
- influenzal 320.0
- Klebsiella pneumoniae 320.82
- late effect — *see* Late, effect, meningitis
- leptospiral (aseptic) 100.81
- Listerella (monocytogenes) 027.0 *[320.7]*
- Listeria monocytogenes 027.0 *[320.7]*
- lymphocytic (acute) (benign) (serous) 049.0
  - choriomeningitis virus 049.0

Meningitis (basal) (basic) (basilar) (brain) (cerebral) (cervical) (congestive) (diffuse) (hemorrhagic) (infantile) (membranous) (metastatic) (nonspecific) (pontine) (progressive) (simple) (spinal) (subacute) (sympathetica) (toxic) — *continued*
- meningococcal (chronic) 036.0
- Mima polymorpha 320.82
- Mollaret's 047.9
- monilial 112.83
- mumps (virus) 072.1
- mycotic NEC 117.9 *[321.1]*
- Neisseria 036.0
- neurosyphilis 094.2
- nonbacterial NEC (*see also* Meningitis, aseptic) 047.9
- nonpyogenic NEC 322.0
- oidiomycosis 112.83
- ossificans 349.2
- Peptococcus 320.81
- Peptostreptococcus 320.81
- pneumococcal 320.1
- poliovirus (*see also* Poliomyolitis) 045.2 ✓5th *[321.2]*
- Proprionibacterium 320.81
- Proteus morganii 320.82
- Pseudomonas (aeruginosa) (pyocyaneus) 320.82
- purulent NEC 320.9
  - specified organism NEC 320.89
- pyogenic NEC 320.9
  - specified organism NEC 320.89
- Salmonella 003.21
- septic NEC 320.9
  - specified organism NEC 320.89
- serosa circumscripta NEC 322.0
- serous NEC (*see also* Meningitis, aseptic) 047.9
  - lymphocytic 049.0
  - syndrome 348.2
- Serratia (marcescens) 320.82
- specified organism NEC 320.89
- sporadic cerebrospinal 036.0
- sporotrichosis 117.1 *[321.1]*
- staphylococcal 320.3
- sterile 997.09
- streptococcal (acute) 320.2
- suppurative 320.9
  - specified organism NEC 320.89
- syphilitic 094.2
  - acute 091.81
  - congenital 090.42
  - secondary 091.81
- torula 117.5 *[321.0]*
- traumatic (complication of injury) 958.8
- Treponema (denticola) (macrodenticum) 320.81
- trypanosomiasis 086.1 *[321.3]*
- tuberculous (*see also* Tuberculosis, meninges) 013.0 ✓5th
- typhoid 002.0 *[320.7]*
- Veillonella 320.81
- Vibrio vulnificus 320.82
- viral, virus NEC (*see also* Meningitis, aseptic) 047.9
- Wallgren's (*see also* Meningitis, aseptic) 047.9

Meningocele (congenital) (spinal) (*see also* Spina bifida) 741.9 ✓5th
- acquired (traumatic) 349.2
- cerebral 742.0
- cranial 742.0

- **Morbus** — *continued*
  - coxae 719.95
    - tuberculous (*see also* Tuberculosis) 015.1 ✓5th
  - hemorrhagicus neonatorum 776.0
  - maculosus neonatorum 772.6
  - renum 593.0
  - senilis (*see also* Osteoarthrosis) 715.9 ✓5th
- **Morel-Kraepelin disease** (*see also* Schizophrenia) 295.9 ✓5th
- **Morel-Moore syndrome** (hyperostosis frontalis interna) 733.3
- **Morel-Morgagni syndrome** (hyperostosis frontalis interna) 733.3
- **Morgagni**
  - cyst, organ, hydatid, or appendage 752.8
    - fallopian tube 752.11
  - disease or syndrome (hyperostosis frontalis interna) 733.3
- **Morgagni-Adams-Stokes syndrome** (syncope with heart block) 426.9
- **Morgagni-Stewart-Morel syndrome** (hyperostosis frontalis interna) 733.3
- **Moria** (*see also* Psychosis) 298.9
- **Morning sickness** 643.0 ✓5th
- **Moron** 317
- **Morphea** (guttate) (linear) 701.0
- **Morphine dependence** (*see also* Dependence) 304.0 ✓5th
- **Morphinism** (*see also* Dependence) 304.0 ✓5th
- **Morphinomania** (*see also* Dependence) 304.0 ✓5th
- **Morphoea** 701.0
- **Morquio** (-Brailsford) (-Ullrich) disease or syndrome (mucopolysaccharidosis IV) 277.5
  - kyphosis 277.5
- **Morris syndrome** (testicular feminization) 257.8
- **Morsus humanus** (open wound) — *see also* Wound, open, by site
  - skin surface intact — *see* Contusion
- **Mortification** (dry) (moist) (*see also* Gangrene) 785.4
- **Morton's**
  - disease 355.6
  - foot 355.6
  - metatarsalgia (syndrome) 355.6
  - neuralgia 355.6
  - neuroma 355.6
  - syndrome (metatarsalgia) (neuralgia) 355.6
  - toe 355.6
- **Morvan's disease** 336.0
- **Mosaicism, mosaic** (chromosomal) 758.9
  - autosomal 758.5
  - sex 758.81
- **Moschcowitz's syndrome** (thrombotic thrombocytopenic purpura) 446.6
- **Mother yaw** 102.0
- **Motion sickness** (from travel, any vehicle) (from roundabouts or swings) 994.6
- **Mottled teeth** (enamel) (endemic) (nonendemic) 520.3
- **Mottling enamel** (endemic) (nonendemic) (teeth) 520.3
- **Mouchet's disease** 732.5
- **Mould(s)** (in vitreous) 117.9
- **Moulders'**
  - bronchitis 502
  - tuberculosis (*see also* Tuberculosis) 011.4 ✓5th
- **Mounier-Kuhn syndrome** 494
- **Mountain**
  - fever — *see* Fever, mountain
  - sickness 993.2
    - with polycythemia, acquired 289.0
    - acute 289.0
  - tick fever 066.1
- **Mouse, joint** (*see also* Loose, body, joint) 718.1 ✓5th
  - knee 717.6
- **Mouth** — *see* condition
- **Movable**
  - coccyx 724.71
  - kidney (*see also* Disease, renal) 593.0
    - congenital 753.3
  - organ or site, congenital NEC — *see* Malposition, congenital
  - spleen 289.59
- **Movement**
  - abnormal (dystonic) (involuntary) 781.0
  - decreased fetal 655.7 ✓5th
  - paradoxical facial 374.43
- **Moya Moya disease** 437.5
- **Mozart's ear** 744.29
- **Mucha's disease** (acute parapsoriasis varioliformis) 696.2
- **Mucha-Haberman syndrome** (acute parapsoriasis varioliformis) 696.2
- **Mu-chain disease** 273.2
- **Mucinosis** (cutaneous) (papular) 701.8
- **Mucocele**
  - appendix 543.9
  - buccal cavity 528.9
  - gallbladder (*see also* Disease, gallbladder) 575.3
  - lacrimal sac 375.43
  - orbit (eye) 376.81
  - salivary gland (any) 527.6
  - sinus (accessory) (nasal) 478.1
  - turbinate (bone) (middle) (nasal) 478.1
  - uterus 621.8
- **Mucocutaneous lymph node syndrome** (acute) (febrile) (infantile) 446.1
- **Mucoenteritis** 564.1
- **Mucolipidosis I, II, III** 272.7
- **Mucopolysaccharidosis** (types 1-6) 277.5
  - cardiopathy 277.5 *[425.7]*
- **Mucormycosis** (lung) 117.7
- **Mucositis** — *see also* Inflammation, by site
  - necroticans agranulocytica 288.0
- **Mucous** — *see also* condition
  - patches (syphilitic) 091.3
    - congenital 090.0
- **Mucoviscidosis** 277.00
  - with meconium obstruction 277.01
- **Mucus**
  - asphyxia or suffocation (*see also* Asphyxia, mucus) 933.1
    - newborn 770.1
  - in stool 792.1
  - plug (*see also* Asphyxia, mucus) 933.1
    - aspiration, of newborn 770.1
    - tracheobronchial 519.1
      - newborn 770.1
- **Muguet** 112.0
- **Mulberry molars** 090.5
- **Mullerian mixed tumor** (M8950/3) — *see* Neoplasm, by site, malignant
- **Multicystic kidney** 753.19
- **Multilobed placenta** — *see* Placenta, abnormal
- **Multiparity** V61.5
  - affecting
    - fetus or newborn 763.89
    - management of
      - labor and delivery 659.4 ✓5th
      - pregnancy V23.3
  - requiring contraceptive management (*see also* Contraception) V25.9
- **Multipartita placenta** — *see* Placenta, abnormal
- **Multiple, multiplex** — *see also* condition
  - birth
    - affecting fetus or newborn 761.5
    - healthy liveborn — *see* Newborn, multiple
  - digits (congenital) 755.00
    - fingers 755.01
    - toes 755.02
  - organ or site NEC — *see* Accessory
  - personality 300.14
  - renal arteries 747.62
- **Mumps** 072.9
  - with complication 072.8
    - specified type NEC 072.79
  - encephalitis 072.2
  - hepatitis 072.71
  - meningitis (aseptic) 072.1
  - meningoencephalitis 072.2
  - oophoritis 072.79
  - orchitis 072.0
  - pancreatitis 072.3
  - polyneuropathy 072.72
  - vaccination, prophylactic (against) V04.6
- **Mumu** (*see also* Infestation, filarial) 125.9
- **Münchausen syndrome** 301.51
- **Münchmeyer's disease or syndrome** (exostosis luxurians) 728.11
- **Mural** — *see* condition
- **Murmur** (cardiac) (heart) (nonorganic) (organic) 785.2
  - abdominal 787.5
  - aortic (valve) (*see also* Endocarditis, aortic) 424.1
  - benign—*omit code*
  - cardiorespiratory 785.2
  - diastolic — *see* condition
  - Flint (*see also* Endocarditis, aortic) 424.1
  - functional—*omit code*
  - Graham Steell (pulmonic regurgitation) (*see also* Endocarditis, pulmonary) 424.3
  - innocent—*omit code*
  - insignificant—*omit code*
  - midsystolic 785.2
  - mitral (valve) — *see* Stenosis
  - physiologic — *see* condition
  - presystolic, mitral — *see* Insufficiency, mitral
  - pulmonic (valve) (*see also* Endocarditis, pulmonary) 424.3
  - Still's (vibratory)—*omit code*
  - systolic (valvular) — *see* condition
  - tricuspid (valve) — *see* Endocarditis, tricuspid
  - undiagnosed 785.2
  - valvular — *see* condition
  - vibratory—*omit code*
- **Murri's disease** (intermittent hemoglobinuria) 283.2
- **Muscae volitantes** 379.24
- **Muscle, muscular** — *see* condition
- **Musculoneuralgia** 729.1

N

	Malignant Primary	Malignant Secondary	Malignant Ca in situ	Benign	Uncertain Behavior	Unspecified
Neoplasm, neoplastic	199.1	199.1	234.9	229.9	238.9	239.9

Notes — 1. The list below gives the code numbers for neoplasms by anatomical site. For each site there are six possible code numbers according to whether the neoplasm in question is malignant, benign, in situ, of uncertain behavior, or of unspecified nature. The description of the neoplasm will often indicate which of the six columns is appropriate; e.g., malignant melanoma of skin, benign fibroadenoma of breast, carcinoma in situ of cervix uteri.

Where such descriptors are not present, the remainder of the Index should be consulted where guidance is given to the appropriate column for each morphological (histological) variety listed; e.g., Mesonephroma — see Neoplasm, malignant; Embryoma — see also Neoplasm, uncertain behavior; Disease, Bowen's — see Neoplasm, skin, in situ. However, the guidance in the Index can be overridden if one of the descriptors mentioned above is present; e.g., malignant adenoma of colon is coded to 153.9 and not to 211.3 as the adjective "malignant" overrides the Index entry "Adenoma — see also Neoplasm, benign."

*2. Sites marked with the sign * (e.g., face NEC*) should be classified to malignant neoplasm of skin of these sites if the variety of neoplasm is a squamous cell carcinoma or an epidermoid carcinoma and to benign neoplasm of skin of these sites if the variety of neoplasm is a papilloma (any type).*

	Malignant					
	Primary	Secondary	Ca in situ	Benign	Uncertain Behavior	Unspecified
Neoplasm, neoplastic — *continued*						
arachnoid (cerebral)	192.1	198.4	—	225.2	237.6	239.7
spinal	192.3	198.4	—	225.4	237.6	239.7
areola (female)	174.0	198.81	233.0	217	238.3	239.3
male	175.0	198.81	233.0	217	238.3	239.3
arm NEC*	195.4	198.89	232.6	229.8	238.8	239.8
artery — *see* Neoplasm, connective tissue						
aryepiglottic fold	148.2	198.89	230.0	210.8	235.1	239.0
hypopharyngeal aspect	148.2	198.89	230.0	210.8	235.1	239.0
laryngeal aspect	161.1	197.3	231.0	212.1	235.6	239.1
marginal zone	148.2	198.89	230.0	210.8	235.1	239.0
arytenoid (cartilage)	161.3	197.3	231.0	212.1	235.6	239.1
fold — *see* Neoplasm, aryepiglottic						
atlas	170.2	198.5	—	213.2	238.0	239.2
atrium, cardiac	164.1	198.89	—	212.7	238.8	239.8
auditory						
canal (external) (skin)	173.2	198.2	232.2	216.2	238.2	239.2
internal	160.1	197.3	231.8	212.0	235.9	239.1
nerve	192.0	198.4	—	225.1	237.9	239.7
tube	160.1	197.3	231.8	212.0	235.9	239.1
opening	147.2	198.89	230.0	210.7	235.1	239.0
auricle, ear	173.2	198.2	232.2	216.2	238.2	239.2
cartilage	171.0	198.89	—	215.0	238.1	239.2
auricular canal (external)	173.2	198.2	232.2	216.2	238.2	239.2
internal	160.1	197.3	231.8	212.0	235.9	239.1
autonomic nerve or nervous system NEC	171.9	198.89	—	215.9	238.1	239.2
axilla, axillary	195.1	198.89	234.8	229.8	238.8	239.8
fold	173.5	198.2	232.5	216.5	238.2	239.2
back NEC*	195.8	198.89	232.5	229.8	238.8	239.8
Bartholin's gland	184.1	198.82	233.3	221.2	236.3	239.5
basal ganglia	191.0	198.3	—	225.0	237.5	239.6
basis pedunculi	191.7	198.3	—	225.0	237.5	239.6
bile or biliary (tract)	156.9	197.8	230.8	211.5	235.3	239.0
canaliculi (biliferi) (intrahepatic)	155.1	197.8	230.8	211.5	235.3	239.0
canals, interlobular	155.1	197.8	230.8	211.5	235.3	239.0
contiguous sites	156.8	—	—	—	—	—
duct or passage (common) (cystic) (extrahepatic)	156.1	197.8	230.8	211.5	235.3	239.0
contiguous sites with gallbladder	156.8	—	—	—	—	—
interlobular	155.1	197.8	230.8	211.5	235.3	239.0
intrahepatic	155.1	197.8	230.8	211.5	235.3	239.0
and extrahepatic	156.9	197.8	230.8	211.5	235.3	239.0
bladder (urinary)	188.9	198.1	233.7	223.3	236.7	239.4
contiguous sites	188.8	—	—	—	—	—
dome	188.1	198.1	233.7	223.3	236.7	239.4
neck	188.5	198.1	233.7	223.3	236.7	239.4
orifice	188.9	198.1	233.7	223.3	236.7	239.4
ureteric	188.6	198.1	233.7	223.3	236.7	239.4
urethral	188.5	198.1	233.7	223.3	236.7	239.4
sphincter	188.8	198.1	233.7	223.3	236.7	239.4
trigone	188.0	198.1	233.7	223.3	236.7	239.4
urachus	188.7	—	233.7	223.3	236.7	239.4
wall	188.9	198.1	233.7	223.3	236.7	239.4
anterior	188.3	198.1	233.7	223.3	236.7	239.4
lateral	188.2	198.1	233.7	223.3	236.7	239.4
posterior	188.4	198.1	233.7	223.3	236.7	239.4
blood vessel — *see* Neoplasm, connective tissue						
bone (periosteum)	170.9	198.5	—	213.9	238.0	239.2

Note — Carcinomas and adenocarcinomas, of any type other than intraosseous or odontogenic, of the sites listed under "Neoplasm, bone" should be considered as constituting metastatic spread from an unspecified primary site and coded to 198.5 for morbidity coding and to 199.1 for underlying cause of death coding.

acetabulum	170.6	198.5	—	213.6	238.0	239.2
acromion (process)	170.4	198.5	—	213.4	238.0	239.2
ankle	170.8	198.5	—	213.8	238.0	239.2
arm NEC	170.4	198.5	—	213.4	238.0	239.2
astragalus	170.8	198.5	—	213.8	238.0	239.2
atlas	170.2	198.5	—	213.2	238.0	239.2

	Malignant			Benign	Uncertain Behavior	Unspecified
	Primary	Secondary	Ca in situ			
Neoplasm, neoplastic — *continued*						
bone (periosteum) — *continued*						
axis	170.2	198.5	—	213.2	238.0	239.2
back NEC	170.2	198.5	—	213.2	238.0	239.2
calcaneus	170.8	198.5	—	213.8	238.0	239.2
calvarium	170.0	198.5	—	213.0	238.0	239.2
carpus (any)	170.5	198.5	—	213.5	238.0	239.2
cartilage NEC	170.9	198.5	—	213.9	238.0	239.2
clavicle	170.3	198.5	—	213.3	238.0	239.2
clivus	170.0	198.5	—	213.0	238.0	239.2
coccygeal vertebra	170.6	198.5	—	213.6	238.0	239.2
coccyx	170.6	198.5	—	213.6	238.0	239.2
costal cartilage	170.3	198.5	—	213.3	238.0	239.2
costovertebral joint	170.3	198.5	—	213.3	238.0	239.2
cranial	170.0	198.5	—	213.0	238.0	239.2
cuboid	170.8	198.5	—	213.8	238.0	239.2
cuneiform	170.9	198.5	—	213.9	238.0	239.2
ankle	170.8	198.5	—	213.8	238.0	239.2
wrist	170.5	198.5	—	213.5	238.0	239.2
digital	170.9	198.5	—	213.9	238.0	239.2
finger	170.5	198.5	—	213.5	238.0	239.2
toe	170.8	198.5	—	213.8	238.0	239.2
elbow	170.4	198.5	—	213.4	238.0	239.2
ethmoid (labyrinth)	170.0	198.5	—	213.0	238.0	239.2
face	170.0	198.5	—	213.0	238.0	239.2
lower jaw	170.1	198.5	—	213.1	238.0	239.2
femur (any part)	170.7	198.5	—	213.7	238.0	239.2
fibula (any part)	170.7	198.5	—	213.7	238.0	239.2
finger (any)	170.5	198.5	—	213.5	238.0	239.2
foot	170.8	198.5	—	213.8	238.0	239.2
forearm	170.4	198.5	—	213.4	238.0	239.2
frontal	170.0	198.5	—	213.0	238.0	239.2
hand	170.5	198.5	—	213.5	238.0	239.2
heel	170.8	198.5	—	213.8	238.0	239.2
hip	170.6	198.5	—	213.6	238.0	239.2
humerus (any part)	170.4	198.5	—	213.4	238.0	239.2
hyoid	170.0	198.5	—	213.0	238.0	239.2
ilium	170.6	198.5	—	213.6	238.0	239.2
innominate	170.6	198.5	—	213.6	238.0	239.2
intervertebral cartilage or disc	170.2	198.5	—	213.2	238.0	239.2
ischium	170.6	198.5	—	213.6	238.0	239.2
jaw (lower)	170.1	198.5	—	213.1	238.0	239.2
upper	170.0	198.5	—	213.0	238.0	239.2
knee	170.7	198.5	—	213.7	238.0	239.2
leg NEC	170.7	198.5	—	213.7	238.0	239.2
limb NEC	170.9	198.5	—	213.9	238.0	239.2
lower (long bones)	170.7	198.5	—	213.7	238.0	239.2
short bones	170.8	198.5	—	213.8	238.0	239.2
upper (long bones)	170.4	198.5	—	213.4	238.0	239.2
short bones	170.5	198.5	—	213.5	238.0	239.2
long	170.9	198.5	—	213.9	238.0	239.2
lower limbs NEC	170.7	198.5	—	213.7	238.0	239.2
upper limbs NEC	170.4	198.5	—	213.4	238.0	239.2
malar	170.0	198.5	—	213.0	238.0	239.2
mandible	170.1	198.5	—	213.1	238.0	239.2
marrow NEC	202.9	198.5	—	—	—	238.7
mastoid	170.0	198.5	—	213.0	238.0	239.2
maxilla, maxillary (superior)	170.0	198.5	—	213.0	238.0	239.2
inferior	170.1	198.5	—	213.1	238.0	239.2
metacarpus (any)	170.5	198.5	—	213.5	238.0	239.2
metatarsus (any)	170.8	198.5	—	213.8	238.0	239.2
navicular (ankle)	170.8	198.5	—	213.8	238.0	239.2
hand	170.5	198.5	—	213.5	238.0	239.2
nose, nasal	170.0	198.5	—	213.0	238.0	239.2
occipital	170.0	198.5	—	213.0	238.0	239.2
orbit	170.0	198.5	—	213.0	238.0	239.2
parietal	170.0	198.5	—	213.0	238.0	239.2
patella	170.8	198.5	—	213.8	238.0	239.2
pelvic	170.6	198.5	—	213.6	238.0	239.2

	Malignant					
	Primary	Secondary	Ca in situ	Benign	Uncertain Behavior	Unspecified
Neoplasm, neoplastic — *continued*						
bone (periosteum) — *continued*						
phalanges	170.9	198.5	—	213.9	238.0	239.2
foot	170.8	198.5	—	213.8	238.0	239.2
hand	170.5	198.5	—	213.5	238.0	239.2
pubic	170.6	198.5	—	213.6	238.0	239.2
radius (any part)	170.4	198.5	—	213.4	238.0	239.2
rib	170.3	198.5	—	213.3	238.0	239.2
sacral vertebra	170.6	198.5	—	213.6	238.0	239.2
sacrum	170.6	198.5	—	213.6	238.0	239.2
scaphoid (of hand)	170.5	198.5	—	213.5	238.0	239.2
of ankle	170.8	198.5	—	213.8	238.0	239.2
scapula (any part)	170.4	198.5	—	213.4	238.0	239.2
sella turcica	170.0	198.5	—	213.0	238.0	239.2
short	170.9	198.5	—	213.9	238.0	239.2
lower limb	170.8	198.5	—	213.8	238.0	239.2
upper limb	170.5	198.5	—	213.5	238.0	239.2
shoulder	170.4	198.5	—	213.4	238.0	239.2
skeleton, skeletal NEC	170.9	198.5	—	213.9	238.0	239.2
skull	170.0	198.5	—	213.0	238.0	239.2
sphenoid	170.0	198.5	—	213.0	238.0	239.2
spine, spinal (column)	170.2	198.5	—	213.2	238.0	239.2
coccyx	170.6	198.5	—	213.6	238.0	239.2
sacrum	170.6	198.5	—	213.6	238.0	239.2
sternum	170.3	198.5	—	213.3	238.0	239.2
tarsus (any)	170.8	198.5	—	213.8	238.0	239.2
temporal	170.0	198.5	—	213.0	238.0	239.2
thumb	170.5	198.5	—	213.5	238.0	239.2
tibia (any part)	170.7	198.5	—	213.7	238.0	239.2
toe (any)	170.8	198.5	—	213.8	238.0	239.2
trapezium	170.5	198.5	—	213.5	238.0	239.2
trapezoid	170.5	198.5	—	213.5	238.0	239.2
turbinate	170.0	198.5	—	213.0	238.0	239.2
ulna (any part)	170.4	198.5	—	213.4	238.0	239.2
unciform	170.5	198.5	—	213.5	238.0	239.2
vertebra (column)	170.2	198.5	—	213.2	238.0	239.2
coccyx	170.6	198.5	—	213.6	238.0	239.2
sacrum	170.6	198.5	—	213.6	238.0	239.2
vomer	170.0	198.5	—	213.0	238.0	239.2
wrist	170.5	198.5	—	213.5	238.0	239.2
xiphoid process	170.3	198.5	—	213.3	238.0	239.2
zygomatic	170.0	198.5	—	213.0	238.0	239.2
book-leaf (mouth)	145.8	198.89	230.0	210.4	235.1	239.0
bowel — *see* Neoplasm, intestine						
brachial plexus	171.2	198.89	—	215.2	238.1	239.2
brain NEC	191.9	198.3	—	225.0	237.5	239.6
basal ganglia	191.0	198.3	—	225.0	237.5	239.6
cerebellopontine angle	191.6	198.3	—	225.0	237.5	239.6
cerebellum NOS	191.6	198.3	—	225.0	237.5	239.6
cerebrum	191.0	198.3	—	225.0	237.5	239.6
choroid plexus	191.5	198.3	—	225.0	237.5	239.6
contiguous sites	191.8	—	—	—	—	—
corpus callosum	191.8	198.3	—	225.0	237.5	239.6
corpus striatum	191.0	198.3	—	225.0	237.5	239.6
cortex (cerebral)	191.0	198.3	—	225.0	237.5	239.6
frontal lobe	191.1	198.3	—	225.0	237.5	239.6
globus pallidus	191.0	198.3	—	225.0	237.5	239.6
hippocampus	191.2	198.3	—	225.0	237.5	239.6
hypothalamus	191.0	198.3	—	225.0	237.5	239.6
internal capsule	191.0	198.3	—	225.0	237.5	239.6
medulla oblongata	191.7	198.3	—	225.0	237.5	239.6
meninges	192.1	198.4	—	225.2	237.6	239.7
midbrain	191.7	198.3	—	225.0	237.5	239.6
occipital lobe	191.4	198.3	—	225.0	237.5	239.6
parietal lobe	191.3	198.3	—	225.0	237.5	239.6
peduncle	191.7	198.3	—	225.0	237.5	239.6
pons	191.7	198.3	—	225.0	237.5	239.6
stem	191.7	198.3	—	225.0	237.5	239.6
tapetum	191.8	198.3	—	225.0	237.5	239.6

	Malignant					
	Primary	Secondary	Ca in situ	Benign	Uncertain Behavior	Unspecified
Neoplasm, neoplastic — *continued*						
carina (bronchus) (trachea)	162.2	197.0	231.2	212.3	235.7	239.1
carotid (artery)	171.0	198.89	—	215.0	238.1	239.2
body	194.5	198.89	—	227.5	237.3	239.7
carpus (any bone)	170.5	198.5	—	213.5	238.0	239.2
cartilage (articular) (joint) NEC — *see also* Neoplasm, bone	170.9	198.5	—	213.9	238.0	239.2
arytenoid	161.3	197.3	231.0	212.1	235.6	239.1
auricular	171.0	198.89	—	215.0	238.1	239.2
bronchi	162.2	197.3	—	212.3	235.7	239.1
connective tissue — *see* Neoplasm, connective tissue						
costal	170.3	198.5	—	213.3	238.0	239.2
cricoid	161.3	197.3	231.0	212.1	235.6	239.1
cuneiform	161.3	197.3	231.0	212.1	235.6	239.1
ear (external)	171.0	198.89	—	215.0	238.1	239.2
ensiform	170.3	198.5	—	213.3	238.0	239.2
epiglottis	161.1	197.3	231.0	212.1	235.6	239.1
anterior surface	146.4	198.89	230.0	210.6	235.1	239.0
eyelid	171.0	198.89	—	215.0	238.1	239.2
intervertebral	170.2	198.5	—	213.2	238.0	239.2
larynx, laryngeal	161.3	197.3	231.0	212.1	235.6	239.1
nose, nasal	160.0	197.3	231.8	212.0	235.9	239.1
pinna	171.0	198.89	—	215.0	238.1	239.2
rib	170.3	198.5	—	213.3	238.0	239.2
semilunar (knee)	170.7	198.5	—	213.7	238.0	239.2
thyroid	161.3	197.3	231.0	212.1	235.6	239.1
trachea	162.0	197.3	231.1	212.2	235.7	239.1
cauda equina	192.2	198.3	—	225.3	237.5	239.7
cavity						
buccal	145.9	198.89	230.0	210.4	235.1	239.0
nasal	160.0	197.3	231.8	212.0	235.9	239.1
oral	145.9	198.89	230.0	210.4	235.1	239.0
peritoneal	158.9	197.6	—	211.8	235.4	239.0
tympanic	160.1	197.3	231.8	212.0	235.9	239.1
cecum	153.4	197.5	230.3	211.3	235.2	239.0
central						
nervous system — *see* Neoplasm, nervous system						
white matter	191.0	198.3	—	225.0	237.5	239.6
cerebellopontine (angle)	191.6	198.3	—	225.0	237.5	239.6
cerebellum, cerebellar	191.6	198.3	—	225.0	237.5	239.6
cerebrum, cerebral (cortex) (hemisphere) (white matter)	191.0	198.3	—	225.0	237.5	239.6
meninges	192.1	198.4	—	225.2	237.6	239.7
peduncle	191.7	198.3	—	225.0	237.5	239.6
ventricle (any)	191.5	198.3	—	225.0	237.5	239.6
cervical region	195.0	198.89	234.8	229.8	238.8	239.8
cervix (cervical) (uteri) (uterus)	180.9	198.82	233.1	219.0	236.0	239.5
canal	180.0	198.82	233.1	219.0	236.0	239.5
contiguous sites	180.8	—	—	—	—	—
endocervix (canal) (gland)	180.0	198.82	233.1	219.0	236.0	239.5
exocervix	180.1	198.82	233.1	219.0	236.0	239.5
external os	180.1	198.82	233.1	219.0	236.0	239.5
internal os	180.0	198.82	233.1	219.0	236.0	239.5
nabothian gland	180.0	198.82	233.1	219.0	236.0	239.5
squamocolumnar junction	180.8	198.82	233.1	219.0	236.0	239.5
stump	180.8	198.82	233.1	219.0	236.0	239.5
cheek	195.0	198.89	234.8	229.8	238.8	239.8
external	173.3	198.2	232.3	216.3	238.2	239.2
inner aspect	145.0	198.89	230.0	210.4	235.1	239.0
internal	145.0	198.89	230.0	210.4	235.1	239.0
mucosa	145.0	198.89	230.0	210.4	235.1	239.0
chest (wall) NEC	195.1	198.89	234.8	229.8	238.8	239.8
chiasma opticum	192.0	198.4	—	225.1	237.9	239.7
chin	173.3	198.2	232.3	216.3	238.2	239.2
choana	147.3	198.89	230.0	210.7	235.1	239.0
cholangiole	155.1	197.8	230.8	211.5	235.3	239.0
choledochal duct	156.1	197.8	230.8	211.5	235.3	239.0
choroid	190.6	198.4	234.0	224.6	238.8	239.8
plexus	191.5	198.3	—	225.0	237.5	239.6

	Malignant					
	Primary	**Secondary**	**Ca in situ**	**Benign**	**Uncertain Behavior**	**Unspecified**
Neoplasm, neoplastic — *continued*						
ciliary body	190.0	198.4	234.0	224.0	238.8	239.8
clavicle	170.3	198.5	—	213.3	238.0	239.2
clitoris	184.3	198.82	233.3	221.2	236.3	239.5
clivus	170.0	198.5	—	213.0	238.0	239.2
cloacogenic zone	154.8	197.5	230.7	211.4	235.5	239.0
coccygeal						
body or glomus	194.6	198.89	—	227.6	237.3	239.7
vertebra	170.6	198.5	—	213.6	238.0	239.2
coccyx	170.6	198.5	—	213.6	238.0	239.2
colon — *see also* Neoplasm, intestine, large and rectum	154.0	197.5	230.4	211.4	235.2	239.0
column, spinal — *see* Neoplasm, spine						
columnella	173.3	198.2	232.3	216.3	238.2	239.2
commissure						
labial, lip	140.6	198.89	230.0	210.4	235.1	239.0
laryngeal	161.0	197.3	231.0	212.1	235.6	239.1
common (bile) duct	156.1	197.8	230.8	211.5	235.3	239.0
concha	173.2	198.2	232.2	216.2	238.2	239.2
nose	160.0	197.3	231.8	212.0	235.9	239.1
conjunctiva	190.3	198.4	234.0	224.3	238.8	239.8
connective tissue NEC	171.9	198.89	—	215.9	238.1	239.2

Note — For neoplasms of connective tissue (blood vessel, bursa, fascia, ligament, muscle, peripheral nerves, sympathetic and parasympathetic nerves and ganglia, synovia, tendon, etc.) or of morphological types that indicate connective tissue, code according to the list under "Neoplasm, connective tissue;" for sites that do not appear in this list, code to neoplasm of that site; e.g.,

liposarcoma, shoulder 171.2

leiomyosarcoma, stomach 151.9

neurofibroma, chest wall 215.4

Morphological types that indicate connective tissue appear in their proper place in the alphabetic index with the instruction "see Neoplasm, connective tissue…."

	Primary	Secondary	Ca in situ	Benign	Uncertain Behavior	Unspecified
abdomen	171.5	198.89	—	215.5	238.1	239.2
abdominal wall	171.5	198.89	—	215.5	238.1	239.2
ankle	171.3	198.89	—	215.3	238.1	239.2
antecubital fossa or space	171.2	198.89	—	215.2	238.1	239.2
arm	171.2	198.89	—	215.2	238.1	239.2
auricle (ear)	171.0	198.89	—	215.0	238.1	239.2
axilla	171.4	198.89	—	215.4	238.1	239.2
back	171.7	198.89	—	215.7	238.1	239.2
breast (female) (*see also* Neoplasm, breast)	174.9	198.81	233.0	217	238.3	239.3
male	175.9	198.81	233.0	217	238.3	239.3
buttock	171.6	198.89	—	215.6	238.1	239.2
calf	171.3	198.89	—	215.3	238.1	239.2
cervical region	171.0	198.89	—	215.0	238.1	239.2
cheek	171.0	198.89	—	215.0	238.1	239.2
chest (wall)	171.4	198.89	—	215.4	238.1	239.2
chin	171.0	198.89	—	215.0	238.1	239.2
contiguous sites	171.8	—	—	—	—	—
diaphragm	171.4	198.89	—	215.4	238.1	239.2
ear (external)	171.0	198.89	—	215.0	238.1	239.2
elbow	171.2	198.89	—	215.2	238.1	239.2
extrarectal	171.6	198.89	—	215.6	238.1	239.2
extremity	171.8	198.89	—	215.8	238.1	239.2
lower	171.3	198.89	—	215.3	238.1	239.2
upper	171.2	198.89	—	215.2	238.1	239.2
eyelid	171.0	198.89	—	215.0	238.1	239.2
face	171.0	198.89	—	215.0	238.1	239.2
finger	171.2	198.89	—	215.2	238.1	239.2
flank	171.7	198.89	—	215.7	238.1	239.2
foot	171.3	198.89	—	215.3	238.1	239.2
forearm	171.2	198.89	—	215.2	238.1	239.2
forehead	171.0	198.89	—	215.0	238.1	239.2
gluteal region	171.6	198.89	—	215.6	238.1	239.2
great vessels NEC	171.4	198.89	—	215.4	238.1	239.2
groin	171.6	198.89	—	215.6	238.1	239.2
hand	171.2	198.89	—	215.2	238.1	239.2

	Malignant					
	Primary	Secondary	Ca in situ	Benign	Uncertain Behavior	Unspecified
Neoplasm, neoplastic — *continued*						
connective tissue NEC — *continued*						
head	171.0	198.89	—	215.0	238.1	239.2
heel	171.3	198.89	—	215.3	238.1	239.2
hip	171.3	198.89	—	215.3	238.1	239.2
hypochondrium	171.5	198.89	—	215.5	238.1	239.2
iliopsoas muscle	171.6	198.89	—	215.5	238.1	239.2
infraclavicular region	171.4	198.89	—	215.4	238.1	239.2
inguinal (canal) (region)	171.6	198.89	—	215.6	238.1	239.2
intrathoracic	171.4	198.89	—	215.4	238.1	239.2
ischorectal fossa	171.6	198.89	—	215.6	238.1	239.2
jaw	143.9	198.89	230.0	210.4	235.1	239.0
knee	171.3	198.89	—	215.3	238.1	239.2
leg	171.3	198.89	—	215.3	238.1	239.2
limb NEC	171.9	198.89	—	215.8	238.1	239.2
lower	171.3	198.89	—	215.3	238.1	239.2
upper	171.2	198.89	—	215.2	238.1	239.2
nates	171.6	198.89	—	215.6	238.1	239.2
neck	171.0	198.89	—	215.0	238.1	239.2
orbit	190.1	198.4	234.0	224.1	238.8	239.8
pararectal	171.6	198.89	—	215.6	238.1	239.2
para-urethral	171.6	198.89	—	215.6	238.1	239.2
paravaginal	171.6	198.89	—	215.6	238.1	239.2
pelvis (floor)	171.6	198.89	—	215.6	238.1	239.2
pelvo-abdominal	171.8	198.89	—	215.8	238.1	239.2
perineum	171.6	198.89	—	215.6	238.1	239.2
perirectal (tissue)	171.6	198.89	—	215.6	238.1	239.2
periurethral (tissue)	171.6	198.89	—	215.6	238.1	239.2
popliteal fossa or space	171.3	198.89	—	215.3	238.1	239.2
presacral	171.6	198.89	—	215.6	238.1	239.2
psoas muscle	171.5	198.89	—	215.5	238.1	239.2
pterygoid fossa	171.0	198.89	—	215.0	238.1	239.2
rectovaginal septum or wall	171.6	198.89	—	215.6	238.1	239.2
rectovesical	171.6	198.89	—	215.6	238.1	239.2
retroperitoneum	158.0	197.6	—	211.8	235.4	239.0
sacrococcygeal region	171.6	198.89	—	215.6	238.1	239.2
scalp	171.0	198.89	—	215.0	238.1	239.2
scapular region	171.4	198.89	—	215.4	238.1	239.2
shoulder	171.2	198.89	—	215.2	238.1	239.2
skin (dermis) NEC	173.9	198.2	232.9	216.9	238.2	239.2
submental	171.0	198.89	—	215.0	238.1	239.2
supraclavicular region	171.0	198.89	—	215.0	238.1	239.2
temple	171.0	198.89	—	215.0	238.1	239.2
temporal region	171.0	198.89	—	215.0	238.1	239.2
thigh	171.3	198.89	—	215.3	238.1	239.2
thoracic (duct) (wall)	171.4	198.89	—	215.4	238.1	239.2
thorax	171.4	198.89	—	215.4	238.1	239.2
thumb	171.2	198.89	—	215.2	238.1	239.2
toe	171.3	198.89	—	215.3	238.1	239.2
trunk	171.7	198.89	—	215.7	238.1	239.2
umbilicus	171.5	198.89	—	215.5	238.1	239.2
vesicorectal	171.6	198.89	—	215.6	238.1	239.2
wrist	171.2	198.89	—	215.2	238.1	239.2
conus medullaris	192.2	198.3	—	225.3	237.5	239.7
cord (true) (vocal)	161.0	197.3	231.0	212.1	235.6	239.1
false	161.1	197.3	231.0	212.1	235.6	239.1
spermatic	187.6	198.82	233.6	222.8	236.6	239.5
spinal (cervical) (lumbar) (thoracic)	192.2	198.3	—	225.3	237.5	239.7
cornea (limbus)	190.4	198.4	234.0	224.4	238.8	239.8
corpus						
albicans	183.0	198.6	233.3	220	236.2	239.5
callosum, brain	191.8	198.3	—	225.0	237.5	239.6
cavernosum	187.3	198.82	233.5	222.1	236.6	239.5
gastric	151.4	197.8	230.2	211.1	235.2	239.0
penis	187.3	198.82	233.5	222.1	236.6	239.5
striatum, cerebrum	191.0	198.3	—	225.0	237.5	239.6
uteri	182.0	198.82	233.2	219.1	236.0	239.5
isthmus	182.1	198.82	233.2	219.1	236.0	239.5

	Malignant Primary	Malignant Secondary	Malignant Ca in situ	Benign	Uncertain Behavior	Unspecified
Neoplasm, neoplastic — *continued*						
cortex						
adrenal	194.0	198.7	234.8	227.0	237.2	239.7
cerebral	191.0	198.3	—	225.0	237.5	239.6
costal cartilage	170.3	198.5	—	213.3	238.0	239.2
costovertebral joint	170.3	198.5	—	213.3	238.0	239.2
Cowper's gland	189.3	198.1	233.9	223.81	236.99	239.5
cranial (fossa, any)	191.9	198.3	—	225.0	237.5	239.6
meninges	192.1	198.4	—	225.2	237.6	239.7
nerve (any)	192.0	198.4	—	225.1	237.9	239.7
craniobuccal pouch	194.3	198.89	234.8	227.3	237.0	239.7
craniopharyngeal (duct) (pouch)	194.3	198.89	234.8	227.3	237.0	239.7
cricoid	148.0	198.89	230.0	210.8	235.1	239.0
cartilage	161.3	197.3	231.0	212.1	235.6	239.1
cricopharynx	148.0	198.89	230.0	210.8	235.1	239.0
crypt of Morgagni	154.8	197.5	230.7	211.4	235.2	239.0
crystalline lens	190.0	198.4	234.0	224.0	238.8	239.8
cul-de-sac (Douglas')	158.8	197.6	—	211.8	235.4	239.0
cuneiform cartilage	161.3	197.3	231.0	212.1	235.6	239.1
cutaneous — *see* Neoplasm, skin						
cutis — *see* Neoplasm, skin						
cystic (bile) duct (common)	156.1	197.8	230.8	211.5	235.3	239.0
dermis — *see* Neoplasm, skin						
diaphragm	171.4	198.89	—	215.4	238.1	239.2
digestive organs, system, tube, or tract NEC	159.9	197.8	230.9	211.9	235.5	239.0
contiguous sites with peritoneum	159.8	—	—	—	—	—
disc, intervertebral	170.2	198.5	—	213.2	238.0	239.2
disease, generalized	199.0	199.0	234.9	229.9	238.9	199.0
disseminated	199.0	199.0	234.9	229.9	238.9	199.0
Douglas' cul-de-sac or pouch	158.8	197.6	—	211.8	235.4	239.0
duodenojejunal junction	152.8	197.4	230.7	211.2	235.2	239.0
duodenum	152.0	197.4	230.7	211.2	235.2	239.0
dura (cranial) (mater)	192.1	198.4	—	225.2	237.6	239.7
cerebral	192.1	198.4	—	225.2	237.6	239.7
spinal	192.3	198.4	—	225.4	237.6	239.7
ear (external)	173.2	198.2	232.2	216.2	238.2	239.2
auricle or auris	173.2	198.2	232.2	216.2	238.2	239.2
canal, external	173.2	198.2	232.2	216.2	238.2	239.2
cartilage	171.0	198.89	—	215.0	238.1	239.2
external meatus	173.2	198.2	232.2	216.2	238.2	239.2
inner	160.1	197.3	231.8	212.0	235.9	239.1
lobule	173.2	198.2	232.2	216.2	238.2	239.2
middle	160.1	197.3	231.8	212.0	235.9	239.1
contiguous sites with accessory sinuses or nasal cavities	160.8	—	—	—	—	—
skin	173.2	198.2	232.2	216.2	238.2	239.2
earlobe	173.2	198.2	232.2	216.2	238.2	239.2
ejaculatory duct	187.8	198.82	233.6	222.8	236.6	239.5
elbow NEC*	195.4	198.89	232.6	229.8	238.8	239.8
endocardium	164.1	198.89	—	212.7	238.8	239.8
endocervix (canal) (gland)	180.0	198.82	233.1	219.0	236.0	239.5
endocrine gland NEC	194.9	198.89	—	227.9	237.4	239.7
pluriglandular NEC	194.8	198.89	234.8	227.8	237.4	239.7
endometrium (gland) (stroma)	182.0	198.82	233.2	219.1	236.0	239.5
ensiform cartilage	170.3	198.5	—	213.3	238.0	239.2
enteric — *see* Neoplasm, intestine						
ependyma (brain)	191.5	198.3	—	225.0	237.5	239.6
epicardium	164.1	198.89	—	212.7	238.8	239.8
epididymis	187.5	198.82	233.6	222.3	236.6	239.5
epidural	192.9	198.4	—	225.9	237.9	239.7
epiglottis	161.1	197.3	231.0	212.1	235.6	239.1
anterior aspect of surface	146.4	198.89	230.0	210.6	235.1	239.0
cartilage	161.3	197.3	231.0	212.1	235.6	239.1
free border (margin)	146.4	198.89	230.0	210.6	235.1	239.0
junctional region	146.5	198.89	230.0	210.6	235.1	239.0
posterior (laryngeal) surface	161.1	197.3	231.0	212.1	235.6	239.1
suprahyoid portion	161.1	197.3	231.0	212.1	235.6	239.1

	Malignant Primary	Malignant Secondary	Malignant Ca in situ	Benign	Uncertain Behavior	Unspecified
Neoplasm, neoplastic — *continued*						
esophagogastric junction	151.0	197.8	230.2	211.1	235.2	239.0
esophagus	150.9	197.8	230.1	211.0	235.5	239.0
abdominal	150.2	197.8	230.1	211.0	235.5	239.0
cervical	150.0	197.8	230.1	211.0	235.5	239.0
contiguous sites	150.8	—	—	—	—	—
distal (third)	150.5	197.8	230.1	211.0	235.5	239.0
lower (third)	150.5	197.8	230.1	211.0	235.5	239.0
middle (third)	150.4	197.8	230.1	211.0	235.5	239.0
proximal (third)	150.3	197.8	230.1	211.0	235.5	239.0
specified part NEC	150.8	197.8	230.1	211.0	235.5	239.0
thoracic	150.1	197.8	230.1	211.0	235.5	239.0
upper (third)	150.3	197.8	230.1	211.0	235.5	239.0
ethmoid (sinus)	160.3	197.3	231.8	212.0	235.9	239.1
bone or labyrinth	170.0	198.5	—	213.0	238.0	239.2
Eustachian tube	160.1	197.3	231.8	212.0	235.9	239.1
exocervix	180.1	198.82	233.1	219.0	236.0	239.5
external						
meatus (ear)	173.2	198.2	232.2	216.2	238.2	239.2
os, cervix uteri	180.1	198.82	233.1	219.0	236.0	239.5
extradural	192.9	198.4	—	225.9	237.9	239.7
extrahepatic (bile) duct	156.1	197.8	230.8	211.5	235.3	239.0
contiguous sites with gallbladder	156.8	—	—	—	—	—
extraocular muscle	190.1	198.4	234.0	224.1	238.8	239.8
extrarectal	195.3	198.89	234.8	229.8	238.8	239.8
extremity*	195.8	198.89	232.8	229.8	238.8	239.8
lower*	195.5	198.89	232.7	229.8	238.8	239.8
upper*	195.4	198.89	232.6	229.8	238.8	239.8
eye NEC	190.9	198.4	234.0	224.9	238.8	239.8
contiguous sites	190.8	—	—	—	—	—
specified sites NEC	190.8	198.4	234.0	224.8	238.8	239.8
eyeball	190.0	198.4	234.0	224.0	238.8	239.8
eyebrow	173.3	198.2	232.3	216.3	238.2	239.2
eyelid (lower) (skin) (upper)	173.1	198.2	232.1	216.1	238.2	239.2
cartilage	171.0	198.89	—	215.0	238.1	239.2
face NEC*	195.0	198.89	232.3	229.8	238.8	239.8
fallopian tube (accessory)	183.2	198.82	233.3	221.0	236.3	239.5
falx (cerebelli) (cerebri)	192.1	198.4	—	225.2	237.6	239.7
fascia — *see also* Neoplasm, connective tissue						
palmar	171.2	198.89	—	215.2	238.1	239.2
plantar	171.3	198.89	—	215.3	238.1	239.2
fatty tissue — *see* Neoplasm, connective tissue						
fauces, faucial NEC	146.9	198.89	230.0	210.6	235.1	239.0
pillars	146.2	198.89	230.0	210.6	235.1	239.0
tonsil	146.0	198.89	230.0	210.5	235.1	239.0
femur (any part)	170.7	198.5	—	213.7	238.0	239.2
fetal membrane	181	198.82	233.2	219.8	236.1	239.5
fibrous tissue — *see* Neoplasm, connective tissue						
fibula (any part)	170.7	198.5	—	213.7	238.0	239.2
filum terminale	192.2	198.3	—	225.3	237.5	239.7
finger NEC*	195.4	198.89	232.6	229.8	238.8	239.8
flank NEC*	195.8	198.89	232.5	229.8	238.8	239.8
follicle, nabothian	180.0	198.82	233.1	219.0	236.0	239.5
foot NEC*	195.5	198.89	232.7	229.8	238.8	239.8
forearm NEC*	195.4	198.89	232.6	229.8	238.8	239.8
forehead (skin)	173.3	198.2	232.3	216.3	238.2	239.2
foreskin	187.1	198.82	233.5	222.1	236.6	239.5
fornix						
pharyngeal	147.3	198.89	230.0	210.7	235.1	239.0
vagina	184.0	198.82	233.3	221.1	236.3	239.5
fossa (of)						
anterior (cranial)	191.9	198.3	—	225.0	237.5	239.6
cranial	191.9	198.3	—	225.0	237.5	239.6
ischiorectal	195.3	198.89	234.8	229.8	238.8	239.8
middle (cranial)	191.9	198.3	—	225.0	237.5	239.6
pituitary	194.3	198.89	234.8	227.3	237.0	239.7
posterior (cranial)	191.9	198.3	—	225.0	237.5	239.6
pterygoid	171.0	198.89	—	215.0	238.1	239.2

	Malignant					
	Primary	Secondary	Ca in situ	Benign	Uncertain Behavior	Unspecified
Neoplasm, neoplastic — *continued*						
fossa (of) — *continued*						
pyriform	148.1	198.89	230.0	210.8	235.1	239.0
Rosenmüller	147.2	198.89	230.0	210.7	235.1	239.0
tonsillar	146.1	198.89	230.0	210.6	235.1	239.0
fourchette	184.4	198.82	233.3	221.2	236.3	239.5
frenulum						
labii — *see* Neoplasm, lip, internal						
linguae	141.3	198.89	230.0	210.1	235.1	239.0
frontal						
bone	170.0	198.5	—	213.0	238.0	239.2
lobe, brain	191.1	198.3	—	225.0	237.5	239.6
meninges	192.1	198.4	—	225.2	237.6	239.7
pole	191.1	198.3	—	225.0	237.5	239.6
sinus	160.4	197.3	231.8	212.0	235.9	239.1
fundus						
stomach	151.3	197.8	230.2	211.1	235.2	239.0
uterus	182.0	198.82	233.2	219.1	236.0	239.5
gall duct (extrahepatic)	156.1	197.8	230.8	211.5	235.3	239.0
intrahepatic	155.1	197.8	230.8	211.5	235.3	239.0
gallbladder	156.0	197.8	230.8	211.5	235.3	239.0
contiguous sites with extrahepatic bile ducts	156.8	—	—	—	—	—
ganglia (*see also* Neoplasm, connective tissue)	171.9	198.89	—	215.9	238.1	239.2
basal	191.0	198.3	—	225.0	237.5	239.6
ganglion (*see also* Neoplasm, connective tissue)	171.9	198.89	—	215.9	238.1	239.2
cranial nerve	192.0	198.4	—	225.1	237.9	239.7
Gartner's duct	184.0	198.82	233.3	221.1	236.3	239.5
gastric — *see* Neoplasm, stomach						
gastrocolic	159.8	197.8	230.9	211.9	235.5	239.0
gastroesophageal junction	151.0	197.8	230.2	211.1	235.2	239.0
gastrointestinal (tract) NEC	159.9	197.8	230.9	211.9	235.5	239.0
generalized	199.0	199.0	234.9	229.9	238.9	199.0
genital organ or tract						
female NEC	184.9	198.82	233.3	221.9	236.3	239.5
contiguous sites	184.8	—	—	—	—	—
specified site NEC	184.8	198.82	233.3	221.8	236.3	239.5
male NEC	187.9	198.82	233.6	222.9	236.6	239.5
contiguous sites	187.8	—	—	—	—	—
specified site NEC	187.8	198.82	233.6	222.8	236.6	239.5
genitourinary tract						
female	184.9	198.82	233.3	221.9	236.3	239.5
male	187.9	198.82	233.6	222.9	236.6	239.5
gingiva (alveolar) (marginal)	143.9	198.89	230.0	210.4	235.1	239.0
lower	143.1	198.89	230.0	210.4	235.1	239.0
mandibular	143.1	198.89	230.0	210.4	235.1	239.0
maxillary	143.0	198.89	230.0	210.4	235.1	239.0
upper	143.0	198.89	230.0	210.4	235.1	239.0
gland, glandular (lymphatic) (system) — *see also* Neoplasm, lymph gland						
endocrine NEC	194.9	198.89	—	227.9	237.4	239.7
salivary — *see* Neoplasm, salivary, gland						
glans penis	187.2	198.82	233.5	222.1	236.6	239.5
globus pallidus	191.0	198.3	—	225.0	237.5	239.6
glomus						
coccygeal	194.6	198.89	—	227.6	237.3	239.7
jugularis	194.6	198.89	—	227.6	237.3	239.7
glosso-epiglottic fold(s)	146.4	198.89	230.0	210.6	235.1	239.0
glossopalatine fold	146.2	198.89	230.0	210.6	235.1	239.0
glossopharyngeal sulcus	146.1	198.89	230.0	210.6	235.1	239.0
glottis	161.0	197.3	231.0	212.1	235.6	239.1
gluteal region*	195.3	198.89	232.5	229.8	238.8	239.8
great vessels NEC	171.4	198.89	—	215.4	238.1	239.2
groin NEC*	195.3	198.89	232.5	229.8	238.8	239.8
gum	143.9	198.89	230.0	210.4	235.1	239.0
contiguous sites	143.8	—	—	—	—	—
lower	143.1	198.89	230.0	210.4	235.1	239.0
upper	143.0	198.89	230.0	210.4	235.1	239.0

	Malignant					
	Primary	Secondary	Ca in situ	Benign	Uncertain Behavior	Unspecified
Neoplasm, neoplastic — *continued*						
hand NEC*	195.4	198.89	232.6	229.8	238.8	239.8
head NEC*	195.0	198.89	232.4	229.8	238.8	239.8
heart	164.1	198.89	—	212.7	238.8	239.8
contiguous sites with mediastinum or thymus	164.8	—	—	—	—	—
heel NEC*	195.5	198.89	232.7	229.8	238.8	239.8
helix	173.2	198.2	232.2	216.2	238.2	239.2
hematopoietic, hemopoietic tissue NEC	202.8	198.89	—	—	—	238.7
hemisphere, cerebral	191.0	198.3	—	225.0	237.5	239.6
hemorrhoidal zone	154.2	197.5	230.5	211.4	235.5	239.0
hepatic	155.2	197.7	230.8	211.5	235.3	239.0
duct (bile)	156.1	197.8	230.8	211.5	235.3	239.0
flexure (colon)	153.0	197.5	230.3	211.3	235.2	239.0
primary	155.0	—	—	—	—	—
hilus of lung	162.2	197.0	231.2	212.3	235.7	239.1
hip NEC*	195.5	198.89	232.7	229.8	238.8	239.8
hippocampus, brain	191.2	198.3	—	225.0	237.5	239.6
humerus (any part)	170.4	198.5	—	213.4	238.0	239.2
hymen	184.0	198.82	233.3	221.1	236.3	239.5
hypopharynx, hypopharyngeal NEC	148.9	198.89	230.0	210.8	235.1	239.0
contiguous sites	148.8	—	—	—	—	—
postcricoid region	148.0	198.89	230.0	210.8	235.1	239.0
posterior wall	148.3	198.89	230.0	210.8	235.1	239.0
pyriform fossa (sinus)	148.1	198.89	230.0	210.8	235.1	239.0
specified site NEC	148.8	198.89	230.0	210.8	235.1	239.0
wall	148.9	198.89	230.0	210.8	235.1	239.0
posterior	148.3	198.89	230.0	210.8	235.1	239.0
hypophysis	194.3	198.89	234.8	227.3	237.0	239.7
hypothalamus	191.0	198.3	—	225.0	237.5	239.6
ileocecum, ileocecal (coil) (junction) (valve)	153.4	197.5	230.3	211.3	235.2	239.0
ileum	152.2	197.4	230.7	211.2	235.2	239.0
ilium	170.6	198.5	—	213.6	238.0	239.2
immunoproliferative NEC	203.8	—	—	—	—	—
infraclavicular (region)*	195.1	198.89	232.5	229.8	238.8	239.8
inguinal (region)*	195.3	198.89	232.5	229.8	238.8	239.8
insula	191.0	198.3	—	225.0	237.5	239.6
insular tissue (pancreas)	157.4	197.8	230.9	211.7	235.5	239.0
brain	191.0	198.3	—	225.0	237.5	239.6
interarytenoid fold	148.2	198.89	230.0	210.8	235.1	239.0
hypopharyngeal aspect	148.2	198.89	230.0	210.8	235.1	239.0
laryngeal aspect	161.1	197.3	231.0	212.1	235.6	239.1
marginal zone	148.2	198.89	230.0	210.8	235.1	239.0
interdental papillae	143.9	198.89	230.0	210.4	235.1	239.0
lower	143.1	198.89	230.0	210.4	235.1	239.0
upper	143.0	198.89	230.0	210.4	235.1	239.0
internal						
capsule	191.0	198.3	—	225.0	237.5	239.6
os (cervix)	180.0	198.82	233.1	219.0	236.0	239.5
intervertebral cartilage or disc	170.2	198.5	—	213.2	238.0	239.2
intestine, intestinal	159.0	197.8	230.7	211.9	235.2	239.0
large	153.9	197.5	230.3	211.3	235.2	239.0
appendix	153.5	197.5	230.3	211.3	235.2	239.0
caput coli	153.4	197.5	230.3	211.3	235.2	239.0
cecum	153.4	197.5	230.3	211.3	235.2	239.0
colon	153.9	197.5	230.3	211.3	235.2	239.0
and rectum	154.0	197.5	230.4	211.4	235.2	239.0
ascending	153.6	197.5	230.3	211.3	235.2	239.0
caput	153.4	197.5	230.3	211.3	235.2	239.0
contiguous sites	153.8	—	—	—	—	—
descending	153.2	197.5	230.3	211.3	235.2	239.0
distal	153.2	197.5	230.3	211.3	235.2	239.0
left	153.2	197.5	230.3	211.3	235.2	239.0
pelvic	153.3	197.5	230.3	211.3	235.2	239.0
right	153.6	197.5	230.3	211.3	235.2	239.0
sigmoid (flexure)	153.3	197.5	230.3	211.3	235.2	239.0
transverse	153.1	197.5	230.3	211.3	235.2	239.0
contiguous sites	153.8	—	—	—	—	—

	Malignant Primary	Malignant Secondary	Malignant Ca in situ	Benign	Uncertain Behavior	Unspecified
Neoplasm, neoplastic — *continued*						
intestine, intestinal — *continued*						
large — *continued*						
hepatic flexure	153.0	197.5	230.3	211.3	235.2	239.0
ileocecum, ileocecal (coil) (valve)	153.4	197.5	230.3	211.3	235.2	239.0
sigmoid flexure (lower) (upper)	153.3	197.5	230.3	211.3	235.2	239.0
splenic flexure	153.7	197.5	230.3	211.3	235.2	239.0
small	152.9	197.4	230.7	211.2	235.2	239.0
contiguous sites	152.8	—	—	—	—	—
duodenum	152.0	197.4	230.7	211.2	235.2	239.0
ileum	152.2	197.4	230.7	211.2	235.2	239.0
jejunum	152.1	197.4	230.7	211.2	235.2	239.0
tract NEC	159.0	197.8	230.7	211.9	235.2	239.0
intra-abdominal	195.2	198.89	234.8	229.8	238.8	239.8
intracranial NEC	191.9	198.3	—	225.0	237.5	239.6
intrahepatic (bile) duct	155.1	197.8	230.8	211.5	235.3	239.0
intraocular	190.0	198.4	234.0	224.0	238.8	239.8
intraorbital	190.1	198.4	234.0	224.1	238.8	239.8
intrasellar	194.3	198.89	234.8	227.3	237.0	239.7
intrathoracic (cavity) (organs NEC)	195.1	198.89	234.8	229.8	238.8	239.8
contiguous sites with respiratory organs	165.8	—	—	—	—	—
iris	190.0	198.4	234.0	224.0	238.8	239.8
ischiorectal (fossa)	195.3	198.89	234.8	229.8	238.8	239.8
ischium	170.6	198.5	—	213.6	238.0	239.2
island of Reil	191.0	198.3	—	225.0	237.5	239.6
islands or islets of Langerhans	157.4	197.8	230.9	211.7	235.5	239.0
isthmus uteri	182.1	198.82	233.2	219.1	236.0	239.5
jaw	195.0	198.89	234.8	229.8	238.8	239.8
bone	170.1	198.5	—	213.1	238.0	239.2
carcinoma	143.9	—	—	—	—	—
lower	143.1	—	—	—	—	—
upper	143.0	—	—	—	—	—
lower	170.1	198.5	—	213.1	238.0	239.2
upper	170.0	198.5	—	213.0	238.0	239.2
carcinoma (any type) (lower) (upper)	195.0	—	—	—	—	—
skin	173.3	198.2	232.3	216.3	238.2	239.2
soft tissues	143.9	198.89	230.0	210.4	235.1	239.0
lower	143.1	198.89	230.0	210.4	235.1	239.0
upper	143.0	198.89	230.0	210.4	235.1	239.0
jejunum	152.1	197.4	230.7	211.2	235.2	239.0
joint NEC (*see also* Neoplasm, bone)	170.9	198.5	—	213.9	238.0	239.2
acromioclavicular	170.4	198.5	—	213.4	238.0	239.2
bursa or synovial membrane — *see* Neoplasm, connective tissue						
costovertebral	170.3	198.5	—	213.3	238.0	239.2
sternocostal	170.3	198.5	—	213.3	238.0	239.2
temporomandibular	170.1	198.5	—	213.1	238.0	239.2
junction						
anorectal	154.8	197.5	230.7	211.4	235.5	239.0
cardioesophageal	151.0	197.8	230.2	211.1	235.2	239.0
esophagogastric	151.0	197.8	230.2	211.1	235.2	239.0
gastroesophageal	151.0	197.8	230.2	211.1	235.2	239.0
hard and soft palate	145.5	198.89	230.0	210.4	235.1	239.0
ileocecal	153.4	197.5	230.3	211.3	235.2	239.0
pelvirectal	154.0	197.5	230.4	211.4	235.2	239.0
pelviureteric	189.1	198.0	233.9	223.1	236.91	239.5
rectosigmoid	154.0	197.5	230.4	211.4	235.2	239.0
squamocolumnar, of cervix	180.8	198.82	233.1	219.0	236.0	239.5
kidney (parenchyma)	189.0	198.0	233.9	223.0	236.91	239.5
calyx	189.1	198.0	233.9	223.1	236.91	239.5
hilus	189.1	198.0	233.9	223.1	236.91	239.5
pelvis	189.1	198.0	233.9	223.1	236.91	239.5
knee NEC*	195.5	198.89	232.7	229.8	238.8	239.8

	Malignant Primary	Malignant Secondary	Malignant Ca in situ	Benign	Uncertain Behavior	Unspecified
Neoplasm, neoplastic — *continued*						
labia (skin)	184.4	198.82	233.3	221.2	236.3	239.5
majora	184.1	198.82	233.3	221.2	236.3	239.5
minora	184.2	198.82	233.3	221.2	236.3	239.5
labial — *see also* Neoplasm, lip						
sulcus (lower) (upper)	145.1	198.89	230.0	210.4	235.1	239.0
labium (skin)	184.4	198.82	233.3	221.2	236.3	239.5
majus	184.1	198.82	233.3	221.2	236.3	239.5
minus	184.2	198.82	233.3	221.2	236.3	239.5
lacrimal						
canaliculi	190.7	198.4	234.0	224.7	238.8	239.8
duct (nasal)	190.7	198.4	234.0	224.7	238.8	239.8
gland	190.2	198.4	234.0	224.2	238.8	239.8
punctum	190.7	198.4	234.0	224.7	238.8	239.8
sac	190.7	198.4	234.0	224.7	238.8	239.8
Langerhans, islands or islets	157.4	197.8	230.9	211.7	235.5	239.0
laryngopharynx	148.9	198.89	230.0	210.8	235.1	239.0
larynx, laryngeal NEC	161.9	197.3	231.0	212.1	235.6	239.1
aryepiglottic fold	161.1	197.3	231.0	212.1	235.6	239.1
cartilage (arytenoid) (cricoid) (cuneiform) (thyroid)	161.3	197.3	231.0	212.1	235.6	239.1
commissure (anterior) (posterior)	161.0	197.3	231.0	212.1	235.6	239.1
contiguous sites	161.8	—	—	—	—	—
extrinsic NEC	161.1	197.3	231.0	212.1	235.6	239.1
meaning hypopharyanx	148.9	198.89	230.0	210.8	235.1	239.0
interarytenoid fold	161.1	197.3	231.0	212.1	235.6	239.1
intrinsic	161.0	197.3	231.0	212.1	235.6	239.1
ventricular band	161.1	197.3	231.0	212.1	235.6	239.1
leg NEC*	195.5	198.89	232.7	229.8	238.8	239.8
lens, crystalline	190.0	198.4	234.0	224.0	238.8	239.8
lid (lower) (upper)	173.1	198.2	232.1	216.1	238.2	239.2
ligament — *see also* Neoplasm, connective tissue						
broad	183.3	198.82	233.3	221.0	236.3	239.5
Mackenrodt's	183.8	198.82	233.3	221.8	236.3	239.5
non-uterine — *see* Neoplasm, connective tissue						
round	183.5	198.82	—	221.0	236.3	239.5
sacro-uterine	183.4	198.82	—	221.0	236.3	239.5
uterine	183.4	198.82	—	221.0	236.3	239.5
utero-ovarian	183.8	198.82	233.3	221.8	236.3	239.5
uterosacral	183.4	198.82	—	221.0	236.3	239.5
limb*	195.8	198.89	232.8	229.8	238.8	239.8
lower*	195.5	198.89	232.7	229.8	238.8	239.8
upper*	195.4	198.89	232.6	229.8	238.8	239.8
limbus or cornea	190.4	198.4	234.0	224.4	238.8	239.8
lingual NEC (*see also* Neoplasm, tongue)	141.9	198.89	230.0	210.1	235.1	239.0
lingula, lung	162.3	197.0	231.2	212.3	235.7	239.1
lip (external) (lipstick area) (vermillion border)	140.9	198.89	230.0	210.0	235.1	239.0
buccal aspect — *see* Neoplasm, lip, internal						
commissure	140.6	198.89	230.0	210.4	235.1	239.0
contiguous sites	140.8	—	—	—	—	—
with oral cavity or pharynx	149.8	—	—	—	—	—
frenulum — *see* Neoplasm, lip, internal						
inner aspect — *see* Neoplasm, lip, internal						
internal (buccal) (frenulum) (mucosa) (oral)	140.5	198.89	230.0	210.0	235.1	239.0
lower	140.4	198.89	230.0	210.0	235.1	239.0
upper	140.3	198.89	230.0	210.0	235.1	239.0
lower	140.1	198.89	230.0	210.0	235.1	239.0
internal (buccal) (frenulum) (mucosa) (oral)	140.4	198.89	230.0	210.0	235.1	239.0
mucosa — *see* Neoplasm, lip, internal						
oral aspect — *see* Neoplasm, lip, internal						
skin (commissure) (lower) (upper)	173.0	198.2	232.0	216.0	238.2	239.2
upper	140.0	198.89	230.0	210.0	235.1	239.0
internal (buccal) (frenulum) (mucosa) (oral)	140.3	198.89	230.0	210.0	235.1	239.0
liver	155.2	197.7	230.8	211.5	235.3	239.0
primary	155.0	—	—	—	—	—
lobe						
azygos	162.3	197.0	231.2	212.3	235.7	239.1
frontal	191.1	198.3	—	225.0	237.5	239.6
lower	162.5	197.0	231.2	212.3	235.7	239.1

	Malignant					
	Primary	Secondary	Ca in situ	Benign	Uncertain Behavior	Unspecified
Neoplasm, neoplastic — *continued*						
lobe — *continued*						
middle	162.4	197.0	231.2	212.3	235.7	239.1
occipital	191.4	198.3	—	225.0	237.5	239.6
parietal	191.3	198.3	—	225.0	237.5	239.6
temporal	191.2	198.3	—	225.0	237.5	239.6
upper	162.3	197.0	231.2	212.3	235.7	239.1
lumbosacral plexus	171.6	198.4	—	215.6	238.1	239.2
lung	162.9	197.0	231.2	212.3	235.7	239.1
azygos lobe	162.3	197.0	231.2	212.3	235.7	239.1
carina	162.2	197.0	231.2	212.3	235.7	239.1
contiguous sites with bronchus or trachea	162.8	—	—	—	—	—
hilus	162.2	197.0	231.2	212.3	235.7	239.1
lingula	162.3	197.0	231.2	212.3	235.7	239.1
lobe NEC	162.9	197.0	231.2	212.3	235.7	239.1
lower lobe	162.5	197.0	231.2	212.3	235.7	239.1
main bronchus	162.2	197.0	231.2	212.3	235.7	239.1
middle lobe	162.4	197.0	231.2	212.3	235.7	239.1
upper lobe	162.3	197.0	231.2	212.3	235.7	239.1
lymph, lymphatic						
channel NEC (*see also* Neoplasm, connective tissue)	171.9	198.89	—	215.9	238.1	239.2
gland (secondary)	—	196.9	—	229.0	238.8	239.8
abdominal	—	196.2	—	229.0	238.8	239.8
aortic	—	196.2	—	229.0	238.8	239.8
arm	—	196.3	—	229.0	238.8	239.8
auricular (anterior) (posterior)	—	196.0	—	229.0	238.8	239.8
axilla, axillary	—	196.3	—	229.0	238.8	239.8
brachial	—	196.3	—	229.0	238.8	239.8
bronchial	—	196.1	—	229.0	238.8	239.8
bronchopulmonary	—	196.1	—	229.0	238.8	239.8
celiac	—	196.2	—	229.0	238.8	239.8
cervical	—	196.0	—	229.0	238.8	239.8
cervicofacial	—	196.0	—	229.0	238.8	239.8
Cloquet	—	196.5	—	229.0	238.8	239.8
colic	—	196.2	—	229.0	238.8	239.8
common duct	—	196.2	—	229.0	238.8	239.8
cubital	—	196.3	—	229.0	238.8	239.8
diaphragmatic	—	196.1	—	229.0	238.8	239.8
epigastric, inferior	—	196.6	—	229.0	238.8	239.8
epitrochlear	—	196.3	—	229.0	238.8	239.8
esophageal	—	196.1	—	229.0	238.8	239.8
face	—	196.0	—	229.0	238.8	239.8
femoral	—	196.5	—	229.0	238.8	239.8
gastric	—	196.2	—	229.0	238.8	239.8
groin	—	196.5	—	229.0	238.8	239.8
head	—	196.0	—	229.0	238.8	239.8
hepatic	—	196.2	—	229.0	238.8	239.8
hilar (pulmonary)	—	196.1	—	229.0	238.8	239.8
splenic	—	196.2	—	229.0	238.8	239.8
hypogastric	—	196.6	—	229.0	238.8	239.8
ileocolic	—	196.2	—	229.0	238.8	239.8
iliac	—	196.6	—	229.0	238.8	239.8
infraclavicular	—	196.3	—	229.0	238.8	239.8
inguina, inguinal	—	196.5	—	229.0	238.8	239.8
innominate	—	196.1	—	229.0	238.8	239.8
intercostal	—	196.1	—	229.0	238.8	239.8
intestinal	—	196.2	—	229.0	238.8	239.8
intrabdominal	—	196.2	—	229.0	238.8	239.8
intrapelvic	—	196.6	—	229.0	238.8	239.8
intrathoracic	—	196.1	—	229.0	238.8	239.9
jugular	—	196.0	—	229.0	238.8	239.8
leg	—	196.5	—	229.0	238.8	239.8
limb						
lower	—	196.5	—	229.0	238.8	239.8
upper	—	196.3	—	229.0	238.8	239.8
lower limb	—	196.5	—	229.0	238.8	239.8
lumbar	—	196.2	—	229.0	238.8	239.8
mandibular	—	196.0	—	229.0	238.8	239.8

	Malignant Primary	Malignant Secondary	Malignant Ca in situ	Benign	Uncertain Behavior	Unspecified
Neoplasm, neoplastic — *continued*						
lymph, lymphatic — *continued*						
gland (secondary) — *continued*						
mediastinal	—	196.1	—	229.0	238.8	239.8
mesenteric (inferior) (superior)	—	196.2	—	229.0	238.8	239.8
midcolic	—	196.2	—	229.0	238.8	239.8
multiple sites in categories 196.0-196.6	—	196.8	—	229.0	238.8	239.8
neck	—	196.0	—	229.0	238.8	239.8
obturator	—	196.6	—	229.0	238.8	239.8
occipital	—	196.0	—	229.0	238.8	239.8
pancreatic	—	196.2	—	229.0	238.8	239.8
para-aortic	—	196.2	—	229.0	238.8	239.8
paracervical	—	196.6	—	229.0	238.8	239.8
parametrial	—	196.6	—	229.0	238.8	239.8
parasternal	—	196.1	—	229.0	238.8	239.8
parotid	—	196.0	—	229.0	238.8	239.8
pectoral	—	196.3	—	229.0	238.8	239.8
pelvic	—	196.6	—	229.0	238.8	239.8
peri-aortic	—	196.2	—	229.0	238.8	239.8
peripancreatic	—	196.2	—	229.0	238.8	239.8
popliteal	—	196.5	—	229.0	238.8	239.8
porta hepatis	—	196.2	—	229.0	238.8	239.8
portal	—	196.2	—	229.0	238.8	239.8
preauricular	—	196.0	—	229.0	238.8	239.8
prelaryngeal	—	196.0	—	229.0	238.8	239.8
presymphysial	—	196.6	—	229.0	238.8	239.8
pretracheal	—	196.0	—	229.0	238.8	239.8
primary (any site) NEC	202.9	—	—	—	—	—
pulmonary (hiler)	—	196.1	—	229.0	238.8	239.8
pyloric	—	196.2	—	229.0	238.8	239.8
retroperitoneal	—	196.2	—	229.0	238.8	239.8
retropharyngeal	—	196.0	—	229.0	238.8	239.8
Rosenmüller's	—	196.5	—	229.0	238.8	239.8
sacral	—	196.6	—	229.0	238.8	239.8
scalene	—	196.0	—	229.0	238.8	239.8
site NEC	—	196.9	—	229.0	238.8	239.8
splenic (hilar)	—	196.2	—	229.0	238.8	239.8
subclavicular	—	196.3	—	229.0	238.8	239.8
subinguinal	—	196.5	—	229.0	238.8	239.8
sublingual	—	196.0	—	229.0	238.8	239.8
submandibular	—	196.0	—	229.0	238.8	239.8
submaxillary	—	196.0	—	229.0	238.8	239.8
submental	—	196.0	—	229.0	238.8	239.8
subscapular	—	196.3	—	229.0	238.8	239.8
supraclavicular	—	196.0	—	229.0	238.8	239.8
thoracic	—	196.1	—	229.0	238.8	239.8
tibial	—	196.5	—	229.0	238.8	239.8
tracheal	—	196.1	—	229.0	238.8	239.8
tracheobronchial	—	196.1	—	229.0	238.8	239.8
upper limb	—	196.3	—	229.0	238.8	239.8
Virchow's	—	196.0	—	229.0	238.8	239.8
node — *see also* Neoplasm, lymph gland primary NEC	202.9	—	—	—	—	—
vessel (*see also* Neoplasm, connective tissue)	171.9	198.89	—	215.9	238.1	239.2
Mackenrodt's ligament	183.8	198.82	233.3	221.8	236.3	239.5
malar	170.0	198.5	—	213.0	238.0	239.2
region — *see* Neoplasm, cheek						
mammary gland — *see* Neoplasm, breast						
mandible	170.1	198.5	—	213.1	238.0	239.2
alveolar						
mucose	143.1	198.89	230.0	210.4	235.1	239.0
ridge or process	170.1	198.5	—	213.1	238.0	239.2
carcinoma	143.1	—	—	—	—	—
carcinoma	143.1	—	—	—	—	—
marrow (bone) NEC	202.9	198.5	—	—	—	238.7
mastectomy site (skin)	173.5	198.2	—	—	—	—
specified as breast tissue	174.8	198.81	—	—	—	—
mastoid (air cells) (antrum) (cavity)	160.1	197.3	231.8	212.0	235.9	239.1
bone or process	170.0	198.5	—	213.0	238.0	239.2

	Malignant			Benign	Uncertain Behavior	Unspecified
	Primary	Secondary	Ca in situ			
Neoplasm, neoplastic — *continued*						
maxilla, maxillary (superior)	170.0	198.5	—	213.0	238.0	239.2
alveolar						
mucosa	143.0	198.89	230.0	210.4	235.1	239.0
ridge or process	170.0	198.5	—	213.0	238.0	239.2
carcinoma	143.0	—	—	—	—	—
antrum	160.2	197.3	231.8	212.0	235.9	239.1
carcinoma	143.0	—	—	—	—	—
inferior — *see* Neoplasm, mandible						
sinus	160.2	197.3	231.8	212.0	235.9	239.1
meatus, external (ear)	173.2	198.2	232.2	216.2	238.2	239.2
Meckel's diverticulum	152.3	197.4	230.7	211.2	235.2	239.0
mediastinum, mediastinal	164.9	197.1	—	212.5	235.8	239.8
anterior	164.2	197.1	—	212.5	235.8	239.8
contiguous sites with heart and thymus	164.8	—	—	—	—	—
posterior	164.3	197.1	—	212.5	235.8	239.8
medulla						
adrenal	194.0	198.7	234.8	227.0	237.2	239.7
oblongata	191.7	198.3	—	225.0	237.5	239.6
meibomian gland	173.1	198.2	232.1	216.1	238.2	239.2
melanoma — *see* Melanoma						
meninges (brain) (cerebral) (cranial) (intracranial)	192.1	198.4	—	225.2	237.6	239.7
spinal (cord)	192.3	198.4	—	225.4	237.6	239.7
meniscus, knee joint (lateral) (medial)	170.7	198.5	—	213.7	238.0	239.2
mesentery, mesenteric	158.8	197.6	—	211.8	235.4	239.0
mesoappendix	158.8	197.6	—	211.8	235.4	239.0
mesocolon	158.8	197.6	—	211.8	235.4	239.0
mesopharynx — *see* Neoplasm, oropharynx						
mesosalpinx	183.3	198.82	233.3	221.0	236.3	239.5
mesovarium	183.3	198.82	233.3	221.0	236.3	239.5
metacarpus (any bone)	170.5	198.5	—	213.5	238.0	239.2
metastatic NEC — *see also* Neoplasm, by site, secondary	—	199.1	—	—	—	—
metatarsus (any bone)	170.8	198.5	—	213.8	238.0	239.2
midbrain	191.7	198.3	—	225.0	237.5	239.6
milk duct — *see* Neoplasm, breast						
mons						
pubis	184.4	198.82	233.3	221.2	236.3	239.5
veneris	184.4	198.82	233.3	221.2	236.3	239.5
motor tract	192.9	198.4	—	225.9	237.9	239.7
brain	191.9	198.3	—	225.0	237.5	239.6
spinal	192.2	198.3	—	225.3	237.5	239.7
mouth	145.9	198.89	230.0	210.4	235.1	239.0
contiguous sites	145.8	—	—	—	—	—
floor	144.9	198.89	230.0	210.3	235.1	239.0
anterior portion	144.0	198.89	230.0	210.3	235.1	239.0
contiguous sites	144.8	—	—	—	—	—
lateral portion	144.1	198.89	230.0	210.3	235.1	239.0
roof	145.5	198.89	230.0	210.4	235.1	239.0
specified part NEC	145.8	198.89	230.0	210.4	235.1	239.0
vestibule	145.1	198.89	230.0	210.4	235.1	239.0
mucosa						
alveolar (ridge or process)	143.9	198.89	230.0	210.4	235.1	239.0
lower	143.1	198.89	230.0	210.4	235.1	239.0
upper	143.0	198.89	230.0	210.4	235.1	239.0
buccal	145.0	198.89	230.0	210.4	235.1	239.0
cheek	145.0	198.89	230.0	210.4	235.1	239.0
lip — *see* Neoplasm, lip, internal						
nasal	160.0	197.3	231.8	212.0	235.9	239.1
oral	145.0	198.89	230.0	210.4	235.1	239.0
Müllerian duct						
female	184.8	198.82	233.3	221.8	236.3	239.5
male	187.8	198.82	233.6	222.8	236.6	239.5
multiple sites NEC	199.0	199.0	234.9	229.9	238.9	199.0
muscle — *see also* Neoplasm, connective tissue extraocular	190.1	198.4	234.0	224.1	238.8	239.8
myocardium	164.1	198.89	—	212.7	238.8	239.8
myometrium	182.0	198.82	233.2	219.1	236.0	239.5
myopericardium	164.1	198.89	—	212.7	238.8	239.8

	Malignant Primary	Malignant Secondary	Malignant Ca in situ	Benign	Uncertain Behavior	Unspecified
Neoplasm, neoplastic — *continued*						
nabothian gland (follicle)	180.0	198.82	233.1	219.0	236.0	239.5
nail	173.9	198.2	232.9	216.9	238.2	239.2
finger	173.6	198.2	232.6	216.6	238.2	239.2
toe	173.7	198.2	232.7	216.7	238.2	239.2
nares, naris (anterior) (posterior)	160.0	197.3	231.8	212.0	235.9	239.1
nasal — *see* Neoplasm, nose						
nasolabial groove	173.3	198.2	232.3	216.3	238.2	239.2
nasolacrimal duct	190.7	198.4	234.0	224.7	238.8	239.8
nasopharynx, nasopharyngeal	147.9	198.89	230.0	210.7	235.1	239.0
contiguous sites	147.8	—	—	—	—	—
floor	147.3	198.89	230.0	210.7	235.1	239.0
roof	147.0	198.89	230.0	210.7	235.1	239.0
specified site NEC	147.8	198.89	230.0	210.7	235.1	239.0
wall	147.9	198.89	230.0	210.7	235.1	239.0
anterior	147.3	198.89	230.0	210.7	235.1	239.0
lateral	147.2	198.89	230.0	210.7	235.1	239.0
posterior	147.1	198.89	230.0	210.7	235.1	239.0
superior	147.0	198.89	230.0	210.7	235.1	239.0
nates	173.5	198.2	232.5	216.5	238.2	239.2
neck NEC*	195.0	198.89	234.8	229.8	238.8	239.8
nerve (autonomic) (ganglion) (parasympathetic) (peripheral) (sympathetic) — *see also* Neoplasm, connective tissue						
abducens	192.0	198.4	—	225.1	237.9	239.7
accessory (spinal)	192.0	198.4	—	225.1	237.9	239.7
acoustic	192.0	198.4	—	225.1	237.9	239.7
auditory	192.0	198.4	—	225.1	237.9	239.7
brachial	171.2	198.89	—	215.2	238.1	239.2
cranial (any)	192.0	198.4	—	225.1	237.9	239.7
facial	192.0	198.4	—	225.1	237.9	239.7
femoral	171.3	198.89	—	215.3	238.1	239.2
glossopharyngeal	192.0	198.4	—	225.1	237.9	239.7
hypoglossal	192.0	198.4	—	225.1	237.9	239.7
intercostal	171.4	198.89	—	215.4	238.1	239.2
lumbar	171.7	198.89	—	215.7	238.1	239.2
median	171.2	198.89	—	215.2	238.1	239.2
obturator	171.3	198.89	—	215.3	238.1	239.2
oculomotor	192.0	198.4	—	225.1	237.9	239.7
olfactory	192.0	198.4	—	225.1	237.9	239.7
optic	192.0	198.4	—	225.1	237.9	239.7
peripheral NEC	171.9	198.89	—	215.9	238.1	239.2
radial	171.2	198.89	—	215.2	238.1	239.2
sacral	171.6	198.89	—	215.6	238.1	239.2
sciatic	171.3	198.89	—	215.3	238.1	239.2
spinal NEC	171.9	198.89	—	215.9	238.1	239.2
trigeminal	192.0	198.4	—	225.1	237.9	239.7
trochlear	192.0	198.4	—	225.1	237.9	239.7
ulnar	171.2	198.89	—	215.2	238.1	239.2
vagus	192.0	198.4	—	225.1	237.9	239.7
nervous system (central) NEC	192.9	198.4	—	225.9	237.9	239.7
autonomic NEC	171.9	198.89	—	215.9	238.1	239.2
brain — *see also* Neoplasm, brain membrane or meninges	192.1	198.4	—	225.2	237.6	239.7
contiguous sites	192.8	—	—	—	—	—
parasympathetic NEC	171.9	198.89	—	215.9	238.1	239.2
sympathetic NEC	171.9	198.89	—	215.9	238.1	239.2
nipple (female)	174.0	198.81	233.0	217	238.3	239.3
male	175.0	198.81	233.0	217	238.3	239.3
nose, nasal	195.0	198.89	234.8	229.8	238.8	239.8
ala (external)	173.3	198.2	232.3	216.3	238.2	239.2
bone	170.0	198.5	—	213.0	238.0	239.2
cartilage	160.0	197.3	231.8	212.0	235.9	239.1
cavity	160.0	197.3	231.8	212.0	235.9	239.1
contiguous sites with accessory sinuses or middle ear	160.8	—	—	—	—	—
choana	147.3	198.89	230.0	210.7	235.1	239.0
external (skin)	173.3	198.2	232.3	216.3	238.2	239.2
fossa	160.0	197.3	231.8	212.0	235.9	239.1

	Malignant Primary	Malignant Secondary	Malignant Ca in situ	Benign	Uncertain Behavior	Unspecified
Neoplasm, neoplastic — *continued*						
nose, nasal — *continued*						
internal	160.0	197.3	231.8	212.0	235.9	239.1
mucosa	160.0	197.3	231.8	212.0	235.9	239.1
septum	160.0	197.3	231.8	212.0	235.9	239.1
posterior margin	147.3	198.89	230.0	210.7	235.1	239.0
sinus — *see* Neoplasm, sinus						
skin	173.3	198.2	232.3	216.3	238.2	239.2
turbinate (mucosa)	160.0	197.3	231.8	212.0	235.9	239.1
bone	170.0	198.5	—	213.0	238.0	239.2
vestibule	160.0	197.3	231.8	212.0	235.9	239.1
nostril	160.0	197.3	231.8	212.0	235.9	239.1
nucleus pulposus	170.2	198.5	—	213.2	238.0	239.2
occipital						
bone	170.0	198.5	—	213.0	238.0	239.2
lobe or pole, brain	191.4	198.3	—	225.0	237.5	239.6
odontogenic — *see* Neoplasm, jaw bone						
oesophagus — *see* Neoplasm, esophagus						
olfactory nerve or bulb	192.0	198.4	—	225.1	237.9	239.7
olive (brain)	191.7	198.3	—	225.0	237.5	239.6
omentum	158.8	197.6	—	211.8	235.4	239.0
operculum (brain)	191.0	198.3	—	225.0	237.5	239.6
optic nerve, chiasm, or tract	192.0	198.4	—	225.1	237.9	239.7
oral (cavity)	145.9	198.89	230.0	210.4	235.1	239.0
contiguous sites with lip or pharynx	149.8	—	—	—	—	—
ill-defined	149.9	198.89	230.0	210.4	235.1	239.0
mucosa	145.9	198.89	230.0	210.4	235.1	239.0
orbit	190.1	198.4	234.0	224.1	238.8	239.8
bone	170.0	198.5	—	213.0	238.0	239.2
eye	190.1	198.4	234.0	224.1	238.8	239.8
soft parts	190.1	198.4	234.0	224.1	238.8	239.8
organ of Zuckerkandl	194.6	198.89	—	227.6	237.3	239.7
oropharynx	146.9	198.89	230.0	210.6	235.1	239.0
branchial cleft (vestige)	146.8	198.89	230.0	210.6	235.1	239.0
contiguous sites	146.8	—	—	—	—	—
junctional region	146.5	198.89	230.0	210.6	235.1	239.0
lateral wall	146.6	198.89	230.0	210.6	235.1	239.0
pillars of fauces	146.2	198.89	230.0	210.6	235.1	239.0
posterior wall	146.7	198.89	230.0	210.6	235.1	239.0
specified part NEC	146.8	198.89	230.0	210.6	235.1	239.0
vallecula	146.3	198.89	230.0	210.6	235.1	239.0
os						
external	180.1	198.82	233.1	219.0	236.0	239.5
internal	180.0	198.82	233.1	219.0	236.0	239.5
ovary	183.0	198.6	233.3	220	236.2	239.5
oviduct	183.2	198.82	233.3	221.0	236.3	239.5
palate	145.5	198.89	230.0	210.4	235.1	239.0
hard	145.2	198.89	230.0	210.4	235.1	239.0
junction of hard and soft palate	145.5	198.89	230.0	210.4	235.1	239.0
soft	145.3	198.89	230.0	210.4	235.1	239.0
nasopharyngeal surface	147.3	198.89	230.0	210.7	235.1	239.0
posterior surface	147.3	198.89	230.0	210.7	235.1	239.0
superior surface	147.3	198.89	230.0	210.7	235.1	239.0
palatoglossal arch	146.2	198.89	230.0	210.6	235.1	239.0
palatopharyngeal arch	146.2	198.89	230.0	210.6	235.1	239.0
pallium	191.0	198.3	—	225.0	237.5	239.6
palpebra	173.1	198.2	232.1	216.1	238.2	239.2
pancreas	157.9	197.8	230.9	211.6	235.5	239.0
body	157.1	197.8	230.9	211.6	235.5	239.0
contiguous sites	157.8	—	—	—	—	—
duct (of Santorini) (of Wirsung)	157.3	197.8	230.9	211.6	235.5	239.0
ectopic tissue	157.8	197.8	230.9	211.6	235.5	239.0
head	157.0	197.8	230.9	211.6	235.5	239.0
islet cells	157.4	197.8	230.9	211.7	235.5	239.0
neck	157.8	197.8	230.9	211.6	235.5	239.0
tail	157.2	197.8	230.9	211.6	235.5	239.0
para-aortic body	194.6	198.89	—	227.6	237.3	239.7
paraganglion NEC	194.6	198.89	—	227.6	237.3	239.7

	Malignant					
	Primary	**Secondary**	**Ca in situ**	**Benign**	**Uncertain Behavior**	**Unspecified**
Neoplasm, neoplastic — *continued*						
parametrium	183.4	198.82	—	221.0	236.3	239.5
paranephric	158.0	197.6	—	211.8	235.4	239.0
pararectal	195.3	198.89	—	229.8	238.8	239.8
parasagittal (region)	195.0	198.89	234.8	229.8	238.8	239.8
parasellar	192.9	198.4	—	225.9	237.9	239.7
parathyroid (gland)	194.1	198.89	234.8	227.1	237.4	239.7
paraurethral	195.3	198.89	—	229.8	238.8	239.8
gland	189.4	198.1	233.9	223.89	236.99	239.5
paravaginal	195.3	198.89	—	229.8	238.8	239.8
parenchyma, kidney	189.0	198.0	233.9	223.0	236.91	239.5
parietal						
bone	170.0	198.5	—	213.0	238.0	239.2
lobe, brain	191.3	198.3	—	225.0	237.5	239.6
paroophoron	183.3	198.82	233.3	221.0	236.3	239.5
parotid (duct) (gland)	142.0	198.89	230.0	210.2	235.0	239.0
parovarium	183.3	198.82	233.3	221.0	236.3	239.5
patella	170.8	198.5	—	213.8	238.0	239.2
peduncle, cerebral	191.7	198.3	—	225.0	237.5	239.6
pelvirectal junction	154.0	197.5	230.4	211.4	235.2	239.0
pelvis, pelvic	195.3	198.89	234.8	229.8	238.8	239.8
bone	170.6	198.5	—	213.6	238.0	239.2
floor	195.3	198.89	234.8	229.8	238.8	239.8
renal	189.1	198.0	233.9	223.1	236.91	239.5
viscera	195.3	198.89	234.8	229.8	238.8	239.8
wall	195.3	198.89	234.8	229.8	238.8	239.8
pelvo-abdominal	195.8	198.89	234.8	229.8	238.8	239.8
penis	187.4	198.82	233.5	222.1	236.6	239.5
body	187.3	198.82	233.5	222.1	236.6	239.5
corpus (cavernosum)	187.3	198.82	233.5	222.1	236.6	239.5
glans	187.2	198.82	233.5	222.1	236.6	239.5
skin NEC	187.4	198.82	233.5	222.1	236.6	239.5
periadrenal (tissue)	158.0	197.6	—	211.8	235.4	239.0
perianal (skin)	173.5	198.2	232.5	216.5	238.2	239.2
pericardium	164.1	198.89	—	212.7	238.8	239.8
perinephric	158.0	197.6	—	211.8	235.4	239.0
perineum	195.3	198.89	234.8	229.8	238.8	239.8
periodontal tissue NEC	143.9	198.89	230.0	210.4	235.1	239.0
periosteum — *see* Neoplasm, bone						
peripancreatic	158.0	197.6	—	211.8	235.4	239.0
peripheral nerve NEC	171.9	198.89	—	215.9	238.1	239.2
perirectal (tissue)	195.3	198.89	—	229.8	238.8	239.8
perirenal (tissue)	158.0	197.6	—	211.8	235.4	239.0
peritoneum, peritoneal (cavity)	158.9	197.6	—	211.8	235.4	239.0
contiguous sites	158.8	—	—	—	—	—
with digestive organs	159.8	—	—	—	—	—
parietal	158.8	197.6	—	211.8	235.4	239.0
pelvic	158.8	197.6	—	211.8	235.4	239.0
specified part NEC	158.8	197.6	—	211.8	235.4	239.0
peritonsillar (tissue)	195.0	198.89	234.8	229.8	238.8	239.8
periurethral tissue	195.3	198.89	—	229.8	238.8	239.8
phalanges	170.9	198.5	—	213.9	238.0	239.2
foot	170.8	198.5	—	213.8	238.0	239.2
hand	170.5	198.5	—	213.5	238.0	239.2
pharynx, pharyngeal	149.0	198.89	230.0	210.9	235.1	239.0
bursa	147.1	198.89	230.0	210.7	235.1	239.0
fornix	147.3	198.89	230.0	210.7	235.1	239.0
recess	147.2	198.89	230.0	210.7	235.1	239.0
region	149.0	198.89	230.0	210.9	235.1	239.0
tonsil	147.1	198.89	230.0	210.7	235.1	239.0
wall (lateral) (posterior)	149.0	198.89	230.0	210.9	235.1	239.0
pia mater (cerebral) (cranial)	192.1	198.4	—	225.2	237.6	239.7
spinal	192.3	198.4	—	225.4	237.6	239.7
pillars of fauces	146.2	198.89	230.0	210.6	235.1	239.0
pineal (body) (gland)	194.4	198.89	234.8	227.4	237.1	239.7
pinna (ear) NEC	173.2	198.2	232.2	216.2	238.2	239.2
cartilage	171.0	198.89	—	215.0	238.1	239.2
piriform fossa or sinus	148.1	198.89	230.0	210.8	235.1	239.0

	Malignant			Benign	Uncertain Behavior	Unspecified
	Primary	Secondary	Ca in situ			
Neoplasm, neoplastic — *continued*						
pituitary (body) (fossa) (gland) (lobe)	194.3	198.89	234.8	227.3	237.0	239.7
placenta	181	198.82	233.2	219.8	236.1	239.5
pleura, pleural (cavity)	163.9	197.2	—	212.4	235.8	239.1
contiguous sites	163.8	—	—	—	—	—
parietal	163.0	197.2	—	212.4	235.8	239.1
visceral	163.1	197.2	—	212.4	235.8	239.1
plexus						
brachial	171.2	198.89	—	215.2	238.1	239.2
cervical	171.0	198.89	—	215.0	238.1	239.2
choroid	191.5	198.3	—	225.0	237.5	239.6
lumbosacral	171.6	198.89	—	215.6	238.1	239.2
sacral	171.6	198.89	—	215.6	238.1	239.2
pluri-endocrine	194.8	198.89	234.8	227.8	237.4	239.7
pole						
frontal	191.1	198.3	—	225.0	237.5	239.6
occipital	191.4	198.3	—	225.0	237.5	239.6
pons (varolii)	191.7	198.3	—	225.0	237.5	239.6
popliteal fossa or space*	195.5	198.89	234.8	229.8	238.8	239.8
postcricoid (region)	148.0	198.89	230.0	210.8	235.1	239.0
posterior fossa (cranial)	191.6	198.3	—	225.0	237.5	239.6
postnasal space	147.9	198.89	230.0	210.7	235.1	239.0
prepuce	187.1	198.82	233.5	222.1	236.6	239.5
prepylorus	151.1	197.8	230.2	211.1	235.2	239.0
presacral (region)	195.3	198.89	—	229.8	238.8	239.8
prostate (gland)	185	198.82	233.4	222.2	236.5	239.5
utricle	189.3	198.1	233.9	223.81	236.99	239.5
pterygoid fossa	171.0	198.89	—	215.0	238.1	239.2
pubic bone	170.6	198.5	—	213.6	238.0	239.2
pudenda, pudendum (female)	184.4	198.82	233.3	221.2	236.3	239.5
pulmonary	162.9	197.0	231.2	212.3	235.7	239.1
putamen	191.0	198.3	—	225.0	237.5	239.6
pyloric						
antrum	151.2	197.8	230.2	211.1	235.2	239.0
canal	151.1	197.8	230.2	211.1	235.2	239.0
pylorus	151.1	197.8	230.2	211.1	235.2	239.0
pyramid (brain)	191.7	198.3	—	225.0	237.5	239.6
pyriform fossa or sinus	148.1	198.89	230.0	210.8	235.1	239.0
radius (any part)	170.4	198.5	—	213.4	238.0	239.2
Rathke's pouch	194.3	198.89	234.8	227.3	237.0	239.7
rectosigmoid (colon) (junction)	154.0	197.5	230.4	211.4	235.2	239.0
contiguous sites with anus or rectum	154.8	—	—	—	—	—
rectouterine pouch	158.8	197.6	—	211.8	235.4	239.0
rectovaginal septum or wall	195.3	198.89	234.8	229.8	238.8	239.8
rectovesical septum	195.3	198.89	234.8	229.8	238.8	239.8
rectum (ampulla)	154.1	197.5	230.4	211.4	235.2	239.0
and colon	154.0	197.5	230.4	211.4	235.2	239.0
contiguous sites with anus or rectosigmoid junction	154.8	—	—	—	—	—
renal	189.0	198.0	233.9	223.0	236.91	239.5
calyx	189.1	198.0	233.9	223.1	236.91	239.5
hilus	189.1	198.0	233.9	223.1	236.91	239.5
parenchyma	189.0	198.0	233.9	223.0	236.91	239.5
pelvis	189.1	198.0	233.9	223.1	236.91	239.5
respiratory						
organs or system NEC	165.9	197.3	231.9	212.9	235.9	239.1
contiguous sites with intrathoracic organs	165.8	—	—	—	—	—
specified sites NEC	165.8	197.3	231.8	212.8	235.9	239.1
tract NEC	165.9	197.3	231.9	212.9	235.9	239.1
upper	165.0	197.3	231.9	212.9	235.9	239.1
retina	190.5	198.4	234.0	224.5	238.8	239.8
retrobulbar	190.1	198.4	—	224.1	238.8	239.8
retrocecal	158.0	197.6	—	211.8	235.4	239.0
retromolar (area) (triangle) (trigone)	145.6	198.89	230.0	210.4	235.1	239.0
retro-orbital	195.0	198.89	234.8	229.8	238.8	239.8
retroperitoneal (space) (tissue)	158.0	197.6	—	211.8	235.4	239.0
contiguous sites	158.8	—	—	—	—	—
retroperitoneum	158.0	197.6	—	211.8	235.4	239.0
contiguous sites	158.8	—	—	—	—	—
retropharyngeal	149.0	198.89	230.0	210.9	235.1	239.0
retrovesical (septum)	195.3	198.89	234.8	229.8	238.8	239.8

	Malignant					
	Primary	Secondary	Ca in situ	Benign	Uncertain Behavior	Unspecified
Neoplasm, neoplastic — *continued*						
rhinencephalon	191.0	198.3	—	225.0	237.5	239.6
rib	170.3	198.5	—	213.3	238.0	239.2
Rosenmüller's fossa	147.2	198.89	230.0	210.7	235.1	239.0
round ligament	183.5	198.82	—	221.0	236.3	239.5
sacrococcyx, sacrococcygeal	170.6	198.5	—	213.6	238.0	239.2
region	195.3	198.89	234.8	229.8	238.8	239.8
sacrouterine ligament	183.4	198.82	—	221.0	236.3	239.5
sacrum, sacral (vertebra)	170.6	198.5	—	213.6	238.0	239.2
salivary gland or duct (major)	142.9	198.89	230.0	210.2	235.0	239.0
contiguous sites	142.8	—	—	—	—	—
minor NEC	145.9	198.89	230.0	210.4	235.1	239.0
parotid	142.0	198.89	230.0	210.2	235.0	239.0
pluriglandular	142.8	198.89	230.0	210.2	235.0	239.0
sublingual	142.2	198.89	230.0	210.2	235.0	239.0
submandibular	142.1	198.89	230.0	210.2	235.0	239.0
submaxillary	142.1	198.89	230.0	210.2	235.0	239.0
salpinx (uterine)	183.2	198.82	233.3	221.0	236.3	239.5
Santorini's duct	157.3	197.8	230.9	211.6	235.5	239.0
scalp	173.4	198.2	232.4	216.4	238.2	239.2
scapula (any part)	170.4	198.5	—	213.4	238.0	239.2
scalpular region	195.1	198.89	234.8	229.8	238.8	239.8
scar NEC (*see also* Neoplasm, skin)	173.9	198.2	232.9	216.9	238.2	239.2
sciatic nerve	171.3	198.89	—	215.3	238.1	239.2
sclera	190.0	198.4	234.0	224.0	238.8	239.8
scrotum (skin)	187.7	198.82	233.6	222.4	236.6	239.5
sebaceous gland — *see* Neoplasm, skin						
sella turcica	194.3	198.89	234.8	227.3	237.0	239.7
bone	170.0	198.5	—	213.0	238.0	239.2
semilunar cartilage (knee)	170.7	198.5	—	213.7	238.0	239.2
seminal vesicle	187.8	198.82	233.6	222.8	236.6	239.5
septum						
nasal	160.0	197.3	231.8	212.0	235.9	239.1
posterior margin	147.3	198.89	230.0	210.7	235.1	239.0
rectovaginal	195.3	198.89	234.8	229.8	238.8	239.8
rectovesical	195.3	198.89	234.8	229.8	238.8	239.8
urethrovaginal	184.9	198.82	233.3	221.9	236.3	239.5
vesicovaginal	184.9	198.82	233.3	221.9	236.3	239.5
shoulder NEC*	195.4	198.89	232.6	229.8	238.8	239.8
sigmoid flexure (lower) (upper)	153.3	197.5	230.3	211.3	235.2	239.0
sinus (accessory)	160.9	197.3	231.8	212.0	235.9	239.1
bone (any)	170.0	198.5	—	213.0	238.0	239.2
contiguous sites with middle ear or nasal cavities	160.8	—	—	—	—	—
ethmodial	160.3	197.3	231.8	212.0	235.9	239.1
frontal	160.4	197.3	231.8	212.0	235.9	239.1
maxillary	160.2	197.3	231.8	212.0	235.9	239.1
nasal, paranasal NEC	160.9	197.3	231.8	212.0	235.9	239.1
pyriform	148.1	198.89	230.0	210.8	235.1	239.0
sphenoidal	160.5	197.3	231.8	212.0	235.9	239.1
skeleton, skeletal NEC	170.9	198.5	—	213.9	238.0	239.2
Skene's gland	189.4	198.1	233.9	223.89	236.99	239.5
skin NEC	173.9	198.2	232.9	216.9	238.2	239.2
abdominal wall	173.5	198.2	232.5	216.5	238.2	239.2
ala nasi	173.3	198.2	232.3	216.3	238.2	239.2
ankle	173.7	198.2	232.7	216.7	238.2	239.2
antecubital space	173.6	198.2	232.6	216.6	238.2	239.2
anus	173.5	198.2	232.5	216.5	238.2	239.2
arm	173.6	198.2	232.6	216.6	238.2	239.2
auditory canal (external)	173.2	198.2	232.2	216.2	238.2	239.2
auricle (ear)	173.2	198.2	232.2	216.2	238.2	239.2
auricular canal (external)	173.2	198.2	232.2	216.2	238.2	239.2
axilla, axillary fold	173.5	198.2	232.5	216.5	238.2	239.2
back	173.5	198.2	232.5	216.5	238.2	239.2
breast	173.5	198.2	232.5	216.5	238.2	239.2
brow	173.3	198.2	232.3	216.3	238.2	239.2
buttock	173.5	198.2	232.5	216.5	238.2	239.2
calf	173.7	198.2	232.7	216.7	238.2	239.2
canthus (eye) (inner) (outer)	173.1	198.2	232.1	216.1	238.2	239.2
cervical region	173.4	198.2	232.4	216.4	238.2	239.2

	Malignant					
	Primary	Secondary	Ca in situ	Benign	Uncertain Behavior	Unspecified
Neoplasm, neoplastic — *continued*						
skin NEC — *continued*						
cheek (external)	173.3	198.2	232.3	216.3	238.2	239.2
chest (wall)	173.5	198.2	232.5	216.5	238.2	239.2
chin	173.3	198.2	232.3	216.3	238.2	239.2
clavicular area	173.5	198.2	232.5	216.5	238.2	239.2
clitoris	184.3	198.82	233.3	221.2	236.3	239.5
columnella	173.3	198.2	232.3	216.3	238.2	239.2
concha	173.2	198.2	232.2	216.2	238.2	239.2
contiguous sites	173.8	—	—	—	—	—
ear (external)	173.2	198.2	232.2	216.2	238.2	239.2
elbow	173.6	198.2	232.6	216.6	238.2	239.2
eyebrow	173.3	198.2	232.3	216.3	238.2	239.2
eyelid	173.1	198.2	232.1	216.1	238.2	239.2
face NEC	173.3	198.2	232.3	216.3	238.2	239.2
female genital organs (external)	184.4	198.82	233.3	221.2	236.3	239.5
clitoris	184.3	198.82	233.3	221.2	236.3	239.5
labium NEC	184.4	198.82	233.3	221.2	236.3	239.5
majus	184.1	198.82	233.3	221.2	236.3	239.5
minus	184.2	198.82	233.3	221.2	236.3	239.5
pudendum	184.4	198.82	233.3	221.2	236.3	239.5
vulva	184.4	198.82	233.3	221.2	236.3	239.5
finger	173.6	198.2	232.6	216.6	238.2	239.2
flank	173.5	198.2	232.5	216.5	238.2	239.2
foot	173.7	198.2	232.7	216.7	238.2	239.2
forearm	173.6	198.2	232.6	216.6	238.2	239.2
forehead	173.3	198.2	232.3	216.3	238.2	239.2
glabella	173.3	198.2	232.3	216.3	238.2	239.2
gtuteal region	173.5	198.2	232.5	216.5	238.2	239.2
groin	173.5	198.2	232.5	216.5	238.2	239.2
hand	173.6	198.2	232.6	216.6	238.2	239.2
head NEC	173.4	198.2	232.4	216.4	238.2	239.2
heel	173.7	198.2	232.7	216.7	238.2	239.2
helix	173.2	198.2	232.2	216.2	238.2	239.2
hip	173.7	198.2	232.7	216.7	238.2	239.2
infraclavicular region	173.5	198.2	232.5	216.5	238.2	239.2
inguinal region	173.5	198.2	232.5	216.5	238.2	239.2
jaw	173.3	198.2	232.3	216.3	238.2	239.2
knee	173.7	198.2	232.7	216.7	238.2	239.2
labia						
majora	184.1	198.82	233.3	221.2	236.3	239.5
minora	184.2	198.82	233.3	221.2	236.3	239.5
leg	173.7	198.2	232.7	216.7	238.2	239.2
lid (lower) (upper)	173.1	198.2	232.1	216.1	238.2	239.2
limb NEC	173.9	198.2	232.9	216.9	238.2	239.5
lower	173.7	198.2	232.7	216.7	238.2	239.2
upper	173.6	198.2	232.6	216.6	238.2	239.2
lip (lower) (upper)	173.0	198.2	232.0	216.0	238.2	239.2
male genital organs	187.9	198.82	233.6	222.9	236.6	239.5
penis	187.4	198.82	233.5	222.1	236.6	239.5
prepuce	187.1	198.82	233.5	222.1	236.6	239.5
scrotum	187.7	198.82	233.6	222.4	236.6	239.5
mastectomy site	173.5	198.2	—	—	—	—
specified as breast tissue	174.8	198.81	—	—	—	—
meatus, acoustic (external)	173.2	198.2	232.2	216.2	238.2	239.2
melanoma — *see* Melanoma						
nates	173.5	198.2	232.5	216.5	238.2	239.2
neck	173.4	198.2	232.4	216.4	238.2	239.2
nose (external)	173.3	198.2	232.3	216.3	238.2	239.2
palm	173.6	198.2	232.6	216.6	238.2	239.2
palpebra	173.1	198.2	232.1	216.1	238.2	239.2
penis NEC	187.4	198.82	233.5	222.1	236.6	239.5
perianal	173.5	198.2	232.5	216.5	238.2	239.2
perineum	173.5	198.2	232.5	216.5	238.2	239.2
pinna	173.2	198.2	232.2	216.2	238.2	239.2
plantar	173.7	198.2	232.7	216.7	238.2	239.2
popliteal fossa or space	173.7	198.2	232.7	216.7	238.2	239.2
prepuce	187.1	198.82	233.5	222.1	236.6	239.5

	Malignant Primary	Malignant Secondary	Malignant Ca in situ	Benign	Uncertain Behavior	Unspecified
Neoplasm, neoplastic — *continued*						
subcutaneous (nodule) (tissue) NEC — *see* Neoplasm, connective tissue						
subdural	192.1	198.4	—	225.2	237.6	239.7
subglottis, subglottic	161.2	197.3	231.0	212.1	235.6	239.1
sublingual	144.9	198.89	230.0	210.3	235.1	239.0
gland or duct	142.2	198.89	230.0	210.2	235.0	239.0
submandibular gland	142.1	198.89	230.0	210.2	235.0	239.0
submaxillary gland or duct	142.1	198.89	230.0	210.2	235.0	239.0
submental	195.0	198.89	234.8	229.8	238.8	239.8
subpleural	162.9	197.0	—	212.3	235.7	239.1
substernal	164.2	197.1	—	212.5	235.8	239.8
sudoriferous, sudoriparous gland, site unspecified	173.9	198.2	232.9	216.9	238.2	239.2
specified site — *see* Neoplasm, skin						
supraclavicular region	195.0	198.89	234.8	229.8	238.8	239.8
supraglottis	161.1	197.3	231.0	212.1	235.6	239.1
suprarenal (capsule) (cortex) (gland) (medulla)	194.0	198.7	234.8	227.0	237.2	239.7
suprasellar (region)	191.9	198.3	—	225.0	237.5	239.6
sweat gland (apocrine) (eccrine), site unspecified	173.9	198.2	232.9	216.9	238.2	239.2
specified site — *see* Neoplasm, skin						
sympathetic nerve or nervous system NEC	171.9	198.89	—	215.9	238.1	239.2
symphysis pubis	170.6	198.5	—	213.6	238.0	239.2
synovial membrane — *see* Neoplasm, connective tissue						
tapetum, brain	191.8	198.3	—	225.0	237.5	239.6
tarsus (any bone)	170.8	198.5	—	213.8	238.0	239.2
temple (skin)	173.3	198.2	232.3	216.3	238.2	239.2
temporal						
bone	170.0	198.5	—	213.0	238.0	239.2
lobe or pole	191.2	198.3	—	225.0	237.5	239.6
region	195.0	198.89	234.8	229.8	238.8	239.8
skin	173.3	198.2	232.3	216.3	238.2	239.2
tendon (sheath) — *see* Neoplasm, connective tissue						
tentorium (cerebelli)	192.1	198.4	—	225.2	237.6	239.7
testis, testes (descended) (scrotal)	186.9	198.82	233.6	222.0	236.4	239.5
ectopic	186.0	198.82	233.6	222.0	236.4	239.5
retained	186.0	198.82	233.6	222.0	236.4	239.5
undescended	186.0	198.82	233.6	222.0	236.4	239.5
thalamus	191.0	198.3	—	225.0	237.5	239.6
thigh NEC*	195.5	198.89	234.8	229.8	238.8	239.8
thorax, thoracic (cavity) (organs NEC)	195.1	198.89	234.8	229.8	238.8	239.8
duct	171.4	198.89	—	215.4	238.1	239.2
wall NEC	195.1	198.89	234.8	229.8	238.8	239.8
throat	149.0	198.89	230.0	210.9	235.1	239.0
thumb NEC*	195.4	198.89	232.6	229.8	238.8	239.8
thymus (gland)	164.0	198.89	—	212.6	235.8	239.8
contiguous sites with heart and mediastinum	164.8	—	—	—	—	—
thyroglossal duct	193	198.89	234.8	226	237.4	239.7
thyroid (gland)	193	198.89	234.8	226	237.4	239.7
cartilage	161.3	197.3	231.0	212.1	235.6	239.1
tibia (any part)	170.7	198.5	—	213.7	238.0	239.2
toe NEC*	195.5	198.89	232.7	229.8	238.8	239.8
tongue	141.9	198.89	230.0	210.1	235.1	239.0
anterior (two-thirds) NEC	141.4	198.89	230.0	210.1	235.1	239.0
dorsal surface	141.1	198.89	230.0	210.1	235.1	239.0
ventral surface	141.3	198.89	230.0	210.1	235.1	239.0
base (dorsal surface)	141.0	198.89	230.0	210.1	235.1	239.0
border (lateral)	141.2	198.89	230.0	210.1	235.1	239.0
contiguous sites	141.8	—	—	—	—	—
dorsal surface NEC	141.1	198.89	230.0	210.1	235.1	239.0
fixed part NEC	141.0	198.89	230.0	210.1	235.1	239.0
foreamen cecum	141.1	198.89	230.0	210.1	235.1	239.0
frenulum linguae	141.3	198.89	230.0	210.1	235.1	239.0
junctional zone	141.5	198.89	230.0	210.1	235.1	239.0
margin (lateral)	141.2	198.89	230.0	210.1	235.1	239.0
midline NEC	141.1	198.89	230.0	210.1	235.1	239.0
mobile part NEC	141.4	198.89	230.0	210.1	235.1	239.0
posterior (third)	141.0	198.89	230.0	210.1	235.1	239.0
root	141.0	198.89	230.0	210.1	235.1	239.0

	Malignant					
	Primary	Secondary	Ca in situ	Benign	Uncertain Behavior	Unspecified
Neoplasm, neoplastic — *continued*						
tongue — *continued*						
surface (dorsal)	141.1	198.89	230.0	210.1	235.1	239.0
base	141.0	198.89	230.0	210.1	235.1	239.0
ventral	141.3	198.89	230.0	210.1	235.1	239.0
tip	141.2	198.89	230.0	210.1	235.1	239.0
tonsil	141.6	198.89	230.0	210.1	235.1	239.0
tonsil	146.0	198.89	230.0	210.5	235.1	239.0
fauces, faucial	146.0	198.89	230.0	210.5	235.1	239.0
lingual	141.6	198.89	230.0	210.1	235.1	239.0
palatine	146.0	198.89	230.0	210.5	235.1	239.0
pharyngeal	147.1	198.89	230.0	210.7	235.1	239.0
pillar (anterior) (posterior)	146.2	198.89	230.0	210.6	235.1	239.0
tonsillar fossa	146.1	198.89	230.0	210.6	235.1	239.0
tooth socket NEC	143.9	198.89	230.0	210.4	235.1	239.0
trachea (cartilage) (mucosa)	162.0	197.3	231.1	212.2	235.7	239.1
contiguous sites with bronchus or lung	162.8	—	—	—	—	—
tracheobronchial	162.8	197.3	231.1	212.2	235.7	239.1
contiguous sites with lung	162.8	—	—	—	—	—
tragus	173.2	198.2	232.2	216.2	238.2	239.2
trunk NEC*	195.8	198.89	232.5	229.8	238.8	239.8
tubo-ovarian	183.8	198.82	233.3	221.8	236.3	239.5
tunica vaginalis	187.8	198.82	233.6	222.8	236.6	239.5
turbinate (bone)	170.0	198.5	—	213.0	238.0	239.2
nasal	160.0	197.3	231.8	212.0	235.9	239.1
tympanic cavity	160.1	197.3	231.8	212.0	235.9	239.1
ulna (any part)	170.4	198.5	—	213.4	238.0	239.2
umbilicus, umbilical	173.5	198.2	232.5	216.5	238.2	239.2
uncus, brain	191.2	198.3	—	225.0	237.5	239.6
unknown site or unspecified	199.1	199.1	234.9	229.9	238.9	239.9
urachus	188.7	198.1	233.7	223.3	236.7	239.4
ureter, ureteral	189.2	198.1	233.9	223.2	236.91	239.5
orifice (bladder)	188.6	198.1	233.7	223.3	236.7	239.4
ureter-bladder (junction)	188.6	198.1	233.7	223.3	236.7	239.4
urethra, urethral (gland)	189.3	198.1	233.9	223.81	236.99	239.5
orifice, internal	188.5	198.1	233.7	223.3	236.7	239.4
urethrovaginal (septum)	184.9	198.82	233.3	221.9	236.3	239.5
urinary organ or system NEC	189.9	198.1	233.9	223.9	236.99	239.5
bladder — *see* Neoplasm, bladder						
contiguous sites	189.8	—	—	—	—	—
specified sites NEC	189.8	198.1	233.9	223.89	236.99	239.5
utero-ovarian	183.8	198.82	233.3	221.8	236.3	239.5
ligament	183.3	198.82	—	221.0	236.3	239.5
uterosacral ligament	183.4	198.82	—	221.0	236.3	239.5
uterus, uteri, uterine	179	198.82	233.2	219.9	236.0	239.5
adnexa NEC	183.9	198.82	233.3	221.8	236.3	239.5
contiguous sites	183.8	—	—	—	—	—
body	182.0	198.82	233.2	219.1	236.0	239.5
contiguous sites	182.8	—	—	—	—	—
cervix	180.9	198.82	233.1	219.0	236.0	239.5
cornu	182.0	198.82	233.2	219.1	236.0	239.5
corpus	182.0	198.82	233.2	219.1	236.0	239.5
endocervix (canal) (gland)	180.0	198.82	233.1	219.0	236.0	239.5
endometrium	182.0	198.82	233.2	219.1	236.0	239.5
exocervix	180.1	198.82	233.1	219.0	236.0	239.5
external os	180.1	198.82	233.1	219.0	236.0	239.5
fundus	182.0	198.82	233.2	219.1	236.0	239.5
internal os	180.0	198.82	233.1	219.0	236.0	239.5
isthmus	182.1	198.82	233.2	219.1	236.0	239.5
ligament	183.4	198.82	—	221.0	236.3	239.5
broad	183.3	198.82	233.3	221.0	236.3	239.5
round	183.5	198.82	—	221.0	236.3	239.5
lower segment	182.1	198.82	233.2	219.1	236.0	239.5
myometrium	182.0	198.82	233.2	219.1	236.0	239.5
squamocolumnar junction	180.8	198.82	233.1	219.0	236.0	239.5
tube	183.2	198.82	233.3	221.0	236.3	239.5

	Malignant Primary	Malignant Secondary	Malignant Ca in situ	Benign	Uncertain Behavior	Unspecified
Neoplasm, neoplastic — *continued*						
utricle, prostatic	189.3	198.1	233.9	223.81	236.99	239.5
uveal tract	190.0	198.4	234.0	224.0	238.8	239.8
uvula	145.4	198.89	230.0	210.4	235.1	239.0
vagina, vaginal (fornix) (vault) (wall)	184.0	198.82	233.3	221.1	236.3	239.5
vaginovesical	184.9	198.82	233.3	221.9	236.3	239.5
septum	194.9	198.82	233.3	221.9	236.3	239.5
vallecula (epiglottis)	146.3	198.89	230.0	210.6	235.1	239.0
vascular — *see* Neoplasm, connective tissue						
vas deferens	187.6	198.82	233.6	222.8	236.6	239.5
Vater's ampulla	156.2	197.8	230.8	211.5	235.3	239.0
vein, venous — *see* Neoplasm, connective tissue						
vena cava (abdominal) (inferior)	171.5	198.89	—	215.5	238.1	239.2
superior	171.4	198.89	—	215.4	238.1	239.2
ventricle (cerebral) (floor) (fourth) (lateral) (third)	191.5	198.3	—	225.0	237.5	239.6
cardiac (left) (right)	164.1	198.89	—	212.7	238.8	239.8
ventricular band of larynx	161.1	197.3	231.0	212.1	235.6	239.1
ventriculus — *see* Neoplasm, stomach						
vermillion border — *see* Neoplasm, lip						
vermis, cerebellum	191.6	198.3	—	225.0	237.5	239.6
vertebra (column)	170.2	198.5	—	213.2	238.0	239.2
coccyx	170.6	198.5	—	213.6	238.0	239.2
sacrum	170.6	198.5	—	213.6	238.0	239.2
vesical — *see* Neoplasm, bladder						
vesicle, seminal	187.8	198.82	233.6	222.8	236.6	239.5
vesicocervical tissue	184.9	198.82	233.3	221.9	236.3	239.5
vesicorectal	195.3	198.89	234.8	229.8	238.8	239.8
vesicovaginal	184.9	198.82	233.3	221.9	236.3	239.5
septum	184.9	198.82	233.3	221.9	236.3	239.5
vessel (blood) — *see* Neoplasm, connective tissue						
vestibular gland, greater	184.1	198.82	233.3	221.2	236.3	239.5
vestibule						
mouth	145.1	198.89	230.0	210.4	235.1	239.0
nose	160.0	197.3	231.8	212.0	235.9	239.1
Virchow's gland	—	196.0	—	229.0	238.8	239.8
viscera NEC	195.8	198.89	234.8	229.8	238.8	239.8
vocal cords (true)	161.0	197.3	231.0	212.1	235.6	239.1
false	161.1	197.3	231.0	212.1	235.6	239.1
vomer	170.0	198.5	—	213.0	238.0	239.2
vulva	184.4	198.82	233.3	221.2	236.3	239.5
vulvovaginal gland	184.4	198.82	233.3	221.2	236.3	239.5
Waldeyer's ring	149.1	198.89	230.0	210.9	235.1	239.0
Wharton's duct	142.1	198.89	230.0	210.2	235.0	239.0
white matter (central) (cerebral)	191.0	198.3	—	225.0	237.5	239.6
windpipe	162.0	197.3	231.1	212.2	235.7	239.1
Wirsung's duct	157.3	197.8	230.9	211.6	235.5	239.0
wolffian (body) (duct)						
female	184.8	198.82	233.3	221.8	236.3	239.5
male	187.8	198.82	233.6	222.8	236.6	239.5
womb — *see* Neoplasm, uterus						
wrist NEC*	195.4	198.89	232.6	229.8	238.8	239.8
xiphoid process	170.3	198.5	—	213.3	238.0	239.2
Zuckerkandl's organ	194.6	198.89	—	227.6	237.3	239.7

Note — Except where otherwise indicated, the varieties of nevus in the list below that are followed by a morphology code number (M- - - -/0) should be coded by site as for "Neoplasm, skin, benign."

O

Note — Use the following fifth-digit subclassification with category 715:

0 site unspecified
1 shoulder region
2 upper arm
3 forearm
4 hand
5 pelvic region and thigh
6 lower leg
7 ankle and foot
8 other specified sites except spine
9 multiple sites

P

Pacemaker syndrome 429.4
Pachyderma, pachydermia 701.8
- laryngis 478.5
- laryngitis 478.79
- larynx (verrucosa) 478.79

Pachydermatitis 701.8
Pachydermatocele (congenital) 757.39
- acquired 701.8

Pachydermatosis 701.8
Pachydermoperiostitis
- secondary 731.2

Pachydermoperiostosis
- primary idiopathic 757.39
- secondary 731.2

Pachymeningitis (adhesive) (basal) (brain) (cerebral) (cervical) (chronic) (circumscribed) (external) (fibrous) (hemorrhagic) (hypertrophic) (internal) (purulent) (spinal) (suppurative) (*see also* Meningitis) 322.9
- gonococcal 098.82

Pachyonychia (congenital) 757.5
- acquired 703.8

Pachyperiosteodermia
- primary or idiopathic 757.39
- secondary 731.2

Pachyperiostosis
- primary or idiopathic 757.39
- secondary 731.2

Pacinian tumor (M9507/0) — *see* Neoplasm, skin, benign
Pads, knuckle or Garrod's 728.79
Paget's disease (osteitis deformans) 731.0
- with infiltrating duct carcinoma of the breast (M8541/3) — *see* Neoplasm, breast, malignant
- bone 731.0
  - osteosarcoma in (M9184/3) — *see* Neoplasm, bone, malignant
- breast (M8540/3) 174.0
- extramammary (M8542/3) — *see also* Neoplasm, skin, malignant
  - anus 154.3
    - skin 173.5
- malignant (M8540/3)
  - breast 174.0
  - specified site NEC (M8542/3) — *see* Neoplasm, skin, malignant
  - unspecified site 174.0
- mammary (M8540/3) 174.0
- necrosis of bone 731.0
- nipple (M8540/3) 174.0
- osteitis deformans 731.0

Paget-Schroetter syndrome (intermittent venous claudication) 453.8
Pain(s)

> *The following fifth-digit subclassification is to be used for code 789.0:*
> *0 unspecified site*
> *1 right upper quadrant*
> *2 left upper quadrant*
> *3 right lower quadrant*
> *4 left lower quadrant*
> *5 periumbilic*
> *6 epigastric*
> *7 generalized*
> *9 other specified site*
> *Multiple sites*

- abdominal 789.0 [5th]
- adnexa (uteri) 625.9
- alimentary, due to vascular insufficiency 557.9
- anginoid (*see also* Pain, precordial) 786.51
- anus 569.42
- arch 729.5
- arm 729.5
- back (postural) 724.5
  - low 724.2
  - psychogenic 307.89
- bile duct 576.9
- bladder 788.9
- bone 733.90
- breast 611.71
  - psychogenic 307.89
- broad ligament 625.9
- cartilage NEC 733.90
- cecum 789.0 [5th]
- cervicobrachial 723.3
- chest (central) 786.50
  - atypical 786.59
  - midsternal 786.51
  - musculoskeletal 786.59
  - noncardiac 786.59
  - substernal 786.51
  - wall (anterior) 786.52
- coccyx 724.79
- colon 789.0 [5th]
- common duct 576.9
- coronary — *see* Angina
- costochondral 786.52
- diaphragm 786.52
- due to (presence of) any device, implant, or graft classifiable to 996.0-996.5 — *see* Complications, due to (presence of) any device, implant, or graft classified to 996.0-996.5 NEC
- ear (*see also* Otalgia) 388.70
- epigastric, epigastrium 789.0 [5th]
- extremity (lower) (upper) 729.5
- eye 379.91
- face, facial 784.0
  - atypical 350.2
  - nerve 351.8
- false (labor) 644.1 [5th]
- female genital organ NEC 625.9
  - psychogenic 307.89
- finger 729.5
- flank 789.0 [5th]
- foot 729.5
- gallbladder 575.9
- gas (intestinal) 787.3
- gastric 536.8
- generalized 780.9
- genital organ
  - female 625.9
  - male 608.9
  - psychogenic 307.89
- groin 789.0 [5th]
- growing 781.9
- hand 729.5
- head (*see also* Headache) 784.0
- heart (*see also* Pain, precordial) 786.51
- infraorbital (*see also* Neuralgia, trigeminal) 350.1
- intermenstrual 625.2
- jaw 526.9
- joint 719.40
  - ankle 719.47
  - elbow 719.42
  - foot 719.47
  - hand 719.44
  - hip 719.45
  - knee 719.46

Pain(s) — *continued*
- joint— *continued*
  - multiple sites 719.49
  - pelvic region 719.45
  - psychogenic 307.89
  - shoulder (region) 719.41
  - specified site NEC 719.48
  - wrist 719.43
- kidney 788.0
- labor, false or spurious 644.1 [5th]
- laryngeal 784.1
- leg 729.5
- limb 729.5
- low back 724.2
- lumbar region 724.2
- mastoid (*see also* Otalgia) 388.70
- maxilla 526.9
- metacarpophalangeal (joint) 719.44
- metatarsophalangeal (joint) 719.47
- mouth 528.9
- muscle 729.1
  - intercostal 786.59
- nasal 478.1
- nasopharynx 478.29
- neck NEC 723.1
  - psychogenic 307.89
- nerve NEC 729.2
- neuromuscular 729.1
- nose 478.1
- ocular 379.91
- ophthalmic 379.91
- orbital region 379.91
- osteocopic 733.90
- ovary 625.9
  - psychogenic 307.89
- over heart (*see also* Pain, precordial) 786.51
- ovulation 625.2
- pelvic (female) 625.9
  - male NEC 789.0 [5th]
    - psychogenic 307.89
  - psychogenic 307.89
- penis 607.9
  - psychogenic 307.89
- pericardial (*see also* Pain, precordial) 786.51
- perineum
  - female 625.9
  - male 608.9
- pharynx 478.29
- pleura, pleural, pleuritic 786.52
- postoperative — *see* Pain, by site
- preauricular 388.70
- precordial (region) 786.51
  - psychogenic 307.89
- psychogenic 307.80
  - cardiovascular system 307.89
  - gastrointestinal system 307.89
  - genitourinary system 307.89
  - heart 307.89
  - musculoskeletal system 307.89
  - respiratory system 307.89
  - skin 306.3
- radicular (spinal) (*see also* Radiculitis) 729.2
- rectum 569.42
- respiration 786.52
- retrosternal 786.51
- rheumatic NEC 729.0
  - muscular 729.1
- rib 786.50
- root (spinal) (*see also* Radiculitis) 729.2
- round ligament (stretch) 625.9
- sacroiliac 724.6

P–U

- **Pain**(s) — *continued*
  - sciatic 724.3
  - scrotum 608.9
    - psychogenic 307.89
  - seminal vesicle 608.9
  - sinus 478.1
  - skin 782.0
  - spermatic cord 608.9
  - spinal root (*see also* Radiculitis) 729.2
  - stomach 536.8
    - psychogenic 307.89
  - substernal 786.51
  - temporomandibular (joint) 524.62
  - temporomaxillary joint 524.62
  - testis 608.9
    - psychogenic 307.89
  - thoracic spine 724.1
    - with radicular and visceral pain 724.4
  - throat 784.1
  - tibia 733.90
  - toe 729.5
  - tongue 529.6
  - tooth 525.9
  - trigeminal (*see also* Neuralgia, trigeminal) 350.1
  - umbilicus 789.0 [5th]
  - ureter 788.0
  - urinary (organ) (system) 788.0
  - uterus 625.9
    - psychogenic 307.89
  - vagina 625.9
  - vertebrogenic (syndrome) 724.5
  - vesical 788.9
  - vulva 625.9
  - xiphoid 733.90
- **Painful** — *see also* Pain
  - arc syndrome 726.19
  - coitus
    - female 625.0
    - male 608.89
    - psychogenic 302.76
  - ejaculation (semen) 608.89
    - psychogenic 302.79
  - erection 607.3
  - feet syndrome 266.2
  - menstruation 625.3
    - psychogenic 306.52
  - micturition 788.1
  - ophthalmoplegia 378.55
  - respiration 786.52
  - scar NEC 709.2
  - urination 788.1
  - wire sutures 998.89
- **Painters' colic** 984.9
  - specified type of lead — *see* Table of Drugs and Chemicals
- **Palate** — *see* condition
- **Palatoplegia** 528.9
- **Palatoschisis** (*see also* Cleft, palate) 749.00
- **Palilalia** 784.69
- **Palindromic arthritis** (*see also* Rheumatism, palindromic) 719.3 [5th]
- **Palliative care** V66.7
- **Pallor** 782.61
  - temporal, optic disc 377.15
- **Palmar** — *see also* condition
  - fascia — *see* condition
- **Palpable**
  - cecum 569.89
  - kidney 593.89
  - liver 573.9
  - lymph nodes 785.6
  - ovary 620.8
  - prostate 602.9
  - spleen (*see also* Splenomegaly) 789.2
  - uterus 625.8
- **Palpitation** (heart) 785.1
  - psychogenic 306.2
- **Palsy** (*see also* Paralysis) 344.9
  - atrophic diffuse 335.20
  - Bell's 351.0
    - newborn 767.5
  - birth 767.7
  - brachial plexus 353.0
    - fetus or newborn 767.6
  - brain — *see also* Palsy, cerebral
    - noncongenital or noninfantile 344.89
      - due to vascular lesion — *see* Late effect(s) (of) cerebrovascular disease
      - late effect — *see* Late effect(s) (of) cerebrovascular disease
    - syphilitic 094.89
      - congenital 090.49
  - bulbar (chronic) (progressive) 335.22
    - pseudo NEC 335.23
    - supranuclear NEC 344.89
  - cerebral (congenital) (infantile) (spastic) 343.9
    - athetoid 333.7
    - diplegic 343.0
      - due to previous vascular lesion — *see* Late effect(s) (of) cerebrovascular disease
      - late effect — *see* Late effect(s) (of) cerebrovascular disease
    - hemiplegic 343.1
    - monoplegic 343.3
    - noncongenital or noninfantile 437.8
      - due to previous vascular lesion — *see* Late effect(s) (of) cerebrovascular disease
      - late effect — *see* Late effect(s) (of) cerebrovascular disease
    - paraplegic 343.0
    - quadriplegic 343.2
    - spastic, not congenital or infantile 344.89
    - syphilitic 094.89
      - congenital 090.49
    - tetraplegic 343.2
  - cranial nerve — *see also* Disorder, nerve, cranial
    - multiple 352.6
  - creeping 335.21
  - divers' 993.3
  - Erb's (birth injury) 767.6
  - facial 351.0
    - newborn 767.5
  - glossopharyngeal 352.2
  - Klumpke (-Déjérine) 767.6
  - lead 984.9
    - specified type of lead — *see* Table of Drugs and Chemicals
  - median nerve (tardy) 354.0
  - peroneal nerve (acute) (tardy) 355.3
  - progressive supranuclear 333.0
  - pseudobulbar NEC 335.23
  - radial nerve (acute) 354.3
  - seventh nerve 351.0
    - newborn 767.5
  - shaking (*see also* Parkinsonism) 332.0
- **Palsy** (*see also* Paralysis) — *continued*
  - spastic (cerebral) (spinal) 343.9
    - hemiplegic 343.1
  - specified nerve NEC — *see* Disorder, nerve
  - supranuclear NEC 356.8
    - progressive 333.0
  - ulnar nerve (tardy) 354.2
  - wasting 335.21
- **Paltauf-Sternberg disease** 201.9 [5th]
- **Paludism** — *see* Malaria
- **Panama fever** 084.0
- **Panaris** (with lymphangitis) 681.9
  - finger 681.02
  - toe 681.11
- **Panaritium** (with lymphangitis) 681.9
  - finger 681.02
  - toe 681.11
- **Panarteritis** (nodosa) 446.0
  - brain or cerebral 437.4
- **Pancake heart** 793.2
  - with cor pulmonale (chronic) 416.9
- **Pancarditis** (acute) (chronic) 429.89
  - with
    - rheumatic
      - fever (active) (acute) (chronic) (subacute) 391.8
        - inactive or quiescent 398.99
  - rheumatic, acute 391.8
    - chronic or inactive 398.99
- **Pancoast's syndrome or tumor** (carcinoma, pulmonary apex) (M8010/3) 162.3
- **Pancoast-Tobias syndrome** (M8010/3) (carcinoma, pulmonary apex) 162.3
- **Pancolitis** 556.6
- **Pancreas, pancreatic** — *see* condition
- **Pancreatitis** 577.0
  - acute (edematous) (hemorrhagic) (recurrent) 577.0
  - annular 577.0
  - apoplectic 577.0
  - calcereous 577.0
  - chronic (infectious) 577.1
    - recurrent 577.1
  - cystic 577.2
  - fibrous 577.8
  - gangrenous 577.0
  - hemorrhagic (acute) 577.0
  - interstitial (chronic) 577.1
    - acute 577.0
  - malignant 577.0
  - mumps 072.3
  - painless 577.1
  - recurrent 577.1
  - relapsing 577.1
  - subacute 577.0
  - suppurative 577.0
  - syphilitic 095.8
- **Pancreatolithiasis** 577.8
- **Pancytolysis** 289.9
- **Pancytopenia** (acquired) 284.8
  - with malformations 284.0
  - congenital 284.0
- **Panencephalitis** — *see also* Encephalitis
  - subacute, sclerosing 046.2
- **Panhematopenia** 284.8
  - congenital 284.0
  - constitutional 284.0
  - splenic, primary 289.4

Note — Except where otherwise indicated, the morphological varieties of papilloma in the list below should be coded by site as for "Neoplasm, benign".

- **Perforation, perforative** (nontraumatic) — *continued*
  - broad ligament
    - with
      - abortion — *see* Abortion, by type, with damage to pelvic organs
      - ectopic pregnancy (*see also* categories 633.0-633.9) 639.2
      - molar pregnancy (*see also* categories 630-632) 639.2
    - following
      - abortion 639.2
      - ectopic or molar pregnancy 639.2
    - obstetrical trauma 665.6 [5th]
  - by
    - device, implant, or graft — *see* Complications, mechanical
    - foreign body left accidentally in operation wound 998.4
    - instrument (any) during a procedure, accidental 998.2
  - cecum 540.0
    - with peritoneal abscess 540.1
  - cervix (uteri) — *see also* Injury, internal, cervix
    - with
      - abortion — *see* Abortion, by type, with damage to pelvic organs
      - ectopic pregnancy (*see also* categories 633.0-633.9) 639.2
      - molar pregnancy (*see also* categories 630-632) 639.2
    - following
      - abortion 639.2
      - ectopic or molar pregnancy 639.2
    - obstetrical trauma 665.3 [5th]
  - colon 569.83
  - common duct (bile) 576.3
  - cornea (*see also* Ulcer, cornea) 370.00
    - due to ulceration 370.06
  - cystic duct 575.4
  - diverticulum (*see also* Diverticula) 562.10
    - small intestine 562.00
  - duodenum, duodenal (ulcer) — *see* Ulcer, duodenum, with perforation
  - ear drum — *see* Perforation, tympanum
  - enteritis — *see* Enteritis
  - esophagus 530.4
  - ethmoidal sinus (*see also* Sinusitis, ethmoidal) 473.2
  - foreign body (external site) — *see also* Wound, open, by site, complicated
    - internal site, by ingested object — *see* Foreign body
  - frontal sinus (*see also* Sinusitis, frontal) 473.1
  - gallbladder or duct (*see also* Disease, gallbladder) 575.4
  - gastric (ulcer) — *see* Ulcer, stomach, with perforation
  - heart valve — *see* Endocarditis
  - ileum (*see also* Perforation, intestine) 569.83
  - instrumental
    - external — *see* Wound, open, by site
    - pregnant uterus, complicating delivery 665.9 [5th]
    - surgical (accidental) (blood vessel) (nerve) (organ) 998.2
  - intestine 569.83
    - with
      - abortion — *see* Abortion, by type, with damage to pelvic organs
      - ectopic pregnancy (*see also* categories 633.0-633.9) 639.2
      - molar pregnancy (*see also* categories 630-632) 639.2
    - fetus or newborn 777.6
    - obstetrical trauma 665.5 [5th]
    - ulcerative NEC 569.83
  - jejunum, jejunal 569.83
    - ulcer — *see* Ulcer, gastrojejunal, with perforation
  - mastoid (antrum) (cell) 383.89
  - maxillary sinus (*see also* Sinusitis, maxillary) 473.0
  - membrana tympani — *see* Perforation, tympanum
  - nasal
    - septum 478.1
      - congenital 748.1
      - syphilitic 095.8
    - sinus (*see also* Sinusitis) 473.9
      - congenital 748.1
  - palate (hard) 526.89
    - soft 528.9
      - syphilitic 095.8
    - syphilitic 095.8
  - palatine vault 526.89
    - syphilitic 095.8
      - congenital 090.5
  - pelvic
    - floor
      - with
        - abortion — *see* Abortion, by type, with damage to pelvic organs
        - ectopic pregnancy (*see also* categories 633.0-633.9) 639.2
        - molar pregnancy (*see also* categories 630-632) 639.2
      - obstetrical trauma 664.1 [5th]
    - organ
      - with
        - abortion — *see* Abortion, by type, with damage to pelvic organs
        - ectopic pregnancy (*see also* categories 633.0-633.9) 639.2
        - molar pregnancy (*see also* categories 630-632) 639.2
      - following
        - abortion 639.2
        - ectopic or molar pregnancy 639.2
      - obstetrical trauma 665.5 [5th]
  - perineum — *see* Laceration, perineum
  - periurethral tissue
    - with
      - abortion — *see* Abortion, by type, with damage to pelvic organs
      - ectopic pregnancy (*see also* categories 630-632) 639.2
      - molar pregnancy (*see also* categories 630-632) 639.2
  - pharynx 478.29
  - pylorus, pyloric (ulcer) — *see* Ulcer, stomach, with perforation
  - rectum 569.49
  - sigmoid 569.83
  - sinus (accessory) (chronic) (nasal) (*see also* Sinusitis) 473.9
  - sphenoidal sinus (*see also* Sinusitis, sphenoidal) 473.3
  - stomach (due to ulcer) — *see* Ulcer, stomach, with perforation
  - surgical (accidental) (by instrument) (blood vessel) (nerve) (organ) 998.2
  - traumatic
    - external — *see* Wound, open, by site
    - eye (*see also* Penetrating wound, ocular) 871.7
    - internal organ — *see* Injury, internal, by site
  - tympanum (membrane) (persistent posttraumatic) (postinflammatory) 384.20
    - with
      - otitis media — *see* Otitis media
    - attic 384.22
    - central 384.21
    - healed 384.81
    - marginal NEC 384.23
    - multiple 384.24
    - pars flaccida 384.22
    - total 384.25
    - traumatic — *see* Wound, open, ear, drum
  - typhoid, gastrointestinal 002.0
  - ulcer — *see* Ulcer, by site, with perforation
  - ureter 593.89
  - urethra
    - with
      - abortion — *see* Abortion, by type, with damage to pelvic organs
      - ectopic pregnancy (*see also* categories 633.0-633.9) 639.2
      - molar pregnancy (*see also* categories 630-632) 639.2
    - following
      - abortion 639.2
      - ectopic or molar pregnancy 639.2
    - obstetrical trauma 665.5 [5th]
  - uterus — *see also* Injury, internal, uterus
    - with
      - abortion — *see* Abortion, by type, with damage to pelvic organs
      - ectopic pregnancy (*see also* categories 633.0-633.9) 639.2
      - molar pregnancy (*see also* categories 630-632) 639.2
    - by intrauterine contraceptive device 996.32
    - following
      - abortion 639.2
      - ectopic or molar pregnancy 639.2
    - obstetrical trauma — *see* Injury, internal, uterus, obstetrical trauma
  - uvula 528.9
    - syphilitic 095.8
  - vagina — *see* Laceration, vagina
  - viscus NEC 799.8
    - traumatic 868.00
      - with open wound into cavity 868.10
- **Periadenitis mucosa necrotica recurrens** 528.2
- **Periangiitis** 446.0
- **Periantritis** 535.4 [5th]

- **Periostitis** (circumscribed) (diffuse) (infective) 730.3 ✓5th

> *Note — Use the following fifth-digit subclassification with category 730:*
>
> *0 site unspecified*
> *1 shoulder region*
> *2 upper arm*
> *3 forearm*
> *4 hand*
> *5 pelvic region and thigh*
> *6 lower leg*
> *7 ankle and foot*
> *8 other specified sites*
> *9 multiple sites*

  - with osteomyelitis (*see also* Osteomyelitis) 730.2 ✓5th
    - acute or subacute 730.0 ✓5th
    - chronic or old 730.1 ✓5th
  - albuminosa, albuminosus 730.3 ✓5th
  - alveolar 526.5
  - alveolodental 526.5
  - dental 526.5
  - gonorrheal 098.89
  - hyperplastica, generalized 731.2
  - jaw (lower) (upper) 526.4
  - monomelic 733.99
  - orbital 376.02
  - syphilitic 095.5
    - congenital 090.0 *[730.8]* ✓5th
    - secondary 091.61
  - tuberculous (*see also* Tuberculosis, bone) 015.9 ✓5th *[730.8]* ✓5th
  - yaws (early) (hypertrophic) (late) 102.6
- **Periostosis** (*see also* Periostitis) 730.3 ✓5th
  - with osteomyelitis (*see also* Osteomyelitis) 730.2 ✓5th
    - acute or subacute 730.0 ✓5th
    - chronic or old 730.1 ✓5th
  - hyperplastic 756.59
- **Periphlebitis** (*see also* Phlebitis) 451.9
  - lower extremity 451.2
    - deep (vessels) 451.19
    - superficial (vessels) 451.0
  - portal 572.1
  - retina 362.18
  - superficial (vessels) 451.0
  - tuberculous (*see also* Tuberculosis) 017.9 ✓5th
    - retina 017.3 ✓5th *[362.18]*
- **Peripneumonia** — *see* Pneumonia
- **Periproctitis** 569.49
- **Periprostatitis** (*see also* Prostatitis) 601.9
- **Perirectal** — *see* condition
- **Perirenal** — *see* condition
- **Perisalpingitis** (*see also* Salpingo-oophoritis) 614.2
- **Perisigmoiditis** 569.89
- **Perisplenitis** (infectional) 289.59
- **Perispondylitis** — *see* Spondylitis
- **Peristalsis reversed or visible** 787.4
- **Peritendinitis** (*see also* Tenosynovitis) 726.90
  - adhesive (shoulder) 726.0
- **Perithelioma** (M9150/1) — *see* Pericytoma
- **Peritoneum, peritoneal** — *see* condition
- **Peritonitis** (acute) (adhesive) (fibrinous) (hemorrhagic) (idiopathic) (localized) (perforative) (primary) (with adhesions) (with effusion) 567.9
  - with or following
    - abortion — *see* Abortion, by type, with sepsis
    - abscess 567.2
    - appendicitis 540.0
      - with peritoneal abscess 540.1
    - ectopic pregnancy (*see also* categories 633.0-633.9) 639.0
    - molar pregnancy (*see also* categories 630-632) 639.0
  - aseptic 998.7
  - bacterial 567.2
  - bile, biliary 567.8
  - chemical 998.7
  - chlamydial 099.56
  - chronic proliferative 567.8
  - congenital NEC 777.6
  - diaphragmatic 567.2
  - diffuse NEC 567.2
  - diphtheritic 032.83
  - disseminated NEC 567.2
  - due to
    - bile 567.8
    - foreign
      - body or object accidentally left during a procedure (instrument) (sponge) (swab) 998.4
      - substance accidentally left during a procedure (chemical) (powder) (talc) 998.7
    - talc 998.7
    - urine 567.8
  - fibrinopurulent 567.2
  - fibrinous 567.2
  - fibrocaseous (*see also* Tuberculosis) 014.0 ✓5th
  - fibropurulent 567.2
  - general, generalized (acute) 567.2
  - gonococcal 098.86
  - in infective disease NEC 136.9 *[567.0]*
  - meconium (newborn) 777.6
  - pancreatic 577.8
  - paroxysmal, benign 277.3
  - pelvic
    - female (acute) 614.5
      - chronic NEC 614.7
        - with adhesions 614.6
      - puerperal, postpartum, childbirth 670
    - male (acute) 567.2
  - periodic (familial) 277.3
  - phlegmonous 567.2
  - pneumococcal 567.1
  - postabortal 639.0
  - proliferative, chronic 567.8
  - puerperal, postpartum, childbirth 670
  - purulent 567.2
  - septic 567.2
  - staphylococcal 567.2
  - streptococcal 567.2
  - subdiaphragmatic 567.2
  - subphrenic 567.2
  - suppurative 567.2
  - syphilitic 095.2
    - congenital 090.0 *[567.0]*
  - talc 998.7
  - tuberculous (*see also* Tuberculosis) 014.0 ✓5th
  - urine 567.8
- **Peritonsillar** — *see* condition
- **Peritonsillitis** 475
- **Perityphlitis** (*see also* Appendicitis) 541
- **Periureteritis** 593.89
- **Periurethral** — *see* condition
- **Periurethritis** (gangrenous) 597.89
- **Periuterine** — *see* condition
- **Perivaginitis** (*see also* Vaginitis) 616.10
- **Perivasculitis, retinal** 362.18
- **Perivasitis** (chronic) 608.4
- **Perivesiculitis** (seminal) (*see also* Vesiculitis) 608.0
- **Perlèche** 686.8
  - due to
    - moniliasis 112.0
    - riboflavin deficiency 266.0
- **Pernicious** — *see* condition
- **Pernio, perniosis** 991.5
- **Persecution**
  - delusion 297.9
  - social V62.4
- **Perseveration** (tonic) 784.69
- **Persistence, persistent** (congenital) 759.89
  - anal membrane 751.2
  - arteria stapedia 744.04
  - atrioventricular canal 745.69
  - bloody ejaculate 792.2
  - branchial cleft 744.41
  - bulbus cordis in left ventricle 745.8
  - canal of Cloquet 743.51
  - capsule (opaque) 743.51
  - cilioretinal artery or vein 743.51
  - cloaca 751.5
  - communication — *see* Fistula, congenital
  - convolutions
    - aortic arch 747.21
    - fallopian tube 752.19
    - oviduct 752.19
    - uterine tube 752.19
  - double aortic arch 747.21
  - ductus
    - arteriosus 747.0
    - Botalli 747.0
  - fetal
    - circulation 747.89
    - form of cervix (uteri) 752.49
    - hemoglobin (hereditary) ("Swiss variety") 282.7
    - pulmonary hypertension 747.89
  - foramen
    - Botalli 745.5
    - ovale 745.5
  - Gartner's duct 752.11
  - hemoglobin, fetal (hereditary) (HPFH) 282.7
  - hyaloid
    - artery (generally incomplete) 743.51
    - system 743.51
  - hymen (tag)
    - in pregnancy or childbirth 654.8 ✓5th
      - causing obstructed labor 660.2 ✓5th
  - lanugo 757.4
  - left
    - posterior cardinal vein 747.49
    - root with right arch of aorta 747.21
    - superior vena cava 747.49
  - Meckel's diverticulum 751.0
  - mesonephric duct 752.8
    - fallopian tube 752.11

- **Pili**
  - annulati or torti (congenital) 757.4
  - incarnati 704.8
- **Pill roller hand** (intrinsic) 736.09
- **Pilomatrixoma** (M8110/0) — *see* Neoplasm, skin, benign
- **Pilonidal** — *see* condition
- **Pimple** 709.8
- **Pinched nerve** — *see* Neuropathy, entrapment
- **Pineal body or gland** — *see* condition
- **Pinealoblastoma** (M9362/3) 194.4
- **Pinealoma** (M9360/1) 237.1
  - malignant (M9360/3) 194.4
- **Pineoblastoma** (M9362/3) 194.4
- **Pineocytoma** (M9361/1) 237.1
- **Pinguecula** 372.51
- **Pinhole meatus** (*see also* Stricture, urethra) 598.9
- **Pink**
  - disease 985.0
  - eye 372.03
  - puffer 492.8
- **Pinkus' disease** (lichen nitidus) 697.1
- **Pinpoint**
  - meatus (*see also* Stricture, urethra) 598.9
  - os (uteri) (*see also* Stricture, cervix) 622.4
- **Pinselhaare** (congenital) 757.4
- **Pinta** 103.9
  - cardiovascular lesions 103.2
  - chancre (primary) 103.0
  - erythematous plaques 103.1
  - hyperchromic lesions 103.1
  - hyperkeratosis 103.1
  - lesions 103.9
    - cardiovascular 103.2
    - hyperchromic 103.1
    - intermediate 103.1
    - late 103.2
    - mixed 103.3
    - primary 103.0
    - skin (achromic) (cicatricial) (dyschromic) 103.2
      - hyperchromic 103.1
      - mixed (achromic and hyperchromic) 103.3
  - papule (primary) 103.0
  - skin lesions (achromic) (cicatricial) (dyschromic) 103.2
    - hyperchromic 103.1
    - mixed (achromic and hyperchromic) 103.3
  - vitiligo 103.2
- **Pintid** 103.0
- **Pinworms** (disease) (infection) (infestation) 127.4
- **Piry fever** 066.8
- **Pistol wound** — *see* Gunshot wound
- **Pit, lip** (mucus), congenital 750.25
- **Pitchers' elbow** 718.82
- **Pithecoid pelvis** 755.69
  - with disproportion (fetopelvic) 653.2 [5th]
    - affecting fetus or newborn 763.1
    - causing obstructed labor 660.1 [5th]
- **Pithiatism** 300.11
- **Pitted** — *see also* Pitting
  - teeth 520.4
- **Pitting** (edema) (*see also* Edema) 782.3
  - lip 782.3
  - nail 703.8
    - congenital 757.5
- **Pituitary gland** — *see* condition
- **Pituitary snuff-takers' disease** 495.8
- **Pityriasis** 696.5
  - alba 696.5
  - capitis 690.11
  - circinata (et maculata) 696.3
  - Hebra's (exfoliative dermatitis) 695.89
  - lichenoides et varioliformis 696.2
  - maculata (et circinata) 696.3
  - nigra 111.1
  - pilaris 757.39
    - acquired 701.1
    - Hebra's 696.4
  - rosea 696.3
  - rotunda 696.3
  - rubra (Hebra) 695.89
    - pilaris 696.4
  - sicca 690.18
  - simplex 690.18
  - specified type NEC 696.5
  - streptogenes 696.5
  - versicolor 111.0
    - scrotal 111.0
- **Placenta, placental**
  - ablatio 641.2 [5th]
    - affecting fetus or newborn 762.1
  - abnormal, abnormality 656.7 [5th]
    - with hemorrhage 641.8 [5th]
      - affecting fetus or newborn 762.1
    - affecting fetus or newborn 762.2
  - abruptio 641.2 [5th]
    - affecting fetus or newborn 762.1
  - accessory lobe — *see* Placenta, abnormal
  - accreta (without hemorrhage) 667.0 [5th]
    - with hemorrhage 666.0 [5th]
  - adherent (without hemorrhage) 667.0 [5th]
    - with hemorrhage 666.0 [5th]
  - apoplexy — *see* Placenta, separation
  - battledore — *see* Placenta, abnormal
  - bilobate — *see* Placenta, abnormal
  - bipartita — *see* Placenta, abnormal
  - carneous mole 631
  - centralis — *see* Placenta, previa
  - circumvallata — *see* Placenta, abnormal
  - cyst (amniotic) — *see* Placenta, abnormal
  - deficiency — *see* Placenta, insufficiency
  - degeneration — *see* Placenta, insufficiency
  - detachment (partial) (premature) (with hemorrhage) 641.2 [5th]
    - affecting fetus or newborn 762.1
  - dimidiata — *see* Placenta, abnormal
  - disease 656.7 [5th]
    - affecting fetus or newborn 762.2
  - duplex — *see* Placenta, abnormal
  - dysfunction — *see* Placenta, insufficiency
  - fenestrata — *see* Placenta, abnormal
  - fibrosis — *see* Placenta, abnormal
  - fleshy mole 631
  - hematoma — *see* Placenta, abnormal
  - hemorrhage NEC — *see* Placenta, separation
  - hormone disturbance or malfunction — *see* Placenta, abnormal
  - hyperplasia — *see* Placenta, abnormal
  - increta (without hemorrhage) 667.0 [5th]
    - with hemorrhage 666.0 [5th]
  - infarction 656.7 [5th]
    - affecting fetus or newborn 762.2
  - insertion, vicious — *see* Placenta, previa
  - insufficiency
    - affecting
      - fetus or newborn 762.2
      - management of pregnancy 656.5 [5th]
  - lateral — *see* Placenta, previa
  - low implantation or insertion — *see* Placenta, previa
  - low-lying — *see* Placenta, previa
  - malformation — *see* Placenta, abnormal
  - malposition — *see* Placenta, previa
  - marginalis, marginata — *see* Placenta, previa
  - marginal sinus (hemorrhage) (rupture) 641.2 [5th]
    - affecting fetus or newborn 762.1
  - membranacea — *see* Placenta, abnormal
  - multilobed — *see* Placenta, abnormal
  - multipartita — *see* Placenta, abnormal
  - necrosis — *see* Placenta, abnormal
  - percreta (without hemorrhage) 667.0 [5th]
    - with hemorrhage 666.0 [5th]
  - polyp 674.4 [5th]
  - previa (central) (centralis) (complete) (lateral) (marginal) (marginalis) (partial) (partialis) (total) (with hemorrhage) 641.1 [5th]
    - affecting fetus or newborn 762.0
    - noted
      - before labor, without hemorrhage (with cesarean delivery) 641.0 [5th]
      - during pregnancy (without hemorrhage) 641.0 [5th]
    - without hemorrhage (before labor and delivery) (during pregnancy) 641.0 [5th]
  - retention (with hemorrhage) 666.0 [5th]
    - fragments, complicating puerperium (delayed hemorrhage) 666.2 [5th]
      - without hemorrhage 667.1 [5th]
    - postpartum, puerperal 666.2 [5th]
    - without hemorrhage 667.0 [5th]
  - separation (normally implanted) (partial) (premature) (with hemorrhage) 641.2 [5th]
    - affecting fetus or newborn 762.1
  - septuplex — *see* Placenta, abnormal
  - small — *see* Placenta, insufficiency
  - softening (premature) — *see* Placenta, abnormal
  - spuria — *see* Placenta, abnormal
  - succenturiata — *see* Placenta, abnormal
  - syphilitic 095.8
  - transfusion syndromes 762.3
  - transmission of chemical substance — *see* Absorption, chemical, through placenta
  - trapped (with hemorrhage) 666.0 [5th]
    - without hemorrhage 667.0 [5th]
  - trilobate — *see* Placenta, abnormal
  - tripartita — *see* Placenta, abnormal
  - triplex — *see* Placenta, abnormal
  - varicose vessel — *see* Placenta, abnormal
  - vicious insertion — *see* Placenta, previa
- **Placentitis**
  - affecting fetus or newborn 762.7
  - complicating pregnancy 658.4 [5th]
- **Plagiocephaly** (skull) 754.0
- **Plague** 020.9
  - abortive 020.8
  - ambulatory 020.8
  - bubonic 020.0
  - cellulocutaneous 020.1

- **Positive** — *continued*
  - serology
    - AIDS virus V08
      - inconclusive 795.71
    - HIV V08
      - inconclusive 795.71
    - human immunodeficiency virus V08
      - inconclusive 795.71
    - syphilis 097.1
      - with signs or symptoms — *see* Syphilis, by site and stage
      - false 795.6
  - skin test 795.4
    - tuberculin (without active tuberculosis) 795.5
  - VDRL 097.1
    - with signs or symptoms — *see* Syphilis, by site and stage
    - false 795.6
  - Wassermann reaction 097.1
    - false 795.6
- **Postcardiotomy syndrome** 429.4
- **Postcaval ureter** 753.4
- **Postcholecystectomy syndrome** 576.0
- **Postclimacteric bleeding** 627.1
- **Postcommissurotomy syndrome** 429.4
- **Postconcussional syndrome** 310.2
- **Postcontusional syndrome** 310.2
- **Postcricoid region** — *see* condition
- **Post-dates** (pregnancy) 645
- **Postencephalitic** — *see also* condition
  - syndrome 310.8
- **Posterior** — *see* condition
- **Posterolateral sclerosis** (spinal cord) — *see* Degeneration, combined
- **Postexanthematous** — *see* condition
- **Postfebrile** — *see* condition
- **Postgastrectomy dumping syndrome** 564.2
- **Posthemiplegic chorea** 344.89
- **Posthemorrhagic anemia** (chronic) 280.0
  - acute 285.1
  - newborn 776.5
- **Posthepatitis syndrome** 780.79
- **Postherpetic neuralgia** (intercostal) (syndrome) (zoster) 053.19
  - geniculate ganglion 053.11
  - ophthalmica 053.19
  - trigeminal 053.12
- **Posthitis** 607.1
- **Postimmunization complication or reaction** — *see* Complications, vaccination
- **Postinfectious** — *see* condition
- **Postinfluenzal syndrome** 780.79
- **Postlaminectomy syndrome** 722.80
  - cervical, cervicothoracic 722.81
  - kyphosis 737.12
  - lumbar, lumbosacral 722.83
  - thoracic, thoracolumbar 722.82
- **Postleukotomy syndrome** 310.0
- **Postlobectomy syndrome** 310.0
- **Postmastectomy lymphedema** (syndrome) 457.0
- **Postmaturity, postmature** (fetus or newborn) 766.2
  - affecting management of pregnancy 645
  - syndrome 766.2
- **Postmeasles** — *see also* condition
  - complication 055.8
    - specified NEC 055.79
- **Postmenopausal**
  - endometrium (atrophic) 627.8
    - suppurative (*see also* Endometritis) 615.9
  - hormone replacement therapy V07.4
- **Postnasal drip** — *see* Sinusitis
- **Postnatal** — *see* condition
- **Postoperative** — *see also* condition
  - confusion state 293.9
  - psychosis 293.9
  - status NEC (*see also* Status (post)) V45.89
- **Postpancreatectomy hyperglycemia** 251.3
- **Postpartum** — *see also* condition
  - observation
    - immediately after delivery V24.0
    - routine follow-up V24.2
- **Postperfusion syndrome** NEC 999.8
  - bone marrow 996.85
- **Postpoliomyelitic** — *see* condition
- **Postsurgery status** NEC (*see also* Status (post)) V45.89
- **Post-term** (pregnancy) 645
  - infant (294 days or more gestation) 766.2
- **Posttraumatic** — *see* condition
- **Posttraumatic brain syndrome, nonpsychotic** 310.2
- **Post-typhoid abscess** 002.0
- **Postures, hysterical** 300.11
- **Postvaccinal reaction or complication** — *see* Complications, vaccination
- **Postvagotomy syndrome** 564.2
- **Postvalvulotomy syndrome** 429.4
- **Postvasectomy sperm count** V25.8
- **Potain's disease** (pulmonary edema) 514
- **Potain's syndrome** (gastrectasis with dyspepsia) 536.1
- **Pott's**
  - curvature (spinal) (*see also* Tuberculosis) 015.0 5th *[737.43]*
  - disease or paraplegia (*see also* Tuberculosis) 015.0 5th *[730.88]*
  - fracture (closed) 824.4
    - open 824.5
  - gangrene 440.24
  - osteomyelitis (*see also* Tuberculosis) 015.0 5th *[730.88]*
  - spinal curvature (*see also* Tuberculosis) 015.0 5th *[737.43]*
  - tumor, puffy (*see also* Osteomyelitis) 730.2 5th
- **Potter's**
  - asthma 502
  - disease 753.0
  - facies 754.0
  - lung 502
  - syndrome (with renal agenesis) 753.0
- **Pouch**
  - bronchus 748.3
  - Douglas' — *see* condition
  - esophagus, esophageal (congenital) 750.4
    - acquired 530.6
  - gastric 537.1
  - Hartmann's (abnormal sacculation of gallbladder neck) 575.8
  - pharynx, pharyngeal (congenital) 750.27
- **Poulet's disease** 714.2
- **Poultrymen's itch** 133.8
- **Poverty** V60.2
- **Prader-Labhart-Willi-Fanconi syndrome** (hypogenital dystrophy with diabetic tendency) 759.81
- **Prader-Willi syndrome** (hypogenital dystrophy with diabetic tendency) 759.81
- **Preachers' voice** 784.49
- **Pre-AIDS** — *see* Human immunodeficiency virus (disease) (illness) (infection)
- **Preauricular appendage** 744.1
- **Prebetalipoproteinemia** (acquired) (essential) (familial) (hereditary) (primary) (secondary) 272.1
  - with chylomicronemia 272.3
- **Precipitate labor** 661.3 5th
  - affecting fetus or newborn 763.6
- **Preclimacteric bleeding** 627.0
  - menorrhagia 627.0
- **Precocious**
  - adrenarche 259.1
  - menarche 259.1
  - menstruation 626.8
  - pubarche 259.1
  - puberty NEC 259.1
  - sexual development NEC 259.1
  - thelarche 259.1
- **Precocity, sexual** (constitutional) (cryptogenic) (female) (idiopathic) (male) NEC 259.1
  - with adrenal hyperplasia 255.2
- **Precordial pain** 786.51
  - psychogenic 307.89
- **Predeciduous teeth** 520.2
- **Prediabetes, prediabetic** 790.2
  - complicating pregnancy, childbirth, or puerperium 648.8 5th
    - fetus or newborn 775.8
- **Predislocation status of hip, at birth** (*see also* Subluxation, congenital, hip) 754.32
- **Pre-eclampsia** (mild) 642.4 5th
  - with pre-existing hypertension 642.7 5th
  - affecting fetus or newborn 760.0
  - severe 642.5 5th
  - superimposed on pre-existing hypertensive disease 642.7 5th
- **Preeruptive color change, teeth, tooth** 520.8
- **Preexcitation** 426.7
  - atrioventricular conduction 426.7
  - ventricular 426.7
- **Preglaucoma** 365.00
- **Pregnancy** (single) (uterine) (without sickness) V22.2

> *Note — Use the following fifth-digit subclassification with categories 640-648, 651-676:*
>
> *0 unspecified as to episode of care*
> *1 delivered, with or without mention of antepartum condition*
> *2 delivered, with mention of postpartum complication*
> *3 antepartum condition or complication*
> *4 postpartum condition or complication*

  - abdominal (ectopic) 633.0
    - affecting fetus or newborn 761.4
  - abnormal NEC 646.9 5th
  - ampullar — *see* Pregnancy, tubal
  - broad ligament — *see* Pregnancy, cornual
  - cervical — *see* Pregnancy, cornual
  - combined (extrauterine and intrauterine) — *see* Pregnancy, cornual

- **Problem** (with) — *continued*
  - head — *continued*
    - mechanical V48.2
    - motor V48.2
    - movement of V48.2
    - sensory V48.4
    - specified condition NEC V48.8
  - hearing V41.2
  - high-risk sexual behavior V69.2
  - influencing health status NEC V49.8
  - internal organ NEC V47.9
    - deficiency V47.0
    - mechanical or motor V47.1
  - interpersonal NEC V62.81
  - jealousy, child 313.3
  - learning V40.0
  - legal V62.5
  - life circumstance NEC V62.89
  - lifestyle V69.9
    - specified NEC V69.8
  - limb V49.9
    - deficiency V49.0
    - disfigurement V49.4
    - mechanical V49.1
    - motor V49.2
    - movement, involving
      - musculoskeletal system V49.1
      - nervous system V49.2
    - sensory V49.3
    - specified condition NEC V49.5
  - litigation V62.5
  - living alone V60.3
  - loneliness NEC V62.89
  - marital V61.10
    - involving
      - divorce V61.0
      - estrangement V61.0
      - psychosexual disorder 302.9
      - sexual function V41.7
  - mastication V41.6
  - medical care, within family V61.49
  - mental V40.9
    - specified NEC V40.2
  - mental hygiene, adult V40.9
  - multiparity V61.5
  - nail biting, child 307.9
  - neck V48.9
    - deficiency V48.1
    - disfigurement V48.7
    - mechanical V48.3
    - motor V48.3
    - movement V48.3
    - sensory V48.5
    - specified condition NEC V48.8
  - neurological NEC 781.9
  - none (feared complaint unfounded) V65.5
  - occupational V62.2
  - parent-child V61.20
  - partner V61.10
  - personal NEC V62.89
    - interpersonal conflict NEC V62.81
  - personality (*see also* Disorder, personality) 301.9
  - phase of life V62.89
  - placenta, affecting management of pregnancy 656.9 ✓5th
    - specified type NEC 656.8 ✓5th
  - poverty V60.2
  - presence of sick or handicapped person in family or household V61.49
  - psychiatric 300.9

- **Problem** (with) — *continued*
  - psychosocial V62.9
    - specified type NEC V62.89
  - relational NEC V62.81
  - relationship, childhood 313.3
  - religious or spiritual belief
    - other than medical care V62.89
    - regarding medical care V62.6
  - self-damaging behavior V69.8
  - sexual
    - behavior, high-risk V69.2
    - function NEC V41.7
  - sibling relational V61.8
  - sight V41.0
  - sleep disorder, child 307.40
  - smell V41.5
  - speech V40.1
  - spite reaction, child (*see also* Disturbance, conduct) 312.0 ✓5th
  - spoiled child reaction (*see also* Disturbance, conduct) 312.1 ✓5th
  - swallowing V41.6
  - tantrum, child (*see also* Disturbance, conduct) 312.1 ✓5th
  - taste V41.5
  - thumb sucking, child 307.9
  - tic, child 307.21
  - trunk V48.9
    - deficiency V48.1
    - disfigurement V48.7
    - mechanical V48.3
    - motor V48.3
    - movement V48.3
    - sensory V48.5
    - specified condition NEC V48.8
  - unemployment V62.0
  - urinary NEC V47.4
  - voice production V41.4
- **Procedure** (surgical) not done NEC V64.3
  - because of
    - contraindication V64.1
    - patient's decision V64.2
      - for reasons of conscience or religion V62.6
    - specified reason NEC V64.3
- **Procidentia**
  - anus (sphincter) 569.1
  - rectum (sphincter) 569.1
  - stomach 537.89
  - uteri 618.1
- **Proctalgia** 569.42
  - fugax 564.6
  - spasmodic 564.6
    - psychogenic 307.89
- **Proctitis** 569.49
  - amebic 006.8
  - chlamydial 099.52
  - gonococcal 098.7
  - granulomatous 555.1
  - idiopathic 556.2
    - with ulcerative sigmoiditis 556.3
  - tuberculous (*see also* Tuberculosis) 014.8 ✓5th
  - ulcerative (chronic) (nonspecific) 556.2
    - with ulcerative sigmoiditis 556.3
- **Proctocele**
  - female (without uterine prolapse) 618.0
    - with uterine prolapse 618.4
      - complete 618.3
      - incomplete 618.2
  - male 569.49

- **Proctocolitis, idiopathic** 556.2
  - with ulcerative sigmoiditis 556.3
- **Proctoptosis** 569.1
- **Proctosigmoiditis** 569.89
  - ulcerative (chronic) 556.3
- **Proctospasm** 564.6
  - psychogenic 306.4
- **Prodromal-AIDS** — *see* Human immunodeficiency virus (disease) (illness) (infection)
- **Profichet's disease or syndrome** 729.9
- **Progeria** (adultorum) (syndrome) 259.8
- **Prognathism** (mandibular) (maxillary) 524.10
- **Progonoma** (melanotic) (M9363/0) — *see* Neoplasm, by site, benign
- **Progressive** — *see* condition
- **Prolapse, prolapsed**
  - anus, anal (canal) (sphincter) 569.1
  - arm or hand, complicating delivery 652.7 ✓5th
    - causing obstructed labor 660.0 ✓5th
      - affecting fetus or newborn 763.1
    - fetus or newborn 763.1
  - bladder (acquired) (mucosa) (sphincter)
    - congenital (female) (male) 756.71
    - female 618.0
    - male 596.8
  - breast implant (prosthetic) 996.54
  - cecostomy 569.69
  - cecum 569.89
  - cervix, cervical (stump) (hypertrophied) 618.1
    - anterior lip, obstructing labor 660.2 ✓5th
      - affecting fetus or newborn 763.1
    - congenital 752.49
    - postpartal (old) 618.1
  - ciliary body 871.1
  - colon (pedunculated) 569.89
  - colostomy 569.69
  - conjunctiva 372.73
  - cord — *see* Prolapse, umbilical cord
  - disc (intervertebral) — *see* Displacement, intervertebral disc
  - duodenum 537.89
  - eye implant (orbital) 996.59
    - lens (ocular) 996.53
  - fallopian tube 620.4
  - fetal extremity, complicating delivery 652.8 ✓5th
    - causing obstructed labor 660.0 ✓5th
    - fetus or newborn 763.1
  - funis — *see* Prolapse, umbilical cord
  - gastric (mucosa) 537.89
  - genital, female 618.9
    - specified NEC 618.8
  - globe 360.81
  - ileostomy bud 569.69
  - intervertebral disc — *see* Displacement, intervertebral disc
  - intestine (small) 569.89
  - iris 364.8
    - traumatic 871.1
  - kidney (*see also* Disease, renal) 593.0
    - congenital 753.3
  - laryngeal muscles or ventricle 478.79
  - leg, complicating delivery 652.8 ✓5th
    - causing obstructed labor 660.0 ✓5th
    - fetus or newborn 763.1
  - liver 573.8
  - meatus urinarius 599.5
  - mitral valve 424.0
  - ocular lens implant 996.53

> *Note — Use the following fifth-digit subclassification with categories 296.0-296.6:*
>
> *0 unspecified*
> *1 mild*
> *2 moderate*
> *3 severe, without mention of psychotic behavior*
> *4 severe, specified as with psychotic behavior*
> *5 in partial or unspecified remission*
> *6 in full remission*

> *Note — Use the following fifth-digit subclassification with category 299:*
>
> *0 current or active state*
> *1 residual state*

Q

R

S

- **Sprain, strain** (joint) (ligament) (muscle) (tendon) — *continued*
  - symphysis — *continued*
    - mandibular 848.1
      - old 524.69
    - pubis 848.5
  - talofibular 845.09
  - tarsal 845.10
  - tarsometatarsal 845.11
  - temporomandibular 848.1
    - old 524.69
  - teres
    - ligamentum femoris 843.8
    - major or minor 840.8
  - thigh (proximal end) 843.9
    - and hip 843.9
    - distal end 844.9
  - thoracic (spine) 847.1
  - thorax 848.8
  - thumb 842.10
  - thyroid cartilage or region 848.2
  - tibia (proximal end) 844.9
    - distal end 845.00
  - tibiofibular
    - distal 845.03
    - superior 844.3
  - toe(s) 845.10
  - trachea 848.8
  - trapezoid 840.8
  - ulna, ulnar (proximal end) 841.9
    - collateral 841.1
    - distal end 842.00
  - ulnohumeral 841.3
  - vertebrae (*see also* Sprain, spine) 847.9
    - cervical, cervicodorsal, cervicothoracic 847.0
  - wrist (cuneiform) (scaphoid) (semilunar) 842.00
  - xiphoid cartilage 848.49
- **Sprengel's deformity** (congenital) 755.52
- **Spring fever** 309.23
- **Sprue** 579.1
  - celiac 579.0
  - idiopathic 579.0
  - meaning thrush 112.0
  - nontropical 579.0
  - tropical 579.1
- **Spur** — *see also* Exostosis
  - bone 726.91
    - calcaneal 726.73
  - calcaneal 726.73
  - iliac crest 726.5
  - nose (septum) 478.1
    - bone 726.91
  - septal 478.1
- **Spuria placenta** — *see* Placenta, abnormal
- **Spurway's syndrome** (brittle bones and blue sclera) 756.51
- **Sputum, abnormal** (amount) (color) (excessive) (odor) (purulent) 786.4
  - bloody 786.3
- **Squamous** — *see also* condition
  - cell metaplasia
    - bladder 596.8
    - cervix — *see* condition
  - epithelium in
    - cervical canal (congenital) 752.49
    - uterine mucosa (congenital) 752.3
- **Squamous** — *see also* condition — *continued*
  - metaplasia
    - bladder 596.8
    - cervix — *see* condition
- **Squashed nose** 738.0
  - congenital 754.0
- **Squeeze, divers'** 993.3
- **Squint** (*see also* Strabismus) 378.9
  - accommodative (*see also* Esotropia) 378.00
  - concomitant (*see also* Heterotropia) 378.30
- **Stab** — *see also* Wound, open, by site
  - internal organs — *see* Injury, internal, by site, with open wound
- **Staggering gait** 781.2
  - hysterical 300.11
- **Staghorn calculus** 592.0
- **Stähl's**
  - ear 744.29
  - pigment line (cornea) 371.11
- **Stähli's pigment lines** (cornea) 371.11
- **Stain**
  - port wine 757.32
  - tooth, teeth (hard tissues) 521.7
    - due to
      - accretions 523.6
      - deposits (betel) (black) (green) (materia alba) (orange) (tobacco) 523.6
      - metals (copper) (silver) 521.7
      - nicotine 523.6
      - pulpal bleeding 521.7
      - tobacco 523.6
- **Stammering** 307.0
- **Standstill**
  - atrial 426.6
  - auricular 426.6
  - cardiac (*see also* Arrest, cardiac) 427.5
  - sinoatrial 426.6
  - sinus 426.6
  - ventricular (*see also* Arrest, cardiac) 427.5
- **Stannosis** 503
- **Stanton's disease** (melioidosis) 025
- **Staphylitis** (acute) (catarrhal) (chronic) (gangrenous) (membranous) (suppurative) (ulcerative) 528.3
- **Staphylococcemia** 038.10
  - aureus 038.11
  - specified organism NEC 038.19
- **Staphylococcus, staphylococcal** — *see* condition
- **Staphyloderma** (skin) 686.00
- **Staphyloma** 379.11
  - anterior, localized 379.14
  - ciliary 379.11
  - cornea 371.73
  - equatorial 379.13
  - posterior 379.12
  - posticum 379.12
  - ring 379.15
  - sclera NEC 379.11
- **Starch eating** 307.52
- **Stargardt's disease** 362.75
- **Starvation** (inanition) (due to lack of food) 994.2
  - edema 262
  - voluntary NEC 307.1
- **Stasis**
  - bile (duct) (*see also* Disease, biliary) 576.8
  - bronchus (*see also* Bronchitis) 490
  - cardiac (*see also* Failure, heart, congestive) 428.0
  - cecum 564.89
- **Stasis** — *continued*
  - colon 564.89
  - dermatitis (*see also* Varix, with stasis dermatitis) 454.1
  - duodenal 536.8
  - eczema (*see also* Varix, with stasis dermatitis) 454.1
  - foot 991.4
  - gastric 536.3
  - ileocecal coil 564.89
  - ileum 564.89
  - intestinal 564.89
  - jejunum 564.89
  - kidney 586
  - liver 571.9
    - cirrhotic — *see* Cirrhosis, liver
  - lymphatic 457.8
  - pneumonia 514
  - portal 571.9
  - pulmonary 514
  - rectal 564.89
  - renal 586
    - tubular 584.5
  - stomach 536.3
  - ulcer
    - with varicose veins 454.0
    - without varicose veins 459.81
  - urine NEC (*see also* Retention, urine) 788.20
  - venous 459.81
- **State**
  - affective and paranoid, mixed, organic psychotic 294.8
  - agitated 307.9
    - acute reaction to stress 308.2
  - anxiety (neurotic) (*see also* Anxiety) 300.00
    - specified type NEC 300.09
  - apprehension (*see also* Anxiety) 300.00
    - specified type NEC 300.09
  - climacteric, female 627.2
    - following induced menopause 627.4
  - clouded
    - epileptic (*see also* Epilepsy) 345.9 ✓5th
    - paroxysmal (idiopathic) (*see also* Epilepsy) 345.9 ✓5th
  - compulsive (mixed) (with obsession) 300.3
  - confusional 298.9
    - acute 293.0
      - with
        - arteriosclerotic dementia 290.41
        - presenile brain disease 290.11
        - senility 290.3
      - alcoholic 291.0
      - drug-induced 292.81
    - epileptic 293.0
    - postoperative 293.9
    - reactive (emotional stress) (psychological trauma) 298.2
    - subacute 293.1
  - constitutional psychopathic 301.9
  - convulsive (*see also* Convulsions) 780.39
  - depressive NEC 311
    - induced by drug 292.84
    - neurotic 300.4
  - dissociative 300.15
  - hallucinatory 780.1
    - induced by drug 292.12
  - hyperdynamic beta-adrenergic circulatory 429.82
  - locked-in 344.81
  - menopausal 627.2
    - artificial 627.4
    - following induced menopause 627.4

T

- **Tetanus, tetanic** (cephalic) (convulsions) 037
  - with
    - abortion — *see* Abortion, by type, with sepsis
    - ectopic pregnancy (*see also* categories 633.0-633.9) 639.0
    - molar pregnancy (*see* categories 630-632) 639.0
  - following
    - abortion 639.0
    - ectopic or molar pregnancy 639.0
  - inoculation V03.7
    - reaction (due to serum) — *see* Complications, vaccination
  - neonatorum 771.3
  - puerperal, postpartum, childbirth 670
- **Tetany, tetanic** 781.7
  - alkalosis 276.3
  - associated with rickets 268.0
  - convulsions 781.7
    - hysterical 300.11
  - functional (hysterical) 300.11
  - hyperkinetic 781.7
    - hysterical 300.11
  - hyperpnea 786.01
    - hysterical 300.11
    - psychogenic 306.1
  - hyperventilation 786.01
    - hysterical 300.11
    - psychogenic 306.1
  - hypocalcemic, neonatal 775.4
  - hysterical 300.11
  - neonatal 775.4
  - parathyroid (gland) 252.1
  - parathyroprival 252.1
  - postoperative 252.1
  - postthyroidectomy 252.1
  - pseudotetany 781.7
    - hysterical 300.11
  - psychogenic 306.1
    - specified as conversion reaction 300.11
- **Tetralogy of Fallot** 745.2
- **Tetraplegia** — *see* Quadriplegia
- **Thailand hemorrhagic fever** 065.4
- **Thalassanemia** 282.4
- **Thalassemia** (alpha) (beta) (disease) (Hb-C) (Hb-D) (Hb-E) (Hb-H) (Hb-I) (Hb-S) (high fetal gene) (high fetal hemoglobin) (intermedia) (major) (minima) (minor) (mixed) (sickle-cell) (trait) (with other hemoglobinopathy) 282.4
- **Thalessemic variants** 282.4
- **Thaysen-Gee disease** (nontropical sprue) 579.0
- **Thecoma** (M8600/0) 220
  - malignant (M8600/3) 183.0
- **Thelarche, precocious** 259.1
- **Thelitis** 611.0
  - puerperal, postpartum 675.0 (5th)
- **Therapeutic** — *see* condition
- **Therapy** V57.9
  - blood transfusion, without reported diagnosis V58.2
  - breathing V57.0
  - chemotherapy V58.1
    - fluoride V07.31
    - prophylactic NEC V07.39
  - dialysis (intermittent) (treatment)
    - extracorporeal V56.0

- **Therapy** — *continued*
  - dialysis (intermittent) (treatment) — *continued*
    - peritoneal V56.8
    - renal V56.0
    - specified type NEC V56.8
  - exercise NEC V57.1
    - breathing V57.0
  - extracorporeal dialysis (renal) V56.0
  - fluoride prophylaxis V07.31
  - hemodialysis V56.0
  - occupational V57.21
  - orthoptic V57.4
  - orthotic V57.81
  - peritoneal dialysis V56.8
  - physical NEC V57.1
  - postmenopausal hormone replacement V07.4
  - radiation V58.0
  - speech V57.3
  - vocational V57.22
- **Thermalgesia** 782.0
- **Thermalgia** 782.0
- **Thermanalgesia** 782.0
- **Thermanesthesia** 782.0
- **Thermic** — *see* condition
- **Thermography** (abnormal) 793.9
  - breast 793.8
- **Thermoplegia** 992.0
- **Thesaurismosis**
  - amyloid 277.3
  - bilirubin 277.4
  - calcium 275.40
  - cystine 270.0
  - glycogen (*see also* Disease, glycogen storage) 271.0
  - kerasin 272.7
  - lipoid 272.7
  - melanin 255.4
  - phosphatide 272.7
  - urate 274.9
- **Thiaminic deficiency** 265.1
  - with beriberi 265.0
- **Thibierge-Weissenbach syndrome** (cutaneous systemic sclerosis) 710.1
- **Thickening**
  - bone 733.99
    - extremity 733.99
  - breast 611.79
  - hymen 623.3
  - larynx 478.79
  - nail 703.8
    - congenital 757.5
  - periosteal 733.99
  - pleura (*see also* Pleurisy) 511.0
  - skin 782.8
  - subepiglottic 478.79
  - tongue 529.8
  - valve, heart — *see* Endocarditis
- **Thiele syndrome** 724.6
- **Thigh** — *see* condition
- **Thinning vertebra** (*see also* Osteoporosis) 733.00
- **Thirst, excessive** 783.5
  - due to deprivation of water 994.3
- **Thomsen's disease** 359.2
- **Thomson's disease** (congenital poikiloderma) 757.33
- **Thoracic** — *see also* condition
  - kidney 753.3
  - outlet syndrome 353.0
  - stomach — *see* Hernia, diaphragm

- **Thoracogastroschisis** (congenital) 759.89
- **Thoracopagus** 759.4
- **Thoracoschisis** 756.3
- **Thorax** — *see* condition
- **Thorn's syndrome** (*see also* Disease, renal) 593.9
- **Thornwaldt's, Tornwaldt's**
  - bursitis (pharyngeal) 478.29
  - cyst 478.26
  - disease (pharyngeal bursitis) 478.29
- **Thorson-Biörck syndrome** (malignant carcinoid) 259.2
- **Threadworm** (infection) (infestation) 127.4
- **Threatened**
  - abortion or miscarriage 640.0 (5th)
    - with subsequent abortion (*see also* Abortion, spontaneous) 634.9 (5th)
    - affecting fetus 762.1
  - labor 644.1 (5th)
    - affecting fetus or newborn 761.8
    - premature 644.0 (5th)
  - miscarriage 640.0 (5th)
    - affecting fetus 762.1
  - premature
    - delivery 644.2 (5th)
      - affecting fetus or newborn 761.8
    - labor 644.0 (5th)
      - before 22 completed weeks' gestation 640.0 (5th)
- **Three-day fever** 066.0
- **Threshers' lung** 495.0
- **Thrix annulata** (congenital) 757.4
- **Throat** — *see* condition
- **Thrombasthenia** (Glanzmann's) (hemorrhagic) (hereditary) 287.1
- **Thromboangiitis** 443.1
  - obliterans (general) 443.1
    - cerebral 437.1
    - vessels
      - brain 437.1
      - spinal cord 437.1
- **Thromboarteritis** — *see* Arteritis
- **Thromboasthenia** (Glanzmann's) (hemorrhagic) (hereditary) 287.1
- **Thrombocytasthenia** (Glanzmann's) 287.1
- **Thrombocythemia** (essential) (hemorrhagic) (primary) (M9962/1) 238.7
  - idiopathic (M9962/1) 238.7
- **Thrombocytopathy** (dystrophic)(granulopenic) 287.1
- **Thrombocytopenia, thrombocytopenic** 287.5
  - with giant hemangioma 287.3
  - amegakaryocytic, congenital 287.3
  - congenital 287.3
  - cyclic 287.3
  - dilutional 287.4
  - due to
    - drugs 287.4
    - extracorporeal circulation of blood 287.4
    - massive blood transfusion 287.4
    - platelet alloimmunization 287.4
  - essential 287.3
  - hereditary 287.3
  - Kasabach-Merritt 287.3

- **Tracheopharyngitis** (acute) 465.8
  - chronic 478.9
    - due to external agent — *see* Condition, respiratory, chronic, due to
  - due to external agent — *see* Inflammation, respiratory, upper, due to
- **Tracheostenosis** 519.1
  - congenital 748.3
- **Tracheostomy**
  - attention to V55.0
  - complication 519.00
    - hemorrhage 519.09
    - infection 519.01
    - malfunctioning 519.02
    - obstruction 519.09
    - sepsis 519.01
  - status V44.0
  - stenosis 519.02
- **Trachoma, trachomatous** 076.9
  - active (stage) 076.1
  - contraction of conjunctiva 076.1
  - dubium 076.0
  - healed or late effect 139.1
  - initial (stage) 076.0
  - Türck's (chronic catarrhal laryngitis) 476.0
- **Trachyphonia** 784.49
- **Training**
  - orthoptic V57.4
  - orthotic V57.81
- **Train sickness** 994.6
- **Trait**
  - hemoglobin
    - abnormal NEC 282.7
      - with thalassemia 282.4
    - C (*see also* Disease, hemoglobin, C) 282.7
      - with elliptocytosis 282.7
    - S (Hb-S) 282.5
  - Lepore 282.4
    - with other abnormal hemoglobin NEC 282.4
  - paranoid 301.0
  - sickle-cell 282.5
    - with
      - elliptocytosis 282.5
      - spherocytosis 282.5
- **Traits, paranoid** 301.0
- **Tramp** V60.0
- **Trance** 780.09
  - hysterical 300.13
- **Transaminasemia** 790.4
- **Transfusion, blood**
  - donor V59.01
    - stem cells V59.02
  - incompatible 999.6
  - reaction or complication — *see* Complications, transfusion
  - syndrome
    - fetomaternal 772.0
    - twin-to-twin
      - blood loss (donor twin) 772.0
      - recipient twin 776.4
  - without reported diagnosis V58.2
- **Transient** — *see also* condition
  - alteration of awareness 780.02
  - blindness 368.12
  - deafness (ischemic) 388.02
  - global amnesia 437.7
  - person (homeless) NEC V60.0
- **Transitional, lumbosacral joint of vertebra** 756.19
- **Translocation**
  - autosomes NEC 758.5
    - 13-15 758.1
    - 16-18 758.2
    - 21 or 22 758.0
    - balanced in normal individual 758.4
    - D_1 758.1
    - E_3 758.2
    - G 758.0
  - balanced autosomal in normal individual 758.4
  - chromosomes NEC 758.89
  - Down's syndrome 758.0
- **Translucency, iris** 364.53
- **Transmission of chemical substances through the placenta** (affecting fetus or newborn) 760.70
  - alcohol 760.71
  - anti-infective agents 760.74
  - cocaine 760.75
  - "crack" 760.75
  - diethylstilbestrol [DES] 760.76
  - hallucinogenic agents 760.73
  - medicinal agents NEC 760.79
  - narcotics 760.72
  - obstetric anesthetic or analgesic drug 763.5
  - specified agent NEC 760.79
  - suspected, affecting management of pregnancy 655.5 [5th]
- **Transplant**(ed)
  - bone V42.4
    - marrow V42.81
  - complication — *see also* Complications, due to (presence of) any device, implant, or graft classified to 996.0-996.5 NEC
    - bone marrow 996.85
    - corneal graft NEC 996.79
      - infection or inflammation 996.69
      - reaction 996.51
      - rejection 996.51
    - organ (failure) (immune or nonimmune cause) (infection) (rejection) 996.80
      - bone marrow 996.85
      - heart 996.83
      - intestines 996.89
      - kidney 996.81
      - liver 996.82
      - lung 996.84
      - pancreas 996.86
      - specified NEC 996.89
    - skin NEC 996.79
      - infection or inflammation 996.69
      - rejection 996.52
        - artificial 996.55
        - decellularized allodermis 996.55
  - cornea V42.5
  - hair V50.0
  - heart V42.1
    - valve V42.2
  - intestine V42.89
  - kidney V42.0
  - liver V42.7
  - lung V42.6
  - organ V42.9
    - specified NEC V42.89
  - pancreas V42.83
  - peripheral stem cells V42.82
  - skin V42.3
- **Transplant**(ed) — *continued*
  - stem cells, peripheral V42.82
  - tissue V42.9
    - specified NEC V42.89
- **Transplants, ovarian, endometrial** 617.1
- **Transposed** — *see* Transposition
- **Transposition** (congenital) — *see also* Malposition, congenital
  - abdominal viscera 759.3
  - aorta (dextra) 745.11
  - appendix 751.5
  - arterial trunk 745.10
  - colon 751.5
  - great vessels (complete) 745.10
    - both originating from right ventricle 745.11
    - corrected 745.12
    - double outlet right ventricle 745.11
    - incomplete 745.11
    - partial 745.11
    - specified type NEC 745.19
  - heart 746.87
    - with complete transposition of viscera 759.3
  - intestine (large) (small) 751.5
  - pulmonary veins 747.49
  - reversed jejunal (for bypass) (status) V45.3
  - stomach 750.7
    - with general transposition of viscera 759.3
  - teeth, tooth 524.3
  - vessels (complete) 745.10
    - partial 745.11
  - viscera (abdominal) (thoracic) 759.3
- **Trans-sexualism** 302.50
  - with
    - asexual history 302.51
    - heterosexual history 302.53
    - homosexual history 302.52
- **Transverse** — *see also* condition
  - arrest (deep), in labor 660.3 [5th]
    - affecting fetus or newborn 763.1
  - lie 652.3 [5th]
    - before labor, affecting fetus or newborn 761.7
    - causing obstructed labor 660.0 [5th]
      - affecting fetus or newborn 763.1
    - during labor, affecting fetus or newborn 763.1
- **Transvestism, transvestitism** (transvestic fetishism) 302.3
- **Trapped placenta** (with hemorrhage) 666.0 [5th]
  - without hemorrhage 667.0 [5th]
- **Trauma, traumatism** (*see also* Injury, by site) 959.9
  - birth — *see* Birth, injury NEC
  - causing hemorrhage of pregnancy or delivery 641.8 [5th]
  - complicating
    - abortion — *see* Abortion, by type, with damage to pelvic organs
    - ectopic pregnancy (*see also* categories 633.0-633.9) 639.2
    - molar pregnancy (*see also* categories 630-632) 639.2
  - during delivery NEC 665.9 [5th]
  - following
    - abortion 639.2
    - ectopic or molar pregnancy 639.2
  - maternal, during pregnancy, affecting fetus or newborn 760.5
  - neuroma — *see* Injury, nerve, by site
  - previous major, affecting management of pregnancy, childbirth, or puerperium V23.8 [5th]

Trauma, traumatism (*see also* Injury, by site) — *continued*
- psychic (current) — *see also* Reaction, adjustment
  - previous (history) V15.49
- psychologic, previous (affecting health) V15.49
- transient paralysis — *see* Injury, nerve, by site

Traumatic — *see* condition
Treacher Collins' syndrome (incomplete facial dysostosis) 756.0
Treitz's hernia — *see* Hernia, Treitz's
Trematode infestation NEC 121.9
Trematodiasis NEC 121.9
Trembles 988.8
Trembling paralysis (*see also* Parkinsonism) 332.0
Tremor 781.0
- essential (benign) 333.1
- familial 333.1
- flapping (liver) 572.8
- hereditary 333.1
- hysterical 300.11
- intention 333.1
- mercurial 985.0
- muscle 728.85
- Parkinson's (*see also* Parkinsonism) 332.0
- psychogenic 306.0
  - specified as conversion reaction 300.11
- senilis 797
- specified type NEC 333.1

Trench
- fever 083.1
- foot 991.4
- mouth 101
- nephritis — *see* Nephritis, acute

Treponema pallidum infection (*see also* Syphilis) 097.9
Treponematosis 102.9
- due to
  - T. pallidum — *see* Syphilis
  - T. pertenue (yaws) (*see also* Yaws) 102.9

Triad
- Kartagener's 759.3
- Reiter's (complete) (incomplete) 099.3
- Saint's (*see also* Hernia, diaphragm) 553.3

Trichiasis 704.2
- cicatricial 704.2
- eyelid 374.05
  - with entropion (*see also* Entropion) 374.00

Trichinella spiralis (infection) (infestation) 124
Trichinelliasis 124
Trichinellosis 124
Trichiniasis 124
Trichinosis 124
Trichobezoar 938
- intestine 936
- stomach 935.2

Trichocephaliasis 127.3
Trichocephalosis 127.3
Trichocephalus infestation 127.3
Trichoclasis 704.2
Trichoepithelioma (M8100/0) — *see also* Neoplasm, skin, benign
- breast 217
- genital organ NEC — *see* Neoplasm, by site, benign
- malignant (M8100/3) — *see* Neoplasm, skin, malignant

Trichofolliculoma (M8101/0) — *see* Neoplasm, skin, benign
Tricholemmoma (M8102/0) — *see* Neoplasm, skin, benign
Trichomatosis 704.2
Trichomoniasis 131.9
- bladder 131.09
- cervix 131.09
- intestinal 007.3
- prostate 131.03
- seminal vesicle 131.09
- specified site NEC 131.8
- urethra 131.02
- urogenitalis 131.00
- vagina 131.01
- vulva 131.01
- vulvovaginal 131.01

Trichomycosis 039.0
- axillaris 039.0
- nodosa 111.2
- nodularis 111.2
- rubra 039.0

Trichonocardiosis (axillaris) (palmellina) 039.0
Trichonodosis 704.2
Trichophytid, trichophyton infection (*see also* Dermatophytosis) 110.9
Trichophytide — *see* Dermatophytosis
Trichophytobezoar 938
- intestine 936
- stomach 935.2

Trichophytosis — *see* Dermatophytosis
Trichoptilosis 704.2
Trichorrhexis (nodosa) 704.2
Trichosporosis nodosa 111.2
Trichostasis spinulosa (congenital) 757.4
Trichostrongyliasis (small intestine) 127.6
Trichostrongylosis 127.6
Trichostrongylus (instabilis) infection 127.6
Trichotillomania 312.39
Trichromat, anomalous (congenital) 368.59
Trichromatopsia, anomalous (congenital) 368.59
Trichuriasis 127.3
Trichuris trichiuria (any site) (infection) (infestation) 127.3
Tricuspid (valve) — *see* condition
Trifid — *see also* Accessory
- kidney (pelvis) 753.3
- tongue 750.13

Trigeminal neuralgia (*see also* Neuralgia, trigeminal) 350.1
Trigeminoencephaloangiomatosis 759.6
Trigeminy 427.89
- postoperative 997.1

Trigger finger (acquired) 727.03
- congenital 756.89

Trigonitis (bladder) (chronic) (pseudomembranous) 595.3
- tuberculous (*see also* Tuberculosis) 016.1 [5th]

Trigonocephaly 756.0
Trihexosidosis 272.7
Trilobate placenta — *see* Placenta, abnormal
Trilocular heart 745.8
Tripartita placenta — *see* Placenta, abnormal
Triple — *see also* Accessory
- kidneys 753.3
- uteri 752.2
- X female 758.81

Triplegia 344.89
- congenital or infantile 343.8

Triplet
- affected by maternal complications of pregnancy 761.5
- healthy liveborn — *see* Newborn, multiple
- pregnancy (complicating delivery) NEC 651.1 [5th]
  - with fetal loss and retention of one or more fetus(es) 651.4 [5th]

Triplex placenta — *see* Placenta, abnormal
Triplication — *see* Accessory
Trismus 781.0
- neonatorum 771.3
- newborn 771.3

Trisomy (syndrome) NEC 758.5
- 13 (partial) 758.1
- 16-18 758.2
- 18 (partial) 758.2
- 21 (partial) 758.0
- 22 758.0
- autosomes NEC 758.5
- D_1 758.1
- E_3 758.2
- G (group) 758.0
- group D_1 758.1
- group E 758.2
- group G 758.0

Tritanomaly 368.53
Tritanopia 368.53
Troisier-Hanot-Chauffard syndrome (bronze diabetes) 275.0
Trombidiosis 133.8
Trophedema (hereditary) 757.0
- congenital 757.0

Trophoblastic disease (*see also* Hydatidiform mole) 630
- previous, affecting management of pregnancy V23.1

Tropholymphedema 757.0
Trophoneurosis NEC 356.9
- arm NEC 354.9
- disseminated 710.1
- facial 349.89
- leg NEC 355.8
- lower extremity NEC 355.8
- upper extremity NEC 354.9

Tropical — *see also* condition
- maceration feet (syndrome) 991.4
- wet foot (syndrome) 991.4

Trouble — *see also* Disease
- bowel 569.9
- heart — *see* Disease, heart
- intestine 569.9
- kidney (*see also* Disease, renal) 593.9
- nervous 799.2
- sinus (*see also* Sinusitis) 473.9

Trousseau's syndrome (thrombophlebitis migrans) 453.1
Truancy, childhood — *see also* Disturbance, conduct
- socialized 312.2 [5th]
- undersocialized, unsocialized 312.1 [5th]

Truncus
- arteriosus (persistent) 745.0
- common 745.0
- communis 745.0

Trunk — *see* condition

Trychophytide — *see* Dermatophytosis

Trypanosoma infestation — *see* Trypanosomiasis

Trypanosomiasis 086.9
- with meningoencephalitis 086.9 *[323.2]*
- African 086.5
  - due to Trypanosoma 086.5
    - gambiense 086.3
    - rhodesiense 086.4
- American 086.2
  - with
    - heart involvement 086.0
    - other organ involvement 086.1
  - without mention of organ involvement 086.2
- Brazilian — *see* Trypanosomiasis, American
- Chagas' — *see* Trypanosomiasis, American
- due to Trypanosoma
  - cruzi — *see* Trypanosomiasis, American
  - gambiense 086.3
  - rhodesiense 086.4
- gambiensis, Gambian 086.3
- North American — *see* Trypanosomiasis, American
- rhodesiensis, Rhodesian 086.4
- South American — *see* Trypanosomiasis, American

T-shaped incisors 520.2

Tsutsugamushi fever 081.2

Tube, tubal, tubular — *see also* condition
- ligation, admission for V25.2

Tubercle — *see also* Tuberculosis
- brain, solitary 013.2 ✓5th
- Darwin's 744.29
- epithelioid noncaseating 135
- Ghon, primary infection 010.0 ✓5th

Tuberculid, tuberculide (indurating) (lichenoid) (miliary) (papulonecrotic) (primary) (skin) (subcutaneous) (*see also* Tuberculosis) 017.0 ✓5th

Tuberculoma — *see also* Tuberculosis
- brain (any part) 013.2 ✓5th
- meninges (cerebral) (spinal) 013.1 ✓5th
- spinal cord 013.4 ✓5th

Tuberculosis, tubercular, tuberculous (calcification) (calcified) (caseous) (chromogenic acid-fast bacilli) (congenital) (degeneration) (disease) (fibrocaseous) (fistula) (gangrene) (interstitial) (isolated circumscribed lesions) (necrosis) (parenchymatous) (ulcerative) 011.9 ✓5th

> *Note — Use the following fifth-digit subclassification with categories 010-018:*
>
> *0 unspecified*
>
> *1 bacteriological or histological examination not done*
>
> *2 bacteriological or histological examination unknown (at present)*
>
> *3 tubercle bacilli found (in sputum) by microscopy*
>
> *4 tubercle bacilli not found (in sputum) by microscopy, but found by bacterial culture*
>
> *5 tubercle bacilli not found by bacteriological examination, but tuberculosis confirmed histologically*
>
> *6 tubercle bacilli not found by bacteriological or histological examination, but tuberculosis confirmed by other methods [inoculation of animals]*
>
> *For tuberculous conditions specified as late effects or sequelae, see category 137.*

- abdomen 014.8 ✓5th
  - lymph gland 014.8 ✓5th
- abscess 011.9 ✓5th
  - arm 017.9 ✓5th
  - bone (*see also* Osteomyelitis, due to, tuberculosis) 015.9 ✓5th *[730.8]* ✓5th
    - hip 015.1 ✓5th *[730.85]*
    - knee 015.2 ✓5th *[730.86]*
    - sacrum 015.0 ✓5th *[730.88]*
    - specified site NEC 015.7 ✓5th *[730.88]*
    - spinal 015.0 ✓5th *[730.88]*
    - vertebra 015.0 ✓5th *[730.88]*
  - brain 013.3 ✓5th
  - breast 017.9 ✓5th
  - Cowper's gland 016.5 ✓5th
  - dura (mater) 013.8 ✓5th
    - brain 013.3 ✓5th
    - spinal cord 013.5 ✓5th
  - epidural 013.8 ✓5th
    - brain 013.3 ✓5th
    - spinal cord 013.5 ✓5th
  - frontal sinus — *see* Tuberculosis, sinus
  - genital organs NEC 016.9 ✓5th
    - female 016.7 ✓5th
    - male 016.5 ✓5th
  - genitourinary NEC 016.9 ✓5th
  - gland (lymphatic) — *see* Tuberculosis, lymph gland
  - hip 015.1 ✓5th
  - iliopsoas 015.0 ✓5th *[730.88]*
  - intestine 014.8 ✓5th
  - ischiorectal 014.8 ✓5th
  - joint 015.9 ✓5th
    - hip 015.1 ✓5th
    - knee 015.2 ✓5th
    - specified joint NEC 015.8 ✓5th
    - vertebral 015.0 ✓5th *[730.88]*
  - kidney 016.0 ✓5th *[590.81]*
  - knee 015.2 ✓5th

Tuberculosis, tubercular, tuberculous (calcification) (calcified) (caseous) (chromogenic acid-fast bacilli) (congenital) (degeneration) (disease) (fibrocaseous) (fistula) (gangrene) (interstitial) (isolated circumscribed lesions) (necrosis) (parenchymatous) (ulcerative) — *continued*
- abscess — *continued*
  - lumbar 015.0 ✓5th *[730.88]*
  - lung 011.2 ✓5th
    - primary, progressive 010.8 ✓5th
  - meninges (cerebral) (spinal) 013.0 ✓5th
  - pelvic 016.9 ✓5th
    - female 016.7 ✓5th
    - male 016.5 ✓5th
  - perianal 014.8 ✓5th
    - fistula 014.8 ✓5th
  - perinephritic 016.0 ✓5th *[590.81]*
  - perineum 017.9 ✓5th
  - perirectal 014.8 ✓5th
  - psoas 015.0 ✓5th *[730.88]*
  - rectum 014.8 ✓5th
  - retropharyngeal 012.8 ✓5th
  - sacrum 015.0 ✓5th *[730.88]*
  - scrofulous 017.2 ✓5th
  - scrotum 016.5 ✓5th
  - skin 017.0 ✓5th
    - primary 017.0 ✓5th
  - spinal cord 013.5 ✓5th
  - spine or vertebra (column) 015.0 ✓5th *[730.88]*
  - strumous 017.2 ✓5th
  - subdiaphragmatic 014.8 ✓5th
  - testis 016.5 ✓5th
  - thigh 017.9 ✓5th
  - urinary 016.3 ✓5th
    - kidney 016.0 ✓5th *[590.81]*
  - uterus 016.7 ✓5th
- accessory sinus — *see* Tuberculosis, sinus
- Addison's disease 017.6 ✓5th
- adenitis (*see also* Tuberculosis, lymph gland) 017.2 ✓5th
- adenoids 012.8 ✓5th
- adenopathy (*see also* Tuberculosis, lymph gland) 017.2 ✓5th
  - tracheobronchial 012.1 ✓5th
    - primary progressive 010.8 ✓5th
- adherent pericardium 017.9 ✓5th *[420.0]*
- adnexa (uteri) 016.7 ✓5th
- adrenal (capsule) (gland) 017.6 ✓5th
- air passage NEC 012.8 ✓5th
- alimentary canal 014.8 ✓5th
- anemia 017.9 ✓5th
- ankle (joint) 015.8 ✓5th
  - bone 015.5 ✓5th *[730.87]*
- anus 014.8 ✓5th
- apex (*see also* Tuberculosis, pulmonary) 011.9 ✓5th
- apical (*see also* Tuberculosis, pulmonary) 011.9 ✓5th
- appendicitis 014.8 ✓5th
- appendix 014.8 ✓5th
- arachnoid 013.0 ✓5th
- artery 017.9 ✓5th
- arthritis (chronic) (synovial) 015.9 ✓5th *[711.40]*
  - ankle 015.8 ✓5th *[730.87]*
  - hip 015.1 ✓5th *[711.45]*
  - knee 015.2 ✓5th *[711.46]*
  - specified site NEC 015.8 ✓5th *[711.48]*
  - spine or vertebra (column) 015.0 ✓5th *[720.81]*
  - wrist 015.8 ✓5th *[730.83]*

Tuberculosis, tubercular, tuberculous (calcification) (calcified) (caseous) (chromogenic acid-fast bacilli) (congenital) (degeneration) (disease) (fibrocaseous) (fistula) (gangrene) (interstitial) (isolated circumscribed lesions) (necrosis) (parenchymatous) (ulcerative) — *continued*

- articular — *see* Tuberculosis, joint
- ascites 014.0 ✓5th
- asthma (*see also* Tuberculosis, pulmonary) 011.9 ✓5th
- axilla, axillary 017.2 ✓5th
  - gland 017.2 ✓5th
- bilateral (*see also* Tuberculosis, pulmonary) 011.9 ✓5th
- bladder 016.1 ✓5th
- bone (*see also* Osteomyelitis, due to, tuberculosis) 015.9 ✓5th *[730.8]* ✓5th
  - hip 015.1 ✓5th *[730.85]*
  - knee 015.2 ✓5th *[730.86]*
  - limb NEC 015.5 ✓5th *[730.88]*
  - sacrum 015.0 ✓5th *[730.88]*
  - specified site NEC 015.7 ✓5th *[730.88]*
  - spinal or vertebral column 015.0 ✓5th *[730.88]*
- bowel 014.8 ✓5th
  - miliary 018.9 ✓5th
- brain 013.2 ✓5th
- breast 017.9 ✓5th
- broad ligament 016.7 ✓5th
- bronchi, bronchial, bronchus 011.3 ✓5th
  - ectasia, ectasis 011.5 ✓5th
  - fistula 011.3 ✓5th
    - primary, progressive 010.8 ✓5th
  - gland 012.1 ✓5th
    - primary, progressive 010.8 ✓5th
  - isolated 012.2 ✓5th
  - lymph gland or node 012.1 ✓5th
    - primary, progressive 010.8 ✓5th
- bronchiectasis 011.5 ✓5th
- bronchitis 011.3 ✓5th
- bronchopleural 012.0 ✓5th
- bronchopneumonia, bronchopneumonic 011.6 ✓5th
- bronchorrhagia 011.3 ✓5th
- bronchotracheal 011.3 ✓5th
  - isolated 012.2 ✓5th
- bronchus — *see* Tuberculosis, bronchi
- bronze disease (Addison's) 017.6 ✓5th
- buccal cavity 017.9 ✓5th
- bulbourethral gland 016.5 ✓5th
- bursa (*see also* Tuberculosis, joint) 015.9 ✓5th
- cachexia NEC (*see also* Tuberculosis, pulmonary) 011.9 ✓5th
- cardiomyopathy 017.9 ✓5th *[425.8]*
- caries (*see also* Tuberculosis, bone) 015.9 ✓5th *[730.8]* ✓5th
- cartilage (*see also* Tuberculosis, bone) 015.9 ✓5th *[730.8]* ✓5th
  - intervertebral 015.0 ✓5th *[730.88]*
- catarrhal (*see also* Tuberculosis, pulmonary) 011.9 ✓5th
- cecum 014.8 ✓5th
- cellular tissue (primary) 017.0 ✓5th
- cellulitis (primary) 017.0 ✓5th
- central nervous system 013.9 ✓5th
  - specified site NEC 013.8 ✓5th
- cerebellum (current) 013.2 ✓5th
- cerebral (current) 013.2 ✓5th
  - meninges 013.0 ✓5th

Tuberculosis, tubercular, tuberculous (calcification) (calcified) (caseous) (chromogenic acid-fast bacilli) (congenital) (degeneration) (disease) (fibrocaseous) (fistula) (gangrene) (interstitial) (isolated circumscribed lesions) (necrosis) (parenchymatous) (ulcerative) — *continued*

- cerebrospinal 013.6 ✓5th
  - meninges 013.0 ✓5th
- cerebrum (current) 013.2 ✓5th
- cervical 017.2 ✓5th
  - gland 017.2 ✓5th
  - lymph nodes 017.2 ✓5th
- cervicitis (uteri) 016.7 ✓5th
- cervix 016.7 ✓5th
- chest (*see also* Tuberculosis, pulmonary) 011.9 ✓5th
- childhood type or first infection 010.0 ✓5th
- choroid 017.3 ✓5th *[363.13]*
- choroiditis 017.3 ✓5th *[363.13]*
- ciliary body 017.3 ✓5th *[364.11]*
- colitis 014.8 ✓5th
- colliers' 011.4 ✓5th
- colliquativa (primary) 017.0 ✓5th
- colon 014.8 ✓5th
  - ulceration 014.8 ✓5th
- complex, primary 010.0 ✓5th
- complicating pregnancy, childbirth, or puerperium 647.3 ✓5th
  - affecting fetus or newborn 760.2
- congenital 771.2
- conjunctiva 017.3 ✓5th *[370.31]*
- connective tissue 017.9 ✓5th
  - bone — *see* Tuberculosis, bone
- contact V01.1
- converter (tuberculin skin test) (without disease) 795.5
- cornea (ulcer) 017.3 ✓5th *[370.31]*
- Cowper's gland 016.5 ✓5th
- coxae 015.1 ✓5th *[730.85]*
- coxalgia 015.1 ✓5th *[730.85]*
- cul-de-sac of Douglas 014.8 ✓5th
- curvature, spine 015.0 ✓5th *[737.40]*
- cutis (colliquativa) (primary) 017.0 ✓5th
- cyst, ovary 016.6 ✓5th
- cystitis 016.1 ✓5th
- dacryocystitis 017.3 ✓5th *[375.32]*
- dactylitis 015.5 ✓5th
- diarrhea 014.8 ✓5th
- diffuse (*see also* Tuberculosis, miliary) 018.9 ✓5th
  - lung — *see* Tuberculosis, pulmonary
  - meninges 013.0 ✓5th
- digestive tract 014.8 ✓5th
- disseminated (*see also* Tuberculosis, miliary) 018.9 ✓5th
  - meninges 013.0 ✓5th
- duodenum 014.8 ✓5th
- dura (mater) 013.9 ✓5th
  - abscess 013.8 ✓5th
    - cerebral 013.3 ✓5th
    - spinal 013.5 ✓5th
- dysentery 014.8 ✓5th
- ear (inner) (middle) 017.4 ✓5th
  - bone 015.6 ✓5th
  - external (primary) 017.0 ✓5th
  - skin (primary) 017.0 ✓5th
- elbow 015.8 ✓5th
- emphysema — *see* Tuberculosis, pulmonary
- empyema 012.0 ✓5th

Tuberculosis, tubercular, tuberculous (calcification) (calcified) (caseous) (chromogenic acid-fast bacilli) (congenital) (degeneration) (disease) (fibrocaseous) (fistula) (gangrene) (interstitial) (isolated circumscribed lesions) (necrosis) (parenchymatous) (ulcerative) — *continued*

- encephalitis 013.6 ✓5th
- endarteritis 017.9 ✓5th
- endocarditis (any valve) 017.9 ✓5th *[424.91]*
- endocardium (any valve) 017.9 ✓5th *[424.91]*
- endocrine glands NEC 017.9 ✓5th
- endometrium 016.7 ✓5th
- enteric, enterica 014.8 ✓5th
- enteritis 014.8 ✓5th
- enterocolitis 014.8 ✓5th
- epididymis 016.4 ✓5th
- epididymitis 016.4 ✓5th
- epidural abscess 013.8 ✓5th
  - brain 013.3 ✓5th
  - spinal cord 013.5 ✓5th
- epiglottis 012.3 ✓5th
- episcleritis 017.3 ✓5th *[379.00]*
- erythema (induratum) (nodosum) (primary) 017.1 ✓5th
- esophagus 017.8 ✓5th
- Eustachian tube 017.4 ✓5th
- exposure to V01.1
- exudative 012.0 ✓5th
  - primary, progressive 010.1 ✓5th
- eye 017.3 ✓5th
  - glaucoma 017.3 ✓5th *[365.62]*
- eyelid (primary) 017.0 ✓5th
  - lupus 017.0 ✓5th *[373.4]*
- fallopian tube 016.6 ✓5th
- fascia 017.9 ✓5th
- fauces 012.8 ✓5th
- finger 017.9 ✓5th
- first infection 010.0 ✓5th
- fistula, perirectal 014.8 ✓5th
- Florida 011.6 ✓5th
- foot 017.9 ✓5th
- funnel pelvis 137.3
- gallbladder 017.9 ✓5th
- galloping (*see also* Tuberculosis, pulmonary) 011.9 ✓5th
- ganglionic 015.9 ✓5th
- gastritis 017.9 ✓5th
- gastrocolic fistula 014.8 ✓5th
- gastroenteritis 014.8 ✓5th
- gastrointestinal tract 014.8 ✓5th
- general, generalized 018.9 ✓5th
  - acute 018.0 ✓5th
  - chronic 018.8 ✓5th
- genital organs NEC 016.9 ✓5th
  - female 016.7 ✓5th
  - male 016.5 ✓5th
- genitourinary NEC 016.9 ✓5th
- genu 015.2 ✓5th
- glandulae suprarenalis 017.6 ✓5th
- glandular, general 017.2 ✓5th
- glottis 012.3 ✓5th
- grinders' 011.4 ✓5th
- groin 017.2 ✓5th
- gum 017.9 ✓5th
- hand 017.9 ✓5th

Tuberculosis, tubercular, tuberculous (calcification) (calcified) (caseous) (chromogenic acid-fast bacilli) (congenital) (degeneration) (disease) (fibrocaseous) (fistula) (gangrene) (interstitial) (isolated circumscribed lesions) (necrosis) (parenchymatous) (ulcerative) — *continued*

- pneumonia, pneumonic 011.6 ✓5th
- pneumothorax 011.7 ✓5th
- polyserositis 018.9 ✓5th
  - acute 018.0 ✓5th
  - chronic 018.8 ✓5th
- potters' 011.4 ✓5th
- prepuce 016.5 ✓5th
- primary 010.9 ✓5th
  - complex 010.0 ✓5th
  - complicated 010.8 ✓5th
    - with pleurisy or effusion 010.1 ✓5th
  - progressive 010.8 ✓5th
    - with pleurisy or effusion 010.1 ✓5th
  - skin 017.0 ✓5th
- proctitis 014.8 ✓5th
- prostate 016.5 ✓5th *[601.4]*
- prostatitis 016.5 ✓5th *[601.4]*
- pulmonaris (*see also* Tuberculosis, pulmonary) 011.9 ✓5th
- pulmonary (artery) (incipient) (malignant) (multiple round foci) (pernicious) (reinfection stage) 011.9 ✓5th
  - cavitated or with cavitation 011.2 ✓5th
    - primary, progressive 010.8 ✓5th
  - childhood type or first infection 010.0 ✓5th
  - chromogenic acid-fast bacilli 795.3
  - fibrosis or fibrotic 011.4 ✓5th
  - infiltrative 011.0 ✓5th
    - primary, progressive 010.9 ✓5th
  - nodular 011.1 ✓5th
  - specified NEC 011.8 ✓5th
  - sputum positive only 795.3
  - status following surgical collapse of lung NEC 011.9 ✓5th
- pyelitis 016.0 ✓5th *[590.81]*
- pyelonephritis 016.0 ✓5th *[590.81]*
- pyemia — *see* Tuberculosis, miliary
- pyonephrosis 016.0 ✓5th
- pyopneumothorax 012.0 ✓5th
- pyothorax 012.0 ✓5th
- rectum (with abscess) 014.8 ✓5th
  - fistula 014.8 ✓5th
- reinfection stage (*see also* Tuberculosis, pulmonary) 011.9 ✓5th
- renal 016.0 ✓5th
- renis 016.0 ✓5th
- reproductive organ 016.7 ✓5th
- respiratory NEC (*see also* Tuberculosis, pulmonary) 011.9 ✓5th
  - specified site NEC 012.8 ✓5th
- retina 017.3 ✓5th *[363.13]*
- retroperitoneal (lymph gland or node) 014.8 ✓5th
  - gland 014.8 ✓5th
- retropharyngeal abscess 012.8 ✓5th
- rheumatism 015.9 ✓5th
- rhinitis 012.8 ✓5th
- sacroiliac (joint) 015.8 ✓5th
- sacrum 015.0 ✓5th *[730.88]*
- salivary gland 017.9 ✓5th
- salpingitis (acute) (chronic) 016.6 ✓5th
- sandblasters' 011.4 ✓5th
- sclera 017.3 ✓5th *[379.09]*
- scoliosis 015.0 ✓5th *[737.43]*

Tuberculosis, tubercular, tuberculous (calcification) (calcified) (caseous) (chromogenic acid-fast bacilli) (congenital) (degeneration) (disease) (fibrocaseous) (fistula) (gangrene) (interstitial) (isolated circumscribed lesions) (necrosis) (parenchymatous) (ulcerative) — *continued*

- scrofulous 017.2 ✓5th
- scrotum 016.5 ✓5th
- seminal tract or vesicle 016.5 ✓5th *[608.81]*
- senile NEC (*see also* Tuberculosis, pulmonary) 011.9 ✓5th
- septic NEC (*see also* Tuberculosis, miliary) 018.9 ✓5th
- shoulder 015.8 ✓5th
  - blade 015.7 ✓5th *[730.8]* ✓5th
- sigmoid 014.8 ✓5th
- sinus (accessory) (nasal) 012.8 ✓5th
  - bone 015.7 ✓5th *[730.88]*
  - epididymis 016.4 ✓5th
- skeletal NEC (*see also* Osteomyelitis, due to tuberculosis) 015.9 ✓5th *[730.8]* ✓5th
- skin (any site) (primary) 017.0 ✓5th
- small intestine 014.8 ✓5th
- soft palate 017.9 ✓5th
- spermatic cord 016.5 ✓5th
- spinal
  - column 015.0 ✓5th *[730.88]*
  - cord 013.4 ✓5th
  - disease 015.0 ✓5th *[730.88]*
  - medulla 013.4 ✓5th
  - membrane 013.0 ✓5th
  - meninges 013.0 ✓5th
- spine 015.0 ✓5th *[730.88]*
- spleen 017.7 ✓5th
- splenitis 017.7 ✓5th
- spondylitis 015.0 ✓5th *[720.81]*
- spontaneous pneumothorax — *see* Tuberculosis, pulmonary
- sternoclavicular joint 015.8 ✓5th
- stomach 017.9 ✓5th
- stonemasons' 011.4 ✓5th
- struma 017.2 ✓5th
- subcutaneous tissue (cellular) (primary) 017.0 ✓5th
- subcutis (primary) 017.0 ✓5th
- subdeltoid bursa 017.9 ✓5th
- submaxillary 017.9 ✓5th
  - region 017.9 ✓5th
- supraclavicular gland 017.2 ✓5th
- suprarenal (capsule) (gland) 017.6 ✓5th
- swelling, joint (*see also* Tuberculosis, joint) 015.9 ✓5th
- symphysis pubis 015.7 ✓5th *[730.88]*
- synovitis 015.9 ✓5th *[727.01]*
  - hip 015.1 ✓5th *[727.01]*
  - knee 015.2 ✓5th *[727.01]*
  - specified site NEC 015.8 ✓5th *[727.01]*
  - spine or vertebra 015.0 ✓5th *[727.01]*
- systemic — *see* Tuberculosis, miliary
- tarsitis (eyelid) 017.0 ✓5th *[373.4]*
  - ankle (bone) 015.5 ✓5th *[730.87]*
- tendon (sheath) — *see* Tuberculosis, tenosynovitis
- tenosynovitis 015.9 ✓5th *[727.01]*
  - hip 015.1 ✓5th *[727.01]*
  - knee 015.2 ✓5th *[727.01]*
  - specified site NEC 015.8 ✓5th *[727.01]*
  - spine or vertebra 015.0 ✓5th *[727.01]*
- testis 016.5 ✓5th *[608.81]*
- throat 012.8 ✓5th

Tuberculosis, tubercular, tuberculous (calcification) (calcified) (caseous) (chromogenic acid-fast bacilli) (congenital) (degeneration) (disease) (fibrocaseous) (fistula) (gangrene) (interstitial) (isolated circumscribed lesions) (necrosis) (parenchymatous) (ulcerative) — *continued*

- thymus gland 017.9 ✓5th
- thyroid gland 017.5 ✓5th
- toe 017.9 ✓5th
- tongue 017.9 ✓5th
- tonsil (lingual) 012.8 ✓5th
- tonsillitis 012.8 ✓5th
- trachea, tracheal 012.8 ✓5th
  - gland 012.1 ✓5th
    - primary, progressive 010.8 ✓5th
  - isolated 012.2 ✓5th
- tracheobronchial 011.3 ✓5th
  - glandular 012.1 ✓5th
    - primary, progressive 010.8 ✓5th
  - isolated 012.2 ✓5th
  - lymph gland or node 012.1 ✓5th
    - primary, progressive 010.8 ✓5th
- tubal 016.6 ✓5th
- tunica vaginalis 016.5 ✓5th
- typhlitis 014.8 ✓5th
- ulcer (primary) (skin) 017.0 ✓5th
  - bowel or intestine 014.8 ✓5th
  - specified site NEC — *see* Tuberculosis, by site
- unspecified site — *see* Tuberculosis, pulmonary
- ureter 016.2 ✓5th
- urethra, urethral 016.3 ✓5th
- urinary organ or tract 016.3 ✓5th
  - kidney 016.0 ✓5th
- uterus 016.7 ✓5th
- uveal tract 017.3 ✓5th *[363.13]*
- uvula 017.9 ✓5th
- vaccination, prophylactic (against) V03.2
- vagina 016.7 ✓5th
- vas deferens 016.5 ✓5th
- vein 017.9 ✓5th
- verruca (primary) 017.0 ✓5th
- verrucosa (cutis) (primary) 017.0 ✓5th
- vertebra (column) 015.0 ✓5th *[730.88]*
- vesiculitis 016.5 ✓5th *[608.81]*
- viscera NEC 014.8 ✓5th
- vulva 016.7 ✓5th *[616.51]*
- wrist (joint) 015.8 ✓5th
  - bone 015.5 ✓5th *[730.83]*

Tuberculum

- auriculae 744.29
- occlusal 520.2
- paramolare 520.2

Tuberous sclerosis (brain) 759.5

Tubo-ovarian — *see* condition

Tuboplasty, after previous sterilization V26.0

Tubotympanitis 381.10

Tularemia 021.9

- with
  - conjunctivitis 021.3
  - pneumonia 021.2
- bronchopneumonic 021.2
- conjunctivitis 021.3
- cryptogenic 021.1
- disseminated 021.8
- enteric 021.1

U

V

- **Vaccination**
  - complication or reaction — *see* Complications, vaccination
  - not done (contraindicated) V64.0
    - because of patient's decision V64.2
  - prophylactic (against) V05.9
    - arthropod-borne viral
      - disease NEC V05.1
      - encephalitis V05.0
    - chicken pox V05.4
    - cholera (alone) V03.0
      - with typhoid-paratyphoid (cholera + TAB) V06.0
    - common cold V04.7
    - diphtheria (alone) V03.5
      - with
        - poliomyelitis (DTP + polio) V06.3
        - tetanus V06.5
          - pertussis combined [DTP] V06.1
        - typhoid-paratyphoid (DTP + TAB) V06.2
    - disease (single) NEC V05.9
      - bacterial NEC V03.9
        - specified type NEC V03.89
      - combination NEC V06.9
        - specified type NEC V06.8
      - specified type NEC V05.8
    - encephalitis, viral, arthropod-borne V05.0
    - Hemophilus influenzae, type B [Hib] V03.81
    - hepatitis, viral V05.3
    - influenza V04.8
      - with
        - Streptococcus pneumoniae [pneumococcus] V06.6
    - lileishmaniasis V05.2
    - measles (alone) V04.2
      - with mumps-rubella (MMR) V06.4
    - mumps (alone) V04.6
      - with measles and rubella (MMR) V06.4
    - pertussis alone V03.6
    - plague V03.3
    - poliomyelitis V04.0
      - with diphtheria-tetanus-pertussis (DTP + polio) V06.3
    - rabies V04.5
    - rubella (alone) V04.3
      - with measles and mumps (MMR) V06.4
    - smallpox V04.1
    - Streptococcus pneumoniae [pneumococcus] V03.82
      - with
        - influenza V06.6
    - tetanus toxoid (alone) V03.7
      - with diphtheria [Td] V06.5
        - with
          - pertussis (DTP) V06.1
            - with poliomyelitis (DTP + polio) V06.3
    - tuberculosis (BCG) V03.2
    - tularemia V03.4
    - typhoid-paratyphoid (TAB) (alone) V03.1
      - with diphtheria-tetanus-pertussis (TAB + DTP) V06.2
    - varicella V05.4
    - viral
      - encephalitis, arthropod-borne V05.0
      - hepatitis V05.3
    - yellow fever V04.4
- **Vaccinia** (generalized) 999.0
  - congenital 771.2
  - conjunctiva 999.3
  - eyelids 999.0 *[373.5]*
  - localized 999.3
  - nose 999.3
  - not from vaccination 051.0
    - eyelid 051.0 *[373.5]*
  - sine vaccinatione 051.0
  - without vaccination 051.0
- **Vacuum**
  - extraction of fetus or newborn 763.3
  - in sinus (accessory) (nasal) (*see also* Sinusitis) 473.9
- **Vagabond** V60.0
- **Vagabondage** V60.0
- **Vagabonds' disease** 132.1
- **Vagina, vaginal** — *see* condition
- **Vaginalitis** (tunica) 608.4
- **Vaginismus** (reflex) 625.1
  - functional 306.51
  - hysterical 300.11
  - psychogenic 306.51
- **Vaginitis** (acute) (chronic) (circumscribed) (diffuse) (emphysematous) (Hemophilus vaginalis) (nonspecific) (nonvenereal) (ulcerative) 616.10
  - with
    - abortion — *see* Abortion, by type, with sepsis
    - ectopic pregnancy (*see also* categories 633.0-633.9) 639.0
    - molar pregnancy (*see also* categories 630-632) 639.0
  - adhesive, congenital 752.49
  - atrophic, postmenopausal 627.3
  - bacterial 616.10
  - blennorrhagic (acute) 098.0
    - chronic or duration of 2 months or over 098.2
  - candidal 112.1
  - chlamydial 099.53
  - complicating pregnancy or puerperium 646.6 [5th]
    - affecting fetus or newborn 760.8
  - congenital (adhesive) 752.49
  - due to
    - C. albicans 112.1
    - Trichomonas (vaginalis) 131.01
  - following
    - abortion 639.0
    - ectopic or molar pregnancy 639.0
  - gonococcal (acute) 098.0
    - chronic or duration of 2 months or over 098.2
  - granuloma 099.2
  - Monilia 112.1
  - mycotic 112.1
  - pinworm 127.4 *[616.11]*
  - postirradiation 616.10
  - postmenopausal atrophic 627.3
  - senile (atrophic) 627.3
  - syphilitic (early) 091.0
    - late 095.8
  - trichomonal 131.01
  - tuberculous (*see also* Tuberculosis) 016.7 [5th]
  - venereal NEC 099.8
- **Vaginosis** — *see* Vaginitis
- **Vagotonia** 352.3
- **Vagrancy** V60.0
- **Vallecula** — *see* condition
- **Valley fever** 114.0
- **Valsuani's disease** (progressive pernicious anemia, puerperal) 648.2 [5th]
- **Valve, valvular** (formation) — *see also* condition
  - cerebral ventricle (communicating) in situ V45.2
  - cervix, internal os 752.49
  - colon 751.5
  - congenital NEC — *see* Atresia
  - formation congenital NEC — *see* Atresia
  - heart defect — *see* Anomaly, heart, valve
  - ureter 753.29
    - pelvic junction 753.21
    - vesical orifice 753.22
  - urethra 753.6
- **Valvulitis** (chronic) (*see also* Endocarditis) 424.90
  - rheumatic (chronic) (inactive) (with chorea) 397.9
    - active or acute (aortic) (mitral) (pulmonary) (tricuspid) 391.1
  - syphilitic NEC 093.20
    - aortic 093.22
    - mitral 093.21
    - pulmonary 093.24
    - tricuspid 093.23
- **Valvulopathy** — *see* Endocarditis
- **van Bogaert's leukoencephalitis** (sclerosing) (subacute) 046.2
- **van Bogaert-Nijssen** (-Peiffer) disease 330.0
- **van Buchem's syndrome** (hyperostosis corticalis) 733.3
- **van Creveld-von Gierke disease** (glycogenosis I) 271.0
- **van den Bergh's disease** (enterogenous cyanosis) 289.7
- **van der Hoeve's syndrome** (brittle bones and blue sclera, deafness) 756.51
- **van der Hoeve-Halbertsma-Waardenburg syndrome** (ptosis-epicanthus) 270.2
- **van der Hoeve-Waardenburg-Gualdi syndrome** (ptosis-epicanthus) 270.2
- **Vanillism** 692.89
- **Vanishing lung** 492.0
- **Vanishing twin** 651.33
- **van Neck** (-Odelberg) disease or syndrome (juvenile osteochondrosis) 732.1
- **Vapor asphyxia or suffocation** NEC 987.9
  - specified agent — *see* Table of Drugs and Chemicals
- **Vaquez's disease** (M9950/1) 238.4
- **Vaquez-Osler disease** (polycythemia vera) (M9950/1) 238.4
- **Variance, lethal ball, prosthetic heart valve** 996.02
- **Variants, thalassemic** 282.4
- **Variations in hair color** 704.3
- **Varicella** 052.9
  - with
    - complication 052.8
      - specified NEC 052.7
    - pneumonia 052.1
  - vaccination and inoculation (prophylactic) V05.4
- **Varices** — *see* Varix
- **Varicocele** (scrotum) (thrombosed) 456.4
  - ovary 456.5
  - perineum 456.6
  - spermatic cord (ulcerated) 456.4

W

Note — For fracture with open wound, see Fracture.

For laceration, traumatic rupture, tear or penetrating wound of internal organs, such as heart, lung, liver, kidney, pelvic organs, etc., whether or not accompanied by open wound or fracture in the same region, see Injury, internal.

For contused wound, see Contusion. For crush injury, see Crush. For abrasion, insect bite (nonvenomous), blister, or scratch, see Injury, superficial.

Complicated includes wounds with:

delayed healing
delayed treatment
foreign body
primary infection

For late effect of open wound, see Late, effect, wound, open, by site.

> *Note — Multiple open wounds of sites classifiable to the same four-digit category should be classified to that category unless they are in different limbs.*
>
> *Multiple open wounds of sites classifiable to different four-digit categories, or to different limbs, should be coded separately.*

X

Y

Yaws — *continued*

Z

SECTION 2

ALPHABETIC INDEX TO POISONING AND EXTERNAL CAUSES OF ADVERSE EFFECTS OF DRUGS AND OTHER CHEMICAL SUBSTANCES

TABLE OF DRUGS AND CHEMICALS

This table contains a classification of drugs and other chemical substances to identify poisoning states and external causes of adverse effects.

Each of the listed substances in the table is assigned a code according to the poisoning classification (960-989). These codes are used when there is a statement of poisoning, overdose, wrong substance given or taken, or intoxication.

The table also contains a listing of external causes of adverse effects. An adverse effect is a pathologic manifestation due to ingestion or exposure to drugs or other chemical substances (e.g., dermatitis, hypersensitivity reaction, aspirin gastritis). The adverse effect is to be identified by the appropriate code found in Section 1, Index to Diseases and Injuries. An external cause code can then be used to identify the circumstances involved. The table headings pertaining to external causes are defined below:

Accidental poisoning (E850-E869) — accidental overdose of drug, wrong substance given or taken, drug taken inadvertently, accidents in the usage of drugs and biologicals in medical and surgical procedures, and to show external causes of poisonings classifiable to 980-989.

Therapeutic use (E930-E949) — a correct substance properly administered in therapeutic or prophylactic dosage as the external cause of adverse effects.

Suicide attempt (E950-E952) — instances in which self-inflicted injuries or poisonings are involved.

Assault (E961-E962) — injury or poisoning inflicted by another person with the intent to injure or kill.

Undetermined (E980-E982) — to be used when the intent of the poisoning or injury cannot be determined whether it was intentional or accidental.

The American Hospital Formulary Service list numbers are included in the table to help classify new drugs not identified in the table by name. The AHFS list numbers are keyed to the continually revised American Hospital Formulary Service (AHFS).* These listings are found in the table under the main term **Drug**.

Excluded from the table are radium and other radioactive substances. The classification of adverse effects and complications pertaining to these substances will be found in Section 1, Index to Diseases and Injuries, and Section 3, Index to External Causes of Injuries.

Although certain substances are indexed with one or more subentries, the majority are listed according to one use or state. It is recognized that many substances may be used in various ways, in medicine and in industry, and may cause adverse effects whatever the state of the agent (solid, liquid, or fumes arising from a liquid). In cases in which the reported data indicates a use or state not in the table, or which is clearly different from the one listed, an attempt should be made to classify the substance in the form which most nearly expresses the reported facts.

* American Hospital Formulary Service, 2 vol. (Washington, D.C.: American Society of Hospital Pharmacists, 1959--)

		External Cause (E-Code)				
Substance	**Poisoning**	**Accident**	**Therapeutic Use**	**Suicide Attempt**	**Assault**	**Un-determined**
1-propanol	980.3	E860.4	—	E950.9	E962.1	E980.9
2-propanol	980.2	E860.3	—	E950.9	E962.1	E980.9
2, 4-D (dichlorophenoxyacetic acid)	989.4	E863.5	—	E950.6	E962.1	E980.7
2, 4-toluene diisocyanate	983.0	E864.0	—	E950.7	E962.1	E980.6
2, 4, 5-T (trichlorophenoxyacetic acid)	989.2	E863.5	—	E950.6	E962.1	E980.7
14-hydroxydihydromorphinone	965.09	E850.2	E935.2	E950.0	E962.0	E980.0
A						
ABOB	961.7	E857	E931.7	E950.4	E962.0	E980.4
Abrus (seed)	988.2	E865.3	—	E950.9	E962.1	E980.9
Absinthe	980.0	E860.1	—	E950.9	E962.1	E980.9
beverage	980.0	E860.0	—	E950.9	E962.1	E980.9
Acenocoumarin, acenocoumarol	964.2	E858.2	E934.2	E950.4	E962.0	E980.4
Acepromazine	969.1	E853.0	E939.1	E950.3	E962.0	E980.3
Acetal	982.8	E862.4	—	E950.9	E962.1	E980.9
Acetaldehyde (vapor)	987.8	E869.8	—	E952.8	E962.2	E982.8
liquid	989.89	E866.8	—	E950.9	E962.1	E980.9
Acetaminophen	965.4	E850.4	E935.4	E950.0	E962.0	E980.0
Acetaminosalol	965.1	E850.3	E935.3	E950.0	E962.0	E980.0
Acetanilid(e)	965.4	E850.4	E935.4	E950.0	E962.0	E980.0
Acetarsol, acetarsone	961.1	E857	E931.1	E950.4	E962.0	E980.4
Acetazolamide	974.2	E858.5	E944.2	E950.4	E962.0	E980.4
Acetic						
acid	983.1	E864.1	—	E950.7	E962.1	E980.6
with sodium acetate (ointment)	976.3	E858.7	E946.3	E950.4	E962.0	E980.4
irrigating solution	974.5	E858.5	E944.5	E950.4	E962.0	E980.4
lotion	976.2	E858.7	E946.2	E950.4	E962.0	E980.4
anhydride	983.1	E864.1	—	E950.7	E962.1	E980.6
ether (vapor)	982.8	E862.4	—	E950.9	E962.1	E980.9
Acetohexamide	962.3	E858.0	E932.3	E950.4	E962.0	E980.4
Acetomenaphthone	964.3	E858.2	E934.3	E950.4	E962.0	E980.4
Acetomorphine	965.01	E850.0	E935.0	E950.0	E962.0	E980.0
Acetone (oils) (vapor)	982.8	E862.4	—	E950.9	E962.1	E980.9
Acetophenazine (maleate)	969.1	E853.0	E939.1	E950.3	E962.0	E980.3
Acetophenetidin	965.4	E850.4	E935.4	E950.0	E962.0	E980.0
Acetophenone	982.0	E862.4	—	E950.9	E962.1	E980.9
Acetorphine	965.09	E850.2	E935.2	E950.0	E962.0	E980.0
Acetosulfone (sodium)	961.8	E857	E931.8	E950.4	E962.0	E980.4
Acetrizoate (sodium)	977.8	E858.8	E947.8	E950.4	E962.0	E980.4
Acetylcarbromal	967.3	E852.2	E937.3	E950.2	E962.0	E980.2
Acetylcholine (chloride)	971.0	E855.3	E941.0	E950.4	E962.0	E980.4
Acetylcysteine	975.5	E858.6	E945.5	E950.4	E962.0	E980.4
Acetyldigitoxin	972.1	E858.3	E942.1	E950.4	E962.0	E980.4
Acetyldihydrocodeine	965.09	E850.2	E935.2	E950.0	E962.0	E980.0
Acetyldihydrocodeinone	965.09	E850.2	E935.2	E950.0	E962.0	E980.0
Acetylene (gas) (industrial)	987.1	E868.1	—	E951.8	E962.2	E981.8
incomplete combustion of—*see* Carbon monoxide, fuel, utility						
tetrachloride (vapor)	982.3	E862.4	—	E950.9	E962.1	E980.9
Acetyliodosalicylic acid	965.1	E850.3	E935.3	E950.0	E962.0	E980.0
Acetylphenylhydrazine	965.8	E850.8	E935.8	E950.0	E962.0	E980.0
Acetylsalicylic acid	965.1	E850.3	E935.3	E950.0	E962.0	E980.0
Achromycin	960.4	E856	E930.4	E950.4	E962.0	E980.4
ophthalmic preparation	976.5	E858.7	E946.5	E950.4	E962.0	E980.4
topical NEC	976.0	E858.7	E946.0	E950.4	E962.0	E980.4
Acidifying agents	963.2	E858.1	E933.2	E950.4	E962.0	E980.4
Acids (corrosive) NEC	983.1	E864.1	—	E950.7	E962.1	E980.6
Aconite (wild)	988.2	E865.4	—	E950.9	E962.1	E980.9
Aconitine (liniment)	976.8	E858.7	E946.8	E950.4	E962.0	E980.4
Aconitum ferox	988.2	E865.4	—	E950.9	E962.1	E980.9
Acridine	983.0	E864.0	—	E950.7	E962.1	E980.6
vapor	987.8	E869.8	—	E952.8	E962.2	E982.8
Acriflavine	961.9	E857	E931.9	E950.4	E962.0	E980.4
Acrisorcin	976.0	E858.7	E946.0	E950.4	E962.0	E980.4
Acrolein (gas)	987.8	E869.8	—	E952.8	E962.2	E982.8
liquid	989.89	E866.8	—	E950.9	E962.1	E980.9
Actaea spicata	988.2	E865.4	—	E950.9	E962.1	E980.9
Acterol	961.5	E857	E931.5	E950.4	E962.0	E980.4
ACTH	962.4	E858.0	E932.4	E950.4	E962.0	E980.4
Acthar	962.4	E858.0	E932.4	E950.4	E962.0	E980.4
Actinomycin (C) (D)	960.7	E856	E930.7	E950.4	E962.0	E980.4
Adalin (acetyl)	967.3	E852.2	E937.3	E950.2	E962.0	E980.2

Substance	Poisoning	External Cause (E-Code)				
		Accident	Therapeutic Use	Suicide Attempt	Assault	Undetermined
Adenosine (phosphate)	977.8	E858.8	E947.8	E950.4	E962.0	E980.4
Adhesives	989.89	E866.6	—	E950.9	E962.1	E980.9
ADH	962.5	E858.0	E932.5	E950.4	E962.0	E980.4
Adicillin	960.0	E856	E930.0	E950.4	E962.0	E980.4
Adiphenine	975.1	E855.6	E945.1	E950.4	E962.0	E980.4
Adjunct, pharmaceutical	977.4	E858.8	E947.4	E950.4	E962.0	E980.4
Adrenal (extract, cortex or medulla) (glucocorticoids) (hormones) (mineralocorticoids)	962.0	E858.0	E932.0	E950.4	E962.0	E980.4
ENT agent	976.6	E858.7	E946.6	E950.4	E962.0	E980.4
ophthalmic preparation	976.5	E858.7	E946.5	E950.4	E962.0	E980.4
topical NEC	976.0	E858.7	E946.0	E950.4	E962.0	E980.4
Adrenalin	971.2	E855.5	E941.2	E950.4	E962.0	E980.4
Adrenergic blocking agents	971.3	E855.6	E941.3	E950.4	E962.0	E980.4
Adrenergics	971.2	E855.5	E941.2	E950.4	E962.0	E980.4
Adrenochrome (derivatives)	972.8	E858.3	E942.8	E950.4	E962.0	E980.4
Adrenocorticotropic hormone	962.4	E858.0	E932.4	E950.4	E962.0	E980.4
Adrenocorticotropin	962.4	E858.0	E932.4	E950.4	E962.0	E980.4
Adriamycin	960.7	E856	E930.7	E950.4	E962.0	E980.4
Aerosol spray—*see* Sprays						
Aerosporin	960.8	E856	E930.8	E950.4	E962.0	E980.4
ENT agent	976.6	E858.7	E946.6	E950.4	E962.0	E980.4
ophthalmic preparation	976.5	E858.7	E946.5	E950.4	E962.0	E980.4
topical NEC	976.0	E858.7	E946.0	E950.4	E962.0	E980.4
Aethusa cynapium	988.2	E865.4	—	E950.9	E962.1	E980.9
Afghanistan black	969.6	E854.1	E939.6	E950.3	E962.0	E980.3
Aflatoxin	989.7	E865.9	—	E950.9	E962.1	E980.9
African boxwood	988.2	E865.4	—	E950.9	E962.1	E980.9
Agar (-agar)	973.3	E858.4	E943.3	E950.4	E962.0	E980.4
Agricultural agent NEC	989.89	E863.9	—	E950.6	E962.1	E980.7
Agrypnal	967.0	E851	E937.0	E950.1	E962.0	E980.1
Air contaminant(s), source or type not specified	987.9	E869.9	—	E952.9	E962.2	E982.9
specified type—*see* specific substance						
Akee	988.2	E865.4	—	E950.9	E962.1	E980.9
Akrinol	976.0	E858.7	E946.0	E950.4	E962.0	E980.4
Alantolactone	961.6	E857	E931.6	E950.4	E962.0	E980.4
Albamycin	960.8	E856	E930.8	E950.4	E962.0	E980.4
Albumin (normal human serum)	964.7	E858.2	E934.7	E950.4	E962.0	E980.4
Alcohol	980.9	E860.9	—	E950.9	E962.1	E980.9
absolute	980.0	E860.1	—	E950.9	E962.1	E980.9
beverage	980.0	E860.0	E947.8	E950.9	E962.1	E980.9
amyl	980.3	E860.4	—	E950.9	E962.1	E980.9
antifreeze	980.1	E860.2	—	E950.9	E962.1	E980.9
butyl	980.3	E860.4	—	E950.9	E962.1	E980.9
dehydrated	980.0	E860.1	—	E950.9	E862.1	E980.9
beverage	980.0	E860.0	E947.8	E950.9	E962.1	E980.9
denatured	980.0	E860.1	—	E950.9	E962.1	E980.9
deterrents	977.3	E858.8	E947.3	E950.4	E962.0	E980.4
diagnostic (gastric function)	977.8	E858.8	E947.8	E950.4	E962.0	E980.4
ethyl	980.0	E860.1	—	E950.9	E962.1	E980.9
beverage	980.0	E860.0	E947.8	E950.9	E962.1	E980.9
grain	980.0	E860.1	—	E950.9	E962.1	E980.9
beverage	980.0	E860.0	E947.8	E950.9	E962.1	E980.9
industrial	980.9	E860.9	—	E950.9	E962.1	E980.9
isopropyl	980.2	E860.3	—	E950.9	E962.1	E980.9
methyl	980.1	E860.2	—	E950.9	E962.1	E980.9
preparation for consumption	980.0	E860.0	E947.8	E950.9	E962.1	E980.9
propyl	980.3	E860.4	—	E950.9	E962.1	E980.9
secondary	980.2	E860.3	—	E950.9	E962.1	E980.9
radiator	980.1	E860.2	—	E950.9	E962.1	E980.9
rubbing	980.2	E860.3	—	E950.9	E962.1	E980.9
specified type NEC	980.8	E860.8	—	E950.9	E962.1	E980.9
surgical	980.9	E860.9	—	E950.9	E962.1	E980.9
vapor (from any type of alcohol)	987.8	E869.8	—	E952.8	E962.2	E982.8
wood	980.1	E860.2	—	E950.9	E962.1	E980.9
Alcuronium chloride	975.2	E858.6	E945.2	E950.4	E962.0	E980.4
Aldactone	974.4	E858.5	E944.4	E950.4	E962.0	E980.4
Aldicarb	989.3	E863.2	—	E950.6	E962.1	E980.7
Aldomet	972.6	E858.3	E942.6	E950.4	E962.0	E980.4
Aldosterone	962.0	E858.0	E932.0	E950.4	E962.0	E980.4
Aldrin (dust)	989.2	E863.0	—	E950.6	E962.1	E980.7
Aleve — *see* Naproxen						
Algeldrate	973.0	E858.4	E943.0	E950.4	E962.0	E980.4
Alidase	963.4	E858.1	E933.4	E950.4	E962.0	E980.4

Substance	Poisoning	External Cause (E-Code) Accident	Therapeutic Use	Suicide Attempt	Assault	Undetermined
Aliphatic thiocyanates	989.0	E866.8	—	E950.9	E962.1	E980.9
Alkaline antiseptic solution (aromatic)	976.6	E858.7	E946.6	E950.4	E962.0	E980.4
Alkalinizing agents (medicinal)	963.3	E858.1	E933.3	E950.4	E962.0	E980.4
Alkalis, caustic	983.2	E864.2	—	E950.7	E962.1	E980.6
Alkalizing agents (medicinal)	963.3	E858.1	E933.3	E950.4	E962.0	E980.4
Alka-seltzer	965.1	E850.3	E935.3	E950.0	E962.0	E980.0
Alkavervir	972.6	E858.3	E942.6	E950.4	E962.0	E980.4
Allegron	969.0	E854.0	E939.0	E950.3	E962.0	E980.3
Allobarbital, allobarbitone	967.0	E851	E937.0	E950.1	E962.0	E980.1
Allopurinol	974.7	E858.5	E944.7	E950.4	E962.0	E980.4
Allylestrenol	962.2	E858.0	E932.2	E950.4	E962.0	E980.4
Allylisopropylacetylurea	967.8	E852.8	E937.8	E950.2	E962.0	E980.2
Allylisopropylmalonylurea	967.0	E851	E937.0	E950.1	E962.0	E980.1
Allyltribromide	967.3	E852.2	E937.3	E950.2	E962.0	E980.2
Aloe, aloes, aloin	973.1	E858.4	E943.1	E950.4	E962.0	E980.4
Aloxidone	966.0	E855.0	E936.0	E950.4	E962.0	E980.4
Aloxiprin	965.1	E850.3	E935.3	E950.0	E962.0	E980.0
Alpha amylase	963.4	E858.1	E933.4	E950.4	E962.0	E980.4
Alphaprodine (hydrochloride)	965.09	E850.2	E935.2	E950.0	E962.0	E980.0
Alpha tocopherol	963.5	E858.1	E933.5	E950.4	E962.0	E980.4
Alseroxylon	972.6	E858.3	E942.6	E950.4	E962.0	E980.4
Alum (ammonium) (potassium)	983.2	E864.2	—	E950.7	E962.1	E980.6
medicinal (astringent) NEC	976.2	E858.7	E946.2	E950.4	E962.0	E980.4
Aluminium, aluminum (gel) (hydroxide)	973.0	E858.4	E943.0	E950.4	E962.0	E980.4
acetate solution	976.2	E858.7	E946.2	E950.4	E962.0	E980.4
aspirin	965.1	E850.3	E935.3	E950.0	E962.0	E980.0
carbonate	973.0	E858.4	E943.0	E950.4	E962.0	E980.4
glycinate	973.0	E858.4	E943.0	E950.4	E962.0	E980.4
nicotinate	972.2	E858.3	E942.2	E950.4	E962.0	E980.4
ointment (surgical) (topical)	976.3	E858.7	E946.3	E950.4	E962.0	E980.4
phosphate	973.0	E858.4	E943.0	E950.4	E962.0	E980.4
subacetate	976.2	E858.7	E946.2	E950.4	E962.0	E980.4
topical NEC	976.3	E858.7	E946.3	E950.4	E962.0	E980.4
Alurate	967.0	E851	E937.0	E950.1	E962.0	E980.1
Alverine (citrate)	975.1	E858.6	E945.1	E950.4	E962.0	E980.4
Alvodine	965.09	E850.2	E935.2	E950.0	E962.0	E980.0
Amanita phalloides	988.1	E865.5	—	E950.9	E962.1	E980.9
Amantadine (hydrochloride)	966.4	E855.0	E936.4	E950.4	E962.0	E980.4
Ambazone	961.9	E857	E931.9	E950.4	E962.0	E980.4
Ambenonium	971.0	E855.3	E941.0	E950.4	E962.0	E980.4
Ambutonium bromide	971.1	E855.4	E941.1	E950.4	E962.0	E980.4
Ametazole	977.8	E858.8	E947.8	E950.4	E962.0	E980.4
Amethocaine (infiltration) (topical)	968.5	E855.2	E938.5	E950.4	E962.0	E980.4
nerve block (peripheral) (plexus)	968.6	E855.2	E938.6	E950.4	E962.0	E980.4
spinal	968.7	E855.2	E938.7	E950.4	E962.0	E980.4
Amethopterin	963.1	E858.1	E933.1	E950.4	E962.0	E980.4
Amfepramone	977.0	E858.8	E947.0	E950.4	E962.0	E980.4
Amidon	965.02	E850.1	E935.1	E950.0	E962.0	E980.0
Amidopyrine	965.5	E850.5	E935.5	E950.0	E962.0	E980.0
Aminacrine	976.0	E858.7	E946.0	E950.4	E962.0	E980.4
Aminitrozole	961.5	E857	E931.5	E950.4	E962.0	E980.4
Aminoacetic acid	974.5	E858.5	E944.5	E950.4	E962.0	E980.4
Amino acids	974.5	E858.5	E944.5	E950.4	E962.0	E980.4
Aminocaproic acid	964.4	E858.2	E934.4	E950.4	E962.0	E980.4
Aminoethylisothiourium	963.8	E858.1	E933.8	E950.4	E962.0	E980.4
Aminoglutethimide	966.3	E855.0	E936.3	E950.4	E962.0	E980.4
Aminometradine	974.3	E858.5	E944.3	E950.4	E962.0	E980.4
Aminopentamide	971.1	E855.4	E941.1	E950.4	E962.0	E980.4
Aminophenazone	965.5	E850.5	E935.5	E950.0	E962.0	E980.0
Aminophenol	983.0	E864.0	—	E950.7	E962.1	E980.6
Aminophenylpyridone	969.5	E853.8	E939.5	E950.3	E962.0	E980.3
Aminophyllin	975.7	E858.6	E945.7	E950.4	E962.0	E980.4
Aminopterin	963.1	E858.1	E933.1	E950.4	E962.0	E980.4
Aminopyrine	965.5	E850.5	E935.5	E950.0	E962.0	E980.0
Aminosalicylic acid	961.8	E857	E931.8	E950.4	E962.0	E980.4
Amiphenazole	970.1	E854.3	E940.1	E950.4	E962.0	E980.4
Amiquinsin	972.6	E858.3	E942.6	E950.4	E962.0	E980.4
Amisometradine	974.3	E858.5	E944.3	E950.4	E962.0	E980.4
Amitriptyline	969.0	E854.0	E939.0	E950.3	E962.0	E980.3
Ammonia (fumes) (gas) (vapor)	987.8	E869.8	—	E952.8	E962.2	E982.8
liquid (household) NEC	983.2	E861.4	—	E950.7	E962.1	E980.6
spirit, aromatic	970.8	E854.3	E940.8	E950.4	E962.0	E980.4

Substance	Poisoning	External Cause (E-Code) Accident	Therapeutic Use	Suicide Attempt	Assault	Undetermined
Ammoniated mercury	976.0	E858.7	E946.0	E950.4	E962.0	E980.4
Ammonium						
carbonate	983.2	E864.2	—	E950.7	E962.1	E980.6
chloride (acidifying agent)	963.2	E858.1	E933.2	E950.4	E962.0	E980.4
expectorant	975.5	E858.6	E945.5	E950.4	E962.0	E980.4
compounds (household) NEC	983.2	E861.4	—	E950.7	E962.1	E980.6
fumes (any usage)	987.8	E869.8	—	E952.8	E962.2	E982.8
industrial	983.2	E864.2	—	E950.7	E962.1	E980.6
ichthyosulfonate	976.4	E858.7	E946.4	E950.4	E962.0	E980.4
mandelate	961.9	E857	E931.9	E950.4	E962.0	E980.4
Amobarbital	967.0	E851	E937.0	E950.1	E962.0	E980.1
Amodiaquin(e)	961.4	E857	E931.4	E950.4	E962.0	E980.4
Amopyroquin(e)	961.4	E857	E931.4	E950.4	E962.0	E980.4
Amphenidone	969.5	E853.8	E939.5	E950.3	E962.0	E980.3
Amphetamine	969.7	E854.2	E939.7	E950.3	E962.0	E980.3
Amphomycin	960.8	E856	E930.8	E950.4	E962.0	E980.4
Amphotericin B	960.1	E856	E930.1	E950.4	E962.0	E980.4
topical	976.0	E858.7	E946.0	E950.4	E962.0	E980.4
Ampicillin	960.0	E856	E930.0	E950.4	E962.0	E980.4
Amprotropine	971.1	E855.4	E941.1	E950.4	E962.0	E980.4
Amygdalin	977.8	E858.8	E947.8	E950.4	E962.0	E980.4
Amyl						
acetate (vapor)	982.8	E862.4	—	E950.9	E962.1	E980.9
alcohol	980.3	E860.4	—	E950.9	E962.1	E980.9
nitrite (medicinal)	972.4	E858.3	E942.4	E950.4	E962.0	E980.4
Amylase (alpha)	963.4	E858.1	E933.4	E950.4	E962.0	E980.4
Amylene hydrate	980.8	E860.8	—	E950.9	E962.1	E980.9
Amylobarbitone	967.0	E851	E937.0	E950.1	E962.0	E980.1
Amylocaine	968.9	E855.2	E938.9	E950.4	E962.0	E980.4
infiltration (subcutaneous)	968.5	E855.2	E938.5	E950.4	E962.0	E980.4
nerve block (peripheral) (plexus)	968.6	E855.2	E938.6	E950.4	E962.0	E980.4
spinal	968.7	E855.2	E938.7	E950.4	E962.0	E980.4
topical (surface)	968.5	E855.2	E938.5	E950.4	E962.0	E980.4
Amytal (sodium)	967.0	E851	E937.0	E950.1	E962.0	E980.1
Analeptics	970.0	E854.3	E940.0	E950.4	E962.0	E980.4
Analgesics	965.9	E850.9	E935.9	E950.0	E962.0	E980.0
aromatic NEC	965.4	E850.4	E935.4	E950.0	E962.0	E980.0
non-narcotic NEC	965.7	E850.7	E935.7	E950.0	E962.0	E980.0
specified NEC	965.8	E850.8	E935.8	E950.0	E962.0	E980.0
Anamirta cocculus	988.2	E865.3	—	E950.9	E962.1	E980.9
Ancillin	960.0	E856	E930.0	E950.4	E962.0	E980.4
Androgens (anabolic congeners)	962.1	E858.0	E932.1	E950.4	E962.0	E980.4
Androstalone	962.1	E858.0	E932.1	E950.4	E962.0	E980.4
Androsterone	962.1	E858.0	E932.1	E950.4	E962.0	E980.4
Anemone pulsatilla	988.2	E865.4	—	E950.9	E962.1	E980.9
Anesthesia, anesthetic (general) NEC	968.4	E855.1	E938.4	E950.4	E962.0	E980.4
block (nerve) (plexus)	968.6	E855.2	E938.6	E950.4	E962.0	E980.4
gaseous NEC	968.2	E855.1	E938.2	E950.4	E962.0	E980.4
halogenated hydrocarbon derivatives NEC	968.2	E855.1	E938.2	E950.4	E962.0	E980.4
infiltration (intradermal) (subcutaneous) (submucosal)	968.5	E855.2	E938.5	E950.4	E962.0	E980.4
intravenous	968.3	E855.1	E938.3	E950.4	E962.0	E980.4
local NEC	968.9	E855.2	E938.9	E950.4	E962.0	E980.4
nerve blocking (peripheral) (plexus)	968.6	E855.2	E938.6	E950.4	E962.0	E980.4
rectal NEC	968.3	E855.1	E938.3	E950.4	E962.0	E980.4
spinal	968.7	E855.2	E938.7	E950.4	E962.0	E980.4
surface	968.5	E855.2	E938.5	E950.4	E962.0	E980.4
topical	968.5	E855.2	E938.5	E950.4	E962.0	E980.4
Aneurine	963.5	E858.1	E933.5	E950.4	E962.0	E980.4
Anginine — *see* Glyceryl trinitrate						
Angio-Conray	977.8	E858.8	E947.8	E950.4	E962.0	E980.4
Angiotensin	971.2	E855.5	E941.2	E950.4	E962.0	E980.4
Anhydrohydroxyprogesterone	962.2	E858.0	E932.2	E950.4	E962.0	E980.4
Anhydron	974.3	E858.5	E944.3	E950.4	E962.0	E980.4
Anileridine	965.09	E850.2	E935.2	E950.0	E962.0	E980.0
Aniline (dye) (liquid)	983.0	E864.0	—	E950.7	E962.1	E980.6
analgesic	965.4	E850.4	E935.4	E950.0	E962.0	E980.0
derivatives, therapeutic NEC	965.4	E850.4	E935.4	E950.0	E962.0	E980.0
vapor	987.8	E869.8	—	E952.8	E962.2	E982.8
Anisindione	964.2	E858.2	E934.2	E950.4	E962.0	E980.4
Anisotropine	971.1	E855.4	E941.1	E950.4	E962.0	E980.4
Anorexic agents	977.0	E858.8	E947.0	E950.4	E962.0	E980.4
Ant (bite) (sting)	989.5	E905.5	—	E950.9	E962.1	E980.9
Antabuse	977.3	E858.8	E947.3	E950.4	E962.0	E980.4

Substance	Poisoning	External Cause (E-Code)				
		Accident	Therapeutic Use	Suicide Attempt	Assault	Un-determined
Antacids	973.0	E858.4	E943.0	E950.4	E962.0	E980.4
Antazoline	963.0	E858.1	E933.0	E950.4	E962.0	E980.4
Anthelmintics	961.6	E857	E931.6	E950.4	E962.0	E980.4
Anthralin	976.4	E858.7	E946.4	E950.4	E962.0	E980.4
Anthramycin	960.7	E856	E930.7	E950.4	E962.0	E980.4
Antiadrenergics	971.3	E855.6	E941.3	E950.4	E962.0	E980.4
Antiallergic agents	963.0	E858.1	E933.0	E950.4	E962.0	E980.4
Antianemic agents NEC	964.1	E858.2	E934.1	E950.4	E962.0	E980.4
Antiaris toxicaria	988.2	E865.4	—	E950.9	E962.1	E980.9
Antiarteriosclerotic agents	972.2	E858.3	E942.2	E950.4	E962.0	E980.4
Antiasthmatics	975.7	E858.6	E945.7	E950.4	E962.0	E980.4
Antibiotics	960.9	E856	E930.9	E950.4	E962.0	E980.4
antifungal	960.1	E856	E930.1	E950.4	E962.0	E980.4
antimycobacterial	960.6	E856	E930.6	E950.4	E962.0	E980.4
antineoplastic	960.7	E856	E930.7	E950.4	E962.0	E980.4
cephalosporin (group)	960.5	E856	E930.5	E950.4	E962.0	E980.4
chloramphenicol (group)	960.2	E856	E930.2	E950.4	E962.0	E980.4
macrolides	960.3	E856	E930.3	E950.4	E962.0	E980.4
specified NEC	960.8	E856	E930.8	E950.4	E962.0	E980.4
tetracycline (group)	960.4	E856	E930.4	E950.4	E962.0	E980.4
Anticancer agents NEC	963.1	E858.1	E933.1	E950.4	E962.0	E980.4
antibiotics	960.7	E856	E930.7	E950.4	E962.0	E980.4
Anticholinergics	971.1	E855.4	E941.1	E950.4	E962.0	E980.4
Anticholinesterase (organophosphorus) (reversible)	971.0	E855.3	E941.0	E950.4	E962.0	E980.4
Anticoagulants	964.2	E858.2	E934.2	E950.4	E962.0	E980.4
antagonists	964.5	E858.2	E934.5	E950.4	E962.0	E980.4
Anti-common cold agents NEC	975.6	E858.6	E945.6	E950.4	E962.0	E980.4
Anticonvulsants NEC	966.3	E855.0	E936.3	E950.4	E962.0	E980.4
Antidepressants	969.0	E854.0	E939.0	E950.3	E962.0	E980.3
Antidiabetic agents	962.3	E858.0	E932.3	E950.4	E962.0	E980.4
Antidiarrheal agents	973.5	E858.4	E943.5	E950.4	E962.0	E980.4
Antidiuretic hormone	962.5	E858.0	E932.5	E950.4	E962.0	E980.4
Antidotes NEC	977.2	E858.8	E947.2	E950.4	E962.0	E980.4
Antiemetic agents	963.0	E858.1	E933.0	E950.4	E962.0	E980.4
Antiepilepsy agent NEC	966.3	E855.0	E936.3	E950.4	E962.0	E980.4
Antifertility pills	962.2	E858.0	E932.2	E950.4	E962.0	E980.4
Antiflatulents	973.8	E858.4	E943.8	E950.4	E962.0	E980.4
Antifreeze	989.89	E866.8	—	E950.9	E962.1	E980.9
alcohol	980.1	E860.2	—	E950.9	E962.1	E980.9
ethylene glycol	982.8	E862.4	—	E950.9	E962.1	E980.9
Antifungals (nonmedicinal) (sprays)	989.4	E863.6	—	E950.6	E962.1	E980.7
medicinal NEC	961.9	E857	E931.9	E950.4	E962.0	E980.4
antibiotic	960.1	E856	E930.1	E950.4	E962.0	E980.4
topical	976.0	E858.7	E946.0	E950.4	E962.0	E980.4
Antigastric secretion agents	973.0	E858.4	E943.0	E950.4	E962.0	E980.4
Antihelmintics	961.6	E857	E931.6	E950.4	E962.0	E980.4
Antihemophilic factor (human)	964.7	E858.2	E934.7	E950.4	E962.0	E980.4
Antihistamine	963.0	E858.1	E933.0	E950.4	E962.0	E980.4
Antihypertensive agents NEC	972.6	E858.3	E942.6	E950.4	E962.0	E980.4
Anti-infectives NEC	961.9	E857	E931.9	E950.4	E962.0	E980.4
antibiotics	960.9	E856	E930.9	E950.4	E962.0	E980.4
specified NEC	960.8	E856	E930.8	E950.4	E962.0	E980.4
anthelmintic	961.6	E857	E931.6	E950.4	E962.0	E980.4
antimalarial	961.4	E857	E931.4	E950.4	E962.0	E980.4
antimycobacterial NEC	961.8	E857	E931.8	E950.4	E962.0	E980.4
antibiotics	960.6	E856	E930.6	E950.4	E962.0	E980.4
antiprotozoal NEC	961.5	E857	E931.5	E950.4	E962.0	E980.4
blood	961.4	E857	E931.4	E950.4	E962.0	E980.4
antiviral	961.7	E857	E931.7	E950.4	E962.0	E980.4
arsenical	961.1	E857	E931.1	E950.4	E962.0	E980.4
ENT agents	976.6	E858.7	E946.6	E950.4	E962.0	E980.4
heavy metals NEC	961.2	E857	E931.2	E950.4	E962.0	E980.4
local	976.0	E858.7	E946.0	E950.4	E962.0	E980.4
ophthalmic preparation	976.5	E858.7	E946.5	E950.4	E962.0	E980.4
topical NEC	976.0	E858.7	E946.0	E950.4	E962.0	E980.4
Anti-inflammatory agents (topical)	976.0	E858.7	E946.0	E950.4	E962.0	E980.4
Antiknock (tetraethyl lead)	984.1	E862.1	—	E950.9	E962.1	E980.9
Antilipemics	972.2	E858.3	E942.2	E950.4	E962.0	E980.4
Antimalarials	961.4	E857	E931.4	E950.4	E962.0	E980.4

		External Cause (E-Code)				
Substance	**Poisoning**	**Accident**	**Therapeutic Use**	**Suicide Attempt**	**Assault**	**Undetermined**
Antimony (compounds) (vapor) NEC	985.4	E866.2	—	E950.9	E962.1	E980.9
anti-infectives	961.2	E857	E931.2	E950.4	E962.0	E980.4
pesticides (vapor)	985.4	E863.4	—	E950.6	E962.2	E980.7
potassium tartrate	961.2	E857	E931.2	E950.4	E962.0	E980.4
tartrated	961.2	E857	E931.2	E950.4	E962.0	E980.4
Antimuscarinic agents	971.1	E855.4	E941.1	E950.4	E962.0	E980.4
Antimycobacterials NEC	961.8	E857	E931.8	E950.4	E962.0	E980.4
antibiotics	960.6	E856	E930.6	E950.4	E962.0	E980.4
Antineoplastic agents	963.1	E858.1	E933.1	E950.4	E962.0	E980.4
antibiotics	960.7	E856	E930.7	E950.4	E962.0	E980.4
Anti-Parkinsonism agents	966.4	E855.0	E936.4	E950.4	E962.0	E980.4
Antiphlogistics	965.69	E850.6	E935.6	E950.0	E962.0	E980.0
Antiprotozoals NEC	961.5	E857	E931.5	E950.4	E962.0	E980.4
blood	961.4	E857	E931.4	E950.4	E962.0	E980.4
Antipruritics (local)	976.1	E858.7	E946.1	E950.4	E962.0	E980.4
Antipsychotic agents NEC	969.3	E853.8	E939.3	E950.3	E962.0	E980.3
Antipyretics	965.9	E850.9	E935.9	E950.0	E962.0	E980.0
specified NEC	965.8	E850.8	E935.8	E950.0	E962.0	E980.0
Antipyrine	965.5	E850.5	E935.5	E950.0	E962.0	E980.0
Antirabies serum (equine)	979.9	E858.8	E949.9	E950.4	E962.0	E980.4
Antirheumatics	965.69	E850.6	E935.6	E950.0	E962.0	E980.0
Antiseborrheics	976.4	E858.7	E946.4	E950.4	E962.0	E980.4
Antiseptics (external) (medicinal)	976.0	E858.7	E946.0	E950.4	E962.0	E980.4
Antistine	963.0	E858.1	E933.0	E950.4	E962.0	E980.4
Antithyroid agents	962.8	E858.0	E932.8	E950.4	E962.0	E980.4
Antitoxin, any	979.9	E858.8	E949.9	E950.4	E962.0	E980.4
Antituberculars	961.8	E857	E931.8	E950.4	E962.0	E980.4
antibiotics	960.6	E856	E930.6	E950.4	E962.0	E980.4
Antitussives	975.4	E858.6	E945.4	E950.4	E962.0	E980.4
Antivaricose agents (sclerosing)	972.7	E858.3	E942.7	E950.4	E962.0	E980.4
Antivenin (crotaline) (spider-bite)	979.9	E858.8	E949.9	E950.4	E962.0	E980.4
Antivert	963.0	E858.1	E933.0	E950.4	E962.0	E980.4
Antivirals NEC	961.7	E857	E931.7	E950.4	E962.0	E980.4
Ant poisons — *see* Pesticides						
Antrol	989.4	E863.4	—	E950.6	E962.1	E980.7
fungicide	989.4	E863.6	—	E950.6	E962.1	E980.7
Apomorphine hydrochloride (emetic)	973.6	E858.4	E943.6	E950.4	E962.0	E980.4
Appetite depressants, central	977.0	E858.8	E947.0	E950.4	E962.0	E980.4
Apresoline	972.6	E858.3	E942.6	E950.4	E962.0	E980.4
Aprobarbital, aprobarbitone	967.0	E851	E937.0	E950.1	E962.0	E980.1
Apronalide	967.8	E852.8	E937.8	E950.2	E962.0	E980.2
Aqua fortis	983.1	E864.1	—	E950.7	E962.1	E980.6
Arachis oil (topical)	976.3	E858.7	E946.3	E950.4	E962.0	E980.4
cathartic	973.2	E858.4	E943.2	E950.4	E962.0	E980.4
Aralen	961.4	E857	E931.4	E950.4	E962.0	E980.4
Arginine salts	974.5	E858.5	E944.5	E950.4	E962.0	E980.4
Argyrol	976.0	E858.7	E946.0	E950.4	E962.0	E980.4
ENT agent	976.6	E858.7	E946.6	E950.4	E962.0	E980.4
ophthalmic preparation	976.5	E858.7	E946.5	E950.4	E962.0	E980.4
Aristocort	962.0	E858.0	E932.0	E950.4	E962.0	E980.4
ENT agent	976.6	E858.7	E946.6	E950.4	E962.0	E980.4
ophthalmic preparation	976.5	E858.7	E946.5	E950.4	E962.0	E980.4
topical NEC	976.0	E858.7	E946.0	E950.4	E962.0	E980.4
Aromatics, corrosive	983.0	E864.0	—	E950.7	E962.1	E980.6
disinfectants	983.0	E861.4	—	E950.7	E962.1	E980.6
Arsenate of lead (insecticide)	985.1	E863.4	—	E950.8	E962.1	E980.8
herbicide	985.1	E863.5	—	E950.8	E962.1	E980.8
Arsenic, arsenicals (compounds) (dust) (fumes) (vapor) NEC	985.1	E866.3	—	E950.8	E962.1	E980.8
anti-infectives	961.1	E857	E931.1	E950.4	E962.0	E980.4
pesticide (dust) (fumes)	985.1	E863.4	—	E950.8	E962.1	E980.8
Arsine (gas)	985.1	E866.3	—	E950.8	E962.1	E980.8
Arsphenamine (silver)	961.1	E857	E931.1	E950.4	E962.0	E980.4
Arsthinol	961.1	E857	E931.1	E950.4	E962.0	E980.4
Artane	971.1	E855.4	E941.1	E950.4	E962.0	E980.4
Arthropod (venomous) NEC	989.5	E905.5	—	E950.9	E962.1	E980.9
Asbestos	989.81	E866.8	—	E950.9	E962.1	E980.9
Ascaridole	961.6	E857	E931.6	E950.4	E962.0	E980.4
Ascorbic acid	963.5	E858.1	E933.5	E950.4	E962.0	E980.4
Asiaticoside	976.0	E858.7	E946.0	E950.4	E962.0	E980.4
Aspidium (oleoresin)	961.6	E857	E931.6	E950.4	E962.0	E980.4
Aspirin	965.1	E850.3	E935.3	E950.0	E962.0	E980.0

Substance	Poisoning	External Cause (E-Code) Accident	Therapeutic Use	Suicide Attempt	Assault	Undetermined
Astringents (local)	976.2	E858.7	E946.2	E950.4	E962.0	E980.4
Atabrine	961.3	E857	E931.3	E950.4	E962.0	E980.4
Ataractics	969.5	E853.8	E939.5	E950.3	E962.0	E980.3
Atonia drug, intestinal	973.3	E858.4	E943.3	E950.4	E962.0	E980.4
Atophan	974.7	E858.5	E944.7	E950.4	E962.0	E980.4
Atropine	971.1	E855.4	E941.1	E950.4	E962.0	E980.4
Attapulgite	973.5	E858.4	E943.5	E950.4	E962.0	E980.4
Attenuvax	979.4	E858.8	E949.4	E950.4	E962.0	E980.4
Aureomycin	960.4	E856	E930.4	E950.4	E962.0	E980.4
ophthalmic preparation	976.5	E858.7	E946.5	E950.4	E962.0	E980.4
topical NEC	976.0	E858.7	E946.0	E950.4	E962.0	E980.4
Aurothioglucose	965.69	E850.6	E935.6	E950.0	E962.0	E980.0
Aurothioglycanide	965.69	E850.6	E935.6	E950.0	E962.0	E980.0
Aurothiomalate	965.69	E850.6	E935.6	E950.0	E962.0	E980.0
Automobile fuel	981	E862.1	—	E950.9	E962.1	E980.9
Autonomic nervous system agents NEC	971.9	E855.9	E941.9	E950.4	E962.0	E980.4
Avlosulfon	961.8	E857	E931.8	E950.4	E962.0	E980.4
Avomine	967.8	E852.8	E937.8	E950.2	E962.0	E980.2
Azacyclonol	969.5	E853.8	E939.5	E950.3	E962.0	E980.3
Azapetine	971.3	E855.6	E941.3	E950.4	E962.0	E980.4
Azaribine	963.1	E858.1	E933.1	E950.4	E962.0	E980.4
Azaserine	960.7	E856	E930.7	E950.4	E962.0	E980.4
Azathioprine	963.1	E858.1	E933.1	E950.4	E962.0	E980.4
Azosulfamide	961.0	E857	E931.0	E950.4	E962.0	E980.4
Azulfidine	961.0	E857	E931.0	E950.4	E962.0	E980.4
Azuresin	977.8	E858.8	E947.8	E950.4	E962.0	E980.4
B						
Bacimycin	976.0	E858.7	E946.0	E950.4	E962.0	E980.4
ophthalmic preparation	976.5	E858.7	E946.5	E950.4	E962.0	E980.4
Bacitracin	960.8	E856	E930.8	E950.4	E962.0	E980.4
ENT agent	976.6	E858.7	E946.6	E950.4	E962.0	E980.4
ophthalmic preparation	976.5	E858.7	E946.5	E950.4	E962.0	E980.4
topical NEC	976.0	E858.7	E946.0	E950.4	E962.0	E980.4
Baking soda	963.3	E858.1	E933.3	E950.4	E962.0	E980.4
BAL	963.8	E858.1	E933.8	E950.4	E962.0	E980.4
Bamethan (sulfate)	972.5	E858.3	E942.5	E950.4	E962.0	E980.4
Bamipine	963.0	E858.1	E933.0	E950.4	E962.0	E980.4
Baneberry	988.2	E865.4	—	E950.9	E962.1	E980.9
Banewort	988.2	E865.4	—	E950.9	E962.1	E980.9
Barbenyl	967.0	E851	E937.0	E950.1	E962.0	E980.1
Barbital, barbitone	967.0	E851	E937.0	E950.1	E962.0	E980.1
Barbiturates, barbituric acid	967.0	E851	E937.0	E950.1	E962.0	E980.1
anesthetic (intravenous)	968.3	E855.1	E938.3	E950.4	E962.0	E980.4
Barium (carbonate) (chloride) (sulfate)	985.8	E866.4	—	E950.9	E962.1	E980.9
diagnostic agent	977.8	E858.8	E947.8	E950.4	E962.0	E980.4
pesticide	985.8	E863.4	—	E950.6	E962.1	E980.7
rodenticide	985.8	E863.7	—	E950.6	E962.1	E980.7
Barrier cream	976.3	E858.7	E946.3	E950.4	E962.0	E980.4
Battery acid or fluid	983.1	E864.1	—	E950.7	E962.1	E980.6
Bay rum	980.8	E860.8	—	E950.9	E962.1	E980.9
BCG vaccine	978.0	E858.8	E948.0	E950.4	E962.0	E980.4
Bearsfoot	988.2	E865.4	—	E950.9	E962.1	E980.9
Beclamide	966.3	E855.0	E936.3	E950.4	E962.0	E980.4
Bee (sting) (venom)	989.5	E905.3	—	E950.9	E962.1	E980.9
Belladonna (alkaloids)	971.1	E855.4	E941.1	E950.4	E962.0	E980.4
Bemegride	970.0	E854.3	E940.0	E950.4	E962.0	E980.4
Benactyzine	969.8	E855.8	E939.8	E950.3	E962.0	E980.3
Benadryl	963.0	E858.1	E933.0	E950.4	E962.0	E980.4
Bendrofluazide	974.3	E858.5	E944.3	E950.4	E962.0	E980.4
Bendroflumethiazide	974.3	E858.5	E944.3	E950.4	E962.0	E980.4
Benemid	974.7	E858.5	E944.7	E950.4	E962.0	E980.4
Benethamine penicillin G	960.0	E856	E930.0	E950.4	E962.0	E980.4
Benisone	976.0	E858.7	E946.0	E950.4	E962.0	E980.4
Benoquin	976.8	E858.7	E946.8	E950.4	E962.0	E980.4
Benoxinate	968.5	E855.2	E938.5	E950.4	E962.0	E980.4
Bentonite	976.3	E858.7	E946.3	E950.4	E962.0	E980.4
Benzalkonium (chloride)	976.0	E858.7	E946.0	E950.4	E962.0	E980.4
ophthalmic preparation	976.5	E858.7	E946.5	E950.4	E962.0	E980.4
Benzamidosalicylate (calcium)	961.8	E857	E931.8	E950.4	E962.0	E980.4
Benzathine penicillin	960.0	E856	E930.0	E950.4	E962.0	E980.4
Benzcarbimine	963.1	E858.1	E933.1	E950.4	E962.0	E980.4
Benzedrex	971.2	E855.5	E941.2	E950.4	E962.0	E980.4

Substance	Poisoning	External Cause (E-Code) Accident	Therapeutic Use	Suicide Attempt	Assault	Undetermined
Benzedrine (amphetamine)	969.7	E854.2	E939.7	E950.3	E962.0	E980.3
Benzene (acetyl) (dimethyl) (methyl) (solvent) (vapor)	982.0	E862.4	—	E950.9	E962.1	E980.9
hexachloride (gamma) (insecticide) (vapor)	989.2	E863.0	—	E950.6	E962.1	E980.7
Benzethonium	976.0	E858.7	E946.0	E950.4	E962.0	E980.4
Benzhexol (chloride)	966.4	E855.0	E936.4	E950.4	E962.0	E980.4
Benzilonium	971.1	E855.4	E941.1	E950.4	E962.0	E980.4
Benzin(e) — *see* Ligroin						
Benziodarone	972.4	E858.3	E942.4	E950.4	E962.0	E980.4
Benzocaine	968.5	E855.2	E938.5	E950.4	E962.0	E980.4
Benzodiapin	969.4	E853.2	E939.4	E950.3	E962.0	E980.3
Benzodiazepines (tranquilizers) NEC	969.4	E853.2	E939.4	E950.3	E962.0	E980.3
Benzoic acid (with salicylic acid) (anti-infective)	976.0	E858.7	E946.0	E950.4	E962.0	E980.4
Benzoin	976.3	E858.7	E946.3	E950.4	E962.0	E980.4
Benzol (vapor)	982.0	E862.4	—	E950.9	E962.1	E980.9
Benzomorphan	965.09	E850.2	E935.2	E950.0	E962.0	E980.0
Benzonatate	975.4	E858.6	E945.4	E950.4	E962.0	E980.4
Benzothiadiazides	974.3	E858.5	E944.3	E950.4	E962.0	E980.4
Benzoylpas	961.8	E857	E931.8	E950.4	E962.0	E980.4
Benzperidol	969.5	E853.8	E939.5	E950.3	E962.0	E980.3
Benzphetamine	977.0	E858.8	E947.0	E950.4	E962.0	E980.4
Benzpyrinium	971.0	E855.3	E941.0	E950.4	E962.0	E980.4
Benzquinamide	963.0	E858.1	E933.0	E950.4	E962.0	E980.4
Benzthiazide	974.3	E858.5	E944.3	E950.4	E962.0	E980.4
Benztropine	971.1	E855.4	E941.1	E950.4	E962.0	E980.4
Benzyl						
acetate	982.8	E862.4	—	E950.9	E962.1	E980.9
benzoate (anti-infective)	976.0	E858.7	E946.0	E950.4	E962.0	E980.4
morphine	965.09	E850.2	E935.2	E950.0	E962.0	E980.0
penicillin	960.0	E856	E930.0	E950.4	E962.0	E980.4
Bephenium hydroxynapthoate	961.6	E857	E931.6	E950.4	E962.0	E980.4
Bergamot oil	989.89	E866.8	—	E950.9	E962.1	E980.9
Berries, poisonous	988.2	E865.3	—	E950.9	E962.1	E980.9
Beryllium (compounds) (fumes)	985.3	E866.4	—	E950.9	E962.1	E980.9
Beta-carotene	976.3	E858.7	E946.3	E950.4	E962.0	E980.4
Beta-Chlor	967.1	E852.0	E937.1	E950.2	E962.0	E980.2
Betamethasone	962.0	E858.0	E932.0	E950.4	E962.0	E980.4
topical	976.0	E858.7	E946.0	E950.4	E962.0	E980.4
Betazole	977.8	E858.8	E947.8	E950.4	E962.0	E980.4
Bethanechol	971.0	E855.3	E941.0	E950.4	E962.0	E980.4
Bethanidine	972.6	E858.3	E942.6	E950.4	E962.0	E980.4
Betula oil	976.3	E858.7	E946.3	E950.4	E962.0	E980.4
Bhang	969.6	E854.1	E939.6	E950.3	E962.0	E980.3
Bialamicol	961.5	E857	E931.5	E950.4	E962.0	E980.4
Bichloride of mercury — *see* Mercury, chloride						
Bichromates (calcium) (crystals) (potassium) (sodium)	983.9	E864.3	—	E950.7	E962.1	E980.6
fumes	987.8	E869.8	—	E952.8	E962.2	E982.8
Biguanide derivatives, oral	962.3	E858.0	E932.3	E950.4	E962.0	E980.4
Biligrafin	977.8	E858.8	E947.8	E950.4	E962.0	E980.4
Bilopaque	977.8	E858.8	E947.8	E950.4	E962.0	E980.4
Bioflavonoids	972.8	E858.3	E942.8	E950.4	E962.0	E980.4
Biological substance NEC	979.9	E858.8	E949.9	E950.4	E962.0	E980.4
Biperiden	966.4	E855.0	E936.4	E950.4	E962.0	E980.4
Bisacodyl	973.1	E858.4	E943.1	E950.4	E962.0	E980.4
Bishydroxycoumarin	964.2	E858.2	E934.2	E950.4	E962.0	E980.4
Bismarsen	961.1	E857	E931.1	E950.4	E962.0	E980.4
Bismuth (compounds) NEC	985.8	E866.4	—	E950.9	E962.1	E980.9
anti-infectives	961.2	E857	E931.2	E950.4	E962.0	E980.4
subcarbonate	973.5	E858.4	E943.5	E950.4	E962.0	E980.4
sulfarsphenamine	961.1	E857	E931.1	E950.4	E962.0	E980.4
Bithionol	961.6	E857	E931.6	E950.4	E962.0	E980.4
Bitter almond oil	989.0	E866.8	—	E950.9	E962.1	E980.9
Bittersweet	988.2	E865.4	—	E950.9	E962.1	E980.9
Black						
flag	989.4	E863.4	—	E950.6	E962.1	E980.7
henbane	988.2	E865.4	—	E950.9	E962.1	E980.9
leaf (40)	989.4	E863.4	—	E950.6	E962.1	E980.7
widow spider (bite)	989.5	E905.1	—	E950.9	E962.1	E980.9
antivenin	979.9	E858.8	E949.9	E950.4	E962.0	E980.4
Blast furnace gas (carbon monoxide from)	986	E868.8	—	E952.1	E962.2	E982.1
Bleach NEC	983.9	E864.3	—	E950.7	E962.1	E980.6
Bleaching solutions	983.9	E864.3	—	E950.7	E962.1	E980.6

Substance	Poisoning	External Cause (E-Code) Accident	Therapeutic Use	Suicide Attempt	Assault	Un-determined
Bleomycin (sulfate)	960.7	E856	E930.7	E950.4	E962.0	E980.4
Blockain	968.9	E855.2	E938.9	E950.4	E962.0	E980.4
infiltration (subcutaneous)	968.5	E855.2	E938.5	E950.4	E962.0	E980.4
nerve block (peripheral) (plexus)	968.6	E855.2	E938.6	E950.4	E962.0	E980.4
topical (surface)	968.5	E855.2	E938.5	E950.4	E962.0	E980.4
Blood (derivatives) (natural) (plasma) (whole)	964.7	E858.2	E934.7	E950.4	E962.0	E980.4
affecting agent	964.9	E858.2	E934.9	E950.4	E962.0	E980.4
specified NEC	964.8	E858.2	E934.8	E950.4	E962.0	E980.4
substitute (macromolecular)	964.8	E858.2	E934.8	E950.4	E962.0	E980.4
Blue velvet	965.09	E850.2	E935.2	E950.0	E962.0	E980.0
Bone meal	989.89	E866.5	—	E950.9	E962.1	E980.9
Bonine	963.0	E858.1	E933.0	E950.4	E962.0	E980.4
Boracic acid	976.0	E858.7	E946.0	E950.4	E962.0	E980.4
ENT agent	976.6	E858.7	E946.6	E950.4	E962.0	E980.4
ophthalmic preparation	976.5	E858.7	E946.5	E950.4	E962.0	E980.4
Borate (cleanser) (sodium)	989.6	E861.3	—	E950.9	E962.1	E980.9
Borax (cleanser)	989.6	E861.3	—	E950.9	E962.1	E980.9
Boric acid	976.0	E858.7	E946.0	E950.4	E962.0	E980.4
ENT agent	976.6	E858.7	E946.6	E950.4	E962.0	E980.4
ophthalmic preparation	976.5	E858.7	E946.5	E950.4	E962.0	E980.4
Boron hydride NEC	989.89	E866.8	—	E950.9	E962.1	E980.9
fumes or gas	987.8	E869.8	—	E952.8	E962.2	E982.8
Brake fluid vapor	987.8	E869.8	—	E952.8	E962.2	E982.8
Brass (compounds) (fumes)	985.8	E866.4	—	E950.9	E962.1	E980.9
Brasso	981	E861.3	—	E950.9	E962.1	E980.9
Bretylium (tosylate)	972.6	E858.3	E942.6	E950.4	E962.0	E980.4
Brevital (sodium)	968.3	E855.1	E938.3	E950.4	E962.0	E980.4
British antilewisite	963.8	E858.1	E933.8	E950.4	E962.0	E980.4
Bromal (hydrate)	967.3	E852.2	E937.3	E950.2	E962.0	E980.2
Bromelains	963.4	E858.1	E933.4	E950.4	E962.0	E980.4
Bromides NEC	967.3	E852.2	E937.3	E950.2	E962.0	E980.2
Bromine (vapor)	987.8	E869.8	—	E952.8	E962.2	E982.8
compounds (medicinal)	967.3	E852.2	E937.3	E950.2	E962.0	E980.2
Bromisovalum	967.3	E852.2	E937.3	E950.2	E962.0	E980.2
Bromobenzyl cyanide	987.5	E869.3	—	E952.8	E962.2	E982.8
Bromodiphenhydramine	963.0	E858.1	E933.0	E950.4	E962.0	E980.4
Bromoform	967.3	E852.2	E937.3	E950.2	E962.0	E980.2
Bromophenol blue reagent	977.8	E858.8	E947.8	E950.4	E962.0	E980.4
Bromosalicylhydroxamic acid	961.8	E857	E931.8	E950.4	E962.0	E980.4
Bromo-seltzer	965.4	E850.4	E935.4	E950.0	E962.0	E980.0
Brompheniramine	963.0	E858.1	E933.0	E950.4	E962.0	E980.4
Bromural	967.3	E852.2	E937.3	E950.2	E962.0	E980.2
Brown spider (bite) (venom)	989.5	E905.1	—	E950.9	E962.1	E980.9
Brucia	988.2	E865.3	—	E950.9	E962.1	E980.9
Brucine	989.1	E863.7	—	E950.6	E962.1	E980.7
Brufen — *see* Ibuprofen						
Brunswick green — *see* Copper						
Bryonia (alba) (dioica)	988.2	E865.4	—	E950.9	E962.1	E980.9
Buclizine	969.5	E853.8	E939.5	E950.3	E962.0	E980.3
Bufferin	965.1	E850.3	E935.3	E950.0	E962.0	E980.0
Bufotenine	969.6	E854.1	E939.6	E950.3	E962.0	E980.3
Buphenine	971.2	E855.5	E941.2	E950.4	E962.0	E980.4
Bupivacaine	968.9	E855.2	E938.9	E950.4	E962.0	E980.4
infiltration (subcutaneous)	968.5	E855.2	E938.5	E950.4	E962.0	E980.4
nerve block (peripheral) (plexus)	968.6	E855.2	E938.6	E950.4	E962.0	E980.4
Busulfan	963.1	E858.1	E933.1	E950.4	E962.0	E980.4
Butabarbital (sodium)	967.0	E851	E937.0	E950.1	E962.0	E980.1
Butabarbitone	967.0	E851	E937.0	E950.1	E962.0	E980.1
Butabarpal	967.0	E851	E937.0	E950.1	E962.0	E980.1
Butacaine	968.5	E855.2	E938.5	E950.4	E962.0	E980.4
Butallylonal	967.0	E851	E937.0	E950.1	E962.0	E980.1
Butane (distributed in mobile container)	987.0	E868.0	—	E951.1	E962.2	E981.1
distributed through pipes	987.0	E867	—	E951.0	E962.2	E981.0
incomplete combustion of — *see* Carbon monoxide, butane						
Butanol	980.3	E860.4	—	E950.9	E962.1	E980.9
Butanone	982.8	E862.4	—	E950.9	E962.1	E980.9
Butaperazine	969.1	E853.0	E939.1	E950.3	E962.0	E980.3
Butazolidin	965.5	E850.5	E935.5	E950.0	E962.0	E980.0
Butethal	967.0	E851	E937.0	E950.1	E962.0	E980.1
Butethamate	971.1	E855.4	E941.1	E950.4	E962.0	E980.4
Buthalitone (sodium)	968.3	E855.1	E938.3	E950.4	E962.0	E980.4

Substance	Poisoning	External Cause (E-Code) Accident	Therapeutic Use	Suicide Attempt	Assault	Undetermined
Butisol (sodium)	967.0	E851	E937.0	E950.1	E962.0	E980.1
Butobarbital, butobarbitone	967.0	E851	E937.0	E950.1	E962.0	E980.1
Butriptyline	969.0	E854.0	E939.0	E950.3	E962.0	E980.3
Buttercups	988.2	E865.4	—	E950.9	E962.1	E980.9
Butter of antimony — *see* Antimony						
Butyl						
acetate (secondary)	982.8	E862.4	—	E950.9	E962.1	E980.9
alcohol	980.3	E860.4	—	E950.9	E962.1	E980.9
carbinol	980.8	E860.8	—	E950.9	E962.1	E980.9
carbitol	982.8	E862.4	—	E950.9	E962.1	E980.9
cellosolve	982.8	E862.4	—	E950.9	E962.1	E980.9
chloral (hydrate)	967.1	E852.0	E937.1	E950.2	E962.0	E980.2
formate	982.8	E862.4	—	E950.9	E962.1	E980.9
scopolammonium bromide	971.1	E855.4	E941.1	E950.4	E962.0	E980.4
Butyn	968.5	E855.2	E938.5	E950.4	E962.0	E980.4
Butyrophenone (-based tranquilizers)	969.2	E853.1	E939.2	E950.3	E962.0	E980.3
C						
Cacodyl, cacodylic acid — *see* Arsenic						
Cactinomycin	960.7	E856	E930.7	E950.4	E962.0	E980.4
Cade oil	976.4	E858.7	E946.4	E950.4	E962.0	E980.4
Cadmium (chloride) (compounds) (dust) (fumes) (oxide)	985.5	E866.4	—	E950.9	E962.1	E980.9
sulfide (medicinal) NEC	976.4	E858.7	E946.4	E950.4	E962.0	E980.4
Caffeine	969.7	E854.2	E939.7	E950.3	E962.0	E980.3
Calabar bean	988.2	E865.4	—	E950.9	E962.1	E980.9
Caladium seguinium	988.2	E865.4	—	E950.9	E962.1	E980.9
Calamine (liniment) (lotion)	976.3	E858.7	E946.3	E950.4	E962.0	E980.4
Calciferol	963.5	E858.1	E933.5	E950.4	E962.0	E980.4
Calcium (salts) NEC	974.5	E858.5	E944.5	E950.4	E962.0	E980.4
acetylsalicylate	965.1	E850.3	E935.3	E950.0	E962.0	E980.0
benzamidosalicylate	961.8	E857	E931.8	E950.4	E962.0	E980.4
carbaspirin	965.1	E850.3	E935.3	E950.0	E962.0	E980.0
carbimide (citrated)	977.3	E858.8	E947.3	E950.4	E962.0	E980.4
carbonate (antacid)	973.0	E858.4	E943.0	E950.4	E962.0	E980.4
cyanide (citrated)	977.3	E858.8	E947.3	E950.4	E962.0	E980.4
dioctyl sulfosuccinate	973.2	E858.4	E943.2	E950.4	E962.0	E980.4
disodium edathamil	963.8	E858.1	E933.8	E950.4	E962.0	E980.4
disodium edetate	963.8	E858.1	E933.8	E950.4	E962.0	E980.4
EDTA	963.8	E858.1	E933.8	E950.4	E962.0	E980.4
hydrate, hydroxide	983.2	E864.2	—	E950.7	E962.1	E980.6
mandelate	961.9	E857	E931.9	E950.4	E962.0	E980.4
oxide	983.2	E864.2	—	E950.7	E962.1	E980.6
Calomel — *see* Mercury, chloride						
Caloric agents NEC	974.5	E858.5	E944.5	E950.4	E962.0	E980.4
Calusterone	963.1	E858.1	E933.1	E950.4	E962.0	E980.4
Camoquin	961.4	E857	E931.4	E950.4	E962.0	E980.4
Camphor (oil)	976.1	E858.7	E946.1	E950.4	E962.0	E980.4
Candeptin	976.0	E858.7	E946.0	E950.4	E962.0	E980.4
Candicidin	976.0	E858.7	E946.0	E950.4	E962.0	E980.4
Cannabinols	969.6	E854.1	E939.6	E950.3	E962.0	E980.3
Cannabis (derivatives) (indica) (sativa)	969.6	E854.1	E939.6	E950.3	E962.0	E980.3
Canned heat	980.1	E860.2	—	E950.9	E962.1	E980.9
Cantharides, cantharidin, cantharis	976.8	E858.7	E946.8	E950.4	E962.0	E980.4
Capillary agents	972.8	E858.3	E942.8	E950.4	E962.0	E980.4
Capreomycin	960.6	E856	E930.6	E950.4	E962.0	E980.4
Captodiame, captodiamine	969.5	E853.8	E939.5	E950.3	E962.0	E980.3
Caramiphen (hydrochloride)	971.1	E855.4	E941.1	E950.4	E962.0	E980.4
Carbachol	971.0	E855.3	E941.0	E950.4	E962.0	E980.4
Carbacrylamine resins	974.5	E858.5	E944.5	E950.4	E962.0	E980.4
Carbamate (sedative)	967.8	E852.8	E937.8	E950.2	E962.0	E980.2
herbicide	989.3	E863.5	—	E950.6	E962.1	E980.7
insecticide	989.3	E863.2	—	E950.6	E962.1	E980.7
Carbamazepine	966.3	E855.0	E936.3	E950.4	E962.0	E980.4
Carbamic esters	967.8	E852.8	E937.8	E950.2	E962.0	E980.2
Carbamide	974.4	E858.5	E944.4	E950.4	E962.0	E980.4
topical	976.8	E858.7	E946.8	E950.4	E962.0	E980.4
Carbamylcholine chloride	971.0	E855.3	E941.0	E950.4	E962.0	E980.4
Carbarsone	961.1	E857	E931.1	E950.4	E962.0	E980.4
Carbaryl	989.3	E863.2	—	E950.6	E962.1	E980.7
Carbaspirin	965.1	E850.3	E935.3	E950.0	E962.0	E980.0
Carbazochrome	972.8	E858.3	E942.8	E950.4	E962.0	E980.4
Carbenicillin	960.0	E856	E930.0	E950.4	E962.0	E980.4
Carbenoxolone	973.8	E858.4	E943.8	E950.4	E962.0	E980.4

Substance	Poisoning	External Cause (E-Code)				
		Accident	Therapeutic Use	Suicide Attempt	Assault	Un-determined
Carbetapentane	975.4	E858.6	E945.4	E950.4	E962.0	E980.4
Carbimazole	962.8	E858.0	E932.8	E950.4	E962.0	E980.4
Carbinol	980.1	E860.2	—	E950.9	E962.1	E980.9
Carbinoxamine	963.0	E858.1	E933.0	E950.4	E962.0	E980.4
Carbitol	982.8	E862.4	—	E950.9	E962.1	E980.9
Carbocaine	968.9	E855.2	E938.9	E950.4	E962.0	E980.4
infiltration (subcutaneous)	968.5	E855.2	E938.5	E950.4	E962.0	E980.4
nerve block (peripheral) (plexus)	968.6	E855.2	E938.6	E950.4	E962.0	E980.4
topical (surface)	968.5	E855.2	E938.5	E950.4	E962.0	E980.4
Carbol-fuchsin solution	976.0	E858.7	E946.0	E950.4	E962.0	E980.4
Carbolic acid (*see also* Phenol)	983.0	E864.0	—	E950.7	E962.1	E980.6
Carbomycin	960.8	E856	E930.8	E950.4	E962.0	E980.4
Carbon						
bisulfide (liquid) (vapor)	982.2	E862.4	—	E950.9	E962.1	E980.9
dioxide (gas)	987.8	E869.8	—	E952.8	E962.2	E982.8
disulfide (liquid) (vapor)	982.2	E862.4	—	E950.9	E962.1	E980.9
monoxide (from incomplete combustion of) (in) NEC	986	E868.9	—	E952.1	E962.2	E982.1
blast furnace gas	986	E868.8	—	E952.1	E962.2	E982.1
butane (distributed in mobile container)	986	E868.0	—	E951.1	E962.2	E981.1
distributed through pipes	986	E867	—	E951.0	E962.2	E981.0
charcoal fumes	986	E868.3	—	E952.1	E962.2	E982.1
coal						
gas (piped)	986	E867	—	E951.0	E962.2	E981.0
solid (in domestic stoves, fireplaces)	986	E868.3	—	E952.1	E962.2	E982.1
coke (in domestic stoves, fireplaces)	986	E868.3	—	E952.1	E962.2	E982.1
exhaust gas (motor) not in transit	986	E868.2	—	E952.0	E962.2	E982.0
combustion engine, any not in watercraft	986	E868.2	—	E952.0	E962.2	E982.0
farm tractor, not in transit	986	E868.2	—	E952.0	E962.2	E982.0
gas engine	986	E868.2	—	E952.0	E962.2	E982.0
motor pump	986	E868.2	—	E952.0	E962.2	E982.0
motor vehicle, not in transit	986	E868.2	—	E952.0	E962.2	E982.0
fuel (in domestic use)	986	E868.3	—	E952.1	E962.2	E982.1
gas (piped)	986	E867	—	E951.0	E962.2	E981.0
in mobile container	986	E868.0	—	E951.1	E962.2	E981.1
utility	986	E868.1	—	E951.8	E962.2	E981.1
in mobile container	986	E868.0	—	E951.1	E962.2	E981.1
piped (natural)	986	E867	—	E951.0	E962.2	E981.0
illuminating gas	986	E868.1	—	E951.8	E962.2	E981.8
industrial fuels or gases, any	986	E868.8	—	E952.1	E962.2	E982.1
kerosene (in domestic stoves, fireplaces)	986	E868.3	—	E952.1	E962.2	E982.1
kiln gas or vapor	986	E868.8	—	E952.1	E962.2	E982.1
motor exhaust gas, not in transit	986	E868.2	—	E952.0	E962.2	E982.0
piped gas (manufactured) (natural)	986	E867	—	E951.0	E962.2	E981.0
producer gas	986	E868.8	—	E952.1	E962.2	E982.1
propane (distributed in mobile container)	986	E868.0	—	E951.1	E962.2	E981.1
distributed through pipes	986	E867	—	E951.0	E962.2	E981.0
specified source NEC	986	E868.8	—	E952.1	E962.2	E982.1
stove gas	986	E868.1	—	E951.8	E962.2	E981.8
piped	986	E867	—	E951.0	E962.2	E981.0
utility gas	986	E868.1	—	E951.8	E962.2	E981.8
piped	986	E867	—	E951.0	E962.2	E981.0
water gas	986	E868.1	—	E951.8	E962.2	E981.8
wood (in domestic stoves, fireplaces)	986	E868.3	—	E952.1	E962.2	E982.1
tetrachloride (vapor) NEC	987.8	E869.8	—	E952.8	E962.2	E982.8
liquid (cleansing agent) NEC	982.1	E861.3	—	E950.9	E962.1	E980.9
solvent	982.1	E862.4	—	E950.9	E962.1	E980.9
Carbonic acid (gas)	987.8	E869.8	—	E952.8	E962.2	E982.8
anhydrase inhibitors	974.2	E858.5	E944.2	E950.4	E962.0	E980.4
Carbowax	976.3	E858.7	E946.3	E950.4	E962.0	E980.4
Carbrital	967.0	E851	E937.0	E950.1	E962.0	E980.1
Carbromal (derivatives)	967.3	E852.2	E937.3	E950.2	E962.0	E980.2
Cardiac						
depressants	972.0	E858.3	E942.0	E950.4	E962.0	E980.4
rhythm regulators	972.0	E858.3	E942.0	E950.4	E962.0	E980.4
Cardiografin	977.8	E858.8	E947.8	E950.4	E962.0	E980.4
Cardio-green	977.8	E858.8	E947.8	E950.4	E962.0	E980.4
Cardiotonic glycosides	972.1	E858.3	E942.1	E950.4	E962.0	E980.4
Cardiovascular agents NEC	972.9	E858.3	E942.9	E950.4	E962.0	E980.4
Cardrase	974.2	E858.5	E944.2	E950.4	E962.0	E980.4
Carfusin	976.0	E858.7	E946.0	E950.4	E962.0	E980.4
Carisoprodol	968.0	E855.1	E938.0	E950.4	E962.0	E980.4
Carmustine	963.1	E858.1	E933.1	E950.4	E962.0	E980.4
Carotene	963.5	E858.1	E933.5	E950.4	E962.0	E980.4

		External Cause (E-Code)				
Substance	**Poisoning**	**Accident**	**Therapeutic Use**	**Suicide Attempt**	**Assault**	**Un-determined**
Carphenazine (maleate)	969.1	E853.0	E939.1	E950.3	E962.0	E980.3
Carter's Little Pills	973.1	E858.4	E943.1	E950.4	E962.0	E980.4
Cascara (sagrada)	973.1	E858.4	E943.1	E950.4	E962.0	E980.4
Cassava	988.2	E865.4	—	E950.9	E962.1	E980.9
Castellani's paint	976.0	E858.7	E946.0	E950.4	E962.0	E980.4
Castor						
bean	988.2	E865.3	—	E950.9	E962.1	E980.9
oil	973.1	E858.4	E943.1	E950.4	E962.0	E980.4
Caterpillar (sting)	989.5	E905.5	—	E950.9	E962.1	E980.9
Catha (edulis)	970.8	E854.3	E940.8	E950.4	E962.0	E980.4
Cathartics NEC	973.3	E858.4	E943.3	E950.4	E962.0	E980.4
contact	973.1	E858.4	E943.1	E950.4	E962.0	E980.4
emollient	973.2	E858.4	E943.2	E950.4	E962.0	E980.4
intestinal irritants	973.1	E858.4	E943.1	E950.4	E962.0	E980.4
saline	973.3	E858.4	E943.3	E950.4	E962.0	E980.4
Cathomycin	960.8	E856	E930.8	E950.4	E962.0	E980.4
Caustic(s)	983.9	E864.4	—	E950.7	E962.1	E980.6
alkali	983.2	E864.2	—	E950.7	E962.1	E980.6
hydroxide	983.2	E864.2	—	E950.7	E962.1	E980.6
potash	983.2	E864.2	—	E950.7	E962.1	E980.6
soda	983.2	E864.2	—	E950.7	E962.1	E980.6
specified NEC	983.9	E864.3	—	E950.7	E962.1	E980.6
Ceepryn	976.0	E858.7	E946.0	E950.4	E962.0	E980.4
ENT agent	976.6	E858.7	E946.6	E950.4	E962.0	E980.4
lozenges	976.6	E858.7	E946.6	E950.4	E962.0	E980.4
Celestone	962.0	E858.0	E932.0	E950.4	E962.0	E980.4
topical	976.0	E858.7	E946.0	E950.4	E962.0	E980.4
Cellosolve	982.8	E862.4	—	E950.9	E962.1	E980.9
Cell stimulants and proliferants	976.8	E858.7	E946.8	E950.4	E962.0	E980.4
Cellulose derivatives, cathartic	973.3	E858.4	E943.3	E950.4	E962.0	E980.4
nitrates (topical)	976.3	E858.7	E946.3	E950.4	E962.0	E980.4
Centipede (bite)	989.5	E905.4	—	E950.9	E962.1	E980.9
Central nervous system						
depressants	968.4	E855.1	E938.4	E950.4	E962.0	E980.4
anesthetic (general) NEC	968.4	E855.1	E938.4	E950.4	E962.0	E980.4
gases NEC	968.2	E855.1	E938.2	E950.4	E962.0	E980.4
intravenous	968.3	E855.1	E938.3	E950.4	E962.0	E980.4
barbiturates	967.0	E851	E937.0	E950.1	E962.0	E980.1
bromides	967.3	E852.2	E937.3	E950.2	E962.0	E980.2
cannabis sativa	969.6	E854.1	E939.6	E950.3	E962.0	E980.3
chloral hydrate	967.1	E852.0	E937.1	E950.2	E962.0	E980.2
hallucinogenics	969.6	E854.1	E939.6	E950.3	E962.0	E980.3
hypnotics	967.9	E852.9	E937.9	E950.2	E962.0	E980.2
specified NEC	967.8	E852.8	E937.8	E950.2	E962.0	E980.2
muscle relaxants	968.0	E855.1	E938.0	E950.4	E962.0	E980.4
paraldehyde	967.2	E852.1	E937.2	E950.2	E962.0	E980.2
sedatives	967.9	E852.9	E937.9	E950.2	E962.0	E980.2
mixed NEC	967.6	E852.5	E937.6	E950.2	E962.0	E980.2
specified NEC	967.8	E852.8	E937.8	E950.2	E962.0	E980.2
muscle-tone depressants	968.0	E855.1	E938.0	E950.4	E962.0	E980.4
stimulants	970.9	E854.3	E940.9	E950.4	E962.0	E980.4
amphetamines	969.7	E854.2	E939.7	E950.3	E962.0	E980.3
analeptics	970.0	E854.3	E940.0	E950.4	E962.0	E980.4
antidepressants	969.0	E854.0	E939.0	E950.3	E962.0	E980.3
opiate antagonists	970.1	E854.3	E940.0	E950.4	E962.0	E980.4
specified NEC	970.8	E854.3	E940.8	E950.4	E962.0	E980.4
Cephalexin	960.5	E856	E930.5	E950.4	E962.0	E980.4
Cephaloglycin	960.5	E856	E930.5	E950.4	E962.0	E980.4
Cephaloridine	960.5	E856	E930.5	E950.4	E962.0	E980.4
Cephalosporins NEC	960.5	E856	E930.5	E950.4	E962.0	E980.4
N (adicillin)	960.0	E856	E930.0	E950.4	E962.0	E980.4
Cephalothin (sodium)	960.5	E856	E930.5	E950.4	E962.0	E980.4
Cerbera (odallam)	988.2	E865.4	—	E950.9	E962.1	E980.9
Cerberin	972.1	E858.3	E942.1	E950.4	E962.0	E980.4
Cerebral stimulants	970.9	E854.3	E940.9	E950.4	E962.0	E980.4
psychotherapeutic	969.7	E854.2	E939.7	E950.3	E962.0	E980.3
specified NEC	970.8	E854.3	E940.8	E950.4	E962.0	E980.4
Cetalkonium (chloride)	976.0	E858.7	E946.0	E950.4	E962.0	E980.4
Cetoxime	963.0	E858.1	E933.0	E950.4	E962.0	E980.4
Cetrimide	976.2	E858.7	E946.2	E950.4	E962.0	E980.4
Cetylpyridinium	976.0	E858.7	E946.0	E950.4	E962.0	E980.4
ENT agent	976.6	E858.7	E946.6	E950.4	E962.0	E980.4
lozenges	976.6	E858.7	E946.6	E950.4	E962.0	E980.4

		External Cause (E-Code)				
Substance	**Poisoning**	**Accident**	**Therapeutic Use**	**Suicide Attempt**	**Assault**	**Un-determined**
Cevadilla — *see* Sabadilla						
Cevitamic acid	963.5	E858.1	E933.5	E950.4	E962.0	E980.4
Chalk, precipitated	973.0	E858.4	E943.0	E950.4	E962.0	E980.4
Charcoal						
fumes (carbon monoxide)	986	E868.3	—	E952.1	E962.2	E982.1
industrial	986	E868.8	—	E952.1	E962.2	E982.1
medicinal (activated)	973.0	E858.4	E943.0	E950.4	E962.0	E980.4
Chelating agents NEC	977.2	E858.8	E947.2	E950.4	E962.0	E980.4
Chelidonium majus	988.2	E865.4	—	E950.9	E962.1	E980.9
Chemical substance	989.9	E866.9	—	E950.9	E962.1	E980.9
specified NEC	989.89	E866.8	—	E950.9	E962.1	E980.9
Chenopodium (oil)	961.6	E857	E931.6	E950.4	E962.0	E980.4
Cherry laurel	988.2	E865.4	—	E950.9	E962.1	E980.9
Chiniofon	961.3	E857	E931.3	E950.4	E962.0	E980.4
Chlophedianol	975.4	E858.6	E945.4	E950.4	E962.0	E980.4
Chloral (betaine) (formamide) (hydrate)	967.1	E852.0	E937.1	E950.2	E962.0	E980.2
Chloralamide	967.1	E852.0	E937.1	E950.2	E962.0	E980.2
Chlorambucil	963.1	E858.1	E933.1	E950.4	E962.0	E980.4
Chloramphenicol	960.2	E856	E930.2	E950.4	E962.0	E980.4
ENT agent	976.6	E858.7	E946.6	E950.4	E962.0	E980.4
ophthalmic preparation	976.5	E858.7	E946.5	E950.4	E962.0	E980.4
topical NEC	976.0	E858.7	E946.0	E950.4	E962.0	E980.4
Chlorate(s) (potassium) (sodium) NEC	983.9	E864.3	—	E950.7	E962.1	E980.6
herbicides	989.4	E863.5	—	E950.6	E962.1	E980.7
Chlorcylizine	963.0	E858.1	E933.0	E950.4	E962.0	E980.4
Chlordan(e) (dust)	989.2	E863.0	—	E950.6	E962.1	E980.7
Chlordantoin	976.0	E858.7	E946.0	E950.4	E962.0	E980.4
Chlordiazepoxide	969.4	E853.2	E939.4	E950.3	E962.0	E980.3
Chloresium	976.8	E858.7	E946.8	E950.4	E962.0	E980.4
Chlorethiazol	967.1	E852.0	E937.1	E950.2	E962.0	E980.2
Chlorethyl — *see* Ethyl, chloride						
Chloretone	967.1	E852.0	E937.1	E950.2	E962.0	E980.2
Chlorex	982.3	E862.4	—	E950.9	E962.1	E980.9
Chlorhexadol	967.1	E852.0	E937.1	E950.2	E962.0	E980.2
Chlorhexidine (hydrochloride)	976.0	E858.7	E946.0	E950.4	E962.0	E980.4
Chlorhydroxyquinolin	976.0	E858.7	E946.0	E950.4	E962.0	E980.4
Chloride of lime (bleach)	983.9	E864.3	—	E950.7	E962.1	E980.6
Chlorinated						
camphene	989.2	E863.0	—	E950.6	E962.1	E980.7
diphenyl	989.89	E866.8	—	E950.9	E962.1	E980.9
hydrocarbons NEC	989.2	E863.0	—	E950.6	E962.1	E980.7
solvent	982.3	E862.4	—	E950.9	E962.1	E980.9
lime (bleach)	983.9	E864.3	—	E950.7	E962.1	E980.6
naphthalene — *see* Naphthalene						
pesticides NEC	989.2	E863.0	—	E950.6	E962.1	E980.7
soda — *see* Sodium, hypochlorite						
Chlorine (fumes) (gas)	987.6	E869.8	—	E952.8	E962.2	E982.8
bleach	983.9	E864.3	—	E950.7	E962.1	E980.6
compounds NEC	983.9	E864.3	—	E950.7	E962.1	E980.6
disinfectant	983.9	E861.4	—	E950.7	E962.1	E980.6
releasing agents NEC	983.9	E864.3	—	E950.7	E962.1	E980.6
Chlorisondamine	972.3	E858.3	E942.3	E950.4	E962.0	E980.4
Chlormadinone	962.2	E858.0	E932.2	E950.4	E962.0	E980.4
Chlormerodrin	974.0	E858.5	E944.0	E950.4	E962.0	E980.4
Chlormethiazole	967.1	E852.0	E937.1	E950.2	E962.0	E980.2
Chlormethylenecycline	960.4	E856	E930.4	E950.4	E962.0	E980.4
Chlormezanone	969.5	E853.8	E939.5	E950.3	E962.0	E980.3
Chloroacetophenone	987.5	E869.3	—	E952.8	E962.2	E982.8
Chloroaniline	983.0	E864.0	—	E950.7	E962.1	E980.6
Chlorobenzene, chlorobenzol	982.0	E862.4	—	E950.9	E962.1	E980.9
Chlorobutanol	967.1	E852.0	E937.1	E950.2	E962.0	E980.2
Chlorodinitrobenzene	983.0	E864.0	—	E950.7	E962.1	E980.6
dust or vapor	987.8	E869.8	—	E952.8	E962.2	E982.8
Chloroethane — *see* Ethyl, chloride						
Chloroform (fumes) (vapor)	987.8	E869.8	—	E952.8	E962.2	E982.8
anesthetic (gas)	968.2	E855.1	E938.2	E950.4	E962.0	E980.4
liquid NEC	968.4	E855.1	E938.4	E950.4	E962.0	E980.4
solvent	982.3	E862.4	—	E950.9	E962.1	E980.9
Chloroguanide	961.4	E857	E931.4	E950.4	E962.0	E980.4

		External Cause (E-Code)				
Substance	Poisoning	Accident	Therapeutic Use	Suicide Attempt	Assault	Un-determined
Chloromycetin	960.2	E856	E930.2	E950.4	E962.0	E980.4
ENT agent	976.6	E858.7	E946.6	E950.4	E962.0	E980.4
ophthalmic preparation	976.5	E858.7	E946.5	E950.4	E962.0	E980.4
otic solution	976.6	E858.7	E946.6	E950.4	E962.0	E980.4
topical NEC	976.0	E858.7	E946.0	E950.4	E962.0	E980.4
Chloronitrobenzene	983.0	E864.0	—	E950.7	E962.1	E980.6
dust or vapor	987.8	E869.8	—	E952.8	E962.2	E982.8
Chlorophenol	983.0	E864.0	—	E950.7	E962.1	E980.6
Chlorophenothane	989.2	E863.0	—	E950.6	E962.1	E980.7
Chlorophyll (derivatives)	976.8	E858.7	E946.8	E950.4	E962.0	E980.4
Chloropicrin (fumes)	987.8	E869.8	—	E952.8	E962.2	E982.8
fumigant	989.4	E863.8	—	E950.6	E962.1	E980.7
fungicide	989.4	E863.6	—	E950.6	E962.1	E980.7
pesticide (fumes)	989.4	E863.4	—	E950.6	E962.1	E980.7
Chloroprocaine	968.9	E855.2	E938.9	E950.4	E962.0	E980.4
infiltration (subcutaneous)	968.5	E855.2	E938.5	E950.4	E962.0	E980.4
nerve block (peripheral) (plexus)	968.6	E855.2	E938.6	E950.4	E962.0	E980.4
Chloroptic	976.5	E858.7	E946.5	E950.4	E962.0	E980.4
Chloropurine	963.1	E858.1	E933.1	E950.4	E962.0	E980.4
Chloroquine (hydrochloride) (phosphate)	961.4	E857	E931.4	E950.4	E962.0	E980.4
Chlorothen	963.0	E858.1	E933.0	E950.4	E962.0	E980.4
Chlorothiazide	974.3	E858.5	E944.3	E950.4	E962.0	E980.4
Chlorotrianisene	962.2	E858.0	E932.2	E950.4	E962.0	E980.4
Chlorovinyldichloroarsine	985.1	E866.3	—	E950.8	E962.1	E980.8
Chloroxylenol	976.0	E858.7	E946.0	E950.4	E962.0	E980.4
Chlorphenesin (carbamate)	968.0	E855.1	E938.0	E950.4	E962.0	E980.4
topical (antifungal)	976.0	E858.7	E946.0	E950.4	E962.0	E980.4
Chlorpheniramine	963.0	E858.1	E933.0	E950.4	E962.0	E980.4
Chlorphenoxamine	966.4	E855.0	E936.4	E950.4	E962.0	E980.4
Chlorphentermine	977.0	E858.8	E947.0	E950.4	E962.0	E980.4
Chlorproguanil	961.4	E857	E931.4	E950.4	E962.0	E980.4
Chlorpromazine	969.1	E853.0	E939.1	E950.3	E962.0	E980.3
Chlorpropamide	962.3	E858.0	E932.3	E950.4	E962.0	E980.4
Chlorprothixene	969.3	E853.8	E939.3	E950.3	E962.0	E980.3
Chlorquinaldol	976.0	E858.7	E946.0	E950.4	E962.0	E980.4
Chlortetracycline	960.4	E856	E930.4	E950.4	E962.0	E980.4
Chlorthalidone	974.4	E858.5	E944.4	E950.4	E962.0	E980.4
Chlortrianisene	962.2	E858.0	E932.2	E950.4	E962.0	E980.4
Chlor-Trimeton	963.0	E858.1	E933.0	E950.4	E962.0	E980.4
Chlorzoxazone	968.0	E855.1	E938.0	E950.4	E962.0	E980.4
Choke damp	987.8	E869.8	—	E952.8	E962.2	E982.8
Cholebrine	977.8	E858.8	E947.8	E950.4	E962.0	E980.4
Cholera vaccine	978.2	E858.8	E948.2	E950.4	E962.0	E980.4
Cholesterol-lowering agents	972.2	E858.3	E942.2	E950.4	E962.0	E980.4
Cholestyramine (resin)	972.2	E858.3	E942.2	E950.4	E962.0	E980.4
Cholic acid	973.4	E858.4	E943.4	E950.4	E962.0	E980.4
Choline						
dihydrogen citrate	977.1	E858.8	E947.1	E950.4	E962.0	E980.4
salicylate	965.1	E850.3	E935.3	E950.0	E962.0	E980.0
theophyllinate	974.1	E858.5	E944.1	E950.4	E962.0	E980.4
Cholinergics	971.0	E855.3	E941.0	E950.4	E962.0	E980.4
Cholografin	977.8	E858.8	E947.8	E950.4	E962.0	E980.4
Chorionic gonadotropin	962.4	E858.0	E932.4	E950.4	E962.0	E980.4
Chromates	983.9	E864.3	—	E950.7	E962.1	E980.6
dust or mist	987.8	E869.8	—	E952.8	E962.2	E982.8
lead	984.0	E866.0	—	E950.9	E962.1	E980.9
paint	984.0	E861.5	—	E950.9	E962.1	E980.9
Chromic acid	983.9	E864.3	—	E950.7	E962.1	E980.6
dust or mist	987.8	E869.8	—	E952.8	E962.2	E982.8
Chromium	985.6	E866.4	—	E950.9	E962.1	E980.9
compounds — *see* Chromates						
Chromonar	972.4	E858.3	E942.4	E950.4	E962.0	E980.4
Chromyl chloride	983.9	E864.3	—	E950.7	E962.1	E980.6
Chrysarobin (ointment)	976.4	E858.7	E946.4	E950.4	E962.0	E980.4
Chrysazin	973.1	E858.4	E943.1	E950.4	E962.0	E980.4
Chymar	963.4	E858.1	E933.4	E950.4	E962.0	E980.4
ophthalmic preparation	976.5	E858.7	E946.5	E950.4	E962.0	E980.4
Chymotrypsin	963.4	E858.1	E933.4	E950.4	E962.0	E980.4
ophthalmic preparation	976.5	E858.7	E946.5	E950.4	E962.0	E980.4
Cicuta maculata or virosa	988.2	E865.4	—	E950.9	E962.1	E980.9
Cigarette lighter fluid	981	E862.1	—	E950.9	E962.1	E980.9

Substance	Poisoning	External Cause (E-Code) Accident	Therapeutic Use	Suicide Attempt	Assault	Un-determined
Cinchocaine (spinal)	968.7	E855.2	E938.7	E950.4	E962.0	E980.4
topical (surface)	968.5	E855.2	E938.5	E950.4	E962.0	E980.4
Cinchona	961.4	E857	E931.4	E950.4	E962.0	E980.4
Cinchonine alkaloids	961.4	E857	E931.4	E950.4	E962.0	E980.4
Cinchophen	974.7	E858.5	E944.7	E950.4	E962.0	E980.4
Cinnarizine	963.0	E858.1	E933.0	E950.4	E962.0	E980.4
Citanest	968.9	E855.2	E938.9	E950.4	E962.0	E980.4
infiltration (subcutaneous)	968.5	E855.2	E938.5	E950.4	E962.0	E980.4
nerve block (peripheral) (plexus)	968.6	E855.2	E938.6	E950.4	E962.0	E980.4
Citric acid	989.89	E866.8	—	E950.9	E962.1	E980.9
Citrovorum factor	964.1	E858.2	E934.1	E950.4	E962.0	E980.4
Claviceps purpurea	988.2	E865.4	—	E950.9	E962.1	E980.9
Cleaner, cleansing agent NEC	989.89	E861.3	—	E950.9	E962.1	E980.9
of paint or varnish	982.8	E862.9	—	E950.9	E962.1	E980.9
Clematis vitalba	988.2	E865.4	—	E950.9	E962.1	E980.9
Clemizole	963.0	E858.1	E933.0	E950.4	E962.0	E980.4
penicillin	960.0	E856	E930.0	E950.4	E962.0	E980.4
Clidinium	971.1	E855.4	E941.1	E950.4	E962.0	E980.4
Clindamycin	960.8	E856	E930.8	E950.4	E962.0	E980.4
Cliradon	965.09	E850.2	E935.2	E950.0	E962.0	E980.0
Clocortolone	962.0	E858.0	E932.0	E950.4	E962.0	E980.4
Clofedanol	975.4	E858.6	E945.4	E950.4	E962.0	E980.4
Clofibrate	972.2	E858.3	E942.2	E950.4	E962.0	E980.4
Clomethiazole	967.1	E852.0	E937.1	E950.2	E962.0	E980.2
Clomiphene	977.8	E858.8	E947.8	E950.4	E962.0	E980.4
Clonazepam	969.4	E853.2	E939.4	E950.3	E962.0	E980.3
Clonidine	972.6	E858.3	E942.6	E950.4	E962.0	E980.4
Clopamide	974.3	E858.5	E944.3	E950.4	E962.0	E980.4
Clorazepate	969.4	E853.2	E939.4	E950.3	E962.0	E980.3
Clorexolone	974.4	E858.5	E944.4	E950.4	E962.0	E980.4
Clorox (bleach)	983.9	E864.3	—	E950.7	E962.1	E980.6
Clortermine	977.0	E858.8	E947.0	E950.4	E962.0	E980.4
Clotrimazole	976.0	E858.7	E946.0	E950.4	E962.0	E980.4
Cloxacillin	960.0	E856	E930.0	E950.4	E962.0	E980.4
Coagulants NEC	964.5	E858.2	E934.5	E950.4	E962.0	E980.4
Coal (carbon monoxide from) — *see also* Carbon, monoxide, coal						
oil — *see* Kerosene						
tar NEC	983.0	E864.0	—	E950.7	E962.1	E980.6
fumes	987.8	E869.8	—	E952.8	E962.2	E982.8
medicinal (ointment)	976.4	E858.7	E946.4	E950.4	E962.0	E980.4
analgesics NEC	965.5	E850.5	E935.5	E950.0	E962.0	E980.0
naphtha (solvent)	981	E862.0	—	E950.9	E962.1	E980.9
Cobalt (fumes) (industrial)	985.8	E866.4	—	E950.9	E962.1	E980.9
Cobra (venom)	989.5	E905.0	—	E950.9	E962.1	E980.9
Coca (leaf)	970.8	E854.3	E940.8	E950.4	E962.0	E980.4
Cocaine (hydrochloride) (salt)	968.5	E855.2	E938.5	E950.4	E962.0	E980.4
Coccidioidin	977.8	E858.8	E947.8	E950.4	E962.0	E980.4
Cocculus indicus	988.2	E865.3	—	E950.9	E962.1	E980.9
Cochineal	989.89	E866.8	—	E950.9	E962.1	E980.9
medicinal products	977.4	E858.8	E947.4	E950.4	E962.0	E980.4
Codeine	965.09	E850.2	E935.2	E950.0	E962.0	E980.0
Coffee	989.89	E866.8	—	E950.9	E962.1	E980.9
Cogentin	971.1	E855.4	E941.1	E950.4	E962.0	E980.4
Coke fumes or gas (carbon monoxide)	986	E868.3	—	E952.1	E962.2	E982.1
industrial use	986	E868.8	—	E952.1	E962.2	E982.1
Colace	973.2	E858.4	E943.2	E950.4	E962.0	E980.4
Colchicine	974.7	E858.5	E944.7	E950.4	E962.0	E980.4
Colchicum	988.2	E865.3	—	E950.9	E962.1	E980.9
Cold cream	976.3	E858.7	E946.3	E950.4	E962.0	E980.4
Colestipol	972.2	E858.3	E942.2	E950.4	E962.0	E980.4
Colistimethate	960.8	E856	E930.8	E950.4	E962.0	E980.4
Colistin	960.8	E856	E930.8	E950.4	E962.0	E980.4
Collagen	977.8	E866.8	E947.8	E950.9	E962.1	E980.9
Collagenase	976.8	E858.7	E946.8	E950.4	E962.0	E980.4
Collodion (flexible)	976.3	E858.7	E946.3	E950.4	E962.0	E980.4
Colocynth	973.1	E858.4	E943.1	E950.4	E962.0	E980.4
Coloring matter — *see* Dye(s)						
Combustion gas — *see* Carbon, monoxide						
Compazine	969.1	E853.0	E939.1	E950.3	E962.0	E980.3

Substance	Poisoning	External Cause (E-Code) Accident	Therapeutic Use	Suicide Attempt	Assault	Undetermined
Compound						
42 (warfarin)	989.4	E863.7	—	E950.6	E962.1	E980.7
269 (endrin)	989.2	E863.0	—	E950.6	E962.1	E980.7
497 (dieldrin)	989.2	E863.0	—	E950.6	E962.1	E980.7
1080 (sodium fluoroacetate)	989.4	E863.7	—	E950.6	E962.1	E980.7
3422 (parathion)	989.3	E863.1	—	E950.6	E962.1	E980.7
3911 (phorate)	989.3	E863.1	—	E950.6	E962.1	E980.7
3956 (toxaphene)	989.2	E863.0	—	E950.6	E962.1	E980.7
4049 (malathion)	989.3	E863.1	—	E950.6	E962.1	E980.7
4124 (dicapthon)	989.4	E863.4	—	E950.6	E962.1	E980.7
E (cortisone)	962.0	E858.0	E932.0	E950.4	E962.0	E980.4
F (hydrocortisone)	962.0	E858.0	E932.0	E950.4	E962.0	E980.4
Congo red	977.8	E858.8	E947.8	E950.4	E962.0	E980.4
Coniine, conine	965.7	E850.7	E935.7	E950.0	E962.0	E980.0
Conium (maculatum)	988.2	E865.4	—	E950.9	E962.1	E980.9
Conjugated estrogens (equine)	962.2	E858.0	E932.2	E950.4	E962.0	E980.4
Contac	975.6	E858.6	E945.6	E950.4	E962.0	E980.4
Contact lens solution	976.5	E858.7	E946.5	E950.4	E962.0	E980.4
Contraceptives (oral)	962.2	E858.0	E932.2	E950.4	E962.0	E980.4
vaginal	976.8	E858.7	E946.8	E950.4	E962.0	E980.4
Contrast media (roentgenographic)	977.8	E858.8	E947.8	E950.4	E962.0	E980.4
Convallaria majalis	988.2	E865.4	—	E950.9	E962.1	E980.9
Copper (dust) (fumes) (salts) NEC	985.8	E866.4	—	E950.9	E962.1	E980.9
arsenate, arsenite	985.1	E866.3	—	E950.8	E962.1	E980.8
insecticide	985.1	E863.4	—	E950.8	E962.1	E980.8
emetic	973.6	E858.4	E943.6	E950.4	E962.0	E980.4
fungicide	985.8	E863.6	—	E950.6	E962.1	E980.7
insecticide	985.8	E863.4	—	E950.6	E962.1	E980.7
oleate	976.0	E858.7	E946.0	E950.4	E962.0	E980.4
sulfate	983.9	E864.3	—	E950.7	E962.1	E980.6
fungicide	983.9	E863.6	—	E950.7	E962.1	E980.6
cupric	973.6	E858.4	E943.6	E950.4	E962.0	E980.4
cuprous	983.9	E864.3	—	E950.7	E962.1	E980.6
Copperhead snake (bite) (venom)	989.5	E905.0	—	E950.9	E962.1	E980.9
Coral (sting)	989.5	E905.6	—	E950.9	E962.1	E980.9
snake (bite) (venom)	989.5	E905.0	—	E950.9	E962.1	E980.9
Cordran	976.0	E858.7	E946.0	E950.4	E962.0	E980.4
Corn cures	976.4	E858.7	E946.4	E950.4	E962.0	E980.4
Cornhusker's lotion	976.3	E858.7	E946.3	E950.4	E962.0	E980.4
Corn starch	976.3	E858.7	E946.3	E950.4	E962.0	E980.4
Corrosive	983.9	E864.4	—	E950.7	E962.1	E980.6
acids NEC	983.1	E864.1	—	E950.7	E962.1	E980.6
aromatics	983.0	E864.0	—	E950.7	E962.1	E980.6
disinfectant	983.0	E861.4	—	E950.7	E962.1	E980.6
fumes NEC	987.9	E869.9	—	E952.9	E962.2	E982.9
specified NEC	983.9	E864.3	—	E950.7	E962.1	E980.6
sublimate — *see* Mercury, chloride						
Cortate	962.0	E858.0	E932.0	E950.4	E962.0	E980.4
Cort-Dome	962.0	E858.0	E932.0	E950.4	E962.0	E980.4
ENT agent	976.6	E858.7	E946.6	E950.4	E962.0	E980.4
ophthalmic preparation	976.5	E858.7	E946.5	E950.4	E962.0	E980.4
topical NEC	976.0	E858.7	E946.0	E950.4	E962.0	E980.4
Cortef	962.0	E858.0	E932.0	E950.4	E962.0	E980.4
ENT agent	976.6	E858.7	E946.6	E950.4	E962.0	E980.4
ophthalmic preparation	976.5	E858.7	E946.5	E950.4	E962.0	E980.4
topical NEC	976.0	E858.7	E946.0	E950.4	E962.0	E980.4
Corticosteroids (fluorinated)	962.0	E858.0	E932.0	E950.4	E962.0	E980.4
ENT agent	976.6	E858.7	E946.6	E950.4	E962.0	E980.4
ophthalmic preparation	976.5	E858.7	E946.5	E950.4	E962.0	E980.4
topical NEC	976.0	E858.7	E946.0	E950.4	E962.0	E980.4
Corticotropin	962.4	E858.0	E932.4	E950.4	E962.0	E980.4
Cortisol	962.0	E858.0	E932.0	E950.4	E962.0	E980.4
ENT agent	976.6	E858.7	E946.6	E950.4	E962.0	E980.4
ophthalmic preparation	976.5	E858.7	E946.5	E950.4	E962.0	E980.4
topical NEC	976.0	E858.7	E946.0	E950.4	E962.0	E980.4
Cortisone derivatives (acetate)	962.0	E858.0	E932.0	E950.4	E962.0	E980.4
ENT agent	976.6	E858.7	E946.6	E950.4	E962.0	E980.4
ophthalmic preparation	976.5	E858.7	E946.5	E950.4	E962.0	E980.4
topical NEC	976.0	E858.7	E946.0	E950.4	E962.0	E980.4
Cortogen	962.0	E858.0	E932.0	E950.4	E962.0	E980.4
ENT agent	976.6	E858.7	E946.6	E950.4	E962.0	E980.4
ophthalmic preparation	976.5	E858.7	E946.5	E950.4	E962.0	E980.4

Substance	Poisoning	External Cause (E-Code) Accident	Therapeutic Use	Suicide Attempt	Assault	Undetermined
Cortone	962.0	E858.0	E932.0	E950.4	E962.0	E980.4
ENT agent	976.6	E858.7	E946.6	E950.4	E962.0	E980.4
ophthalmic preparation	976.5	E858.7	E946.5	E950.4	E962.0	E980.4
Cortril	962.0	E858.0	E932.0	E950.4	E962.0	E980.4
ENT agent	976.6	E858.7	E946.6	E950.4	E962.0	E980.4
ophthalmic preparation	976.5	E858.7	E946.5	E950.4	E962.0	E980.4
topical NEC	976.0	E858.7	E946.0	E950.4	E962.0	E980.4
Cosmetics	989.89	E866.7	—	E950.9	E962.1	E980.9
Cosyntropin	977.8	E858.8	E947.8	E950.4	E962.0	E980.4
Cotarnine	964.5	E858.2	E934.5	E950.4	E962.0	E980.4
Cottonseed oil	976.3	E858.7	E946.3	E950.4	E962.0	E980.4
Cough mixtures (antitussives)	975.4	E858.6	E945.4	E950.4	E962.0	E980.4
containing opiates	965.09	E850.2	E935.2	E950.0	E962.0	E980.0
expectorants	975.5	E858.6	E945.5	E950.4	E962.0	E980.4
Coumadin	964.2	E858.2	E934.2	E950.4	E962.0	E980.4
rodenticide	989.4	E863.7	—	E950.6	E962.1	E980.7
Coumarin	964.2	E858.2	E934.2	E950.4	E962.0	E980.4
Coumetarol	964.2	E858.2	E934.2	E950.4	E962.0	E980.4
Cowbane	988.2	E865.4	—	E950.9	E962.1	E980.9
Cozyme	963.5	E858.1	E933.5	E950.4	E962.0	E980.4
Creolin	983.0	E864.0	—	E950.7	E962.1	E980.6
disinfectant	983.0	E861.4	—	E950.7	E962.1	E980.6
Creosol (compound)	983.0	E864.0	—	E950.7	E962.1	E980.6
Creosote (beechwood) (coal tar)	983.0	E864.0	—	E950.7	E962.1	E980.6
medicinal (expectorant)	975.5	E858.6	E945.5	E950.4	E962.0	E980.4
syrup	975.5	E858.6	E945.5	E950.4	E962.0	E980.4
Cresol	983.0	E864.0	—	E950.7	E962.1	E980.6
disinfectant	983.0	E861.4	—	E950.7	E962.1	E980.6
Cresylic acid	983.0	E864.0	—	E950.7	E962.1	E980.6
Cropropamide	965.7	E850.7	E935.7	E950.0	E962.0	E980.0
with crotethamide	970.0	E854.3	E940.0	E950.4	E962.0	E980.4
Crotamiton	976.0	E858.7	E946.0	E950.4	E962.0	E980.4
Crotethamide	965.7	E850.7	E935.7	E950.0	E962.0	E980.0
with cropropamide	970.0	E854.3	E940.0	E950.4	E962.0	E980.4
Croton (oil)	973.1	E858.4	E943.1	E950.4	E962.0	E980.4
chloral	967.1	E852.0	E937.1	E950.2	E962.0	E980.2
Crude oil	981	E862.1	—	E950.9	E962.1	E980.9
Cryogenine	965.8	E850.8	E935.8	E950.0	E962.0	E980.0
Cryolite (pesticide)	989.4	E863.4	—	E95.06	E962.1	E980.7
Cryptenamine	972.6	E858.3	E942.6	E950.4	E962.0	E980.4
Crystal violet	976.0	E858.7	E946.0	E950.4	E962.0	E980.4
Cuckoopint	988.2	E865.4	—	E950.9	E962.1	E980.9
Cumetharol	964.2	E858.2	E934.2	E950.4	E962.0	E980.4
Cupric sulfate	973.6	E858.4	E943.6	E950.4	E962.0	E980.4
Cuprous sulfate	983.9	E864.3	—	E950.7	E962.1	E980.6
Curare, curarine	975.2	E858.6	E945.2	E950.4	E962.0	E980.4
Cyanic acid — *see* Cyanide(s)						
Cyanide(s) (compounds) (hydrogen) (potassium) (sodium) NEC	989.0	E866.8	—	E950.9	E962.1	E980.9
dust or gas (inhalation) NEC	987.7	E869.8	—	E952.8	E962.2	E982.8
fumigant	989.0	E863.8	—	E950.6	E962.1	E980.7
mercuric — *see* Mercury						
pesticide (dust) (fumes)	989.0	E863.4	—	E950.6	E962.1	E980.7
Cyanocobalamin	964.1	E858.2	E934.1	E950.4	E962.0	E980.4
Cyanogen (chloride) (gas) NEC	987.8	E869.8	—	E952.8	E962.2	E982.8
Cyclaine	968.5	E855.2	E938.5	E950.4	E962.0	E980.4
Cyclamen europaeum	988.2	E865.4	—	E950.9	E962.1	E980.9
Cyclandelate	972.5	E858.3	E942.5	E950.4	E962.0	E980.4
Cyclazocine	965.09	E850.2	E935.2	E950.0	E962.0	E980.0
Cyclizine	963.0	E858.1	E933.0	E950.4	E962.0	E980.4
Cyclobarbital, cyclobarbitone	967.0	E851	E937.0	E950.1	E962.0	E980.1
Cycloguanil	961.4	E857	E931.4	E950.4	E962.0	E980.4
Cyclohexane	982.0	E862.4	—	E950.9	E962.1	E980.9
Cyclohexanol	980.8	E860.8	—	E950.9	E962.1	E980.9
Cyclohexanone	982.8	E862.4	—	E950.9	E962.1	E980.9
Cyclomethycaine	968.5	E855.2	E938.5	E950.4	E962.0	E980.4
Cyclopentamine	971.2	E855.5	E941.2	E950.4	E962.0	E980.4
Cyclopenthiazide	974.3	E858.5	E944.3	E950.4	E962.0	E980.4
Cyclopentolate	971.1	E855.4	E941.1	E950.4	E962.0	E980.4
Cyclophosphamide	963.1	E858.1	E933.1	E950.4	E962.0	E980.4
Cyclopropane	968.2	E855.1	E938.2	E950.4	E962.0	E980.4
Cycloserine	960.6	E856	E930.6	E950.4	E962.0	E980.4

Substance	Poisoning	External Cause (E-Code) Accident	Therapeutic Use	Suicide Attempt	Assault	Undetermined
Cyclothiazide	974.3	E858.5	E944.3	E950.4	E962.0	E980.4
Cycrimine	966.4	E855.0	E936.4	E950.4	E962.0	E980.4
Cymarin	972.1	E858.3	E942.1	E950.4	E962.0	E980.4
Cyproheptadine	963.0	E858.1	E933.0	E950.4	E962.0	E980.4
Cyprolidol	969.0	E854.0	E939.0	E950.3	E962.0	E980.3
Cytarabine	963.1	E858.1	E933.1	E950.4	E962.0	E980.4
Cytisus						
laburnum	988.2	E865.4	—	E950.9	E962.1	E980.9
scoparius	988.2	E865.4	—	E950.9	E962.1	E980.9
Cytomel	962.7	E858.0	E932.7	E950.4	E962.0	E980.4
Cytosine (antineoplastic)	963.1	E858.1	E933.1	E950.4	E962.0	E980.4
Cytoxan	963.1	E858.1	E933.1	E950.4	E962.0	E980.4
D						
Dacarbazine	963.1	E858.1	E933.1	E950.4	E962.0	E980.4
Dactinomycin	960.7	E856	E930.7	E950.4	E962.0	E980.4
DADPS	961.8	E857	E931.8	E950.4	E962.0	E980.4
Dakin's solution (external)	976.0	E858.7	E946.0	E950.4	E962.0	E980.4
Dalmane	969.4	E853.2	E939.4	E950.3	E962.0	E980.3
DAM	977.2	E858.8	E947.2	E950.4	E962.0	E980.4
Danilone	964.2	E858.2	E934.2	E950.4	E962.0	E980.4
Danthron	973.1	E858.4	E943.1	E950.4	E962.0	E980.4
Dantrolene	975.2	E858.6	E945.2	E950.4	E962.0	E980.4
Daphne (gnidium) (mezereum)	988.2	E865.4	—	E950.9	E962.1	E980.9
berry	988.2	E865.3	—	E950.9	E962.1	E980.9
Dapsone	961.8	E857	E931.8	E950.4	E962.0	E980.4
Daraprim	961.4	E857	E931.4	E950.4	E962.0	E980.4
Darnel	988.2	E865.3	—	E950.9	E962.1	E980.9
Darvon	965.8	E850.8	E935.8	E950.0	E962.0	E980.0
Daunorubicin	960.7	E856	E930.7	E950.4	E962.0	E980.4
DBI	962.3	E858.0	E932.3	E950.4	E962.0	E980.4
D-Con (rodenticide)	989.4	E863.7	—	E950.6	E962.1	E980.7
DDS	961.8	E857	E931.8	E950.4	E962.0	E980.4
DDT	989.2	E863.0	—	E950.6	E962.1	E980.7
Deadly nightshade	988.2	E865.4	—	E950.9	E962.1	E980.9
berry	988.2	E865.3	—	E950.9	E962.1	E980.9
Deanol	969.7	E854.2	E939.7	E950.3	E962.0	E980.3
Debrisoquine	972.6	E858.3	E942.6	E950.4	E962.0	E980.4
Decaborane	989.89	E866.8	—	E950.9	E962.1	E980.9
fumes	987.8	E869.8	—	E952.8	E962.2	E982.8
Decadron	962.0	E858.0	E932.0	E950.4	E962.0	E980.4
ENT agent	976.6	E858.7	E946.6	E950.4	E962.0	E980.4
ophthalmic preparation	976.5	E858.7	E946.5	E950.4	E962.0	E980.4
topical NEC	976.0	E858.7	E946.0	E950.4	E962.0	E980.4
Decahydronaphthalene	982.0	E862.4	—	E950.9	E962.1	E980.9
Decalin	982.0	E862.4	—	E950.9	E962.1	E980.9
Decamethonium	975.2	E858.6	E945.2	E950.4	E962.0	E980.4
Decholin	973.4	E858.4	E943.4	E950.4	E962.0	E980.4
sodium (diagnostic)	977.8	E858.8	E947.8	E950.4	E962.0	E980.4
Declomycin	960.4	E856	E930.4	E950.4	E962.0	E980.4
Deferoxamine	963.8	E858.1	E933.8	E950.4	E962.0	E980.4
Dehydrocholic acid	973.4	E858.4	E943.4	E950.4	E962.0	E980.4
DeKalin	982.0	E862.4	—	E950.9	E962.1	E980.9
Delalutin	962.2	E858.0	E932.2	E950.4	E962.0	E980.4
Delphinium	988.2	E865.3	—	E950.9	E962.1	E980.9
Deltasone	962.0	E858.0	E932.0	E950.4	E962.0	E980.4
Deltra	962.0	E858.0	E932.0	E950.4	E962.0	E980.4
Delvinal	967.0	E851	E937.0	E950.1	E962.0	E980.1
Demecarium (bromide)	971.0	E855.3	E941.0	E950.4	E962.0	E980.4
Demeclocycline	960.4	E856	E930.4	E950.4	E962.0	E980.4
Demecolcine	963.1	E858.1	E933.1	E950.4	E962.0	E980.4
Demelanizing agents	976.8	E858.7	E946.8	E950.4	E962.0	E980.4
Demerol	965.09	E850.2	E935.2	E950.0	E962.0	E980.0
Demethylchlortetracycline	960.4	E856	E930.4	E950.4	E962.0	E980.4
Demethyltetracycline	960.4	E856	E930.4	E950.4	E962.0	E980.4
Demeton	989.3	E863.1	—	E950.6	E962.1	E980.7
Demulcents	976.3	E858.7	E946.3	E950.4	E962.0	E980.4
Demulen	962.2	E858.0	E932.2	E950.4	E962.0	E980.4
Denatured alcohol	980.0	E860.1	—	E950.9	E962.1	E980.9
Dendrid	976.5	E858.7	E946.5	E950.4	E962.0	E980.4
Dental agents, topical	976.7	E858.7	E946.7	E950.4	E962.0	E980.4
Deodorant spray (feminine hygiene)	976.8	E858.7	E946.8	E950.4	E962.0	E980.4

Substance	Poisoning	External Cause (E-Code) Accident	Therapeutic Use	Suicide Attempt	Assault	Un-determined
Deoxyribonuclease	963.4	E858.1	E933.4	E950.4	E962.0	E980.4
Depressants						
appetite, central	977.0	E858.8	E947.0	E950.4	E962.0	E980.4
cardiac	972.0	E858.3	E942.0	E950.4	E962.0	E980.4
central nervous system (anesthetic)	968.4	E855.1	E938.4	E950.4	E962.0	E980.4
psychotherapeutic	969.5	E853.9	E939.5	E950.3	E962.0	E980.3
Dequalinium	976.0	E858.7	E946.0	E950.4	E962.0	E980.4
Dermolate	976.2	E858.7	E946.2	E950.4	E962.0	E980.4
DES	962.2	E858.0	E932.2	E950.4	E962.0	E980.4
Desenex	976.0	E858.7	E946.0	E950.4	E962.0	E980.4
Deserpidine	972.6	E858.3	E942.6	E950.4	E962.0	E980.4
Desipramine	969.0	E854.0	E939.0	E950.3	E962.0	E980.3
Deslanoside	972.1	E858.3	E942.1	E950.4	E962.0	E980.4
Desocodeine	965.09	E850.2	E935.2	E950.0	E962.0	E980.0
Desomorphine	965.09	E850.2	E935.2	E950.0	E962.0	E980.0
Desonide	976.0	E858.7	E946.0	E950.4	E962.0	E980.4
Desoxycorticosterone derivatives	962.0	E858.0	E932.0	E950.4	E962.0	E980.4
Desoxyephedrine	969.7	E854.2	E939.7	E950.3	E962.0	E980.3
DET	969.6	E854.1	E939.6	E950.3	E962.0	E980.3
Detergents (ingested) (synthetic)	989.6	E861.0	—	E950.9	E962.1	E980.9
external medication	976.2	E858.7	E946.2	E950.4	E962.0	E980.4
Deterrent, alcohol	977.3	E858.8	E947.3	E950.4	E962.0	E980.4
Detrothyronine	962.7	E858.0	E932.7	E950.4	E962.0	E980.4
Dettol (external medication)	976.0	E858.7	E946.0	E950.4	E962.0	E980.4
Dexamethasone	962.0	E858.0	E932.0	E950.4	E962.0	E980.4
ENT agent	976.6	E858.7	E946.6	E950.4	E962.0	E980.4
ophthalmic preparation	976.5	E858.7	E946.5	E950.4	E962.0	E980.4
topical NEC	976.0	E858.7	E946.0	E950.4	E962.0	E980.4
Dexamphetamine	969.7	E854.2	E939.7	E950.3	E962.0	E980.3
Dexedrine	969.7	E854.2	E939.7	E950.3	E962.0	E980.3
Dexpanthenol	963.5	E858.1	E933.5	E950.4	E962.0	E980.4
Dextran	964.8	E858.2	E934.8	E950.4	E962.0	E980.4
Dextriferron	964.0	E858.2	E934.0	E950.4	E962.0	E980.4
Dextroamphetamine	969.7	E854.2	E939.7	E950.3	E962.0	E980.3
Dextro calcium pantothenate	963.5	E858.1	E933.5	E950.4	E962.0	E980.4
Dextromethorphan	975.4	E858.6	E945.4	E950.4	E962.0	E980.4
Dextromoramide	965.09	E850.2	E935.2	E950.0	E962.0	E980.0
Dextro pantothenyl alcohol	963.5	E858.1	E933.5	E950.4	E962.0	E980.4
topical	976.8	E858.7	E946.8	E950.4	E962.0	E980.4
Dextropropoxyphene (hydrochloride)	965.8	E850.8	E935.8	E950.0	E962.0	E980.0
Dextrorphan	965.09	E850.2	E935.2	E950.0	E962.0	E980.0
Dextrose NEC	974.5	E858.5	E944.5	E950.4	E962.0	E980.4
Dextrothyroxin	962.7	E858.0	E932.7	E950.4	E962.0	E980.4
DFP	971.0	E855.3	E941.0	E950.4	E962.0	E980.4
DHE-45	972.9	E858.3	E942.9	E950.4	E962.0	E980.4
Diabinese	962.3	E858.0	E932.3	E950.4	E962.0	E980.4
Diacetyl monoxime	977.2	E858.8	E947.2	E950.4	E962.0	E980.4
Diacetylmorphine	965.01	E850.0	E935.0	E950.0	E962.0	E980.0
Diagnostic agents	977.8	E858.8	E947.8	E950.4	E962.0	E980.4
Dial (soap)	976.2	E858.7	E946.2	E950.4	E962.0	E980.4
sedative	967.0	E851	E937.0	E950.1	E962.0	E980.1
Diallylbarbituric acid	967.0	E851	E937.0	E950.1	E962.0	E980.1
Diaminodiphenylsulfone	961.8	E857	E931.8	E950.4	E962.0	E980.4
Diamorphine	965.01	E850.0	E935.0	E950.0	E962.0	E980.0
Diamox	974.2	E858.5	E944.2	E950.4	E962.0	E980.4
Diamthazole	976.0	E858.7	E946.0	E950.4	E962.0	E980.4
Diaphenylsulfone	961.8	E857	E931.8	E950.4	E962.0	E980.4
Diasone (sodium)	961.8	E857	E931.8	E950.4	E962.0	E980.4
Diazepam	969.4	E853.2	E939.4	E950.3	E962.0	E980.3
Diazinon	989.3	E863.1	—	E950.6	E962.1	E980.7
Diazomethane (gas)	987.8	E869.8	—	E952.8	E962.2	E982.8
Diazoxide	972.5	E858.3	E942.5	E950.4	E962.0	E980.4
Dibenamine	971.3	E855.6	E941.3	E950.4	E962.0	E980.4
Dibenzheptropine	963.0	E858.1	E933.0	E950.4	E962.0	E980.4
Dibenzyline	971.3	E855.6	E941.3	E950.4	E962.0	E980.4
Diborane (gas)	987.8	E869.8	—	E952.8	E962.2	E982.8
Dibromomannitol	963.1	E858.1	E933.1	E950.4	E962.0	E980.4
Dibucaine (spinal)	968.7	E855.2	E938.7	E950.4	E962.0	E980.4
topical (surface)	968.5	E855.2	E938.5	E950.4	E962.0	E980.4
Dibunate sodium	975.4	E858.6	E945.4	E950.4	E962.0	E980.4
Dibutoline	971.1	E855.4	E941.1	E950.4	E962.0	E980.4

Substance	Poisoning	External Cause (E-Code) Accident	Therapeutic Use	Suicide Attempt	Assault	Undetermined
Dicapthon	989.4	E863.4	—	E950.6	E962.1	E980.7
Dichloralphenazone	967.1	E852.0	E937.1	E950.2	E962.0	E980.2
Dichlorodifluoromethane	987.4	E869.2	—	E952.8	E962.2	E982.8
Dichloroethane	982.3	E862.4	—	E950.9	E962.1	E980.9
Dichloroethylene	982.3	E862.4	—	E950.9	E962.1	E980.9
Dichloroethyl sulfide	987.8	E869.8	—	E952.8	E962.2	E982.8
Dichlorohydrin	982.3	E862.4	—	E950.9	E962.1	E980.9
Dichloromethane (solvent) (vapor)	982.3	E862.4	—	E950.9	E962.1	E980.9
Dichlorophen(e)	961.6	E857	E931.6	E950.4	E962.0	E980.4
Dichlorphenamide	974.2	E858.5	E944.2	E950.4	E962.0	E980.4
Dichlorvos	989.3	E863.1	—	E950.6	E962.1	E980.7
Diclofenac sodium	965.69	E850.6	E935.6	E950.0	E962.0	E980.0
Dicoumarin, dicumarol	964.2	E858.2	E934.2	E950.4	E962.0	E980.4
Dicyanogen (gas)	987.8	E869.8	—	E952.8	E962.2	E982.8
Dicyclomine	971.1	E855.4	E941.1	E950.4	E962.0	E980.4
Dieldrin (vapor)	989.2	E863.0	—	E950.6	E962.1	E980.7
Dienestrol	962.2	E858.0	E932.2	E950.4	E962.0	E980.4
Dietetics	977.0	E858.8	E947.0	E950.4	E962.0	E980.4
Diethazine	966.4	E855.0	E936.4	E950.4	E962.0	E980.4
Diethyl						
barbituric acid	967.0	E851	E937.0	E950.1	E962.0	E980.1
carbamazine	961.6	E857	E931.6	E950.4	E962.0	E980.4
carbinol	980.8	E860.8	—	E950.9	E962.1	E980.9
carbonate	982.8	E862.4	—	E950.9	E962.1	E980.9
ether (vapor) — *see* Ether(s)						
propion	977.0	E858.8	E947.0	E950.4	E962.0	E980.4
stilbestrol	962.2	E858.0	E932.2	E950.4	E962.0	E980.4
Diethylene						
dioxide	982.8	E862.4	—	E950.9	E962.1	E980.9
glycol (monoacetate) (monoethyl ether)	982.8	E862.4	—	E950.9	E962.1	E980.9
Diethylsulfone-diethylmethane	967.8	E852.8	E937.8	E950.2	E962.0	E980.2
Difencloxazine	965.09	E850.2	E935.2	E950.0	E962.0	E980.0
Diffusin	963.4	E858.1	E933.4	E950.4	E962.0	E980.4
Diflos	971.0	E855.3	E941.0	E950.4	E962.0	E980.4
Digestants	973.4	E858.4	E943.4	E950.4	E962.0	E980.4
Digitalin(e)	972.1	E858.3	E942.1	E950.4	E962.0	E980.4
Digitalis glycosides	972.1	E858.3	E942.1	E950.4	E962.0	E980.4
Digitoxin	972.1	E858.3	E942.1	E950.4	E962.0	E980.4
Digoxin	972.1	E858.3	E942.1	E950.4	E962.0	E980.4
Dihydrocodeine	965.09	E850.2	E935.2	E950.0	E962.0	E980.0
Dihydrocodeinone	965.09	E850.2	E935.2	E950.0	E962.0	E980.0
Dihydroergocristine	972.9	E858.3	E942.9	E950.4	E962.0	E980.4
Dihydroergotamine	972.9	E858.3	E942.9	E950.4	E962.0	E980.4
Dihydroergotoxine	972.9	E858.3	E942.9	E950.4	E962.0	E980.4
Dihydrohydroxycodeinone	965.09	E850.2	E935.2	E950.0	E962.0	E980.0
Dihydrohydroxymorphinone	965.09	E850.2	E935.2	E950.0	E962.0	E980.0
Dihydroisocodeine	965.09	E850.2	E935.2	E950.0	E962.0	E980.0
Dihydromorphine	965.09	E850.2	E935.2	E950.0	E962.0	E980.0
Dihydromorphinone	965.09	E850.2	E935.2	E950.0	E962.0	E980.0
Dihydrostreptomycin	960.6	E856	E930.6	E950.4	E962.0	E980.4
Dihydrotachysterol	962.6	E858.0	E932.6	E950.4	E962.0	E980.4
Dihydroxyanthraquinone	973.1	E858.4	E943.1	E950.4	E962.0	E980.4
Dihydroxycodeinone	965.09	E850.2	E935.2	E950.0	E962.0	E980.0
Diiodohydroxyquin	961.3	E857	E931.3	E950.4	E962.0	E980.4
topical	976.0	E858.7	E946.0	E950.4	E962.0	E980.4
Diiodohydroxyquinoline	961.3	E857	E931.3	E950.4	E962.0	E980.4
Dilantin	966.1	E855.0	E936.1	E950.4	E962.0	E980.4
Dilaudid	965.09	E850.2	E935.2	E950.0	E962.0	E980.0
Diloxanide	961.5	E857	E931.5	E950.4	E962.0	E980.4
Dimefline	970.0	E854.3	E940.0	E950.4	E962.0	E980.4
Dimenhydrinate	963.0	E858.1	E933.0	E950.4	E962.0	E980.4
Dimercaprol	963.8	E858.1	E933.8	E950.4	E962.0	E980.4
Dimercaptopropanol	963.8	E858.1	E933.8	E950.4	E962.0	E980.4
Dimetane	963.0	E858.1	E933.0	E950.4	E962.0	E980.4
Dimethicone	976.3	E858.7	E946.3	E950.4	E962.0	E980.4
Dimethindene	963.0	E858.1	E933.0	E950.4	E962.0	E980.4
Dimethisoquin	968.5	E855.2	E938.5	E950.4	E962.0	E980.4
Dimethisterone	962.2	E858.0	E932.2	E950.4	E962.0	E980.4
Dimethoxanate	975.4	E858.6	E945.4	E950.4	E962.0	E980.4
Dimethyl						
arsine, arsinic acid — *see* Arsenic						

Substance	Poisoning	External Cause (E-Code)				
		Accident	Therapeutic Use	Suicide Attempt	Assault	Undetermined
Dimethyl — *continued*						
carbinol	980.2	E860.3	—	E950.9	E962.1	E980.9
diguanide	962.3	E858.0	E932.3	E950.4	E962.0	E980.4
ketone	982.8	E862.4	—	E950.9	E962.1	E980.9
vapor	987.8	E869.8	—	E952.8	E962.2	E982.8
meperidine	965.09	E850.2	E935.2	E950.0	E962.0	E980.0
parathion	989.3	E863.1	—	E950.6	E962.1	E980.7
polysiloxane	973.8	E858.4	E943.8	E950.4	E962.0	E980.4
sulfate (fumes)	987.8	E869.8	—	E952.8	E962.2	E982.8
liquid	983.9	E864.3	—	E950.7	E962.1	E980.6
sulfoxide NEC	982.8	E862.4	—	E950.9	E962.1	E980.9
medicinal	976.4	E858.7	E946.4	E950.4	E962.0	E980.4
triptamine	969.6	E854.1	E939.6	E950.3	E962.0	E980.3
tubocurarine	975.2	E858.6	E945.2	E950.4	E962.0	E980.4
Dindevan	964.2	E858.2	E934.2	E950.4	E962.0	E980.4
Dinitro (-ortho-) cresol (herbicide) (spray)	989.4	E863.5	—	E950.6	E962.1	E980.7
insecticide	989.4	E863.4	—	E950.6	E962.1	E980.7
Dinitrobenzene	983.0	E864.0	—	E950.7	E962.1	E980.6
vapor	987.8	E869.8	—	E952.8	E962.2	E982.8
Dinitro-orthocresol (herbicide)	989.4	E863.5	—	E950.6	E962.1	E980.7
insecticide	989.4	E863.4	—	E950.6	E962.1	E980.7
Dinitrophenol (herbicide) (spray)	989.4	E863.5	—	E950.6	E962.1	E980.7
insecticide	989.4	E863.4	—	E950.6	E962.1	E980.7
Dinoprost	975.0	E858.6	E945.0	E950.4	E962.0	E980.4
Dioctyl sulfosuccinate (calcium) (sodium)	973.2	E858.4	E943.2	E950.4	E962.0	E980.4
Diodoquin	961.3	E857	E931.3	E950.4	E962.0	E980.4
Dione derivatives NEC	966.3	E855.0	E936.3	E950.4	E962.0	E980.4
Dionin	965.09	E850.2	E935.2	E950.0	E962.0	E980.0
Dioxane	982.8	E862.4	—	E950.9	E962.1	E980.9
Dioxin — *see* herbicide						
Dioxyline	972.5	E858.3	E942.5	E950.4	E962.0	E980.4
Dipentene	982.8	E862.4	—	E950.9	E962.1	E980.9
Diphemanil	971.1	E855.4	E941.1	E950.4	E962.0	E980.4
Diphenadione	964.2	E858.2	E934.2	E950.4	E962.0	E980.4
Diphenhydramine	963.0	E858.1	E933.0	E950.4	E962.0	E980.4
Diphenidol	963.0	E858.1	E933.0	E950.4	E962.0	E980.4
Diphenoxylate	973.5	E858.4	E943.5	E950.4	E962.0	E980.4
Diphenylchloroarsine	985.1	E866.3	—	E950.8	E962.1	E980.8
Diphenylhydantoin (sodium)	966.1	E855.0	E936.1	E950.4	E962.0	E980.4
Diphenylpyraline	963.0	E858.1	E933.0	E950.4	E962.0	E980.4
Diphtheria						
antitoxin	979.9	E858.8	E949.9	E950.4	E962.0	E980.4
toxoid	978.5	E858.8	E948.5	E950.4	E962.0	E980.4
with tetanus toxoid	978.9	E858.8	E948.9	E950.4	E962.0	E980.4
with pertussis component	978.6	E858.8	E948.6	E950.4	E962.0	E980.4
vaccine	978.5	E858.8	E948.5	E950.4	E962.0	E980.4
Dipipanone	965.09	E850.2	E935.2	E950.0	E962.0	E980.0
Diplovax	979.5	E858.8	E949.5	E950.4	E962.0	E980.4
Diprophylline	975.1	E858.6	E945.1	E950.4	E962.0	E980.4
Dipyridamole	972.4	E858.3	E942.4	E950.4	E962.0	E980.4
Dipyrone	965.5	E850.5	E935.5	E950.0	E962.0	E980.0
Diquat	989.4	E863.5	—	E950.6	E962.1	E980.7
Disinfectant NEC	983.9	E861.4	—	E950.7	E962.1	E980.6
alkaline	983.2	E861.4	—	E950.7	E962.1	E980.6
aromatic	983.0	E861.4	—	E950.7	E962.1	E980.6
Disipal	966.4	E855.0	E936.4	E950.4	E962.0	E980.4
Disodium edetate	963.8	E858.1	E933.8	E950.4	E962.0	E980.4
Disulfamide	974.4	E858.5	E944.4	E950.4	E962.0	E980.4
Disulfanilamide	961.0	E857	E931.0	E950.4	E962.0	E980.4
Disulfiram	977.3	E858.8	E947.3	E950.4	E962.0	E980.4
Dithiazanine	961.6	E857	E931.6	E950.4	E962.0	E980.4
Dithioglycerol	963.8	E858.1	E933.8	E950.4	E962.0	E980.4
Dithranol	976.4	E858.7	E946.4	E950.4	E962.0	E980.4
Diucardin	974.3	E858.5	E944.3	E950.4	E962.0	E980.4
Diupres	974.3	E858.5	E944.3	E950.4	E962.0	E980.4
Diuretics NEC	974.4	E858.5	E944.4	E950.4	E962.0	E980.4
carbonic acid anhydrase inhibitors	974.2	E858.5	E944.2	E950.4	E962.0	E980.4
mercurial	974.0	E858.5	E944.0	E950.4	E962.0	E980.4
osmotic	974.4	E858.5	E944.4	E950.4	E962.0	E980.4
purine derivatives	974.1	E858.5	E944.1	E950.4	E962.0	E980.4
saluretic	974.3	E858.5	E944.3	E950.4	E962.0	E980.4
Diuril	974.3	E858.5	E944.3	E950.4	E962.0	E980.4
Divinyl ether	968.2	E855.1	E938.2	E950.4	E962.0	E980.4

Substance	Poisoning	External Cause (E-Code): Accident	Therapeutic Use	Suicide Attempt	Assault	Undetermined
D-lysergic acid diethylamide	969.6	E854.1	E939.6	E950.3	E962.0	E980.3
DMCT	960.4	E856	E930.4	E950.4	E962.0	E980.4
DMSO	982.8	E862.4	—	E950.9	E962.1	E980.9
DMT	969.6	E854.1	E939.6	E950.3	E962.0	E980.3
DNOC	989.4	E863.5	—	E950.6	E962.1	E980.7
DOCA	962.0	E858.0	E932.0	E950.4	E962.0	E980.4
Dolophine	965.02	E850.1	E935.1	E950.0	E962.0	E980.0
Doloxene	965.8	E850.8	E935.8	E950.0	E962.0	E980.0
DOM	969.6	E854.1	E939.6	E950.3	E962.0	E980.3
Domestic gas — *see* Gas, utility						
Domiphen (bromide) (lozenges)	976.6	E858.7	E946.6	E950.4	E962.0	E980.4
Dopa (levo)	966.4	E855.0	E936.4	E950.4	E962.0	E980.4
Dopamine	971.2	E855.5	E941.2	E950.4	E962.0	E980.4
Doriden	967.5	E852.4	E937.5	E950.2	E962.0	E980.2
Dormiral	967.0	E851	E937.0	E950.1	E962.0	E980.1
Dormison	967.8	E852.8	E937.8	E950.2	E962.0	E980.2
Dornase	963.4	E858.1	E933.4	E950.4	E962.0	E980.4
Dorsacaine	968.5	E855.2	E938.5	E950.4	E962.0	E980.4
Dothiepin hydrochloride	969.0	E854.0	E939.0	E950.3	E962.0	E980.3
Doxapram	970.0	E854.3	E940.0	E950.4	E962.0	E980.4
Doxepin	969.0	E854.0	E939.0	E950.3	E962.0	E980.3
Doxorubicin	960.7	E856	E930.7	E950.4	E962.0	E980.4
Doxycycline	960.4	E856	E930.4	E950.4	E962.0	E980.4
Doxylamine	963.0	E858.1	E933.0	E950.4	E962.0	E980.4
Dramamine	963.0	E858.1	E933.0	E950.4	E962.0	E980.4
Drano (drain cleaner)	983.2	E864.2	—	E950.7	E962.1	E980.6
Dromoran	965.09	E850.2	E935.2	E950.0	E962.0	E980.0
Dromostanolone	962.1	E858.0	E932.1	E950.4	E962.0	E980.4
Droperidol	969.2	E853.1	E939.2	E950.3	E962.0	E980.3
Drug	977.9	E858.9	E947.9	E950.5	E962.0	E980.5
specified NEC	977.8	E858.8	E947.8	E950.4	E962.0	E980.4
AHFS List						
4:00 antihistamine drugs	963.0	E858.1	E933.0	E950.4	E962.0	E980.4
8:04 amebacides	961.5	E857	E931.5	E950.4	E962.0	E980.4
arsenical anti-infectives	961.1	E857	E931.1	E950.4	E962.0	E980.4
quinoline derivatives	961.3	E857	E931.3	E950.4	E962.0	E980.4
8:08 anthelmintics	961.6	E857	E931.6	E950.4	E962.0	E980.4
quinoline derivatives	961.3	E857	E931.3	E950.4	E962.0	E980.4
8:12.04 antifungal antibiotics	960.1	E856	E930.1	E950.4	E962.0	E980.4
8:12.06 cephalosporins	960.5	E856	E930.5	E950.4	E962.0	E980.4
8:12.08 chloramphenicol	960.2	E856	E930.2	E950.4	E962.0	E980.4
8:12.12 erythromycins	960.3	E856	E930.3	E950.4	E962.0	E980.4
8:12.16 penicillins	960.0	E856	E930.0	E950.4	E962.0	E980.4
8:12.20 streptomycins	960.6	E856	E930.6	E950.4	E962.0	E980.4
8:12.24 tetracyclines	960.4	E856	E930.4	E950.4	E962.0	E980.4
8:12.28 other antibiotics	960.8	E856	E930.8	E950.4	E962.0	E980.4
antimycobacterial	960.6	E856	E930.6	E950.4	E962.0	E980.4
macrolides	960.3	E856	E930.3	E950.4	E962.0	E980.4
8:16 antituberculars	961.8	E857	E931.8	E950.4	E962.0	E980.4
antibiotics	960.6	E856	E930.6	E950.4	E962.0	E980.4
8:18 antivirals	961.7	E857	E931.7	E950.4	E962.0	E980.4
8:20 plasmodicides (antimalarials)	961.4	E857	E931.4	E950.4	E962.0	E980.4
8:24 sulfonamides	961.0	E857	E931.0	E950.4	E962.0	E980.4
8:26 sulfones	961.8	E857	E931.8	E950.4	E962.0	E980.4
8:28 treponemicides	961.2	E857	E931.2	E950.4	E962.0	E980.4
8:32 trichomonacides	961.5	E857	E931.5	E950.4	E962.0	E980.4
quinoline derivatives	961.3	E857	E931.3	E950.4	E962.0	E980.4
nitrofuran derivatives	961.9	E857	E931.9	E950.4	E962.0	E980.4
8:36 urinary germicides	961.9	E857	E931.9	E950.4	E962.0	E980.4
quinoline derivatives	961.3	E857	E931.3	E950.4	E962.0	E980.4
8:40 other anti-infectives	961.9	E857	E931.9	E950.4	E962.0	E980.4
10:00 antineoplastic agents	963.1	E858.1	E933.1	E950.4	E962.0	E980.4
antibiotics	960.7	E856	E930.7	E950.4	E962.0	E980.4
progestogens	962.2	E858.0	E932.2	E950.4	E962.0	E980.4
12:04 parasympathomimetic (cholinergic) agents	971.0	E855.3	E941.0	E950.4	E962.0	E980.4
12:08 parasympatholytic (cholinergic-blocking) agents	971.1	E855.4	E941.1	E950.4	E962.0	E980.4
12:12 Sympathomimetic (adrenergic) agents	971.2	E855.5	E941.2	E950.4	E962.0	E980.4
12:16 sympatholytic (adrenergic-blocking) agents	971.3	E855.6	E941.3	E950.4	E962.0	E980.4
12:20 skeletal muscle relaxants						
central nervous system muscle-tone depressants	968.0	E855.1	E938.0	E950.4	E962.0	E980.4
myoneural blocking agents	975.2	E858.6	E945.2	E950.4	E962.0	E980.4
16:00 blood derivatives	964.7	E858.2	E934.7	E950.4	E962.0	E980.4
20:04 antianemia drugs	964.1	E858.2	E934.1	E950.4	E962.0	E980.4

Substance	Poisoning	External Cause (E-Code)				
		Accident	Therapeutic Use	Suicide Attempt	Assault	Undetermined
Drug — *continued*						
20:04.04 iron preparations	964.0	E858.2	E934.0	E950.4	E962.0	E980.4
20:04.08 liver and stomach preparations	964.1	E858.2	E934.1	E950.4	E962.0	E980.4
20:12.04 anticoagulants	964.2	E858.2	E934.2	E950.4	E962.0	E980.4
20:12.08 antiheparin agents	964.5	E858.2	E934.5	E950.4	E962.0	E980.4
20:12.12 coagulants	964.5	E858.2	E934.5	E950.4	E962.0	E980.4
20:12.16 hemostatics NEC	964.5	E858.2	E934.5	E950.4	E962.0	E980.4
capillary active drugs	972.8	E858.3	E942.8	E950.4	E962.0	E980.4
24:04 cardiac drugs	972.9	E858.3	E942.9	E950.4	E962.0	E980.4
cardiotonic agents	972.1	E858.3	E942.1	E950.4	E962.0	E980.4
rhythm regulators	972.0	E858.3	E942.0	E950.4	E962.0	E980.4
24:06 antilipemic agents	972.2	E858.3	E942.2	E950.4	E962.0	E980.4
thyroid derivatives	962.7	E858.0	E932.7	E950.4	E962.0	E980.4
24:08 hypotensive agents	972.6	E858.3	E942.6	E950.4	E962.0	E980.4
adrenergic blocking agents	971.3	E855.6	E941.3	E950.4	E962.0	E980.4
ganglion blocking agents	972.3	E858.3	E942.3	E950.4	E962.0	E980.4
vasodilators	972.5	E858.3	E942.5	E950.4	E962.0	E980.4
24:12 vasodilating agents NEC	972.5	E858.3	E942.5	E950.4	E962.0	E980.4
coronary	972.4	E858.3	E942.4	E950.4	E962.0	E980.4
nicotinic acid derivatives	972.2	E858.3	E942.2	E950.4	E962.0	E980.4
24:16 sclerosing agents	972.7	E858.3	E942.7	E950.4	E962.0	E980.4
28:04 general anesthetics	968.4	E855.1	E938.4	E950.4	E962.0	E980.4
gaseous anesthetics	968.2	E855.1	E938.2	E950.4	E962.0	E980.4
halothane	968.1	E855.1	E938.1	E950.4	E962.0	E980.4
intravenous anesthetics	968.3	E855.1	E938.3	E950.4	E962.0	E980.4
28:08 analgesics and antipyretics	965.9	E850.9	E935.9	E950.0	E962.0	E980.0
antirheumatics	965.69	E850.6	E935.6	E950.0	E962.0	E980.0
aromatic analgesics	965.4	E850.4	E935.4	E950.0	E962.0	E980.0
non-narcotic NEC	965.7	E850.7	E935.7	E950.0	E962.0	E980.0
opium alkaloids	965.00	E850.2	E935.2	E950.0	E962.0	E980.0
heroin	965.01	E850.0	E935.0	E950.0	E962.0	E980.0
methadone	965.02	E850.1	E935.1	E950.0	E962.0	E980.0
specified type NEC	965.09	E850.2	E935.2	E950.0	E962.0	E980.0
pyrazole derivatives	965.5	E850.5	E935.5	E950.0	E962.0	E980.0
salicylates	965.1	E850.3	E935.3	E950.0	E962.0	E980.0
specified NEC	965.8	E850.8	E935.8	E950.0	E962.0	E980.0
28:10 narcotic antagonists	970.1	E854.3	E940.1	E950.4	E962.0	E980.4
28:12 anticonvulsants	966.3	E855.0	E936.3	E950.4	E962.0	E980.4
barbiturates	967.0	E851	E937.0	E950.1	E962.0	E980.1
benzodiazepine-based tranquilizers	969.4	E853.2	E939.4	E950.3	E962.0	E980.3
bromides	967.3	E852.2	E937.3	E950.2	E962.0	E980.2
hydantoin derivatives	966.1	E855.0	E936.1	E950.4	E962.0	E980.4
oxazolidine (derivatives)	966.0	E855.0	E936.0	E950.4	E962.0	E980.4
succinimides	966.2	E855.0	E936.2	E950.4	E962.0	E980.4
28:16.04 antidepressants	969.0	E854.0	E939.0	E950.3	E962.0	E980.3
28:16.08 tranquilizers	969.5	E853.9	E939.5	E950.3	E962.0	E980.3
benzodiazepine-based	969.4	E853.2	E939.4	E950.3	E962.0	E980.3
butyrophenone-based	969.2	E853.1	E939.2	E950.3	E962.0	E980.3
major NEC	969.3	E853.8	E939.3	E950.3	E962.0	E980.3
phenothiazine-based	969.1	E853.0	E939.1	E950.3	E962.0	E980.3
28:16.12 other psychotherapeutic agents	969.8	E855.8	E939.8	E950.3	E962.0	E980.3
28:20 respiratory and cerebral stimulants	970.9	E854.3	E940.9	E950.4	E962.0	E980.4
analeptics	970.0	E854.3	E940.0	E950.4	E962.0	E980.4
anorexigenic agents	977.0	E858.8	E947.0	E950.4	E962.0	E980.4
psychostimulants	969.7	E854.2	E939.7	E950.3	E962.0	E980.3
specified NEC	970.8	E854.3	E940.8	E950.4	E962.0	E980.4
28:24 sedatives and hypnotics	967.9	E852.9	E937.9	E950.2	E962.0	E980.2
barbiturates	967.0	E851	E937.0	E950.1	E962.0	E980.1
benzodiazepine-based tranquilizers	969.4	E853.2	E939.4	E950.3	E962.0	E980.3
chloral hydrate (group)	967.1	E852.0	E937.1	E950.2	E962.0	E980.2
glutethamide group	967.5	E852.4	E937.5	E950.2	E962.0	E980.2
intravenous anesthetics	968.3	E855.1	E938.3	E950.4	E962.0	E980.4
methaqualone (compounds)	967.4	E852.3	E937.4	E950.2	E962.0	E980.2
paraldehyde	967.2	E852.1	E937.2	E950.2	E962.0	E980.2
phenothiazine-based tranquilizers	969.1	E853.0	E939.1	E950.3	E962.0	E980.3
specified NEC	967.8	E852.8	E937.8	E950.2	E962.0	E980.2
thiobarbiturates	968.3	E855.1	E938.3	E950.4	E962.0	E980.4
tranquilizer NEC	969.5	E853.9	E939.5	E950.3	E962.0	E980.3
36:04 to 36:88 diagnostic agents	977.8	E858.8	E947.8	E950.4	E962.0	E980.4
40:00 electrolyte, caloric, and water balance agents NEC	974.5	E858.5	E944.5	E950.4	E962.0	E980.4
40:04 acidifying agents	963.2	E858.1	E933.2	E950.4	E962.0	E980.4
40:08 alkalinizing agents	963.3	E858.1	E933.3	E950.4	E962.0	E980.4
40:10 ammonia detoxicants	974.5	E858.5	E944.5	E950.4	E962.0	E980.4
40:12 replacement solutions	974.5	E858.5	E944.5	E950.4	E962.0	E980.4
plasma expanders	964.8	E858.2	E934.8	E950.4	E962.0	E980.4

Substance	Poisoning	Accident	Therapeutic Use	Suicide Attempt	Assault	Undetermined
		External Cause (E-Code)				
Drug — *continued*						
40:16 sodium-removing resins	974.5	E858.5	E944.5	E950.4	E962.0	E980.4
40:18 potassium-removing resins	974.5	E858.5	E944.5	E950.4	E962.0	E980.4
40:20 caloric agents	974.5	E858.5	E944.5	E950.4	E962.0	E980.4
40:24 salt and sugar substitutes	974.5	E858.5	E944.5	E950.4	E962.0	E980.4
40:28 diuretics NEC	974.4	E858.5	E944.4	E950.4	E962.0	E980.4
carbonic acid anhydrase inhibitors	974.2	E858.5	E944.2	E950.4	E962.0	E980.4
mercurials	974.0	E858.5	E944.0	E950.4	E962.0	E980.4
purine derivatives	974.1	E858.5	E944.1	E950.4	E962.0	E980.4
saluretics	974.3	E858.5	E944.3	E950.4	E962.0	E980.4
thiazides	974.3	E858.5	E944.3	E950.4	E962.1	E980.4
40:36 irrigating solutions	974.5	E858.5	E944.5	E950.4	E962.0	E980.4
40:40 uricosuric agents	974.7	E858.5	E944.7	E950.4	E962.0	E980.4
44:00 enzymes	963.4	E858.1	E933.4	E950.4	E962.0	E980.4
fibrinolysis-affecting agents	964.4	E858.2	E934.4	E950.4	E962.0	E980.4
gastric agents	973.4	E858.4	E943.4	E950.4	E962.0	E980.4
48:00 expectorants and cough preparations						
antihistamine agents	963.0	E858.1	E933.0	E950.4	E962.0	E980.4
antitussives	975.4	E858.6	E945.4	E950.4	E962.0	E980.4
codeine derivatives	965.09	E850.2	E935.2	E950.0	E962.0	E980.0
expectorants	975.5	E858.6	E945.5	E950.4	E962.0	E980.4
narcotic agents NEC	965.09	E850.2	E935.2	E950.0	E962.0	E980.0
52:04 anti-infectives (EENT)						
ENT agent	976.6	E858.7	E946.6	E950.4	E962.0	E980.4
ophthalmic preparation	976.5	E858.7	E946.5	E950.4	E962.0	E980.4
52:04.04 antibiotics (EENT)						
ENT agent	976.6	E858.7	E946.6	E950.4	E962.0	E980.4
ophthalmic preparation	976.5	E858.7	E946.5	E950.4	E962.0	E980.4
52:04.06 antivirals (EENT)						
ENT agent	976.6	E858.7	E946.6	E950.4	E962.0	E980.4
ophthalmic preparation	976.5	E858.7	E946.5	E950.4	E962.0	E980.4
52:04.08 sulfonamides (EENT)						
ENT agent	976.6	E858.7	E946.6	E950.4	E962.0	E980.4
ophthalmic preparation	976.5	E858.7	E946.5	E950.4	E962.0	E980.4
52:04.12 miscellaneous anti-infectives (EENT)						
ENT agent	976.6	E858.7	E946.6	E950.4	E962.0	E980.4
ophthalmic preparation	976.5	E858.7	E946.5	E950.4	E962.0	E980.4
52:08 anti-inflammatory agents (EENT)						
ENT agent	976.6	E858.7	E946.6	E950.4	E962.0	E980.4
ophthalmic preparation	976.5	E858.7	E946.5	E950.4	E962.0	E980.4
52:10 carbonic anhydrase inhibitors	974.2	E858.5	E944.2	E950.4	E962.0	E980.4
52:12 contact lens solutions	976.5	E858.7	E946.5	E950.4	E962.0	E980.4
52:16 local anesthetics (EENT)	968.5	E855.2	E938.5	E950.4	E962.0	E980.4
52:20 miotics	971.0	E855.3	E941.0	E950.4	E962.0	E980.4
52:24 mydriatics						
adrenergics	971.2	E855.5	E941.2	E950.4	E962.0	E980.4
anticholinergics	971.1	E855.4	E941.1	E950.4	E962.0	E980.4
antimuscarinics	971.1	E855.4	E941.1	E950.4	E962.0	E980.4
parasympatholytics	971.1	E855.4	E941.1	E950.4	E962.0	E980.4
spasmolytics	971.1	E855.4	E941.1	E950.4	E962.0	E980.4
sympathomimetics	971.2	E855.5	E941.2	E950.4	E962.0	E980.4
52:28 mouth washes and gargles	976.6	E858.7	E946.6	E950.4	E962.0	E980.4
52:32 vasoconstrictors (EENT)	971.2	E855.5	E941.2	E950.4	E962.0	E980.4
52:36 unclassified agents (EENT)						
ENT agent	976.6	E858.7	E946.6	E950.4	E962.0	E980.4
ophthalmic preparation	976.5	E858.7	E946.5	E950.4	E962.0	E980.4
56:04 antacids and adsorbents	973.0	E858.4	E943.0	E950.4	E962.0	E980.4
56:08 Antidiarrhea agents	973.5	E858.4	E943.5	E950.4	E962.0	E980.4
56:10 antiflatulents	973.8	E858.4	E943.8	E950.4	E962.0	E980.4
56:12 cathartics NEC	973.3	E858.4	E943.3	E950.4	E962.0	E980.4
emollients	973.2	E858.4	E943.2	E950.4	E962.0	E980.4
irritants	973.1	E858.4	E943.1	E950.4	E962.0	E980.4
56:16 digestants	973.4	E858.4	E943.4	E950.4	E962.0	E980.4
56:20 emetics and antiemetics						
antiemetics	963.0	E858.1	E933.0	E950.4	E962.0	E980.4
emetics	973.6	E858.4	E943.6	E950.4	E962.0	E980.4
56:24 lipotropic agents	977.1	E858.8	E947.1	E950.4	E962.0	E980.4
56:40 miscellaneous G.I. drugs	973.8	E858.4	E943.8	E950.4	E962.0	E980.4
60:00 gold compounds	965.69	E850.6	E935.6	E950.0	E962.0	E980.0
64:00 heavy metal antagonists	963.8	E858.1	E933.8	E950.4	E962.0	E980.4
68:04 adrenals	962.0	E858.0	E932.0	E950.4	E962.0	E980.4
68:08 adrogens	962.1	E858.0	E932.1	E950.4	E962.0	E980.4
68:12 contraceptives, oral	962.2	E858.0	E932.2	E950.4	E962.0	E980.4
68:16 estrogens	962.2	E858.0	E932.2	E950.4	E962.0	E980.4
68:18 gonadotropins	962.4	E858.0	E932.4	E950.4	E962.0	E980.4

Substance	Poisoning	External Cause (E-Code) Accident	Therapeutic Use	Suicide Attempt	Assault	Undetermined
Drug — *continued*						
68:20 insulins and antidiabetic agents	962.3	E858.0	E932.3	E950.4	E962.0	E980.4
68:20.08 insulins	962.3	E858.0	E932.3	E950.4	E962.0	E980.4
68:24 parathyroid	962.6	E858.0	E932.6	E950.4	E962.0	E980.4
68:28 pituitary (posterior)	962.5	E858.0	E932.5	E950.4	E962.0	E980.4
anterior	962.4	E858.0	E932.4	E950.4	E962.0	E980.4
68:32 progestogens	962.2	E858.0	E932.2	E950.4	E962.0	E980.4
68:34 other corpus luteum hormones NEC	962.2	E858.0	E932.2	E950.4	E962.0	E980.4
68:36 thyroid and antithyroid						
antithyroid	962.8	E858.0	E932.8	E950.4	E962.0	E980.4
thyroid (derivatives)	962.7	E858.0	E932.7	E950.4	E962.0	E980.4
72:00 local anesthetics NEC	968.9	E855.2	E938.9	E950.4	E962.0	E980.4
topical (surface)	968.5	E855.2	E938.5	E950.4	E962.0	E980.4
infiltration (intradermal) (subcutaneous) (submucosal)	968.5	E855.2	E938.5	E950.4	E962.0	E980.4
nerve blocking (peripheral) (plexus) (regional)	968.6	E855.2	E938.6	E950.4	E962.0	E980.4
spinal	968.7	E855.2	E938.7	E950.4	E962.0	E980.4
76:00 oxytocics	975.0	E858.6	E945.0	E950.4	E962.0	E980.4
78:00 radioactive agents	990	—	—	—	—	—
80:04 serums NEC	979.9	E858.8	E949.9	E950.4	E962.0	E980.4
immune gamma globulin (human)	964.6	E858.2	E934.6	E950.4	E962.0	E980.4
80:08 toxoids NEC	978.8	E858.8	E948.8	E950.4	E962.0	E980.4
diphtheria	978.5	E858.8	E948.5	E950.4	E962.0	E980.4
and tetanus	978.9	E858.8	E948.9	E950.4	E962.0	E980.4
with pertussis component	978.6	E858.8	E948.6	E950.4	E962.0	E980.4
tetanus	978.4	E858.8	E948.4	E950.4	E962.0	E980.4
and diphtheria	978.9	E858.8	E948.9	E950.4	E962.0	E980.4
with pertussis component	978.6	E858.8	E948.6	E950.4	E962.0	E980.4
80:12 vaccines	979.9	E858.8	E949.9	E950.4	E962.0	E980.4
bacterial NEC	978.8	E858.8	E948.8	E950.4	E962.0	E980.4
with						
other bacterial components	978.9	E858.8	E948.9	E950.4	E962.0	E980.4
pertussis component	978.6	E858.8	E948.6	E950.4	E962.0	E980.4
viral and rickettsial components	979.7	E858.8	E949.7	E950.4	E962.0	E980.4
rickettsial NEC	979.6	E858.8	E949.6	E950.4	E962.0	E980.4
with						
bacterial component	979.7	E858.8	E949.7	E950.4	E962.0	E980.4
pertussis component	978.6	E858.8	E948.6	E950.4	E962.0	E980.4
viral component	979.7	E858.8	E949.7	E950.4	E962.0	E980.4
viral NEC	979.6	E858.8	E949.6	E950.4	E962.0	E980.4
with						
bacterial component	979.7	E858.8	E949.7	E950.4	E962.0	E980.4
pertussis component	978.6	E858.8	E948.6	E950.4	E962.0	E980.4
rickettsial component	979.7	E858.8	E949.7	E950.4	E962.0	E980.4
84:04.04 antibiotics (skin and mucous membrane)	976.0	E858.7	E946.0	E950.4	E962.0	E980.4
84:04.08 fungicides (skin and mucous membrane)	976.0	E858.7	E946.0	E950.4	E962.0	E980.4
84:04.12 scabicides and pediculicides (skin and mucous membrane)	976.0	E858.7	E946.0	E950.4	E962.0	E980.4
84:04.16 miscellaneous local anti-infectives (skin and mucous membrane)	976.0	E858.7	E946.0	E950.4	E962.0	E980.4
84:06 anti-inflammatory agents (skin and mucous membrane)	976.0	E858.7	E946.0	E950.4	E962.0	E980.4
84:08 antipruritics and local anesthetics						
antipruritics	976.1	E858.7	E946.1	E950.4	E962.0	E980.4
local anesthetics	968.5	E855.2	E938.5	E950.4	E962.0	E980.4
84:12 astringents	976.2	E858.7	E946.2	E950.4	E962.0	E980.4
84:16 cell stimulants and proliferants	976.8	E858.7	E946.8	E950.4	E962.0	E980.4
84:20 detergents	976.2	E858.7	E946.2	E950.4	E962.0	E980.4
84:24 emollients, demulcents, and protectants	976.3	E858.7	E946.3	E950.4	E962.0	E980.4
84:28 keratolytic agents	976.4	E858.7	E946.4	E950.4	E962.0	E980.4
84:32 keratoplastic agents	976.4	E858.7	E946.4	E950.4	E962.0	E980.4
84:36 miscellaneous agents (skin and mucous membrane)	976.8	E858.7	E946.8	E950.4	E962.0	E980.4
86:00 spasmolytic agents	975.1	E858.6	E945.1	E950.4	E962.0	E980.4
antiasthmatics	975.7	E858.6	E945.7	E950.4	E962.0	E980.4
papaverine	972.5	E858.3	E942.5	E950.4	E962.0	E980.4
theophylline	974.1	E858.5	E944.1	E950.4	E962.0	E980.4
88:04 vitamin A	963.5	E858.1	E933.5	E950.4	E962.0	E980.4
88:08 vitamin B complex	963.5	E858.1	E933.5	E950.4	E962.0	E980.4
hematopoietic vitamin	964.1	E858.2	E934.1	E950.4	E962.0	E980.4
nicotinic acid derivatives	972.2	E858.3	E942.2	E950.4	E962.0	E980.4
88:12 vitamin C	963.5	E858.1	E933.5	E950.4	E962.0	E980.4
88:16 vitamin D	963.5	E858.1	E933.5	E950.4	E962.0	E980.4
88:20 vitamin E	963.5	E858.1	E933.5	E950.4	E962.0	E980.4
88:24 vitamin K activity	964.3	E858.2	E934.3	E950.4	E962.0	E980.4
88:28 multivitamin preparations	963.5	E858.1	E933.5	E950.4	E962.0	E980.4
92:00 unclassified therapeutic agents	977.8	E858.8	E947.8	E950.4	E962.0	E980.4
Duboisine	971.1	E855.4	E941.1	E950.4	E962.0	E980.4
Dulcolax	973.1	E858.4	E943.1	E950.4	E962.0	E980.4

Substance	Poisoning	External Cause (E-Code) Accident	Therapeutic Use	Suicide Attempt	Assault	Un-determined
Duponol (C) (EP)	976.2	E858.7	E946.2	E950.4	E962.0	E980.4
Durabolin	962.1	E858.0	E932.1	E950.4	E962.0	E980.4
Dyclone	968.5	E855.2	E938.5	E950.4	E962.0	E980.4
Dyclonine	968.5	E855.2	E938.5	E950.4	E962.0	E980.4
Dydrogesterone	962.2	E858.0	E932.2	E950.4	E962.0	E980.4
Dyes NEC	989.89	E866.8	—	E950.9	E962.1	E980.9
diagnostic agents	977.8	E858.8	E947.8	E950.4	E962.0	E980.4
pharmaceutical NEC	977.4	E858.8	E947.4	E950.4	E962.0	E980.4
Dyfols	971.0	E855.3	E941.0	E950.4	E962.0	E980.4
Dymelor	962.3	E858.0	E932.3	E950.4	E962.0	E980.4
Dynamite	989.89	E866.8	—	E950.9	E962.1	E980.9
fumes	987.8	E869.8	—	E952.8	E962.2	E982.8
Dyphylline	975.1	E858.6	E945.1	E950.4	E962.0	E980.4
E						
Ear preparations	976.6	E858.7	E946.6	E950.4	E962.0	E980.4
Echothiopate, ecothiopate	971.0	E855.3	E941.0	E950.4	E962.0	E980.4
Ectylurea	967.8	E852.8	E937.8	E950.2	E962.0	E980.2
Edathamil disodium	963.8	E858.1	E933.8	E950.4	E962.0	E980.4
Edecrin	974.4	E858.5	E944.4	E950.4	E962.0	E980.4
Edetate, disodium (calcium)	963.8	E858.1	E933.8	E950.4	E962.0	E980.4
Edrophonium	971.0	E855.3	E941.0	E950.4	E962.0	E980.4
Elase	976.8	E858.7	E946.8	E950.4	E962.0	E980.4
Elaterium	973.1	E858.4	E943.1	E950.4	E962.0	E980.4
Elder	988.2	E865.4	—	E950.9	E962.1	E980.9
berry (unripe)	988.2	E865.3	—	E950.9	E962.1	E980.9
Electrolytes NEC	974.5	E858.5	E944.5	E950.4	E962.0	E980.4
Electrolytic agent NEC	974.5	E858.5	E944.5	E950.4	E962.0	E980.4
Embramine	963.0	E858.1	E933.0	E950.4	E962.0	E980.4
Emetics	973.6	E858.4	E943.6	E950.4	E962.0	E980.4
Emetine (hydrochloride)	961.5	E857	E931.5	E950.4	E962.0	E980.4
Emollients	976.3	E858.7	E946.3	E950.4	E962.0	E980.4
Emylcamate	969.5	E853.8	E939.5	E950.3	E962.0	E980.3
Encyprate	969.0	E854.0	E939.0	E950.3	E962.0	E980.3
Endocaine	968.5	E855.2	E938.5	E950.4	E962.0	E980.4
Endrin	989.2	E863.0	—	E950.6	E962.1	E980.7
Enflurane	968.2	E855.1	E938.2	E950.4	E962.0	E980.4
Enovid	962.2	E858.0	E932.2	E950.4	E962.0	E980.4
ENT preparations (anti-infectives)	976.6	E858.7	E946.6	E950.4	E962.0	E980.4
Enzodase	963.4	E858.1	E933.4	E950.4	E962.0	E980.4
Enzymes NEC	963.4	E858.1	E933.4	E950.4	E962.0	E980.4
Epanutin	966.1	E855.0	E936.1	E950.4	E962.0	E980.4
Ephedra (tincture)	971.2	E855.5	E941.2	E950.4	E962.0	E980.4
Ephedrine	971.2	E855.5	E941.2	E950.4	E962.0	E980.4
Epiestriol	962.2	E858.0	E932.2	E950.4	E962.0	E980.4
Epilim — *see* Sodium valproate						
Epinephrine	971.2	E855.5	E941.2	E950.4	E962.0	E980.4
Epsom salt	973.3	E858.4	E943.3	E950.4	E962.0	E980.4
Equanil	969.5	E853.8	E939.5	E950.3	E962.0	E980.3
Equisetum (diuretic)	974.4	E858.5	E944.4	E950.4	E962.0	E980.4
Ergometrine	975.0	E858.6	E945.0	E950.4	E962.0	E980.4
Ergonovine	975.0	E858.6	E945.0	E950.4	E962.0	E980.4
Ergot NEC	988.2	E865.4	—	E950.9	E962.1	E980.9
medicinal (alkaloids)	975.0	E858.6	E945.0	E950.4	E962.0	E980.4
Ergotamine (tartrate) (for migraine) NEC	972.9	E858.3	E942.9	E950.4	E962.0	E980.4
Ergotrate	975.0	E858.6	E945.0	E950.4	E962.0	E980.4
Erythrityl tetranitrate	972.4	E858.3	E942.4	E950.4	E962.0	E980.4
Erythrol tetranitrate	972.4	E858.3	E942.4	E950.4	E962.0	E980.4
Erythromycin	960.3	E856	E930.3	E950.4	E962.0	E980.4
ophthalmic preparation	976.5	E858.7	E946.5	E950.4	E962.0	E980.4
topical NEC	976.0	E858.7	E946.0	E950.4	E962.0	E980.4
Eserine	971.0	E855.3	E941.0	E950.4	E962.0	E980.4
Eskabarb	967.0	E851	E937.0	E950.1	E962.0	E980.1
Eskalith	969.8	E855.8	E939.8	E950.3	E962.0	E980.3
Estradiol (cypionate) (dipropionate) (valerate)	962.2	E858.0	E932.2	E950.4	E962.0	E980.4
Estriol	962.2	E858.0	E932.2	E950.4	E962.0	E980.4
Estrogens (with progestogens)	962.2	E858.0	E932.2	E950.4	E962.0	E980.4
Estrone	962.2	E858.0	E932.2	E950.4	E962.0	E980.4
Etafedrine	971.2	E855.5	E941.2	E950.4	E962.0	E980.4
Ethacrynate sodium	974.4	E858.5	E944.4	E950.4	E962.0	E980.4
Ethacrynic acid	974.4	E858.5	E944.4	E950.4	E962.0	E980.4
Ethambutol	961.8	E857	E931.8	E950.4	E962.0	E980.4

Substance	Poisoning	External Cause (E-Code) Accident	Therapeutic Use	Suicide Attempt	Assault	Undetermined
Ethamide	974.2	E858.5	E944.2	E950.4	E962.0	E980.4
Ethamivan	970.0	E854.3	E940.0	E950.4	E962.0	E980.4
Ethamsylate	964.5	E858.2	E934.5	E950.4	E962.0	E980.4
Ethanol	980.0	E860.1	—	E950.9	E962.1	E980.9
beverage	980.0	E860.0	—	E950.9	E962.1	E980.9
Ethchlorvynol	967.8	E852.8	E937.8	E950.2	E962.0	E980.2
Ethebenecid	974.7	E858.5	E944.7	E950.4	E962.0	E980.4
Ether(s) (diethyl) (ethyl) (vapor)	987.8	E869.8	—	E952.8	E962.2	E982.8
anesthetic	968.2	E855.1	E938.2	E950.4	E962.0	E980.4
petroleum — *see* Ligroin						
solvent	982.8	E862.4	—	E950.9	E962.1	E980.9
Ethidine chloride (vapor)	987.8	E869.8	—	E952.8	E962.2	E982.8
liquid (solvent)	982.3	E862.4	—	E950.9	E962.1	E980.9
Ethinamate	967.8	E852.8	E937.8	E950.2	E962.0	E980.2
Ethinylestradiol	962.2	E858.0	E932.2	E950.4	E962.0	E980.4
Ethionamide	961.8	E857	E931.8	E950.4	E962.0	E980.4
Ethisterone	962.2	E858.0	E932.2	E950.4	E962.0	E980.4
Ethobral	967.0	E851	E937.0	E950.1	E962.0	E980.1
Ethocaine (infiltration) (topical)	968.5	E855.2	E938.5	E950.4	E962.0	E980.4
nerve block (peripheral) (plexus)	968.6	E855.2	E938.6	E950.4	E962.0	E980.4
spinal	968.7	E855.2	E938.7	E950.4	E962.0	E980.4
Ethoheptazine (citrate)	965.7	E850.7	E935.7	E950.0	E962.0	E980.0
Ethopropazine	966.4	E855.0	E936.4	E950.4	E962.0	E980.4
Ethosuximide	966.2	E855.0	E936.2	E950.4	E962.0	E980.4
Ethotoin	966.1	E855.0	E936.1	E950.4	E962.0	E980.4
Ethoxazene	961.9	E857	E931.9	E950.4	E962.0	E980.4
Ethoxzolamide	974.2	E858.5	E944.2	E950.4	E962.0	E980.4
Ethyl						
acetate (vapor)	982.8	E862.4	—	E950.9	E962.1	E980.9
alcohol	980.0	E860.1	—	E950.9	E962.1	E980.9
beverage	980.0	E860.0	—	E950.9	E962.1	E980.9
aldehyde (vapor)	987.8	E869.8	—	E952.8	E962.2	E982.8
liquid	989.89	E866.8	—	E950.9	E962.1	E980.9
aminobenzoate	968.5	E855.2	E938.5	E950.4	E962.0	E980.4
biscoumacetate	964.2	E858.2	E934.2	E950.4	E962.0	E980.4
bromide (anesthetic)	968.2	E855.1	E938.2	E950.4	E962.0	E980.4
carbamate (antineoplastic)	963.1	E858.1	E933.1	E950.4	E962.0	E980.4
carbinol	980.3	E860.4	—	E950.9	E962.1	E980.9
chaulmoograte	961.8	E857	E931.8	E950.4	E962.0	E980.4
chloride (vapor)	987.8	E869.8	—	E952.8	E962.2	E982.8
anesthetic (local)	968.5	E855.2	E938.5	E950.4	E962.0	E980.4
inhaled	968.2	E855.1	E938.2	E950.4	E962.0	E980.4
solvent	982.3	E862.4	—	E950.9	E962.1	E980.9
estranol	962.1	E858.0	E932.1	E950.4	E962.0	E980.4
ether — *see* Ether(s)						
formate (solvent) NEC	982.8	E862.4	—	E950.9	E962.1	E980.9
iodoacetate	987.5	E869.3	—	E952.8	E962.2	E982.8
lactate (solvent) NEC	982.8	E862.4	—	E950.9	E962.1	E980.9
methylcarbinol	980.8	E860.8	—	E950.9	E962.1	E980.9
morphine	965.09	E850.2	E935.2	E950.0	E962.0	E980.0
Ethylene (gas)	987.1	E869.8	—	E952.8	E962.2	E982.8
anesthetic (general)	968.2	E855.1	E938.2	E950.4	E962.0	E980.4
chlorohydrin (vapor)	982.3	E862.4	—	E950.9	E962.1	E980.9
dichloride (vapor)	982.3	E862.4	—	E950.9	E962.1	E980.9
glycol(s) (any) (vapor)	982.8	E862.4	—	E950.9	E962.1	E980.9
Ethylidene						
chloride NEC	982.3	E862.4	—	E950.9	E962.1	E980.9
diethyl ether	982.8	E862.4	—	E950.9	E962.1	E980.9
Ethynodiol	962.2	E858.0	E932.2	E950.4	E962.0	E980.4
Etidocaine	968.9	E855.2	E938.9	E950.4	E962.0	E980.4
infiltration (subcutaneous)	968.5	E855.2	E938.5	E950.4	E962.0	E980.4
nerve (peripheral) (plexus)	968.6	E855.2	E938.6	E950.4	E962.0	E980.4
Etilfen	967.0	E851	E937.0	E950.1	E962.0	E980.1
Etomide	965.7	E850.7	E935.7	E950.0	E962.0	E980.0
Etorphine	965.09	E850.2	E935.2	E950.0	E962.0	E980.0
Etoval	967.0	E851	E937.0	E950.1	E962.0	E980.1
Etryptamine	969.0	E854.0	E939.0	E950.3	E962.0	E980.3
Eucaine	968.5	E855.2	E938.5	E950.4	E962.0	E980.4
Eucalyptus (oil) NEC	975.5	E858.6	E945.5	E950.4	E962.0	E980.4
Eucatropine	971.1	E855.4	E941.1	E950.4	E962.0	E980.4
Eucodal	965.09	E850.2	E935.2	E950.0	E962.0	E980.0
Euneryl	967.0	E851	E937.0	E950.1	E962.0	E980.1
Euphthalmine	971.1	E855.4	E941.1	E950.4	E962.0	E980.4

		External Cause (E-Code)				
Substance	**Poisoning**	**Accident**	**Therapeutic Use**	**Suicide Attempt**	**Assault**	**Un-determined**
Eurax	976.0	E858.7	E946.0	E950.4	E962.0	E980.4
Euresol	976.4	E858.7	E946.4	E950.4	E962.0	E980.4
Euthroid	962.7	E858.0	E932.7	E950.4	E962.0	E980.4
Evans blue	977.8	E858.8	E947.8	E950.4	E962.0	E980.4
Evipal	967.0	E851	E937.0	E950.1	E962.0	E980.1
sodium	968.3	E855.1	E938.3	E950.4	E962.0	E980.4
Evipan	967.0	E851	E937.0	E950.1	E962.0	E980.1
sodium	968.3	E855.1	E938.3	E950.4	E962.0	E980.4
Exalgin	965.4	E850.4	E935.4	E950.0	E962.0	E980.0
Excipients, pharmaceutical	977.4	E858.8	E947.4	E950.4	E962.0	E980.4
Exhaust gas — *see* Carbon, monoxide						
Ex-Lax (phenolphthalein)	973.1	E858.4	E943.1	E950.4	E962.0	E980.4
Expectorants	975.5	E858.6	E945.5	E950.4	E962.0	E980.4
External medications (skin) (mucous membrane)	976.9	E858.7	E946.9	E950.4	E962.0	E980.4
dental agent	976.7	E858.7	E946.7	E950.4	E962.0	E980.4
ENT agent	976.6	E858.7	E946.6	E950.4	E962.0	E980.4
ophthalmic prepration	976.5	E858.7	E946.5	E950.4	E962.0	E980.4
specified NEC	976.8	E858.7	E946.8	E950.4	E962.0	E980.4
Eye agents (anti-infective)	976.5	E858.7	E946.5	E950.4	E962.0	E980.4
F						
Factor IX complex (human)	964.5	E858.2	E934.5	E950.4	E962.0	E980.4
Fecal softeners	973.2	E858.4	E943.2	E950.4	E962.0	E980.4
Fenbutrazate	977.0	E858.8	E947.0	E950.4	E962.0	E980.4
Fencamfamin	970.8	E854.3	E940.8	E950.4	E962.0	E980.4
Fenfluramine	977.0	E858.8	E947.0	E950.4	E962.0	E980.4
Fenoprofen	965.61	E850.6	E935.6	E950.0	E962.0	E980.0
Fentanyl	965.09	E850.2	E935.2	E950.0	E962.0	E980.0
Fentazin	969.1	E853.0	E939.1	E950.3	E962.0	E980.3
Fenticlor, fentichlor	976.0	E858.7	E946.0	E950.4	E962.0	E980.4
Fer de lance (bite) (venom)	989.5	E905.0	—	E950.9	E962.1	E980.9
Ferric — *see* Iron						
Ferrocholinate	964.0	E858.2	E934.0	E950.4	E962.0	E980.4
Ferrous fumerate, gluconate, lactate, salt NEC, sulfate (medicinal)	964.0	E858.2	E934.0	E950.4	E962.0	E980.4
Ferrum — *see* Iron						
Fertilizers NEC	989.89	E866.5	—	E950.9	E962.1	E980.4
with herbicide mixture	989.4	E863.5	—	E950.6	E962.1	E980.7
Fibrinogen (human)	964.7	E858.2	E934.7	E950.4	E962.0	E980.4
Fibrinolysin	964.4	E858.2	E934.4	E950.4	E962.0	E980.4
Fibrinolysis-affecting agents	964.4	E858.2	E934.4	E950.4	E962.0	E980.4
Filix mas	961.6	E857	E931.6	E950.4	E962.0	E980.4
Fiorinal	965.1	E850.3	E935.3	E950.0	E962.0	E980.0
Fire damp	987.1	E869.8	—	E952.8	E962.2	E982.8
Fish, nonbacterial or noxious	988.0	E865.2	—	E950.9	E962.1	E980.9
shell	988.0	E865.1	—	E950.9	E962.1	E980.9
Flagyl	961.5	E857	E931.5	E950.4	E962.0	E980.4
Flavoxate	975.1	E858.6	E945.1	E950.4	E962.0	E980.4
Flaxedil	975.2	E858.6	E945.2	E950.4	E962.0	E980.4
Flaxseed (medicinal)	976.3	E858.7	E946.3	E950.4	E962.0	E980.4
Florantyrone	973.4	E858.4	E943.4	E950.4	E962.0	E980.4
Floraquin	961.3	E857	E931.3	E950.4	E962.0	E980.4
Florinef	962.0	E858.0	E932.0	E950.4	E962.0	E980.4
ENT agent	976.6	E858.7	E946.6	E950.4	E962.0	E980.4
ophthalmic preparation	976.5	E858.7	E946.5	E950.4	E962.0	E980.4
topical NEC	976.0	E858.7	E946.0	E950.4	E962.0	E980.4
Flowers of sulfur	976.4	E858.7	E946.4	E950.4	E962.0	E980.4
Floxuridine	963.1	E858.1	E933.1	E950.4	E962.0	E980.4
Flucytosine	961.9	E857	E931.9	E950.4	E962.0	E980.4
Fludrocortisone	962.0	E858.0	E932.0	E950.4	E962.0	E980.4
ENT agent	976.6	E858.7	E946.6	E950.4	E962.0	E980.4
ophthalmic preparation	976.5	E858.7	E946.5	E950.4	E962.0	E980.4
topical NEC	976.0	E858.7	E946.0	E950.4	E962.0	E980.4
Flumethasone	976.0	E858.7	E946.0	E950.4	E962.0	E980.4
Flumethiazide	974.3	E858.5	E944.3	E950.4	E962.0	E980.4
Flumidin	961.7	E857	E931.7	E950.4	E962.0	E980.4
Fluocinolone	976.0	E858.7	E946.0	E950.4	E962.0	E980.4
Fluocortolone	962.0	E858.0	E932.0	E950.4	E962.0	E980.4
Fluohydrocortisone	962.0	E858.0	E932.0	E950.4	E962.0	E980.4
ENT agent	976.6	E858.7	E946.6	E950.4	E962.0	E980.4
ophthalmic preparation	976.5	E858.7	E946.5	E950.4	E962.0	E980.4
topical NEC	976.0	E858.7	E946.0	E950.4	E962.0	E980.4

Substance	Poisoning	External Cause (E-Code) Accident	Therapeutic Use	Suicide Attempt	Assault	Undetermined
Fluonid	976.0	E858.7	E946.0	E950.4	E962.0	E980.4
Fluopromazine	969.1	E853.0	E939.1	E950.3	E962.0	E980.3
Fluoracetate	989.4	E863.7	—	E950.6	E962.1	E980.7
Fluorescein (sodium)	977.8	E858.8	E947.8	E950.4	E962.0	E980.4
Fluoride(s) (pesticides) (sodium) NEC	989.4	E863.4	—	E950.6	E962.1	E980.7
hydrogen — *see* Hydrofluoric acid						
medicinal	976.7	E858.7	E946.7	E950.4	E962.0	E980.4
not pesticide NEC	983.9	E864.4	—	E950.7	E962.1	E980.6
stannous	976.7	E858.7	E946.7	E950.4	E962.0	E980.4
Fluorinated corticosteroids	962.0	E858.0	E932.0	E950.4	E962.0	E980.4
Fluorine (compounds) (gas)	987.8	E869.8	—	E952.8	E962.2	E982.8
salt — *see* Fluoride(s)						
Fluoristan	976.7	E858.7	E946.7	E950.4	E962.0	E980.4
Fluoroacetate	989.4	E863.7	—	E950.6	E962.1	E980.7
Fluorodeoxyuridine	963.1	E858.1	E933.1	E950.4	E962.0	E980.4
Fluorometholone (topical) NEC	976.0	E858.7	E946.0	E950.4	E962.0	E980.4
ophthalmic preparation	976.5	E858.7	E946.5	E950.4	E962.0	E980.4
Fluorouracil	963.1	E858.1	E933.1	E950.4	E962.0	E980.4
Fluothane	968.1	E855.1	E938.1	E950.4	E962.0	E980.4
Fluoxetine hydrochloride	969.0	E854.0	E939.0	E950.3	E962.0	E980.3
Fluoxymesterone	962.1	E858.0	E932.1	E950.4	E962.0	E980.4
Fluphenazine	969.1	E853.0	E939.1	E950.3	E962.0	E980.3
Fluprednisolone	962.0	E858.0	E932.0	E950.4	E962.0	E980.4
Flurandrenolide	976.0	E858.7	E946.0	E950.4	E962.0	E980.4
Flurazepam (hydrochloride)	969.4	E853.2	E939.4	E950.3	E962.0	E980.3
Flurbiprofen	965.61	E850.6	E935.6	E950.0	E962.0	E980.0
Flurobate	976.0	E858.7	E946.0	E950.4	E962.0	E980.4
Flurothyl	969.8	E855.8	E939.8	E950.3	E962.0	E980.3
Fluroxene	968.2	E855.1	E938.2	E950.4	E962.0	E980.4
Folacin	964.1	E858.2	E934.1	E950.4	E962.0	E980.4
Folic acid	964.1	E858.2	E934.1	E950.4	E962.0	E980.4
Follicle stimulating hormone	962.4	E858.0	E932.4	E950.4	E962.0	E980.4
Food, foodstuffs, nonbacterial or noxious	988.9	E865.9	—	E950.9	E962.1	E980.9
berries, seeds	988.2	E865.3	—	E950.9	E962.1	E980.9
fish	988.0	E865.2	—	E950.9	E962.1	E980.9
mushrooms	988.1	E865.5	—	E950.9	E962.1	E980.9
plants	988.2	E865.9	—	E950.9	E962.1	E980.9
specified type NEC	988.2	E865.4	—	E950.9	E962.1	E980.9
shellfish	988.0	E865.1	—	E950.9	E962.1	E980.9
specified NEC	988.8	E865.8	—	E950.9	E962.1	E980.9
Fool's parsley	988.2	E865.4	—	E950.9	E962.1	E980.9
Formaldehyde (solution)	989.89	E861.4	—	E950.9	E962.1	E980.9
fungicide	989.4	E863.6	—	E950.6	E962.1	E980.7
gas or vapor	987.8	E869.8	—	E952.8	E962.2	E982.8
Formalin	989.89	E861.4	—	E950.9	E962.1	E980.9
fungicide	989.4	E863.6	—	E950.6	E962.1	E980.7
vapor	987.8	E869.8	—	E952.8	E962.2	E982.8
Formic acid	983.1	E864.1	—	E950.7	E962.1	E980.6
vapor	987.8	E869.8	—	E952.8	E962.2	E982.8
Fowler's solution	985.1	E866.3	—	E950.8	E962.1	E980.8
Foxglove	988.2	E865.4	—	E950.9	E962.1	E980.9
Fox green	977.8	E858.8	E947.8	E950.4	E962.0	E980.4
Framycetin	960.8	E856	E930.8	E950.4	E962.0	E980.4
Frangula (extract)	973.1	E858.4	E943.1	E950.4	E962.0	E980.4
Frei antigen	977.8	E858.8	E947.8	E950.4	E962.0	E980.4
Freons	987.4	E869.2	—	E952.8	E962.2	E982.8
Fructose	974.5	E858.5	E944.5	E950.4	E962.0	E980.4
Frusemide	974.4	E858.5	E944.4	E950.4	E962.0	E980.4
FSH	962.4	E858.0	E932.4	E950.4	E962.0	E980.4
Fuel						
automobile	981	E862.1	—	E950.9	E962.1	E980.9
exhaust gas, not in transit	986	E868.2	—	E952.0	E962.2	E982.0
vapor NEC	987.1	E869.8	—	E952.8	E962.2	E982.8
gas (domestic use) — *see also* Carbon, monoxide, fuel utility	987.1	E868.1	—	E951.8	E962.2	E981.8
incomplete combustion of — *see* Carbon, monoxide, fuel, utility						
in mobile container	987.0	E868.0	—	E951.1	E962.2	E981.1
piped (natural)	987.1	E867	—	E951.0	E962.2	E981.0
industrial, incomplete combustion	986	E868.3	—	E952.1	E962.2	E982.1
Fugillin	960.8	E856	E930.8	E950.4	E962.0	E980.4
Fulminate of mercury	985.0	E866.1	—	E950.9	E962.1	E980.9
Fulvicin	960.1	E856	E930.1	E950.4	E962.0	E980.4

Substance	Poisoning	Accident	Therapeutic Use	Suicide Attempt	Assault	Undetermined
		External Cause (E-Code)				
Fumadil	960.8	E856	E930.8	E950.4	E962.0	E980.4
Fumagillin	960.8	E856	E930.8	E950.4	E962.0	E980.4
Fumes (from)	987.9	E869.9	—	E952.9	E962.2	E982.9
carbon monoxide — *see* Carbon, monoxide						
charcoal (domestic use)	986	E868.3	—	E952.1	E962.2	E982.1
chloroform — *see* Chloroform						
coke (in domestic stoves, fireplaces)	986	E868.3	—	E952.1	E962.2	E982.1
corrosive NEC	987.8	E869.8	—	E952.8	E962.2	E982.8
ether — *see* Ether(s)						
freons	987.4	E869.2	—	E952.8	E962.2	E982.8
hydrocarbons	987.1	E869.8	—	E952.8	E962.2	E982.8
petroleum (liquefied)	987.0	E868.0	—	E951.1	E962.2	E981.1
distributed through pipes (pure or mixed with air)	987.0	E867	—	E951.0	E962.2	E981.0
lead — *see* Lead						
metals — *see* specified metal						
nitrogen dioxide	987.2	E869.0	—	E952.8	E962.2	E982.8
pesticides — *see* Pesticides						
petroleum (liquefied)	987.0	E868.0	—	E951.1	E962.2	E981.1
distributed through pipes (pure or mixed with air)	987.0	E867	—	E951.0	E962.2	E981.0
polyester	987.8	E869.8	—	E952.8	E962.2	E982.8
specified source, other (*see also* substance specified)	987.8	E869.8	—	E952.8	E962.2	E982.8
sulfur dioxide	987.3	E869.1	—	E952.8	E962.2	E982.8
Fumigants	989.4	E863.8	—	E950.6	E962.1	E980.7
Fungi, noxious, used as food	988.1	E865.5	—	E950.9	E962.1	E980.9
Fungicides (*see also* Antifungals)	989.4	E863.6	—	E950.6	E962.1	E980.7
Fungizone	960.1	E856	E930.1	E950.4	E962.0	E980.4
topical	976.0	E858.7	E946.0	E950.4	E962.0	E980.4
Furacin	976.0	E858.7	E946.0	E950.4	E962.0	E980.4
Furadantin	961.9	E857	E931.9	E950.4	E962.0	E980.4
Furazolidone	961.9	E857	E931.9	E950.4	E962.0	E980.4
Furnace (coal burning) (domestic), gas from	986	E868.3	—	E952.1	E962.2	E982.1
industrial	986	E868.8	—	E952.1	E962.2	E982.1
Furniture polish	989.89	E861.2	—	E950.9	E962.1	E890.9
Furosemide	974.4	E858.5	E944.4	E950.4	E962.0	E980.4
Furoxone	961.9	E857	E931.9	E950.4	E962.0	E980.4
Fusel oil (amyl) (butyl) (propyl)	980.3	E860.4	—	E950.9	E962.1	E980.9
Fusidic acid	960.8	E856	E930.8	E950.4	E962.0	E980.4
G						
Gallamine	975.2	E858.6	E945.2	E950.4	E962.0	E980.4
Gallotannic acid	976.2	E858.7	E946.2	E950.4	E962.0	E980.4
Gamboge	973.1	E858.4	E943.1	E950.4	E962.0	E980.4
Gamimune	964.6	E858.2	E934.6	E950.4	E962.0	E980.4
Gamma-benzene hexachloride (vapor)	989.2	E863.0	—	E950.6	E962.1	E980.7
Gamma globulin	964.6	E858.2	E934.6	E950.4	E962.0	E980.4
Gamulin	964.6	E858.2	E934.6	E950.4	E962.0	E980.4
Ganglionic blocking agents	972.3	E858.3	E942.3	E950.4	E962.0	E980.4
Ganja	969.6	E854.1	E939.6	E950.3	E962.0	E980.3
Garamycin	960.8	E856	E930.8	E950.4	E962.0	E980.4
ophthalmic preparation	976.5	E858.7	E945.5	E950.4	E962.0	E980.4
topical NEC	976.0	E858.7	E946.0	E950.4	E962.0	E980.4
Gardenal	967.0	E851	E937.0	E950.1	E962.0	E980.1
Gardepanyl	967.0	E851	E937.0	E950.1	E962.0	E980.1
Gas	987.9	E869.9	—	E952.9	E962.2	E982.9
acetylene	987.1	E868.1	—	E951.8	E962.2	E981.8
incomplete combustion of — *see* Carbon, monoxide, fuel, utility						
air contaminants, source or type not specified	987.9	E869.9	—	E952.9	E962.2	E982.9
anesthetic (general) NEC	968.2	E855.1	E938.2	E950.4	E962.0	E980.4
blast furnace	986	E868.8	—	E952.1	E962.2	E982.1
butane — *see* Butane						
carbon monoxide — *see* Carbon, monoxide						
chlorine	987.6	E869.8	—	E952.8	E962.2	E982.8
coal — *see* Carbon, monoxide, coal						
cyanide	987.7	E869.8	—	E952.8	E962.2	E982.8
dicyanogen	987.8	E869.8	—	E952.8	E962.2	E982.8
domestic — *see* Gas, utility						
exhaust — *see* Carbon, monoxide, exhaust gas						
from wood- or coal-burning stove or fireplace	986	E868.3	—	E952.1	E962.2	E982.1

Substance	Poisoning	External Cause (E-Code) Accident	Therapeutic Use	Suicide Attempt	Assault	Undetermined
Gas — *continued*						
fuel (domestic use) — *see also* Carbon, monoxide, fuel						
industrial use	986	E868.8	—	E952.1	E962.2	E982.1
utility	987.1	E868.1	—	E951.8	E962.2	E981.8
incomplete combustion of — *see* Carbon, monoxide, fuel, utility						
in mobile container	987.0	E868.0	—	E951.1	E962.2	E981.1
piped (natural)	987.1	E867	—	E951.0	E962.2	E981.0
garage	986	E868.2	—	E952.0	E962.2	E982.0
hydrocarbon NEC	987.1	E869.8	—	E952.8	E962.2	E982.8
incomplete combustion of — *see* Carbon, monoxide, fuel, utility						
liquefied (mobile container)	987.0	E868.0	—	E951.1	E962.2	E981.1
piped	987.0	E867	—	E951.0	E962.2	E981.0
hydrocyanic acid	987.7	E869.8	—	E952.8	E962.2	E982.8
illuminating — *see* Gas, utility						
incomplete combustion, any — *see* Carbon, monoxide						
kiln	986	E868.8	—	E952.1	E962.2	E982.1
lacrimogenic	987.5	E869.3	—	E952.8	E962.2	E982.8
marsh	987.1	E869.8	—	E952.8	E962.2	E982.8
motor exhaust, not in transit	986	E868.8	—	E952.1	E962.2	E982.1
mustard — *see* Mustard, gas						
natural	987.1	E867	—	E951.0	E962.2	E981.0
nerve (war)	987.9	E869.9	—	E952.9	E962.2	E982.9
oils	981	E862.1	—	E950.9	E962.1	E980.9
petroleum (liquefied) (distributed in mobile containers)	987.0	E868.0	—	E951.1	E962.2	E981.1
piped (pure or mixed with air)	987.0	E867	—	E951.1	E962.2	E981.1
piped (manufactured) (natural) NEC	987.1	E867	—	E951.0	E962.2	E981.0
producer	986	E868.8	—	E952.1	E962.2	E982.1
propane — *see* Propane						
refrigerant (freon)	987.4	E869.2	—	E952.8	E962.2	E982.8
not freon	987.9	E869.9	—	E952.9	E962.2	E982.9
sewer	987.8	E869.8	—	E952.8	E962.2	E982.8
specified source NEC (*see also* substance specified)	987.8	E869.8	—	E952.8	E962.2	E982.8
stove — *see* Gas, utility						
tear	987.5	E869.3	—	E952.8	E962.2	E982.8
utility (for cooking, heating, or lighting) (piped) NEC	987.1	E868.1	—	E951.8	E962.2	E981.8
incomplete combustion of — *see* Carbon, monoxide, fuel, utility						
in mobile container	987.0	E868.0	—	E951.1	E962.2	E981.1
piped (natural)	987.1	E867	—	E951.0	E962.2	E981.0
water	987.1	E868.1	—	E951.8	E962.2	E981.8
incomplete combustion of — *see* Carbon, monoxide, fuel, utility						
Gaseous substance — *see* Gas						
Gasoline, gasolene	981	E862.1	—	E950.9	E962.1	E980.9
vapor	987.1	E869.8	—	E952.8	E962.2	E982.8
Gastric enzymes	973.4	E858.4	E943.4	E950.4	E962.0	E980.4
Gastrografin	977.8	E858.8	E947.8	E950.4	E962.0	E980.4
Gastrointestinal agents	973.9	E858.4	E943.9	E950.4	E962.0	E980.4
specified NEC	973.8	E858.4	E943.8	E950.4	E962.0	E980.4
Gaultheria procumbens	988.2	E865.4	—	E950.9	E962.1	E980.9
Gelatin (intravenous)	964.8	E858.2	E934.8	E950.4	E962.0	E980.4
absorbable (sponge)	964.5	E858.2	E934.5	E950.4	E962.0	E980.4
Gelfilm	976.8	E858.7	E946.8	E950.4	E962.0	E980.4
Gelfoam	964.5	E858.2	E934.5	E950.4	E962.0	E980.4
Gelsemine	970.8	E854.3	E940.8	E950.4	E962.0	E980.4
Gelsemium (sempervirens)	988.2	E865.4	—	E950.9	E962.1	E980.9
Gemonil	967.0	E851	E937.0	E950.1	E962.0	E980.1
Gentamicin	960.8	E856	E930.8	E950.4	E962.0	E980.4
ophthalmic preparation	976.5	E858.7	E946.5	E950.4	E962.0	E980.4
topical NEC	976.0	E858.7	E946.0	E950.4	E962.0	E980.4
Gentian violet	976.0	E858.7	E946.0	E950.4	E962.0	E980.4
Gexane	976.0	E858.7	E946.0	E950.4	E962.0	E980.4
Gila monster (venom)	989.5	E905.0	—	E950.9	E962.1	E980.9
Ginger, Jamaica	989.89	E866.8	—	E950.9	E962.1	E980.9
Gitalin	972.1	E858.3	E942.1	E950.4	E962.0	E980.4
Gitoxin	972.1	E858.3	E942.1	E950.4	E962.0	E980.4
Glandular extract (medicinal) NEC	977.9	E858.9	E947.9	E950.5	E962.0	E980.5
Glaucarubin	961.5	E857	E931.5	E950.4	E962.0	E980.4
Globin zinc insulin	962.3	E858.0	E932.3	E950.4	E962.0	E980.4
Glucagon	962.3	E858.0	E932.3	E950.4	E962.0	E980.4
Glucochloral	967.1	E852.0	E937.1	E950.2	E962.0	E980.2
Glucocorticoids	962.0	E858.0	E932.0	E950.4	E962.0	E980.4

Substance	Poisoning	External Cause (E-Code) Accident	Therapeutic Use	Suicide Attempt	Assault	Undetermined
Glucose	974.5	E858.5	E944.5	E950.4	E962.0	E980.4
oxidase reagent	977.8	E858.8	E947.8	E950.4	E962.0	E980.4
Glucosulfone sodium	961.8	E857	E931.8	E950.4	E962.0	E980.4
Glue(s)	989.89	E866.6	—	E950.9	E962.1	E980.9
Glutamic acid (hydrochloride)	973.4	E858.4	E943.4	E950.4	E962.0	E980.4
Glutathione	963.8	E858.1	E933.8	E950.4	E962.0	E980.4
Glutethimide (group)	967.5	E852.4	E937.5	E950.2	E962.0	E980.2
Glycerin (lotion)	976.3	E858.7	E946.3	E950.4	E962.0	E980.4
Glycerol (topical)	976.3	E858.7	E946.3	E950.4	E962.0	E980.4
Glyceryl						
guaiacolate	975.5	E858.6	E945.5	E950.4	E962.0	E980.4
triacetate (topical)	976.0	E858.7	E946.0	E950.4	E962.0	E980.4
trinitrate	972.4	E858.3	E942.4	E950.4	E962.0	E980.4
Glycine	974.5	E858.5	E944.5	E950.4	E962.0	E980.4
Glycobiarsol	961.1	E857	E931.1	E950.4	E962.0	E980.4
Glycols (ether)	982.8	E862.4	—	E950.9	E962.1	E980.9
Glycopyrrolate	971.1	E855.4	E941.1	E950.4	E962.0	E980.4
Glymidine	962.3	E858.0	E932.3	E950.4	E962.0	E980.4
Gold (compounds) (salts)	965.69	E850.6	E935.6	E950.0	E962.0	E980.0
Golden sulfide of antimony	985.4	E866.2	—	E950.9	E962.1	E980.9
Goldylocks	988.2	E865.4	—	E950.9	E962.1	E980.9
Gonadal tissue extract	962.9	E858.0	E932.9	E950.4	E962.0	E980.4
female	962.2	E858.0	E932.2	E950.4	E962.0	E980.4
male	962.1	E858.0	E932.1	E950.4	E962.0	E980.4
Gonadotropin	962.4	E858.0	E932.4	E950.4	E962.0	E980.4
Grain alcohol	980.0	E860.1	—	E950.9	E962.1	E980.9
beverage	980.0	E860.0	—	E950.9	E962.1	E980.9
Gramicidin	960.8	E856	E930.8	E950.4	E962.0	E980.4
Gratiola officinalis	988.2	E865.4	—	E950.9	E962.1	E980.9
Grease	989.89	E866.8	—	E950.9	E962.1	E980.9
Green hellebore	988.2	E865.4	—	E950.9	E962.1	E980.9
Green soap	976.2	E858.7	E946.2	E950.4	E962.0	E980.4
Grifulvin	960.1	E856	E930.1	E950.4	E962.0	E980.4
Griseofulvin	960.1	E856	E930.1	E950.4	E962.0	E980.4
Growth hormone	962.4	E858.0	E932.4	E950.4	E962.0	E980.4
Guaiacol	975.5	E858.6	E945.5	E950.4	E962.0	E980.4
Guaiac reagent	977.8	E858.8	E947.8	E950.4	E962.0	E980.4
Guaifenesin	975.5	E858.6	E945.5	E950.4	E962.0	E980.4
Guaiphenesin	975.5	E858.6	E945.5	E950.4	E962.0	E980.4
Guanatol	961.4	E857	E931.4	E950.4	E962.0	E980.4
Guanethidine	972.6	E858.3	E942.6	E950.4	E962.0	E980.4
Guano	989.89	E866.5	—	E950.9	E962.1	E980.9
Guanochlor	972.6	E858.3	E942.6	E950.4	E962.0	E980.4
Guanoctine	972.6	E858.3	E942.6	E950.4	E962.0	E980.4
Guanoxan	972.6	E858.3	E942.6	E950.4	E962.0	E980.4
H						
Hair treatment agent NEC	976.4	E858.7	E946.4	E950.4	E962.0	E980.4
Halcinonide	976.0	E858.7	E946.0	E950.4	E962.0	E980.4
Halethazole	976.0	E858.7	E946.0	E950.4	E962.0	E980.4
Hallucinogens	969.6	E854.1	E939.6	E950.3	E962.0	E980.3
Haloperidol	969.2	E853.1	E939.2	E950.3	E962.0	E980.3
Haloprogin	976.0	E858.7	E946.0	E950.4	E962.0	E980.4
Halotex	976.0	E858.7	E946.0	E950.4	E962.0	E980.4
Halothane	968.1	E855.1	E938.1	E950.4	E962.0	E980.4
Halquinols	976.0	E858.7	E946.0	E950.4	E962.0	E980.4
Harmonyl	972.6	E858.3	E942.6	E950.4	E962.0	E980.4
Hartmann's solution	974.5	E858.5	E944.5	E950.4	E962.0	E980.4
Hashish	969.6	E854.1	E939.6	E950.3	E962.0	E980.3
Hawaiian wood rose seeds	969.6	E854.1	E939.6	E950.3	E962.0	E980.3
Headache cures, drugs, powders NEC	977.9	E858.9	E947.9	E950.5	E962.0	E980.9
Heavenly Blue (morning glory)	969.6	E854.1	E939.6	E950.3	E962.0	E980.3
Heavy metal						
antagonists	963.8	E858.1	E933.8	E950.4	E962.0	E980.4
anti-infectives	961.2	E857	E931.2	E950.4	E962.0	E980.4
Hedaquinium	976.0	E858.7	E946.0	E950.4	E962.0	E980.4
Hedge hyssop	988.2	E865.4	—	E950.9	E962.1	E980.9
Heet	976.8	E858.7	E946.8	E950.4	E962.0	E980.4
Helenin	961.6	E857	E931.6	E950.4	E962.0	E980.4
Hellebore (black) (green) (white)	988.2	E865.4	—	E950.9	E962.1	E980.9
Hemlock	988.2	E865.4	—	E950.9	E962.1	E980.9

Substance	Poisoning	External Cause (E-Code) Accident	Therapeutic Use	Suicide Attempt	Assault	Undetermined
Hemostatics	964.5	E858.2	E934.5	E950.4	E962.0	E980.4
capillary active drugs	972.8	E858.3	E942.8	E950.4	E962.0	E980.4
Henbane	988.2	E865.4	—	E950.9	E962.1	E980.9
Heparin (sodium)	964.2	E858.2	E934.2	E950.4	E962.0	E980.4
Heptabarbital, heptabarbitone	967.0	E851	E937.0	E950.1	E962.0	E980.1
Heptachlor	989.2	E863.0	—	E950.6	E962.1	E980.7
Heptalgin	965.09	E850.2	E935.2	E950.0	E962.0	E980.0
Herbicides	989.4	E863.5	—	E950.6	E962.1	E980.7
Heroin	965.01	E850.0	E935.0	E950.0	E962.0	E980.0
Herplex	976.5	E858.7	E946.5	E950.4	E962.0	E980.4
HES	964.8	E858.2	E934.8	E950.4	E962.0	E980.4
Hetastarch	964.8	E858.2	E934.8	E950.4	E962.0	E980.4
Hexachlorocyclohexane	989.2	E863.0	—	E950.6	E962.1	E980.7
Hexachlorophene	976.2	E858.7	E946.2	E950.4	E962.0	E980.4
Hexadimethrine (bromide)	964.5	E858.2	E934.5	E950.4	E962.0	E980.4
Hexafluorenium	975.2	E858.6	E945.2	E950.4	E962.0	E980.4
Hexa-germ	976.2	E858.7	E946.2	E950.4	E962.0	E980.4
Hexahydrophenol	980.8	E860.8	—	E950.9	E962.1	E980.9
Hexalin	980.8	E860.8	—	E950.9	E962.1	E980.9
Hexamethonium	972.3	E858.3	E942.3	E950.4	E962.0	E980.4
Hexamethyleneamine	961.9	E857	E931.9	E950.4	E962.0	E980.4
Hexamine	961.9	E857	E931.9	E950.4	E962.0	E980.4
Hexanone	982.8	E862.4	—	E950.9	E962.1	E980.9
Hexapropymate	967.8	E852.8	E937.8	E950.2	E962.0	E980.2
Hexestrol	962.2	E858.0	E932.2	E950.4	E962.0	E980.4
Hexethal (sodium)	967.0	E851	E937.0	E950.1	E962.0	E980.1
Hexetidine	976.0	E858.7	E946.0	E950.4	E962.0	E980.4
Hexobarbital, hexobarbitone	967.0	E851	E937.0	E950.1	E962.0	E980.1
sodium (anesthetic)	968.3	E855.1	E938.3	E950.4	E962.0	E980.4
soluble	968.3	E855.1	E938.3	E950.4	E962.0	E980.4
Hexocyclium	971.1	E855.4	E941.1	E950.4	E962.0	E980.4
Hexoestrol	962.2	E858.0	E932.2	E950.4	E962.0	E980.4
Hexone	982.8	E862.4	—	E950.9	E962.1	E980.9
Hexylcaine	968.5	E855.2	E938.5	E950.4	E962.0	E980.4
Hexylresorcinol	961.6	E857	E931.6	E950.4	E962.0	E980.4
Hinkle's pills	973.1	E858.4	E943.1	E950.4	E962.0	E980.4
Histalog	977.8	E858.8	E947.8	E950.4	E962.0	E980.4
Histamine (phosphate)	972.5	E858.3	E942.5	E950.4	E962.0	E980.4
Histoplasmin	977.8	E858.8	E947.8	E950.4	E962.0	E980.4
Holly berries	988.2	E865.3	—	E950.9	E962.1	E980.9
Homatropine	971.1	E855.4	E941.1	E950.4	E962.0	E980.4
Homo-tet	964.6	E858.2	E934.6	E950.4	E962.0	E980.4
Hormones (synthetic substitute) NEC	962.9	E858.0	E932.9	E950.4	E962.0	E980.4
adrenal cortical steroids	962.0	E858.0	E932.0	E950.4	E962.0	E980.4
antidiabetic agents	962.3	E858.0	E932.3	E950.4	E962.0	E980.4
follicle stimulating	962.4	E858.0	E932.4	E950.4	E962.0	E980.4
gonadotropic	962.4	E858.0	E932.4	E950.4	E962.0	E980.4
growth	962.4	E858.0	E932.4	E950.4	E962.0	E980.4
ovarian (substitutes)	962.2	E858.0	E932.2	E950.4	E962.0	E980.4
parathyroid (derivatives)	962.6	E858.0	E932.6	E950.4	E962.0	E980.4
pituitary (posterior)	962.5	E858.0	E932.5	E950.4	E962.0	E980.4
anterior	962.4	E858.0	E932.4	E950.4	E962.0	E980.4
thyroid (derivative)	962.7	E858.0	E932.7	E950.4	E962.0	E980.4
Hornet (sting)	989.5	E905.3	—	E950.9	E962.1	E980.9
Horticulture agent NEC	989.4	E863.9	—	E950.6	E962.1	E980.7
Hyaluronidase	963.4	E858.1	E933.4	E950.4	E962.0	E980.4
Hyazyme	963.4	E858.1	E933.4	E950.4	E962.0	E980.4
Hycodan	965.09	E850.2	E935.2	E950.0	E962.0	E980.0
Hydantoin derivatives	966.1	E855.0	E936.1	E950.4	E962.0	E980.4
Hydeltra	962.0	E858.0	E932.0	E950.4	E962.0	E980.4
Hydergine	971.3	E855.6	E941.3	E950.4	E962.0	E980.4
Hydrabamine penicillin	960.0	E856	E930.0	E950.4	E962.0	E980.4
Hydralazine, hydrallazine	972.6	E858.3	E942.6	E950.4	E962.0	E980.4
Hydrargaphen	976.0	E858.7	E946.0	E950.4	E962.0	E980.4
Hydrazine	983.9	E864.3	—	E950.7	E962.1	E980.6
Hydriodic acid	975.5	E858.6	E945.5	E950.4	E962.0	E980.4
Hydrocarbon gas	987.1	E869.8	—	E952.8	E962.2	E982.8
incomplete combustion of — *see* Carbon, monoxide, fuel, utility						
liquefied (mobile container)	987.0	E868.0	—	E951.1	E962.2	E981.1
piped (natural)	987.0	E867	—	E951.0	E962.2	E981.0

Substance	Poisoning	External Cause (E-Code) Accident	Therapeutic Use	Suicide Attempt	Assault	Un-determined
Hydrochloric acid (liquid)	983.1	E864.1	—	E950.7	E962.1	E980.6
medicinal	973.4	E858.4	E943.4	E950.4	E962.0	E980.4
vapor	987.8	E869.8	—	E952.8	E962.2	E982.8
Hydrochlorothiazide	974.3	E858.5	E944.3	E950.4	E962.0	E980.4
Hydrocodone	965.09	E850.2	E935.2	E950.0	E962.0	E980.0
Hydrocortisone	962.0	E858.0	E932.0	E950.4	E962.0	E980.4
ENT agent	976.6	E858.7	E946.6	E950.4	E962.0	E980.4
ophthalmic preparation	976.5	E858.7	E946.5	E950.4	E962.0	E980.4
topical NEC	976.0	E858.7	E946.0	E950.4	E962.0	E980.4
Hydrocortone	962.0	E858.0	E932.0	E950.4	E962.0	E980.4
ENT agent	976.6	E858.7	E946.6	E950.4	E962.0	E980.4
ophthalmic preparation	976.5	E858.7	E946.5	E950.4	E962.0	E980.4
topical NEC	976.0	E858.7	E946.0	E950.4	E962.0	E980.4
Hydrocyanic acid — *see* Cyanide(s)						
Hydroflumethiazide	974.3	E858.5	E944.3	E950.4	E962.0	E980.4
Hydrofluoric acid (liquid)	983.1	E864.1	—	E950.7	E962.1	E980.6
vapor	987.8	E869.8	—	E952.8	E962.2	E982.8
Hydrogen	987.8	E869.8	—	E952.8	E962.2	E982.8
arsenide	985.1	E866.3	—	E950.8	E962.1	E980.8
arseniureted	985.1	E866.3	—	E950.8	E962.1	E980.8
cyanide (salts)	989.0	E866.8	—	E950.9	E962.1	E980.9
gas	987.7	E869.8	—	E952.8	E962.2	E982.8
fluoride (liquid)	983.1	E864.1	—	E950.7	E962.1	E980.6
vapor	987.8	E869.8	—	E952.8	E962.2	E982.8
peroxide (solution)	976.6	E858.7	E946.6	E950.4	E962.0	E980.4
phosphureted	987.8	E869.8	—	E952.8	E962.2	E982.8
sulfide (gas)	987.8	E869.8	—	E952.8	E962.2	E982.8
arseniureted	985.1	E866.3	—	E950.8	E962.1	E980.8
sulfureted	987.8	E869.8	—	E952.8	E962.2	E982.8
Hydromorphinol	965.09	E850.2	E935.2	E950.0	E962.0	E980.0
Hydromorphinone	965.09	E850.2	E935.2	E950.0	E962.0	E980.0
Hydromorphone	965.09	E850.2	E935.2	E950.0	E962.0	E980.0
Hydromox	974.3	E858.5	E944.3	E950.4	E962.0	E980.4
Hydrophilic lotion	976.3	E858.7	E946.3	E950.4	E962.0	E980.4
Hydroquinone	983.0	E864.0	—	E950.7	E962.1	E980.6
vapor	987.8	E869.8	—	E952.8	E962.2	E982.8
Hydrosulfuric acid (gas)	987.8	E869.8	—	E952.8	E962.2	E982.8
Hydrous wool fat (lotion)	976.3	E858.7	E946.3	E950.4	E962.0	E980.4
Hydroxide, caustic	983.2	E864.2	—	E950.7	E962.1	E980.6
Hydroxocobalamin	964.1	E858.2	E934.1	E950.4	E962.0	E980.4
Hydroxyamphetamine	971.2	E855.5	E941.2	E950.4	E962.0	E980.4
Hydroxychloroquine	961.4	E857	E931.4	E950.4	E962.0	E980.4
Hydroxydihydrocodeinone	965.09	E850.2	E935.2	E950.0	E962.0	E980.0
Hydroxyethyl starch	964.8	E858.2	E934.8	E950.4	E962.0	E980.4
Hydroxyphenamate	969.5	E853.8	E939.5	E950.3	E962.0	E980.3
Hydroxyphenylbutazone	965.5	E850.5	E935.5	E950.0	E962.0	E980.0
Hydroxyprogesterone	962.2	E858.0	E932.2	E950.4	E962.0	E980.4
Hydroxyquinoline derivatives	961.3	E857	E931.3	E950.4	E962.0	E980.4
Hydroxystilbamidine	961.5	E857	E931.5	E950.4	E962.0	E980.4
Hydroxyurea	963.1	E858.1	E933.1	E950.4	E962.0	E980.4
Hydroxyzine	969.5	E853.8	E939.5	E950.3	E962.0	E980.3
Hyoscine (hydrobromide)	971.1	E855.4	E941.1	E950.4	E962.0	E980.4
Hyoscyamine	971.1	E855.4	E941.1	E950.4	E962.0	E980.4
Hyoscyamus (albus) (niger)	988.2	E865.4	—	E950.9	E962.1	E980.9
Hypaque	977.8	E858.8	E947.8	E950.4	E962.0	E980.4
Hypertussis	964.6	E858.2	E934.6	E950.4	E962.0	E980.4
Hypnotics NEC	967.9	E852.9	E937.9	E950.2	E962.0	E980.2
Hypochlorites — *see* Sodium, hypochlorite						
Hypotensive agents NEC	972.6	E858.3	E942.6	E950.4	E962.0	E980.4
I						
Ibufenac	965.69	E850.6	E935.6	E950.0	E962.0	E980.0
Ibuprofen	965.61	E850.6	E935.6	E950.0	E962.0	E980.0
ICG	977.8	E858.8	E947.8	E950.4	E962.0	E980.4
Ichthammol	976.4	E858.7	E946.4	E950.4	E962.0	E980.4
Ichthyol	976.4	E858.7	E946.4	E950.4	E962.0	E980.4
Idoxuridine	976.5	E858.7	E946.5	E950.4	E962.0	E980.4
IDU	976.5	E858.7	E946.5	E950.4	E962.0	E980.4
Iletin	962.3	E858.0	E932.3	E950.4	E962.0	E980.4
Ilex	988.2	E865.4	—	E950.9	E962.1	E980.9
Illuminating gas — *see* Gas, utility						
Ilopan	963.5	E858.1	E933.5	E950.4	E962.0	E980.4

		External Cause (E-Code)				
Substance	**Poisoning**	**Accident**	**Therapeutic Use**	**Suicide Attempt**	**Assault**	**Un-determined**
Ilotycin	960.3	E856	E930.3	E950.4	E962.0	E980.4
ophthalmic preparation	976.5	E858.7	E946.5	E950.4	E962.0	E980.4
topical NEC	976.0	E858.7	E946.0	E950.4	E962.0	E980.4
Imipramine	969.0	E854.0	E939.0	E950.3	E962.0	E980.3
Immu-G	964.6	E858.2	E934.6	E950.4	E962.0	E980.4
Immuglobin	964.6	E858.2	E934.6	E950.4	E962.0	E980.4
Immune serum globulin	964.6	E858.2	E934.6	E950.4	E962.0	E980.4
Immunosuppressive agents	963.1	E858.1	E933.1	E950.4	E962.0	E980.4
Immu-tetanus	964.6	E858.2	E934.6	E950.4	E962.0	E980.4
Indandione (derivatives)	964.2	E858.2	E934.2	E950.4	E962.0	E980.4
Inderal	972.0	E858.3	E942.0	E950.4	E962.0	E980.4
Indian						
hemp	969.6	E854.1	E939.6	E950.3	E962.0	E980.3
tobacco	988.2	E865.4	—	E950.9	E962.1	E980.9
Indigo carmine	977.8	E858.8	E947.8	E950.4	E962.0	E980.4
Indocin	965.69	E850.6	E935.6	E950.0	E962.0	E980.0
Indocyanine green	977.8	E858.8	E947.8	E950.4	E962.0	E980.4
Indomethacin	965.69	E850.6	E935.6	E950.0	E962.0	E980.0
Industrial						
alcohol	980.9	E860.9	—	E950.9	E962.1	E980.9
fumes	987.8	E869.8	—	E952.8	E962.2	E982.8
solvents (fumes) (vapors)	982.8	E862.9	—	E950.9	E962.1	E980.9
Influenza vaccine	979.6	E858.8	E949.6	E950.4	E962.0	E982.8
Ingested substances NEC	989.9	E866.9	—	E950.9	E962.1	E980.9
INH (isoniazid)	961.8	E857	E931.8	E950.4	E962.0	E980.4
Inhalation, gas (noxious) — *see* Gas						
Ink	989.89	E866.8	—	E950.9	E962.1	E980.9
Innovar	967.6	E852.5	E937.6	E950.2	E962.0	E980.2
Inositol niacinate	972.2	E858.3	E942.2	E950.4	E962.0	E980.4
Inproquone	963.1	E858.1	E933.1	E950.4	E962.0	E980.4
Insect (sting), venomous	989.5	E905.5	—	E950.9	E962.1	E980.9
Insecticides (*see also* Pesticides)	989.4	E863.4	—	E950.6	E962.1	E980.7
chlorinated	989.2	E863.0	—	E950.6	E962.1	E980.7
mixtures	989.4	E863.3	—	E950.6	E962.1	E980.7
organochlorine (compounds)	989.2	E863.0	—	E950.6	E962.1	E980.7
organophosphorus (compounds)	989.3	E863.1	—	E950.6	E962.1	E980.7
Insular tissue extract	962.3	E858.0	E932.3	E950.4	E962.0	E980.4
Insulin (amorphous) (globin) (isophane) (Lente) (NPH) (protamine) (Semilente) (Ultralente) (zinc)	962.3	E858.0	E932.3	E950.4	E962.0	E980.4
Intranarcon	968.3	E855.1	E938.3	E950.4	E962.0	E980.4
Inulin	977.8	E858.8	E947.8	E950.4	E962.0	E980.4
Invert sugar	974.5	E858.5	E944.5	E950.4	E962.0	E980.4
Inza — *see* Naproxen						
Iodide NEC (*see also* Iodine)	976.0	E858.7	E946.0	E950.4	E962.0	E980.4
mercury (ointment)	976.0	E858.7	E946.0	E950.4	E962.0	E980.4
methylate	976.0	E858.7	E946.0	E950.4	E962.0	E980.4
potassium (expectorant) NEC	975.5	E858.6	E945.5	E950.4	E962.0	E980.4
Iodinated glycerol	975.5	E858.6	E945.5	E950.4	E962.0	E980.4
Iodine (antiseptic, external) (tincture) NEC	976.0	E858.7	E946.0	E950.4	E962.0	E980.4
diagnostic	977.8	E858.8	E947.8	E950.4	E962.0	E980.4
for thyroid conditions (antithyroid)	962.8	E858.0	E932.8	E950.4	E962.0	E980.4
vapor	987.8	E869.8	—	E952.8	E962.2	E982.8
Iodized oil	977.8	E858.8	E947.8	E950.4	E962.0	E980.4
Iodobismitol	961.2	E857	E931.2	E950.4	E962.0	E980.4
Iodochlorhydroxyquin	961.3	E857	E931.3	E950.4	E962.0	E980.4
topical	976.0	E858.7	E946.0	E950.4	E962.0	E980.4
Iodoform	976.0	E858.7	E946.0	E950.4	E962.0	E980.4
Iodopanoic acid	977.8	E858.8	E947.8	E950.4	E962.0	E980.4
Iodophthalein	977.8	E858.8	E947.8	E950.4	E962.0	E980.4
Ion exchange resins	974.5	E858.5	E944.5	E950.4	E962.0	E980.4
Iopanoic acid	977.8	E858.8	E947.8	E950.4	E962.0	E980.4
Iophendylate	977.8	E858.8	E947.8	E950.4	E962.0	E980.4
Iothiouracil	962.8	E858.0	E932.8	E950.4	E962.0	E980.4
Ipecac	973.6	E858.4	E943.6	E950.4	E962.0	E980.4
Ipecacuanha	973.6	E858.4	E943.6	E950.4	E962.0	E980.4
Ipodate	977.8	E858.8	E947.8	E950.4	E962.0	E980.4
Ipral	967.0	E851	E937.0	E950.1	E962.0	E980.1
Iproniazid	969.0	E854.0	E939.0	E950.3	E962.0	E980.3
Iron (compounds) (medicinal) (preparations)	964.0	E858.2	E934.0	E950.4	E962.0	E980.4
dextran	964.0	E858.2	E934.0	E950.4	E962.0	E980.4
nonmedicinal (dust) (fumes) NEC	985.8	E866.4	—	E950.9	E962.1	E980.9
Irritant drug	977.9	E858.9	E947.9	E950.5	E962.0	E980.5

Substance	Poisoning	External Cause (E-Code) Accident	Therapeutic Use	Suicide Attempt	Assault	Un-determined
Ismelin	972.6	E858.3	E942.6	E950.4	E962.0	E980.4
Isoamyl nitrite	972.4	E858.3	E942.4	E950.4	E962.0	E980.4
Isobutyl acetate	982.8	E862.4	—	E950.9	E962.1	E980.9
Isocarboxazid	969.0	E854.0	E939.0	E950.3	E962.0	E980.3
Isoephedrine	971.2	E855.5	E941.2	E950.4	E962.0	E980.4
Isoetharine	971.2	E855.5	E941.2	E950.4	E962.0	E980.4
Isofluorophate	971.0	E855.3	E941.0	E950.4	E962.0	E980.4
Isoniazid (INH)	961.8	E857	E931.8	E950.4	E962.0	E980.4
Isopentaquine	961.4	E857	E931.4	E950.4	E962.0	E980.4
Isophane insulin	962.3	E858.0	E932.3	E950.4	E962.0	E980.4
Isopregnenone	962.2	E858.0	E932.2	E950.4	E962.0	E980.4
Isoprenaline	971.2	E855.5	E941.2	E950.4	E962.0	E980.4
Isopropamide	971.1	E855.4	E941.1	E950.4	E962.0	E980.4
Isopropanol	980.2	E860.3	—	E950.9	E962.1	E980.9
topical (germicide)	976.0	E858.7	E946.0	E950.4	E962.0	E980.4
Isopropyl						
acetate	982.8	E862.4	—	E950.9	E962.1	E980.9
alcohol	980.2	E860.3	—	E950.9	E962.1	E980.9
topical (germicide)	976.0	E858.7	E946.0	E950.4	E962.0	E980.4
ether	982.8	E862.4	—	E950.9	E962.1	E980.9
Isoproterenol	971.2	E855.5	E941.2	E950.4	E962.0	E980.4
Isosorbide dinitrate	972.4	E858.3	E942.4	E950.4	E962.0	E980.4
Isothipendyl	963.0	E858.1	E933.0	E950.4	E962.0	E980.4
Isoxazolyl penicillin	960.0	E856	E930.0	E950.4	E962.0	E980.4
Isoxsuprine hydrochloride	972.5	E858.3	E942.5	E950.4	E962.0	E980.4
I-thyroxine sodium	962.7	E858.0	E932.7	E950.4	E962.0	E980.4
J						
Jaborandi (pilocarpus) (extract)	971.0	E855.3	E941.0	E950.4	E962.0	E980.4
Jalap	973.1	E858.4	E943.1	E950.4	E962.0	E980.4
Jamaica						
dogwood (bark)	965.7	E850.7	E935.7	E950.0	E962.0	E980.0
ginger	989.89	E866.8	—	E950.9	E962.1	E980.9
Jatropha	988.2	E865.4	—	E950.9	E962.1	E980.9
curcas	988.2	E865.3	—	E950.9	E962.1	E980.9
Jectofer	964.0	E858.2	E934.0	E950.4	E962.0	E980.4
Jellyfish (sting)	989.5	E905.6	—	E950.9	E962.1	E980.9
Jequirity (bean)	988.2	E865.3	—	E950.9	E962.1	E980.9
Jimson weed	988.2	E865.4	—	E950.9	E962.1	E980.9
seeds	988.2	E865.3	—	E950.9	E962.1	E980.9
Juniper tar (oil) (ointment)	976.4	E858.7	E946.4	E950.4	E962.0	E980.4
K						
Kallikrein	972.5	E858.3	E942.5	E950.4	E962.0	E980.4
Kanamycin	960.6	E856	E930.6	E950.4	E962.0	E980.4
Kantrex	960.6	E856	E930.6	E950.4	E962.0	E980.4
Kaolin	973.5	E858.4	E943.5	E950.4	E962.0	E980.4
Karaya (gum)	973.3	E858.4	E943.3	E950.4	E962.0	E980.4
Kemithal	968.3	E855.1	E938.3	E950.4	E962.0	E980.4
Kenacort	962.0	E858.0	E932.0	E950.4	E962.0	E980.4
Keratolytics	976.4	E858.7	E946.4	E950.4	E962.0	E980.4
Keratoplastics	976.4	E858.7	E946.4	E950.4	E962.0	E980.4
Kerosene, kerosine (fuel) (solvent) NEC	981	E862.1	—	E950.9	E962.1	E980.9
insecticide	981	E863.4	—	E950.6	E962.1	E980.7
vapor	987.1	E869.8	—	E952.8	E962.2	E982.8
Ketamine	968.3	E855.1	E938.3	E950.4	E962.0	E980.4
Ketobemidone	965.09	E850.2	E935.2	E950.0	E962.0	E980.0
Ketols	982.8	E862.4	—	E950.9	E962.1	E980.9
Ketone oils	982.8	E862.4	—	E950.9	E962.1	E980.9
Ketoprofen	965.61	E850.6	E935.6	E950.0	E962.0	E980.0
Kiln gas or vapor (carbon monoxide)	986	E868.8	—	E952.1	E962.2	E982.1
Konsyl	973.3	E858.4	E943.3	E950.4	E962.0	E980.4
Kosam seed	988.2	E865.3	—	E950.9	E962.1	E980.9
Krait (venom)	989.5	E905.0	—	E950.9	E962.1	E980.9
Kwell (insecticide)	989.2	E863.0	—	E950.6	E962.1	E980.7
anti-infective (topical)	976.0	E858.7	E946.0	E950.4	E962.0	E980.4
L						
Laburnum (flowers) (seeds)	988.2	E865.3	—	E950.9	E962.1	E980.9
leaves	988.2	E865.4	—	E950.9	E962.1	E980.9
Lacquers	989.89	E861.6	—	E950.9	E962.1	E980.9
Lacrimogenic gas	987.5	E869.3	—	E952.8	E962.2	E982.8
Lactic acid	983.1	E864.1	—	E950.7	E962.1	E980.6
Lactobacillus acidophilus	973.5	E858.4	E943.5	E950.4	E962.0	E980.4

Substance	Poisoning	External Cause (E-Code) Accident	Therapeutic Use	Suicide Attempt	Assault	Un-determined
Lactoflavin	963.5	E858.1	E933.5	E950.4	E962.0	E980.4
Lactuca (virosa) (extract)	967.8	E852.8	E937.8	E950.2	E962.0	E980.2
Lactucarium	967.8	E852.8	E937.8	E950.2	E962.0	E980.2
Laevulose	974.5	E858.5	E944.5	E950.4	E962.0	E980.4
Lanatoside(C)	972.1	E858.3	E942.1	E950.4	E962.0	E980.4
Lanolin (lotion)	976.3	E858.7	E946.3	E950.4	E962.0	E980.4
Largactil	969.1	E853.0	E939.1	E950.3	E962.0	E980.3
Larkspur	988.2	E865.3	—	E950.9	E962.1	E980.9
Laroxyl	969.0	E854.0	E939.0	E950.3	E962.0	E980.3
Lasix	974.4	E858.5	E944.4	E950.4	E962.0	E980.4
Latex	989.82	E866.8	—	E950.9	E962.1	E980.9
Lathyrus (seed)	988.2	E865.3	—	E950.9	E962.1	E980.9
Laudanum	965.09	E850.2	E935.2	E950.0	E962.0	E980.0
Laudexium	975.2	E858.6	E945.2	E950.4	E962.0	E980.4
Laurel, black or cherry	988.2	E865.4	—	E950.9	E962.1	E980.9
Laurolinium	976.0	E858.7	E946.0	E950.4	E962.0	E980.4
Lauryl sulfoacetate	976.2	E858.7	E946.2	E950.4	E962.0	E980.4
Laxatives NEC	973.3	E858.4	E943.3	E950.4	E962.0	E980.4
emollient	973.2	E858.4	E943.2	E950.4	E962.0	E980.4
L-dopa	966.4	E855.0	E936.4	E950.4	E962.0	E980.4
L-Tryptophan — *see* amino acid						
Lead (dust) (fumes) (vapor) NEC	984.9	E866.0	—	E950.9	E962.1	E980.9
acetate (dust)	984.1	E866.0	—	E950.9	E962.1	E980.9
anti-infectives	961.2	E857	E931.2	E950.4	E962.0	E980.4
antiknock compound (tetraethyl)	984.1	E862.1	—	E950.9	E962.1	E980.9
arsenate, arsenite (dust) (insecticide) (vapor)	985.1	E863.4	—	E950.8	E962.1	E980.8
herbicide	985.1	E863.5	—	E950.8	E962.1	E980.8
carbonate	984.0	E866.0	—	E950.9	E962.1	E980.9
paint	984.0	E861.5	—	E950.9	E962.1	E980.9
chromate	984.0	E866.0	—	E950.9	E962.1	E980.9
paint	984.0	E861.5	—	E950.9	E962.1	E980.9
dioxide	984.0	E866.0	—	E950.9	E962.1	E980.9
inorganic (compound)	984.0	E866.0	—	E950.9	E962.1	E980.9
paint	984.0	E861.5	—	E950.9	E962.1	E980.9
iodide	984.0	E866.0	—	E950.9	E962.1	E980.9
pigment (paint)	984.0	E861.5	—	E950.9	E962.1	E980.9
monoxide (dust)	984.0	E866.0	—	E950.9	E962.1	E980.9
paint	984.0	E861.5	—	E950.9	E962.1	E980.9
organic	984.1	E866.0	—	E950.9	E962.1	E980.9
oxide	984.0	E866.0	—	E950.9	E962.1	E980.9
paint	984.0	E861.5	—	E950.9	E962.1	E980.9
paint	984.0	E861.5	—	E950.9	E962.1	E980.9
salts	984.0	E866.0	—	E950.9	E962.1	E980.9
specified compound NEC	984.8	E866.0	—	E950.9	E962.1	E980.9
tetra-ethyl	984.1	E862.1	—	E950.9	E962.1	E980.9
Lebanese red	969.6	E854.1	E939.6	E950.3	E962.0	E980.3
Lente Iletin (insulin)	962.3	E858.0	E932.3	E950.4	E962.0	E980.4
Leptazol	970.0	E854.3	E940.0	E950.4	E962.0	E980.4
Leritine	965.09	E850.2	E935.2	E950.0	E962.0	E980.0
Letter	962.7	E858.0	E932.7	E950.4	E962.0	E980.4
Lettuce opium	967.8	E852.8	E937.8	E950.2	E962.0	E980.2
Leucovorin (factor)	964.1	E858.2	E934.1	E950.4	E962.0	E980.4
Leukeran	963.1	E858.1	E933.1	E950.4	E962.0	E980.4
Levallorphan	970.1	E854.3	E940.1	E950.4	E962.0	E980.4
Levanil	967.8	E852.8	E937.8	E950.2	E962.0	E980.2
Levarterenol	971.2	E855.5	E941.2	E950.4	E962.0	E980.4
Levodopa	966.4	E855.0	E936.4	E950.4	E962.0	E980.4
Levo-dromoran	965.09	E850.2	E935.2	E950.0	E962.0	E980.0
Levoid	962.7	E858.0	E932.7	E950.4	E962.0	E980.4
Levo-iso-methadone	965.02	E850.1	E935.1	E950.0	E962.0	E980.0
Levomepromazine	967.8	E852.8	E937.8	E950.2	E962.0	E980.2
Levoprome	967.8	E852.8	E937.8	E950.2	E962.0	E980.2
Levopropoxyphene	975.4	E858.6	E945.4	E950.4	E962.0	E980.4
Levorphan, levophanol	965.09	E850.2	E935.2	E950.0	E962.0	E980.0
Levothyroxine (sodium)	962.7	E858.0	E932.7	E950.4	E962.0	E980.4
Levsin	971.1	E855.4	E941.1	E950.4	E962.0	E980.4
Levulose	974.5	E858.5	E944.5	E950.4	E962.0	E980.4
Lewisite (gas)	985.1	E866.3	—	E950.8	E962.1	E980.8
Librium	969.4	E853.2	E939.4	E950.3	E962.0	E980.3
Lidex	976.0	E858.7	E946.0	E950.4	E962.0	E980.4
Lidocaine (infiltration) (topical)	968.5	E855.2	E938.5	E950.4	E962.0	E980.4
nerve block (peripheral) (plexus)	968.6	E855.2	E938.6	E950.4	E962.0	E980.4
spinal	968.7	E855.2	E938.7	E950.4	E962.0	E980.4

Substance	Poisoning	External Cause (E-Code) Accident	Therapeutic Use	Suicide Attempt	Assault	Un-determined
Lighter fluid	981	E862.1	—	E950.9	E962.1	E980.9
Lignocaine (infiltration) (topical)	968.5	E855.2	E938.5	E950.4	E962.0	E980.4
nerve block (peripheral) (plexus)	968.6	E855.2	E938.6	E950.4	E962.0	E980.4
spinal	968.7	E855.2	E938.7	E950.4	E962.0	E980.4
Ligroin(e) (solvent)	981	E862.0	—	E950.9	E962.1	E980.9
vapor	987.1	E869.8	—	E952.8	E962.2	E982.8
Ligustrum vulgare	988.2	E865.3	—	E950.9	E962.1	E980.9
Lily of the valley	988.2	E865.4	—	E950.9	E962.1	E980.9
Lime (chloride)	983.2	E864.2	—	E950.7	E962.1	E980.6
solution, sulferated	976.4	E858.7	E946.4	E950.4	E962.0	E980.4
Limonene	982.8	E862.4	—	E950.9	E962.1	E980.9
Lincomycin	960.8	E856	E930.8	E950.4	E962.0	E980.4
Lindane (insecticide) (vapor)	989.2	E863.0	—	E950.6	E962.1	E980.7
anti-infective (topical)	976.0	E858.7	E946.0	E950.4	E962.0	E980.4
Liniments NEC	976.9	E858.7	E946.9	E950.4	E962.0	E980.4
Linoleic acid	972.2	E858.3	E942.2	E950.4	E962.0	E980.4
Liothyronine	962.7	E858.0	E932.7	E950.4	E962.0	E980.4
Liotrix	962.7	E858.0	E932.7	E950.4	E962.0	E980.4
Lipancreatin	973.4	E858.4	E943.4	E950.4	E962.0	E980.4
Lipo-Lutin	962.2	E858.0	E932.2	E950.4	E962.0	E980.4
Lipotropic agents	977.1	E858.8	E947.1	E950.4	E962.0	E980.4
Liquefied petroleum gases	987.0	E868.0	—	E951.1	E962.2	E981.1
piped (pure or mixed with air)	987.0	E867	—	E951.0	E962.2	E981.0
Liquid						
petrolatum	973.2	E858.4	E943.2	E950.4	E962.0	E980.4
substance	989.9	E866.9	—	E950.9	E962.1	E980.9
specified NEC	989.89	E866.8	—	E950.9	E962.1	E980.9
Lirugen	979.4	E858.8	E949.4	E950.4	E962.0	E980.4
Lithane	969.8	E855.8	E939.8	E950.3	E962.0	E980.3
Lithium	985.8	E866.4	—	E950.9	E962.1	E980.9
carbonate	969.8	E855.8	E939.8	E950.3	E962.0	E980.3
Lithonate	969.8	E855.8	E939.8	E950.3	E962.0	E980.3
Liver (extract) (injection) (preparations)	964.1	E858.2	E934.1	E950.4	E962.0	E980.4
Lizard (bite) (venom)	989.5	E905.0	—	E950.9	E962.1	E980.9
LMD	964.8	E858.2	E934.8	E950.4	E962.0	E980.4
Lobelia	988.2	E865.4	—	E950.9	E962.1	E980.9
Lobeline	970.0	E854.3	E940.0	E950.4	E962.0	E980.4
Locorten	976.0	E858.7	E946.0	E950.4	E962.0	E980.4
Lolium temulentum	988.2	E865.3	—	E950.9	E962.1	E980.9
Lomotil	973.5	E858.4	E943.5	E950.4	E962.0	E980.4
Lomustine	963.1	E858.1	E933.1	E950.4	E962.0	E980.4
Lophophora williamsii	969.6	E854.1	E939.6	E950.3	E962.0	E980.3
Lorazepam	969.4	E853.2	E939.4	E950.3	E962.0	E980.3
Lotions NEC	976.9	E858.7	E946.9	E950.4	E962.0	E980.4
Lotusate	967.0	E851	E937.0	E950.1	E962.0	E980.1
Lowila	976.2	E858.7	E946.2	E950.4	E962.0	E980.4
Loxapine	969.3	E853.8	E939.3	E950.3	E962.0	E980.3
Lozenges (throat)	976.6	E858.7	E946.6	E950.4	E962.0	E980.4
LSD (25)	969.6	E854.1	E939.6	E950.3	E962.0	E980.3
Lubricating oil NEC	981	E862.2	—	E950.9	E962.1	E980.9
Lucanthone	961.6	E857	E931.6	E950.4	E962.0	E980.4
Luminal	967.0	E851	E937.0	E950.1	E962.0	E980.1
Lung irritant (gas) NEC	987.9	E869.9	—	E952.9	E962.2	E982.9
Lutocylol	962.2	E858.0	E932.2	E950.4	E962.0	E980.4
Lutromone	962.2	E858.0	E932.2	E950.4	E962.0	E980.4
Lututrin	975.0	E858.6	E945.0	E950.4	E962.0	E980.4
Lye (concentrated)	983.2	E864.2	—	E950.7	E962.1	E980.6
Lygranum (skin test)	977.8	E858.8	E947.8	E950.4	E962.0	E980.4
Lymecycline	960.4	E856	E930.4	E950.4	E962.0	E980.4
Lymphogranuloma venereum antigen	977.8	E858.8	E947.8	E950.4	E962.0	E980.4
Lynestrenol	962.2	E858.0	E932.2	E950.4	E962.0	E980.4
Lyovac Sodium Edecrin	974.4	E858.5	E944.4	E950.4	E962.0	E980.4
Lypressin	962.5	E858.0	E932.5	E950.4	E962.0	E980.4
Lysergic acid (amide) (diethylamide)	969.6	E854.1	E939.6	E950.3	E962.0	E980.3
Lysergide	969.6	E854.1	E939.6	E950.3	E962.0	E980.3
Lysine vasopressin	962.5	E858.0	E932.5	E950.4	E962.0	E980.4
Lysol	983.0	E864.0	—	E950.7	E962.1	E980.6
Lytta (vitatta)	976.8	E858.7	E946.8	E950.4	E962.0	E980.4
M						
Mace	987.5	E869.3	—	E952.8	E962.2	E982.8
Macrolides (antibiotics)	960.3	E856	E930.3	E950.4	E962.0	E980.4

		External Cause (E-Code)				
Substance	**Poisoning**	**Accident**	**Therapeutic Use**	**Suicide Attempt**	**Assault**	**Undetermined**
Mafenide	976.0	E858.7	E946.0	E950.4	E962.0	E980.4
Magaldrate	973.0	E858.4	E943.0	E950.4	E962.0	E980.4
Magic mushroom	969.6	E854.1	E939.6	E950.3	E962.0	E980.3
Magnamycin	960.8	E856	E930.8	E950.4	E962.0	E980.4
Magnesia magma	973.0	E858.4	E943.0	E950.4	E962.0	E980.4
Magnesium (compounds) (fumes) NEC	985.8	E866.4	—	E950.9	E962.1	E980.9
antacid	973.0	E858.4	E943.0	E950.4	E962.0	E980.4
carbonate	973.0	E858.4	E943.0	E950.4	E962.0	E980.4
cathartic	973.3	E858.4	E943.3	E950.4	E962.0	E980.4
citrate	973.3	E858.4	E943.3	E950.4	E962.0	E980.4
hydroxide	973.0	E858.4	E943.0	E950.4	E962.0	E980.4
oxide	973.0	E858.4	E943.0	E950.4	E962.0	E980.4
sulfate (oral)	973.3	E858.4	E943.3	E950.4	E962.0	E980.4
intravenous	966.3	E855.0	E936.3	E950.4	E962.0	E980.4
trisilicate	973.0	E858.4	E943.0	E950.4	E962.0	E980.4
Malathion (insecticide)	989.3	E863.1	—	E950.6	E962.1	E980.7
Male fern (oleoresin)	961.6	E857	E931.6	E950.4	E962.0	E980.4
Mandelic acid	961.9	E857	E931.9	E950.4	E962.0	E980.4
Manganese compounds (fumes) NEC	985.2	E866.4	—	E950.9	E962.1	E980.9
Mannitol (diuretic) (medicinal) NEC	974.4	E858.5	E944.4	E950.4	E962.0	E980.4
hexanitrate	972.4	E858.3	E942.4	E950.4	E962.0	E980.4
mustard	963.1	E858.1	E933.1	E950.4	E962.0	E980.4
Mannomustine	963.1	E858.1	E933.1	E950.4	E962.0	E980.4
MAO inhibitors	969.0	E854.0	E939.0	E950.3	E962.0	E980.3
Mapharsen	961.1	E857	E931.1	E950.4	E962.0	E980.4
Marcaine	968.9	E855.2	E938.9	E950.4	E962.0	E980.4
infiltration (subcutaneous)	968.5	E855.2	E938.5	E950.4	E962.0	E980.4
nerve block (peripheral) (plexus)	968.6	E855.2	E938.6	E950.4	E962.0	E980.4
Marezine	963.0	E858.1	E933.0	E950.4	E962.0	E980.4
Marihuana, marijuana (derivatives)	969.6	E854.1	E939.6	E950.3	E962.0	E980.3
Marine animals or plants (sting)	989.5	E905.6	—	E950.9	E962.1	E980.9
Marplan	969.0	E854.0	E939.0	E950.3	E962.0	E980.3
Marsh gas	987.1	E869.8	—	E952.8	E962.2	E982.8
Marsilid	969.0	E854.0	E939.0	E950.3	E962.0	E980.3
Matulane	963.1	E858.1	E933.1	E950.4	E962.0	E980.4
Mazindol	977.0	E858.8	E947.0	E950.4	E962.0	E980.4
Meadow saffron	988.2	E865.3	—	E950.9	E962.1	E980.9
Measles vaccine	979.4	E858.8	E949.4	E950.4	E962.0	E980.4
Meat, noxious or nonbacterial	988.8	E865.0	—	E950.9	E962.1	E980.9
Mebanazine	969.0	E854.0	E939.0	E950.3	E962.0	E980.3
Mebaral	967.0	E851	E937.0	E950.1	E962.0	E980.1
Mebendazole	961.6	E857	E931.6	E950.4	E962.0	E980.4
Mebeverine	975.1	E858.6	E945.1	E950.4	E962.0	E980.4
Mebhydroline	963.0	E858.1	E933.0	E950.4	E962.0	E980.4
Mebrophenhydramine	963.0	E858.1	E933.0	E950.4	E962.0	E980.4
Mebutamate	969.5	E853.8	E939.5	E950.3	E962.0	E980.3
Mecamylamine (chloride)	972.3	E858.3	E942.3	E950.4	E962.0	E980.4
Mechlorethamine hydrochloride	963.1	E858.1	E933.1	E950.4	E962.0	E980.4
Meclizene (hydrochloride)	963.0	E858.1	E933.0	E950.4	E962.0	E980.4
Meclofenoxate	970.0	E854.3	E940.0	E950.4	E962.0	E980.4
Meclozine (hydrochloride)	963.0	E858.1	E933.0	E950.4	E962.0	E980.4
Medazepam	969.4	E853.2	E939.4	E950.3	E962.0	E980.3
Medicine, medicinal substance	977.9	E858.9	E947.9	E950.5	E962.0	E980.5
specified NEC	977.8	E858.8	E947.8	E950.4	E962.0	E980.4
Medinal	967.0	E851	E937.0	E950.1	E962.0	E980.1
Medomin	967.0	E851	E937.0	E950.1	E962.0	E980.1
Medroxyprogesterone	962.2	E858.0	E932.2	E950.4	E962.0	E980.4
Medrysone	976.5	E858.7	E946.5	E950.4	E962.0	E980.4
Mefenamic acid	965.7	E850.7	E935.7	E950.0	E962.0	E980.0
Megahallucinogen	969.6	E854.1	E939.6	E950.3	E962.0	E980.3
Megestrol	962.2	E858.0	E932.2	E950.4	E962.0	E980.4
Meglumine	977.8	E858.8	E947.8	E950.4	E962.0	E980.4
Meladinin	976.3	E858.7	E946.3	E950.4	E962.0	E980.4
Melanizing agents	976.3	E858.7	E946.3	E950.4	E962.0	E980.4
Melarsoprol	961.1	E857	E931.1	E950.4	E962.0	E980.4
Melia azedarach	988.2	E865.3	—	E950.9	E962.1	E980.9
Mellaril	969.1	E853.0	E939.1	E950.3	E962.0	E980.3
Meloxine	976.3	E858.7	E946.3	E950.4	E962.0	E980.4
Melphalan	963.1	E858.1	E933.1	E950.4	E962.0	E980.4
Menadiol sodium diphosphate	964.3	E858.2	E934.3	E950.4	E962.0	E980.4
Menadione (sodium bisulfite)	964.3	E858.2	E934.3	E950.4	E962.0	E980.4

		External Cause (E-Code)				
Substance	Poisoning	Accident	Therapeutic Use	Suicide Attempt	Assault	Undetermined
Menaphthone	964.3	E858.2	E934.3	E950.4	E962.0	E980.4
Meningococcal vaccine	978.8	E858.8	E948.8	E950.4	E962.0	E980.4
Menningovax-C	978.8	E858.8	E948.8	E950.4	E962.0	E980.4
Menotropins	962.4	E858.0	E932.4	E950.4	E962.0	E980.4
Menthol NEC	976.1	E858.7	E946.1	E950.4	E962.0	E980.4
Mepacrine	961.3	E857	E931.3	E950.4	E962.0	E980.4
Meparfynol	967.8	E852.8	E937.8	E950.2	E962.0	E980.2
Mepazine	969.1	E853.0	E939.1	E950.3	E962.0	E980.3
Mepenzolate	971.1	E855.4	E941.1	E950.4	E962.0	E980.4
Meperidine	965.09	E850.2	E935.2	E950.0	E962.0	E980.0
Mephenamin(e)	966.4	E855.0	E936.4	E950.4	E962.0	E980.4
Mephenesin (carbamate)	968.0	E855.1	E938.0	E950.4	E962.0	E980.4
Mephenoxalone	969.5	E853.8	E939.5	E950.3	E962.0	E980.3
Mephentermine	971.2	E855.5	E941.2	E950.4	E962.0	E980.4
Mephenytoin	966.1	E855.0	E936.1	E950.4	E962.0	E980.4
Mephobarbital	967.0	E851	E937.0	E950.1	E962.0	E980.1
Mepiperphenidol	971.1	E855.4	E941.1	E950.4	E962.0	E980.4
Mepivacaine	968.9	E855.2	E938.9	E950.4	E962.0	E980.4
infiltration (subcutaneous)	968.5	E855.2	E938.5	E950.4	E962.0	E980.4
nerve block (peripheral) (plexus)	968.6	E855.2	E938.6	E950.4	E962.0	E980.4
topical (surface)	968.5	E855.2	E938.5	E950.4	E962.0	E980.4
Meprednisone	962.0	E858.0	E932.0	E950.4	E962.0	E980.4
Meprobam	969.5	E853.8	E939.5	E950.3	E962.0	E980.3
Meprobamate	969.5	E853.8	E939.5	E950.3	E962.0	E980.3
Mepyramine (maleate)	963.0	E858.1	E933.0	E950.4	E962.0	E980.4
Meralluride	974.0	E858.5	E944.0	E950.4	E962.0	E980.4
Merbaphen	974.0	E858.5	E944.0	E950.4	E962.0	E980.4
Merbromin	976.0	E858.7	E946.0	E950.4	E962.0	E980.4
Mercaptomerin	974.0	E858.5	E944.0	E950.4	E962.0	E980.4
Mercaptopurine	963.1	E858.1	E933.1	E950.4	E962.0	E980.4
Mercumatilin	974.0	E858.5	E944.0	E950.4	E962.0	E980.4
Mercuramide	974.0	E858.5	E944.0	E950.4	E962.0	E980.4
Mercuranin	976.0	E858.7	E946.0	E950.4	E962.0	E980.4
Mercurochrome	976.0	E858.7	E946.0	E950.4	E962.0	E980.4
Mercury, mercuric, mercurous (compounds) (cyanide) (fumes) (nonmedicinal) (vapor) NEC	985.0	E866.1	—	E950.9	E962.1	E980.9
ammoniated	976.0	E858.7	E946.0	E950.4	E962.0	E980.4
anti-infective	961.2	E857	E931.2	E950.4	E962.0	E980.4
topical	976.0	E858.7	E946.0	E950.4	E962.0	E980.4
chloride (antiseptic) NEC	976.0	E858.7	E946.0	E950.4	E962.0	E980.4
fungicide	985.0	E863.6	—	E950.6	E962.1	E980.7
diuretic compounds	974.0	E858.5	E944.0	E950.4	E962.0	E980.4
fungicide	985.0	E863.6	—	E950.6	E962.1	E980.7
organic (fungicide)	985.0	E863.6	—	E950.6	E962.1	E980.7
Merethoxylline	974.0	E858.5	E944.0	E950.4	E962.0	E980.4
Mersalyl	974.0	E858.5	E944.0	E950.4	E962.0	E980.4
Merthiolate (topical)	976.0	E858.7	E946.0	E950.4	E962.0	E980.4
ophthalmic preparation	976.5	E858.7	E946.5	E950.4	E962.0	E980.4
Meruvax	979.4	E858.8	E949.4	E950.4	E962.0	E980.4
Mescal buttons	969.6	E854.1	E939.6	E950.3	E962.0	E980.3
Mescaline (salts)	969.6	E854.1	E939.6	E950.3	E962.0	E980.3
Mesoridazine besylate	969.1	E853.0	E939.1	E950.3	E962.0	E980.3
Mestanolone	962.1	E858.0	E932.1	E950.4	E962.0	E980.4
Mestranol	962.2	E858.0	E932.2	E950.4	E962.0	E980.4
Metacresylacetate	976.0	E858.7	E946.0	E950.4	E962.0	E980.4
Metaldehyde (snail killer) NEC	989.4	E863.4	—	E950.6	E962.1	E980.7
Metals (heavy) (nonmedicinal) NEC	985.9	E866.4	—	E950.9	E962.1	E980.9
dust, fumes, or vapor NEC	985.9	E866.4	—	E950.9	E962.1	E980.9
light NEC	985.9	E866.4	—	E950.9	E962.1	E980.9
dust, fumes, or vapor NEC	985.9	E866.4	—	E950.9	E962.1	E980.9
pesticides (dust) (vapor)	985.9	E863.4	—	E950.6	E962.1	E980.7
Metamucil	973.3	E858.4	E943.3	E950.4	E962.0	E980.4
Metaphen	976.0	E858.7	E946.0	E950.4	E962.0	E980.4
Metaproterenol	975.1	E858.6	E945.1	E950.4	E962.0	E980.4
Metaraminol	972.8	E858.3	E942.8	E950.4	E962.0	E980.4
Metaxalone	968.0	E855.1	E938.0	E950.4	E962.0	E980.4
Metformin	962.3	E858.0	E932.3	E950.4	E962.0	E980.4
Methacycline	960.4	E856	E930.4	E950.4	E962.0	E980.4
Methadone	965.02	E850.1	E935.1	E950.0	E962.0	E980.0
Methallenestril	962.2	E858.0	E932.2	E950.4	E962.0	E980.4
Methamphetamine	969.7	E854.2	E939.7	E950.3	E962.0	E980.3
Methandienone	962.1	E858.0	E932.1	E950.4	E962.0	E980.4

Substance	Poisoning	External Cause (E-Code) Accident	Therapeutic Use	Suicide Attempt	Assault	Undetermined
Methandriol	962.1	E858.0	E932.1	E950.4	E962.0	E980.4
Methandrostenolone	962.1	E858.0	E932.1	E950.4	E962.0	E980.4
Methane gas	987.1	E869.8	—	E952.8	E962.2	E982.8
Methanol	980.1	E860.2	—	E950.9	E962.1	E980.9
vapor	987.8	E869.8	—	E952.8	E962.2	E982.8
Methantheline	971.1	E855.4	E941.1	E950.4	E962.0	E980.4
Methaphenilene	963.0	E858.1	E933.0	E950.4	E962.0	E980.4
Methapyrilene	963.0	E858.1	E933.0	E950.4	E962.0	E980.4
Methaqualone (compounds)	967.4	E852.3	E937.4	E950.2	E962.0	E980.2
Metharbital, metharbitone	967.0	E851	E937.0	E950.1	E962.0	E980.1
Methazolamide	974.2	E858.5	E944.2	E950.4	E962.0	E980.4
Methdilazine	963.0	E858.1	E933.0	E950.4	E962.0	E980.4
Methedrine	969.7	E854.2	E939.7	E950.3	E962.0	E980.3
Methenamine (mandelate)	961.9	E857	E931.9	E950.4	E962.0	E980.4
Methenolone	962.1	E858.0	E932.1	E950.4	E962.0	E980.4
Methergine	975.0	E858.6	E945.0	E950.4	E962.0	E980.4
Methiacil	962.8	E858.0	E932.8	E950.4	E962.0	E980.4
Methicillin (sodium)	960.0	E856	E930.0	E950.4	E962.0	E980.4
Methimazole	962.8	E858.0	E932.8	E950.4	E962.0	E980.4
Methionine	977.1	E858.8	E947.1	E950.4	E962.0	E980.4
Methisazone	961.7	E857	E931.7	E950.4	E962.0	E980.4
Methitural	967.0	E851	E937.0	E950.1	E962.0	E980.1
Methixene	971.1	E855.4	E941.1	E950.4	E962.0	E980.4
Methobarbital, methobarbitone	967.0	E851	E937.0	E950.1	E962.0	E980.1
Methocarbamol	968.0	E855.1	E938.0	E950.4	E962.0	E980.4
Methohexital, methohexitone (sodium)	968.3	E855.1	E938.3	E950.4	E962.0	E980.4
Methoin	966.1	E855.0	E936.1	E950.4	E962.0	E980.4
Methopholine	965.7	E850.7	E935.7	E950.0	E962.0	E980.0
Methorate	975.4	E858.6	E945.4	E950.4	E962.0	E980.4
Methoserpidine	972.6	E858.3	E942.6	E950.4	E962.0	E980.4
Methotrexate	963.1	E858.1	E933.1	E950.4	E962.0	E980.4
Methotrimeprazine	967.8	E852.8	E937.8	E950.2	E962.0	E980.2
Methoxa-Dome	976.3	E858.7	E946.3	E950.4	E962.0	E980.4
Methoxamine	971.2	E855.5	E941.2	E950.4	E962.0	E980.4
Methoxsalen	976.3	E858.7	E946.3	E950.4	E962.0	E980.4
Methoxybenzyl penicillin	960.0	E856	E930.0	E950.4	E962.0	E980.4
Methoxychlor	989.2	E863.0	—	E950.6	E962.1	E980.7
Methoxyflurane	968.2	E855.1	E938.2	E950.4	E962.0	E980.4
Methoxyphenamine	971.2	E855.5	E941.2	E950.4	E962.0	E980.4
Methoxypromazine	969.1	E853.0	E939.1	E950.3	E962.0	E980.3
Methoxypsoralen	976.3	E858.7	E946.3	E950.4	E962.0	E980.4
Methscopolamine (bromide)	971.1	E855.4	E941.1	E950.4	E962.0	E980.4
Methsuximide	966.2	E855.0	E936.2	E950.4	E962.0	E980.4
Methyclothiazide	974.3	E858.5	E944.3	E950.4	E962.0	E980.4
Methyl						
acetate	982.8	E862.4	—	E950.9	E962.1	E980.9
acetone	982.8	E862.4	—	E950.9	E962.1	E980.9
alcohol	980.1	E860.2	—	E950.9	E962.1	E980.9
amphetamine	969.7	E854.2	E939.7	E950.3	E962.0	E980.3
androstanolone	962.1	E858.0	E932.1	E950.4	E962.0	E980.4
atropine	971.1	E855.4	E941.1	E950.4	E962.0	E980.4
benzene	982.0	E862.4	—	E950.9	E962.1	E980.9
bromide (gas)	987.8	E869.8	—	E952.8	E962.2	E982.8
fumigant	987.8	E863.8	—	E950.6	E962.2	E980.7
butanol	980.8	E860.8	—	E950.9	E962.1	E980.9
carbinol	980.1	E860.2	—	E950.9	E962.1	E980.9
cellosolve	982.8	E862.4	—	E950.9	E962.1	E980.9
cellulose	973.3	E858.4	E943.3	E950.4	E962.0	E980.4
chloride (gas)	987.8	E869.8	—	E952.8	E962.2	E982.8
cyclohexane	982.8	E862.4	—	E950.9	E962.1	E980.9
cyclohexanone	982.8	E862.4	—	E950.9	E962.1	E980.9
dihydromorphinone	965.09	E850.2	E935.2	E950.0	E962.0	E980.0
ergometrine	975.0	E858.6	E945.0	E950.4	E962.0	E980.4
ergonovine	975.0	E858.6	E945.0	E950.4	E962.0	E980.4
ethyl ketone	982.8	E862.4	—	E950.9	E962.1	E980.9
hydrazine	983.9	E864.3	—	E950.7	E962.1	E980.6
isobutyl ketone	982.8	E862.4	—	E950.9	E962.1	E980.9
morphine NEC	965.09	E850.2	E935.2	E950.0	E962.0	E980.0
parafynol	967.8	E852.8	E937.8	E950.2	E962.0	E980.2
parathion	989.3	E863.1	—	E950.6	E962.1	E980.7
pentynol NEC	967.8	E852.8	E937.8	E950.2	E962.0	E980.2
peridol	969.2	E853.1	E939.2	E950.3	E962.0	E980.3

Substance	Poisoning	External Cause (E-Code) Accident	Therapeutic Use	Suicide Attempt	Assault	Un-determined
Methyl — *continued*						
phenidate	969.7	E854.2	E939.7	E950.3	E962.0	E980.3
prednisolone	962.0	E858.0	E932.0	E950.4	E962.0	E980.4
ENT agent	976.6	E858.7	E946.6	E950.4	E962.0	E980.4
ophthalmic preparation	976.5	E858.7	E946.5	E950.4	E962.0	E980.4
topical NEC	976.0	E858.7	E946.0	E950.4	E962.0	E980.4
propylcarbinol	980.8	E860.8	—	E950.9	E962.1	E980.9
rosaniline NEC	976.0	E858.7	E946.0	E950.4	E962.0	E980.4
salicylate NEC	976.3	E858.7	E946.3	E950.4	E962.0	E980.4
sulfate (fumes)	987.8	E869.8	—	E952.8	E962.2	E982.8
liquid	983.9	E864.3	—	E950.7	E962.1	E980.6
sulfonal	967.8	E852.8	E937.8	E950.2	E962.0	E980.2
testosterone	962.1	E858.0	E932.1	E950.4	E962.0	E980.4
thiouracil	962.8	E858.0	E932.8	E950.4	E962.0	E980.4
Methylated spirit	980.0	E860.1	—	E950.9	E962.1	E980.9
Methyldopa	972.6	E858.3	E942.6	E950.4	E962.0	E980.4
Methylene						
blue	961.9	E857	E931.9	E950.4	E962.0	E980.4
chloride or dichloride (solvent) NEC	982.3	E862.4	—	E950.9	E962.1	E980.9
Methylhexabital	967.0	E851	E937.0	E950.1	E962.0	E980.1
Methylparaben (ophthalmic)	976.5	E858.7	E946.5	E950.4	E962.0	E980.4
Methyprylon	967.5	E852.4	E937.5	E950.2	E962.0	E980.2
Methysergide	971.3	E855.6	E941.3	E950.4	E962.0	E980.4
Metoclopramide	963.0	E858.1	E933.0	E950.4	E962.0	E980.4
Metofoline	965.7	E850.7	E935.7	E950.0	E962.0	E980.0
Metopon	965.09	E850.2	E935.2	E950.0	E962.0	E980.0
Metronidazole	961.5	E857	E931.5	E950.4	E962.0	E980.4
Metycaine	968.9	E855.2	E938.9	E950.4	E962.0	E980.4
infiltration (subcutaneous)	968.5	E855.2	E938.5	E950.4	E962.0	E980.4
nerve block (peripheral) (plexus)	968.6	E855.2	E938.6	E950.4	E962.0	E980.4
topical (surface)	968.5	E855.2	E938.5	E950.4	E962.0	E980.4
Metyrapone	977.8	E858.8	E947.8	E950.4	E962.0	E980.4
Mevinphos	989.3	E863.1	—	E950.6	E962.1	E980.7
Mezereon (berries)	988.2	E865.3	—	E950.9	E962.1	E980.9
Micatin	976.0	E858.7	E946.0	E950.4	E962.0	E980.4
Miconazole	976.0	E858.7	E946.0	E950.4	E962.0	E980.4
Midol	965.1	E850.3	E935.3	E950.0	E962.0	E980.0
Milk of magnesia	973.0	E858.4	E943.0	E950.4	E962.0	E980.4
Millipede (tropical) (venomous)	989.5	E905.4	—	E950.9	E962.1	E980.9
Miltown	969.5	E853.8	E939.5	E950.3	E962.0	E980.3
Mineral						
oil (medicinal)	973.2	E858.4	E943.2	E950.4	E962.0	E980.4
nonmedicinal	981	E862.1	—	E950.9	E962.1	E980.9
topical	976.3	E858.7	E946.3	E950.4	E962.0	E980.4
salts NEC	974.6	E858.5	E944.6	E950.4	E962.0	E980.4
spirits	981	E862.0	—	E950.9	E962.1	E980.9
Minocycline	960.4	E856	E930.4	E950.4	E962.0	E980.4
Mithramycin (antineoplastic)	960.7	E856	E930.7	E950.4	E962.0	E980.4
Mitobronitol	963.1	E858.1	E933.1	E950.4	E962.0	E980.4
Mitomycin (antineoplastic)	960.7	E856	E930.7	E950.4	E962.0	E980.4
Mitotane	963.1	E858.1	E933.1	E950.4	E962.0	E980.4
Moderil	972.6	E858.3	E942.6	E950.4	E962.0	E980.4
Mogadon — *see* Nitrazepam						
Molindone	969.3	E853.8	E939.3	E950.3	E962.0	E980.3
Monistat	976.0	E858.7	E946.0	E950.4	E962.0	E980.4
Monkshood	988.2	E865.4	—	E950.9	E962.1	E980.9
Monoamine oxidase inhibitors	969.0	E854.0	E939.0	E950.3	E962.0	E980.3
Monochlorobenzene	982.0	E862.4	—	E950.9	E962.1	E980.9
Monosodium glutamate	989.89	E866.8	—	E950.9	E962.1	E980.9
Monoxide, carbon — *see* Carbon, monoxide						
Moperone	969.2	E853.1	E939.2	E950.3	E962.0	E980.3
Morning glory seeds	969.6	E854.1	E939.6	E950.3	E962.0	E980.3
Moroxydine (hydrochloride)	961.7	E857	E931.7	E950.4	E962.0	E980.4
Morphazinamide	961.8	E857	E931.8	E950.4	E962.0	E980.4
Morphinans	965.09	E850.2	E935.2	E950.0	E962.0	E980.0
Morphine NEC	965.09	E850.2	E935.2	E950.0	E962.0	E980.0
antagonists	970.1	E854.3	E940.1	E950.4	E962.0	E980.4
Morpholinylethylmorphine	965.09	E850.2	E935.2	E950.0	E962.0	E980.0
Morrhuate sodium	972.7	E858.3	E942.7	E950.4	E962.0	E980.4
Moth balls (*see also* Pesticides)	989.4	E863.4	—	E950.6	E962.1	E980.7
naphthalene	983.0	E863.4	—	E950.7	E962.1	E980.6
Motor exhaust gas — *see* Carbon, monoxide, exhaust gas						

Substance	Poisoning	External Cause (E-Code)				
		Accident	Therapeutic Use	Suicide Attempt	Assault	Undetermined
Mouth wash	976.6	E858.7	E946.6	E950.4	E962.0	E980.4
Mucolytic agent	975.5	E858.6	E945.5	E950.4	E962.0	E980.4
Mucomyst	975.5	E858.6	E945.5	E950.4	E962.0	E980.4
Mucous membrane agents (external)	976.9	E858.7	E946.9	E950.4	E962.0	E980.4
specified NEC	976.8	E858.7	E946.8	E950.4	E962.0	E980.4
Mumps						
immune globulin (human)	964.6	E858.2	E934.6	E950.4	E962.0	E980.4
skin test antigen	977.8	E858.8	E947.8	E950.4	E962.0	E980.4
vaccine	979.6	E858.8	E949.6	E950.4	E962.0	E980.4
Mumpsvax	979.6	E858.8	E949.6	E950.4	E962.0	E980.4
Muriatic acid — *see* Hydrochloric acid						
Muscarine	971.0	E855.3	E941.0	E950.4	E962.0	E980.4
Muscle affecting agents NEC	975.3	E858.6	E945.3	E950.4	E962.0	E980.4
oxytocic	975.0	E858.6	E945.0	E950.4	E962.0	E980.4
relaxants	975.3	E858.6	E945.3	E950.4	E962.0	E980.4
central nervous system	968.0	E855.1	E938.0	E950.4	E962.0	E980.4
skeletal	975.2	E858.6	E945.2	E950.4	E962.0	E980.4
smooth	975.1	E858.6	E945.1	E950.4	E962.0	E980.4
Mushrooms, noxious	988.1	E865.5	—	E950.9	E962.1	E980.9
Mussel, noxious	988.0	E865.1	—	E950.9	E962.1	E980.9
Mustard (emetic)	973.6	E858.4	E943.6	E950.4	E962.0	E980.4
gas	987.8	E869.8	—	E952.8	E962.2	E982.8
nitrogen	963.1	E858.1	E933.1	E950.4	E962.0	E980.4
Mustine	963.1	E858.1	E933.1	E950.4	E962.0	E980.4
M-vac	979.4	E858.8	E949.4	E950.4	E962.0	E980.4
Mycifradin	960.8	E856	E930.8	E950.4	E962.0	E980.4
topical	976.0	E858.7	E946.0	E950.4	E962.0	E980.4
Mycitracin	960.8	E856	E930.8	E950.4	E962.0	E980.4
ophthalmic preparation	976.5	E858.7	E946.5	E950.4	E962.0	E980.4
Mycostatin	960.1	E856	E930.1	E950.4	E962.0	E980.4
topical	976.0	E858.7	E946.0	E950.4	E962.0	E980.4
Mydriacyl	971.1	E855.4	E941.1	E950.4	E962.0	E980.4
Myelobromal	963.1	E858.1	E933.1	E950.4	E962.0	E980.4
Myleran	963.1	E858.1	E933.1	E950.4	E962.0	E980.4
Myochrysin(e)	965.69	E850.6	E935.6	E950.0	E962.0	E980.0
Myoneural blocking agents	975.2	E858.6	E945.2	E950.4	E962.0	E980.4
Myristica fragrans	988.2	E865.3	—	E950.9	E962.1	E980.9
Myristicin	988.2	E865.3	—	E950.9	E962.1	E980.9
Mysoline	966.3	E855.0	E936.3	E950.4	E962.0	E980.4
N						
Nafcillin (sodium)	960.0	E856	E930.0	E950.4	E962.0	E980.4
Nail polish remover	982.8	E862.4	—	E950.9	E962.1	E980.9
Nalidixic acid	961.9	E857	E931.9	E950.4	E962.0	E980.4
Nalorphine	970.1	E854.3	E940.1	E950.4	E962.0	E980.4
Naloxone	970.1	E854.3	E940.1	E950.4	E962.0	E980.4
Nandrolone (decanoate) (phenproprioate)	962.1	E858.0	E932.1	E950.4	E962.0	E980.4
Naphazoline	971.2	E855.5	E941.2	E950.4	E962.0	E980.4
Naphtha (painter's) (petroleum)	981	E862.0	—	E950.9	E962.1	E980.9
solvent	981	E862.0	—	E950.9	E962.1	E980.9
vapor	987.1	E869.8	—	E952.8	E962.2	E982.8
Naphthalene (chlorinated)	983.0	E864.0	—	E950.7	E962.1	E980.6
insecticide or moth repellent	983.0	E863.4	—	E950.7	E962.1	E980.6
vapor	987.8	E869.8	—	E952.8	E962.2	E982.8
Naphthol	983.0	E864.0	—	E950.7	E962.1	E980.6
Naphthylamine	983.0	E864.0	—	E950.7	E962.1	E980.6
Naprosyn — *see* Naproxen						
Naproxen	965.61	E850.6	E935.6	E950.0	E962.0	E980.0
Narcotic (drug)	967.9	E852.9	E937.9	E950.2	E962.0	E980.2
analgesic NEC	965.8	E850.8	E935.8	E950.0	E962.0	E980.0
antagonist	970.1	E854.3	E940.1	E950.4	E962.0	E980.4
specified NEC	967.8	E852.8	E937.8	E950.2	E962.0	E980.2
Narcotine	975.4	E858.6	E945.4	E950.4	E962.0	E980.4
Nardil	969.0	E854.0	E939.0	E950.3	E962.0	E980.3
Natrium cyanide — *see* Cyanide(s)						
Natural						
blood (product)	964.7	E858.2	E934.7	E950.4	E962.0	E980.4
gas (piped)	987.1	E867	—	E951.0	E962.2	E981.0
incomplete combustion	986	E867	—	E951.0	E962.2	E981.0
Nealbarbital, nealbarbitone	967.0	E851	E937.0	E950.1	E962.0	E980.1
Nectadon	975.4	E858.6	E945.4	E950.4	E962.0	E980.4
Nematocyst (sting)	989.5	E905.6	—	E950.9	E962.1	E980.9
Nembutal	967.0	E851	E937.0	E950.1	E962.0	E980.1

Substance	Poisoning	External Cause (E-Code) Accident	Therapeutic Use	Suicide Attempt	Assault	Un-determined
Neoarsphenamine	961.1	E857	E931.1	E950.4	E962.0	E980.4
Neocinchophen	974.7	E858.5	E944.7	E950.4	E962.0	E980.4
Neomycin	960.8	E856	E930.8	E950.4	E962.0	E980.4
ENT agent	976.6	E858.7	E946.6	E950.4	E962.0	E980.4
ophthalmic preparation	976.5	E858.7	E946.5	E950.4	E962.0	E980.4
topical NEC	976.0	E858.7	E946.0	E950.4	E962.0	E980.4
Neonal	967.0	E851	E937.0	E950.1	E962.0	E980.1
Neoprontosil	961.0	E857	E931.0	E950.4	E962.0	E980.4
Neosalvarsan	961.1	E857	E931.1	E950.4	E962.0	E980.4
Neosilversalvarsan	961.1	E857	E931.1	E950.4	E962.0	E980.4
Neosporin	960.8	E856	E930.8	E950.4	E962.0	E980.4
ENT agent	976.6	E858.7	E946.6	E950.4	E962.0	E980.4
ophthalmic preparation	976.5	E858.7	E946.5	E950.4	E962.0	E980.4
topical NEC	976.0	E858.7	E946.0	E950.4	E962.0	E980.4
Neostigmine	971.0	E855.3	E941.0	E950.4	E962.0	E980.4
Neraval	967.0	E851	E937.0	E950.1	E962.0	E980.1
Neravan	967.0	E851	E937.0	E950.1	E962.0	E980.1
Nerium oleander	988.2	E865.4	—	E950.9	E962.1	E980.9
Nerve gases (war)	987.9	E869.9	—	E952.9	E962.2	E982.9
Nesacaine	968.9	E855.2	E938.9	E950.4	E962.0	E980.4
infiltration (subcutaneous)	968.5	E855.2	E938.5	E950.4	E962.0	E980.4
nerve block (peripheral) (plexus)	968.6	E855.2	E938.6	E950.4	E962.0	E980.4
Neurobarb	967.0	E851	E937.0	E950.1	E962.0	E980.1
Neuroleptics NEC	969.3	E853.8	E939.3	E950.3	E962.0	E980.3
Neutral spirits	980.0	E860.1	—	E950.9	E962.1	E980.9
beverage	980.0	E860.0	—	E950.9	E962.1	E980.9
Niacin, niacinamide	972.2	E858.3	E942.2	E950.4	E962.0	E980.4
Nialamide	969.0	E854.0	E939.0	E950.3	E962.0	E980.3
Nickle(carbonyl)(compounds)(fumes)(tetracarbonyl)(vapor)	985.8	E866.4	—	E950.9	E962.1	E980.9
Niclosamide	961.6	E857	E931.6	E950.4	E962.0	E980.4
Nicomorphine	965.09	E850.2	E935.2	E950.0	E962.0	E980.0
Nicotinamide	972.2	E858.3	E942.2	E950.4	E962.0	E980.4
Nicotine (insecticide) (spray) (sulfate) NEC	989.4	E863.4	—	E950.6	E962.1	E980.7
not insecticide	989.89	E866.8	—	E950.9	E962.1	E980.9
Nicotinic acid (derivatives)	972.2	E858.3	E942.2	E950.4	E962.0	E980.4
Nicotinyl alcohol	972.2	E858.3	E942.2	E950.4	E962.0	E980.4
Nicoumalone	964.2	E858.2	E934.2	E950.4	E962.0	E980.4
Nifenazone	965.5	E850.5	E935.5	E950.0	E962.0	E980.0
Nifuraldezone	961.9	E857	E931.9	E950.4	E962.0	E980.4
Nightshade (deadly)	988.2	E865.4	—	E950.9	E962.1	E980.9
Nikethamide	970.0	E854.3	E940.0	E950.4	E962.0	E980.4
Nilstat	960.1	E856	E930.1	E950.4	E962.0	E980.4
topical	976.0	E858.7	E946.0	E950.4	E962.0	E980.4
Niridazole	961.6	E857	E931.6	E950.4	E962.0	E980.4
Nisentil	965.09	E850.2	E935.2	E950.0	E962.0	E980.0
Nitrates	972.4	E858.3	E942.4	E950.4	E962.0	E980.4
Nitrazepam	969.4	E853.2	E939.4	E950.3	E962.0	E980.3
Nitric						
acid (liquid)	983.1	E864.1	—	E950.7	E962.1	E980.6
vapor	987.8	E869.8	—	E952.8	E962.2	E982.8
oxide (gas)	987.2	E869.0	—	E952.8	E962.2	E982.8
Nitrite, amyl (medicinal) (vapor)	972.4	E858.3	E942.4	E950.4	E962.0	E980.4
Nitroaniline	983.0	E864.0	—	E950.7	E962.1	E980.6
vapor	987.8	E869.8	—	E952.8	E962.2	E982.8
Nitrobenzene, nitrobenzol	983.0	E864.0	—	E950.7	E962.1	E980.6
vapor	987.8	E869.8	—	E952.8	E962.2	E982.8
Nitrocellulose	976.3	E858.7	E946.3	E950.4	E962.0	E980.4
Nitrofuran derivatives	961.9	E857	E931.9	E950.4	E962.0	E980.4
Nitrofurantoin	961.9	E857	E931.9	E950.4	E962.0	E980.4
Nitrofurazone	976.0	E858.7	E946.0	E950.4	E962.0	E980.4
Nitrogen (dioxide) (gas) (oxide)	987.2	E869.0	—	E952.8	E962.2	E982.8
mustard (antineoplastic)	963.1	E858.1	E933.1	E950.4	E962.0	E980.4
Nitroglycerin, nitroglycerol (medicinal)	972.4	E858.3	E942.4	E950.4	E962.0	E980.4
nonmedicinal	989.89	E866.8	—	E950.9	E962.1	E980.9
fumes	987.8	E869.8	—	E952.8	E962.2	E982.8
Nitrohydrochloric acid	983.1	E864.1	—	E950.7	E962.1	E980.6
Nitromersol	976.0	E858.7	E946.0	E950.4	E962.0	E980.4
Nitronaphthalene	983.0	E864.0	—	E950.7	E962.2	E980.6
Nitrophenol	983.0	E864.0	—	E950.7	E962.2	E980.6
Nitrothiazol	961.6	E857	E931.6	E950.4	E962.0	E980.4

Substance	Poisoning	External Cause (E-Code) Accident	Therapeutic Use	Suicide Attempt	Assault	Undetermined
Nitrotoluene, nitrotoluol	983.0	E864.0	—	E950.7	E962.1	E980.6
vapor	987.8	E869.8	—	E952.8	E962.2	E982.8
Nitrous	968.2	E855.1	E938.2	E950.4	E962.0	E980.4
acid (liquid)	983.1	E864.1	—	E950.7	E962.1	E980.6
fumes	987.2	E869.0	—	E952.8	E962.2	E982.8
oxide (anesthetic) NEC	968.2	E855.1	E938.2	E950.4	E962.0	E980.4
Nitrozone	976.0	E858.7	E946.0	E950.4	E962.0	E980.4
Noctec	967.1	E852.0	E937.1	E950.2	E962.0	E980.2
Noludar	967.5	E852.4	E937.5	E950.2	E962.0	E980.2
Noptil	967.0	E851	E937.0	E950.1	E962.0	E980.1
Noradrenalin	971.2	E855.5	E941.2	E950.4	E962.0	E980.4
Noramidopyrine	965.5	E850.5	E935.5	E950.0	E962.0	E980.0
Norepinephrine	971.2	E855.5	E941.2	E950.4	E962.0	E980.4
Norethandrolone	962.1	E858.0	E932.1	E950.4	E962.0	E980.4
Norethindrone	962.2	E858.0	E932.2	E950.4	E962.0	E980.4
Norethisterone	962.2	E858.0	E932.2	E950.4	E962.0	E980.4
Norethynodrel	962.2	E858.0	E932.2	E950.4	E962.0	E980.4
Norlestrin	962.2	E858.0	E932.2	E950.4	E962.0	E980.4
Norlutin	962.2	E858.0	E932.2	E950.4	E962.0	E980.4
Normison — *see* Benzodiazepines						
Normorphine	965.09	E850.2	E935.2	E950.0	E962.0	E980.0
Nortriptyline	969.0	E854.0	E939.0	E950.3	E962.0	E980.3
Noscapine	975.4	E858.6	E945.4	E950.4	E962.0	E980.4
Nose preparations	976.6	E858.7	E946.6	E950.4	E962.0	E980.4
Novobiocin	960.8	E856	E930.8	E950.4	E962.0	E980.4
Novocain (infiltration) (topical)	968.5	E855.2	E938.5	E950.4	E962.0	E980.4
nerve block (peripheral) (plexus)	968.6	E855.2	E938.6	E950.4	E962.0	E980.4
spinal	968.7	E855.2	E938.7	E950.4	E962.0	E980.4
Noxythiolin	961.9	E857	E931.9	E950.4	E962.0	E980.4
NPH Iletin (insulin)	962.3	E858.0	E932.3	E950.4	E962.0	E980.4
Numorphan	965.09	E850.2	E935.2	E950.0	E962.0	E980.0
Nunol	967.0	E851	E937.0	E950.1	E962.0	E980.1
Nupercaine (spinal anesthetic)	968.7	E855.2	E938.7	E950.4	E962.0	E980.4
topical (surface)	968.5	E855.2	E938.5	E950.4	E962.0	E980.4
Nutmeg oil (liniment)	976.3	E858.7	E946.3	E950.4	E962.0	E980.4
Nux vomica	989.1	E863.7	—	E950.6	E962.1	E980.7
Nydrazid	961.8	E857	E931.8	E950.4	E962.0	E980.4
Nylidrin	971.2	E855.5	E941.2	E950.4	E962.0	E980.4
Nystatin	960.1	E856	E930.1	E950.4	E962.0	E980.4
topical	976.0	E858.7	E946.0	E950.4	E962.0	E980.4
Nytol	963.0	E858.1	E933.0	E950.4	E962.0	E980.4
O						
Oblivion	967.8	E852.8	E937.8	E950.2	E962.0	E980.2
Octyl nitrite	972.4	E858.3	E942.4	E950.4	E962.0	E980.4
Oestradiol (cypionate) (dipropionate) (valerate)	962.2	E858.0	E932.2	E950.4	E962.0	E980.4
Oestriol	962.2	E858.0	E932.2	E950.4	E962.0	E980.4
Oestrone	962.2	E858.0	E932.2	E950.4	E962.0	E980.4
Oil (of) NEC	989.89	E866.8	—	E950.9	E962.1	E980.9
bitter almond	989.0	E866.8	—	E950.9	E962.1	E980.9
camphor	976.1	E858.7	E946.1	E950.4	E962.0	E980.4
colors	989.89	E861.6	—	E950.9	E962.1	E980.9
fumes	987.8	E869.8	—	E952.8	E962.2	E982.8
lubricating	981	E862.2	—	E950.9	E962.1	E980.9
specified source, other — *see* substance specified						
vitriol (liquid)	983.1	E864.1	—	E950.7	E962.1	E980.6
fumes	987.8	E869.8	—	E952.8	E962.2	E982.8
wintergreen (bitter) NEC	976.3	E858.7	E946.3	E950.4	E962.0	E980.4
Ointments NEC	976.9	E858.7	E946.9	E950.4	E962.0	E980.4
Oleander	988.2	E865.4	—	E950.9	E962.1	E980.9
Oleandomycin	960.3	E856	E930.3	E950.4	E962.0	E980.4
Oleovitamin A	963.5	E858.1	E933.5	E950.4	E962.0	E980.4
Oleum ricini	973.1	E858.4	E943.1	E950.4	E962.0	E980.4
Olive oil (medicinal) NEC	973.2	E858.4	E943.2	E950.4	E962.0	E980.4
OMPA	989.3	E863.1	—	E950.6	E962.1	E980.7
Oncovin	963.1	E858.1	E933.1	E950.4	E962.0	E980.4
Ophthaine	968.5	E855.2	E938.5	E950.4	E962.0	E980.4
Ophthetic	968.5	E855.2	E938.5	E950.4	E962.0	E980.4
Opiates, opioids, opium NEC	965.00	E850.2	E935.2	E950.0	E962.0	E980.0
antagonists	970.1	E854.3	E940.1	E950.4	E962.0	E980.4
Oracon	962.2	E858.0	E932.2	E950.4	E962.0	E980.4
Oragrafin	977.8	E858.8	E947.8	E950.4	E962.0	E980.4

		External Cause (E-Code)				
Substance	Poisoning	Accident	Therapeutic Use	Suicide Attempt	Assault	Un-determined
Oral contraceptives	962.2	E858.0	E932.2	E950.4	E962.0	E980.4
Orciprenaline	975.1	E858.6	E945.1	E950.4	E962.0	E980.4
Organidin	975.5	E858.6	E945.5	E950.4	E962.0	E980.4
Organophosphates	989.3	E863.1	—	E950.6	E962.1	E980.7
Orimune	979.5	E858.8	E949.5	E950.4	E962.0	E980.4
Orinase	962.3	E858.0	E932.3	E950.4	E962.0	E980.4
Orphenadrine	966.4	E855.0	E936.4	E950.4	E962.0	E980.4
Ortal (sodium)	967.0	E851	E937.0	E950.1	E962.0	E980.1
Orthoboric acid	976.0	E858.7	E946.0	E950.4	E962.0	E980.4
ENT agent	976.6	E858.7	E946.6	E950.4	E962.0	E980.4
ophthalmic preparation	976.5	E858.7	E946.5	E950.4	E962.0	E980.4
Orthocaine	968.5	E855.2	E938.5	E950.4	E962.0	E980.4
Ortho-Novum	962.2	E858.0	E932.2	E950.4	E962.0	E980.4
Orthotolidine (reagent)	977.8	E858.8	E947.8	E950.4	E962.0	E980.4
Osmic acid (liquid)	983.1	E864.1	—	E950.7	E962.1	E980.6
fumes	987.8	E869.8	—	E952.8	E962.2	E982.8
Osmotic diuretics	974.4	E858.5	E944.4	E950.4	E962.0	E980.4
Ouabain	972.1	E858.3	E942.1	E950.4	E962.0	E980.4
Ovarian hormones (synthetic substitutes)	962.2	E858.0	E932.2	E950.4	E962.0	E980.4
Ovral	962.2	E858.0	E932.2	E950.4	E962.0	E980.4
Ovulation suppressants	962.2	E858.0	E932.2	E950.4	E962.0	E980.4
Ovulen	962.2	E858.0	E932.2	E950.4	E962.0	E980.4
Oxacillin (sodium)	960.0	E856	E930.0	E950.4	E962.0	E980.4
Oxalic acid	983.1	E864.1	—	E950.7	E962.1	E980.6
Oxanamide	969.5	E853.8	E939.5	E950.3	E962.0	E980.3
Oxandrolone	962.1	E858.0	E932.1	E950.4	E962.0	E980.4
Oxaprozin	965.61	E850.6	E935.6	E950.0	E962.0	E980.0
Oxazepam	969.4	E853.2	E939.4	E950.3	E962.0	E980.3
Oxazolidine derivatives	966.0	E855.0	E936.0	E950.4	E962.0	E980.4
Ox bile extract	973.4	E858.4	E943.4	E950.4	E962.0	E980.4
Oxedrine	971.2	E855.5	E941.2	E950.4	E962.0	E980.4
Oxeladin	975.4	E858.6	E945.4	E950.4	E962.0	E980.4
Oxethazaine NEC	968.5	E855.2	E938.5	E950.4	E962.0	E980.4
Oxidizing agents NEC	983.9	E864.3	—	E950.7	E962.1	E980.6
Oxolinic acid	961.3	E857	E931.3	E950.4	E962.0	E980.4
Oxophenarsine	961.1	E857	E931.1	E950.4	E962.0	E980.4
Oxsoralen	976.3	E858.7	E946.3	E950.4	E962.0	E980.4
Oxtriphylline	975.7	E858.6	E945.7	E950.4	E962.0	E980.4
Oxybuprocaine	968.5	E855.2	E938.5	E950.4	E962.0	E980.4
Oxybutynin	975.1	E858.6	E945.1	E950.4	E962.0	E980.4
Oxycodone	965.09	E850.2	E935.2	E950.0	E962.0	E980.0
Oxygen	987.8	E869.8	—	E952.8	E962.2	E982.8
Oxylone	976.0	E858.7	E946.0	E950.4	E962.0	E980.4
ophthalmic preparation	976.5	E858.7	E946.5	E950.4	E962.0	E980.4
Oxymesterone	962.1	E858.0	E932.1	E950.4	E962.0	E980.4
Oxymetazoline	971.2	E855.5	E941.2	E950.4	E962.0	E980.4
Oxymetholone	962.1	E858.0	E932.1	E950.4	E962.0	E980.4
Oxymorphone	965.09	E850.2	E935.2	E950.0	E962.0	E980.0
Oxypertine	969.0	E854.0	E939.0	E950.3	E962.0	E980.3
Oxyphenbutazone	965.5	E850.5	E935.5	E950.0	E962.0	E980.0
Oxyphencyclimine	971.1	E855.4	E941.1	E950.4	E962.0	E980.4
Oxyphenisatin	973.1	E858.4	E943.1	E950.4	E962.0	E980.4
Oxyphenonium	971.1	E855.4	E941.1	E950.4	E962.0	E980.4
Oxyquinoline	961.3	E857	E931.3	E950.4	E962.0	E980.4
Oxytetracycline	960.4	E856	E930.4	E950.4	E962.0	E980.4
Oxytocics	975.0	E858.6	E945.0	E950.4	E962.0	E980.4
Oxytocin	975.0	E858.6	E945.0	E950.4	E962.0	E980.4
Ozone	987.8	E869.8	—	E952.8	E962.2	E982.8
P						
PABA	976.3	E858.7	E946.3	E950.4	E962.0	E980.4
Packed red cells	964.7	E858.2	E934.7	E950.4	E962.0	E980.4
Paint NEC	989.89	E861.6	—	E950.9	E962.1	E980.9
cleaner	982.8	E862.9	—	E950.9	E962.1	E980.9
fumes NEC	987.8	E869.8	—	E952.8	E962.1	E982.8
lead (fumes)	984.0	E861.5	—	E950.9	E962.1	E980.9
solvent NEC	982.8	E862.9	—	E950.9	E962.1	E980.9
stripper	982.8	E862.9	—	E950.9	E962.1	E980.9
Palfium	965.09	E850.2	E935.2	E950.0	E962.0	E980.0
Paludrine	961.4	E857	E931.4	E950.4	E962.0	E980.4
PAM	977.2	E855.8	E947.2	E950.4	E962.0	E980.4
Pamaquine (naphthoate)	961.4	E857	E931.4	E950.4	E962.0	E980.4

Substance	Poisoning	External Cause (E-Code)				
		Accident	Therapeutic Use	Suicide Attempt	Assault	Undetermined
Pamprin	965.1	E850.3	E935.3	E950.0	E962.0	E980.0
Panadol	965.4	E850.4	E935.4	E950.0	E962.0	E980.0
Pancreatic dornase (mucolytic)	963.4	E858.1	E933.4	E950.4	E962.0	E980.4
Pancreatin	973.4	E858.4	E943.4	E950.4	E962.0	E980.4
Pancrelipase	973.4	E858.4	E943.4	E950.4	E962.0	E980.4
Pangamic acid	963.5	E858.1	E933.5	E950.4	E962.0	E980.4
Panthenol	963.5	E858.1	E933.5	E950.4	E962.0	E980.4
topical	976.8	E858.7	E946.8	E950.4	E962.0	E980.4
Pantopaque	977.8	E858.8	E947.8	E950.4	E962.0	E980.4
Pantopon	965.00	E850.2	E935.2	E950.0	E962.0	E980.0
Pantothenic acid	963.5	E858.1	E933.5	E950.4	E962.0	E980.4
Panwarfin	964.2	E858.2	E934.2	E950.4	E962.0	E980.4
Papain	973.4	E858.4	E943.4	E950.4	E962.0	E980.4
Papaverine	972.5	E858.3	E942.5	E950.4	E962.0	E980.4
Para-aminobenzoic acid	976.3	E858.7	E946.3	E950.4	E962.0	E980.4
Para-aminophenol derivatives	965.4	E850.4	E935.4	E950.0	E962.0	E980.0
Para-aminosalicylic acid (derivatives)	961.8	E857	E931.8	E950.4	E962.0	E980.4
Paracetaldehyde (medicinal)	967.2	E852.1	E937.2	E950.2	E962.0	E980.2
Paracetamol	965.4	E850.4	E935.4	E950.0	E962.0	E980.0
Paracodin	965.09	E850.2	E935.2	E950.0	E962.0	E980.0
Paradione	966.0	E855.0	E936.0	E950.4	E962.0	E980.4
Paraffin(s) (wax)	981	E862.3	—	E950.9	E962.1	E980.9
liquid (medicinal)	973.2	E858.4	E943.2	E950.4	E962.0	E980.4
nonmedicinal (oil)	981	E962.1	—	E950.9	E962.1	E980.9
Paraldehyde (medicinal)	967.2	E852.1	E937.2	E950.2	E962.0	E980.2
Paramethadione	966.0	E855.0	E936.0	E950.4	E962.0	E980.4
Paramethasone	962.0	E858.0	E932.0	E950.4	E962.0	E980.4
Paraquat	989.4	E863.5	—	E950.6	E962.1	E980.7
Parasympatholytics	971.1	E855.4	E941.1	E950.4	E962.0	E980.4
Parasympathomimetics	971.0	E855.3	E941.0	E950.4	E962.0	E980.4
Parathion	989.3	E863.1	—	E950.6	E962.1	E980.7
Parathormone	962.6	E858.0	E932.6	E950.4	E962.0	E980.4
Parathyroid (derivatives)	962.6	E858.0	E932.6	E950.4	E962.0	E980.4
Paratyphoid vaccine	978.1	E858.8	E948.1	E950.4	E962.0	E980.4
Paredrine	971.2	E855.5	E941.2	E950.4	E962.0	E980.4
Paregoric	965.00	E850.2	E935.2	E950.0	E962.0	E980.0
Pargyline	972.3	E858.3	E942.3	E950.4	E962.0	E980.4
Paris green	985.1	E866.3	—	E950.8	E962.1	E980.8
insecticide	985.1	E863.4	—	E950.8	E962.1	E980.8
Parnate	969.0	E854.0	E939.0	E950.3	E962.0	E980.3
Paromomycin	960.8	E856	E930.8	E950.4	E962.0	E980.4
Paroxypropione	963.1	E858.1	E933.1	E950.4	E962.0	E980.4
Parzone	965.09	E850.2	E935.2	E950.0	E962.0	E980.0
PAS	961.8	E857	E931.8	E950.4	E962.0	E980.4
PCBs	981	E862.3	—	E950.9	E962.1	E980.9
PCP (pentachlorophenol)	989.4	E863.6	—	E950.6	E962.1	E980.7
herbicide	989.4	E863.5	—	E950.6	E962.1	E980.7
insecticide	989.4	E863.4	—	E950.6	E962.1	E980.7
phencyclidine	968.3	E855.1	E938.3	E950.4	E962.0	E980.4
Peach kernel oil (emulsion)	973.2	E858.4	E943.2	E950.4	E962.0	E980.4
Peanut oil (emulsion) NEC	973.2	E858.4	E943.2	E950.4	E962.0	E980.4
topical	976.3	E858.7	E946.3	E950.4	E962.0	E980.4
Pearly Gates (morning glory seeds)	969.6	E854.1	E939.6	E950.3	E962.0	E980.3
Pecazine	969.1	E853.0	E939.1	E950.3	E962.0	E980.3
Pecilocin	960.1	E856	E930.1	E950.4	E962.0	E980.4
Pectin (with kaolin) NEC	973.5	E858.4	E943.5	E950.4	E962.0	E980.4
Pelletierine tannate	961.6	E857	E931.6	E950.4	E962.0	E980.4
Pemoline	969.7	E854.2	E939.7	E950.3	E962.0	E980.3
Pempidine	972.3	E858.3	E942.3	E950.4	E962.0	E980.4
Penamecillin	960.0	E856	E930.0	E950.4	E962.0	E980.4
Penethamate hydriodide	960.0	E856	E930.0	E950.4	E962.0	E980.4
Penicillamine	963.8	E858.1	E933.8	E950.4	E962.0	E980.4
Penicillin (any type)	960.0	E856	E930.0	E950.4	E962.0	E980.4
Penicillinase	963.4	E858.1	E933.4	E950.4	E962.0	E980.4
Pentachlorophenol (fungicide)	989.4	E863.6	—	E950.6	E962.1	E980.7
herbicide	989.4	E863.5	—	E950.6	E962.1	E980.7
insecticide	989.4	E863.4	—	E950.6	E962.1	E980.7
Pentaerythritol	972.4	E858.3	E942.4	E950.4	E962.0	E980.4
chloral	967.1	E852.0	E937.1	E950.2	E962.0	E980.2
tetranitrate NEC	972.4	E858.3	E942.4	E950.4	E962.0	E980.4
Pentagastrin	977.8	E858.8	E947.8	E950.4	E962.0	E980.4
Pentalin	982.3	E862.4	—	E950.9	E962.1	E980.9

Substance	Poisoning	External Cause (E-Code) Accident	Therapeutic Use	Suicide Attempt	Assault	Un-determined
Pentamethonium (bromide)	972.3	E858.3	E942.3	E950.4	E962.0	E980.4
Pentamidine	961.5	E857	E931.5	E950.4	E962.0	E980.4
Pentanol	980.8	E860.8	—	E950.9	E962.1	E980.9
Pentaquine	961.4	E857	E931.4	E950.4	E962.0	E980.4
Pentazocine	965.8	E850.8	E935.8	E950.0	E962.0	E980.0
Penthienate	971.1	E855.4	E941.1	E950.4	E962.0	E980.4
Pentobarbital, pentobarbitone (sodium)	967.0	E851	E937.0	E950.1	E962.0	E980.1
Pentolinium (tartrate)	972.3	E858.3	E942.3	E950.4	E962.0	E980.4
Pentothal	968.3	E855.1	E938.3	E950.4	E962.0	E980.4
Pentylenetetrazol	970.0	E854.3	E940.0	E950.4	E962.0	E980.4
Pentylsalicylamide	961.8	E857	E931.8	E950.4	E962.0	E980.4
Pepsin	973.4	E858.4	E943.4	E950.4	E962.0	E980.4
Peptavlon	977.8	E858.8	E947.8	E950.4	E962.0	E980.4
Percaine (spinal)	968.7	E855.2	E938.7	E950.4	E962.0	E980.4
topical (surface)	968.5	E855.2	E938.5	E950.4	E962.0	E980.4
Perchloroethylene (vapor)	982.3	E862.4	—	E950.9	E962.1	E980.9
medicinal	961.6	E857	E931.6	E950.4	E962.0	E980.4
Percodan	965.09	E850.2	E935.2	E950.0	E962.0	E980.0
Percogesic	965.09	E850.2	E935.2	E950.0	E962.0	E980.0
Percorten	962.0	E858.0	E932.0	E950.4	E962.0	E980.4
Pergonal	962.4	E858.0	E932.4	E950.4	E962.0	E980.4
Perhexiline	972.4	E858.3	E942.4	E950.4	E962.0	E980.4
Periactin	963.0	E858.1	E933.0	E950.4	E962.0	E980.4
Periclor	967.1	E852.0	E937.1	E950.2	E962.0	E980.2
Pericyazine	969.1	E853.0	E939.1	E950.3	E962.0	E980.3
Peritrate	972.4	E858.3	E942.4	E950.4	E962.0	E980.4
Permanganates NEC	983.9	E864.3	—	E950.7	E962.1	E980.6
potassium (topical)	976.0	E858.7	E946.0	E950.4	E962.0	E980.4
Pernocton	967.0	E851	E937.0	E950.1	E962.0	E980.1
Pernoston	967.0	E851	E937.0	E950.1	E962.0	E980.1
Peronin(e)	965.09	E850.2	E935.2	E950.0	E962.0	E980.0
Perphenazine	969.1	E853.0	E939.1	E950.3	E962.0	E980.3
Pertofrane	969.0	E854	E939.0	E950.3	E962.0	E980.3
Pertussis						
immune serum (human)	964.6	E858.2	E934.6	E950.4	E962.0	E980.4
vaccine (with diphtheria toxoid) (with tetanus toxoid)	978.6	E858.8	E948.6	E950.4	E962.0	E980.4
Peruvian balsam	976.8	E858.7	E946.8	E950.4	E962.0	E980.4
Pesticides (dust) (fumes) (vapor)	989.4	E863.4	—	E950.6	E962.1	E980.7
arsenic	985.1	E863.4	—	E950.8	E962.1	E980.8
chlorinated	989.2	E863.0	—	E950.6	E962.1	E980.7
cyanide	989.0	E863.4	—	E950.6	E962.1	E980.7
kerosene	981	E863.4	—	E950.6	E962.1	E980.7
mixture (of compounds)	989.4	E863.3	—	E950.6	E962.1	E980.7
naphthalene	983.0	E863.4	—	E950.7	E962.1	E980.6
organochlorine (compounds)	989.2	E863.0	—	E950.6	E962.1	E980.7
petroleum (distillate) (products) NEC	981	E863.4	—	E950.6	E962.1	E980.7
specified ingredient NEC	989.4	E863.4	—	E950.6	E962.1	E980.7
strychnine	989.1	E863.4	—	E950.6	E962.1	E980.7
thallium	985.8	E863.7	—	E950.6	E962.1	E980.7
Pethidine (hydrochloride)	965.09	E850.2	E935.2	E950.0	E962.0	E980.0
Petrichloral	967.1	E852.0	E937.1	E950.2	E962.0	E980.2
Petrol	981	E862.1	—	E950.9	E962.1	E980.9
vapor	987.1	E869.8	—	E952.8	E962.2	E982.8
Petrolatum (jelly) (ointment)	976.3	E858.7	E946.3	E950.4	E962.0	E980.4
hydrophilic	976.3	E858.7	E946.3	E950.4	E962.0	E980.4
liquid	973.2	E858.4	E943.2	E950.4	E962.0	E980.4
topical	976.3	E858.7	E946.3	E950.4	E962.0	E980.4
nonmedicinal	981	E862.1	—	E950.9	E962.1	E980.9
Petroleum (cleaners) (fuels) (products) NEC	981	E862.1	—	E950.9	E962.1	E980.9
benzin(e) — *see* Ligroin						
ether — *see* Ligroin						
jelly — *see* Petrolatum						
naphtha — *see* Ligroin						
pesticide	981	E863.4	—	E950.6	E962.1	E980.7
solids	981	E862.3	—	E950.9	E962.1	E980.9
solvents	981	E862.0	—	E950.9	E962.1	E980.9
vapor	987.1	E869.8	—	E952.8	E962.2	E982.8
Peyote	969.6	E854.1	E939.6	E950.3	E962.0	E980.3
Phanodorm, phanodorn	967.0	E851	E937.0	E950.1	E962.0	E980.1
Phanquinone, phanquone	961.5	E857	E931.5	E950.4	E962.0	E980.4
Pharmaceutical excipient or adjunct	977.4	E858.8	E947.4	E950.4	E962.0	E980.4
Phenacemide	966.3	E855.0	E936.3	E950.4	E962.0	E980.4
Phenacetin	965.4	E850.4	E935.4	E950.0	E962.0	E980.0

		External Cause (E-Code)				
Substance	**Poisoning**	**Accident**	**Therapeutic Use**	**Suicide Attempt**	**Assault**	**Un-determined**
Phenadoxone	965.09	E850.2	E935.2	E950.0	E962.0	E980.0
Phenaglycodol	969.5	E853.8	E939.5	E950.3	E962.0	E980.3
Phenantoin	966.1	E855.0	E936.1	E950.4	E962.0	E980.4
Phenaphthazine reagent	977.8	E858.8	E947.8	E950.4	E962.0	E980.4
Phenazocine	965.09	E850.2	E935.2	E950.0	E962.0	E980.0
Phenazone	965.5	E850.5	E935.5	E950.0	E962.0	E980.0
Phenazopyridine	976.1	E858.7	E946.1	E950.4	E962.0	E980.4
Phenbenicillin	960.0	E856	E930.0	E950.4	E962.0	E980.4
Phenbutrazate	977.0	E858.8	E947.0	E950.4	E962.0	E980.4
Phencyclidine	968.3	E855.1	E938.3	E950.4	E962.0	E980.4
Phendimetrazine	977.0	E858.8	E947.0	E950.4	E962.0	E980.4
Phenelzine	969.0	E854.0	E939.0	E950.3	E962.0	E980.3
Phenergan	967.8	E852.8	E937.8	E950.2	E962.0	E980.2
Phenethicillin (potassium)	960.0	E856	E930.0	E950.4	E962.0	E980.4
Phenetsal	965.1	E850.3	E935.3	E950.0	E962.0	E980.0
Pheneturide	966.3	E855.0	E936.3	E950.4	E962.0	E980.4
Phenformin	962.3	E858.0	E932.3	E950.4	E962.0	E980.4
Phenglutarimide	971.1	E855.4	E941.1	E950.4	E962.0	E980.4
Phenicarbazide	965.8	E850.8	E935.8	E950.0	E962.0	E980.0
Phenindamine (tartrate)	963.0	E858.1	E933.0	E950.4	E962.0	E980.4
Phenindione	964.2	E858.2	E934.2	E950.4	E962.0	E980.4
Pheniprazine	969.0	E854.0	E939.0	E950.3	E962.0	E980.3
Pheniramine (maleate)	963.0	E858.1	E933.0	E950.4	E962.0	E980.4
Phenmetrazine	977.0	E858.8	E947.0	E950.4	E962.0	E980.4
Phenobal	967.0	E851	E937.0	E950.1	E962.0	E980.1
Phenobarbital	967.0	E851	E937.0	E950.1	E962.0	E980.1
Phenobarbitone	967.0	E851	E937.0	E950.1	E962.0	E980.1
Phenoctide	976.0	E858.7	E946.0	E950.4	E962.0	E980.4
Phenol (derivatives) NEC	983.0	E864.0	—	E950.7	E962.1	E980.6
disinfectant	983.0	E864.0	—	E950.7	E962.1	E980.6
pesticide	989.4	E863.4	—	E950.6	E962.1	E980.7
red	977.8	E858.8	E947.8	E950.4	E962.0	E980.4
Phenolphthalein	973.1	E858.4	E943.1	E950.4	E962.0	E980.4
Phenolsulfonphthalein	977.8	E858.8	E947.8	E950.4	E962.0	E980.4
Phenomorphan	965.09	E850.2	E935.2	E950.0	E962.0	E980.0
Phenonyl	967.0	E851	E937.0	E950.1	E962.0	E980.1
Phenoperidine	965.09	E850.2	E935.2	E950.0	E962.0	E980.0
Phenoquin	974.7	E858.5	E944.7	E950.4	E962.0	E980.4
Phenothiazines (tranquilizers) NEC	969.1	E853.0	E939.1	E950.3	E962.0	E980.3
insecticide	989.3	E863.4	—	E950.6	E962.1	E980.7
Phenoxybenzamine	971.3	E855.6	E941.3	E950.4	E962.0	E980.4
Phenoxymethyl penicillin	960.0	E856	E930.0	E950.4	E962.0	E980.4
Phenprocoumon	964.2	E858.2	E934.2	E950.4	E962.0	E980.4
Phensuximide	966.2	E855.0	E936.2	E950.4	E962.0	E980.4
Phentermine	977.0	E858.8	E947.0	E950.4	E962.0	E980.4
Phentolamine	971.3	E855.6	E941.3	E950.4	E962.0	E980.4
Phenyl						
butazone	965.5	E850.5	E935.5	E950.0	E962.0	E980.0
enediamine	983.0	E864.0	—	E950.7	E962.1	E980.6
hydrazine	983.0	E864.0	—	E950.7	E962.1	E980.6
antineoplastic	963.1	E858.1	E933.1	E950.4	E962.0	E980.4
mercuric compounds — *see* Mercury						
salicylate	976.3	E858.7	E946.3	E950.4	E962.0	E980.4
Phenylephrin	971.2	E855.5	E941.2	E950.4	E962.0	E980.4
Phenylethylbiguanide	962.3	E858.0	E932.3	E950.4	E962.0	E980.4
Phenylpropanolamine	971.2	E855.5	E941.2	E950.4	E962.0	E980.4
Phenylsulfthion	989.3	E863.1	—	E950.6	E962.1	E980.7
Phenyramidol, phenyramidon	965.7	E850.7	E935.7	E950.0	E962.0	E980.0
Phenytoin	966.1	E855.0	E936.1	E950.4	E962.0	E980.4
pHisoHex	976.2	E858.7	E946.2	E950.4	E962.0	E980.4
Pholcodine	965.09	E850.2	E935.2	E950.0	E962.0	E980.0
Phorate	989.3	E863.1	—	E950.6	E962.1	E980.7
Phosdrin	989.3	E863.1	—	E950.6	E962.1	E980.7
Phosgene (gas)	987.8	E869.8	—	E952.8	E962.2	E982.8
Phosphate (tricresyl)	989.89	E866.8	—	E950.9	E962.1	E980.9
organic	989.3	E863.1	—	E950.6	E962.1	E980.7
solvent	982.8	E862.4	—	E950.9	E926.1	E980.9
Phosphine	987.8	E869.8	—	E952.8	E962.2	E982.8
fumigant	987.8	E863.8	—	E950.6	E962.2	E980.7
Phospholine	971.0	E855.3	E941.0	E950.4	E962.0	E980.4
Phosphoric acid	983.1	E864.1	—	E950.7	E962.1	E980.6

Substance	Poisoning	External Cause (E-Code) Accident	Therapeutic Use	Suicide Attempt	Assault	Undetermined
Phosphorus (compounds) NEC	983.9	E864.3	—	E950.7	E962.1	E980.6
rodenticide	983.9	E863.7	—	E950.7	E962.1	E980.6
Phthalimidoglutarimide	967.8	E852.8	E937.8	E950.2	E962.0	E980.2
Phthalylsulfathiazole	961.0	E857	E931.0	E950.4	E962.0	E980.4
Phylloquinone	964.3	E858.2	E934.3	E950.4	E962.0	E980.4
Physeptone	965.02	E850.1	E935.1	E950.0	E962.0	E980.0
Physostigma venenosum	988.2	E865.4	—	E950.9	E962.1	E980.9
Physostigmine	971.0	E855.3	E941.0	E950.4	E962.0	E980.4
Phytolacca decandra	988.2	E865.4	—	E950.9	E962.1	E980.9
Phytomenadione	964.3	E858.2	E934.3	E950.4	E962.0	E980.4
Phytonadione	964.3	E858.2	E934.3	E950.4	E962.0	E980.4
Picric (acid)	983.0	E864.0	—	E950.7	E962.1	E980.6
Picrotoxin	970.0	E854.3	E940.0	E950.4	E962.0	E980.4
Pilocarpine	971.0	E855.3	E941.0	E950.4	E962.0	E980.4
Pilocarpus (jaborandi) extract	971.0	E855.3	E941.0	E950.4	E962.0	E980.4
Pimaricin	960.1	E856	E930.1	E950.4	E962.0	E980.4
Piminodine	965.09	E850.2	E935.2	E950.0	E962.0	E980.0
Pine oil, pinesol (disinfectant)	983.9	E861.4	—	E950.7	E962.1	E980.6
Pinkroot	961.6	E857	E931.6	E950.4	E962.0	E980.4
Pipadone	965.09	E850.2	E935.2	E950.0	E962.0	E980.0
Pipamazine	963.0	E858.1	E933.0	E950.4	E962.0	E980.4
Pipazethate	975.4	E858.6	E945.4	E950.4	E962.0	E980.4
Pipenzolate	971.1	E855.4	E941.1	E950.4	E962.0	E980.4
Piperacetazine	969.1	E853.0	E939.1	E950.3	E962.0	E980.3
Piperazine NEC	961.6	E857	E931.6	E950.4	E962.0	E980.4
estrone sulfate	962.2	E858.0	E932.2	E950.4	E962.0	E980.4
Piper cubeba	988.2	E865.4	—	E950.9	E962.1	E980.9
Piperidione	975.4	E858.6	E945.4	E950.4	E962.0	E980.4
Piperidolate	971.1	E855.4	E941.1	E950.4	E962.0	E980.4
Piperocaine	968.9	E855.2	E938.9	E950.4	E962.0	E980.4
infiltration (subcutaneous)	968.5	E855.2	E938.5	E950.4	E962.0	E980.4
nerve block (peripheral) (plexus)	968.6	E855.2	E938.6	E950.4	E962.0	E980.4
topical (surface)	968.5	E855.2	E938.5	E950.4	E962.0	E980.4
Pipobroman	963.1	E858.1	E933.1	E950.4	E962.0	E980.4
Pipradrol	970.8	E854.3	E940.8	E950.4	E962.0	E980.4
Piscidia (bark) (erythrina)	965.7	E850.7	E935.7	E950.0	E962.0	E980.0
Pitch	983.0	E864.0	—	E950.7	E962.1	E980.6
Pitkin's solution	968.7	E855.2	E938.7	E950.4	E962.0	E980.4
Pitocin	975.0	E858.6	E945.0	E950.4	E962.0	E980.4
Pitressin (tannate)	962.5	E858.0	E932.5	E950.4	E962.0	E980.4
Pituitary extracts (posterior)	962.5	E858.0	E932.5	E950.4	E962.0	E980.4
anterior	962.4	E858.0	E932.4	E950.4	E962.0	E980.4
Pituitrin	962.5	E858.0	E932.5	E950.4	E962.0	E980.4
Placental extract	962.9	E858.0	E932.9	E950.4	E962.0	E980.4
Placidyl	967.8	E852.8	E937.8	E950.2	E962.0	E980.2
Plague vaccine	978.3	E858.8	E948.3	E950.4	E962.0	E980.4
Plant foods or fertilizers NEC	989.89	E866.5	—	E950.9	E962.1	E980.9
mixed with herbicides	989.4	E863.5	—	E950.6	E962.1	E980.7
Plants, noxious, used as food	988.2	E865.9	—	E950.9	E962.1	E980.9
berries and seeds	988.2	E865.3	—	E950.9	E962.1	E980.9
specified type NEC	988.2	E865.4	—	E950.9	E962.1	E980.9
Plasma (blood)	964.7	E858.2	E934.7	E950.4	E962.0	E980.4
expanders	964.8	E858.2	E934.8	E950.4	E962.0	E980.4
Plasmanate	964.7	E858.2	E934.7	E950.4	E962.0	E980.4
Plegicil	969.1	E853.0	E939.1	E950.3	E962.0	E980.3
Podophyllin	976.4	E858.7	E946.4	E950.4	E962.0	E980.4
Podophyllum resin	976.4	E858.7	E946.4	E950.4	E962.0	E980.4
Poison NEC	989.9	E866.9	—	E950.9	E962.1	E980.9
Poisonous berries	988.2	E865.3	—	E950.9	E962.1	E980.9
Pokeweed (any part)	988.2	E865.4	—	E950.9	E962.1	E980.9
Poldine	971.1	E855.4	E941.1	E950.4	E962.0	E980.4
Poliomyelitis vaccine	979.5	E858.8	E949.5	E950.4	E962.0	E980.4
Poliovirus vaccine	979.5	E858.8	E949.5	E950.4	E962.0	E980.4
Polish (car) (floor) (furniture) (metal) (silver)	989.89	E861.2	—	E950.9	E962.1	E980.9
abrasive	989.89	E861.3	—	E950.9	E962.1	E980.9
porcelain	989.89	E861.3	—	E950.9	E962.1	E980.9
Poloxalkol	973.2	E858.4	E943.2	E950.4	E962.0	E980.4
Polyaminostyrene resins	974.5	E858.5	E944.5	E950.4	E962.0	E980.4
Polychlorinated biphenyl — *see* PCBs						
Polycycline	960.4	E856	E930.4	E950.4	E962.0	E980.4
Polyester resin hardener	982.8	E862.4	—	E950.9	E962.1	E980.9
fumes	987.8	E869.8	—	E952.8	E962.2	E982.8

Substance	Poisoning	External Cause (E-Code) Accident	Therapeutic Use	Suicide Attempt	Assault	Undetermined
Polyestradiol (phosphate)	962.2	E858.0	E932.2	E950.4	E962.0	E980.4
Polyethanolamine alkyl sulfate	976.2	E858.7	E946.2	E950.4	E962.0	E980.4
Polyethylene glycol	976.3	E858.7	E946.3	E950.4	E962.0	E980.4
Polyferose	964.0	E858.2	E934.0	E950.4	E962.0	E980.4
Polymyxin B	960.8	E856	E930.8	E950.4	E962.0	E980.4
ENT agent	976.6	E858.7	E946.6	E950.4	E962.0	E980.4
ophthalmic preparation	976.5	E858.7	E946.5	E950.4	E962.0	E980.4
topical NEC	976.0	E858.7	E946.0	E950.4	E962.0	E980.4
Polynoxylin(e)	976.0	E858.7	E946.0	E950.4	E962.0	E980.4
Polyoxymethyleneurea	976.0	E858.7	E946.0	E950.4	E962.0	E980.4
Polytetrafluoroethylene (inhaled)	987.8	E869.8	—	E952.8	E962.2	E982.8
Polythiazide	974.3	E858.5	E944.3	E950.4	E962.0	E980.4
Polyvinylpyrrolidone	964.8	E858.2	E934.8	E950.4	E962.0	E980.4
Pontocaine (hydrochloride) (infiltration) (topical)	968.5	E855.2	E938.5	E950.4	E962.0	E980.4
nerve block (peripheral) (plexus)	968.6	E855.2	E938.6	E950.4	E962.0	E980.4
spinal	968.7	E855.2	E938.7	E950.4	E962.0	E980.4
Pot	969.6	E854.1	E939.6	E950.3	E962.0	E980.3
Potash (caustic)	983.2	E864.2	—	E950.7	E962.1	E980.6
Potassic saline injection (lactated)	974.5	E858.5	E944.5	E950.4	E962.0	E980.4
Potassium (salts) NEC	974.5	E858.5	E944.5	E950.4	E962.0	E980.4
aminosalicylate	961.8	E857	E931.8	E950.4	E962.0	E980.4
arsenite (solution)	985.1	E866.3	—	E950.8	E962.1	E980.8
bichromate	983.9	E864.3	—	E950.7	E962.1	E980.6
bisulfate	983.9	E864.3	—	E950.7	E962.1	E980.6
bromide (medicinal) NEC	967.3	E852.2	E937.3	E950.2	E962.0	E980.2
carbonate	983.2	E864.2	—	E950.7	E962.1	E980.6
chlorate NEC	983.9	E864.3	—	E950.7	E962.1	E980.6
cyanide — *see* Cyanide						
hydroxide	983.2	E864.2	—	E950.7	E962.1	E980.6
iodide (expectorant) NEC	975.5	E858.6	E945.5	E950.4	E962.0	E980.4
nitrate	989.89	E866.8	—	E950.9	E962.1	E980.9
oxalate	983.9	E864.3	—	E950.7	E962.1	E980.6
perchlorate NEC	977.8	E858.8	E947.8	E950.4	E962.0	E980.4
antithyroid	962.8	E858.0	E932.8	E950.4	E962.0	E980.4
permanganate	976.0	E858.7	E946.0	E950.4	E962.0	E980.4
nonmedicinal	983.9	E864.3	—	E950.7	E962.1	E980.6
Povidone-iodine (anti-infective) NEC	976.0	E858.7	E946.0	E950.4	E962.0	E980.4
Practolol	972.0	E858.3	E942.0	E950.4	E962.0	E980.4
Pralidoxime (chloride)	977.2	E858.8	E947.2	E950.4	E962.0	E980.4
Pramoxine	968.5	E855.2	E938.5	E950.4	E962.0	E980.4
Prazosin	972.6	E858.3	E942.6	E950.4	E962.0	E980.4
Prednisolone	962.0	E858.0	E932.0	E950.4	E962.0	E980.4
ENT agent	976.6	E858.7	E946.6	E950.4	E962.0	E980.4
ophthalmic preparation	976.5	E858.7	E946.5	E950.4	E962.0	E980.4
topical NEC	976.0	E858.7	E946.0	E950.4	E962.0	E980.4
Prednisone	962.0	E858.0	E932.0	E950.4	E962.0	E980.4
Pregnanediol	962.2	E858.0	E932.2	E950.4	E962.0	E980.4
Pregneninolone	962.2	E858.0	E932.2	E950.4	E962.0	E980.4
Preludin	977.0	E858.8	E947.0	E950.4	E962.0	E980.4
Premarin	962.2	E858.0	E932.2	E950.4	E962.0	E980.4
Prenylamine	972.4	E858.3	E942.4	E950.4	E962.0	E980.4
Preparation H	976.8	E858.7	E946.8	E950.4	E962.0	E980.4
Preservatives	989.89	E866.8	—	E950.9	E962.1	E980.9
Pride of China	988.2	E865.3	—	E950.9	E962.1	E980.9
Prilocaine	968.9	E855.2	E938.9	E950.4	E962.0	E980.4
infiltration (subcutaneous)	968.5	E855.2	E938.5	E950.4	E962.0	E980.4
nerve block (peripheral) (plexus)	968.6	E855.2	E938.6	E950.4	E962.0	E980.4
Primaquine	961.4	E857	E931.4	E950.4	E962.0	E980.4
Primidone	966.3	E855.0	E936.3	E950.4	E962.0	E980.4
Primula (veris)	988.2	E865.4	—	E950.9	E962.1	E980.9
Prinadol	965.09	E850.2	E935.2	E950.0	E962.0	E980.0
Priscol, Priscoline	971.3	E855.6	E941.3	E950.4	E962.0	E980.4
Privet	988.2	E865.4	—	E950.9	E962.1	E980.9
Privine	971.2	E855.5	E941.2	E950.4	E962.0	E980.4
Pro-Banthine	971.1	E855.4	E941.1	E950.4	E962.0	E980.4
Probarbital	967.0	E851	E937.0	E950.1	E962.0	E980.1
Probenecid	974.7	E858.5	E944.7	E950.4	E962.0	E980.4
Procainamide (hydrochloride)	972.0	E858.3	E942.0	E950.4	E962.0	E980.4
Procaine (hydrochloride) (infiltration) (topical)	968.5	E855.2	E938.5	E950.4	E962.0	E980.4
nerve block (peripheral) (plexus)	968.6	E855.2	E938.6	E950.4	E962.0	E980.4
penicillin G	960.0	E856	E930.0	E950.4	E962.0	E980.4
spinal	968.7	E855.2	E938.7	E950.4	E962.0	E980.4

Substance	Poisoning	External Cause (E-Code) Accident	Therapeutic Use	Suicide Attempt	Assault	Undetermined
Procalmidol	969.5	E853.8	E939.5	E950.3	E962.0	E980.3
Procarbazine	963.1	E858.1	E933.1	E950.4	E962.0	E980.4
Prochlorperazine	969.1	E853.0	E939.1	E950.3	E962.0	E980.3
Procyclidine	966.4	E855.0	E936.4	E950.4	E962.0	E980.4
Producer gas	986	E868.8	—	E952.1	E962.2	E982.1
Profenamine	966.4	E855.0	E936.4	E950.4	E962.0	E980.4
Profenil	975.1	E858.6	E945.1	E950.4	E962.0	E980.4
Progesterones	962.2	E858.0	E932.2	E950.4	E962.0	E980.4
Progestin	962.2	E858.0	E932.2	E950.4	E962.0	E980.4
Progestogens (with estrogens)	962.2	E858.0	E932.2	E950.4	E962.0	E980.4
Progestone	962.2	E858.0	E932.2	E950.4	E962.0	E980.4
Proguanil	961.4	E857	E931.4	E950.4	E962.0	E980.4
Prolactin	962.4	E858.0	E932.4	E950.4	E962.0	E980.4
Proloid	962.7	E858.0	E932.7	E950.4	E962.0	E980.4
Proluton	962.2	E858.0	E932.2	E950.4	E962.0	E980.4
Promacetin	961.8	E857	E931.8	E950.4	E962.0	E980.4
Promazine	969.1	E853.0	E939.1	E950.3	E962.0	E980.3
Promedol	965.09	E850.2	E935.2	E950.0	E962.0	E980.0
Promethazine	967.8	E852.8	E937.8	E950.2	E962.0	E980.2
Promin	961.8	E857	E931.8	E950.4	E962.0	E980.4
Pronestyl (hydrochloride)	972.0	E858.3	E942.0	E950.4	E962.0	E980.4
Pronetalol, pronethalol	972.0	E858.3	E942.0	E950.4	E962.0	E980.4
Prontosil	961.0	E857	E931.0	E950.4	E962.0	E980.4
Propamidine isethionate	961.5	E857	E931.5	E950.4	E962.0	E980.4
Propanal (medicinal)	967.8	E852.8	E937.8	E950.2	E962.0	E980.2
Propane (gas) (distributed in mobile container)	987.0	E868.0	—	E951.1	E962.2	E981.1
distributed through pipes	987.0	E867	—	E951.0	E962.2	E981.0
incomplete combustion of — *see* Carbon monoxide, Propane						
Propanidid	968.3	E855.1	E938.3	E950.4	E962.0	E980.4
Propanol	980.3	E860.4	—	E950.9	E962.1	E980.9
Propantheline	971.1	E855.4	E941.1	E950.4	E962.0	E980.4
Proparacaine	968.5	E855.2	E938.5	E950.4	E962.0	E980.4
Propatyl nitrate	972.4	E858.3	E942.4	E950.4	E962.0	E980.4
Propicillin	960.0	E856	E930.0	E950.4	E962.0	E980.4
Propiolactone (vapor)	987.8	E869.8	—	E952.8	E962.2	E982.8
Propiomazine	967.8	E852.8	E937.8	E950.2	E962.0	E980.2
Propionaldehyde (medicinal)	967.8	E852.8	E937.8	E950.2	E962.0	E980.2
Propionate compound	976.0	E858.7	E946.0	E950.4	E962.0	E980.4
Propion gel	976.0	E858.7	E946.0	E950.4	E962.0	E980.4
Propitocaine	968.9	E855.2	E938.9	E950.4	E962.0	E980.4
infiltration (subcutaneous)	968.5	E855.2	E938.5	E950.4	E962.0	E980.4
nerve block (peripheral) (plexus)	968.6	E855.2	E938.6	E950.4	E962.0	E980.4
Propoxur	989.3	E863.2	—	E950.6	E962.1	E980.7
Propoxycaine	968.9	E855.2	E938.9	E950.4	E962.0	E980.4
infiltration (subcutaneous)	968.5	E855.2	E938.5	E950.4	E962.0	E980.4
nerve block (peripheral) (plexus)	968.6	E855.2	E938.6	E950.4	E962.0	E980.4
topical (surface)	968.5	E855.2	E938.5	E950.4	E962.0	E980.4
Propoxyphene (hydrochloride)	965.8	E850.8	E935.8	E950.0	E962.0	E980.0
Propranolol	972.0	E858.3	E942.0	E950.4	E962.0	E980.4
Propyl						
alcohol	980.3	E860.4	—	E950.9	E962.1	E980.9
carbinol	980.3	E860.4	—	E950.9	E962.1	E980.9
hexadrine	971.2	E855.5	E941.2	E950.4	E962.0	E980.4
iodone	977.8	E858.8	E947.8	E950.4	E962.0	E980.4
thiouracil	962.8	E858.0	E932.8	E950.4	E962.0	E980.4
Propylene	987.1	E869.8	—	E952.8	E962.2	E982.8
Propylparaben (ophthalmic)	976.5	E858.7	E946.5	E950.4	E962.0	E980.4
Proscillaridin	972.1	E858.3	E942.1	E950.4	E962.0	E980.4
Prostaglandins	975.0	E858.6	E945.0	E950.4	E962.0	E980.4
Prostigmin	971.0	E855.3	E941.0	E950.4	E962.0	E980.4
Protamine (sulfate)	964.5	E858.2	E934.5	E950.4	E962.0	E980.4
zinc insulin	962.3	E858.0	E932.3	E950.4	E962.0	E980.4
Protectants (topical)	976.3	E858.7	E946.3	E950.4	E962.0	E980.4
Protein hydrolysate	974.5	E858.5	E944.5	E950.4	E962.0	E980.4
Prothiaden — *see* Dothiepin hydrochloride						
Prothionamide	961.8	E857	E931.8	E950.4	E962.0	E980.4
Prothipendyl	969.5	E853.8	E939.5	E950.3	E962.0	E980.3
Protokylol	971.2	E855.5	E941.2	E950.4	E962.0	E980.4
Protopam	977.2	E858.8	E947.2	E950.4	E962.0	E980.4
Protoveratrine(s) (A) (B)	972.6	E858.3	E942.6	E950.4	E962.0	E980.4

		External Cause (E-Code)				
Substance	Poisoning	Accident	Therapeutic Use	Suicide Attempt	Assault	Un-determined
Protriptyline	969.0	E854.0	E939.0	E950.3	E962.0	E980.3
Provera	962.2	E858.0	E932.2	E950.4	E962.0	E980.4
Provitamin A	963.5	E858.1	E933.5	E950.4	E962.0	E980.4
Proxymetacaine	968.5	E855.2	E938.5	E950.4	E962.0	E980.4
Proxyphylline	975.1	E858.6	E945.1	E950.4	E962.0	E980.4
Prozac — *see* Fluoxetine hydrochloride						
Prunus						
laurocerasus	988.2	E865.4	—	E950.9	E962.1	E980.9
virginiana	988.2	E865.4	—	E950.9	E962.1	E980.9
Prussic acid	989.0	E866.8	—	E950.9	E962.1	E980.9
vapor	987.7	E869.8	—	E952.8	E962.2	E982.8
Pseudoephedrine	971.2	E855.5	E941.2	E950.4	E962.0	E980.4
Psilocin	969.6	E854.1	E939.6	E950.3	E962.0	E980.3
Psilocybin	969.6	E854.1	E939.6	E950.3	E962.0	E980.3
PSP	977.8	E858.8	E947.8	E950.4	E962.0	E980.4
Psychedelic agents	969.6	E854.1	E939.6	E950.3	E962.0	E980.3
Psychodysleptics	969.6	E854.1	E939.6	E950.3	E962.0	E980.3
Psychostimulants	969.7	E854.2	E939.7	E950.3	E962.0	E980.3
Psychotherapeutic agents	969.9	E855.9	E939.9	E950.3	E962.0	E980.3
antidepressants	969.0	E854.0	E939.0	E950.3	E962.0	E980.3
specified NEC	969.8	E855.8	E939.8	E950.3	E962.0	E980.3
tranquilizers NEC	969.5	E853.9	E939.5	E950.3	E962.0	E980.3
Psychotomimetic agents	969.6	E854.1	E939.6	E950.3	E962.0	E980.3
Psychotropic agents	969.9	E854.8	E939.9	E950.3	E962.0	E980.3
specified NEC	969.8	E854.8	E939.8	E950.3	E962.0	E980.3
Psyllium	973.3	E858.4	E943.3	E950.4	E962.0	E980.4
Pteroylglutamic acid	964.1	E858.2	E934.1	E950.4	E962.0	E980.4
Pteroyltriglutamate	963.1	E858.1	E933.1	E950.4	E962.0	E980.4
PTFE	987.8	E869.8	—	E952.8	E962.2	E982.8
Pulsatilla	988.2	E865.4	—	E950.9	E962.1	E980.9
Purex (bleach)	983.9	E864.3	—	E950.7	E962.1	E980.6
Purine diuretics	974.1	E858.5	E944.1	E950.4	E962.0	E980.4
Purinethol	963.1	E858.1	E933.1	E950.4	E962.0	E980.4
PVP	964.8	E858.2	E934.8	E950.4	E962.0	E980.4
Pyrabital	965.7	E850.7	E935.7	E950.0	E962.0	E980.0
Pyramidon	965.5	E850.5	E935.5	E950.0	E962.0	E980.0
Pyrantel (pamoate)	961.6	E857	E931.6	E950.4	E962.0	E980.4
Pyrathiazine	963.0	E858.1	E933.0	E950.4	E962.0	E980.4
Pyrazinamide	961.8	E857	E931.8	E950.4	E962.0	E980.4
Pyrazinoic acid (amide)	961.8	E857	E931.8	E950.4	E962.0	E980.4
Pyrazole (derivatives)	965.5	E850.5	E935.5	E950.0	E962.0	E980.0
Pyrazolone (analgesics)	965.5	E850.5	E935.5	E950.0	E962.0	E980.0
Pyrethrins, pyrethrum	989.4	E863.4	—	E950.6	E962.1	E980.7
Pyribenzamine	963.0	E858.1	E933.0	E950.4	E962.0	E980.4
Pyridine (liquid) (vapor)	982.0	E862.4	—	E950.9	E962.1	E980.9
aldoxime chloride	977.2	E858.8	E947.2	E950.4	E962.0	E980.4
Pyridium	976.1	E858.7	E946.1	E950.4	E962.0	E980.4
Pyridostigmine	971.0	E855.3	E941.0	E950.4	E962.0	E980.4
Pyridoxine	963.5	E858.1	E933.5	E950.4	E962.0	E980.4
Pyrilamine	963.0	E858.1	E933.0	E950.4	E962.0	E980.4
Pyrimethamine	961.4	E857	E931.4	E950.4	E962.0	E980.4
Pyrogallic acid	983.0	E864.0	—	E950.7	E962.1	E980.6
Pyroxylin	976.3	E858.7	E946.3	E950.4	E962.0	E980.4
Pyrrobutamine	963.0	E858.1	E933.0	E950.4	E962.0	E980.4
Pyrrocaine	968.5	E855.2	E938.5	E950.4	E962.0	E980.4
Pyrvinium (pamoate)	961.6	E857	E931.6	E950.4	E962.0	E980.4
PZI	962.3	E858.0	E932.3	E950.4	E962.0	E980.4
Q						
Quaalude	967.4	E852.3	E937.4	E950.2	E962.0	E980.2
Quaternary ammonium derivatives	971.1	E855.4	E941.1	E950.4	E962.0	E980.4
Quicklime	983.2	E864.2	—	E950.7	E962.1	E980.6
Quinacrine	961.3	E857	E931.3	E950.4	E962.0	E980.4
Quinaglute	972.0	E858.3	E942.0	E950.4	E962.0	E980.4
Quinalbarbitone	967.0	E851	E937.0	E950.1	E962.0	E980.1
Quinestradiol	962.2	E858.0	E932.2	E950.4	E962.0	E980.4
Quinethazone	974.3	E858.5	E944.3	E950.4	E962.0	E980.4
Quinidine (gluconate) (polygalacturonate) (salts) (sulfate)	972.0	E858.3	E942.0	E950.4	E962.0	E980.4
Quinine	961.4	E857	E931.4	E950.4	E962.0	E980.4
Quiniobine	961.3	E857	E931.3	E950.4	E962.0	E980.4
Quinolines	961.3	E857	E931.3	E950.4	E962.0	E980.4
Quotane	968.5	E855.2	E938.5	E950.4	E962.0	E980.4

Substance	Poisoning	External Cause (E-Code) Accident	Therapeutic Use	Suicide Attempt	Assault	Undetermined
R						
Rabies						
immune globulin (human)	964.6	E858.2	E934.6	E950.4	E962.0	E980.4
vaccine	979.1	E858.8	E949.1	E950.4	E962.0	E980.4
Racemoramide	965.09	E850.2	E935.2	E950.0	E962.0	E980.0
Racemorphan	965.09	E850.2	E935.2	E950.0	E962.0	E980.0
Radiator alcohol	980.1	E860.2	—	E950.9	E962.1	E980.9
Radio-opaque (drugs) (materials)	977.8	E858.8	E947.8	E950.4	E962.0	E980.4
Ranunculus	988.2	E865.4	—	E950.9	E962.1	E980.9
Rat poison	989.4	E863.7	—	E950.6	E962.1	E980.7
Rattlesnake (venom)	989.5	E905.0	—	E950.9	E962.1	E980.9
Raudixin	972.6	E858.3	E942.6	E950.4	E962.0	E980.4
Rautensin	972.6	E858.3	E942.6	E950.4	E962.0	E980.4
Rautina	972.6	E858.3	E942.6	E950.4	E962.0	E980.4
Rautotal	972.6	E858.3	E942.6	E950.4	E962.0	E980.4
Rauwiloid	972.6	E858.3	E942.6	E950.4	E962.0	E980.4
Rauwoldin	972.6	E858.3	E942.6	E950.4	E962.0	E980.4
Rauwolfia (alkaloids)	972.6	E858.3	E942.6	E950.4	E962.0	E980.4
Realgar	985.1	E866.3	—	E950.8	E962.1	E980.8
Red cells, packed	964.7	E858.2	E934.7	E950.4	E962.0	E980.4
Reducing agents, industrial NEC	983.9	E864.3	—	E950.7	E962.1	E980.6
Refrigerant gas (freon)	987.4	E869.2	—	E952.8	E962.2	E982.8
not freon	987.9	E869.9	—	E952.9	E962.2	E982.9
Regroton	974.4	E858.5	E944.4	E950.4	E962.0	E980.4
Rela	968.0	E855.1	E938.0	E950.4	E962.0	E980.4
Relaxants, skeletal muscle (autonomic)	975.2	E858.6	E945.2	E950.4	E962.0	E980.4
central nervous system	968.0	E855.1	E938.0	E950.4	E962.0	E980.4
Renese	974.3	E858.5	E944.3	E950.4	E962.0	E980.4
Renografin	977.8	E858.8	E947.8	E950.4	E962.0	E980.4
Replacement solutions	974.5	E858.5	E944.5	E950.4	E962.0	E980.4
Rescinnamine	972.6	E858.3	E942.6	E950.4	E962.0	E980.4
Reserpine	972.6	E858.3	E942.6	E950.4	E962.0	E980.4
Resorcin, resorcinol	976.4	E858.7	E946.4	E950.4	E962.0	E980.4
Respaire	975.5	E858.6	E945.5	E950.4	E962.0	E980.4
Respiratory agents NEC	975.8	E858.6	E945.8	E950.4	E962.0	E980.4
Retinoic acid	976.8	E858.7	E946.8	E950.4	E962.0	E980.4
Retinol	963.5	E858.1	E933.5	E950.4	E962.0	E980.4
Rh_0 (D) immune globulin (human)	964.6	E858.2	E934.6	E950.4	E962.0	E980.4
Rhodine	965.1	E850.3	E935.3	E950.0	E962.0	E980.0
RhoGAM	964.6	E858.2	E934.6	E950.4	E962.0	E980.4
Riboflavin	963.5	E858.1	E933.5	E950.4	E962.0	E980.4
Ricin	989.89	E866.8	—	E950.9	E962.1	E980.9
Ricinus communis	988.2	E865.3	—	E950.9	E962.1	E980.9
Rickettsial vaccine NEC	979.6	E858.8	E949.6	E950.4	E962.0	E980.4
with viral and bacterial vaccine	979.7	E858.8	E949.7	E950.4	E962.0	E980.4
Rifampin	960.6	E856	E930.6	E950.4	E962.0	E980.4
Rimifon	961.8	E857	E931.8	E950.4	E962.0	E980.4
Ringer's injection (lactated)	974.5	E858.5	E944.5	E950.4	E962.0	E980.4
Ristocetin	960.8	E856	E930.8	E950.4	E962.0	E980.4
Ritalin	969.7	E854.2	E939.7	E950.3	E962.0	E980.3
Roach killers — *see* Pesticides						
Rocky Mountain spotted fever vaccine	979.6	E858.8	E949.6	E950.4	E962.0	E980.4
Rodenticides	989.4	E863.7	—	E950.6	E962.1	E980.7
Rolaids	973.0	E858.4	E943.0	E950.4	E962.0	E980.4
Rolitetracycline	960.4	E856	E930.4	E950.4	E962.0	E980.4
Romilar	975.4	E858.6	E945.4	E950.4	E962.0	E980.4
Rose water ointment	976.3	E858.7	E946.3	E950.4	E962.0	E980.4
Rotenone	989.4	E863.7	—	E950.6	E962.1	E980.7
Rotoxamine	963.0	E858.1	E933.0	E950.4	E962.0	E980.4
Rough-on-rats	989.4	E863.7	—	E950.6	E962.1	E980.7
Rubbing alcohol	980.2	E860.3	—	E950.9	E962.1	E980.9
Rubella virus vaccine	979.4	E858.8	E949.4	E950.4	E962.0	E980.4
Rubelogen	979.4	E858.8	E949.4	E950.4	E962.0	E980.4
Rubeovax	979.4	E858.8	E949.4	E950.4	E962.0	E980.4
Rubidomycin	960.7	E856	E930.7	E950.4	E962.0	E980.4
Rue	988.2	E865.4	—	E950.9	E962.1	E980.9
Ruta	988.2	E865.4	—	E950.9	E962.1	E980.9
S						
Sabadilla (medicinal)	976.0	E858.7	E946.0	E950.4	E962.0	E980.4
pesticide	989.4	E863.4	—	E950.6	E962.1	E980.7

Substance	Poisoning	Accident	Therapeutic Use	Suicide Attempt	Assault	Undetermined
		External Cause (E-Code)				
Sabin oral vaccine	979.5	E858.8	E949.5	E950.4	E962.0	E980.4
Saccharated iron oxide	964.0	E858.2	E934.0	E950.4	E962.0	E980.4
Saccharin	974.5	E858.5	E944.5	E950.4	E962.0	E980.4
Safflower oil	972.2	E858.3	E942.2	E950.4	E962.0	E980.4
Salbutamol sulfate	975.7	E858.6	E945.7	E950.4	E962.0	E980.4
Salicylamide	965.1	E850.3	E935.3	E950.0	E962.0	E980.0
Salicylate(s)	965.1	E850.3	E935.3	E950.0	E962.0	E980.0
methyl	976.3	E858.7	E946.3	E950.4	E962.0	E980.4
theobromine calcium	974.1	E858.5	E944.1	E950.4	E962.0	E980.4
Salicylazosulfapyridine	961.0	E857	E931.0	E950.4	E962.0	E980.4
Salicylhydroxamic acid	976.0	E858.7	E946.0	E950.4	E962.0	E980.4
Salicylic acid (keratolytic) NEC	976.4	E858.7	E946.4	E950.4	E962.0	E980.4
congeners	965.1	E850.3	E935.3	E950.0	E962.0	E980.0
salts	965.1	E850.3	E935.3	E950.0	E962.0	E980.0
Saliniazid	961.8	E857	E931.8	E950.4	E962.0	E980.4
Salol	976.3	E858.7	E946.3	E950.4	E962.0	E980.4
Salt (substitute) NEC	974.5	E858.5	E944.5	E950.4	E962.0	E980.4
Saluretics	974.3	E858.5	E944.3	E950.4	E962.0	E980.4
Saluron	974.3	E858.5	E944.3	E950.4	E962.0	E980.4
Salvarsan 606 (neosilver) (silver)	961.1	E857	E931.1	E950.4	E962.0	E980.4
Sambucus canadensis	988.2	E865.4	—	E950.9	E962.1	E980.9
berry	988.2	E865.3	—	E950.9	E962.1	E980.9
Sandril	972.6	E858.3	E942.6	E950.4	E962.0	E980.4
Sanguinaria canadensis	988.2	E865.4	—	E950.9	E962.1	E980.9
Saniflush (cleaner)	983.9	E861.3	—	E950.7	E962.1	E980.6
Santonin	961.6	E857	E931.6	E950.4	E962.0	E980.4
Santyl	976.8	E858.7	E946.8	E950.4	E962.0	E980.4
Sarkomycin	960.7	E856	E930.7	E950.4	E962.0	E980.4
Saroten	969.0	E854.0	E939.0	E950.3	E962.0	E980.3
Saturnine — *see* Lead						
Savin (oil)	976.4	E858.7	E946.4	E950.4	E962.0	E980.4
Scammony	973.1	E858.4	E943.1	E950.4	E962.0	E980.4
Scarlet red	976.8	E858.7	E946.8	E950.4	E962.0	E980.4
Scheele's green	985.1	E866.3	—	E950.8	E962.1	E980.8
insecticide	985.1	E863.4	—	E950.8	E962.1	E980.8
Schradan	989.3	E863.1	—	E950.6	E962.1	E980.7
Schweinfurt(h) green	985.1	E866.3	—	E950.8	E962.1	E980.8
insecticide	985.1	E863.4	—	E950.8	E962.1	E980.8
Scilla — *see* Squill						
Sclerosing agents	972.7	E858.3	E942.7	E950.4	E962.0	E980.4
Scopolamine	971.1	E855.4	E941.1	E950.4	E962.0	E980.4
Scouring powder	989.89	E861.3	—	E950.9	E962.1	E980.9
Sea						
anemone (sting)	989.5	E905.6	—	E950.9	E962.1	E980.9
cucumber (sting)	989.5	E905.6	—	E950.9	E962.1	E980.9
snake (bite) (venom)	989.5	E905.0	—	E950.9	E962.1	E980.9
urchin spine (puncture)	989.5	E905.6	—	E950.9	E962.1	E980.9
Secbutabarbital	967.0	E851	E937.0	E950.1	E962.0	E980.1
Secbutabaritone	967.0	E851	E937.0	E950.1	E962.0	E980.1
Secobarbital	967.0	E851	E937.0	E950.1	E962.0	E980.1
Seconal	967.0	E851	E937.0	E950.1	E962.0	E980.1
Secretin	977.8	E858.8	E947.8	E950.4	E962.0	E980.4
Sedatives, nonbarbiturate	967.9	E852.9	E937.9	E950.2	E962.0	E980.2
specified NEC	967.8	E852.8	E937.8	E950.2	E962.0	E980.2
Sedormid	967.8	E852.8	E937.8	E950.2	E962.0	E980.2
Seed (plant)	988.2	E865.3	—	E950.9	E962.1	E980.9
disinfectant or dressing	989.89	E866.5	—	E950.9	E962.1	E980.9
Selenium (fumes) NEC	985.8	E866.4	—	E950.9	E962.1	E980.9
disulfide or sulfide	976.4	E858.7	E946.4	E950.4	E962.0	E980.4
Selsun	976.4	E858.7	E946.4	E950.4	E962.0	E980.4
Senna	973.1	E858.4	E943.1	E950.4	E962.0	E980.4
Septisol	976.2	E858.7	E946.2	E950.4	E962.0	E980.4
Serax	969.4	E853.2	E939.4	E950.3	E962.0	E980.3
Serenesil	967.8	E852.8	E937.8	E950.2	E962.0	E980.2
Serenium (hydrochloride)	961.9	E857	E931.9	E950.4	E962.0	E980.4
Serepax — *see* Oxazepam						
Sernyl	968.3	E855.1	E938.3	E950.4	E962.0	E980.4
Serotonin	977.8	E858.8	E947.8	E950.4	E962.0	E980.4
Serpasil	972.6	E858.3	E942.6	E950.4	E962.0	E980.4
Sewer gas	987.8	E869.8	—	E952.8	E962.2	E982.8
Shampoo	989.6	E861.0	—	E950.9	E962.1	E980.9

		External Cause (E-Code)				
Substance	**Poisoning**	**Accident**	**Therapeutic Use**	**Suicide Attempt**	**Assault**	**Undetermined**
Shellfish, nonbacterial or noxious	988.0	E865.1	—	E950.9	E962.1	E980.9
Silicones NEC	989.83	E866.8	E947.8	E950.9	E962.1	E980.9
Silvadene	976.0	E858.7	E946.0	E950.4	E962.0	E980.4
Silver (compound) (medicinal) NEC	976.0	E858.7	E946.0	E950.4	E962.0	E980.4
anti-infectives	976.0	E858.7	E946.0	E950.4	E962.0	E980.4
arsphenamine	961.1	E857	E931.1	E950.4	E962.0	E980.4
nitrate	976.0	E858.7	E946.0	E950.4	E962.0	E980.4
ophthalmic preparation	976.5	E858.7	E946.5	E950.4	E962.0	E980.4
toughened (keratolytic)	976.4	E858.7	E946.4	E950.4	E962.0	E980.4
nonmedicinal (dust)	985.8	E866.4	—	E950.9	E962.1	E980.9
protein (mild) (strong)	976.0	E858.7	E946.0	E950.4	E962.0	E980.4
salvarsan	961.1	E857	E931.1	E950.4	E962.0	E980.4
Simethicone	973.8	E858.4	E943.8	E950.4	E962.0	E980.4
Sinequan	969.0	E854.0	E939.0	E950.3	E962.0	E980.3
Singoserp	972.6	E858.3	E942.6	E950.4	E962.0	E980.4
Sintrom	964.2	E858.2	E934.2	E950.4	E962.0	E980.4
Sitosterols	972.2	E858.3	E942.2	E950.4	E962.0	E980.4
Skeletal muscle relaxants	975.2	E858.6	E945.2	E950.4	E962.0	E980.4
Skin						
agents (external)	976.9	E858.7	E946.9	E950.4	E962.0	E980.4
specified NEC	976.8	E858.7	E946.8	E950.4	E962.0	E980.4
test antigen	977.8	E858.8	E947.8	E950.4	E962.0	E980.4
Sleep-eze	963.0	E858.1	E933.0	E950.4	E962.0	E980.4
Sleeping draught (drug) (pill) (tablet)	967.9	E852.9	E937.9	E950.2	E962.0	E980.2
Smallpox vaccine	979.0	E858.8	E949.0	E950.4	E962.0	E980.4
Smelter fumes NEC	985.9	E866.4	—	E950.9	E962.1	E980.9
Smog	987.3	E869.1	—	E952.8	E962.2	E982.8
Smoke NEC	987.9	E869.9	—	E952.9	E962.2	E982.9
Smooth muscle relaxant	975.1	E858.6	E945.1	E950.4	E962.0	E980.4
Snail killer	989.4	E863.4	—	E950.6	E962.1	E980.7
Snake (bite) (venom)	989.5	E905.0	—	E950.9	E962.1	E980.9
Snuff	989.89	E866.8	—	E950.9	E962.1	E980.9
Soap (powder) (product)	989.6	E861.1	—	E950.9	E962.1	E980.9
medicinal, soft	976.2	E858.7	E946.2	E950.4	E962.0	E980.4
Soda (caustic)	983.2	E864.2	—	E950.7	E962.1	E980.6
bicarb	963.3	E858.1	E933.3	E950.4	E962.0	E980.4
chlorinated — *see* Sodium, hypochlorite						
Sodium						
acetosulfone	961.8	E857	E931.8	E950.4	E962.0	E980.4
acetrizoate	977.8	E858.8	E947.8	E950.4	E962.0	E980.4
amytal	967.0	E851	E937.0	E950.1	E962.0	E980.1
arsenate — *see* Arsenic						
bicarbonate	963.3	E858.1	E933.3	E950.4	E962.0	E980.4
bichromate	983.9	E864.3	—	E950.7	E962.1	E980.6
biphosphate	963.2	E858.1	E933.2	E950.4	E962.0	E980.4
bisulfate	983.9	E864.3	—	E950.7	E962.1	E980.6
borate (cleanser)	989.6	E861.3	—	E950.9	E962.1	E980.9
bromide NEC	967.3	E852.2	E937.3	E950.2	E962.0	E980.2
cacodylate (nonmedicinal) NEC	978.8	E858.8	E948.8	E950.4	E962.0	E980.4
anti-infective	961.1	E857	E931.1	E950.4	E962.0	E980.4
herbicide	989.4	E863.5	—	E950.6	E962.1	E980.7
calcium edetate	963.8	E858.1	E933.8	E950.4	E962.0	E980.4
carbonate NEC	983.2	E864.2	—	E950.7	E962.1	E980.6
chlorate NEC	983.9	E864.3	—	E950.7	E962.1	E980.6
herbicide	983.9	E863.5	—	E950.7	E962.1	E980.6
chloride NEC	974.5	E858.5	E944.5	E950.4	E962.0	E980.4
chromate	983.9	E864.3	—	E950.7	E962.1	E980.6
citrate	963.3	E858.1	E933.3	E950.4	E962.0	E980.4
cyanide — *see* Cyanide(s)						
cyclamate	974.5	E858.5	E944.5	E950.4	E962.0	E980.4
diatrizoate	977.8	E858.8	E947.8	E950.4	E962.0	E980.4
dibunate	975.4	E858.6	E945.4	E950.4	E962.0	E980.4
dioctyl sulfosuccinate	973.2	E858.4	E943.2	E950.4	E962.0	E980.4
edetate	963.8	E858.1	E933.8	E950.4	E962.0	E980.4
ethacrynate	974.4	E858.5	E944.4	E950.4	E962.0	E980.4
fluoracetate (dust) (rodenticide)	989.4	E863.7	—	E950.6	E962.1	E980.7
fluoride — *see* Fluoride(s)						
free salt	974.5	E858.5	E944.5	E950.4	E962.0	E980.4
glucosulfone	961.8	E857	E931.8	E950.4	E962.0	E980.4
hydroxide	983.2	E864.2	—	E950.7	E962.1	E980.6
hypochlorite (bleach) NEC	983.9	E864.3	—	E950.7	E962.1	E980.6
disinfectant	983.9	E861.4	—	E950.7	E962.1	E980.6
medicinal (anti-infective) (external)	976.0	E858.7	E946.0	E950.4	E962.0	E980.4

Substance	Poisoning	External Cause (E-Code) Accident	Therapeutic Use	Suicide Attempt	Assault	Undetermined
Sodium — *continued*						
hypochlorite (bleach) NEC — *continued*						
vapor	987.8	E869.8	—	E952.8	E962.2	E982.8
hyposulfite	976.0	E858.7	E946.0	E950.4	E962.0	E980.4
indigotindisulfonate	977.8	E858.8	E947.8	E950.4	E962.0	E980.4
iodide	977.8	E858.8	E947.8	E950.4	E962.0	E980.4
iothalamate	977.8	E858.8	E947.8	E950.4	E962.0	E980.4
iron edetate	964.0	E858.2	E934.0	E950.4	E962.0	E980.4
lactate	963.3	E858.1	E933.3	E950.4	E962.0	E980.4
lauryl sulfate	976.2	E858.7	E946.2	E950.4	E962.0	E980.4
L-triiodothyronine	962.7	E858.0	E932.7	E950.4	E962.0	E980.4
metrizoate	977.8	E858.8	E947.8	E950.4	E962.0	E980.4
monofluoracetate (dust) (rodenticide)	989.4	E863.7	—	E950.6	E962.1	E980.7
morrhuate	972.7	E858.3	E942.7	E950.4	E962.0	E980.4
nafcillin	960.0	E856	E930.0	E950.4	E962.0	E980.4
nitrate (oxidizing agent)	983.9	E864.3	—	E950.7	E962.1	E980.6
nitrite (medicinal)	972.4	E858.3	E942.4	E950.4	E962.0	E980.4
nitroferricyanide	972.6	E858.3	E942.6	E950.4	E962.0	E980.4
nitroprusside	972.6	E858.3	E942.6	E950.4	E962.0	E980.4
para-aminohippurate	977.8	E858.8	E947.8	E950.4	E962.0	E980.4
perborate (nonmedicinal) NEC	989.89	E866.8	—	E950.9	E962.1	E980.9
medicinal	976.6	E858.7	E946.6	E950.4	E962.0	E980.4
soap	989.6	E861.1	—	E950.9	E962.1	E980.9
percarbonate — *see* Sodium, perborate						
phosphate	973.3	E858.4	E943.3	E950.4	E962.0	E980.4
polystyrene sulfonate	974.5	E858.5	E944.5	E950.4	E962.0	E980.4
propionate	976.0	E858.7	E946.0	E950.4	E962.0	E980.4
psylliate	972.7	E858.3	E942.7	E950.4	E962.0	E980.4
removing resins	974.5	E858.5	E944.5	E950.4	E962.0	E980.4
salicylate	965.1	E850.3	E935.3	E950.0	E962.0	E980.0
sulfate	973.3	E858.4	E943.3	E950.4	E962.0	E980.4
sulfoxone	961.8	E857	E931.8	E950.4	E962.0	E980.4
tetradecyl sulfate	972.7	E858.3	E942.7	E950.4	E962.0	E980.4
thiopental	968.3	E855.1	E938.3	E950.4	E962.0	E980.4
thiosalicylate	965.1	E850.3	E935.3	E950.0	E962.0	E980.0
thiosulfate	976.0	E858.7	E946.0	E950.4	E962.0	E980.4
tolbutamide	977.8	E858.8	E947.8	E950.4	E962.0	E980.4
tyropanoate	977.8	E858.8	E947.8	E950.4	E962.0	E980.4
valproate	966.3	E855.0	E936.3	E950.4	E962.0	E980.4
Solanine	977.8	E858.8	E947.8	E950.4	E962.0	E980.4
Solanum dulcamara	988.2	E865.4	—	E950.9	E962.1	E980.9
Solapsone	961.8	E857	E931.8	E950.4	E962.0	E980.4
Solasulfone	961.8	E857	E931.8	E950.4	E962.0	E980.4
Soldering fluid	983.1	E864.1	—	E950.7	E962.1	E980.6
Solid substance	989.9	E866.9	—	E950.9	E962.1	E980.9
specified NEC	989.9	E866.8	—	E950.9	E962.1	E980.9
Solvents, industrial	982.8	E862.9	—	E950.9	E962.1	E980.9
naphtha	981	E862.0	—	E950.9	E962.1	E980.9
petroleum	981	E862.0	—	E950.9	E962.1	E980.9
specified NEC	982.8	E862.4	—	E950.9	E962.1	E980.9
Soma	968.0	E855.1	E938.0	E950.4	E962.0	E980.4
Somatotropin	962.4	E858.0	E932.4	E950.4	E962.0	E980.4
Sominex	963.0	E858.1	E933.0	E950.4	E962.0	E980.4
Somnos	967.1	E852.0	E937.1	E950.2	E962.0	E980.2
Somonal	967.0	E851	E937.0	E950.1	E962.0	E980.1
Soneryl	967.0	E851	E937.0	E950.1	E962.0	E980.1
Soothing syrup	977.9	E858.9	E947.9	E950.5	E962.0	E980.5
Sopor	967.4	E852.3	E937.4	E950.2	E962.0	E980.2
Soporific drug	967.9	E852.9	E937.9	E950.2	E962.0	E980.2
specified type NEC	967.8	E852.8	E937.8	E950.2	E962.0	E980.2
Sorbitol NEC	977.4	E858.8	E947.4	E950.4	E962.0	E980.4
Sotradecol	972.7	E858.3	E942.7	E950.4	E962.0	E980.4
Spacoline	975.1	E858.6	E945.1	E950.4	E962.0	E980.4
Spanish fly	976.8	E858.7	E946.8	E950.4	E962.0	E980.4
Sparine	969.1	E853.0	E939.1	E950.3	E962.0	E980.3
Sparteine	975.0	E858.6	E945.0	E950.4	E962.0	E980.4
Spasmolytics	975.1	E858.6	E945.1	E950.4	E962.0	E980.4
anticholinergics	971.1	E855.4	E941.1	E950.4	E962.0	E980.4
Spectinomycin	960.8	E856	E930.8	E950.4	E962.0	E980.4
Speed	969.7	E854.2	E939.7	E950.3	E962.0	E980.3
Spermicides	976.8	E858.7	E946.8	E950.4	E962.0	E980.4
Spider (bite) (venom)	989.5	E905.1	—	E950.9	E962.1	E980.9
antivenin	979.9	E858.8	E949.9	E950.4	E962.0	E980.4

Substance	Poisoning	External Cause (E-Code) Accident	Therapeutic Use	Suicide Attempt	Assault	Undetermined
Spigelia (root)	961.6	E857	E931.6	E950.4	E962.0	E980.4
Spiperone	969.2	E853.1	E939.2	E950.3	E962.0	E980.3
Spiramycin	960.3	E856	E930.3	E950.4	E962.0	E980.4
Spirilene	969.5	E853.8	E939.5	E950.3	E962.0	E980.3
Spirit(s) (neutral) NEC	980.0	E860.1	—	E950.9	E962.1	E980.9
beverage	980.0	E860.0	—	E950.9	E962.1	E980.9
industrial	980.9	E860.9	—	E950.9	E962.1	E980.9
mineral	981	E862.0	—	E950.9	E962.1	E980.9
of salt — *see* Hydrochloric acid						
surgical	980.9	E860.9	—	E950.9	E962.1	E980.9
Spironolactone	974.4	E858.5	E944.4	E950.4	E962.0	E980.4
Sponge, absorbable (gelatin)	964.5	E858.2	E934.5	E950.4	E962.0	E980.4
Sporostacin	976.0	E858.7	E946.0	E950.4	E962.0	E980.4
Sprays (aerosol)	989.89	E866.8	—	E950.9	E962.1	E980.9
cosmetic	989.89	E866.7	—	E950.9	E962.1	E980.9
medicinal NEC	977.9	E858.9	E947.9	E950.5	E962.0	E980.5
pesticides — *see* Pesticides						
specified content — *see* substance specified						
Spurge flax	988.2	E865.4	—	E950.9	E962.1	E980.9
Spurges	988.2	E865.4	—	E950.9	E962.1	E980.9
Squill (expectorant) NEC	975.5	E858.6	E945.5	E950.4	E962.0	E980.4
rat poison	989.4	E863.7	—	E950.6	E962.1	E980.7
Squirting cucumber (cathartic)	973.1	E858.4	E943.1	E950.4	E962.0	E980.4
Stains	989.89	E866.8	—	E950.9	E962.1	E980.9
Stannous — *see also* Tin						
fluoride	976.7	E858.7	E946.7	E950.4	E962.0	E980.4
Stanolone	962.1	E858.0	E932.1	E950.4	E962.0	E980.4
Stanozolol	962.1	E858.0	E932.1	E950.4	E962.0	E980.4
Staphisagria or stavesacre (pediculicide)	976.0	E858.7	E946.0	E950.4	E962.0	E980.4
Stelazine	969.1	E853.0	E939.1	E950.3	E962.0	E980.3
Stemetil	969.1	E853.0	E939.1	E950.3	E962.0	E980.3
Sterculia (cathartic) (gum)	973.3	E858.4	E943.3	E950.4	E962.0	E980.4
Sternutator gas	987.8	E869.8	—	E952.8	E962.2	E982.8
Steroids NEC	962.0	E858.0	E932.0	E950.4	E962.0	E980.4
ENT agent	976.6	E858.7	E946.6	E950.4	E962.0	E980.4
ophthalmic preparation	976.5	E858.7	E946.5	E950.4	E962.0	E980.4
topical NEC	976.0	E858.7	E946.0	E950.4	E962.0	E980.4
Stibine	985.8	E866.4	—	E950.9	E962.1	E980.9
Stibophen	961.2	E857	E931.2	E950.4	E962.0	E980.4
Stilbamide, stilbamidine	961.5	E857	E931.5	E950.4	E962.0	E980.4
Stilbestrol	962.2	E858.0	E932.2	E950.4	E962.0	E980.4
Stimulants (central nervous system)	970.9	E854.3	E940.9	E950.4	E962.0	E980.4
analeptics	970.0	E854.3	E940.0	E950.4	E962.0	E980.4
opiate antagonist	970.1	E854.3	E940.1	E950.4	E962.0	E980.4
psychotherapeutic NEC	969.0	E854.0	E939.0	E950.3	E962.0	E980.3
specified NEC	970.8	E854.3	E940.8	E950.4	E962.0	E980.4
Storage batteries (acid) (cells)	983.1	E864.1	—	E950.7	E962.1	E980.6
Stovaine	968.9	E855.2	E938.9	E950.4	E962.0	E980.4
infiltration (subcutaneous)	968.5	E855.2	E938.5	E950.4	E962.0	E980.4
nerve block (peripheral) (plexus)	968.6	E855.2	E938.6	E950.4	E962.0	E980.4
spinal	968.7	E855.2	E938.7	E950.4	E962.0	E980.4
topical (surface)	968.5	E855.2	E938.5	E950.4	E962.0	E980.4
Stovarsal	961.1	E857	E931.1	E950.4	E962.0	E980.4
Stove gas — *see* Gas, utility						
Stoxil	976.5	E858.7	E946.5	E950.4	E962.0	E980.4
STP	969.6	E854.1	E939.6	E950.3	E962.0	E980.3
Stramonium (medicinal) NEC	971.1	E855.4	E941.1	E950.4	E962.0	E980.4
natural state	988.2	E865.4	—	E950.9	E962.1	E980.9
Streptodornase	964.4	E858.2	E934.4	E950.4	E962.0	E980.4
Streptoduocin	960.6	E856	E930.6	E950.4	E962.0	E980.4
Streptokinase	964.4	E858.2	E934.4	E950.4	E962.0	E980.4
Streptomycin	960.6	E856	E930.6	E950.4	E962.0	E980.4
Streptozocin	960.7	E856	E930.7	E950.4	E962.0	E980.4
Stripper (paint) (solvent)	982.8	E862.9	—	E950.9	E962.1	E980.9
Strobane	989.2	E863.0	—	E950.6	E962.1	E980.7
Strophanthin	972.1	E858.3	E942.1	E950.4	E962.0	E980.4
Strophanthus hispidus or kombe	988.2	E865.4	—	E950.9	E962.1	E980.9
Strychnine (rodenticide) (salts)	989.1	E863.7	—	E950.6	E962.1	E980.7
medicinal NEC	970.8	E854.3	E940.8	E950.4	E962.0	E980.4
Strychnos (ignatii) — *see* Strychnine						
Styramate	968.0	E855.1	E938.0	E950.4	E962.0	E980.4
Styrene	983.0	E864.0	—	E950.7	E962.1	E980.6

Substance	Poisoning	External Cause (E-Code) Accident	Therapeutic Use	Suicide Attempt	Assault	Un-determined
Succinimide (anticonvulsant)	966.2	E855.0	E936.2	E950.4	E962.0	E980.4
mercuric — *see* Mercury						
Succinylcholine	975.2	E858.6	E945.2	E950.4	E962.0	E980.4
Succinylsulfathiazole	961.0	E857	E931.0	E950.4	E962.0	E980.4
Sucrose	974.5	E858.5	E944.5	E950.4	E962.0	E980.4
Sulfacetamide	961.0	E857	E931.0	E950.4	E962.0	E980.4
ophthalmic preparation	976.5	E858.7	E946.5	E950.4	E962.0	E980.4
Sulfachlorpyridazine	961.0	E857	E931.0	E950.4	E962.0	E980.4
Sulfacytine	961.0	E857	E931.0	E950.4	E962.0	E980.4
Sulfadiazine	961.0	E857	E931.0	E950.4	E962.0	E980.4
silver (topical)	976.0	E858.7	E946.0	E950.4	E962.0	E980.4
Sulfadimethoxine	961.0	E857	E931.0	E950.4	E962.0	E980.4
Sulfadimidine	961.0	E857	E931.0	E950.4	E962.0	E980.4
Sulfaethidole	961.0	E857	E931.0	E950.4	E962.0	E980.4
Sulfafurazole	961.0	E857	E931.0	E950.4	E962.0	E980.4
Sulfaguanidine	961.0	E857	E931.0	E950.4	E962.0	E980.4
Sulfamerazine	961.0	E857	E931.0	E950.4	E962.0	E980.4
Sulfameter	961.0	E857	E931.0	E950.4	E962.0	E980.4
Sulfamethizole	961.0	E857	E931.0	E950.4	E962.0	E980.4
Sulfamethoxazole	961.0	E857	E931.0	E950.4	E962.0	E980.4
Sulfamethoxydiazine	961.0	E857	E931.0	E950.4	E962.0	E980.4
Sulfamethoxypyridazine	961.0	E857	E931.0	E950.4	E962.0	E980.4
Sulfamethylthiazole	961.0	E857	E931.0	E950.4	E962.0	E980.4
Sulfamylon	976.0	E858.7	E946.0	E950.4	E962.0	E980.4
Sulfan blue (diagnostic dye)	977.8	E858.8	E947.8	E950.4	E962.0	E980.4
Sulfanilamide	961.0	E857	E931.0	E950.4	E962.0	E980.4
Sulfanilylguanidine	961.0	E857	E931.0	E950.4	E962.0	E980.4
Sulfaphenazole	961.0	E857	E931.0	E950.4	E962.0	E980.4
Sulfaphenylthiazole	961.0	E857	E931.0	E950.4	E962.0	E980.4
Sulfaproxyline	961.0	E857	E931.0	E950.4	E962.0	E980.4
Sulfapyridine	961.0	E857	E931.0	E950.4	E962.0	E980.4
Sulfapyrimidine	961.0	E857	E931.0	E950.4	E962.0	E980.4
Sulfarsphenamine	961.1	E857	E931.1	E950.4	E962.0	E980.4
Sulfasalazine	961.0	E857	E931.0	E950.4	E962.0	E980.4
Sulfasomizole	961.0	E857	E931.0	E950.4	E962.0	E980.4
Sulfasuxidine	961.0	E857	E931.0	E950.4	E962.0	E980.4
Sulfinpyrazone	974.7	E858.5	E944.7	E950.4	E962.0	E980.4
Sulfisoxazole	961.0	E857	E931.0	E950.4	E962.0	E980.4
ophthalmic preparation	976.5	E858.7	E946.5	E950.4	E962.0	E980.4
Sulfomyxin	960.8	E856	E930.8	E950.4	E962.0	E980.4
Sulfonal	967.8	E852.8	E937.8	E950.2	E962.0	E980.2
Sulfonamides (mixtures)	961.0	E857	E931.0	E950.4	E962.0	E980.4
Sulfones	961.8	E857	E931.8	E950.4	E962.0	E980.4
Sulfonethylmethane	967.8	E852.8	E937.8	E950.2	E962.0	E980.2
Sulfonmethane	967.8	E852.8	E937.8	E950.2	E962.0	E980.2
Sulfonphthal, sulfonphthol	977.8	E858.8	E947.8	E950.4	E962.0	E980.4
Sulfonylurea derivatives, oral	962.3	E858.0	E932.3	E950.4	E962.0	E980.4
Sulfoxone	961.8	E857	E931.8	E950.4	E962.0	E980.4
Sulfur, sulfureted, sulfuric, sulfurous, sulfuryl (compounds) NEC	989.89	E866.8	—	E950.9	E962.1	E980.9
acid	983.1	E864.1	—	E950.7	E962.1	E980.6
dioxide	987.3	E869.1	—	E952.8	E962.2	E982.8
ether — *see* Ether(s)						
hydrogen	987.8	E869.8	—	E952.8	E962.2	E982.8
medicinal (keratolytic) (ointment) NEC	976.4	E858.7	E946.4	E950.4	E962.0	E980.4
pesticide (vapor)	989.4	E863.4	—	E950.6	E962.1	E980.7
vapor NEC	987.8	E869.8	—	E952.8	E962.2	E982.8
Sulkowitch's reagent	977.8	E858.8	E947.8	E950.4	E962.0	E980.4
Sulph — *see also* Sulf-						
Sulphadione	961.8	E857	E931.8	E950.4	E962.0	E980.4
Sulthiame, sultiame	966.3	E855.0	E936.3	E950.4	E962.0	E980.4
Superinone	975.5	E858.6	E945.5	E950.4	E962.0	E980.4
Suramin	961.5	E857	E931.5	E950.4	E962.0	E980.4
Surfacaine	968.5	E855.2	E938.5	E950.4	E962.0	E980.4
Surital	968.3	E855.1	E938.3	E950.4	E962.0	E980.4
Sutilains	976.8	E858.7	E946.8	E950.4	E962.0	E980.4
Suxamethonium (bromide) (chloride) (iodide)	975.2	E858.6	E945.2	E950.4	E962.0	E980.4
Suxethonium (bromide)	975.2	E858.6	E945.2	E950.4	E962.0	E980.4
Sweet oil (birch)	976.3	E858.7	E946.3	E950.4	E962.0	E980.4
Sym-dichloroethyl ether	982.3	E862.4	—	E950.9	E962.1	E980.9
Sympatholytics	971.3	E855.6	E941.3	E950.4	E962.0	E980.4

Substance	Poisoning	External Cause (E-Code) Accident	Therapeutic Use	Suicide Attempt	Assault	Undetermined
Sympathomimetics	971.2	E855.5	E941.2	E950.4	E962.0	E980.4
Synalar	976.0	E858.7	E946.0	E950.4	E962.0	E980.4
Synthroid	962.7	E858.0	E932.7	E950.4	E962.0	E980.4
Syntocinon	975.0	E858.6	E945.0	E950.4	E962.0	E950.4
Syrosingopine	972.6	E858.3	E942.6	E950.4	E962.0	E980.4
Systemic agents (primarily)	963.9	E858.1	E933.9	E950.4	E962.0	E980.4
specified NEC	963.8	E858.1	E933.8	E950.4	E962.0	E980.4
T						
Tablets (*see also* specified substance)	977.9	E858.9	E947.9	E950.5	E962.0	E980.5
Tace	962.2	E858.0	E932.2	E950.4	E962.0	E980.4
Tacrine	971.0	E855.3	E941.0	E950.4	E962.0	E980.4
Talbutal	967.0	E851	E937.0	E950.1	E962.0	E980.1
Talc	976.3	E858.7	E946.3	E950.4	E962.0	E980.4
Talcum	976.3	E858.7	E946.3	E950.4	E962.0	E980.4
Tandearil, tanderil	965.5	E850.5	E935.5	E950.0	E962.0	E980.0
Tannic acid	983.1	E864.1	—	E950.7	E962.1	E980.6
medicinal (astringent)	976.2	E858.7	E946.2	E950.4	E962.0	E980.4
Tannin — *see* Tannic acid						
Tansy	988.2	E865.4	—	E950.9	E962.1	E980.9
TAO	960.3	E856	E930.3	E950.4	E962.0	E980.4
Tapazole	962.8	E858.0	E932.8	E950.4	E962.0	E980.4
Tar NEC	983.0	E864.0	—	E950.7	E962.1	E980.6
camphor — *see* Naphthalene						
fumes	987.8	E869.8	—	E952.8	E962.2	E982.8
Taractan	969.3	E853.8	E939.3	E950.3	E962.0	E980.3
Tarantula (venomous)	989.5	E905.1	—	E950.9	E962.1	E980.9
Tartar emetic (anti-infective)	961.2	E857	E931.2	E950.4	E962.0	E980.4
Tartaric acid	983.1	E864.1	—	E950.7	E962.1	E980.6
Tartrated antimony (anti-infective)	961.2	E857	E931.2	E950.4	E962.0	E980.4
TCA —*see* Trichloroacetic acid						
TDI	983.0	E864.0	—	E950.7	E962.1	E980.6
vapor	987.8	E869.8	—	E952.8	E962.2	E982.8
Tear gas	987.5	E869.3	—	E952.8	E962.2	E982.8
Teclothiazide	974.3	E858.5	E944.3	E950.4	E962.0	E980.4
Tegretol	966.3	E855.0	E936.3	E950.4	E962.0	E980.4
Telepaque	977.8	E858.8	E947.8	E950.4	E962.0	E980.4
Tellurium	985.8	E866.4	—	E950.9	E962.1	E980.9
fumes	985.8	E866.4	—	E950.9	E962.1	E980.9
TEM	963.1	E858.1	E933.1	E950.4	E962.0	E980.4
Temazepan — *see* Benzodiazepines						
TEPA	963.1	E858.1	E933.1	E950.4	E962.0	E980.4
TEPP	989.3	E863.1	—	E950.6	E962.1	E980.7
Terbutaline	971.2	E855.5	E941.2	E950.4	E962.0	E980.4
Teroxalene	961.6	E857	E931.6	E950.4	E962.0	E980.4
Terpin hydrate	975.5	E858.6	E945.5	E950.4	E962.0	E980.4
Terramycin	960.4	E856	E930.4	E950.4	E962.0	E980.4
Tessalon	975.4	E858.6	E945.4	E950.4	E962.0	E980.4
Testosterone	962.1	E858.0	E932.1	E950.4	E962.0	E980.4
Tetanus (vaccine)	978.4	E858.8	E948.4	E950.4	E962.0	E980.4
antitoxin	979.9	E858.8	E949.9	E950.4	E962.0	E980.4
immune globulin (human)	964.6	E858.2	E934.6	E950.4	E962.0	E980.4
toxoid	978.4	E858.8	E948.4	E950.4	E962.0	E980.4
with diphtheria toxoid	978.9	E858.8	E948.9	E950.4	E962.0	E980.4
with pertussis	978.6	E858.8	E948.6	E950.4	E962.0	E980.4
Tetrabenazine	969.5	E853.8	E939.5	E950.3	E962.0	E980.3
Tetracaine (infiltration) (topical)	968.5	E855.2	E938.5	E950.4	E962.0	E980.4
nerve block (peripheral) (plexus)	968.6	E855.2	E938.6	E950.4	E962.0	E980.4
spinal	968.7	E855.2	E938.7	E950.4	E962.0	E980.4
Tetrachlorethylene — *see* Tetrachloroethylene						
Tetrachlormethiazide	974.3	E858.5	E944.3	E950.4	E962.0	E980.4
Tetrachloroethane (liquid) (vapor)	982.3	E862.4	—	E950.9	E962.1	E980.9
paint or varnish	982.3	E861.6	—	E950.9	E962.1	E980.9
Tetrachloroethylene (liquid) (vapor)	982.3	E862.4	—	E950.9	E962.1	E980.9
medicinal	961.6	E857	E931.6	E950.4	E962.0	E980.4
Tetrachloromethane — *see* Carbon, tetrachloride						
Tetracycline	960.4	E856	E930.4	E950.4	E962.0	E980.4
ophthalmic preparation	976.5	E858.7	E946.5	E950.4	E962.0	E980.4
topical NEC	976.0	E858.7	E946.0	E950.4	E962.0	E980.4
Tetraethylammonium chloride	972.3	E858.3	E942.3	E950.4	E962.0	E980.4
Tetraethyl lead (antiknock compound)	984.1	E862.1	—	E950.9	E962.1	E980.9
Tetraethyl pyrophosphate	989.3	E863.1	—	E950.6	E962.1	E980.7

		External Cause (E-Code)				
Substance	Poisoning	Accident	Therapeutic Use	Suicide Attempt	Assault	Un-determined
Tetraethylthiuram disulfide	977.3	E858.8	E947.3	E950.4	E962.0	E980.4
Tetrahydroaminoacridine	971.0	E855.3	E941.0	E950.4	E962.0	E980.4
Tetrahydrocannabinol	969.6	E854.1	E939.6	E950.3	E962.0	E980.3
Tetrahydronaphthalene	982.0	E862.4	—	E950.9	E962.1	E980.9
Tetrahydrozoline	971.2	E855.5	E941.2	E950.4	E962.0	E980.4
Tetralin	982.0	E862.4	—	E950.9	E962.1	E980.9
Tetramethylthiuram (disulfide) NEC	989.4	E863.6	—	E950.6	E962.1	E980.7
medicinal	976.2	E858.7	E946.2	E950.4	E962.0	E980.4
Tetronal	967.8	E852.8	E937.8	E950.2	E962.0	E980.2
Tetryl	983.0	E864.0	—	E950.7	E962.1	E980.6
Thalidomide	967.8	E852.8	E937.8	E950.2	E962.0	E980.2
Thallium (compounds) (dust) NEC	985.8	E866.4	—	E950.9	E962.1	E980.9
pesticide (rodenticide)	985.8	E863.7	—	E950.6	E962.1	E980.7
THC	969.6	E854.1	E939.6	E950.3	E962.0	E980.3
Thebacon	965.09	E850.2	E935.2	E950.0	E962.0	E980.0
Thebaine	965.09	E850.2	E935.2	E950.0	E962.0	E980.0
Theobromine (calcium salicylate)	974.1	E858.5	E944.1	E950.4	E962.0	E980.4
Theophylline (diuretic)	974.1	E858.5	E944.1	E950.4	E962.0	E980.4
ethylenediamine	975.7	E858.6	E945.7	E950.4	E962.0	E980.4
Thiabendazole	961.6	E857	E931.6	E950.4	E962.0	E980.4
Thialbarbital, thialbarbitone	968.3	E855.1	E938.3	E950.4	E962.0	E980.4
Thiamine	963.5	E858.1	E933.5	E950.4	E962.0	E980.4
Thiamylal (sodium)	968.3	E855.1	E938.3	E950.4	E962.0	E980.4
Thiazesim	969.0	E854.0	E939.0	E950.3	E962.0	E980.3
Thiazides (diuretics)	974.3	E858.5	E944.3	E950.4	E962.0	E980.4
Thiethylperazine	963.0	E858.1	E933.0	E950.4	E962.0	E980.4
Thimerosal (topical)	976.0	E858.7	E946.0	E950.4	E962.0	E980.4
ophthalmic preparation	976.5	E858.7	E946.5	E950.4	E962.0	E980.4
Thioacetazone	961.8	E857	E931.8	E950.4	E962.0	E980.4
Thiobarbiturates	968.3	E855.1	E938.3	E950.4	E962.0	E980.4
Thiobismol	961.2	E857	E931.2	E950.4	E962.0	E980.4
Thiocarbamide	962.8	E858.0	E932.8	E950.4	E962.0	E980.4
Thiocarbarsone	961.1	E857	E931.1	E950.4	E962.0	E980.4
Thiocarlide	961.8	E857	E931.8	E950.4	E962.0	E980.4
Thioguanine	963.1	E858.1	E933.1	E950.4	E962.0	E980.4
Thiomercaptomerin	974.0	E858.5	E944.0	E950.4	E962.0	E980.4
Thiomerin	974.0	E858.5	E944.0	E950.4	E962.0	E980.4
Thiopental, thiopentone (sodium)	968.3	E855.1	E938.3	E950.4	E962.0	E980.4
Thiopropazate	969.1	E853.0	E939.1	E950.3	E962.0	E980.3
Thioproperazine	969.1	E853.0	E939.1	E950.3	E962.0	E980.3
Thioridazine	969.1	E853.0	E939.1	E950.3	E962.0	E980.3
Thio-TEPA, thiotepa	963.1	E858.1	E933.1	E950.4	E962.0	E980.4
Thiothixene	969.3	E853.8	E939.3	E950.3	E962.0	E980.3
Thiouracil	962.8	E858.0	E932.8	E950.4	E962.0	E980.4
Thiourea	962.8	E858.0	E932.8	E950.4	E962.0	E980.4
Thiphenamil	971.1	E855.4	E941.1	E950.4	E962.0	E980.4
Thiram NEC	989.4	E863.6	—	E950.6	E962.1	E980.7
medicinal	976.2	E858.7	E946.2	E950.4	E962.0	E980.4
Thonzylamine	963.0	E858.1	E933.0	E950.4	E962.0	E980.4
Thorazine	969.1	E853.0	E939.1	E950.3	E962.0	E980.3
Thornapple	988.2	E865.4	—	E950.9	E962.1	E980.9
Throat preparation (lozenges) NEC	976.6	E858.7	E946.6	E950.4	E962.0	E980.4
Thrombin	964.5	E858.2	E934.5	E950.4	E962.0	E980.4
Thrombolysin	964.4	E858.2	E934.4	E950.4	E962.0	E980.4
Thymol	983.0	E864.0	—	E950.7	E962.1	E980.6
Thymus extract	962.9	E858.0	E932.9	E950.4	E962.0	E980.4
Thyroglobulin	962.7	E858.0	E932.7	E950.4	E962.0	E980.4
Thyroid (derivatives) (extract)	962.7	E858.0	E932.7	E950.4	E962.0	E980.4
Thyrolar	962.7	E858.0	E932.7	E950.4	E962.0	E980.4
Thyrothrophin, thyrotropin	977.8	E858.8	E947.8	E950.4	E962.0	E980.4
Thyroxin(e)	962.7	E858.0	E932.7	E950.4	E962.0	E980.4
Tigan	963.0	E858.1	E933.0	E950.4	E962.0	E980.4
Tigloidine	968.0	E855.1	E938.0	E950.4	E962.0	E980.4
Tin (chloride) (dust) (oxide) NEC	985.8	E866.4	—	E950.9	E962.1	E980.9
anti-infectives	961.2	E857	E931.2	E950.4	E962.0	E980.4
Tinactin	976.0	E858.7	E946.0	E950.4	E962.0	E980.4
Tincture, iodine — *see* Iodine						
Tindal	969.1	E853.0	E939.1	E950.3	E962.0	E980.3
Titanium (compounds) (vapor)	985.8	E866.4	—	E950.9	E962.1	E980.9
ointment	976.3	E858.7	E946.3	E950.4	E962.0	E980.4
Titroid	962.7	E858.0	E932.7	E950.4	E962.0	E980.4

Substance	Poisoning	External Cause (E-Code) Accident	Therapeutic Use	Suicide Attempt	Assault	Un-determined
TMTD — *see* Tetramethylthiuram disulfide						
TNT	989.89	E866.8	—	E950.9	E962.1	E980.9
fumes	987.8	E869.8	—	E952.8	E962.2	E982.8
Toadstool	988.1	E865.5	—	E950.9	E962.1	E980.9
Tobacco NEC	989.84	E866.8	—	E950.9	E962.1	E980.9
Indian	988.2	E865.4	—	E950.9	E962.1	E980.9
smoke, second-hand	987.8	E869.4	—	—	—	—
Tocopherol	963.5	E858.1	E933.5	E950.4	E962.0	E980.4
Tocosamine	975.0	E858.6	E945.0	E950.4	E962.0	E980.4
Tofranil	969.0	E854.0	E939.0	E950.3	E962.0	E980.3
Toilet deodorizer	989.8	E866.8	—	E950.9	E962.1	E980.9
Tolazamide	962.3	E858.0	E932.3	E950.4	E962.0	E980.4
Tolazoline	971.3	E855.6	E941.3	E950.4	E962.0	E980.4
Tolbutamide	962.3	E858.0	E932.3	E950.4	E962.0	E980.4
sodium	977.8	E858.8	E947.8	E950.4	E962.0	E980.4
Tolmetin	965.69	E850.6	E935.6	E950.0	E962.0	E980.0
Tolnaftate	976.0	E858.7	E946.0	E950.4	E962.0	E980.4
Tolpropamine	976.1	E858.7	E946.1	E950.4	E962.0	E980.4
Tolserol	968.0	E855.1	E938.0	E950.4	E962.0	E980.4
Toluene (liquid) (vapor)	982.0	E862.4	—	E950.9	E962.1	E980.9
diisocyanate	983.0	E864.0	—	E950.7	E962.1	E980.6
Toluidine	983.0	E864.0	—	E950.7	E962.1	E980.6
vapor	987.8	E869.8	—	E952.8	E962.2	E982.8
Toluol (liquid) (vapor)	982.0	E862.4	—	E950.9	E962.1	E980.9
Tolylene-2,4-diisocyanate	983.0	E864.0	—	E950.7	E962.1	E980.6
Tonics, cardiac	972.1	E858.3	E942.1	E950.4	E962.0	E980.4
Toxaphene (dust) (spray)	989.2	E863.0	—	E950.6	E962.1	E980.7
Toxoids NEC	978.8	E858.8	E948.8	E950.4	E962.0	E980.4
Tractor fuel NEC	981	E862.1	—	E950.9	E962.1	E980.9
Tragacanth	973.3	E858.4	E943.3	E950.4	E962.0	E980.4
Tramazoline	971.2	E855.5	E941.2	E950.4	E962.0	E980.4
Tranquilizers	969.5	E853.9	E939.5	E950.3	E962.0	E980.3
benzodiazepine-based	969.4	E853.2	E939.4	E950.3	E962.0	E980.3
butyrophenone-based	969.2	E853.1	E939.2	E950.3	E962.0	E980.3
major NEC	969.3	E853.8	E939.3	E950.3	E962.0	E980.3
phenothiazine-based	969.1	E853.0	E939.1	E950.3	E962.0	E980.3
specified NEC	969.5	E853.8	E939.5	E950.3	E962.0	E980.3
Trantoin	961.9	E857	E931.9	E950.4	E962.0	E980.4
Tranxene	969.4	E853.2	E939.4	E950.3	E962.0	E980.3
Tranylcypromine (sulfate)	969.0	E854.0	E939.0	E950.3	E962.0	E980.3
Trasentine	975.1	E858.6	E945.1	E950.4	E962.0	E980.4
Travert	974.5	E858.5	E944.5	E950.4	E962.0	E980.4
Trecator	961.8	E857	E931.8	E950.4	E962.0	E980.4
Tretinoin	976.8	E858.7	E946.8	E950.4	E962.0	E980.4
Triacetin	976.0	E858.7	E946.0	E950.4	E962.0	E980.4
Triacetyloleandomycin	960.3	E856	E930.3	E950.4	E962.0	E980.4
Triamcinolone	962.0	E858.0	E932.0	E950.4	E962.0	E980.4
ENT agent	976.6	E858.7	E946.6	E950.4	E962.0	E980.4
ophthalmic preparation	976.5	E858.7	E946.5	E950.4	E962.0	E980.4
topical NEC	976.0	E858.7	E946.0	E950.4	E962.0	E980.4
Triamterene	974.4	E858.5	E944.4	E950.4	E962.0	E980.4
Triaziquone	963.1	E858.1	E933.1	E950.4	E962.0	E980.4
Tribromacetaldehyde	967.3	E852.2	E937.3	E950.2	E962.0	E980.2
Tribromoethanol	968.2	E855.1	E938.2	E950.4	E962.0	E980.4
Tribromomethane	967.3	E852.2	E937.3	E950.2	E962.0	E980.2
Trichlorethane	982.3	E862.4	—	E950.9	E962.1	E980.9
Trichlormethiazide	974.3	E858.5	E944.3	E950.4	E962.0	E980.4
Trichloroacetic acid	983.1	E864.1	—	E950.7	E962.1	E980.6
medicinal (keratolytic)	976.4	E858.7	E946.4	E950.4	E962.0	E980.4
Trichloroethanol	967.1	E852.0	E937.1	E950.2	E962.0	E980.2
Trichloroethylene (liquid) (vapor)	982.3	E862.4	—	E950.9	E962.1	E980.9
anesthetic (gas)	968.2	E855.1	E938.2	E950.4	E962.0	E980.4
Trichloroethyl phosphate	967.1	E852.0	E937.1	E950.2	E962.0	E980.2
Trichlorofluoromethane NEC	987.4	E869.2	—	E952.8	E962.2	E982.8
Trichlorotriethylamine	963.1	E858.1	E933.1	E950.4	E962.0	E980.4
Trichomonacides NEC	961.5	E857	E931.5	E950.4	E962.0	E980.4
Trichomycin	960.1	E856	E930.1	E950.4	E962.0	E980.4
Triclofos	967.1	E852.0	E937.1	E950.2	E962.0	E980.2
Tricresyl phosphate	989.89	E866.8	—	E950.9	E962.1	E980.9
solvent	982.8	E862.4	—	E950.9	E962.1	E980.9
Tricyclamol	966.4	E855.0	E936.4	E950.4	E962.0	E980.4
Tridesilon	976.0	E858.7	E946.0	E950.4	E962.0	E980.4

Substance	Poisoning	External Cause (E-Code) Accident	Therapeutic Use	Suicide Attempt	Assault	Undetermined
Tridihexethyl	971.1	E855.4	E941.1	E950.4	E962.0	E980.4
Tridione	966.0	E855.0	E936.0	E950.4	E962.0	E980.4
Triethanolamine NEC	983.2	E864.2	—	E950.7	E962.1	E980.6
detergent	983.2	E861.0	—	E950.7	E962.1	E980.6
trinitrate	972.4	E858.3	E942.4	E950.4	E962.0	E980.4
Triethanomelamine	963.1	E858.1	E933.1	E950.4	E962.0	E980.4
Triethylene melamine	963.1	E858.1	E933.1	E950.4	E962.0	E980.4
Triethylenephosphoramide	963.1	E858.1	E933.1	E950.4	E962.0	E980.4
Triethylenethiophosphoramide	963.1	E858.1	E933.1	E950.4	E962.0	E980.4
Trifluoperazine	969.1	E853.0	E939.1	E950.3	E962.0	E980.3
Trifluperidol	969.2	E853.1	E939.2	E950.3	E962.0	E980.3
Triflupromazine	969.1	E853.0	E939.1	E950.3	E962.0	E980.3
Trihexyphenidyl	971.1	E855.4	E941.1	E950.4	E962.0	E980.4
Triiodothyronine	962.7	E858.0	E932.7	E950.4	E962.0	E980.4
Trilene	968.2	E855.1	E938.2	E950.4	E962.0	E980.4
Trimeprazine	963.0	E858.1	E933.0	E950.4	E962.0	E980.4
Trimetazidine	972.4	E858.3	E942.4	E950.4	E962.0	E980.4
Trimethadione	966.0	E855.0	E936.0	E950.4	E962.0	E980.4
Trimethaphan	972.3	E858.3	E942.3	E950.4	E962.0	E980.4
Trimethidinium	972.3	E858.3	E942.3	E950.4	E962.0	E980.4
Trimethobenzamide	963.0	E858.1	E933.0	E950.4	E962.0	E980.4
Trimethylcarbinol	980.8	E860.8	—	E950.9	E962.1	E980.9
Trimethylpsoralen	976.3	E858.7	E946.3	E950.4	E962.0	E980.4
Trimeton	963.0	E858.1	E933.0	E950.4	E962.0	E980.4
Trimipramine	969.0	E854.0	E939.0	E950.3	E962.0	E980.3
Trimustine	963.1	E858.1	E933.1	E950.4	E962.0	E980.4
Trinitrin	972.4	E858.3	E942.4	E950.4	E962.0	E980.4
Trinitrophenol	983.0	E864.0	—	E950.7	E962.1	E980.6
Trinitrotoluene	989.89	E866.8	—	E950.9	E962.1	E980.9
fumes	987.8	E869.8	—	E952.8	E962.2	E982.8
Trional	967.8	E852.8	E937.8	E950.2	E962.0	E980.2
Trioxide of arsenic — *see* Arsenic						
Trioxsalen	976.3	E858.7	E946.3	E950.4	E962.0	E980.4
Tripelennamine	963.0	E858.1	E933.0	E950.4	E962.0	E980.4
Triperidol	969.2	E853.1	E939.2	E950.3	E962.0	E980.3
Triprolidine	963.0	E858.1	E933.0	E950.4	E962.0	E980.4
Trisoralen	976.3	E858.7	E946.3	E950.4	E962.0	E980.4
Troleandomycin	960.3	E856	E930.3	E950.4	E962.0	E980.4
Trolnitrate (phosphate)	972.4	E858.3	E942.4	E950.4	E962.0	E980.4
Trometamol	963.3	E858.1	E933.3	E950.4	E962.0	E980.4
Tromethamine	963.3	E858.1	E933.3	E950.4	E962.0	E980.4
Tronothane	968.5	E855.2	E938.5	E950.4	E962.0	E980.4
Tropicamide	971.1	E855.4	E941.1	E950.4	E962.0	E980.4
Troxidone	966.0	E855.0	E936.0	E950.4	E962.0	E980.4
Tryparsamide	961.1	E857	E931.1	E950.4	E962.0	E980.4
Trypsin	963.4	E858.1	E933.4	E950.4	E962.0	E980.4
Tryptizol	969.0	E854.0	E939.0	E950.3	E962.0	E980.3
Tuaminoheptane	971.2	E855.5	E941.2	E950.4	E962.0	E980.4
Tuberculin (old)	977.8	E858.8	E947.8	E950.4	E962.0	E980.4
Tubocurare	975.2	E858.6	E945.2	E950.4	E962.0	E980.4
Tubocurarine	975.2	E858.6	E945.2	E950.4	E962.0	E980.4
Turkish green	969.6	E854.1	E939.6	E950.3	E962.0	E980.3
Turpentine (spirits of) (liquid) (vapor)	982.8	E862.4	—	E950.9	E962.1	E980.9
Tybamate	969.5	E853.8	E939.5	E950.3	E962.0	E980.3
Tyloxapol	975.5	E858.6	E945.5	E950.4	E962.0	E980.4
Tymazoline	971.2	E855.5	E941.2	E950.4	E962.0	E980.4
Typhoid vaccine	978.1	E858.8	E948.1	E950.4	E962.0	E980.4
Typhus vaccine	979.2	E858.8	E949.2	E950.4	E962.0	E980.4
Tyrothricin	976.0	E858.7	E946.0	E950.4	E962.0	E980.4
ENT agent	976.6	E858.7	E946.6	E950.4	E962.0	E980.4
ophthalmic preparation	976.5	E858.7	E946.5	E950.4	E962.0	E980.4
U						
Undecenoic acid	976.0	E858.7	E946.0	E950.4	E962.0	E980.4
Undecylenic acid	976.0	E858.7	E946.0	E950.4	E962.0	E980.4
Unna's boot	976.3	E858.7	E946.3	E950.4	E962.0	E980.4
Uracil mustard	963.1	E858.1	E933.1	E950.4	E962.0	E980.4
Uramustine	963.1	E858.1	E933.1	E950.4	E962.0	E980.4
Urari	975.2	E858.6	E945.2	E950.4	E962.0	E980.4
Urea	974.4	E858.5	E944.4	E950.4	E962.0	E980.4
topical	976.8	E858.7	E946.8	E950.4	E962.0	E980.4
Urethan(e) (antineoplastic)	963.1	E858.1	E933.1	E950.4	E962.0	E980.4

Substance	Poisoning	External Cause (E-Code) Accident	Therapeutic Use	Suicide Attempt	Assault	Undetermined
Urginea (maritima) (scilla) — *see* Squill						
Uric acid metabolism agents NEC	974.7	E858.5	E944.7	E950.4	E962.0	E980.4
Urokinase	964.4	E858.2	E934.4	E950.4	E962.0	E980.4
Urokon	977.8	E858.8	E947.8	E950.4	E962.0	E980.4
Urotropin	961.9	E857	E931.9	E950.4	E962.0	E980.4
Urtica	988.2	E865.4	—	E950.9	E962.1	E980.9
Utility gas — *see* Gas, utility						
V						
Vaccine NEC	979.9	E858.8	E949.9	E950.4	E962.0	E980.4
bacterial NEC	978.8	E858.8	E948.8	E950.4	E962.0	E980.4
with						
other bacterial component	978.9	E858.8	E948.9	E950.4	E962.0	E980.4
pertussis component	978.6	E858.8	E948.6	E950.4	E962.0	E980.4
viral-rickettsial component	979.7	E858.8	E949.7	E950.4	E962.0	E980.4
mixed NEC	978.9	E858.8	E948.9	E950.4	E962.0	E980.4
BCG	978.0	E858.8	E948.0	E950.4	E962.0	E980.4
cholera	978.2	E858.8	E948.2	E950.4	E962.0	E980.4
diphtheria	978.5	E858.8	E948.5	E950.4	E962.0	E980.4
influenza	979.6	E858.8	E949.6	E950.4	E962.0	E980.4
measles	979.4	E858.8	E949.4	E950.4	E962.0	E980.4
Vaccine NEC— *continued*						
meningococcal	978.8	E858.8	E948.8	E950.4	E962.0	E980.4
mumps	979.6	E858.8	E949.6	E950.4	E962.0	E980.4
paratyphoid	978.1	E858.8	E948.1	E950.4	E962.0	E980.4
pertussis (with diphtheria toxoid) (with tetanus toxoid)	978.6	E858.8	E948.6	E950.4	E962.0	E980.4
plague	978.3	E858.8	E948.3	E950.4	E962.0	E980.4
poliomyelitis	979.5	E858.8	E949.5	E950.4	E962.0	E980.4
poliovirus	979.5	E858.8	E949.5	E950.4	E962.0	E980.4
rabies	979.1	E858.8	E949.1	E950.4	E962.0	E980.4
rickettsial NEC	979.6	E858.8	E949.6	E950.4	E962.0	E980.4
with						
bacterial component	979.7	E858.8	E949.7	E950.4	E962.0	E980.4
pertussis component	978.6	E858.8	E948.6	E950.4	E962.0	E980.4
viral component	979.7	E858.8	E949.7	E950.4	E962.0	E980.4
Rocky mountain spotted fever	979.6	E858.8	E949.6	E950.4	E962.0	E980.4
rubella virus	979.4	E858.8	E949.4	E950.4	E962.0	E980.4
sabin oral	979.5	E858.8	E949.5	E950.4	E962.0	E980.4
smallpox	979.0	E858.8	E949.0	E950.4	E962.0	E980.4
tetanus	978.4	E858.8	E948.4	E950.4	E962.0	E980.4
typhoid	978.1	E858.8	E948.1	E950.4	E962.0	E980.4
typhus	979.2	E858.8	E949.2	E950.4	E962.0	E980.4
viral NEC	979.6	E858.8	E949.6	E950.4	E962.0	E980.4
with						
bacterial component	979.7	E858.8	E949.7	E950.4	E962.0	E980.4
pertussis component	978.6	E858.8	E948.6	E950.4	E962.0	E980.4
rickettsial component	979.7	E858.8	E949.7	E950.4	E962.0	E980.4
yellow fever	979.3	E858.8	E949.3	E950.4	E962.0	E980.4
Vaccinia immune globulin (human)	964.6	E858.2	E934.6	E950.4	E962.0	E980.4
Vaginal contraceptives	976.8	E858.7	E946.8	E950.4	E962.0	E980.4
Valethamate	971.1	E855.4	E941.1	E950.4	E962.0	E980.4
Valisone	976.0	E858.7	E946.0	E950.4	E962.0	E980.4
Valium	969.4	E853.2	E939.4	E950.3	E962.0	E980.3
Valmid	967.8	E852.8	E937.8	E950.2	E962.0	E980.2
Vanadium	985.8	E866.4	—	E950.9	E962.1	E980.9
Vancomycin	960.8	E856	E930.8	E950.4	E962.0	E980.4
Vapor (*see also* Gas)	987.9	E869.9	—	E952.9	E962.2	E982.9
kiln (carbon monoxide)	986	E868.8	—	E952.1	E962.2	E982.1
lead — *see* Lead						
specified source NEC (*see also* specific substance)	987.8	E869.8	—	E952.8	E962.2	E982.8
Varidase	964.4	E858.2	E934.4	E950.4	E962.0	E980.4
Varnish	989.89	E861.6	—	E950.9	E962.1	E980.9
cleaner	982.8	E862.9	—	E950.9	E962.1	E980.9
Vaseline	976.3	E858.7	E946.3	E950.4	E962.0	E980.4
Vasodilan	972.5	E858.3	E942.5	E950.4	E962.0	E980.4
Vasodilators NEC	972.5	E858.3	E942.5	E950.4	E962.0	E980.4
coronary	972.4	E858.3	E942.4	E950.4	E962.0	E980.4
Vasopressin	962.5	E858.0	E932.5	E950.4	E962.0	E980.4
Vasopressor drugs	962.5	E858.0	E932.5	E950.4	E962.0	E980.4
Venom, venomous (bite) (sting)	989.5	E905.9	—	E950.9	E962.1	E980.9
arthropod NEC	989.5	E905.5	—	E950.9	E962.1	E980.9
bee	989.5	E905.3	—	E950.9	E962.1	E980.9
centipede	989.5	E905.4	—	E950.9	E962.1	E980.9
hornet	989.5	E905.3	—	E950.9	E962.1	E980.9

		External Cause (E-Code)				
Substance	**Poisoning**	**Accident**	**Therapeutic Use**	**Suicide Attempt**	**Assault**	**Undetermined**
Venom, venomous (bite) (sting) — *continued*						
lizard	989.5	E905.0	—	E950.9	E962.1	E980.9
marine animals or plants	989.5	E905.6	—	E950.9	E962.1	E980.9
millipede (tropical)	989.5	E905.4	—	E950.9	E962.1	E980.9
plant NEC	989.5	E905.7	—	E950.9	E962.1	E980.9
marine	989.5	E905.6	—	E950.9	E962.1	E980.9
scorpion	989.5	E905.2	—	E950.9	E962.1	E980.9
snake	989.5	E905.0	—	E950.9	E962.1	E980.9
specified NEC	989.5	E905.8	—	E950.9	E962.1	E980.9
spider	989.5	E905.1	—	E950.9	E962.1	E980.9
wasp	989.5	E905.3	—	E950.9	E962.1	E980.9
Ventolin — *see* Salbutamol sulfate						
Veramon	967.0	E851	E937.0	E950.1	E962.0	E980.1
Veratrum						
album	988.2	E865.4	—	E950.9	E962.1	E980.9
alkaloids	972.6	E858.3	E942.6	E950.4	E962.0	E980.4
viride	988.2	E865.4	—	E950.9	E962.1	E980.9
Verdigris (*see also* Copper)	985.8	E866.4	—	E950.9	E962.1	E980.9
Veronal	967.0	E851	E937.0	E950.1	E962.0	E980.1
Veroxil	961.6	E857	E931.6	E950.4	E962.0	E980.4
Versidyne	965.7	E850.7	E935.7	E950.0	E962.0	E980.0
Vienna						
green	985.1	E866.3	—	E950.8	E962.1	E980.8
insecticide	985.1	E863.4	—	E950.6	E962.1	E980.7
red	989.89	E866.8	—	E950.9	E962.1	E980.9
pharmaceutical dye	977.4	E858.8	E947.4	E950.4	E962.0	E980.4
Vinbarbital, vinbarbitone	967.0	E851	E937.0	E950.1	E962.0	E980.1
Vinblastine	963.1	E858.1	E933.1	E950.4	E962.0	E980.4
Vincristine	963.1	E858.1	E933.1	E950.4	E962.0	E980.4
Vinesthene, vinethene	968.2	E855.1	E938.2	E950.4	E962.0	E980.4
Vinyl						
bital	967.0	E851	E937.0	E950.1	E962.0	E980.1
ether	968.2	E855.1	E938.2	E950.4	E962.0	E980.4
Vioform	961.3	E857	E931.3	E950.4	E962.0	E980.4
topical	976.0	E858.7	E946.0	E950.4	E962.0	E980.4
Viomycin	960.6	E856	E930.6	E950.4	E962.0	E980.4
Viosterol	963.5	E858.1	E933.5	E950.4	E962.0	E980.4
Viper (venom)	989.5	E905.0	—	E950.9	E962.1	E980.9
Viprynium (embonate)	961.6	E857	E931.6	E950.4	E962.0	E980.4
Virugon	961.7	E857	E931.7	E950.4	E962.0	E980.4
Visine	976.5	E858.7	E946.5	E950.4	E962.0	E980.4
Vitamins NEC	963.5	E858.1	E933.5	E950.4	E962.0	E980.4
B_{12}	964.1	E858.2	E934.1	E950.4	E962.0	E980.4
hematopoietic	964.1	E858.2	E934.1	E950.4	E962.0	E980.4
K	964.3	E858.2	E934.3	E950.4	E962.0	E980.4
Vleminckx's solution	976.4	E858.7	E946.4	E950.4	E962.0	E980.4
Voltaren — *see* Diclofenac sodium						
W						
Warfarin (potassium) (sodium)	964.2	E858.2	E934.2	E950.4	E962.0	E980.4
rodenticide	989.4	E863.7	—	E950.6	E962.1	E980.7
Wasp (sting)	989.5	E905.3	—	E950.9	E962.1	E980.9
Water						
balance agents NEC	974.5	E858.5	E944.5	E950.4	E962.0	E980.4
gas	987.1	E868.1	—	E951.8	E962.2	E981.8
incomplete combustion of — *see* Carbon, monoxide, fuel, utility						
hemlock	988.2	E865.4	—	E950.9	E962.1	E980.9
moccasin (venom)	989.5	E905.0	—	E950.9	E962.1	E980.9
Wax (paraffin) (petroleum)	981	E862.3	—	E950.9	E962.1	E980.9
automobile	989.89	E861.2	—	E950.9	E962.1	E980.9
floor	981	E862.0	—	E950.9	E962.1	E980.9
Weed killers NEC	989.4	E863.5	—	E950.6	E962.1	E980.7
Welldorm	967.1	E852.0	E937.1	E950.2	E962.0	E980.2
White						
arsenic — *see* Arsenic						
hellebore	988.2	E865.4	—	E950.9	E962.1	E980.9
lotion (keratolytic)	976.4	E858.7	E946.4	E950.4	E962.0	E980.4
spirit	981	E862.0	—	E950.9	E962.1	E980.9
Whitewashes	989.89	E861.6	—	E950.9	E962.1	E980.9
Whole blood	964.7	E858.2	E934.7	E950.4	E962.0	E980.4

Substance	Poisoning	External Cause (E-Code) Accident	Therapeutic Use	Suicide Attempt	Assault	Undetermined
Wild						
black cherry	988.2	E865.4	—	E950.9	E962.1	E980.9
poisonous plants NEC	988.2	E865.4	—	E950.9	E962.1	E980.9
Window cleaning fluid	989.89	E861.3	—	E950.9	E962.1	E980.9
Wintergreen (oil)	976.3	E858.7	E946.3	E950.4	E962.0	E980.4
Witch hazel	976.2	E858.7	E946.2	E950.4	E962.0	E980.4
Wood						
alcohol	980.1	E860.2	—	E950.9	E962.1	E980.9
spirit	980.1	E860.2	—	E950.9	E962.1	E980.9
Woorali	975.2	E858.6	E945.2	E950.4	E962.0	E980.4
Wormseed, American	961.6	E857	E931.6	E950.4	E962.0	E980.4
X						
Xanthine diuretics	974.1	E858.5	E944.1	E950.4	E962.0	E980.4
Xanthocillin	960.0	E856	E930.0	E950.4	E962.0	E980.4
Xanthotoxin	976.3	E858.7	E946.3	E950.4	E962.0	E980.4
Xylene (liquid) (vapor)	982.0	E862.4	—	E950.9	E962.1	E980.9
Xylocaine (infiltration) (topical)	968.5	E855.2	E938.5	E950.4	E962.0	E980.4
nerve block (peripheral) (plexus)	968.6	E855.2	E938.6	E950.4	E962.0	E980.4
spinal	968.7	E855.2	E938.7	E950.4	E962.0	E980.4
Xylol (liquid) (vapor)	982.0	E862.4	—	E950.9	E962.1	E980.9
Xylometazoline	971.2	E855.5	E941.2	E950.4	E962.0	E980.4
Y						
Yellow						
fever vaccine	979.3	E858.8	E949.3	E950.4	E962.0	E980.4
jasmine	988.2	E865.4	—	E950.9	E962.1	E980.9
Yew	988.2	E865.4	—	E950.9	E962.1	E980.9
Z						
Zactane	965.7	E850.7	E935.7	E950.0	E962.0	E980.0
Zaroxolyn	974.3	E858.5	E944.3	E950.4	E962.0	E980.4
Zephiran (topical)	976.0	E858.7	E946.0	E950.4	E962.0	E980.4
ophthalmic preparation	976.5	E858.7	E946.5	E950.4	E962.0	E980.4
Zerone	980.1	E860.2	—	E950.9	E962.1	E980.9
Zinc (compounds) (fumes) (salts) (vapor) NEC	985.8	E866.4	—	E950.9	E962.1	E980.9
anti-infectives	976.0	E858.7	E946.0	E950.4	E962.0	E980.4
antivaricose	972.7	E858.3	E942.7	E950.4	E962.0	E980.4
bacitracin	976.0	E858.7	E946.0	E950.4	E962.0	E980.4
chloride	976.2	E858.7	E946.2	E950.4	E962.0	E980.4
gelatin	976.3	E858.7	E946.3	E950.4	E962.0	E980.4
oxide	976.3	E858.7	E946.3	E950.4	E962.0	E980.4
peroxide	976.0	E858.7	E946.0	E950.4	E962.0	E980.4
pesticides	985.8	E863.4	—	E950.6	E962.1	E980.7
phosphide (rodenticide)	985.8	E863.7	—	E950.6	E962.1	E980.7
stearate	976.3	E858.7	E946.3	E950.4	E962.0	E980.4
sulfate (antivaricose)	972.7	E858.3	E942.7	E950.4	E962.0	E980.4
ENT agent	976.6	E858.7	E946.6	E950.4	E962.0	E980.4
ophthalmic solution	976.5	E858.7	E946.5	E950.4	E962.0	E980.4
topical NEC	976.0	E858.7	E946.0	E950.4	E962.0	E980.4
undecylenate	976.0	E858.7	E946.0	E950.4	E962.0	E980.4
Zoxazolamine	968.0	E855.1	E938.0	E950.4	E962.0	E980.4
Zygadenus (venenosus)	988.2	E865.4	—	E950.9	E962.1	E980.9

SECTION 3

ALPHABETIC INDEX TO EXTERNAL CAUSES OF INJURY AND POISONING (E CODE)

This section contains the index to the codes which classify environmental events, circumstances, and other conditions as the cause of injury and other adverse effects. Where a code from the section Supplementary Classification of External Causes of Injury and Poisoning (E800-E998) is applicable, it is intended that the E code shall be used in addition to a code from the main body of the classification, Chapters 1 to 17.

The alphabetic index to the E codes is organized by main terms which describe the *accident, circumstance, event,* or specific *agent* which caused the injury or other adverse effect.

Note — Transport accidents (E800-E848) include accidents involving:

aircraft and space craft (E840-E845)
watercraft (E830-E838)
motor vehicle (E810-E825)
railway (E800-E807)
other road vehicles (E826-E829)

For definitions and examples related to transport accidents — see Supplementary Classification of External Causes of Injury and Poisoning (E800–E999).

The fourth-digit subdivisions for use with categories E800–E848 to identify the injured person are found at the end of this section.

For identifying the place in which an accident or poisoning occurred (circumstances classifiable to categories E850-E869 and E880-E928) — see the listing in this section under "Accident, occurring."

See the Table of Drugs and Chemicals (Section 2 of this volume) for identifying the specific agent involved in drug overdose or a wrong substance given or taken in error, and for intoxication or poisoning by a drug or other chemical substance.

The specific adverse effect, reaction, or localized toxic effect to a correct drug or substance properly administered in therapeutic or prophylactic dosage should be classified according to the nature of the adverse effect (e.g., allergy, dermatitis, tachycardia) listed in Section 1 of this volume.

A

Accident (to) — *continued*
railway — *continued*
involving — *continued*
fall (*see also* Fall, from, railway rolling stock) E804 ✓4th
fire (*see also* Explosion, railway engine) E803 ✓4th
hitting by, being struck by
object falling in, on, from, rolling stock, train, vehicle E806 ✓4th
rolling stock, train, vehicle E805 ✓4th
overturning, railway rolling stock, train, vehicle (*see also* Derailment, railway) E802 ✓4th
running off rails, railway (*see also* Derailment, railway) E802 ✓4th
specified circumstances NEC E806 ✓4th
train or vehicle hit by
avalanche E909.2
falling object (earth, rock, tree) E806 ✓4th
due to cataclysm — *see* categories E908, E909
landslide E909.2
ski(ing) E885
jump E884.9
lift or tow (with chair or gondola) E847
snow vehicle, motor driven (not on public highway) E820 ✓4th
on public highway — *see* catagories E810-E819
spacecraft E845 ✓4th
specified cause NEC E928.8
street car E829 ✓4th
traffic NEC E819 ✓4th
vehicle NEC (with pedestrian) E848
battery powered
airport passenger vehicle E846
truck (baggage) (mail) E846
powered commercial or industrial (with other vehicle or object within commercial or industrial premises) E846
watercraft E838 ✓4th
with
drowning or submersion resulting from
accident other than to watercraft E832 ✓4th
accident to watercraft E830 ✓4th
injury, except drowning or submersion, resulting from
accident other than to watercraft — *see* categories E833-E838
accident to watercraft E831 ✓4th
due to, caused by, cataclysm — *see* categories E908, E909
machinery E836 ✓4th
Acid throwing E961
Acosta syndrome E902.0
Aeroneurosis E902.1
Aero-otitis media — *see* Effects of, air pressure
Aerosinusitis — *see* Effects of, air pressure
After-effect, late — *see* Late effect
Air
blast in war operations E993
embolism (traumatic) NEC E928.9
in
infusion or transfusion E874.1
perfusion E874.2
sickness E903
Alpine sickness E902.0
Altitude sickness — *see* Effects of, air pressure
Anaphylactic shock, anaphylaxis (*see also* Table of Drugs and Chemicals) E947.9
due to bite or sting (venomous) — *see* Bite, venomous
Andes disease E902.0
Apoplexy
heat — *see* Heat
Arachnidism E905.1
Arson E968.0
Asphyxia, asphyxiation
by
chemical in war operations E997.2
explosion — *see* Explosion
food (bone) (regurgitated food) (seed) E911
foreign object, except food E912
fumes in war operations E997.2
gas — *see also* Table of Drugs and Chemicals
in war operations E997.2
legal
execution E978
intervention (tear) E972
tear E972
mechanical means (*see also* Suffocation) E913.9
from
conflagration — *see* Conflagration
fire — *see also* Fire
in war operations E990.9
ignition — *see* Ignition
Aspiration
foreign body — *see* Foreign body, aspiration
mucus, not of newborn (with asphyxia, obstruction respiratory passage, suffocation) E912
phlegm (with asphyxia, obstruction respiratory passage, suffocation) E912
vomitus (with asphyxia, obstruction respiratory passage, suffocation) (*see also* Foreign body, aspiration, food) E911
Assassination (attempt) (*see also* Assault) E968.9
Assault (homicidal) (by) (in) E968.9
acid E961
swallowed E962.1
air gun E968.6
BB gun E968.6
bite (of human being) E968.8
bomb ((placed in) car or house) E965.8
antipersonnel E965.5
letter E965.7
petrol E965.6
brawl (hand) (fists) (foot) E960.0
burning, burns (by fire) E968.0
acid E961
swallowed E962.1
caustic, corrosive substance E961
swallowed E962.1
chemical from swallowing caustic, corrosive substance NEC E962.1
hot liquid E968.3
scalding E968.3
vitriol E961
swallowed E962.1
caustic, corrosive substance E961
swallowed E962.1
cut, any part of body E966
dagger E966
drowning E964
explosive(s) E965.9
bomb (*see also* Assault, bomb) E965.8
dynamite E965.8
fight (hand) (fists) (foot) E960.0
with weapon E968.9
Assault (homicidal) (by) (in) — *continued*
fight (hand) (fists) (foot) — *continued*
with weapon — *continued*
blunt or thrown E968.2
cutting or piercing E966
firearm — *see* Shooting, homicide
fire E968.0
firearm(s) — *see* Shooting, homicide
garrotting E963
gunshot (wound) — *see* Shooting, homicide
hanging E963
injury NEC E968.9
knife E966
late effect of E969
ligature E963
poisoning E962.9
drugs or medicinals E962.0
gas(es) or vapors, except drugs and medicinals E962.2
solid or liquid substances, except drugs and medicinals E962.1
puncture, any part of body E966
pushing
before moving object, train, vehicle E968.5
from high place E968.1
rape E960.1
scalding E968.3
shooting — *see* Shooting, homicide
sodomy E960.1
stab, any part of body E966
strangulation E963
submersion E964
suffocation E963
transport vehicle E968.5
violence NEC E968.9
vitriol E961
swallowed E962.1
weapon E968.9
blunt or thrown E968.2
cutting or piercing E966
firearm — *see* Shooting, homicide
wound E968.9
cutting E966
gunshot — *see* Shooting, homicide
knife E966
piercing E966
puncture E966
stab E966
Attack by animal NEC E906.9
Avalanche E909.2
falling on or hitting
motor vehicle (in motion) (on public highway) E909.2
railway train E909.2
Aviator's disease E902.1

B

Barotitis, barodontalgia, barosinusitis, barotrauma (otitic) (sinus) — *see* Effects of, air pressure
Battered
baby or child (syndrome) — *see* Abuse, child; category E967
person other than baby or child — *see* Assault
Bayonet wound (*see also* Cut, by bayonet) E920.3
in
legal intervention E974
war operations E995
Bean in nose E912
Bed set on fire NEC E898.0

> *Note — In the case of collisions between different types of vehicles, persons and objects, priority in classification is in the following order:*
> *Aircraft*
> *Watercraft*
> *Motor vehicle*
> *Railway vehicle*
> *Pedal Cycle*
> *Animal-drawn vehicle*
> *Animal being ridden*
> *Streetcar or other nonmotor road vehicle*
> *Other vehicle*
> *Pedestrian or person using pedestrian conveyance*
> *Object (except where falling from or set in motion by vehicle etc. listed above)*
>
> *In the listing below, the combinations are listed only under the vehicle etc. having priority. For definitions, see Supplementary Classification of External Causes of Injury and Poisoning (E800-E999) Volume 1, page E-1 – E-2.*

D

- **Fire** (accidental) (caused by great heat from appliance (electrical), hot object or hot substance) (secondary, resulting from explosion) — *continued*
  - late effect of NEC E929.4
  - lumber (uncontrolled) E892
  - mine (uncontrolled) E892
  - prairie (uncontrolled) E892
  - self-inflicted (unspecified whether accidental or intentional) E988.1
    - stated as intentional, purposeful E958.1
  - specified NEC E898.1
    - with
      - conflagration — *see* Conflagration
      - ignition (of)
        - clothing — *see* Ignition, clothes
        - highly inflammable material (benzine) (fat) (gasoline) (kerosene) (paraffin) (petrol) E894
  - started by other person
    - stated as
      - with intent to injure or kill E968.0
      - undetermined whether or not with intent to injure or kill E988.1
  - suicide (attempted) E958.1
    - late effect of E959
  - tunnel (uncontrolled) E892
- **Fireball effects from nuclear explosion in war operations** E996
- **Fireworks** (explosion) E923.0
- **Flash burns from explosion** (*see also* Explosion) E923.9
- **Flood** (any injury) (resulting from storm) E908.2
  - caused by collapse of dam or manmade structure E909.3
- **Forced landing** (aircraft) E840 ✓4th
- **Foreign body, object or material** (entrance into (accidental))
  - air passage (causing injury) E915
    - with asphyxia, obstruction, suffocation E912
      - food or vomitus E911
    - nose (with asphyxia, obstruction, suffocation) E912
      - causing injury without asphyxia, obstruction, suffocation E915
  - alimentary canal (causing injury) (with obstruction) E915
    - with asphyxia, obstruction respiratory passage, suffocation E912
      - food E911
    - mouth E915
      - with asphyxia, obstruction, suffocation E912
        - food E911
    - pharynx E915
      - with asphyxia, obstruction, suffocation E912
        - food E911
  - apiration (with asphyxia, obstruction respiratory passage, suffocation) E912
    - causing injury without asphyxia, obstruction respiratory passage, suffocation E915
    - food (regurgitated) (vomited) E911
      - causing injury without asphyxia, obstruction respiratory passage, suffocation E915
    - mucus (not of newborn) E912
    - phlegm E912
  - bladder (causing injury or obstruction) E915
  - bronchus, bronchi — *see* Foreign body, air passages
  - conjunctival sac E914
  - digestive system — *see* Foreign body, alimentary canal
- **Foreign body, object or material** (entrance into (accidental)) — *continued*
  - ear (causing injury or obstruction) E915
  - esophagus (causing injury or obstruction) (*see also* Foreign body, alimentary canal) E915
  - eye (any part) E914
  - eyelid E914
  - hairball (stomach) (with obstruction) E915
  - ingestion — *see* Foreign body, alimentary canal
  - inhalation — *see* Foreign body, aspiration
  - intestine (causing injury or obstruction) E915
  - iris E914
  - lacrimal apparatus E914
  - larynx — *see* Foreign body, air passage
  - late effect of NEC E929.8
  - lung — *see* Foreign body, air passage
  - mouth — *see* Foreign body, alimentary canal, mouth
  - nasal passage — *see* Foreign body, air passage, nose
  - nose — *see* Foreign body, air passage, nose
  - ocular muscle E914
  - operation wound (left in) — *see* Misadventure, foreign object
  - orbit E914
  - pharynx — *see* Foreign body, alimentary canal, pharynx
  - rectum (causing injury or obstruction) E915
  - stomach (hairball) (causing injury or obstruction) E915
  - tear ducts or glands E914
  - trachea — *see* Foreign body, air passage
  - urethra (causing injury or obstruction) E915
  - vagina (causing injury or obstruction) E915
- **Found dead, injured**
  - from exposure (to) — *see* Exposure
  - on
    - public highway E819 ✓4th
    - railway right of way E807 ✓4th
- **Fracture** (circumstances unknown or unspecified) E887
  - due to specified external means — *see* manner of accident
  - late effect of NEC E929.3
  - occuring in water transport NEC E835 ✓4th
- **Freezing** — *see* Cold, exposure to
- **Frostbite** E901.0
  - due to manmade conditions E901.1
- **Frozen** — *see* Cold, exposure to

G

- **Garrotting, homicidal** (attempted) E963
- **Gored** E906.8
- **Gunshot wound** (*see also* Shooting) E922.9

H

- **Hailstones, injury by** E904.3
- **Hairball** (stomach) (with obstruction) E915
- **Hanged himself** (*see also* Hanging, self-inflicted) E983.0
- **Hang gliding** E842 ✓4th
- **Hanging** (accidental) E913.8
  - caused by other person
    - in accidental circumstances E913.8
    - stated as
      - intentional, homicidal E963
      - undetermined whether accidental or intentional E983.0
  - homicide (attempt) E963
  - in bed or cradle E913.0
- **Hanging** (accidental) — *continued*
  - legal execution E978
  - self-inflicted (unspecified whether accidental or intentional) E983.0
    - in accidental circumstances E913.8
    - stated as intentional, purposeful E953.0
  - stated as undetermined whether accidental or intentional E983.0
  - suicidal (attempt) E953.0
- **Heat** (apoplexy) (collapse) (cramps) (effects of) (excessive) (exhaustion) (fever) (prostration) (stroke) E900.9
  - due to
    - manmade conditions (as listed in E900.1, except boat, ship, watercraft) E900.1
    - weather (conditions) E900.0
  - from
    - electric heating appartus causing burning E924.8
    - nuclear explosion in war operations E996
  - generated in, boiler, engine, evaporator, fire room of boat, ship, watercraft E838 ✓4th
  - inappropriate in local application or packing in medical or surgical procedure E873.5
  - late effect of NEC E989
- **Hemorrhage**
  - delayed following medical or surgical treatment without mention of misadventure — *see* Reaction, abnormal
  - during medical or surgical treatment as misadventure — *see* Misadventure, cut
- **High**
  - altitude, effects E902.9
  - level of radioactivity, effects — *see* Radiation
  - pressure effects — *see also* Effects of, air pressure
    - from rapid descent in water (causing caisson or divers' disease, palsy, or paralysis) E902.2
  - temperature, effects — *see* Heat
- **Hit, hitting** (accidental) by
  - aircraft (propeller) (without accident to aircraft) E844 ✓4th
    - unpowered E842 ✓4th
  - avalanche E909.2
  - being thrown against object in or part of
    - motor vehicle (in motion) (on public highway) E818 ✓4th
      - not on public highway E825 ✓4th
    - nonmotor road vehicle NEC E829 ✓4th
    - street car E829 ✓4th
  - boat, ship, watercraft
    - after fall from watercraft E838 ✓4th
      - damaged, involved in accident E831 ✓4th
    - while swimming, water skiing E838 ✓4th
  - bullet (*see also* Shooting) E922.9
    - from air gun E922.4
    - in war operations E991.2
      - rubber E991.0
  - flare, Verey pistol (*see also* Shooting) E922.8
  - hailstones E904.3
  - landslide E909.2
  - law-enforcing agent (on duty) E975
    - with blunt object (baton) (night stick) (stave) (truncheon) E973
  - machine — *see* Accident, machine
  - missile
    - firearm (*see also* Shooting) E922.9
    - in war operations — *see* War operations, missile
  - motor vehicle (on public highway) (traffic accident) E814 ✓4th
    - not on public highway, nontraffic accident E822 ✓4th
  - nonmotor road vehicle NEC E829 ✓4th

N

O

P

R

T

V

W

FOURTH DIGIT SUBDIVISIONS FOR THE EXTERNAL CAUSE (E) CODE

RAILWAY ACCIDENTS (E800-E807)

The following fourth-digit subdivisions are for use with categories E800-E807 to identify the injured person:

.0 Railway employee

Any person who by virtue of his employment in connection with a railway, whether by the railway company or not, is at increased risk of involvement in a railway accident, such as:

catering staff on train
driver
guard
porter
postal staff on train
railway fireman
shunter
sleeping car attendant

.1 Passenger on railway

Any authorized person traveling on a train, except a railway employee

Excludes: intending passenger waiting at station (.8)
unauthorized rider on railway vehicle (.8)

.2 Pedestrian

See definition (r), Vol. 1, page E-2

.3 Pedal cyclist

See definition (p), Vol. 1, page E-2

.8 Other specified person

Intending passenger waiting at station
Unauthorized rider on railway vehicle

.9 Unspecified person

MOTOR VEHICLE TRAFFIC AND NONTRAFFIC ACCIDENTS (E810-E825)

The following fourth-digit subdivisions are for use with categories E810-E819 and E820-E825 to identify the injured person:

.0 Driver of motor vehicle other than motorcycle

See definition (l), Vol. 1, page E-2

.1 Passenger in motor vehicle other than motorcycle

See definition (l), Vol. 1, page E-2

.2 Motorcyclist

See definition (l), Vol. 1, page E-2

.3 Passenger on motorcycle

See definition (l), Vol. 1, page E-2

.4 Occupant of streetcar

.5 Rider of animal; occupant of animal-drawn vehicle

.6 Pedal cyclist

See definition (p), Vol. 1, page E-2

.7 Pedestrian

See definition (r), Vol. 1, page E-2

.8 Other specified person

Occupant of vehicle other than above
Person in railway train involved in accident
Unauthorized rider of motor vehicle

.9 Unspecified person

OTHER ROAD VEHICLE ACCIDENTS (E826-E829)

(animal-drawn vehicle, streetcar, pedal cycle, and other nonmotor road vehicle accidents)

The following fourth-digit subdivisions are for use with categories E826-E829 to identify the injured person:

.0 Pedestrian

See definition (r), Vol. 1, page E-2

.1 Pedal cyclist (does not apply to codes E827, E828, E829)

See definition (p), Vol. 1, page E-2

.2 Rider of animal (does not apply to code E829)

.3 Occupant of animal-drawn vehicle (does not apply to codes E828, E829)

.4 Occupant of streetcar

.8 Other specified person

.9 Unspecified person

WATER TRANSPORT ACCIDENTS (E830-E838)

The following fourth-digit subdivisions are for use with categories E830-E838 to identify the injured person:

.0 Occupant of small boat, unpowered

.1 Occupant of small boat, powered

See definition (t), Vol. 1, page E-2

Excludes: water skier (.4)

.2 Occupant of other watercraft—crew

Persons:
- engaged in operation of watercraft
- providing passenger services [cabin attendants, ship's physician, catering personnel]
- working on ship during voyage in other capacity [musician in band, operators of shops and beauty parlors]

.3 Occupant of other watercraft—other than crew

Passenger
Occupant of lifeboat, other than crew, after abandoning ship

.4 Water skier

.5 Swimmer

.6 Dockers, stevedores

Longshoreman employed on the dock in loading and unloading ships

.8 Other specified person

Immigration and custom officials on board ship
Person:
- accompanying passenger or member of crew
- visiting boat

Pilot (guiding ship into port)

.9 Unspecified person

AIR AND SPACE TRANSPORT ACCIDENTS (E840-E845)

The following fourth-digit subdivisions are for use with categories E840-E845 to identify the injured person:

.0 Occupant of spacecraft

.1 Occupant of military aircraft, any

Crew
Passenger (civilian) (military)
Troops
} in military aircraft [air force] [army] [national guard] [navy]

Excludes: occupants of aircraft operated under jurisdiction of police departments (.5)
parachutist (.7)

.2 Crew of commercial aircraft (powered) in surface to surface transport

.3 Other occupant of commercial aircraft (powered) in surface to surface transport

Flight personnel:
- not part of crew
- on familiarization flight

Passenger on aircraft (powered) NOS

.4 Occupant of commercial aircraft (powered) in surface to air transport

Occupant [crew] [passenger] of aircraft (powered) engaged in activities, such as:
- aerial spraying (crops) (fire retardants)
- air drops of emergency supplies
- air drops of parachutists, except from military craft
- crop dusting
- lowering of construction material [bridge or telephone pole]
- sky writing

.5 Occupant of other powered aircraft

Occupant [crew] [passenger] of aircraft (powered) engaged in activities, such as:
- aerobatic flying
- aircraft racing
- rescue operation
- storm surveillance
- traffic surveillance

Occupant of private plane NOS

.6 Occupant of unpowered aircraft, except parachutist

Occupant of aircraft classifiable to E842

.7 Parachutist (military) (other)

Person making voluntary descent

Excludes: person making descent after accident to aircraft (.1-.6)

.8 Ground crew, airline employee

Persons employed at airfields (civil) (military) or launching pads, not occupants of aircraft

.9 Other person

NOTES

NOTES

NOTES

NOTES

NOTES

NOTES

NOTES

NOTES

NOTES

NOTES

NOTES

NOTES

NOTES

NOTES

1. INFECTIOUS AND PARASITIC DISEASES (001-139)

Note: Categories for "late effects" of infectious and parasitic diseases are to be found at 137-139.

Includes: diseases generally recognized as communicable or transmissible as well as a few diseases of unknown but possibly infectious origin

Excludes: *acute respiratory infections (460-466)*
carrier or suspected carrier of infectious organism (V02.0-V02.9)
certain localized infections
influenza (487.0-487.8)

INTESTINAL INFECTIOUS DISEASES (001-009)

Excludes: *helminthiases (120.0-129)*

001 Cholera

001.0 Due to Vibrio cholerae

001.1 Due to Vibrio cholerae el tor

001.9 Cholera, unspecified

002 Typhoid and paratyphoid fevers

002.0 Typhoid fever
Typhoid (fever) (infection) [any site]

002.1 Paratyphoid fever A

002.2 Paratyphoid fever B

002.3 Paratyphoid fever C

002.9 Paratyphoid fever, unspecified

003 Other salmonella infections

Includes: infection or food poisoning by Salmonella [any serotype]

003.0 Salmonella gastroenteritis
Salmonellosis

003.1 Salmonella septicemia

✓5th **003.2 Localized salmonella infections**

003.20 Localized salmonella infection, unspecified

003.21 Salmonella meningitis

003.22 Salmonella pneumonia

003.23 Salmonella arthritis

003.24 Salmonella osteomyelitis

003.29 Other

003.8 Other specified salmonella infections

003.9 Salmonella infection, unspecified

004 Shigellosis

Includes: bacillary dysentery

004.0 Shigella dysenteriae
Infection by group A Shigella (Schmitz) (Shiga)

004.1 Shigella flexneri
Infection by group B Shigella

004.2 Shigella boydii
Infection by group C Shigella

004.3 Shigella sonnei
Infection by group D Shigella

004.8 Other specified Shigella infections

004.9 Shigellosis, unspecified

005 Other food poisoning (bacterial)

Excludes: *salmonella infections (003.0-003.9)*
toxic effect of:
food contaminants (989.7)
noxious foodstuffs (988.0-988.9)

005.0 Staphylococcal food poisoning
Staphylococcal toxemia specified as due to food

005.1 Botulism
Food poisoning due to Clostridium botulinum

005.2 Food poisoning due to Clostridium perfringens [C. welchii]
Enteritis necroticans

005.3 Food poisoning due to other Clostridia

005.4 Food poisoning due to Vibrio parahaemolyticus

✓5th **005.8 Other bacterial food poisoning**

Excludes: *salmonella food poisoning (003.0-003.9)*

005.81 Food poisoning due to Vibrio vulnificus

005.89 Other bacterial food poisoning
Food poisoning due to Bacillus cereus

005.9 Food poisoning, unspecified

006 Amebiasis

Includes: infection due to Entamoeba histolytica

Excludes: *amebiasis due to organisms other than Entamoeba histolytica (007.8)*

006.0 Acute amebic dysentery without mention of abscess
Acute amebiasis

006.1 Chronic intestinal amebiasis without mention of abscess
Chronic:
amebiasis
amebic dysentery

006.2 Amebic nondysenteric colitis

006.3 Amebic liver abscess
Hepatic amebiasis

006.4 Amebic lung abscess
Amebic abscess of lung (and liver)

006.5 Amebic brain abscess
Amebic abscess of brain (and liver) (and lung)

006.6 Amebic skin ulceration
Cutaneous amebiasis

006.8 Amebic infection of other sites
Amebic:
appendicitis
balanitis
Ameboma

Excludes: *specific infections by free-living amebae (136.2)*

006.9 Amebiasis, unspecified
Amebiasis NOS

007 Other protozoal intestinal diseases

Includes: protozoal:
colitis
diarrhea
dysentery

007.0 Balantidiasis
Infection by Balantidium coli

007.1 Giardiasis
Infection by Giardia lamblia
Lambliasis

007.2 Coccidiosis
Infection by Isospora belli and Isospora hominis
Isosporiasis

007.3 Intestinal trichomoniasis

007.4 Cryptosporidiosis

➡ **AHA Coding Clinic:** 4Q, '97, 30

007.8 Other specified protozoal intestinal diseases
Amebiasis due to organisms other than Entamoeba histolytica

007.9 Unspecified protozoal intestinal disease
Flagellate diarrhea
Protozoal dysentery NOS

008 Intestinal infections due to other organisms

Includes: any condition classifiable to 009.0-009.3 with mention of the responsible organisms

Excludes: *food poisoning by these organisms (005.0-005.9)*

✓5th **008.0 Escherichia coli [E. coli]**

➡ **AHA Coding Clinic:** 4Q, '92, 17

008.00 E. coli, unspecified
E. coli enteritis NOS

008.01 Enteropathogenic E. coli

008.02 Enterotoxigenic E. coli

008.03 Enteroinvasive E. coli

008.04 Enterohemorrhagic E. coli

008.09 Other intestinal E. coli infections

008.1 Arizona group of paracolon bacilli

008.2 Aerobacter aerogenes
Enterobacter aerogenes

008.3 Proteus (mirabilis) (morganii)

✓5th **008.4 Other specified bacteria**

➡ **AHA Coding Clinic:** 4Q, '92, 18

008.41 Staphylococcus
Staphylococcal enterocolitis

➡ **CC Excl:** 001.1, 002.0, 002.9, 003.0, 004.9, 005.0-005.2, 006.0-006.2, 006.9, 007.1-007.9, 008.00-008.49, 008.5, 008.61-008.69, 008.8, 009.0, 014.80-014.86, 112.85, 129, 487.8, 536.3, 536.8, 555.0-555.9, 556.0-556.9, 557.0-557.9, 558.2, 558.9, 564.1, 775.0-775.9, 777.5, 777.8

008.42 Pseudomonas

➡
CC Excl: see Code 008.41

➡ **AHA Coding Clinic:** 2Q, '89, 10

008.43 Campylobacter

➡ **CC Excl:** see Code 008.41

008.44 Yersinia enterocolitica

➡ **CC Excl:** see Code 008.41

008.45 Clostridium difficile
Pseudomembranous colitis

➡ **CC Excl:** see Code 008.41

008.46 Other anaerobes
Anaerobic enteritis NOS
Bacteroides (fragilis)
Gram-negative anaerobes

➡ **CC Excl:** see Code 008.41

008.47 Other gram-negative bacteria
Gram-negative enteritis NOS

Excludes: *gram-negative anaerobes (008.46)*

➡ **CC Excl:** see Code 008.41

008.49 Other
➡ **CC Excl:** see Code 008.41
➡ **AHA Coding Clinic:** 2Q, '89, 10; 1Q, '88, 6

008.5 Bacterial enteritis, unspecified

✓5th **008.6** Enteritis due to specified virus
➡ **AHA Coding Clinic:** 4Q, '92, 18

008.61 Rotavirus

008.62 Adenovirus

008.63 Norwalk virus
Norwalk-like agent

008.64 Other small round viruses [SRV's]
Small round virus NOS

008.65 Calcivirus

008.66 Astrovirus

008.67 Enterovirus NEC
Coxsackie virus
Echovirus

Excludes: *poliovirus (045.0-045.9)*

008.69 Other viral enteritis
Torovirus

008.8 Other organism, not elsewhere classified
Viral:
enteritis NOS
gastroenteritis

Excludes: *influenza with involvement of gastrointestinal tract (487.8)*

009 Ill-defined intestinal infections

Excludes: *diarrheal disease or intestinal infection due to specified organism (001.0-008.8)*
diarrhea following gastrointestinal surgery (564.4)
intestinal malabsorption (579.0-579.9)
ischemic enteritis (557.0-557.9)
other noninfectious gastroenteritis and colitis (558.1-558.9)
regional enteritis (555.0-555.9)
ulcerative colitis (556)

009.0 Infectious colitis, enteritis, and gastroenteritis
Colitis, Enteritis, Gastroenteritis } septic
Dysentery:
NOS
catarrhal
hemorrhagic

009.1 Colitis, enteritis, and gastroenteritis of presumed infectious origin

Excludes: *colitis NOS (558.9)*
enteritis NOS (558.9)
gastroenteritis NOS (558.9)

009.2 Infectious diarrhea
Diarrhea:
dysenteric
epidemic
Infectious diarrheal disease NOS

009.3 Diarrhea of presumed infectious origin

Excludes: *diarrhea NOS (787.91)*

➡ **AHA Coding Clinic:** N-D, '87, 7

TUBERCULOSIS (010-018)

Includes: infection by Mycobacterium tuberculosis (human) (bovine)

Excludes: *congenital tuberculosis (771.2)*
late effects of tuberculosis (137.0-137.4)

The following fifth-digit subclassification is for use with categories 010-018:

0 **unspecified**
1 **bacteriological or histological examination not done**
2 **bacteriological or histological examination unknown (at present)**
3 **tubercle bacilli found (in sputum) by microscopy**
4 **tubercle bacilli not found (in sputum) by microscopy, but found by bacterial culture**
5 **tubercle bacilli not found by bacteriological examination, but tuberculosis confirmed histologically**
6 **tubercle bacilli not found by bacteriological or histological examination but tuberculosis confirmed by other methods [inoculation of animals]**

§ 010 Primary tuberculous infection

✓5th **010.0** Primary tuberculous infection

Excludes: *nonspecific reaction to tuberculin skin test without active tuberculosis (795.5)*
positive:
PPD (795.5)
tuberculin skin test without active tuberculosis (795.5)

✓5th **010.1** Tuberculous pleurisy in primary progressive tuberculosis

§ Requires fifth-digit. See above, this page for codes and definitions.

✓5th **010.8** **Other primary progressive tuberculosis**

Excludes: *tuberculous erythema nodosum (017.1)*

✓5th **010.9** **Primary tuberculous infection, unspecified**

§ 011 Pulmonary tuberculosis

Use additional code to identify any associated silicosis (502)

✓5th **011.0** **Tuberculosis of lung, infiltrative**

➡ **CC Excl:** 011.00-011.96, 012.00-012.86, 017.90-017.96, 018.00-018.96, 031.0, 031.2, 031.8-031.9, 041.81-041.89, 041.9, 137.0, 139.8, 480.0-487.1, 494, 495.0-495.9, 496, 500-505, 506.0-506.9, 507.0-507.8, 508.0-508.9, 517.1, 518.89

✓5th **011.1** **Tuberculosis of lung, nodular**

➡ **CC Excl:** see Code 011.0

✓5th **011.2** **Tuberculosis of lung with cavitation**

➡ **CC Excl:** see Code 011.0

✓5th **011.3** **Tuberculosis of bronchus**

Excludes: *isolated bronchial tuberculosis (012.2)*

➡ **CC Excl:** see Code 011.0

✓5th **011.4** **Tuberculous fibrosis of lung**

➡ **CC Excl:** see Code 011.0

✓5th **011.5** **Tuberculous bronchiectasis**

➡ **CC Excl:** see Code 011.0

✓5th **011.6** **Tuberculous pneumonia [any form]**

➡ **CC Excl: For codes 011.60-011.65:** see Code 011.0

➡ **CC Excl: For code 011.66:** 011.66, 139.8, 480.0-487.1, 494, 495.0-495.9, 496, 500-505, 506.0-506.9, 507.0-507.8, 508.0-508.9, 517.1, 518.89

✓5th **011.7** **Tuberculous pneumothorax**

➡ **CC Excl:** see Code 011.0

✓5th **011.8** **Other specified pulmonary tuberculosis**

➡ **CC Excl:** see Code 011.0

✓5th **011.9** **Pulmonary tuberculosis, unspecified**

Respiratory tuberculosis NOS
Tuberculosis of lung NOS

➡ **CC Excl:** see Code 011.0

§ 012 Other respiratory tuberculosis

Excludes: *respiratory tuberculosis, unspecified (011.9)*

✓5th **012.0** **Tuberculous pleurisy**

Tuberculosis of pleura
Tuberculous empyema
Tuberculous hydrothorax

Excludes: *pleurisy with effusion without mention of cause (511.9)*
tuberculous pleurisy in primary progressive tuberculosis (010.1)

➡ **CC Excl:** see Code 011.0

✓5th **012.1** **Tuberculosis of intrathoracic lymph nodes**

Tuberculosis of lymph nodes:
- hilar
- mediastinal
- tracheobronchial

Tuberculous tracheobronchial adenopathy

Excludes: *that specified as primary (010.0-010.9)*

➡ **CC Excl:** see Code 011.0

✓5th **012.2** **Isolated tracheal or bronchial tuberculosis**

✓5th **012.3** **Tuberculous laryngitis**

Tuberculosis of glottis

✓5th **012.8** **Other specified respiratory tuberculosis**

Tuberculosis of:
- mediastinum
- nasopharynx

Tuberculosis of:
- nose (septum)
- sinus [any nasal]

§ 013 Tuberculosis of meninges and central nervous system

✓5th **013.0** **Tuberculous meningitis**

Tuberculosis of meninges (cerebral) (spinal)

Tuberculous:
- leptomeningitis
- meningoencephalitis

Excludes: *tuberculoma of meninges (013.1)*

➡ **CC Excl:** 003.21, 013.00-013.16, 013.40-013.56, 013.80-013.96, 017.90-017.96, 031.2, 031.8-031.9, 036.0, 041.81-041.89, 041.9, 047.0-047.9, 049.0-049.1, 053.0, 054.72, 072.1, 090.42, 091.81, 094.2, 098.89, 100.81, 112.83, 114.2, 115.01, 115.11, 115.91, 130.0, 137.1, 139.8, 320.0-320.9, 321.0-321.8, 322.0-322.9, 349.89, 349.9, 357.0

§ Requires fifth-digit. See page 3 for codes and definitions.

✓5th **013.1** **Tuberculoma of meninges**

➡ **CC Excl:** see Code 013.0

✓5th ☐ **013.2** **Tuberculoma of brain**

Tuberculosis of brain (current disease)

➡ **CC Excl:** 013.20-013.36, 013.60-013.96, 017.90-017.96, 031.2, 031.8-031.9, 041.81-041.89, 041.9, 137.1, 139.8

✓5th ☐ **013.3** **Tuberculous abscess of brain**

➡ **CC Excl:** see Code 013.2

✓5th ☐ **013.4** **Tuberculoma of spinal cord**

➡ **CC Excl:** 013.00-013.16, 013.40-013.56, 013.80-013.96, 017.90-017.96, 031.2, 031.8-031.9, 041.81-041.89, 041.9, 137.1, 139.8

✓5th ☐ **013.5** **Tuberculous abscess of spinal cord**

➡ **CC Excl:** see Code 013.4

✓5th ☐ **013.6** **Tuberculous encephalitis or myelitis**

➡ **CC Excl:** 013.20-013.36, 013.60-013.96, 017.90-017.96, 031.2, 031.8-031.9, 041.81-041.89, 041.9, 137.1, 139.8

✓5th ☐ **013.8** **Other specified tuberculosis of central nervous system**

➡ **CC Excl:** 013.80-013.96, 017.90-017.96, 031.2, 031.8-031.9, 041.81-041.89, 041.9, 137.1, 139.8

✓5th **013.9** **Unspecified tuberculosis of central nervous system**

Tuberculosis of central nervous system NOS

➡ **CC Excl:** see Code 013.8

§ 014 Tuberculosis of intestines, peritoneum, and mesenteric glands

✓5th **014.0** **Tuberculous peritonitis**

Tuberculous ascites

➡ **CC Excl:** 014.00-014.86, 017.90-017.96, 031.2, 031.8-031.9, 041.81-041.89, 041.9, 139.8

✓5th **014.8** **Other**

Tuberculosis (of):
- anus
- intestine (large) (small)
- mesenteric glands
- rectum
- retroperitoneal (lymph nodes)

Tuberculous enteritis

➡ **CC Excl: For Code 014.80:** see Code 014.0

➡ **CC Excl: For Code 014.81:** 014.81, 139.8

➡ **CC Excl: For Code 014.82:** 014.00-014.86, 017.90-017.96, 031.2, 031.8-031.9, 041.81-041.89, 041.9, 139.8

➡ **CC Excl: For Code 014.83-014.86:** see Code 014.82

§ 015 Tuberculosis of bones and joints

Use additional code to identify manifestation, as:
tuberculous:
- arthropathy (711.4)
- necrosis of bone (730.8)
- osteitis (730.8)
- osteomyelitis (730.8)
- synovitis (727.01)
- tenosynovitis (727.01)

✓5th **015.0** **Vertebral column**

Pott's disease

Use additional code to identify manifestation, as:
- curvature of spine [Pott's] (737.4)
- kyphosis (737.4)
- spondylitis (720.81)

✓5th **015.1** **Hip**

✓5th **015.2** **Knee**

✓5th ☐ **015.5** **Limb bones**

Tuberculous dactylitis

✓5th ☐ **015.6** **Mastoid**

Tuberculous mastoiditis

✓5th ☐ **015.7** **Other specified bone**

✓5th **015.8** **Other specified joint**

✓5th **015.9** **Tuberculosis of unspecified bones and joints**

§ 016 Tuberculosis of genitourinary system

✓5th **016.0** **Kidney**

Renal tuberculosis

Use additional code to identify manifestation, as:
tuberculous:
- nephropathy (583.81)
- pyelitis (590.81)
- pyelonephritis (590.81)

➡ **CC Excl:** 016.00-016.36, 016.90-016.96, 017.90-017.96, 031.2, 031.8-031.9, 041.81-041.89, 041.9, 137.2, 139.8

✓5th ☐ **016.1** **Bladder**

➡ **CC Excl:** see Code 016.0

✓5th ☐ **016.2** **Ureter**

➡ **CC Excl:** see Code 016.0

✓5th ☐ **016.3** **Other urinary organs**

➡ **CC Excl:** see Code 016.0

§ Requires fifth-digit. See page 3 for codes and definitions.

✓5th ☐ **016.4 Epididymis** ♂

➡ **CC Excl:** 016.40-016.56, 016.90-016.96, 017.90-017.96, 031.2, 031.8-031.9, 041.81-041.89, 041.9, 137.2, 139.8

✓5th ☐ **016.5 Other male genital organs** ♂

Use additional code to identify manifestation, as:
tuberculosis of:
prostate (601.4)
seminal vesicle (608.81)
testis (608.81)

➡ **CC Excl:** see Code 016.4

✓5th ☐ **016.6 Tuberculous oophoritis and salpingitis** ♀

➡ **CC Excl:** 016.60-016.96, 017.90-017.96, 031.2, 031.8-031.9, 041.81-041.89, 041.9, 137.2, 139.8

✓5th ☐ **016.7 Other female genital organs** ♀

Tuberculous:
cervicitis
endometritis

➡ **CC Excl:** see Code 016.6

✓5th **016.9 Genitourinary tuberculosis, unspecified**

➡ **CC Excl:** 016.90-016.96, 017.90-017.96, 031.2, 031.8-031.9, 041.81-041.89, 041.9, 137.2, 139.8

§ 017 Tuberculosis of other organs

✓5th **017.0 Skin and subcutaneous cellular tissue**

Lupus:
exedens
vulgaris
Scrofuloderma

Tuberculosis:
colliquativa
cutis
lichenoides
papulonecrotica
verrucosa cutis

Excludes: *lupus erythematosus (695.4)*
disseminated (710.0)
lupus NOS (710.0)
nonspecific reaction to tuberculin skin test without active tuberculosis (795.5)
positive:
PPD (795.5)
tuberculin skin test without active tuberculosis (795.5)

✓5th **017.1 Erythema nodosum with hypersensitivity reaction in tuberculosis**

Bazin's disease
Erythema:
induratum
nodosum, tuberculous
Tuberculosis indurativa

Excludes: *erythema nodosum NOS (695.2)*

✓5th **017.2 Peripheral lymph nodes**

Scrofula
Scrofulous abscess
Tuberculous adenitis

Excludes: *tuberculosis of lymph nodes:*
bronchial and mediastinal (012.1)
mesenteric and retroperitoneal (014.8)
tuberculous tracheobronchial adenopathy (012.1)

➡ **CC Excl:** 017.20-017.26, 017.90-017.96, 031.2, 031.8-031.9, 041.81-041.89, 041.9, 139.8

✓5th **017.3 Eye**

Use additional code to identify manifestation, as:
tuberculous:
chorioretinitis, disseminated (363.13)
episcleritis (379.09)
interstitial keratitis (370.59)
iridocyclitis, chronic (364.11)
keratoconjunctivitis (phlyctenular) (370.31)

➡ **CC Excl:** 017.30-017.36, 017.90-017.96, 031.2, 031.8-031.9, 041.81-041.89, 041.9, 139.8

✓5th **017.4 Ear**

Tuberculosis of ear
Tuberculous otitis media

Excludes: *tuberculous mastoiditis (015.6)*

➡ **CC Excl:** 017.40-017.46, 017.90-017.96, 031.2, 031.8-031.9, 041.81-041.89, 041.9, 139.8

✓5th **017.5 Thyroid gland**

➡ **CC Excl:** 017.50-017.56, 017.90-017.96, 031.2, 031.8-031.9, 041.81-041.89, 041.9, 139.8

✓5th **017.6 Adrenal glands**

Addison's disease, tuberculous

➡ **CC Excl:** 017.60-017.66, 017.90-017.96, 031.2, 031.8-031.9, 041.81-041.89, 041.9, 139.8

✓5th **017.7 Spleen**

➡ **CC Excl:** 017.70-017.76, 017.90-017.96, 031.2, 031.8-031.9, 041.81-041.89, 041.9, 139.8

✓5th ☐ **017.8 Esophagus**

➡ **CC Excl:** 017.80-017.96, 031.2, 031.8-031.9, 041.81-041.89, 041.9, 139.8

✓5th ☐ **017.9 Other specified organs**

Use additional code to identify manifestation, as:
tuberculosis of:
endocardium [any valve] (424.91)
myocardium (422.0)
pericardium (420.0)

➡ **CC Excl:** 017.90-017.96, 031.2, 031.8-031.9, 041.81-041.89, 041.9, 139.8

§ Requires fifth-digit. See page 3 for codes and definitions.

§ 018 Miliary tuberculosis

Includes: tuberculosis:
disseminated
generalized
miliary, whether of a single specified site, multiple sites, or unspecified site
polyserositis

✓5th **018.0 Acute miliary tuberculosis**

➡ **CC Excl:** 017.90-017.96, 018.00-018.96, 031.2, 031.8-031.9, 041.81-041.89, 041.9, 139.8

✓5th **018.8 Other specified miliary tuberculosis**

➡ **CC Excl:** see Code 018.0

✓5th **018.9 Miliary tuberculosis, unspecified**

➡ **CC Excl:** see Code 018.0

ZOONOTIC BACTERIAL DISEASES (020-027)

020 Plague

Includes: infection by Yersinia [Pasteurella] pestis

020.0 Bubonic

020.1 Cellulocutaneous

020.2 Septicemic

020.3 Primary pneumonic

020.4 Secondary pneumonic

020.5 Pneumonic, unspecified

020.8 Other specified types of plague

Abortive plague
Ambulatory plague
Pestis minor

020.9 Plague, unspecified

021 Tularemia

Includes: deerfly fever
infection by Francisella [Pasteurella] tularensis
rabbit fever

021.0 Ulceroglandular tularemia

021.1 Enteric tularemia

Tularemia:
cryptogenic
intestinal
typhoidal

021.2 Pulmonary tularemia

Bronchopneumonic tularemia

021.3 Oculoglandular tularemia

021.8 Other specified tularemia

Tularemia:
generalized or disseminated
glandular

021.9 Unspecified tularemia

022 Anthrax

022.0 Cutaneous anthrax

Malignant pustule

022.1 Pulmonary anthrax

Respiratory anthrax
Wool-sorters' disease

022.2 Gastrointestinal anthrax

022.3 Anthrax septicemia

022.8 Other specified manifestations of anthrax

022.9 Anthrax, unspecified

023 Brucellosis

Includes: fever:
Malta
Mediterranean
undulant

023.0 Brucella melitensis

023.1 Brucella abortus

023.2 Brucella suis

023.3 Brucella canis

023.8 Other brucellosis

Infection by more than one organism

023.9 Brucellosis, unspecified

024 Glanders

Infection by:
Actinobacillus mallei
Malleomyces mallei
Pseudomonas mallei
Farcy
Malleus

025 Melioidosis

Infection by:
Malleomyces pseudomallei
Pseudomonas pseudomallei
Whitmore's bacillus
Pseudoglanders

§ Requires fifth-digit. See page 3 for codes and definitions.

026 Rat-bite fever

026.0 Spirillary fever
Rat-bite fever due to Spirillum minor [S. minus]
Sodoku

026.1 Streptobacillary fever
Epidemic arthritic erythema
Haverhill fever
Rat-bite fever due to Streptobacillus moniliformis

026.9 Unspecified rat-bite fever

027 Other zoonotic bacterial diseases

027.0 Listeriosis
Infection } by Listeria monocytogenes
Septicemia }
Use additional code to identify manifestation, as meningitis (320.7)

Excludes: *congenital listeriosis (771.2)*

027.1 Erysipelothrix infection
Erysipeloid (of Rosenbach)
Infection } by Erysipelothrix insidiosa [E. rhusiopathiae]
Septicemia }

027.2 Pasteurellosis
Pasteurella pseudotuberculosis infection } by Pasteurella multocida [P. septica]
Mesenteric adenitis }
Septic infection (cat bite) (dog bite) }

Excludes: *infection by:*
Francisella [Pasteurella] tularensis (021.0-021.9)
Yersinia [Pasteurella] pestis (020.0-020.9)

027.8 Other specified zoonotic bacterial diseases

027.9 Unspecified zoonotic bacterial disease

OTHER BACTERIAL DISEASES (030-041)

Excludes: *bacterial venereal diseases (098.0-099.9)*
bartonellosis (088.0)

030 Leprosy

Includes: Hansen's disease
infection by Mycobacterium leprae

030.0 Lepromatous [type L]
Lepromatous leprosy (macular) (diffuse) (infiltrated) (nodular) (neuritic)

030.1 Tuberculoid [type T]
Tuberculoid leprosy (macular) (maculoanesthetic) (major) (minor) (neuritic)

030.2 Indeterminate [group I]
Indeterminate [uncharacteristic] leprosy (macular) (neuritic)

030.3 Borderline [group B]
Borderline or dimorphous leprosy (infiltrated) (neuritic)

030.8 Other specified leprosy

030.9 Leprosy, unspecified

031 Diseases due to other mycobacteria

031.0 Pulmonary
Battey disease
Infection by Mycobacterium:
avium
intracellulare [Battey bacillus]
kansasii

➡ **CC Excl:** 011.00-011.96, 012.00-012.86, 017.90-017.96, 031.0, 031.2, 031.8-031.9, 041.81-041.89, 041.9, 137.0, 139.8, 480.0-480.9, 481, 482.0-482.9, 483.0, 483.1, 483.8, 484.1-484.8, 485-486, 487.0-487.1, 494, 495.0-495.9, 496, 500-505, 506.0-506.9, 507.0-507.8, 508.0-508.9, 517.1, 518.89

031.1 Cutaneous
Buruli ulcer
Infection by Mycobacterium:
marinum [M. balnei]
ulcerans

031.2 Disseminated
Disseminated mycobacterium avium-intracellulare complex (DMAC)
Mycobacterium avium-intracellulare complex (MAC) bacteremia

➡ **AHA Coding Clinic:** 4Q, '97, 31

031.8 Other specified mycobacterial diseases

031.9 Unspecified diseases due to mycobacteria
Atypical mycobacterium infection NOS

032 Diphtheria

Includes: infection by Corynebacterium diphtheriae

032.0 Faucial diphtheria
Membranous angina, diphtheritic

032.1 Nasopharyngeal diphtheria

032.2 Anterior nasal diphtheria

032.3 Laryngeal diphtheria
Laryngotracheitis, diphtheritic

✓5th **032.8 Other specified diphtheria**

032.81 Conjunctival diphtheria
Pseudomembranous diphtheritic conjunctivitis

032.82 Diphtheritic myocarditis

032.83 Diphtheritic peritonitis

032.84 Diphtheritic cystitis

032.85 Cutaneous diphtheria

032.89 Other

032.9 Diphtheria, unspecified

033 Whooping cough

Includes: pertussis

Use additional code to identify any associated pneumonia (484.3)

033.0 Bordetella pertussis [B. pertussis]

033.1 Bordetella parapertussis [B. parapertussis]

033.8 Whooping cough due to other specified organism

Bordetella bronchiseptica [B. bronchiseptica]

033.9 Whooping cough, unspecified organism

034 Streptococcal sore throat and scarlet fever

034.0 Streptococcal sore throat

Septic:	Streptococcal:
angina	angina
sore throat	laryngitis
	pharyngitis
	tonsillitis

034.1 Scarlet fever

Scarlatina

Excludes: *parascarlatina (057.8)*

035 Erysipelas

Excludes: *postpartum or puerperal erysipelas (670)*

036 Meningococcal infection

036.0 Meningococcal meningitis

Cerebrospinal fever (meningococcal)	Meningitis:
	cerebrospinal
	epidemic

➡ **CC Excl:** 003.21, 013.00-013.16, 036.0, 036.89, 036.9, 041.81-041.89, 041.9, 047.0-047.9, 049.0-049.1, 053.0, 054.72, 072.1, 090.42, 091.81, 094.2, 098.89, 100.81, 112.83, 114.2, 115.01, 115.11, 115.91, 130.0, 139.8, 320.0-320.9, 321.0-321.8, 322.0-322.9, 349.89, 349.9, 357.0

036.1 Meningococcal encephalitis

➡ **CC Excl:** 036.1, 036.89, 036.9, 041.81-041.89, 041.9, 139.8

036.2 Meningococcemia

Meningococcal septicemia

➡ **CC Excl:** 003.1, 020.2, 036.2, 036.89, 036.9, 038.0, 038.10-038.11, 038.19, 038.2-038.9, 041.81-041.89, 041.9, 054.5, 139.8

036.3 Waterhouse-Friderichsen syndrome, meningococcal

Meningococcal hemorrhagic adrenalitis
Meningococcic adrenal syndrome
Waterhouse-Friderichsen syndrome NOS

➡ **CC Excl:** 036.3, 036.89, 036.9, 041.81-041.89, 041.9, 139.8

✓5th **036.4** Meningococcal carditis

036.40 Meningococcal carditis, unspecified

➡ **CC Excl:** 036.40, 036.89, 036.9, 041.81-041.89, 041.9, 139.8

036.41 Meningococcal pericarditis

➡ **CC Excl:** 036.41, 036.89, 036.9, 041.81-041.89, 041.9, 139.8

036.42 Meningococcal endocarditis

➡ **CC Excl:** 036.42, 036.89, 036.9, 041.81-041.89, 041.9, 139.8

036.43 Meningococcal myocarditis

➡ **CC Excl:** 036.43, 041.81-041.89, 041.9, 139.8

✓5th **036.8** Other specified meningococcal infections

036.81 Meningococcal optic neuritis

➡ **CC Excl:** 036.81, 036.89, 036.9, 041.81-041.89, 041.9, 139.8

036.82 Meningococcal arthropathy

➡ **CC Excl:** 036.82, 036.89, 036.9, 041.81-041.89, 041.9, 139.8

036.89 Other

➡ **CC Excl:** 036.89, 036.9, 041.81-041.89, 041.9, 139.8

036.9 Meningococcal infection, unspecified

Meningococcal infection NOS

➡ **CC Excl:** see Code 036.89

037 Tetanus

Excludes: *tetanus:*
complicating:
abortion (634-638 with .0, 639.0)
ectopic or molar pregnancy (639.0)
neonatorum (771.3)
puerperal (670)

➡ **CC Excl:** 037, 139.8

038 Septicemia

Excludes: *bacteremia (790.7)*
during labor (659.3)
following ectopic or molar pregnancy (639.0)
following infusion, injection, transfusion, or vaccination (999.3)
postpartum, puerperal (670)
that complicating abortion (634-638 with .0, 639.0)

➡ **AHA Coding Clinic:** 4Q, '88, 10; 3Q, '88, 12

✔ **St. Anthony's Clinical Coder:** see Chapter 5

038.0 **Streptococcal septicemia**

➡ **CC Excl:** 003.1, 020.2, 036.2, 038.0, 038.10-038.11, 038.19, 040.89, 041.00-041.89, 041.9, 054.5, 139.8, V09.90-V09.91

DRG 416

✓5th **038.1** **Staphylococcal septicemia**

➡ **AHA Coding Clinic:** 4Q, '97, 32

038.10 **Staphylococcal septicemia, unspecified**

➡ **CC Excl:** 003.1, 020.2, 036.2, 038.0-038.9, 040.89, 041.00-041.05, 041.09-041.11, 041.19, 041.2-041.7, 041.81-041.86, 041.89, 041.9, 054.5, 139.8, V09.0-V09.91

038.11 **Staphylococcus aureus septicemia**

➡ **CC Excl:** see Code 038.10

038.19 **Other staphylococcal septicemia**

➡ **CC Excl:** see Code 038.10

DRG 416

038.2 **Pneumococcal septicemia [Streptococcus pneumoniae septicemia]**

➡ **CC Excl:** see Code 038.0

➡ **AHA Coding Clinic:** 2Q, '96, 5; 1Q, '91, 13

038.3 **Septicemia due to anaerobes**

Septicemia due to bacteroides

Excludes: *gas gangrene (040.0)*
that due to anaerobic streptococci (038.0)

➡ **CC Excl:** see Code 038.0

✓5th **038.4** **Septicemia due to other gram-negative organisms**

038.40 **Gram-negative organism, unspecified**

Gram-negative septicemia NOS

➡ **CC Excl:** see Code 038.0

038.41 **Hemophilus influenzae [H. influenzae]**

➡ **CC Excl:** see Code 038.0

038.42 **Escherichia coli [E. coli]**

➡ **CC Excl:** see Code 038.0

DRG 416

038.43 **Pseudomonas**

➡ **CC Excl:** see Code 038.0

038.44 **Serratia**

➡ **CC Excl:** see Code 038.0

038.49 **Other**

➡ **CC Excl:** see Code 038.0

DRG 416

038.8 **Other specified septicemias**

Excludes: *septicemia (due to):*
anthrax (022.3)
gonococcal (098.89)
herpetic (054.5)
meningococcal (036.2)
septicemic plague (020.2)

➡ **CC Excl:** see Code 038.0

DRG 416

038.9 **Unspecified septicemia**

Septicemia NOS

Excludes: *bacteremia NOS (790.7)*

➡ **CC Excl:** see Code 038.0

➡ **AHA Coding Clinic:** 1Q, '98, 5; 3Q, '96, 16; 2Q, '96, 6

DRG 416

039 Actinomycotic infections

Includes: actinomycotic mycetoma
infection by Actinomycetales, such as species of Actinomyces, Actinomadura, Nocardia, Streptomyces
maduromycosis (actinomycotic)
schizomycetoma (actinomycotic)

039.0 **Cutaneous**

Erythrasma
Trichomycosis axillaris

039.1 **Pulmonary**

Thoracic actinomycosis

039.2 **Abdominal**

039.3 **Cervicofacial**

039.4 **Madura foot**

Excludes: *madura foot due to mycotic infection (117.4)*

039.8 **Of other specified sites**

039.9 **Of unspecified site**

Actinomycosis NOS
Maduromycosis NOS
Nocardiosis NOS

040 Other bacterial diseases

Excludes: *bacteremia NOS (790.7)*
bacterial infection NOS (041.9)

040.0 **Gas gangrene**

Gas bacillus infection or gangrene
Infection by Clostridium:
histolyticum
oedematiens
perfringens [welchii]
septicum
sordellii
Malignant edema
Myonecrosis, clostridial
Myositis, clostridial

➡ **CC Excl:** 040.0, 139.8

➡ **AHA Coding Clinic:** 1Q, '95, 11

040.1 Rhinoscleroma

040.2 Whipple's disease
Intestinal lipodystrophy

040.3 Necrobacillosis

040.8 Other specified bacterial diseases

040.81 Tropical pyomyositis

040.89 Other
➡ **AHA Coding Clinic:** N-D, '86, 7

041 Bacterial infection in conditions classified elsewhere and of unspecified site

Note: This category is provided to be used as an additional code to identify the bacterial agent in diseases classified elsewhere. This category will also be used to classify bacterial infections of unspecified nature or site.

Excludes: *bacteremia NOS (790.7)*
septicemia (038.0-038.9)

041.0 Streptococcus

041.00 Streptococcus, unspecified

041.01 Group A

041.02 Group B

041.03 Group C

041.04 Group D [Enterococcus]

041.05 Group G

041.09 Other Streptococcus

041.1 Staphylococcus

041.10 Staphylococcus, unspecified

041.11 Staphylococcus aureus
➡ **AHA Coding Clinic:** 4Q, '97, 32

041.19 Other Staphylococcus

041.2 Pneumococcus

041.3 Friedländer's bacillus
Infection by Klebsiella pneumoniae

041.4 Escherichia coli [E. coli]

041.5 Hemophilus influenzae [H. influenzae]

041.6 Proteus (mirabilis) (morganii)

041.7 Pseudomonas

041.8 Other specified bacterial infections

041.81 Mycoplasma
Eaton's agent
Pleuropneumonia-like organisms [PPLO]

041.82 Bacillus fragilis

041.83 Clostridium perfringens

041.84 Other anaerobes
Bacteroides (fragilis)
Gram-negative anaerobes

Excludes: *Helicobacter pylori (041.86)*

041.85 Other gram-negative organisms
Aerobacter aerogenes
Gram-negative bacteria NOS
Mima polymorpha
Serratia

Excludes: *gram-negative anaerobes (041.84)*

041.86 Helicobacter pylori (H. pylori)
➡ **AHA Coding Clinic:** 4Q, '95, 60

041.89 Other specified bacteria

041.9 Bacterial infection, unspecified
➡ **AHA Coding Clinic:** 2Q, '91, 9

HUMAN IMMUNODEFICIENCY VIRUS (HIV) INFECTION (042)

042 Human immunodeficiency virus [HIV] disease

Acquired immune deficiency syndrome
Acquired immunodeficiency syndrome
AIDS
AIDS-like syndrome
AIDS-related complex
ARC
HIV infection, symptomatic

Use additional code(s) to identify all manifestations of HIV

Use additional code to identify HIV-2 infection (079.53)

Excludes: *asymptomatic HIV infection status (V08)*
exposure to HIV virus (V01.7)
nonspecific serologic evidence of HIV (795.71)

➡ **CC Excl:** 042, 139.8

➡ **AHA Coding Clinic:** 4Q, '97, 30, 31; 1Q, '93, 21; 2Q, '92, 11; 3Q, '90, 17; J-A, '87, 8

POLIOMYELITIS AND OTHER NON-ARTHROPOD-BORNE VIRAL DISEASES OF CENTRAL NERVOUS SYSTEM (045-049)

045 Acute poliomyelitis

Excludes: *late effects of acute poliomyelitis (138)*

The following fifth-digit subclassification is for use with category 045:

- 0 **poliovirus, unspecified type**
- 1 **poliovirus type I**
- 2 **poliovirus type II**
- 3 **poliovirus type III**

✓5th **045.0 Acute paralytic poliomyelitis specified as bulbar**

Infantile paralysis (acute) } specified as bulbar
Poliomyelitis (acute) (anterior) } specified as bulbar
Polioencephalitis (acute) (bulbar)
Polioencephalomyelitis (acute) (anterior) (bulbar)

✓5th **045.1 Acute poliomyelitis with other paralysis**

Paralysis:
- acute atrophic, spinal
- infantile, paralytic

Poliomyelitis (acute) anterior, epidemic } with paralysis except bulbar

✓5th **045.2 Acute nonparalytic poliomyelitis**

Poliomyelitis (acute) anterior, epidemic } specified as nonparalytic

✓5th **045.9 Acute poliomyelitis, unspecified**

Infantile paralysis; Poliomyelitis (acute) anterior, epidemic } unspecified whether paralytic or nonparalytic

046 Slow virus infection of central nervous system

046.0 Kuru

046.1 Jakob-Creutzfeldt disease

Subacute spongiform encephalopathy

046.2 Subacute sclerosing panencephalitis

Dawson's inclusion body encephalitis
Van Bogaert's sclerosing leukoencephalitis

➡ **CC Excl:** 046.2, 139.8

046.3 Progressive multifocal leukoencephalopathy

Multifocal leukoencephalopathy NOS

046.8 Other specified slow virus infection of central nervous system

046.9 Unspecified slow virus infection of central nervous system

047 Meningitis due to enterovirus

Includes: meningitis:
- abacterial
- aseptic
- viral

Excludes: *meningitis due to:*
- *adenovirus (049.1)*
- *arthropod-borne virus (060.0-066.9)*
- *leptospira (100.81)*
- *virus of:*
  - *herpes simplex (054.72)*
  - *herpes zoster (053.0)*
  - *lymphocytic choriomeningitis (049.0)*
  - *mumps (072.1)*
  - *poliomyelitis (045.0-045.9)*
- *any other infection specifically classified elsewhere*

047.0 Coxsackie virus

047.1 ECHO virus

Meningo-eruptive syndrome

047.8 Other specified viral meningitis

047.9 Unspecified viral meningitis

Viral meningitis NOS

048 Other enterovirus diseases of central nervous system

Boston exanthem

049 Other non-arthropod-borne viral diseases of central nervous system

Excludes: *late effects of viral encephalitis (139.0)*

049.0 Lymphocytic choriomeningitis

Lymphocytic:
- meningitis (serous) (benign)
- meningoencephalitis (serous) (benign)

049.1 Meningitis due to adenovirus

049.8 Other specified non-arthropod-borne viral diseases of central nervous system

Encephalitis:
- acute:
  - inclusion body
  - necrotizing
- epidemic

Encephalitis:
- lethargica
- Rio Bravo
- von Economo's disease

049.9 Unspecified non-arthropod-borne viral diseases of central nervous system

Viral encephalitis NOS

VIRAL DISEASES ACCOMPANIED BY EXANTHEM (050-057)

Excludes: *arthropod-borne viral diseases (060.0-066.9)*
Boston exanthem (048)

050 Smallpox

050.0 Variola major
Hemorrhagic (pustular) smallpox
Malignant smallpox
Purpura variolosa

050.1 Alastrim
Variola minor

050.2 Modified smallpox
Varioloid

050.9 Smallpox, unspecified

051 Cowpox and paravaccinia

051.0 Cowpox
Vaccinia not from vaccination

Excludes: *vaccinia (generalized) (from vaccination) (999.0)*

051.1 Pseudocowpox
Milkers' node

051.2 Contagious pustular dermatitis
Ecthyma contagiosum
Orf

051.9 Paravaccinia, unspecified

052 Chickenpox

052.0 Postvaricella encephalitis
Postchickenpox encephalitis
➡ **CC Excl:** 051.9, 052.0, 052.7-052.9, 078.88-078.89, 079.81, 079.88-079.89, 079.98-079.99, 139.8

052.1 Varicella (hemorrhagic) pneumonitis
➡ **CC Excl:** 051.9, 052.1, 052.7-052.9, 078.88-078.89, 079.81, 079.88-079.89, 079.98-079.99, 139.8

052.7 With other specified complications
➡ **CC Excl:** 051.9, 052.7-052.9, 078.88-078.89, 079.81, 079.88-079.89, 079.98-079.99, 139.8

052.8 With unspecified complication
➡ **CC Excl:** see Code 052.7

052.9 Varicella without mention of complication
Chickenpox NOS
Varicella NOS
➡ **CC Excl:** see Code 052.7

053 Herpes zoster

Includes: shingles
zona

053.0 With meningitis
➡ **CC Excl:** 003.21, 013.00-013.16, 036.0, 047.0-047.9, 049.0-049.1, 053.0-053.19, 053.79, 053.8-053.9, 054.72, 054.79, 054.8-054.9, 072.1, 078.88-078.89, 079.81, 079.88-079.89, 079.98-079.99, 090.42, 091.81, 094.2, 098.89, 100.81, 112.83, 114.2, 115.01, 115.11, 115.91, 130.0, 139.8, 320.0-320.9, 321.0-321.8, 322.0-322.9, 349.89, 349.9, 357.0

✓5th **053.1 With other nervous system complications**

053.10 With unspecified nervous system complication
➡ **CC Excl:** 053.0-053.19, 053.79, 053.8-053.9, 054.72, 054.79, 054.8-054.9, 078.88-078.89, 079.81, 079.88-079.89, 079.98-079.99, 139.8

053.11 Geniculate herpes zoster
Herpetic geniculate ganglionitis
➡ **CC Excl:** see Code 053.10

053.12 Postherpetic trigeminal neuralgia
➡ **CC Excl:** see Code 053.10

053.13 Postherpetic polyneuropathy
➡ **CC Excl:** see Code 053.10

053.19 Other
➡ **CC Excl:** see Code 053.10

✓5th **053.2 With ophthalmic complications**

053.20 Herpes zoster dermatitis of eyelid
Herpes zoster ophthalmicus

053.21 Herpes zoster keratoconjunctivitis

053.22 Herpes zoster iridocyclitis

053.29 Other

✓5th **053.7 With other specified complications**

053.71 Otitis externa due to herpes zoster

053.79 Other
➡ **CC Excl:** 053.0-053.9, 054.0-054.71, 054.73, 054.79, 054.8-054.9, 078.88-078.89, 079.81, 079.81, 079.81, 079.88-079.89, 079.98-079.99, 139.8

053.8 With unspecified complication
➡ **CC Excl:** see Code 053.79

053.9 Herpes zoster without mention of complication
Herpes zoster NOS

054 Herpes simplex

Excludes: *congenital herpes simplex (771.2)*

054.0 Eczema herpeticum
Kaposi's varicelliform eruption

✓5th **054.1** Genital herpes

054.10 Genital herpes, unspecified
Herpes progenitalis

054.11 Herpetic vulvovaginitis ♀

054.12 Herpetic ulceration of vulva ♀

054.13 Herpetic infection of penis ♂

054.19 Other

054.2 Herpetic gingivostomatitis

054.3 Herpetic meningoencephalitis
Herpes encephalitis   Simian B disease
➡ **CC Excl:** 054.3, 054.79, 054.8-054.9, 139.8

✓5th **054.4** With ophthalmic complications

054.40 With unspecified ophthalmic complication

054.41 Herpes simplex dermatitis of eyelid

054.42 Dendritic keratitis

054.43 Herpes simplex disciform keratitis

054.44 Herpes simplex iridocyclitis

054.49 Other

054.5 Herpetic septicemia
➡ **CC Excl:** 003.1, 020.2, 036.2, 038.0, 038.10-038.11, 038.19, 038.2-038.9, 054.5, 054.79, 054.8-054.9, 139.8

054.6 Herpetic whitlow
Herpetic felon

✓5th **054.7** With other specified complications

054.71 Visceral herpes simplex
➡ **CC Excl:** 054.71, 054.72, 054.79, 054.8-054.9, 139.8

054.72 Herpes simplex meningitis
➡ **CC Excl:** 003.21, 013.00-013.16, 036.0, 047.0-047.9, 049.0-049.1, 053.0, 054.72, 054.79, 054.8-054.9, 072.1, 090.42, 091.81, 094.2, 098.89, 100.81, 112.83, 114.2, 115.01, 115.11, 115.91, 130.0, 139.8, 320.0-320.9, 321.0-321.8, 322.0-322.9, 349.89, 349.9, 357.0

054.73 Herpes simplex otitis externa

054.79 Other
➡ **CC Excl:** 054.79, 054.8-054.9, 078.88-078.89, 079.81, 079.88-079.89, 079.98-079.99, 139.8

054.8 With unspecified complication
➡ **CC Excl:** see Code 054.79

054.9 Herpes simplex without mention of complication

055 Measles

Includes: morbilli
rubeola

055.0 Postmeasles encephalitis
➡ **CC Excl:** 055.0, 055.79, 055.8-055.9, 078.88-078.89, 079.81,079.88-079.89, 079.98-079.99, 139.8

055.1 Postmeasles pneumonia
➡ **CC Excl:** 055.1, 055.79, 055.8-055.9, 078.88-078.89, 079.81, 079.88-079.89, 079.98-079.99, 139.8

055.2 Postmeasles otitis media
➡ **CC Excl:** 055.2, 055.79, 055.8-055.9, 078.88-078.89, 079.81, 079.88-079.89, 079.98-079.99, 139.8

✓5th **055.7** With other specified complications

055.71 Measles keratoconjunctivitis
Measles keratitis
➡ **CC Excl:** 055.71, 055.79, 055.8-055.9, 078.88-078.89, 079.81, 079.88-079.89, 079.98-079.99, 139.8

055.79 Other
➡ **CC Excl:** 055.79, 055.8-055.9, 078.88-078.89, 079.81, 079.88-079.89, 079.98-079.99, 139.8

055.8 With unspecified complication
➡ **CC Excl:** 055.79, 055.8-055.9, 056.09, 078.88-078.89, 079.81, 079.88-079.89, 079.98-079.99, 139.8

055.9 Measles without mention of complication

056 Rubella

Includes: German measles

Excludes: *congenital rubella (771.0)*

✓5th **056.0 With neurological complications**

056.00 With unspecified neurological complication

➡ **CC Excl:** 056.00-056.09, 056.79, 056.8-056.9, 078.88-078.89, 079.81, 079.88-079.89, 079.98-079.99, 139.8

056.01 Encephalomyelitis due to rubella

Encephalitis } due to rubella
Meningoencephalitis } due to rubella

➡ **CC Excl:** see Code 056.00

056.09 Other

➡ **CC Excl:** see Code 056.00

✓5th **056.7 With other specified complications**

056.71 Arthritis due to rubella

➡ **CC Excl:** 056.71-056.9, 078.88-078.89, 079.81, 079.88-079.89, 079.98-079.99, 139.8

056.79 Other

➡ **CC Excl:** see Code 056.00

056.8 With unspecified complications

➡ **CC Excl:** 056.00, 056.01, 056.79, 056.8-056.9, 078.88-078.89, 079.81, 079.88-079.89, 079.98-079.99, 139.8

056.9 Rubella without mention of complication

057 Other viral exanthemata

057.0 Erythema infectiosum [fifth disease]

057.8 Other specified viral exanthemata

Dukes (-Filatow) disease
Exanthema subitum [sixth disease]
Fourth disease
Parascarlatina
Pseudoscarlatina
Roseola infantum

057.9 Viral exanthem, unspecified

ARTHROPOD-BORNE VIRAL DISEASES (060-066)

Use additional code to identify any associated meningitis (321.2)

Excludes: *late effects of viral encephalitis (139.0)*

060 Yellow fever

060.0 Sylvatic

Yellow fever:
jungle
sylvan

060.1 Urban

060.9 Yellow fever, unspecified

061 Dengue

Breakbone fever

Excludes: *hemorrhagic fever caused by dengue virus (065.4)*

062 Mosquito-borne viral encephalitis

062.0 Japanese encephalitis

Japanese B encephalitis

062.1 Western equine encephalitis

062.2 Eastern equine encephalitis

Excludes: *Venezuelan equine encephalitis (066.2)*

062.3 St. Louis encephalitis

062.4 Australian encephalitis

Australian arboencephalitis
Australian X disease
Murray Valley encephalitis

062.5 California virus encephalitis

Encephalitis:
California
La Crosse
Tahyna fever

062.8 Other specified mosquito-borne viral encephalitis

Encephalitis by Ilheus virus

062.9 Mosquito-borne viral encephalitis, unspecified

063 Tick-borne viral encephalitis

Includes: diphasic meningoencephalitis

063.0 Russian spring-summer [taiga] encephalitis

063.1 Louping ill

063.2 Central European encephalitis

063.8 Other specified tick-borne viral encephalitis

Langat encephalitis
Powassan encephalitis

063.9 Tick-borne viral encephalitis, unspecified

064 Viral encephalitis transmitted by other and unspecified arthropods

Arthropod-borne viral encephalitis, vector unknown
Negishi virus encephalitis

Excludes: *viral encephalitis NOS (049.9)*

065 Arthropod-borne hemorrhagic fever

065.0 Crimean hemorrhagic fever [CHF Congo virus]
Central Asian hemorrhagic fever

065.1 Omsk hemorrhagic fever

065.2 Kyasanur Forest disease

065.3 Other tick-borne hemorrhagic fever

065.4 Mosquito-borne hemorrhagic fever
Chikungunya hemorrhagic fever
Dengue hemorrhagic fever

Excludes: *Chikungunya fever (066.3)*
dengue (061)
yellow fever (060.0-060.9)

065.8 Other specified arthropod-borne hemorrhagic fever
Mite-borne hemorrhagic fever

065.9 Arthropod-borne hemorrhagic fever, unspecified
Arbovirus hemorrhagic fever NOS

066 Other arthropod-borne viral diseases

066.0 Phlebotomus fever
Changuinola fever
Sandfly fever

066.1 Tick-borne fever
Nairobi sheep disease
Tick fever:
American mountain
Colorado
Tick fever:
Kemerovo
Quaranfil

066.2 Venezuelan equine fever
Venezuelan equine encephalitis

066.3 Other mosquito-borne fever
Fever (viral):
Bunyamwera
Bwamba
Chikungunya
Guama
Mayaro
Mucambo
O'nyong-nyong
Fever (viral):
Oropouche
Pixuna
Rift valley
Ross river
Wesselsbron
West Nile
Zika

Excludes: *dengue (061)*
yellow fever (060.0-060.9)

066.8 Other specified arthropod-borne viral diseases
Chandipura fever
Piry fever

066.9 Arthropod-borne viral disease, unspecified
Arbovirus infection NOS

OTHER DISEASES DUE TO VIRUSES AND CHLAMYDIAE (070-079)

070 Viral hepatitis

Includes: viral hepatitis (acute) (chronic)

Excludes: *cytomegalic inclusion virus hepatitis (078.5)*

The following fifth-digit subclassification is for use with categories 070.2 and 070.3:

0 acute or unspecified, without mention of hepatitis delta
1 acute or unspecified, with hepatitis delta
2 chronic, without mention of hepatitis delta
3 chronic, with hepatitis delta

070.0 Viral hepatitis A with hepatic coma

070.1 Viral hepatitis A without mention of hepatic coma
Infectious hepatitis

✓5th **070.2 Viral hepatitis B with hepatic coma**

➡ **CC Excl: For Codes 070.20-070.21:** 070.22-070.23, 070.32-070.33, 070.44, 070.54, 079.81

➡ **CC Excl: For Code 070.22-070.23:** 070.0-070.9, 078.88-078.89, 079.81, 079.81, 079.81, 079.88-079.89, 079.98-079.99, 139.8

➡ **AHA Coding Clinic:** 4Q, '91, 28

✓5th **070.3 Viral hepatitis B without mention of hepatic coma**
Serum hepatitis

➡ **CC Excl: For Codes 070.30-070.31:** see Code 070.20

➡ **CC Excl: For Codes 070.32-070.33:** see Code 070.22

➡ **AHA Coding Clinic:** 1Q, '93, 28; 4Q, '91, 28

✓5th **070.4 Other specified viral hepatitis with hepatic coma**

➡ **AHA Coding Clinic:** 4Q, '91, 28

070.41 Acute or unspecified hepatitis C with hepatic coma

➡ **CC Excl:For codes 070.41-070.43:** see Code 070.20

070.42 Hepatitis delta without mention of active hepatitis B disease with hepatic coma
Hepatitis delta with hepatitis B carrier state

070.43 Hepatitis E with hepatic coma

070.44 Chronic hepatitis C with hepatic coma
➡ **CC Excl:** see Code 070.22

070.49 Other specified viral hepatitis with hepatic coma
➡ **CC Excl:** see Code 070.20

✓5th **070.5** Other specified viral hepatitis without mention of hepatic coma
➡ **AHA Coding Clinic:** 4Q, '91, 28

070.51 Acute or unspecified hepatitis C without mention of hepatic coma
➡ **CC Excl: For codes 070.51-070.53:** see Code 070.20

070.52 Hepatitis delta without mention of active hepatitis B disease or hepatic coma

070.53 Hepatitis E without mention of hepatic coma

070.54 Chronic hepatitis C without mention of hepatic coma
➡ **CC Excl:** see Code 070.20

070.59 Other specified viral hepatitis without mention of hepatic coma
➡ **CC Excl:** see Code 070.20

070.6 Unspecified viral hepatitis with hepatic coma
➡ **CC Excl:** see Code 070.20

070.9 Unspecified viral hepatitis without mention of hepatic coma
Viral hepatitis NOS
➡ **CC Excl:** see Code 070.20

071 Rabies

Hydrophobia
Lyssa

072 Mumps

072.0 Mumps orchitis ♂
➡ **CC Excl:** 072.0, 072.79, 072.8-072.9, 078.88-078.89, 079.81, 079.81, 079.81, 079.88-079.89, 079.98-079.99, 139.8

072.1 Mumps meningitis
➡ **CC Excl:** 003.21, 013.00-013.16, 036.0, 047.0-047.9, 049.0-049.1, 053.0, 054.72, 072.1, 072.79, 072.8-072.9, 078.88-078.89, 079.81, 079.81, 079.81, 079.88-079.89, 079.98-079.99, 090.42, 091.81, 094.2, 098.89, 100.81, 112.83, 114.2, 115.01, 115.11, 115.91, 130.0, 139.8, 320.0-320.9, 321.0-321.8, 322.0-322.9, 349.89, 349.9, 357.0

072.2 Mumps encephalitis
Mumps meningoencephalitis
➡ **CC Excl:** 072.2, 072.79, 072.8-072.9, 078.88-078.89, 079.81, 079.81, 079.81, 079.88-079.89, 079.98-079.99, 139.8

072.3 Mumps pancreatitis
➡ **CC Excl:** 072.3, 072.79, 072.8-072.9, 078.88-078.89, 079.81, 079.81, 079.81, 079.88-079.89, 079.98-079.99, 139.8

✓5th **072.7** Mumps with other specified complications

072.71 Mumps hepatitis
➡ **CC Excl:** 072.71, 072.79, 072.8-072.9, 078.88-078.89, 079.81, 079.81, 079.81, 079.88-079.89, 079.98-079.99, 139.8

072.72 Mumps polyneuropathy
➡ **CC Excl:** 072.72, 072.79, 072.8-072.9, 078.88-078.89, 079.81, 079.81, 079.81, 079.88-079.89, 079.98-079.99, 139.8

072.79 Other
➡ **CC Excl:** 072.79, 072.8-072.9, 078.88-078.89, 079.81, 079.81, 079.81, 079.88-079.89, 079.98-079.99, 139.8

072.8 Mumps with unspecified complication
➡ **CC Excl:** 072.79, 072.8-072.9, 078.88-078.89, 079.81, 079.81, 079.81, 079.88-079.89, 079.98-079.99

072.9 Mumps without mention of complication
Epidemic parotitis
Infectious parotitis

073 Ornithosis

Includes: parrot fever
psittacosis

073.0 With pneumonia
Lobular pneumonitis due to ornithosis

073.7 With other specified complications

073.8 With unspecified complication

073.9 Ornithosis, unspecified

074 Specific diseases due to Coxsackie virus

Excludes: *Coxsackie virus:*
infection NOS (079.2)
meningitis (047.0)

074.0 Herpangina
Vesicular pharyngitis

074.1 Epidemic pleurodynia
Bornholm disease
Devil's grip
Epidemic:
myalgia
myositis

✓5th **074.2** Coxsackie carditis

074.20 Coxsackie carditis, unspecified

074.21 Coxsackie pericarditis

074.22 Coxsackie endocarditis

074.23 Coxsackie myocarditis
Aseptic myocarditis of newborn

074.3 Hand, foot, and mouth disease
Vesicular stomatitis and exanthem

074.8 Other specified diseases due to Coxsackie virus
Acute lymphonodular pharyngitis

075 Infectious mononucleosis

Glandular fever
Monocytic angina
Pfeiffer's disease

➡ **AHA Coding Clinic:** M-A, '87, 8

076 Trachoma

Excludes: *late effect of trachoma (139.1)*

076.0 Initial stage
Trachoma dubium

076.1 Active stage
Granular conjunctivitis (trachomatous)
Trachomatous:
follicular conjunctivitis
pannus

076.9 Trachoma, unspecified
Trachoma NOS

077 Other diseases of conjunctiva due to viruses and Chlamydiae

Excludes: *ophthalmic complications of viral diseases classified elsewhere*

077.0 Inclusion conjunctivitis
Paratrachoma
Swimming pool conjunctivitis

Excludes: *inclusion blennorrhea (neonatal) (771.6)*

077.1 Epidemic keratoconjunctivitis
Shipyard eye

077.2 Pharyngoconjunctival fever
Viral pharyngoconjunctivitis

077.3 Other adenoviral conjunctivitis
Acute adenoviral follicular conjunctivitis

077.4 Epidemic hemorrhagic conjunctivitis
Apollo:
conjunctivitis
disease
Conjunctivitis due to enterovirus type 70
Hemorrhagic conjunctivitis (acute) (epidemic)

077.8 Other viral conjunctivitis
Newcastle conjunctivitis

✓5th **077.9** Unspecified diseases of conjunctiva due to viruses and Chlamydiae

077.98 Due to Chlamydiae

077.99 Due to viruses
Viral conjunctivitis NOS

078 Other diseases due to viruses and Chlamydiae

Excludes: *viral infection NOS (079.0-079.9)*
viremia NOS (790.8)

078.0 Molluscum contagiosum

✓5th **078.1** Viral warts
Viral warts due to Human papillomavirus

➡ **AHA Coding Clinic:** 2Q, '97, 9

078.10 Viral warts, unspecified
Condyloma NOS
Verruca:
NOS
vulgaris
Warts (infectious)

078.11 Condyloma acuminatum

078.19 Other specified viral warts
Genital warts NOS
Verruca:
plana
plantaris

078.2 Sweating fever
Miliary fever
Sweating disease

078.3 Cat-scratch disease
Benign lymphoreticulosis (of inoculation)
Cat-scratch fever

078.4 Foot and mouth disease
Aphthous fever
Epizootic:
aphthae
stomatitis

078.5 Cytomegaloviral disease
Cytomegalic inclusion disease
Salivary gland virus disease

Use additional code to identify manifestation, as:
cytomegalic inclusion virus:
hepatitis (573.1)
pneumonia (484.1)

Excludes: *congenital cytomegalovirus infection (771.1)*

➡ **AHA Coding Clinic:** 2Q, '93, 11; 1Q, '89, 9

078.6 Hemorrhagic nephrosonephritis
Hemorrhagic fever:
epidemic
Korean
Hemorrhagic fever:
Russian
with renal syndrome

078.7 Arenaviral hemorrhagic fever

Hemorrhagic fever:
- Argentine
- Bolivian

Hemorrhagic fever:
- Junin virus
- Machupo virus

✓5th **078.8 Other specified diseases due to viruses and Chlamydiae**

Excludes: *epidemic diarrhea (009.2)*
lymphogranuloma venereum (099.1)

078.81 Epidemic vertigo

078.82 Epidemic vomiting syndrome

Winter vomiting disease

078.88 Other specified diseases due to Chlamydiae

078.89 Other specified diseases due to viruses

Epidemic cervical myalgia
Marburg disease
Tanapox

079 Viral and chlamydial infection in conditions classified elsewhere and of unspecified site

Note: This category is provided to be used as an additional code to identify the viral agent in diseases classifiable elsewhere. This category will also be used to classify virus infection of unspecified nature or site.

079.0 Adenovirus

079.1 ECHO virus

079.2 Coxsackie virus

079.3 Rhinovirus

079.4 Human papillomavirus

➡ **AHA Coding Clinic:** 2Q, '97, 9; 4Q, '93, 22

✓5th **079.5 Retrovirus**

Excludes: *human immunodeficiency virus, type 1 [HIV-1] (042)*
human T-cell lymphotrophic virus, type III [HTLV-III] (042)
lymphadenopathy-associated virus [LAV] (042)

079.50 Retrovirus, unspecified

079.51 Human T-cell lymphotrophic virus, type I [HTLV-I]

079.52 Human T-cell lymphotrophic virus, type II [HTLV-II]

079.53 Human immunodeficiency virus, type 2 [HIV 2]

079.59 Other specified retrovirus

079.6 Respiratory syncytial virus (RSV)

➡ **AHA Coding Clinic:** 4Q, '96, 27, 28

✓5th **079.8 Other specified viral and chlamydial infections**

➡ **AHA Coding Clinic:** 1Q, '88, 12

079.81 Hantavirus infection

➡ **AHA Coding Clinic:** 4Q, '95, 60

079.88 Other specified chlamydial infection

079.89 Other specified viral infection

✓5th **079.9 Unspecified viral and chlamydial infections**

Excludes: *viremia NOS (790.8)*

➡ **AHA Coding Clinic:** 2Q, '91, 8

079.98 Unspecified chlamydial infection

Chlamydial infection NOS

079.99 Unspecified viral infection

Viral infection NOS

RICKETTSIOSES AND OTHER ARTHROPOD-BORNE DISEASES (080-088)

Excludes: *arthropod-borne viral diseases (060.0-066.9)*

080 Louse-borne [epidemic] typhus

Typhus (fever):
- classical
- epidemic

Typhus (fever):
- exanthematic NOS
- louse-borne

081 Other typhus

081.0 Murine [endemic] typhus

Typhus (fever):
- endemic
- flea-borne

081.1 Brill's disease

Brill-Zinsser disease
Recrudescent typhus (fever)

081.2 Scrub typhus

Japanese river fever
Kedani fever
Mite-borne typhus
Tsutsugamushi

081.9 Typhus, unspecified

Typhus (fever) NOS

082 Tick-borne rickettsioses

082.0 Spotted fevers

Rocky mountain spotted fever
São Paulo fever

082.1 Boutonneuse fever

African tick typhus
India tick typhus
Kenya tick typhus
Marseilles fever
Mediterranean tick fever

082.2 North Asian tick fever

Siberian tick typhus

082.3 Queensland tick typhus

082.8 Other specified tick-borne rickettsioses

Lone star fever

082.9 Tick-borne rickettsiosis, unspecified

Tick-borne typhus NOS

083 Other rickettsioses

083.0 Q fever

083.1 Trench fever
Quintan fever
Wolhynian fever

083.2 Rickettsialpox
Vesicular rickettsiosis

083.8 Other specified rickettsioses

083.9 Rickettsiosis, unspecified

084 Malaria

Note: Subcategories 084.0-084.6 exclude the listed conditions with mention of pernicious complications (084.8-084.9).

Excludes: *congenital malaria (771.2)*

084.0 Falciparum malaria [malignant tertian]
Malaria (fever):
by Plasmodium falciparum
subtertian

084.1 Vivax malaria [benign tertian]
Malaria (fever) by Plasmodium vivax

084.2 Quartan malaria
Malaria (fever) by Plasmodium malariae
Malariae malaria

084.3 Ovale malaria
Malaria (fever) by Plasmodium ovale

084.4 Other malaria
Monkey malaria

084.5 Mixed malaria
Malaria (fever) by more than one parasite

084.6 Malaria, unspecified
Malaria (fever) NOS

084.7 Induced malaria
Therapeutically induced malaria

Excludes: *accidental infection from syringe, blood transfusion, etc. (084.0-084.6, above, according to parasite species)*
transmission from mother to child during delivery (771.2)

084.8 Blackwater fever
Hemoglobinuric:
fever (bilious)
malaria
Malarial hemoglobinuria

084.9 Other pernicious complications of malaria
Algid malaria
Cerebral malaria

Use additional code to identify complication, as:
malarial:
hepatitis (573.2)
nephrosis (581.81)

085 Leishmaniasis

085.0 Visceral [kala-azar]
Dumdum fever
Infection by Leishmania:
donovani
infantum
Leishmaniasis:
dermal, post-kala-azar
Mediterranean
visceral (Indian)

085.1 Cutaneous, urban
Aleppo boil
Baghdad boil
Delhi boil
Infection by Leishmania tropica (minor)
Leishmaniasis, cutaneous:
dry form
late
recurrent
ulcerating
Oriental sore

085.2 Cutaneous, Asian desert
Infection by Leishmania tropica major
Leishmaniasis, cutaneous:
acute necrotizing
rural
wet form
zoonotic form

085.3 Cutaneous, Ethiopian
Infection by Leishmania ethiopica
Leishmaniasis, cutaneous:
diffuse
lepromatous

085.4 Cutaneous, American
Chiclero ulcer
Infection by Leishmania mexicana
Leishmaniasis tegumentaria diffusa

085.5 Mucocutaneous (American)
Espundia
Infection by Leishmania braziliensis
Uta

085.9 Leishmaniasis, unspecified

086 Trypanosomiasis

Use additional code to identify manifestations, as:
trypanosomiasis:
encephalitis (323.2)
meningitis (321.3)

086.0 Chagas' disease with heart involvement
American trypanosomiasis } with heart involvement
Infection by Trypanosoma cruzi } with heart involvement
Any condition classifiable to 086.2 } with heart involvement

➡ **CC Excl:** 086.0, 139.8

086.1 Chagas' disease with other organ involvement

American trypanosomiasis | Infection by Trypanosoma cruzi | Any condition classifiable to 086.2 } with involvement of organ other than heart

086.2 Chagas' disease without mention of organ involvement

American trypanosomiasis
Infection by Trypanosoma cruzi

086.3 Gambian trypanosomiasis

Gambian sleeping sickness
Infection by Trypanosoma gambiense

086.4 Rhodesian trypanosomiasis

Infection by Trypanosoma rhodesiense
Rhodesian sleeping sickness

086.5 African trypanosomiasis, unspecified

Sleeping sickness NOS

086.9 Trypanosomiasis, unspecified

087 Relapsing fever

Includes: recurrent fever

087.0 Louse-borne

087.1 Tick-borne

087.9 Relapsing fever, unspecified

088 Other arthropod-borne diseases

088.0 Bartonellosis

Carrión's disease
Oroya fever
Verruga peruana

✓5th **088.8 Other specified arthropod-borne diseases**

088.81 Lyme disease

Erythema chronicum migrans

➡ **AHA Coding Clinic:** 4Q, '91, 15; 3Q, '90, 14; 2Q, '89, 10

088.82 Babesiosis

Babesiasis

088.89 Other

088.9 Arthropod-borne disease, unspecified

SYPHILIS AND OTHER VENEREAL DISEASES (090-099)

Excludes: *nonvenereal endemic syphilis (104.0)*
urogenital trichomoniasis (131.0)

090 Congenital syphilis

090.0 Early congenital syphilis, symptomatic

Congenital syphilitic:
- choroiditis
- coryza (chronic)
- hepatomegaly
- mucous patches
- periostitis
- splenomegaly

Syphilitic (congenital):
- epiphysitis
- osteochondritis
- pemphigus

Any congenital syphilitic condition specified as early or manifest less than two years after birth

090.1 Early congenital syphilis, latent

Congenital syphilis without clinical manifestations, with positive serological reaction and negative spinal fluid test, less than two years after birth

090.2 Early congenital syphilis, unspecified

Congenital syphilis NOS, less than two years after birth

090.3 Syphilitic interstitial keratitis

Syphilitic keratitis:
- parenchymatous
- punctata profunda

Excludes: *interstitial keratitis NOS (370.50)*

✓5th **090.4 Juvenile neurosyphilis**

Use additional code to identify any associated mental disorder

090.40 Juvenile neurosyphilis, unspecified

Congenital neurosyphilis
Dementia paralytica juvenilis
Juvenile:
- general paresis
- tabes
- taboparesis

➡ **CC Excl:** 090.0-090.9, 091.0-091.9, 092.0, 092.9, 093.0-093.9, 094.0-094.9, 095.0-095.9, 096, 097.0-097.9, 099.40-099.59, 099.8, 099.9, 139.8

090.41 Congenital syphilitic encephalitis

➡ **CC Excl:** see Code 090.40

090.42 Congenital syphilitic meningitis

➡ **CC Excl:** 003.21, 013.00-013.16, 036.0, 047.0-047.9, 049.0-049.1, 053.0, 054.72, 072.1, 090.0-090.9, 091.0-091.9, 092.0, 092.9, 093.0-093.9, 094.0-094.9, 095.0-095.9, 096, 097.0-097.9, 098.89, 099.40-099.59, 099.8, 099.9, 100.81, 112.83, 114.2, 115.01, 115.11, 115.91, 130.0, 139.8, 320.0-320.9, 321.0-321.8, 322.0-322.9, 349.89, 349.9, 357.0

090.49 **Other**

➡ **CC Excl:** 090.0-090.9, 091.0-091.9, 092.0, 092.9, 093.0-093.9, 094.0-094.9, 095.0-095.9, 096, 097.0-097.9, 099.40-099.59, 099.8, 099.9, 139.8

090.5 **Other late congenital syphilis, symptomatic**

Gumma due to congenital syphilis
Hutchinson's teeth
Syphilitic saddle nose
Any congenital syphilitic condition specified as late or manifest two years or more after birth

090.6 **Late congenital syphilis, latent**

Congenital syphilis without clinical manifestations, with positive serological reaction and negative spinal fluid test, two years or more after birth

090.7 **Late congenital syphilis, unspecified**

Congenital syphilis NOS, two years or more after birth

090.9 **Congenital syphilis, unspecified**

091 Early syphilis, symptomatic

Excludes: *early cardiovascular syphilis (093.0-093.9)*
early neurosyphilis (094.0-094.9)

091.0 **Genital syphilis (primary)**

Genital chancre

091.1 **Primary anal syphilis**

091.2 **Other primary syphilis**

Primary syphilis of:
breast
fingers
lip
tonsils

091.3 **Secondary syphilis of skin or mucous membranes**

Condyloma latum
Secondary syphilis of:
anus
mouth
pharynx
skin
tonsils
vulva

091.4 **Adenopathy due to secondary syphilis**

Syphilitic adenopathy (secondary)
Syphilitic lymphadenitis (secondary)

✓5th **091.5** **Uveitis due to secondary syphilis**

091.50 **Syphilitic uveitis, unspecified**

091.51 **Syphilitic chorioretinitis (secondary)**

091.52 **Syphilitic iridocyclitis (secondary)**

✓5th **091.6** **Secondary syphilis of viscera and bone**

091.61 **Secondary syphilitic periostitis**

091.62 **Secondary syphilitic hepatitis**

Secondary syphilis of liver

091.69 **Other viscera**

091.7 **Secondary syphilis, relapse**

Secondary syphilis, relapse (treated) (untreated)

✓5th **091.8** **Other forms of secondary syphilis**

091.81 **Acute syphilitic meningitis (secondary)**

091.82 **Syphilitic alopecia**

091.89 **Other**

091.9 **Unspecified secondary syphilis**

092 Early syphilis, latent

Includes: syphilis (acquired) without clinical manifestations, with positive serological reaction and negative spinal fluid test, less than two years after infection

092.0 **Early syphilis, latent, serological relapse after treatment**

092.9 **Early syphilis, latent, unspecified**

093 Cardiovascular syphilis

093.0 **Aneurysm of aorta, specified as syphilitic**

Dilatation of aorta, specified as syphilitic

➡ **CC Excl:** see Code 090.49

093.1 **Syphilitic aortitis**

➡ **CC Excl:** see Code 090.49

✓5th **093.2** **Syphilitic endocarditis**

093.20 **Valve, unspecified**

Syphilitic ostial coronary disease

➡ **CC Excl:** see Code 090.49

093.21 **Mitral valve**

➡ **CC Excl:** see Code 090.49

093.22 **Aortic valve**

Syphilitic aortic incompetence or stenosis

➡ **CC Excl:** see Code 090.49

093.23 **Tricuspid valve**

➡ **CC Excl:** see Code 090.49

093.24 **Pulmonary valve**

➡ **CC Excl:** see Code 090.49

✓5th **093.8** **Other specified cardiovascular syphilis**

093.81 **Syphilitic pericarditis**
➡ **CC Excl:** see Code 090.49

093.82 **Syphilitic myocarditis**
➡ **CC Excl:** see Code 090.49

093.89 **Other**
➡ **CC Excl:** see Code 090.49

093.9 **Cardiovascular syphilis, unspecified**
➡ **CC Excl:** see Code 090.49

094 Neurosyphilis

Use additional code to identify any associated mental disorder

094.0 **Tabes dorsalis**
Locomotor ataxia (progressive)
Posterior spinal sclerosis (syphilitic)
Tabetic neurosyphilis

Use additional code to identify manifestation, as:
neurogenic arthropathy [Charcot's joint disease] (713.5)

➡ **CC Excl:** see Code 090.49

094.1 **General paresis**
Dementia paralytica
General paralysis (of the insane) (progressive)
Paretic neurosyphilis
Taboparesis

➡ **CC Excl:** see Code 090.49

094.2 **Syphilitic meningitis**
Meningovascular syphilis

Excludes: *acute syphilitic meningitis (secondary) (091.81)*

➡ **CC Excl:** 003.21, 013.00-013.16, 036.0, 047.0-047.9, 049.0-049.1, 053.0, 054.72, 072.1, 090.0-090.9, 091.0-091.9, 092.0, 092.9, 093.0-093.9, 094.0-094.9, 095.0-095.9, 096, 097.0-097.9, 098.89, 099.40-099.59, 099.8, 099.9, 100.81, 112.83, 114.2, 115.01, 115.11, 115.91, 130.0, 139.8, 320.0-320.9, 321.0-321.8, 322.0-322.9, 349.89, 349.9, 357.0

094.3 **Asymptomatic neurosyphilis**
➡ **CC Excl:** 090.0-090.9, 091.0-091.9, 092.0, 092.9, 093.0-093.9, 094.0-094.9, 095.0-095.9, 096, 097.0-097.9, 099.40-099.59, 099.8, 099.9, 139.8

✓5th **094.8** **Other specified neurosyphilis**

094.81 **Syphilitic encephalitis**
➡ **CC Excl:** see Code 094.3

094.82 **Syphilitic Parkinsonism**

094.83 **Syphilitic disseminated retinochoroiditis**

094.84 **Syphilitic optic atrophy**

094.85 **Syphilitic retrobulbar neuritis**

094.86 **Syphilitic acoustic neuritis**

094.87 **Syphilitic ruptured cerebral aneurysm**
➡ **CC Excl:** see Code 094.3

094.89 **Other**
➡ **CC Excl:** see Code 094.3

094.9 **Neurosyphilis, unspecified**
Gumma (syphilitic) } of central nervous system NOS
Syphilis (early) (late) } of central nervous system NOS
Syphiloma } of central nervous system NOS

➡ **CC Excl:** see Code 094.3

095 Other forms of late syphilis, with symptoms

Includes: gumma (syphilitic)
syphilis, late, tertiary, or unspecified stage

095.0 **Syphilitic episcleritis**

095.1 **Syphilis of lung**

095.2 **Syphilitic peritonitis**

095.3 **Syphilis of liver**

095.4 **Syphilis of kidney**

095.5 **Syphilis of bone**

095.6 **Syphilis of muscle**
Syphilitic myositis

095.7 **Syphilis of synovium, tendon, and bursa**
Syphilitic:
bursitis
synovitis

095.8 **Other specified forms of late symptomatic syphilis**

Excludes: *cardiovascular syphilis (093.0-093.9)*
neurosyphilis (094.0-094.9)

095.9 **Late symptomatic syphilis, unspecified**

096 Late syphilis, latent

Syphilis (acquired) without clinical manifestations, with positive serological reaction and negative spinal fluid test, two years or more after infection

097 Other and unspecified syphilis

097.0 **Late syphilis, unspecified**

097.1 **Latent syphilis, unspecified**
Positive serological reaction for syphilis

097.9 **Syphilis, unspecified**
Syphilis (acquired) NOS

Excludes: *syphilis NOS causing death under two years of age (090.9)*

098 Gonococcal infections

098.0 **Acute, of lower genitourinary tract**
Gonococcal:
Bartholinitis (acute)
urethritis (acute)
vulvovaginitis (acute)
Gonorrhea (acute):
NOS
genitourinary (tract) NOS

➡ **CC Excl:** 098.0-098.39, 098.89, 099.40-099.59, 099.8, 099.9, 139.8

✓5th **098.1** **Acute, of upper genitourinary tract**

098.10 **Gonococcal infection (acute) of upper genitourinary tract, site unspecified**
➡ **CC Excl:** see Code 098.0

098.11 **Gonococcal cystitis (acute)**
Gonorrhea (acute) of bladder
➡ **CC Excl:** see Code 098.0

098.12 **Gonococcal prostatitis (acute)** ♂
➡ **CC Excl:** see Code 098.0

098.13 **Gonococcal epididymo-orchitis (acute)** ♂
Gonococcal orchitis (acute)
➡ **CC Excl:** see Code 098.0

098.14 **Gonococcal seminal vesiculitis (acute)** ♂
Gonorrhea (acute) of seminal vesicle
➡ **CC Excl:** see Code 098.0

098.15 **Gonococcal cervicitis (acute)** ♀
Gonorrhea (acute) of cervix
➡ **CC Excl:** see Code 098.0

098.16 **Gonococcal endometritis (acute)** ♀
Gonorrhea (acute) of uterus
➡ **CC Excl:** see Code 098.0

098.17 **Gonococcal salpingitis, specified as acute** ♀
➡ **CC Excl:** see Code 098.0

098.19 **Other**
➡ **CC Excl:** see Code 098.0

098.2 **Chronic, of lower genitourinary tract**
Gonococcal:
Bartholinitis
urethritis
vulvovaginitis
Gonorrhea:
NOS
genitourinary (tract)
Any condition classifiable to 098.0
} specified as chronic or with duration of two months or more

✓5th **098.3** **Chronic, of upper genitourinary tract**
Includes: any condition classifiable to 098.1 stated as chronic or with a duration of two months or more

098.30 **Chronic gonococcal infection of upper genitourinary tract, site unspecified**

098.31 **Gonococcal cystitis, chronic**
Any condition classifiable to 098.11, specified as chronic
Gonorrhea of bladder, chronic

098.32 **Gonococcal prostatitis, chronic** ♂
Any condition classifiable to 098.12, specified as chronic

098.33 **Gonococcal epididymo-orchitis, chronic** ♂
Any condition classifiable to 098.13, specified as chronic
Chronic gonococcal orchitis

098.34 **Gonococcal seminal vesiculitis, chronic** ♂
Any condition classifiable to 098.14, specified as chronic
Gonorrhea of seminal vesicle, chronic

098.35 **Gonococcal cervicitis, chronic** ♀
Any condition classifiable to 098.15, specified as chronic
Gonorrhea of cervix, chronic

098.36 **Gonococcal endometritis, chronic** ♀
Any condition classifiable to 098.16, specified as chronic

098.37 **Gonococcal salpingitis (chronic)** ♀

098.39 **Other**

✓5th **098.4** **Gonococcal infection of eye**

098.40 **Gonococcal conjunctivitis (neonatorum)**
Gonococcal ophthalmia (neonatorum)

098.41 **Gonococcal iridocyclitis**

098.42 **Gonococcal endophthalmia**

098.43 **Gonococcal keratitis**

098.49 **Other**

✓5th **098.5 Gonococcal infection of joint**

098.50 Gonococcal arthritis
Gonococcal infection of joint NOS

098.51 Gonococcal synovitis and tenosynovitis

098.52 Gonococcal bursitis

098.53 Gonococcal spondylitis

098.59 Other
Gonococcal rheumatism

098.6 Gonococcal infection of pharynx

098.7 Gonococcal infection of anus and rectum
Gonococcal proctitis

✓5th **098.8 Gonococcal infection of other specified sites**

098.81 Gonococcal keratosis (blennorrhagica)

098.82 Gonococcal meningitis

098.83 Gonococcal pericarditis

098.84 Gonococcal endocarditis

098.85 Other gonococcal heart disease

098.86 Gonococcal peritonitis

098.89 Other
Gonococcemia

099 Other venereal diseases

099.0 Chancroid
Bubo (inguinal):
chancroidal
due to Hemophilus ducreyi
Chancre:
Ducrey's
simple
soft
Ulcus molle (cutis) (skin)

099.1 Lymphogranuloma venereum
Climatic or tropical bubo
(Durand-) Nicolas-Favre disease
Esthiomene
Lymphogranuloma inguinale

099.2 Granuloma inguinale
Donovanosis
Granuloma pudendi (ulcerating)
Granuloma venereum
Pudendal ulcer

099.3 Reiter's disease
Reiter's syndrome

Use additional code for associated:
arthropathy (711.1)
conjunctivitis (372.33)

✓5th **099.4 Other nongonococcal urethritis [NGU]**

099.40 Unspecified
Nonspecific urethritis

099.41 Chlamydia trachomatis

099.49 Other specified organism

✓5th **099.5 Other venereal diseases due to Chlamydia trachomatis**

Excludes: *Chlamydia trachomatis infection of conjunctiva (076.0-076.9, 077.0, 077.9)*
Lymphogranuloma venereum (099.1)

099.50 Unspecified site

099.51 Pharynx

099.52 Anus and rectum

099.53 Lower genitourinary sites
Use additional code to specify site of infection, such as:
bladder (595.4)
cervix (616.0)
vagina and vulva (616.11)

Excludes: *urethra (099.41)*

099.54 Other genitourinary sites
Use additional code to specify site of infection, such as:
pelvic inflammatory disease NOS (614.9)
testis and epididymis (604.91)

099.55 Unspecified genitourinary site

099.56 Peritoneum
Perihepatitis

099.59 Other specified site

099.8 Other specified venereal diseases

099.9 Venereal disease, unspecified

OTHER SPIROCHETAL DISEASES (100-104)

100 Leptospirosis

100.0 Leptospirosis icterohemorrhagica
Leptospiral or spirochetal jaundice (hemorrhagic)
Weil's disease

✓5th **100.8 Other specified leptospiral infections**

100.81 Leptospiral meningitis (aseptic)

100.89 Other

Fever:	Infection by Leptospira:
Fort Bragg	australis
pretibial	bataviae
swamp	pyrogenes

100.9 Leptospirosis, unspecified

101 Vincent's angina

Acute necrotizing ulcerative:
- gingivitis
- stomatitis

Fusospirochetal pharyngitis
Spirochetal stomatitis
Trench mouth
Vincent's:
- gingivitis
- infection [any site]

102 Yaws

Includes: frambesia
pian

102.0 Initial lesions

Chancre of yaws
Frambesia, initial or primary
Initial frambesial ulcer
Mother yaw

102.1 Multiple papillomata and wet crab yaws

Butter yaws
Frambesioma
Pianoma
Plantar or palmar papilloma of yaws

102.2 Other early skin lesions

Cutaneous yaws, less than five years after infection
Early yaws (cutaneous) (macular) (papular) (maculopapular) (micropapular)
Frambeside of early yaws

102.3 Hyperkeratosis

Ghoul hand
Hyperkeratosis, palmar or plantar (early) (late) due to yaws
Worm-eaten soles

102.4 Gummata and ulcers

Gummatous frambeside
Nodular late yaws (ulcerated)

102.5 Gangosa

Rhinopharyngitis mutilans

102.6 Bone and joint lesions

Goundou; Gumma, bone; Gummatous osteitis or periostitis — of yaws (late)
Hydrarthrosis; Osteitis; Periostitis (hypertrophic) — of yaws (early) (late)

102.7 Other manifestations

Juxta-articular nodules of yaws
Mucosal yaws

102.8 Latent yaws

Yaws without clinical manifestations, with positive serology

102.9 Yaws, unspecified

103 Pinta

103.0 Primary lesions

Chancre (primary); Papule (primary); Pintid — of pinta [carate]

103.1 Intermediate lesions

Erythematous plaques; Hyperchromic lesions; Hyperkeratosis — of pinta [carate]

103.2 Late lesions

Cardiovascular lesions; Skin lesions: achromic, cicatricial, dyschromic; Vitiligo — of pinta [carate]

103.3 Mixed lesions

Achromic and hyperchromic skin lesions of pinta [carate]

103.9 Pinta, unspecified

104 Other spirochetal infection

104.0 Nonvenereal endemic syphilis

Bejel
Njovera

104.8 Other specified spirochetal infections

Excludes: *relapsing fever (087.0-087.9)*
syphilis (090.0-097.9)

104.9 Spirochetal infection, unspecified

MYCOSES (110-118)

Use additional code to identify manifestation, as:
- arthropathy (711.6)
- meningitis (321.0-321.1)
- otitis externa (380.15)

Excludes: *infection by Actinomycetales, such as species of Actinomyces, Actinomadura, Nocardia, Streptomyces (039.0-039.9)*

110 Dermatophytosis

Includes: infection by species of Epidermophyton, Microsporum, and Trichophyton
tinea, any type except those in 111

110.0 Of scalp and beard
Kerion
Sycosis, mycotic
Trichophytic tinea [black dot tinea], scalp

110.1 Of nail
Dermatophytic onychia
Onychomycosis
Tinea unguium

110.2 Of hand
Tinea manuum

110.3 Of groin and perianal area
Dhobie itch
Eczema marginatum
Tinea cruris

110.4 Of foot
Athlete's foot
Tinea pedis

110.5 Of the body
Herpes circinatus
Tinea imbricata [Tokelau]

110.6 Deep seated dermatophytosis
Granuloma trichophyticum
Majocchi's granuloma

110.8 Of other specified sites

110.9 Of unspecified site
Favus NOS
Microsporic tinea NOS
Ringworm NOS

111 Dermatomycosis, other and unspecified

111.0 Pityriasis versicolor
Infection by Malassezia [Pityrosporum] furfur
Tinea flava
Tinea versicolor

111.1 Tinea nigra
Infection by Cladosporium species
Keratomycosis nigricans
Microsporosis nigra
Pityriasis nigra
Tinea palmaris nigra

111.2 Tinea blanca
Infection by Trichosporon (beigelii) cutaneum
White piedra

111.3 Black piedra
Infection by Piedraia hortai

111.8 Other specified dermatomycoses

111.9 Dermatomycosis, unspecified

112 Candidiasis

Includes: infection by Candida species
moniliasis

Excludes: neonatal monilial infection (771.7)

112.0 Of mouth
Thrush (oral)
➡ **CC Excl:** 112.0-112.9, 117.9, 139.8

112.1 Of vulva and vagina ♀
Candidal vulvovaginitis
Monilial vulvovaginitis

112.2 Of other urogenital sites
Candidal balanitis
➡ **AHA Coding Clinic:** 4Q, '96, 33

112.3 Of skin and nails
Candidal intertrigo
Candidal onychia
Candidal perionyxis [paronychia]

112.4 Of lung
Candidal pneumonia
➡ **CC Excl:** see Code 112.0

112.5 Disseminated
Systemic candidiasis
➡ **CC Excl:** see Code 112.0
➡ **AHA Coding Clinic:** 2Q, '89, 10

✓5th **112.8 Of other specified sites**

112.81 Candidal endocarditis
➡ **CC Excl:** see Code 112.0

112.82 Candidal otitis externa
Otomycosis in moniliasis
➡ **CC Excl:** see Code 112.0

112.83 Candidal meningitis
➡ **CC Excl:** 003.21, 013.00-013.16, 036.0, 047.0-047.9, 049.0-049.1, 053.0, 054.72, 072.1, 090.42, 091.81, 094.2, 098.89, 100.81, 112.0-112.9, 114.2, 115.01, 115.11, 115.91, 117.9, 130.0, 139.8, 320.0-320.9, 321.0-321.8, 322.0-322.9, 349.89, 349.9, 357.0

112.84 Candidal esophagitis
➡ **AHA Coding Clinic:** 4Q, '92, 19

112.85 Candidal enteritis
➡ **AHA Coding Clinic:** 4Q, '92, 19

112.89 Other
➡ **AHA Coding Clinic:** 1Q, '92, 17; 3Q, '91, 20

112.9 Of unspecified site

114 Coccidioidomycosis

Includes: infection by Coccidioides (immitis)
Posada-Wernicke disease

114.0 Primary coccidioidomycosis (pulmonary)

Acute pulmonary coccidioidomycosis
Coccidioidomycotic pneumonitis
Desert rheumatism
Pulmonary coccidioidomycosis
San Joaquin Valley fever

➡ **CC Excl:** 114.0, 114.3, 114.4-114.5, 114.9, 117.9, 139.8

114.1 Primary extrapulmonary coccidioidomycosis

Chancriform syndrome
Primary cutaneous coccidioidomycosis

114.2 Coccidioidal meningitis

➡ **CC Excl:** 003.21, 013.00-013.16, 036.0, 047.0-047.9, 049.0-049.1, 053.0, 054.72, 072.1, 090.42, 091.81, 094.2, 098.89, 100.81, 112.83, 114.2-114.9, 115.01, 115.11, 115.91, 117.9, 130.0, 139.8, 320.0-320.9, 321.0-321.8, 322.0-322.9, 349.89, 349.9, 357.0

114.3 Other forms of progressive coccidioidomycosis

Coccidioidal granuloma
Disseminated coccidioidomycosis

➡ **CC Excl:** 114.3, 114.9, 117.9, 139.8

114.4 Chronic pulmonary coccidioidomycosis

114.5 Pulmonary coccidioidomycosis, unspecified

114.9 Coccidioidomycosis, unspecified

➡ **CC Excl:** see Code 114.3

115 Histoplasmosis

The following fifth-digit subclassification is for use with category 115:

- 0 **without mention of manifestation**
- 1 **meningitis**
- 2 **retinitis**
- 3 **pericarditis**
- 4 **endocarditis**
- 5 **pneumonia**
- 9 **other**

✓5th [14] **115.0 Infection by Histoplasma capsulatum**

American histoplasmosis
Darling's disease
Reticuloendothelial cytomycosis
Small form histoplasmosis

➡ **CC Excl: For Code 115.00:** 115.00, 115.09, 115.90, 115.99, 117.9, 139.8

➡ **CC Excl: For Code 115.01:** 003.21, 013.00-013.16, 036.0, 047.0-047.9, 049.0-049.1, 053.0, 054.72, 072.1, 090.42, 091.81, 094.2, 098.89, 100.81, 112.83, 114.2, 115.00-115.01, 115.09, 115.11, 115.90-115.91, 115.99, 117.9, 130.0, 139.8, 320.0-320.9, 321.0-321.8, 322.0-322.9, 349.89, 349.9, 357.0

➡ **CC Excl: For Code 115.02:** 115.00, 115.02, 115.09, 115.90, 115.92, 115.99, 117.9, 139.8

➡ **CC Excl: For Code 115.03:** 115.00, 115.03, 115.09, 115.90, 115.93, 115.99, 117.9, 139.8

➡ **CC Excl: For Code 115.04:** 115.00, 115.04, 115.09, 115.90, 115.94, 115.99, 117.9, 139.8

➡ **CC Excl: For Code 115.05:** 115.00, 115.05, 115.09, 115.90, 115.95, 115.99, 117.9, 139.8, 480.0-480.9, 481, 482.0-482.7, 482.81-482.84, 482.89, 482.9, 483.0, 483.1, 483.8, 484.1-484.8, 485-486, 487.0-487.1, 494, 495.0-495.9, 496, 500-505, 506.0-506.9, 507.0-507.8, 508.0-508.9, 517.1, 518.89

✓5th **115.1 Infection by Histoplasma duboisii**

African histoplasmosis
Large form histoplasmosis

➡ **CC Excl: For Code 115.10:** 115.10, 115.19, 115.90, 115.99, 117.9, 139.8

➡ **CC Excl: For Code 115.11:** 003.21, 013.00-013.16, 036.0, 047.0-047.9, 049.0-049.1, 053.0, 054.72, 072.1, 090.42, 091.81, 094.2, 098.89, 100.81, 112.83, 114.2, 115.01, 115.10-115.11, 115.19, 115.90-115.91, 115.99, 117.9, 130.0, 139.8, 320.0-320.9, 321.0-321.8, 322.0-322.9, 349.89, 349.9, 357.0

➡ **CC Excl: For Code 115.12:** 115.10, 115.12, 115.19, 115.90, 115.92, 115.99, 117.9, 139.8

➡ **CC Excl: For Code 115.13:** 115.10, 115.13, 115.19, 115.90, 115.93, 115.99, 117.9, 139.8

➡ **CC Excl: For Code 115.14:** 115.10, 115.14, 115.19, 115.90, 115.94, 115.99, 117.9, 139.8

➡ **CC Excl: For Code 115.15:** 115.05, 115.10, 115.15, 115.19, 115.90, 115.95, 115.99, 117.9, 139.8, 480.0-480.9, 481, 482.0-482.7, 482.81-482.83, 482.89, 482.9, 483.0, 483.1, 483.8, 484.1-484.8, 485-486, 487.0-487.1, 494, 495.0-495.9, 496, 500-505, 506.0-506.9, 507.0-507.8, 508.0-508.9, 517.1, 518.89

➡ **CC Excl: For Code 115.19:** 115.10, 115.19, 115.90, 115.99, 117.9, 139.8

[14] CC Coding = 0-5

✓5th **115.9 Histoplasmosis, unspecified**

Histoplasmosis NOS

➡ **CC Excl: For Code 115.90:** 115.90, 115.99, 117.9, 139.8

➡ **CC Excl: For Code 115.91:** 003.21, 013.00-013.16, 036.0, 047.0-047.9, 049.0-049.1, 053.0, 054.72, 072.1, 090.42, 091.81, 094.2, 098.89, 100.81, 112.83, 114.2, 115.01, 115.11, 115.91, 115.99, 117.9, 130.0, 139.8, 320.0-320.9, 321.0-321.8, 322.0-322.9, 349.89, 349.9, 357.0

➡ **CC Excl: For Code 115.92:** 115.92, 115.99, 117.9, 139.8

➡ **CC Excl: For Code 115.93:** 115.93, 115.99, 117.9, 139.8

➡ **CC Excl: For Code 115.94:** 115.94, 115.99, 117.9, 139.8

➡ **CC Excl: For Code 115.95:** 115.05, 115.15, 115.95, 115.99, 117.9, 139.8

➡ **CC Excl: For Code 115.99:** 115.99, 117.9, 139.8

116 Blastomycotic infection

116.0 Blastomycosis

Blastomycotic dermatitis
Chicago disease
Cutaneous blastomycosis
Disseminated blastomycosis
Gilchrist's disease
Infection by Blastomyces [Ajellomyces] dermatitidis
North American blastomycosis
Primary pulmonary blastomycosis

➡ **CC Excl:** 116.0, 117.9, 139.8

116.1 Paracoccidioidomycosis

Brazilian blastomycosis
Infection by Paracoccidioides [Blastomyces] brasiliensis
Lutz-Splendore-Almeida disease
Mucocutaneous-lymphangitic paracoccidioidomycosis
Pulmonary paracoccidioidomycosis
South American blastomycosis
Visceral paracoccidioidomycosis

➡ **CC Excl:** 116.1, 117.9, 139.8

116.2 Lobomycosis

Infections by Loboa [Blastomyces] loboi
Keloidal blastomycosis
Lobo's disease

117 Other mycoses

117.0 Rhinosporidiosis

Infection by Rhinosporidium seeberi

117.1 Sporotrichosis

Cutaneous sporotrichosis
Disseminated sporotrichosis
Infection by Sporothrix [Sporotrichum] schenckii
Lymphocutaneous sporotrichosis
Pulmonary sporotrichosis
Sporotrichosis of the bones

117.2 Chromoblastomycosis

Chromomycosis
Infection by Cladosporidium carrionii, Fonsecaea compactum, Fonsecaea pedrosoi, Phialophora verrucosa

117.3 Aspergillosis

Infection by Aspergillus species, mainly A. fumigatus, A. flavus group, A. terreus group

➡ **CC Excl:** 117.3, 117.9, 139.8

➡ **AHA Coding Clinic:** 4Q, '97, 40

117.4 Mycotic mycetomas

Infection by various genera and species of Ascomycetes and Deuteromycetes, such as Acremonium [Cephalosporium] falciforme, Neotestudina rosatii, Madurella grisea, Madurella mycetomii, Pyrenochaeta romeroi, Zopfia [Leptosphaeria] senegalensis
Madura foot, mycotic
Maduromycosis, mycotic

Excludes: *actinomycotic mycetomas (039.0-039.9)*

➡ **CC Excl:** 117.4, 117.9, 139.8

117.5 Cryptococcosis

Busse-Buschke's disease
European cryptococcosis
Infection by Cryptococcus neoformans
Pulmonary cryptococcosis
Systemic cryptococcosis
Torula

➡ **CC Excl:** 117.5, 117.9, 139.8

117.6 Allescheriosis [Petriellidosis]

Infections by Allescheria [Petriellidium] boydii [Monosporium apiospermum]

Excludes: *mycotic mycetoma (117.4)*

➡ **CC Excl:** 117.6, 117.9, 139.8

117.7 Zygomycosis [Phycomycosis or Mucormycosis]

Infection by species of Absidia, Basidiobolus, Conidiobolus, Cunninghamella, Entomophthora, Mucor, Rhizopus, Saksenaea

➡ **CC Excl:** 117.7, 117.9, 139.8

117.8 Infection by dematiacious fungi [Phaehyphomycosis]

Infection by dematiacious fungi, such as Cladosporium trichoides [bantianum], Dreschlera hawaiiensis, Phialophora gougerotii, Phialophora jeanselmi

117.9 Other and unspecified mycoses

118 Opportunistic mycoses

Infection of skin, subcutaneous tissues, and/or organs by a wide variety of fungi generally considered to be pathogenic to compromised hosts only (e.g., infection by species of Alternaria, Dreschlera, Fusarium)

➡ **CC Excl:** 117.9, 118, 139.8

HELMINTHIASES (120-129)

120 Schistosomiasis [bilharziasis]

120.0 Schistosoma haematobium

Vesical schistosomiasis NOS

120.1 Schistosoma mansoni

Intestinal schistosomiasis NOS

120.2 Schistosoma japonicum

Asiatic schistosomiasis NOS
Katayama disease or fever

120.3 Cutaneous

Cercarial dermatitis
Infection by cercariae of Schistosoma
Schistosome dermatitis
Swimmers' itch

120.8 Other specified schistosomiasis

Infection by Schistosoma:
bovis
intercalatum
mattheii
Infection by Schistosoma spindale
Schistosomiasis chestermani

120.9 Schistosomiasis, unspecified

Blood flukes NOS
Hemic distomiasis

121 Other trematode infections

121.0 Opisthorchiasis

Infection by:
cat liver fluke
Opisthorchis (felineus) (tenuicollis) (viverrini)

121.1 Clonorchiasis

Biliary cirrhosis due to clonorchiasis
Chinese liver fluke disease
Hepatic distomiasis due to Clonorchis sinensis
Oriental liver fluke disease

121.2 Paragonimiasis

Infection by Paragonimus
Lung fluke disease (oriental)
Pulmonary distomiasis

121.3 Fascioliasis

Infection by Fasciola:
gigantica
hepatica
Liver flukes NOS
Sheep liver fluke infection

121.4 Fasciolopsiasis

Infection by Fasciolopsis (buski)
Intestinal distomiasis

121.5 Metagonimiasis

Infection by Metagonimus yokogawai

121.6 Heterophyiasis

Infection by:
Heterophyes heterophyes
Stellantchasmus falcatus

121.8 Other specified trematode infections

Infection by:
Dicrocoelium dendriticum
Echinostoma ilocanum
Gastrodiscoides hominis

121.9 Trematode infection, unspecified

Distomiasis NOS
Fluke disease NOS

122 Echinococcosis

Includes: echinococciasis
hydatid disease
hydatidosis

122.0 Echinococcus granulosus infection of liver

122.1 Echinococcus granulosus infection of lung

122.2 Echinococcus granulosus infection of thyroid

122.3 Echinococcus granulosus infection, other

122.4 Echinococcus granulosus infection, unspecified

122.5 Echinococcus multilocularis infection of liver

122.6 Echinococcus multilocularis infection, other

122.7 Echinococcus multilocularis infection, unspecified

122.8 Echinococcosis, unspecified, of liver

122.9 Echinococcosis, other and unspecified

123 Other cestode infection

123.0 Taenia solium infection, intestinal form

Pork tapeworm (adult) (infection)

123.1 Cysticercosis

Cysticerciasis
Infection by Cysticercus cellulosae [larval form of Taenia solium]

➡ **AHA Coding Clinic:** 2Q, '97, 8

123.2 Taenia saginata infection

Beef tapeworm (infection)
Infection by Taeniarhynchus saginatus

123.3 Taeniasis, unspecified

123.4 Diphyllobothriasis, intestinal

Diphyllobothrium (adult) (latum) (pacificum) infection
Fish tapeworm (infection)

123.5 Sparganosis [larval diphyllobothriasis]
Infection by:
Diphyllobothrium larvae
Sparganum (mansoni) (proliferum)
Spirometra larvae

123.6 Hymenolepiasis
Dwarf tapeworm (infection)
Hymenolepis (diminuta) (nana) infection
Rat tapeworm (infection)

123.8 Other specified cestode infection
Diplogonoporus (grandis) infection
Dipylidium (caninum) infection
Dog tapeworm (infection)

123.9 Cestode infection, unspecified
Tapeworm (infection) NOS

124 Trichinosis
Trichinella spiralis infection
Trichinellosis
Trichiniasis

125 Filarial infection and dracontiasis

125.0 Bancroftian filariasis
Chyluria, Elephantiasis, Infection, Lymphadenitis, Lymphangitis — due to Wuchereria bancrofti
Wuchereriasis

125.1 Malayan filariasis
Brugia filariasis, Chyluria, Elephantiasis, Infection, Lymphadenitis, Lymphangitis — due to Brugia [Wuchereria] malayi

125.2 Loiasis
Eyeworm disease of Africa
Loa loa infection

125.3 Onchocerciasis
Onchocerca volvulus infection
Onchocercosis

125.4 Dipetalonemiasis
Infection by:
Acanthocheilonema perstans
Dipetalonema perstans

125.5 Mansonella ozzardi infection
Filariasis ozzardi

125.6 Other specified filariasis
Dirofilaria infection
Infection by:
Acanthocheilonema streptocerca
Dipetalonema streptocerca

125.7 Dracontiasis
Guinea-worm infection
Infection by Dracunculus medinensis

125.9 Unspecified filariasis

126 Ancylostomiasis and necatoriasis
Includes: cutaneous larva migrans due to Ancylostoma
hookworm (disease) (infection)
uncinariasis

126.0 Ancylostoma duodenale

126.1 Necator americanus

126.2 Ancylostoma braziliense

126.3 Ancylostoma ceylanicum

126.8 Other specified Ancylostoma

126.9 Ancylostomiasis and necatoriasis, unspecified
Creeping eruption NOS
Cutaneous larva migrans NOS

127 Other intestinal helminthiases

127.0 Ascariasis
Ascaridiasis
Infection by Ascaris lumbricoides
Roundworm infection

127.1 Anisakiasis
Infection by Anisakis larva

127.2 Strongyloidiasis
Infection by Strongyloides stercoralis

Excludes: *trichostrongyliasis (127.6)*

127.3 Trichuriasis
Infection by Trichuris trichiuria
Trichocephaliasis
Whipworm (disease) (infection)

127.4 Enterobiasis
Infection by Enterobius vermicularis
Oxyuriasis
Oxyuris vermicularis infection
Pinworm (disease) (infection)
Threadworm infection

127.5 Capillariasis
Infection by Capillaria philippinensis

Excludes: *infection by Capillaria hepatica (128.8)*

127.6 Trichostrongyliasis
Infection by Trichostrongylus species

127.7 Other specified intestinal helminthiasis
Infection by:
Oesophagostomum apiostomum and related species
Ternidens diminutus
other specified intestinal helminth
Physalopteriasis

127.8 Mixed intestinal helminthiasis
Infection by intestinal helminths classified to more than one of the categories 120.0-127.7
Mixed helminthiasis NOS

127.9 Intestinal helminthiasis, unspecified

128 Other and unspecified helminthiases

128.0 Toxocariasis
Larva migrans visceralis
Toxocara (canis) (cati) infection
Visceral larva migrans syndrome

128.1 Gnathostomiasis
Infection by Gnathostoma spinigerum and related species

128.8 Other specified helminthiasis
Infection by:
Angiostrongylus cantonensis
Capillaria hepatica
other specified helminth

128.9 Helminth infection, unspecified
Helminthiasis NOS
Worms NOS

129 Intestinal parasitism, unspecified

OTHER INFECTIOUS AND PARASITIC DISEASES (130-136)

130 Toxoplasmosis

Includes: infection by toxoplasma gondii
toxoplasmosis (acquired)

Excludes: *congenital toxoplasmosis (771.2)*

130.0 Meningoencephalitis due to toxoplasmosis
Encephalitis due to acquired toxoplasmosis
➡ **CC Excl:** 130.0, 130.7-130.9, 139.8

130.1 Conjunctivitis due to toxoplasmosis
➡ **CC Excl:** 130.1, 130.7-130.9, 139.8

130.2 Chorioretinitis due to toxoplasmosis
Focal retinochoroiditis due to acquired toxoplasmosis
➡ **CC Excl:** 130.2, 130.7-130.9, 139.8

130.3 Myocarditis due to toxoplasmosis
➡ **CC Excl:** 130.3, 130.7-130.9, 139.8

130.4 Pneumonitis due to toxoplasmosis
➡ **CC Excl:** 130.4, 130.7-130.9, 139.8, 480.0-480.9, 481, 482.0-482.7, 482.81-482.83, 482.89, 482.9, 483.0, 483.1, 483.8, 484.1-484.8, 485-486, 487.0-487.1, 494, 495.0-495.9, 496, 500-505, 506.0-506.9, 507.0-507.8, 508.0-508.9, 517.1, 518.89

130.5 Hepatitis due to toxoplasmosis
➡ **CC Excl:** 130.5-130.9, 139.8

130.7 Toxoplasmosis of other specified sites
➡ **CC Excl:** 130.7-130.9, 139.8

130.8 Multisystemic disseminated toxoplasmosis
Toxoplasmosis of multiple sites
➡ **CC Excl:** see Code 130.7

130.9 Toxoplasmosis, unspecified

131 Trichomoniasis

Includes: infection due to Trichomonas (vaginalis)

✓5th **131.0 Urogenital trichomoniasis**

131.00 Urogenital trichomoniasis, unspecified
Fluor (vaginalis), Leukorrhea (vaginalis) } trichomonal or due to Trichomonas (vaginalis)

131.01 Trichomonal vulvovaginitis ♀
Vaginitis, trichomonal or due to Trichomonas (vaginalis)

131.02 Trichomonal urethritis

131.03 Trichomonal prostatitis ♂

131.09 Other

131.8 Other specified sites

Excludes: *intestinal (007.3)*

131.9 Trichomoniasis, unspecified

132 Pediculosis and phthirus infestation

132.0 Pediculus capitis [head louse]

132.1 Pediculus corporis [body louse]

132.2 Phthirus pubis [pubic louse]
Pediculus pubis

132.3 Mixed infestation
Infestation classifiable to more than one of the categories 132.0-132.2

132.9 Pediculosis, unspecified

133 Acariasis

133.0 Scabies
Infestation by Sarcoptes scabiei
Norwegian scabies
Sarcoptic itch

133.8 Other acariasis
Chiggers
Infestation by:
Demodex folliculorum
Trombicula

133.9 Acariasis, unspecified
Infestation by mites NOS

134 Other infestation

134.0 Myiasis
Infestation by:
Dermatobia (hominis)
fly larvae
Gasterophilus (intestinalis)
Infestation by:
maggots
Oestrus ovis

134.1 Other arthropod infestation
Infestation by:
chigoe
sand flea
Tunga penetrans
Jigger disease
Scarabiasis
Tungiasis

134.2 Hirudiniasis
Hirudiniasis (external) (internal)
Leeches (aquatic) (land)

134.8 Other specified infestations

134.9 Infestation, unspecified
Infestation (skin) NOS
Skin parasites NOS

135 Sarcoidosis

Besnier-Boeck-Schaumann disease
Lupoid (miliary) of Boeck
Lupus pernio (Besnier)
Lymphogranulomatosis, benign (Schaumann's)
Sarcoid (any site):
NOS
Boeck
Darier-Roussy
Uveoparotid fever

➡ **CC Excl:** 135, 139.8

136 Other and unspecified infectious and parasitic diseases

136.0 Ainhum
Dactylolysis spontanea

136.1 Behçet's syndrome

136.2 Specific infections by free-living amebae
Meningoencephalitis due to Naegleria

136.3 Pneumocystosis
Pneumonia due to Pneumocystis carinii

➡ **CC Excl:** 136.3, 139.8, 480.0-480.9, 481, 482.0-482.7, 482.81-482.83, 482.89, 482.9, 483.0, 483.1, 483.8, 484.1-484.8, 485-486, 487.0-487.1, 494, 495.0-495.9, 496, 500-505, 506.0-506.9, 507.0-507.8, 508.0-508.9, 517.1, 518.89

136.4 Psorospermiasis

136.5 Sarcosporidiosis
Infection by Sarcocystis lindemanni

136.8 Other specified infectious and parasitic diseases
Candiru infestation

136.9 Unspecified infectious and parasitic diseases
Infectious disease NOS
Parasitic disease NOS

➡ **AHA Coding Clinic:** 2Q, '91, 8

LATE EFFECTS OF INFECTIOUS AND PARASITIC DISEASES (137-139)

137 Late effects of tuberculosis

Note: This category is to be used to indicate conditions classifiable to 010-018 as the cause of late effects, which are themselves classified elsewhere. The "late effects" include those specified as such, as sequelae, or as due to old or inactive tuberculosis, without evidence of active disease.

137.0 Late effects of respiratory or unspecified tuberculosis

➡ **CC Excl:** 137.0, 139.8

137.1 Late effects of central nervous system tuberculosis

➡ **CC Excl:** 137.1, 139.8

137.2 Late effects of genitourinary tuberculosis

➡ **CC Excl:** 137.2, 139.8

137.3 Late effects of tuberculosis of bones and joints

137.4 Late effects of tuberculosis of other specified organs

138 Late effects of acute poliomyelitis

Note: This category is to be used to indicate conditions classifiable to 045 as the cause of late effects, which are themselves classified elsewhere. The "late effects" include conditions specified as such, or as sequelae, or as due to old or inactive poliomyelitis, without evidence of active disease.

➡ **CC Excl:** 138, 139.8

139 Late effects of other infectious and parasitic diseases

Note: This category is to be used to indicate conditions classifiable to categories 001-009, 020-041, 046-136 as the cause of late effects, which are themselves classified elsewhere. The "late effects" include conditions specified as such; they also include sequelae of diseases classifiable to the above categories if there is evidence that the disease itself is no longer present.

139.0 **Late effects of viral encephalitis**

Late effects of conditions classifiable to 049.8-049.9, 062-064

139.1 **Late effects of trachoma**

Late effects of conditions classifiable to 076

139.8 **Late effects of other and unspecified infectious and parasitic diseases**

➡ **AHA Coding Clinic:** 4Q, '91, 15; 3Q, '90, 14; M-A, '87, 8

2. NEOPLASMS (140-239)

Notes:

1. Content

This chapter contains the following broad groups:

140–195 Malignant neoplasms, stated or presumed to be primary, of specified sites, except of lymphatic and hematopoietic tissue
196–198 Malignant neoplasms, stated or presumed to be secondary, of specified sites
199 Malignant neoplasms, without specification of site
200–208 Malignant neoplasms, stated or presumed to be primary, of lymphatic and hematopoietic tissue
210–229 Benign neoplasms
230–234 Carcinoma in situ
235–238 Neoplasms of uncertain behavior [see Note above category 235]
239 Neoplasms of unspecified nature

2. Functional activity

All neoplasms are classified in this chapter, whether or not functionally active. An additional code from Chapter 3 may be used to identify such functional activity associated with any neoplasm, e.g.:

catecholamine-producing malignant pheochromocytoma of adrenal:
code 194.0, additional code 255.6
basophil adenoma of pituitary with Cushing's syndrome:
code 227.3, additional code 255.0

3. Morphology [Histology]

For those wishing to identify the histological type of neoplasms, a comprehensive coded nomenclature, which comprises the morphology rubrics of the ICD-Oncology, is given on pages App-1–App-6.

4. Malignant neoplasms overlapping site boundaries

Categories 140-195 are for the classification of primary malignant neoplasms according to their point of origin. A malignant neoplasm that overlaps two or more subcategories within a three-digit rubric and whose point of origin cannot be determined should be classified to the subcategory .8 "Other." For example, "carcinoma involving tip and ventral surface of tongue" should be assigned to 141.8. On the other hand, "carcinoma of tip of tongue, extending to involve the ventral surface" should be coded to 141.2, as the point of origin, the tip, is known. Three subcategories (149.8, 159.8, 165.8) have been provided for malignant neoplasms that overlap the boundaries of three-digit rubrics within certain systems. Overlapping malignant neoplasms that cannot be classified as indicated above should be assigned to the appropriate subdivision of category 195 (Malignant neoplasm of other and ill-defined sites).

➡ **AHA Coding Clinic:** 2Q, '90, 7

MALIGNANT NEOPLASM OF LIP, ORAL CAVITY, AND PHARYNX (140-149)

Excludes: *carcinoma in situ (230.0)*

140 Malignant neoplasm of lip

Excludes: *skin of lip (173.0)*

140.0 Upper lip, vermilion border
Upper lip:
NOS
external
lipstick area

140.1 Lower lip, vermilion border
Lower lip:
NOS
external
lipstick area

140.3 Upper lip, inner aspect
Upper lip:
buccal aspect
frenulum
mucosa
oral aspect

140.4 Lower lip, inner aspect
Lower lip:
buccal aspect
frenulum
mucosa
oral aspect

140.5 Lip, unspecified, inner aspect
Lip, not specified whether upper or lower:
buccal aspect
frenulum
mucosa
oral aspect

140.6 Commissure of lip
Labial commissure

140.8 Other sites of lip
Malignant neoplasm of contiguous or overlapping sites of lip whose point of origin cannot be determined

140.9 Lip, unspecified, vermilion border
Lip, not specified as upper or lower:
NOS
external
lipstick area

141 Malignant neoplasm of tongue

141.0 Base of tongue
Dorsal surface of base of tongue
Fixed part of tongue NOS

141.1 Dorsal surface of tongue
Anterior two-thirds of tongue, dorsal surface
Dorsal tongue NOS
Midline of tongue

Excludes: *dorsal surface of base of tongue (141.0)*

141.2 Tip and lateral border of tongue

141.3 Ventral surface of tongue
Anterior two-thirds of tongue, ventral surface
Frenulum linguae

141.4 Anterior two-thirds of tongue, part unspecified
Mobile part of tongue NOS

141.5 **Junctional zone**
Border of tongue at junction of fixed and mobile parts at insertion of anterior tonsillar pillar

141.6 **Lingual tonsil**

141.8 **Other sites of tongue**
Malignant neoplasm of contiguous or overlapping sites of tongue whose point of origin cannot be determined

141.9 **Tongue, unspecified**
Tongue NOS

142 Malignant neoplasm of major salivary glands

Includes: salivary ducts

Excludes: *malignant neoplasm of minor salivary glands:*
NOS (145.9)
buccal mucosa (145.0)
soft palate (145.3)
tongue (141.0-141.9)
tonsil, palatine (146.0)

142.0 **Parotid gland**

142.1 **Submandibular gland**
Submaxillary gland

142.2 **Sublingual gland**

142.8 **Other major salivary glands**
Malignant neoplasm of contiguous or overlapping sites of salivary glands and ducts whose point of origin cannot be determined

142.9 **Salivary gland, unspecified**
Salivary gland (major) NOS

143 Malignant neoplasm of gum

Includes: alveolar (ridge) mucosa
gingiva (alveolar) (marginal)
interdental papillae

Excludes: *malignant odontogenic neoplasms (170.0-170.1)*

143.0 **Upper gum**

143.1 **Lower gum**

143.8 **Other sites of gum**
Malignant neoplasm of contiguous or overlapping sites of gum whose point of origin cannot be determined

143.9 **Gum, unspecified**

144 Malignant neoplasm of floor of mouth

144.0 **Anterior portion**
Anterior to the premolar-canine junction

144.1 **Lateral portion**

144.8 **Other sites of floor of mouth**
Malignant neoplasm of contiguous or overlapping sites of floor of mouth whose point of origin cannot be determined

144.9 **Floor of mouth, part unspecified**

145 Malignant neoplasm of other and unspecified parts of mouth

Excludes: *mucosa of lips (140.0-140.9)*

145.0 **Cheek mucosa**
Buccal mucosa
Cheek, inner aspect

145.1 **Vestibule of mouth**
Buccal sulcus (upper) (lower)
Labial sulcus (upper) (lower)

145.2 **Hard palate**

145.3 **Soft palate**

Excludes: *nasopharyngeal [posterior] [superior] surface of soft palate (147.3)*

145.4 **Uvula**

145.5 **Palate, unspecified**
Junction of hard and soft palate
Roof of mouth

145.6 **Retromolar area**

145.8 **Other specified parts of mouth**
Malignant neoplasm of contiguous or overlapping sites of mouth whose point of origin cannot be determined

145.9 **Mouth, unspecified**
Buccal cavity NOS
Minor salivary gland, unspecified site
Oral cavity NOS

146 Malignant neoplasm of oropharynx

146.0 **Tonsil**
Tonsil:
NOS
faucial
palatine

Excludes: *lingual tonsil (141.6)*
pharyngeal tonsil (147.1)

146.1 **Tonsillar fossa**

146.2 **Tonsillar pillars (anterior) (posterior)**
Faucial pillar
Glossopalatine fold
Palatoglossal arch
Palatopharyngeal arch

146.3 Vallecula
Anterior and medial surface of the pharyngoepiglottic fold

146.4 Anterior aspect of epiglottis
Epiglottis, free border [margin]
Glossoepiglottic fold(s)

Excludes: *epiglottis:*
NOS (161.1)
suprahyoid portion (161.1)

146.5 Junctional region
Junction of the free margin of the epiglottis, the aryepiglottic fold, and the pharyngoepiglottic fold

146.6 Lateral wall of oropharynx

146.7 Posterior wall of oropharynx

146.8 Other specified sites of oropharynx
Branchial cleft
Malignant neoplasm of contiguous or overlapping sites of oropharynx whose point of origin cannot be determined

146.9 Oropharynx, unspecified

147 Malignant neoplasm of nasopharynx

147.0 Superior wall
Roof of nasopharynx

147.1 Posterior wall
Adenoid
Pharyngeal tonsil

147.2 Lateral wall
Fossa of Rosenmüller
Opening of auditory tube
Pharyngeal recess

147.3 Anterior wall
Floor of nasopharynx
Nasopharyngeal [posterior] [superior] surface of soft palate
Posterior margin of nasal septum and choanae

147.8 Other specified sites of nasopharynx
Malignant neoplasm of contiguous or overlapping sites of nasopharynx whose point of origin cannot be determined

147.9 Nasopharynx, unspecified
Nasopharyngeal wall NOS

148 Malignant neoplasm of hypopharynx

148.0 Postcricoid region

148.1 Pyriform sinus
Pyriform fossa

148.2 Aryepiglottic fold, hypopharyngeal aspect
Aryepiglottic fold or interarytenoid fold:
NOS
marginal zone

Excludes: *aryepiglottic fold or interarytenoid fold, laryngeal aspect (161.1)*

148.3 Posterior hypopharyngeal wall

148.8 Other specified sites of hypopharynx
Malignant neoplasm of contiguous or overlapping sites of hypopharynx whose point of origin cannot be determined

148.9 Hypopharynx, unspecified
Hypopharyngeal wall NOS
Hypopharynx NOS

149 Malignant neoplasm of other and ill-defined sites within the lip, oral cavity, and pharynx

149.0 Pharynx, unspecified

149.1 Waldeyer's ring

149.8 Other
Malignant neoplasms of lip, oral cavity, and pharynx whose point of origin cannot be assigned to any one of the categories 140-148

Excludes: *"book leaf" neoplasm [ventral surface of tongue and floor of mouth] (145.8)*

149.9 Ill-defined

MALIGNANT NEOPLASM OF DIGESTIVE ORGANS AND PERITONEUM (150-159)

Excludes: *carcinoma in situ (230.1-230.9)*

150 Malignant neoplasm of esophagus

150.0 Cervical esophagus
➡ **CC Excl:** 150.0-150.9, 159.0, 159.8-159.9, 176.3, 195.8, 199.0-199.1, 239.0, 239.8-239.9

150.1 Thoracic esophagus
➡ **CC Excl:** see Code 150.0

150.2 Abdominal esophagus

Excludes: *adenocarcinoma (151.0)*
cardio-esophageal junction (151.0)

➡ **CC Excl:** see Code 150.0

150.3 Upper third of esophagus
Proximal third of esophagus
➡ **CC Excl:** see Code 150.0

150.4 **Middle third of esophagus**
➡ **CC Excl:** see Code 150.0

150.5 **Lower third of esophagus**
Distal third of esophagus

Excludes: *adenocarcinoma (151.0)*
cardio-esophageal junction (151.0)

➡ **CC Excl:** see Code 150.0

150.8 **Other specified part**
Malignant neoplasm of contiguous or overlapping sites of esophagus whose point of origin cannot be determined
➡ **CC Excl:** see Code 150.0

150.9 **Esophagus, unspecified**
➡ **CC Excl:** see Code 150.0

151 Malignant neoplasm of stomach

151.0 **Cardia**
Cardiac orifice
Cardio-esophageal junction

Excludes: *squamous cell carcinoma (150.2, 150.5)*

➡ **CC Excl:** 151.0-151.9, 159.0, 159.8-159.9, 176.3, 195.8, 199.0-199.1, 239.0, 239.8-239.9

151.1 **Pylorus**
Prepylorus
Pyloric canal
➡ **CC Excl:** see Code 151.0

151.2 **Pyloric antrum**
Antrum of stomach NOS
➡ **CC Excl:** see Code 151.0

151.3 **Fundus of stomach**
➡ **CC Excl:** see Code 151.0

151.4 **Body of stomach**
➡ **CC Excl:** see Code 151.0

151.5 **Lesser curvature, unspecified**
Lesser curvature, not classifiable to 151.1-151.4
➡ **CC Excl:** see Code 151.0

151.6 **Greater curvature, unspecified**
Greater curvature, not classifiable to 151.0-151.4
➡ **CC Excl:** see Code 151.0

151.8 **Other specified sites of stomach**
Anterior wall, not classifiable to 151.0-151.4
Posterior wall, not classifiable to 151.0-151.4
Malignant neoplasm of contiguous or overlapping sites of stomach whose point of origin cannot be determined
➡ **CC Excl:** see Code 151.0

151.9 **Stomach, unspecified**
Carcinoma ventriculi
Gastric cancer
➡ **CC Excl:** see Code 151.0

152 Malignant neoplasm of small intestine, including duodenum

152.0 **Duodenum**
➡ **CC Excl:** 152.0, 152.8-152.9, 159.0, 159.8-159.9, 176.3, 195.8, 199.0-199.1, 239.0, 239.8-239.9

152.1 **Jejunum**
➡ **CC Excl:** 152.1, 152.8-152.9, 159.0, 159.8-159.9, 176.3, 195.8, 199.0-199.1, 239.0, 239.8-239.9

152.2 **Ileum**

Excludes: *ileocecal valve (153.4)*

➡ **CC Excl:** 152.2, 152.8-152.9, 159.0, 159.8-159.9, 176.3, 195.8, 199.0-199.1, 239.0, 239.8-239.9

152.3 **Meckel's diverticulum**
➡ **CC Excl:** 152.3-152.9, 159.0, 159.8-159.9, 176.3, 195.8, 199.0-199.1, 239.0, 239.8-239.9

152.8 **Other specified sites of small intestine**
Duodenojejunal junction
Malignant neoplasm of contiguous or overlapping sites of small intestine whose point of origin cannot be determined
➡ **CC Excl:** 152.8-152.9, 159.0, 159.8-159.9, 176.3, 195.8, 199.0-199.1, 239.0, 239.8-239.9

152.9 **Small intestine, unspecified**
➡ **CC Excl:** see Code 152.8

153 Malignant neoplasm of colon

153.0 **Hepatic flexure**
➡ **CC Excl:** 153.0, 153.8-153.9, 159.0, 159.8-159.9, 176.3, 195.8, 199.0-199.1, 239.0, 239.8-239.9

153.1 **Transverse colon**
➡ **CC Excl:** 153.1, 153.8-153.9, 159.0, 159.8-159.9, 176.3, 195.8, 199.0-199.1, 239.0, 239.8-239.9

153.2 **Descending colon**
Left colon
➡ **CC Excl:** 153.2, 153.8-153.9, 159.0, 159.8-159.9, 176.3, 195.8, 199.0-199.1, 239.0, 239.8-239.9

153.3 **Sigmoid colon**
Sigmoid (flexure)

Excludes: *rectosigmoid junction (154.0)*

➡ **CC Excl:** 153.3, 153.8-153.9, 159.0, 159.8-159.9, 176.3, 195.8, 199.0-199.1, 239.0, 239.8-239.9

153.4 Cecum

Ileocecal valve

➡ **CC Excl:** 153.4, 153.8-153.9, 159.0, 159.8-159.9, 176.3, 195.8, 199.0-199.1, 239.0, 239.8-239.9

153.5 Appendix

➡ **CC Excl:** 153.5, 153.8-153.9, 159.0, 159.8-159.9, 176.3, 195.8, 199.0-199.1, 239.0, 239.8-239.9

153.6 Ascending colon

Right colon

➡ **CC Excl:** 153.6, 153.8-153.9, 159.0, 159.8-159.9, 176.3, 195.8, 199.0-199.1, 239.0, 239.8-239.9

153.7 Splenic flexure

➡ **CC Excl:** 153.7-153.9, 159.0, 159.8-159.9, 176.3, 195.8, 199.0-199.1, 239.0, 239.8-239.9

153.8 Other specified sites of large intestine

Malignant neoplasm of contiguous or overlapping sites of colon whose point of origin cannot be determined

Excludes: *ileocecal valve (153.4)*
rectosigmoid junction (154.0)

➡ **CC Excl:** 153.8-153.9, 159.0, 159.8-159.9, 176.3, 195.8, 199.0-199.1, 239.0, 239.8-239.9

153.9 Colon, unspecified

Large intestine NOS

➡ **CC Excl:** see Code 153.8

154 Malignant neoplasm of rectum, rectosigmoid junction, and anus

154.0 Rectosigmoid junction

Colon with rectum
Rectosigmoid (colon)

➡ **CC Excl:** 154.0, 154.8, 159.0, 159.8-159.9, 176.3, 195.8, 199.0-199.1, 239.0, 239.8-239.9

154.1 Rectum

Rectal ampulla

➡ **CC Excl:** 154.1, 154.8, 159.0, 159.8-159.9, 176.3, 195.8, 199.0-199.1, 239.0, 239.8-239.9

154.2 Anal canal

Anal sphincter

Excludes: *skin of anus (172.5, 173.5)*

➡ **CC Excl:** 154.2-154.8, 159.0, 159.8-159.9, 176.3, 195.8, 199.0-199.1, 239.0, 239.8-239.9

154.3 Anus, unspecified

Excludes: *anus:*
margin (172.5, 173.5)
skin (172.5, 173.5)
perianal skin (172.5, 173.5)

➡ **CC Excl:** see Code 154.2

154.8 Other

Anorectum
Cloacogenic zone
Malignant neoplasm of contiguous or overlapping sites of rectum, rectosigmoid junction, and anus whose point of origin cannot be determined

➡ **CC Excl:** 154.8, 159.0, 159.8-159.9, 176.3, 195.8, 199.0-199.1, 239.0, 239.8-239.9

155 Malignant neoplasm of liver and intrahepatic bile ducts

155.0 Liver, primary

Carcinoma:
liver, specified as primary
hepatocellular
liver cell
Hepatoblastoma

➡ **CC Excl:**155.0-155.2, 159.0, 159.8-159.9, 176.3, 195.8, 199.0-199.1, 239.0, 239.8-239.9

155.1 Intrahepatic bile ducts

Canaliculi biliferi
Interlobular:
bile ducts
biliary canals
Intrahepatic:
biliary passages
canaliculi
gall duct

Excludes: *hepatic duct (156.1)*

➡ **CC Excl:** see Code 155.0

155.2 Liver, not specified as primary or secondary

➡ **CC Excl:** see Code 155.0

156 Malignant neoplasm of gallbladder and extrahepatic bile ducts

156.0 Gallbladder

➡ **CC Excl:** 156.0, 156.8-156.9, 159.0, 159.8-159.9, 176.3, 195.8, 199.0-199.1, 239.0, 239.8-239.9

156.1 Extrahepatic bile ducts

Biliary duct or passage NOS
Common bile duct
Cystic duct
Hepatic duct
Sphincter of Oddi

➡ **CC Excl:** 156.1, 156.8-156.9, 159.0, 159.8-159.9, 176.3, 195.8, 199.0-199.1, 239.0, 239.8-239.9

156.2 Ampulla of Vater

➡ **CC Excl:** 156.2-156.9, 159.0, 159.8-159.9, 176.3, 195.8, 199.0-199.1, 239.0, 239.8-239.9

156.8 Other specified sites of gallbladder and extrahepatic bile ducts

Malignant neoplasm of contiguous or overlapping sites of gallbladder and extrahepatic bile ducts whose point of origin cannot be determined

➡ **CC Excl:** 156.8-156.9, 159.0, 159.8-159.9, 176.3, 195.8, 199.0-199.1, 239.0, 239.8-239.9

156.9 Biliary tract, part unspecified

Malignant neoplasm involving both intrahepatic and extrahepatic bile ducts

➡ **CC Excl:** see Code 156.8

157 Malignant neoplasm of pancreas

157.0 Head of pancreas

➡ **CC Excl:** 157.0-157.9, 159.0, 159.8-159.9, 176.3, 195.8, 199.0-199.1, 239.0, 239.8-239.9

157.1 Body of pancreas

➡ **CC Excl:** see Code 157.0

157.2 Tail of pancreas

➡ **CC Excl:** see Code 157.0

157.3 Pancreatic duct

Duct of:
  Santorini
  Wirsung

➡ **CC Excl:** see Code 157.0

157.4 Islets of Langerhans

Islets of Langerhans, any part of pancreas

Use additional code to identify any functional activity

➡ **CC Excl:** see Code 157.0

157.8 Other specified sites of pancreas

Ectopic pancreatic tissue
Malignant neoplasm of contiguous or overlapping sites of pancreas whose point of origin cannot be determined

➡ **CC Excl:** see Code 157.0

157.9 Pancreas, part unspecified

➡ **CC Excl:** see Code 157.0

➡ **AHA Coding Clinic:** 4Q, '89, 11

158 Malignant neoplasm of retroperitoneum and peritoneum

158.0 Retroperitoneum

Periadrenal tissue
Perinephric tissue
Perirenal tissue
Retrocecal tissue

158.8 Specified parts of peritoneum

Cul-de-sac (of Douglas)
Mesentery
Mesocolon
Omentum
Peritoneum:
  parietal
  pelvic
Rectouterine pouch
Malignant neoplasm of contiguous or overlapping sites of retroperitoneum and peritoneum whose point of origin cannot be determined

158.9 Peritoneum, unspecified

159 Malignant neoplasm of other and ill-defined sites within the digestive organs and peritoneum

159.0 Intestinal tract, part unspecified

Intestine NOS

159.1 Spleen, not elsewhere classified

Angiosarcoma } of spleen
Fibrosarcoma } of spleen

Excludes: *Hodgkin's disease (201.0-201.9)*
lymphosarcoma (200.1)
reticulosarcoma (200.0)

159.8 Other sites of digestive system and intra-abdominal organs

Malignant neoplasm of digestive organs and peritoneum whose point of origin cannot be assigned to any one of the categories 150-158

Excludes: *anus and rectum (154.8)*
cardio-esophageal junction (151.0)
colon and rectum (154.0)

159.9 Ill-defined

Alimentary canal or tract NOS
Gastrointestinal tract NOS

Excludes: *abdominal NOS (195.2)*
intra-abdominal NOS (195.2)

MALIGNANT NEOPLASM OF RESPIRATORY AND INTRATHORACIC ORGANS (160-165)

Excludes: *carcinoma in situ (231.0-231.9)*

160 Malignant neoplasm of nasal cavities, middle ear, and accessory sinuses

160.0 Nasal cavities

Cartilage of nose
Conchae, nasal
Internal nose
Septum of nose
Vestibule of nose

Excludes: *nasal bone (170.0)*
nose NOS (195.0)
olfactory bulb (192.0)
posterior margin of septum and choanae (147.3)
skin of nose (172.3, 173.3)
turbinates (170.0)

160.1 Auditory tube, middle ear, and mastoid air cells

Antrum tympanicum
Eustachian tube
Tympanic cavity

Excludes: *auditory canal (external) (172.2, 173.2)*
bone of ear (meatus) (170.0)
cartilage of ear (171.0)
ear (external) (skin) (172.2, 173.2)

160.2 Maxillary sinus

Antrum (Highmore) (maxillary)

160.3 Ethmoidal sinus

160.4 Frontal sinus

160.5 Sphenoidal sinus

160.8 Other

Malignant neoplasm of contiguous or overlapping sites of nasal cavities, middle ear, and accessory sinuses whose point of origin cannot be determined

160.9 Accessory sinus, unspecified

161 Malignant neoplasm of larynx

161.0 Glottis

Intrinsic larynx
Laryngeal commissure (anterior) (posterior)
True vocal cord
Vocal cord NOS

161.1 Supraglottis

Aryepiglottic fold or interarytenoid fold, laryngeal aspect
Epiglottis (suprahyoid portion) NOS
Extrinsic larynx
False vocal cords
Posterior (laryngeal) surface of epiglottis
Ventricular bands

Excludes: *anterior aspect of epiglottis (146.4)*
aryepiglottic fold or interarytenoid fold:
NOS (148.2)
hypopharyngeal aspect (148.2)
marginal zone (148.2)

161.2 Subglottis

161.3 Laryngeal cartilages

Cartilage:
arytenoid
cricoid
Cartilage:
cuneiform
thyroid

161.8 Other specified sites of larynx

Malignant neoplasm of contiguous or overlapping sites of larynx whose point of origin cannot be determined

161.9 Larynx, unspecified

162 Malignant neoplasm of trachea, bronchus, and lung

162.0 Trachea

Cartilage } of trachea
Mucosa } of trachea

162.2 Main bronchus

Carina
Hilus of lung

➡ **CC Excl:** 162.2, 162.8-162.9, 165.8-165.9, 176.4, 195.8, 199.0-199.1, 239.1, 239.8-239.9

162.3 Upper lobe, bronchus or lung

➡ **CC Excl:** 162.3, 162.8-162.9, 165.8-165.9, 176.4, 195.8, 199.0-199.1, 239.1, 239.8-239.9

162.4 Middle lobe, bronchus or lung

➡ **CC Excl:** 162.4, 162.8-162.9, 165.8-165.9, 176.4, 195.8, 199.0-199.1, 239.1, 239.8-239.9

162.5 Lower lobe, bronchus or lung

➡ **CC Excl:** 162.5-162.9, 165.8-165.9, 176.4, 195.8, 199.0-199.1, 239.1, 239.8-239.9

162.8 Other parts of bronchus or lung

Malignant neoplasm of contiguous or overlapping sites of bronchus or lung whose point of origin cannot be determined

➡ **CC Excl:** 162.8-162.9, 165.8-165.9, 176.4, 195.8, 199.0-199.1, 239.1, 239.8-239.9

162.9 Bronchus and lung, unspecified

➡ **CC Excl:** see Code 162.8

➡ **AHA Coding Clinic:** 2Q, '97, 3; 4Q, '96, 48

163 Malignant neoplasm of pleura

163.0 Parietal pleura

➡ **CC Excl:** 163.0-163.9, 165.8-165.9, 195.8, 199.0-199.1, 239.1, 239.8-239.9

163.1 Visceral pleura

➡ **CC Excl:** see Code 163.0

163.8 Other specified sites of pleura

Malignant neoplasm of contiguous or overlapping sites of pleura whose point of origin cannot be determined

➡ **CC Excl:** see Code 163.0

163.9 Pleura, unspecified

➡ **CC Excl:** see Code 163.0

164 Malignant neoplasm of thymus, heart, and mediastinum

164.0 Thymus

➡ **CC Excl:** 164.0

164.1 Heart

Endocardium
Epicardium
Myocardium
Pericardium

Excludes: *great vessels (171.4)*

➡ **CC Excl:** 164.1

164.2 Anterior mediastinum

➡ **CC Excl:** 164.2-164.9, 165.8-165.9, 195.8, 199.0-199.1, 239.1, 239.8-239.9

164.3 **Posterior mediastinum**

➡ **CC Excl:** see Code 164.2

164.8 **Other**

Malignant neoplasm of contiguous or overlapping sites of thymus, heart, and mediastinum whose point of origin cannot be determined

➡ **CC Excl:** see Code 164.2

164.9 **Mediastinum, part unspecified**

➡ **CC Excl:** see Code 164.2

165 Malignant neoplasm of other and ill-defined sites within the respiratory system and intrathoracic organs

165.0 **Upper respiratory tract, part unspecified**

165.8 **Other**

Malignant neoplasm of respiratory and intrathoracic organs whose point of origin cannot be assigned to any one of the categories 160-164

165.9 **Ill-defined sites within the respiratory system**

Respiratory tract NOS

Excludes: *intrathoracic NOS (195.1)*
thoracic NOS (195.1)

MALIGNANT NEOPLASM OF BONE, CONNECTIVE TISSUE, SKIN, AND BREAST (170-176)

Excludes: *carcinoma in situ:*
breast (233.0)
skin (232.0-232.9)

170 Malignant neoplasm of bone and articular cartilage

Includes: cartilage (articular) (joint)
periosteum

Excludes: *bone marrow NOS (202.9)*
cartilage:
ear (171.0)
eyelid (171.0)
larynx (161.3)
nose (160.0)
synovia (171.0-171.9)

170.0 **Bones of skull and face, except mandible**

Bone:
ethmoid
frontal
malar
nasal
occipital
orbital
parietal

Bone:
sphenoid
temporal
zygomatic
Maxilla (superior)
Turbinate
Upper jaw bone
Vomer

Excludes: *carcinoma, any type except intraosseous or odontogenic:*
jaw bone (lower) (170.1)
maxilla, maxillary (sinus) (160.2)
upper jaw bone (143.0)

170.1 **Mandible**

Inferior maxilla
Jaw bone NOS
Lower jaw bone

Excludes: *carcinoma, any type except intraosseous or odontogenic:*
jaw bone NOS (143.9)
lower (143.1)
upper jaw bone (170.0)

170.2 **Vertebral column, excluding sacrum and coccyx**

Spinal column
Spine
Vertebra

Excludes: *sacrum and coccyx (170.6)*

170.3 **Ribs, sternum, and clavicle**

Costal cartilage
Costovertebral joint
Xiphoid process

170.4 **Scapula and long bones of upper limb**

Acromion
Bones NOS of upper limb
Humerus
Radius
Ulna

170.5 **Short bones of upper limb**

Carpal
Cuneiform, wrist
Metacarpal
Navicular, of hand
Phalanges of hand
Pisiform
Scaphoid (of hand)
Semilunar or lunate
Trapezium
Trapezoid
Unciform

170.6 **Pelvic bones, sacrum, and coccyx**

Coccygeal vertebra
Ilium
Ischium
Pubic bone
Sacral vertebra

170.7 **Long bones of lower limb**

Bones NOS of lower limb
Femur
Fibula
Tibia

170.8 **Short bones of lower limb**

Astragalus [talus]
Calcaneus
Cuboid
Cuneiform, ankle
Metatarsal
Navicular (of ankle)
Patella
Phalanges of foot
Tarsal

170.9 **Bone and articular cartilage, site unspecified**

171 Malignant neoplasm of connective and other soft tissue

Includes: blood vessel
bursa
fascia
fat
ligament, except uterine
muscle
peripheral, sympathetic, and parasympathetic nerves and ganglia
synovia
tendon (sheath)

Excludes: *cartilage (of):*
articular (170.0-170.9)
larynx (161.3)
nose (160.0)
connective tissue:
breast (174.0-175.9)
internal organs — code to malignant neoplasm of the site [e.g., leiomyosarcoma of stomach, 151.9]
heart (164.1)
uterine ligament (183.4)

171.0 Head, face, and neck

Cartilage of:
ear
eyelid

171.2 Upper limb, including shoulder

Arm
Finger
Forearm
Hand

171.3 Lower limb, including hip

Foot
Leg
Popliteal space
Thigh
Toe

171.4 Thorax

Axilla
Diaphragm
Great vessels

Excludes: *heart (164.1)*
mediastinum (164.2-164.9)
thymus (164.0)

171.5 Abdomen

Abdominal wall
Hypochondrium

Excludes: *peritoneum (158.8)*
retroperitoneum (158.0)

171.6 Pelvis

Buttock
Groin
Inguinal region
Perineum

Excludes: *pelvic peritoneum (158.8)*
retroperitoneum (158.0)
uterine ligament, any (183.3-183.5)

171.7 Trunk, unspecified

Back NOS
Flank NOS

171.8 Other specified sites of connective and other soft tissue

Malignant neoplasm of contiguous or overlapping sites of connective tissue whose point of origin cannot be determined

171.9 Connective and other soft tissue, site unspecified

172 Malignant melanoma of skin

Includes: melanocarcinoma
melanoma (skin) NOS

Excludes: *skin of genital organs (184.0-184.9, 187.1-187.9)*
sites other than skin — code to malignant neoplasm of the site

172.0 Lip

Excludes: *vermilion border of lip (140.0-140.1, 140.9)*

172.1 Eyelid, including canthus

172.2 Ear and external auditory canal

Auricle (ear)
Auricular canal, external
External [acoustic] meatus
Pinna

172.3 Other and unspecified parts of face

Cheek (external)
Chin
Eyebrow
Forehead
Nose, external
Temple

172.4 Scalp and neck

172.5 Trunk, except scrotum

Axilla
Breast
Buttock
Groin
Perianal skin
Perineum
Umbilicus

Excludes: *anal canal (154.2)*
anus NOS (154.3)
scrotum (187.7)

172.6 Upper limb, including shoulder

Arm
Finger
Forearm
Hand

172.7 Lower limb, including hip

Ankle
Foot
Heel
Knee
Leg
Popliteal area
Thigh
Toe

172.8 Other specified sites of skin

Malignant melanoma of contiguous or overlapping sites of skin whose point of origin cannot be determined

172.9 Melanoma of skin, site unspecified

173 Other malignant neoplasm of skin

Includes: malignant neoplasm of:
- sebaceous glands
- sudoriferous, sudoriparous glands
- sweat glands

Excludes: *Kaposi's sarcoma (176.0-176.9)*
malignant melanoma of skin (172.0-172.9)
skin of genital organs (184.0-184.9, 187.1-187.9)

➡ **AHA Coding Clinic:** 2Q, '96, 12

173.0 Skin of lip

Excludes: *vermilion border of lip (140.0-140.1, 140.9)*

173.1 Eyelid, including canthus

Excludes: *cartilage of eyelid (171.0)*

173.2 Skin of ear and external auditory canal

Auricle (ear)
Auricular canal, external
External meatus
Pinna

Excludes: *cartilage of ear (171.0)*

173.3 Skin of other and unspecified parts of face

Cheek, external
Chin
Eyebrow
Forehead
Nose, external
Temple

173.4 Scalp and skin of neck

173.5 Skin of trunk, except scrotum

Axillary fold
Perianal skin
Skin of:
- abdominal wall
- anus
- back
- breast
- buttock
- chest wall
- groin
- perineum

Umbilicus

Excludes: *anal canal (154.2)*
anus NOS (154.3)
skin of scrotum (187.7)

173.6 Skin of upper limb, including shoulder

Arm
Finger
Forearm
Hand

173.7 Skin of lower limb, including hip

Ankle
Foot
Heel
Knee
Leg
Popliteal area
Thigh
Toe

173.8 Other specified sites of skin

Malignant neoplasm of contiguous or overlapping sites of skin whose point of origin cannot be determined

173.9 Skin, site unspecified

174 Malignant neoplasm of female breast ♀

Includes: breast (female)
- connective tissue
- soft parts

Paget's disease of:
- breast
- nipple

Excludes: *skin of breast (172.5, 173.5)*

➡ **AHA Coding Clinic:** 3Q, '97, 8; 4Q, '89, 11

174.0 Nipple and areola

174.1 Central portion

174.2 Upper-inner quadrant

174.3 Lower-inner quadrant

174.4 Upper-outer quadrant

174.5 Lower-outer quadrant

174.6 Axillary tail

174.8 Other specified sites of female breast

Ectopic sites
Inner breast
Lower breast
Midline of breast
Outer breast
Upper breast
Malignant neoplasm of contiguous or overlapping sites of breast whose point of origin cannot be determined

174.9 Breast (female), unspecified

175 Malignant neoplasm of male breast ♂

Excludes: *skin of breast (172.5, 173.5)*

175.0 Nipple and areola

175.9 Other and unspecified sites of male breast

Ectopic breast tissue, male

176 Kaposi's sarcoma

➡ **AHA Coding Clinic:** 4Q, '91, 24

176.0 Skin

176.1 Soft tissue

Includes: blood vessel
- connective tissue
- fascia
- ligament
- lymphatic(s) NEC
- muscle

Excludes: *lymph glands and nodes (176.5)*

176.2 Palate

176.3 Gastrointestinal sites

176.4 **Lung**
➡ **CC Excl:** 162.8-162.9, 165.8-165.9, 176.4, 195.8, 199.0-199.1, 239.1, 239.8-239.9

176.5 **Lymph nodes**
➡ **CC Excl:** 176.5, 195.8, 196.0-196.9, 199.0-199.1, 239.8-239.9

176.8 **Other specified sites**
Includes: oral cavity NEC

176.9 **Unspecified**
Viscera NOS

MALIGNANT NEOPLASM OF GENITOURINARY ORGANS (179-189)

Excludes: *carcinoma in situ (233.1-233.9)*

179 Malignant neoplasm of uterus, part unspecified ♀

180 Malignant neoplasm of cervix uteri ♀
Includes: invasive malignancy [carcinoma]

Excludes: *carcinoma in situ (233.1)*

180.0 **Endocervix**
Cervical canal NOS
Endocervical canal
Endocervical gland

180.1 **Exocervix**

180.8 **Other specified sites of cervix**
Cervical stump
Squamocolumnar junction of cervix
Malignant neoplasm of contiguous or overlapping sites of cervix uteri whose point of origin cannot be determined

180.9 **Cervix uteri, unspecified**

181 Malignant neoplasm of placenta ♀
Choriocarcinoma NOS
Chorioepithelioma NOS

Excludes: *chorioadenoma (destruens) (236.1)*
hydatidiform mole (630)
malignant (236.1)
invasive mole (236.1)
male choriocarcinoma NOS (186.0-186.9)

182 Malignant neoplasm of body of uterus ♀

Excludes: *carcinoma in situ (233.2)*

182.0 **Corpus uteri, except isthmus**
Cornu
Endometrium
Fundus
Myometrium

182.1 **Isthmus**
Lower uterine segment

182.8 **Other specified sites of body of uterus**
Malignant neoplasm of contiguous or overlapping sites of body of uterus whose point of origin cannot be determined

Excludes: *uterus NOS (179)*

183 Malignant neoplasm of ovary and other uterine adnexa ♀

Excludes: *Douglas' cul-de-sac (158.8)*

183.0 **Ovary**
Use additional code to identify any functional activity

183.2 **Fallopian tube**
Oviduct
Uterine tube

183.3 **Broad ligament**
Mesovarium
Parovarian region

183.4 **Parametrium**
Uterine ligament NOS
Uterosacral ligament

183.5 **Round ligament**

183.8 **Other specified sites of uterine adnexa**
Tubo-ovarian
Utero-ovarian
Malignant neoplasm of contiguous or overlapping sites of ovary and other uterine adnexa whose point of origin cannot be determined

183.9 **Uterine adnexa, unspecified**

184 Malignant neoplasm of other and unspecified female genital organs ♀

Excludes: *carcinoma in situ (233.3)*

184.0 **Vagina**
Gartner's duct
Vaginal vault

184.1 **Labia majora**
Greater vestibular [Bartholin's] gland

184.2 **Labia minora**

184.3 **Clitoris**

184.4 **Vulva, unspecified**
External female genitalia NOS
Pudendum

184.8 **Other specified sites of female genital organs**
Malignant neoplasm of contiguous or overlapping sites of female genital organs whose point of origin cannot be determined

184.9 **Female genital organ, site unspecified**
Female genitourinary tract NOS

185 Malignant neoplasm of prostate ♂

Excludes: *seminal vesicles (187.8)*

186 Malignant neoplasm of testis ♂

Use additional code to identify any functional activity

186.0 Undescended testis

Ectopic testis
Retained testis

186.9 Other and unspecified testis

Testis:
- NOS
- descended
- scrotal

187 Malignant neoplasm of penis and other male genital organs ♂

187.1 Prepuce

Foreskin

187.2 Glans penis

187.3 Body of penis

Corpus cavernosum

187.4 Penis, part unspecified

Skin of penis NOS

187.5 Epididymis

187.6 Spermatic cord

Vas deferens

187.7 Scrotum

Skin of scrotum

187.8 Other specified sites of male genital organs

Seminal vesicle
Tunica vaginalis
Malignant neoplasm of contiguous or overlapping sites of penis and other male genital organs whose point of origin cannot be determined

187.9 Male genital organ, site unspecified

Male genital organ or tract NOS

188 Malignant neoplasm of bladder

Excludes: *carcinoma in situ (233.7)*

188.0 Trigone of urinary bladder

188.1 Dome of urinary bladder

188.2 Lateral wall of urinary bladder

188.3 Anterior wall of urinary bladder

188.4 Posterior wall of urinary bladder

188.5 Bladder neck

Internal urethral orifice

188.6 Ureteric orifice

188.7 Urachus

188.8 Other specified sites of bladder

Malignant neoplasm of contiguous or overlapping sites of bladder whose point of origin cannot be determined

188.9 Bladder, part unspecified

Bladder wall NOS

189 Malignant neoplasm of kidney and other and unspecified urinary organs

189.0 Kidney, except pelvis

Kidney NOS
Kidney parenchyma

➡ **CC Excl:** 189.0-189.1, 189.8-189.9, 195.8, 199.0-199.1, 239.5, 239.8-239.9

189.1 Renal pelvis

Renal calyces
Ureteropelvic junction

➡ **CC Excl:** see Code 189.0

189.2 Ureter

Excludes: *ureteric orifice of bladder (188.6)*

➡ **CC Excl:** 189.2, 189.8-189.9, 195.8, 199.0-199.1, 239.5, 239.8-239.9

189.3 Urethra

Excludes: *urethral orifice of bladder (188.5)*

189.4 Paraurethral glands

189.8 Other specified sites of urinary organs

Malignant neoplasm of contiguous or overlapping sites of kidney and other urinary organs whose point of origin cannot be determined

189.9 Urinary organ, site unspecified

Urinary system NOS

MALIGNANT NEOPLASM OF OTHER AND UNSPECIFIED SITES (190-199)

Excludes: *carcinoma in situ (234.0-234.9)*

190 Malignant neoplasm of eye

Excludes: *carcinoma in situ (234.0)*
eyelid (skin) (172.1, 173.1)
cartilage (171.0)
optic nerve (192.0)
orbital bone (170.0)

190.0 Eyeball, except conjunctiva, cornea, retina, and choroid
Ciliary body
Crystalline lens
Iris
Sclera
Uveal tract

190.1 Orbit
Connective tissue of orbit
Extraocular muscle
Retrobulbar

Excludes: *bone of orbit (170.0)*

190.2 Lacrimal gland

190.3 Conjunctiva

190.4 Cornea

190.5 Retina

190.6 Choroid

190.7 Lacrimal duct
Lacrimal sac
Nasolacrimal duct

190.8 Other specified sites of eye
Malignant neoplasm of contiguous or overlapping sites of eye whose point of origin cannot be determined

190.9 Eye, part unspecified

191 Malignant neoplasm of brain

Excludes: *cranial nerves (192.0)*
retrobulbar area (190.1)

191.0 Cerebrum, except lobes and ventricles
Basal ganglia
Cerebral cortex
Corpus striatum
Globus pallidus
Hypothalamus
Thalamus

➡ **CC Excl:** 191.0-191.9, 192.0-192.1, 192.8-192.9, 195.8, 199.0-199.1, 239.6-239.9

191.1 Frontal lobe
➡ **CC Excl:** see Code 191.0

191.2 Temporal lobe
Hippocampus
Uncus

➡ **CC Excl:** see Code 191.0

191.3 Parietal lobe
➡ **CC Excl:** see Code 191.0

191.4 Occipital lobe
➡ **CC Excl:** see Code 191.0

191.5 Ventricles
Choroid plexus
Floor of ventricle

➡ **CC Excl:** see Code 191.0

191.6 Cerebellum NOS
Cerebellopontine angle

➡ **CC Excl:** see Code 191.0

191.7 Brain stem
Cerebral peduncle
Medulla oblongata
Midbrain
Pons

➡ **CC Excl:** see Code 191.0

191.8 Other parts of brain
Corpus callosum
Tapetum
Malignant neoplasm of contiguous or overlapping sites of brain whose point of origin cannot be determined

➡ **CC Excl:** see Code 191.0

191.9 Brain, unspecified
Cranial fossa NOS

➡ **CC Excl:** see Code 191.0

192 Malignant neoplasm of other and unspecified parts of nervous system

Excludes: *peripheral, sympathetic, and parasympathetic nerves and ganglia (171.0-171.9)*

192.0 Cranial nerves
Olfactory bulb

➡ **CC Excl:** 192.0, 192.8-192.9, 195.8, 199.0-199.1, 239.6-239.9

192.1 Cerebral meninges
Dura (mater)
Falx (cerebelli) (cerebri)
Meninges NOS
Tentorium

➡ **CC Excl:** 192.1, 192.8-192.9, 195.8, 199.0-199.1, 239.6-239.9

192.2 Spinal cord
Cauda equina

➡ **CC Excl:** 192.2, 192.8-192.9, 195.8, 199.0-199.1, 239.6-239.9

192.3 Spinal meninges
➡ **CC Excl:** 192.3-192.9, 195.8, 199.0-199.1, 239.6-239.9

192.8 Other specified sites of nervous system
Malignant neoplasm of contiguous or overlapping sites of other parts of nervous system whose point of origin cannot be determined

➡ **CC Excl:** 191.0-191.9, 192.0-192.9, 195.8, 199.0-199.1, 239.6-239.9

192.9 Nervous system, part unspecified
Nervous system (central) NOS

Excludes: *meninges NOS (192.1)*

193 Malignant neoplasm of thyroid gland

Sipple's syndrome
Thyroglossal duct

Use additional code to identify any functional activity

194 Malignant neoplasm of other endocrine glands and related structures

Use additional code to identify any functional activity

Excludes: *islets of Langerhans (157.4)*
ovary (183.0)
testis (186.0-186.9)
thymus (164.0)

194.0 Adrenal gland

Adrenal cortex
Adrenal medulla
Suprarenal gland

194.1 Parathyroid gland

194.3 Pituitary gland and craniopharyngeal duct

Craniobuccal pouch
Hypophysis
Rathke's pouch
Sella turcica

➡ **AHA Coding Clinic:** J-A, '85, 9

194.4 Pineal gland

194.5 Carotid body

194.6 Aortic body and other paraganglia

Coccygeal body
Glomus jugulare
Para-aortic body

194.8 Other

Pluriglandular involvement NOS

Note: If the sites of multiple involvements are known, they should be coded separately.

194.9 Endocrine gland, site unspecified

195 Malignant neoplasm of other and ill-defined sites

Includes: malignant neoplasms of contiguous sites, not elsewhere classified, whose point of origin cannot be determined

Excludes: *malignant neoplasm:*
lymphatic and hematopoietic tissue (200.0-208.9)
secondary sites (196.0-198.8)
unspecified site (199.0-199.1)

195.0 Head, face, and neck

Cheek NOS
Jaw NOS
Nose NOS
Supraclavicular region NOS

195.1 Thorax

Axilla
Chest (wall) NOS
Intrathoracic NOS

195.2 Abdomen

Intra-abdominal NOS

➡ **AHA Coding Clinic:** 2Q, '97, 3

195.3 Pelvis

Groin
Inguinal region NOS
Presacral region
Sacrococcygeal region
Sites overlapping systems within pelvis, as:
rectovaginal (septum)
rectovesical (septum)

195.4 Upper limb

195.5 Lower limb

195.8 Other specified sites

Back NOS
Flank NOS
Trunk NOS

196 Secondary and unspecified malignant neoplasm of lymph nodes

Excludes: *any malignant neoplasm of lymph nodes, specified as primary (200.0-202.9)*
Hodgkin's disease (201.0-201.9)
lymphosarcoma (200.1)
other forms of lymphoma (202.0-202.9)
reticulosarcoma (200.0)

➡ **AHA Coding Clinic:** 2Q, '92, 3

196.0 Lymph nodes of head, face, and neck

Cervical
Cervicofacial
Scalene
Supraclavicular

➡ **CC Excl:** 176.5, 195.8, 196.0-196.9, 199.0-199.1, 239.8-239.9

196.1 Intrathoracic lymph nodes

Bronchopulmonary
Intercostal
Mediastinal
Tracheobronchial

➡ **CC Excl:** see Code 196.0

196.2 Intra-abdominal lymph nodes

Intestinal
Mesenteric
Retroperitoneal

➡ **CC Excl:** see Code 196.0

196.3 Lymph nodes of axilla and upper limb

Brachial
Epitrochlear
Infraclavicular
Pectoral

➡ **CC Excl:** see Code 196.0

196.5 Lymph nodes of inguinal region and lower limb

Femoral
Groin
Popliteal
Tibial

➡ **CC Excl:** see Code 196.0

196.6 **Intrapelvic lymph nodes**
Hypogastric
Iliac
Obturator
Parametrial
➡ **CC Excl:** see Code 196.0

196.8 **Lymph nodes of multiple sites**
➡ **CC Excl:** see Code 196.0

196.9 **Site unspecified**
Lymph nodes NOS
➡ **CC Excl:** see Code 196.0

197 Secondary malignant neoplasm of respiratory and digestive systems

Excludes: *lymph node metastasis (196.0-196.9)*

197.0 **Lung**
Bronchus
➡ **CC Excl:** 195.8, 197.0, 197.3, 198.89, 199.0-199.1, 239.8-239.9

197.1 **Mediastinum**
➡ **CC Excl:** 195.8, 197.1, 197.3, 198.89, 199.0-199.1, 239.8-239.9

197.2 **Pleura**
➡ **CC Excl:** 195.8, 197.2-197.3, 198.89, 199.0-199.1, 239.8-239.9
➡ **AHA Coding Clinic:** 4Q, '89, 11

197.3 **Other respiratory organs**
Trachea
➡ **CC Excl:** 195.8, 197.0-197.3, 198.89, 199.0-199.1, 239.8-239.9

197.4 **Small intestine, including duodenum**
➡ **CC Excl:** 195.8, 197.4, 197.8, 198.89, 199.0-199.1, 239.8-239.9

197.5 **Large intestine and rectum**
➡ **CC Excl:** 195.8, 197.5, 197.8, 198.89, 199.0-199.1, 239.8-239.9

197.6 **Retroperitoneum and peritoneum**
➡ **CC Excl:** 195.8, 197.6, 197.8, 198.89, 199.0-199.1, 239.8-239.9
➡ **AHA Coding Clinic:** 4Q, '89, 11

197.7 **Liver, specified as secondary**
➡ **CC Excl:** 195.8, 197.7-197.8, 198.89, 199.0-199.1, 239.8-239.9

197.8 **Other digestive organs and spleen**
➡ **CC Excl:** 195.8, 197.4-197.8, 198.89, 199.0-199.1, 239.8-239.9
➡ **AHA Coding Clinic:** 2Q, '97, 3; 2Q, '92, 3

198 Secondary malignant neoplasm of other specified sites

Excludes: *lymph node metastasis (196.0-196.9)*

198.0 **Kidney**
➡ **CC Excl:** 195.8, 198.0-198.1, 198.89, 199.0-199.1, 239.8-239.9

198.1 **Other urinary organs**
➡ **CC Excl:** see Code 198.0

198.2 **Skin**
Skin of breast
➡ **CC Excl:** 195.8, 198.2, 198.89, 199.0-199.1, 239.8-239.9

198.3 **Brain and spinal cord**
➡ **CC Excl:** 195.8, 198.3, 198.89, 199.0-199.1, 239.8-239.9

198.4 **Other parts of nervous system**
Meninges (cerebral) (spinal)
➡ **CC Excl:** 195.8, 198.4, 198.89, 199.0-199.1, 239.8-239.9
➡ **AHA Coding Clinic:** J-F, '87, 7

198.5 **Bone and bone marrow**
➡ **CC Excl:** 195.8, 198.5, 198.89, 199.0-199.1, 239.8-239.9
➡ **AHA Coding Clinic:** 2Q, '92, 3; 1Q, '91, 16; 4Q, '89, 10
DRG 239

198.6 **Ovary** ♀
➡ **CC Excl:** 195.8, 198.6, 198.89, 199.0-199.1, 239.8-239.9

198.7 **Adrenal gland**
Suprarenal gland
➡ **CC Excl:** 195.8, 198.7, 198.89, 199.0-199.1, 239.8-239.9

✓5th **198.8** **Other specified sites**

198.81 **Breast**

Excludes: *skin of breast (198.2)*

➡ **CC Excl:** 195.8, 198.81, 198.89, 199.0-199.1, 239.8-239.9

198.82 **Genital organs**

➡ **CC Excl:** 195.8, 198.82, 198.89, 199.0-199.1, 239.8-239.9

198.89 **Other**

Excludes: *retroperitoneal lymph nodes (196.2)*

➡ **CC Excl:** 195.8, 198.89, 199.0-199.1, 239.8-239.9

➡ **AHA Coding Clinic:** 2Q, '97, 4

199 Malignant neoplasm without specification of site

199.0 **Disseminated**

Carcinomatosis
Generalized:
  cancer
  malignancy
Multiple cancer
} unspecified site (primary) (secondary)

➡ **CC Excl:** see Code 198.89

➡ **AHA Coding Clinic:** 4Q, '89, 10

199.1 **Other**

Cancer
Carcinoma
Malignancy
} unspecified site (primary) (secondary)

MALIGNANT NEOPLASM OF LYMPHATIC AND HEMATOPOIETIC TISSUE (200-208)

Excludes: *secondary neoplasm of:*
bone marrow (198.5)
spleen (197.8)
secondary and unspecified neoplasm of lymph nodes (196.0-196.9)

The following fifth-digit subclassification is for use with categories 200-202:

0 unspecified site, extranodal and solid organ sites
1 lymph nodes of head, face, and neck
2 intrathoracic lymph nodes
3 intra-abdominal lymph nodes
4 lymph nodes of axilla and upper limb
5 lymph nodes of inguinal region and lower limb
6 intrapelvic lymph nodes
7 spleen
8 lymph nodes of multiple sites

§ 200 Lymphosarcoma and reticulosarcoma

➡ **AHA Coding Clinic:** 2Q, '92, 3; N-D, '86, 5

✓5th **200.0** **Reticulosarcoma**

Lymphoma (malignant):
  histiocytic (diffuse):
    nodular
    pleomorphic cell type
  reticulum cell type
Reticulum cell sarcoma:
  NOS
  pleomorphic cell type

➡ **CC Excl: For code 200.00:** 200.00-200.08, 239.8-239.9

➡ **CC Excl: For code 200.01:** 200.00, 200.01, 200.08, 239.8-239.9

➡ **CC Excl: For code 200.02:** 200.00, 200.02, 200.08, 239.8-239.9

➡ **CC Excl: For code 200.03:** 200.00, 200.03, 200.08, 239.8-239.9

➡ **CC Excl: For code 200.04:** 200.00, 200.04, 200.08, 239.8-239.9

➡ **CC Excl: For code 200.05:** 200.00, 200.05, 200.08, 239.8-239.9

➡ **CC Excl: For code 200.06:** 200.00, 200.06, 200.08, 239.8-239.9

➡ **CC Excl: For code 200.07:** 200.00, 200.07-200.08, 239.8-239.9

➡ **CC Excl: For code 200.08:** 200.00-200.08, 239.8-239.9

§ Requires fifth-digit. See above, page this for codes and definitions.

✓5th **200.1 Lymphosarcoma**

Lymphoblastoma (diffuse)
Lymphoma (malignant):
lymphoblastic (diffuse)
lymphocytic (cell type) (diffuse)
lymphosarcoma type
Lymphosarcoma:
NOS
diffuse NOS
lymphoblastic (diffuse)
lymphocytic (diffuse)
prolymphocytic

Excludes: *lymphosarcoma:*
follicular or nodular (202.0)
mixed cell type (200.8)
lymphosarcoma cell leukemia (207.8)

➡ **CC Excl: For code 200.10:** 200.10-200.18, 239.8-239.9

➡ **CC Excl: For code 200.11:** 200.10, 200.11, 200.18, 239.8-239.9

➡ **CC Excl: For code 200.12:** 200.10, 200.12, 200.18, 239.8-239.9

➡ **CC Excl: For code 200.13:** 200.10, 200.13, 200.18, 239.8-239.9

➡ **CC Excl: For code 200.14:** 200.10, 200.14, 200.18, 239.8-239.9

➡ **CC Excl: For code 200.15:** 200.10, 200.15, 200.18, 239.8-239.9

➡ **CC Excl: For code 200.16:** 200.10, 200.16, 200.18, 239.8-239.9

➡ **CC Excl: For code 200.17:** 200.10, 200.17-200.18, 239.8-239.9

➡ **CC Excl: For code 200.18:** 200.10-200.18, 239.8-239.9

✓5th **200.2 Burkitt's tumor or lymphoma**

Malignant lymphoma, Burkitt's type

➡ **CC Excl: For code 200.20:** 200.20-200.28, 239.8-239.9

➡ **CC Excl: For code 200.21:** 200.20, 200.21, 200.28, 239.8-239.9

➡ **CC Excl: For code 200.22:** 200.20, 200.22, 200.28, 239.8-239.9

➡ **CC Excl: For code 200.23:** 200.20, 200.23, 200.28, 239.8-239.9

➡ **CC Excl: For code 200.24:** 200.20, 200.24, 200.28, 239.8-239.9

➡ **CC Excl: For code 200.25:** 200.20, 200.25, 200.28, 239.8-239.9

➡ **CC Excl: For code 200.26:** 200.20, 200.26, 200.28, 239.8-239.9

➡ **CC Excl: For code 200.27:** 200.20, 200.27-200.28, 239.8-239.9

➡ **CC Excl: For code 200.28:** 200.20-200.28, 239.8-239.9

✓5th **200.8 Other named variants**

Lymphoma (malignant):
lymphoplasmacytoid type
mixed lymphocytic-histiocytic (diffuse)
Lymphosarcoma, mixed cell type (diffuse)
Reticulolymphosarcoma (diffuse)

➡ **CC Excl: For code 200.80:** 200.80-200.88, 239.8-239.9

➡ **CC Excl: For code 200.81:** 200.80, 200.81, 200.88, 239.8-239.9

➡ **CC Excl: For code 200.82:** 200.80, 200.82, 200.88, 239.8-239.9

➡ **CC Excl: For code 200.83:** 200.80, 200.83, 200.88, 239.8-239.9

➡ **CC Excl: For code 200.84:** 200.80, 200.84, 200.88, 239.8-239.9

➡ **CC Excl: For code 200.85:** 200.80, 200.85, 200.88, 239.8-239.9

➡ **CC Excl: For code 200.86:** 200.80, 200.86, 200.88, 239.8-239.9

➡ **CC Excl: For code 200.87:** 200.80, 200.87-200.88, 239.8-239.9

➡ **CC Excl: For code 200.88:** 200.80-200.88, 239.8-239.9

§ 201 Hodgkin's disease

➡ **AHA Coding Clinic:** 2Q, '92, 3; N-D, '86, 5

✓5th **201.0 Hodgkin's paragranuloma**

➡ **CC Excl: For code 201.00:** 201.00-201.08, 201.90, 239.8-239.9

➡ **CC Excl: For code 201.01:** 201.00, 201.01, 201.08, 201.90-201.91, 239.8-239.9

➡ **CC Excl: For code 201.02:** 201.00, 201.02, 201.08, 201.90, 201.92, 239.8-239.9

➡ **CC Excl: For code 201.03:** 201.00, 201.03, 201.08, 201.90, 201.93, 239.8-239.9

➡ **CC Excl: For code 201.04:** 201.00, 201.04, 201.08, 201.90, 201.94, 239.8-239.9

➡ **CC Excl: For code 201.05:** 201.00, 201.05, 201.08, 201.90, 201.95, 239.8-239.9

➡ **CC Excl: For code 201.06:** 201.00, 201.06, 201.08, 201.90, 201.96, 239.8-239.9

➡ **CC Excl: For code 201.07:** 201.00, 201.07-201.08, 201.90, 201.97, 239.8-239.9

➡ **CC Excl: For code 201.08:** 201.00-201.08, 201.90, 201.98, 239.8-239.9

§ Requires fifth-digit. See page 50 for codes and definitions.

✓5th **201.1 Hodgkin's granuloma**

➡ **CC Excl: For code 201.10:** 201.10-201.18, 201.90, 201.98, 239.8-239.9

➡ **CC Excl: For code 201.11:** 201.10, 201.11, 201.18, 201.90-201.91, 201.98, 239.8-239.9

➡ **CC Excl: For code 201.12:** 201.10, 201.12, 201.18, 201.90, 201.92, 201.98, 239.8-239.9

➡ **CC Excl: For code 201.13:** 201.10, 201.13, 201.18, 201.90, 201.93, 201.98, 239.8-239.9

➡ **CC Excl: For code 201.14:** 201.10, 201.14, 201.18, 201.90, 201.94, 201.98, 239.8-239.9

➡ **CC Excl: For code 201.15:** 201.10, 201.15, 201.18, 201.90, 201.95, 201.98, 239.8-239.9

➡ **CC Excl: For code 201.16:** 201.10, 201.16, 201.18, 201.90, 201.96, 201.98, 239.8-239.9

➡ **CC Excl: For code 201.17:** 201.10, 201.17-201.18, 201.90, 201.97-201.98, 239.8-239.9

➡ **CC Excl: For code 201.18:** 201.10-201.18, 201.90, 201.98, 239.8-239.9

✓5th **201.2 Hodgkin's sarcoma**

➡ **CC Excl: For code 201.20:** 201.20-201.28, 201.90, 201.98, 239.8-239.9

➡ **CC Excl: For code 201.21:** 201.20, 201.21, 201.28, 201.90-201.91, 201.98, 239.8-239.9

➡ **CC Excl: For code 201.22:** 201.20, 201.22, 201.28, 201.90, 201.92, 201.98, 239.8-239.9

➡ **CC Excl: For code 201.23:** 201.20, 201.23, 201.28, 201.90, 201.93, 201.98, 239.8-239.9

➡ **CC Excl: For code 201.24:** 201.20, 201.24, 201.28, 201.90, 201.94, 201.98, 239.8-239.9

➡ **CC Excl: For code 201.25:** 201.20, 201.25, 201.28, 201.90, 201.95, 201.98, 239.8-239.9

➡ **CC Excl: For code 201.26:** 201.20, 201.26, 201.28, 201.90, 201.96, 201.98, 239.8-239.9

➡ **CC Excl: For code 201.27:** 201.20, 201.27-201.28, 201.90, 201.97-201.98, 239.8-239.9

➡ **CC Excl: For code 201.28:** 201.20-201.28, 201.90, 201.98, 239.8-239.9

✓5th **201.4 Lymphocytic-histiocytic predominance**

➡ **CC Excl: For code 201.40:** 201.40-201.48, 201.90, 201.98, 239.8-239.9

➡ **CC Excl: For code 201.41:** 201.40, 201.41, 201.48, 201.90-201.91, 201.98, 239.8-239.9

➡ **CC Excl: For code 201.42:** 201.40, 201.42, 201.48, 201.90, 201.92, 201.98, 239.8-239.9

➡ **CC Excl: For code 201.43:** 201.40, 201.43, 201.48, 201.90, 201.93, 201.98, 239.8-239.9

➡ **CC Excl: For code 201.44:** 201.40, 201.44, 201.48, 201.90, 201.94, 201.98, 239.8-239.9

➡ **CC Excl: For code 201.45:** 201.40, 201.45, 201.48, 201.90, 201.95, 201.98, 239.8-239.9

➡ **CC Excl: For code 201.46:** 201.40, 201.46, 201.48, 201.90, 201.96, 201.98, 239.8-239.9

➡ **CC Excl: For code 201.47:** 201.40, 201.47-201.48, 201.90, 201.97-201.98, 239.8-239.9

➡ **CC Excl: For code 201.48:** 201.40-201.48, 201.90, 201.98, 239.8-239.9

✓5th **201.5 Nodular sclerosis**

Hodgkin's disease, nodular sclerosis:
- NOS
- cellular phase

➡ **CC Excl: For code 201.50:** 201.50-201.58, 201.90, 201.98, 239.8-239.9

➡ **CC Excl: For code 201.51:** 201.50, 201.51, 201.58, 201.90-201.91, 201.98, 239.8-239.9

➡ **CC Excl: For code 201.52:** 201.50, 201.52, 201.58, 201.90, 201.92, 201.98, 239.8-239.9

➡ **CC Excl: For code 201.53:** 201.50, 201.53, 201.58, 201.90, 201.93, 201.98, 239.8-239.9

➡ **CC Excl: For code 201.54:** 201.50, 201.54, 201.58, 201.90, 201.94, 201.98, 239.8-239.9

➡ **CC Excl: For code 201.55:** 201.50, 201.55, 201.58, 201.90, 201.95, 201.98, 239.8-239.9

➡ **CC Excl: For code 201.56:** 201.50, 201.56, 201.58, 201.90, 201.96, 201.98, 239.8-239.9

➡ **CC Excl: For code 201.57:** 201.50, 201.57-201.58, 201.90, 201.97-201.98, 239.8-239.9

➡ **CC Excl: For code 201.58:** 201.50-201.58, 201.90, 201.98, 239.8-239.9

✓5th **201.6** **Mixed cellularity**

➡ **CC Excl: For code 201.60:** 201.60-201.68, 201.90, 201.98, 239.8-239.9

➡ **CC Excl: For code 201.61:** 201.60, 201.61, 201.68, 201.90-201.91, 201.98, 239.8-239.9

➡ **CC Excl: For code 201.62:** 201.60, 201.62, 201.68, 201.90, 201.92, 201.98, 239.8-239.9

➡ **CC Excl: For code 201.63:** 201.60, 201.63, 201.68, 201.90, 201.93, 201.98, 239.8-239.9

➡ **CC Excl: For code 201.64:** 201.60, 201.64, 201.68, 201.90, 201.94, 201.98, 239.8-239.9

➡ **CC Excl: For code 201.65:** 201.60, 201.65, 201.68, 201.90, 201.95, 201.98, 239.8-239.9

➡ **CC Excl: For code 201.66:** 201.60, 201.66, 201.68, 201.90, 201.96, 201.98, 239.8-239.9

➡ **CC Excl: For code 201.67:** 201.60, 201.67-201.68, 201.90, 201.97-201.98, 239.8-239.9

➡ **CC Excl: For code 201.68:** 201.60-201.68, 201.90, 201.98, 239.8-239.9

✓5th **201.7** **Lymphocytic depletion**

Hodgkin's disease, lymphocytic depletion:
- NOS
- diffuse fibrosis
- reticular type

➡ **CC Excl: For code 201.70:** 201.70-201.78, 201.90, 201.98, 239.8-239.9

➡ **CC Excl: For code 201.71:** 201.70, 201.71, 201.78, 201.91, 201.98, 239.8-239.9

➡ **CC Excl: For code 201.72:** 201.70, 201.72, 201.78, 201.92, 201.98, 239.8-239.9

➡ **CC Excl: For code 201.73:** 201.70, 201.73, 201.78, 201.93, 201.98, 239.8-239.9

➡ **CC Excl: For code 201.74:** 201.70, 201.74, 201.78, 201.94, 201.98, 239.8-239.9

➡ **CC Excl: For code 201.75:** 201.70, 201.75, 201.78, 201.95, 201.98, 239.8-239.9

➡ **CC Excl: For code 201.76:** 201.70, 201.76, 201.78, 201.96, 201.98, 239.8-239.9

➡ **CC Excl: For code 201.77:** 201.70, 201.77-201.78, 201.97-201.98, 239.8-239.9

➡ **CC Excl: For code 201.78:** 201.70-201.78, 201.98, 239.8-239.9

✓5th **201.9** **Hodgkin's disease, unspecified**

Hodgkin's:
- disease NOS
- lymphoma NOS

Malignant:
- lymphogranuloma
- lymphogranulomatosis

➡ **CC Excl: For code 201.90:** 201.90-201.98, 239.8-239.9

➡ **CC Excl: For code 201.91:** 201.90, 201.91, 201.98, 239.8-239.9

➡ **CC Excl: For code 201.92:** 201.90, 201.92, 201.98, 239.8-239.9

➡ **CC Excl: For code 201.93:** 201.90, 201.93, 201.98, 239.8-239.9

➡ **CC Excl: For code 201.94:** 201.90, 201.94, 201.98, 239.8-239.9

➡ **CC Excl: For code 201.95:** 201.90, 201.95, 201.98, 239.8-239.9

➡ **CC Excl: For code 201.96:** 201.90, 201.96, 201.98, 239.8-239.9

➡ **CC Excl: For code 201.97:** 201.90, 201.97-201.98, 239.8-239.9

➡ **CC Excl: For code 201.98:** 201.90-201.98, 239.8-239.9

§ 202 Other malignant neoplasms of lymphoid and histiocytic tissue

➡ **AHA Coding Clinic:** 2Q, '92, 3; N-D, '86, 5

✓5th **202.0** **Nodular lymphoma**

Brill-Symmers disease
Lymphoma:
- follicular (giant)
- lymphocytic, nodular

Lymphosarcoma:
- follicular (giant)
- nodular

Reticulosarcoma,
- follicular or nodular

➡ **CC Excl: For code 202.00:** 202.00-202.08, 202.80, 202.90, 239.8-239.9

➡ **CC Excl: For code 202.01:** 202.00, 202.01, 202.08, 202.81, 202.91, 239.8-239.9

➡ **CC Excl: For code 202.02:** 202.00, 202.02, 202.08, 202.82, 202.92, 239.8-239.9

➡ **CC Excl: For code 202.03:** 202.00, 202.03, 202.08, 202.83, 202.93, 239.8-239.9

➡ **CC Excl: For code 202.04:** 202.00, 202.04, 202.08, 202.84, 202.94, 239.8-239.9

➡ **CC Excl: For code 202.05:** 202.00, 202.05, 202.08, 202.85, 202.95, 239.8-239.9

➡ **CC Excl: For code 202.06:** 202.00, 202.06, 202.08, 202.86, 202.96, 239.8-239.9

➡ **CC Excl: For code 202.07:** 202.00, 202.07-202.08, 202.87, 202.97, 239.8-239.9

➡ **CC Excl: For code 202.08:** 202.00-202.08, 202.88, 202.98, 239.8-239.9

§ Requires fifth-digit. See page 50 for codes and definitions.

✓5th **202.1 Mycosis fungoides**

➡ **CC Excl: For code 202.10:** 202.10-202.18, 202.80, 202.90, 239.8-239.9

➡ **CC Excl: For code 202.11:** 202.10, 202.11, 202.18, 202.81, 202.91, 239.8-239.9

➡ **CC Excl: For code 202.12:** 202.10, 202.12, 202.18, 202.82, 202.92, 239.8-239.9

➡ **CC Excl: For code 202.13:** 202.10, 202.13, 202.18, 202.83, 202.93, 239.8-239.9

➡ **CC Excl: For code 202.14:** 202.10, 202.14, 202.18, 202.84, 202.94, 239.8-239.9

➡ **CC Excl: For code 202.15:** 202.10, 202.15, 202.18, 202.85, 202.95, 239.8-239.9

➡ **CC Excl: For code 202.16:** 202.10, 202.16, 202.18, 202.86, 202.96, 239.8-239.9

➡ **CC Excl: For code 202.17:** 202.10, 202.17-202.18, 202.87, 202.97, 239.8-239.9

➡ **CC Excl: For code 202.18:** 202.10-202.18, 202.88, 202.98, 239.8-239.9

➡ **AHA Coding Clinic:** 2Q, '92, 4

✓5th **202.2 Sézary's disease**

➡ **CC Excl: For code 202.20:** 202.20-202.28, 202.80, 202.90, 239.8-239.9

➡ **CC Excl: For code 202.21:** 202.20, 202.21, 202.28, 202.81, 202.91, 239.8-239.9

➡ **CC Excl: For code 202.22:** 202.20, 202.22, 202.28, 202.82, 202.92, 239.8-239.9

➡ **CC Excl: For code 202.23:** 202.20, 202.23, 202.28, 202.83, 202.93, 239.8-239.9

➡ **CC Excl: For code 202.24:** 202.20, 202.24, 202.28, 202.84, 202.94, 239.8-239.9

➡ **CC Excl: For code 202.25:** 202.20, 202.25, 202.28, 202.85, 202.95, 239.8-239.9

➡ **CC Excl: For code 202.26:** 202.20, 202.26, 202.28, 202.86, 202.96, 239.8-239.9

➡ **CC Excl: For code 202.27:** 202.20, 202.27-202.28, 202.87, 202.97, 239.8-239.9

➡ **CC Excl: For code 202.28:** 202.20-202.28, 202.88, 202.98, 239.8-239.9

✓5th **202.3 Malignant histiocytosis**

Histiocytic medullary reticulosis
Malignant:
  reticuloendotheliosis
  reticulosis

➡ **CC Excl: For code 202.30:** 202.30-202.38, 202.80, 202.90, 239.8-239.9

➡ **CC Excl: For code 202.31:** 202.30, 202.31, 202.38, 202.81, 202.91, 239.8-239.9

➡ **CC Excl: For code 202.32:** 202.30, 202.32, 202.38, 202.82, 202.92, 239.8-239.9

➡ **CC Excl: For code 202.33:** 202.30, 202.33, 202.38, 202.83, 202.93, 239.8-239.9

➡ **CC Excl: For code 202.34:** 202.30, 202.34, 202.38, 202.84, 202.94, 239.8-239.9

➡ **CC Excl: For code 202.35:** 202.30, 202.35, 202.38, 202.85, 202.95, 239.8-239.9

➡ **CC Excl: For code 202.36:** 202.30, 202.36, 202.38, 202.86, 202.96, 239.8-239.9

➡ **CC Excl: For code 202.37:** 202.30, 202.37-202.38, 202.87, 202.97, 239.8-239.9

➡ **CC Excl: For code 202.38:** 202.30-202.38, 202.88, 202.98, 239.8-239.9

✓5th **202.4 Leukemic reticuloendotheliosis**

Hairy-cell leukemia

➡ **CC Excl: For code 202.40:** 202.40-202.48, 202.80, 202.90, 239.8-239.9

➡ **CC Excl: For code 202.41:** 202.40, 202.41, 202.48, 202.81, 202.91, 239.8-239.9

➡ **CC Excl: For code 202.42:** 202.40, 202.42, 202.48, 202.82, 202.92, 239.8-239.9

➡ **CC Excl: For code 202.43:** 202.40, 202.43, 202.48, 202.83, 202.93, 239.8-239.9

➡ **CC Excl: For code 202.44:** 202.40, 202.44, 202.48, 202.84, 202.94, 239.8-239.9

➡ **CC Excl: For code 202.45:** 202.40, 202.45, 202.48, 202.85, 202.95, 239.8-239.9

➡ **CC Excl: For code 202.46:** 202.40, 202.46, 202.48, 202.86, 202.96, 239.8-239.9

➡ **CC Excl: For code 202.47:** 202.40, 202.47-202.48, 202.87, 202.97, 239.8-239.9

➡ **CC Excl: For code 202.48:** 202.40-202.48, 202.88, 202.98, 239.8-239.9

✓5th **202.5 Letterer-Siwe disease**

Acute:
- differentiated progressive histiocytosis
- histiocytosis X (progressive)
- infantile reticuloendotheliosis
- reticulosis of infancy

Excludes: *Hand-Schüller-Christian disease (277.8)*
histiocytosis (acute) (chronic) (277.8)
histiocytosis X (chronic) (277.8)

➡ **CC Excl: For code 202.50:** 202.50-202.58, 202.80, 202.90, 239.8-239.9

➡ **CC Excl: For code 202.51:** 202.50, 202.51, 202.58, 202.81, 202.91, 239.8-239.9

➡ **CC Excl: For code 202.52:** 202.50, 202.52, 202.58, 202.82, 202.92, 239.8-239.9

➡ **CC Excl: For code 202.53:** 202.50, 202.53, 202.58, 202.83, 202.93, 239.8-239.9

➡ **CC Excl: For code 202.54:** 202.50, 202.54, 202.58, 202.84, 202.94, 239.8-239.9

➡ **CC Excl: For code 202.55:** 202.50, 202.55, 202.58, 202.85, 202.95, 239.8-239.9

➡ **CC Excl: For code 202.56:** 202.50, 202.56, 202.58, 202.86, 202.96, 239.8-239.9

➡ **CC Excl: For code 202.57:** 202.50, 202.57-202.58, 202.87, 202.97, 239.8-239.9

➡ **CC Excl: For code 202.58:** 202.50-202.58, 202.88, 202.98, 239.8-239.9

✓5th **202.6 Malignant mast cell tumors**

Malignant:
- mastocytoma
- mastocytosis

Mast cell sarcoma
Systemic tissue mast cell disease

Excludes: *mast cell leukemia (207.8)*

➡ **CC Excl: For code 202.60:** 202.60-202.68, 202.80, 202.90, 239.8-239.9

➡ **CC Excl: For code 202.61:** 202.60, 202.61, 202.68, 202.81, 202.91, 239.8-239.9

➡ **CC Excl: For code 202.62:** 202.60, 202.62, 202.68, 202.82, 202.92, 239.8-239.9

➡ **CC Excl: For code 202.63:** 202.60, 202.63, 202.68, 202.83, 202.93, 239.8-239.9

➡ **CC Excl: For code 202.64:** 202.60, 202.64, 202.68, 202.84, 202.94, 239.8-239.9

➡ **CC Excl: For code 202.65:** 202.60, 202.65, 202.68, 202.85, 202.95, 239.8-239.9

➡ **CC Excl: For code 202.66:** 202.60, 202.66, 202.68, 202.86, 202.96, 239.8-239.9

➡ **CC Excl: For code 202.67:** 202.60, 202.67-202.68, 202.87, 202.97, 239.8-239.9

➡ **CC Excl: For code 202.68:** 202.60-202.68, 202.88, 202.98, 239.8-239.9

✓5th **202.8 Other lymphomas**

Lymphoma (malignant):
- NOS
- diffuse

Excludes: *benign lymphoma (229.0)*

➡ **CC Excl: For code 202.80:** 202.80-202.88, 202.90, 239.8-239.9

➡ **CC Excl: For code 202.81:** 202.80, 202.81, 202.88, 202.91, 239.8-239.9

➡ **CC Excl: For code 202.82:** 202.80, 202.82, 202.88, 202.92, 239.8-239.9

➡ **CC Excl: For code 202.83:** 202.80, 202.83, 202.88, 202.93, 239.8-239.9

➡ **CC Excl: For code 202.84:** 202.80, 202.84, 202.88, 202.94, 239.8-239.9

➡ **CC Excl: For code 202.85:** 202.80, 202.85, 202.88, 202.95, 239.8-239.9

➡ **CC Excl: For code 202.86:** 202.80, 202.86, 202.88, 202.96, 239.8-239.9

➡ **CC Excl: For code 202.87:** 202.80, 202.87-202.88, 202.97, 239.8-239.9

➡ **CC Excl: For code 202.88:** 202.80-202.88, 202.98, 239.8-239.9

➡ **AHA Coding Clinic:** 2Q, '92, 4

✓5th **202.9 Other and unspecified malignant neoplasms of lymphoid and histiocytic tissue**

Malignant neoplasm of bone marrow NOS

➡ **CC Excl: For code 202.90:** 202.90-202.98, 239.8-239.9

➡ **CC Excl: For code 202.91:** 202.90, 202.91, 202.98, 239.8-239.9

➡ **CC Excl: For code 202.92:** 202.90, 202.92, 202.98, 239.8-239.9

➡ **CC Excl: For code 202.93:** 202.90, 202.93, 202.98, 239.8-239.9

➡ **CC Excl: For code 202.94:** 202.90, 202.94, 202.98, 239.8-239.9

➡ **CC Excl: For code 202.95:** 202.90, 202.95, 202.98, 239.8-239.9

➡ **CC Excl: For code 202.96:** 202.90, 202.96, 202.98, 239.8-239.9

➡ **CC Excl: For code 202.97:** 202.90, 202.97-202.98, 239.8-239.9

➡ **CC Excl: For code 202.98:** 202.90-202.98, 239.8-239.9

203 Multiple myeloma and immunoproliferative neoplasms

The following fifth-digit subclassification is for use with category 203:

0 without mention of remission
1 in remission

➡ **AHA Coding Clinic:** 4Q, '91, 26

✓5th **203.0 Multiple myeloma**

Kahler's disease
Myelomatosis

Excludes: *solitary myeloma (238.6)*

➡ **CC Excl:** 203.00-203.81, 204.00-204.91, 205.00-205.91, 206.00-206.91, 207.00-207.81, 208.00-208.91, 239.8-239.9

➡ **AHA Coding Clinic:** 4Q, '89, 10

✓5th **203.1 Plasma cell leukemia**

Plasmacytic leukemia

➡ **CC Excl:** see Code 203.0

✓5th **203.8 Other immunoproliferative neoplasms**

➡ **CC Excl:** see Code 203.0

➡ **AHA Coding Clinic:** 4Q, '90, 26; S-O, '86, 12

204 Lymphoid leukemia

Includes: leukemia:
- lymphatic
- lymphoblastic

leukemia:
- lymphocytic
- lymphogenous

The following fifth-digit subclassification is for use with category 204:

0 without mention of remission
1 in remission

➡ **AHA Coding Clinic:** 4Q, '91, 26

✓5th **204.0 Acute**

Excludes: *acute exacerbation of chronic lymphoid leukemia (204.1)*

➡ **CC Excl:** see Code 203.0

✓5th **204.1 Chronic**

➡ **CC Excl:** see Code 203.0

✓5th **204.2 Subacute**

➡ **CC Excl:** see Code 203.0

✓5th **204.8 Other lymphoid leukemia**

Aleukemic leukemia:
- lymphatic
- lymphocytic
- lymphoid

➡ **CC Excl:** see Code 203.0

✓5th **204.9 Unspecified lymphoid leukemia**

➡ **CC Excl:** see Code 203.0

205 Myeloid leukemia

Includes: leukemia:
- granulocytic
- myeloblastic
- myelocytic
- myelogenous

leukemia:
- myelomonocytic
- myelosclerotic
- myelosis

The following fifth-digit subclassification is for use with category 205:

0 without mention of remission
1 in remission

➡ **AHA Coding Clinic:** 4Q, '91, 26

✓5th **205.0 Acute**

Acute promyelocytic leukemia

Excludes: *acute exacerbation of chronic myeloid leukemia (205.1)*

➡ **CC Excl:** see Code 203.0

✓5th **205.1 Chronic**

Eosinophilic leukemia
Neutrophilic leukemia

➡ **CC Excl:** see Code 203.0

➡ **AHA Coding Clinic:** J-A, '85, 13

✓5th **205.2 Subacute**

➡ **CC Excl:** see Code 203.0

✓5th **205.3 Myeloid sarcoma**

Chloroma
Granulocytic sarcoma

➡ **CC Excl:** see Code 203.0

✓5th **205.8 Other myeloid leukemia**

Aleukemic leukemia:
- granulocytic
- myelogenous
- myeloid

Aleukemic myelosis

➡ **CC Excl:** see Code 203.0

✓5th **205.9 Unspecified myeloid leukemia**

➡ **CC Excl:** see Code 203.0

206 Monocytic leukemia

Includes: leukemia:
histiocytic
monoblastic
monocytoid

The following fifth-digit subclassification is for use with category 206:

0 **without mention of remission**
1 **in remission**

➡ **AHA Coding Clinic:** 4Q, '91, 26

✓5th **206.0** **Acute**

Excludes: *acute exacerbation of chronic monocytic leukemia (206.1)*

➡ **CC Excl:** see Code 203.0

✓5th **206.1** **Chronic**

➡ **CC Excl:** see Code 203.0

✓5th **206.2** **Subacute**

➡ **CC Excl:** see Code 203.0

✓5th **206.8** **Other monocytic leukemia**

Aleukemic:
monocytic leukemia
monocytoid leukemia

➡ **CC Excl:** see Code 203.0

✓5th **206.9** **Unspecified monocytic leukemia**

➡ **CC Excl:** see Code 203.0

207 Other specified leukemia

Excludes: *leukemic reticuloendotheliosis (202.4)*
plasma cell leukemia (203.1)

The following fifth-digit subclassification is for use with category 207:

0 **without mention of remission**
1 **in remission**

➡ **AHA Coding Clinic:** 4Q, '91, 26

✓5th **207.0** **Acute erythremia and erythroleukemia**

Acute erythremic myelosis
Di Guglielmo's disease
Erythremic myelosis

➡ **CC Excl:** see Code 203.0

✓5th **207.1** **Chronic erythremia**

Heilmeyer-Schöner disease

➡ **CC Excl:** see Code 203.0

✓5th **207.2** **Megakaryocytic leukemia**

Megakaryocytic myelosis
Thrombocytic leukemia

➡ **CC Excl:** see Code 203.0

✓5th **207.8** **Other specified leukemia**

Lymphosarcoma cell leukemia

➡ **CC Excl:** see Code 203.0

208 Leukemia of unspecified cell type

The following fifth-digit subclassification is for use with category 208:

0 **without mention of remission**
1 **in remission**

➡ **AHA Coding Clinic:** 4Q, '91, 26; M-A, '87, 12

✓5th **208.0** **Acute**

Acute leukemia NOS
Blast cell leukemia
Stem cell leukemia

Excludes: *acute exacerbation of chronic unspecified leukemia (208.1)*

➡ **CC Excl:** see Code 203.0

✓5th **208.1** **Chronic**

Chronic leukemia NOS

➡ **CC Excl:** see Code 203.0

✓5th **208.2** **Subacute**

Subacute leukemia NOS

➡ **CC Excl:** see Code 203.0

✓5th **208.8** **Other leukemia of unspecified cell type**

➡ **CC Excl:** see Code 203.0

✓5th **208.9** **Unspecified leukemia**

Leukemia NOS

➡ **CC Excl:** see Code 203.0

BENIGN NEOPLASMS (210-229)

210 Benign neoplasm of lip, oral cavity, and pharynx

Excludes: *cyst (of):*
jaw (526.0-526.2, 526.89)
oral soft tissue (528.4)
radicular (522.8)

210.0 **Lip**

Frenulum labii
Lip (inner aspect) (mucosa) (vermilion border)

Excludes: *labial commissure (210.4)*
skin of lip (216.0)

210.1 **Tongue**

Lingual tonsil

210.2 Major salivary glands

Gland:
- parotid
- sublingual
- submandibular

Excludes: *benign neoplasms of minor salivary glands:*
NOS (210.4)
buccal mucosa (210.4)
lips (210.0)
palate (hard) (soft) (210.4)
tongue (210.1)
tonsil, palatine (210.5)

210.3 Floor of mouth

210.4 Other and unspecified parts of mouth

Gingiva	Oral mucosa
Gum (upper) (lower)	Palate (hard) (soft)
Labial commissure	Uvula
Oral cavity NOS	

Excludes: *benign odontogenic neoplasms of bone (213.0-213.1)*
developmental odontogenic cysts (526.0)
mucosa of lips (210.0)
nasopharyngeal [posterior] [superior] surface of soft palate (210.7)

210.5 Tonsil

Tonsil (faucial) (palatine)

Excludes: *lingual tonsil (210.1)*
pharyngeal tonsil (210.7)
tonsillar:
fossa (210.6)
pillars (210.6)

210.6 Other parts of oropharynx

Branchial cleft or vestiges
Epiglottis, anterior aspect
Fauces NOS
Mesopharynx NOS
Tonsillar:
- fossa
- pillars

Vallecula

Excludes: *epiglottis:*
NOS (212.1)
suprahyoid portion (212.1)

210.7 Nasopharynx

Adenoid tissue	Pharyngeal tonsil
Lymphadenoid tissue	Posterior nasal septum

210.8 Hypopharynx

Arytenoid fold	Postcricoid region
Laryngopharynx	Pyriform fossa

210.9 Pharynx, unspecified

Throat NOS

211 Benign neoplasm of other parts of digestive system

211.0 Esophagus

211.1 Stomach

Body, Cardia, Fundus } of stomach
Cardiac orifice
Pylorus

211.2 Duodenum, jejunum, and ileum

Small intestine NOS

Excludes: *ampulla of Vater (211.5)*
ileocecal valve (211.3)

211.3 Colon

Appendix	Ileocecal valve
Cecum	Large intestine NOS

Excludes: *rectosigmoid junction (211.4)*

DRG 188

211.4 Rectum and anal canal

Anal canal or sphincter	Rectosigmoid junction
Anus NOS	

Excludes: *anus:*
margin (216.5)
skin (216.5)
perianal skin (216.5)

211.5 Liver and biliary passages

Ampulla of Vater	Gallbladder
Common bile duct	Hepatic duct
Cystic duct	Sphincter of Oddi

211.6 Pancreas, except islets of Langerhans

211.7 Islets of Langerhans

Islet cell tumor

Use additional code to identify any functional activity

211.8 Retroperitoneum and peritoneum

Mesentery	Omentum
Mesocolon	Retroperitoneal tissue

211.9 Other and unspecified site

Alimentary tract NOS	Intestinal tract NOS
Digestive system NOS	Intestine NOS
Gastrointestinal tract NOS	Spleen, not elsewhere classified

212 Benign neoplasm of respiratory and intrathoracic organs

212.0 Nasal cavities, middle ear, and accessory sinuses

Cartilage of nose
Eustachian tube
Nares
Septum of nose
Sinus:
 ethmoidal
 frontal
 maxillary
 sphenoidal

Excludes: *auditory canal (external) (216.2)*
bone of:
 ear (213.0)
 nose [turbinates] (213.0)
cartilage of ear (215.0)
ear (external) (skin) (216.2)
nose NOS (229.8)
 skin (216.3)
olfactory bulb (225.1)
polyp of:
 accessory sinus (471.8)
 ear (385.30-385.35)
 nasal cavity (471.0)
posterior margin of septum and choanae (210.7)

212.1 Larynx

Cartilage:
 arytenoid
 cricoid
 cuneiform
 thyroid
Epiglottis (suprahyoid portion) NOS
Glottis
Vocal cords (false) (true)

Excludes: *epiglottis, anterior aspect (210.6)*
polyp of vocal cord or larynx (478.4)

212.2 Trachea

212.3 Bronchus and lung

Carina
Hilus of lung

212.4 Pleura

212.5 Mediastinum

212.6 Thymus

212.7 Heart

Excludes: *great vessels (215.4)*

212.8 Other specified sites

212.9 Site unspecified

Respiratory organ NOS
Upper respiratory tract NOS

Excludes: *intrathoracic NOS (229.8)*
thoracic NOS (229.8)

213 Benign neoplasm of bone and articular cartilage

Includes: cartilage (articular) (joint)
periosteum

Excludes: *cartilage of:*
 ear (215.0)
 eyelid (215.0)
 larynx (212.1)
 nose (212.0)
exostosis NOS (726.91)
synovia (215.0-215.9)

213.0 Bones of skull and face

Excludes: *lower jaw bone (213.1)*

213.1 Lower jaw bone

213.2 Vertebral column, excluding sacrum and coccyx

213.3 Ribs, sternum, and clavicle

213.4 Scapula and long bones of upper limb

213.5 Short bones of upper limb

213.6 Pelvic bones, sacrum, and coccyx

213.7 Long bones of lower limb

213.8 Short bones of lower limb

213.9 Bone and articular cartilage, site unspecified

214 Lipoma

Includes: angiolipoma
fibrolipoma
hibernoma
lipoma (fetal) (infiltrating) (intramuscular)
myelolipoma
myxolipoma

214.0 Skin and subcutaneous tissue of face

214.1 Other skin and subcutaneous tissue

214.2 Intrathoracic organs

214.3 Intra-abdominal organs

214.4 Spermatic cord ♂

214.8 Other specified sites

➡ **AHA Coding Clinic:** 3Q, '94, 7

214.9 Lipoma, unspecified site

215 Other benign neoplasm of connective and other soft tissue

Includes: blood vessel, bursa, fascia, ligament, muscle, peripheral, sympathetic, and parasympathetic nerves and ganglia, synovia, tendon (sheath)

Excludes: *cartilage:*
articular (213.0-213.9)
larynx (212.1)
nose (212.0)
connective tissue of:
breast (217)
internal organ, except lipoma and hemangioma — code to benign neoplasm of the site
lipoma (214.0-214.9)

215.0 Head, face, and neck

215.2 Upper limb, including shoulder

215.3 Lower limb, including hip

215.4 Thorax

Excludes: *heart (212.7)*
mediastinum (212.5)
thymus (212.6)

215.5 Abdomen

Abdominal wall
Hypochondrium

215.6 Pelvis

Buttock
Groin
Inguinal region
Perineum

Excludes: *uterine:*
leiomyoma (218.0-218.9)
ligament, any (221.0)

215.7 Trunk, unspecified

Back NOS
Flank NOS

215.8 Other specified sites

215.9 Site unspecified

216 Benign neoplasm of skin

Includes: blue nevus, dermatofibroma, hydrocystoma, pigmented nevus, syringoadenoma, syringoma

Excludes: *skin of genital organs (221.0-222.9)*

216.0 Skin of lip

Excludes: *vermilion border of lip (210.0)*

216.1 Eyelid, including canthus

Excludes: *cartilage of eyelid (215.0)*

216.2 Ear and external auditory canal

Auricle (ear)
Auricular canal, external
External meatus
Pinna

Excludes: *cartilage of ear (215.0)*

216.3 Skin of other and unspecified parts of face

Cheek, external
Eyebrow
Nose, external
Temple

216.4 Scalp and skin of neck

216.5 Skin of trunk, except scrotum

Axillary fold
Perianal skin
Skin of:
- abdominal wall
- anus
- back
- breast

Skin of:
- buttock
- chest wall
- groin
- perineum

Umbilicus

Excludes: *anal canal (211.4)*
anus NOS (211.4)
skin of scrotum (222.4)

216.6 Skin of upper limb, including shoulder

216.7 Skin of lower limb, including hip

216.8 Other specified sites of skin

216.9 Skin, site unspecified

217 Benign neoplasm of breast

Breast (male) (female):
- connective tissue
- glandular tissue
- soft parts

Excludes: *adenofibrosis (610.2)*
benign cyst of breast (610.0)
fibrocystic disease (610.1)
skin of breast (216.5)

218 Uterine leiomyoma ♀

Includes: fibroid (bleeding) (uterine)
uterine:
- fibromyoma
- myoma

218.0 Submucous leiomyoma of uterus

218.1 Intramural leiomyoma of uterus

Interstitial leiomyoma of uterus

218.2 Subserous leiomyoma of uterus

Subperitoneal leiomyoma of uterus

218.9 Leiomyoma of uterus, unspecified

219 Other benign neoplasm of uterus ♀

219.0 Cervix uteri

219.1 Corpus uteri
Endometrium
Fundus
Myometrium

219.8 Other specified parts of uterus

219.9 Uterus, part unspecified

220 Benign neoplasm of ovary ♀

Use additional code to identify any functional activity (256.0-256.1)

Excludes: *cyst:*
corpus albicans (620.2)
corpus luteum (620.1)
endometrial (617.1)
follicular (atretic) (620.0)
graafian follicle (620.0)
ovarian NOS (620.2)
retention (620.2)

221 Benign neoplasm of other female genital organs ♀

Includes: adenomatous polyp
benign teratoma

Excludes: *cyst:*
epoophoron (752.11)
fimbrial (752.11)
Gartner's duct (752.11)
parovarian (752.11)

221.0 Fallopian tube and uterine ligaments
Oviduct
Parametrium
Uterine ligament (broad) (round) (uterosacral)
Uterine tube

221.1 Vagina

221.2 Vulva
Clitoris
External female genitalia NOS
Greater vestibular [Bartholin's] gland
Labia (majora) (minora)
Pudendum

Excludes: *Bartholin's (duct) (gland) cyst (616.2)*

221.8 Other specified sites of female genital organs

221.9 Female genital organ, site unspecified
Female genitourinary tract NOS

222 Benign neoplasm of male genital organs ♂

222.0 Testis
Use additional code to identify any functional activity

222.1 Penis
Corpus cavernosum
Glans penis
Prepuce

222.2 Prostate

Excludes: *adenomatous hyperplasia of prostate (600)*
prostatic:
adenoma (600)
enlargement (600)
hypertrophy (600)

222.3 Epididymis

222.4 Scrotum
Skin of scrotum

222.8 Other specified sites of male genital organs
Seminal vesicle
Spermatic cord

222.9 Male genital organ, site unspecified
Male genitourinary tract NOS

223 Benign neoplasm of kidney and other urinary organs

223.0 Kidney, except pelvis
Kidney NOS

Excludes: *renal:*
calyces (223.1)
pelvis (223.1)

223.1 Renal pelvis

223.2 Ureter

Excludes: *ureteric orifice of bladder (223.3)*

223.3 Bladder

✓5th **223.8 Other specified sites of urinary organs**

223.81 Urethra

Excludes: *urethral orifice of bladder (223.3)*

223.89 Other
Paraurethral glands

223.9 Urinary organ, site unspecified
Urinary system NOS

224 Benign neoplasm of eye

Excludes: *cartilage of eyelid (215.0)*
eyelid (skin) (216.1)
optic nerve (225.1)
orbital bone (213.0)

224.0 Eyeball, except conjunctiva, cornea, retina, and choroid
Ciliary body
Iris
Sclera
Uveal tract

224.1 **Orbit**

Excludes: *bone of orbit (213.0)*

224.2 **Lacrimal gland**

224.3 **Conjunctiva**

224.4 **Cornea**

224.5 **Retina**

Excludes: *hemangioma of retina (228.03)*

224.6 **Choroid**

224.7 **Lacrimal duct**

Lacrimal sac
Nasolacrimal duct

224.8 **Other specified parts of eye**

224.9 **Eye, part unspecified**

225 Benign neoplasm of brain and other parts of nervous system

Excludes: *hemangioma (228.02)*
neurofibromatosis (237.7)
peripheral, sympathetic, and parasympathetic nerves and ganglia (215.0-215.9)
retrobulbar (224.1)

225.0 **Brain**

225.1 **Cranial nerves**

225.2 **Cerebral meninges**

Meninges NOS
Meningioma (cerebral)

225.3 **Spinal cord**

Cauda equina

225.4 **Spinal meninges**

Spinal meningioma

225.8 **Other specified sites of nervous system**

225.9 **Nervous system, part unspecified**

Nervous system (central) NOS

Excludes: *meninges NOS (225.2)*

226 Benign neoplasm of thyroid glands

Use additional code to identify any functional activity

227 Benign neoplasm of other endocrine glands and related structures

Use additional code to identify any functional activity

Excludes: *ovary (220)*
pancreas (211.6)
testis (222.0)

227.0 **Adrenal gland**

Suprarenal gland

227.1 **Parathyroid gland**

227.3 **Pituitary gland and craniopharyngeal duct (pouch)**

Craniobuccal pouch
Hypophysis
Rathke's pouch
Sella turcica

➡ **AHA Coding Clinic:** J-A, '85, 9

227.4 **Pineal gland**

Pineal body

227.5 **Carotid body**

227.6 **Aortic body and other paraganglia**

Coccygeal body
Glomus jugulare
Para-aortic body

227.8 **Other**

227.9 **Endocrine gland, site unspecified**

228 Hemangioma and lymphangioma, any site

Includes: angioma (benign) (cavernous) (congenital) NOS
cavernous nevus
glomus tumor
hemangioma (benign) (congenital)

Excludes: *benign neoplasm of spleen, except hemangioma and lymphangioma (211.9)*
glomus jugulare (227.6)
nevus:
NOS (216.0-216.9)
blue or pigmented (216.0-216.9)
vascular (757.32)

➡ **AHA Coding Clinic:** 4Q, '88, 6

✓5th **228.0** **Hemangioma, any site**

228.00 **Of unspecified site**

228.01 **Of skin and subcutaneous tissue**

228.02 **Of intracranial structures**

228.03 **Of retina**

228.04 **Of intra-abdominal structures**

Peritoneum
Retroperitoneal tissue

228.09 **Of other sites**
Systemic angiomatosis
➡ **AHA Coding Clinic:** 3Q, '91, 20

228.1 **Lymphangioma, any site**
Congenital lymphangioma
Lymphatic nevus

229 Benign neoplasm of other and unspecified sites

229.0 **Lymph nodes**

Excludes: *lymphangioma (228.1)*

229.8 **Other specified sites**
Intrathoracic NOS
Thoracic NOS

229.9 **Site unspecified**

CARCINOMA IN SITU (230-234)

Includes: Bowen's disease
erythroplasia
Queyrat's erythroplasia

Excludes: *leukoplakia — see Alphabetic Index*

230 Carcinoma in situ of digestive organs

230.0 **Lip, oral cavity, and pharynx**
Gingiva
Hypopharynx
Mouth [any part]
Nasopharynx
Oropharynx
Salivary gland or duct
Tongue

Excludes: *aryepiglottic fold or interarytenoid fold, laryngeal aspect (231.0)*
epiglottis:
NOS (231.0)
suprahyoid portion (231.0)
skin of lip (232.0)

230.1 **Esophagus**

230.2 **Stomach**
Body, Cardia, Fundus } of stomach
Cardiac orifice
Pylorus

230.3 **Colon**
Appendix
Cecum
Ileocecal valve
Large intestine NOS

Excludes: *rectosigmoid junction (230.4)*

230.4 **Rectum**
Rectosigmoid junction

230.5 **Anal canal**
Anal sphincter

230.6 **Anus, unspecified**

Excludes: *anus:*
margin (232.5)
skin (232.5)
perianal skin (232.5)

230.7 **Other and unspecified parts of intestine**
Duodenum
Ileum
Jejunum
Small intestine NOS

Excludes: *ampulla of Vater (230.8)*

230.8 **Liver and biliary system**
Ampulla of Vater
Common bile duct
Cystic duct
Gallbladder
Hepatic duct
Sphincter of Oddi

230.9 **Other and unspecified digestive organs**
Digestive organ NOS
Gastrointestinal tract NOS
Pancreas
Spleen

231 Carcinoma in situ of respiratory system

231.0 **Larynx**
Cartilage:
arytenoid
cricoid
cuneiform
thyroid
Epiglottis:
NOS
posterior surface
suprahyoid portion
Vocal cords (false) (true)

Excludes: *aryepiglottic fold or interarytenoid fold:*
NOS (230.0)
hypopharyngeal aspect (230.0)
marginal zone (230.0)

231.1 **Trachea**

231.2 **Bronchus and lung**
Carina
Hilus of lung

231.8 **Other specified parts of respiratory system**
Accessory sinuses
Middle ear
Nasal cavities
Pleura

Excludes: *ear (external) (skin) (232.2)*
nose NOS (234.8)
skin (232.3)

231.9 **Respiratory system, part unspecified**
Respiratory organ NOS

232 Carcinoma in situ of skin

Includes: pigment cells

232.0 **Skin of lip**

Excludes: *vermilion border of lip (230.0)*

232.1 **Eyelid, including canthus**

232.2 **Ear and external auditory canal**

232.3 **Skin of other and unspecified parts of face**

232.4 **Scalp and skin of neck**

232.5 **Skin of trunk, except scrotum**

Anus, margin
Axillary fold
Perianal skin
Skin of:
  abdominal wall
  anus
  back
Skin of:
  breast
  buttock
  chest wall
  groin
  perineum
Umbilicus

Excludes: *anal canal (230.5)*
anus NOS (230.6)
skin of genital organs (233.3, 233.5-233.6)

232.6 **Skin of upper limb, including shoulder**

232.7 **Skin of lower limb, including hip**

232.8 **Other specified sites of skin**

232.9 **Skin, site unspecified**

233 Carcinoma in situ of breast and genitourinary system

233.0 **Breast**

Excludes: *Paget's disease (174.0-174.9)*
skin of breast (232.5)

233.1 **Cervix uteri** ♀

➡ **AHA Coding Clinic:** 3Q, '92, 7; 3Q, '92, 8; 1Q, '91, 11

233.2 **Other and unspecified parts of uterus** ♀

233.3 **Other and unspecified female genital organs** ♀

233.4 **Prostate** ♂

233.5 **Penis** ♂

233.6 **Other and unspecified male genital organs** ♂

233.7 **Bladder**

233.9 **Other and unspecified urinary organs**

234 Carcinoma in situ of other and unspecified sites

234.0 **Eye**

Excludes: *cartilage of eyelid (234.8)*
eyelid (skin) (232.1)
optic nerve (234.8)
orbital bone (234.8)

234.8 **Other specified sites**

Endocrine gland [any]

234.9 **Site unspecified**

Carcinoma in situ NOS

NEOPLASMS OF UNCERTAIN BEHAVIOR (235-238)

Note: Categories 235-238 classify by site certain histo-morphologically well-defined neoplasms, the subsequent behavior of which cannot be predicted from the present appearance.

235 Neoplasm of uncertain behavior of digestive and respiratory systems

235.0 **Major salivary glands**

Gland:
  parotid
  sublingual
  submandibular

Excludes: *minor salivary glands (235.1)*

235.1 **Lip, oral cavity, and pharynx**

Gingiva
Hypopharynx
Minor salivary glands
Mouth
Nasopharynx
Oropharynx
Tongue

Excludes: *aryepiglottic fold or interarytenoid fold, laryngeal aspect (235.6)*
epiglottis:
  NOS (235.6)
  suprahyoid portion (235.6)
skin of lip (238.2)

235.2 **Stomach, intestines, and rectum**

235.3 **Liver and biliary passages**

Ampulla of Vater
Bile ducts [any]
Gallbladder
Liver

235.4 **Retroperitoneum and peritoneum**

235.5 **Other and unspecified digestive organs**

Anal:
  canal
  sphincter
Anus NOS
Esophagus
Pancreas
Spleen

Excludes: *anus:*
  margin (238.2)
  skin (238.2)
perianal skin (238.2)

235.6 **Larynx**

Excludes: *aryepiglottic fold or interarytenoid fold:*
  NOS (235.1)
  hypopharyngeal aspect (235.1)
  marginal zone (235.1)

235.7 **Trachea, bronchus, and lung**

235.8 **Pleura, thymus, and mediastinum**

235.9 **Other and unspecified respiratory organs**
Accessory sinuses
Middle ear
Nasal cavities
Respiratory organ NOS

Excludes: *ear (external) (skin) (238.2)*
nose (238.8)
skin (238.2)

236 Neoplasm of uncertain behavior of genitourinary organs

236.0 **Uterus** ♀

236.1 **Placenta** ♀
Chorioadenoma (destruens)
Invasive mole
Malignant hydatid(iform) mole

236.2 **Ovary** ♀
Use additional code to identify any functional activity

236.3 **Other and unspecified female genital organs** ♀

236.4 **Testis** ♂
Use additional code to identify any functional activity

236.5 **Prostate** ♂

236.6 **Other and unspecified male genital organs** ♂

236.7 **Bladder**

✓5th **236.9** **Other and unspecified urinary organs**

236.90 **Urinary organ, unspecified**

236.91 **Kidney and ureter**

236.99 **Other**

237 Neoplasm of uncertain behavior of endocrine glands and nervous system

237.0 **Pituitary gland and craniopharyngeal duct**
Use additional code to identify any functional activity

237.1 **Pineal gland**

237.2 **Adrenal gland**
Suprarenal gland
Use additional code to identify any functional activity

237.3 **Paraganglia**
Aortic body
Carotid body
Coccygeal body
Glomus jugulare

237.4 **Other and unspecified endocrine glands**
Parathyroid gland
Thyroid gland

237.5 **Brain and spinal cord**

237.6 **Meninges**
Meninges:
NOS
cerebral
spinal

✓5th **237.7** **Neurofibromatosis**
von Recklinghausen's disease

237.70 **Neurofibromatosis, unspecified**

237.71 **Neurofibromatosis, Type 1 [von Recklinghausen's disease]**

237.72 **Neurofibromatosis, Type 2 [acoustic neurofibromatosis]**

237.9 **Other and unspecified parts of nervous system**
Cranial nerves

Excludes: *peripheral, sympathetic, and parasympathetic nerves and ganglia (238.1)*

238 Neoplasm of uncertain behavior of other and unspecified sites and tissues

238.0 **Bone and articular cartilage**

Excludes: *cartilage:*
ear (238.1)
eyelid (238.1)
larynx (235.6)
nose (235.9)
synovia (238.1)

238.1 **Connective and other soft tissue**
Peripheral, sympathetic, and parasympathetic nerves and ganglia

Excludes: *cartilage (of):*
articular (238.0)
larynx (235.6)
nose (235.9)
connective tissue of breast (238.3)

238.2 **Skin**

Excludes: *anus NOS (235.5)*
skin of genital organs (236.3, 236.6)
vermilion border of lip (235.1)

238.3 **Breast**

Excludes: *skin of breast (238.2)*

238.4 Polycythemia vera

238.5 Histiocytic and mast cells

Mast cell tumor NOS
Mastocytoma NOS

238.6 Plasma cells

Plasmacytoma NOS
Solitary myeloma

238.7 Other lymphatic and hematopoietic tissues

Disease:
lymphoproliferative (chronic) NOS
myeloproliferative (chronic) NOS
Idiopathic thrombocythemia
Megakaryocytic myelosclerosis
Myelodysplastic syndrome
Myelosclerosis with myeloid metaplasia
Panmyelosis (acute)

Excludes: *myelofibrosis (289.8)*
myelosclerosis NOS (289.8)
myelosis:
NOS (205.9)
megakaryocytic (207.2)

➡ **AHA Coding Clinic:** 1Q, '97, 5; 2Q, '89, 8

238.8 Other specified sites

Eye
Heart

Excludes: *eyelid (skin) (238.2)*
cartilage (238.1)

238.9 Site unspecified

NEOPLASMS OF UNSPECIFIED NATURE (239)

239 Neoplasms of unspecified nature

Note: Category 239 classifies by site neoplasms of unspecified morphology and behavior. The term "mass," unless otherwise stated, is not to be regarded as a neoplastic growth.

Includes: "growth" NOS
neoplasm NOS
new growth NOS
tumor NOS

239.0 Digestive system

Excludes: *anus:*
margin (239.2)
skin (239.2)
perianal skin (239.2)

239.1 Respiratory system

239.2 Bone, soft tissue, and skin

Excludes: *anal canal (239.0)*
anus NOS (239.0)
bone marrow (202.9)
cartilage:
larynx (239.1)
nose (239.1)
connective tissue of breast (239.3)
skin of genital organs (239.5)
vermilion border of lip (239.0)

239.3 Breast

Excludes: *skin of breast (239.2)*

239.4 Bladder

239.5 Other genitourinary organs

239.6 Brain

Excludes: *cerebral meninges (239.7)*
cranial nerves (239.7)

239.7 Endocrine glands and other parts of nervous system

Excludes: *peripheral, sympathetic, and parasympathetic nerves and ganglia (239.2)*

239.8 Other specified sites

Excludes: *eyelid (skin) (239.2)*
cartilage (239.2)
great vessels (239.2)
optic nerve (239.7)

239.9 Site unspecified

3. ENDOCRINE, NUTRITIONAL AND METABOLIC DISEASES, AND IMMUNITY DISORDERS (240-279)

Excludes: *endocrine and metabolic disturbances specific to the fetus and newborn (775.0-775.9)*

Note: All neoplasms, whether functionally active or not, are classified in Chapter 2. Codes in Chapter 3 (i.e., 242.8, 246.0, 251-253, 255-259) may be used to identify such functional activity associated with any neoplasm, or by ectopic endocrine tissue.

DISORDERS OF THYROID GLAND (240-246)

240 Simple and unspecified goiter

240.0 Goiter, specified as simple

Any condition classifiable to 240.9, specified as simple

240.9 Goiter, unspecified

Enlargement of thyroid
Goiter or struma:
- NOS
- diffuse colloid
- endemic

Goiter or struma:
- hyperplastic
- nontoxic (diffuse)
- parenchymatous
- sporadic

Excludes: *congenital (dyshormonogenic) goiter (246.1)*

241 Nontoxic nodular goiter

Excludes: *adenoma of thyroid (226)*
cystadenoma of thyroid (226)

241.0 Nontoxic uninodular goiter

Thyroid nodule
Uninodular goiter (nontoxic)

241.1 Nontoxic multinodular goiter

Multinodular goiter (nontoxic)

241.9 Unspecified nontoxic nodular goiter

Adenomatous goiter
Nodular goiter (nontoxic) NOS
Struma nodosa (simplex)

242 Thyrotoxicosis with or without goiter

Excludes: *neonatal thyrotoxicosis (775.3)*

The following fifth-digit subclassification is for use with category 242:

0 without mention of thyrotoxic crisis or storm
1 with mention of thyrotoxic crisis or storm

✓5th **242.0 Toxic diffuse goiter**

Basedow's disease
Exophthalmic or toxic goiter NOS
Graves' disease
Primary thyroid hyperplasia

➡ **CC Excl:** 017.50-017.56, 017.90-017.96, 240.0, 240.9, 241.0-241.9, 242.00-242.91,243, 244.0-244.9, 245.0-245.9, 246.0-246.9, 259.8-259.9

✓5th **242.1 Toxic uninodular goiter**

Thyroid nodule } toxic or with hyperthyroidism
Uninodular goiter }

➡ **CC Excl:** see Code 242.0

✓5th **242.2 Toxic multinodular goiter**

Secondary thyroid hyperplasia

➡ **CC Excl:** see Code 242.0

✓5th **242.3 Toxic nodular goiter, unspecified**

Adenomatous goiter }
Nodular goiter } toxic or with hyperthyroidism
Struma nodosa }

Any condition classifiable to 241.9 specified as toxic or with hyperthyroidism

➡ **CC Excl:** see Code 242.0

✓5th **242.4 Thyrotoxicosis from ectopic thyroid nodule**

➡ **CC Excl:** see Code 242.0

✓5th **242.8 Thyrotoxicosis of other specified origin**

Overproduction of thyroid-stimulating hormone [TSH]
Thyrotoxicosis:
- factitia from ingestion of excessive thyroid material

Use additional E code to identify cause if drug-induced

➡ **CC Excl:** see Code 242.0

✓5th **242.9 Thyrotoxicosis without mention of goiter or other cause**

Hyperthyroidism NOS Thyrotoxicosis NOS

➡ **CC Excl:** see Code 242.0

243 Congenital hypothyroidism

Congenital thyroid insufficiency
Cretinism (athyrotic) (endemic)

Use additional code to identify associated mental retardation

Excludes: *congenital (dyshormonogenic) goiter (246.1)*

240–289.9

244 Acquired hypothyroidism

Includes: athyroidism (acquired)
hypothyroidism (acquired)
myxedema (adult) (juvenile)
thyroid (gland) insufficiency (acquired)

244.0 Postsurgical hypothyroidism

244.1 Other postablative hypothyroidism

Hypothyroidism following therapy, such as irradiation

244.2 Iodine hypothyroidism

Hypothyroidism resulting from administration or ingestion of iodide

Use additional E code to identify drug

244.3 Other iatrogenic hypothyroidism

Hypothyroidism resulting from:
P-aminosalicylic acid [PAS]
Phenylbutazone
Resorcinol
Iatrogenic hypothyroidism NOS

Use additional E code to identify drug

244.8 Other specified acquired hypothyroidism

Secondary hypothyroidism NEC

➡ **AHA Coding Clinic:** J-A, '85, 9

244.9 Unspecified hypothyroidism

Hypothyroidism } primary or NOS
Myxedema } primary or NOS

➡ **AHA Coding Clinic:** 4Q, '96, 29

245 Thyroiditis

245.0 Acute thyroiditis

Abscess of thyroid
Thyroiditis:
nonsuppurative, acute
pyogenic
suppurative

Use additional code to identify organism

245.1 Subacute thyroiditis

Thyroiditis:
de Quervain's
giant cell

Thyroiditis:
granulomatous
viral

245.2 Chronic lymphocytic thyroiditis

Hashimoto's disease
Struma lymphomatosa

Thyroiditis:
autoimmune
lymphocytic (chronic)

245.3 Chronic fibrous thyroiditis

Struma fibrosa
Thyroiditis:
invasive (fibrous)
ligneous
Riedel's

245.4 Iatrogenic thyroiditis

Use additional E code to identify cause

245.8 Other and unspecified chronic thyroiditis

Chronic thyroiditis:
NOS
nonspecific

245.9 Thyroiditis, unspecified

Thyroiditis NOS

246 Other disorders of thyroid

246.0 Disorders of thyrocalcitonin secretion

Hypersecretion of calcitonin or thyrocalcitonin

246.1 Dyshormonogenic goiter

Congenital (dyshormonogenic) goiter
Goiter due to enzyme defect in synthesis of thyroid hormone
Goitrous cretinism (sporadic)

246.2 Cyst of thyroid

Excludes: *cystadenoma of thyroid (226)*

246.3 Hemorrhage and infarction of thyroid

246.8 Other specified disorders of thyroid

Abnormality of thyroid-binding globulin
Atrophy of thyroid

Hyper-TBG-nemia
Hypo-TBG-nemia

246.9 Unspecified disorder of thyroid

DISEASES OF OTHER ENDOCRINE GLANDS (250-259)

250 Diabetes mellitus

Excludes: *gestational diabetes (648.8)*
hyperglycemia NOS (790.6)
neonatal diabetes mellitus (775.1)
nonclinical diabetes (790.2)

The following fifth-digit subclassification is for use with category 250:

0 type II [non-insulin dependent type] [NIDDM type] [adult-onset type] or unspecified type, not stated as uncontrolled
Fifth-digit 0 is for use for type II, adult-onset diabetic patients, even if the patient requires insulin

1 type I [insulin dependent type] [IDDM type] [juvenile type], not stated as uncontrolled

2 type II [non-insulin dependent type] [NIDDM type] [adult-onset type] or unspecified type, uncontrolled
Fifth-digit 2 is for use for type II, adult-onset diabetic patients, even if the patient requires insulin

3 type I [insulin dependent type] [IDDM type] [juvenile type], uncontrolled

➡ **AHA Coding Clinic:** 4Q, '97, 32; 2Q, '97, 14; 3Q, '96, 5; 4Q, '93, 19; 2Q, '92, 5; 3Q, '91, 3; 2Q, '90, 22; N-D, '85, 11

✓5th [20a]**250.0 Diabetes mellitus without mention of complication**
Diabetes mellitus without mention of complication or manifestation classifiable to 250.1-250.9
Diabetes (mellitus) NOS

➡ **CC Excl: For Code 250.01:** 250.00-250.93, 251.0-251.3, 259.8-259.9

➡ **CC Excl: For Code 250.02:** 250.00-250.93, 251.0-251.3, 259.8-259.9

➡ **CC Excl: For Code 250.03:** see Code 250.02

➡ **AHA Coding Clinic:** 4Q, '97, 32

✓5th **250.1 Diabetes with ketoacidosis**
Diabetic:
acidosis } without mention of coma
ketosis }

➡ **CC Excl: For Code 250.11:** 250.02-250.03, 250.12-250.13, 250.22-250.23, 250.32-250.33, 250.42-250.43, 250.52-250.53, 250.62-250.63, 250.72-250.73, 250.82-250.83, 250.92-250.93

➡ **CC Excl: For Code 250.12:** see Code 250.02

➡ **CC Excl: For Code 250.13:** see Code 250.02

✓5th □ **250.2 Diabetes with hyperosmolarity**
Hyperosmolar (nonketotic) coma

➡ **CC Excl: For Code 250.21:** see Code 250.11

➡ **CC Excl: For Code 250.22:** see Code 250.02

➡ **CC Excl: For Code 250.23:** see Code 250.02

➡ **AHA Coding Clinic:** 4Q, '93, 19

✓5th □ **250.3 Diabetes with other coma**
Diabetic coma (with ketoacidosis)
Diabetic hypoglycemic coma
Insulin coma NOS

Excludes: *diabetes with hyperosmolar coma (250.2)*

➡ **CC Excl: For Code 250.31:** see Code 250.11

➡ **CC Excl: For Code 250.32:** see Code 250.02

➡ **CC Excl: For Code 250.33:** see Code 250.02

✓5th □ **250.4 Diabetes with renal manifestations**
Use additional code to identify manifestation, as:
diabetic:
nephropathy NOS (583.81)
nephrosis (581.81)
intercapillary glomerulosclerosis (581.81)
Kimmelstiel-Wilson syndrome (581.81)

➡ **CC Excl: For Code 250.41:** see Code 250.11

➡ **CC Excl: For Code 250.42:** see Code 250.02

➡ **CC Excl: For Code 250.43:** see Code 250.02

➡ **AHA Coding Clinic:** S-O, '84, 3

✓5th □ **250.5 Diabetes with ophthalmic manifestations**
Use additional code to identify manifestation, as:
diabetic:
blindness (369.00-369.9)
cataract (366.41)
glaucoma (365.44)
retinal edema (362.83)
retinopathy (362.01-362.02)

➡ **CC Excl: For Code 250.51:** see Code 250.11

➡ **CC Excl: For Code 250.52:** see Code 250.02

➡ **CC Excl: For Code 250.53:** see Code 250.02

➡ **AHA Coding Clinic:** S-O, '85, 11

✓5th □ **250.6 Diabetes with neurological manifestations**
Use additional code to identify manifestation, as:
diabetic:
amyotrophy (358.1)
mononeuropathy (354.0-355.9)
neurogenic arthropathy (713.5)
peripheral autonomic neuropathy (337.1)
polyneuropathy (357.2)

➡ **CC Excl: For Code 250.61:** see Code 250.11

➡ **CC Excl: For Code 250.62:** see Code 250.02

➡ **CC Excl: For Code 250.63:** see Code 250.02

➡ **AHA Coding Clinic:** 2Q, '93, 6; 2Q, '92, 15; N-D, '84, 9

[20a] Questionable admission = 0-1

✓5th ☐ **250.7 Diabetes with peripheral circulatory disorders**

Use additional code to identify manifestation, as:
diabetic:
gangrene (785.4)
peripheral angiopathy (443.81)

➡ **CC Excl: For Code 250.71:** see Code 250.11

➡ **CC Excl: For Code 250.72:** see Code 250.02

➡ **CC Excl: For Code 250.73:** see Code 250.02

➡ **AHA Coding Clinic:** 3Q, '94, 5; 2Q, '94, 17; 3Q, '90, 15

✓5th ☐ **250.8 Diabetes with other specified manifestations**

Diabetic hypoglycemia
Hypoglycemic shock

Use additional code to identify manifestation, as:
diabetic bone changes (731.8)

Use additional E code to identify cause if drug-induced

➡ **CC Excl: For Code 250.81:** see Code 250.11

➡ **CC Excl: For Code 250.82:** see Code 250.02

➡ **CC Excl: For Code 250.83:** see Code 250.02

➡ **AHA Coding Clinic:** 4Q, '97, 43; 2Q, '97, 16; 4Q, '93, 20

➡ **AHA Coding Clinic: For code 250.80:** 2Q, '94, 13

✓5th **250.9 Diabetes with unspecified complication**

➡ **CC Excl: For Code 250.91:** see Code 250.11

➡ **CC Excl: For Code 250.92:** see Code 250.02

➡ **CC Excl: For Code 250.93:** see Code 250.02

➡ **AHA Coding Clinic:** 2Q, '92, 15

251 Other disorders of pancreatic internal secretion

251.0 Hypoglycemic coma

Iatrogenic hyperinsulinism
Non-diabetic insulin coma

Use additional E code to identify cause if drug-induced

Excludes: *hypoglycemic coma in diabetes mellitus (250.3)*

➡ **CC Excl:** see Code 250.10

➡ **AHA Coding Clinic:** M-A, '85, 8

251.1 Other specified hypoglycemia

Hyperinsulinism:
NOS
ectopic
functional
Hyperplasia of pancreatic islet beta cells NOS

Use additional E code to identify cause if drug-induced

Excludes: *hypoglycemia in diabetes mellitus (250.8)*
hypoglycemia in infant of diabetic mother (775.0)
hypoglycemic coma (251.0)
neonatal hypoglycemia (775.6)

251.2 Hypoglycemia, unspecified

Hypoglycemia:
NOS
reactive
spontaneous

Excludes: *hypoglycemia:*
with coma (251.0)
in diabetes mellitus (250.8)
leucine-induced (270.3)

➡ **AHA Coding Clinic:** M-A, '85, 8

251.3 Postsurgical hypoinsulinemia

Hypoinsulinemia following complete or partial pancreatectomy
Postpancreatectomy hyperglycemia

➡ **CC Excl:** see Code 250.10

➡ **AHA Coding Clinic:** 3Q, '91, 6

251.4 Abnormality of secretion of glucagon

Hyperplasia of pancreatic islet alpha cells with glucagon excess

251.5 Abnormality of secretion of gastrin

Hyperplasia of pancreatic alpha cells with gastrin excess
Zollinger-Ellison syndrome

251.8 Other specified disorders of pancreatic internal secretion

➡ **AHA Coding Clinic:** 3Q, '91, 6

251.9 Unspecified disorder of pancreatic internal secretion

Islet cell hyperplasia NOS

252 Disorders of parathyroid gland

252.0 Hyperparathyroidism

Hyperplasia of parathyroid
Osteitis fibrosa cystica generalisata
von Recklinghausen's disease of bone

Excludes: *ectopic hyperparathyroidism (259.3)*
secondary hyperparathyroidism (of renal origin) (588.8)

252.1 Hypoparathyroidism
Parathyroiditis (autoimmune)
Tetany:
parathyroid
parathyroprival

Excludes: *pseudohypoparathyroidism (275.4)*
pseudopseudohypoparathyroidism (275.4)
tetany NOS (781.7)
transitory neonatal hypoparathyroidism (775.4)

➡ **CC Excl:** 252.0-252.9, 259.8-259.9

252.8 Other specified disorders of parathyroid gland
Cyst } of parathyroid gland
Hemorrhage }

252.9 Unspecified disorder of parathyroid gland

253 Disorders of the pituitary gland and its hypothalamic control

Includes: the listed conditions whether the disorder is in the pituitary or the hypothalamus

Excludes: *Cushing's syndrome (255.0)*

253.0 Acromegaly and gigantism
Overproduction of growth hormone

253.1 Other and unspecified anterior pituitary hyperfunction
Forbes-Albright syndrome

Excludes: *overproduction of:*
ACTH (255.3)
thyroid-stimulating hormone [TSH] (242.8)

➡ **AHA Coding Clinic:** J-A, '85, 9

253.2 Panhypopituitarism
Cachexia, pituitary
Necrosis of pituitary (postpartum)
Pituitary insufficiency NOS
Sheehan's syndrome
Simmonds' disease

Excludes: *iatrogenic hypopituitarism (253.7)*

➡ **CC Excl:** 253.0-253.9, 259.8-259.9

253.3 Pituitary dwarfism
Isolated deficiency of (human) growth hormone [HGH]
Lorain-Levi dwarfism

253.4 Other anterior pituitary disorders
Isolated or partial deficiency of an anterior pituitary hormone, other than growth hormone
Prolactin deficiency

➡ **AHA Coding Clinic:** J-A, '85, 9

253.5 Diabetes insipidus
Vasopressin deficiency

Excludes: *nephrogenic diabetes insipidus (588.1)*

➡ **CC Excl:** 253.1-253.2, 253.4-253.9, 259.8-259.9

253.6 Other disorders of neurohypophysis
Syndrome of inappropriate secretion of antidiuretic hormone [ADH]

Excludes: *ectopic antidiuretic hormone secretion (259.3)*

253.7 Iatrogenic pituitary disorders
Hypopituitarism:
hormone-induced
hypophysectomy-induced
postablative
radiotherapy-induced

Use additional E code to identify cause

253.8 Other disorders of the pituitary and other syndromes of diencephalohypophyseal origin
Abscess of pituitary
Adiposogenital dystrophy
Cyst of Rathke's pouch
Fröhlich's syndrome

Excludes: *craniopharyngioma (237.0)*

253.9 Unspecified
Dyspituitarism

254 Diseases of thymus gland

Excludes: *aplasia or dysplasia with immunodeficiency (279.2)*
hypoplasia with immunodeficiency (279.2)
myasthenia gravis (358.0)

254.0 Persistent hyperplasia of thymus
Hypertrophy of thymus

254.1 Abscess of thymus

➡ **CC Excl:** 254.0-254.1, 254.8-254.9, 259.8-259.9

254.8 Other specified diseases of thymus gland
Atrophy } of thymus
Cyst }

Excludes: *thymoma (212.6)*

254.9 Unspecified disease of thymus gland

255 Disorders of adrenal glands

Includes: the listed conditions whether the basic disorder is in the adrenals or is pituitary-induced

255.0 Cushing's syndrome

Adrenal hyperplasia due to excess ACTH
Cushing's syndrome:
 NOS
 iatrogenic
 idiopathic
 pituitary-dependent
Ectopic ACTH syndrome
Iatrogenic syndrome of excess cortisol
Overproduction of cortisol

Use additional E code to identify cause if drug-induced

Excludes: *congenital adrenal hyperplasia (255.2)*

➡ **CC Excl:** 255.0-255.2, 259.8-259.9

255.1 Hyperaldosteronism

Aldosteronism (primary) (secondary)
Bartter's syndrome
Conn's syndrome

255.2 Adrenogenital disorders

Adrenogenital syndromes, virilizing or feminizing, whether acquired or associated with congenital adrenal hyperplasia consequent on inborn enzyme defects in hormone synthesis
Achard-Thiers syndrome
Congenital adrenal hyperplasia
Female adrenal pseudohermaphroditism
Male:
 macrogenitosomia praecox
 sexual precocity with adrenal hyperplasia
Virilization (female) (suprarenal)

Excludes: *adrenal hyperplasia due to excess ACTH (255.0)*
isosexual virilization (256.4)

255.3 Other corticoadrenal overactivity

Acquired benign adrenal androgenic overactivity
Overproduction of ACTH

➡ **CC Excl:** 017.60-017.66, 017.90-017.96, 255.3-255.9, 259.8-259.9

255.4 Corticoadrenal insufficiency

Addisonian crisis
Addison's disease NOS
Adrenal:
 atrophy (autoimmune)
 calcification
Adrenal:
 crisis
 hemorrhage
 infarction
 insufficiency NOS

Excludes: *tuberculous Addison's disease (017.6)*

➡ **CC Excl:** see Code 255.3

✔ **St. Anthony's Clinical Coder:** see Chapter 5

255.5 Other adrenal hypofunction

Adrenal medullary insufficiency

Excludes: *Waterhouse-Friderichsen syndrome (meningococcal) (036.3)*

➡ **CC Excl:** see Code 255.3

255.6 Medulloadrenal hyperfunction

Catecholamine secretion by pheochromocytoma

➡ **CC Excl:** see Code 255.3

255.8 Other specified disorders of adrenal glands

Abnormality of cortisol-binding globulin

255.9 Unspecified disorder of adrenal glands

256 Ovarian dysfunction ♀

256.0 Hyperestrogenism

256.1 Other ovarian hyperfunction

Hypersecretion of ovarian androgens

➡ **AHA Coding Clinic:** 3Q, '95, 15

256.2 Postablative ovarian failure

Ovarian failure:
 iatrogenic
 postirradiation
 postsurgical

256.3 Other ovarian failure

Premature menopause NOS
Primary ovarian failure

256.4 Polycystic ovaries

Isosexual virilization
Stein-Leventhal syndrome

256.8 Other ovarian dysfunction

256.9 Unspecified ovarian dysfunction

257 Testicular dysfunction ♂

257.0 Testicular hyperfunction

Hypersecretion of testicular hormones

257.1 Postablative testicular hypofunction

Testicular hypofunction:
 iatrogenic
 postirradiation
 postsurgical

257.2 Other testicular hypofunction

Defective biosynthesis of testicular androgen
Eunuchoidism:
 NOS
 hypogonadotropic
Failure:
 Leydig's cell, adult
 seminiferous tubule, adult
Testicular hypogonadism

Excludes: *azoospermia (606.0)*

257.8 Other testicular dysfunction

Goldberg-Maxwell syndrome
Male pseudohermaphroditism with testicular feminization
Testicular feminization

257.9 Unspecified testicular dysfunction

258 Polyglandular dysfunction and related disorders

258.0 Polyglandular activity in multiple endocrine adenomatosis

Wermer's syndrome

➡ **CC Excl:** 240.0, 240.9, 241.0-241.9, 242.00-242.91, 243, 244.0-244.9, 245.0-245.9, 246.0-246.9, 250.00-250.93, 251.0-251.9, 252.0-252.9, 253.0-253.9, 254.0-254.9, 255.0-255.9, 256.0-256.9, 257.0-257.9, 258.0-258.9, 259.0-259.9

258.1 Other combinations of endocrine dysfunction

Lloyd's syndrome
Schmidt's syndrome

➡ **CC Excl:** see Code 258.0

258.8 Other specified polyglandular dysfunction

➡ **CC Excl:** see Code 258.0

258.9 Polyglandular dysfunction, unspecified

➡ **CC Excl:** see Code 258.0

259 Other endocrine disorders

259.0 Delay in sexual development and puberty, not elsewhere classified

Delayed puberty

259.1 Precocious sexual development and puberty, not elsewhere classified A: 0–17

Sexual precocity:
- NOS
- constitutional
- cryptogenic
- idiopathic

259.2 Carcinoid syndrome

Hormone secretion by carcinoid tumors

➡ **CC Excl:** 259.2-259.3, 259.8-259.9

259.3 Ectopic hormone secretion, not elsewhere classified

Ectopic:
- antidiuretic hormone secretion [ADH]
- hyperparathyroidism

Excludes: *ectopic ACTH syndrome (255.0)*

➡ **AHA Coding Clinic:** N-D, '85, 4

259.4 Dwarfism, not elsewhere classified

Dwarfism:
- NOS
- constitutional

Excludes: *dwarfism:*
- *achondroplastic (756.4)*
- *intrauterine (759.7)*
- *nutritional (263.2)*
- *pituitary (253.3)*
- *renal (588.0)*

progeria (259.8)

259.8 Other specified endocrine disorders

Pineal gland dysfunction
Werner's syndrome
Progeria

259.9 Unspecified endocrine disorder

Disturbance:
- endocrine NOS
- hormone NOS

Infantilism NOS

NUTRITIONAL DEFICIENCIES (260-269)

Excludes: *deficiency anemias (280.0-281.9)*

260 Kwashiorkor

Nutritional edema with dyspigmentation of skin and hair

➡ **CC Excl:** 260-262, 263.0-263.9

261 Nutritional marasmus

Nutritional atrophy
Severe malnutrition NOS
Severe calorie deficiency

➡ **CC Excl:** see Code 260

262 Other severe protein-calorie malnutrition

Nutritional edema without mention of dyspigmentation of skin and hair

➡ **CC Excl:** see Code 260

➡ **AHA Coding Clinic:** 4Q, '92, 24

263 Other and unspecified protein-calorie malnutrition

➡ **AHA Coding Clinic:** 4Q, '92, 24

263.0 Malnutrition of moderate degree

➡ **CC Excl:** see Code 260

263.1 Malnutrition of mild degree

➡ **CC Excl:** see Code 260

263.2 Arrested development following protein-calorie malnutrition

Nutritional dwarfism
Physical retardation due to malnutrition

➡ **CC Excl:** see Code 260

263.8 **Other protein-calorie malnutrition**

➡ **CC Excl:** see Code 260

263.9 **Unspecified protein-calorie malnutrition**

Dystrophy due to malnutrition
Malnutrition (calorie) NOS

Excludes: *nutritional deficiency NOS (269.9)*

➡ **CC Excl:** see Code 260

➡ **AHA Coding Clinic:** N-D, '84, 19

✔ **St. Anthony's Clinical Coder:** see Chapter 5

264 Vitamin A deficiency

264.0 **With conjunctival xerosis**

264.1 **With conjunctival xerosis and Bitot's spot**

Bitot's spot in the young child

264.2 **With corneal xerosis**

264.3 **With corneal ulceration and xerosis**

264.4 **With keratomalacia**

264.5 **With night blindness**

264.6 **With xerophthalmic scars of cornea**

264.7 **Other ocular manifestations of vitamin A deficiency**

Xerophthalmia due to vitamin A deficiency

264.8 **Other manifestations of vitamin A deficiency**

Follicular keratosis } due to vitamin A deficiency
Xeroderma }

264.9 **Unspecified vitamin A deficiency**

Hypovitaminosis A NOS

265 Thiamine and niacin deficiency states

265.0 **Beriberi**

265.1 **Other and unspecified manifestations of thiamine deficiency**

Other vitamin B_1 deficiency states

265.2 **Pellagra**

Deficiency:
- niacin (-tryptophan)
- nicotinamide
- nicotinic acid
- vitamin PP

Pellagra (alcoholic)

266 Deficiency of B-complex components

266.0 **Ariboflavinosis**

Riboflavin [vitamin B_2] deficiency

266.1 **Vitamin B_6 deficiency**

Deficiency:
- pyridoxal
- pyridoxamine
- pyridoxine

Vitamin B_6 deficiency syndrome

Excludes: *vitamin B_6-responsive sideroblastic anemia (285.0)*

266.2 **Other B-complex deficiencies**

Deficiency:
- cyanocobalamin
- folic acid
- vitamin B_{12}

Excludes: *combined system disease with anemia (281.0-281.1)*
deficiency anemias (281.0-281.9)
subacute degeneration of spinal cord with anemia (281.0-281.1)

266.9 **Unspecified vitamin B deficiency**

267 Ascorbic acid deficiency

Deficiency of vitamin C
Scurvy

Excludes: *scorbutic anemia (281.8)*

268 Vitamin D deficiency

Excludes: *vitamin D-resistant:*
osteomalacia (275.3)
rickets (275.3)

268.0 **Rickets, active**

Excludes: *celiac rickets (579.0)*
renal rickets (588.0)

268.1 **Rickets, late effect**

Any condition specified as due to rickets and stated to be a late effect or sequela of rickets

Use additional code to identify the nature of late effect

268.2 **Osteomalacia, unspecified**

268.9 **Unspecified vitamin D deficiency**

Avitaminosis D

269 Other nutritional deficiencies

269.0 **Deficiency of vitamin K**

Excludes: *deficiency of coagulation factor due to vitamin K deficiency (286.7)*
vitamin K deficiency of newborn (776.0)

➡ **CC Excl:** 269.0

269.1 Deficiency of other vitamins
Deficiency:
vitamin E
vitamin P

269.2 Unspecified vitamin deficiency
Multiple vitamin deficiency NOS

269.3 Mineral deficiency, not elsewhere classified
Deficiency:
calcium, dietary
iodine

Excludes: *deficiency:*
calcium NOS (275.4)
potassium (276.8)
sodium (276.1)

269.8 Other nutritional deficiency

Excludes: *failure to thrive (783.4)*
feeding problems (783.3)
newborn (779.3)

269.9 Unspecified nutritional deficiency

OTHER METABOLIC AND IMMUNITY DISORDERS (270-279)

Use additional code to identify any associated mental retardation

270 Disorders of amino-acid transport and metabolism

Excludes: *abnormal findings without manifest disease (790.0-796.9)*
disorders of purine and pyrimidine metabolism (277.1-277.2)
gout (274.0-274.9)

270.0 Disturbances of amino-acid transport
Cystinosis
Cystinuria
Fanconi (-de Toni) (-Debré) syndrome
Glycinuria (renal)
Hartnup disease

270.1 Phenylketonuria [PKU]
Hyperphenylalaninemia

270.2 Other disturbances of aromatic amino-acid metabolism
Albinism
Alkaptonuria
Alkaptonuric ochronosis
Disturbances of metabolism of tyrosine and tryptophan
Homogentisic acid defects
Hydroxykynureninuria
Hypertyrosinemia
Indicanuria
Kynureninase defects
Oasthouse urine disease
Ochronosis
Tyrosinosis
Tyrosinuria
Waardenburg syndrome

Excludes: *vitamin B_6-deficiency syndrome (266.1)*

270.3 Disturbances of branched-chain amino-acid metabolism
Disturbances of metabolism of leucine, isoleucine, and valine
Hypervalinemia
Intermittent branched-chain ketonuria
Leucine-induced hypoglycemia
Leucinosis
Maple syrup urine disease

270.4 Disturbances of sulphur-bearing amino-acid metabolism
Cystathioninemia
Cystathioninuria
Disturbances of metabolism of methionine, homocystine, and cystathionine
Homocystinuria
Hypermethioninemia
Methioninemia

270.5 Disturbances of histidine metabolism
Carnosinemia
Histidinemia
Hyperhistidinemia
Imidazole aminoaciduria

270.6 Disorders of urea cycle metabolism
Argininosuccinic aciduria
Citrullinemia
Disorders of metabolism of ornithine, citrulline, argininosuccinic acid, arginine, and ammonia
Hyperammonemia
Hyperornithinemia

270.7 Other disturbances of straight-chain amino-acid metabolism
Glucoglycinuria
Glycinemia (with methylmalonic acidemia)
Hyperglycinemia
Hyperlysinemia
Pipecolic acidemia
Saccharopinuria
Other disturbances of metabolism of glycine, threonine, serine, glutamine, and lysine

270.8 Other specified disorders of amino-acid metabolism
Alaninemia
Ethanolaminuria
Glycoprolinuria
Hydroxyprolinemia
Hyperprolinemia
Iminoacidopathy
Prolinemia
Prolinuria
Sarcosinemia

270.9 Unspecified disorder of amino-acid metabolism

271 Disorders of carbohydrate transport and metabolism

Excludes: *abnormality of secretion of glucagon (251.4)*
diabetes mellitus (250.0-250.9)
hypoglycemia NOS (251.2)
mucopolysaccharidosis (277.5)

271.0 Glycogenosis
Amylopectinosis
Glucose-6-phosphatase deficiency
Glycogen storage disease
McArdle's disease
Pompe's disease
von Gierke's disease

➡ **AHA Coding Clinic:** 1Q, '98, 5

271.1 Galactosemia

Galactose-1-phosphate uridyl transferase deficiency
Galactosuria

271.2 Hereditary fructose intolerance

Essential benign fructosuria
Fructosemia

271.3 Intestinal disaccharidase deficiencies and disaccharide malabsorption

Intolerance or malabsorption (congenital) (of):
- glucose-galactose
- lactose
- sucrose-isomaltose

271.4 Renal glycosuria

Renal diabetes

271.8 Other specified disorders of carbohydrate transport and metabolism

Essential benign pentosuria
Fucosidosis
Glycolic aciduria
Hyperoxaluria (primary)
Mannosidosis
Oxalosis
Xylosuria
Xylulosuria

271.9 Unspecified disorder of carbohydrate transport and metabolism

272 Disorders of lipoid metabolism

Excludes: *localized cerebral lipidoses (330.1)*

272.0 Pure hypercholesterolemia

Familial hypercholesterolemia
Fredrickson Type IIa hyperlipoproteinemia
Hyperbetalipoproteinemia
Hyperlipidemia, Group A
Low-density-lipoid-type [LDL] hyperlipoproteinemia

272.1 Pure hyperglyceridemia

Endogenous hyperglyceridemia
Fredrickson Type IV hyperlipoproteinemia
Hyperlipidemia, Group B
Hyperprebetalipoproteinemia
Hypertriglyceridemia, essential
Very-low-density-lipoid-type [VLDL] hyperlipoproteinemia

272.2 Mixed hyperlipidemia

Broad- or floating-betalipoproteinemia
Fredrickson Type IIb or III hyperlipoproteinemia
Hypercholesterolemia with endogenous hyperglyceridemia
Hyperbetalipoproteinemia with prebetalipoproteinemia
Tubo-eruptive xanthoma
Xanthoma tuberosum

272.3 Hyperchylomicronemia

Bürger-Grütz syndrome
Fredrickson type I or V hyperlipoproteinemia
Hyperlipidemia, Group D
Mixed hyperglyceridemia

272.4 Other and unspecified hyperlipidemia

Alpha-lipoproteinemia
Combined hyperlipidemia
Hyperlipidemia NOS
Hyperlipoproteinemia NOS

272.5 Lipoprotein deficiencies

Abetalipoproteinemia
Bassen-Kornzweig syndrome
High-density lipoid deficiency
Hypoalphalipoproteinemia
Hypobetalipoproteinemia (familial)

272.6 Lipodystrophy

Barraquer-Simons disease
Progressive lipodystrophy

Use additional E code to identify cause if iatrogenic

Excludes: *intestinal lipodystrophy (040.2)*

272.7 Lipidoses

Chemically-induced lipidosis
Disease:
- Anderson's
- Fabry's
- Gaucher's
- I cell [mucolipidosis I]
- lipoid storage NOS
- Niemann-Pick
- pseudo-Hurler's or mucolipidosis III
- triglyceride storage, Type I or II
- Wolman's or triglyceride storage, Type III

Mucolipidosis II
Primary familial xanthomatosis

Excludes: *cerebral lipidoses (330.1)*
Tay-Sachs disease (330.1)

272.8 Other disorders of lipoid metabolism

Hoffa's disease or liposynovitis prepatellaris
Launois-Bensaude's lipomatosis
Lipoid dermatoarthritis

272.9 Unspecified disorder of lipoid metabolism

273 Disorders of plasma protein metabolism

Excludes: *agammaglobulinemia and hypogammaglobulinemia (279.0-279.2)*
coagulation defects (286.0-286.9)
hereditary hemolytic anemias (282.0-282.9)

273.0 Polyclonal hypergammaglobulinemia

Hypergammaglobulinemic purpura:
- benign primary
- Waldenström's

273.1 Monoclonal paraproteinemia
Benign monoclonal hypergammaglobulinemia [BMH]
Monoclonal gammopathy:
NOS
associated with lymphoplasmacytic dyscrasias
benign
Paraproteinemia:
benign (familial)
secondary to malignant or inflammatory disease

273.2 Other paraproteinemias
Cryoglobulinemic:
purpura
vasculitis
Mixed cryoglobulinemia

273.3 Macroglobulinemia
Macroglobulinemia (idiopathic) (primary)
Waldenström's macroglobulinemia
➡ **CC Excl:** 273.0-273.9

273.8 Other disorders of plasma protein metabolism
Abnormality of transport protein
Bisalbuminemia

273.9 Unspecified disorder of plasma protein metabolism

274 Gout

Excludes: *lead gout (984.0-984.9)*

➡ **AHA Coding Clinic:** 2Q, '95, 4

274.0 Gouty arthropathy

✓5th **274.1 Gouty nephropathy**

274.10 Gouty nephropathy, unspecified

274.11 Uric acid nephrolithiasis

274.19 Other

✓5th **274.8 Gout with other specified manifestations**

274.81 Gouty tophi of ear

274.82 Gouty tophi of other sites
Gouty tophi of heart

274.89 Other
Use additional code to identify manifestations, as:
gouty:
iritis (364.11)
neuritis (357.4)

274.9 Gout, unspecified

275 Disorders of mineral metabolism

Excludes: *abnormal findings without manifest disease (790.0-796.9)*

275.0 Disorders of iron metabolism
Bronzed diabetes
Hemochromatosis
Pigmentary cirrhosis (of liver)

Excludes: *anemia:*
iron deficiency (280.0-280.9)
sideroblastic (285.0)

➡ **AHA Coding Clinic:** 2Q, '97, 11

275.1 Disorders of copper metabolism
Hepatolenticular degeneration
Wilson's disease

275.2 Disorders of magnesium metabolism
Hypermagnesemia
Hypomagnesemia

275.3 Disorders of phosphorus metabolism
Familial hypophosphatemia
Hypophosphatasia
Vitamin D-resistant:
osteomalacia
rickets

✓5th **275.4 Disorders of calcium metabolism**

Excludes: *parathyroid disorders (252.0-252.9)*
vitamin D deficiency (268.0-268.9)

➡ **AHA Coding Clinic:** 4Q, '97, 33

275.40 Unspecified disorder of calcium metabolism

275.41 Hypocalcemia

275.42 Hypercalcemia

275.49 Other disorders of calcium metabolism
Nephrocalcinosis
Pseudohypoparathyroidism
Pseudopseudohypoparathyroidism

275.8 Other specified disorders of mineral metabolism

275.9 Unspecified disorder of mineral metabolism

276 Disorders of fluid, electrolyte, and acid-base balance

Excludes: *diabetes insipidus (253.5)*
familial periodic paralysis (359.3)

276.0 Hyperosmolality and/or hypernatremia
Sodium [Na] excess
Sodium [Na] overload
➡ **CC Excl:** 276.0-276.9

276.1 Hyposmolality and/or hyponatremia
Sodium [Na] deficiency
➡ **CC Excl:** see Code 276.0
DRG 296
✔ **St. Anthony's Clinical Coder:** see Chapter 5

276.2 Acidosis

Acidosis:
- NOS
- lactic
- metabolic
- respiratory

Excludes: *diabetic acidosis (250.1)*

➡ **CC Excl:** see Code 276.0

➡ **AHA Coding Clinic:** J-F, '87, 15

✔ **St. Anthony's Clinical Coder:** see Chapter 5

276.3 Alkalosis

Alkalosis:
- NOS
- metabolic
- respiratory

➡ **CC Excl:** see Code 276.0

✔ **St. Anthony's Clinical Coder:** see Chapter 5

276.4 Mixed acid-base balance disorder

Hypercapnia with mixed acid-base disorder

➡ **CC Excl:** see Code 276.0

276.5 Volume depletion

Dehydration
Depletion of volume of plasma or extracellular fluid
Hypovolemia

Excludes: *hypovolemic shock:*
postoperative (998.0)
traumatic (958.4)

➡ **CC Excl:** see Code 276.0

➡ **AHA Coding Clinic:** 4Q, '97, 30; 2Q, '88, 9

DRG 296

✔ **St. Anthony's Clinical Coder:** see Chapter 5

276.6 Fluid overload

Fluid retention

Excludes: *ascites (789.5)*
localized edema (782.3)

➡ **CC Excl:** see Code 276.0

276.7 Hyperpotassemia

Hyperkalemia
Potassium [K]:
- excess
- intoxication
- overload

➡ **CC Excl:** see Code 276.0

276.8 Hypopotassemia

Hypokalemia
Potassium [K] deficiency

276.9 Electrolyte and fluid disorders not elsewhere classified

Electrolyte imbalance
Hypochloremia
Hyperchloremia

Excludes: *electrolyte imbalance:*
associated with hyperemesis gravidarum (643.1)
complicating labor and delivery (669.0)
following abortion and ectopic or molar pregnancy (634-638 with .4, 639.4)

➡ **CC Excl:** see Code 276.0

➡ **AHA Coding Clinic:** J-F, '87, 15

277 Other and unspecified disorders of metabolism

✓5th **277.0 Cystic fibrosis**

Fibrocystic disease of the pancreas
Mucoviscidosis

➡ **AHA Coding Clinic:** 4Q, '90, 16; 3Q, '90, 18

277.00 Without mention of meconium ileus

➡ **CC Excl:** 277.00-277.01

277.01 With meconium ileus A: 0

Meconium:
- ileus (of newborn)
- obstruction of intestine in mucoviscidosis

➡ **CC Excl:** see Code 277.00

277.1 Disorders of porphyrin metabolism

Hematoporphyria
Hematoporphyrinuria
Hereditary coproporphyria
Porphyria
Porphyrinuria
Protocoproporphyria
Protoporphyria
Pyrroloporphyria

277.2 Other disorders of purine and pyrimidine metabolism

Hypoxanthine-guanine-phosphoribosyltransferase deficiency [HG-PRT deficiency]
Lesch-Nyhan syndrome
Xanthinuria

Excludes: *gout (274.0-274.9)*
orotic aciduric anemia (281.4)

277.3 Amyloidosis

Amyloidosis:
- NOS
- inherited systemic
- nephropathic
- neuropathic (Portuguese) (Swiss)
- secondary

Benign paroxysmal peritonitis
Familial Mediterranean fever
Hereditary cardiac amyloidosis

277.4 Disorders of bilirubin excretion

Hyperbilirubinemia:
- congenital
- constitutional

Syndrome:
- Crigler-Najjar
- Dubin-Johnson
- Gilbert's
- Rotor's

Excludes: *hyperbilirubinemias specific to the perinatal period (774.0-774.7)*

277.5 Mucopolysaccharidosis

Gargoylism
Hunter's syndrome
Hurler's syndrome
Lipochondrodystrophy
Maroteaux-Lamy syndrome
Morquio-Brailsford disease
Osteochondrodystrophy
Sanfilippo's syndrome
Scheie's syndrome

277.6 Other deficiencies of circulating enzymes

Alpha 1-antitrypsin deficiency
Hereditary angioedema

277.8 Other specified disorders of metabolism

Hand-Schüller-Christian disease
Histiocytosis (acute) (chronic)
Histiocytosis X (chronic)

Excludes: *histiocytosis:*
- *acute differentiated progressive (202.5)*
- *X, acute (progressive) (202.5)*

➡ **AHA Coding Clinic:** S-O, '87, 9

277.9 Unspecified disorder of metabolism

Enzymopathy NOS

278 Obesity and other hyperalimentation

Excludes: *hyperalimentation NOS (783.6)*
poisoning by vitamins NOS (963.5)
polyphagia (783.6)

✓5th **278.0 Obesity**

Excludes: *adiposogenital dystrophy (253.8)*
obesity of endocrine origin NOS (259.9)

278.00 Obesity, unspecified

Obesity NOS

278.01 Morbid obesity

278.1 Localized adiposity

Fat pad

278.2 Hypervitaminosis A

278.3 Hypercarotinemia

278.4 Hypervitaminosis D

278.8 Other hyperalimentation

279 Disorders involving the immune mechanism

✓5th **279.0 Deficiency of humoral immunity**

279.00 Hypogammaglobulinemia, unspecified

Agammaglobulinemia NOS

279.01 Selective IgA immunodeficiency

279.02 Selective IgM immunodeficiency

➡ **CC Excl:** 279.02-279.9

279.03 Other selective immunoglobulin deficiencies

Selective deficiency of IgG

➡ **CC Excl:** see Code 279.02

279.04 Congenital hypogammaglobulinemia

Agammaglobulinemia:
- Bruton's type
- X-linked

➡ **CC Excl:** see Code 279.02

279.05 Immunodeficiency with increased IgM

Immunodeficiency with hyper-IgM:
- autosomal recessive
- X-linked

➡ **CC Excl:** see Code 279.02

279.06 Common variable immunodeficiency

Dysgammaglobulinemia (acquired) (congenital) (primary)
Hypogammaglobulinemia:
- acquired primary
- congenital non-sex-linked
- sporadic

➡ **CC Excl:** see Code 279.02

279.09 Other

Transient hypogammaglobulinemia of infancy

➡ **CC Excl:** see Code 279.02

✓5th **279.1 Deficiency of cell-mediated immunity**

279.10 Immunodeficiency with predominant T-cell defect, unspecified

➡ **CC Excl:** see Code 279.02
➡ **AHA Coding Clinic:** S-O, '87, 10

279.11 DiGeorge's syndrome

Pharyngeal pouch syndrome
Thymic hypoplasia

➡ **CC Excl:** see Code 279.02

279.12 Wiskott-Aldrich syndrome

➡ **CC Excl:** see Code 279.02

279.13 **Nezelof's syndrome**

Cellular immunodeficiency with abnormal immunoglobulin deficiency

➡ **CC Excl:** see Code 279.02

279.19 **Other**

Excludes: *ataxia-telangiectasia (334.8)*

➡ **CC Excl:** see Code 279.02

279.2 **Combined immunity deficiency**

Agammaglobulinemia:
- autosomal recessive
- Swiss-type
- x-linked recessive

Severe combined immunodeficiency [SCID]

Thymic:
- alymphoplasia
- aplasia or dysplasia with immunodeficiency

Excludes: *thymic hypoplasia (279.11)*

➡ **CC Excl:** see Code 279.02

279.3 **Unspecified immunity deficiency**

➡ **CC Excl:** see Code 279.02

279.4 **Autoimmune disease, not elsewhere classified**

Autoimmune disease NOS

Excludes: *transplant failure or rejection (996.80-996.89)*

➡ **CC Excl:** see Code 279.02

279.8 **Other specified disorders involving the immune mechanism**

Single complement [C_1-C_9] deficiency or dysfunction

➡ **CC Excl:** see Code 279.02

279.9 **Unspecified disorder of immune mechanism**

➡ **CC Excl:** see Code 279.02

➡ **AHA Coding Clinic:** 3Q, '92, 13; 3Q, '92, 14

4. DISEASES OF THE BLOOD AND BLOOD-FORMING ORGANS (280-289)

Excludes: *anemia complicating pregnancy or the puerperium (648.2)*

280 Iron deficiency anemias

Includes: anemia:
asiderotic
hypochromic-microcytic
sideropenic

Excludes: *familial microcytic anemia (282.4)*

280.0 Secondary to blood loss (chronic)

Normocytic anemia due to blood loss

Excludes: *acute posthemorrhagic anemia (285.1)*

➡ **CC Excl:** 280.0-280.9, 281.0-281.9, 282.0-282.9, 283.0-283.9, 284.0, 284.8, 285.0-285.9, 289.8-289.9

✔ **St. Anthony's Clinical Coder:** see Chapter 5

280.1 Secondary to inadequate dietary iron intake

280.8 Other specified iron deficiency anemias

Paterson-Kelly syndrome
Plummer-Vinson syndrome
Sideropenic dysphagia

280.9 Iron deficiency anemia, unspecified

Anemia:
achlorhydric
chlorotic
idiopathic hypochromic
iron [Fe] deficiency NOS

281 Other deficiency anemias

281.0 Pernicious anemia

Anemia:
Addison's
Biermer's
congenital pernicious

Congenital intrinsic factor [Castle's] deficiency

Excludes: *combined system disease without mention of anemia (266.2)*
subacute degeneration of spinal cord without mention of anemia (266.2)

281.1 Other vitamin B_{12} deficiency anemia

Anemia:
vegan's
vitamin B_{12} deficiency (dietary)
due to selective vitamin B_{12} malabsorption with proteinuria

Syndrome:
Imerslund's
Imerslund-Gräsbeck

Excludes: *combined system disease without mention of anemia (266.2)*
subacute degeneration of spinal cord without mention of anemia (266.2)

281.2 Folate-deficiency anemia

Congenital folate malabsorption
Folate or folic acid deficiency anemia:
NOS
dietary
drug-induced
Goat's milk anemia
Nutritional megaloblastic anemia (of infancy)

Use additional E code to identify drug

281.3 Other specified megaloblastic anemias, not elsewhere classified

Combined B_{12} and folate-deficiency anemia
Refractory megaloblastic anemia

281.4 Protein-deficiency anemia

Amino-acid-deficiency anemia

➡ **CC Excl:** see Code 280.0

281.8 Anemia associated with other specified nutritional deficiency

Scorbutic anemia

➡ **CC Excl:** see Code 280.0

281.9 Unspecified deficiency anemia

Anemia:
dimorphic
macrocytic
megaloblastic NOS

Anemia:
nutritional NOS
simple chronic

282 Hereditary hemolytic anemias

282.0 Hereditary spherocytosis

Acholuric (familial) jaundice
Congenital hemolytic anemia (spherocytic)
Congenital spherocytosis
Minkowski-Chauffard syndrome
Spherocytosis (familial)

Excludes: *hemolytic anemia of newborn (773.0-773.5)*

282.1 Hereditary elliptocytosis

Elliptocytosis (congenital)
Ovalocytosis (congenital) (hereditary)

282.2 Anemias due to disorders of glutathione metabolism

Anemia:
6-phosphogluconic dehydrogenase deficiency
enzyme deficiency, drug-induced
erythrocytic glutathione deficiency
glucose-6-phosphate dehydrogenase [G-6-PD] deficiency
glutathione-reductase deficiency
hemolytic nonspherocytic (hereditary), type I
Disorder of pentose phosphate pathway
Favism

282.3 Other hemolytic anemias due to enzyme deficiency

Anemia:
- hemolytic nonspherocytic (hereditary), type II
- hexokinase deficiency
- pyruvate kinase [PK] deficiency
- triosephosphate isomerase deficiency

282.4 Thalassemias

Cooley's anemia
Hereditary leptocytosis
Mediterranean anemia (with other hemoglobinopathy)
Microdrepanocytosis
Sickle-cell thalassemia
Thalassemia (alpha) (beta) (intermedia) (major) (minima) (minor) (mixed) (trait) (with other hemoglobinopathy)
Thalassemia-Hb-S disease

Excludes: *sickle-cell:*
anemia (282.60-282.69)
trait (282.5)

➡ **CC Excl:** see Code 280.0

282.5 Sickle-cell trait

Hb-AS genotype
Hemoglobin S [Hb-S] trait
Heterozygous:
- hemoglobin S
- Hb-S

Excludes: *that with other hemoglobinopathy (282.60-282.69)*
that with thalassemia (282.4)

✓5th **282.6 Sickle-cell anemia**

Excludes: *sickle-cell thalassemia (282.4)*
sickle-cell trait (282.5)

282.60 Sickle-cell anemia, unspecified

➡ **CC Excl:** see Code 280.0

➡ **AHA Coding Clinic:** 2Q, '97, 11

282.61 Hb-S disease without mention of crisis

➡ **CC Excl:** see Code 280.0

282.62 Hb-S disease with mention of crisis

Sickle-cell crisis NOS

➡ **CC Excl:** see Code 280.0

➡ **AHA Coding Clinic:** 2Q, '91, 15

282.63 Sickle-cell/Hb-C disease

Hb-S/Hb-C disease

➡ **CC Excl:** see Code 280.0

282.69 Other

Disease:
- Hb-S/Hb-D
- Hb-S/Hb-E

Disease:
- sickle-cell/Hb-D
- sickle-cell/Hb-E

➡ **CC Excl:** see Code 280.0

282.7 Other hemoglobinopathies

Abnormal hemoglobin NOS
Congenital Heinz-body anemia
Disease:
- Hb-Bart's
- hemoglobin C [Hb-C]
- hemoglobin D [Hb-D]
- hemoglobin E [Hb-E]
- hemoglobin Zurich [Hb-Zurich]

Hemoglobinopathy NOS
Hereditary persistence of fetal hemoglobin [HPFH]
Unstable hemoglobin hemolytic disease

Excludes: *familial polycythemia (289.6)*
hemoglobin M [Hb-M] disease (289.7)
high-oxygen-affinity hemoglobin (289.0)

282.8 Other specified hereditary hemolytic anemias

Stomatocytosis

282.9 Hereditary hemolytic anemia, unspecified

Hereditary hemolytic anemia NOS

283 Acquired hemolytic anemias

283.0 Autoimmune hemolytic anemias

Autoimmune hemolytic disease (cold type) (warm type)
Chronic cold hemagglutinin disease
Cold agglutinin disease or hemoglobinuria
Hemolytic anemia:
- cold type (secondary) (symptomatic)
- drug-induced
- warm type (secondary) (symptomatic)

Use additional E code to identify cause if drug-induced

Excludes: *Evans' syndrome (287.3)*
hemolytic disease of newborn (773.0-773.5)

➡ **CC Excl:** see Code 280.0

✓5th **283.1 Non-autoimmune hemolytic anemias**

283.10 Non-autoimmune hemolytic anemia, unspecified

➡ **CC Excl:** 280.0-280.9, 281.0-281.9, 282.0-282.9, 283.0-283.9, 284.0-284.9, 285.0-285.9, 289.8-289.9

283.11 Hemolytic-uremic syndrome

➡ **CC Excl:** see Code 283.10

283.19 Other non-autoimmune hemolytic anemias

Hemolytic anemia:
- mechanical
- microangiopathic
- toxic

Use additional E code to identify cause

➡ **CC Excl:** see Code 283.10

283.2 Hemoglobinuria due to hemolysis from external causes

Acute intravascular hemolysis
Hemoglobinuria:
- from exertion
- march
- paroxysmal (cold) (nocturnal)
- due to other hemolysis

Marchiafava-Micheli syndrome

Use additional E code to identify cause

➡ **CC Excl:** see Code 280.0

283.9 Acquired hemolytic anemia, unspecified

Acquired hemolytic anemia NOS
Chronic idiopathic hemolytic anemia

➡ **CC Excl:** see Code 280.0

284 Aplastic anemia

284.0 Constitutional aplastic anemia

Aplasia, (pure) red cell:
- congenital
- of infants
- primary

Blackfan-Diamond syndrome
Familial hypoplastic anemia
Fanconi's anemia
Pancytopenia with malformations

➡ **CC Excl:** see Code 280.0

➡ **AHA Coding Clinic:** 1Q, '91, 14

284.8 Other specified aplastic anemias

Aplastic anemia (due to):
- chronic systemic disease
- drugs
- infection
- radiation
- toxic (paralytic)

Pancytopenia (acquired)
Red cell aplasia (acquired) (adult) (pure) (with thymoma)

Use additional E code to identify cause

➡ **CC Excl:** see Code 280.0

➡ **AHA Coding Clinic:** 1Q, '97, 5; 1Q, '92, 15; 1Q, '91, 14

284.9 Aplastic anemia, unspecified

Anemia:
- aplastic (idiopathic) NOS
- aregenerative
- hypoplastic NOS

Anemia:
- nonregenerative
- refractory

Medullary hypoplasia

➡ **CC Excl:** see Code 280.0

285 Other and unspecified anemias

285.0 Sideroblastic anemia

Anemia:
- hypochromic with iron loading
- sideroachrestic
- sideroblastic
  - acquired
  - congenital
  - hereditary
  - primary
  - refractory
  - secondary (drug-induced) (due to disease)
  - sex-linked hypochromic
  - vitamin B_6-responsive
- Pyridoxine-responsive (hypochromic) anemia

Use additional E code to identify cause if drug induced

➡ **CC Excl:** see Code 280.0

285.1 Acute posthemorrhagic anemia

Anemia due to acute blood loss

Excludes: *anemia due to chronic blood loss (280.0)*
blood loss anemia NOS (280.0)

➡ **CC Excl:** 280.0-280.9, 281.0-281.9, 282.0-282.9, 283.0-283.9, 284.0, 284.8, 285.0-285.9, 289.8-289.9, 958.2

➡ **AHA Coding Clinic:** 2Q, '92, 15

✔ **St. Anthony's Clinical Coder:** see Chapter 5

285.8 Other specified anemias

Anemia:
- dyserythropoietic (congenital)
- dyshematopoietic (congenital)
- leukoerythroblastic
- von Jaksch's

Infantile pseudoleukemia

➡ **AHA Coding Clinic:** 1Q, '91, 16

285.9 Anemia, unspecified

Anemia:
- NOS
- essential
- normocytic, not due to blood loss

Anemia:
- profound
- progressive
- secondary

Oligocythemia

Excludes: *anemia (due to):*
- *blood loss:*
  - *acute (285.1)*
  - *chronic or unspecified (280.0)*
- *iron deficiency (280.0-280.9)*

➡ **AHA Coding Clinic:** 2Q, '92, 16; M-A, '85, 13; N-D, '84, 1

286 Coagulation defects

286.0 Congenital factor VIII disorder

Antihemophilic globulin [AHG] deficiency
Factor VIII (functional) deficiency
Hemophilia:
- NOS
- A
- classical
- familial
- hereditary

Subhemophilia

Excludes: *factor VIII deficiency with vascular defect (286.4)*

➡ **CC Excl:** 286.0-286.9, 287.0-287.9, 289.8-289.9

286.1 Congenital factor IX disorder

Christmas disease
Deficiency:
- factor IX (functional)
- plasma thromboplastin component [PTC]

Hemophilia B

➡ **CC Excl:** see Code 286.0

286.2 Congenital factor XI deficiency

Hemophilia C
Plasma thromboplastin antecedent [PTA] deficiency
Rosenthal's disease

➡ **CC Excl:** see Code 286.0

286.3 Congenital deficiency of other clotting factors

Congenital afibrinogenemia
Deficiency:
- AC globulin
- factor:
  - I [fibrinogen]
  - II [prothrombin]
  - V [labile]
  - VII [stable]
  - X [Stuart-Prower]
  - XII [Hageman]
  - XIII [fibrin stabilizing]

Deficiency:
- Laki-Lorand factor
- proaccelerin

Disease:
- Owren's
- Stuart-Prower

Dysfibrinogenemia (congenital)
Dysprothrombinemia (constitutional)
Hypoproconvertinemia
Hypoprothrombinemia (hereditary)
Parahemophilia

➡ **CC Excl:** see Code 286.0

286.4 von Willebrand's disease

Angiohemophilia (A) (B)
Constitutional thrombopathy
Factor VIII deficiency with vascular defect
Pseudohemophilia type B
Vascular hemophilia
von Willebrand's (-Jürgens') disease

Excludes: *factor VIII deficiency:*
NOS (286.0)
with functional defect (286.0)
hereditary capillary fragility (287.8)

➡ **CC Excl:** see Code 286.0

286.5 Hemorrhagic disorder due to circulating anticoagulants

Antithrombinemia
Antithromboplastinemia
Antithromboplastinogenemia
Hyperheparinemia
Increase in:
- anti-VIIIa
- anti-IXa
- anti-Xa
- anti-XIa
- antithrombin

Systemic lupus erythematosus [SLE] inhibitor

Use additional E code to identify cause if drug-induced

➡ **CC Excl:** see Code 286.0

➡ **AHA Coding Clinic:** 3Q, '92, 15; 3Q, '90, 14

286.6 Defibrination syndrome

Afibrinogenemia, acquired
Consumption coagulopathy
Diffuse or disseminated intravascular coagulation [DIC syndrome]
Fibrinolytic hemorrhage, acquired
Hemorrhagic fibrinogenolysis
Pathologic fibrinolysis
Purpura:
- fibrinolytic
- fulminans

Excludes: *that complicating:*
abortion (634-638 with .1, 639.1)
pregnancy or the puerperium (641.3, 666.3)
disseminated intravascular coagulation in newborn (776.2)

➡ **CC Excl:** see Code 286.0

286.7 Acquired coagulation factor deficiency

Deficiency of coagulation factor due to:
- liver disease
- vitamin K deficiency

Hypoprothrombinemia, acquired

Use additional E-code to identify cause, if drug induced

Excludes: *vitamin K deficiency of newborn (776.0)*

➡ **CC Excl:** see Code 286.0

286.9 Other and unspecified coagulation defects

Defective coagulation NOS
Deficiency, coagulation factor NOS
Delay, coagulation
Disorder:
- coagulation
- hemostasis

Excludes: *abnormal coagulation profile (790.92)*
hemorrhagic disease of newborn (776.0)
that complicating:
- *abortion (634-638 with .1, 639.1)*
- *pregnancy or the puerperium (641.3, 666.3)*

➡ **CC Excl:** see Code 286.0

287 Purpura and other hemorrhagic conditions

Excludes: *hemorrhagic thrombocythemia (238.7)*
purpura fulminans (286.6)

287.0 Allergic purpura

Peliosis rheumatica
Purpura:
- anaphylactoid
- autoimmune
- Henoch's
- nonthrombocytopenic:
  - hemorrhagic
  - idiopathic
- rheumatica
- Schönlein-Henoch
- vascular

Vasculitis, allergic

Excludes: *hemorrhagic purpura (287.3)*
purpura annularis telangiectodes (709.1)

➡ **CC Excl:** see Code 286.0

287.1 Qualitative platelet defects

Thrombasthenia (hemorrhagic) (hereditary)
Thrombocytasthenia
Thrombocytopathy (dystrophic)
Thrombopathy (Bernard-Soulier)

Excludes: *von Willebrand's disease (286.4)*

➡ **CC Excl:** see Code 286.0

287.2 Other nonthrombocytopenic purpuras

Purpura:
- NOS
- senile
- simplex

➡ **CC Excl:** see Code 286.0

287.3 Primary thrombocytopenia

Evans' syndrome
Megakaryocytic hypoplasia
Purpura, thrombocytopenic
- congenital
- hereditary
- idiopathic

Thrombocytopenia:
- congenital
- hereditary
- primary

Tidal platelet dysgenesis

Excludes: *thrombotic thrombocytopenic purpura (446.6)*
transient thrombocytopenia of newborn (776.1)

➡ **CC Excl:** see Code 286.0

287.4 Secondary thrombocytopenia

Posttransfusion purpura
Thrombocytopenia (due to):
- dilutional
- drugs
- extracorporeal circulation of blood
- massive blood transfusion
- platelet alloimmunization

Use additional E code to identify cause

Excludes: *transient thrombocytopenia of newborn (776.1)*

➡ **CC Excl:** see Code 286.0

287.5 Thrombocytopenia, unspecified

➡ **CC Excl:** see Code 286.0

287.8 Other specified hemorrhagic conditions

Capillary fragility (hereditary)
Vascular pseudohemophilia

➡ **CC Excl:** see Code 286.0

287.9 Unspecified hemorrhagic conditions

Hemorrhagic diathesis (familial)

➡ **CC Excl:** see Code 286.0

288 Diseases of white blood cells

Excludes: *leukemia (204.0-208.9)*

288.0 Agranulocytosis

Infantile genetic agranulocytosis
Kostmann's syndrome
Neutropenia:
- NOS
- cyclic

Neutropenia:
- drug-induced
- immune
- periodic
- toxic

Neutropenic splenomegaly

Use additional E code to identify drug or other cause

Excludes: *transitory neonatal neutropenia (776.7)*

➡ **CC Excl:** 288.0-288.9, 289.8-289.9

➡ **AHA Coding Clinic:** 3Q, '96, 16; 2Q, '96, 6

✔ **St. Anthony's Clinical Coder:** see Chapter 5

288.1 Functional disorders of polymorphonuclear neutrophils

Chronic (childhood) granulomatous disease
Congenital dysphagocytosis
Job's syndrome
Lipochrome histiocytosis (familial)
Progressive septic granulomatosis

➡ **CC Excl:** see Code 288.0

288.2 Genetic anomalies of leukocytes

Anomaly (granulation) (granulocyte) or syndrome:
- Alder's (-Reilly)
- Chédiak-Steinbrinck (-Higashi)
- Jordan's
- May-Hegglin
- Pelger-Huet

Hereditary:
- hypersegmentation
- hyposegmentation
- leukomelanopathy

288.3 Eosinophilia

Eosinophilia
- allergic
- hereditary
- idiopathic
- secondary

Eosinophilic leukocytosis

Excludes: *Löffler's syndrome (518.3)*
pulmonary eosinophilia (518.3)

288.8 Other specified disease of white blood cells

Leukemoid reaction
- lymphocytic
- monocytic
- myelocytic

Leukocytosis
Lymphocytopenia
Lymphocytosis (symptomatic)
Lymphopenia
Monocytosis (symptomatic)
Plasmacytosis

Excludes: *immunity disorders (279.0-279.9)*

➡ **AHA Coding Clinic:** M-A, '87, 12

288.9 Unspecified disease of white blood cells

289 Other diseases of blood and blood-forming organs

289.0 Polycythemia, secondary

High-oxygen-affinity hemoglobin
Polycythemia:
- acquired
- benign
- due to:
  - fall in plasma volume
  - high altitude

Polycythemia:
- emotional
- erythropoietin
- hypoxemic
- nephrogenous
- relative
- spurious
- stress

Excludes: *polycythemia:*
neonatal (776.4)
primary (238.4)
vera (238.4)

289.1 Chronic lymphadenitis

Chronic:
- adenitis } any lymph node, except mesenteric
- lymphadenitis }

Excludes: *acute lymphadenitis (683)*
mesenteric (289.2)
enlarged glands NOS (785.6)

289.2 Nonspecific mesenteric lymphadenitis

Mesenteric lymphadenitis (acute) (chronic)

289.3 Lymphadenitis, unspecified, except mesenteric

➡ **AHA Coding Clinic:** 2Q, '92, 8

289.4 Hypersplenism

"Big spleen" syndrome
Dyssplenism
Hypersplenia

Excludes: *primary splenic neutropenia (288.0)*

✓5th 289.5 Other diseases of spleen

289.50 Disease of spleen, unspecified

289.51 Chronic congestive splenomegaly

289.59 Other

Lien migrans
Perisplenitis
Splenic:
- abscess
- atrophy
- cyst

Splenic:
- fibrosis
- infarction
- rupture, nontraumatic

Splenitis
Wandering spleen

Excludes: *bilharzial splenic fibrosis (120.0-120.9)*
hepatolienal fibrosis (571.5)
splenomegaly NOS (789.2)

289.6 Familial polycythemia

Familial:
- benign polycythemia
- erythrocytosis

289.7 Methemoglobinemia

Congenital NADH [DPNH]-methemoglobin-reductase deficiency
Hemoglobin M [Hb-M] disease
Methemoglobinemia:
  NOS
  acquired (with sulfhemoglobinemia)
  hereditary
  toxic
Stokvis' disease
Sulfhemoglobinemia

Use additional E code to identify cause

289.8 Other specified diseases of blood and blood-forming organs

Hypergammaglobulinemia
Myelofibrosis
Pseudocholinesterase deficiency

➡ **AHA Coding Clinic:** 2Q, '89, 8; M-A, '87, 12

289.9 Unspecified diseases of blood and blood-forming organs

Blood dyscrasia NOS
Erythroid hyperplasia

➡ **AHA Coding Clinic:** M-A, '85, 14

5. MENTAL DISORDERS (290-319)

In the International Classification of Diseases, 9th Revision (*ICD-9*), the corresponding Chapter V, "Mental Disorders," includes a glossary which defines the contents of each category. The introduction to Chapter V in *ICD-9* indicates that the glossary is intended so that psychiatrists can make the diagnosis based on the descriptions provided rather than from the category titles. Lay coders are instructed to code whatever diagnosis the physician records.

Chapter 5, "Mental Disorders," in *ICD-9-CM* uses the standard classification format with inclusion and exclusion terms, omitting the glossary as part of the main text.

The mental disorders section of *ICD-9-CM* has been expanded to incorporate additional psychiatric disorders not listed in *ICD-9*. The glossary from *ICD-9* does not contain all these terms. It now appears in Appendix B, which also contains descriptions and definitions for the terms added in *ICD-9-CM*. Some of these were provided by the American Psychiatric Association's Task Force on Nomenclature and Statistics who are preparing the *Diagnostic and Statistical Manual,* Third Edition (DSM-III), and others from *A Psychiatric Glossary.*

The American Psychiatric Association provided invaluable assistance in modifying Chapter 5 of *ICD-9-CM* to incorporate detail useful to American clinicians and gave permission to use material from the aforementioned sources.

1. Manual of the *International Statistical Classification of Diseases, Injuries, and Causes of Death,* 9th Revision, World Health Organization, Geneva, Switzerland, 1975.
2. American Psychiatric Association, Task Force on Nomenclature and Statistics, Robert L. Spitzer, M.D., Chairman.
3. *A Psychiatric Glossary,* Fourth Edition, American Psychiatric Association, Washington, D.C., 1975.

PSYCHOSES (290-299)

Excludes: *mental retardation (317-319)*

ORGANIC PSYCHOTIC CONDITIONS (290-294)

Includes: psychotic organic brain syndrome

Excludes: *nonpsychotic syndromes of organic etiology (310.0-310.9)*
psychoses classifiable to 295-298 and without impairment of orientation, comprehension, calculation, learning capacity, and judgement, but associated with physical disease, injury, or condition affecting the brain [e.g., following childbirth] (295.0-298.8)

➡ **AHA Coding Clinic:** 1Q, '88, 3

290 Senile and presenile organic psychotic conditions

Code first the associated neurological condition

Excludes: *dementia not classified as senile, presenile, or arteriosclerotic (294.1)*
psychoses classifiable to 295-298 occurring in the senium without dementia or delirium (295.0-298.8)
senility with mental changes of nonpsychotic severity (310.1)
transient organic psychotic conditions (293.0-293.9)

290.0 Senile dementia, uncomplicated A:15–124

Senile dementia:
NOS
simple type

Excludes: *mild memory disturbances, not amounting to dementia, associated with senile brain disease (310.1)*
senile dementia with:
delirium or confusion (290.3)
delusional [paranoid] features (290.20)
depressive features (290.21)

✓5th **290.1 Presenile dementia** A:15–124

Brain syndrome with presenile brain disease

Excludes: *arteriosclerotic dementia (290.40-290.43)*
dementia associated with other cerebral conditions (294.1)

➡ **AHA Coding Clinic:** N-D, '84, 20

290.10 Presenile dementia, uncomplicated

Presenile dementia:
NOS
simple type

290.11 Presenile dementia with delirium

Presenile dementia with acute confusional state

290.12 Presenile dementia with delusional features

Presenile dementia, paranoid type

290.13 Presenile dementia with depressive features

Presenile dementia, depressed type

✓5th **290.2 Senile dementia with delusional or depressive features** A:15–124

Excludes: *senile dementia:*
NOS (290.0)
with delirium and/or confusion (290.3)

290.20 Senile dementia with delusional features
Senile dementia, paranoid type
Senile psychosis NOS

290.21 Senile dementia with depressive features

290.3 Senile dementia with delirium A:15–124
Senile dementia with acute confusional state

Excludes: *senile:*
dementia NOS (290.0)
psychosis NOS (290.20)

✓5th **290.4 Arteriosclerotic dementia** A:15–124
Multi-infarct dementia or psychosis

Use additional code to identify cerebral atherosclerosis (437.0)

Excludes: *suspected cases with no clear evidence of arteriosclerosis (290.9)*

290.40 Arteriosclerotic dementia, uncomplicated
Arteriosclerotic dementia:
NOS
simple type

290.41 Arteriosclerotic dementia with delirium
Arteriosclerotic dementia with acute confusional state

290.42 Arteriosclerotic dementia with delusional features
Arteriosclerotic dementia, paranoid type

290.43 Arteriosclerotic dementia with depressive features
Arteriosclerotic dementia, depressed type

290.8 Other specified senile psychotic conditions
Presbyophrenic psychosis

290.9 Unspecified senile psychotic condition A:15–124

291 Alcoholic psychoses

Excludes: *alcoholism without psychosis (303.0-303.9)*

➡ **AHA Coding Clinic:** S-O, '86, 3

291.0 Alcohol withdrawal delirium
Alcoholic delirium   Delirium tremens

Excludes: *alcohol withdrawal (291.81)*

➡ **CC Excl:** 291.0-291.9, 292.0-292.9, 293.0-293.7, 293.84, 293.9, 294.0-294.9, 303.00-303.93, 304.00-304.91, 305.00-305.03, 305.20-305.93, 790.3

➡ **AHA Coding Clinic:** 2Q, '91, 11

291.1 Alcohol amnestic syndrome
Alcoholic polyneuritic psychosis
Korsakoff's psychosis, alcoholic
Wernicke-Korsakoff syndrome (alcoholic)

➡ **CC Excl:** see Code 291.0

291.2 Other alcoholic dementia
Alcoholic dementia NOS
Alcoholism associated with dementia NOS
Chronic alcoholic brain syndrome

➡ **CC Excl:** see Code 291.0

✔ **St. Anthony's Clinical Coder:** see Chapter 5

291.3 Alcohol withdrawal hallucinosis
Alcoholic:
hallucinosis (acute)
psychosis with hallucinosis

Excludes: *alcohol withdrawal with delirium (291.0)*
schizophrenia (295.0-295.9) and paranoid states (297.0-297.9) taking the form of chronic hallucinosis with clear consciousness in an alcoholic

➡ **CC Excl:** see Code 291.0

➡ **AHA Coding Clinic:** 2Q, '91, 11

291.4 Idiosyncratic alcohol intoxication
Pathologic:
alcohol intoxication
drunkenness

Excludes: *acute alcohol intoxication (305.0)*
in alcoholism (303.0)
simple drunkenness (305.0)

➡ **CC Excl:** see Code 291.0

291.5 Alcoholic jealousy
Alcoholic:
paranoia
psychosis, paranoid type

Excludes: *nonalcoholic paranoid states (297.0-297.9)*
schizophrenia, paranoid type (295.3)

✓5th **291.8 Other specified alcoholic psychosis**

291.81 Alcohol withdrawal
Alcohol:
abstinence syndrome or symptoms
withdrawal syndrome or symptoms

Excludes: *alcohol withdrawal:*
delirium (291.0)
hallucinosis (291.3)
delirium tremens (291.0)

➡ **CC Excl:** 291.0-291.9, 292.0-292.9, 293.0-293.9, 294.0-294.9, 303.00-303.93, 304.00-304.93, 305.00-305.03, 305.20-305.93, 790.3

➡ **AHA Coding Clinic:** 4Q, '96, 28; 2Q, '91, 11

291.89 Other
➡ **CC Excl:** see Code 291.81

291.9 Unspecified alcoholic psychosis
Alcoholic:
mania NOS
psychosis NOS
Alcoholism (chronic) with psychosis
➡ **CC Excl:** see Code 291.0

292 Drug psychoses

Includes: drug-induced mental disorders
organic brain syndrome associated with consumption of drugs

Use additional code for any associated drug dependence (304.0-304.9)

Use additional E code to identify drug

➡ **AHA Coding Clinic:** 2Q, '91, 11; S-O, '86, 3

292.0 Drug withdrawal syndrome
Drug:
abstinence syndrome or symptoms
withdrawal syndrome or symptoms
➡ **CC Excl:** see Code 291.0
➡ **AHA Coding Clinic:** 1Q, '97, 12

✓5th **292.1 Paranoid and/or hallucinatory states induced by drugs**

292.11 Drug-induced organic delusional syndrome
Paranoid state induced by drugs
➡ **CC Excl:** see Code 291.0

292.12 Drug-induced hallucinosis
Hallucinatory state induced by drugs

Excludes: *states following LSD or other hallucinogens, lasting only a few days or less ["bad trips"] (305.3)*

➡ **CC Excl:** see Code 291.0

292.2 Pathological drug intoxication
Drug reaction: NOS, idiosyncratic, pathologic } resulting in brief psychotic states

Excludes: *expected brief psychotic reactions to hallucinogens ["bad trips"] (305.3)*
physiological side-effects of drugs (e.g., dystonias)

➡ **CC Excl:** see Code 291.0

✓5th **292.8 Other specified drug-induced mental disorders**

292.81 Drug-induced delirium
➡ **CC Excl:** see Code 291.0

292.82 Drug-induced dementia
➡ **CC Excl:** see Code 291.0

292.83 Drug-induced amnestic syndrome
➡ **CC Excl:** see Code 291.0

292.84 Drug-induced organic affective syndrome
Depressive state induced by drugs
➡ **CC Excl:** see Code 291.0

292.89 Other
Drug-induced organic personality syndrome
➡ **CC Excl:** see Code 291.0

292.9 Unspecified drug-induced mental disorder
Organic psychosis NOS due to or associated with drugs
➡ **CC Excl:** see Code 291.0

293 Transient organic psychotic conditions

Code first the associated physical or neurological condition

Includes: transient organic mental disorders not associated with alcohol or drugs

Excludes: *confusional state or delirium superimposed on senile dementia (290.3)*
dementia due to:
alcohol (291.0-291.9)
arteriosclerosis (290.40-290.43)
drugs (292.82)
senility (290.0)

293.0 Acute delirium

Acute:
- confusional state
- infective psychosis
- organic reaction
- posttraumatic organic psychosis
- psycho-organic syndrome

Acute psychosis associated with endocrine, metabolic, or cerebrovascular disorder

Epileptic:
- confusional state
- twilight state

293.1 Subacute delirium

Subacute:
- confusional state
- infective psychosis
- organic reaction
- posttraumatic organic psychosis

Subacute:
- psycho-organic syndrome
- psychosis associated with endocrine or metabolic disorder

✓5th **293.8 Other specified transient organic mental disorders**

293.81 Organic delusional syndrome

Transient organic psychotic condition, paranoid type

➡ **CC Excl:** 291.0-291.7, 291.81, 291.89, 291.9, 292.0-292.9, 293.0-293.7, 293.84, 293.9, 294.0-294.9, 303.00-303.93, 304.00-304.93, 305.00-305.03, 305.20-305.93, 790.3

293.82 Organic hallucinosis syndrome

Transient organic psychotic condition, hallucinatory type

➡ **CC Excl:** see Code 293.81

293.83 Organic affective syndrome

Transient organic psychotic condition, depressive type

➡ **CC Excl:** see Code 293.81

293.84 Organic anxiety syndrome

➡ **CC Excl:** 291.0-291.9, 292.0-292.9, 293.0-293.9, 294.0-294.9, 303.00-303.93, 304.00-304.93, 305.00-305.03, 305.20-305.93, 790.3

➡ **AHA Coding Clinic:** 4Q, '96, 29

293.89 Other

293.9 Unspecified transient organic mental disorder

Organic psychosis:
- infective NOS
- posttraumatic NOS
- transient NOS

Psycho-organic syndrome

294 Other organic psychotic conditions (chronic)

Includes: organic psychotic brain syndromes (chronic), not elsewhere classified

➡ **AHA Coding Clinic:** M-A, '85, 12

294.0 Amnestic syndrome

Korsakoff's psychosis or syndrome (nonalcoholic)

Excludes: *alcoholic:*
- *amnestic syndrome (291.1)*
- *Korsakoff's psychosis (291.1)*

294.1 Dementia in conditions classified elsewhere

Code first any underlying physical condition, as:

dementia in:
- Alzheimer's disease (331.0)
- cerebral lipidoses (330.1)
- epilepsy (345.0-345.9)
- general paresis [syphilis] (094.1)
- hepatolenticular degeneration (275.1)
- Huntington's chorea (333.4)
- Jakob-Creutzfeldt disease (046.1)
- multiple sclerosis (340)
- Pick's disease of the brain (331.1)
- polyarteritis nodosa (446.0)
- syphilis (094.1)

Excludes: *dementia:*
- *arteriosclerotic (290.40-290.43)*
- *presenile (290.10-290.13)*
- *senile (290.0)*

epileptic psychosis NOS (294.8)

➡ **AHA Coding Clinic:** N-D, '85, 5

294.8 Other specified organic brain syndromes (chronic)

Epileptic psychosis NOS

Mixed paranoid and affective organic psychotic states

Use additional code for associated epilepsy (345.0-345.9)

Excludes: *mild memory disturbances, not amounting to dementia (310.1)*

294.9 Unspecified organic brain syndrome (chronic)

Organic psychosis (chronic)

OTHER PSYCHOSES (295-299)

Use additional code to identify any associated physical disease, injury, or condition affecting the brain with psychoses classifiable to 295-298

295 Schizophrenic disorders

Includes: schizophrenia of the types described in 295.0-295.9 occurring in children

Excludes: *childhood type schizophrenia (299.9)*
infantile autism (299.0)

The following fifth-digit subclassification is for use with category 295:

- **0 unspecified**
- **1 subchronic**
- **2 chronic**
- **3 subchronic with acute exacerbation**
- **4 chronic with acute exacerbation**
- **5 in remission**

✓5th [3] **295.0 Simple type**
Schizophrenia simplex

Excludes: *latent schizophrenia (295.5)*

➡ **CC Excl: For codes 295.00-295.04:** 295.00-295.95, 296.00-296.99, 297.0-297.9, 298.0-298.9, 299.00-299.91, 300.00-300.9, 301.0-301.9, 306.0-306.9, 307.0-307.9, 308.0-308.9, 309.0-309.9, 310.0-310.9, 311, 312.00-312.9, 313.0-313.9, 314.00-314.9, 315.00-315.9, 316-317, 318.0-318.2, 319

✓5th [3] **295.1 Disorganized type**
Hebephrenia
Hebephrenic type schizophrenia

➡ **CC Excl: For codes 295.10-295.14:** see Code 295.0

✓5th [11] **295.2 Catatonic type**

Catatonic (schizophrenia):
- agitation
- excitation
- excited type
- stupor
- withdrawn type

Schizophrenic:
- catalepsy
- catatonia
- flexibilitas cerea

➡ **CC Excl: For codes 295.21-295.24:** see Code 295.0

✓5th [3] **295.3 Paranoid type**
Paraphrenic schizophrenia

Excludes: *involutional paranoid state (297.2)*
paranoia (297.1)
paraphrenia (297.2)

➡ **CC Excl: For codes 295.30-295.34:** see Code 295.0

DRG 430: For codes 295.30, 295.32, 295.34

✓5th [3] **295.4 Acute schizophrenic episode**
Oneirophrenia
Schizophreniform:
- attack
- disorder
- psychosis, confusional type

Excludes: *acute forms of schizophrenia of:*
- *catatonic type (295.2)*
- *hebephrenic type (295.1)*
- *paranoid type (295.3)*
- *simple type (295.0)*
- *undifferentiated type (295.8)*

➡ **CC Excl: For codes 295.40-295.44:** see Code 295.0

✓5th **295.5 Latent schizophrenia**

Latent schizophrenic reaction
Schizophrenia:
- borderline
- incipient

Schizophrenia:
- prepsychotic
- prodromal
- pseudoneurotic
- pseudopsychopathic

Excludes: *schizoid personality (301.20-301.22)*

✓5th [3] **295.6 Residual schizophrenia**
Chronic undifferentiated schizophrenia
Restzustand (schizophrenic)
Schizophrenic residual state

➡ **CC Excl: For codes 295.60-295.64:** see Code 295.0

DRG 430: For code 295.64

✓5th [3] **295.7 Schizo-affective type**
Cyclic schizophrenia
Mixed schizophrenic and affective psychosis
Schizo-affective psychosis
Schizophreniform psychosis, affective type

➡ **CC Excl: For codes 295.70-295.74:** see Code 295.0

DRG 430: For codes 295.70 and 295.74

✓5th [3] **295.8 Other specified types of schizophrenia**
Acute (undifferentiated) schizophrenia
Atypical schizophrenia
Cenesthopathic schizophrenia

Excludes: *infantile autism (299.0)*

➡ **CC Excl: For codes 295.80-295.84:** see Code 295.0

✓5th [3] **295.9 Unspecified schizophrenia**

Schizophrenia:
- NOS
- mixed NOS
- undifferentiated NOS

Schizophrenic reaction
- NOS

Schizophreniform
- psychosis NOS

➡ **CC Excl: For codes 295.90-295.94:** see Code 295.0

➡ **AHA Coding Clinic:** 3Q, '95, 6

DRG 430: For code 295.90

296 Affective psychoses

Includes: episodic affective disorders

Excludes: *neurotic depression (300.4)*
reactive depressive psychosis (298.0)
reactive excitation (298.1)

The following fifth-digit subclassification is for use with categories 296.0-296.6:

0 unspecified
1 mild
2 moderate
3 severe, without mention of psychotic behavior
4 severe, specified as with psychotic behavior
5 in partial or unspecified remission
6 in full remission

➡ **AHA Coding Clinic:** M-A, '85, 14

[3] CC Coding = 0-4
[11] CC Coding = 1-4

✓5th [5] □ **296.0 Manic disorder, single episode**

Hypomania (mild) NOS
Hypomanic psychosis
Mania (monopolar) NOS
Manic-depressive psychosis or reaction:
hypomanic
manic
} single episode or unspecified

Excludes: *circular type, if there was a previous attack of depression (296.4)*

➡ **CC Excl: For code 296.04:** see Code 295.0

✓5th [5] □ **296.1 Manic disorder, recurrent episode**

Any condition classifiable to 296.0, stated to be recurrent

Excludes: *circular type, if there was a previous attack of depression (296.4)*

➡ **CC Excl: For code 296.14:** see Code 295.0

✓5th □ **296.2 Major depressive disorder, single episode**

Depressive psychosis
Endogenous depression
Involutional melancholia
Manic-depressive psychosis or reaction, depressed type
Monopolar depression
Psychotic depression
} single episode or unspecified

Excludes: *circular type, if previous attack was of manic type (296.5)*
depression NOS (311)
reactive depression (neurotic) (300.4)
psychotic (298.0)

DRG 430: For codes 296.20, 296.23 and 296.24

✓5th [5] □ **296.3 Major depressive disorder, recurrent episode**

Any condition classifiable to 296.2, stated to be recurrent

Excludes: *circular type, if previous attack was of manic type (296.5)*
depression NOS (311)
reactive depression (neurotic) (300.4)
psychotic (298.0)

➡ **CC Excl: For code 296.34:** see Code 295.0

DRG 430: For codes 296.30, 296.33 and 296.34

✓5th [5] □ **296.4 Bipolar affective disorder, manic**

Bipolar disorder, now manic
Manic-depressive psychosis, circular type but currently manic

Excludes: *brief compensatory or rebound mood swings (296.99)*

➡ **CC Excl: For code 296.44:** see Code 295.0

DRG 430: For codes 296.40, 296.44

✓5th [5] □ **296.5 Bipolar affective disorder, depressed**

Bipolar disorder, now depressed
Manic-depressive psychosis, circular type but currently depressed

Excludes: *brief compensatory or rebound mood swings (296.99)*

➡ **CC Excl: For code 296.54:** see Code 295.0

DRG 430: For code 296.50

✓5th [5] □ **296.6 Bipolar affective disorder, mixed**

Manic-depressive psychosis, circular type, mixed

➡ **CC Excl: For code 296.64:** see Code 295.0

□ **296.7 Bipolar affective disorder, unspecified**

Atypical bipolar affective disorder NOS
Manic-depressive psychosis, circular type, current condition not specified as either manic or depressive

DRG 430

✓5th □ **296.8 Manic-depressive psychosis, other and unspecified**

296.80 Manic-depressive psychosis, unspecified

Manic-depressive:
reaction NOS
syndrome NOS

296.81 Atypical manic disorder

296.82 Atypical depressive disorder

296.89 Other

Manic-depressive psychosis, mixed type

✓5th □ **296.9 Other and unspecified affective psychoses**

Excludes: *psychogenic affective psychoses (298.0-298.8)*

296.90 Unspecified affective psychosis

Affective psychosis NOS
Melancholia NOS

296.99 Other specified affective psychoses

Mood swings:
brief compensatory
rebound

297 Paranoid states (Delusional disorders)

Includes: paranoid disorders

Excludes: *acute paranoid reaction (298.3)*
alcoholic jealousy or paranoid state (291.5)
paranoid schizophrenia (295.3)

297.0 Paranoid state, simple

[5] CC Coding = 4

297.1 Paranoia
Chronic paranoid psychosis
Sander's disease
Systematized delusions

Excludes: *paranoid personality disorder (301.0)*

297.2 Paraphrenia
Involutional paranoid state
Late paraphrenia
Paraphrenia (involutional)

297.3 Shared paranoid disorder
Folie á deux
Induced psychosis or paranoid disorder

297.8 Other specified paranoid states
Paranoia querulans
Sensitiver Beziehungswahn

Excludes: *acute paranoid reaction or state (298.3)*
senile paranoid state (290.20)

297.9 Unspecified paranoid state
Paranoid:
disorder NOS
psychosis NOS
reaction NOS
state NOS

298 Other nonorganic psychoses

Includes: psychotic conditions due to or provoked by:
emotional stress
environmental factors as major part of etiology

298.0 Depressive type psychosis
Psychogenic depressive psychosis
Psychotic reactive depression
Reactive depressive psychosis

Excludes: *manic-depressive psychosis, depressed type (296.2-296.3)*
neurotic depression (300.4)
reactive depression NOS (300.4)

➡ **CC Excl:** see Code 295.0

298.1 Excitative type psychosis
Acute hysterical psychosis
Psychogenic excitation
Reactive excitation

Excludes: *manic-depressive psychosis, manic type (296.0-296.1)*

298.2 Reactive confusion
Psychogenic confusion
Psychogenic twilight state

Excludes: *acute confusional state (293.0)*

298.3 Acute paranoid reaction
Acute psychogenic paranoid psychosis
Bouffée délirante

Excludes: *paranoid states (297.0-297.9)*

➡ **CC Excl:** see Code 295.0

298.4 Psychogenic paranoid psychosis
Protracted reactive paranoid psychosis

➡ **CC Excl:** see Code 295.0

298.8 Other and unspecified reactive psychosis
Brief reactive psychosis NOS
Hysterical psychosis
Psychogenic psychosis NOS
Psychogenic stupor

Excludes: *acute hysterical psychosis (298.1)*

298.9 Unspecified psychosis
Atypical psychosis
Psychosis NOS

DRG 430

299 Psychoses with origin specific to childhood

Includes: pervasive developmental disorders

Excludes: *adult type psychoses occurring in childhood, as:*
affective disorders (296.0-296.9)
manic-depressive disorders (296.0-296.9)
schizophrenia (295.0-295.9)

The following fifth-digit subclassification is for use with category 299:

0 current or active state
1 residual state

✓5th **299.0 Infantile autism**
Childhood autism
Infantile psychosis
Kanner's syndrome

Excludes: *disintegrative psychosis (299.1)*
Heller's syndrome (299.1)
schizophrenic syndrome of childhood (299.9)

➡ **CC Excl: For code 299.00:** see Code 295.0

✓5th [1] **299.1 Disintegrative psychosis**
Heller's syndrome

Use additional code to identify any associated neurological disorder

Excludes: *infantile autism (299.0)*
schizophrenic syndrome of childhood (299.9)

➡ **CC Excl: For code 299.10:** see Code 295.0

[1] CC Coding = 0

✓5th [1] **299.8 Other specified early childhood psychoses**
Atypical childhood psychosis
Borderline psychosis of childhood

Excludes: simple stereotypies without psychotic disturbance (307.3)

➡ **CC Excl: For code 299.80:** see Code 295.0

✓5th [1] **299.9 Unspecified**
Child psychosis NOS
Schizophrenia, childhood type NOS
Schizophrenic syndrome of childhood NOS

Excludes: schizophrenia of adult type occurring in childhood (295.0-295.9)

➡ **CC Excl: For code 299.90:** see Code 295.0

NEUROTIC DISORDERS, PERSONALITY DISORDERS, AND OTHER NONPSYCHOTIC MENTAL DISORDERS (300-316)

300 Neurotic disorders

✓5th **300.0 Anxiety states**

Excludes: anxiety in:
acute stress reaction (308.0)
transient adjustment reaction (309.24)
neurasthenia (300.5)
psychophysiological disorders (306.0-306.9)
separation anxiety (309.21)

300.00 Anxiety state, unspecified
Anxiety:
neurosis
reaction
state (neurotic)
Atypical anxiety disorder

300.01 Panic disorder
Panic:
attack
state

300.02 Generalized anxiety disorder

300.09 Other

✓5th **300.1 Hysteria**

Excludes: adjustment reaction (309.0-309.9)
anorexia nervosa (307.1)
gross stress reaction (308.0-308.9)
hysterical personality (301.50-301.59)
psychophysiologic disorders (306.0-306.9)

300.10 Hysteria, unspecified

300.11 Conversion disorder
Astasia-abasia, hysterical
Conversion hysteria or reaction
Hysterical:
blindness
deafness
paralysis

➡ **AHA Coding Clinic:** N-D, '85, 15

300.12 Psychogenic amnesia
Hysterical amnesia

300.13 Psychogenic fugue
Hysterical fugue

300.14 Multiple personality
Dissociative identity disorder

300.15 Dissociative disorder or reaction, unspecified

300.16 Factitious illness with psychological symptoms
Compensation neurosis
Ganser's syndrome, hysterical

300.19 Other and unspecified factitious illness
Factitious illness (with physical symptoms) NOS

Excludes: multiple operations or hospital addiction syndrome (301.51)

✓5th **300.2 Phobic disorders**

Excludes: anxiety state not associated with a specific situation or object (300.00-300.09)
obsessional phobias (300.3)

300.20 Phobia, unspecified
Anxiety-hysteria NOS
Phobia NOS

300.21 Agoraphobia with panic attacks
Fear of:
open spaces } with panic attacks
streets } with panic attacks
travel } with panic attacks

300.22 Agoraphobia without mention of panic attacks
Any condition classifiable to 300.21 without mention of panic attacks

300.23 Social phobia
Fear of:
eating in public
public speaking
washing in public

300.29 Other isolated or simple phobias
Acrophobia
Animal phobias
Claustrophobia
Fear of crowds

[1] CC Coding = 0

300.3 Obsessive-compulsive disorders

Anancastic neurosis
Compulsive neurosis
Obsessional phobia [any]

Excludes: *obsessive-compulsive symptoms occurring in:*
endogenous depression (296.2-296.3)
organic states (e.g., encephalitis)
schizophrenia (295.0-295.9)

300.4 Neurotic depression

Anxiety depression
Depression with anxiety
Depressive reaction
Dysthymic disorder
Neurotic depressive state
Reactive depression

Excludes: *adjustment reaction with depressive symptoms (309.0-309.1)*
depression NOS (311)
manic-depressive psychosis, depressed type (296.2-296.3)
reactive depressive psychosis (298.0)

300.5 Neurasthenia

Fatigue neurosis
Nervous debility
Psychogenic:
asthenia
general fatigue

Use additional code to identify any associated physical disorder

Excludes: *anxiety state (300.00-300.09)*
neurotic depression (300.4)
psychophysiological disorders (306.0-306.9)
specific nonpsychotic mental disorders following organic brain damage (310.0–310.9)

300.6 Depersonalization syndrome

Depersonalization disorder
Derealization (neurotic)
Neurotic state with depersonalization episode

Excludes: *depersonalization associated with:*
anxiety (300.00-300.09)
depression (300.4)
manic-depressive disorder or psychosis (296.0-296.9)
schizophrenia (295.0-295.9)

300.7 Hypochondriasis

Body dysmorphic disorder

Excludes: *hypochondriasis in:*
hysteria (300.10-300.19)
manic-depressive psychosis, depressed type (296.2-296.3)
neurasthenia (300.5)
obsessional disorder (300.3)
schizophrenia (295.0-295.9)

✓5th **300.8 Other neurotic disorders**

300.81 Somatization disorder

Briquet's disorder
Severe somatoform disorder

300.82 Undifferentiated somatoform disorder

Atypical somatoform disorder
Somatoform disorder NOS

➡ **AHA Coding Clinic:** 4Q, '96, 29

300.89 Other

Occupational neurosis, including writers' cramp
Psychasthenia
Psychasthenic neurosis

300.9 Unspecified neurotic disorder

Neurosis NOS
Psychoneurosis NOS

301 Personality disorders

Includes: character neurosis

Use additional code to identify any associated neurosis or psychosis, or physical condition

Excludes: *nonpsychotic personality disorder associated with organic brain syndromes (310.0-310.9)*

301.0 Paranoid personality disorder

Fanatic personality
Paranoid personality (disorder)
Paranoid traits

Excludes: *acute paranoid reaction (298.3)*
alcoholic paranoia (291.5)
paranoid schizophrenia (295.3)
paranoid states (297.0-297.9)

✓5th **301.1 Affective personality disorder**

Excludes: *affective psychotic disorders (296.0-296.9)*
neurasthenia (300.5)
neurotic depression (300.4)

301.10 Affective personality disorder, unspecified

301.11 Chronic hypomanic personality disorder

Chronic hypomanic disorder
Hypomanic personality

301.12 Chronic depressive personality disorder

Chronic depressive disorder
Depressive character or personality

301.13 Cyclothymic disorder

Cycloid personality
Cyclothymia
Cyclothymic personality

✓5th **301.2 Schizoid personality disorder**

Excludes: *schizophrenia (295.0-295.9)*

301.20 Schizoid personality disorder, unspecified

301.21 Introverted personality

301.22 Schizotypal personality

301.3 Explosive personality disorder

Aggressive:
- personality
- reaction

Aggressiveness
Emotional instability (excessive)
Pathological emotionality
Quarrelsomeness

Excludes: *dyssocial personality (301.7)*
hysterical neurosis (300.10-300.19)

301.4 Compulsive personality disorder

Anancastic personality
Obsessional personality

Excludes: *obsessive-compulsive disorder (300.3)*
phobic state (300.20-300.29)

✓5th **301.5 Histrionic personality disorder**

Excludes: *hysterical neurosis (300.10-300.19)*

301.50 Histrionic personality disorder, unspecified

Hysterical personality NOS

301.51 Chronic factitious illness with physical symptoms

Hospital addiction syndrome
Multiple operations syndrome
Munchausen syndrome

301.59 Other histrionic personality disorder

Personality:
- emotionally unstable
- labile
- psychoinfantile

301.6 Dependent personality disorder

Asthenic personality
Inadequate personality
Passive personality

Excludes: *neurasthenia (300.5)*
passive-aggressive personality (301.84)

301.7 Antisocial personality disorder

Amoral personality
Asocial personality
Dyssocial personality
Personality disorder with predominantly sociopathic or asocial manifestation

Excludes: *disturbance of conduct without specifiable personality disorder (312.0-312.9)*
explosive personality (301.3)

✓5th **301.8 Other personality disorders**

301.81 Narcissistic personality

301.82 Avoidant personality

301.83 Borderline personality

301.84 Passive-aggressive personality

301.89 Other

Personality:
- eccentric
- "haltlose" type
- immature

Personality:
- masochistic
- psychoneurotic

Excludes: *psychoinfantile personality (301.59)*

301.9 Unspecified personality disorder

Pathological personality NOS
Personality disorder NOS
Psychopathic:
- constitutional state
- personality (disorder)

302 Sexual deviations and disorders

Excludes: *sexual disorder manifest in:*
organic brain syndrome (290.0-294.9, 310.0-310.9)
psychosis (295.0-298.9)

302.0 Ego-dystonic homosexuality

Ego-dystonic lesbianism
Homosexual conflict disorder

Excludes: *homosexual pedophilia (302.2)*

302.1 Zoophilia

Bestiality

302.2 Pedophilia

302.3 Transvestism

Excludes: *trans-sexualism (302.5)*

302.4 Exhibitionism

✓5th **302.5 Trans-sexualism**

Excludes: *transvestism (302.3)*

302.50 With unspecified sexual history

302.51 With asexual history

302.52 With homosexual history

302.53 With heterosexual history

302.6 Disorders of psychosexual identity

Feminism in boys
Gender identity disorder of childhood

Excludes: *gender identity disorder in adult (302.85)*
homosexuality (302.0)
trans-sexualism (302.50-302.53)
transvestism (302.3)

✓5th **302.7 Psychosexual dysfunction**

Excludes: *impotence of organic origin (607.84)*
normal transient symptoms from ruptured hymen
transient or occasional failures of erection due to fatigue, anxiety, alcohol, or drugs

302.70 Psychosexual dysfunction, unspecified

302.71 With inhibited sexual desire

302.72 With inhibited sexual excitement
Frigidity Impotence

302.73 With inhibited female orgasm ♀

302.74 With inhibited male orgasm ♂

302.75 With premature ejaculation ♂

302.76 With functional dyspareunia ♀
Dyspareunia, psychogenic

302.79 With other specified psychosexual dysfunctions

✓5th **302.8 Other specified psychosexual disorders**

302.81 Fetishism

302.82 Voyeurism

302.83 Sexual masochism

302.84 Sexual sadism

302.85 Gender identity disorder of adolescent or adult life A: 15-124

302.89 Other
Nymphomania Satyriasis

302.9 Unspecified psychosexual disorder
Pathologic sexuality NOS Sexual deviation NOS

303 Alcohol dependence syndrome

Use additional code to identify any associated condition, as:
alcoholic psychoses (291.0-291.9)
drug dependence (304.0-304.9)
physical complications of alcohol, such as:
cerebral degeneration (331.7)
cirrhosis of liver (571.2)
epilepsy (345.0-345.9)
gastritis (535.3)
hepatitis (571.1)
liver damage NOS (571.3)

Excludes: *drunkenness NOS (305.0)*

The following fifth-digit subclassification is for use with category 303:

0 **unspecified**
1 **continuous**
2 **episodic**
3 **in remission**

➡ **AHA Coding Clinic:** 3Q, '95, 6; 2Q, '91, 9; 4Q, '88, 8; S-O, '86, 3

✓5th [2] **303.0 Acute alcoholic intoxication**
Acute drunkenness in alcoholism

➡ **CC Excl: For codes 303.00-303.02:** 291.0-291.7, 291.81, 291.89, 291.9, 292.0-292.9, 303.00-303.93, 304.00-304.91, 305.00-305.03, 305.20-305.93, 790.3

✓ **St. Anthony's Clinical Coder: For Codes 303.00-303.02:** see Chapter 5

✓5th [2] **303.9 Other and unspecified alcohol dependence**
Chronic alcoholism Dipsomania

➡ **CC Excl: For codes 303.90-303.92:** see Code 303.0

➡ **AHA Coding Clinic:** 2Q, '89, 9

✓ **St. Anthony's Clinical Coder: For Codes 303.90-303.92:** see Chapter 5

304 Drug dependence

Excludes: *nondependent abuse of drugs (305.1-305.9)*

The following fifth-digit subclassification is for use with category 304:

0 **unspecified**
1 **continuous**
2 **episodic**
3 **in remission**

➡ **AHA Coding Clinic:** 2Q, '91, 10; 4Q, '88, 8; S-O, '86, 3

[2] CC Coding = 0-2

✓5th [2] **304.0 Opioid type dependence**

Heroin
Meperidine
Methadone
Morphine
Opium
Opium alkaloids and their derivatives
Synthetics with morphine-like effects

➡ **CC Excl: For codes 304.00-304.02:** see Code 303.0

✓5th [2] **304.1 Barbiturate and similarly acting sedative or hypnotic dependence**

Barbiturates
Nonbarbiturate sedatives and tranquilizers with a similar effect:
- chlordiazepoxide
- diazepam
- glutethimide
- meprobamate
- methaqualone

➡ **CC Excl: For codes 304.10-304.12:** see Code 303.0

✓5th [2] **304.2 Cocaine dependence**

Coca leaves and derivatives

➡ **CC Excl: For codes 304.20-304.22:** see Code 303.0

✓5th **304.3 Cannabis dependence**

Hashish
Hemp
Marihuana

✓5th [2] **304.4 Amphetamine and other psychostimulant dependence**

Methylphenidate
Phenmetrazine

➡ **CC Excl: For codes 304.40-304.42:** see Code 303.0

✓5th [2] **304.5 Hallucinogen dependence**

Dimethyltryptamine [DMT]
Lysergic acid diethylamide [LSD] and derivatives
Mescaline
Psilocybin

➡ **CC Excl: For codes 304.50-304.52:** see Code 303.0

✓5th [2] **304.6 Other specified drug dependence**

Absinthe addiction
Glue sniffing

Excludes: *tobacco dependence (305.1)*

➡ **CC Excl: For codes 304.60-304.62:** see Code 303.0

✓5th [2] **304.7 Combinations of opioid type drug with any other**

➡ **CC Excl: For codes 304.70-304.72:** see Code 303.0

✓5th [2] **304.8 Combinations of drug dependence excluding opioid type drug**

➡ **CC Excl: For codes 304.80-304.82:** see Code 303.0

➡ **AHA Coding Clinic:** M-A, '86, 12

✓5th [2] **304.9 Unspecified drug dependence**

Drug addiction NOS
Drug dependence NOS

➡ **CC Excl: For codes 304.90-304.92:** see Code 303.0

305 Nondependent abuse of drugs

Note: Includes cases where a person, for whom no other diagnosis is possible, has come under medical care because of the maladaptive effect of a drug on which he is not dependent and that he has taken on his own initiative to the detriment of his health or social functioning.

Excludes: *alcohol dependence syndrome (303.0-303.9)*
drug dependence (304.0-304.9)
drug withdrawal syndrome (292.0)
poisoning by drugs or medicinal substances (960.0-979.9)

The following fifth-digit subclassification is for use with codes 305.0, 305.2-305.9:

0 unspecified
1 continuous
2 episodic
3 in remission

➡ **AHA Coding Clinic:** 2Q, '91, 10; 4Q, '88, 8; S-O, '86, 3

✓5th **305.0 Alcohol abuse**

Drunkenness NOS
Excessive drinking of alcohol NOS
"Hangover" (alcohol)
Inebriety NOS

Excludes: *acute alcohol intoxication in alcoholism (303.0)*
alcoholic psychoses (291.0-291.9)

➡ **CC Excl: For codes 305.00-305.02:** see Code 303.0

305.1 Tobacco use disorder

Tobacco dependence

Excludes: *history of tobacco use (V15.82)*

➡ **AHA Coding Clinic:** 2Q, '96, 10; N-D, '84, 12

✓5th **305.2 Cannabis abuse**

[2] CC Coding = 0-2

✓5th [2] **305.3 Hallucinogen abuse**

Acute intoxication from hallucinogens ["bad trips"]
LSD reaction

➡ **CC Excl: For codes 305.30-305.32:** see Code 303.0

✓5th [2] **305.4 Barbiturate and similarly acting sedative or hypnotic abuse**

➡ **CC Excl: For codes 305.40-305.42:** see Code 303.0

✓5th [2] **305.5 Opioid abuse**

➡ **CC Excl: For codes 305.50-305.52:** see Code 303.0

✓5th [2] **305.6 Cocaine abuse**

➡ **CC Excl: For codes 305.60-305.62:** see Code 303.0

➡ **AHA Coding Clinic:** 1Q, '93, 25

✓5th [2] **305.7 Amphetamine or related acting sympathomimetic abuse**

➡ **CC Excl: For codes 305.70-305.72:** see Code 303.0

✓5th **305.8 Antidepressant type abuse**

✓5th [2] **305.9 Other, mixed, or unspecified drug abuse**

"Laxative habit"
Misuse of drugs NOS
Nonprescribed use of drugs or patent medicinals

➡ **CC Excl: For codes 305.90-305.92:** see Code 303.0

306 Physiological malfunction arising from mental factors

Includes: psychogenic:
physical symptoms } not involving tissue damage
physiological manifestations } not involving tissue damage

Excludes: *hysteria (300.11-300.19)*
physical symptoms secondary to a psychiatric disorder classified elsewhere
psychic factors associated with physical conditions involving tissue damage classified elsewhere (316)
specific nonpsychotic mental disorders following organic brain damage (310.0-310.9)

306.0 Musculoskeletal

Psychogenic paralysis
Psychogenic torticollis

Excludes: *Gilles de la Tourette's syndrome (307.23)*
paralysis as hysterical or conversion reaction (300.11)
tics (307.20-307.22)

306.1 Respiratory

Psychogenic:
air hunger
cough
hiccough

Psychogenic:
hyperventilation
yawning

Excludes: *psychogenic asthma (316 and 493.9)*

306.2 Cardiovascular

Cardiac neurosis
Cardiovascular neurosis
Neurocirculatory asthenia
Psychogenic cardiovascular disorder

Excludes: *psychogenic paroxysmal tachycardia (316 and 427.2)*

➡ **AHA Coding Clinic:** J-A, '85, 14

306.3 Skin

Psychogenic pruritus

Excludes: *psychogenic:*
alopecia (316 and 704.00)
dermatitis (316 and 692.9)
eczema (316 and 691.8 or 692.9)
urticaria (316 and 708.0-708.9)

306.4 Gastrointestinal

Aerophagy
Cyclical vomiting, psychogenic
Diarrhea, psychogenic
Nervous gastritis
Psychogenic dyspepsia

Excludes: *cyclical vomiting NOS (536.2)*
globus hystericus (300.11)
mucous colitis (316 and 564.1)
psychogenic:
cardiospasm (316 and 530.0)
duodenal ulcer (316 and 532.0-532.9)
gastric ulcer (316 and 531.0-531.9)
peptic ulcer NOS (316 and 533.0-533.9)
vomiting NOS (307.54)

➡ **AHA Coding Clinic:** 2Q, '89, 11

✓5th **306.5 Genitourinary**

Excludes: *enuresis, psychogenic (307.6)*
frigidity (302.72)
impotence (302.72)
psychogenic dyspareunia (302.76)

306.50 Psychogenic genitourinary malfunction, unspecified

306.51 Psychogenic vaginismus ♀

Functional vaginismus

306.52 Psychogenic dysmenorrhea ♀

306.53 Psychogenic dysuria

306.59 Other

➡ **AHA Coding Clinic:** M-A, '87, 11

[2] CC Coding = 0-2

306.6 **Endocrine**

306.7 **Organs of special sense**

Excludes: *hysterical blindness or deafness (300.11)*
psychophysical visual disturbances (368.16)

306.8 **Other specified psychophysiological malfunction**
Bruxism
Teeth grinding

306.9 **Unspecified psychophysiological malfunction**
Psychophysiologic disorder NOS
Psychosomatic disorder NOS

307 Special symptoms or syndromes, not elsewhere classified

Note: This category is intended for use if the psychopathology is manifested by a single specific symptom or group of symptoms which is not part of an organic illness or other mental disorder classifiable elsewhere.

Excludes: *those due to mental disorders classified elsewhere*
those of organic origin

307.0 **Stammering and stuttering**

Excludes: *dysphasia (784.5)*
lisping or lalling (307.9)
retarded development of speech (315.31-315.39)

307.1 **Anorexia nervosa**

Excludes: *eating disturbance NOS (307.50)*
feeding problem (783.3)
of nonorganic origin (307.59)
loss of appetite (783.0)
of nonorganic origin (307.59)

➡ **CC Excl:** 306.4, 306.8-306.9, 307.1, 307.50-307.59, 309.22

➡ **AHA Coding Clinic:** 4Q, '89, 11

✔ **St. Anthony's Clinical Coder:** see Chapter 5

✓5th **307.2** **Tics**

Excludes: *nail-biting or thumb-sucking (307.9)*
stereotypies occurring in isolation (307.3)
tics of organic origin (333.3)

307.20 **Tic disorder, unspecified**

307.21 **Transient tic disorder of childhood**

307.22 **Chronic motor tic disorder**

307.23 **Gilles de la Tourette's disorder**
Motor-verbal tic disorder

307.3 **Stereotyped repetitive movements**
Body-rocking
Head banging
Spasmus nutans
Stereotypies NOS

Excludes: *tics (307.20-307.23)*
of organic origin (333.3)

✓5th **307.4** **Specific disorders of sleep of nonorganic origin**

Excludes: *narcolepsy (347)*
those of unspecified cause (780.50-780.59)

307.40 **Nonorganic sleep disorder, unspecified**

307.41 **Transient disorder of initiating or maintaining sleep**
Hyposomnia, Insomnia, Sleeplessness } associated with acute or intermittent emotional reactions or conflicts

307.42 **Persistent disorder of initiating or maintaining sleep**
Hyposomnia, insomnia, or sleeplessness associated with:
- anxiety
- conditioned arousal
- depression (major) (minor)
- psychosis

307.43 **Transient disorder of initiating or maintaining wakefulness**
Hypersomnia associated with acute or intermittent emotional reactions or conflicts

307.44 **Persistent disorder of initiating or maintaining wakefulness**
Hypersomnia associated with depression (major) (minor)

307.45 **Phase-shift disruption of 24-hour sleep-wake cycle**
Irregular sleep-wake rhythm, nonorganic origin
Jet lag syndrome
Rapid time-zone change
Shifting sleep-work schedule

307.46 **Somnambulism or night terrors**

307.47 **Other dysfunctions of sleep stages or arousal from sleep**
Nightmares:
- NOS
- REM-sleep type

Sleep drunkness

307.48 **Repetitive intrusions of sleep**
Repetitive intrusion of sleep with:
- atypical polysomnographic features
- environmental disturbances
- repeated REM-sleep interruptions

307.49 Other
"Short-sleeper"
Subjective insomnia complaint

✓5th **307.5 Other and unspecified disorders of eating**

Excludes: *anorexia:*
nervosa (307.1)
of unspecified cause (783.0)
overeating, of unspecified cause (783.6)
vomiting:
NOS (787.0)
cyclical (536.2)
psychogenic (306.4)

307.50 Eating disorder, unspecified

307.51 Bulimia
Overeating of nonorganic origin

307.52 Pica
Perverted appetite of nonorganic origin

307.53 Psychogenic rumination
Regurgitation, of nonorganic origin, of food with reswallowing

Excludes: *obsessional rumination (300.3)*

307.54 Psychogenic vomiting

307.59 Other
Infantile feeding disturbances } of nonorganic origin
Loss of appetite } of nonorganic origin

307.6 Enuresis
Enuresis (primary) (secondary) of nonorganic origin

Excludes: *enuresis of unspecified cause (788.3)*

307.7 Encopresis
Encopresis (continuous) (discontinuous) of nonorganic origin

Excludes: *encopresis of unspecified cause (787.6)*

✓5th **307.8 Psychalgia**

307.80 Psychogenic pain, site unspecified

307.81 Tension headache

Excludes: *headache:*
NOS (784.0)
migraine (346.0-346.9)

➡ **AHA Coding Clinic:** N-D, '85, 16

307.89 Other
Psychogenic backache

Excludes: *pains not specifically attributable to a psychological cause (in):*
back (724.5)
joint (719.4)
limb (729.5)
lumbago (724.2)
rheumatic (729.0)

307.9 Other and unspecified special symptoms or syndromes, not elsewhere classified
Hair-plucking
Lalling
Lisping
Masturbation
Nail-biting
Thumb-sucking

308 Acute reaction to stress

Includes: catastrophic stress
combat fatigue
gross stress reaction (acute)
transient disorders in response to exceptional physical or mental stress which usually subside within hours or days

Excludes: *adjustment reaction or disorder (309.0-309.9)*
chronic stress reaction (309.1-309.9)

308.0 Predominant disturbance of emotions
Anxiety } as acute reaction to exceptional [gross] stress
Emotional crisis } as acute reaction to exceptional [gross] stress
Panic state } as acute reaction to exceptional [gross] stress

308.1 Predominant disturbance of consciousness
Fugues as acute reaction to exceptional [gross] stress

308.2 Predominant psychomotor disturbance
Agitation states } as acute reaction to exceptional [gross] stress
Stupor } as acute reaction to exceptional [gross] stress

308.3 Other acute reactions to stress
Acute situational disturbance
Brief or acute posttraumatic stress disorder

Excludes: *prolonged posttraumatic emotional disturbance (309.81)*

308.4 Mixed disorders as reaction to stress

308.9 Unspecified acute reaction to stress

309 Adjustment reaction

Includes: adjustment disorders
reaction (adjustment) to chronic stress

Excludes: *acute reaction to major stress (308.0-308.9)*
neurotic disorders (300.0-300.9)

309.0 Brief depressive reaction
Adjustment disorder with depressed mood
Grief reaction

Excludes: *affective psychoses (296.0-296.9)*
neurotic depression (300.4)
prolonged depressive reaction (309.1)
psychogenic depressive psychosis (298.0)

309.1 Prolonged depressive reaction

Excludes: *affective psychoses (296.0-296.9)*
brief depressive reaction (309.0)
neurotic depression (300.4)
psychogenic depressive psychosis (298.0)

✓5th **309.2 With predominant disturbance of other emotions**

309.21 Separation anxiety disorder

309.22 Emancipation disorder of adolescence and early adult life

309.23 Specific academic or work inhibition

309.24 Adjustment reaction with anxious mood

309.28 Adjustment reaction with mixed emotional features
Adjustment reaction with anxiety and depression

309.29 Other
Culture shock

309.3 With predominant disturbance of conduct
Conduct disturbance } as adjustment reaction
Destructiveness }

Excludes: *destructiveness in child (312.9)*
disturbance of conduct NOS (312.9)
dyssocial behavior without manifest psychiatric disorder (V71.01-V71.02)
personality disorder with predominantly sociopathic or asocial manifestations (301.7)

309.4 With mixed disturbance of emotions and conduct

✓5th **309.8 Other specified adjustment reactions**

309.81 Prolonged posttraumatic stress disorder
Chronic posttraumatic stress disorder
Concentration camp syndrome

Excludes: *posttraumatic brain syndrome:*
nonpsychotic (310.2)
psychotic (293.0-293.9)

309.82 Adjustment reaction with physical symptoms

309.83 Adjustment reaction with withdrawal
Elective mutism as adjustment reaction
Hospitalism (in children) NOS

309.89 Other

309.9 Unspecified adjustment reaction
Adaptation reaction NOS Adjustment reaction NOS

310 Specific nonpsychotic mental disorders due to organic brain damage

Excludes: *neuroses, personality disorders, or other nonpsychotic conditions occurring in a form similar to that seen with functional disorders but in association with a physical condition (300.0-300.9, 301.0-301.9)*

310.0 Frontal lobe syndrome
Lobotomy syndrome
Postleucotomy syndrome [state]

Excludes: *postcontusion syndrome (310.2)*

310.1 Organic personality syndrome
Cognitive or personality change of other type, of nonpsychotic severity
Mild memory disturbance
Organic psychosyndrome of nonpsychotic severity
Presbyophrenia NOS
Senility with mental changes of nonpsychotic severity

310.2 Postconcussion syndrome
Postcontusion syndrome or encephalopathy
Posttraumatic brain syndrome, nonpsychotic
Status postcommotio cerebri

Excludes: *frontal lobe syndrome (310.0)*
postencephalitic syndrome (310.8)
any organic psychotic conditions following head injury (293.0-294.0)

➡ **AHA Coding Clinic:** 4Q, '90, 24

310.8 Other specified nonpsychotic mental disorders following organic brain damage
Other focal (partial) organic psychosyndromes
Postencephalitic syndrome

310.9 Unspecified nonpsychotic mental disorder following organic brain damage

311 Depressive disorder, not elsewhere classified

Depressive disorder NOS Depression NOS
Depressive state NOS

Excludes: *acute reaction to major stress with depressive symptoms (308.0)*
affective personality disorder (301.10-301.13)
affective psychoses (296.0-296.9)
brief depressive reaction (309.0)
depressive states associated with stressful events (309.0-309.1)
disturbance of emotions specific to childhood and adolescence, with misery and unhappiness (313.1)
mixed adjustment reaction with depressive symptoms (309.4)
neurotic depression (300.4)
prolonged depressive adjustment reaction (309.1)
psychogenic depressive psychosis (298.0)

312 Disturbance of conduct, not elsewhere classified

Excludes: *adjustment reaction with disturbance of conduct (309.3)*
drug dependence (304.0-304.9)
dyssocial behavior without manifest psychiatric disorder (V71.01-V71.02)
personality disorder with predominantly sociopathic or asocial manifestations (301.7)
sexual deviations (302.0-302.9)

The following fifth-digit subclassification is for use with categories 312.0-312.2:

0 unspecified
1 mild
2 moderate
3 severe

✓5th □ **312.0 Undersocialized conduct disorder, aggressive type**

Aggressive outburst
Anger reaction
Unsocialized aggressive disorder

✓5th □ **312.1 Undersocialized conduct disorder, unaggressive type**

Childhood truancy, unsocialized
Solitary stealing
Tantrums

✓5th □ **312.2 Socialized conduct disorder**

Childhood truancy, socialized
Group delinquency

Excludes: *gang activity without manifest psychiatric disorder (V71.01)*

✓5th □ **312.3 Disorders of impulse control, not elsewhere classified**

312.30 Impulse control disorder, unspecified

312.31 Pathological gambling

312.32 Kleptomania

312.33 Pyromania

312.34 Intermittent explosive disorder

312.35 Isolated explosive disorder

312.39 Other

□ **312.4 Mixed disturbance of conduct and emotions**

Neurotic delinquency

Excludes: *compulsive conduct disorder (312.3)*

✓5th **312.8 Other specified disturbances of conduct, not elsewhere classified**

312.81 Conduct disorder, childhood onset type

312.82 Conduct disorder, adolescent onset type

312.89 Other conduct disorder

312.9 Unspecified disturbance of conduct

Delinquency (juvenile)

313 Disturbance of emotions specific to childhood and adolescence

Excludes: *adjustment reaction (309.0-309.9)*
emotional disorder of neurotic type (300.0-300.9)
masturbation, nail-biting, thumb-sucking, and other isolated symptoms (307.0-307.9)

313.0 Overanxious disorder

Anxiety and fearfulness } of childhood and adolescence
Overanxious disorder }

Excludes: *abnormal separation anxiety (309.21)*
anxiety states (300.00-300.09)
hospitalism in children (309.83)
phobic state (300.20-300.29)

313.1 Misery and unhappiness disorder

Excludes: *depressive neurosis (300.4)*

✓5th **313.2 Sensitivity, shyness, and social withdrawal disorder**

Excludes: *infantile autism (299.0)*
schizoid personality (301.20-301.22)
schizophrenia (295.0-295.9)

313.21 Shyness disorder of childhood

Sensitivity reaction of childhood or adolescence

313.22 Introverted disorder of childhood

Social withdrawal } of childhood or adolescence
Withdrawal reaction }

313.23 Elective mutism

Excludes: *elective mutism as adjustment reaction (309.83)*

313.3 Relationship problems
Sibling jealousy

Excludes: *relationship problems associated with aggression, destruction, or other forms of conduct disturbance (312.0-312.9)*

✓5th **313.8 Other or mixed emotional disturbances of childhood or adolescence**

313.81 Oppositional disorder

313.82 Identity disorder

313.83 Academic underachievement disorder

313.89 Other A:0–17

313.9 Unspecified emotional disturbance of childhood or adolescence A:0–17

314 Hyperkinetic syndrome of childhood

Excludes: *hyperkinesis as symptom of underlying disorder—code the underlying disorder*

✓5th **314.0 Attention deficit disorder**
Adult
Child

314.00 Without mention of hyperactivity
Predominantly inattentive type

➡ **AHA Coding Clinic:** 1Q, '97, 8

314.01 With hyperactivity
Combined type
Overactivity NOS
Predominantly hyperative/impulsive type
Simple disturbance of attention with overactivity

➡ **AHA Coding Clinic:** 1Q, '97, 8

314.1 Hyperkinesis with developmental delay
Developmental disorder of hyperkinesis

Use additional code to identify any associated neurological disorder

314.2 Hyperkinetic conduct disorder
Hyperkinetic conduct disorder without developmental delay

Excludes: *hyperkinesis with significant delays in specific skills (314.1)*

314.8 Other specified manifestations of hyperkinetic syndrome

314.9 Unspecified hyperkinetic syndrome
Hyperkinetic reaction of childhood or adolescence NOS
Hyperkinetic syndrome NOS

315 Specific delays in development

Excludes: *that due to a neurological disorder (320.0-389.9)*

✓5th **315.0 Specific reading disorder**

315.00 Reading disorder, unspecified

315.01 Alexia

315.02 Developmental dyslexia

315.09 Other
Specific spelling difficulty

315.1 Specific arithmetical disorder
Dyscalculia

315.2 Other specific learning difficulties

Excludes: *specific arithmetical disorder (315.1)*
specific reading disorder (315.00-315.09)

✓5th **315.3 Developmental speech or language disorder**

315.31 Developmental language disorder
Developmental aphasia
Expressive language disorder
Word deafness

Excludes: *acquired aphasia (784.3)*
elective mutism (309.83, 313.0, 313.23)

315.32 Receptive language disorder (mixed)
Receptive expressive language disorder

➡ **AHA Coding Clinic:** 4Q, '96, 30

315.39 Other
Developmental articulation disorder
Dyslalia

Excludes: *lisping and lalling (307.9)*
stammering and stuttering (307.0)

315.4 Coordination disorder
Clumsiness syndrome
Dyspraxia syndrome
Specific motor development disorder

315.5 Mixed development disorder

315.8 Other specified delays in development

315.9 Unspecified delay in development
Developmental disorder NOS

316 Psychic factors associated with diseases classified elsewhere

Psychologic factors in physical conditions classified elsewhere

Use additional code to identify the associated physical condition, as:
- psychogenic:
  - asthma (493.9)
  - dermatitis (692.9)
  - duodenal ulcer (532.0-532.9)
  - eczema (691.8, 692.9)
  - gastric ulcer (531.0-531.9)
  - mucous colitis (564.1)
  - paroxysmal tachycardia (427.2)
  - ulcerative colitis (556)
  - urticaria (708.0-708.9)
- psychosocial dwarfism (259.4)

Excludes: *physical symptoms and physiological malfunctions, not involving tissue damage, of mental origin (306.0-306.9)*

MENTAL RETARDATION (317-319)

Use additional code(s) to identify any associated psychiatric or physical condition(s)

317 Mild mental retardation

High-grade defect
IQ 50-70
Mild mental subnormality

318 Other specified mental retardation

318.0 Moderate mental retardation

IQ 35-49
Moderate mental subnormality

318.1 Severe mental retardation

IQ 20-34
Severe mental subnormality

318.2 Profound mental retardation

IQ under 20
Profound mental subnormality

319 Unspecified mental retardation

Mental deficiency NOS
Mental subnormality NOS

6. DISEASES OF THE NERVOUS SYSTEM AND SENSE ORGANS (320-389)

INFLAMMATORY DISEASES OF THE CENTRAL NERVOUS SYSTEM (320-326)

320 Bacterial meningitis

Includes: arachnoiditis, leptomeningitis, meningitis, meningoencephalitis, meningomyelitis, pachymeningitis } bacterial

➡ **AHA Coding Clinic:** J-F, '87, 6

320.0 Hemophilus meningitis

Meningitis due to Hemophilus influenzae [H. influenzae]

➡ **CC Excl:** 003.21, 013.00-013.16, 036.0, 047.0-047.9, 049.0-049.1, 053.0, 054.72, 072.1, 090.42, 091.81, 094.2, 098.89, 100.81, 112.83, 114.2, 115.01, 115.11, 115.91, 130.0, 250.60-250.63, 250.80-250.93, 320.0-320.9, 321.0-321.8, 322.0-322.9, 349.89, 349.9, 357.0

320.1 Pneumococcal meningitis

➡ **CC Excl:** see Code 320.0

320.2 Streptococcal meningitis

➡ **CC Excl:** see Code 320.0

320.3 Staphylococcal meningitis

➡ **CC Excl:** see Code 320.0

320.7 *Meningitis in other bacterial diseases classified elsewhere*

Code first underlying disease as:
- actinomycosis (039.8)
- listeriosis (027.0)
- typhoid fever (002.0)
- whooping cough (033.0-033.9)

Excludes: *meningitis (in):*
- *epidemic (036.0)*
- *gonococcal (098.82)*
- *meningococcal (036.0)*
- *salmonellosis (003.21)*
- *syphilis:*
  - *NOS (094.2)*
  - *congenital (090.42)*
  - *meningovascular (094.2)*
  - *secondary (091.81)*
- *tuberculous (013.0)*

➡ **CC Excl:** see Code 320.0

✓5th **320.8 Meningitis due to other specified bacteria**

➡ **CC Excl:** see Code 320.0

320.81 Anaerobic meningitis

Bacteroides (fragilis)
Gram-negative anaerobes

320.82 Meningitis due to gram-negative bacteria, not elsewhere classified

Aerobacter aerogenes
Escherichia coli [E. coli]
Friedländer bacillus
Klebsiella pneumoniae
Proteus morganii
Pseudomonas

Excludes: *gram-negative anaerobes (320.81)*

320.89 Meningitis due to other specified bacteria

Bacillus pyocyaneus

320.9 Meningitis due to unspecified bacterium

Meningitis:
- bacterial NOS
- purulent NOS

Meningitis:
- pyogenic NOS
- suppurative NOS

➡ **CC Excl:** see Code 320.0

321 Meningitis due to other organisms

Includes: arachnoiditis, leptomeningitis, meningtis, pachymeningitis } due to organisms other than bacteria

➡ **AHA Coding Clinic:** J-F, '87, 6

321.0 *Cryptococcal meningitis*

Code first underlying disease (117.5)

➡ **CC Excl:** see Code 320.0

321.1 *Meningitis in other fungal diseases*

Code first underlying disease (110.0-118)

Excludes: *meningitis in:*
- *candidiasis (112.83)*
- *coccidioidomycosis (114.2)*
- *histoplasmosis (115.01, 115.11, 115.91)*

➡ **CC Excl:** see Code 320.0

321.2 ***Meningitis due to viruses not elsewhere classified***

Code first underlying disease as:
meningitis due to arbovirus (060.0-066.9)

Excludes: *meningitis (due to):*
abacterial (047.0-047.9)
adenovirus (049.1)
aseptic NOS (047.9)
Coxsackie (virus) (047.0)
ECHO virus (047.1)
enterovirus (047.0-047.9)
herpes simplex virus (054.72)
herpes zoster virus (053.0)
lymphocytic choriomeningitis virus (049.0)
mumps (072.1)
viral NOS (047.9)
meningo-eruptive syndrome (047.1)

➡ **CC Excl:** 003.21, 013.00-013.16, 036.0, 047.0-047.9, 049.0-049.1, 053.0, 054.72, 072.1, 090.42, 091.81, 094.2, 098.89, 100.81, 112.83, 114.2, 115.01, 115.11, 115.91, 130.0, 320.0-320.9, 321.0-321.8, 322.0-322.9, 349.89, 349.9, 357.0

321.3 ***Meningitis due to trypanosomiasis***

Code first underlying disease (086.0-086.9)

➡ **CC Excl:** 003.21, 013.00-013.16, 036.0, 047.0-047.9, 049.0-049.1, 053.0, 054.72, 072.1, 090.42, 091.81, 094.2, 098.89, 100.81, 112.83, 114.2, 115.01, 115.11, 115.91, 130.0, 250.60-250.63, 250.80-250.93, 320.0-320.9, 321.0-321.8, 322.0-322.9, 349.89, 349.9, 357.0

321.4 ***Meningitis in sarcoidosis***

Code first underlying disease (135)

➡ **CC Excl:** see Code 321.3

321.8 ***Meningitis due to other nonbacterial organisms classified elsewhere***

Code first underlying disease

Excludes: *leptospiral meningitis (100.81)*

➡ **CC Excl:** see Code 321.3

322 Meningitis of unspecified cause

Includes: arachnoiditis, leptomeningitis, meningitis, pachymeningitis } with no organism specified as cause

➡ **AHA Coding Clinic:** J-F, '87, 6

322.0 **Nonpyogenic meningitis**

Meningitis with clear cerebrospinal fluid

➡ **CC Excl:** see Code 321.3

322.1 **Eosinophilic meningitis**

➡ **CC Excl:** see Code 321.3

322.2 **Chronic meningitis**

➡ **CC Excl:**see Code 321.3

322.9 **Meningitis, unspecified**

➡ **CC Excl:** see Code 321.3

323 Encephalitis, myelitis, and encephalomyelitis

Includes: acute disseminated encephalomyelitis
meningoencephalitis, except bacterial
meningomyelitis, except bacterial
myelitis (acute):
ascending
transverse

Excludes: *bacterial:*
meningoencephalitis (320.0-320.9)
meningomyelitis (320.0-320.9)

323.0 ***Encephalitis in viral diseases classified elsewhere***

Code first underlying disease as:
cat-scratch disease (078.3)
infectious mononucleosis (075)
ornithosis (073.7)

Excludes: *encephalitis (in):*
arthropod-borne viral (062.0-064)
herpes simplex (054.3)
mumps (072.2)
other viral diseases of central nervous system (049.8-049.9)
poliomyelitis (045.0-045.9)
rubella (056.01)
slow virus infections of central nervous system (046.0-046.9)
viral NOS (049.9)

323.1 ***Encephalitis in rickettsial diseases classified elsewhere***

Code first underlying disease (080-083.9)

323.2 ***Encephalitis in protozoal diseases classified elsewhere***

Code first underlying disease as:
malaria (084.0-084.9)
trypanosomiasis (086.0-086.9)

323.4 ***Other encephalitis due to infection classified elsewhere***

Code first underlying disease

Excludes: *encephalitis (in):*
meningococcal (036.1)
syphilis:
NOS (094.81)
congenital (090.41)
toxoplasmosis (130.0)
tuberculosis (013.6)
meningoencephalitis due to free-living ameba [Naegleria] (136.2)

323.5 Encephalitis following immunization procedures

Encephalitis } postimmunization or postvaccinal
Encephalomyelitis }

Use additional E code to identify vaccine

323.6 Postinfectious encephalitis

Code first underlying disease

Excludes: *encephalitis:*
postchickenpox (052.0)
postmeasles (055.0)

323.7 Toxic encephalitis

Code first underlying disease as:
carbon tetrachloride (982.1)
hydroxyquinoline derivatives (961.3)
lead (984.0-984.9)
mercury (985.0)
thallium (985.8)

➡ **AHA Coding Clinic:** 2Q, '97, 8

323.8 Other causes of encephalitis

323.9 Unspecified cause of encephalitis

324 Intracranial and intraspinal abscess

324.0 Intracranial abscess

Abscess (embolic):
cerebellar
cerebral

Abscess (embolic) of brain [any part]:
epidural
extradural
otogenic
subdural

Excludes: *tuberculous (013.3)*

➡ **CC Excl:** 006.5, 013.20-013.36, 250.60-250.63, 250.80-250.93, 324.0-324.9, 325, 348.8-348.9

324.1 Intraspinal abscess

Abscess (embolic) of spinal cord [any part]:
epidural
extradural
subdural

Excludes: *tuberculous (013.5)*

➡ **CC Excl:** 006.5, 013.20-013.36, 250.60-250.63, 250.80-250.93, 324.1

324.9 Of unspecified site

Extradural or subdural abscess NOS

➡ **CC Excl:** 006.5, 013.20-013.36, 250.60-250.63, 250.80-250.93, 324.0-324.9, 325

325 Phlebitis and thrombophlebitis of intracranial venous sinuses

Embolism
Endophlebitis
Phlebitis, septic or suppurative
Thrombophlebitis
Thrombosis
} of cavernous, lateral, or other intracranial or unspecified intracranial venous sinus

Excludes: *that specified as:*
complicating pregnancy, childbirth, or the puerperium (671.5)
of nonpyogenic origin (437.6)

➡ **CC Excl:** see Code 324.9

326 Late effects of intracranial abscess or pyogenic infection

Note: This category is to be used to indicate conditions whose primary classification is to 320-325 [excluding 320.7, 321.0-321.8, 323.0-323.4, 323.6-323.7] as the cause of late effects, themselves classifiable elsewhere. The "late effects" include conditions specified as such, or as sequelae, which may occur at any time after the resolution of the causal condition.

Use additional code to identify condition, as:
hydrocephalus (331.4)
paralysis (342.0-342.9, 344.0-344.9)

HEREDITARY AND DEGENERATIVE DISEASES OF THE CENTRAL NERVOUS SYSTEM (330-337)

Excludes: *hepatolenticular degeneration (275.1)*
multiple sclerosis (340)
other demyelinating diseases of central nervous system (341.0-341.9)

330 Cerebral degenerations usually manifest in childhood

Use additional code to identify associated mental retardation

330.0 Leukodystrophy

Krabbe's disease
Leukodystrophy:
NOS
globoid cell

Leukodystrophy:
metachromatic
sudanophilic
Pelizaeus-Merzbacher disease
Sulfatide lipidosis

330.1 Cerebral lipidoses

Amaurotic (familial) idiocy
Disease:
Batten
Jansky-Bielschowsky

Disease:
Kufs'
Spielmeyer-Vogt
Tay-Sachs
Gangliosidosis

330.2 Cerebral degeneration in generalized lipidoses

Code first underlying disease as:
Fabry's disease (272.7)
Gaucher's disease (272.7)
Niemann-Pick disease (272.7)
sphingolipidosis (272.7)

330.3 Cerebral degeneration of childhood in other diseases classified elsewhere

Code first underlying disease as:
Hunter's disease (277.5)
mucopolysaccharidosis (277.5)

330.8 Other specified cerebral degenerations in childhood

Alpers' disease or gray-matter degeneration
Infantile necrotizing encephalomyelopathy
Leigh's disease
Subacute necrotizing encephalopathy or encephalomyelopathy

➡ **AHA Coding Clinic:** N-D, '85, 5

330.9 Unspecified cerebral degeneration in childhood

331 Other cerebral degenerations

331.0 Alzheimer's disease

➡ **AHA Coding Clinic:** N-D, '84, 20

331.1 Pick's disease

331.2 Senile degeneration of brain

Excludes: *senility NOS (797)*

331.3 Communicating hydrocephalus

Excludes: *congenital hydrocephalus (741.0, 742.3)*

➡ **AHA Coding Clinic:** S-O, '85, 12

331.4 Obstructive hydrocephalus

Acquired hydrocephalus NOS

Excludes: *congenital hydrocephalus (741.0, 742.3)*

➡ **CC Excl:** 250.60-250.63, 250.80-250.93, 331.3-331.7, 331.89, 331.9, 348.8-348.9, 741.00-741.03, 742.3-742.4, 742.59, 742.8-742.9

331.7 Cerebral degeneration in diseases classified elsewhere

Code first underlying disease as:
alcoholism (303.0-303.9)
beriberi (265.0)
cerebrovascular disease (430-438)
congenital hydrocephalus (741.0, 742.3)
neoplastic disease (140.0-239.9)
myxedema (244.0-244.9)
vitamin B_{12} deficiency (266.2)

Excludes: *cerebral degeneration in:*
Jakob-Creutzfeldt disease (046.1)
progressive multifocal leukoencephalopathy (046.3)
subacute spongiform encephalopathy (046.1)

✓5th **331.8 Other cerebral degeneration**

331.81 Reye's syndrome A: 0–17

331.89 Other

Cerebral ataxia

331.9 Cerebral degeneration, unspecified

332 Parkinson's disease

332.0 Paralysis agitans

Parkinsonism or Parkinson's disease:
NOS
idiopathic
primary

➡ **AHA Coding Clinic:** M-A, '87, 7

332.1 Secondary Parkinsonism

Parkinsonism due to drugs

Use additional E code to identify drug if drug-induced

Excludes: *Parkinsonism (in):*
Huntington's disease (333.4)
progressive supranuclear palsy (333.0)
Shy-Drager syndrome (333.0)
syphilitic (094.82)

333 Other extrapyramidal disease and abnormal movement disorders

Includes: other forms of extrapyramidal, basal ganglia, or striatopallidal disease

Excludes: *abnormal movements of head NOS (781.0)*

333.0 Other degenerative diseases of the basal ganglia

Atrophy or degeneration:
olivopontocerebellar [Déjérine-Thomas syndrome]
pigmentary pallidal [Hallervorden-Spatz disease]
striatonigral
Parkinsonian syndrome associated with:
idiopathic orthostatic hypotension
symptomatic orthostatic hypotension
Progressive supranuclear ophthalmoplegia
Shy-Drager syndrome

➡ **AHA Coding Clinic:** 2Q, '96, 8

333.1 Essential and other specified forms of tremor

Benign essential tremor Familial tremor

Use additional E code to identify drug if drug-induced

Excludes: *tremor NOS (781.0)*

333.2 Myoclonus

Familial essential myoclonus
Progressive myoclonic epilepsy
Unverricht-Lundborg disease

Use additional E code to identify drug if drug-induced

➡ **AHA Coding Clinic:** 3Q, '97, 4; M-A, '87, 12

333.3 Tics of organic origin

Use additional E code to identify drug if drug-induced

Excludes: *Gilles de la Tourette's syndrome (307.23)*
habit spasm (307.22)
tic NOS (307.20)

333.4 Huntington's chorea

333.5 Other choreas

Hemiballism(us)
Paroxysmal choreo-athetosis

Use additional E code to identify drug if drug-induced

Excludes: *Sydenham's or rheumatic chorea (392.0-392.9)*

333.6 Idiopathic torsion dystonia

Dystonia:
- deformans progressiva
- musculorum deformans

(Schwalbe-) Ziehen-Oppenheim disease

333.7 Symptomatic torsion dystonia

Athetoid cerebral palsy [Vogt's disease]
Double athetosis (syndrome)

Use additional E code to identify drug if drug-induced

✓5th **333.8 Fragments of torsion dystonia**

Use additional E code to identify drug if drug-induced

333.81 Blepharospasm

333.82 Orofacial dyskinesia

333.83 Spasmodic torticollis

Excludes: *torticollis:*
- *NOS (723.5)*
- *hysterical (300.11)*
- *psychogenic (306.0)*

333.84 Organic writers' cramp

Excludes: *psychogenic (300.89)*

333.89 Other

✓5th **333.9 Other and unspecified extrapyramidal diseases and abnormal movement disorders**

333.90 Unspecified extrapyramidal disease and abnormal movement disorder

333.91 Stiff-man syndrome

333.92 Neuroleptic malignant syndrome

Use additional E code to identify drug if drug-induced

➡ **AHA Coding Clinic:** 4Q, '94, 37

333.93 Benign shuddering attacks

➡ **AHA Coding Clinic:** 4Q, '94, 37

333.99 Other

Restless legs

➡ **AHA Coding Clinic:** M-A, '87, 7

334 Spinocerebellar disease

Excludes: *olivopontocerebellar degeneration (333.0)*
peroneal muscular atrophy (356.1)

334.0 Friedreich's ataxia

334.1 Hereditary spastic paraplegia

334.2 Primary cerebellar degeneration

Cerebellar ataxia:
- Marie's
- Sanger-Brown

Dyssynergia cerebellaris myoclonica
Primary cerebellar degeneration:
- NOS
- hereditary
- sporadic

➡ **AHA Coding Clinic:** M-A, '87, 9

334.3 **Other cerebellar ataxia**
Cerebellar ataxia NOS
Use additional E code to identify drug if drug-induced

334.4 ***Cerebellar ataxia in diseases classified elsewhere***
Code first underlying disease as:
alcoholism (303.0-303.9)
myxedema (244.0-244.9)
neoplastic disease (140.0-239.9)

334.8 **Other spinocerebellar diseases**
Ataxia-telangiectasia [Louis-Bar syndrome]
Corticostriatal-spinal degeneration

334.9 **Spinocerebellar disease, unspecified**

335 Anterior horn cell disease

335.0 **Werdnig-Hoffmann disease**
Infantile spinal muscular atrophy
Progressive muscular atrophy of infancy
➡ **CC Excl:** 250.60-250.63, 250.80-250.93, 334.8-334.9, 335.0, 335.10-335.9, 336.0-336.9, 337.0-337.9, 349.89, 349.9

✓5th **335.1** **Spinal muscular atrophy**

335.10 **Spinal muscular atrophy, unspecified**
➡ **CC Excl:** see Code 335.0

335.11 **Kugelberg-Welander disease**
Spinal muscular atrophy:
familial
juvenile
➡ **CC Excl:** see Code 335.0

335.19 **Other**
Adult spinal muscular atrophy
➡ **CC Excl:** see Code 335.0

✓5th **335.2** **Motor neuron disease**

335.20 **Amyotrophic lateral sclerosis** **A: 15–124**
Motor neuron disease (bulbar) (mixed type)
➡ **CC Excl:** see Code 335.0
➡ **AHA Coding Clinic:** 4Q, '95, 81

335.21 **Progressive muscular atrophy**
Duchenne-Aran muscular atrophy
Progressive muscular atrophy (pure)
➡ **CC Excl:** see Code 335.0

335.22 **Progressive bulbar palsy**
➡ **CC Excl:** see Code 335.0

335.23 **Pseudobulbar palsy**
➡ **CC Excl:** see Code 335.0

335.24 **Primary lateral sclerosis**
➡ **CC Excl:** see Code 335.0

335.29 **Other**
➡ **CC Excl:** see Code 335.0

335.8 **Other anterior horn cell diseases**
➡ **CC Excl:** see Code 335.0

335.9 **Anterior horn cell disease, unspecified**
➡ **CC Excl:** see Code 335.0

336 Other diseases of spinal cord

336.0 **Syringomyelia and syringobulbia**
➡ **AHA Coding Clinic:** 1Q, '89, 10

336.1 **Vascular myelopathies**
Acute infarction of spinal cord (embolic) (nonembolic)
Arterial thrombosis of spinal cord
Edema of spinal cord
Hematomyelia
Subacute necrotic myelopathy

336.2 ***Subacute combined degeneration of spinal cord in diseases classified elsewhere***
Code first underlying disease as:
pernicious anemia (281.0)
other vitamin B_{12} deficiency anemia (281.1)
vitamin B_{12} deficiency (266.2)

336.3 ***Myelopathy in other diseases classified elsewhere***
Code first underlying disease as:
myelopathy in neoplastic disease (140.0-239.9)

Excludes: *myelopathy in:*
intervertebral disc disorder (722.70-722.73)
spondylosis (721.1, 721.41-721.42, 721.91)

336.8 **Other myelopathy**
Myelopathy:
drug-induced
radiation-induced
Use additional E code to identify cause

336.9 **Unspecified disease of spinal cord**
Cord compression NOS Myelopathy NOS

Excludes: *myelitis (323.0-323.9)*
spinal (canal) stenosis (723.0, 724.00-724.09)

337 Disorders of the autonomic nervous system

Includes: disorders of peripheral autonomic, sympathetic, parasympathetic, or vegetative system

Excludes: *familial dysautonomia [Riley-Day syndrome] (742.8)*

337.0 Idiopathic peripheral autonomic neuropathy

Carotid sinus syncope or syndrome
Cervical sympathetic dystrophy or paralysis

337.1 *Peripheral autonomic neuropathy in disorders classified elsewhere*

Code first underlying disease as:
amyloidosis (277.3)
diabetes (250.6)

➡ **AHA Coding Clinic:** 2Q, '93, 6; N-D, '84, 9

✓5th **337.2 Reflex sympathetic dystrophy**

337.20 Reflex sympathetic dystrophy, unspecified

337.21 Reflex sympathetic dystrophy of upper limb

337.22 Reflex sympathetic dystrophy of lower limb

337.29 Reflex sympathetic dystrophy of other specified site

337.3 Autonomic dysreflexia

Use additional code to identify the underlying cause, such as:
decubitus ulcer (707.0)
fecal impactation (560.39)
urinary tract infection (599.0)

➡ **CC Excl:** see Code 335.0

337.9 Unspecified disorder of autonomic nervous system

OTHER DISORDERS OF THE CENTRAL NERVOUS SYSTEM (340-349)

340 Multiple sclerosis A: 15–124

Disseminated or multiple sclerosis:
NOS
brain stem
cord
generalized

➡ **CC Excl:** 250.60-250.63, 250.80-250.93, 340, 341.8-341.9

341 Other demyelinating diseases of central nervous system

341.0 Neuromyelitis optica

341.1 Schilder's disease

Baló's concentric sclerosis
Encephalitis periaxialis:
concentrica [Baló's]
diffusa [Schilder's]

341.8 Other demyelinating diseases of central nervous system

Central demyelination of corpus callosum
Central pontine myelinosis
Marchiafava (-Bignami) disease

➡ **AHA Coding Clinic:** N-D, '87, 6

341.9 Demyelinating disease of central nervous system, unspecified

342 Hemiplegia and hemiparesis

Note: This category is to be used when hemiplegia (complete) (incomplete) is reported without further specification, or is stated to be old or long-standing but of unspecified cause. The category is also for use in multiple coding to identify these types of hemiplegia resulting from any cause.

Excludes: *congenital (343.1)*
hemiplegia due to late effect of cerebrovascular accident (438.20-438.22)
infantile NOS (343.4)

The following fifth-digits are for use with codes 342.0-342.9:

0 affecting unspecified side
1 affecting dominant side
2 affecting nondominant side

✓5th **342.0 Flaccid hemiplegia**

✓5th **342.1 Spastic hemiplegia**

✓5th **342.8 Other specified hemiplegia**

✓5th **342.9 Hemiplegia, unspecified**

343 Infantile cerebral palsy

Includes: cerebral:
palsy NOS
spastic infantile paralysis
congenital spastic paralysis (cerebral)
Little's disease
paralysis (spastic) due to birth injury:
intracranial
spinal

Excludes: *hereditary cerebral paralysis, such as:*
hereditary spastic paraplegia (334.1)
Vogt's disease (333.7)
spastic paralysis specified as noncongenital or noninfantile (344.0-344.9)

343.0 Diplegic

Congenital diplegia
Congenital paraplegia

343.1 Hemiplegic

Congenital hemiplegia

Excludes: *infantile hemiplegia NOS (343.4)*

343.2 Quadriplegic

Tetraplegic

➡ **CC Excl:** 250.60-250.63, 250.80-250.93, 342.00-342.92, 343.0-343.9, 344.00-344.61, 344.9, 348.8-348.9, 349.89, 349.9, 742.59, 742.8-742.9

343.3 Monoplegic

343.4 Infantile hemiplegia

Infantile hemiplegia (postnatal) NOS

343.8 Other specified infantile cerebral palsy

343.9 Infantile cerebral palsy, unspecified

Cerebral palsy NOS

344 Other paralytic syndromes

Note: This category is to be used when the listed conditions are reported without further specification or are stated to be old or long-standing but of unspecified cause. The category is also for use in multiple coding to identify these conditions resulting from any cause.

Includes: paralysis (complete) (incomplete), except as classifiable to 342 and 343

Excludes: *congenital or infantile cerebral palsy (343.0-343.9)*
hemiplegia (342.0-342.9)
congenital or infantile (343.1, 343.4)

✓5th **344.0 Quadriplegia and quadriparesis**

344.00 Quadriplegia, unspecified
➡ **CC Excl:** see Code 343.2

344.01 C1-C4, complete
➡ **CC Excl:** see Code 343.2

344.02 C1-C4, incomplete
➡ **CC Excl:** see Code 343.2

344.03 C5-C7, complete
➡ **CC Excl:** see Code 343.2

344.04 C5-C7, incomplete
➡ **CC Excl:** see Code 343.2

344.09 Other
➡ **CC Excl:** see Code 343.2

344.1 Paraplegia
Paralysis of both lower limbs
Paraplegia (lower)
➡ **AHA Coding Clinic:** M-A, '87, 10

344.2 Diplegia of upper limbs
Diplegia (upper)
Paralysis of both upper limbs

✓5th **344.3 Monoplegia of lower limb**
Paralysis of lower limb

Excludes: *monoplegia of lower limb due to late effect of cerebrovascular accident (438.40-438.42)*

344.30 Affecting unspecified side

344.31 Affecting dominant side

344.32 Affecting nondominant side

✓5th **344.4 Monoplegia of upper limb**
Paralysis of upper limb

Excludes: *monoplegia of upper limb due to late effect of cerebrovascular accident (438.30-438.32)*

344.40 Affecting unspecified side

344.41 Affecting dominant side

344.42 Affecting nondominant side

344.5 Unspecified monoplegia

✓5th **344.6 Cauda equina syndrome**

344.60 Without mention of neurogenic bladder

344.61 With neurogenic bladder
Acontractile bladder
Autonomic hyperreflexia of bladder
Cord bladder
Detrusor hyperreflexia
➡ **AHA Coding Clinic:** M-J, '87, 12; M-A, '87, 10

✓5th **344.8 Other specified paralytic syndromes**

344.81 Locked-in state

344.89 Other specified paralytic syndrome

344.9 Paralysis, unspecified

345 Epilepsy

Excludes: *progressive myoclonic epilepsy (333.2)*

The following fifth-digit subclassification is for use with categories 345.0, .1, .4-.9:

0 without mention of intractable epilepsy
1 with intractable epilepsy

➡ **AHA Coding Clinic:** 1Q, '93, 24; 2Q, '92, 8

✓5th [4] **345.0 Generalized nonconvulsive epilepsy**
Absences:
atonic
typical
Minor epilepsy
Petit mal
Pykno-epilepsy
Seizures:
akinetic
atonic

➡ **CC Excl: For code 345.01:** 250.60-250.63, 345.00-345.91, 348.8-348.9, 349.89, 349.9

✔ **St. Anthony's Clinical Coder: For Code 345.01:** see Chapter 5

✓5th **345.1 Generalized convulsive epilepsy**
Epileptic seizures:
clonic
myoclonic
tonic
tonic-clonic
Grand mal
Major epilepsy

Excludes: *convulsions:*
NOS (780.3)
infantile (780.3)
newborn (779.0)
infantile spasms (345.6)

➡ **CC Excl:** see code 345.01
➡ **AHA Coding Clinic:** 3Q, '97, 4

345.2 Petit mal status
Epileptic absence status
➡ **CC Excl:** 250.60-250.63, 250.80-250.93, 345.00-345.91, 348.8-348.9, 349.89, 349.9

[4] CC Coding = 1

345.3 Grand mal status

Status epilepticus NOS

Excludes: *epilepsia partialis continua (345.7)*
status:
psychomotor (345.7)
temporal lobe (345.7)

➡ **CC Excl:** see Code 345.2

✓5th [4] **345.4 Partial epilepsy, with impairment of consciousness**

Epilepsy:
limbic system
partial:
secondarily generalized
with memory and ideational disturbances
psychomotor
psychosensory
temporal lobe
Epileptic automatism

➡ **CC Excl: For code 345.41:** 250.60-250.63, 345.00-345.91, 348.8-348.9, 349.89, 349.9

✓5th [4] **345.5 Partial epilepsy, without mention of impairment of consciousness**

Epilepsy:
Bravais-Jacksonian NOS
focal (motor) NOS
Jacksonian NOS
motor partial
partial NOS

Epilepsy:
sensory-induced
somatomotor
somatosensory
visceral
visual

➡ **CC Excl: For code 345.51:** see Code 345.4

✓5th [4] **345.6 Infantile spasms**

Hypsarrhythmia
Lightning spasms
Salaam attacks

Excludes: *salaam tic (781.0)*

➡ **CC Excl: For code 345.61:** see Code 345.4

✓5th [4] **345.7 Epilepsia partialis continua**

Kojevnikov's epilepsy

➡ **CC Excl: For code 345.71:** see Code 345.4

✓5th [4] **345.8 Other forms of epilepsy**

Epilepsy:
cursive [running]
gelastic

➡ **CC Excl: For code 345.81:** see Code 345.4

✓5th [4] **345.9 Epilepsy, unspecified**

Epileptic convulsions, fits, or seizures NOS

Excludes: *convulsive seizure or fit NOS (780.3)*

➡ **CC Excl: For code 345.91:** see Code 345.4

346 Migraine

The following fifth-digit subclassification is for use with category 346:

0 without mention of intractable migraine
1 with intractable migraine, so stated

✓5th **346.0 Classical migraine**

Migraine preceded or accompanied by transient focal neurological phenomena
Migraine with aura

✓5th **346.1 Common migraine**

Atypical migraine
Sick headache

✓5th **346.2 Variants of migraine**

Cluster headache
Histamine cephalgia
Horton's neuralgia
Migraine:
abdominal
basilar

Migraine:
lower half
retinal
Neuralgia:
ciliary
migrainous

✓5th **346.8 Other forms of migraine**

Migraine:
hemiplegic
ophthalmoplegic

✓5th **346.9 Migraine, unspecified**

➡ **AHA Coding Clinic:** N-D, '85, 16

347 Cataplexy and narcolepsy

348 Other conditions of brain

348.0 Cerebral cysts

Arachnoid cyst
Porencephalic cyst
Porencephaly, acquired
Pseudoporencephaly

Excludes: *porencephaly (congenital) (742.4)*

348.1 Anoxic brain damage

Use additional E code to identify cause

Excludes: *that occurring in:*
abortion (634-638 with .7, 639.8)
ectopic or molar pregnancy (639.8)
labor or delivery (668.2, 669.4)
that of newborn (767.0, 768.0-768.9, 772.1-772.2)

➡ **CC Excl:** 250.60-250.63, 250.80-250.93, 348.1-348.2, 349.89, 349.9

348.2 Benign intracranial hypertension

Pseudotumor cerebri

Excludes: *hypertensive encephalopathy (437.2)*

348.3 Encephalopathy, unspecified

➡ **AHA Coding Clinic:** 3Q, '97, 4

[4] CC Coding = 1

348.4 Compression of brain
Compression } brain (stem)
Herniation }
Posterior fossa compression syndrome
➡ **AHA Coding Clinic:** 4Q, '94, 37

348.5 Cerebral edema

348.8 Other conditions of brain
Cerebral:
calcification
fungus
➡ **AHA Coding Clinic:** S-O, '87, 9

348.9 Unspecified condition of brain

349 Other and unspecified disorders of the nervous system

349.0 Reaction to spinal or lumbar puncture
Headache following lumbar puncture
➡ **AHA Coding Clinic:** 3Q, '90, 18

349.1 Nervous system complications from surgically implanted device

Excludes: *immediate postoperative complications (997.00-997.09)*
mechanical complications of nervous system device (996.2)

➡ **CC Excl:** 250.60-250.63, 250.80-250.93, 349.1, 349.89, 349.9

349.2 Disorders of meninges, not elsewhere classified
Adhesions, meningeal (cerebral) (spinal)
Cyst, spinal meninges
Meningocele, acquired
Pseudomeningocele, acquired
➡ **AHA Coding Clinic:** 3Q, '94, 4

✓5th **349.8 Other specified disorders of nervous system**

349.81 Cerebrospinal fluid rhinorrhea

Excludes: *cerebrospinal fluid otorrhea (388.61)*

➡ **CC Excl:** 250.60-250.63, 250.80-250.93, 349.81, 349.89, 349.9

349.82 Toxic encephalopathy
Use additional E code to identify cause
➡ **CC Excl:** 013.60-013.66, 017.90-017.96, 036.1, 049.8-049.9, 052.0, 054.3, 062.0-062.9, 063.0-063.9, 072.2, 090.41, 094.81, 130.0, 250.60-250.63, 250.80-250.93, 323.0-323.9, 348.3, 348.8-348.9, 349.82-349.89, 349.9

349.89 Other

349.9 Unspecified disorders of nervous system
Disorder of nervous system (central) NOS

DISORDERS OF THE PERIPHERAL NERVOUS SYSTEM (350-359)

Excludes: *diseases of:*
acoustic [8th] nerve (388.5)
oculomotor [3rd, 4th, 6th] nerves (378.0-378.9)
optic [2nd] nerve (377.0-377.9)
peripheral autonomic nerves (337.0-337.9)
neuralgia } NOS or "rheumatic" (729.2)
neuritis }
radiculitis }
peripheral neuritis in pregnancy (646.4)

350 Trigeminal nerve disorders

Includes: disorders of 5th cranial nerve

350.1 Trigeminal neuralgia
Tic douloureux
Trifacial neuralgia
Trigeminal neuralgia NOS

Excludes: *postherpetic (053.12)*

350.2 Atypical face pain

350.8 Other specified trigeminal nerve disorders

350.9 Trigeminal nerve disorder, unspecified

351 Facial nerve disorders

Includes: disorders of 7th cranial nerve

Excludes: *that in newborn (767.5)*

351.0 Bell's palsy
Facial palsy

351.1 Geniculate ganglionitis
Geniculate ganglionitis NOS

Excludes: *herpetic (053.11)*

351.8 Other facial nerve disorders
Facial myokymia
Melkersson's syndrome

351.9 Facial nerve disorder, unspecified

352 Disorders of other cranial nerves

352.0 Disorders of olfactory [1st] nerve

352.1 Glossopharyngeal neuralgia

352.2 Other disorders of glossopharyngeal [9th] nerve

352.3 **Disorders of pneumogastric [10th] nerve**
Disorders of vagal nerve

Excludes: *paralysis of vocal cords or larynx (478.30-478.34)*

352.4 **Disorders of accessory [11th] nerve**

352.5 **Disorders of hypoglossal [12th] nerve**

352.6 **Multiple cranial nerve palsies**
Collet-Sicard syndrome
Polyneuritis cranialis

352.9 **Unspecified disorder of cranial nerves**

353 Nerve root and plexus disorders

Excludes: *conditions due to:*
intervertebral disc disorders (722.0-722.9)
spondylosis (720.0-721.9)
vertebrogenic disorders (723.0-724.9)

353.0 **Brachial plexus lesions**
Cervical rib syndrome
Costoclavicular syndrome
Scalenus anticus syndrome
Thoracic outlet syndrome

Excludes: *brachial neuritis or radiculitis NOS (723.4)*
that in newborn (767.6)

353.1 **Lumbosacral plexus lesions**

353.2 **Cervical root lesions, not elsewhere classified**

353.3 **Thoracic root lesions, not elsewhere classified**

353.4 **Lumbosacral root lesions, not elsewhere classified**

353.5 **Neuralgic amyotrophy**
Parsonage-Aldren-Turner syndrome

353.6 **Phantom limb (syndrome)**

353.8 **Other nerve root and plexus disorders**

353.9 **Unspecified nerve root and plexus disorder**

354 Mononeuritis of upper limb and mononeuritis multiplex

354.0 **Carpal tunnel syndrome**
Median nerve entrapment
Partial thenar atrophy

354.1 **Other lesion of median nerve**
Median nerve neuritis

354.2 **Lesion of ulnar nerve**
Cubital tunnel syndrome
Tardy ulnar nerve palsy

354.3 **Lesion of radial nerve**
Acute radial nerve palsy
➡ **AHA Coding Clinic:** N-D, '87, 6

354.4 **Causalgia of upper limb**

Excludes: *causalgia:*
NOS (355.9)
lower limb (355.71)

354.5 **Mononeuritis multiplex**
Combinations of single conditions classifiable to 354 or 355

354.8 **Other mononeuritis of upper limb**

354.9 **Mononeuritis of upper limb, unspecified**

355 Mononeuritis of lower limb and unspecified site

355.0 **Lesion of sciatic nerve**

Excludes: *sciatica NOS (724.3)*

➡ **AHA Coding Clinic:** 2Q, '89, 12

355.1 **Meralgia paresthetica**
Lateral cutaneous femoral nerve of thigh compression or syndrome

355.2 **Other lesion of femoral nerve**

355.3 **Lesion of lateral popliteal nerve**
Lesion of common peroneal nerve

355.4 **Lesion of medial popliteal nerve**

355.5 **Tarsal tunnel syndrome**

355.6 **Lesion of plantar nerve**
Morton's metatarsalgia, neuralgia, or neuroma

✓5th **355.7** **Other mononeuritis of lower limb**

355.71 **Causalgia of lower limb**

Excludes: *causalgia:*
NOS (355.9)
upper limb (354.4)

355.79 **Other mononeuritis of lower limb**

355.8 **Mononeuritis of lower limb, unspecified**

355.9 **Mononeuritis of unspecified site**
Causalgia NOS

Excludes: *causalgia:*
lower limb (355.71)
upper limb (354.4)

356 Hereditary and idiopathic peripheral neuropathy

356.0 **Hereditary peripheral neuropathy**
Déjérine-Sottas disease

356.1 **Peroneal muscular atrophy**
Charcot-Marie-Tooth disease
Neuropathic muscular atrophy

356.2 **Hereditary sensory neuropathy**

356.3 **Refsum's disease**
Heredopathia atactica polyneuritiformis

356.4 **Idiopathic progressive polyneuropathy**

356.8 **Other specified idiopathic peripheral neuropathy**
Supranuclear paralysis

356.9 **Unspecified**

357 Inflammatory and toxic neuropathy

357.0 **Acute infective polyneuritis**
Guillain-Barré syndrome
Postinfectious polyneuritis

➡ **CC Excl:** 003.21, 013.00-013.16, 036.0, 036.89, 036.9, 041.81-041.89, 041.9, 047.0-047.9, 049.0-049.1, 053.0, 054.72, 072.1, 090.42, 091.81, 094.2, 098.89, 100.81, 112.83, 114.2, 115.01, 115.11, 115.91, 130.0, 139.8, 320.0-320.9, 321.0-321.8, 322.0-322.9, 349.89, 349.9, 357.0

357.1 ***Polyneuropathy in collagen vascular disease***
Code first underlying disease as:
disseminated lupus erythematosus (710.0)
polyarteritis nodosa (446.0)
rheumatoid arthritis (714.0)

357.2 ***Polyneuropathy in diabetes***
Code first underlying disease (250.6)

➡ **AHA Coding Clinic:** 2Q, '92, 15

357.3 ***Polyneuropathy in malignant disease***
Code first underlying disease (140.0-208.9)

357.4 ***Polyneuropathy in other diseases classified elsewhere***
Code first underlying disease as:
amyloidosis (277.3)
beriberi (265.0)
deficiency of B vitamins (266.0-266.9)
diphtheria (032.0-032.9)
hypoglycemia (251.2)
pellagra (265.2)
porphyria (277.1)
sarcoidosis (135)
uremia (585)

Excludes: *polyneuropathy in:*
herpes zoster (053.13)
mumps (072.72)

357.5 **Alcoholic polyneuropathy**

357.6 **Polyneuropathy due to drugs**
Use additional E code to identify drug

357.7 **Polyneuropathy due to other toxic agents**
Use additional E code to identify toxic agent

357.8 **Other**
Chronic inflammatory demyelinating polyneuritis

357.9 **Unspecified**

358 Myoneural disorders

358.0 **Myasthenia gravis**

➡ **CC Excl:** 250.60-250.63, 250.80-250.93, 349.89, 349.9, 358.0-358.1

358.1 ***Myasthenic syndromes in diseases classified elsewhere***
Amyotrophy } from stated cause classified elsewhere
Eaton-Lambert syndrome } from stated cause classified elsewhere

Code first underlying disease as:
botulism (005.1)
diabetes mellitus (250.6)
hypothyroidism (244.0-244.9)
malignant neoplasm (140.0-208.9)
pernicious anemia (281.0)
thyrotoxicosis (242.0-242.9)

➡ **CC Excl:** see Code 358.0

358.2 **Toxic myoneural disorders**
Use additional E code to identify toxic agent

358.8 **Other specified myoneural disorders**

358.9 **Myoneural disorders, unspecified**

359 Muscular dystrophies and other myopathies

Excludes: *idiopathic polymyositis (710.4)*

359.0 **Congenital hereditary muscular dystrophy**
Benign congenital myopathy
Central core disease
Centronuclear myopathy
Myotubular myopathy
Nemaline body disease

Excludes: *arthrogryposis multiplex congenita (754.89)*

➡ **CC Excl:** 250.60-250.63, 250.80-250.93, 349.89, 349.9, 359.0-359.1

359.1 Hereditary progressive muscular dystrophy

Muscular dystrophy:
- NOS
- distal
- Duchenne
- Erb's
- fascioscapulohumeral

Muscular dystrophy:
- Gower's
- Landouzy-Déjérine
- limb-girdle
- ocular
- oculopharyngeal

➡ **CC Excl:** see Code 359.0

359.2 Myotonic disorders

Dystrophia myotonica
Eulenburg's disease
Myotonia congenita
Paramyotonia congenita
Steinert's disease
Thomsen's disease

359.3 Familial periodic paralysis

Hypokalemic familial periodic paralysis

359.4 Toxic myopathy

Use additional E code to identify toxic agent

359.5 Myopathy in endocrine diseases classified elsewhere

Code first underlying disease as:
- Addison's disease (255.4)
- Cushing's syndrome (255.0)
- hypopituitarism (253.2)
- myxedema (244.0-244.9)
- thyrotoxicosis (242.0-242.9)

359.6 Symptomatic inflammatory myopathy in diseases classified elsewhere

Code first underlying disease as:
- amyloidosis (277.3)
- disseminated lupus erythematosus (710.0)
- malignant neoplasm (140.0-208.9)
- polyarteritis nodosa (446.0)
- rheumatoid arthritis (714.0)
- sarcoidosis (135)
- scleroderma (710.1)
- Sjögren's disease (710.2)

359.8 Other myopathies

➡ **AHA Coding Clinic:** 3Q, '90, 17

359.9 Myopathy, unspecified

DISORDERS OF THE EYE AND ADNEXA (360-379)

360 Disorders of the globe

Includes: disorders affecting multiple structures of eye

✓5th **360.0 Purulent endophthalmitis**

360.00 Purulent endophthalmitis, unspecified

360.01 Acute endophthalmitis

360.02 Panophthalmitis

360.03 Chronic endophthalmitis

360.04 Vitreous abscess

✓5th **360.1 Other endophthalmitis**

360.11 Sympathetic uveitis

360.12 Panuveitis

360.13 Parasitic endophthalmitis NOS

360.14 Ophthalmia nodosa

360.19 Other

Phacoanaphylactic endophthalmitis

✓5th **360.2 Degenerative disorders of globe**

360.20 Degenerative disorder of globe, unspecified

360.21 Progressive high (degenerative) myopia

Malignant myopia

360.23 Siderosis

360.24 Other metallosis

Chalcosis

360.29 Other

Excludes: *xerophthalmia (264.7)*

✓5th **360.3 Hypotony of eye**

360.30 Hypotony, unspecified

360.31 Primary hypotony

360.32 Ocular fistula causing hypotony

360.33 Hypotony associated with other ocular disorders

360.34 Flat anterior chamber

✓5th **360.4 Degenerated conditions of globe**

360.40 Degenerated globe or eye, unspecified

360.41 Blind hypotensive eye

Atrophy of globe
Phthisis bulbi

360.42 Blind hypertensive eye

Absolute glaucoma

360.43 Hemophthalmos, except current injury

Excludes: *traumatic (871.0-871.9, 921.0-921.9)*

360.44 Leucocoria

✓5th **360.5 Retained (old) intraocular foreign body, magnetic**

Excludes: *current penetrating injury with magnetic foreign body (871.5)*
retained (old) foreign body of orbit (376.6)

360.50 Foreign body, magnetic, intraocular, unspecified

360.51 Foreign body, magnetic, in anterior chamber

360.52 Foreign body, magnetic, in iris or ciliary body

360.53 Foreign body, magnetic, in lens

360.54 Foreign body, magnetic, in vitreous

360.55 Foreign body, magnetic, in posterior wall

360.59 Foreign body, magnetic, in other or multiple sites

✓5th **360.6 Retained (old) intraocular foreign body, nonmagnetic**

Retained (old) foreign body:
NOS
nonmagnetic

Excludes: *current penetrating injury with (nonmagnetic) foreign body (871.6)*
retained (old) foreign body in orbit (376.6)

360.60 Foreign body, intraocular, unspecified

360.61 Foreign body in anterior chamber

360.62 Foreign body in iris or ciliary body

360.63 Foreign body in lens

360.64 Foreign body in vitreous

360.65 Foreign body in posterior wall

360.69 Foreign body in other or multiple sites

✓5th **360.8 Other disorders of globe**

360.81 Luxation of globe

360.89 Other

360.9 Unspecified disorder of globe

361 Retinal detachments and defects

✓5th **361.0 Retinal detachment with retinal defect**

Rhegmatogenous retinal detachment

Excludes: *detachment of retinal pigment epithelium (362.42-362.43)*
retinal detachment (serous) (without defect) (361.2)

361.00 Retinal detachment with retinal defect, unspecified

361.01 Recent detachment, partial, with single defect

361.02 Recent detachment, partial, with multiple defects

361.03 Recent detachment, partial, with giant tear

361.04 Recent detachment, partial, with retinal dialysis

Dialysis (juvenile) of retina (with detachment)

361.05 Recent detachment, total or subtotal

361.06 Old detachment, partial

Delimited old retinal detachment

361.07 Old detachment, total or subtotal

✓5th **361.1 Retinoschisis and retinal cysts**

Excludes: *juvenile retinoschisis (362.73)*
microcystoid degeneration of retina (362.62)
parasitic cyst of retina (360.13)

361.10 Retinoschisis, unspecified

361.11 Flat retinoschisis

361.12 Bullous retinoschisis

361.13 Primary retinal cysts

361.14 Secondary retinal cysts

361.19 Other

Pseudocyst of retina

361.2 Serous retinal detachment

Retinal detachment without retinal defect

Excludes: *central serous retinopathy (362.41)*
retinal pigment epithelium detachment (362.42-362.43)

✓5th **361.3 Retinal defects without detachment**

Excludes: *chorioretinal scars after surgery for detachment (363.30-363.35)*
peripheral retinal degeneration without defect (362.60-362.66)

361.30 **Retinal defect, unspecified**
Retinal break(s) NOS

361.31 **Round hole of retina without detachment**

361.32 **Horseshoe tear of retina without detachment**
Operculum of retina without mention of detachment

361.33 **Multiple defects of retina without detachment**

✓5th **361.8** **Other forms of retinal detachment**

361.81 **Traction detachment of retina**
Traction detachment with vitreoretinal organization

361.89 **Other**

361.9 **Unspecified retinal detachment**
➡ **AHA Coding Clinic:** N-D, '87, 10

362 Other retinal disorders

Excludes: *chorioretinal scars (363.30-363.35)*
chorioretinitis (363.0-363.2)

✓5th ***362.0*** ***Diabetic retinopathy***
Code first diabetes (250.5)

362.01 ***Background diabetic retinopathy***
Diabetic retinal microaneurysms
Diabetic retinopathy NOS

362.02 ***Proliferative diabetic retinopathy***
➡ **AHA Coding Clinic:** 3Q, '96, 5

✓5th **362.1** **Other background retinopathy and retinal vascular changes**

362.10 **Background retinopathy, unspecified**

362.11 **Hypertensive retinopathy**
➡ **AHA Coding Clinic:** 3Q, '90, 3

362.12 **Exudative retinopathy**
Coats' syndrome

362.13 **Changes in vascular appearance**
Vascular sheathing of retina
Use additional code for any associated atherosclerosis (440.8)

362.14 **Retinal microaneurysms NOS**

362.15 **Retinal telangiectasia**

362.16 **Retinal neovascularization NOS**
Neovascularization:
choroidal
subretinal

362.17 **Other intraretinal microvascular abnormalities**
Retinal varices

362.18 **Retinal vasculitis**
Eales' disease
Retinal:
arteritis
endarteritis
Retinal:
perivasculitis
phlebitis

✓5th **362.2** **Other proliferative retinopathy**

362.21 **Retrolental fibroplasia**

362.29 **Other nondiabetic proliferative retinopathy**
➡ **AHA Coding Clinic:** 3Q, '96, 5

✓5th **362.3** **Retinal vascular occlusion**

362.30 **Retinal vascular occlusion, unspecified**

362.31 **Central retinal artery occlusion**

362.32 **Arterial branch occlusion**

362.33 **Partial arterial occlusion**
Hollenhorst plaque
Retinal microembolism

362.34 **Transient arterial occlusion**
Amaurosis fugax

362.35 **Central retinal vein occlusion**
➡ **AHA Coding Clinic:** 2Q, '93, 6

362.36 **Venous tributary (branch) occlusion**

362.37 **Venous engorgement**
Occlusion:
incipient } of retinal vein
partial

✓5th **362.4** **Separation of retinal layers**

Excludes: *retinal detachment (serous) (361.2)*
rhegmatogenous (361.00-361.07)

362.40 **Retinal layer separation, unspecified**

362.41 **Central serous retinopathy**

362.42 **Serous detachment of retinal pigment epithelium**
Exudative detachment of retinal pigment epithelium

362.43 **Hemorrhagic detachment of retinal pigment epithelium**

✓5th **362.5** **Degeneration of macula and posterior pole**

Excludes: *degeneration of optic disc (377.21-377.24)*
hereditary retinal degeneration [dystrophy] (362.70-362.77)

362.50 **Macular degeneration (senile), unspecified**

362.51 Nonexudative senile macular degeneration
Senile macular degeneration:
atrophic
dry

362.52 Exudative senile macular degeneration
Kuhnt-Junius degeneration
Senile macular degeneration:
disciform
wet

362.53 Cystoid macular degeneration
Cystoid macular edema

362.54 Macular cyst, hole, or pseudohole

362.55 Toxic maculopathy
Use additional E code to identify drug if drug induced

362.56 Macular puckering
Preretinal fibrosis

362.57 Drusen (degenerative)

✓5th **362.6 Peripheral retinal degenerations**

Excludes: *hereditary retinal degeneration [dystrophy] (362.70-362.77)*
retinal degeneration with retinal defect (361.00-361.07)

362.60 Peripheral retinal degeneration, unspecified

362.61 Paving stone degeneration

362.62 Microcystoid degeneration
Blessig's cysts
Iwanoff's cysts

362.63 Lattice degeneration
Palisade degeneration of retina

362.64 Senile reticular degeneration

362.65 Secondary pigmentary degeneration
Pseudoretinitis pigmentosa

362.66 Secondary vitreoretinal degenerations

✓5th **362.7 Hereditary retinal dystrophies**

362.70 Hereditary retinal dystrophy, unspecified

362.71 Retinal dystrophy in systemic or cerebroretinal lipidoses
Code first underlying disease as:
cerebroretinal lipidoses (330.1)
systemic lipidoses (272.7)

362.72 Retinal dystrophy in other systemic disorders and syndromes
Code first underlying disease as:
Bassen-Kornzweig syndrome (272.5)
Refsum's disease (356.3)

362.73 Vitreoretinal dystrophies
Juvenile retinoschisis

362.74 Pigmentary retinal dystrophy
Retinal dystrophy, albipunctate
Retinitis pigmentosa

362.75 Other dystrophies primarily involving the sensory retina
Progressive cone (-rod) dystrophy
Stargardt's disease

362.76 Dystrophies primarily involving the retinal pigment epithelium
Fundus flavimaculatus
Vitelliform dystrophy

362.77 Dystrophies primarily involving Bruch's membrane
Dystrophy:
hyaline
pseudoinflammatory foveal
Hereditary drusen

✓5th **362.8 Other retinal disorders**

Excludes: *chorioretinal inflammations (363.0-363.2)*
chorioretinal scars (363.30-363.35)

362.81 Retinal hemorrhage
Hemorrhage:
preretinal
retinal (deep) (superficial)
subretinal

➡ **AHA Coding Clinic:** 4Q, '96, 43

362.82 Retinal exudates and deposits

362.83 Retinal edema
Retinal:
cotton wool spots
edema (localized) (macular) (peripheral)

362.84 Retinal ischemia

362.85 Retinal nerve fiber bundle defects

362.89 Other retinal disorders

362.9 Unspecified retinal disorder

363 Chorioretinal inflammations, scars, and other disorders of choroid

✓5th **363.0 Focal chorioretinitis and focal retinochoroiditis**

Excludes: *focal chorioretinitis or retinochoroiditis in:*
histoplasmosis (115.02, 115.12, 115.92)
toxoplasmosis (130.2)
congenital infection (771.2)

363.00 Focal chorioretinitis, unspecified
Focal:
choroiditis or chorioretinitis NOS
retinitis or retinochoroiditis NOS

363.01 Focal choroiditis and chorioretinitis, juxtapapillary

363.03 Focal choroiditis and chorioretinitis of other posterior pole

363.04 Focal choroiditis and chorioretinitis, peripheral

363.05 Focal retinitis and retinochoroiditis, juxtapapillary
Neuroretinitis

363.06 Focal retinitis and retinochoroiditis, macular or paramacular

363.07 Focal retinitis and retinochoroiditis of other posterior pole

363.08 Focal retinitis and retinochoroiditis, peripheral

✓5th **363.1 Disseminated chorioretinitis and disseminated retinochoroiditis**

Excludes: *disseminated choroiditis or chorioretinitis in secondary syphilis (091.51)*
neurosyphilitic disseminated retinitis or retinochoroiditis (094.83)
retinal (peri)vasculitis (362.18)

363.10 Disseminated chorioretinitis, unspecified
Disseminated:
choroiditis or chorioretinitis NOS
retinitis or retinochoroiditis NOS

363.11 Disseminated choroiditis and chorioretinitis, posterior pole

363.12 Disseminated choroiditis and chorioretinitis, peripheral

363.13 Disseminated choroiditis and chorioretinitis, generalized
Code also any underlying disease, as:
tuberculosis (017.3)

363.14 Disseminated retinitis and retinochoroiditis, metastatic

363.15 Disseminated retinitis and retinochoroiditis, pigment epitheliopathy
Acute posterior multifocal placoid pigment epitheliopathy

✓5th **363.2 Other and unspecified forms of chorioretinitis and retinochoroiditis**

Excludes: *panophthalmitis (360.02)*
sympathetic uveitis (360.11)
uveitis NOS (364.3)

363.20 Chorioretinitis, unspecified
Choroiditis NOS
Retinitis NOS
Uveitis, posterior NOS

363.21 Pars planitis
Posterior cyclitis

363.22 Harada's disease

✓5th **363.3 Chorioretinal scars**
Scar (postinflammatory) (postsurgical) (posttraumatic):
choroid
retina

363.30 Chorioretinal scar, unspecified

363.31 Solar retinopathy

363.32 Other macular scars

363.33 Other scars of posterior pole

363.34 Peripheral scars

363.35 Disseminated scars

✓5th **363.4 Choroidal degenerations**

363.40 Choroidal degeneration, unspecified
Choroidal sclerosis NOS

363.41 Senile atrophy of choroid

363.42 Diffuse secondary atrophy of choroid

363.43 Angioid streaks of choroid

✓5th **363.5 Hereditary choroidal dystrophies**
Hereditary choroidal atrophy:
partial [choriocapillaris]
total [all vessels]

363.50 Hereditary choroidal dystrophy or atrophy, unspecified

363.51 Circumpapillary dystrophy of choroid, partial

363.52 Circumpapillary dystrophy of choroid, total
Helicoid dystrophy of choroid

363.53 Central dystrophy of choroid, partial
Dystrophy, choroidal:
central areolar
circinate

363.54 Central choroidal atrophy, total
Dystrophy, choroidal:
central gyrate
serpiginous

363.55 Choroideremia

363.56 Other diffuse or generalized dystrophy, partial
Diffuse choroidal sclerosis

363.57 Other diffuse or generalized dystrophy, total
Generalized gyrate atrophy, choroid

✓5th **363.6 Choroidal hemorrhage and rupture**

363.61 Choroidal hemorrhage, unspecified

363.62 Expulsive choroidal hemorrhage

363.63 Choroidal rupture

✓5th **363.7 Choroidal detachment**

363.70 Choroidal detachment, unspecified

363.71 Serous choroidal detachment

363.72 Hemorrhagic choroidal detachment

363.8 Other disorders of choroid

363.9 Unspecified disorder of choroid

364 Disorders of iris and ciliary body

✓5th **364.0 Acute and subacute iridocyclitis**
Anterior uveitis, Cyclitis, Iridocyclitis, Iritis } acute, subacute

Excludes: *gonococcal (098.41)*
herpes simplex (054.44)
herpes zoster (053.22)

364.00 Acute and subacute iridocyclitis, unspecified

364.01 Primary iridocyclitis

364.02 Recurrent iridocyclitis

364.03 Secondary iridocyclitis, infectious

364.04 Secondary iridocyclitis, noninfectious
Aqueous:
cells
fibrin
flare

364.05 Hypopyon

✓5th **364.1 Chronic iridocyclitis**

Excludes: *posterior cyclitis (363.21)*

364.10 Chronic iridocyclitis, unspecified

364.11 Chronic iridocyclitis in diseases classified elsewhere
Code first underlying disease as:
sarcoidosis (135)
tuberculosis (017.3)

Excludes: *syphilitic iridocyclitis (091.52)*

✓5th **364.2 Certain types of iridocyclitis**

Excludes: *posterior cyclitis (363.21)*
sympathetic uveitis (360.11)

364.21 Fuchs' heterochromic cyclitis

364.22 Glaucomatocyclitic crises

364.23 Lens-induced iridocyclitis

364.24 Vogt-Koyanagi syndrome

364.3 Unspecified iridocyclitis
Uveitis NOS

✓5th **364.4 Vascular disorders of iris and ciliary body**

364.41 Hyphema
Hemorrhage of iris or ciliary body

364.42 Rubeosis iridis
Neovascularization of iris or ciliary body

✓5th **364.5 Degenerations of iris and ciliary body**

364.51 Essential or progressive iris atrophy

364.52 Iridoschisis

364.53 Pigmentary iris degeneration
Acquired heterochromia, Pigment dispersion syndrome, Translucency } of iris

364.54 Degeneration of pupillary margin
Atrophy of sphincter, Ectropion of pigment epithelium } of iris

364.55 Miotic cysts of pupillary margin

364.56 Degenerative changes of chamber angle

364.57 Degenerative changes of ciliary body

364.59 Other iris atrophy
Iris atrophy (generalized) (sector shaped)

✓5th **364.6 Cysts of iris, ciliary body, and anterior chamber**

Excludes: *miotic pupillary cyst (364.55)*
parasitic cyst (360.13)

364.60 Idiopathic cysts

364.61 Implantation cysts
Epithelial down-growth, anterior chamber
Implantation cysts (surgical) (traumatic)

364.62 Exudative cysts of iris or anterior chamber

364.63 Primary cyst of pars plana

364.64 Exudative cyst of pars plana

✓5th **364.7 Adhesions and disruptions of iris and ciliary body**

Excludes: *flat anterior chamber (360.34)*

364.70 Adhesions of iris, unspecified
Synechiae (iris) NOS

364.71 Posterior synechiae

364.72 Anterior synechiae

364.73 Goniosynechiae
Peripheral anterior synechiae

364.74 Pupillary membranes
Iris bombé
Pupillary:
occlusion
seclusion

364.75 Pupillary abnormalities
Deformed pupil
Ectopic pupil
Rupture of sphincter, pupil

364.76 Iridodialysis
➡ **AHA Coding Clinic:** J-A, '85, 16

364.77 Recession of chamber angle

364.8 Other disorders of iris and ciliary body
Prolapse of iris NOS

Excludes: *prolapse of iris in recent wound (871.1)*

364.9 Unspecified disorder of iris and ciliary body

365 Glaucoma

Excludes: *blind hypertensive eye [absolute glaucoma] (360.42)*
congenital glaucoma (743.20-743.22)

✓5th **365.0 Borderline glaucoma [glaucoma suspect]**

365.00 Preglaucoma, unspecified

365.01 Open angle with borderline findings
Open angle with:
borderline intraocular pressure
cupping of optic discs

365.02 Anatomical narrow angle

365.03 Steroid responders

365.04 Ocular hypertension

✓5th **365.1 Open-angle glaucoma**

365.10 Open-angle glaucoma, unspecified
Wide-angle glaucoma NOS

365.11 Primary open angle glaucoma
Chronic simple glaucoma

365.12 Low tension glaucoma

365.13 Pigmentary glaucoma

365.14 Glaucoma of childhood
Infantile or juvenile glaucoma

365.15 Residual stage of open angle glaucoma

✓5th **365.2 Primary angle-closure glaucoma**

365.20 Primary angle-closure glaucoma, unspecified

365.21 Intermittent angle-closure glaucoma
Angle-closure glaucoma:
interval
subacute

365.22 Acute angle-closure glaucoma

365.23 Chronic angle-closure glaucoma

365.24 Residual stage of angle-closure glaucoma

✓5th **365.3 Corticosteroid-induced glaucoma**

365.31 Glaucomatous stage

365.32 Residual stage

✓5th **365.4 Glaucoma associated with congenital anomalies, dystrophies, and systemic syndromes**

365.41 Glaucoma associated with chamber angle anomalies
Code first associated disorder, as:
Axenfeld's anomaly (743.44)
Rieger's anomaly or syndrome (743.44)

365.42 Glaucoma associated with anomalies of iris
Code first associated disorder, as:
aniridia (743.45)
essential iris atrophy (364.51)

365.43 ***Glaucoma associated with other anterior segment anomalies***

Code first associated disorder, as:
microcornea (743.41)

365.44 ***Glaucoma associated with systemic syndromes***

Code first associated disease, as:
neurofibromatosis (237.7)
Sturge-Weber (-Dimitri) syndrome (759.6)

✓5th **365.5** **Glaucoma associated with disorders of the lens**

365.51 **Phacolytic glaucoma**

Use additional code for associated hypermature cataract (366.18)

365.52 **Pseudoexfoliation glaucoma**

Use additional code for associated pseudoexfoliation of capsule (366.11)

365.59 **Glaucoma associated with other lens disorders**

Use additional code for associated disorder, as:
dislocation of lens (379.33-379.34)
spherophakia (743.36)

✓5th **365.6** **Glaucoma associated with other ocular disorders**

365.60 **Glaucoma associated with unspecified ocular disorder**

365.61 **Glaucoma associated with pupillary block**

Use additional code for associated disorder, as:
seclusion of pupil [iris bombé] (364.74)

365.62 **Glaucoma associated with ocular inflammations**

Use additional code for associated disorder, as:
glaucomatocyclitic crises (364.22)
iridocyclitis (364.0-364.3)

365.63 **Glaucoma associated with vascular disorders**

Use additional code for associated disorder, as:
central retinal vein occlusion (362.35)
hyphema (364.41)

365.64 **Glaucoma associated with tumors or cysts**

Use additional code for associated disorder, as:
benign neoplasm (224.0-224.9)
epithelial down-growth (364.61)
malignant neoplasm (190.0-190.9)

365.65 **Glaucoma associated with ocular trauma**

Use additional code for associated condition, as:
contusion of globe (921.3)
recession of chamber angle (364.77)

✓5th **365.8** **Other specified forms of glaucoma**

365.81 **Hypersecretion glaucoma**

365.82 **Glaucoma with increased episcleral venous pressure**

365.89 **Other specified glaucoma**

365.9 **Unspecified glaucoma**

366 Cataract

Excludes: *congenital cataract (743.30-743.34)*

✓5th **366.0** **Infantile, juvenile, and presenile cataract**

366.00 **Nonsenile cataract, unspecified**

366.01 **Anterior subcapsular polar cataract**

366.02 **Posterior subcapsular polar cataract**

366.03 **Cortical, lamellar, or zonular cataract**

366.04 **Nuclear cataract**

366.09 **Other and combined forms of nonsenile cataract**

✓5th **366.1** **Senile cataract** A: 15–124

366.10 **Senile cataract, unspecified**

366.11 **Pseudoexfoliation of lens capsule**

366.12 **Incipient cataract**

Cataract:
coronary
immature NOS
punctate

Water clefts

366.13 **Anterior subcapsular polar senile cataract**

366.14 **Posterior subcapsular polar senile cataract**

366.15 **Cortical senile cataract**

366.16 **Nuclear sclerosis**
Cataracta brunescens
Nuclear cataract

366.17 **Total or mature cataract**

366.18 **Hypermature cataract**
Morgagni cataract

366.19 **Other and combined forms of senile cataract**

✓5th **366.2** **Traumatic cataract**

366.20 **Traumatic cataract, unspecified**

366.21 **Localized traumatic opacities**
Vossius' ring

366.22 **Total traumatic cataract**

366.23 **Partially resolved traumatic cataract**

✓5th **366.3** **Cataract secondary to ocular disorders**

366.30 **Cataracta complicata, unspecified**

366.31 **Glaucomatous flecks (subcapsular)**
Code first underlying glaucoma (365.0-365.9)

366.32 **Cataract in inflammatory disorders**
Code first underlying condition, as:
chronic choroiditis (363.0-363.2)

366.33 **Cataract with neovascularization**
Code first underlying condition, as:
chronic iridocyclitis (364.10)

366.34 **Cataract in degenerative disorders**
Sunflower cataract
Code first underlying condition, as:
chalcosis (360.24)
degenerative myopia (360.21)
pigmentary retinal dystrophy (362.74)

✓5th **366.4** **Cataract associated with other disorders**

366.41 ***Diabetic cataract***
Code first diabetes (250.5)

366.42 ***Tetanic cataract***
Code first underlying disease as:
calcinosis (275.4)
hypoparathyroidism (252.1)

366.43 ***Myotonic cataract***
Code first underlying disorder (359.2)

366.44 ***Cataract associated with other syndromes***
Code first underlying condition, as:
craniofacial dysostosis (756.0)
galactosemia (271.1)

366.45 **Toxic cataract**
Drug-induced cataract
Use additional E code to identify drug or other toxic substance

366.46 **Cataract associated with radiation and other physical influences**
Use additional E code to identify cause

✓5th **366.5** **After-cataract**

366.50 **After-cataract, unspecified**
Secondary cataract NOS

366.51 **Soemmering's ring**

366.52 **Other after-cataract, not obscuring vision**

366.53 **After-cataract, obscuring vision**

366.8 **Other cataract**
Calcification of lens

366.9 **Unspecified cataract**

367 Disorders of refraction and accommodation

367.0 **Hypermetropia**
Far-sightedness Hyperopia

367.1 **Myopia**
Near-sightedness

✓5th **367.2** **Astigmatism**

367.20 **Astigmatism, unspecified**

367.21 **Regular astigmatism**

367.22 **Irregular astigmatism**

✓5th **367.3** **Anisometropia and aniseikonia**

367.31 **Anisometropia**

367.32 **Aniseikonia**

367.4 **Presbyopia**

✓5th **367.5 Disorders of accommodation**

367.51 Paresis of accommodation
Cycloplegia

367.52 Total or complete internal ophthalmoplegia

367.53 Spasm of accommodation

✓5th **367.8 Other disorders of refraction and accommodation**

367.81 Transient refractive change

367.89 Other
Drug-induced } disorders of refraction
Toxic } and accommodation

367.9 Unspecified disorder of refraction and accommodation

368 Visual disturbances

Excludes: *electrophysiological disturbances (794.11-794.14)*

✓5th **368.0 Amblyopia ex anopsia**

368.00 Amblyopia, unspecified

368.01 Strabismic amblyopia
Suppression amblyopia

368.02 Deprivation amblyopia

368.03 Refractive amblyopia

✓5th **368.1 Subjective visual disturbances**

368.10 Subjective visual disturbance, unspecified

368.11 Sudden visual loss

368.12 Transient visual loss
Concentric fading
Scintillating scotoma

368.13 Visual discomfort
Asthenopia
Eye strain
Photophobia

368.14 Visual distortions of shape and size
Macropsia
Metamorphopsia
Micropsia

368.15 Other visual distortions and entoptic phenomena
Photopsia
Refractive:
diplopia
polyopia
Visual halos

368.16 Psychophysical visual disturbances
Visual:
agnosia
disorientation syndrome
hallucinations

368.2 Diplopia
Double vision

✓5th **368.3 Other disorders of binocular vision**

368.30 Binocular vision disorder, unspecified

368.31 Suppression of binocular vision

368.32 Simultaneous visual perception without fusion

368.33 Fusion with defective stereopsis

368.34 Abnormal retinal correspondence

✓5th **368.4 Visual field defects**

368.40 Visual field defects, unspecified

368.41 Scotoma involving central area
Scotoma:
central
centrocecal
paracentral

368.42 Scotoma of blind spot area
Enlarged:
angioscotoma
blind spot
Paracecal scotoma

368.43 Sector or arcuate defects
Scotoma:
arcuate
Bjerrum
Seidel

368.44 Other localized visual field defect
Scotoma:
NOS
ring
Visual field defect:
nasal step
peripheral

368.45 Generalized contraction or constriction

368.46 Homonymous bilateral field defects
Hemianopsia (altitudinal) (homonymous)
Quadrant anopia

368.47 Heteronymous bilateral field defects
Hemianopsia:
binasal
bitemporal

✓5th **368.5 Color vision deficiencies**
Color blindness

368.51 Protan defect
Protanomaly
Protanopia

368.52 Deutan defect
Deuteranomaly
Deuteranopia

368.53 Tritan defect
Tritanomaly
Tritanopia

368.54 **Achromatopsia**
Monochromatism (cone) (rod)

368.55 **Acquired color vision deficiencies**

368.59 **Other color vision deficiencies**

✓5th **368.6** **Night blindness**
Hemeralopia   Nyctalopia

368.60 **Night blindness, unspecified**

368.61 **Congenital night blindness**
Hereditary night blindness
Oguchi's disease

368.62 **Acquired night blindness**

Excludes: *that due to vitamin A deficiency (264.5)*

368.63 **Abnormal dark adaptation curve**
Abnormal threshold } of cones or rods
Delayed adaptation } of cones or rods

368.69 **Other night blindness**

368.8 **Other specified visual disturbances**
Blurred vision NOS

368.9 **Unspecified visual disturbance**

369 Blindness and low vision

Note: Visual impairment refers to a functional limitation of the eye (e.g., limited visual acuity or visual field). It should be distinguished from visual disability, indicating a limitation of the abilities of the individual (e.g., limited reading skills, vocational skills), and from visual handicap, indicating a limitation of personal and socioeconomic independence (e.g., limited mobility, limited employability).

The levels of impairment defined in the table on page 133 are based on the recommendations of the WHO Study Group on Prevention of Blindness (Geneva, November 6-10, 1972; WHO Technical Report Series 518), and of the International Council of Ophthalmology (1976).

Note that definitions of blindness vary in different settings.

For international reporting WHO defines blindness as profound impairment. This definition can be applied to blindness of one eye (369.1, 369.6) and to blindness of the individual (369.0).

For determination of benefits in the U.S.A., the definition of legal blindness as severe impairment is often used. This definition applies to blindness of the individual only.

Excludes: *correctable impaired vision due to refractive errors (367.0-367.9)*

✓5th **369.0** **Profound impairment, both eyes**

369.00 **Impairment level not further specified**
Blindness:
NOS according to WHO definition
both eyes

369.01 **Better eye: total impairment; lesser eye: total impairment**

369.02 **Better eye: near-total impairment; lesser eye: not further specified**

369.03 **Better eye: profound impairment; lesser eye: total impairment**

369.04 **Better eye: near-total impairment; lesser eye: near-total impairment**

369.05 **Better eye: profound impairment; lesser eye: not further specified**

369.06 **Better eye: profound impairment; lesser eye: total impairment**

369.07 **Better eye: profound impairment; lesser eye: near-total impairment**

369.08 **Better eye: profound impairment; lesser eye: profound impairment**

✓5th **369.1** **Moderate or severe impairment, better eye, profound impairment lesser eye**

369.10 **Impairment level not further specified**
Blindness, one eye, low vision other eye

369.11 **Better eye: severe impairment; lesser eye: blind, not further specified**

369.12 **Better eye: severe impairment; lesser eye: total impairment**

369.13 **Better eye: severe impairment; lesser eye: near-total impairment**

369.14 **Better eye: severe impairment; lesser eye: profound impairment**

369.15 **Better eye: moderate impairment; lesser eye: blind, not further specified**

369.16 **Better eye: moderate impairment; lesser eye: total impairment**

369.17 **Better eye: moderate impairment; lesser eye: near-total impairment**

369.18 **Better eye: moderate impairment; lesser eye: profound impairment**

✓5th **369.2** **Moderate or severe impairment, both eyes**

369.20 **Impairment level not further specified**
Low vision, both eyes NOS

369.21 **Better eye: severe impairment; lesser eye: not further specified**

369.22 **Better eye: severe impairment; lesser eye: severe impairment**

369.23 **Better eye: moderate impairment; lesser eye: not further specified**

369.24 **Better eye: moderate impairment; lesser eye: severe impairment**

369.25 **Better eye: moderate impairment; lesser eye: moderate impairment**

369.3 **Unqualified visual loss, both eyes**

Excludes: *blindness NOS:*
legal [U.S.A. definition] (369.4)
WHO definition (369.00)

☐ **369.4** **Legal blindness, as defined in U.S.A.**
Blindness NOS according to U.S.A. definition

Excludes: *legal blindness with specification of impairment level (369.01-369.08, 369.11-369.14, 369.21-369.22)*

✓5th **369.6** **Profound impairment, one eye**

369.60 **Impairment level not further specified**
Blindness, one eye

369.61 **One eye: total impairment; other eye: not specified**

369.62 **One eye: total impairment; other eye: near-normal vision**

369.63 **One eye: total impairment; other eye: normal vision**

369.64 **One eye: near-total impairment; other eye: not specified**

369.65 **One eye: near-total impairment; other eye: near-normal vision**

369.66 **One eye: near-total impairment; other eye: normal vision**

369.67 **One eye: profound impairment; other eye: not specified**

369.68 **One eye: profound impairment; other eye: near-normal vision**

369.69 **One eye: profound impairment; other eye: normal vision**

✓5th **369.7** **Moderate or severe impairment, one eye**

369.70 **Impairment level not further specified**
Low vision, one eye

369.71 **One eye: severe impairment; other eye: not specified**

369.72 **One eye: severe impairment; other eye: near-normal vision**

369.73 **One eye: severe impairment; other eye: normal vision**

369.74 **One eye: moderate impairment; other eye: not specified**

369.75 **One eye: moderate impairment; other eye: near-normal vision**

369.76 **One eye: moderate impairment; other eye: normal vision**

369.8 **Unqualified visual loss, one eye**

369.9 **Unspecified visual loss**

Classification		LEVELS OF VISUAL IMPAIRMENT	Additional descriptors which may be encountered
"legal"	WHO	Visual acuity and/or visual field limitation (whichever is worse)	
	(NEAR-) NORMAL VISION	RANGE OF NORMAL VISION 20/10 20/13 20/16 20/20 20/25 2.0 1.6 1.25 1.0 0.8	
	(NEAR-) NORMAL VISION	NEAR-NORMAL VISION 20/30 20/40 20/50 20/60 0.7 0.6 0.5 0.4 0.3	
	LOW VISION	MODERATE VISUAL IMPAIRMENT 20/70 20/80 20/100 20/125 20/160 0.25 0.20 0.16 0.12	Moderate low vision
LEGAL BLINDNESS (U.S.A.) both eyes	LOW VISION	SEVERE VISUAL IMPAIRMENT 20/200 20/250 20/320 20/400 0.10 0.08 0.06 0.05 Visual field: 20 degrees or less	Severe low vision, "Legal" blindness
LEGAL BLINDNESS (U.S.A.) both eyes	BLINDNESS (WHO) one or both eyes	PROFOUND VISUAL IMPAIRMENT 20/500 20/630 20/800 20/1000 0.04 0.03 0.025 0.02 Count fingers at: less than 3m (10 ft.) Visual field: 10 degrees or less	Profound low vision, Moderate blindness
LEGAL BLINDNESS (U.S.A.) both eyes	BLINDNESS (WHO) one or both eyes	NEAR-TOTAL VISUAL IMPAIRMENT Visual acuity: less than 0.02 (20/1000) Count fingers at: 1m (3 ft.) or less Hand movements: 5m (15 ft.) or less Light projection, light perception Visual field: 5 degrees or less	Severe blindness, Near-total blindness
LEGAL BLINDNESS (U.S.A.) both eyes	BLINDNESS (WHO) one or both eyes	TOTAL VISUAL IMPAIRMENT No light perception (NLP)	Total blindness

Visual acuity refers to best achievable acuity with correction.
Non-listed Snellen fractions may be classified by converting to the nearest decimal equivalent, e.g. 10/200 = 0.05, 6/30 = 0.20.
CF (count fingers) without designation of distance, may be classified to profound impairment.
HN (hand motion) without designation of distance, may be classified to near-total impairment.
Visual field measurements refer to the largest field diameter for a 1/100 white test object.

370 Keratitis

✓5th **370.0 Corneal ulcer**

Excludes: *that due to vitamin A deficiency (264.3)*

370.00 Corneal ulcer, unspecified

370.01 Marginal corneal ulcer

370.02 Ring corneal ulcer

370.03 Central corneal ulcer

370.04 Hypopyon ulcer
Serpiginous ulcer

370.05 Mycotic corneal ulcer

370.06 Perforated corneal ulcer

370.07 Mooren's ulcer

✓5th **370.2 Superficial keratitis without conjunctivitis**

Excludes: *dendritic [herpes simplex] keratitis (054.42)*

370.20 Superficial keratitis, unspecified

370.21 Punctate keratitis
Thygeson's superficial punctate keratitis

370.22 Macular keratitis
Keratitis:
- areolar
- nummular
- stellate
- striate

370.23 Filamentary keratitis

370.24 Photokeratitis
Snow blindness
Welders' keratitis
➡ **AHA Coding Clinic:** 3Q, '96, 6

✓5th **370.3 Certain types of keratoconjunctivitis**

370.31 Phlyctenular keratoconjunctivitis
Phlyctenulosis
Use additional code for any associated tuberculosis (017.3)

370.32 Limbar and corneal involvement in vernal conjunctivitis
Use additional code for vernal conjunctivitis (372.13)

370.33 Keratoconjunctivitis sicca, not specified as Sjögren's

Excludes: *Sjögren's syndrome (710.2)*

370.34 Exposure keratoconjunctivitis
➡ **AHA Coding Clinic:** 3Q, '96, 6

370.35 Neurotrophic keratoconjunctivitis

✓5th **370.4 Other and unspecified keratoconjunctivitis**

370.40 Keratoconjunctivitis, unspecified
Superficial keratitis with conjunctivitis NOS

370.44 **Keratitis or keratoconjunctivitis in exanthema**

Code first underlying condition (050.0-052.9)

Excludes: *herpes simplex (054.43)*
herpes zoster (053.21)
measles (055.71)

370.49 **Other**

Excludes: *epidemic keratoconjunctivitis (077.1)*

✓5th **370.5** **Interstitial and deep keratitis**

370.50 **Interstitial keratitis, unspecified**

370.52 **Diffuse interstitial keratitis**
Cogan's syndrome

370.54 **Sclerosing keratitis**

370.55 **Corneal abscess**

370.59 **Other**

Excludes: *disciform herpes simplex keratitis (054.43)*
syphilitic keratitis (090.3)

✓5th **370.6** **Corneal neovascularization**

370.60 **Corneal neovascularization, unspecified**

370.61 **Localized vascularization of cornea**

370.62 **Pannus (corneal)**

370.63 **Deep vascularization of cornea**

370.64 **Ghost vessels (corneal)**

370.8 **Other forms of keratitis**

370.9 **Unspecified keratitis**

371 Corneal opacity and other disorders of cornea

✓5th **371.0** **Corneal scars and opacities**

Excludes: *that due to vitamin A deficiency (264.6)*

371.00 **Corneal opacity, unspecified**
Corneal scar NOS

371.01 **Minor opacity of cornea**
Corneal nebula

371.02 **Peripheral opacity of cornea**
Corneal macula not interfering with central vision

371.03 **Central opacity of cornea**
Corneal:
leucoma } interfering with central vision
macula }

371.04 **Adherent leucoma**

371.05 **Phthisical cornea**

Code first underlying tuberculosis (017.3)

✓5th **371.1** **Corneal pigmentations and deposits**

371.10 **Corneal deposit, unspecified**

371.11 **Anterior pigmentations**
Stähli's lines

371.12 **Stromal pigmentations**
Hematocornea

371.13 **Posterior pigmentations**
Krukenberg spindle

371.14 **Kayser-Fleischer ring**

371.15 **Other deposits associated with metabolic disorders**

371.16 **Argentous deposits**

✓5th **371.2** **Corneal edema**

371.20 **Corneal edema, unspecified**

371.21 **Idiopathic corneal edema**

371.22 **Secondary corneal edema**

371.23 **Bullous keratopathy**

371.24 **Corneal edema due to wearing of contact lenses**

✓5th **371.3** **Changes of corneal membranes**

371.30 **Corneal membrane change, unspecified**

371.31 **Folds and rupture of Bowman's membrane**

371.32 **Folds in Descemet's membrane**

371.33 **Rupture in Descemet's membrane**

✓5th **371.4** **Corneal degenerations**

371.40 **Corneal degeneration, unspecified**

371.41 **Senile corneal changes**
Arcus senilis   Hassall-Henle bodies

371.42 **Recurrent erosion of cornea**

Excludes: *Mooren's ulcer (370.07)*

371.43 Band-shaped keratopathy

371.44 Other calcerous degenerations of cornea

371.45 Keratomalacia NOS

Excludes: *that due to vitamin A deficiency (264.4)*

371.46 Nodular degeneration of cornea
Salzmann's nodular dystrophy

371.48 Peripheral degenerations of cornea
Marginal degeneration of cornea [Terrien's]

371.49 Other
Discrete colliquative keratopathy

✓5th **371.5** Hereditary corneal dystrophies

371.50 Corneal dystrophy, unspecified

371.51 Juvenile epithelial corneal dystrophy

371.52 Other anterior corneal dystrophies
Corneal dystrophy:
- microscopic cystic
- ring-like

371.53 Granular corneal dystrophy

371.54 Lattice corneal dystrophy

371.55 Macular corneal dystrophy

371.56 Other stromal corneal dystrophies
Crystalline corneal dystrophy

371.57 Endothelial corneal dystrophy
Combined corneal dystrophy
Cornea guttata
Fuchs' endothelial dystrophy

371.58 Other posterior corneal dystrophies
Polymorphous corneal dystrophy

✓5th **371.6** Keratoconus

371.60 Keratoconus, unspecified

371.61 Keratoconus, stable condition

371.62 Keratoconus, acute hydrops

✓5th **371.7** Other corneal deformities

371.70 Corneal deformity, unspecified

371.71 Corneal ectasia

371.72 Descemetocele

371.73 Corneal staphyloma

✓5th **371.8** Other corneal disorders

371.81 Corneal anesthesia and hypoesthesia

371.82 Corneal disorder due to contact lens

Excludes: *corneal edema due to contact lens (371.24)*

371.89 Other

371.9 Unspecified corneal disorder

372 Disorders of conjunctiva

Excludes: *keratoconjunctivitis (370.3-370.4)*

✓5th **372.0** Acute conjunctivitis

372.00 Acute conjunctivitis, unspecified

372.01 Serous conjunctivitis, except viral

Excludes: *viral conjunctivitis NOS (077.9)*

372.02 Acute follicular conjunctivitis
Conjunctival folliculosis NOS

Excludes: *conjunctivitis:*
- *adenoviral (acute follicular) (077.3)*
- *epidemic hemorrhagic (077.4)*
- *inclusion (077.0)*
- *Newcastle (077.8)*

epidemic keratoconjunctivitis (077.1)
pharyngoconjunctival fever (077.2)

372.03 Other mucopurulent conjunctivitis
Catarrhal conjunctivitis

Excludes: *blennorrhea neonatorum (gonococcal) (098.40)*
neonatal conjunctivitis (771.6)
ophthalmia neonatorum NOS (771.6)

372.04 Pseudomembranous conjunctivitis
Membranous conjunctivitis

Excludes: *diphtheritic conjunctivitis (032.81)*

372.05 Acute atopic conjunctivitis

✓5th **372.1** Chronic conjunctivitis

372.10 Chronic conjunctivitis, unspecified

372.11 Simple chronic conjunctivitis

372.12 Chronic follicular conjunctivitis

372.13 Vernal conjunctivitis
➡ **AHA Coding Clinic:** 3Q, '96, 8

372.14 Other chronic allergic conjunctivitis
➡ **AHA Coding Clinic:** 3Q, '96, 8

372.15 ***Parasitic conjunctivitis***
Code first underlying disease as:
filariasis (125.0-125.9)
mucocutaneous leishmaniasis (085.5)

✓5th **372.2** Blepharoconjunctivitis

372.20 Blepharoconjunctivitis, unspecified

372.21 Angular blepharoconjunctivitis

372.22 Contact blepharoconjunctivitis

✓5th **372.3** Other and unspecified conjunctivitis

372.30 Conjunctivitis, unspecified

372.31 ***Rosacea conjunctivitis***
Code first underlying rosacea dermatitis (695.3)

372.33 ***Conjunctivitis in mucocutaneous disease***
Code first underlying disease as:
erythema multiforme (695.1)
Reiter's disease (099.3)

Excludes: *ocular pemphigoid (694.61)*

372.39 Other

✓5th **372.4** Pterygium

Excludes: *pseudopterygium (372.52)*

372.40 Pterygium, unspecified

372.41 Peripheral pterygium, stationary

372.42 Peripheral pterygium, progressive

372.43 Central pterygium

372.44 Double pterygium

372.45 Recurrent pterygium

✓5th **372.5** Conjunctival degenerations and deposits

372.50 Conjunctival degeneration, unspecified

372.51 Pinguecula

372.52 Pseudopterygium

372.53 Conjunctival xerosis

Excludes: *conjunctival xerosis due to vitamin A deficiency (264.0, 264.1, 264.7)*

372.54 Conjunctival concretions

372.55 Conjunctival pigmentations
Conjunctival argyrosis

372.56 Conjunctival deposits

✓5th **372.6** Conjunctival scars

372.61 Granuloma of conjunctiva

372.62 Localized adhesions and strands of conjunctiva

372.63 Symblepharon
Extensive adhesions of conjunctiva

372.64 Scarring of conjunctiva
Contraction of eye socket (after enucleation)

✓5th **372.7** Conjunctival vascular disorders and cysts

372.71 Hyperemia of conjunctiva

372.72 Conjunctival hemorrhage
Hyposphagma
Subconjunctival hemorrhage

372.73 Conjunctival edema
Chemosis of conjunctiva
Subconjunctival edema

372.74 Vascular abnormalities of conjunctiva
Aneurysm(ata) of conjunctiva

372.75 Conjunctival cysts

372.8 Other disorders of conjunctiva

372.9 Unspecified disorder of conjunctiva

373 Inflammation of eyelids

✓5th **373.0** Blepharitis

Excludes: *blepharoconjunctivitis (372.20-372.22)*

373.00 Blepharitis, unspecified

373.01 Ulcerative blepharitis

373.02 Squamous blepharitis

✓5th **373.1** **Hordeolum and other deep inflammation of eyelid**

373.11 **Hordeolum externum**
Hordeolum NOS
Stye

373.12 **Hordeolum internum**
Infection of meibomian gland

373.13 **Abscess of eyelid**
Furuncle of eyelid

373.2 **Chalazion**
Meibomian (gland) cyst

Excludes: *infected meibomian gland (373.12)*

✓5th **373.3** **Noninfectious dermatoses of eyelid**

373.31 **Eczematous dermatitis of eyelid**

373.32 **Contact and allergic dermatitis of eyelid**

373.33 **Xeroderma of eyelid**

373.34 **Discoid lupus erythematosus of eyelid**

373.4 ***Infective dermatitis of eyelid of types resulting in deformity***
Code first underlying disease as:
leprosy (030.0-030.9)
lupus vulgaris (tuberculous) (017.0)
yaws (102.0-102.9)

373.5 ***Other infective dermatitis of eyelid***
Code first underlying disease as:
actinomycosis (039.3)
impetigo (684)
mycotic dermatitis (110.0-111.9)
vaccinia (051.0)
postvaccination (999.0)

Excludes: *herpes:*
simplex (054.41)
zoster (053.20)

373.6 ***Parasitic infestation of eyelid***
Code first underlying disease as:
leishmaniasis (085.0-085.9)
loiasis (125.2)
onchocerciasis (125.3)
pediculosis (132.0)

373.8 **Other inflammations of eyelids**

373.9 **Unspecified inflammation of eyelid**

374 Other disorders of eyelids

✓5th **374.0** **Entropion and trichiasis of eyelid**

374.00 **Entropion, unspecified**

374.01 **Senile entropion** A:15–124

374.02 **Mechanical entropion**

374.03 **Spastic entropion**

374.04 **Cicatricial entropion**

374.05 **Trichiasis without entropion**

✓5th **374.1** **Ectropion**

374.10 **Ectropion, unspecified**

374.11 **Senile ectropion** A:15–124

374.12 **Mechanical ectropion**

374.13 **Spastic ectropion**

374.14 **Cicatricial ectropion**

✓5th **374.2** **Lagophthalmos**

374.20 **Lagophthalmos, unspecified**

374.21 **Paralytic lagophthalmos**

374.22 **Mechanical lagophthalmos**

374.23 **Cicatricial lagophthalmos**

✓5th **374.3** **Ptosis of eyelid**

374.30 **Ptosis of eyelid, unspecified**
➡ **AHA Coding Clinic:** 2Q, '96, 11

374.31 **Paralytic ptosis**

374.32 **Myogenic ptosis**

374.33 **Mechanical ptosis**

374.34 **Blepharochalasis**
Pseudoptosis

✓5th **374.4** **Other disorders affecting eyelid function**

Excludes: *blepharoclonus (333.81)*
blepharospasm (333.81)
facial nerve palsy (351.0)
third nerve palsy or paralysis (378.51-378.52)
tic (psychogenic) (307.20-307.23)
organic (333.3)

374.41 **Lid retraction or lag**

374.43 **Abnormal innervation syndrome**
Jaw-blinking
Paradoxical facial movements

374.44 **Sensory disorders**

374.45 **Other sensorimotor disorders**
Deficient blink reflex

374.46 **Blepharophimosis**
Ankyloblepharon

✓5th **374.5** **Degenerative disorders of eyelid and periocular area**

374.50 **Degenerative disorder of eyelid, unspecified**

374.51 ***Xanthelasma***
Xanthoma (planum) (tuberosum) of eyelid
Code first underlying condition (272.0-272.9)

374.52 **Hyperpigmentation of eyelid**
Chloasma
Dyspigmentation

374.53 **Hypopigmentation of eyelid**
Vitiligo of eyelid

374.54 **Hypertrichosis of eyelid**

374.55 **Hypotrichosis of eyelid**
Madarosis of eyelid

374.56 **Other degenerative disorders of skin affecting eyelid**

✓5th **374.8** **Other disorders of eyelid**

374.81 **Hemorrhage of eyelid**

Excludes: *black eye (921.0)*

374.82 **Edema of eyelid**
Hyperemia of eyelid

374.83 **Elephantiasis of eyelid**

374.84 **Cysts of eyelids**
Sebaceous cyst of eyelid

374.85 **Vascular anomalies of eyelid**

374.86 **Retained foreign body of eyelid**

374.87 **Dermatochalasis**

374.89 **Other disorders of eyelid**

374.9 **Unspecified disorder of eyelid**

375 Disorders of lacrimal system

✓5th **375.0** **Dacryoadenitis**

375.00 **Dacryoadenitis, unspecified**

375.01 **Acute dacryoadenitis**

375.02 **Chronic dacryoadenitis**

375.03 **Chronic enlargement of lacrimal gland**

✓5th **375.1** **Other disorders of lacrimal gland**

375.11 **Dacryops**

375.12 **Other lacrimal cysts and cystic degeneration**

375.13 **Primary lacrimal atrophy**

375.14 **Secondary lacrimal atrophy**

375.15 **Tear film insufficiency, unspecified**
Dry eye syndrome
➡ **AHA Coding Clinic:** 3Q, '96, 6

375.16 **Dislocation of lacrimal gland**

✓5th **375.2** **Epiphora**

375.20 **Epiphora, unspecified as to cause**

375.21 **Epiphora due to excess lacrimation**

375.22 **Epiphora due to insufficient drainage**

✓5th **375.3** **Acute and unspecified inflammation of lacrimal passages**

Excludes: *neonatal dacryocystitis (771.6)*

375.30 **Dacryocystitis, unspecified**

375.31 **Acute canaliculitis, lacrimal**

375.32 **Acute dacryocystitis**
Acute peridacryocystitis

375.33 **Phlegmonous dacryocystitis**

✓5th **375.4** **Chronic inflammation of lacrimal passages**

375.41 **Chronic canaliculitis**

375.42 **Chronic dacryocystitis**

375.43 **Lacrimal mucocele**

✓5th **375.5** **Stenosis and insufficiency of lacrimal passages**

375.51 **Eversion of lacrimal punctum**

375.52 **Stenosis of lacrimal punctum**

375.53 **Stenosis of lacrimal canaliculi**

375.54 **Stenosis of lacrimal sac**

375.55 **Obstruction of nasolacrimal duct, neonatal**

Excludes: *congenital anomaly of nasolacrimal duct (743.65)*

375.56 Stenosis of nasolacrimal duct, acquired

375.57 Dacryolith

✓5th **375.6** Other changes of lacrimal passages

375.61 Lacrimal fistula

375.69 Other

✓5th **375.8** Other disorders of lacrimal system

375.81 Granuloma of lacrimal passages

375.89 Other

375.9 Unspecified disorder of lacrimal system

376 Disorders of the orbit

✓5th **376.0** Acute inflammation of orbit

376.00 Acute inflammation of orbit, unspecified

376.01 Orbital cellulitis
Abscess of orbit

376.02 Orbital periostitis

376.03 Orbital osteomyelitis

376.04 Tenonitis

✓5th **376.1** Chronic inflammatory disorders of orbit

376.10 Chronic inflammation of orbit, unspecified

376.11 Orbital granuloma
Pseudotumor (inflammatory) of orbit

376.12 Orbital myositis

376.13 *Parasitic infestation of orbit*

Code first underlying disease as:
hydatid infestation of orbit (122.3, 122.6, 122.9)
myiasis of orbit (134.0)

✓5th ***376.2*** *Endocrine exophthalmos*

Code first underlying thyroid disorder (242.0-242.9)

376.21 *Thyrotoxic exophthalmos*

376.22 *Exophthalmic ophthalmoplegia*

✓5th **376.3** Other exophthalmic conditions

376.30 Exophthalmos, unspecified

376.31 Constant exophthalmos

376.32 Orbital hemorrhage

376.33 Orbital edema or congestion

376.34 Intermittent exophthalmos

376.35 Pulsating exophthalmos

376.36 Lateral displacement of globe

✓5th **376.4** Deformity of orbit

376.40 Deformity of orbit, unspecified

376.41 Hypertelorism of orbit

376.42 Exostosis of orbit

376.43 Local deformities due to bone disease

376.44 Orbital deformities associated with craniofacial deformities

376.45 Atrophy of orbit

376.46 Enlargement of orbit

376.47 Deformity due to trauma or surgery

✓5th **376.5** Enophthalmos

376.50 Enophthalmos, unspecified as to cause

376.51 Enophthalmos due to atrophy of orbital tissue

376.52 Enophthalmos due to trauma or surgery

376.6 Retained (old) foreign body following penetrating wound of orbit
Retrobulbar foreign body

✓5th **376.8** Other orbital disorders

376.81 Orbital cysts
Encephalocele of orbit

376.82 Myopathy of extraocular muscles

376.89 Other

376.9 Unspecified disorder of orbit

377 Disorders of optic nerve and visual pathways

✓5th **377.0** Papilledema

377.00 Papilledema, unspecified
➡ **CC Excl:** 017.30-017.36, 017.90-017.96, 036.81, 250.50-250.53, 250.80-250.93, 377.00-377.03, 377.14, 377.24, 379.8, 379.90, 379.99, 743.8-743.9

377.01 Papilledema associated with increased intracranial pressure
➡ **CC Excl:** see Code 377.00

377.02 **Papilledema associated with decreased ocular pressure**
➡ **CC Excl:** see Code 377.00

377.03 **Papilledema associated with retinal disorder**

377.04 **Foster-Kennedy syndrome**

✓5th **377.1** **Optic atrophy**

377.10 **Optic atrophy, unspecified**

377.11 **Primary optic atrophy**

Excludes: *neurosyphilitic optic atrophy (094.84)*

377.12 **Postinflammatory optic atrophy**

377.13 **Optic atrophy associated with retinal dystrophies**

377.14 **Glaucomatous atrophy [cupping] of optic disc**

377.15 **Partial optic atrophy**
Temporal pallor of optic disc

377.16 **Hereditary optic atrophy**
Optic atrophy:
dominant hereditary
Leber's

✓5th **377.2** **Other disorders of optic disc**

377.21 **Drusen of optic disc**

377.22 **Crater-like holes of optic disc**

377.23 **Coloboma of optic disc**

377.24 **Pseudopapilledema**

✓5th **377.3** **Optic neuritis**

Excludes: *meningococcal optic neuritis (036.81)*

377.30 **Optic neuritis, unspecified**

377.31 **Optic papillitis**

377.32 **Retrobulbar neuritis (acute)**

Excludes: *syphilitic retrobulbar neuritis (094.85)*

377.33 **Nutritional optic neuropathy**

377.34 **Toxic optic neuropathy**
Toxic amblyopia

377.39 **Other**

Excludes: *ischemic optic neuropathy (377.41)*

✓5th **377.4** **Other disorders of optic nerve**

377.41 **Ischemic optic neuropathy**

377.42 **Hemorrhage in optic nerve sheaths**

377.49 **Other**
Compression of optic nerve

✓5th **377.5** **Disorders of optic chiasm**

377.51 **Associated with pituitary neoplasms and disorders**

377.52 **Associated with other neoplasms**

377.53 **Associated with vascular disorders**

377.54 **Associated with inflammatory disorders**

✓5th **377.6** **Disorders of other visual pathways**

377.61 **Associated with neoplasms**

377.62 **Associated with vascular disorders**

377.63 **Associated with inflammatory disorders**

✓5th **377.7** **Disorders of visual cortex**

Excludes: *visual:*
agnosia (368.16)
hallucinations (368.16)
halos (368.15)

377.71 **Associated with neoplasms**

377.72 **Associated with vascular disorders**

377.73 **Associated with inflammatory disorders**

377.75 **Cortical blindness**

377.9 **Unspecified disorder of optic nerve and visual pathways**

378 Strabismus and other disorders of binocular eye movements

Excludes: *nystagmus and other irregular eye movements (379.50-379.59)*

✓5th **378.0** **Esotropia**
Convergent concomitant strabismus

Excludes: *intermittent esotropia (378.20-378.22)*

378.00 **Esotropia, unspecified**

378.01 **Monocular esotropia**

378.02 Monocular esotropia with A pattern

378.03 Monocular esotropia with V pattern

378.04 Monocular esotropia with other noncomitancies
Monocular esotropia with X or Y pattern

378.05 Alternating esotropia

378.06 Alternating esotropia with A pattern

378.07 Alternating esotropia with V pattern

378.08 Alternating esotropia with other noncomitancies
Alternating esotropia with X or Y pattern

✓5th **378.1** Exotropia
Divergent concomitant strabismus

Excludes: *intermittent exotropia (378.20, 378.23-378.24)*

378.10 Exotropia, unspecified

378.11 Monocular exotropia

378.12 Monocular exotropia with A pattern

378.13 Monocular exotropia with V pattern

378.14 Monocular exotropia with other noncomitancies
Monocular exotropia with X or Y pattern

378.15 Alternating exotropia

378.16 Alternating exotropia with A pattern

378.17 Alternating exotropia with V pattern

378.18 Alternating exotropia with other noncomitancies
Alternating exotropia with X or Y pattern

✓5th **378.2** Intermittent heterotropia

Excludes: *vertical heterotropia (intermittent) (378.31)*

378.20 Intermittent heterotropia, unspecified
Intermittent:
esotropia NOS
exotropia NOS

378.21 Intermittent esotropia, monocular

378.22 Intermittent esotropia, alternating

378.23 Intermittent exotropia, monocular

378.24 Intermittent exotropia, alternating

✓5th **378.3** Other and unspecified heterotropia

378.30 Heterotropia, unspecified

378.31 Hypertropia
Vertical heterotropia (constant) (intermittent)

378.32 Hypotropia

378.33 Cyclotropia

378.34 Monofixation syndrome
Microtropia

378.35 Accommodative component in esotropia

✓5th **378.4** Heterophoria

378.40 Heterophoria, unspecified

378.41 Esophoria

378.42 Exophoria

378.43 Vertical heterophoria

378.44 Cyclophoria

378.45 Alternating hyperphoria

✓5th **378.5** Paralytic strabismus

378.50 Paralytic strabismus, unspecified

378.51 Third or oculomotor nerve palsy, partial

378.52 Third or oculomotor nerve palsy, total
➡ **AHA Coding Clinic:** 2Q, '89, 12

378.53 Fourth or trochlear nerve palsy

378.54 Sixth or abducens nerve palsy

378.55 External ophthalmoplegia
➡ **AHA Coding Clinic:** 2Q, '89, 12

378.56 Total ophthalmoplegia

✓5th **378.6** Mechanical strabismus

378.60 Mechanical strabismus, unspecified

378.61 Brown's (tendon) sheath syndrome

378.62 Mechanical strabismus from other musculofascial disorders

378.63 Limited duction associated with other conditions

✓5th **378.7** **Other specified strabismus**

378.71 **Duane's syndrome**

378.72 **Progressive external ophthalmoplegia**

378.73 **Strabismus in other neuromuscular disorders**

✓5th **378.8** **Other disorders of binocular eye movements**

Excludes: *nystagmus (379.50-379.56)*

378.81 **Palsy of conjugate gaze**

378.82 **Spasm of conjugate gaze**

378.83 **Convergence insufficiency or palsy**

378.84 **Convergence excess or spasm**

378.85 **Anomalies of divergence**

378.86 **Internuclear ophthalmoplegia**

378.87 **Other dissociated deviation of eye movements**
Skew deviation

378.9 **Unspecified disorder of eye movements**
Ophthalmoplegia NOS Strabismus NOS

379 Other disorders of eye

✓5th **379.0** **Scleritis and episcleritis**

Excludes: *syphilitic episcleritis (095.0)*

379.00 **Scleritis, unspecified**
Episcleritis NOS

379.01 **Episcleritis periodica fugax**

379.02 **Nodular episcleritis**

379.03 **Anterior scleritis**

379.04 **Scleromalacia perforans**

379.05 **Scleritis with corneal involvement**
Scleroperikeratitis

379.06 **Brawny scleritis**

379.07 **Posterior scleritis**
Sclerotenonitis

379.09 **Other**
Scleral abscess

✓5th **379.1** **Other disorders of sclera**

Excludes: *blue sclera (743.47)*

379.11 **Scleral ectasia**
Scleral staphyloma NOS

379.12 **Staphyloma posticum**

379.13 **Equatorial staphyloma**

379.14 **Anterior staphyloma, localized**

379.15 **Ring staphyloma**

379.16 **Other degenerative disorders of sclera**

379.19 **Other**

✓5th **379.2** **Disorders of vitreous body**

379.21 **Vitreous degeneration**
Vitreous:
cavitation
detachment
liquefaction

379.22 **Crystalline deposits in vitreous**
Asteroid hyalitis Synchysis scintillans

379.23 **Vitreous hemorrhage**
➡ **AHA Coding Clinic:** 3Q, '91, 15

379.24 **Other vitreous opacities**
Vitreous floaters

379.25 **Vitreous membranes and strands**

379.26 **Vitreous prolapse**

379.29 **Other disorders of vitreous**

Excludes: *vitreous abscess (360.04)*

✓5th **379.3** **Aphakia and other disorders of lens**

Excludes: *after-cataract (366.50-366.53)*

379.31 **Aphakia**

Excludes: *cataract extraction status (V45.61)*

379.32 **Subluxation of lens**

379.33 **Anterior dislocation of lens**

379.34 **Posterior dislocation of lens**

379.39 **Other disorders of lens**

✓5th **379.4** **Anomalies of pupillary function**

379.40 **Abnormal pupillary function, unspecified**

379.41 **Anisocoria**

379.42 **Miosis (persistent), not due to miotics**

379.43 **Mydriasis (persistent), not due to mydriatics**

379.45 **Argyll Robertson pupil, atypical**
Argyll Robertson phenomenon or pupil, nonsyphilitic

Excludes: *Argyll Robertson pupil (syphilitic) (094.89)*

379.46 **Tonic pupillary reaction**
Adie's pupil or syndrome

379.49 **Other**
Hippus
Pupillary paralysis

✓5th **379.5** **Nystagmus and other irregular eye movements**

379.50 **Nystagmus, unspecified**

379.51 **Congenital nystagmus**

379.52 **Latent nystagmus**

379.53 **Visual deprivation nystagmus**

379.54 **Nystagmus associated with disorders of the vestibular system**

379.55 **Dissociated nystagmus**

379.56 **Other forms of nystagmus**

379.57 **Deficiencies of saccadic eye movements**
Abnormal optokinetic response

379.58 **Deficiencies of smooth pursuit movements**

379.59 **Other irregularities of eye movements**
Opsoclonus

379.8 **Other specified disorders of eye and adnexa**

✓5th **379.9** **Unspecified disorder of eye and adnexa**

379.90 **Disorder of eye, unspecified**

379.91 **Pain in or around eye**

379.92 **Swelling or mass of eye**

379.93 **Redness or discharge of eye**

379.99 **Other ill-defined disorders of eye**

Excludes: *blurred vision NOS (368.8)*

DISEASES OF THE EAR AND MASTOID PROCESS (380-389)

380 Disorders of external ear

✓5th **380.0** **Perichondritis of pinna**
Perichondritis of auricle

380.00 **Perichondritis of pinna, unspecified**

380.01 **Acute perichondritis of pinna**

380.02 **Chronic perichondritis of pinna**

✓5th **380.1** **Infective otitis externa**

380.10 **Infective otitis externa, unspecified**
Otitis externa (acute):
- NOS
- circumscribed
- diffuse
- hemorrhagica
- infective NOS

380.11 **Acute infection of pinna**

Excludes: *furuncular otitis externa (680.0)*

380.12 **Acute swimmers' ear**
Beach ear Tank ear

380.13 ***Other acute infections of external ear***
Code first underlying disease, as:
- erysipelas (035)
- impetigo (684)
- seborrheic dermatitis (690.10-690.18)

Excludes: *herpes simplex (054.73)*
herpes zoster (053.71)

380.14 **Malignant otitis externa**

380.15 ***Chronic mycotic otitis externa***
Code first underlying disease as:
- aspergillosis (117.3)
- otomycosis NOS (111.9)

Excludes: *candidal otitis externa (112.82)*

380.16 **Other chronic infective otitis externa**
Chronic infective otitis externa NOS

✓5th **380.2** **Other otitis externa**

380.21 **Cholesteatoma of external ear**
Keratosis obturans of external ear (canal)

Excludes: *cholesteatoma NOS (385.30-385.35)*
postmastoidectomy (383.32)

380.22 **Other acute otitis externa**
Acute otitis externa:
- actinic
- chemical
- contact
- eczematoid
- reactive

380.23 **Other chronic otitis externa**
Chronic otitis externa NOS

✓5th **380.3 Noninfectious disorders of pinna**

380.30 Disorder of pinna, unspecified

380.31 Hematoma of auricle or pinna

380.32 Acquired deformities of auricle or pinna

Excludes: *cauliflower ear (738.7)*

380.39 Other

Excludes: *gouty tophi of ear (274.81)*

380.4 Impacted cerumen

Wax in ear

✓5th **380.5 Acquired stenosis of external ear canal**

Collapse of external ear canal

380.50 Acquired stenosis of external ear canal, unspecified as to cause

380.51 Secondary to trauma

380.52 Secondary to surgery

380.53 Secondary to inflammation

✓5th **380.8 Other disorders of external ear**

380.81 Exostosis of external ear canal

380.89 Other

380.9 Unspecified disorder of external ear

381 Nonsuppurative otitis media and Eustachian tube disorders

✓5th **381.0 Acute nonsuppurative otitis media**

Acute tubotympanic catarrh
Otitis media, acute or subacute:
- catarrhal
- exudative
- transudative
- with effusion

Excludes: *otitic barotrauma (993.0)*

381.00 Acute nonsuppurative otitis media, unspecified

381.01 Acute serous otitis media

Acute or subacute secretory otitis media

381.02 Acute mucoid otitis media

Acute or subacute seromucinous otitis media
Blue drum syndrome

381.03 Acute sanguinous otitis media

381.04 Acute allergic serous otitis media

381.05 Acute allergic mucoid otitis media

381.06 Acute allergic sanguinous otitis media

✓5th **381.1 Chronic serous otitis media**

Chronic tubotympanic catarrh

381.10 Chronic serous otitis media, simple or unspecified

381.19 Other

Serosanguinous chronic otitis media

✓5th **381.2 Chronic mucoid otitis media**

Glue ear

Excludes: *adhesive middle ear disease (385.10-385.19)*

381.20 Chronic mucoid otitis media, simple or unspecified

381.29 Other

Mucosanguinous chronic otitis media

381.3 Other and unspecified chronic nonsuppurative otitis media

Otitis media, chronic:
- allergic
- exudative
- secretory
- seromucinous
- transudative
- with effusion

381.4 Nonsuppurative otitis media, not specified as acute or chronic

Otitis media:
- allergic
- catarrhal
- exudative
- mucoid
- secretory
- seromucinous
- serous
- transudative
- with effusion

✓5th **381.5 Eustachian salpingitis**

381.50 Eustachian salpingitis, unspecified

381.51 Acute Eustachian salpingitis

381.52 Chronic Eustachian salpingitis

✓5th **381.6 Obstruction of Eustachian tube**

Stenosis } of Eustachian tube
Stricture }

381.60 Obstruction of Eustachian tube, unspecified

381.61 Osseous obstruction of Eustachian tube

Obstruction of Eustachian tube from cholesteatoma, polyp, or other osseous lesion

381.62 Intrinsic cartilagenous obstruction of Eustachian tube

381.63 **Extrinsic cartilagenous obstruction of Eustachian tube**
Compression of Eustachian tube

381.7 **Patulous Eustachian tube**

✓5th **381.8** **Other disorders of Eustachian tube**

381.81 **Dysfunction of Eustachian tube**

381.89 **Other**

381.9 **Unspecified Eustachian tube disorder**

382 Suppurative and unspecified otitis media

✓5th **382.0** **Acute suppurative otitis media**
Otitis media, acute:
necrotizing NOS
purulent

382.00 **Acute suppurative otitis media without spontaneous rupture of ear drum**

382.01 **Acute suppurative otitis media with spontaneous rupture of ear drum**

382.02 ***Acute suppurative otitis media in diseases classified elsewhere***
Code first underlying disease as:
influenza (487.8)
scarlet fever (034.1)

Excludes: *postmeasles otitis (055.2)*

382.1 **Chronic tubotympanic suppurative otitis media**
Benign chronic suppurative otitis media } (with anterior perforation of ear drum)
Chronic tubotympanic disease } (with anterior perforation of ear drum)

382.2 **Chronic atticoantral suppurative otitis media**
Chronic atticoantral disease } (with posterior or superior marginal perforation of ear drum)
Persistent mucosal disease } (with posterior or superior marginal perforation of ear drum)

382.3 **Unspecified chronic suppurative otitis media**
Chronic purulent otitis media

Excludes: *tuberculous otitis media (017.4)*

382.4 **Unspecified suppurative otitis media**
Purulent otitis media NOS

382.9 **Unspecified otitis media**
Otitis media:
NOS
acute NOS
chronic NOS

383 Mastoiditis and related conditions

✓5th **383.0** **Acute mastoiditis**
Abscess of mastoid
Empyema of mastoid

383.00 **Acute mastoiditis without complications**

383.01 **Subperiosteal abscess of mastoid**
➡ **CC Excl:** 015.60-015.66, 017.40-017.46, 017.90-017.96, 383.00-383.9, 388.71-388.72, 388.8-388.9, 744.00, 744.02, 744.09, 744.29, 744.3

383.02 **Acute mastoiditis with other complications**
Gradenigo's syndrome

383.1 **Chronic mastoiditis**
Caries of mastoid
Fistula of mastoid

Excludes: *tuberculous mastoiditis (015.6)*

✓5th **383.2** **Petrositis**
Coalescing osteitis } of petrous bone
Inflammation } of petrous bone
Osteomyelitis } of petrous bone

383.20 **Petrositis, unspecified**

383.21 **Acute petrositis**

383.22 **Chronic petrositis**

✓5th **383.3** **Complications following mastoidectomy**

383.30 **Postmastoidectomy complication, unspecified**
➡ **CC Excl:** see Code 383.01

383.31 **Mucosal cyst of postmastoidectomy cavity**

383.32 **Recurrent cholesteatoma of postmastoidectomy cavity**

383.33 **Granulations of postmastoidectomy cavity**
Chronic inflammation of postmastoidectomy cavity

✓5th **383.8** **Other disorders of mastoid**

383.81 **Postauricular fistula**
➡ **CC Excl:** see Code 383.01

383.89 **Other**

383.9 **Unspecified mastoiditis**

384 Other disorders of tympanic membrane

✓5th **384.0** **Acute myringitis without mention of otitis media**

384.00 **Acute myringitis, unspecified**
Acute tympanitis NOS

384.01 **Bullous myringitis**
Myringitis bullosa hemorrhagica

384.09 **Other**

384.1 **Chronic myringitis without mention of otitis media**
Chronic tympanitis

✓5th **384.2** **Perforation of tympanic membrane**
Perforation of ear drum:
NOS
persistent posttraumatic
postinflammatory

Excludes: *otitis media with perforation of tympanic membrane (382.00-382.9)*
traumatic perforation [current injury] (872.61)

384.20 **Perforation of tympanic membrane, unspecified**

384.21 **Central perforation of tympanic membrane**

384.22 **Attic perforation of tympanic membrane**
Pars flaccida

384.23 **Other marginal perforation of tympanic membrane**

384.24 **Multiple perforations of tympanic membrane**

384.25 **Total perforation of tympanic membrane**

✓5th **384.8** **Other specified disorders of tympanic membrane**

384.81 **Atrophic flaccid tympanic membrane**
Healed perforation of ear drum

384.82 **Atrophic nonflaccid tympanic membrane**

384.9 **Unspecified disorder of tympanic membrane**

385 Other disorders of middle ear and mastoid

Excludes: *mastoiditis (383.0-383.9)*

✓5th **385.0** **Tympanosclerosis**

385.00 **Tympanosclerosis, unspecified as to involvement**

385.01 **Tympanosclerosis involving tympanic membrane only**

385.02 **Tympanosclerosis involving tympanic membrane and ear ossicles**

385.03 **Tympanosclerosis involving tympanic membrane, ear ossicles, and middle ear**

385.09 **Tympanosclerosis involving other combination of structures**

✓5th **385.1** **Adhesive middle ear disease**
Adhesive otitis
Otitis media:
chronic adhesive
fibrotic

Excludes: *glue ear (381.20-381.29)*

385.10 **Adhesive middle ear disease, unspecified as to involvement**

385.11 **Adhesions of drum head to incus**

385.12 **Adhesions of drum head to stapes**

385.13 **Adhesions of drum head to promontorium**

385.19 **Other adhesions and combinations**

✓5th **385.2** **Other acquired abnormality of ear ossicles**

385.21 **Impaired mobility of malleus**
Ankylosis of malleus

385.22 **Impaired mobility of other ear ossicles**
Ankylosis of ear ossicles, except malleus

385.23 **Discontinuity or dislocation of ear ossicles**

385.24 **Partial loss or necrosis of ear ossicles**

✓5th **385.3** **Cholesteatoma of middle ear and mastoid**
Cholesterosis } of (middle) ear
Epidermosis }
Keratosis }
Polyp }

Excludes: *cholesteatoma:*
external ear canal (380.21)
recurrent of postmastoidectomy cavity (383.32)

385.30 **Cholesteatoma, unspecified**

385.31 **Cholesteatoma of attic**

385.32 **Cholesteatoma of middle ear**

385.33 **Cholesteatoma of middle ear and mastoid**

385.35 **Diffuse cholesteatosis**

✓5th **385.8** **Other disorders of middle ear and mastoid**

385.82 **Cholesterin granuloma**

385.83 **Retained foreign body of middle ear**

385.89 **Other**

385.9 **Unspecified disorder of middle ear and mastoid**

386 Vertiginous syndromes and other disorders of vestibular system

Excludes: *vertigo NOS (780.4)*

➡ **AHA Coding Clinic:** M-A, '85, 12

✓5th **386.0 Ménière's disease**

Endolymphatic hydrops
Lermoyez's syndrome
Ménière's syndrome or vertigo

386.00 Méniére's disease, unspecified
Méniére's disease (active)

386.01 Active Ménière's disease, cochleovestibular

386.02 Active Ménière's disease, cochlear

386.03 Active Ménière's disease, vestibular

386.04 Inactive Ménière's disease
Ménière's disease in remission

✓5th **386.1 Other and unspecified peripheral vertigo**

Excludes: *epidemic vertigo (078.81)*

386.10 Peripheral vertigo, unspecified

386.11 Benign paroxysmal positional vertigo
Benign paroxysmal positional nystagmus

386.12 Vestibular neuronitis
Acute (and recurrent) peripheral vestibulopathy

386.19 Other
Aural vertigo
Otogenic vertigo

386.2 Vertigo of central origin
Central positional nystagmus
Malignant positional vertigo

✓5th **386.3 Labyrinthitis**

386.30 Labyrinthitis, unspecified

386.31 Serous labyrinthitis
Diffuse labyrinthitis

386.32 Circumscribed labyrinthitis
Focal labyrinthitis

386.33 Suppurative labyrinthitis
Purulent labyrinthitis

386.34 Toxic labyrinthitis

386.35 Viral labyrinthitis

✓5th **386.4 Labyrinthine fistula**

386.40 Labyrinthine fistula, unspecified

386.41 Round window fistula

386.42 Oval window fistula

386.43 Semicircular canal fistula

386.48 Labyrinthine fistula of combined sites

✓5th **386.5 Labyrinthine dysfunction**

386.50 Labyrinthine dysfunction, unspecified

386.51 Hyperactive labyrinth, unilateral

386.52 Hyperactive labyrinth, bilateral

386.53 Hypoactive labyrinth, unilateral

386.54 Hypoactive labyrinth, bilateral

386.55 Loss of labyrinthine reactivity, unilateral

386.56 Loss of labyrinthine reactivity, bilateral

386.58 Other forms and combinations

386.8 Other disorders of labyrinth

386.9 Unspecified vertiginous syndromes and labyrinthine disorders

387 Otosclerosis

Includes: otospongiosis

387.0 Otosclerosis involving oval window, nonobliterative

387.1 Otosclerosis involving oval window, obliterative

387.2 Cochlear otosclerosis
Otosclerosis involving:
otic capsule
round window

387.8 Other otosclerosis

387.9 Otosclerosis, unspecified

388 Other disorders of ear

✓5th **388.0 Degenerative and vascular disorders of ear**

388.00 Degenerative and vascular disorders, unspecified

388.01 Presbyacusis

388.02 Transient ischemic deafness

✓5th **388.1 Noise effects on inner ear**

388.10 Noise effects on inner ear, unspecified

388.11 Acoustic trauma (explosive) to ear
Otitic blast injury

388.12 Noise-induced hearing loss

388.2 Sudden hearing loss, unspecified

✓5th **388.3** Tinnitus

388.30 Tinnitus, unspecified

388.31 Subjective tinnitus

388.32 Objective tinnitus

✓5th **388.4** Other abnormal auditory perception

388.40 Abnormal auditory perception, unspecified

388.41 Diplacusis

388.42 Hyperacusis

388.43 Impairment of auditory discrimination

388.44 Recruitment

388.5 Disorders of acoustic nerve

Acoustic neuritis
Degeneration } of acoustic or eighth nerve
Disorder } of acoustic or eighth nerve

Excludes: *acoustic neuroma (225.1)*
syphilitic acoustic neuritis (094.86)

➡ **AHA Coding Clinic:** M-A, '87, 8

✓5th **388.6** Otorrhea

388.60 Otorrhea, unspecified
Discharging ear NOS

388.61 Cerebrospinal fluid otorrhea

Excludes: *cerebrospinal fluid rhinorrhea (349.81)*

388.69 Other
Otorrhagia

✓5th **388.7** Otalgia

388.70 Otalgia, unspecified
Earache NOS

388.71 Otogenic pain

388.72 Referred pain

388.8 Other disorders of ear

388.9 Unspecified disorder of ear

389 Hearing loss

✓5th **389.0** Conductive hearing loss
Conductive deafness

389.00 Conductive hearing loss, unspecified

389.01 Conductive hearing loss, external ear

389.02 Conductive hearing loss, tympanic membrane

389.03 Conductive hearing loss, middle ear

389.04 Conductive hearing loss, inner ear

389.08 Conductive hearing loss of combined types

✓5th **389.1** Sensorineural hearing loss
Perceptive hearing loss or deafness

Excludes: *abnormal auditory perception (388.40-388.44)*
psychogenic deafness (306.7)

389.10 Sensorineural hearing loss, unspecified

➡ **AHA Coding Clinic:** 1Q, '93, 29

389.11 Sensory hearing loss

389.12 Neural hearing loss

389.14 Central hearing loss

389.18 Sensorineural hearing loss of combined types

389.2 Mixed conductive and sensorineural hearing loss
Deafness or hearing loss of type classifiable to 389.0 with type classifiable to 389.1

389.7 Deaf mutism, not elsewhere classifiable
Deaf, nonspeaking

389.8 Other specified forms of hearing loss

389.9 Unspecified hearing loss
Deafness NOS

7. DISEASES OF THE CIRCULATORY SYSTEM (390-459)

ACUTE RHEUMATIC FEVER (390-392)

390 Rheumatic fever without mention of heart involvement

Arthritis, rheumatic, acute or subacute
Rheumatic fever (active) (acute)
Rheumatism, articular, acute or subacute

Excludes: *that with heart involvement (391.0-391.9)*

391 Rheumatic fever with heart involvement

Excludes: *chronic heart diseases of rheumatic origin (393.0-398.9) unless rheumatic fever is also present or there is evidence of recrudescence or activity of the rheumatic process*

391.0 Acute rheumatic pericarditis

Rheumatic:
fever (active) (acute) with pericarditis
pericarditis (acute)
Any condition classifiable to 390 with pericarditis

Excludes: *that not specified as rheumatic (420.0-420.9)*

391.1 Acute rheumatic endocarditis

Rheumatic:
endocarditis, acute
fever (active) (acute) with endocarditis or valvulitis
valvulitis acute
Any condition classifiable to 390 with endocarditis or valvulitis

391.2 Acute rheumatic myocarditis

Rheumatic fever (active) (acute) with myocarditis
Any condition classifiable to 390 with myocarditis

391.8 Other acute rheumatic heart disease

Rheumatic:
fever (active) (acute) with other or multiple types of heart involvement
pancarditis, acute
Any condition classifiable to 390 with other or multiple types of heart involvement

391.9 Acute rheumatic heart disease, unspecified

Rheumatic:
carditis, acute
fever (active) (acute) with unspecified type of heart involvement
heart disease, active or acute
Any condition classifiable to 390 with unspecified type of heart involvement

392 Rheumatic chorea

Includes: Sydenham's chorea

Excludes: *chorea:*
NOS (333.5)
Huntington's (333.4)

392.0 With heart involvement

Rheumatic chorea with heart involvement of any type classifiable to 391

392.9 Without mention of heart involvement

CHRONIC RHEUMATIC HEART DISEASE (393-398)

393 Chronic rheumatic pericarditis

Adherent pericardium, rheumatic
Chronic rheumatic:
mediastinopericarditis
myopericarditis

Excludes: *pericarditis NOS or not specified as rheumatic (423.0-423.9)*

394 Diseases of mitral valve

Excludes: *that with aortic valve involvement (396.0-396.9)*

394.0 Mitral stenosis

Mitral (valve):
obstruction (rheumatic)
stenosis NOS

➡ **CC Excl:** 390, 391.8-391.9, 394.0-394.9, 396.0-396.9, 397.9, 398.90, 398.99, 424.0, 459.89, 459.9

394.1 Rheumatic mitral insufficiency

Rheumatic mitral:
incompetence
regurgitation

Excludes: *that not specified as rheumatic (424.0)*

➡ **CC Excl:** see Code 394.0

394.2 Mitral stenosis with insufficiency

Mitral stenosis with incompetence or regurgitation

➡ **CC Excl:** see Code 394.0

394.9 Other and unspecified mitral valve diseases

Mitral (valve):
disease (chronic)
failure

➡ **CC Excl:** see Code 394.0

395 Diseases of aortic valve

Excludes: *that not specified as rheumatic (424.1)*
that with mitral valve involvement (396.0-396.9)

395.0 Rheumatic aortic stenosis

Rheumatic aortic (valve) obstruction

➡ **CC Excl:** 390, 391.8-391.9, 395.0-395.9, 396.0-396.9, 397.9, 398.90, 398.99, 424.1, 459.89, 459.9

395.1 Rheumatic aortic insufficiency

Rheumatic aortic:
- incompetence
- regurgitation

➡ **CC Excl:** see Code 395.0

395.2 Rheumatic aortic stenosis with insufficiency

Rheumatic aortic stenosis with incompetence or regurgitation

➡ **CC Excl:** see Code 395.0

395.9 Other and unspecified rheumatic aortic diseases

Rheumatic aortic (valve) disease

➡ **CC Excl:** see Code 395.0

396 Diseases of mitral and aortic valves

Includes: involvement of both mitral and aortic valves, whether specified as rheumatic or not

➡ **AHA Coding Clinic:** N-D, '87, 8

396.0 Mitral valve stenosis and aortic valve stenosis

Atypical aortic (valve) stenosis
Mitral and aortic (valve) obstruction (rheumatic)

➡ **CC Excl:** 390, 391.8-391.9, 394.0-394.9, 395.0-395.9, 396.0-396.9, 397.9, 398.90, 398.99, 424.0-424.1, 459.89, 459.9

396.1 Mitral valve stenosis and aortic valve insufficiency

➡ **CC Excl:** see Code 396.0

396.2 Mitral valve insufficiency and aortic valve stenosis

➡ **CC Excl:** see Code 396.0

396.3 Mitral valve insufficiency and aortic valve insufficiency

Mitral and aortic (valve):
- incompetence
- regurgitation

➡ **CC Excl:** see Code 396.0

396.8 Multiple involvement of mitral and aortic valves

Stenosis and insufficiency of mitral or aortic valve with stenosis or insufficiency, or both, of the other valve

➡ **CC Excl:** see Code 396.0

396.9 Mitral and aortic valve diseases, unspecified

➡ **CC Excl:** see Code 396.0

397 Diseases of other endocardial structures

397.0 Diseases of tricuspid valve

Tricuspid (valve) (rheumatic):
- disease
- insufficiency
- obstruction
- regurgitation
- stenosis

➡ **CC Excl:** 397.0, 398.90, 398.99, 424.2, 459.89, 459.9

397.1 Rheumatic diseases of pulmonary valve

Excludes: *that not specified as rheumatic (424.3)*

➡ **CC Excl:** 397.1, 398.90, 398.99, 424.3, 459.89, 459.9

397.9 Rheumatic diseases of endocardium, valve unspecified

Rheumatic:
- endocarditis (chronic)
- valvulitis (chronic)

Excludes: *that not specified as rheumatic (424.90-424.99)*

➡ **CC Excl:** 390, 391.1, 391.8-391.9, 394.0-394.9, 395.0-395.9, 397.1, 397.9, 398.90, 398.99, 421.0-421.9, 424.0-424.99, 459.89, 459.9

398 Other rheumatic heart disease

398.0 Rheumatic myocarditis

Rheumatic degeneration of myocardium

Excludes: *myocarditis not specified as rheumatic (429.0)*

➡ **CC Excl:** 390, 391.2-391.9, 398.0, 398.90, 398.99, 422.0, 422.90-422.99, 429.0, 429.71, 429.79, 459.89, 459.9

✓5th **398.9 Other and unspecified rheumatic heart diseases**

398.90 Rheumatic heart disease, unspecified

Rheumatic:
- carditis
- heart disease NOS

Excludes: *carditis not specified as rheumatic (429.89)*
heart disease NOS not specified as rheumatic (429.9)

398.91 Rheumatic heart failure (congestive)

Rheumatic left ventricular failure

➡ **CC Excl:** 398.90-398.99, 402.01, 402.11, 402.91, 428.0-428.9, 459.89, 459.9

398.99 Other

HYPERTENSIVE DISEASE (401-405)

Excludes: *that complicating pregnancy, childbirth, or the puerperium (642.0-642.9)*
that involving coronary vessels (410.00-414.9)

➡ **AHA Coding Clinic:** 3Q, '90, 3; 2Q, '89, 12; S-O, '87, 9; J-A, '84, 11

401 Essential hypertension

Includes: high blood pressure
hyperpiesia
hyperpiesis
hypertension (arterial) (essential) (primary) (systemic)
hypertensive vascular:
degeneration
disease

Excludes: *elevated blood pressure without diagnosis of hypertension (796.2)*
pulmonary hypertension (416.0-416.9)
that involving vessels of:
brain (430-438)
eye (362.11)

➡ **AHA Coding Clinic:** 2Q, '92, 5

401.0 Malignant

➡ **CC Excl:** 401.0-401.9, 402.00-402.91, 403.00-403.91, 404.00-404.93, 405.01-405.99, 459.89, 459.9

➡ **AHA Coding Clinic:** 1Q, '91, 16

401.1 Benign

401.9 Unspecified

➡ **AHA Coding Clinic:** 4Q, '97, 37

402 Hypertensive heart disease

Includes: hypertensive:
cardiomegaly
cardiopathy
cardiovascular disease
heart (disease) (failure)
any condition classifiable to 428, 429.0-429.3, 429.8, 429.9 due to hypertension

➡ **AHA Coding Clinic:** 2Q, '93, 9; N-D, '84, 18

✓5th **402.0 Malignant**

402.00 Without congestive heart failure

➡ **CC Excl:** see Code 401.0

402.01 With congestive heart failure

➡ **CC Excl:** 398.91, 401.0-401.9, 402.00-402.91, 403.00-403.91, 404.00-404.93, 405.01-405.99, 428.0-428.9, 459.89, 459.9

✓ **St. Anthony's Clinical Coder:** see Chapters 5, 6 & 7

✓5th **402.1 Benign**

402.10 Without congestive heart failure

402.11 With congestive heart failure

➡ **CC Excl:** see Code 402.01

✓ **St. Anthony's Clinical Coder:** see Chapters 5, 6 & 7

✓5th **402.9 Unspecified**

402.90 Without congestive heart failure

402.91 With congestive heart failure

➡ **CC Excl:** see Code 402.01

➡ **AHA Coding Clinic:** 1Q, '93, 19; 2Q, '89, 12

DRG 127

✓ **St. Anthony's Clinical Coder:** see Chapters 5, 6 & 7

403 Hypertensive renal disease

Includes: arteriolar nephritis
arteriosclerosis of:
kidney
renal arterioles
arteriosclerotic nephritis (chronic) (interstitial)
hypertensive:
nephropathy
renal failure
uremia (chronic)
nephrosclerosis
renal sclerosis with hypertension
any condition classifiable to 585, 586, or 587 with any condition classifiable to 401

Excludes: *acute renal failure (584.5-584.9)*
renal disease stated as not due to hypertension
renovascular hypertension (405.0-405.9 with fifth-digit 1)

The following fifth-digit subclassification is for use with category 403:

0 without mention of renal failure
1 with renal failure

➡ **AHA Coding Clinic:** 4Q, '92, 22; 2Q, '92, 5

✓5th **403.0 Malignant**

➡ **CC Excl:** 401.0-401.9, 402.00-402.91, 403.00-403.91, 404.00-404.93, 405.01-405.99, 459.89, 459.9

✓5th [4] **403.1** Benign

➡ **CC Excl: For code 403.11:** see Code 403.0

✓5th [4] **403.9** Unspecified

➡ **CC Excl: For code 403.91:** see Code 403.0

DRG 316: For code 403.91

404 Hypertensive heart and renal disease

Includes: disease:
cardiorenal
cardiovascular renal
any condition classifiable to 402 with any condition classifiable to 403

The following fifth-digit subclassification is for use with category 404:

- **0 without mention of congestive heart failure or renal failure**
- **1 with congestive heart failure**
- **2 with renal failure**
- **3 with congestive heart failure and renal failure**

✓5th **404.0** Malignant

➡ **CC Excl:** see Code 403.0

✔ **St. Anthony's Clinical Coder: For code 404.01:** see Chapters 5, 6 & 7

✓5th [15] **404.1** Benign

➡ **CC Excl: For codes 404.11-404.13:** see Code 403.0

✓5th [15] **404.9** Unspecified

➡ **CC Excl: For codes 404.91-404.93:** see Code 403.0

405 Secondary hypertension

✓5th **405.0** Malignant

405.01 Renovascular

➡ **CC Excl:** 401.0-401.9, 402.00-402.91, 403.00-403.91, 404.00-404.93, 405.01-405.99, 459.89, 459.9

405.09 Other

➡ **CC Excl:** see Code 405.01

✓5th **405.1** Benign

405.11 Renovascular

405.19 Other

✓5th **405.9** Unspecified

405.91 Renovascular

405.99 Other

[4] CC Coding =1
[15] CC Coding =1

ISCHEMIC HEART DISEASE (410-414)

Includes: that with mention of hypertension

Use additional code to identify presence of hypertension (401.0-405.9)

➡ **AHA Coding Clinic:** J-A, '84, 5

410 Acute myocardial infarction A: 15–124

Includes: cardiac infarction
coronary (artery):
embolism
occlusion
rupture
thrombosis
infarction of heart, myocardium, or ventricle
rupture of heart, myocardium, or ventricle
any condition classifiable to 414.1-414.9 specified as acute or with a stated duration of 8 weeks or less

The following fifth-digit subclassification is for use with category 410:

0 episode of care unspecified
Use when the source document does not contain sufficient information for the assignment of fifth digit 1 or 2.

1 initial episode of care
Use fifth-digit 1 to designate the first episode of care (regardless of facility site) for a newly diagnosed myocardial infarction. The fifth-digit 1 is assigned regardless of the number of times a patient may be transferred during the initial episode of care.

2 subsequent episode of care
Use fifth-digit 2 to designate an episode of care following the initial episode when the patient is admitted for further observation, evaluation or treatment for a myocardial infarction that has received initial treatment, but is still less than 8 weeks old.

➡ **AHA Coding Clinic:** 4Q, '97, 37; 3Q, '95, 9; 4Q, '92, 24; 1Q, '92,10; 3Q, '91, 18; 1Q, '91, 14; 3Q, '89, 3

✓5th **410.0** Of anterolateral wall

➡ **CC Excl: For code 410.01:** 410.00-410.92, 459.89, 459.9

✔ **St. Anthony's Clinical Coder: For code 410.01:** see Chapter 5

✓5th **410.1** Of other anterior wall

Infarction:
anterior (wall) NOS
anteroapical
anteroseptal
} (with contiguous portion of intraventricular septum)

➡ **CC Excl: For code 410.11:** see Code 410.0

DRG 121 and DRG 122: For code 410.11

✔ **St. Anthony's Clinical Coder: For code 410.11:** see Chapter 5

✓5th **410.2** **Of inferolateral wall**

➡ **CC Excl: For code 410.21:** see Code 410.0

✔ **St. Anthony's Clinical Coder: For code 410.21:** see Chapter 5

✓5th **410.3** **Of inferoposterior wall**

➡ **CC Excl: For code 410.31:** see Code 410.0

✔ **St. Anthony's Clinical Coder: For code 410.31:** see Chapter 5

✓5th **410.4** **Of other inferior wall**

Infarction:
diaphragmatic wall NOS } (with contiguous portion of
inferior (wall) NOS } intraventricular septum)

➡ **CC Excl: For code 410.41:** see Code 410.0

➡ **AHA Coding Clinic:** 3Q, '97, 10

DRG 121 and DRG 122: For code 410.41

✔ **St. Anthony's Clinical Coder: For code 410.41:** see Chapter 5

✓5th **410.5** **Of other lateral wall**

Infarction:
apical-lateral
basal-lateral

Infarction:
high lateral
posterolateral

➡ **CC Excl: For code 410.51:** see Code 410.0

✔ **St. Anthony's Clinical Coder: For code 410.51:** see Chapter 5

✓5th **410.6** **True posterior wall infarction**

Infarction:
posterobasal
strictly posterior

➡ **CC Excl: For code 410.61:** see Code 410.0

✔ **St. Anthony's Clinical Coder: For code 410.61:** see Chapter 5

✓5th **410.7** **Subendocardial infarction**

Nontransmural infarction

➡ **CC Excl: For code 410.71:** see Code 410.0

DRG 121 and DRG 122: For code 410.71

✔ **St. Anthony's Clinical Coder: For code 410.71:** see Chapter 5

✓5th **410.8** **Of other specified sites**

Infarction of:
atrium
papillary muscle
septum alone

➡ **CC Excl: For code 410.81:** see Code 410.0

✔ **St. Anthony's Clinical Coder: For code 410.81:** see Chapter 5

✓5th **410.9** **Unspecified site**

Acute myocardial infarction NOS
Coronary occlusion NOS

➡ **CC Excl: For code 410.91:** see Code 410.0

➡ **AHA Coding Clinic:** 1Q, '92, 9

DRG 121 and DRG 122: For code 410.91

✔ **St. Anthony's Clinical Coder: For code 410.91:** see Chapter 5

411 Other acute and subacute forms of ischemic heart disease — A: 15–124

➡ **AHA Coding Clinic:** 4Q, '94, 55; 3Q, '91, 24

411.0 **Postmyocardial infarction syndrome**

Dressler's syndrome

➡ **CC Excl:** 411.0, 411.81, 411.89, 459.89, 459.9

✔ **St. Anthony's Clinical Coder:** see Chapters 5, 6 & 7

411.1 **Intermediate coronary syndrome**

Impending infarction
Preinfarction angina
Preinfarction syndrome
Unstable angina

Excludes: *angina (pectoris) (413.9)*
decubitus (413.0)

➡ **CC Excl:** 410.00-410.92, 411.1-411.89, 413.0-413.9 414.8-414.9, 459.89, 459.9

➡ **AHA Coding Clinic:** 2Q, '96, 10; 3Q, '91, 24; 1Q, '91, 14; 3Q, '90, 6; 4Q, '89, 10

DRG 140

✔ **St. Anthony's Clinical Coder:** see Chapters 5 & 7

✓5th **411.8** **Other**

➡ **AHA Coding Clinic:** 3Q, '91, 18; 3Q, '89, 4

✔ **St. Anthony's Clinical Coder:** see Chapters 5 & 7

411.81 **Coronary occlusion without myocardial infarction**

Coronary (artery):
embolism } without or not
occlusion } resulting in
thrombosis } myocardial infarction

Excludes: *occlusion without infarction due to atherosclerosis (414.00-414.05)*

➡ **CC Excl:** 410.00-410.92, 411.0-411.89, 413.0-413.9, 414.8-414.9, 459.89, 459.9

➡ **AHA Coding Clinic:** 3Q, '91, 24; 1Q, '91, 14

411.89 **Other**

Coronary insufficiency (acute)
Subendocardial ischemia

➡ **CC Excl:** see Code 411.81

➡ **AHA Coding Clinic:** 1Q, '92, 9

DRG 140

412 Old myocardial infarction — A: 15–124

Healed myocardial infarction
Past myocardial infarction diagnosed on ECG [EKG] or other special investigation, but currently presenting no symptoms

➡ **AHA Coding Clinic:** 2Q, '91, 22; 3Q, '90, 7

413 Angina pectoris — A: 15–124

413.0 **Angina decubitus**

Nocturnal angina

➡ **CC Excl:** 410.00-410.92, 411.1-411.89, 413.0-413.9, 414.8-414.9, 459.89, 459.9

413.1 **Prinzmetal angina**

Variant angina pectoris

➡ **CC Excl:** see Code 413.0

413.9 **Other and unspecified angina pectoris**

Angina:
  NOS
  cardiac
  of effort
Anginal syndrome
Status anginosus
Stenocardia
Syncope anginosa

Excludes: *preinfarction angina (411.1)*

➡ **CC Excl:** see Code 413.0

➡ **AHA Coding Clinic:** 3Q, '91, 16; 3Q, '90, 6

DRG 140

✔ **St. Anthony's Clinical Coder:** see Chapter 5

414 Other forms of chronic ischemic heart disease

Excludes: *arteriosclerotic cardiovascular disease [ASCVD] (429.2)*
cardiovascular:
  arteriosclerosis or sclerosis (429.2)
  degeneration or disease (429.2)

✓5th **414.0** **Coronary atherosclerosis** A: 15–124

Arteriosclerotic heart disease [ASHD]
Atherosclerotic heart disease
Coronary (artery):
  arteriosclerosis
  arteritis or endarteritis
  atheroma
  sclerosis
  stricture

Excludes: *embolism, occlusion NOS, thrombus } of graft (996.72)*

➡ **AHA Coding Clinic:** 2Q, '97, 13; 2Q, '95, 17; 4Q, '94, 49; 2Q, '94, 13; 1Q, '94, 6; 3Q, '90, 6

414.00 **Of unspecified type of vessel, native or graft**

➡ **AHA Coding Clinic:** 3Q, '97, 15; 4Q, '96, 31

DRG 132

414.01 **Of native coronary artery**

➡ **AHA Coding Clinic:** 3Q, '97, 15; 4Q, '96, 31

DRG 132

414.02 **Of autologous biological bypass graft**

414.03 **Of nonautologous biological bypass graft**

414.04 **Of artery bypass graft**

Internal mammary artery

414.05 **Of unspecified type of bypass graft**

Bypass graft NOS

➡ **AHA Coding Clinic:** 3Q, '97, 15; 4Q, '96, 31

✓5th **414.1** **Aneurysm of heart**

414.10 **Of heart (wall)**

Aneurysm (arteriovenous):
  mural
  ventricular

✔ **St. Anthony's Clinical Coder:** see Chapter 6

414.11 **Of coronary vessels**

Aneurysm (arteriovenous) of coronary vessels

✔ **St. Anthony's Clinical Coder:** see Chapter 6

414.19 **Other**

Arteriovenous fistula, acquired, of heart

414.8 **Other specified forms of chronic ischemic heart disease**

Chronic coronary insufficiency
Ischemia, myocardial (chronic)
Any condition classifiable to 410 specified as chronic, or presenting with symptoms after 8 weeks from date of infarction

Excludes: *coronary insufficiency (acute) (411.89)*

➡ **AHA Coding Clinic:** 1Q, '92, 10; 3Q, '90, 7; 3Q, '90, 15; 2Q, '90, 19

414.9 **Chronic ischemic heart disease, unspecified**

Ischemic heart disease NOS

DISEASES OF PULMONARY CIRCULATION (415-417)

415 Acute pulmonary heart disease

415.0 **Acute cor pulmonale**

Excludes: *cor pulmonale NOS (416.9)*

➡ **CC Excl:** 415.0, 416.8-416.9, 459.89, 459.9

✔ **St. Anthony's Clinical Coder:** see Chapters 5 & 7

✓5th **415.1** **Pulmonary embolism and infarction**

Pulmonary (artery) (vein):
  apoplexy
  embolism
  infarction (hemorrhagic)
  thrombosis

Excludes: *that complicating:*
  abortion (634-638 with .6, 639.6)
  ectopic or molar pregnancy (639.6)
  pregnancy, childbirth, or the puerperium (673.0-673.8)

➡ **AHA Coding Clinic:** 4Q, '90, 25

✔ **St. Anthony's Clinical Coder:** see Chapters 6 & 7

415.11 **Iatrogenic pulmonary embolism and infarction**

➡ **CC Excl:** 415.11, 415.19, 459.89, 459.9

➡ **AHA Coding Clinic:** 4Q, '95, 58

415.19 **Other pulmonary embolism and infarction**

➡ **CC Excl:** 415.11, 415.19, 459.89, 459.9

416 Chronic pulmonary heart disease

416.0 **Primary pulmonary hypertension**

Idiopathic pulmonary arteriosclerosis
Pulmonary hypertension (essential) (idiopathic) (primary)

➡ **CC Excl:** 416.0, 416.8-416.9, 417.8-417.9, 459.89, 459.9

416.1 **Kyphoscoliotic heart disease**

416.8 Other chronic pulmonary heart diseases
Pulmonary hypertension, secondary

416.9 Chronic pulmonary heart disease, unspecified
Chronic cardiopulmonary disease
Cor pulmonale (chronic) NOS

417 Other diseases of pulmonary circulation

417.0 Arteriovenous fistula of pulmonary vessels

Excludes: *congenital arteriovenous fistula (747.3)*

417.1 Aneurysm of pulmonary artery

Excludes: *congenital aneurysm (747.3)*

417.8 Other specified diseases of pulmonary circulation
Pulmonary:
arteritis
endarteritis
Rupture } of pulmonary vessel
Stricture } of pulmonary vessel

417.9 Unspecified disease of pulmonary circulation

OTHER FORMS OF HEART DISEASE (420-429)

420 Acute pericarditis

Includes: acute:
mediastinopericarditis
myopericarditis
pericardial effusion
pleuropericarditis
pneumopericarditis

Excludes: *acute rheumatic pericarditis (391.0)*
postmyocardial infarction syndrome [Dressler's] (411.0)

420.0 *Acute pericarditis in diseases classified elsewhere*
Code first underlying disease as:
actinomycosis (039.8)
amebiasis (006.8)
nocardiosis (039.8)
tuberculosis (017.9)
uremia (585)

Excludes: *pericarditis (acute) (in):*
Coxsackie (virus) (074.21)
gonococcal (098.83)
histoplasmosis (115.0-115.9 with fifth-digit 3)
meningococcal infection (036.41)
syphilitic (093.81)

➡ **CC Excl:** 391.0, 393, 420.0-420.99, 423.8-423.9, 459.89, 459.9

✔ **St. Anthony's Clinical Coder:** see Chapter 7

✓5th **420.9** Other and unspecified acute pericarditis
✔ **St. Anthony's Clinical Coder:** see Chapters 5 & 7

420.90 Acute pericarditis, unspecified
Pericarditis (acute):
NOS
infective NOS
sicca

➡ **CC Excl:** see Code 420.0

➡ **AHA Coding Clinic:** 2Q, '89, 12

420.91 Acute idiopathic pericarditis
Pericarditis, acute:
benign
nonspecific
viral

➡ **CC Excl:** see Code 420.0

420.99 Other
Pericarditis (acute):
pneumococcal
purulent
staphylococcal
Pericarditis (acute):
streptococcal
suppurative
Pneumopyopericardium
Pyopericardium

Excludes: *pericarditis in diseases classified elsewhere (420.0)*

➡ **CC Excl:** see Code 420.0

421 Acute and subacute endocarditis

421.0 Acute and subacute bacterial endocarditis
Endocarditis (acute) (chronic) (subacute):
bacterial
infective NOS
lenta
malignant
purulent
Endocarditis (acute) (chronic) (subacute):
septic
ulcerative
vegetative
Infective aneurysm
Subacute bacterial endocarditis [SBE]

Use additional code to identify infectious organism [e.g., Streptococcus 041.0, Staphylococcus 041.1]

➡ **CC Excl:** 391.1, 397.9, 421.0-421.9, 424.90-424.99, 459.89, 459.9

➡ **AHA Coding Clinic:** 1Q, '91, 15

✔ **St. Anthony's Clinical Coder:** see Chapter 7

421.1 **Acute and subacute infective endocarditis in diseases classified elsewhere**

Code first underlying disease as:
blastomycosis (116.0)
Q fever (083.0)
typhoid (fever) (002.0)

Excludes: *endocarditis (in):*
Coxsackie (virus) (074.22)
gonococcal (098.84)
histoplasmosis (115.0-115.9 with fifth-digit 4)
meningococcal infection (036.42)
monilial (112.81)

➡ **CC Excl:** see Code 421.0

421.9 **Acute endocarditis, unspecified**

Endocarditis, Myoendocarditis, Periendocarditis } acute or subacute

Excludes: *acute rheumatic endocarditis (391.1)*

➡ **CC Excl:** see Code 421.0

✔ **St. Anthony's Clinical Coder:** see Chapter 7

422 Acute myocarditis

Excludes: *acute rheumatic myocarditis (391.2)*

✔ **St. Anthony's Clinical Coder:** see Chapter 7

422.0 **Acute myocarditis in diseases classified elsewhere**

Code first underlying disease as:
myocarditis (acute):
influenzal (487.8)
tuberculous (017.9)

Excludes: *myocarditis (acute) (due to):*
aseptic, of newborn (074.23)
Coxsackie (virus) (074.23)
diphtheritic (032.82)
meningococcal infection (036.43)
syphilitic (093.82)
toxoplasmosis (130.3)

➡ **CC Excl:** 391.2, 398.0, 422.0-422.99, 429.0, 429.71, 429.79, 459.89, 459.9

✓5th **422.9** **Other and unspecified acute myocarditis**

422.90 **Acute myocarditis, unspecified**

Acute or subacute (interstitial) myocarditis

➡ **CC Excl:** see Code 422.0

✔ **St. Anthony's Clinical Coder:** see Chapters 5 & 7

422.91 **Idiopathic myocarditis**

Myocarditis (acute or subacute):
Fiedler's
giant cell
isolated (diffuse) (granulomatous)
nonspecific granulomatous

➡ **CC Excl:** see Code 422.0

422.92 **Septic myocarditis**

Myocarditis, acute or subacute:
pneumococcal
staphylococcal

Use additional code to identify infectious organism [e.g., Staphylococcus 041.1]

Excludes: *myocarditis, acute or subacute:*
in bacterial diseases classified elsewhere (422.0)
streptococcal (391.2)

➡ **CC Excl:** see Code 422.0

✔ **St. Anthony's Clinical Coder:** see Chapters 5 & 7

422.93 **Toxic myocarditis**

➡ **CC Excl:** see Code 422.0

✔ **St. Anthony's Clinical Coder:** see Chapters 5 & 7

422.99 **Other**

➡ **CC Excl:** see Code 422.0

✔ **St. Anthony's Clinical Coder:** see Chapters 5 & 7

423 Other diseases of pericardium

Excludes: *that specified as rheumatic (393)*

423.0 **Hemopericardium**

➡ **CC Excl:** 423.0-423.9, 459.89, 459.9

✔ **St. Anthony's Clinical Coder:** see Chapter 7

423.1 **Adhesive pericarditis**

Adherent pericardium
Fibrosis of pericardium
Milk spots
Pericarditis:
adhesive
obliterative
Soldiers' patches

➡ **CC Excl:** see Code 423.0

423.2 **Constrictive pericarditis**

Concato's disease
Pick's disease of heart (and liver)

➡ **CC Excl:** see Code 423.0

423.8 **Other specified diseases of pericardium**

Calcification, Fistula } of pericardium

➡ **AHA Coding Clinic:** 2Q, '89, 12

423.9 **Unspecified disease of pericardium**

424 Other diseases of endocardium

Excludes: *bacterial endocarditis (421.0-421.9)*
rheumatic endocarditis (391.1, 394.0-397.9)
syphilitic endocarditis (093.20-093.24)

424.0 Mitral valve disorders

Mitral (valve):
- incompetence, insufficiency, regurgitation } NOS; of specified cause, except rheumatic

Excludes: *mitral (valve):*
disease (394.9)
failure (394.9)
stenosis (394.0)
the listed conditions:
specified as rheumatic (394.1)
unspecified as to cause but with mention of:
diseases of aortic valve (396.0-396.9)
mitral stenosis or obstruction (394.2)

➡ **CC Excl:** 394.0-394.9, 396.0-396.9, 424.0, 459.89, 459.9

➡ **AHA Coding Clinic:** N-D, '87, 8; N-D, '84, 8

424.1 Aortic valve disorders

Aortic (valve):
- incompetence, insufficiency, regurgitation, stenosis } NOS; of specified cause, except rheumatic

Excludes: *hypertrophic subaortic stenosis (425.1)*
that specified as rheumatic (395.0-395.9)
that of unspecified cause but with mention of diseases of mitral valve (396.0-396.9)

➡ **CC Excl:** 395.0-395.9, 396.0-396.9, 424.1, 459.89, 459.9

➡ **AHA Coding Clinic:** 4Q, '88, 8; N-D, '87, 8

424.2 Tricuspid valve disorders, specified as nonrheumatic

Tricuspid valve:
- incompetence, insufficiency, regurgitation, stenosis } of specified cause, except rheumatic

Excludes: *rheumatic or of unspecified cause (397.0)*

➡ **CC Excl:** 397.0, 424.2, 459.89, 459.9

424.3 Pulmonary valve disorders

Pulmonic:
- incompetence NOS
- insufficiency NOS

Pulmonic:
- regurgitation NOS
- stenosis NOS

Excludes: *that specified as rheumatic (397.1)*

➡ **CC Excl:** 397.1, 424.3, 459.89, 459.9

✓5th **424.9 Endocarditis, valve unspecified**

424.90 Endocarditis, valve unspecified, unspecified cause

Endocarditis (chronic):
- NOS
- nonbacterial thrombotic

Valvular:
- incompetence, insufficiency, regurgitation, stenosis } of unspecified valve, unspecified cause

Valvulitis (chronic)

➡ **CC Excl:** 424.90-424.99, 459.89, 459.9

✓ **St. Anthony's Clinical Coder:** see Chapter 7

424.91 Endocarditis in diseases classified elsewhere

Code first underlying disease as:
- atypical verrucous endocarditis [Libman-Sacks] (710.0)
- disseminated lupus erythematosus (710.0)
- tuberculosis (017.9)

Excludes: *syphilitic (093.20-093.24)*

➡ **CC Excl:** see Code 424.90

✓ **St. Anthony's Clinical Coder:** see Chapter 7

424.99 Other

Any condition classifiable to 424.90 with specified cause, except rheumatic

Excludes: *endocardial fibroelastosis (425.3)*
that specified as rheumatic (397.9)

➡ **CC Excl:** see Code 424.90

425 Cardiomyopathy

Includes: myocardiopathy

425.0 Endomyocardial fibrosis

➡ **CC Excl:** 425.0-425.9, 459.89, 459.9

425.1 Hypertrophic obstructive cardiomyopathy

Hypertrophic subaortic stenosis (idiopathic)

➡ **CC Excl:** see Code 425.0

425.2 Obscure cardiomyopathy of Africa

Becker's disease
Idiopathic mural endomyocardial disease

➡ **CC Excl:** see Code 425.0

✓ **St. Anthony's Clinical Coder:** see Chapter 7

425.3 Endocardial fibroelastosis

Elastomyofibrosis

➡ **CC Excl:** see156 Code 425.0

✓ **St. Anthony's Clinical Coder:** see Chapter 7

425.4 Other primary cardiomyopathies

Cardiomyopathy:
- NOS
- congestive
- constrictive
- familial
- hypertrophic

Cardiomyopathy:
- idiopathic
- nonobstructive
- obstructive
- restrictive

Cardiovascular collagenosis

➡ **CC Excl:** see Code 425.0

➡ **AHA Coding Clinic:** 4Q, '97, 55; 2Q, '90, 19

✔ **St. Anthony's Clinical Coder:** see Chapters 5 & 7

425.5 Alcoholic cardiomyopathy

➡ **CC Excl:** see Code 425.0

✔ **St. Anthony's Clinical Coder:** see Chapters 5 & 7

425.7 Nutritional and metabolic cardiomyopathy

Code first underlying disease as:
- amyloidosis (277.3)
- beriberi (265.0)
- cardiac glycogenosis (271.0)
- mucopolysaccharidosis (277.5)
- thyrotoxicosis (242.0–242.9)

Excludes: *gouty tophi of heart (274.82)*

➡ **CC Excl:** see Code 425.0

✔ **St. Anthony's Clinical Coder:** see Chapter 7

425.8 Cardiomyopathy in other diseases classified elsewhere

Code first underlying disease as:
- Friedreich's ataxia (334.0)
- myotonia atrophica (359.2)
- progressive muscular dystrophy (359.1)
- sarcoidosis (135)

Excludes: *cardiomyopathy in Chagas' disease (086.0)*

➡ **CC Excl:** see Code 425.0

➡ **AHA Coding Clinic:** 2Q, '93, 9

✔ **St. Anthony's Clinical Coder:** see Chapters 5 & 7

425.9 Secondary cardiomyopathy, unspecified

➡ **CC Excl:** see Code 425.0

✔ **St. Anthony's Clinical Coder:** see Chapters 5 & 7

426 Conduction disorders

426.0 Atrioventricular block, complete

Third degree atrioventricular block

➡ **CC Excl:** 426.0-426.9, 427.0-427.5, 427.89, 459.89, 459.9

✔ **St. Anthony's Clinical Coder:** see Chapter 6

✓5th **426.1 Atrioventricular block, other and unspecified**

426.10 Atrioventricular block, unspecified

Atrioventricular [AV] block (incomplete) (partial)

✔ **St. Anthony's Clinical Coder:** see Chapter 6

426.11 First degree atrioventricular block

Incomplete atrioventricular block, first degree
Prolonged P-R interval NOS

426.12 Mobitz (type) II atrioventricular block

Incomplete atrioventricular block:
- Mobitz (type) II
- second degree, Mobitz (type) II

➡ **CC Excl:** see Code 426.0

✔ **St. Anthony's Clinical Coder:** see Chapter 6

426.13 Other second degree atrioventricular block

Incomplete atrioventricular block:
- Mobitz (type) I [Wenckebach's]
- second degree:
  - NOS
  - Mobitz (type) I
- with 2:1 atrioventricular response [block]

Wenckebach's phenomenon

➡ **CC Excl:** see Code 426.0

✔ **St. Anthony's Clinical Coder:** see Chapter 6

426.2 Left bundle branch hemiblock

Block:
- left anterior fascicular
- left posterior fascicular

426.3 Other left bundle branch block

Left bundle branch block:
- NOS
- anterior fascicular with posterior fascicular
- complete
- main stem

✔ **St. Anthony's Clinical Coder:** see Chapter 6

426.4 Right bundle branch block

✓5th **426.5 Bundle branch block, other and unspecified**

426.50 Bundle branch block, unspecified

426.51 Right bundle branch block and left posterior fascicular block

✔ **St. Anthony's Clinical Coder:** see Chapter 6

426.52 Right bundle branch block and left anterior fascicular block

✔ **St. Anthony's Clinical Coder:** see Chapter 6

426.53 Other bilateral bundle branch block

Bifascicular block NOS
Bilateral bundle branch block NOS
Right bundle branch with left bundle branch block (incomplete) (main stem)

➡ **CC Excl:** see Code 426.0

✔ **St. Anthony's Clinical Coder:** see Chapter 6

426.54 Trifascicular block

➡ **CC Excl:** see Code 426.0

✔ **St. Anthony's Clinical Coder:** see Chapter 6

426.6 Other heart block

Intraventricular block:
- NOS
- diffuse
- myofibrillar

Sinoatrial block
Sinoauricular block

➡ **CC Excl:** see Code 426.0

426.7 Anomalous atrioventricular excitation

Atrioventricular conduction:
- accelerated
- accessory
- pre-excitation

Ventricular pre-excitation
Wolff-Parkinson-White syndrome

➡ **CC Excl:** see Code 426.0

✓5th **426.8 Other specified conduction disorders**

426.81 Lown-Ganong-Levine syndrome

Syndrome of short P-R interval, normal QRS complexes, and supraventricular tachycardias

➡ **CC Excl:** see Code 426.0

426.89 Other

Dissociation:
- atrioventricular [AV]
- interference
- isorhythmic

Nonparoxysmal AV nodal tachycardia

➡ **CC Excl:** see Code 426.0

426.9 Conduction disorder, unspecified

Heart block NOS
Stokes-Adams syndrome

➡ **CC Excl:** see Code 426.0

427 Cardiac dysrhythmias

Excludes: *that complicating:*
- *abortion (634-638 with .7, 639.8)*
- *ectopic or molar pregnancy (639.8)*
- *labor or delivery (668.1, 669.4)*

427.0 Paroxysmal supraventricular tachycardia

Paroxysmal tachycardia:
- atrial [PAT]
- atrioventricular [AV]
- junctional
- nodal

➡ **CC Excl:** see Code 426.0

DRG 138

✓ **St. Anthony's Clinical Coder:** see Chapter 6

427.1 Paroxysmal ventricular tachycardia

Ventricular tachycardia (paroxysmal)

➡ **CC Excl:** see Code 426.0

➡ **AHA Coding Clinic:** 3Q, '95, 9; M-A, '86, 11

DRG 138

✓ **St. Anthony's Clinical Coder:** see Chapters 5, 6 & 7

427.2 Paroxysmal tachycardia, unspecified

Bouveret-Hoffmann syndrome
Paroxysmal tachycardia:
- NOS
- essential

➡ **CC Excl:** see Code 426.0

✓ **St. Anthony's Clinical Coder:** see Chapters 5 & 6

✓5th **427.3 Atrial fibrillation and flutter**

427.31 Atrial fibrillation

➡ **CC Excl:** see Code 426.0

➡ **AHA Coding Clinic:** 3Q, '95, 8

DRG 138

✓ **St. Anthony's Clinical Coder:** see Chapters 5 & 6

427.32 Atrial flutter

➡ **CC Excl:** see Code 426.0

DRG 138

✓ **St. Anthony's Clinical Coder:** see Chapters 5 & 6

✓5th **427.4 Ventricular fibrillation and flutter**

427.41 Ventricular fibrillation

➡ **CC Excl:** see Code 426.0

✓ **St. Anthony's Clinical Coder:** see Chapters 5 & 6

427.42 Ventricular flutter

➡ **CC Excl:** see Code 426.0

✓ **St. Anthony's Clinical Coder:** see Chapter 6

427.5 Cardiac arrest

Cardiorespiratory arrest

➡ **CC Excl:** 427.0-427.5, 459.89, 459.9

➡ **AHA Coding Clinic:** 3Q, '95, 8; 2Q, '88, 8

✓ **St. Anthony's Clinical Coder:** see Chapters 5, 6 & 7

✓5th **427.6 Premature beats**

427.60 Premature beats, unspecified

Ectopic beats
Extrasystoles
Extrasystolic arrhythmia
Premature contractions or systoles NOS

427.61 Supraventricular premature beats

Atrial premature beats, contractions, or systoles

427.69 Other

Ventricular premature beats, contractions, or systoles

✓5th **427.8 Other specified cardiac dysrhythmias**

427.81 Sinoatrial node dysfunction

Sinus bradycardia:
- persistent
- severe

Syndrome:
- sick sinus
- tachycardia-bradycardia

Excludes: *sinus bradycardia NOS (427.89)*

DRG 138

427.89 **Other**

Rhythm disorder:
  coronary sinus
  ectopic
  nodal

Wandering (atrial) pacemaker

Excludes: *carotid sinus syncope (337.0)*
reflex bradycardia (337.0)
tachycardia NOS (785.0)

DRG 138

427.9 **Cardiac dysrhythmia, unspecified**

Arrhythmia (cardiac) NOS

➡ **AHA Coding Clinic:** 2Q, '89, 10

428 Heart failure

Excludes: *following cardiac surgery (429.4)*
rheumatic (398.91)
that complicating:
  abortion (634-638 with .7, 639.8)
  ectopic or molar pregnancy (639.8)
  labor or delivery (668.1, 669.4)
that due to hypertension (402.0-402.9 with fifth-digit 1)

➡ **AHA Coding Clinic:** 2Q, '90, 16; 2Q, '90, 19; 2Q, '89, 10; 3Q, '88, 3

428.0 **Congestive heart failure**

Congestive heart disease
Right heart failure (secondary to left heart failure)

➡ **CC Excl:** 398.91, 402.01, 402.11, 402.91, 428.0-428.9, 459.89, 459.9, 518.4

➡ **AHA Coding Clinic:** 4Q, '97, 55; 3Q, '97, 10; 3Q, '96, 9; 3Q, '91, 18; 3Q, '91, 19; 2Q, '89, 12

DRG 121 and 127

✔ **St. Anthony's Clinical Coder:** see Chapters 5, 6 & 7

428.1 **Left heart failure**

Acute edema of lung } with heart disease
Acute pulmonary edema } NOS or heart failure
Cardiac asthma
Left ventricular failure

➡ **CC Excl:** 398.91, 402.01, 402.11, 402.91, 428.0-428.9, 459.89, 459.9

✔ **St. Anthony's Clinical Coder:** see Chapters 5, 6 & 7

428.9 **Heart failure, unspecified**

Cardiac failure NOS
Heart failure NOS
Myocardial failure NOS
Weak heart

➡ **CC Excl:** see Code 428.1

✔ **St. Anthony's Clinical Coder:** see Chapters 5, 6 & 7

429 Ill-defined descriptions and complications of heart disease

429.0 **Myocarditis, unspecified**

Myocarditis: } (with mention of arteriosclerosis)
  NOS
  chronic (interstitial)
  fibroid
  senile

Use additional code to identify presence of arteriosclerosis

Excludes: *acute or subacute (422.0-422.9)*
rheumatic (398.0)
  acute (391.2)
that due to hypertension (402.0-402.9)

429.1 **Myocardial degeneration**

Degeneration of heart or myocardium: } (with mention of arteriosclerosis)
  fatty
  mural
  muscular
Myocardial:
  degeneration
  disease

Use additional code to identify presence of arteriosclerosis

Excludes: *that due to hypertension (402.0-402.9)*

429.2 **Cardiovascular disease, unspecified** **A: 15–124**

Arteriosclerotic cardiovascular disease [ASCVD]
Cardiovascular arteriosclerosis
Cardiovascular: } (with mention of arteriosclerosis)
  degeneration
  disease
  sclerosis

Use additional code to identify presence of arteriosclerosis

Excludes: *that due to hypertension (402.0-402.9)*

429.3 **Cardiomegaly**

Cardiac:
  dilatation
  hypertrophy
Ventricular dilatation

Excludes: *that due to hypertension (402.0-402.9)*

429.4 **Functional disturbances following cardiac surgery**

Cardiac insufficiency } following cardiac surgery or
Heart failure } due to prosthesis
Postcardiotomy syndrome
Postvalvulotomy syndrome

Excludes: *cardiac failure in the immediate postoperative period (997.1)*

➡ **CC Excl:** 429.4, 429.71, 429.79, 459.89, 459.9

➡ **AHA Coding Clinic:** N-D, '85, 6

✔ **St. Anthony's Clinical Coder:** see Chapter 7

429.5 **Rupture of chordae tendineae**

➡ **CC Excl:** 429.5, 429.71, 429.79, 459.89, 459.9

✔ **St. Anthony's Clinical Coder:** see Chapters 6 & 7

429.6 **Rupture of papillary muscle**

➡ **CC Excl:** 429.6, 429.71, 429.79, 429.81, 459.89, 459.9

✔ **St. Anthony's Clinical Coder:** see Chapters 6 & 7

✓5th **429.7 Certain sequelae of myocardial infarction, not elsewhere classified** A: 15–124

Use additional code to identify the associated myocardial infarction:
with onset of 8 weeks or less (410.00-410.92)
with onset of more than 8 weeks (414.8)

Excludes: *congenital defects of heart (745, 746)*
coronary aneurysm (414.11)
disorders of papillary muscle (429.6, 429.81)
postmyocardial infarction syndrome (411.0)
rupture of chordae tendineae (429.5)

➡ **AHA Coding Clinic:** 3Q, '89, 5

✔ **St. Anthony's Clinical Coder:** see Chapter 7

429.71 Acquired cardiac septal defect

Excludes: *acute septal infarction (410.00-410.92)*

➡ **CC Excl:** 422.0-422.99, 429.0, 429.4-429.9, 745.0-745.9, 746.89, 746.9, 747.89, 747.9, 759.7-759.89

429.79 Other

Mural thrombus (atrial) (ventricular) acquired, following myocardial infarction

➡ **CC Excl:** see Code 429.71

➡ **AHA Coding Clinic:** 1Q, '92, 10

✓5th **429.8 Other ill-defined heart diseases**

429.81 Other disorders of papillary muscle

Papillary muscle:
atrophy
degeneration
dysfunction
incompetence
incoordination
scarring

➡ **CC Excl:** 429.6, 429.71, 429.79, 429.81, 459.89, 459.9

✔ **St. Anthony's Clinical Coder:** see Chapters 6 & 7

429.82 Hyperkinetic heart disease

➡ **CC Excl:** 429.71, 429.79, 429.82, 459.89, 459.9

✔ **St. Anthony's Clinical Coder:** see Chapter 6

429.89 Other

Carditis

Excludes: *that due to hypertension (402.0-402.9)*

➡ **AHA Coding Clinic:** 1Q, '92, 10

429.9 Heart disease, unspecified

Heart disease (organic) NOS
Morbus cordis NOS

Excludes: *that due to hypertension (402.0-402.9)*

➡ **AHA Coding Clinic:** 1Q, '93, 19

CEREBROVASCULAR DISEASE (430-438)

Includes: with mention of hypertension (conditions classifiable to 401-405)

Use additional code to identify presence of hypertension

Excludes: *any condition classifiable to 430-434, 436, 437 occurring during pregnancy, childbirth, or the puerperium, or specified as puerperal (674.0)*

➡ **AHA Coding Clinic:** 1Q, '93, 27; 3Q, '90, 3; 2Q, '89, 8; M-A, '85, 6

430 Subarachnoid hemorrhage

Meningeal hemorrhage
Ruptured:
berry aneurysm
(congenital) cerebral aneurysm NOS

Excludes: *syphilitic ruptured cerebral aneurysm (094.87)*

➡ **CC Excl:** 430, 431, 432.0-432.9, 459.89, 459.9, 780.01, 780.03, 800.00-800.99, 801.00-801.99, 803.00-803.99, 804.00-804.96, 850.0-850.9, 851.00-851.99, 852.00-852.19, 852.21-852.59, 853.00-853.19, 854.00-854.19

431 Intracerebral hemorrhage

Hemorrhage (of):
basilar
bulbar
cerebellar
cerebral
cerebromeningeal
cortical
internal capsule
intrapontine
pontine
subcortical
ventricular

Rupture of blood vessel in brain

➡ **CC Excl:** see Code 430

DRG 014

432 Other and unspecified intracranial hemorrhage

432.0 Nontraumatic extradural hemorrhage

Nontraumatic epidural hemorrhage

➡ **CC Excl:** see Code 430

432.1 Subdural hemorrhage

Subdural hematoma, nontraumatic

➡ **CC Excl:** see Code 430

432.9 Unspecified intracranial hemorrhage

Intracranial hemorrhage NOS

433 Occlusion and stenosis of precerebral arteries A: 15–124

Includes:
embolism, narrowing, obstruction, thrombosis } of basilar, carotid, and vertebral arteries

Excludes: *insufficiency NOS of precerebral arteries (435.0-435.9)*

The following fifth-digit subclassification is for use with category 433:

0 without mention of cerebral infarction
1 with cerebral infarction

➡ **AHA Coding Clinic:** 2Q, '95, 14; 3Q, '90, 16

✓5th **433.0 Basilar artery**
➡ **CC Excl: For code 433.01:** 250.70-250.93, 433.00-433.91, 435.90, 459.89, 459.9

✓5th **433.1 Carotid artery**
➡ **CC Excl: For code 433.11:** 250.70-250.93, 433.00-433.91, 459.89, 459.9

✓5th **433.2 Vertebral artery**
➡ **CC Excl: For code 433.21:** 250.70-250.93, 433.00-433.91, 435.1, 459.89, 459.9

✓5th **433.3 Multiple and bilateral**
➡ **CC Excl: For code 433.31:** see Code 433.11

✓5th **433.8 Other specified precerebral artery**
➡ **CC Excl: For code 433.81:** see Code 433.01

✓5th **433.9 Unspecified precerebral artery**
Precerebral artery NOS
➡ **CC Excl: For code 433.91:** see Code 433.01

434 Occlusion of cerebral arteries A: 15–124

The following fifth-digit subclassification is for use with category 434:

0 without mention of cerebral infarction
1 with cerebral infarction

➡ **AHA Coding Clinic:** 2Q, '95, 14

✓5th **434.0 Cerebral thrombosis**
Thrombosis of cerebral arteries
➡ **CC Excl: For code 434.01:** 250.70-250.93, 434.00-434.91, 436, 459.89, 459.9

✓5th **434.1 Cerebral embolism**
➡ **CC Excl: For code 434.11:** see Code 434.01
➡ **AHA Coding Clinic:** 3Q, '97, 11
DRG 014: For Code 434.11

✓5th [8] **434.9 Cerebral artery occlusion, unspecified**
➡ **CC Excl: For code 434.91:** see Code 434.01
DRG 014: For Code 434.91

435 Transient cerebral ischemia

Includes: cerebrovascular insufficiency (acute) with transient focal neurological signs and symptoms
insufficiency of basilar, carotid, and vertebral arteries
spasm of cerebral arteries

Excludes: *acute cerebrovascular insufficiency NOS (437.1)*
that due to any condition classifiable to 433 (433.0-433.9)

435.0 Basilar artery syndrome

435.1 Vertebral artery syndrome

435.2 Subclavian steal syndrome

435.3 Vertebrobasilar artery syndrome
➡ **AHA Coding Clinic:** 4Q, '95, 60

435.8 Other specified transient cerebral ischemias A: 15–124

435.9 Unspecified transient cerebral ischemia A: 15–124
Impending cerebrovascular accident
Intermittent cerebral ischemia
Transient ischemic attack [TIA]

436 Acute, but ill-defined, cerebrovascular disease A: 15–124

Apoplexy, apoplectic:	Cerebral seizure
NOS	Cerebrovascular accident [CVA] NOS
attack	Stroke
cerebral	
seizure	

Excludes: *any condition classifiable to categories 430-435*

➡ **CC Excl:** 250.70-250.93, 430-431, 432.0-432.9, 434.00-434.91, 436, 459.89, 459.9, 780.01, 780.03, 800.00-800.99, 801.00-801.99, 803.00-803.99, 804.00-804.96, 850.0-850.9, 851.00-851.99, 852.00-852.19, 852.21-852.59, 853.00-853.19, 854.00-854.19

DRG 014

437 Other and ill-defined cerebrovascular disease

437.0 Cerebral atherosclerosis A: 15–124
Atheroma of cerebral arteries
Cerebral arteriosclerosis

437.1 Other generalized ischemic cerebrovascular disease
Acute cerebrovascular insufficiency NOS
Cerebral ischemia (chronic)

437.2 Hypertensive encephalopathy
➡ **CC Excl:** 250.70-250.93, 437.2, 459.89, 459.9
➡ **AHA Coding Clinic:** J-A, '84, 14

437.3 Cerebral aneurysm, nonruptured
Internal carotid artery, intracranial portion
Internal carotid artery NOS

Excludes: *congenital cerebral aneurysm, nonruptured (747.81)*
internal carotid artery, extracranial portion (442.81)

[8] Nonspecific PDX = 0

437.4 Cerebral arteritis

➡ **CC Excl:** 250.70-250.93, 437.4, 459.89, 459.9

437.5 Moyamoya disease

➡ **CC Excl:** 250.70-250.93, 437.5, 459.89, 459.9

437.6 Nonpyogenic thrombosis of intracranial venous sinus

Excludes: *pyogenic (325)*

➡ **CC Excl:** 250.70-250.93, 437.6, 459.89, 459.9

437.7 Transient global amnesia

➡ **AHA Coding Clinic:** 4Q, '92, 20

437.8 Other

437.9 Unspecified

Cerebrovascular disease or lesion NOS

438 Late effects of cerebrovascular disease

Note: This category is to be used to indicate conditions in 430-437 as the cause of late effects. The "late effects" include conditions specified as such, or as sequelae, which may occur at any time after the onset of the causal condition.

➡ **AHA Coding Clinic:** 4Q, '97, 35, 37; 4Q, '92, 21; N-D,'86, 12; M-A, '86, 7

438.0 Cognitive deficits

✓5th **438.1** Speech and language deficits

438.10 Speech and language deficits, unspecified

438.11 Aphasia

➡ **AHA Coding Clinic:** 4Q, '97, 36

438.12 Dysphasia

438.19 Other speech and language deficits

✓5th **438.2** Hemiplegia/hemiparesis

438.20 Hemiplegia affecting unspecified side

438.21 Hemiplegia affecting dominant side

438.22 Hemiplegia affecting nondominant side

✓5th **438.3** Monoplegia of upper limb

438.30 Monoplegia of upper limb affecting unspecified side

438.31 Monoplegia of upper limb affecting dominant side

438.32 Monoplegia of upper limb affecting nondominant side

✓5th **438.4** Monoplegia of lower limb

438.40 Monoplegia of lower limb affecting unspecified side

438.41 Monoplegia of lower limb affecting dominant side

438.42 Monoplegia of lower limb affecting nondominant side

✓5th **438.5** Other paralytic syndrome

Use additional code to identify type of paralytic syndrome, such as:
locked-in-state (344.81)
quadriplegia (344.00-344.09)

Excludes: *late effects of cerebrovascular accident with:*
hemiplegia/hemiparesis (438.20-438.22)
monoplegia of lower limb (438.40-438.42)
monoplegia of upper limb (438.30-438.32)

438.50 Other paralytic syndrome affecting unspecified side

438.51 Other paralytic syndrome affecting dominant side

438.52 Other paralytic syndrome affecting nondominant side

438.53 Other paralytic syndrome, bilateral

✓5th **438.8** Other late effect of cerebrovascular disease

438.81 Apraxia

438.82 Dysphagia

438.89 Other late effects of cerebrovascular disease

Use additional code to identify the late effect

438.9 Unspecified late effects of cerebrovascular disease

DISEASES OF ARTERIES, ARTERIOLES, AND CAPILLARIES (440-448)

440 Atherosclerosis A: 15–124

Includes: arteriolosclerosis
arteriosclerosis (obliterans) (senile)
arteriosclerotic vascular disease
atheroma
degeneration:
arterial
arteriovascular
vascular
endarteritis deformans or obliterans
senile:
arteritis
endarteritis

Excludes: *atherosclerosis of bypass graft of the extremities (440.30-440.32)*

440.0 Of aorta

➡ **AHA Coding Clinic:** 2Q, '93, 7; 2Q, '93, 8

440.1 Of renal artery

Excludes: *atherosclerosis of renal arterioles (403.00-403.91)*

✓5th **440.2 Of native arteries of the extremities**

Excludes: *atherosclerosis of bypass graft of the extremities (440.30-440.32)*

➡ **AHA Coding Clinic:** 4Q, '94, 49; 4Q, '93, 27; 4Q, '92, 25; 3Q, '90, 15; M-A, '87, 6

440.20 Atherosclerosis of the extremities, unspecified

440.21 Atherosclerosis of the extremities with intermittent claudication

440.22 Atherosclerosis of the extremities with rest pain

Includes: any condition classifiable to 440.21

440.23 Atherosclerosis of the extremities with ulceration

Includes: any condition classifiable to 440.21 and 440.22

440.24 Atherosclerosis of the extremities with gangrene

Includes: any condition classifiable to 440.21, 440.22, and 440.23 with ischemic gangrene 785.4

Excludes: *gas gangrene 040.0*

➡ **CC Excl:** 440.24, 780.9, 785.4, 799.8

➡ **AHA Coding Clinic:** 4Q, '95, 54; 1Q, '95, 11

440.29 Other atherosclerosis of native arteries of extremities

✓5th **440.3 Of bypass graft of the extremities**

Excludes: *atherosclerosis of native artery of the extremity (440.21-440.24)*
embolism [occlusion NOS] [thrombus] of graft (996.74)

➡ **AHA Coding Clinic:** 4Q, '94, 49

440.30 Of unspecified graft

440.31 Of autologous vein bypass graft

440.32 Of nonautologous biological bypass graft

440.8 Of other specified arteries

Excludes: *basilar (433.0)*
carotid (433.1)
cerebral (437.0)
coronary (414.00-414.05)
mesenteric (557.1)
precerebral (433.0-433.9)
pulmonary (416.0)
vertebral (433.2)

440.9 Generalized and unspecified atherosclerosis

Arteriosclerotic vascular disease NOS

Excludes: *arteriosclerotic cardiovascular disease [ASCVD] (429.2)*

441 Aortic aneurysm and dissection A: 15–124

Excludes: *syphilitic aortic aneurysm (093.0)*
traumatic aortic aneurysm (901.0, 902.0)

✓5th **441.0 Dissection of aorta**

Dissecting aneurysm of aorta (ruptured)

➡ **AHA Coding Clinic:** 4Q, '89, 10

✔ **St. Anthony's Clinical Coder:** see Chapters 5 & 6

441.00 Unspecified site

➡ **CC Excl:** 250.70-250.93, 441.00-441.9, 459.89, 459.9

441.01 Thoracic

➡ **CC Excl:** see Code 441.00

441.02 Abdominal

➡ **CC Excl:** see Code 441.00

441.03 Thoracoabdominal

➡ **CC Excl:** see Code 441.00

441.1 Thoracic aneurysm, ruptured

➡ **CC Excl:** see Code 441.00

441.2 Thoracic aneurysm without mention of rupture

➡ **AHA Coding Clinic:** 3Q, '92, 10

441.3 Abdominal aneurysm, ruptured

➡ **CC Excl:** see Code 441.00

441.4 Abdominal aneurysm without mention of rupture

➡ **AHA Coding Clinic:** 3Q, '92, 10

441.5 Aortic aneurysm of unspecified site, ruptured

Rupture of aorta NOS

➡ **CC Excl:** see Code 441.00

✔ **St. Anthony's Clinical Coder:** see Chapter 5

441.6 Thoracoabdominal aneurysm, ruptured

➡ **CC Excl:** see Code 441.00

441.7 Thoracoabdominal aneurysm, without mention of rupture

☐ **441.9 Aortic aneurysm of unspecified site without mention of rupture**

Aneurysm } of aorta
Dilatation } of aorta
Hyaline necrosis } of aorta

442 Other aneurysm A: 15–124

Includes: aneurysm (ruptured) (cirsoid) (false) (varicose)
aneurysmal varix

Excludes: *arteriovenous aneurysm or fistula:*
acquired (447.0)
congenital (747.60-747.69)
traumatic (900.0-904.9)

442.0 Of artery of upper extremity

442.1 Of renal artery

442.2 Of iliac artery

442.3 Of artery of lower extremity

Aneurysm:
femoral } artery
popliteal }

✓5th **442.8 Of other specified artery**

442.81 Artery of neck

Aneurysm of carotid artery (common) (external) (internal, extracranial portion)

Excludes: *internal carotid artery, intracranial portion (437.3)*

442.82 Subclavian artery

442.83 Splenic artery

442.84 Other visceral artery

Aneurysm:
celiac } artery
gastroduodenal
gastroepiploic
hepatic
pancreaticoduodenal
superior mesenteric

442.89 Other

Aneurysm:
mediastinal } artery
spinal }

Excludes: *cerebral (nonruptured) (437.3)*
congenital (747.81)
ruptured (430)
coronary (414.11)
heart (414.10)
pulmonary (417.1)

442.9 Of unspecified site

443 Other peripheral vascular disease

443.0 Raynaud's syndrome

Raynaud's:
disease
phenomenon (secondary)

Use additional code to identify gangrene (785.4)

443.1 Thromboangiitis obliterans [Buerger's disease]

Presenile gangrene

✓5th **443.8 Other specified peripheral vascular diseases**

443.81 Peripheral angiopathy in diseases classified elsewhere

Code first underlying disease as:
diabetes mellitus (250.7)

443.89 Other

Acrocyanosis
Acroparesthesia:
simple [Schultze's type]
vasomotor [Nothnagel's type]
Erythrocyanosis
Erythromelalgia

Excludes: *chilblains (991.5)*
frostbite (991.0-991.3)
immersion foot (991.4)

443.9 Peripheral vascular disease, unspecified

Intermittent claudication NOS
Peripheral:
angiopathy NOS
vascular disease NOS
Spasm of artery

Excludes: *atherosclerosis of the arteries of the extremities (440.20-440.22)*
spasm of cerebral artery (435.0-435.9)

444 Arterial embolism and thrombosis

Includes: infarction:
embolic
thrombotic
occlusion

Excludes: *that complicating:*
abortion (634-638 with .6, 639.6)
ectopic or molar pregnancy (639.6)
pregnancy, childbirth, or the puerperium (673.0-673.8)

➡ **AHA Coding Clinic:** 2Q, '92, 11

444.0 Of abdominal aorta

Aortic bifurcation syndrome
Aortoiliac obstruction
Leriche's syndrome
Saddle embolus

➡ **CC Excl:** 250.70-250.93, 444.0, 444.89, 444.9, 459.89, 459.9

➡ **AHA Coding Clinic:** 2Q, '93, 7; 4Q, '90, 27

444.1 Of thoracic aorta

Embolism or thrombosis of aorta (thoracic)

➡ **CC Excl:** 250.70-250.93, 444.1, 444.89, 444.9, 459.89, 459.9

✓5th **444.2 Of arteries of the extremities**

➡ **AHA Coding Clinic:** M-A, '87, 6

444.21 Upper extremity

➡ **CC Excl:** 250.70-250.93, 444.21, 444.89, 444.9, 459.89, 459.9

444.22 Lower extremity

Arterial embolism or thrombosis:
femoral
peripheral NOS
popliteal

Excludes: *iliofemoral (444.81)*

➡ **CC Excl:** 250.70-250.93, 444.22, 444.89, 444.9, 459.89, 459.9

➡ **AHA Coding Clinic:** 3Q, '90, 16

✓5th **444.8 Of other specified artery**

444.81 Iliac artery

➡ **CC Excl:** 250.70-250.93, 444.81-444.9, 459.89, 459.9

444.89 Other

Excludes: *basilar (433.0)*
carotid (433.1)
cerebral (434.0-434.9)
coronary (410.00-410.92)
mesenteric (557.0)
ophthalmic (362.30-362.34)
precerebral (433.0-433.9)
pulmonary (415.19)
renal (593.81)
retinal (362.30-362.34)
vertebral (433.2)

➡ **CC Excl:** 250.70-250.93, 444.89, 444.9, 459.89, 459.9

444.9 Of unspecified artery

➡ **CC Excl:** see Code 444.89

446 Polyarteritis nodosa and allied conditions

446.0 Polyarteritis nodosa

Disseminated necrotizing periarteritis
Necrotizing angiitis
Panarteritis (nodosa)
Periarteritis (nodosa)

➡ **CC Excl:** 250.70-250.93, 446.0-446.7, 459.89, 459.9

446.1 Acute febrile mucocutaneous lymph node syndrome [MCLS]

Kawasaki disease

✓5th **446.2 Hypersensitivity angiitis**

Excludes: *antiglomerular basement membrane disease without pulmonary hemorrhage (583.89)*

446.20 Hypersensitivity angiitis, unspecified

➡ **CC Excl:** see Code 446.0

446.21 Goodpasture's syndrome

Antiglomerular basement membrane antibody-mediated nephritis with pulmonary hemorrhage

Use additional code to identify renal disease (583.81)

➡ **CC Excl:** see Code 446.0

446.29 Other specified hypersensitivity angiitis

➡ **CC Excl:** see Code 446.0

446.3 Lethal midline granuloma

Malignant granuloma of face

➡ **CC Excl:** see Code 446.0

446.4 Wegener's granulomatosis

Necrotizing respiratory granulomatosis
Wegener's syndrome

➡ **CC Excl:** see Code 446.0

446.5 Giant cell arteritis

Cranial arteritis
Horton's disease
Temporal arteritis

➡ **CC Excl:** see Code 446.0

446.6 Thrombotic microangiopathy

Moschcowitz's syndrome
Thrombotic thrombocytopenic purpura

➡ **CC Excl:** see Code 446.0

446.7 Takayasu's disease

Aortic arch arteritis
Pulseless disease

➡ **CC Excl:** see Code 446.0

447 Other disorders of arteries and arterioles

447.0 Arteriovenous fistula, acquired

Arteriovenous aneurysm, acquired

Excludes: *cerebrovascular (437.3)*
coronary (414.19)
pulmonary (417.0)
surgically created arteriovenous shunt or fistula:
complication (996.1, 996.61-996.62)
status or presence (V45.1)
traumatic (900.0-904.9)

447.1 Stricture of artery

➡ **AHA Coding Clinic:** 2Q, '93, 8; M-A, '87, 6

447.2 Rupture of artery

Erosion, Fistula, except arteriovenous, Ulcer } of artery

Excludes: *traumatic rupture of artery (900.0-904.9)*

447.3 **Hyperplasia of renal artery**
Fibromuscular hyperplasia of renal artery

447.4 **Celiac artery compression syndrome**
Celiac axis syndrome
Marable's syndrome

447.5 **Necrosis of artery**

447.6 **Arteritis, unspecified**
Aortitis NOS
Endarteritis NOS

Excludes: *arteritis, endarteritis:*
aortic arch (446.7)
cerebral (437.4)
coronary (414.00-414.05)
deformans (440.0-440.9)
obliterans (440.0-440.9)
pulmonary (417.8)
senile (440.0-440.9)
polyarteritis NOS (446.0)
syphilitic aortitis (093.1)

447.8 **Other specified disorders of arteries and arterioles**
Fibromuscular hyperplasia of arteries, except renal

447.9 **Unspecified disorders of arteries and arterioles**

448 Disease of capillaries

448.0 **Hereditary hemorrhagic telangiectasia**
Rendu-Osler-Weber disease

448.1 **Nevus, non-neoplastic**
Nevus:
araneus
senile
spider
stellar

Excludes: *neoplastic (216.0-216.9)*
port wine (757.32)
strawberry (757.32)

448.9 **Other and unspecified capillary diseases**
Capillary:
hemorrhage
hyperpermeability
thrombosis

Excludes: *capillary fragility (hereditary) (287.8)*

DISEASES OF VEINS AND LYMPHATICS, AND OTHER DISEASES OF CIRCULATORY SYSTEM (451-459)

451 Phlebitis and thrombophlebitis

Includes: endophlebitis
inflammation, vein
periphlebitis
suppurative phlebitis

Use additional E code to identify drug if drug-induced

Excludes: *that complicating:*
abortion (634-638 with .7, 639.8)
ectopic or molar pregnancy (639.8)
pregnancy, childbirth, or the puerperium (671.0-671.9)
that due to or following:
implant or catheter device (996.61-996.62)
infusion, perfusion, or transfusion (999.2)

➡ **AHA Coding Clinic:** 1Q, '92, 16

451.0 **Of superficial vessels of lower extremities**
Saphenous vein (greater) (lesser)
➡ **CC Excl:** 250.70-250.93, 451.0-451.9, 459.89, 459.9
➡ **AHA Coding Clinic:** 3Q, '91, 16
✔ **St. Anthony's Clinical Coder:** see Chapter 5

✓5th **451.1** **Of deep vessels of lower extremities**

451.11 **Femoral vein (deep) (superficial)**
➡ **CC Excl:** see Code 451.0
✔ **St. Anthony's Clinical Coder:** see Chapter 5

451.19 **Other**
Femoropopliteal vein
Popliteal vein
Tibial vein
➡ **CC Excl:** see Code 451.0

451.2 **Of lower extremities, unspecified**
➡ **CC Excl:** see Code 451.0

✓5th **451.8** **Of other sites**

Excludes: *intracranial venous sinus (325)*
nonpyogenic (437.6)
portal (vein) (572.1)

451.81 **Iliac vein**
➡ **CC Excl:** see Code 451.0

451.82 **Of superficial veins of upper extremities**
Antecubital vein
Basilic vein
Cephalic vein

451.83 **Of deep veins of upper extremities**
Brachial vein
Radial vein
Ulnar vein

451.84 **Of upper extremities, unspecified**

451.89 **Other**
Axillary vein
Jugular vein
Subclavian vein
Thrombophlebitis of breast (Mondor's disease)

451.9 **Of unspecified site**

452 Portal vein thrombosis
Portal (vein) obstruction

Excludes: *hepatic vein thrombosis (453.0)*
phlebitis of portal vein (572.1)

➡ **CC Excl:** 250.70-250.93, 452, 453.8-453.9, 459.89, 459.9

453 Other venous embolism and thrombosis

Excludes: *that complicating:*
abortion (634-638 with .7, 639.8)
ectopic or molar pregnancy (639.8)
pregnancy, childbirth, or the puerperium (671.0-671.9)
that with inflammation, phlebitis, and thrombophlebitis (451.0-451.9)

➡ **AHA Coding Clinic:** 1Q, '92, 16

453.0 **Budd-Chiari syndrome**
Hepatic vein thrombosis
➡ **CC Excl:** 250.70-250.93, 453.0, 453.8-453.9, 459.89, 459.9

453.1 **Thrombophlebitis migrans**
➡ **CC Excl:** 250.70-250.93, 453.1, 453.8-453.9, 459.89, 459.9

453.2 **Of vena cava**
➡ **CC Excl:** 250.70-250.93, 453.2, 453.8-453.9, 459.89, 459.9

453.3 **Of renal vein**
➡ **CC Excl:** 250.70-250.93, 453.3, 453.8-453.9, 459.89, 459.9

453.8 **Of other specified veins**

Excludes: *cerebral (434.0-434.9)*
coronary (410.00-410.92)
intracranial venous sinus (325)
nonpyogenic (437.6)
mesenteric (557.0)
portal (452)
precerebral (433.0-433.9)
pulmonary (415.19)

➡ **CC Excl:** 250.70-250.93, 453.8-453.9, 459.89, 459.9
➡ **AHA Coding Clinic:** 1Q, '92, 16
DRG 130

453.9 **Of unspecified site**
Embolism of vein
Thrombosis (vein)
➡ **CC Excl:** see Code 453.8

454 Varicose veins of lower extremities A: 15–124

Excludes: *that complicating pregnancy, childbirth, or the puerperium (671.0)*

➡ **AHA Coding Clinic:** 2Q, '91, 20

454.0 **With ulcer**
Varicose ulcer (lower extremity, any part)
Varicose veins with ulcer of lower extremity [any part] or of unspecified site
Any condition classifiable to 454.9 with ulcer or specified as ulcerated

454.1 **With inflammation**
Stasis dermatitis
Varicose veins with inflammation of lower extremity [any part] or of unspecified site
Any condition classifiable to 454.9 with inflammation or specified as inflamed

454.2 **With ulcer and inflammation**
Varicose veins with ulcer and inflammation of lower extremity [any part] or of unspecified site
Any condition classifiable to 454.9 with ulcer and inflammation

454.9 **Without mention of ulcer or inflammation**
Phlebectasia, Varicose veins, Varix } of lower extremity [any part] or of unspecified site

455 Hemorrhoids

Includes: hemorrhoids (anus) (rectum)
piles
varicose veins, anus or rectum

Excludes: *that complicating pregnancy, childbirth, or the puerperium (671.8)*

455.0 **Internal hemorrhoids without mention of complication**

455.1 **Internal thrombosed hemorrhoids**

455.2 **Internal hemorrhoids with other complication**
Internal hemorrhoids:
bleeding
prolapsed
strangulated
ulcerated

DRG 188

455.3 **External hemorrhoids without mention of complication**

455.4 **External thrombosed hemorrhoids**

455.5 **External hemorrhoids with other complication**
External hemorrhoids:
bleeding
prolapsed
strangulated
ulcerated

455.6 Unspecified hemorrhoids without mention of complication
Hemorrhoids NOS

455.7 Unspecified thrombosed hemorrhoids
Thrombosed hemorrhoids, unspecified whether internal or external

455.8 Unspecified hemorrhoids with other complication
Hemorrhoids, unspecified whether internal or external:
- bleeding
- prolapsed
- strangulated
- ulcerated

455.9 Residual hemorrhoidal skin tags
Skin tags, anus or rectum

456 Varicose veins of other sites

456.0 Esophageal varices with bleeding
➡ **CC Excl:** 251.5, 456.0, 456.20, 459.89, 459.9, 530.2, 530.7, 530.82, 531.00-531.91, 532.00-532.91, 533.00-533.91, 534.00-534.91, 535.01, 535.11, 535.21, 535.31, 535.41, 535.51, 535.61, 537.83, 562.02-562.03, 562.12-562.13, 569.3, 569.85, 578.0-578.9
✔ **St. Anthony's Clinical Coder:** see Chapter 5

456.1 Esophageal varices without mention of bleeding

✓5th **456.2 Esophageal varices in diseases classified elsewhere**
Code first underlying disease as:
cirrhosis of liver (571.0-571.9)
portal hypertension (572.3)

456.20 With bleeding
➡ **CC Excl:** 456.0, 456.20, 459.89, 459.9, 530.82
➡ **AHA Coding Clinic:** N-D, '85, 14

456.21 Without mention of bleeding

456.3 Sublingual varices

456.4 Scrotal varices ♂
Varicocele

456.5 Pelvic varices
Varices of broad ligament

456.6 Vulval varices ♀
Varices of perineum

Excludes: *that complicating pregnancy, childbirth, or the puerperium (671.1)*

456.8 Varices of other sites
Varicose veins of nasal septum (with ulcer)

Excludes: *placental varices (656.7)*
retinal varices (362.17)
varicose ulcer of unspecified site (454.0)
varicose veins of unspecified site (454.9)

457 Noninfectious disorders of lymphatic channels

457.0 Postmastectomy lymphedema syndrome A: 15–124
Elephantiasis } due to mastectomy
Obliteration of lymphatic vessel } due to mastectomy

457.1 Other lymphedema
Elephantiasis (nonfilarial) NOS
Lymphangiectasis
Lymphedema:
- acquired (chronic)
- praecox
- secondary

Obliteration, lymphatic vessel

Excludes: *elephantiasis (nonfilarial):*
congenital (757.0)
eyelid (374.83)
vulva (624.8)

457.2 Lymphangitis
Lymphangitis:
- NOS
- chronic
- subacute

Excludes: *acute lymphangitis (682.0-682.9)*

457.8 Other noninfectious disorders of lymphatic channels
Chylocele (nonfilarial)
Chylous:
- ascites
- cyst

Lymph node or vessel:
- fistula
- infarction
- rupture

Excludes: *chylocele:*
filarial (125.0-125.9)
tunica vaginalis (nonfilarial) (608.84)

457.9 Unspecified noninfectious disorder of lymphatic channels

458 Hypotension

Includes: hypopiesis

Excludes: *cardiovascular collapse (785.50)*
maternal hypotension syndrome (669.2)
shock (785.50-785.59)
Shy-Drager syndrome (333.0)

458.0 Orthostatic hypotension

Hypotension:
orthostatic (chronic)
postural

458.1 Chronic hypotension

Permanent idiopathic hypotension

458.2 Iatrogenic hypotension

Postoperative hypotension

➡ **AHA Coding Clinic:** 4Q, '95, 57

458.8 Other specified hypotension

➡ **AHA Coding Clinic:** 4Q, '97, 37

458.9 Hypotension, unspecified

Hypotension (arterial) NOS

✔ **St. Anthony's Clinical Coder:** see Chapter 6

459 Other disorders of circulatory system

459.0 Hemorrhage, unspecified

Rupture of blood vessel NOS
Spontaneous hemorrhage NEC

Excludes: *hemorrhage:*
gastrointestinal NOS (578.9)
in newborn NOS (772.9)
secondary or recurrent following trauma (958.2)
traumatic rupture of blood vessel (900.0-904.9)

➡ **CC Excl:** 459.0, 459.89, 459.9

➡ **AHA Coding Clinic:** 4Q, '90, 26

459.1 Postphlebitic syndrome

➡ **AHA Coding Clinic:** 2Q, '91, 20

459.2 Compression of vein

Stricture of vein
Vena cava syndrome (inferior) (superior)

✓5th **459.8 Other specified disorders of circulatory system**

459.81 Venous (peripheral) insufficiency, unspecified

Chronic venous insufficiency NOS

Use additional code for any associated ulceration (707.1-707.9)

➡ **AHA Coding Clinic:** 2Q, '91, 20

459.89 Other

Collateral circulation (venous), any site
Phlebosclerosis
Venofibrosis

459.9 Unspecified circulatory system disorder

8. DISEASES OF THE RESPIRATORY SYSTEM (460-519)

Use additional code to identify infectious organism

ACUTE RESPIRATORY INFECTIONS (460-466)

Excludes: *pneumonia and influenza (480.0-487.8)*

460 Acute nasopharyngitis [common cold]

Coryza (acute)
Nasal catarrh, acute
Nasopharyngitis:
  NOS
  acute
  infective NOS
Rhinitis:
  acute
  infective

Excludes: *nasopharyngitis, chronic (472.2)*
pharyngitis:
  acute or unspecified (462)
  chronic (472.1)
rhinitis:
  allergic (477.0-477.9)
  chronic or unspecified (472.0)
sore throat:
  acute or unspecified (462)
  chronic (472.1)

461 Acute sinusitis

Includes: abscess, empyema, infection, inflammation, suppuration } acute, of sinus (accessory) (nasal)

Excludes: *chronic or unspecified sinusitis (473.0-473.9)*

461.0 Maxillary
Acute antritis

461.1 Frontal

461.2 Ethmoidal

461.3 Sphenoidal

461.8 Other acute sinusitis
Acute pansinusitis

461.9 Acute sinusitis, unspecified
Acute sinusitis NOS

462 Acute pharyngitis

Acute sore throat NOS
Pharyngitis (acute):
  NOS
  gangrenous
  infective
  phlegmonous
  pneumococcal
Pharyngitis (acute):
  staphylococcal
  suppurative
  ulcerative
Sore throat (viral) NOS
Viral pharyngitis

Excludes: *abscess:*
  peritonsillar [quinsy] (475)
  pharyngeal NOS (478.29)
  retropharyngeal (478.24)
chronic pharyngitis (472.1)
infectious mononucleosis (075)
that specified as (due to):
  Coxsackie (virus) (074.0)
  gonococcus (098.6)
  herpes simplex (054.79)
  influenza (487.1)
  septic (034.0)
  streptococcal (034.0)

➡ **AHA Coding Clinic:** S-O, '85, 8

463 Acute tonsillitis

Tonsillitis (acute):
  NOS
  follicular
  gangrenous
  infective
  pneumococcal
Tonsillitis (acute):
  septic
  staphylococcal
  suppurative
  ulcerative
  viral

Excludes: *chronic tonsillitis (474.0)*
hypertrophy of tonsils (474.1)
peritonsillar abscess [quinsy] (475)
sore throat:
  acute or NOS (462)
  septic (034.0)
streptococcal tonsillitis (034.0)

464 Acute laryngitis and tracheitis

Excludes: *that associated with influenza (487.1)*
that due to Streptococcus (034.0)

464.0 Acute laryngitis
Laryngitis (acute):
  NOS
  edematous
  Hemophilus influenzae [H. influenzae]
Laryngitis (acute):
  pneumococcal
  septic
  suppurative
  ulcerative

Excludes: *chronic laryngitis (476.0-476.1)*
influenzal laryngitis (487.1).

✓5th **464.1 Acute tracheitis**

Tracheitis (acute):
- NOS
- catarrhal
- viral

Excludes: *chronic tracheitis (491.8)*

464.10 Without mention of obstruction

464.11 With obstruction

➡ **CC Excl:** 012.20-012.86, 017.90-017.96, 464.10-464.31, 519.8-519.9

✓5th **464.2 Acute laryngotracheitis**

Laryngotracheitis (acute)
Tracheitis (acute) with laryngitis (acute)

Excludes: *chronic laryngotracheitis (476.1)*

464.20 Without mention of obstruction

464.21 With obstruction

➡ **CC Excl:** see Code 464.11

✓5th **464.3 Acute epiglottitis**

Viral epiglottitis

Excludes: *epiglottitis, chronic (476.1)*

464.30 Without mention of obstruction

464.31 With obstruction

➡ **CC Excl:** see Code 464.11

464.4 Croup

Croup syndrome

465 Acute upper respiratory infections of multiple or unspecified sites

Excludes: *upper respiratory infection due to:*
- *influenza (487.1)*
- *Streptococcus (034.0)*

465.0 Acute laryngopharyngitis

465.8 Other multiple sites

Multiple URI

465.9 Unspecified site

Acute URI NOS
Upper respiratory infection (acute)

466 Acute bronchitis and bronchiolitis

Includes: that with:
- bronchospasm
- obstruction

466.0 Acute bronchitis

Bronchitis, acute or subacute:
- fibrinous
- membranous
- pneumococcal
- purulent
- septic
- viral
- with tracheitis

Croupous bronchitis
Tracheobronchitis, acute

➡ **AHA Coding Clinic:** 4Q, '96, 28; 4Q, '91, 24

✓5th **466.1 Acute bronchiolitis**

Bronchiolitis (acute)
Capillary pneumonia

466.11 Due to respiratory syncytial virus (RSV)

➡ **AHA Coding Clinic:** 4Q, '96, 27

466.19 Due to other infectious organisms

Use additional code to identify organism

OTHER DISEASES OF THE UPPER RESPIRATORY TRACT (470-478)

470 Deviated nasal septum

Deflected septum (nasal) (acquired)

Excludes: *congenital (754.0)*

471 Nasal polyps

Excludes: *adenomatous polyps (212.0)*

471.0 Polyp of nasal cavity

Polyp:
- choanal
- nasopharyngeal

471.1 Polypoid sinus degeneration

Woakes' syndrome or ethmoiditis

471.8 Other polyp of sinus

Polyp of sinus:
- accessory
- ethmoidal

Polyp of sinus:
- maxillary
- sphenoidal

471.9 Unspecified nasal polyp

Nasal polyp NOS

472 Chronic pharyngitis and nasopharyngitis

472.0 Chronic rhinitis

Ozena
Rhinitis:
- NOS
- atrophic
- granulomatous

Rhinitis:
- hypertrophic
- obstructive
- purulent
- ulcerative

Excludes: *allergic rhinitis (477.0-477.9)*

472.1 Chronic pharyngitis

Chronic sore throat
Pharyngitis:
- atrophic
- granular (chronic)
- hypertrophic

472.2 Chronic nasopharyngitis

Excludes: *acute or unspecified nasopharyngitis (460)*

473 Chronic sinusitis

Includes: abscess, empyema, infection, suppuration } (chronic) of sinus (accessory) (nasal)

Excludes: *acute sinusitis (461.0-461.9)*

473.0 Maxillary
Antritis (chronic)

473.1 Frontal

473.2 Ethmoidal

Excludes: *Woakes' ethmoiditis (471.1)*

473.3 Sphenoidal

473.8 Other chronic sinusitis
Pansinusitis (chronic)

473.9 Unspecified sinusitis (chronic)
Sinusitis (chronic) NOS

474 Chronic disease of tonsils and adenoids

✓5th **474.0 Chronic tonsillitis and adenoiditis**

Excludes: *acute or unspecified tonsillitis (463)*

➡ **AHA Coding Clinic:** 4Q, '97, 38

474.00 Chronic tonsillitis

474.01 Chronic adenoiditis

474.02 Chronic tonsillitis and adenoiditis

✓5th **474.1 Hypertrophy of tonsils and adenoids**

Enlargement, Hyperplasia, Hypertrophy } of tonsils or adenoids

Excludes: *that with:*
adenoiditis (474.01)
adenoiditis and tonsillitis (474.02)
tonsillitis (474.00)

474.10 Tonsils with adenoids

474.11 Tonsils alone

474.12 Adenoids alone

474.2 Adenoid vegetations

474.8 Other chronic disease of tonsils and adenoids
Amygdalolith
Calculus, tonsil
Cicatrix of tonsil (and adenoid)
Tonsillar tag
Ulcer, tonsil

474.9 Unspecified chronic disease of tonsils and adenoids
Disease (chronic) of tonsils (and adenoids)

475 Peritonsillar abscess
Abscess of tonsil
Peritonsillar cellulitis
Quinsy

Excludes: *tonsillitis:*
acute or NOS (463)
chronic (474.0)

➡ **CC Excl:** 475, 519.8-519.9

476 Chronic laryngitis and laryngotracheitis

476.0 Chronic laryngitis
Laryngitis:
catarrhal
hypertrophic
sicca

476.1 Chronic laryngotracheitis
Laryngitis, chronic, with tracheitis (chronic)
Tracheitis, chronic, with laryngitis

Excludes: *chronic tracheitis (491.8)*
laryngitis and tracheitis, acute or unspecified (464.0-464.4)

477 Allergic rhinitis

Includes: allergic rhinitis (nonseasonal) (seasonal)
hay fever
spasmodic rhinorrhea

Excludes: *allergic rhinitis with asthma (bronchial) (493.0)*

477.0 Due to pollen
Pollinosis

477.8 Due to other allergen

477.9 Cause unspecified
➡ **AHA Coding Clinic:** 2Q, '97, 9

478 Other diseases of upper respiratory tract

478.0 Hypertrophy of nasal turbinates

478.1 Other diseases of nasal cavity and sinuses

Abscess, Necrosis, Ulcer } of nose (septum)
Cyst or mucocele of sinus (nasal)
Rhinolith

Excludes: *varicose ulcer of nasal septum (456.8)*

✓5th **478.2 Other diseases of pharynx, not elsewhere classified**

478.20 Unspecified disease of pharynx

478.21 Cellulitis of pharynx or nasopharynx
➡ **CC Excl:** 478.20-478.24, 519.8-519.9

478.22 Parapharyngeal abscess
➡ **CC Excl:** see Code 478.21

478.24 Retropharyngeal abscess
➡ **CC Excl:** see Code 478.21

478.25 Edema of pharynx or nasopharynx

478.26 Cyst of pharynx or nasopharynx

478.29 Other
Abscess of pharynx or nasopharynx

Excludes: *ulcerative pharyngitis (462)*

✓5th **478.3 Paralysis of vocal cords or larynx**

478.30 Paralysis, unspecified
Laryngoplegia Paralysis of glottis
➡ **CC Excl:** 478.30-478.34, 478.5, 478.70, 519.8-519.9

478.31 Unilateral, partial
➡ **CC Excl:** see Code 478.30

478.32 Unilateral, complete
➡ **CC Excl:** see Code 478.30

478.33 Bilateral, partial
➡ **CC Excl:** see Code 478.30

478.34 Bilateral, complete
➡ **CC Excl:** see Code 478.30

478.4 Polyp of vocal cord or larynx

Excludes: *adenomatous polyps (212.1)*

478.5 Other diseases of vocal cords

Abscess, Cellulitis, Granuloma, Leukoplakia } of vocal cords
Chorditis (fibrinous) (nodosa) (tuberosa)
Singers' nodes

478.6 Edema of larynx
Edema (of):
glottis
subglottic
supraglottic

✓5th **478.7 Other diseases of larynx, not elsewhere classified**

478.70 Unspecified disease of larynx

478.71 Cellulitis and perichondritis of larynx

478.74 Stenosis of larynx

478.75 Laryngeal spasm
Laryngismus (stridulus)

478.79 Other

Abscess, Necrosis, Obstruction, Pachyderma, Ulcer } of larynx

Excludes: *ulcerative laryngitis (464.0)*

478.8 Upper respiratory tract hypersensitivity reaction, site unspecified

Excludes: *hypersensitivity reaction of lower respiratory tract, as:*
extrinsic allergic alveolitis (495.0-495.9)
pneumoconiosis (500-505)

478.9 Other and unspecified diseases of upper respiratory tract
Abscess, Cicatrix } of trachea

PNEUMONIA AND INFLUENZA (480-487)

Excludes: *pneumonia:*
allergic or eosinophilic (518.3)
aspiration:
NOS (507.0)
newborn (770.1)
solids and liquids (507.0-507.8)
congenital (770.0)
lipoid (507.1)
passive (514)
rheumatic (390)

480 Viral pneumonia

480.0 Pneumonia due to adenovirus

480.1 Pneumonia due to respiratory syncytial virus
➡ **AHA Coding Clinic:** 4Q, '96, 28; 1Q, '88, 12

480.2 Pneumonia due to parainfluenza virus

480.8 Pneumonia due to other virus not elsewhere classified

Excludes: *congenital rubella pneumonitis (771.0)*
influenza with pneumonia, any form (487.0)
pneumonia complicating viral diseases classified elsewhere (484.1-484.8)

480.9 Viral pneumonia, unspecified

481 Pneumococcal pneumonia [Streptococcus pneumoniae pneumonia]

Lobar pneumonia, organism unspecified

➡ **CC Excl:** 011.00-011.96, 012.00-012.86, 017.90-017.96, 021.2, 031.0, 039.1, 115.05, 115.15, 115.95, 122.1, 130.4, 136.3, 480.0-486, 487.0-487.1, 494-508.9, 517.1, 517.8, 518.89, 519.8-519.9, 748.61

➡ **AHA Coding Clinic:** 4Q, '92, 19; 1Q, '92, 18; 1Q, '91, 13; 1Q, '88, 13; M-A, '85, 6

DRG 089

482 Other bacterial pneumonia

➡ **AHA Coding Clinic:** 4Q, '93, 39

482.0 Pneumonia due to Klebsiella pneumoniae

➡ **CC Excl:** see Code 481

DRG 079

482.1 Pneumonia due to Pseudomonas

➡ **CC Excl:** see Code 481

DRG 079

482.2 Pneumonia due to Hemophilus influenzae [H. influenzae]

➡ **CC Excl:** see Code 481

✓5th **482.3 Pneumonia due to Streptococcus**

Excludes: *Streptococcus pneumoniae pneumonia (481)*

➡ **AHA Coding Clinic:** 1Q, '88, 13

482.30 Streptococcus, unspecified

➡ **CC Excl:** see Code 481

482.31 Group A

➡ **CC Excl:** see Code 481

482.32 Group B

➡ **CC Excl:** see Code 481

482.39 Other Streptococcus

➡ **CC Excl:** see Code 481

✓5th **482.4 Pneumonia due to Staphylococcus**

➡ **AHA Coding Clinic:** 3Q, '91, 16

DRG 079

482.40 Pneumonia due to Staphylococcus, unspecified

➡ **CC Excl:** see Code 481

482.41 Pneumonia due to Staphylococcus aureus

➡ **CC Excl:** see Code 481

482.49 Other Staphylococcus pneumonia

➡ **CC Excl:** see Code 481

✓5th **482.8 Pneumonia due to other specified bacteria**

Excludes: *pneumonia complicating infectious disease classified elsewhere (484.1-484.8)*

482.81 Anaerobes

Bacteroides (melaninogenicus)
Gram-negative anaerobes

➡ **CC Excl:** see Code 481

482.82 Escherichia coli [E. coli]

➡ **CC Excl:** see Code 481

482.83 Other gram-negative bacteria

Gram-negative pneumonia NOS
Proteus
Serratia marcescens

Excludes: *gram-negative anaerobes (482.81)*
Legionnaires' disease (482.84)

➡ **CC Excl:** see Code 481

➡ **AHA Coding Clinic:** 3Q, '94, 9

DRG 079

482.84 Legionnaires' disease

➡ **CC Excl:** 011.00-011.06, 011.10-011.16, 011.20-011.26, 011.30-011.36, 011.40-011.46, 011.50-011.56, 011.60-011.66, 011.70-011.76, 011.80-011.86, 011.90-011.96, 012.00-012.06, 012.10-012.16, 012.80-012.86, 017.90-017.96, 021.2, 031.0, 039.1, 115.05, 115.15, 115.95, 122.1, 130.4, 136.3, 480.0-480.2, 480.8-480.9, 481, 482.0-482.2, 482.30-482.32, 482.39, 482.4, 482.81-482.84, 482.89, 482.9, 483.0-483.1, 483.8, 484.1, 484.3, 484.5-484.8, 485, 486, 487.0-487.1, 494, 495.0-495.9, 496, 500, 501, 502, 503, 504, 505, 506.0-506.4, 506.9, 507.0-507.1, 507.8, 508.0-508.1, 508.8, 508.9, 517.1-517.8, 518.89, 519.8, 519.9, 748.61

➡ **AHA Coding Clinic:** 4Q, '97, 40

482.89 Other specified bacteria

➡ **CC Excl:** see Code 481

➡ **AHA Coding Clinic:** 2Q, '97, 6

DRG 079

482.9 Bacterial pneumonia unspecified

➡ **CC Excl:** see Code 481

➡ **AHA Coding Clinic:** 2Q, '97, 6; 1Q, '94, 17

483 Pneumonia due to other specified organism

➡ **AHA Coding Clinic:** N-D, '87, 5

483.0 Mycoplasma pneumoniae

Eaton's agent
Pleuropneumonia-like organisms [PPLO]

➡ **CC Excl:** see Code 481

483.1 Chlamydia

➡ **CC Excl:** 011.00-011.06, 011.10-011.16, 011.20-011.26, 011.30-011.36, 011.40-011.46, 011.50-011.56, 011.60-011.66, 011.70-011.76, 011.80-011.86, 011.90-011.96, 012.00-012.06, 012.10-012.16, 012.80-012.86, 017.90-017.96, 021.2, 031.0, 039.1, 115.05, 115.15, 115.95, 122.1, 130.4, 136.3, 480.0-480.2, 480.8-480.9, 481, 482.0-482.2, 482.30-482.32, 482.39, 482.4, 482.81-482.84, 482.89, 482.9, 483.0-483.1, 483.8, 484.1, 484.3, 484.5-484.8, 485, 486, 487.0-487.1, 494, 495.0-495.9, 496, 500-505, 506.0-506.4, 506.9, 507.0-507.1, 507.8, 508.0-508.1, 508.8-508.9, 517.1, 517.8, 518.89, 519.8, 519.9, 748.61

➡ **AHA Coding Clinic:** 4Q, '96, 31

483.8 Other specified organism

➡ **CC Excl:** see Code 481

484 Pneumonia in infectious diseases classified elsewhere

Excludes: *influenza with pneumonia, any form (487.0)*

484.1 Pneumonia in cytomegalic inclusion disease

Code first underlying disease as: (078.5)

➡ **CC Excl:** see Code 481

484.3 Pneumonia in whooping cough

Code first underlying disease as: (033.0-033.9)

➡ **CC Excl:** see Code 481

484.5 Pneumonia in anthrax

Code first underlying disease (022.1)

➡ **CC Excl:** see Code 481

484.6 Pneumonia in aspergillosis

Code first underlying disease (117.3)

➡ **CC Excl:** see Code 481

➡ **AHA Coding Clinic:** 4Q, '97, 40

484.7 Pneumonia in other systemic mycoses

Code first underlying disease

Excludes: *pneumonia in:*
candidiasis (112.4)
coccidioidomycosis (114.0)
histoplasmosis (115.0-115.9 with fifth-digit 5)

➡ **CC Excl:** see Code 481

484.8 Pneumonia in other infectious diseases classified elsewhere

Code first underlying disease as:
Q fever (083.0)
typhoid fever (002.0)

Excludes: *pneumonia in:*
actinomycosis (039.1)
measles (055.1)
nocardiosis (039.1)
ornithosis (073.0)
Pneumocystis carinii (136.3)
salmonellosis (003.22)
toxoplasmosis (130.4)
tuberculosis (011.6)
tularemia (021.2)
varicella (052.1)

➡ **CC Excl:** see Code 481

485 Bronchopneumonia, organism unspecified

Bronchopneumonia:
hemorrhagic
terminal
Pleurobronchopneumonia
Pneumonia:
lobular
segmental

Excludes: *bronchiolitis (acute) (466.11-466.19)*
chronic (491.8)
lipoid pneumonia (507.1)

➡ **CC Excl:** see Code 481

486 Pneumonia, organism unspecified

Excludes: *hypostatic or passive pneumonia (514)*
influenza with pneumonia, any form (487.0)
inhalation or aspiration pneumonia due to foreign materials (507.0-507.8)
pneumonitis due to fumes and vapors (506.0)

➡ **CC Excl:** see Code 481

➡ **AHA Coding Clinic:** 1Q, '98, 8; 3Q, '97, 9; 3Q, '94, 10; 3Q, '88, 11

DRG 089

✔ **St. Anthony's Clinical Coder:** see Chapter 5

487 Influenza

Excludes: *Hemophilus influenzae [H. influenzae]:*
infection NOS (041.5)
laryngitis (464.0)
meningitis (320.0)
pneumonia (482.2)

487.0 With pneumonia
Influenza with pneumonia, any form
Influenzal:
bronchopneumonia
pneumonia

➡ **CC Excl:** see Code 481

487.1 With other respiratory manifestations
Influenza NOS
Influenzal:
laryngitis
pharyngitis
respiratory infection (upper) (acute)

487.8 With other manifestations
Encephalopathy due to influenza
Influenza with involvement of gastrointestinal tract

Excludes: *"intestinal flu" [viral gastroenteritis] (008.8)*

CHRONIC OBSTRUCTIVE PULMONARY DISEASE AND ALLIED CONDITIONS (490-496)

➡ **AHA Coding Clinic:** 3Q, '88, 5

490 Bronchitis, not specified as acute or chronic

Bronchitis NOS:
catarrhal
with tracheitis NOS
Tracheobronchitis NOS

Excludes: *bronchitis:*
allergic NOS (493.9)
asthmatic NOS (493.9)
due to fumes and vapors (506.0)

491 Chronic bronchitis

Excludes: *chronic obstructive asthma (493.2)*

491.0 Simple chronic bronchitis
Catarrhal bronchitis, chronic
Smokers' cough

491.1 Mucopurulent chronic bronchitis
Bronchitis (chronic) (recurrent):
fetid
mucopurulent
purulent

➡ **CC Excl:** 491.1-491.9, 493.20-493.21

➡ **AHA Coding Clinic:** 3Q, '88, 12

✓5th **491.2 Obstructive chronic bronchitis**
Bronchitis:
asthmatic, chronic
emphysematous
obstructive (chronic) (diffuse)
Bronchitis with:
chronic airway obstruction
emphysema

Excludes: *asthmatic bronchitis (acute) (NOS) (493.9)*
chronic obstructive asthma (493.2)

➡ **AHA Coding Clinic:** 3Q, '97, 9; 4Q, '91, 25; 2Q, '91, 21

491.20 Without mention of acute exacerbation
Chronic asthmatic bronchitis
Emphysema with chronic bronchitis

➡ **CC Excl:** see Code 491.1

491.21 With acute exacerbation
Acute bronchitis with chronic obstructive pulmonary disease [COPD]
Acute and chronic obstructive bronchitis
Chronic asthmatic bronchitis with acute exacerbation
Emphysema with both acute and chronic bronchitis

➡ **CC Excl:** see Code 491.1

➡ **AHA Coding Clinic:** 2Q, '96, 10

DRG 088

491.8 Other chronic bronchitis
Chronic:
tracheitis
tracheobronchitis

➡ **CC Excl:** see Code 491.1

491.9 Unspecified chronic bronchitis

➡ **CC Excl:** see Code 491.1

✔ **St. Anthony's Clinical Coder:** see Chapter 5

492 Emphysema

➡ **AHA Coding Clinic:** 2Q, '91, 21

492.0 Emphysematous bleb
Giant bullous emphysema
Ruptured emphysematous bleb
Tension pneumatocele
Vanishing lung

492.8 Other emphysema
Emphysema (lung or pulmonary):
NOS
centriacinar
centrilobular
obstructive
panacinar
panlobular
unilateral
vesicular
MacLeod's syndrome
Swyer-James syndrome
Unilateral hyperlucent lung

Excludes: *emphysema:*
with both acute and chronic bronchitis (491.21)
with chronic bronchitis (491.20)
compensatory (518.2)
due to fumes and vapors (506.4)
interstitial (518.1)
newborn (770.2)
mediastinal (518.1)
surgical (subcutaneous) (998.81)
traumatic (958.7)

➡ **CC Excl:** 492.0, 492.8, 493.20-493.21

✔ **St. Anthony's Clinical Coder:** see Chapter 5

[4] CC Coding = 1

493 Asthma

Excludes: *wheezing NOS (786.07)*

The following fifth-digit subclassification is for use with category 493:

0 without mention of status asthmaticus
1 with status asthmaticus

➡ **AHA Coding Clinic:** 1Q, '91, 13; 3Q, '88, 9; J-A, '85, 8; N-D, '84, 17

✓5th [4] **493.0 Extrinsic asthma**

Asthma:
- allergic with stated cause
- atopic
- childhood
- hay
- platinum

Hay fever with asthma

Excludes: *asthma:*
- *allergic NOS (493.9)*
- *detergent (507.8)*
- *miners' (500)*
- *wood (495.8)*

➡ **CC Excl: For code 493.01:** 493.00-493.91, 517.8, 518.89, 519.8-519.9

✓5th [4] **493.1 Intrinsic asthma**

Late-onset asthma

➡ **CC Excl: For code 493.11:** see Code 493.0

✓5th **493.2 Chronic obstructive asthma**

Asthma with chronic obstructive pulmonary disease [COPD]

Excludes: *chronic asthmatic bronchitis (491.2)*
chronic obstructive bronchitis (491.2)

➡ **CC Excl:** 491.1-491.9, 492.0, 492.8, 493.00-493.91, 517.8, 518.89, 519.8-519.9

➡ **AHA Coding Clinic:** 2Q, '91, 21; 2Q, '90, 20

DRG 088: For code 493.20

✓5th [4] **493.9 Asthma, unspecified**

Asthma (bronchial) (allergic NOS)

Bronchitis:
- allergic
- asthmatic

➡ **CC Excl: For code 493.91:** 493.00-493.91, 517.8, 518.89, 519.8-519.9

➡ **AHA Coding Clinic:** 4Q, '97, 40

➡ **AHA Coding Clinic: For code 493.90:** 1Q, '97, 7

494 Bronchiectasis

Bronchiectasis (fusiform) (postinfectious) (recurrent)
Bronchiolectasis

Excludes: *congenital (748.61)*
tuberculous bronchiectasis (current disease) (011.5)

➡ **CC Excl:** 017.90-017.96, 487.1, 494, 496, 506.1, 506.4, 506.9, 748.61

✓ **St. Anthony's Clinical Coder:** see Chapter 5

495 Extrinsic allergic alveolitis

Includes: allergic alveolitis and pneumonitis due to inhaled organic dust particles of fungal, thermophilic actinomycete, or other origin

495.0 Farmers' lung

➡ **CC Excl:** 011.00-011.96, 012.00-012.16, 012.80-012.86, 017.90-017.96, 021.2, 031.0, 039.1, 115.05, 115.15, 115.95, 122.1, 130.4, 136.3, 480.0-480.9, 481, 482.0-482.7, 482.81-482.84, 482.89, 482.9, 483.0, 483.1, 483.8, 484.1-484.8, 485-486, 487.0-487.1, 494, 495.0-495.9, 496, 500-505, 506.0-506.9, 507.0-507.8, 508.0-508.9, 517.1, 517.8, 518.89, 519.8-519.9, 748.61

495.1 Bagassosis

➡ **CC Excl:** see Code 495.0

495.2 Bird-fanciers' lung

Budgerigar-fanciers' disease or lung
Pigeon-fanciers' disease or lung

➡ **CC Excl:** see Code 495.0

495.3 Suberosis

Cork-handlers' disease or lung

➡ **CC Excl:** see Code 495.0

495.4 Malt workers' lung

Alveolitis due to Aspergillus clavatus

➡ **CC Excl:** see Code 495.0

495.5 Mushroom workers' lung

➡ **CC Excl:** see Code 495.0

495.6 Maple bark-strippers' lung

Alveolitis due to Cryptostroma corticale

➡ **CC Excl:** see Code 495.0

495.7 "Ventilation" pneumonitis

Allergic alveolitis due to fungal, thermophilic actinomycete, and other organisms growing in ventilation [air conditioning] systems

➡ **CC Excl:** see Code 495.0

495.8 Other specified allergic alveolitis and pneumonitis

Cheese-washers' lung
Coffee workers' lung
Fish-meal workers' lung
Furriers' lung
Grain-handlers' disease or lung
Pituitary snuff-takers' disease
Sequoiosis or red-cedar asthma
Wood asthma

➡ **CC Excl:** see Code 495.0

495.9 Unspecified allergic alveolitis and pneumonitis

Alveolitis, allergic (extrinsic)
Hypersensitivity pneumonitis

➡ **CC Excl:** see Code 495.0

[4] CC Coding = 1

496 Chronic airway obstruction, not elsewhere classified A: 15–124

Note: This code is not to be used with any code from categories 491-493

Chronic:
nonspecific lung disease
obstructive lung disease
obstructive pulmonary disease [COPD] NOS

Excludes: *chronic obstructive lung disease [COPD] specified (as) (with):*
allergic alveolitis (495.0-495.9)
asthma (493.2)
bronchiectasis (494)
bronchitis (491.20-491.21)
with emphysema (491.20-491.21)
emphysema (492.0-492.8)

➡ **CC Excl:** 017.90-017.96, 487.1, 494, 496, 506.1, 506.4, 506.9, 748.61

DRG 088

✔ **St. Anthony's Clinical Coder:** see Chapter 5

PNEUMOCONIOSES AND OTHER LUNG DISEASES DUE TO EXTERNAL AGENTS (500-508)

500 Coal workers' pneumoconiosis A: 15–124

Anthracosilicosis
Anthracosis
Black lung disease
Coal workers' lung
Miners' asthma

501 Asbestosis A: 15–124

502 Pneumoconiosis due to other silica or silicates

Pneumoconiosis due to talc
Silicotic fibrosis (massive) of lung
Silicosis (simple) (complicated)

503 Pneumoconiosis due to other inorganic dust

Aluminosis (of lung)
Bauxite fibrosis (of lung)
Berylliosis
Graphite fibrosis (of lung)
Siderosis
Stannosis

504 Pneumonopathy due to inhalation of other dust

Byssinosis
Cannabinosis
Flax-dressers' disease

Excludes: *allergic alveolitis (495.0-495.9)*
asbestosis (501)
bagassosis (495.1)
farmers' lung (495.0)

505 Pneumoconiosis, unspecified

506 Respiratory conditions due to chemical fumes and vapors

Use additional E code to identify cause

506.0 Bronchitis and pneumonitis due to fumes and vapors

Chemical bronchitis (acute)

➡ **CC Excl:** 011.00-011.96, 012.10-012.16, 012.80-012.86, 017.90-017.96, 021.2, 031.0, 039.1, 115.05, 115.15, 115.95, 122.1, 130.4, 136.3, 480.0-480.9, 481, 482.0-482.7, 482.81-482.84, 482.89, 482.9, 483.0, 483.1, 483.8, 484.1-484.8, 485-486, 487.0-487.1, 494, 495.0-495.9, 496, 500-505, 506.0-506.9, 507.0-507.8, 508.0-508.9, 517.1, 517.8, 518.89, 519.8-519.9, 748.61

506.1 Acute pulmonary edema due to fumes and vapors

Chemical pulmonary edema (acute)

Excludes: *acute pulmonary edema NOS (518.4)*
chronic or unspecified pulmonary edema (514)

➡ **CC Excl:** see Code 506.0

506.2 Upper respiratory inflammation due to fumes and vapors

506.3 Other acute and subacute respiratory conditions due to fumes and vapors

506.4 Chronic respiratory conditions due to fumes and vapors

Emphysema (diffuse) (chronic), Obliterative bronchiolitis (chronic) (subacute), Pulmonary fibrosis (chronic) — due to inhalation of chemical fumes and vapors

506.9 Unspecified respiratory conditions due to fumes and vapors

Silo-fillers' disease

507 Pneumonitis due to solids and liquids

Excludes: *fetal aspiration pneumonitis (770.1)*

➡ **AHA Coding Clinic:** 3Q, '91, 16

507.0 Due to inhalation of food or vomitus

Aspiration pneumonia (due to):
- NOS
- food (regurgitated)
- gastric secretions
- milk
- saliva
- vomitus

➡ **CC Excl:** see Code 506.0

➡ **AHA Coding Clinic:** 1Q, '89, 10

DRG 079

507.1 Due to inhalation of oils and essences

Lipoid pneumonia (exogenous)

Excludes: *endogenous lipoid pneumonia (516.8)*

➡ **CC Excl:** see Code 506.0

507.8 Due to other solids and liquids

Detergent asthma

➡ **CC Excl:** see Code 506.0

508 Respiratory conditions due to other and unspecified external agents

Use additional E code to identify cause

508.0 Acute pulmonary manifestations due to radiation

Radiation pneumonitis

➡ **CC Excl:** see Code 506.0

508.1 Chronic and other pulmonary manifestations due to radiation

Fibrosis of lung following radiation

➡ **CC Excl:** see Code 506.0

508.8 Respiratory conditions due to other specified external agents

508.9 Respiratory conditions due to unspecified external agent

OTHER DISEASES OF RESPIRATORY SYSTEM (510-519)

510 Empyema

Use additional code to identify infectious organism (041.0-041.9)

Excludes: *abscess of lung (513.0)*

510.0 With fistula

Fistula:
- bronchocutaneous
- bronchopleural
- hepatopleural

Fistula:
- mediastinal
- pleural
- thoracic

Any condition classifiable to 510.9 with fistula

➡ **CC Excl:** 510.0, 510.9, 517.8, 518.89, 519.8-519.9

510.9 Without mention of fistula

Abscess:
- pleura
- thorax

Empyema (chest) (lung) (pleura)

Fibrinopurulent pleurisy

Pleurisy:
- purulent
- septic
- seropurulent
- suppurative

Pyopneumothorax

Pyothorax

➡ **CC Excl:** see Code 510.0

511 Pleurisy

Excludes: *malignant pleural effusion (197.2)*
pleurisy with mention of tuberculosis, current disease (012.0)

511.0 Without mention of effusion or current tuberculosis

Adhesion, lung or pleura

Calcification of pleura

Pleurisy (acute) (sterile):
- diaphragmatic
- fibrinous
- interlobar

Pleurisy:
- NOS
- pneumococcal
- staphylococcal
- streptococcal

Thickening of pleura

➡ **AHA Coding Clinic:** 3Q, '94, 5

511.1 **With effusion, with mention of a bacterial cause other than tuberculosis**

Pleurisy with effusion (exudative) (serous):
- pneumococcal
- staphylococcal
- streptococcal
- other specified nontuberculous bacterial cause

➡ **CC Excl:** 011.00-011.96, 012.00-012.16, 012.80-012.86, 017.90-017.96, 511.0-511.9, 517.8, 518.89, 519.8-519.9

511.8 **Other specified forms of effusion, except tuberculous**

Encysted pleurisy
Hemopneumothorax
Hemothorax
Hydropneumothorax
Hydrothorax

Excludes: *traumatic (860.2-860.5)*

➡ **CC Excl:** see Code 511.1

➡ **AHA Coding Clinic:** 1Q, '97, 10

511.9 **Unspecified pleural effusion**

Pleural effusion NOS
Pleurisy:
- exudative
- serofibrinous

Pleurisy:
- serous
- with effusion NOS

➡ **CC Excl:** see Code 511.1

➡ **AHA Coding Clinic:** 3Q, '91, 19; 4Q, '89, 11

✔ **St. Anthony's Clinical Coder:** see Chapter 5

512 Pneumothorax

512.0 **Spontaneous tension pneumothorax**

➡ **CC Excl:** 512.0-512.1, 512.8, 517.8, 518.89, 519.8-519.9

➡ **AHA Coding Clinic:** 3Q, '94, 5

512.1 **Iatrogenic pneumothorax**

Postoperative pneumothorax

➡ **CC Excl:** see Code 512.0

512.8 **Other spontaneous pneumothorax**

Pneumothorax:
- NOS
- acute
- chronic

Excludes: *pneumothorax:*
- *congenital (770.2)*
- *traumatic (860.0-860.1, 860.4-860.5)*
- *tuberculous, current disease (011.7)*

➡ **CC Excl:** see Code 512.0

➡ **AHA Coding Clinic:** 2Q, '93, 3

✔ **St. Anthony's Clinical Coder:** see Chapter 5

513 Abscess of lung and mediastinum

513.0 **Abscess of lung**

Abscess (multiple) of lung
Gangrenous or necrotic pneumonia
Pulmonary gangrene or necrosis

➡ **CC Excl:** 006.4, 011.00-011.96, 012.00-012.16, 012.80-012.86, 017.90-017.96, 513.0, 519.8-519.9

513.1 **Abscess of mediastinum**

➡ **CC Excl:** 513.1, 519.8-519.9

514 Pulmonary congestion and hypostasis

Hypostatic:
- bronchopneumonia
- pneumonia

Passive pneumonia
Pulmonary congestion (chronic) (passive)
Pulmonary edema:
- NOS
- chronic

Excludes: *acute pulmonary edema:*
- *NOS (518.4)*
- *with mention of heart disease or failure (428.1)*

➡ **AHA Coding Clinic:** 3Q, '88, 5

▽ **DRG 087**

515 Postinflammatory pulmonary fibrosis

Cirrhosis of lung
Fibrosis of lung (atrophic) (confluent) (massive) (perialveolar) (peribronchial)
Induration of lung
} chronic or unspecified

➡ **CC Excl:** 011.00-011.96, 012.00-012.16, 012.80-012.86, 017.90-017.96, 494, 495.0-495.9, 496, 500-505, 506.0-506.9, 507.0-507.8, 508.0-508.9, 515, 516.0-516.9, 517.2, 517.8, 518.89, 519.8-519.9, 748.61

516 Other alveolar and parietoalveolar pneumonopathy

516.0 **Pulmonary alveolar proteinosis**

➡ **CC Excl:** see Code 515

516.1 ***Idiopathic pulmonary hemosiderosis***

Essential brown induration of lung

Code first underlying disease (275.0)

➡ **CC Excl:** see Code 515

516.2 **Pulmonary alveolar microlithiasis**

➡ **CC Excl:** see Code 515

516.3 **Idiopathic fibrosing alveolitis**

Alveolar capillary block
Diffuse (idiopathic) (interstitial) pulmonary fibrosis
Hamman-Rich syndrome

➡ **CC Excl:** see Code 515

516.8 **Other specified alveolar and parietoalveolar pneumonopathies**

Endogenous lipoid pneumonia
Interstitial pneumonia (desquamative) (lymphoid)

Excludes: *lipoid pneumonia, exogenous or unspecified (507.1)*

➡ **CC Excl:** see Code 515

➡ **AHA Coding Clinic:** 1Q, '92, 12

516.9 **Unspecified alveolar and parietoalveolar pneumonopathy**

➡ **CC Excl:** see Code 515

517 Lung involvement in conditions classified elsewhere

Excludes: *rheumatoid lung (714.81)*

517.1 ***Rheumatic pneumonia***

Code first underlying disease (390)

➡ **CC Excl:** 011.00-011.96, 012.00-012.16, 012.80-012.86, 017.90-017.96, 480.0-480.9, 481, 482.0-482.7, 482.81-482.84, 482.89, 482.9, 483.0, 483.1, 483.8, 484.1-484.8, 485-486, 487.0-487.1, 494, 495.0-495.9, 496, 500-505, 506.0-506.9, 507.0-507.8, 508.0-508.9, 515, 516.0-516.9, 517.1-517.8, 518.89, 519.8-519.9, 748.61

517.2 ***Lung involvement in systemic sclerosis***

Code first underlying disease (710.1)

➡ **CC Excl:** 011.00-011.96, 012.00-012.16, 012.80-012.86, 017.90-017.96, 494, 495.0-495.9, 496, 500-505, 506.0-506.9, 507.0-507.8, 508.0-508.9, 515, 516.0-516.9, 517.2, 517.8, 518.89, 519.8-519.9, 748.61

517.8 ***Lung involvement in other diseases classified elsewhere***

Code first underlying disease as:
amyloidosis (277.3)
polymyositis (710.4)
sarcoidosis (135)
Sjögren's disease (710.2)
systemic lupus erythematosus (710.0)

Excludes: *syphilis (095.1)*

➡ **CC Excl:** see Code 517.2

518 Other diseases of lung

518.0 **Pulmonary collapse**

Atelectasis
Collapse of lung
Middle lobe syndrome

Excludes: *atelectasis:*
congenital (partial) (770.5)
primary (770.4)
tuberculous, current disease (011.8)

➡ **CC Excl:** 518.0, 519.8-519.9

➡ **AHA Coding Clinic:** 4Q, '90, 25

✔ **St. Anthony's Clinical Coder:** see Chapter 5

518.1 **Interstitial emphysema**

Mediastinal emphysema

Excludes: *surgical (subcutaneous) emphysema (998.81)*
that in fetus or newborn (770.2)
traumatic emphysema (958.7)

➡ **CC Excl:** 518.1, 519.8-519.9

518.2 **Compensatory emphysema**

518.3 **Pulmonary eosinophilia**

Eosinophilic asthma
Löffler's syndrome
Pneumonia:
allergic
eosinophilic
Tropical eosinophilia

518.4 **Acute edema of lung, unspecified**

Acute pulmonary edema NOS
Pulmonary edema, postoperative

Excludes: *pulmonary edema:*
acute, with mention of heart disease or failure (428.1)
chronic or unspecified (514)
due to external agents (506.0-508.9)

➡ **CC Excl:** 398.91, 428.0-428.9, 518.4, 519.8-519.9

DRG 087

518.5 **Pulmonary insufficiency following trauma and surgery**

Adult respiratory distress syndrome
Pulmonary insufficiency following:
shock
surgery
trauma
Shock lung

Excludes: *adult respiratory distress syndrome associated with other conditions (518.82)*
pneumonia:
aspiration (507.0)
hypostatic (514)
respiratory failure in other conditions (518.81, 518.83-518.84)

➡ **CC Excl:** 518.5, 519.8-519.9

➡ **AHA Coding Clinic:** 3Q, '88, 3; 3Q, '88, 7; S-O, '87, 1

518.6 **Allergic bronchopulmonary aspergillosis**
➡ **CC Excl:** 518.6, 519.8-519.9
➡ **AHA Coding Clinic:** 4Q, '97, 40

✓5th **518.8** **Other diseases of lung**

518.81 **Acute respiratory failure**
Respiratory failure NOS

Excludes: *acute and chronic respiratory failure (518.84)*
acute respiratory distress (518.82)
chronic respiratory failure (518.83)
respiratory arrest (799.1)
respiratory failure, newborn (770.8)

➡ **CC Excl:** 518.81-518.89, 519.8-519.9, 799.1
➡ **AHA Coding Clinic:** 3Q, '91, 14; 2Q, '91, 3; 2Q, '90, 20; 3Q, '88, 7; 3Q, '88, 10; S-O, '87, 1
DRG 087
✓ **St. Anthony's Clinical Coder:** see Chapter 5

518.82 **Other pulmonary insufficiency, not elsewhere classified**
Acute respiratory distress
Acute respiratory insufficiency
Adult respiratory distress syndrome NEC

Excludes: *adult respiratory distress syndrome associated with trauma or surgery (518.5)*
pulmonary insufficiency following trauma or surgery (518.5)
respiratory distress:
newborn (770.8)
NOS (786.09)
syndrome, newborn (769)
shock lung (518.5)

➡ **CC Excl:** see Code 518.81
➡ **AHA Coding Clinic:** 2Q, '91, 21; 3Q, '88, 7

518.83 **Chronic respiratory failure**
➡ **CC Excl:** see Code 518.81

518.84 **Acute and chronic respiratory failure**
Acute on chronic respiratory failure
➡ **CC Excl:** see Code 518.81

518.89 **Other diseases of lung, not elsewhere classified**
Broncholithiasis
Calcification of lung
Lung disease NOS
Pulmolithiasis
➡ **AHA Coding Clinic:** 3Q, '90, 18; 4Q, '88, 6

519 Other diseases of respiratory system

✓5th **519.0** **Tracheostomy complications**

519.00 **Tracheostomy complication, unspecified**
➡ **CC Excl:** 519.0-519.1, 519.8-519.9

519.01 **Infection of tracheostomy**
Use additional code to identify type of infection, such as:
abscess or cellulitis of neck (682.1)
septicemia (038.0-038.9)
Use additional code to identify organism (041.00-041.9)
➡ **CC Excl:** see Code 519.00

519.02 **Mechanical complication of tracheostomy**
Tracheal stenosis due to tracheostomy
➡ **CC Excl:** see Code 519.00

519.09 **Other tracheostomy complication**
Hemorrhage due to tracheostomy
Tracheoesophageal fistula due to tracheostomy
➡ **CC Excl:** see Code 519.00

519.1 **Other diseases of trachea and bronchus, not elsewhere classified**
Calcification, Stenosis, Ulcer } of bronchus or trachea
➡ **AHA Coding Clinic:** 3Q, '88, 6

519.2 **Mediastinitis**
➡ **CC Excl:** 519.2-519.3, 519.8-519.9

519.3 **Other diseases of mediastinum, not elsewhere classified**
Fibrosis, Hernia, Retraction } of mediastinum

519.4 **Disorders of diaphragm**
Diaphragmitis
Paralysis of diaphragm
Relaxation of diaphragm

Excludes: *congenital defect of diaphragm (756.6)*
diaphragmatic hernia (551-553 with .3)
congenital (756.6)

519.8 **Other diseases of respiratory system, not elsewhere classified**
➡ **AHA Coding Clinic:** 4Q, '89, 12

519.9 **Unspecified disease of respiratory system**
Respiratory disease (chronic) NOS

9. DISEASES OF THE DIGESTIVE SYSTEM (520-579)

DISEASES OF ORAL CAVITY, SALIVARY GLANDS, AND JAWS (520-529)

520 Disorders of tooth development and eruption

520.0 Anodontia

Absence of teeth (complete) (congenital) (partial)
Hypodontia
Oligodontia

Excludes: *acquired absence of teeth (525.1)*

520.1 Supernumerary teeth

Distomolar
Fourth molar
Mesiodens
Paramolar
Supplemental teeth

Excludes: *supernumerary roots (520.2)*

520.2 Abnormalities of size and form

Concrescence, Fusion, Gemination } of teeth
Dens evaginatus
Dens in dente
Dens invaginatus
Enamel pearls
Macrodontia
Microdontia
Peg-shaped [conical] teeth
Supernumerary roots
Taurodontism
Tuberculum paramolare

Excludes: *that due to congenital syphilis (090.5)*
tuberculum Carabelli, which is regarded as a normal variation

520.3 Mottled teeth

Dental fluorosis
Mottling of enamel
Nonfluoride enamel opacities

520.4 Disturbances of tooth formation

Aplasia and hypoplasia of cementum
Dilaceration of tooth
Enamel hypoplasia (neonatal) (postnatal) (prenatal)
Horner's teeth
Hypocalcification of teeth
Regional odontodysplasia
Turner's tooth

Excludes: *Hutchinson's teeth and mulberry molars in congenital syphilis (090.5)*
mottled teeth (520.3)

520.5 Hereditary disturbances in tooth structure, not elsewhere classified

Amelogenesis, Dentinogenesis, Odontogenesis } imperfecta
Dentinal dysplasia
Shell teeth

520.6 Disturbances in tooth eruption

Teeth:
- embedded
- impacted
- natal
- neonatal
- primary [deciduous]:
  - persistent
  - shedding, premature

Tooth eruption:
- late
- obstructed
- premature

Excludes: *exfoliation of teeth (attributable to disease of surrounding tissues) (525.0-525.1)*
impacted or embedded teeth with abnormal position of such teeth or adjacent teeth (524.3)

520.7 Teething syndrome

520.8 Other specified disorders of tooth development and eruption

Color changes during tooth formation
Pre-eruptive color changes

Excludes: *posteruptive color changes (521.7)*

520.9 Unspecified disorder of tooth development and eruption

521 Diseases of hard tissues of teeth

521.0 Dental caries

Caries (of):
- arrested
- cementum
- dentin (acute) (chronic)
- enamel (acute) (chronic) (incipient)

Infantile melanodontia
Odontoclasia
White spot lesions of teeth

521.1 Excessive attrition

Approximal wear
Occlusal wear

521.2 Abrasion

Abrasion: dentifrice, habitual, occupational, ritual, traditional; Wedge defect NOS } of teeth

521.3 Erosion

Erosion of teeth:
- NOS
- due to:
  - medicine
  - persistent vomiting
- idiopathic
- occupational

521.4 Pathological resorption

Internal granuloma of pulp
Resorption of tooth or root (external) (internal)

521.5 Hypercementosis
Cementation hyperplasia

521.6 Ankylosis of teeth

521.7 Posteruptive color changes
Staining [discoloration] of teeth:
NOS
due to:
drugs
metals
pulpal bleeding

Excludes: *accretions [deposits] on teeth (523.6)*
pre-eruptive color changes (520.8)

521.8 Other specified diseases of hard tissues of teeth
Irradiated enamel
Sensitive dentin

521.9 Unspecified disease of hard tissues of teeth

522 Diseases of pulp and periapical tissues

522.0 Pulpitis
Pulpal:
abscess
polyp
Pulpitis:
acute
chronic (hyperplastic)
(ulcerative)
suppurative

522.1 Necrosis of the pulp
Pulp gangrene

522.2 Pulp degeneration
Denticles
Pulp calcifications
Pulp stones

522.3 Abnormal hard tissue formation in pulp
Secondary or irregular dentin

522.4 Acute apical periodontitis of pulpal origin

522.5 Periapical abscess without sinus
Abscess:
dental
dentoalveolar

Excludes: *periapical abscess with sinus (522.7)*

522.6 Chronic apical periodontitis
Apical or periapical granuloma
Apical periodontitis NOS

522.7 Periapical abscess with sinus
Fistula:
alveolar process
dental

522.8 Radicular cyst
Cyst:
apical (periodontal)
periapical
radiculodental
residual radicular

Excludes: *lateral developmental or lateral periodontal cyst (526.0)*

522.9 Other and unspecified diseases of pulp and periapical tissues

523 Gingival and periodontal diseases

523.0 Acute gingivitis

Excludes: *acute necrotizing ulcerative gingivitis (101)*
herpetic gingivostomatitis (054.2)

523.1 Chronic gingivitis
Gingivitis (chronic):
NOS
desquamative
hyperplastic
simple marginal
ulcerative
Gingivostomatitis

Excludes: *herpetic gingivostomatitis (054.2)*

523.2 Gingival recession
Gingival recession (generalized) (localized) (postinfective) (postoperative)

523.3 Acute periodontitis
Acute:
pericementitis
pericoronitis
Paradontal abscess
Periodontal abscess

Excludes: *acute apical periodontitis (522.4)*
periapical abscess (522.5, 522.7)

523.4 Chronic periodontitis
Alveolar pyorrhea
Chronic pericoronitis
Pericementitis (chronic)
Periodontitis:
NOS
complex
simplex

Excludes: *chronic apical periodontitis (522.6)*

523.5 Periodontosis

523.6 Accretions on teeth
Dental calculus:
subgingival
supragingival
Deposits on teeth:
betel
materia alba
soft
tartar
tobacco

523.8 Other specified periodontal diseases

Giant cell:
  epulis
  peripheral granuloma
Gingival:
  cysts
  enlargement NOS
  fibromatosis
Gingival polyp
Periodontal lesions due to traumatic occlusion
Peripheral giant cell granuloma

Excludes: *leukoplakia of gingiva (528.6)*

523.9 Unspecified gingival and periodontal disease

524 Dentofacial anomalies, including malocclusion

✓5th **524.0 Major anomalies of jaw size**

Excludes: *hemifacial atrophy or hypertrophy (754.0)*
unilateral condylar hyperplasia or hypoplasia of mandible (526.89)

524.00 Unspecified anomaly

524.01 Maxillary hyperplasia

524.02 Mandibular hyperplasia

524.03 Maxillary hypoplasia

524.04 Mandibular hypoplasia

524.05 Macrogenia

524.06 Microgenia

524.09 Other specified anomaly

✓5th **524.1 Anomalies of relationship of jaw to cranial base**

524.10 Unspecified anomaly

Prognathism
Retrognathism

524.11 Maxillary asymmetry

524.12 Other jaw asymmetry

524.19 Other specified anomaly

524.2 Anomalies of dental arch relationship

Crossbite (anterior)
  (posterior)
Disto-occlusion
Mesio-occlusion
Midline deviation
Open bite (anterior)
  (posterior)
Overbite (excessive):
  deep
  horizontal
  vertical
Overjet
Posterior lingual occlusion of mandibular teeth
Soft tissue impingement

Excludes: *hemifacial atrophy or hypertrophy (754.0)*
unilateral condylar hyperplasia or hypoplasia of mandible (526.89)

524.3 Anomalies of tooth position

Crowding, Diastema, Displacement, Rotation, Spacing, abnormal, Transposition — of tooth, teeth
Impacted or embedded teeth with abnormal position of such teeth or adjacent teeth

524.4 Malocclusion, unspecified

524.5 Dentofacial functional abnormalities

Abnormal jaw closure
Malocclusion due to:
  abnormal swallowing
  mouth breathing
  tongue, lip, or finger habits

✓5th **524.6 Temporomandibular joint disorders**

Excludes: *current temporomandibular joint:*
dislocation (830.0-830.1)
strain (848.1)

524.60 Temporomandibular joint disorders, unspecified

Temporomandibular joint-pain-dysfunction syndrome [TMJ]

524.61 Adhesions and ankylosis (bony or fibrous)

524.62 Arthralgia of temporomandibular joint

524.63 Articular disc disorder (reducing or non-reducing)

524.69 Other specified temporomandibular joint disorders

✓5th **524.7 Dental alveolar anomalies**

524.70 Unspecified alveolar anomaly

524.71 Alveolar maxillary hyperplasia

524.72 Alveolar mandibular hyperplasia

524.73 Alveolar maxillary hypoplasia

524.74 Alveolar mandibular hypoplasia

524.79 Other specified alveolar anomaly

524.8 Other specified dentofacial anomalies

524.9 Unspecified dentofacial anomalies

525 Other diseases and conditions of the teeth and supporting structures

525.0 Exfoliation of teeth due to systemic causes

525.1 Loss of teeth due to accident, extraction, or local periodontal disease
Acquired absence of teeth

525.2 Atrophy of edentulous alveolar ridge

525.3 Retained dental root

525.8 Other specified disorders of the teeth and supporting structures
Enlargement of alveolar ridge NOS
Irregular alveolar process

525.9 Unspecified disorder of the teeth and supporting structures

526 Diseases of the jaws

526.0 Developmental odontogenic cysts
Cyst:
- dentigerous
- eruption
- follicular
- lateral developmental

Cyst:
- lateral periodontal
- primordial

Keratocyst

Excludes: *radicular cyst (522.8)*

526.1 Fissural cysts of jaw
Cyst:
- globulomaxillary
- incisor canal
- median anterior maxillary
- median palatal
- nasopalatine
- palatine of papilla

Excludes: *cysts of oral soft tissues (528.4)*

526.2 Other cysts of jaws
Cyst of jaw:
- NOS
- aneurysmal

Cyst of jaw:
- hemorrhagic
- traumatic

526.3 Central giant cell (reparative) granuloma

Excludes: *peripheral giant cell granuloma (523.8)*

526.4 Inflammatory conditions
Abscess, Osteitis, Osteomyelitis (neonatal), Periostitis } of jaw (acute) (chronic) (suppurative)
Sequestrum of jaw bone

Excludes: *alveolar osteitis (526.5)*

526.5 Alveolitis of jaw
Alveolar osteitis
Dry socket

✓5th **526.8 Other specified diseases of the jaws**

526.81 Exostosis of jaw
Torus mandibularis
Torus palatinus

526.89 Other
Cherubism
Fibrous dysplasia, Latent bone cyst, Osteoradionecrosis } of jaw(s)
Unilateral condylar hyperplasia or hypoplasia of mandible

526.9 Unspecified disease of the jaws

527 Diseases of the salivary glands

527.0 Atrophy

527.1 Hypertrophy

527.2 Sialoadenitis
Parotitis:
- NOS
- allergic
- toxic

Sialoangitis
Sialodochitis

Excludes: *epidemic or infectious parotitis (072.0-072.9)*
uveoparotid fever (135)

527.3 Abscess
➡ **CC Excl:** 527.0-527.9, 537.89, 537.9

527.4 Fistula

Excludes: *congenital fistula of salivary gland (750.24)*

➡ **CC Excl:** see Code 527.3

527.5 Sialolithiasis
Calculus, Stone } of salivary gland or duct
Sialodocholithiasis

527.6 Mucocele
Mucous:
- extravasation cyst of salivary gland
- retention cyst of salivary gland

Ranula

527.7 Disturbance of salivary secretion
Hyposecretion
Ptyalism
Sialorrhea
Xerostomia

527.8 Other specified diseases of the salivary glands
Benign lymphoepithelial lesion of salivary gland
Sialectasia
Sialosis
Stenosis, Stricture } of salivary duct

527.9 Unspecified disease of the salivary glands

528 Diseases of the oral soft tissues, excluding lesions specific for gingiva and tongue

528.0 Stomatitis

Stomatitis:
- NOS
- ulcerative

Vesicular stomatitis

Excludes: *stomatitis:*
- *acute necrotizing ulcerative (101)*
- *aphthous (528.2)*
- *gangrenous (528.1)*
- *herpetic (054.2)*
- *Vincent's (101)*

528.1 Cancrum oris

Gangrenous stomatitis
Noma

528.2 Oral aphthae

Aphthous stomatitis
Canker sore
Periadenitis mucosa necrotica recurrens
Recurrent aphthous ulcer
Stomatitis herpetiformis

Excludes: *herpetic stomatitis (054.2)*

528.3 Cellulitis and abscess

Cellulitis of mouth (floor)
Ludwig's angina
Oral fistula

Excludes: *abscess of tongue (529.0)*
cellulitis or abscess of lip (528.5)
fistula (of):
- *dental (522.7)*
- *lip (528.5)*

gingivitis (523.0-523.1)

➡ **CC Excl:** 528.0, 528.3, 529.0, 529.2

528.4 Cysts

Dermoid cyst, Epidermoid cyst, Epstein's pearl, Lymphoepithelial cyst, Nasoalveolar cyst, Nasolabial cyst } of mouth

Excludes: *cyst:*
- *gingiva (523.8)*
- *tongue (529.8)*

528.5 Diseases of lips

Abscess, Cellulitis, Fistula, Hypertrophy } of lip(s)

Cheilitis:
- NOS
- angular

Cheilodynia
Cheilosis

Excludes: *actinic cheilitis (692.79)*
congenital fistula of lip (750.25)
leukoplakia of lips (528.6)

➡ **AHA Coding Clinic:** S-O, '86, 10

528.6 Leukoplakia of oral mucosa, including tongue

Leukokeratosis of oral mucosa
Leukoplakia of:
- gingiva
- lips
- tongue

Excludes: *carcinoma in situ (230.0, 232.0)*
leukokeratosis nicotina palati (528.7)

528.7 Other disturbances of oral epithelium, including tongue

Erythroplakia, Focal epithelial hyperplasia, Leukoedema } of mouth or tongue
Leukokeratosis nicotina palati

Excludes: *carcinoma in situ (230.0, 232.0)*
leukokeratosis NOS (702)

528.8 Oral submucosal fibrosis, including of tongue

528.9 Other and unspecified diseases of the oral soft tissues

Cheek and lip biting
Denture sore mouth
Denture stomatitis
Melanoplakia
Papillary hyperplasia of palate
Eosinophilic granuloma, Irritative hyperplasia, Pyogeumnic granuloma, Ulcer (traumatic) } of oral mucosa

529 Diseases and other conditions of the tongue

529.0 Glossitis

Abscess, Ulceration (traumatic) } of tongue

Excludes: *glossitis:*
- *benign migratory (529.1)*
- *Hunter's (529.4)*
- *median rhomboid (529.2)*
- *Moeller's (529.4)*

529.1 Geographic tongue

Benign migratory glossitis
Glossitis areata exfoliativa

529.2 Median rhomboid glossitis

529.3 Hypertrophy of tongue papillae

Black hairy tongue
Coated tongue
Hypertrophy of foliate papillae
Lingua villosa nigra

529.4 Atrophy of tongue papillae

Bald tongue
Glazed tongue
Glossitis:
- Hunter's
- Moeller's

Glossodynia exfoliativa
Smooth atrophic tongue

529.5 Plicated tongue

Fissured, Furrowed, Scrotal } tongue

Excludes: *fissure of tongue, congenital (750.13)*

529.6 Glossodynia

Glossopyrosis
Painful tongue

Excludes: *glossodynia exfoliativa (529.4)*

529.8 Other specified conditions of the tongue

Atrophy, Crenated, Enlargement, Hypertrophy } (of) tongue
Glossocele
Glossoptosis

Excludes: *erythroplasia of tongue (528.7)*
leukoplakia of tongue (528.6)
macroglossia (congenital) (750.15)
microglossia (congenital) (750.16)
oral submucosal fibrosis (528.8)

529.9 Unspecified condition of the tongue

DISEASES OF ESOPHAGUS, STOMACH, AND DUODENUM (530-537)

530 Diseases of esophagus

Excludes: *esophageal varices (456.0-456.2)*

530.0 Achalasia and cardiospasm

Achalasia (of cardia)
Aperistalsis of esophagus
Megaesophagus

Excludes: *congenital cardiospasm (750.7)*

✓5th **530.1 Esophagitis**

Abscess of esophagus
Esophagitis:
- NOS
- chemical
- peptic
- postoperative
- regurgitant

Use additional E code to identify cause if induced by chemical

Excludes: *tuberculous esophagitis (017.8)*

530.10 Esophagitis, unspecified

530.11 Reflux esophagitis

➡ **AHA Coding Clinic:** 4Q, '95, 82

530.19 Other esophagitis

530.2 Ulcer of esophagus

Ulcer of esophagus:
- fungal
- peptic

Ulcer of esophagus due to ingestion of:
- aspirin
- chemicals
- medicines

Use additional E code to identify cause if induced by chemical or drug

530.3 Stricture and stenosis of esophagus

Compression of esophagus
Obstruction of esophagus

Excludes: *congenital stricture of esophagus (750.3)*

➡ **AHA Coding Clinic:** 2Q, '97, 3; 1Q, '88, 13

530.4 Perforation of esophagus

Rupture of esophagus

Excludes: *traumatic perforation of esophagus (862.22, 862.32, 874.4-874.5)*

➡ **CC Excl:** 530.4, 530.7-530.9

530.5 Dyskinesia of esophagus

Corkscrew esophagus
Curling esophagus
Esophagospasm
Spasm of esophagus

Excludes: *cardiospasm (530.0)*

➡ **AHA Coding Clinic:** 1Q, '88, 13; N-D, '84, 19

530.6 Diverticulum of esophagus, acquired

Diverticulum, acquired:
- epiphrenic
- pharyngoesophageal
- pulsion
- subdiaphragmatic
- traction
- Zenker's (hypopharyngeal)

Esophageal pouch, acquired
Esophagocele, acquired

Excludes: *congenital diverticulum of esophagus (750.4)*

➡ **AHA Coding Clinic:** J-F, '85, 3

530.7 Gastroesophageal laceration-hemorrhage syndrome

Mallory-Weiss syndrome

➡ **CC Excl:** 251.5, 456.0, 530.2, 530.4, 530.7-530.9, 531.00-531.91, 532.00-532.91, 533.00-533.91, 534.00-534.91, 535.01, 535.11, 535.21, 535.31, 535.41, 535.51, 535.61, 537.83, 562.02-562.03, 562.12-562.13, 569.3, 569.85, 578.0-578.9

✓5th **530.8 Other specified disorders of esophagus**

530.81 Esophageal reflux

Gastroesophageal reflux

Excludes: *reflux esophagitis (530.11)*

530.82 Esophageal hemorrhage

Excludes: *hemorrhage due to esophageal varices (456.0-456.2)*

➡ **CC Excl:** 251.5, 456.0, 456.20, 459.89-459.9, 530.2, 530.7, 530.82, 531.00-531.21, 531.30-531.31, 531.40-531.91, 532.00-532.91, 533.00-533.91, 534.00-534.51, 534.61, 534.70-534.91, 535.01-535.11, 535.21, 535.31, 535.41, 535.51, 535.61, 537.83, 562.02-562.03, 562.12-562.13, 569.3, 569.85, 578.0-578.9, 634.60

530.83 Esophageal leukoplakia

530.84 Tracheoesophageal fistula

Excludes: *congenital tracheoesophageal fistula (750.3)*

➡ **CC Excl:** 530.4, 530.7, 530.81, 530.83-530.9

530.89 Other

Excludes: *Paterson-Kelly syndrome (280.8)*

530.9 Unspecified disorder of esophagus

531 Gastric ulcer

Includes: ulcer (peptic):
- prepyloric
- pylorus
- stomach

Use additional E code to identify drug if drug-induced

Excludes: *peptic ulcer NOS (533.0-533.9)*

The following fifth-digit subclassification is for use with category 531:

0 without mention of obstruction
1 with obstruction

➡ **AHA Coding Clinic:** 1Q, '91, 15; 4Q, '90, 27

✓5th **531.0** Acute with hemorrhage

➡ **CC Excl:** 251.5, 456.0, 530.2, 530.7, 530.82, 531.00-531.91, 532.00-532.91, 533.00-533.91, 534.00-534.91, 535.01, 535.11, 535.21, 535.31, 535.41, 535.51, 535.61, 537.83, 537.89, 537.9, 562.02-562.03, 562.12-562.13, 569.3, 569.85, 578.0-578.9

➡ **AHA Coding Clinic:** N-D, '84, 15

DRG 174: For code 531.00

✓5th **531.1** Acute with perforation

➡ **CC Excl:** see Code 531.0

✓5th **531.2** Acute with hemorrhage and perforation

➡ **CC Excl:** see Code 531.0

✓5th [4] **531.3** Acute without mention of hemorrhage or perforation

➡ **CC Excl: For code 531.31:** see code 531.0

✓5th **531.4** Chronic or unspecified with hemorrhage

➡ **CC Excl:** see Code 531.0

➡ **AHA Coding Clinic:** 4Q, '90, 22

DRG 174: For code 531.40

✓5th **531.5** Chronic or unspecified with perforation

➡ **CC Excl:** see Code 531.0

✓5th **531.6** Chronic or unspecified with hemorrhage and perforation

➡ **CC Excl:** see Code 531.0

✓5th [4] **531.7** Chronic without mention of hemorrhage or perforation

➡ **CC Excl: For code 531.71:** see Code 531.0

✓5th [4] **531.9** Unspecified as acute or chronic, without mention of hemorrhage or perforation

➡ **CC Excl: For code 531.91:** see Code 531.0

532 Duodenal ulcer

Includes: erosion (acute) of duodenum
ulcer (peptic):
- duodenum
- postpyloric

Use additional E code to identify drug if drug-induced

Excludes: *peptic ulcer NOS (533.0-533.9)*

The following fifth-digit subclassification is for use with category 532:

0 without mention of obstruction
1 with obstruction

➡ **AHA Coding Clinic:** 4Q, '90, 27

✓5th **532.0** Acute with hemorrhage

➡ **CC Excl:** 251.5, 456.0, 530.2, 530.7, 530.82, 531.00-531.91, 532.00-532.91, 533.00-533.91, 534.00-534.91, 535.01, 535.11, 535.21, 535.31, 535.41, 535.51, 535.61, 537.3, 537.83, 537.89, 537.9, 562.02-562.03, 562.12-562.13, 569.3, 569.85, 578.0-578.9

➡ **AHA Coding Clinic:** 4Q, '90, 22

DRG 174: For code 532.00

✓5th **532.1** Acute with perforation

➡ **CC Excl:** see Code 532.0

✓5th **532.2** Acute with hemorrhage and perforation

➡ **CC Excl:** see Code 532.0

[4] CC Coding = 1

✓5th [4] **532.3** **Acute without mention of hemorrhage or perforation**
➡ **CC Excl: For code 532.31:** see Code 532.0

✓5th **532.4** **Chronic or unspecified with hemorrhage**
➡ **CC Excl:** see Code 532.0
DRG 174: For code 532.40

✓5th **532.5** **Chronic or unspecified with perforation**
➡ **CC Excl:** see Code 532.0

✓5th **532.6** **Chronic or unspecified with hemorrhage and perforation**
➡ **CC Excl:** see Code 532.0

✓5th [4] **532.7** **Chronic without mention of hemorrhage or perforation**
➡ **CC Excl: For code 532.71:** see Code 532.0

✓5th [4] **532.9** **Unspecified as acute or chronic, without mention of hemorrhage or perforation**
➡ **CC Excl: For code 532.91:** see Code 532.0

533 Peptic ulcer, site unspecified

Includes: gastroduodenal ulcer NOS
peptic ulcer NOS
stress ulcer NOS

Use additional E code to identify drug if drug-induced

Excludes: *peptic ulcer:*
duodenal (532.0-532.9)
gastric (531.0-531.9)

The following fifth-digit subclassification is for use with category 533:

0 without mention of obstruction
1 with obstruction

➡ **AHA Coding Clinic:** 4Q, '90, 27

✓5th **533.0** **Acute with hemorrhage**
➡ **CC Excl:** see Code 532.0

✓5th **533.1** **Acute with perforation**
➡ **CC Excl:** see Code 532.0

✓5th **533.2** **Acute with hemorrhage and perforation**
➡ **CC Excl:** see Code 532.0

✓5th [4] **533.3** **Acute without mention of hemorrhage and perforation**
➡ **CC Excl: For code 533.31:** see Code 532.0

✓5th **533.4** **Chronic or unspecified with hemorrhage**
➡ **CC Excl:** see Code 532.0

✓5th **533.5** **Chronic or unspecified with perforation**
➡ **CC Excl:** see Code 532.0

✓5th **533.6** **Chronic or unspecified with hemorrhage and perforation**
➡ **CC Excl:** see Code 532.0

✓5th [4] **533.7** **Chronic without mention of hemorrhage or perforation**
➡ **CC Excl: For code 533.71:** see Code 532.0
➡ **AHA Coding Clinic:** 2Q, '89, 16

✓5th [4] **533.9** **Unspecified as acute or chronic, without mention of hemorrhage or perforation**
➡ **CC Excl: For code 533.91:** see Code 532.0

534 Gastrojejunal ulcer

Includes: ulcer (peptic) or erosion:
anastomotic
gastrocolic
gastrointestinal
gastrojejunal
jejunal
marginal
stomal

Excludes: *primary ulcer of small intestine (569.82)*

The following fifth-digit subclassification is for use with category 534:

0 without mention of obstruction
1 with obstruction

➡ **AHA Coding Clinic:** 4Q, '90, 27

✓5th **534.0** **Acute with hemorrhage**
➡ **CC Excl:** 251.5, 456.0, 530.2, 530.7, 530.82, 531.00-531.91, 532.00-532.91, 533.00-533.91, 534.00-534.91, 535.01, 535.11, 535.21, 535.31, 535.41, 535.51, 535.61, 537.83, 537.89, 537.9, 562.02-562.03, 562.12-562.13, 569.3, 569.85, 578.0-578.9

✓5th **534.1** **Acute with perforation**
➡ **CC Excl:** see Code 534.0

✓5th **534.2** **Acute with hemorrhage and perforation**
➡ **CC Excl:** see Code 534.0

✓5th [4] **534.3** **Acute without mention of hemorrhage or perforation**
➡ **CC Excl: For code 534.31:** see Code 534.0

✓5th **534.4** **Chronic or unspecified with hemorrhage**
➡ **CC Excl:** see Code 534.0

[4] CC Coding = 1

✓5th **534.5 Chronic or unspecified with perforation**

➡ **CC Excl:** see Code 534.0

✓5th **534.6 Chronic or unspecified with hemorrhage and perforation**

➡ **CC Excl:** see Code 534.0

✓5th [4] **534.7 Chronic without mention of hemorrhage or perforation**

➡ **CC Excl: For code 534.71:** see Code 534.0

✓5th [4] **534.9 Unspecified as acute or chronic, without mention of hemorrhage or perforation**

➡ **CC Excl: For code 534.91:** see Code 534.0

535 Gastritis and duodenitis

The following fifth-digit subclassification is for use with category 535:

0 **without mention of hemorrhage**
1 **with hemorrhage**

➡ **AHA Coding Clinic:** 4Q, '91, 25

✓5th [4] **535.0 Acute gastritis**

➡ **CC Excl: For code 535.01:** 251.5, 456.0, 530.2, 530.7, 530.82, 531.00-531.91, 532.00-532.91, 533.00-533.91, 534.00-534.91, 535.01, 535.11, 535.21, 535.31, 535.41, 535.51, 535.61, 537.83, 562.02-562.03, 562.12-562.13, 569.3, 569.85, 578.0-578.9

➡ **AHA Coding Clinic:** 2Q, '92, 8; N-D, '86, 9

✓5th [4] **535.1 Atrophic gastritis**

Gastritis:
atrophic-hyperplastic
chronic (atrophic)

➡ **CC Excl: For code 535.11:** see Code 535.01

✓5th [4] **535.2 Gastric mucosal hypertrophy**

Hypertrophic gastritis

➡ **CC Excl: For code 535.21:** see Code 535.01

✓5th [4] **535.3 Alcoholic gastritis**

➡ **CC Excl: For code 535.31:** see Code 535.01

✓5th [4] **535.4 Other specified gastritis**

Gastritis:
allergic
bile induced
irritant
superficial
toxic

➡ **CC Excl: For code 535.41:** see Code 535.01

➡ **AHA Coding Clinic:** 4Q, '90, 27

✓5th [4] **535.5 Unspecified gastritis and gastroduodenitis**

➡ **CC Excl: For code 535.51:** see Code 535.01

✓5th [4] **535.6 Duodenitis**

➡ **CC Excl: For code 535.61:** see Code 535.01

536 Disorders of function of stomach

Excludes: *functional disorders of stomach specified as psychogenic (306.4)*

536.0 Achlorhydria

536.1 Acute dilatation of stomach

Acute distention of stomach

➡ **CC Excl:** 536.1

536.2 Persistent vomiting

Habit vomiting
Persistent vomiting [not of pregnancy]
Uncontrollable vomiting

Excludes: *excessive vomiting in pregnancy (643.0-643.9)*
vomiting NOS (787.0)

536.3 Gastroparesis

➡ **AHA Coding Clinic:** 4Q, '94, 42

✓5th **536.4 Gastrostomy complications**

536.40 Gastrostomy complication, unspecified

➡ **CC Excl:** 536.40-536.49, 997.4, 997.91, 997.99, 998.81-998.9

536.41 Infection of gastrostomy

Use additional code to specify type of infection, such as:
abscess or cellulitis of abdomen (682.2)
septicemia (038.0-038.9)
Use additional code to identify organism (041.00-041.9)

➡ **CC Excl:** see Code 536.40

536.42 Mechanical complication of gastrostomy

➡ **CC Excl:** see Code 536.40

536.49 Other gastrostomy complications

➡ **CC Excl:** see Code 536.40

536.8 Dyspepsia and other specified disorders of function of stomach

Achylia gastrica
Hourglass contraction of stomach
Hyperacidity
Hyperchlorhydria
Hypochlorhydria
Indigestion

Excludes: *achlorhydria (536.0)*
heartburn (787.1)

➡ **AHA Coding Clinic:** 2Q, '93, 6; 2Q, '89, 16; N-D, '84, 9

536.9 Unspecified functional disorder of stomach

Functional gastrointestinal:
disorder
disturbance
irritation

537 Other disorders of stomach and duodenum

537.0 Acquired hypertrophic pyloric stenosis

Constriction, Obstruction, Stricture } of pylorus, acquired or adult

Excludes: *congenital or infantile pyloric stenosis (750.5)*

➡ **CC Excl:** 536.3-536.9, 537.0, 537.3, 750.5, 750.8-750.9, 751.1, 751.5

➡ **AHA Coding Clinic:** J-F, '85, 14

[4] CC Coding = 1

537.1 Gastric diverticulum

Excludes: *congenital diverticulum of stomach (750.7)*

➡ **AHA Coding Clinic:** J-F, '85, 4

537.2 Chronic duodenal ileus

537.3 Other obstruction of duodenum

Cicatrix, Stenosis, Stricture, Volvulus } of duodenum

Excludes: *congenital obstruction of duodenum (751.1)*

➡ **CC Excl:** 537.3, 750.8-750.9, 751.1, 751.5

537.4 Fistula of stomach or duodenum

Gastrocolic fistula
Gastrojejunocolic fistula

➡ **CC Excl:** 537.4, 750.9, 751.5

537.5 Gastroptosis

537.6 Hourglass stricture or stenosis of stomach

Cascade stomach

Excludes: *congenital hourglass stomach (750.7)*
hourglass contraction of stomach (536.8)

✓5th **537.8 Other specified disorders of stomach and duodenum**

➡ **AHA Coding Clinic:** 4Q, '91, 25

537.81 Pylorospasm

Excludes: *congenital pylorospasm (750.5)*

537.82 Angiodysplasia of stomach and duodenum without mention of hemorrhage

➡ **AHA Coding Clinic:** 3Q, '96, 10; 4Q, '90, 4

537.83 Angiodysplasia of stomach and duodenum with hemorrhage

➡ **CC Excl:** 251.5, 456.0, 530.2, 530.7, 530.82, 531.00-531.91, 532.00-532.91, 533.00-533.91, 534.00-534.91, 535.01, 535.11, 535.21, 535.31, 535.41, 535.51, 535.61, 537.83, 562.02-562.03, 562.12-562.13, 569.3, 569.85, 578.0-578.9

537.89 Other

Gastric or duodenal:
- prolapse
- rupture

Intestinal metaplasia of gastric mucosa
Passive congestion of stomach

Excludes: *diverticula of duodenum (562.00-562.01)*
gastrointestinal hemorrhage (578.0-578.9)

537.9 Unspecified disorder of stomach and duodenum

APPENDICITIS (540-543)

540 Acute appendicitis

➡ **AHA Coding Clinic:** N-D, '84, 19

540.0 With generalized peritonitis

Appendicitis (acute):
- fulminating
- gangrenous
- obstructive

Cecitis (acute)
Rupture of appendix

} with:
- perforation
- peritonitis (generalized)
- rupture

Excludes: *acute appendicitis with peritoneal abscess (540.1)*

➡ **CC Excl:** 537.89, 537.9, 540.0-540.9, 541-542, 543.0, 543.9

540.1 With peritoneal abscess

Abscess of appendix
With generalized peritonitis

➡ **CC Excl:** see Code 540.0

540.9 Without mention of peritonitis

Acute:
- appendicitis:
  - fulminating
  - gangrenous
  - inflamed
  - obstructive
- cecitis

} without mention of perforation, peritonitis, or rupture

➡ **CC Excl:** see Code 540.0

➡ **AHA Coding Clinic:** 4Q, '97, 52

541 Appendicitis, unqualified

➡ **AHA Coding Clinic:** 2Q, '90, 26

542 Other appendicitis

Appendicitis:
- chronic
- recurrent

Appendicitis:
- relapsing
- subacute

Excludes: *hyperplasia (lymphoid) of appendix (543.0)*

543 Other diseases of appendix

543.0 Hyperplasia of appendix (lymphoid)

543.9 Other and unspecified diseases of appendix

Appendicular or appendiceal:
colic
concretion
fistula
Diverticulum, Fecalith, Intussusception, Mucocele, Stercolith } of appendix

HERNIA OF ABDOMINAL CAVITY (550-553)

Includes: hernia:
acquired
congenital, except diaphragmatic or hiatal

550 Inguinal hernia

Includes: bubonocele
inguinal hernia (direct) (double) (indirect) (oblique) (sliding)
scrotal hernia

The following fifth-digit subclassification is for use with category 550:

0 **unilateral or unspecified (not specified as recurrent)**
Unilateral NOS
1 **unilateral or unspecified, recurrent**
2 **bilateral (not specified as recurrent)**
Bilateral NOS
3 **bilateral, recurrent**

✓5th **550.0 Inguinal hernia, with gangrene**
Inguinal hernia with gangrene (and obstruction)
➡ **CC Excl:** 537.89, 537.9, 550.00-550.93, 552.8-552.9, 553.8-553.9

✓5th **550.1 Inguinal hernia, with obstruction, without mention of gangrene**
Inguinal hernia with mention of incarceration, irreducibility, or strangulation
➡ **CC Excl:** see Code 550.0

✓5th **550.9 Inguinal hernia, without mention of obstruction or gangrene**
Inguinal hernia NOS

551 Other hernia of abdominal cavity, with gangrene

Includes: that with gangrene (and obstruction)

✓5th **551.0 Femoral hernia with gangrene**

551.00 Unilateral or unspecified (not specified as recurrent)
Femoral hernia NOS with gangrene
➡ **CC Excl:** 537.89, 537.9, 551.00-551.03, 552.8-552.9, 553.00-553.03, 553.8-553.9

551.01 Unilateral or unspecified, recurrent
➡ **CC Excl:** see Code 551.00

551.02 Bilateral (not specified as recurrent)
➡ **CC Excl:** see Code 551.00

551.03 Bilateral, recurrent
➡ **CC Excl:** see Code 551.00

551.1 Umbilical hernia with gangrene
Parumbilical hernia specified as gangrenous
➡ **CC Excl:** 537.89, 537.9, 551.1-551.29, 552.1-552.29, 552.8-552.9, 553.1-553.29, 553.8-553.9

✓5th **551.2 Ventral hernia with gangrene**

551.20 Ventral, unspecified, with gangrene
➡ **CC Excl:** see Code 551.1

551.21 Incisional, with gangrene
Hernia:
postoperative, recurrent, ventral } specified as gangrenous
➡ **CC Excl:** see Code 551.1

551.29 Other
Epigastric hernia specified as gangrenous
➡ **CC Excl:** see Code 551.1

551.3 Diaphragmatic hernia with gangrene
Hernia:
hiatal (esophageal) (sliding), paraesophageal, Thoracic stomach } specified as gangrenous

Excludes: *congenital diaphragmatic hernia (756.6)*

➡ **CC Excl:** 551.3, 552.3, 552.8-552.9, 553.3, 553.8-553.9

551.8 Hernia of other specified sites, with gangrene
Any condition classifiable to 553.8 if specified as gangrenous
➡ **CC Excl:** 537.89, 537.9, 550.00-550.93, 551.00-551.9, 552.00-552.9, 553.00-553.9

551.9 Hernia of unspecified site, with gangrene
Any condition classifiable to 553.9 if specified as gangrenous
➡ **CC Excl:** see Code 551.8

552 Other hernia of abdominal cavity, with obstruction, but without mention of gangrene

Excludes: *that with mention of gangrene (551.0-551.9)*

✓5th **552.0 Femoral hernia with obstruction**
Femoral hernia specified as incarcerated, irreducible, strangulated, or causing obstruction

552.00 Unilateral or unspecified (not specified as recurrent)
➡ **CC Excl:** 537.89, 537.9, 551.00-551.03, 552.00-552.03, 552.8-552.9, 553.00-553.03, 553.8-553.9

552.01 Unilateral or unspecified, recurrent
➡ **CC Excl:** see Code 552.00

552.02 Bilateral (not specified as recurrent)
➡ **CC Excl:** see Code 552.00

552.03 Bilateral, recurrent
➡ **CC Excl:** see Code 552.00

552.1 Umbilical hernia with obstruction
Parumbilical hernia specified as incarcerated, irreducible, strangulated, or causing obstruction
➡ **CC Excl:** 551.1-551.29, 552.1-552.29, 552.8-552.9, 553.8-553.9

✓5th **552.2 Ventral hernia with obstruction**
Ventral hernia specified as incarcerated, irreducible, strangulated, or causing obstruction

552.20 Ventral, unspecified, with obstruction
➡ **CC Excl:** see Code 552.1

552.21 Incisional, with obstruction
Hernia:
postoperative } specified as incarcerated, irreducible, strangulated, or causing obstruction
recurrent, ventral }
➡ **CC Excl:** see Code 552.1

552.29 Other
Epigastric hernia specified as incarcerated, irreducible, strangulated, or causing obstruction
➡ **CC Excl:** see Code 552.1

552.3 Diaphragmatic hernia with obstruction
Hernia:
hiatal (esophageal) (sliding) } specified as incarcerated, irreducible, strangulated, or causing obstruction
paraesophageal }
Thoracic stomach }

Excludes: *congenital diaphragmatic hernia (756.6)*
➡ **CC Excl:** 551.3, 552.3-552.9, 553.3-553.9

552.8 Hernia of other specified sites, with obstruction
Any condition classifiable to 553.8 if specified as incarcerated, irreducible, strangulated, or causing obstruction
➡ **CC Excl:** 550.00-550.93, 551.00-551.9, 552.00-552.9, 553.00-553.9

552.9 Hernia of unspecified site, with obstruction
Any condition classifiable to 553.9 if specified as incarcerated, irreducible, strangulated, or causing obstruction
➡ **CC Excl:** see Code 552.8

553 Other hernia of abdominal cavity without mention of obstruction or gangrene

Excludes: *the listed conditions with mention of:*
gangrene (and obstruction) (551.0-551.9)
obstruction (552.0-552.9)

✓5th **553.0 Femoral hernia**

553.00 Unilateral or unspecified (not specified as recurrent)
Femoral hernia NOS

553.01 Unilateral or unspecified, recurrent

553.02 Bilateral (not specified as recurrent)

553.03 Bilateral, recurrent

553.1 Umbilical hernia
Parumbilical hernia

✓5th **553.2 Ventral hernia**

553.20 Ventral, unspecified
➡ **AHA Coding Clinic:** 3Q, '96, 15

553.21 Incisional
Hernia:
postoperative
recurrent, ventral

553.29 Other
Hernia:
epigastric
spigelian

553.3 Diaphragmatic hernia

Hernia:
hiatal (esophageal) (sliding)
paraesophageal
Thoracic stomach

Excludes: *congenital:*
diaphragmatic hernia (756.6)
hiatal hernia (750.6)
esophagocele (530.6)

553.8 Hernia of other specified sites

Hernia:
ischiatic
ischiorectal
lumbar
obturator
pudendal
retroperitoneal
sciatic
Other abdominal hernia of specified site

Excludes: *vaginal enterocele (618.6)*

553.9 Hernia of unspecified site

Enterocele
Epiplocele
Hernia:
NOS
interstitial
intestinal
intra-abdominal
Rupture (nontraumatic)
Sarcoepiplocele

NONINFECTIOUS ENTERITIS AND COLITIS (555-558)

555 Regional enteritis

Includes: Crohn's disease
Granulomatous enteritis

Excludes: *ulcerative colitis (556)*

555.0 Small intestine

Ileitis:
regional
segmental
terminal
Regional enteritis or Crohn's disease of:
duodenum
ileum
jejunum

555.1 Large intestine

Colitis:
granulomatous
regional
transmural
Regional enteritis or Crohn's disease of:
colon
large bowel
rectum

555.2 Small intestine with large intestine

Regional ileocolitis

555.9 Unspecified site

Crohn's disease NOS
Regional enteritis NOS

➡ **AHA Coding Clinic:** 4Q, '97, 42; 2Q, '97, 3

556 Ulcerative colitis

556.0 Ulcerative (chronic) enterocolitis

556.1 Ulcerative (chronic) ileocolitis

556.2 Ulcerative (chronic) proctitis

556.3 Ulcerative (chronic) proctosigmoiditis

556.4 Pseudopolyposis of colon

556.5 Left-sided ulcerative (chronic) colitis

556.6 Universal ulcerative (chronic) colitis

Pancolitis

556.8 Other ulcerative colitis

556.9 Ulcerative colitis, unspecified

Ulcerative enteritis NOS

557 Vascular insufficiency of intestine

Excludes: *necrotizing enterocolitis of the newborn (777.5)*

557.0 Acute vascular insufficiency of intestine

Acute:
hemorrhagic enterocolitis
ischemic colitis, enteritis, or enterocolitis
massive necrosis of intestine
Bowel infarction
Embolism of mesenteric artery
Fulminant enterocolitis
Hemorrhagic necrosis of intestine
Infarction of appendices epiploicae
Intestinal gangrene
Intestinal infarction (acute) (agnogenic) (hemorrhagic) (nonocclusive)
Mesenteric infarction (embolic) (thrombotic)
Necrosis of intestine
Terminal hemorrhagic enteropathy
Thrombosis of mesenteric artery

➡ **CC Excl:** 557.0-557.1

DRG 188

557.1 Chronic vascular insufficiency of intestine

Angina, abdominal
Chronic ischemic colitis, enteritis, or enterocolitis
Ischemic stricture of intestine
Mesenteric:
angina
artery syndrome (superior)
vascular insufficiency

➡ **AHA Coding Clinic:** N-D, '86, 11; N-D, '84, 7

557.9 Unspecified vascular insufficiency of intestine

Alimentary pain due to vascular insufficiency
Ischemic colitis, enteritis, or enterocolitis NOS

DRG 188

558 Other noninfectious gastroenteritis and colitis

Excludes: *infectious:*
colitis, enteritis, or gastroenteritis (009.0-009.1)
diarrhea (009.2-009.3)

558.1 Gastroenteritis and colitis due to radiation

Radiation enterocolitis

➡ **CC Excl:** 558.1

558.2 Toxic gastroenteritis and colitis

Use additional E code to identify cause

➡ **CC Excl:** 558.2

558.9 Other and unspecified noninfectious gastroenteritis and colitis

Colitis, Enteritis, Gastroenteritis, Ileitis, Jejunitis, Sigmoiditis } NOS, allergic dietetic, or noninfectious

➡ **AHA Coding Clinic:** N-D, '87, 7

OTHER DISEASES OF INTESTINES AND PERITONEUM (560-569)

560 Intestinal obstruction without mention of hernia

Excludes: *duodenum (537.2-537.3)*
inguinal hernia with obstruction (550.1)
intestinal obstruction complicating hernia (552.0-552.9)
mesenteric:
embolism (557.0)
infarction (557.0)
thrombosis (557.0)
neonatal intestinal obstruction (277.01, 777.1-777.2, 777.4)

560.0 Intussusception

Intussusception (colon) (intestine) (rectum)
Invagination of intestine or colon

Excludes: *intussusception of appendix (543.9)*

➡ **CC Excl:** 560.0-560.9, 569.89, 569.9

560.1 Paralytic ileus

Adynamic ileus
Ileus (of intestine) (of bowel) (of colon)
Paralysis of intestine or colon

Excludes: *gallstone ileus (560.31)*

➡ **CC Excl:** see Code 560.0

➡ **AHA Coding Clinic:** J-F, '87, 13

✔ **St. Anthony's Clinical Coder:** see Chapter 5

560.2 Volvulus

Knotting, Strangulation, Torsion, Twist } of intestine, bowel, or colon

➡ **CC Excl:** see Code 560.0

✓5th **560.3 Impaction of intestine**

560.30 Impaction of intestine, unspecified

Impaction of colon

➡ **CC Excl:** see Code 560.0

560.31 Gallstone ileus

Obstruction of intestine by gallstone

➡ **CC Excl:** see Code 560.0

560.39 Other

Concretion of intestine
Enterolith
Fecal impaction

➡ **CC Excl:** see Code 560.0

✓5th **560.8 Other specified intestinal obstruction**

560.81 Intestinal or peritoneal adhesions with obstruction (postoperative) (postinfection)

Excludes: *adhesions without obstruction (568.0)*

➡ **CC Excl:** see Code 560.0

➡ **AHA Coding Clinic:** 4Q, '95, 55; 3Q, '95, 6; N-D, '87, 9

560.89 Other

Mural thickening causing obstruction

Excludes: *ischemic stricture of intestine (557.1)*

➡ **CC Excl:** see Code 560.0

➡ **AHA Coding Clinic:** 2Q, '97, 3; 1Q, '88, 6

560.9 Unspecified intestinal obstruction

Enterostenosis
Obstruction, Occlusion, Stenosis, Stricture } of intestine or colon

Excludes: *congenital stricture or stenosis of intestine (751.1-751.2)*

➡ **CC Excl:** see Code 560.0

562 Diverticula of intestine

Use additional code to identify any associated:
peritonitis (567.0-567.9)

Excludes: *congenital diverticulum of colon (751.5)*
diverticulum of appendix (543.9)
Meckel's diverticulum (751.0)

➡ **AHA Coding Clinic:** 4Q, '91, 25; J-F, '85, 1

✓5th **562.0 Small intestine**

562.00 **Diverticulosis of small intestine (without mention of hemorrhage)**
Diverticulosis:
duodenum, ileum, jejunum } without mention of diverticulitis

562.01 **Diverticulitis of small intestine (without mention of hemorrhage)**
Diverticulitis (with diverticulosis):
duodenum
ileum
jejunum
small intestine

562.02 **Diverticulosis of small intestine with hemorrhage**
➡ **CC Excl:** 251.5, 456.0, 530.2, 530.7, 530.82, 531.00-531.91, 532.00-532.91, 533.00-533.91, 534.00-534.91, 535.01, 535.11, 535.21, 535.31, 535.41, 535.51, 535.61, 537.83, 562.02-562.03, 562.12-562.13, 569.3, 569.85, 578.0-578.9

562.03 **Diverticulitis of small intestine with hemorrhage**
➡ **CC Excl:** see Code 562.02

✓5th **562.1** **Colon**

562.10 **Diverticulosis of colon (without mention of hemorrhage)**
Diverticulosis:
NOS
intestine (large)
Diverticular disease (colon)
} without mention of diverticulitis
➡ **AHA Coding Clinic:** 4Q, '90, 21

562.11 **Diverticulitis of colon (without mention of hemorrhage)**
Diverticulitis (with diverticulosis):
NOS
colon
intestine (large)
➡ **AHA Coding Clinic:** 1Q, '96, 14

562.12 **Diverticulosis of colon with hemorrhage**
➡ **CC Excl:** see Code 562.02
DRG 174

562.13 **Diverticulitis of colon with hemorrhage**
➡ **CC Excl:** see Code 562.02

564 Functional digestive disorders, not elsewhere classified

Excludes: *functional disorders of stomach (536.0-536.9)*
those specified as psychogenic (306.4)

564.0 **Constipation**

564.1 **Irritable colon**
Colitis:
adaptive
membranous
mucous
Enterospasm
Irritable bowel syndrome
Spastic colon
➡ **AHA Coding Clinic:** 1Q, '88, 6

564.2 **Postgastric surgery syndromes**
Dumping syndrome
Jejunal syndrome
Postgastrectomy syndrome
Postvagotomy syndrome

Excludes: *malnutrition following gastrointestinal surgery (579.3)*
postgastrojejunostomy ulcer (534.0-534.9)
➡ **AHA Coding Clinic:** 1Q, '95, 11

564.3 **Vomiting following gastrointestinal surgery**
Vomiting (bilious) following gastrointestinal surgery

564.4 **Other postoperative functional disorders**
Diarrhea following gastrointestinal surgery

Excludes: *colostomy and enterostomy complications (569.60-569.69)*

564.5 **Functional diarrhea**

Excludes: *diarrhea:*
NOS (787.91)
psychogenic (306.4)

564.6 **Anal spasm**
Proctalgia fugax

564.7 **Megacolon, other than Hirschsprung's**
Dilatation of colon

Excludes: *megacolon:*
congenital [Hirschsprung's] (751.3)
toxic (556)

✓5th **564.8** **Other specified functional disorders of intestine**

Excludes: *malabsorption (579.0-579.9)*
➡ **AHA Coding Clinic:** 1Q, '88, 6

564.81 **Neurogenic bowel**

564.89 **Other functional disorders of intestine**
Atony of colon

564.9 **Unspecified functional disorder of intestine**

565 Anal fissure and fistula
➡ **CC Excl:** 566

565.0 **Anal fissure**
Tear of anus, nontraumatic

Excludes: *traumatic (863.89, 863.99)*

565.1 Anal fistula

Fistula:
- anorectal
- rectal
- rectum to skin

Excludes: *fistula of rectum to internal organs — see Alphabetic Index*
ischiorectal fistula (566)
rectovaginal fistula (619.1)

566 Abscess of anal and rectal regions

Abscess:
- ischiorectal
- perianal
- perirectal

Cellulitis:
- anal
- perirectal
- rectal

Ischiorectal fistula

➡ **CC Excl:** 566

567 Peritonitis

Excludes: *peritonitis:*
- *benign paroxysmal (277.3)*
- *pelvic, female (614.5, 614.7)*
- *periodic familial (277.3)*
- *puerperal (670)*
- *with or following:*
  - *abortion (634-638 with .0, 639.0)*
  - *appendicitis (540.0-540.1)*
  - *ectopic or molar pregnancy (639.0)*

✔ **St. Anthony's Clinical Coder:** see Chapter 5

567.0 *Peritonitis in infectious diseases classified elsewhere*

Code first underlying disease

Excludes: *peritonitis:*
- *gonococcal (098.86)*
- *syphilitic (095.2)*
- *tuberculous (014.0)*

➡ **CC Excl:** 567.0-567.9, 569.89, 569.9

567.1 Pneumococcal peritonitis

➡ **CC Excl:** see Code 567.0

567.2 Other suppurative peritonitis

Abscess (of):
- abdominopelvic
- mesenteric
- omentum
- peritoneum
- retrocecal
- retroperitoneal
- subdiaphragmatic

Abscess (of):
- subhepatic
- subphrenic

Peritonitis (acute):
- general
- pelvic, male
- subphrenic
- suppurative

➡ **CC Excl:** see Code 567.0

DRG 188

567.8 Other specified peritonitis

Chronic proliferative peritonitis
Fat necrosis of peritoneum
Mesenteric saponification
Peritonitis due to:
- bile
- urine

➡ **CC Excl:** see Code 567.0

567.9 Unspecified peritonitis

Peritonitis:
- NOS
- of unspecified cause

➡ **CC Excl:** see Code 567.0

568 Other disorders of peritoneum

568.0 Peritoneal adhesions (postoperative) (postinfection)

Adhesions (of):
- abdominal (wall)
- diaphragm
- intestine
- male pelvis

Adhesions (of):
- mesenteric
- omentum
- stomach

Adhesive bands

Excludes: *adhesions:*
- *pelvic, female (614.6)*
- *with obstruction:*
  - *duodenum (537.3)*
  - *intestine (560.81)*

➡ **AHA Coding Clinic:** 4Q, '95, 55; 3Q, '95, 7; S-O, '85, 11

✓5th **568.8 Other specified disorders of peritoneum**

568.81 Hemoperitoneum (nontraumatic)

➡ **CC Excl:** 568.81

568.82 Peritoneal effusion (chronic)

Excludes: *ascites NOS (789.5)*

568.89 Other

Peritoneal:
- cyst
- granuloma

568.9 Unspecified disorder of peritoneum

569 Other disorders of intestine

569.0 Anal and rectal polyp

Anal and rectal polyp NOS

Excludes: *adenomatous anal and rectal polyp (211.4)*

569.1 Rectal prolapse

Procidentia:
- anus (sphincter)
- rectum (sphincter)

Proctoptosis

Prolapse:
- anal canal
- rectal mucosa

Excludes: *prolapsed hemorrhoids (455.2, 455.5)*

569.2 Stenosis of rectum and anus

Stricture of anus (sphincter)

569.3 Hemorrhage of rectum and anus

Excludes: *gastrointestinal bleeding NOS (578.9)*
melena (578.1)

➡ **CC Excl:** 251.5, 456.0, 530.2, 530.7, 530.82, 531.00-531.91, 532.00-532.91, 533.00-533.91, 534.00-534.91, 535.01, 535.11, 535.21, 535.31, 535.41, 535.51, 535.61, 537.83, 562.02-562.03, 562.12-562.13, 569.3, 569.85, 578.0-578.9

✓5th **569.4 Other specified disorders of rectum and anus**

569.41 Ulcer of anus and rectum

Solitary ulcer / Stercoral ulcer } of anus (sphincter) or rectum (sphincter)

569.42 Anal or rectal pain

➡ **AHA Coding Clinic:** 1Q, '96, 13

569.49 Other

Granuloma / Rupture } of rectum (sphincter)
Hypertrophy of anal papillae
Proctitis NOS

Excludes: *fistula of rectum to:*
internal organs — see Alphabetic Index
skin (565.1)
hemorrhoids (455.0-455.9)
incontinence of sphincter ani (787.6)

569.5 Abscess of intestine

Excludes: *appendiceal abscess (540.1)*

➡ **CC Excl:** 569.5

✓5th **569.6 Colostomy and enterostomy complications**

➡ **AHA Coding Clinic:** 4Q, '95, 58

569.60 Colostomy and enterostomy complication, unspecified

➡ **CC Excl:** 569.60-569.69

569.61 Infection of colostomy or enterostomy

Use additional code to specify type of infection, such as:
abscess or cellulitis of abdomen (682.2)
septicemia (038.0-038.9)

Use additional code to identify organism (041.00-041.9)

➡ **CC Excl:** see code 596.60

569.62 Mechanical complication of colostomy and enterostomy

Malfunction of colostomy and enterostomy

➡ **CC Excl:** 536.40-536.49, 569.60-569.69, 997.4, 997.91, 997.99, 998.81-998.9

569.69 Other complication

Fistula
Hernia
Prolapse

➡ **CC Excl:** see code 596.60

✓5th **569.8 Other specified disorders of intestine**

➡ **AHA Coding Clinic:** 4Q, '91, 25

569.81 Fistula of intestine, excluding rectum and anus

Fistula:
abdominal wall
enterocolic
enteroenteric
ileorectal

Excludes: *fistula of intestine to internal organs — see Alphabetic Index*
persistent postoperative fistula (998.6)

569.82 Ulceration of intestine

Primary ulcer of intestine
Ulceration of colon

Excludes: *that with perforation (569.83)*

569.83 Perforation of intestine

➡ **CC Excl:** 569.83

569.84 Angiodysplasia of intestine (without mention of hemorrhage)

➡ **AHA Coding Clinic:** 3Q, '96, 10; 4Q, '90, 4; 4Q, '90, 21

569.85 Angiodysplasia of intestine with hemorrhage

➡ **CC Excl:** 251.5, 456.0, 530.2, 530.7, 530.82, 531.00-531.91, 532.00-532.91, 533.00-533.91, 534.00-534.91, 535.01, 535.11, 535.21, 535.31, 535.41, 535.51, 535.61, 537.83, 562.02-562.03, 562.12-562.13, 569.3, 569.85, 578.0-578.9

569.89 Other

Enteroptosis
Granuloma / Prolapse } of intestine
Pericolitis
Perisigmoiditis
Visceroptosis

Excludes: *gangrene of intestine, mesentery, or omentum (557.0)*
hemorrhage of intestine NOS (578.9)
obstruction of intestine (560.0-560.9)

569.9 Unspecified disorder of intestine

OTHER DISEASES OF DIGESTIVE SYSTEM (570-579)

570 Acute and subacute necrosis of liver

Acute hepatic failure
Acute or subacute hepatitis, not specified as infective
Necrosis of liver (acute) (diffuse) (massive) (subacute)
Parenchymatous degeneration of liver
Yellow atrophy (liver) (acute) (subacute)

Excludes: *icterus gravis of newborn (773.0-773.2)*
serum hepatitis (070.2-070.3)
that with:
abortion (634-638 with .7, 639.8)
ectopic or molar pregnancy (639.8)
pregnancy, childbirth, or the puerperium (646.7)
viral hepatitis (070.0-070.9)

➡ **CC Excl:** 570, 573.4-573.9

571 Chronic liver disease and cirrhosis

571.0 Alcoholic fatty liver A: 15–124

571.1 Acute alcoholic hepatitis A: 15–124
Acute alcoholic liver disease

571.2 Alcoholic cirrhosis of liver A: 15–124
Florid cirrhosis
Laennec's cirrhosis (alcoholic)

➡ **CC Excl:** 571.2, 573.8-573.9
➡ **AHA Coding Clinic:** N-D, '85, 14

571.3 Alcoholic liver damage, unspecified A: 15–124

✓5th **571.4 Chronic hepatitis**

Excludes: *viral hepatitis (acute) (chronic) (070.0-070.9)*

571.40 Chronic hepatitis, unspecified

571.41 Chronic persistent hepatitis

571.49 Other
Chronic hepatitis:
active
aggressive
Recurrent hepatitis

➡ **CC Excl:** 571.49, 571.5-571.9, 573.8-573.9

571.5 Cirrhosis of liver without mention of alcohol
Cirrhosis of liver:
NOS
cryptogenic
macronodular
micronodular
Cirrhosis of liver:
posthepatitic
postnecrotic
Healed yellow atrophy (liver)
Portal cirrhosis

➡ **CC Excl:** see Code 571.49

571.6 Biliary cirrhosis
Chronic nonsuppurative destructive cholangitis
Cirrhosis:
cholangitic
cholestatic

➡ **CC Excl:** see Code 571.49

571.8 Other chronic nonalcoholic liver disease
Chronic yellow atrophy (liver)
Fatty liver, without mention of alcohol

➡ **AHA Coding Clinic:** 2Q, '96, 12

571.9 Unspecified chronic liver disease without mention of alcohol

572 Liver abscess and sequelae of chronic liver disease

572.0 Abscess of liver

Excludes: *amebic liver abscess (006.3)*

➡ **CC Excl:** 006.3, 572.0-572.1, 573.8-573.9

572.1 Portal pyemia
Phlebitis of portal vein
Portal thrombophlebitis
Pylephlebitis
Pylethrombophlebitis

➡ **CC Excl:** see Code 572.0

572.2 Hepatic coma
Hepatic encephalopathy
Hepatocerebral intoxication
Portal-systemic encephalopathy

➡ **CC Excl:** 572.2, 573.8-573.9
➡ **AHA Coding Clinic:** 3Q, '95, 14

572.3 Portal hypertension

572.4 Hepatorenal syndrome

Excludes: *that following delivery (674.8)*

➡ **CC Excl:** 572.4, 573.8-573.9

572.8 Other sequelae of chronic liver disease

573 Other disorders of liver

Excludes: *amyloid or lardaceous degeneration of liver (277.3)*
congenital cystic disease of liver (751.62)
glycogen infiltration of liver (271.0)
hepatomegaly NOS (789.1)
portal vein obstruction (452)

573.0 Chronic passive congestion of liver

573.1 ***Hepatitis in viral diseases classified elsewhere***

Code first underlying disease as:
Coxsackie virus disease (074.8)
cytomegalic inclusion virus disease (078.5)
infectious mononucleosis (075)

Excludes: *hepatitis (in):*
mumps (072.71)
viral (070.0-070.9)
yellow fever (060.0-060.9)

➡ **CC Excl:** 573.1-573.3, 573.8-573.9

573.2 ***Hepatitis in other infectious diseases classified elsewhere***

Code first underlying disease as:
malaria (084.9)

Excludes: *hepatitis in:*
late syphilis (095.3)
secondary syphilis (091.62)
toxoplasmosis (130.5)

➡ **CC Excl:** see Code 573.1

573.3 **Hepatitis, unspecified**
Toxic (noninfectious) hepatitis
Use additional E code to identify cause

➡ **CC Excl:** see Code 573.1
➡ **AHA Coding Clinic:** 4Q, '90, 26

573.4 **Hepatic infarction**

➡ **CC Excl:** 570, 573.4-573.9

573.8 **Other specified disorders of liver**
Hepatoptosis

573.9 **Unspecified disorder of liver**

574 Cholelithiasis

The following fifth-digit subclassification is for use with category 574:

0 without mention of obstruction
1 with obstruction

✓5th **574.0** **Calculus of gallbladder with acute cholecystitis** **A: 15–124**

Biliary calculus / Calculus of cystic duct / Cholelithiasis } with acute cholecystitis
Any condition classifiable to 574.2 with acute cholecystitis

➡ **CC Excl: For code 574.00:** 574.00-574.21, 574.40, 574.60-574.61, 574.80-574.81, 575.0, 575.10-575.12, 576.8-576.9
➡ **CC Excl: For code 574.01:** 574.00-574.21, 574.60-574.61, 574.80-574.81, 575.0, 575.10-575.12, 576.8-576.9
➡ **AHA Coding Clinic:** 4Q, '96, 32

✓5th **574.1** **Calculus of gallbladder with other cholecystitis** **A: 15–124**

Biliary calculus / Calculus of cystic duct / Cholelithiasis } with cholecystitis
Cholecystitis with cholelithiasis NOS
Any condition classifiable to 574.2 with cholecystitis (chronic)

➡ **CC Excl:** see Code 574.01
➡ **AHA Coding Clinic:** 4Q, '96, 32, 69; 2Q, '96, 13

✓5th [4] **574.2** **Calculus of gallbladder without mention of cholecystitis** **A: 15–124**

Biliary:
calculus NOS
colic NOS
Calculus of cystic duct
Cholelithiasis NOS
Colic (recurrent) of gallbladder
Gallstone (impacted)

➡ **CC Excl: For code 574.21:** see Code 574.01
➡ **AHA Coding Clinic:** For code 574.20: 1Q, '88, 14

✓5th **574.3** **Calculus of bile duct with acute cholecystitis** **A: 15–124**

Calculus of bile duct [any] / Choledocholithiasis } with acute cholecystitis
Any condition classifiable to 574.5 with acute cholecystitis

➡ **CC Excl:** 574.30-574.51, 574.60-574.61, 574.70-574.71, 574.80-574.81, 574.90-574.91, 575.0, 575.10-575.12, 576.8-576.9

✓5th **574.4** **Calculus of bile duct with other cholecystitis** **A: 15–124**

Calculus of bile duct [any] / Choledocholithiasis } with cholecystitis (chronic)
Any condition classifiable to 574.5 with cholecystitis (chronic)

➡ **CC Excl:** see Code 574.3

✓5th **574.5** **Calculus of bile duct without mention of cholecystitis** **A: 15–124**

Calculus of:
bile duct [any]
common duct
hepatic duct
Choledocholithiasis
Hepatic:
colic (recurrent)
lithiasis

➡ **CC Excl:** see Code 574.3
➡ **AHA Coding Clinic:** 3Q, '94, 11

✓5th **574.6** **Calculus of gallbladder and bile duct with acute cholecystitis** **A: 15–124**

Any condition classifiable to 574.0 and 574.3

➡ **CC Excl:** 574.60-574.61, 575.0, 575.10-575.12, 575.9, 576.8-576.9

✓5th **574.7** **Calculus of gallbladder and bile duct with other cholecystitis** **A: 15–124**

Any condition classifiable to 574.1 and 574.4

➡ **CC Excl:** 574.30-574.31, 574.40-574.41, 574.50-574.51, 574.60-574.61, 574.70-574.71, 574.80-574.81, 574.90-574.91, 575.0, 575.10-575.12, 576.8-576.9

✓5th **574.8** **Calculus of gallbladder and bile duct with acute and chronic cholecystitis** **A: 15–124**

Any condition classifiable to 574.6 and 574.7

➡ **CC Excl:** 574.80-574.81, 575.0, 575.10-575.12, 575.9, 576.8-576.9
➡ **AHA Coding Clinic:** 4Q, '96, 32

✓5th **574.9** **Calculus of gallbladder and bile duct without cholecystitis** **A: 15–124**

Any condition classifiable to 574.2 and 574.5

➡ **CC Excl:** see Code 574.7

[4] CC Coding = 1

575 Other disorders of gallbladder

575.0 Acute cholecystitis A: 15–124

Abscess of gallbladder
Angiocholecystitis
Cholecystitis:
  emphysematous (acute)
  gangrenous
  suppurative
Empyema of gallbladder
Gangrene of gallbladder
} without mention of calculus

Excludes: *that with:*
acute and chronic cholecystitis (575.12)
choledocholithiasis (574.3)
choledocholithiasis and cholelithiasis (574.6)
cholelithiasis (574.0)

➡ **CC Excl:** 574.60-574.61, 574.80-574.81, 575.0, 575.10-575.12, 576.8-576.9

➡ **AHA Coding Clinic:** 3Q, '91, 17

✓5th **575.1 Other cholecystitis** A: 15–124

Cholecystitis:
  NOS
  chronic
} without mention of calculus

Excludes: *that with:*
choledocholithiasis (574.4)
choledocholithiasis and cholelithiasis (574.8)
cholelithiasis (574.1)

➡ **CC Excl:** 575.0, 575.10-575.12, 575.9, 576.8-576.9

575.10 Cholecystitis, unspecified
Cholecystitis NOS

575.11 Chronic cholecystitis

575.12 Acute and chronic cholecystitis
➡ **AHA Coding Clinic:** 4Q, '97, 52; 4Q, '96, 32

575.2 Obstruction of gallbladder A: 15–124

Occlusion
Stenosis
Stricture
} of cystic duct or gallbladder without mention of calculus

Excludes: *that with calculus (574.0-574.2 with fifth-digit 1)*

➡ **CC Excl:** 575.2-575.9, 576.8-576.9

575.3 Hydrops of gallbladder A: 15–124

Mucocele of gallbladder

➡ **CC Excl:** see Code 575.2

➡ **AHA Coding Clinic:** 2Q, '89, 13

575.4 Perforation of gallbladder

Rupture of cystic duct or gallbladder

➡ **CC Excl:** see Code 575.2

575.5 Fistula of gallbladder

Fistula:
  cholecystoduodenal
  cholecystoenteric

➡ **CC Excl:** see Code 575.2

575.6 Cholesterolosis of gallbladder

Strawberry gallbladder

➡ **AHA Coding Clinic:** 4Q, '90, 17

575.8 Other specified disorders of gallbladder

Adhesions
Atrophy
Cyst
Hypertrophy
Nonfunctioning
Ulcer
} (of) { cystic duct, gallbladder
Biliary dyskinesia

Excludes: *nonvisualization of gallbladder (793.3)*

➡ **AHA Coding Clinic:** 4Q, '90, 26; 2Q, '89, 13

575.9 Unspecified disorder of gallbladder

576 Other disorders of biliary tract

Excludes: *that involving the:*
cystic duct (575.0-575.9)
gallbladder (575.0-575.9)

576.0 Postcholecystectomy syndrome A: 15–124

➡ **AHA Coding Clinic:** 1Q, '88, 10

576.1 Cholangitis

Cholangitis:	Cholangitis:
NOS	recurrent
acute	sclerosing
ascending	secondary
chronic	stenosing
primary	suppurative

➡ **CC Excl:** 576.1, 576.8-576.9

✔ **St. Anthony's Clinical Coder:** see Chapter 5

576.2 Obstruction of bile duct

Occlusion
Stenosis
Stricture
} of bile duct, except cystic duct, without mention of calculus

Excludes: *congenital (751.61)*
that with calculus (574.3-574.5 with fifth-digit 1)

576.3 Perforation of bile duct

Rupture of bile duct, except cystic duct

➡ **CC Excl:** 576.3-576.4, 576.8-576.9

576.4 Fistula of bile duct

Choledochoduodenal fistula

➡ **CC Excl:** see Code 576.3

576.5 Spasm of sphincter of Oddi

576.8 Other specified disorders of biliary tract

Adhesions
Atrophy
Cyst
Hypertrophy
Stasis
Ulcer
} of bile duct [any]

Excludes: *congenital choledochal cyst (751.69)*

576.9 Unspecified disorder of biliary tract

577 Diseases of pancreas

577.0 Acute pancreatitis A: 15–124

Abscess of pancreas
Necrosis of pancreas:
  acute
  infective
Pancreatitis:
  NOS
  acute (recurrent)
  apoplectic
  hemorrhagic
  subacute
  suppurative

Excludes: *mumps pancreatitis (072.3)*

➡ **CC Excl:** 577.0-577.1, 577.8-577.9

➡ **AHA Coding Clinic:** 2Q, '96, 13; 2Q, '89, 9

✔ **St. Anthony's Clinical Coder:** see Chapter 5

577.1 Chronic pancreatitis A: 15–124

Chronic pancreatitis:
  NOS
  infectious
  interstitial
Pancreatitis:
  painless
  recurrent
  relapsing

➡ **AHA Coding Clinic:** 2Q, '96, 13; 3Q, '94, 11

577.2 Cyst and pseudocyst of pancreas A: 15–124

➡ **CC Excl:** 577.2, 577.8-577.9

577.8 Other specified diseases of pancreas

Atrophy, Calculus, Cirrhosis, Fibrosis } of pancreas
Pancreatic:
  infantilism
  necrosis:
    NOS
    aseptic
    fat
Pancreatolithiasis

Excludes: *fibrocystic disease of pancreas (277.00-277.01)*
islet cell tumor of pancreas (211.7)
pancreatic steatorrhea (579.4)

577.9 Unspecified disease of pancreas

578 Gastrointestinal hemorrhage

Excludes: *that with mention of:*
angiodysplasia of stomach and duodenum (537.83)
angiodysplasia of intestine (569.85)
diverticulitis, intestine:
  large (562.13)
  small (562.03)
diverticulosis, intestine:
  large (562.12)
  small (562.02)
gastritis and duodenitis (535.0-535.6)
ulcer:
  duodenal, gastric, gastrojejunal or peptic (531.00-534.91)

➡ **AHA Coding Clinic:** 2Q, '92, 9; 4Q, '90, 20

✔ **St. Anthony's Clinical Coder:** see Chapter 5

578.0 Hematemesis

Vomiting of blood

➡ **CC Excl:** 251.5, 456.0, 530.2, 530.7, 530.82, 531.00-531.91, 532.00-532.91, 533.00-533.91, 534.00-534.91, 535.01, 535.11, 535.21, 535.31, 535.41, 535.51, 535.61, 537.83, 562.02-562.03, 562.12-562.13, 569.3, 569.85, 578.0-578.9

578.1 Blood in stool

Melena

Excludes: *melena of the newborn (772.4, 777.3)*
occult blood (792.1)

➡ **CC Excl:** see Code 578.0

➡ **AHA Coding Clinic:** 2Q, '92, 8

DRG 174

578.9 Hemorrhage of gastrointestinal tract, unspecified

Gastric hemorrhage
Intestinal hemorrhage

➡ **CC Excl:** see Code 578.0

➡ **AHA Coding Clinic:** N-D, '86, 9

DRG 174

579 Intestinal malabsorption

579.0 Celiac disease

Celiac:
  crisis
  infantilism
  rickets
Gee (-Herter) disease
Gluten enteropathy
Idiopathic steatorrhea
Nontropical sprue

579.1 Tropical sprue

Sprue:
  NOS
  tropical
Tropical steatorrhea

579.2 Blind loop syndrome

Postoperative blind loop syndrome

579.3 Other and unspecified postsurgical nonabsorption

Hypoglycemia, Malnutrition } following gastrointestinal surgery

➡ **CC Excl:** 579.3-579.9

579.4 Pancreatic steatorrhea

579.8 Other specified intestinal malabsorption

Enteropathy:
  exudative
  protein-losing
Steatorrhea (chronic)

579.9 Unspecified intestinal malabsorption

Malabsorption syndrome NOS

10. DISEASES OF THE GENITOURINARY SYSTEM (580-629)

NEPHRITIS, NEPHROTIC SYNDROME, AND NEPHROSIS (580-589)

Excludes: *hypertensive renal disease (403.00-403.91)*

580 Acute glomerulonephritis

Includes: acute nephritis

580.0 With lesion of proliferative glomerulonephritis

Acute (diffuse) proliferative glomerulonephritis
Acute poststreptococcal glomerulonephritis

➡ **CC Excl:** 016.00-016.06, 016.30-016.36, 016.90-016.96, 017.90-017.96, 098.10, 098.19, 098.30-098.31, 098.89, 112.2, 131.00, 131.8-131.9, 250.40-250.43, 250.80-250.93, 274.10, 274.19, 580.0-580.9, 581.0-581.9, 582.0-582.9, 583.0-583.9, 584.5-584.9, 585-587, 588.0-588.9, 589.0-589.9, 590.00-590.9, 591, 593.0-593.2, 593.89, 593.9, 599.7-599.9

580.4 With lesion of rapidly progressive glomerulonephritis

Acute nephritis with lesion of necrotizing glomerulitis

➡ **CC Excl:** see Code 580.0

✓5th **580.8 With other specified pathological lesion in kidney**

580.81 Acute glomerulonephritis in diseases classified elsewhere

Code first underlying disease as:
infectious hepatitis (070.0-070.9)
mumps (072.79)
subacute bacterial endocarditis (421.0)
typhoid fever (002.0)

➡ **CC Excl:** see Code 580.0

580.89 Other

Glomerulonephritis, acute, with lesion of:
exudative nephritis
interstitial (diffuse) (focal) nephritis

➡ **CC Excl:** 016.00-016.06, 016.30-016.36, 016.90-016.96, 017.90-017.96, 098.10, 098.19, 098.30-098.31, 098.89, 112.2, 131.00, 131.8-131.9, 274.10, 274.19, 580.0-580.9, 581.0-581.9, 582.0-582.9, 583.0-583.9, 584.5-584.9, 585-587, 588.0-588.9, 589.0-589.9, 590.00-590.9, 591, 593.0-593.2, 593.89, 593.9, 599.7-599.9

580.9 Acute glomerulonephritis with unspecified pathological lesion in kidney

Glomerulonephritis: NOS, hemorrhagic; Nephritis; Nephropathy — specified as acute

➡ **CC Excl:** 016.00-016.06, 016.30-016.36, 016.90-016.96, 017.90-017.96, 098.10, 098.19, 098.30-098.31, 098.89, 112.2, 131.00, 131.8-131.9, 250.40-250.43, 250.80-250.93, 274.10, 274.19, 580.0-580.9, 581.0-581.9, 582.0-582.9, 583.0-583.9, 584.5-584.9, 585-587, 588.0-588.9, 589.0-589.9, 590.00-590.09, 591, 593.0-593.2, 593.89, 593.9, 599.7-599.9

581 Nephrotic syndrome

581.0 With lesion of proliferative glomerulonephritis

➡ **CC Excl:** see Code 580.9

581.1 With lesion of membranous glomerulonephritis

Epimembranous nephritis
Idiopathic membranous glomerular disease
Nephrotic syndrome with lesion of:
focal glomerulosclerosis
sclerosing membranous glomerulonephritis
segmental hyalinosis

➡ **CC Excl:** see Code 580.9

581.2 With lesion of membranoproliferative glomerulonephritis

Nephrotic syndrome with lesion (of):
endothelial; hypocomplementemic persistent; lobular; mesangiocapillary; mixed membranous and proliferative — glomerulonephritis

➡ **CC Excl:** see Code 580.9

581.3 With lesion of minimal change glomerulonephritis

Foot process disease
Lipoid nephrosis
Minimal change:
glomerular disease
glomerulitis
nephrotic syndrome

➡ **CC Excl:** see Code 580.9

✓5th **581.8 With other specified pathological lesion in kidney**

581.81 *Nephrotic syndrome in diseases classified elsewhere*

Code first underlying disease as:
amyloidosis (277.3)
diabetes mellitus (250.4)
malaria (084.9)
polyarteritis (446.0)
systemic lupus erythematosus (710.0)

Excludes: *nephrosis in epidemic hemorrhagic fever (078.6)*

➡ **CC Excl:** see Code 580.9

581.89 Other

Glomerulonephritis with edema and lesion of:
exudative nephritis
interstitial (diffuse) (focal) nephritis

➡ **CC Excl:** see Code 580.9

581.9 Nephrotic syndrome with unspecified pathological lesion in kidney

Glomerulonephritis with edema NOS
Nephritis:
nephrotic NOS
with edema NOS
Nephrosis NOS
Renal disease with edema NOS

➡ **CC Excl:** see Code 580.9

582 Chronic glomerulonephritis

Includes: chronic nephritis

582.0 With lesion of proliferative glomerulonephritis

Chronic (diffuse) proliferative glomerulonephritis

582.1 With lesion of membranous glomerulonephritis

Chronic glomerulonephritis:
membranous
sclerosing
Focal glomerulosclerosis
Segmental hyalinosis

582.2 With lesion of membranoproliferative glomerulonephritis

Chronic glomerulonephritis:
endothelial
hypocomplementemic persistent
lobular
membranoproliferative
mesangiocapillary
mixed membranous and proliferative

582.4 With lesion of rapidly progressive glomerulonephritis

Chronic nephritis with lesion of necrotizing glomerulitis

✓5th **582.8 With other specified pathological lesion in kidney**

582.81 *Chronic glomerulonephritis in diseases classified elsewhere*

Code first underlying disease as:
amyloidosis (277.3)
systemic lupus erythematosus (710.0)

582.89 Other

Chronic glomerulonephritis with lesion of:
exudative nephritis
interstitial (diffuse) (focal) nephritis

582.9 Chronic glomerulonephritis with unspecified pathological lesion in kidney

Glomerulonephritis:
NOS
hemorrhagic
Nephritis
Nephropathy
} specified as chronic

583 Nephritis and nephropathy, not specified as acute or chronic

Includes: "renal disease" so stated, not specified as acute or chronic but with stated pathology or cause

583.0 With lesion of proliferative glomerulonephritis

Proliferative:
glomerulonephritis (diffuse) NOS
nephritis NOS
nephropathy NOS

583.1 With lesion of membranous glomerulonephritis

Membranous:
glomerulonephritis NOS
nephritis NOS
Membranous nephropathy NOS

583.2 With lesion of membranoproliferative glomerulonephritis

Membranoproliferative:
glomerulonephritis NOS
nephritis NOS
nephropathy NOS
Nephritis NOS, with lesion of:
hypocomplementemic persistent
lobular
mesangiocapillary
mixed membranous and proliferative
} glomerulonephritis

583.4 With lesion of rapidly progressive glomerulonephritis

Necrotizing or rapidly progressive:
glomerulitis NOS
glomerulonephritis NOS
nephritis NOS
nephropathy NOS
Nephritis, unspecified, with lesion of necrotizing glomerulitis

➡ **CC Excl:** see Code 580.9

583.6 **With lesion of renal cortical necrosis**

Nephritis NOS } with (renal) cortical necrosis
Nephropathy NOS }
Renal cortical necrosis NOS

583.7 **With lesion of renal medullary necrosis**

Nephritis NOS } with (renal) medullary [papillary] necrosis
Nephropathy NOS }

✓5th **583.8** **With other specified pathological lesion in kidney**

583.81 ***Nephritis and nephropathy, not specified as acute or chronic, in diseases classified elsewhere***

Code first underlying disease as:
amyloidosis (277.3)
diabetes mellitus (250.4)
gonococcal infection (098.19)
Goodpasture's syndrome (446.21)
systemic lupus erythematosus (710.0)
tuberculosis (016.0)

Excludes: *gouty nephropathy (274.10)*
syphilitic nephritis (095.4)

583.89 **Other**

Glomerulitis, Glomerulonephritis, Nephritis, Nephropathy, Renal disease } with lesion of:
exudative nephritis
interstitial nephritis

583.9 **With unspecified pathological lesion in kidney**

Glomerulitis, Glomerulonephritis, Nephritis, Nephropathy } NOS

Excludes: *nephropathy complicating pregnancy, labor, or the puerperium (642.0 642.9, 646.2)*
renal disease NOS with no stated cause (593.9)

584 **Acute renal failure**

Excludes: *following labor and delivery (669.3)*
posttraumatic (958.5)
that complicating:
abortion (634-638 with .3, 639.3)
ectopic or molar pregnancy (639.3)

➡ **AHA Coding Clinic:** 1Q, '93, 18; 2Q, '92, 5

584.5 **With lesion of tubular necrosis**

Lower nephron nephrosis
Renal failure with (acute) tubular necrosis
Tubular necrosis:
NOS
acute

➡ **CC Excl:** 250.40-250.43, 250.80-250.93, 274.10, 274.19, 580.0-580.9, 581.0-581.9, 582.0-582.9, 583.0-583.9, 584.5-584.9, 585-587, 588.0-588.9, 589.0-589.9, 590.00-590.9, 591, 593.0-593.2, 593.89, 593.9, 599.7-599.9, 753.0, 753.20-753.23, 753.29, 753.3, 753.9

✔ **St. Anthony's Clinical Coder:** see Chapters 5 & 6

584.6 **With lesion of renal cortical necrosis**

➡ **CC Excl:** see Code 584.5

✔ **St. Anthony's Clinical Coder:** see Chapters 5 & 6

584.7 **With lesion of renal medullary [papillary] necrosis**

Necrotizing renal papillitis

➡ **CC Excl:** see Code 584.5

✔ **St. Anthony's Clinical Coder:** see Chapters 5 & 6

584.8 **With other specified pathological lesion in kidney**

➡ **CC Excl:** 250.40-250.43, 250.80-250.93, 274.10, 274.19, 580.0-580.9, 581.0-581.9, 582.0-582.9, 583.0-583.9, 584.5-584.9, 585-587, 588.0-588.9, 589.0-589.9, 590.00-590.9, 591, 593.0-593.2, 593.89, 593.9, 599.7-599.9

➡ **AHA Coding Clinic:** N-D, '85, 1

✔ **St. Anthony's Clinical Coder:** see Chapters 5 & 6

584.9 **Acute renal failure, unspecified**

➡ **CC Excl:** 250.40-250.43, 250.80-250.93, 274.10, 274.19, 580.0-580.9, 581.0-581.9, 582.0-582.9, 583.0-583.9, 584.5-584.9, 585-587, 588.0-588.9, 589.0-589.9, 590.00-590.9, 591, 593.0-593.2, 593.89, 593.9, 599.7-599.9, 753.0, 753.20-753.23, 753.29, 753.3, 753.9

➡ **AHA Coding Clinic:** 3Q, '96, 9; 4Q, '88, 1

DRG 316

✔ **St. Anthony's Clinical Coder:** see Chapters 5 & 6

585 **Chronic renal failure**

Chronic uremia

Use additional code to identify manifestation as:
uremic:
neuropathy (357.4)
pericarditis (420.0)

Excludes: *that with any condition classifiable to 401 (403.0-403.9 with fifth-digit 1)*

➡ **CC Excl:** see Code 584.9

➡ **AHA Coding Clinic:** 3Q, '96, 9; 1Q, '93, 18; 4Q, '89, 1; N-D, '85, 15; S-O, '84, 3

DRG 316

586 Renal failure, unspecified

Uremia NOS

Excludes: *following labor and delivery (669.3)*
posttraumatic renal failure (958.5)
that complicating:
abortion (634-638 with .3, 639.3)
ectopic or molar pregnancy (639.3)
uremia:
extrarenal (788.9)
prerenal (788.9)
with any condition classifiable to 401 (403.0-403.9 with fifth-digit 1)

➡ **AHA Coding Clinic:** 1Q, '93, 18

DRG 316

587 Renal sclerosis, unspecified

Atrophy of kidney
Contracted kidney
Renal:
cirrhosis
fibrosis

Excludes: *nephrosclerosis (arteriolar) (arteriosclerotic) (403.00-403.92)*
with hypertension (403.00-403.92)

588 Disorders resulting from impaired renal function

588.0 Renal osteodystrophy

Azotemic osteodystrophy
Phosphate-losing tubular disorders
Renal:
dwarfism
infantilism
rickets

588.1 Nephrogenic diabetes insipidus

Excludes: *diabetes insipidus NOS (253.5)*

588.8 Other specified disorders resulting from impaired renal function

Hypokalemic nephropathy
Secondary hyperparathyroidism (of renal origin)

Excludes: *secondary hypertension (405.0-405.9)*

588.9 Unspecified disorder resulting from impaired renal function

589 Small kidney of unknown cause

589.0 Unilateral small kidney

589.1 Bilateral small kidneys

589.9 Small kidney, unspecified

OTHER DISEASES OF URINARY SYSTEM (590-599)

590 Infections of kidney

Use additional code to identify organism such as Escherichia coli [E. coli] (041.4)

✓5th **590.0 Chronic pyelonephritis**

Chronic pyelitis
Chronic pyonephrosis

Code also any associated vesicoureteral reflux (593.70-593.73)

590.00 Without lesion of renal medullary necrosis

590.01 With lesion of renal medullary necrosis

✓5th **590.1 Acute pyelonephritis**

Acute pyelitis
Acute pyonephrosis

590.10 Without lesion of renal medullary necrosis

➡ **CC Excl:** 016.00-016.06, 016.30-016.36, 016.90-016.96, 017.90-017.96, 098.10, 098.19, 098.30-098.31, 098.89, 112.2, 131.00, 131.8-131.9, 250.40-250.43, 250.80-250.93, 274.10, 274.19, 580.0-580.9, 581.0-581.9, 582.0-582.9, 583.0-583.9, 584.5-584.9, 585-587, 588.0-588.9, 589.0-589.9, 590.00-590.9, 591, 593.0-593.2, 593.89, 593.9, 599.0, 599.7-599.9

DRG 320

590.11 With lesion of renal medullary necrosis

➡ **CC Excl:** see Code 590.10

590.2 Renal and perinephric abscess

Abscess:
kidney
nephritic
perirenal
Carbuncle of kidney

➡ **CC Excl:** see Code 590.10

590.3 Pyeloureteritis cystica

Infection of renal pelvis and ureter
Ureteritis cystica

➡ **CC Excl:** 016.00-016.06, 016.30-016.36, 016.90-016.96, 017.90-017.96, 098.10, 098.19, 098.30-098.31, 098.89, 112.2, 131.00, 131.8-131.9, 274.10, 274.19, 580.0-580.9, 581.0-581.9, 582.0-582.9, 583.0-583.9, 584.5-584.9, 585-587, 588.0-588.9, 589.0-589.9, 590.00-590.9 591, 593.0-593.2, 593.89, 593.9, 599.0, 599.7-599.9

✓5th **590.8 Other pyelonephritis or pyonephrosis, not specified as acute or chronic**

590.80 Pyelonephritis, unspecified
Pyelitis NOS Pyelonephritis NOS
➡ **CC Excl:** see Code 590.3
➡ **AHA Coding Clinic:** 4Q, '97, 40

590.81 Pyelitis or pyelonephritis in diseases classified elsewhere
Code first underlying disease as:
tuberculosis (016.0)
➡ **CC Excl:** see Code 590.3

590.9 Infection of kidney, unspecified
Excludes: *urinary tract infection NOS (599.0)*
➡ **CC Excl:** see Code 590.3

591 Hydronephrosis

Hydrocalycosis
Hydronephrosis
Hydroureteronephrosis

Excludes: *congenital hydronephrosis (753.29)*
hydroureter (593.5)

➡ **CC Excl:** see Code 590.3

592 Calculus of kidney and ureter

Excludes: *nephrocalcinosis (275.4)*

592.0 Calculus of kidney
Nephrolithiasis NOS
Renal calculus or stone
Staghorn calculus
Stone in kidney

Excludes: *uric acid nephrolithiasis (274.11)*

592.1 Calculus of ureter
Ureteric stone Ureterolithiasis
➡ **CC Excl:** 592.0-592.9, 593.1-593.5, 593.89, 593.9, 594.0-594.9, 599.6-599.9
➡ **AHA Coding Clinic:** 1Q, '98, 10; 4Q, '97, 40

592.9 Urinary calculus, unspecified
➡ **AHA Coding Clinic:** 4Q, '97, 40

593 Other disorders of kidney and ureter

593.0 Nephroptosis
Floating kidney Mobile kidney

593.1 Hypertrophy of kidney

593.2 Cyst of kidney, acquired
Cyst (multiple) (solitary) of kidney, not congenital
Peripelvic (lymphatic) cyst

Excludes: *calyceal or pyelogenic cyst of kidney (591)*
congenital cyst of kidney (753.1)
polycystic (disease of) kidney (753.1)

593.3 Stricture or kinking of ureter
Angulation } of ureter (postoperative)
Constriction } of ureter (postoperative)
Stricture of pelviureteric junction

593.4 Other ureteric obstruction
Idiopathic retroperitoneal fibrosis
Occlusion NOS of ureter

Excludes: *that due to calculus (592.1)*
➡ **AHA Coding Clinic:** 2Q, '97, 4

593.5 Hydroureter

Excludes: *congenital hydroureter (753.22)*
hydroureteronephrosis (591)

➡ **CC Excl:** 593.3-593.5, 593.89, 593.9, 595.0-595.9, 596.8-596.9, 599.0, 599.6-599.9, 753.4-753.5, 753.9

593.6 Postural proteinuria
Benign postural proteinuria
Orthostatic proteinuria

Excludes: *proteinuria NOS (791.0)*

✓5th **593.7 Vesicoureteral reflux**
Use additional code to identify:
chronic pyelonephritis (590.00-590.01)
renal agenesis (753.0)
renal dysplasia (753.15)
➡ **AHA Coding Clinic:** 4Q, '94, 42

593.70 Unspecified or without reflux nephropathy

593.71 With reflux nephropathy, unilateral

593.72 With reflux nephropathy, bilateral

593.73 With reflux nephropathy NOS

✓5th **593.8 Other specified disorders of kidney and ureter**

593.81 Vascular disorders of kidney
Renal (artery):
embolism
hemorrhage
thrombosis
Renal infarction

593.82 Ureteral fistula
Intestinoureteral fistula

Excludes: *fistula between ureter and female genital tract (619.0)*

593.89 Other
Adhesions, kidney or ureter
Periureteritis
Polyp of ureter
Pyelectasia
Ureterocele

Excludes: *tuberculosis of ureter (016.2)*
ureteritis cystica (590.3)

593.9 Unspecified disorder of kidney and ureter
Renal disease NOS
Salt-losing nephritis or syndrome

Excludes: *cystic kidney disease (753.1)*
nephropathy, so stated (583.0-583.9)
renal disease:
acute (580.0-580.9)
arising in pregnancy or the puerperium (642.1-642.2, 642.4-642.7, 646.2)
chronic (582.0-582.9)
not specified as acute or chronic, but with stated pathology or cause (583.0-583.9)

➡ **AHA Coding Clinic:** 1Q, '93, 17

594 Calculus of lower urinary tract

594.0 Calculus in diverticulum of bladder

594.1 Other calculus in bladder
Urinary bladder stone

Excludes: *staghorn calculus (592.0)*

594.2 Calculus in urethra

594.8 Other lower urinary tract calculus
➡ **AHA Coding Clinic:** J-F, '85, 16

594.9 Calculus of lower urinary tract, unspecified

Excludes: *calculus of urinary tract NOS (592.9)*

595 Cystitis

Use additional code to identify organism such as Escherichia coli [E. coli] (041.4)

Excludes: *prostatocystitis (601.3)*

595.0 Acute cystitis

Excludes: *trigonitis (595.3)*

➡ **CC Excl:** 016.10-016.16, 016.30-016.36, 016.90-016.96, 017.90-017.96, 098.0, 098.11, 098.2, 098.39, 098.89, 112.2, 131.00, 131.8-131.9, 593.3-593.5, 593.89, 593.9, 595.0-595.9, 596.8-596.9, 599.0, 599.6-599.9

✔ **St. Anthony's Clinical Coder:** see Chapter 5

595.1 Chronic interstitial cystitis
Hunner's ulcer
Panmural fibrosis of bladder
Submucous cystitis

➡ **CC Excl:** see Code 595.0

595.2 Other chronic cystitis
Chronic cystitis NOS
Subacute cystitis

Excludes: *trigonitis (595.3)*

➡ **CC Excl:** see Code 595.0

✔ **St. Anthony's Clinical Coder:** see Chapter 5

595.3 Trigonitis
Follicular cystitis
Trigonitis (acute) (chronic)
Urethrotrigonitis

595.4 Cystitis in diseases classified elsewhere
Code first underlying disease as:
actinomycosis (039.8)
amebiasis (006.8)
bilharziasis (120.0-120.9)
Echinococcus infestation (122.3, 122.6)

Excludes: *cystitis:*
diphtheritic (032.84)
gonococcal (098.11, 098.31)
monilial (112.2)
trichomonal (131.09)
tuberculous (016.1)

➡ **CC Excl:** see Code 595.0

✓5th **595.8 Other specified types of cystitis**

595.81 Cystitis cystica
➡ **CC Excl:** see Code 595.0

595.82 Irradiation cystitis
Use additional E code to identify cause
➡ **CC Excl:** see Code 595.0

595.89 Other
Abscess of bladder
Cystitis:
bullous
emphysematous
glandularis

➡ **CC Excl:** see Code 595.0

595.9 Cystitis, unspecified

➡ **CC Excl:** see Code 595.0

596 Other disorders of bladder

Use additional code to identify urinary incontinence (625.6, 788.30-788.39)

➡ **AHA Coding Clinic:** M-A, '87, 10

596.0 Bladder neck obstruction

Contracture (acquired) / Obstruction (acquired) / Stenosis (acquired) } of bladder neck or vesicourethral orifice

Excludes: *congenital (753.6)*

➡ **CC Excl:** 185, 188.0-188.9, 189.3-189.9, 596.0, 596.4, 596.51-596.59, 596.8-596.9, 600, 601.0-601.9, 602.0-602.9

596.1 Intestinovesical fistula

Fistula:
- enterovesical
- vesicocolic

Fistula:
- vesicoenteric
- vesicorectal

➡ **CC Excl:** 098.0, 098.2, 098.39, 098.89, 596.1-596.2, 596.8-596.9, 599.7-599.9, 788.1

596.2 Vesical fistula, not elsewhere classsified

Fistula:
- bladder NOS
- urethrovesical

Fistula:
- vesicocutaneous
- vesicoperineal

Excludes: *fistula between bladder and female genital tract (619.0)*

➡ **CC Excl:** see Code 596.1

✔ **St. Anthony's Clinical Coder:** see Chapter 5

596.3 Diverticulum of bladder

Diverticulitis / Diverticulum (acquired) (false) } of bladder

Excludes: *that with calculus in diverticulum of bladder (594.0)*

596.4 Atony of bladder

High compliance bladder

Hypotonicity / Inertia } of bladder

Excludes: *neurogenic bladder (596.54)*

➡ **CC Excl:** 596.4, 596.51-596.59, 596.8-596.9, 599.7-599.9, 788.1

✓5th **596.5 Other functional disorders of bladder**

Excludes: *cauda equina syndrome with neurogenic bladder (344.61)*

596.51 Hypertonicity of bladder

Hyperactivity

596.52 Low bladder compliance

596.53 Paralysis of bladder

596.54 Neurogenic bladder NOS

596.55 Detrusor sphincter dyssynergia

596.59 Other functional disorder of bladder

Detrusor instability

596.6 Rupture of bladder, nontraumatic

➡ **CC Excl:** 596.6-596.9, 599.7-599.9, 788.1

596.7 Hemorrhage into bladder wall

Hyperemia of bladder

Excludes: *acute hemorrhagic cystitis (595.0)*

➡ **CC Excl:** see Code 596.6

596.8 Other specified disorders of bladder

Bladder:
- calcified
- contracted

Bladder:
- hemorrhage
- hypertrophy

Excludes: *cystocele, female (618.0, 618.2-618.4)*
hernia or prolapse of bladder, female (618.0, 618.2-618.4)

596.9 Unspecified disorder of bladder

597 Urethritis, not sexually transmitted, and urethral syndrome

Excludes: *nonspecific urethritis, so stated (099.4)*

597.0 Urethral abscess

Abscess of:
- bulbourethral gland
- Cowper's gland
- Littré's gland

Abscess:
- periurethral
- urethral (gland)

Periurethral cellulitis

Excludes: *urethral caruncle (599.3)*

➡ **CC Excl:** 098.0, 098.2, 098.39, 098.89, 099.40-099.49, 112.2, 131.00, 131.02, 131.8-131.9, 597.0-597.89, 598.00-598.01, 598.8-598.9, 599.0, 599.6-599.9, 607.1-607.83, 607.89, 607.9, 608.4, 608.81, 608.85, 608.89, 752.61-752.65, 752.69, 752.8-752.9, 753.6-753.9, 788.1

✓5th **597.8 Other urethritis**

597.80 Urethritis, unspecified

597.81 Urethral syndrome NOS

597.89 **Other**

Adenitis, Skene's glands
Cowperitis
Meatitis, urethral
Ulcer, urethra (meatus)
Verumontanitis

Excludes: *trichomonal (131.02)*

598 Urethral stricture

Use additional code to identify urinary incontinence (625.6, 788.30-788.39)

Includes: pinhole meatus
stricture of urinary meatus

Excludes: *congenital stricture of urethra and urinary meatus (753.6)*

✓5th **598.0** **Urethral stricture due to infection**

598.00 **Due to unspecified infection**

598.01 ***Due to infective diseases classified elsewhere***

Code first underlying disease as:
gonococcal infection (098.2)
schistosomiasis (120.0-120.9)
syphilis (095.8)

598.1 **Traumatic urethral stricture**

Stricture of urethra:
late effect of injury
postobstetric

Excludes: *postoperative following surgery on genitourinary tract (598.2)*

➡ **CC Excl:** 098.0, 098.2, 098.39, 098.89, 131.02, 598.1-598.9, 599.6-599.9, 752.61-752.65, 752.69, 753.6-753.9, 788.1

598.2 **Postoperative urethral stricture**

Postcatheterization stricture of urethra

➡ **CC Excl:** see Code 598.1

➡ **AHA Coding Clinic:** 3Q, '97, 6

598.8 **Other specified causes of urethral stricture**

598.9 **Urethral stricture, unspecified**

599 Other disorders of urethra and urinary tract

599.0 **Urinary tract infection, site not specified**

Pyuria

Use additional code to identify organism such as Escherichia coli [E. coli] (041.4)

Excludes: *Candidiasis of urinary tract (112.2)*

➡ **CC Excl:** 098.2, 098.39, 098.89, 099.40-099.49, 112.2, 131.00, 131.8-131.9, 590.10-590.9, 591, 593.89, 593.9, 595.0-595.9, 599.0, 599.6-599.9, 788.1, 996.64

➡ **AHA Coding Clinic:** 1Q, '98, 5; 2Q, '96, 7; 1Q, '92, 13

DRG 320

✓ **St. Anthony's Clinical Coder:** see Chapter 5

599.1 **Urethral fistula**

Fistula:
urethroperineal
urethrorectal
Urinary fistula NOS

Excludes: *fistula:*
urethroscrotal (608.89)
urethrovaginal (619.0)
urethrovesicovaginal (619.0)

➡ **AHA Coding Clinic:** 3Q, '97, 6

599.2 **Urethral diverticulum**

599.3 **Urethral caruncle**

Polyp of urethra

599.4 **Urethral false passage**

➡ **CC Excl:** 597.0-597.89, 598.00-598.9, 599.1-599.9, 607.1-607.83, 607.89, 607.9, 608.4, 608.81, 608.85, 608.89, 752.61-752.65, 752.69, 752.8-752.9, 753.9, 788.1

599.5 **Prolapsed urethral mucosa**

Prolapse of urethra
Urethrocele

Excludes: *urethrocele, female (618.0, 618.2-618.4)*

599.6 **Urinary obstruction, unspecified**

Obstructive uropathy NOS
Urinary (tract) obstruction NOS

Use additional code to identify urinary incontinence (625.6, 788.30-788.39)

Excludes: *obstructive nephropathy NOS (593.89)*

➡ **CC Excl:** 185, 188.0-188.9, 189.2-189.9, 274.11, 344.61, 592.1, 592.9, 593.1-593.5, 593.89, 593.9, 594.0-594.9, 595.0-595.9, 596.0, 596.51-596.59, 596.8-596.9, 597.0-597.89, 598.00-598.9, 599.0-599.9, 600, 601.0-601.9, 602.0-602.9, 753.0-753.9, 788.1

✓ **St. Anthony's Clinical Coder:** see Chapter 5

599.7 **Hematuria**

Hematuria (benign) (essential)

Excludes: *hemoglobinuria (791.2)*

➡ **CC Excl:** 592.0-592.9, 593.1-593.2, 593.89, 593.9, 594.0-594.9, 596.6-596.7, 599.7-599.9

➡ **AHA Coding Clinic:** 3Q, '95, 8

✓ **St. Anthony's Clinical Coder:** see Chapter 5

✓5th **599.8** **Other specified disorders of urethra and urinary tract**

Use additonal code to identify urinary incontinence (625.6, 788.30-788.39)

Excludes: *symptoms and other conditions classifiable to 788.0-788.2, 788.4-788.9, 791.0-791.9*

599.81 **Urethral hypermobility**

599.82 **Intrinsic (urethral) sphincter deficiency [ISD]**

➡ **AHA Coding Clinic:** 2Q, '96, 15

599.83 **Urethral instability**

599.84 **Other specified disorders of urethra**

Rupture of urethra (nontraumatic)
Urethral:
cyst
granuloma

599.89 **Other specified disorders of urinary tract**

599.9 **Unspecified disorder of urethra and urinary tract**

DISEASES OF MALE GENITAL ORGANS (600-608)

600 Hyperplasia of prostate ♂ A: 15–124

Adenofibromatous hypertrophy, Adenoma (benign), Enlargement (benign), Fibroadenoma, Fibroma, Hypertrophy (benign), Myoma } of prostate
Median bar (prostate)
Prostatic obstruction NOS

Use additional code to identify urinary incontinence (788.30-788.39)

Excludes: *benign neoplasms of prostate (222.2)*

➡ **AHA Coding Clinic:** 3Q, '94, 12; 3Q, '92, 7; N-D, '86, 10

601 Inflammatory diseases of prostate ♂ A: 15–124

Use additional code to identify organism, such as Staphylococcus (041.1), or Streptococcus (041.0)

601.0 **Acute prostatitis**

➡ **CC Excl:** 098.12, 098.32, 098.89, 112.2, 131.00, 131.03, 131.8-131.9, 600, 601.0-601.9, 602.0-602.9

✔ **St. Anthony's Clinical Coder:** see Chapter 5

601.1 **Chronic prostatitis**

601.2 **Abscess of prostate**

➡ **CC Excl:** see Code 601.0

601.3 **Prostatocystitis**

➡ **CC Excl:** see Code 601.0

601.4 ***Prostatitis in diseases classified elsewhere***

Code first underlying disease as:
actinomycosis (039.8)
blastomycosis (116.0)
syphilis (095.8)
tuberculosis (016.5)

Excludes: *prostatitis:*
gonococcal (098.12, 098.32)
monilial (112.2)
trichomonal (131.03)

601.8 **Other specified inflammatory diseases of prostate**

Prostatitis:
cavitary
diverticular
granulomatous

601.9 **Prostatitis, unspecified**

Prostatitis NOS

602 Other disorders of prostate ♂ A: 15–124

602.0 **Calculus of prostate**

Prostatic stone

602.1 **Congestion or hemorrhage of prostate**

➡ **CC Excl:** see Code 601.0

602.2 **Atrophy of prostate**

602.8 **Other specified disorders of prostate**

Fistula, Infraction, Stricture } of prostate
Periprostatic adhesions

602.9 **Unspecified disorder of prostate**

603 Hydrocele

Includes: hydrocele of spermatic cord, testis, or tunica vaginalis

Excludes: *congenital (778.6)*

603.0 **Encysted hydrocele**

603.1 **Infected hydrocele**

Use additional code to identify organism

➡ **CC Excl:** 112.2, 131.00, 131.8-131.9, 603.0-603.9

✔ **St. Anthony's Clinical Coder:** see Chapter 5

603.8 **Other specified types of hydrocele**

603.9 **Hydrocele, unspecified**

604 Orchitis and epididymitis ♂

Use additional code to identify organism such as Escherichia coli [E. coli] (041.4), Staphylococcus (041.1), or Streptococcus (041.0)

604.0 **Orchitis, epididymitis, and epididymo-orchitis, with abscess**

Abscess of epididymis or testis

➡ **CC Excl:** 072.0, 098.13-098.14, 098.33-098.34, 098.89, 112.2, 131.00, 131.8-131.9, 604.0-604.99

✔ **St. Anthony's Clinical Coder:** Chapter 5

✓5th **604.9 Other orchitis, epididymitis, and epididymo-orchitis, without mention of abscess**

604.90 Orchitis and epididymitis, unspecified

604.91 Orchitis and epididymitis in diseases classified elsewhere

Code first underlying disease as:
diphtheria (032.89)
filariasis (125.0-125.9)
syphilis (095.8)

Excludes: *orchitis:*
gonococcal (098.13, 098.33)
mumps (072.0)
tuberculous (016.5)
tuberculous epididymitis (016.4)

604.99 Other

605 Redundant prepuce and phimosis ♂

Adherent prepuce
Paraphimosis
Phimosis (congenital)
Tight foreskin

606 Infertility, male ♂ A: 15–124

➡ **AHA Coding Clinic:** 2Q, '96, 9

606.0 Azoospermia

Absolute infertility
Infertility due to:
germinal (cell) aplasia
spermatogenic arrest (complete)

606.1 Oligospermia

Infertility due to:
germinal cell desquamation
hypospermatogenesis
incomplete spermatogenic arrest

606.8 Infertility due to extratesticular causes

Infertility due to:
drug therapy
infection
obstruction of efferent ducts
radiation
systemic disease

606.9 Male infertility, unspecified

607 Disorders of penis ♂

Excludes: *phimosis (605)*

607.0 Leukoplakia of penis

Kraurosis of penis

Excludes: *carcinoma in situ of penis (233.5)*
erythroplasia of Queyrat (233.5)

607.1 Balanoposthitis

Balanitis

Use additional code to identify organism

607.2 Other inflammatory disorders of penis

Abscess, Boil, Carbuncle, Cellulitis } of corpus cavernosum or penis
Cavernitis (penis)

Use additional code to identify organism

Excludes: *herpetic infection (054.13)*

607.3 Priapism

Painful erection

✓5th **607.8 Other specified disorders of penis**

607.81 Balanitis xerotica obliterans

Induratio penis plastica

607.82 Vascular disorders of penis

Embolism, Hematoma (nontraumatic), Hemorrhage, Thrombosis } of corpus cavernosum or penis

607.83 Edema of penis

607.84 Impotence of organic origin A: 15–124

Excludes: *nonorganic or unspecified (302.72)*

607.89 Other

Atrophy, Fibrosis, Hypertrophy, Ulcer (chronic) } of corpus cavernosum or penis

607.9 Unspecified disorder of penis

608 Other disorders of male genital organs ♂

608.0 Seminal vesiculitis

Abscess, Cellulitis } of seminal vesicle
Vesiculitis (seminal)

Use additional code to identify organism

Excludes: *gonococcal infection (098.14, 098.34)*

608.1 Spermatocele

608.2 Torsion of testis

Torsion of:
epididymis
spermatic cord
testicle

608.3 Atrophy of testis

608.4 Other inflammatory disorders of male genital organs

Abscess, Boil, Carbuncle, Cellulitis } of scrotum, spermatic cord, testis [except abscess], tunica vaginalis, or vas deferens

Vasitis

Use additional code to identify organism

Excludes: *abscess of testis (604.0)*

✓5th **608.8 Other specified disorders of male genital organs**

608.81 Disorders of male genital organs in diseases classified elsewhere

Code first underlying disease as:
filariasis (125.0-125.9)
tuberculosis (016.5)

608.83 Vascular disorders

Hematoma (nontraumatic), Hemorrhage, Thrombosis } of seminal vesicle, spermatic cord, testis, scrotum, tunica vaginalis, or vas deferens

Hematocele NOS, male

608.84 Chylocele of tunica vaginalis

608.85 Stricture

Stricture of:
spermatic cord
tunica vaginalis
vas deferens

608.86 Edema

608.89 Other

Atrophy, Fibrosis, Hypertrophy, Ulcer } of seminal vesicle, spermatic cord, testis, scrotum, tunica vaginalis, or vas deferens

Excludes: *atrophy of testis (608.3)*

608.9 Unspecified disorder of male genital organs

DISORDERS OF BREAST (610-611)

610 Benign mammary dysplasias

610.0 Solitary cyst of breast

Cyst (solitary) of breast

610.1 Diffuse cystic mastopathy A: 15–124

Chronic cystic mastitis
Cystic breast
Fibrocystic disease of breast

610.2 Fibroadenosis of breast

Fibroadenosis of breast:
NOS
chronic
cystic
diffuse
periodic
segmental

610.3 Fibrosclerosis of breast

610.4 Mammary duct ectasia

Comedomastitis
Duct ectasia
Mastitis:
periductal
plasma cell

610.8 Other specified benign mammary dysplasias

Mazoplasia
Sebaceous cyst of breast

610.9 Benign mammary dysplasia, unspecified

611 Other disorders of breast

Excludes: *that associated with lactation or the puerperium (675.0-676.9)*

611.0 Inflammatory disease of breast

Abscess (acute) (chronic) (nonpuerperal) of:
areola
breast
Mammillary fistula
Mastitis (acute) (subacute) (nonpuerperal):
NOS
infective
retromammary
submammary

Excludes: *carbuncle of breast (680.2)*
chronic cystic mastitis (610.1)
neonatal infective mastitis (771.5)
thrombophlebitis of breast [Mondor's disease] (451.89)

611.1 Hypertrophy of breast

Gynecomastia
Hypertrophy of breast:
NOS
massive pubertal

611.2 Fissure of nipple

611.3 Fat necrosis of breast

Fat necrosis (segmental) of breast

611.4 Atrophy of breast

611.5 Galactocele

611.6 Galactorrhea not associated with childbirth

✓5th **611.7 Signs and symptoms in breast**

611.71 Mastodynia

Pain in breast

611.72 Lump or mass in breast

➡ **CC Excl:** 610.0-610.9, 611.0-611.9

611.79 Other

Induration of breast
Inversion of nipple
Nipple discharge
Retraction of nipple

611.8 Other specified disorders of breast

Hematoma (nontraumatic) } of breast
Infarction } of breast
Occlusion of breast duct
Subinvolution of breast (postlactational) (postpartum)

611.9 Unspecified breast disorder

INFLAMMATORY DISEASE OF FEMALE PELVIC ORGANS (614-616)

Use additional code to identify organism, such as Staphylococcus (041.1), or Streptococcus (041.0)

Excludes: *that associated with pregnancy, abortion, childbirth, or the puerperium (630-676.9)*

614 Inflammatory disease of ovary, fallopian tube, pelvic cellular tissue, and peritoneum ♀

Excludes: *endometritis (615.0-615.9)*
major infection following delivery (670)
that complicating:
abortion (634-638 with .0, 639.0)
ectopic or molar pregnancy (639.0)
pregnancy or labor (646.6)

614.0 Acute salpingitis and oophoritis

Any condition classifiable to 614.2, specified as acute or subacute

➡ **CC Excl:** 016.60-016.96, 017.90-017.96, 098.15-098.17, 098.35-098.37, 098.89, 112.2, 131.00, 131.8-131.9, 614.0-614.9, 615.0-615.9, 616.8-616.9, 625.8-625.9, 629.8-629.9, 752.8-752.9

614.1 Chronic salpingitis and oophoritis

Hydrosalpinx
Salpingitis:
follicularis
isthmica nodosa

Any condition classifiable to 614.2, specified as chronic

614.2 Salpingitis and oophoritis not specified as acute, subacute, or chronic

Abscess (of):
fallopian tube
ovary
tubo-ovarian
Oophoritis
Perioophoritis
Perisalpingitis
Pyosalpinx
Salpingitis
Salpingo-oophoritis
Tubo-ovarian inflammatory disease

Excludes: *gonococcal infection (chronic) (098.37)*
acute (098.17)
tuberculous (016.6)

614.3 Acute parametritis and pelvic cellulitis

Acute inflammatory pelvic disease
Any condition classifiable to 614.4, specified as acute

➡ **CC Excl:** see Code 614.0

614.4 Chronic or unspecified parametritis and pelvic cellulitis

Abscess (of):
broad ligament } chronic or NOS
parametrium } chronic or NOS
pelvis, female } chronic or NOS
pouch of Douglas } chronic or NOS
Chronic inflammatory pelvic disease
Pelvic cellulitis, female

Excludes: *tuberculous (016.7)*

614.5 Acute or unspecified pelvic peritonitis, female

➡ **CC Excl:** see Code 614.0

614.6 Pelvic peritoneal adhesions, female (postoperative) (postinfection)

Adhesions:
peritubal
tubo-ovarian

Use additional code to identify any associated infertility (628.2)

➡ **AHA Coding Clinic:** 3Q, '95, 7

614.7 Other chronic pelvic peritonitis, female

Excludes: *tuberculous (016.7)*

614.8 Other specified inflammatory disease of female pelvic organs and tissues

614.9 Unspecified inflammatory disease of female pelvic organs and tissues

Pelvic infection or inflammation, female NOS
Pelvic inflammatory disease [PID]

✔ **St. Anthony's Clinical Coder:** see Chapter 5

615 Inflammatory diseases of uterus, except cervix ♀

Excludes: *following delivery (670)*
hyperplastic endometritis (621.3)
that complicating:
abortion (634-638 with .0, 639.0)
ectopic or molar pregnancy (639.0)
pregnancy or labor (646.6)

615.0 Acute

Any condition classifiable to 615.9, specified as acute or subacute

➡ **CC Excl:** 016.60-016.96, 017.90-017.96, 098.15-098.17, 098.35-098.37, 098.89, 112.2, 131.00, 131.8-131.9, 614.0-614.9, 615.0-615.9, 616.0, 616.8-616.9, 621.8-621.9, 625.8-625.9, 629.8-629.9, 752.8-752.9

✔ **St. Anthony's Clinical Coder:** see Chapter 5

615.1 Chronic

Any condition classifiable to 615.9, specified as chronic

615.9 Unspecified inflammatory disease of uterus

Endometritis
Endomyometritis
Metritis
Myometritis
Perimetritis
Pyometra
Uterine abscess

616 Inflammatory disease of cervix, vagina, and vulva ♀

Excludes: *that complicating:*
abortion (634-638 with .0, 639.0)
ectopic or molar pregnancy (639.0)
pregnancy, childbirth, or the puerperium (646.6)

616.0 Cervicitis and endocervicitis

Cervicitis, Endocervicitis } with or without mention of erosion or ectropion
Nabothian (gland) cyst or follicle

Excludes: *erosion or ectropion without mention of cervicitis (622.0)*

✓5th **616.1 Vaginitis and vulvovaginitis**

616.10 Vaginitis and vulvovaginitis, unspecified

Vaginitis:
NOS
postirradiation
Vulvitis NOS
Vulvovaginitis NOS

Use additional code to identify organism, such as Escherichia coli [E. coli] (041.4), Staphylococcus (041.1), or Streptococcus (041.0)

Excludes: *noninfective leukorrhea (623.5)*
postmenopausal or senile vaginitis (627.3)

616.11 Vaginitis and vulvovaginitis in diseases classified elsewhere

Code first underlying disease as:
pinworm vaginitis (127.4)

Excludes: *herpetic vulvovaginitis (054.11)*
monilial vulvovaginitis (112.1)
trichomonal vaginitis or vulvovaginitis (131.01)

616.2 Cyst of Bartholin's gland

Bartholin's duct cyst

616.3 Abscess of Bartholin's gland

Vulvovaginal gland abscess

➡ **CC Excl:** 016.70-016.96, 017.90-017.96, 112.1-112.2, 131.00-131.01, 131.8-131.9, 616.10-616.9, 624.3-624.9, 625.8-625.9, 629.8-629.9, 752.8-752.9

✔ **St. Anthony's Clinical Coder:** see Chapter 5

616.4 Other abscess of vulva

Abscess, Carbuncle, Furuncle } of vulva

➡ **CC Excl:** see Code 616.3

✓5th **616.5 Ulceration of vulva**

616.50 Ulceration of vulva, unspecified

Ulcer NOS of vulva

616.51 Ulceration of vulva in diseases classified elsewhere

Code first underlying disease as:
Behçet's syndrome (136.1)
tuberculosis (016.7)

Excludes: *vulvar ulcer (in):*
gonococcal (098.0)
herpes simplex (054.12)
syphilitic (091.0)

616.8 Other specified inflammatory diseases of cervix, vagina, and vulva

Caruncle, vagina or labium
Ulcer, vagina

Excludes: *noninflammatory disorders of:*
cervix (622.0-622.9)
vagina (623.0-623.9)
vulva (624.0-624.9)

616.9 Unspecified inflammatory disease of cervix, vagina, and vulva

OTHER DISORDERS OF FEMALE GENITAL TRACT (617-629)

617 Endometriosis ♀

617.0 Endometriosis of uterus

Adenomyosis
Endometriosis:
cervix
internal
myometrium

Excludes: *stromal endometriosis (236.0)*

617.1 Endometriosis of ovary

Chocolate cyst of ovary
Endometrial cystoma of ovary

617.2 Endometriosis of fallopian tube

617.3 Endometriosis of pelvic peritoneum

Endometriosis:
broad ligament
cul-de-sac (Douglas')
Endometriosis:
parametrium
round ligament

617.4 Endometriosis of rectovaginal septum and vagina

617.5 Endometriosis of intestine
Endometriosis:
appendix
colon
rectum

617.6 Endometriosis in scar of skin

617.8 Endometriosis of other specified sites
Endometriosis:
bladder
lung
Endometriosis:
umbilicus
vulva

617.9 Endometriosis, site unspecified

618 Genital prolapse ♀

Use additional code to identify urinary incontinence (625.6, 788.31, 788.33-788.39)

Excludes: *that complicating pregnancy, labor, or delivery (654.4)*

618.0 Prolapse of vaginal walls without mention of uterine prolapse
Cystocele
Cystourethrocele
Proctocele, female
Rectocele
Urethrocele, female
Vaginal prolapse
} without mention of uterine prolapse

Excludes: *that with uterine prolapse (618.2-618.4)*
enterocele (618.6)
vaginal vault prolapse following hysterectomy (618.5)

618.1 Uterine prolapse without mention of vaginal wall prolapse
Descensus uteri
Uterine prolapse:
NOS
complete
Uterine prolapse:
first degree
second degree
third degree

Excludes: *that with mention of cystocele, urethrocele, or rectocele (618.2-618.4)*

618.2 Uterovaginal prolapse, incomplete

618.3 Uterovaginal prolapse, complete

618.4 Uterovaginal prolapse, unspecified

618.5 Prolapse of vaginal vault after hysterectomy

618.6 Vaginal enterocele, congenital or acquired
Pelvic enterocele, congenital or acquired

618.7 Old laceration of muscles of pelvic floor

618.8 Other specified genital prolapse
Incompetence or weakening of pelvic fundus
Relaxation of vaginal outlet or pelvis

618.9 Unspecified genital prolapse

619 Fistula involving female genital tract ♀

Excludes: *vesicorectal and intestinovesical fistula (596.1)*

619.0 Urinary-genital tract fistula, female
Fistula:
cervicovesical
ureterovaginal
urethrovaginal
urethrovesicovaginal
Fistula:
uteroureteric
uterovesical
vesicocervicovaginal
vesicovaginal.

619.1 Digestive-genital tract fistula, female
Fistula:
intestinouterine
intestinovaginal
rectovaginal
Fistula:
rectovulval
sigmoidovaginal
uterorectal

619.2 Genital tract-skin fistula, female
Fistula:
uterus to abdominal wall
vaginoperineal

619.8 Other specified fistulas involving female genital tract
Fistula:
cervix
cul-de-sac (Douglas')
Fistula:
uterus
vagina

619.9 Unspecified fistula involving female genital tract

620 Noninflammatory disorders of ovary, fallopian tube, and broad ligament ♀

Excludes: *hydrosalpinx (614.1)*

620.0 Follicular cyst of ovary
Cyst of graafian follicle

620.1 Corpus luteum cyst or hematoma
Corpus luteum hemorrhage or rupture
Lutein cyst

620.2 Other and unspecified ovarian cyst
Cyst:
NOS
corpus albicans
retention NOS
serous
theca-lutein
} of ovary
Simple cystoma of ovary

Excludes: *cystadenoma (benign) (serous) (220)*
developmental cysts (752.0)
neoplastic cysts (220)
polycystic ovaries (256.4)
Stein-Leventhal syndrome (256.4)

620.3 Acquired atrophy of ovary and fallopian tube
Senile involution of ovary

620.4 Prolapse or hernia of ovary and fallopian tube
Displacement of ovary and fallopian tube
Salpingocele

620.5 Torsion of ovary, ovarian pedicle, or fallopian tube
Torsion:
accessory tube
hydatid of Morgagni

620.6 Broad ligament laceration syndrome
Masters-Allen syndrome

620.7 Hematoma of broad ligament
Hematocele, broad ligament

➡ **CC Excl:** 620.6-620.9, 625.8-625.9, 629.8-629.9, 752.8-752.9

620.8 Other noninflammatory disorders of ovary, fallopian tube, and broad ligament
Cyst, Polyp } of broad ligament or fallopian tube
Infarction, Rupture } of ovary or fallopian tube
Hematosalpinx

Excludes: *hematosalpinx in ectopic pregnancy (639.2)*
peritubal adhesions (614.6)
torsion of ovary, ovarian pedicle, or fallopian tube (620.5)

620.9 Unspecified noninflammatory disorder of ovary, fallopian tube, and broad ligament

621 Disorders of uterus, not elsewhere classified ♀

621.0 Polyp of corpus uteri
Polyp:
endometrium
uterus NOS

Excludes: *cervical polyp NOS (622.7)*

621.1 Chronic subinvolution of uterus

Excludes: *puerperal (674.8)*

621.2 Hypertrophy of uterus
Bulky or enlarged uterus

Excludes: *puerperal (674.8)*

621.3 Endometrial cystic hyperplasia
Hyperplasia (adenomatous) (cystic) (glandular) of endometrium
Hyperplastic endometritis

621.4 Hematometra
Hemometra

Excludes: *that in congenital anomaly (752.2-752.3)*

621.5 Intrauterine synechiae
Adhesions of uterus
Band(s) of uterus

621.6 Malposition of uterus
Anteversion, Retroflexion, Retroversion } of uterus

Excludes: *malposition complicating pregnancy, labor, or delivery (654.3-654.4)*
prolapse of uterus (618.1-618.4)

621.7 Chronic inversion of uterus

Excludes: *current obstetrical trauma (665.2)*
prolapse of uterus (618.1-618.4)

621.8 Other specified disorders of uterus, not elsewhere classified
Atrophy, acquired; Cyst; Fibrosis NOS; Old laceration (postpartum); Ulcer } of uterus

Excludes: *bilharzial fibrosis (120.0-120.9)*
endometriosis (617.0)
fistulas (619.0-619.8)
inflammatory diseases (615.0-615.9)

621.9 Unspecified disorder of uterus

622 Noninflammatory disorders of cervix ♀

Excludes: *abnormality of cervix complicating pregnancy, labor, or delivery (654.5-654.6)*
fistula (619.0-619.8)

622.0 Erosion and ectropion of cervix
Eversion, Ulcer } of cervix

Excludes: *that in chronic cervicitis (616.0)*

622.1 Dysplasia of cervix (uteri)
Anaplasia of cervix
Cervical atypism

Excludes: *carcinoma in situ of cervix (233.1)*
cervical intraepithelial neoplasia III [CIN III] (233.1)

➡ **AHA Coding Clinic:** 1Q, '91, 11

622.2 Leukoplakia of cervix (uteri)

Excludes: *carcinoma in situ of cervix (233.1)*

622.3 Old laceration of cervix
Adhesions, Band(s), Cicatrix (postpartum) } of cervix

Excludes: *current obstetrical trauma (665.3)*

622.4 Stricture and stenosis of cervix

Atresia (acquired), Contracture, Occlusion — of cervix
Pinpoint os uteri

Excludes: *congenital (752.49)*
that complicating labor (654.6)

622.5 Incompetence of cervix

Excludes: *complicating pregnancy (654.5)*
that affecting fetus or newborn (761.0)

622.6 Hypertrophic elongation of cervix

622.7 Mucous polyp of cervix

Polyp NOS of cervix

Excludes: *adenomatous polyp of cervix (219.0)*

622.8 Other specified noninflammatory disorders of cervix

Atrophy (senile), Cyst, Fibrosis, Hemorrhage — of cervix

Excludes: *endometriosis (617.0)*
fistula (619.0-619.8)
inflammatory diseases (616.0)

622.9 Unspecified noninflammatory disorder of cervix

623 Noninflammatory disorders of vagina ♀

Excludes: *abnormality of vagina complicating pregnancy, labor, or delivery (654.7)*
congenital absence of vagina (752.49)
congenital diaphragm or bands (752.49)
fistulas involving vagina (619.0-619.8)

623.0 Dysplasia of vagina

Excludes: *carcinoma in situ of vagina (233.3)*

623.1 Leukoplakia of vagina

623.2 Stricture or atresia of vagina

Adhesions (postoperative) (postradiation) of vagina
Occlusion of vagina
Stenosis, vagina

Use additional E code to identify any external cause

Excludes: *congenital atresia or stricture (752.49)*

623.3 Tight hymenal ring

Rigid hymen, Tight hymenal ring, Tight introitus — acquired or congenital

Excludes: *imperforate hymen (752.42)*

623.4 Old vaginal laceration

Excludes: *old laceration involving muscles of pelvic floor (618.7)*

623.5 Leukorrhea, not specified as infective

Leukorrhea NOS of vagina
Vaginal discharge NOS

Excludes: *trichomonal (131.00)*

623.6 Vaginal hematoma

Excludes: *current obstetrical trauma (665.7)*

623.7 Polyp of vagina

623.8 Other specified noninflammatory disorders of vagina

Cyst, Hemorrhage — of vagina

623.9 Unspecified noninflammatory disorder of vagina

624 Noninflammatory disorders of vulva and perineum ♀

Excludes: *abnormality of vulva and perineum complicating pregnancy, labor, or delivery (654.8)*
condyloma acuminatum (078.1)
fistulas involving:
perineum — see Alphabetic Index
vulva (619.0-619.8)
vulval varices (456.6)
vulvar involvement in skin conditions (690-709.9)

624.0 Dystrophy of vulva

Kraurosis, Leukoplakia — of vulva

Excludes: *carcinoma in situ of vulva (233.3)*

624.1 Atrophy of vulva

624.2 Hypertrophy of clitoris

Excludes: *that in endocrine disorders (255.2, 256.1)*

624.3 Hypertrophy of labia

Hypertrophy of vulva NOS

624.4 Old laceration or scarring of vulva

624.5 Hematoma of vulva

Excludes: *that complicating delivery (664.5)*

624.6 Polyp of labia and vulva

624.8 Other specified noninflammatory disorders of vulva and perineum

Cyst, Edema, Stricture } of vulva

624.9 Unspecified noninflammatory disorder of vulva and perineum

625 Pain and other symptoms associated with female genital organs ♀

625.0 Dyspareunia

Excludes: *psychogenic dyspareunia (302.76)*

625.1 Vaginismus

Colpospasm
Vulvismus

Excludes: *psychogenic vaginismus (306.51)*

625.2 Mittelschmerz

Intermenstrual pain
Ovulation pain

625.3 Dysmenorrhea

Painful menstruation

Excludes: *psychogenic dysmenorrhea (306.52)*

625.4 Premenstrual tension syndromes

Menstrual:
- migraine
- molimen

Premenstrual syndrome
Premenstrual tension NOS

625.5 Pelvic congestion syndrome

Congestion-fibrosis syndrome
Taylor's syndrome

625.6 Stress incontinence, female

Excludes: *mixed incontinence (788.33)*
stress incontinence, male (788.32)

625.8 Other specified symptoms associated with female genital organs

➡ **AHA Coding Clinic:** N-D, '85, 16

625.9 Unspecified symptom associated with female genital organs

626 Disorders of menstruation and other abnormal bleeding from female genital tract ♀

Excludes: *menopausal and premenopausal bleeding (627.0)*
pain and other symptoms associated with menstrual cycle (625.2-625.4)
postmenopausal bleeding (627.1)

626.0 Absence of menstruation

Amenorrhea (primary) (secondary)

626.1 Scanty or infrequent menstruation

Hypomenorrhea
Oligomenorrhea

626.2 Excessive or frequent menstruation

Heavy periods
Menometrorrhagia
Menorrhagia
Polymenorrhea

Excludes: *premenopausal (627.0)*
that in puberty (626.3)

626.3 Puberty bleeding

Excessive bleeding associated with onset of menstrual periods
Pubertal menorrhagia

626.4 Irregular menstrual cycle

Irregular:
- bleeding NOS
- menstruation
- periods

626.5 Ovulation bleeding

Regular intermenstrual bleeding

626.6 Metrorrhagia

Bleeding unrelated to menstrual cycle
Irregular intermenstrual bleeding

626.7 Postcoital bleeding

626.8 Other

Dysfunctional or functional uterine hemorrhage NOS
Menstruation:
- retained
- suppression of

626.9 Unspecified

627 Menopausal and postmenopausal disorders ♀

627.0 Premenopausal menorrhagia

Excessive bleeding associated with onset of menopause
Menorrhagia:
- climacteric
- menopausal
- preclimacteric

627.1 Postmenopausal bleeding

627.2 Menopausal or female climacteric states

Symptoms, such as flushing, sleeplessness, headache, lack of concentration, associated with the menopause

627.3 Postmenopausal atrophic vaginitis

Senile (atrophic) vaginitis

627.4 States associated with artificial menopause

Postartificial menopause syndromes
Any condition classifiable to 627.1, 627.2, or 627.3 which follows induced menopause

627.8 Other specified menopausal and postmenopausal disorders

Excludes: premature menopause NOS (256.3)

627.9 Unspecified menopausal and postmenopausal disorder

628 Infertility, female ♀

Includes: primary and secondary sterility

➡ **AHA Coding Clinic:** 2Q, '96, 9

628.0 Associated with anovulation

Anovulatory cycle

Use additional code for any associated Stein-Leventhal syndrome (256.4)

628.1 Of pituitary-hypothalamic origin

Code first underlying disease as:
adiposogenital dystrophy (253.8)
anterior pituitary disorder (253.0-253.4)

628.2 Of tubal origin

Infertility associated with congenital anomaly of tube

Tubal:
block
occlusion
stenosis

Use additional code for any associated peritubal adhesions (614.6)

628.3 Of uterine origin

Infertility associated with congenital anomaly of uterus

Nonimplantation

Use additional code for any associated tuberculous endometritis (016.7)

628.4 Of cervical or vaginal origin

Infertility associated with:
anomaly or cervical mucus
congenital structural anomaly
dysmucorrhea

628.8 Of other specified origin

628.9 Of unspecified origin

629 Other disorders of female genital organs ♀

629.0 Hematocele, female, not elsewhere classified

Excludes: hematocele or hematoma:
broad ligament (620.7)
fallopian tube (620.8)
that associated with ectopic pregnancy (633.0-633.9)
uterus (621.4)
vagina (623.6)
vulva (624.5)

629.1 Hydrocele, canal of Nuck

Cyst of canal of Nuck (acquired)

Excludes: congenital (752.41)

629.8 Other specified disorders of female genital organs

629.9 Unspecified disorder of female genital organs

Habitual aborter without current pregnancy

11. COMPLICATIONS OF PREGNANCY, CHILDBIRTH, AND THE PUERPERIUM (630-677)

ECTOPIC AND MOLAR PREGNANCY (630-633)

Use additional code from category 639 to identify any complications

630 Hydatidiform mole ♀ A: 12–55

Trophoblastic disease NOS
Vesicular mole

Excludes: *chorioadenoma (destruens) (236.1)*
chorionepithelioma (181)
malignant hydatidiform mole (236.1)

631 Other abnormal product of conception ♀ A: 12–55

Blighted ovum
Mole:
 NOS
 carneous
Mole:
 fleshy
 stone

632 Missed abortion ♀ A: 12–55

Early fetal death before completion of 22 weeks' gestation with retention of dead fetus
Retained products of conception, not following spontaneous or induced abortion or delivery

Excludes: *failed induced abortion (638.0-638.9)*
fetal death (intrauterine) (late) (656.4)
missed delivery (656.4)
that with abnormal product of conception (630, 631)

633 Ectopic pregnancy ♀ A: 12–55

Includes: ruptured ectopic pregnancy

633.0 Abdominal pregnancy

Intraperitoneal pregnancy

633.1 Tubal pregnancy

Fallopian pregnancy
Rupture of (fallopian) tube due to pregnancy
Tubal abortion

➡ **AHA Coding Clinic:** 2Q, '90, 27

633.2 Ovarian pregnancy

633.8 Other ectopic pregnancy

Pregnancy:
 cervical
 combined
 cornual
Pregnancy:
 intraligamentous
 mesometric
 mural

633.9 Unspecified ectopic pregnancy

OTHER PREGNANCY WITH ABORTIVE OUTCOME (634-639)

The following fourth-digit subdivisions are for use with categories 634-638:

.0 Complicated by genital tract and pelvic infection

Endometritis
Salpingo-oophoritis
Sepsis NOS
Septicemia NOS
Any condition classifiable to 639.0, with condition classifiable to 634-638

Excludes: *urinary tract infection (634-638 with .7)*

.1 Complicated by delayed or excessive hemorrhage

Afibrinogenemia
Defibrination syndrome
Intravascular hemolysis
Any condition classifiable to 639.1, with condition classifiable to 634-638

.2 Complicated by damage to pelvic organs and tissues

Laceration, perforation, or tear of:
 bladder
 uterus
Any condition classifiable to 639.2, with condition classifiable to 634-638

.3 Complicated by renal failure

Oliguria
Uremia
Any condition classifiable to 639.3, with condition classifiable to 634-638

.4 Complicated by metabolic disorder

Electrolyte imbalance with conditions classifiable to 634-638

.5 Complicated by shock

Circulatory collapse
Shock (postoperative) (septic)
Any condition classifiable to 639.5, with condition classifiable to 634-638

.6 Complicated by embolism

Embolism:
 NOS
 amniotic fluid
 pulmonary
Any condition classifiable to 639.6, with condition classifiable to 634-638

.7 With other specified complications

Cardiac arrest or failure
Urinary tract infection
Any condition classifiable to 639.8, with condition classifiable to 634-638

.8 With unspecified complications

.9 Without mention of complication

§ 634 Spontaneous abortion ♀ A: 12–55

Includes: miscarriage
spontaneous abortion

✓5th **634.0 Complicated by genital tract and pelvic infection**
➡ **CC Excl:** 634.00-634.92, 635.00-635.92, 636.00-636.92, 637.00-637.92, 638.0-638.9, 640.00-640.93, 641.00-641.23, 646.80-646.93, 648.90-648.94, 650, 669.40-669.44, 669.80-669.94

✓5th **634.1 Complicated by delayed or excessive hemorrhage**
➡ **CC Excl:** see Code 634.0

✓5th **634.2 Complicated by damage to pelvic organs or tissues**
➡ **CC Excl:** see Code 634.0

✓5th **634.3 Complicated by renal failure**
➡ **CC Excl:** see Code 634.0

✓5th **634.4 Complicated by metabolic disorder**
➡ **CC Excl:** see Code 634.0

✓5th **634.5 Complicated by shock**
➡ **CC Excl:** see Code 634.0

✓5th **634.6 Complicated by embolism**
➡ **CC Excl:** see Code 634.0

✓5th **634.7 With other specified complications**
➡ **CC Excl:** see Code 634.0

✓5th **634.8 With unspecified complication**
➡ **CC Excl:** see Code 634.0

✓5th **634.9 Without mention of complication**
➡ **CC Excl:** see Code 634.0

§ 635 Legally induced abortion ♀ A: 12–55

Includes: abortion or termination of pregnancy:
elective
legal
therapeutic

Excludes: *menstrual extraction or regulation (V25.3)*

✓5th **635.0 Complicated by genital tract and pelvic infection**

✓5th **635.1 Complicated by delayed or excessive hemorrhage**

✓5th **635.2 Complicated by damage to pelvic organs or tissues**

✓5th **635.3 Complicated by renal failure**

✓5th **635.4 Complicated by metabolic disorder**

✓5th **635.5 Complicated by shock**

✓5th **635.6 Complicated by embolism**

✓5th **635.7 With other specified complications**

✓5th **635.8 With unspecified complication**

✓5th **635.9 Without mention of complication**

§ 636 Illegally induced abortion ♀ A: 12–55

Includes: abortion:
criminal
illegal
self-induced

✓5th **636.0 Complicated by genital tract and pelvic infection**

✓5th **636.1 Complicated by delayed or excessive hemorrhage**

✓5th **636.2 Complicated by damage to pelvic organs or tissues**

✓5th **636.3 Complicated by renal failure**

✓5th **636.4 Complicated by metabolic disorder**

✓5th **636.5 Complicated by shock**

✓5th **636.6 Complicated by embolism**

✓5th **636.7 With other specified complications**

✓5th **636.8 With unspecified complication**

✓5th **636.9 Without mention of complication**

§ 637 Unspecified abortion ♀ A: 12–55

Includes: abortion NOS
retained products of conception following abortion, not classifiable elsewhere

✓5th **637.0 Complicated by genital tract and pelvic infection**

✓5th **637.1 Complicated by delayed or excessive hemorrhage**

✓5th **637.2 Complicated by damage to pelvic organs or tissues**

✓5th **637.3 Complicated by renal failure**

✓5th **637.4 Complicated by metabolic disorder**

✓5th **637.5 Complicated by shock**

✓5th **637.6 Complicated by embolism**

✓5th **637.7 With other specified complications**

✓5th **637.8 With unspecified complication**

✓5th **637.9 Without mention of complication**

§Requires fifth-digit to identify stage:
0 unspecified
1 incomplete
2 complete

638 Failed attempted abortion ♀ A: 12–55

Includes: failure of attempted induction of (legal) abortion

Excludes: *incomplete abortion (634.0-637.9)*

638.0 Complicated by genital tract and pelvic infection

638.1 Complicated by delayed or excessive hemorrhage

638.2 Complicated by damage to pelvic organs or tissues

638.3 Complicated by renal failure

638.4 Complicated by metabolic disorder

638.5 Complicated by shock

638.6 Complicated by embolism

638.7 With other specified complications

638.8 With unspecified complication

638.9 Without mention of complication

639 Complications following abortion and ectopic and molar pregnancies ♀ A: 12–55

Note: This category is provided for use when it is required to classify separately the complications classifiable to the fourth-digit level in categories 634-638; for example:
a) when the complication itself was responsible for an episode of medical care, the abortion, ectopic or molar pregnancy itself having been dealt with at a previous episode
b) when these conditions are immediate complications of ectopic or molar pregnancies classifiable to 630-633 where they cannot be identified at fourth-digit level.

639.0 Genital tract and pelvic infection

Endometritis
Parametritis
Pelvic peritonitis
Salpingitis
Salpingo-oophoritis
Sepsis NOS
Septicemia NOS
} following conditions classifiable to 630-638

Excludes: *urinary tract infection (639.8)*

➡ **CC Excl:** 639.0, 639.2-639.9, 640.00-640.93, 641.00-641.23, 646.80-646.93, 648.90-648.94, 650, 669.40-669.44, 669.80-669.94

639.1 Delayed or excessive hemorrhage

Afibrinogenemia
Defibrination syndrome
Intravascular hemolysis
} following conditions classifiable to 630-638

➡ **CC Excl:** 639.1-639.9, 640.00-640.93, 641.00-641.23, 646.80-646.93, 648.90-648.94, 650, 669.40-669.44, 669.80-669.94

639.2 Damage to pelvic organs and tissues

Laceration, perforation, or tear of:
- bladder
- bowel
- broad ligament
- cervix
- periurethral tissue
- uterus
- vagina

} following conditions classifiable to 630-638

➡ **CC Excl:** 639.2-639.9, 640.00-640.93, 641.00-641.23, 646.80-646.93, 648.90-648.94, 650, 669.40-669.44, 669.80-669.94

639.3 Renal failure

Oliguria
Renal:
- failure (acute)
- shutdown
- tubular necrosis

Uremia
} following conditions classifiable to 630-638

➡ **CC Excl:** see Code 639.2

639.4 Metabolic disorders

Electrolyte imbalance following conditions classifiable to 630-638

➡ **CC Excl:** see Code 639.2

639.5 Shock

Circulatory collapse
Shock (postoperative) (septic)
} following conditions classifiable to 630-638

➡ **CC Excl:** see Code 639.2

639.6 Embolism

Embolism:
- NOS
- air
- amniotic fluid
- blood-clot
- fat
- pulmonary
- pyemic
- septic
- soap

} following conditions classifiable to 630-638

➡ **CC Excl:** see Code 639.2

639.8 Other specified complications following abortion or ectopic and molar pregnancy

Acute yellow atrophy or necrosis of liver; Cardiac arrest or failure; Cerebral anoxia; Urinary tract infection — following conditions classifiable to 630-638

➡ **CC Excl:** see Code 639.2

639.9 Unspecified complication following abortion or ectopic and molar pregnancy

Complication(s) not further specified following conditions classifiable to 630-638

➡ **CC Excl:** see Code 639.2

COMPLICATIONS MAINLY RELATED TO PREGNANCY (640-648)

Includes: the listed conditions even if they arose or were present during labor, delivery, or the puerperium

The following fifth-digit subclassification is for use with categories 640-648 to denote the current episode of care:

0 unspecified as to episode of care or not applicable

1 delivered, with or without mention of antepartum condition

Antepartum condition with delivery

Delivery NOS; Intrapartum obstetric condition; Pregnancy, delivered — (with mention of antepartum complication during current episode of care)

2 delivered, with mention of postpartum complication

Delivery with mention of puerperal complication during current episode of care

3 antepartum condition or complication

Antepartum obstetric condition, not delivered during the current episode of care

4 postpartum condition or complication

Postpartum or puerperal obstetric condition or complication following delivery that occurred:
- during previous episode of care
- outside hospital, with subsequent admission for observation or care

➡ **AHA Coding Clinic:** 2Q, '90, 11

§ 640 Hemorrhage in early pregnancy ♀ A: 12–55

Includes: hemorrhage before completion of 22 weeks' gestation

✓5th **640.0 Threatened abortion**
[0,1,3]

➡ **CC Excl:** 640.00-640.93, 641.00-641.13, 646.80-646.93, 648.90-648.94, 650, 669.40-669.44, 669.80-669.94

✓5th **640.8 Other specified hemorrhage in early pregnancy**
[0,1,3]

➡ **CC Excl:** see Code 640.0

✓5th **640.9 Unspecified hemorrhage in early pregnancy**
[0,1,3]

➡ **CC Excl:** see Code 640.0

§ 641 Antepartum hemorrhage, abruptio placentae, and placenta previa ♀ A: 12–55

✓5th [8] **641.0 Placenta previa without hemorrhage**
[0,1,3]

Low implantation of placenta; Placenta previa noted: during pregnancy; before labor (and delivered by cesarean delivery) — without hemorrhage

➡ **CC Excl:** see Code 640.0

✓5th [8] **641.1 Hemorrhage from placenta previa**
[0,1,3]

Low-lying placenta; Placenta previa: incomplete, marginal, partial, total — NOS or with hemorrhage (intrapartum)

Excludes: *hemorrhage from vasa previa (663.5)*

➡ **CC Excl:** see Code 640.0

✓5th [8] **641.2 Premature separation of placenta**
[0,1,3]

Ablatio placentae
Abruptio placentae
Accidental antepartum hemorrhage
Couvelaire uterus
Detachment of placenta (premature)
Premature separation of normally implanted placenta

✓5th [8] **641.3 Antepartum hemorrhage associated with coagulation defects**
[0,1,3]

Antepartum or intrapartum hemorrhage associated with:
- afibrinogenemia
- hyperfibrinolysis
- hypofibrinogenemia

➡ **CC Excl:** 641.30-641.93, 646.80-646.93, 648.90-648.94, 650, 669.40-669.44, 669.80-669.94

✓5th [8] **641.8 Other antepartum hemorrhage**
[0,1,3]

Antepartum or intrapartum hemorrhage associated with:
- trauma
- uterine leiomyoma

➡ **CC Excl:** see Code 641.3

§ Requires fifth-digit. Valid digits are in [brackets] under each code. See above, this page for definitions.
[8] Nonspecific PDX = 0

✓5th **641.9 Unspecified antepartum hemorrhage**
[0,1,3]
Hemorrhage:
antepartum NOS
intrapartum NOS
of pregnancy NOS

➡ **CC Excl:** see Code 641.3

§ 642 Hypertension complicating pregnancy, childbirth, and the puerperium ♀ A: 12–55

✓5th [8] **642.0 Benign essential hypertension complicating pregnancy, childbirth, and the puerperium**
[0–4]
Hypertension:
benign essential
chronic NOS
essential
pre-existing NOS
} specified as complicating, or as a reason for obstetric care during pregnancy, childbirth, or the puerperium

✓5th [8] **642.1 Hypertension secondary to renal disease, complicating pregnancy, childbirth, and the puerperium**
[0–4]
Hypertension secondary to renal disease, specified as complicating, or as a reason for obstetric care during pregnancy, childbirth, or the puerperium

✓5th [8] **642.2 Other pre-existing hypertension complicating pregnancy, childbirth, and the puerperium**
[0–4]
Hypertensive:
heart and renal disease
heart disease
renal disease
Malignant hypertension
} specified as complicating, or as a reason for obstetric care during pregnancy, childbirth, or the puerperium

✓5th [8] **642.3 Transient hypertension of pregnancy**
[0–4]
Gestational hypertension
Transient hypertension, so described, in pregnancy, childbirth, or the puerperium

➡ **AHA Coding Clinic:** 3Q, '90, 4

✓5th [8] **642.4 Mild or unspecified pre-eclampsia**
[0–4]
Hypertension in pregnancy, childbirth, or the puerperium, not specified as pre-existing, with either albuminuria or edema, or both; mild or unspecified

Pre-eclampsia:
NOS
mild

Toxemia (pre-eclamptic):
NOS
mild

Excludes: *albuminuria in pregnancy, without mention of hypertension (646.2)*
edema in pregnancy, without mention of hypertension (646.1)

➡ **CC Excl:** 642.00-642.94, 646.10-646.14, 646.80-646.93, 648.90-648.94, 650, 669.40-669.44, 669.80-669.94

✓5th [8] **642.5 Severe pre-eclampsia**
[0–4]
Hypertension in pregnancy, childbirth, or the puerperium, not specified as pre-existing, with either albuminuria or edema, or both; specified as severe
Pre-eclampsia, severe
Toxemia (pre-eclamptic), severe

➡ **CC Excl:** see Code 642.4

➡ **AHA Coding Clinic:** N-D, '85, 3

✓5th [8] **642.6 Eclampsia**
[0–4]
Toxemia:
eclamptic
with convulsions

➡ **CC Excl:** see Code 642.4

✓5th [8] **642.7 Pre-eclampsia or eclampsia superimposed on pre-existing hypertension**
[0–4]
Conditions classifiable to 642.4-642.6, with conditions classifiable to 642.0-642.2

➡ **CC Excl:** see Code 642.4

✓5th [8] **642.9 Unspecified hypertension complicating pregnancy, childbirth, or the puerperium**
[0–4]
Hypertension NOS, without mention of albuminuria or edema, complicating pregnancy, childbirth, or the puerperium

§ 643 Excessive vomiting in pregnancy ♀ A: 12–55

Includes: hyperemesis
vomiting:
persistent
vicious
} arising during pregnancy
hyperemesis gravidarum

✓5th [8] **643.0 Mild hyperemesis gravidarum**
[0,1,3]
Hyperemesis gravidarum, mild or unspecified, starting before the end of the 22nd week of gestation

✓5th [8] **643.1 Hyperemesis gravidarum with metabolic disturbance**
[0,1,3]
Hyperemesis gravidarum, starting before the end of the 22nd week of gestation, with metabolic disturbance, such as:
carbohydrate depletion
dehydration
electrolyte imbalance

✓5th [8] **643.2 Late vomiting of pregnancy**
[0,1,3]
Excessive vomiting starting after 22 completed weeks of gestation

✓5th [8] **643.8 Other vomiting complicating pregnancy**
[0,1,3]
Vomiting due to organic disease or other cause, specified as complicating pregnancy, or as a reason for obstetric care during pregnancy

Use additional code to specify cause

§ Requires fifth-digit. Valid digits are in [brackets] under each code. See page 228 for definitions.
[8] Nonspecific PDX = 0

✓5th [8] **643.9 Unspecified vomiting of pregnancy**
[0,1,3]
Vomiting as a reason for care during pregnancy, length of gestation unspecified

§ 644 Early or threatened labor ♀ A: 12–55

✓5th [8] □ **644.0 Threatened premature labor**
[0,3]
Premature labor after 22 weeks, but before 37 completed weeks of gestation without delivery

Excludes: *that occurring before 22 completed weeks of gestation (640.0)*

➡ **CC Excl:** 644.00-644.21, 646.80-646.93, 648.90-648.94, 650, 669.40-669.44, 669.80-669.94

✓5th [8] □ **644.1 Other threatened labor**
[0,3]
False labor:
NOS
after 37 completed weeks of gestation
Threatened labor NOS
} without delivery

➡ **CC Excl:** see Code 644.0

✓5th [8] □ **644.2 Early onset of delivery**
[0–1]
Onset (spontaneous) of delivery
Premature labor with onset of delivery
} before 37 completed weeks of gestation

➡ **AHA Coding Clinic:** 2Q, '91, 16

[8] **§ 645 Prolonged pregnancy** ♀ A: 12–55
[0,1,3]
Postterm pregnancy
Pregnancy which has advanced beyond 42 weeks of gestation

✓5th Use 0 as fourth-digit for category 645

➡ **AHA Coding Clinic:** 4Q, '91, 26

§ 646 Other complications of pregnancy, not elsewhere classified ♀ A: 12–55

Use additional code(s) to further specify complication

➡ **AHA Coding Clinic:** 4Q, '95, 59

✓5th [8] **646.0 Papyraceous fetus**
[0,1,3]

✓5th [8] **646.1 Edema or excessive weight gain in pregnancy, without mention of hypertension**
[0–4]
Gestational edema
Maternal obesity syndrome

Excludes: *that with mention of hypertension (642.0-642.9)*

✓5th [8] **646.2 Unspecified renal disease in pregnancy, without mention of hypertension**
[0–4]
Albuminuria
Nephropathy NOS
Renal disease NOS
Uremia
Gestational proteinuria
} in pregnancy or the puerperium, without mention of hypertension

Excludes: *that with mention of hypertension (642.0-642.9)*

✓5th [8] **646.3 Habitual aborter**
[0,1,3]

Excludes: *with current abortion (634.0-634.9)*
without current pregnancy (629.9)

✓5th [8] **646.4 Peripheral neuritis in pregnancy**
[0–4]

✓5th [8] **646.5 Asymptomatic bacteriuria in pregnancy**
[0–4]

✓5th [8] **646.6 Infections of genitourinary tract in pregnancy**
[0–4]
Conditions classifiable to 590, 595, 597, 599.0, 616 complicating pregnancy, childbirth, or the puerperium
Conditions classifiable to 614-615 complicating pregnancy or labor

Excludes: *major puerperal infection (670)*

➡ **CC Excl:** 646.60-646.64, 646.80-646.93, 648.90-648.94, 650, 669.40-669.44, 669.80-669.94

✓5th [8] **646.7 Liver disorders in pregnancy**
[0,1,3]
Acute yellow atrophy of liver (obstetric) (true)
Icterus gravis
Necrosis of liver
} of pregnancy

Excludes: *hepatorenal syndrome following delivery (674.8)*
viral hepatitis (647.6)

➡ **CC Excl:** 646.70-646.93, 648.90-648.94, 650, 669.40-669.44, 669.80-669.94

✓5th [8] **646.8 Other specified complications of pregnancy**
[0–4]
Fatigue during pregnancy
Herpes gestationis
Insufficient weight gain of pregnancy

✓5th [8] **646.9 Unspecified complication of pregnancy**
[0,1,3]

§ Requires fifth-digit. Valid digits are in [brackets] under each code. See page 228 for definitions.
[8] Nonspecific PDX = 0

§ 647 Infectious and parasitic conditions in the mother classifiable elsewhere, but complicating pregnancy, childbirth, or the puerperium ♀ A: 12–55

Use additional code(s) to further specify complication

Includes: the listed conditions when complicating the pregnant state, aggravated by the pregnancy, or when a main reason for obstetric care

Excludes: *those conditions in the mother known or suspected to have affected the fetus (655.0-655.9)*

✓5th [8] **647.0** **Syphilis**
[0–4] Conditions classifiable to 090-097

✓5th [8] **647.1** **Gonorrhea**
[0–4] Conditions classifiable to 098

✓5th [8] **647.2** **Other venereal diseases**
[0–4] Conditions classifiable to 099

✓5th [8] **647.3** **Tuberculosis**
[0–4] Conditions classifiable to 010-018

➡ **CC Excl:** 646.80-646.93, 647.30-647.34, 648.90-648.94, 650, 669.40-669.44, 669.80-669.94

✓5th [8] **647.4** **Malaria**
[0–4] Conditions classifiable to 084

➡ **CC Excl:** 646.80-646.93, 647.40-647.44, 648.90-648.94, 650, 669.40-669.44, 669.80-669.94

✓5th [8] **647.5** **Rubella**
[0–4] Conditions classifiable to 056

✓5th [8] **647.6** **Other viral diseases**
[0–4] Conditions classifiable to 042 and 050-079, except 056

➡ **AHA Coding Clinic:** J-F, '85, 15

✓5th [8] **647.8** **Other specified infectious and parasitic diseases**
[0–4]

✓5th **647.9** **Unspecified infection or infestation**
[0–4]

§ 648 Other current conditions in the mother classifiable elsewhere, but complicating pregnancy, childbirth, or the puerperium ♀ A: 12–55

Use additional code(s) to identify the condition

Includes: the listed conditions when complicating the pregnant state, aggravated by the pregnancy, or when a main reason for obstetric care

Excludes: *those conditions in the mother known or suspected to have affected the fetus (655.0-665.9)*

✓5th [8] **648.0** **Diabetes mellitus**
[0–4] Conditions classifiable to 250

Excludes: *gestational diabetes (648.8)*

➡ **CC Excl:** 646.80-646.93, 648.00-648.04, 648.90-648.94, 650, 669.40-669.44, 669.80-669.94

➡ **AHA Coding Clinic:** 3Q, '91, 5

✓5th [8] **648.1** **Thyroid dysfunction**
[0–4] Conditions classifiable to 240-246

✓5th [8] **648.2** **Anemia**
[0–4] Conditions classifiable to 280-285

➡ **CC Excl:** 646.80-646.93, 648.20-648.24, 648.90-648.94, 650, 669.40-669.44, 669.80-669.94

✓5th [8] **648.3** **Drug dependence**
[0–4] Conditions classifiable to 304

➡ **CC Excl:** 646.80-646.93, 648.30-648.34, 648.90-648.94, 650, 669.40-669.44, 669.80-669.94

➡ **AHA Coding Clinic:** 4Q, '88, 8

✓5th [8] **648.4** **Mental disorders**
[0–4] Conditions classifiable to 290-303, 305-316, 317-319

➡ **AHA Coding Clinic:** 4Q, '95, 63

✓5th [8] **648.5** **Congenital cardiovascular disorders**
[0–4] Conditions classifiable to 745-747

➡ **CC Excl:** 646.80-646.93, 648.50-648.64, 648.90-648.94, 650, 669.40-669.44, 669.80-669.94

✓5th [8] **648.6** **Other cardiovascular diseases**
[0–4] Conditions classifiable to 390-398, 410-429

Excludes: *cerebrovascular disorders in the puerperium (674.0)*
venous complications (671.0-671.9)

➡ **CC Excl:** see Code 648.5

✓5th [8] **648.7** **Bone and joint disorders of back, pelvis, and lower limbs**
[0–4]

Conditions classifiable to 720-724, and those classifiable to 711-719 or 725-738, specified as affecting the lower limbs

§ Requires fifth-digit. Valid digits are in [brackets] under each code. See page 228 for definitions.
[8] Nonspecific PDX = 0

✓5th [8] **648.8** **Abnormal glucose tolerance**
[0–4]
Conditions classifiable to 790.2
Gestational diabetes

➡ **AHA Coding Clinic:** 3Q, '91, 5

✓5th [8] **648.9** **Other current conditions classifiable elsewhere**
[0–4]
Conditions classifiable to 440-459
Nutritional deficiencies [conditions classifiable to 260-269]

NORMAL DELIVERY, AND OTHER INDICATIONS FOR CARE IN PREGNANCY, LABOR, AND DELIVERY (650-659)

650 Normal delivery ♀ A: 12–55

Delivery requiring minimal or no assistance, with or without episiotomy, without fetal manipulation [e.g., rotation version] or instrumentation [forceps] of spontaneous, cephalic, vaginal, full-term, single, live born infant. This code is for use as a single diagnosis code and is not to be used with any other code in the range 630-676.

Use additional code to indicate outcome of delivery (V27.0)

Excludes: *breech delivery (assisted) (spontaneous) NOS (652.2)*
delivery by vacuum extractor, forceps, cesarean section, or breech extraction, without specified complication (669.5-669.7)

➡ **AHA Coding Clinic:** 4Q, '95, 59

The following fifth-digit subclassification is for use with categories 651-659 to denote the current episode of care:

0 **unspecified as to episode of care or not applicable**
1 **delivered, with or without mention of antepartum condition**
2 **delivered, with mention of postpartum complication**
3 **antepartum condition or complication**
4 **postpartum condition or complication**

§ 651 Multiple gestation ♀ A: 12–55

✓5th [8] **651.0** **Twin pregnancy**
[0,1,3]

✓5th [8] **651.1** **Triplet pregnancy**
[0,1,3]

✓5th [8] **651.2** **Quadruplet pregnancy**
[0,1,3]

✓5th [8] **651.3** **Twin pregnancy with fetal loss and retention of one fetus**
[0,1,3]

✓5th [8] **651.4** **Triplet pregnancy with fetal loss and retention of one or more fetus(es)**
[0,1,3]

✓5th [8] **651.5** **Quadruplet pregnancy with fetal loss and retention of one or more fetus(es)**
[0,1,3]

✓5th [8] **651.6** **Other multiple pregnancy with fetal loss and retention of one or more fetus(es)**
[0,1,3]

✓5th [8] **651.8** **Other specified multiple gestation**
[0,1,3]

✓5th **651.9** **Unspecified multiple gestation**
[0,1,3]

§ 652 Malposition and malpresentation of fetus ♀ A: 12–55

Code also any associated obstructed labor (660.0)

✓5th [8] **652.0** **Unstable lie**
[0,1,3]

✓5th [8] **652.1** **Breech or other malpresentation successfully converted to cephalic presentation**
[0,1,3]
Cephalic version NOS

✓5th [8] **652.2** **Breech presentation without mention of version**
[0,1,3]
Breech delivery (assisted) (spontaneous) NOS
Buttocks presentation
Complete breech
Frank breech

Excludes: footling presentation (652.8)
incomplete breech (652.8)

✓5th [8] **652.3** **Transverse or oblique presentation**
[0,1,3]
Oblique lie
Transverse lie

Excludes: *transverse arrest of fetal head (660.3)*

✓5th [8] **652.4** **Face or brow presentation**
[0,1,3]
Mentum presentation

✓5th [8] **652.5** **High head at term**
[0,1,3]
Failure of head to enter pelvic brim

✓5th [8] **652.6** **Multiple gestation with malpresentation of one fetus or more**
[0,1,3]

✓5th [8] **652.7** **Prolapsed arm**
[0,1,3]

✓5th [8] **652.8** **Other specified malposition or malpresentation**
[0,1,3]
Compound presentation

✓5th **652.9** **Unspecified malposition or malpresentation**
[0,1,3]

§ 653 Disproportion ♀ A: 12–55

Code also any associated obstructed labor (660.1)

✓5th [8] **653.0** **Major abnormality of bony pelvis, not further specified**
[0,1,3]
Pelvic deformity NOS

✓5th [8] **653.1** **Generally contracted pelvis**
[0,1,3]
Contracted pelvis NOS

✓5th [8] **653.2** **Inlet contraction of pelvis**
[0,1,3]
Inlet contraction (pelvis)

✓5th [8] **653.3** **Outlet contraction of pelvis**
[0,1,3]
Outlet contraction (pelvis)

§ Requires fifth-digit. Valid digits are in [brackets] under each code. See above, this page for definitions.
[8] Nonspecific PDX = 0

✓5th [8] **653.4 Fetopelvic disproportion**
[0,1,3]
Cephalopelvic disproportion NOS
Disproportion of mixed maternal and fetal origin, with normally formed fetus

✓5th [8] **653.5 Unusually large fetus causing disproportion**
[0,1,3]
Disproportion of fetal origin with normally formed fetus
Fetal disproportion NOS

Excludes: *that when the reason for medical care was concern for the fetus (656.6)*

✓5th [8] **653.6 Hydrocephalic fetus causing disproportion**
[0,1,3]

Excludes: *that when the reason for medical care was concern for the fetus (655.0)*

✓5th [8] **653.7 Other fetal abnormality causing disproportion**
[0,1,3]
Conjoined twins
Fetal:
- ascites
- hydrops

Fetal:
- myelomeningocele
- sacral teratoma
- tumor

✓5th [8] **653.8 Disproportion of other origin**
[0,1,3]

Excludes: *shoulder (girdle) dystocia (660.4)*

✓5th **653.9 Unspecified disproportion**
[0,1,3]

§ 654 Abnormality of organs and soft tissues of pelvis ♀ A: 12–55

Includes: the listed conditions during pregnancy, childbirth, or the puerperium

Code also any associated obstructed labor (660.2)

✓5th [8] **654.0 Congenital abnormalities of uterus**
[0–4]
Double uterus
Uterus bicornis

✓5th [8] **654.1 Tumors of body of uterus**
[0–4]
Uterine fibroids

✓5th [8] **654.2 Previous cesarean delivery**
[0,1,3]
Uterine scar from previous cesarean delivery

➡ **AHA Coding Clinic:** 1Q, '92, 8

✓5th [8] **654.3 Retroverted and incarcerated gravid uterus**
[0–4]

✓5th [8] **654.4 Other abnormalities in shape or position of gravid uterus and of neighboring structures**
[0–4]
Cystocele
Pelvic floor repair
Pendulous abdomen
Prolapse of gravid uterus
Rectocele
Rigid pelvic floor

✓5th [8] **654.5 Cervical incompetence**
[0–4]
Presence of Shirodkar suture with or without mention of cervical incompetence

✓5th [8] **654.6 Other congenital or acquired abnormality of cervix**
[0–4]
Cicatricial cervix
Polyp of cervix
Previous surgery to cervix
Rigid cervix (uteri)
Stenosis or stricture of cervix
Tumor of cervix

✓5th [8] **654.7 Congenital or acquired abnormality of vagina**
[0–4]
Previous surgery to vagina
Septate vagina
Stenosis of vagina (acquired) (congenital)
Stricture of vagina
Tumor of vagina

✓5th [8] **654.8 Congenital or acquired abnormality of vulva**
[0–4]
Fibrosis of perineum
Persistent hymen
Previous surgery to perineum or vulva
Rigid perineum
Tumor of vulva

Excludes: *varicose veins of vulva (671.1)*

✓5th **654.9 Other and unspecified**
[0–4]
Uterine scar NEC

§ 655 Known or suspected fetal abnormality affecting management of mother ♀ A: 12–55

Includes: the listed conditions in the fetus as a reason for observation or obstetrical care of the mother, or for termination of pregnancy

➡ **AHA Coding Clinic:** 3Q, '90, 4

✓5th [8] **655.0 Central nervous system malformation in fetus**
[0,1,3]
Fetal or suspected fetal:
- anencephaly
- hydrocephalus
- spina bifida (with myelomeningocele)

✓5th [8] **655.1 Chromosomal abnormality in fetus**
[0,1,3]

✓5th [8] **655.2 Hereditary disease in family possibly affecting fetus**
[0,1,3]

✓5th [8] **655.3 Suspected damage to fetus from viral disease in the mother**
[0,1,3]
Suspected damage to fetus from maternal rubella

✓5th [8] **655.4 Suspected damage to fetus from other disease in the mother**
[0,1,3]
Suspected damage to fetus from maternal:
- alcohol addiction
- listeriosis
- toxoplasmosis

✓5th [8] **655.5 Suspected damage to fetus from drugs**
[0,1,3]

§ Requires fifth-digit. Valid digits are in [brackets] under each code. See page 232 for definitions.
[8] Nonspecific PDX = 0

✓5th [8] **655.6** **Suspected damage to fetus from radiation**
[0,1,3]

✓5th [8] **655.7** **Decreased fetal movements**
[0,1,3]
➡ **AHA Coding Clinic:** 4Q, '97, 41

✓5th [8] **655.8** **Other known or suspected fetal abnormality, not elsewhere classified**
[0,1,3]
Suspected damage to fetus from:
environmental toxins
intrauterine contraceptive device

✓5th **655.9** **Unspecified**
[0,1,3]

§ 656 Other fetal and placental problems affecting management of mother ♀ A: 12–55

➡ **AHA Coding Clinic:** 3Q, '90, 4

✓5th [8] **656.0** **Fetal-maternal hemorrhage**
[0,1,3]
Leakage (microscopic) of fetal blood into maternal circulation

✓5th [8] **656.1** **Rhesus isoimmunization**
[0,1,3]
Anti-D [Rh] antibodies
Rh incompatibility

✓5th [8] **656.2** **Isoimmunization from other and unspecified blood-group incompatibility**
[0,1,3]
ABO isoimmunization

✓5th [8] **656.3** **Fetal distress**
[0,1,3]
Fetal metabolic acidemia

Excludes: *abnormal fetal acid-base balance (656.8)*
abnormality in fetal heart rate or rhythm (659.7)
fetal bradycardia (659.7)
fetal distress NOS (656.8)
fetal tachycardia (659.7)
meconium in liquor (656.8)

➡ **AHA Coding Clinic:** N-D, '86, 4

✓5th [8] **656.4** **Intrauterine death**
[0,1,3]
Fetal death:
NOS
after completion of 22 weeks' gestation
late
Missed delivery

Excludes: *missed abortion (632)*

✓5th [8] **656.5** **Poor fetal growth**
[0,1,3]
"Light-for-dates"
"Placental insufficiency"
"Small-for-dates"

✓5th [8] **656.6** **Excessive fetal growth**
[0,1,3]
"Large-for-dates"

✓5th [8] **656.7** **Other placental conditions**
[0,1,3]
Abnormal placenta
Placental infarct

Excludes: *placental polyp (674.4)*
placentitis (658.4)

✓5th [8] **656.8** **Other specified fetal and placental problems**
[0,1,3]
Abnormal acid-base balance
Intrauterine acidosis
Lithopedion
Meconium in liquor

✓5th [8] **656.9** **Unspecified fetal and placental problem**
[0,1,3]

[8] § 657 Polyhydramnios ♀ A: 12–55

[0,1,3]
Hydramnios

✓5th Use 0 as fourth-digit for category 657

➡ **AHA Coding Clinic:** 4Q, '91, 26

§ 658 Other problems associated with amniotic cavity and membranes ♀ A: 12–55

Excludes: *amniotic fluid embolism (673.1)*

✓5th [8] **658.0** **Oligohydramnios**
[0,1,3]
Oligohydramnios without mention of rupture of membranes

✓5th [8] **658.1** **Premature rupture of membranes**
[0,1,3]
Rupture of amniotic sac less than 24 hours prior to the onset of labor

✓5th [8] **658.2** **Delayed delivery after spontaneous or unspecified rupture of membranes**
[0,1,3]
Prolonged rupture of membranes NOS
Rupture of amniotic sac 24 hours or more prior to the onset of labor

✓5th [8] **658.3** **Delayed delivery after artificial rupture of membranes**
[0,1,3]

✓5th [8] **658.4** **Infection of amniotic cavity**
[0,1,3]
Amnionitis
Chorioamnionitis
Membranitis
Placentitis

✓5th [8] **658.8** **Other**
[0,1,3]
Amnion nodosum
Amniotic cyst

✓5th **658.9** **Unspecified**
[0,1,3]

§ 659 Other indications for care or intervention related to labor and delivery, not elsewhere classified ♀ A: 12–55

✓5th [8] **659.0** **Failed mechanical induction**
[0,1,3]
Failure of induction of labor by surgical or other instrumental methods

✓5th [8] **659.1** **Failed medical or unspecified induction**
[0,1,3]
Failed induction NOS
Failure of induction of labor by medical methods, such as oxytoxic drugs

✓5th [8] **659.2** **Maternal pyrexia during labor, unspecified**
[0,1,3]

✓5th [8] **659.3** **Generalized infection during labor**
[0,1,3]
Septicemia during labor
➡ **CC Excl:** 646.80-646.93, 648.90-648.94, 650, 659.30-659.33, 669.40-669.44, 669.80-669.94

§ Requires fifth-digit. Valid digits are in [brackets] under each code. See page 232 for definitions.
[8] Nonspecific PDX = 0

✓5th [8] **659.4** **Grand multiparity**
[0,1,3]

Excludes: *supervision only, in pregnancy (V23.3)*
without current pregnancy (V61.5)

✓5th [8] **659.5** **Elderly primigravida**
[0,1,3]
First pregnancy in a woman who will be 35 years of age or older at expected date of delivery

Excludes: *supervision only, in pregnancy (V23.81)*

✓5th [8] **659.6** **Elderly multigravida**
[0,1,3]
Second or more pregnancy in a woman who will be 35 years of age or older at expected date of delivery

Excludes: *elderly primigravida (659.5)*
supervision only, in pregnancy (V23.82)

✓5th **659.7** **Abnormality in fetal heart rate/rhythm**
[0,1,3]
Depressed fetal heart tones
Fetal:
bradycardia
tachycardia
Fetal heart rate decelerations
Non-reassuring fetal heart rate or rhythm

✓5th [8] **659.8** **Other specified indications for care or intervention related to labor and delivery**
[0,1,3]
Pregnancy in a female less than 16 years old at expected date of delivery
Very young maternal age

✓5th **659.9** **Unspecified indication for care or intervention related to labor and delivery**
[0,1,3]

COMPLICATIONS OCCURRING MAINLY IN THE COURSE OF LABOR AND DELIVERY (660-669)

The following fifth-digit subclassification is for use with categories 660-669 to denote the current episode of care:

0 unspecified as to episode of care or not applicable
1 delivered, with or without mention of antepartum condition
2 delivered, with mention of postpartum complication
3 antepartum condition or complication
4 postpartum condition or complication

§ 660 Obstructed labor ♀ A: 12–55

✓5th [8] **660.0** **Obstruction caused by malposition of fetus at onset of labor**
[0,1,3]
Any condition classifiable to 652, causing obstruction during labor

Use additional code from 652.0-652.9 to identify condition

✓5th [8] **660.1** **Obstruction by bony pelvis**
[0,1,3]
Any condition classifiable to 653, causing obstruction during labor

Use additional code from 653.0-653.9 to identify condition

✓5th [8] **660.2** **Obstruction by abnormal pelvic soft tissues**
[0,1,3]
Prolapse of anterior lip of cervix
Any condition classifiable to 654, causing obstruction during labor

Use additional code from 654.0-654.9 to identify condition

✓5th [8] **660.3** **Deep transverse arrest and persistent occipitoposterior position**
[0,1,3]

✓5th [8] **660.4** **Shoulder (girdle) dystocia**
[0,1,3]
Impacted shoulders

✓5th [8] **660.5** **Locked twins**
[0,1,3]

✓5th [8] **660.6** **Failed trial of labor, unspecified**
[0,1,3]
Failed trial of labor, without mention of condition or suspected condition

✓5th [8] **660.7** **Failed forceps or vacuum extractor, unspecified**
[0,1,3]
Application of ventouse or forceps, without mention of condition

✓5th [8] **660.8** **Other causes of obstructed labor**
[0,1,3]

✓5th [8] **660.9** **Unspecified obstructed labor**
[0,1,3]
Dystocia:
NOS
fetal NOS
maternal NOS

§ 661 Abnormality of forces of labor ♀ A: 12–55

✓5th [8] **661.0** **Primary uterine inertia**
[0,1,3]
Failure of cervical dilation
Hypotonic uterine dysfunction, primary
Prolonged latent phase of labor

✓5th [8] **661.1** **Secondary uterine inertia**
[0,1,3]
Arrested active phase of labor
Hypotonic uterine dysfunction, secondary

✓5th [8] **661.2** **Other and unspecified uterine inertia**
[0,1,3]
Desultory labor
Irregular labor
Poor contractions
Slow slope active phase of labor

✓5th [8] **661.3** **Precipitate labor**
[0,1,3]

✓5th [8] **661.4** **Hypertonic, incoordinate, or prolonged uterine contractions**
[0,1,3]
Cervical spasm
Contraction ring (dystocia)
Dyscoordinate labor
Hourglass contraction of uterus
Hypertonic uterine dysfunction
Incoordinate uterine action
Retraction ring (Bandl's) (pathological)
Tetanic contractions
Uterine dystocia NOS
Uterine spasm

✓5th **661.9** **Unspecified abnormality of labor**
[0,1,3]

§ 662 Long labor ♀ A: 12–55

✓5th [8] **662.0** **Prolonged first stage**
[0,1,3]

✓5th [8] **662.1** **Prolonged labor, unspecified**
[0,1,3]

✓5th [8] **662.2** **Prolonged second stage**
[0,1,3]

✓5th [8] **662.3** **Delayed delivery of second twin, triplet, etc.**
[0,1,3]

§ Requires fifth-digit. Valid digits are in [brackets] under each code. See above, this page for definitions.
[8] Nonspecific PDX = 0

§ 663 Umbilical cord complications ♀ A: 12–55

✓5th [8] **663.0** **Prolapse of cord**
[0,1,3]
Presentation of cord

✓5th [8] **663.1** **Cord around neck, with compression**
[0,1,3]
Cord tightly around neck

✓5th [8] **663.2** **Other and unspecified cord entanglement, with compression**
[0,1,3]
Entanglement of cords of twins in mono-amniotic sac
Knot in cord (with compression)

✓5th [8] **663.3** **Other and unspecified cord entanglement, without mention of compression**
[0,1,3]

✓5th [8] **663.4** **Short cord**
[0,1,3]

✓5th [8] **663.5** **Vasa previa**
[0,1,3]
Velamentous insertion of umbilical cord

✓5th [8] **663.6** **Vascular lesions of cord**
[0,1,3]
Bruising of cord
Hematoma of cord
Thrombosis of vessels of cord

✓5th [8] **663.8** **Other umbilical cord complications**
[0,1,3]

✓5th **663.9** **Unspecified umbilical cord complication**
[0,1,3]

§ 664 Trauma to perineum and vulva during delivery ♀ A: 12–55

Includes: damage from instruments
that from extension of episiotomy

➡ **AHA Coding Clinic:** 1Q, '92, 11; N-D, '84, 10

✓5th [8] **664.0** **First-degree perineal laceration**
[0,1,4]
Perineal laceration, rupture, or tear involving:
- fourchette
- hymen
- labia
- skin
- vagina
- vulva

✓5th [8] **664.1** **Second-degree perineal laceration**
[0,1,4]
Perineal laceration, rupture, or tear (following episiotomy) involving:
- pelvic floor
- perineal muscles
- vaginal muscles

Excludes: *that involving anal sphincter (664.2)*

✓5th [8] **664.2** **Third-degree perineal laceration**
[0,1,4]
Perineal laceration, rupture, or tear (following episiotomy) involving:
- anal sphincter
- rectovaginal septum
- sphincter NOS

Excludes: *that with anal or rectal mucosal laceration (664.3)*

✓5th [8] **664.3** **Fourth-degree perineal laceration**
[0,1,4]
Perineal laceration, rupture, or tear as classifiable to 664.2 and involving also:
- anal mucosa
- rectal mucosa

✓5th [8] **664.4** **Unspecified perineal laceration**
[0,1,4]
Central laceration

➡ **AHA Coding Clinic:** 1Q, '92, 8

✓5th [8] **664.5** **Vulval and perineal hematoma**
[0,1,4]

✓5th [8] **664.8** **Other specified trauma to perineum and vulva**
[0,1,4]

✓5th **664.9** **Unspecified trauma to perineum and vulva**
[0,1,4]

§ 665 Other obstetrical trauma ♀ A: 12–55

Includes: damage from instruments

➡ **AHA Coding Clinic:** N-D, '84, 10

✓5th [8] **665.0** **Rupture of uterus before onset of labor**
[0,1,3]

➡ **CC Excl:** 646.80-646.93, 648.90, 650, 665.00-665.11, 665.50-665.54, 665.70-665.71, 665.73, 665.80-665.94, 669.40-669.44, 669.80-669.94

✓5th [8] **665.1** **Rupture of uterus during labor**
[0,1]
Rupture of uterus NOS

➡ **CC Excl:** see Code 665.0

✓5th [8] **665.2** **Inversion of uterus**
[0,2,4]

✓5th [8] **665.3** **Laceration of cervix**
[0,1,4]

✓5th [8] **665.4** **High vaginal laceration**
[0,1,4]
Laceration of vaginal wall or sulcus without mention of perineal laceration

✓5th [8] **665.5** **Other injury to pelvic organs**
[0,1,4]
Injury to:
- bladder
- urethra

§ Requires fifth-digit. Valid digits are in [brackets] under each code. See page 235 for definitions.
[8] Nonspecific PDX = 0

✓5th [8] **665.6 Damage to pelvic joints and ligaments**
[0,1,4]
Avulsion of inner symphyseal cartilage
Damage to coccyx
Separation of symphysis (pubis)

➡ **AHA Coding Clinic:** N-D, '84, 12

✓5th [8] **665.7 Pelvic hematoma**
[0-2,4]
Hematoma of vagina

✓5th [8] **665.8 Other specified obstetrical trauma**
[0–4]

✓5th **665.9 Unspecified obstetrical trauma**
[0–4]

§ 666 Postpartum hemorrhage ♀ A: 12–55

➡ **AHA Coding Clinic:** 1Q, '88, 14

✓5th [8] **666.0 Third-stage hemorrhage**
[0,2,4]
Hemorrhage associated with retained, trapped, or adherent placenta
Retained placenta NOS

✓5th [8] **666.1 Other immediate postpartum hemorrhage**
[0,2,4]
Atony of uterus
Hemorrhage within the first 24 hours following delivery of placenta
Postpartum hemorrhage (atonic) NOS

✓5th [8] **666.2 Delayed and secondary postpartum hemorrhage**
[0,2,4]
Hemorrhage:
- after the first 24 hours following delivery
- associated with retained portions of placenta or membranes

Postpartum hemorrhage specified as delayed or secondary
Retained products of conception NOS, following delivery

✓5th [8, 13] **666.3 Postpartum coagulation defects**
[0,2,4]
Postpartum:
- afibrinogenemia
- fibrinolysis

➡ **CC Excl: For Codes 666.32-666.34:** 646.80-646.93, 648.90-648.94, 650, 666.00-666.34, 669.40-669.44, 669.80-669.94

§ 667 Retained placenta or membranes, without hemorrhage ♀ A: 12–55

➡ **AHA Coding Clinic:** 1Q, '88, 14

✓5th [8] **667.0 Retained placenta without hemorrhage**
[0,2,4]
Placenta accreta } without hemorrhage
Retained placenta:
- NOS } without hemorrhage
- total } without hemorrhage

✓5th [8] **667.1 Retained portions of placenta or membranes, without hemorrhage**
[0,2,4]
Retained products of conception following delivery, without hemorrhage

§ 668 Complications of the administration of anesthetic or other sedation in labor and delivery ♀ A: 12–55

Use additional code(s) to further specify complication

Includes: complications arising from the administration of a general or local anesthetic, analgesic, or other sedation in labor and delivery

Excludes: *reaction to spinal or lumbar puncture (349.0)*
spinal headache (349.0)

✓5th [8] **668.0 Pulmonary complications**
[0–4]
Inhalation [aspiration] of stomach contents or secretions } following anesthesia or other sedation in labor or delivery
Mendelson's syndrome } following anesthesia or other sedation in labor or delivery
Pressure collapse of lun } following anesthesia or other sedation in labor or delivery

➡ **CC Excl:** 646.80-646.93, 648.90-648.94, 650, 668.00-668.04, 669.40-669.44, 669.80-669.94

✓5th [8] **668.1 Cardiac complications**
[0–4]
Cardiac arrest or failure following anesthesia or other sedation in labor and delivery

➡ **CC Excl:** 646.80-646.93, 648.90-648.94, 650, 668.10-668.14, 669.40-669.44, 669.80-669.94

✓5th [8] **668.2 Central nervous system complications**
[0–4]
Cerebral anoxia following anesthesia or other sedation in labor and delivery

➡ **CC Excl:** 646.80-646.93, 648.90-648.94, 650, 668.20-668.24, 669.40-669.44, 669.80-669.94

✓5th [8] **668.8 Other complications of anesthesia or other sedation in labor and delivery**
[0–4]

➡ **CC Excl:** 646.80-646.93, 648.90-648.94, 650, 668.80-94, 669.40-669.44, 669.80-669.94

✓5th **668.9 Unspecified complication of anesthesia and other sedation**
[0–4]

➡ **CC Excl:** see Code 668.8

§ 669 Other complications of labor and delivery, not elsewhere classified ♀ A: 12–55

✓5th [8] **669.0 Maternal distress**
[0–4]
Metabolic disturbance in labor and delivery

✓5th [8] **669.1 Shock during or following labor and delivery**
[0–4]
Obstetric shock

➡ **CC Excl:** 646.80-646.93, 648.90-648.94, 650, 669.10-669.14, 669.40-669.44, 669.80-669.94

✓5th [8] **669.2 Maternal hypotension syndrome**
[0–4]

§ Requires fifth-digit. Valid digits are in [brackets] under each code. See page 235 for definitions.
[8] Nonspecific PDX = 0
[13] CC Coding = 2 or 4

✓5th [8] **669.3** **Acute renal failure following labor and delivery**
[0,2,4]

➡ **CC Excl:** 646.80-646.93, 648.90-648.94, 650, 669.30-669.44, 669.80-669.94

✓5th [8] **669.4** **Other complications of obstetrical surgery and procedures**
[0–4]

Cardiac: arrest, failure; Cerebral anoxia — following cesarean or other obstetrical surgery or procedure, including delivery NOS

Excludes: *complications of obstetrical surgical wounds (674.1-674.3)*

✓5th [8] **669.5** **Forceps or vacuum extractor delivery without mention of indication**
[0,1]

Delivery by ventouse, without mention of indication

✓5th [8] **669.6** **Breech extraction, without mention of indication**
[0,1]

Excludes: *breech delivery NOS (652.2)*

✓5th [8] **669.7** **Cesarean delivery, without mention of indication**
[0,1]

✓5th [8] **669.8** **Other complications of labor and delivery**
[0–4]

✓5th **669.9** **Unspecified complication of labor and delivery**
[0–4]

COMPLICATIONS OF THE PUERPERIUM (670-677)

Note: Categories 671 and 673-676 include the listed conditions even if they occur during pregnancy or childbirth.

The following fifth-digit subclassification is for use with categories 670-676 to denote the current episode of care:

- **0 unspecified as to episode of care or not applicable**
- **1 delivered, with or without mention of antepartum condition**
- **2 delivered, with mention of postpartum complication**
- **3 antepartum condition or complication**
- **4 postpartum condition or complication**

[8]§ **670 Major puerperal infection** ♀ A: 12–55
[0,2,4]

Puerperal:
- endometritis
- fever (septic)
- pelvic:
  - cellulitis
  - sepsis

Puerperal:
- peritonitis
- pyemia
- salpingitis
- septicemia

✓5th Use 0 as fourth-digit for category 670

Excludes: *infection following abortion (639.0)*
minor genital tract infection following delivery (646.6)
puerperal fever NOS (672)
puerperal pyrexia NOS (672)
puerperal pyrexia of unknown origin (672)
urinary tract infection following delivery (646.6)

➡ **CC Excl:** 646.80-646.93, 648.90-648.94, 650, 669.40-669.44, 669.80-669.94, 670.00-670.04

➡ **AHA Coding Clinic:** 4Q, '91, 26

§ **671 Venous complications in pregnancy and the puerperium** ♀ A: 12–55

✓5th [8] **671.0** **Varicose veins of legs**
[0–4]

Varicose veins NOS

✓5th [8] **671.1** **Varicose veins of vulva and perineum**
[0–4]

✓5th [8] **671.2** **Superficial thrombophlebitis**
[0–4]

Thrombophlebitis (superficial)

➡ **CC Excl:** 646.80-646.93, 648.90-648.94, 650, 669.40-669.44, 669.80-669.94, 671.20-671.94

✓5th [8] **671.3** **Deep phlebothrombosis, antepartum**
[0,1,3]

Deep-vein thrombosis, antepartum

➡ **CC Excl:** see Code 671.2

✓5th [8] **671.4** **Deep phlebothrombosis, postpartum**
[0,2,4]

Deep-vein thrombosis, postpartum
Pelvic thrombophlebitis, postpartum
Phlegmasia alba dolens (puerperal)

➡ **CC Excl:** see Code 671.2

✓5th [8] **671.5** **Other phlebitis and thrombosis**
[0–4]

Cerebral venous thrombosis
Thrombosis of intracranial venous sinus

✓5th [8] **671.8** **Other venous complications**
[0–4]

Hemorrhoids

✓5th **671.9** **Unspecified venous complication**
[0–4]

Phlebitis NOS
Thrombosis NOS

[8]§ **672 Pyrexia of unknown origin during the puerperium** ♀ A: 12–55
[0,2,4]

Postpartum fever NOS
Puerperal fever NOS
Puerperal pyrexia NOS

✓5th Use 0 as fourth-digit for category 672

➡ **AHA Coding Clinic:** 4Q, '91, 26

§ Requires fifth-digit. Valid digits are in [brackets] under each code. See above, this page for definitions.
[8] Nonspecific PDX = 0

§ 673 Obstetrical pulmonary embolism ♀ A: 12–55

Includes: pulmonary emboli in pregnancy, childbirth, or the puerperium, or specified as puerperal

Excludes: *embolism following abortion (639.6)*

✓5th [8] **673.0 Obstetrical air embolism**
[0–4]

➡ **CC Excl:** 646.80-646.93, 648.90-648.94, 650, 669.40-669.44, 669.80-669.94, 673.00-673.84,

✓5th [8] **673.1 Amniotic fluid embolism**
[0–4]

➡ **CC Excl:** see Code 673.0

✓5th [8] **673.2 Obstetrical blood-clot embolism**
[0–4] Puerperal pulmonary embolism NOS

➡ **CC Excl:** see Code 673.0

✓5th [8] **673.3 Obstetrical pyemic and septic embolism**
[0–4]

➡ **CC Excl:** see Code 673.0

✓5th [8] **673.8 Other pulmonary embolism**
[0–4] Fat embolism

➡ **CC Excl:** see Code 673.0

§ 674 Other and unspecified complications of the puerperium, not elsewhere classified ♀ A: 12–55

✓5th [8] **674.0 Cerebrovascular disorders in the puerperium**
[0–4] Any condition classifiable to 430-434, 436-437 occurring during pregnancy, childbirth, or the puerperium, or specified as puerperal

Excludes: *intracranial venous sinus thrombosis (671.5)*

➡ **CC Excl:** 646.80-646.93, 648.90-648.94, 650, 669.40-669.44, 669.80-669.94, 674.00-674.04

✓5th [8,10] **674.1 Disruption of cesarean wound**
[0,2,4] Dehiscence or disruption of uterine wound

➡ **CC Excl: For Codes 674.10-674.12:** 646.80-646.93, 648.90-648.94, 650, 669.40-669.44, 669.80-669.94, 674.10, 674.34

✓5th [8] **674.2 Disruption of perineal wound**
[0,2,4] Breakdown of perineum
Secondary perineal tear
Disruption of wound of:
- episiotomy
- perineal laceration

➡ **CC Excl:** see Code 674.1

➡ **AHA Coding Clinic: For code 674.24:** 1Q, '97, 9

✓5th [8] **674.3 Other complications of obstetrical surgical wounds**
[0,2,4] Hematoma, Hemorrhage, Infection } of cesarean section or perineal wound

Excludes: *damage from instruments in delivery (664.0-665.9)*

✓5th [8] **674.4 Placental polyp**
[0,2,4]

✓5th [8] **674.8 Other**
[0,2,4] Hepatorenal syndrome, following delivery
Postpartum:
- cardiomyopathy
- subinvolution of uterus
- uterine hypertrophy

✓5th **674.9 Unspecified**
[0,2,4] Sudden death of unknown cause during the puerperium

§ 675 Infections of the breast and nipple associated with childbirth ♀ A: 12–55

Includes: the listed conditions during pregnancy, childbirth, or the puerperium

✓5th [8] **675.0 Infections of nipple**
[0–4] Abscess of nipple

✓5th [2,8] **675.1 Abscess of breast**
[0–4] Abscess:
- mammary
- subareolar
- submammary

Mastitis:
- purulent
- retromammary
- submammary

➡ **CC Excl: For codes 675.10-675.12:** 646.80-646.93, 648.90-648.94, 650, 669.40-669.44, 669.80-669.94, 675.00-675.94

✓5th [8] **675.2 Nonpurulent mastitis**
[0–4] Lymphangitis of breast
Mastitis:
- NOS
- interstitial
- parenchymatous

✓5th [8] **675.8 Other specified infections of the breast and nipple**
[0–4]

✓5th [8] **675.9 Unspecified infection of the breast and nipple**
[0–4]

§ Requires fifth-digit. Valid digits are in [brackets] under each code. See page 238 for definitions.
[8] Nonspecific PDX = 0
[10] CC Coding = 0 or 2

§ 676 Other disorders of the breast associated with childbirth and disorders of lactation ♀ A: 12–55

Includes: the listed conditions during pregnancy, the puerperium, or lactation

✓5th [8] **676.0 Retracted nipple**
[0–4]

✓5th [8] **676.1 Cracked nipple**
[0–4]
Fissure of nipple

✓5th [8] **676.2 Engorgement of breasts**
[0–4]

✓5th [8] **676.3 Other and unspecified disorder of breast**
[0–4]

✓5th [8] **676.4 Failure of lactation**
[0–4]
Agalactia

[8] **676.5 Suppressed lactation**
[0–4]

✓5th [8] **676.6 Galactorrhea**
[0–4]

Excludes: *galactorrhea not associated with childbirth (611.6)*

✓5th [8] **676.8 Other disorders of lactation**
[0–4]
Galactocele

✓5th **676.9 Unspecified disorder of lactation**
[0–4]

677 Late effect of complication of pregnancy, childbirth, and the puerperium ♀ A: 12–55

Note: This category is to be used to indicate conditions in 632-648.9 and 651-676.9 as the cause of the late effect, themselves classifiable elsewhere. The "late effects" include conditions specified as such, or as sequelae, which may occur at any time after the puerperium.

Code also any sequelae

➡ **AHA Coding Clinic:** 1Q, '97, 9; 4Q, '94, 42

§ Requires fifth-digit. Valid digits are in [brackets] under each code. See page 238 for definitions.
[8] Nonspecific PDX = 0

12. DISEASES OF THE SKIN AND SUBCUTANEOUS TISSUE (680-709)

INFECTIONS OF SKIN AND SUBCUTANEOUS TISSUE (680-686)

Excludes: *certain infections of skin classified under "Infectious and Parasitic Diseases," such as:*
erysipelas (035)
erysipeloid of Rosenbach (027.1)
herpes:
simplex (054.0-054.9)
zoster (053.0-053.9)
molluscum contagiosum (078.0)
viral warts (078.1)

680 Carbuncle and furuncle

Includes: boil
furunculosis

680.0 **Face**

Ear [any part]
Face [any part, except eye]
Nose (septum)
Temple (region)

Excludes: *eyelid (373.13)*
lacrimal apparatus (375.31)
orbit (376.01)

➡ **CC Excl:** 017.00-017.06, 017.90-017.96, 040.89, 041.00-041.89, 041.9, 680.0, 680.8-680.9, 686.00-686.01, 686.09, 686.1-686.9, 705.83, 709.8, V09.0-V09.91

680.1 **Neck**

➡ **CC Excl:** 017.00-017.06, 017.90-017.96, 040.89, 041.00-041.89, 041.9, 680.1, 680.8-680.9, 686.00-686.01, 686.09, 686.1-686.9, 705.83, 709.8, V09.0-V09.91

680.2 **Trunk**

Abdominal wall
Back [any part, except buttocks]
Breast
Chest wall
Flank
Groin
Pectoral region
Perineum
Umbilicus

Excludes: *buttocks (680.5)*
external genital organs:
female (616.4)
male (607.2, 608.4)

➡ **CC Excl:** 017.00-017.06, 017.90-017.96, 040.89, 041.00-041.89, 041.9, 680.2, 680.8-680.9, 686.00-686.01, 686.09, 686.1-686.9, 705.83, 709.8, V09.0-V09.91

680.3 **Upper arm and forearm**

Arm [any part, except hand]
Axilla
Shoulder

➡ **CC Excl:** 017.00-017.06, 017.90-017.96, 040.89, 041.00-041.89, 041.9, 680.3, 680.8-680.9, 686.00-686.01, 686.09, 686.1-686.9, 705.83, 709.8, V09.0-V09.91

680.4 **Hand**

Finger [any]
Thumb
Wrist

➡ **CC Excl:** 017.00-017.06, 017.90-017.96, 040.89, 041.00-041.89, 041.9, 680.4, 680.8-680.9, 686.00-686.01, 686.09, 686.1-686.9, 705.83, 709.8, V09.0-V09.91

680.5 **Buttock**

Anus
Gluteal region

➡ **CC Excl:** 017.00-017.06, 017.90-017.96, 040.89, 041.00-041.89, 041.9, 680.5, 680.8-680.9, 686.00-686.01, 686.09, 686.1-686.9, 705.83, 709.8, V09.0-V09.91

680.6 **Leg, except foot**

Ankle
Hip
Knee
Thigh

➡ **CC Excl:** 017.00-017.06, 017.90-017.96, 040.89, 041.00-041.89, 041.9, 680.6, 680.8-680.9, 686.00-686.01, 686.09, 686.1-686.9, 705.83, 709.8, V09.0-V09.91

680.7 **Foot**

Heel
Toe

➡ **CC Excl:** 017.00-017.06, 017.90-017.96, 040.89, 041.00-041.89, 041.9, 680.7-680.9, 686.00-686.01, 686.09, 686.1-686.9, 705.83, 709.8, V09.0-V09.91

680.8 **Other specified sites**

Head [any part, except face]
Scalp

Excludes: *external genital organs:*
female (616.4)
male (607.2, 608.4)

➡ **CC Excl:** 017.00-017.06, 017.90-017.96, 040.89, 041.00-041.89, 041.9, 680.8-680.9, 686.00-686.01, 686.09, 686.1-686.9, 705.83, 709.8, V09.0-V09.91

680.9 **Unspecified site**

Boil NOS
Carbuncle NOS
Furuncle NOS

➡ **CC Excl:** see Code 680.8

✔ **St. Anthony's Clinical Coder:** see Chapter 5

681 Cellulitis and abscess of finger and toe

Use additional code to identify organism such as Staphylococcus (041.1)

Includes: that with lymphangitis

➡ **AHA Coding Clinic:** 2Q, '91, 5; J-F, '87, 12

✓5th **681.0** **Finger**

681.00 **Cellulitis and abscess, unspecified**

681.01 **Felon**

Pulp abscess
Whitlow

Excludes: *herpetic whitlow (054.6)*

681.02 Onychia and paronychia of finger

Panaritium } of finger
Perionychia

✓5th **681.1 Toe**

681.10 Cellulitis and abscess, unspecified

681.11 Onychia and paronychia of toe

Panaritium } of toe
Perionychia

681.9 Cellulitis and abscess of unspecified digit

Infection of nail NOS

682 Other cellulitis and abscess

Use additional code to identify organism such as Staphylococcus (041.1)

Includes: abscess (acute) } (with lymphangitis) except of finger or toe
cellulitis (diffuse)
lymphangitis, acute

Excludes: *lymphangitis (chronic) (subacute) (457.2)*

➡ **AHA Coding Clinic:** 2Q, '91, 5; J-F, '87, 12

682.0 Face

Cheek, external	Nose, external
Chin	Submandibular
Forehead	Temple (region)

Excludes: *ear [any part] (380.10-380.16)*
eyelid (373.13)
lacrimal apparatus (375.31)
lip (528.5)
mouth (528.3)
nose (internal) (478.1)
orbit (376.01)

➡ **CC Excl:** 017.00-017.06, 017.90-017.96, 040.89, 041.00-041.89, 041.9, 682.0, 682.8-682.9, 686.00-686.01, 686.09, 686.1-686.9, 705.83, 709.8, V09.0-V09.91

682.1 Neck

➡ **CC Excl:** 017.00-017.06, 017.90-017.96, 040.89, 041.00-041.89, 041.9, 682.1, 682.8-682.9, 686.00-686.01, 686.09, 686.1-686.9, 705.83, 709.8, V09.0-V09.91

682.2 Trunk

Abdominal wall	Groin
Back [any part, except buttock]	Pectoral region
	Perineum
Chest wall	Umbilicus, except newborn
Flank	

Excludes: *anal and rectal regions (566)*
breast:
NOS (611.0)
puerperal (675.1)
external genital organs:
female (616.3-616.4)
male (604.0, 607.2, 608.4)
umbilicus, newborn (771.4)

➡ **CC Excl:** 017.00-017.06, 017.90-017.96, 040.89, 041.00-041.89, 041.9, 682.2, 682.8-682.9, 686.00-686.01, 686.09, 686.1-686.9, 705.83, 709.8, V09.0-V09.91

682.3 Upper arm and forearm

Arm [any part, except hand]
Axilla
Shoulder

Excludes: *hand (682.4)*

➡ **CC Excl:** 017.00-017.06, 017.90-017.96, 040.89, 041.00-041.89, 041.9, 682.3, 682.8-682.9, 686.00-686.01, 686.09, 686.1-686.9, 705.83, 709.8, V09.0-V09.91

682.4 Hand, except fingers and thumb

Wrist

Excludes: *finger and thumb (681.00-681.02)*

682.5 Buttock

Gluteal region

Excludes: *anal and rectal regions (566)*

➡ **CC Excl:** 017.00-017.06, 017.90-017.96, 040.89, 041.00-041.89, 041.9, 682.5, 682.8-682.9, 686.00-686.01, 686.09, 686.1-686.9, 705.83, 709.8, V09.0-V09.91

682.6 Leg, except foot

Ankle	Knee
Hip	Thigh

➡ **CC Excl:** 017.00-017.06, 017.90-017.96, 040.89, 041.00-041.89, 041.9, 682.6, 682.8-682.9, 686.00-686.01, 686.09, 686.1-686.9, 705.83, 709.8, V09.0-V09.91

682.7 Foot, except toes

Heel

Excludes: *toe (681.10-681.11)*

➡ **CC Excl:** 017.00-017.06, 017.90-017.96, 040.89, 041.00-041.89, 041.9, 682.7-682.9, 686.00-686.01, 686.09, 686.1-686.9, 705.83, 709.8, V09.0-V09.91

682.8 Other specified sites
Head [except face] Scalp

Excludes: *face (682.0)*

➡ **CC Excl:** 017.00-017.06, 017.90-017.96, 040.89, 041.00-041.89, 041.9, 682.8-682.9, 686.00-686.01, 686.09, 686.1-686.9, 705.83, 709.8, V09.0-V09.91

682.9 Unspecified site
Abscess NOS
Cellulitis NOS
Lymphangitis, acute NOS

Excludes: *lymphangitis NOS (457.2)*

➡ **CC Excl:** see Code 682.8

✔ **St. Anthony's Clinical Coder:** see Chapter 5

683 Acute lymphadenitis

Adenitis, acute } lymph gland or node, except mesenteric
Lymphadenitis, acute } lymph gland or node, except mesenteric

Use additional code to identify organism such as Staphylococcus (041.1)

Excludes: *enlarged glands NOS (785.6)*
lymphadenitis:
chronic or subacute, except mesenteric (289.1)
mesenteric (acute) (chronic) (subacute) (289.2)
unspecified (289.3)

684 Impetigo

Impetiginization of other dermatoses
Impetigo (contagiosa) [any site] [any organism]:
bullous
circinate
neonatorum
simplex
Pemphigus neonatorum

Excludes: *impetigo herpetiformis (694.3)*

➡ **CC Excl:** 684, 686.00-686.01, 686.09, 686.1-686.9, 709.8

685 Pilonidal cyst

Includes: fistula } coccygeal or pilonidal
sinus } coccygeal or pilonidal

685.0 With abscess
➡ **CC Excl:** 685.0-685.1, 709.8

685.1 Without mention of abscess

686 Other local infections of skin and subcutaneous tissue

Use additional code to identify any infectious organism (041.0-041.8)

✓5th **686.0** Pyoderma
Dermatitis:
purulent
septic
suppurative

686.00 Pyoderma, unspecified

686.01 Pyoderma gangrenosum
➡ **AHA Coding Clinic:** 4Q, '97, 42

686.09 Other pyoderma

686.1 Pyogenic granuloma
Granuloma:
septic
suppurative
telangiectaticum

Excludes: *pyogenic granuloma of oral mucosa (528.9)*

686.8 Other specified local infections of skin and subcutaneous tissue
Bacterid (pustular)
Dermatitis vegetans
Ecthyma
Perlèche

Excludes: *dermatitis infectiosa eczematoides (690.8)*
panniculitis (729.30-729.39)

686.9 Unspecified local infection of skin and subcutaneous tissue
Fistula of skin NOS
Skin infection NOS

Excludes: *fistula to skin from internal organs — see Alphabetic Index*

OTHER INFLAMMATORY CONDITIONS OF SKIN AND SUBCUTANEOUS TISSUE (690-698)

Excludes: *panniculitis (729.30-729.39)*

690 Erythematosquamous dermatosis

Excludes: *eczematous dermatitis of eyelid (373.31)*
parakeratosis variegata (696.2)
psoriasis (696.0-696.1)
seborrheic keratosis (702)

✓5th **690.1** Seborrheic dermatitis
➡ **AHA Coding Clinic:** 4Q, '95, 58

690.10 Seborrheic dermatitis, unspecified
Seborrheic dermatitis NOS

690.11 Seborrhea capitis A: 0–17
Cradle cap

690.12 Seborrheic infantile dermatitis A: 0–17

690.18 Other seborrheic dermatitis

690.8 Other erythematosquamous dermatosis

691 Atopic dermatitis and related conditions

691.0 Diaper or napkin rash

Ammonia dermatitis
Diaper or napkin:
- dermatitis
- erythema
- rash

Psoriasiform napkin eruption

691.8 Other atopic dermatitis and related conditions

Atopic dermatitis
Besnier's prurigo
Eczema:
- atopic
- flexural
- intrinsic (allergic)

Neurodermatitis:
- atopic
- diffuse (of Brocq)

692 Contact dermatitis and other eczema

Includes: dermatitis:
- NOS
- contact
- occupational
- venenata

eczema (acute) (chronic):
- NOS
- allergic
- erythematous
- occupational

Excludes: *allergy NOS (995.3)*
contact dermatitis of eyelids (373.32)
dermatitis due to substances taken internally (693.0-693.9)
eczema of external ear (380.22)
perioral dermatitis (695.3)
urticarial reactions (708.0-708.9, 995.1)

692.0 Due to detergents

692.1 Due to oils and greases

692.2 Due to solvents

Dermatitis due to solvents of:
- chlorocompound group
- cyclohexane group
- ester group
- glycol group
- hydrocarbon group
- ketone group

692.3 Due to drugs and medicines in contact with skin

Dermatitis (allergic) (contact) due to:
- arnica
- fungicides
- iodine
- keratolytics
- mercurials
- neomycin
- pediculocides
- phenols
- scabicides
- any drug applied to skin

Dermatitis medicamentosa due to drug applied to skin

Use additional E code to identify drug

Excludes: *allergy NOS due to drugs (995.2)*
dermatitis due to ingested drugs (693.0)
dermatitis medicamentosa NOS (693.0)

692.4 Due to other chemical products

Dermatitis due to:
- acids
- adhesive plaster
- alkalis
- caustics
- dichromate

Dermatitis due to:
- insecticide
- nylon
- plastic
- rubber

➡ **AHA Coding Clinic:** 2Q, '89, 16

692.5 Due to food in contact with skin

Dermatitis, contact, due to:
- cereals
- fish
- flour

Dermatitis, contact, due to:
- fruit
- meat
- milk

Excludes: *dermatitis due to:*
dyes (692.89)
ingested foods (693.1)
preservatives (692.89)

692.6 Due to plants [except food]

Dermatitis due to:
- lacquer tree [Rhus verniciflua]
- poison:
  - ivy [Rhus toxicodendron]
  - oak [Rhus diversiloba]
  - sumac [Rhus venenata]
  - vine [Rhus radicans]
- primrose [Primula]
- ragweed [Senecio jacobae]
- other plants in contact with the skin

Excludes: *allergy NOS due to pollen (477.0)*
nettle rash (708.8)

✓5th **692.7 Due to solar radiation**

692.70 Unspecified dermatitis due to sun

692.71 Sunburn

692.72 Acute dermatitis due to solar radiation

Berloque dermatitis
Photoallergic response
Phototoxic response
Polymorphous light eruption
Acute solar skin damage NOS

Use additional E code to identify drug if drug induced

Excludes: *sunburn (692.71)*

692.73 Actinic reticuloid and actinic granuloma

692.74 Other chronic dermatitis due to solar radiation

Chronic solar skin damage NOS
Solar elastosis

Excludes: *actinic [solar] keratosis (702.0)*

692.79 Other dermatitis due to solar radiation

Hydroa aestivale
Photodermatitis } (due to sun)
Photosensitiveness } (due to sun)
Solar skin damage NOS

✓5th **692.8 Due to other specified agents**

692.81 Dermatitis due to cosmetics

692.82 Dermatitis due to other radiation

Infrared rays
Light, except from sun
Radiation NOS
Ultraviolet rays, except from sun
X-rays

Excludes: *that due to solar radiation (692.70-692.79)*

692.83 Dermatitis due to metals

Jewelry

692.89 Other

Dermatitis due to:
cold weather
dyes
furs
hot weather
preservatives

Excludes: *allergy NOS due to animal hair, dander (animal), or dust (477.8)*
sunburn (692.71)

692.9 Unspecified cause

Dermatitis:
NOS
contact NOS
venenata NOS
Eczema NOS

693 Dermatitis due to substances taken internally

Excludes: *adverse effect NOS of drugs and medicines (995.2)*
allergy NOS (995.3)
contact dermatitis (692.0-692.9)
urticarial reactions (708.0-708.9, 995.1)

693.0 Due to drugs and medicines

Dermatitis medicamentosa NOS

Use additional E code to identify drug

Excludes: *that due to drugs in contact with skin (692.3)*

693.1 Due to food

693.8 Due to other specified substances taken internally

693.9 Due to unspecified substance taken internally

Excludes: *dermatitis NOS (692.9)*

694 Bullous dermatoses

694.0 Dermatitis herpetiformis

Dermatosis herpetiformis
Duhring's disease
Hydroa herpetiformis

Excludes: *herpes gestationis (646.8)*
dermatitis herpetiformis:
juvenile (694.2)
senile (694.5)

694.1 Subcorneal pustular dermatosis

Sneddon-Wilkinson disease or syndrome

694.2 Juvenile dermatitis herpetiformis

Juvenile pemphigoid

694.3 Impetigo herpetiformis

694.4 Pemphigus

Pemphigus:
NOS
erythematosus
foliaceus
malignant
vegetans
vulgaris

Excludes: *pemphigus neonatorum (684)*

➡ **CC Excl:** 694.4-694.9, 709.8

694.5 Pemphigoid

Benign pemphigus NOS
Bullous pemphigoid
Herpes circinatus bullosus
Senile dermatitis herpetiformis

➡ **CC Excl:** see Code 694.4

✓5th **694.6 Benign mucous membrane pemphigoid**
Cicatricial pemphigoid
Mucosynechial atrophic bullous dermatitis

694.60 Without mention of ocular involvement

694.61 With ocular involvement
Ocular pemphigus

694.8 Other specified bullous dermatoses

Excludes: *herpes gestationis (646.8)*

694.9 Unspecified bullous dermatoses

695 Erythematous conditions

695.0 Toxic erythema

Erythema venenatum

➡ **CC Excl:** 695.0-695.4, 709.8

695.1 Erythema multiforme

Erythema iris
Herpes iris
Lyell's syndrome
Scalded skin syndrome
Stevens-Johnson syndrome
Toxic epidermal necrolysis

695.2 Erythema nodosum

Excludes: *tuberculous erythema nodosum (017.1)*

695.3 Rosacea

Acne:
erythematosa
rosacea
Perioral dermatitis
Rhinophyma

695.4 Lupus erythematosus

Lupus:
erythematodes (discoid)
erythematosus (discoid), not disseminated

Excludes: *lupus (vulgaris) NOS (017.0)*
systemic [disseminated] lupus erythematosus (710.0)

✓5th **695.8 Other specified erythematous conditions**

695.81 Ritter's disease

Dermatitis exfoliativa neonatorum

695.89 Other

Erythema intertrigo
Intertrigo
Pityriasis rubra (Hebra)

Excludes: *mycotic intertrigo (111.0-111.9)*

➡ **AHA Coding Clinic:** S-O, '86, 10

695.9 Unspecified erythematous condition
Erythema NOS
Erythroderma (secondary)

696 Psoriasis and similar disorders

696.0 Psoriatic arthropathy

➡ **CC Excl:** 015.80-015.96, 017.90-017.96, 036.82, 056.71, 098.50-098.51, 098.59-098.89, 696.0, 711.00-711.99, 712.10-712.99, 713.0-713.8, 714.0, 715.00, 715.09-715.10, 715.18, 715.20-715.98, 716.00-716.99, 718.00-718.08, 719.00-719.09, 719.10, 719.18-719.19, 719.20-719.99

696.1 Other psoriasis
Acrodermatitis continua
Dermatitis repens
Psoriasis:
NOS
any type, except arthropathic

Excludes: *psoriatic arthropathy (696.0)*

696.2 Parapsoriasis

Parakeratosis variegata
Parapsoriasis lichenoides chronica
Pityriasis lichenoides et varioliformis

696.3 Pityriasis rosea

Pityriasis circinata (et maculata)

696.4 Pityriasis rubra pilaris

Devergie's disease
Lichen ruber acuminatus

Excludes: *pityriasis rubra (Hebra) (695.89)*

696.5 Other and unspecified pityriasis
Pityriasis:
NOS
alba
streptogenes

Excludes: *pityriasis:*
simplex (690.18)
versicolor (111.0)

696.8 Other

697 Lichen

Excludes: *lichen:*
obtusus corneus (698.3)
pilaris (congenital) (757.39)
ruber acuminatus (696.4)
sclerosus et atrophicus (701.0)
scrofulosus (017.0)
simplex chronicus (698.3)
spinulosus (congenital) (757.39)
urticatus (698.2)

697.0 Lichen planus

Lichen:
planopilaris
ruber planus

697.1 Lichen nitidus

Pinkus' disease

697.8 Other lichen, not elsewhere classified

Lichen:
- ruber moniliforme
- striata

697.9 Lichen, unspecified

698 Pruritus and related conditions

Excludes: *pruritus specified as psychogenic (306.3)*

698.0 Pruritus ani

Perianal itch

698.1 Pruritus of genital organs

698.2 Prurigo

Lichen urticatus
Prurigo:
- NOS
- Hebra's
- mitis
- simplex

Urticaria papulosa (Hebra)

Excludes: *prurigo nodularis (698.3)*

698.3 Lichenification and lichen simplex chronicus

Hyde's disease
Neurodermatitis (circumscripta) (local)
Prurigo nodularis

Excludes: *neurodermatitis, diffuse (of Brocq) (691.8)*

698.4 Dermatitis factitia [artefacta]

Dermatitis ficta
Neurotic excoriation

Use additional code to identify any associated mental disorder

698.8 Other specified pruritic conditions

Pruritus:
- hiemalis
- senilis

Winter itch

698.9 Unspecified pruritic disorder

Itch NOS
Pruritus NOS

OTHER DISEASES OF SKIN AND SUBCUTANEOUS TISSUE (700-709)

Excludes: *conditions confined to eyelids (373.0-374.9)*
congenital conditions of skin, hair, and nails (757.0-757.9)

700 Corns and callosities

Callus
Clavus

701 Other hypertrophic and atrophic conditions of skin

Excludes: *dermatomyositis (710.3)*
hereditary edema of legs (757.0)
scleroderma (generalized) (710.1)

701.0 Circumscribed scleroderma

Addison's keloid
Dermatosclerosis, localized
Lichen sclerosus et atrophicus
Morphea
Scleroderma, circumscribed or localized

701.1 Keratoderma, acquired

Acquired:
- ichthyosis
- keratoderma palmaris et plantaris

Elastosis perforans serpiginosa
Hyperkeratosis:
- NOS
- follicularis in cutem penetrans
- palmoplantaris climacterica

Keratoderma:
- climactericum
- tylodes, progressive

Keratosis (blennorrhagica)

Excludes: *Darier's disease [keratosis follicularis] (congenital) (757.39)*
keratosis:
- *arsenical (692.4)*
- *gonococcal (098.81)*

701.2 Acquired acanthosis nigricans

Keratosis nigricans

701.3 Striae atrophicae

Atrophic spots of skin
Atrophoderma maculatum
Atrophy blanche (of Milian)
Degenerative colloid atrophy
Senile degenerative atrophy
Striae distensae

701.4 Keloid scar

Cheloid
Hypertrophic scar
Keloid

701.5 Other abnormal granulation tissue

Excessive granulation

701.8 Other specified hypertrophic and atrophic conditions of skin

Acrodermatitis atrophicans chronica
Atrophia cutis senilis
Atrophoderma neuriticum
Confluent and reticulate papillomatosis
Cutis laxa senilis
Elastosis senilis
Folliculitis ulerythematosa reticulata
Gougerot-Carteaud syndrome or disease

701.9 Unspecified hypertrophic and atrophic conditions of skin
Atrophoderma

702 Other dermatoses

Excludes: *carcinoma in situ (232.0-232.9)*

702.0 Actinic keratosis
➡ **AHA Coding Clinic:** 1Q, '92, 18

✓5th **702.1 Seborrheic keratosis**

702.11 Inflamed seborrheic keratosis

702.19 Other seborrheic keratosis
Seborrheic keratosis NOS

702.8 Other specified dermatoses

703 Diseases of nail

Excludes: *congenital anomalies (757.5)*
onychia and paronychia (681.02, 681.11)

703.0 Ingrowing nail
Ingrowing nail with infection
Unguis incarnatus

Excludes: *infection, nail NOS (681.9)*

703.8 Other specified diseases of nail
Dystrophia unguium
Hypertrophy of nail
Koilonychia
Leukonychia (punctata)
(striata)
Onychauxis
Onychogryposis
Onycholysis

703.9 Unspecified disease of nail

704 Diseases of hair and hair follicles

Excludes: *congenital anomalies (757.4)*

✓5th **704.0 Alopecia**

Excludes: *madarosis (374.55)*
syphilitic alopecia (091.82)

704.00 Alopecia, unspecified
Baldness
Loss of hair

704.01 Alopecia areata
Ophiasis

704.02 Telogen effluvium

704.09 Other
Folliculitis decalvans
Hypotrichosis:
NOS
postinfectional NOS
Pseudopelade

704.1 Hirsutism
Hypertrichosis:
NOS
lanuginosa, acquired
Polytrichia

Excludes: *hypertrichosis of eyelid (374.54)*

704.2 Abnormalities of the hair
Atrophic hair
Clastothrix
Fragilitas crinium
Trichiasis:
NOS
cicatrical
Trichorrhexis (nodosa)

Excludes: *trichiasis of eyelid (374.05)*

704.3 Variations in hair color
Canities (premature)
Grayness, hair
(premature)
Heterochromia of hair
Poliosis:
NOS
circumscripta, acquired

704.8 Other specified diseases of hair and hair follicles
Folliculitis:
NOS
abscedens et suffodiens
pustular
Perifolliculitis:
NOS
capitis abscedens et
suffodiens
scalp
Sycosis:
NOS
barbae [not parasitic]
lupoid
vulgaris

704.9 Unspecified disease of hair and hair follicles

705 Disorders of sweat glands

705.0 Anhidrosis
Hypohidrosis
Oligohidrosis

705.1 Prickly heat
Heat rash
Miliaria rubra (tropicalis)
Sudamina

✓5th **705.8 Other specified disorders of sweat glands**

705.81 Dyshidrosis
Cheiropompholyx
Pompholyx

705.82 Fox-Fordyce disease

705.83 Hidradenitis
Hidradenitis suppurativa

705.89 Other
Bromhidrosis
Chromhidrosis
Granulosis rubra nasi
Urhidrosis

Excludes: *hidrocystoma (216.0-216.9)*
hyperhidrosis (780.8)

705.9 Unspecified disorder of sweat glands
Disorder of sweat glands NOS

706 Diseases of sebaceous glands

706.0 Acne varioliformis

Acne:
frontalis
necrotica

706.1 Other acne

Acne:
NOS
conglobata
cystic
pustular
vulgaris

Blackhead
Comedo

Excludes: *acne rosacea (695.3)*

706.2 Sebaceous cyst

Atheroma, skin
Keratin cyst
Wen

706.3 Seborrhea

Excludes: *seborrhea:*
capitis (690.11)
sicca (690.18)
seborrheic keratosis (702)

706.8 Other specified diseases of sebaceous glands

Asteatosis (cutis)
Xerosis cutis

706.9 Unspecified disease of sebaceous glands

707 Chronic ulcer of skin

Includes: non-infected sinus of skin
non-healing ulcer

Excludes: *specific infections classified under "Infectious and Parasitic Diseases" (001.0-136.9)*
varicose ulcer (454.0, 454.2)

707.0 Decubitus ulcer

Bed sore
Decubitus ulcer [any site]
Plaster ulcer
Pressure ulcer

➡ **CC Excl:** 707.0, 707.8-707.9, 709.8

➡ **AHA Coding Clinic:** 1Q, '96, 15; 3Q, '90, 15; N-D, '87, 9

✔ **St. Anthony's Clinical Coder:** see Chapter 5

707.1 Ulcer of lower limbs, except decubitus

Ulcer, chronic: neurogenic, trophic } of lower limb

Excludes: *that with atherosclerosis of the extremities (440.23)*

➡ **CC Excl:** 440.23, 707.1-707.9, 709.8

707.8 Chronic ulcer of other specified sites

Ulcer, chronic: neurogenic, trophic } of other specified sites

707.9 Chronic ulcer of unspecified site

Chronic ulcer NOS
Trophic ulcer NOS
Tropical ulcer NOS
Ulcer of skin NOS

708 Urticaria

Excludes: *edema:*
angioneurotic (995.1)
Quincke's (995.1)
hereditary angioedema (277.6)
urticaria:
giant (995.1)
papulosa (Hebra) (698.2)
pigmentosa (juvenile) (congenital) (757.33)

708.0 Allergic urticaria

708.1 Idiopathic urticaria

708.2 Urticaria due to cold and heat

Thermal urticaria

708.3 Dermatographic urticaria

Dermatographia
Factitial urticaria

708.4 Vibratory urticaria

708.5 Cholinergic urticaria

708.8 Other specified urticaria

Nettle rash
Urticaria:
chronic
recurrent periodic

708.9 Urticaria, unspecified

Hives NOS

709 Other disorders of skin and subcutaneous tissue

✓5th **709.0 Dyschromia**

Excludes: *albinism (270.2)*
pigmented nevus (216.0-216.9)
that of eyelid (374.52-374.53)

709.00 Dyschromia, unspecified

709.01 Vitiligo

709.09 Other

709.1 Vascular disorders of skin

Angioma serpiginosum
Purpura (primary) annularis telangiectodes

709.2 Scar conditions and fibrosis of skin

Adherent scar (skin)
Cicatrix
Disfigurement (due to scar)
Fibrosis, skin NOS
Scar NOS

Excludes: *keloid scar (701.4)*

➡ **AHA Coding Clinic:** N-D, '84, 19

709.3 Degenerative skin disorders

Calcinosis:
- circumscripta
- cutis

Colloid milium
Degeneration, skin
Deposits, skin
Senile dermatosis NOS
Subcutaneous calcification

709.4 Foreign body granuloma of skin and subcutaneous tissue

Excludes: *residual foreign body without granuloma of skin and subcutaneous tissue (729.6)*
that of muscle (728.82)

709.8 Other specified disorders of skin

Epithelial hyperplasia
Menstrual dermatosis
Vesicular eruption

➡ **AHA Coding Clinic:** N-D, '87, 6

709.9 Unspecified disorder of skin and subcutaneous tissue

Dermatosis NOS

13. DISEASES OF THE MUSCULOSKELETAL SYSTEM AND CONNECTIVE TISSUE (710-739)

The following fifth-digit subclassification is for use with categories 711-712, 715-716, 718-719, and 730:

0 site unspecified

1 shoulder region
- Acromioclavicular joint(s)
- Glenohumeral joint(s)
- Sternoclavicular joint(s)
- Clavicle
- Scapula

2 upper arm
- Elbow joint
- Humerus

3 forearm
- Radius
- Ulna
- Wrist joint

4 hand
- Carpus
- Metacarpus
- Phalanges [fingers]

5 pelvic region and thigh
- Buttock
- Femur
- Hip (joint)

6 lower leg
- Fibula
- Knee joint
- Patella
- Tibia

7 ankle and foot
- Ankle joint
- Digits [toes]
- Metatarsus
- Phalanges, foot
- Tarsus
- Other joints in foot

8 other specified sites
- Head
- Neck
- Ribs
- Skull
- Trunk
- Vertebral column

9 multiple sites

ARTHROPATHIES AND RELATED DISORDERS (710-719)

Excludes: *disorders of spine (720.0-724.9)*

710 Diffuse diseases of connective tissue

Includes: all collagen diseases whose effects are not mainly confined to a single system

Use additional code to identify manifestation, as:
- lung involvement (517.8)
- myopathy (359.6)

Excludes: *those affecting mainly the cardiovascular system, i.e., polyarteritis nodosa and allied conditions (446.0-446.7)*

710.0 Systemic lupus erythematosus

Disseminated lupus erythematosus
Libman-Sacks disease

Use additional code to identify manifestation, as:
- endocarditis (424.91)
- nephritis (583.81)
  - chronic (582.81)
- nephrotic syndrome (581.81)

Excludes: *lupus erythematosus (discoid) NOS (695.4)*

➡ **CC Excl:** 710.0

➡ **AHA Coding Clinic:** 2Q, '97, 8

710.1 Systemic sclerosis

Acrosclerosis
CRST syndrome
Progressive systemic sclerosis
Scleroderma

Excludes: *circumscribed scleroderma (701.0)*

➡ **CC Excl:** 710.1

710.2 Sicca syndrome

Keratoconjunctivitis sicca
Sjögren's disease

710.3 Dermatomyositis

Poikilodermatomyositis
Polymyositis with skin involvement

➡ **CC Excl:** 710.3

710.4 Polymyositis

➡ **CC Excl:** 710.4

710.5 Eosinophilia myalgia syndrome

Toxic oil syndrome

Use additional E code to identify drug if drug induced

➡ **CC Excl:** 292.0-292.9, 293.0-293.7, 293.84, 293.9, 710.5

➡ **AHA Coding Clinic:** 4Q, '92, 21

710.8 Other specified diffuse diseases of connective tissue

Multifocal fibrosclerosis (idiopathic) NEC
Systemic fibrosclerosing syndrome

➡ **CC Excl:** 710.8

➡ **AHA Coding Clinic:** M-A, '87, 12

710.9 Unspecified diffuse connective tissue disease

Collagen disease NOS

711 Arthropathy associated with infections

Includes: arthritis, arthropathy, polyarthritis, polyarthropathy } associated with conditions classifiable below

Excludes: *rheumatic fever (390)*

The following fifth-digit subclassification is for use with category 711; valid digits are in [brackets] under each code. See page 251 for definitions:

0 site unspecified
1 shoulder region
2 upper arm
3 forearm
4 hand
5 pelvic region and thigh
6 lower leg
7 ankle and foot
8 other specified sites
9 multiple sites

➡ **AHA Coding Clinic:** 1Q, '92, 17

✓5th **711.0 Pyogenic arthritis**
[0–9]

Arthritis or polyarthritis (due to):
- coliform [Escherichia coli]
- Hemophilus influenzae [H. influenzae]
- pneumococcal
- Pseudomonas
- staphylococcal
- streptococcal

Pyarthrosis

Use additional code to identify infectious organism (041.0-041.8)

➡ **CC Excl: For code 711.00:** 015.80-015.96, 017.90-017.96, 036.82, 056.71, 098.50-098.51, 098.59, 098.89, 711.00-711.99, 712.10-712.99, 713.0-713.8, 714.0, 715.00, 715.09-715.10, 715.18-715.98, 716.00-716.99, 718.00-718.08, 719.00-719.10, 719.18-719.99

➡ **CC Excl: For code 711.01:** 015.80-015.96, 017.90-017.96, 036.82, 056.71, 098.50-098.51, 098.59, 098.89, 711.00-711.01, 711.08-711.11, 711.18-711.21, 711.28-711.31, 711.38-711.41, 711.48-711.51, 711.58-711.61, 711.68-711.71, 711.78-711.81, 711.88-711.91, 711.98-711.99, 712.10-712.11, 712.18-712.21, 712.28-712.31, 712.38-712.81, 712.88-712.91, 712.98-712.99, 713.0-713.8, 714.0, 715.00, 715.09-715.11, 715.18-715.21, 715.28-715.31, 715.38, 715.91, 715.98, 716.00-716.01, 716.08-716.11, 716.18-716.21, 716.28-716.31, 716.38-716.41, 716.48-716.51, 716.58-716.61, 716.68-716.81, 716.88-716.91, 716.98-716.99, 718.00-718.01, 718.08, 719.00-719.01, 719.08-719.11, 719.18-719.21, 719.28-719.31, 719.38-719.41, 719.48-719.51, 719.58-719.61, 719.68-719.70, 719.78-719.81, 719.88-719.91, 719.98-719.99

➡ **CC Excl: For code 711.02:** 015.80-015.96, 017.90-017.96, 036.82, 056.71, 098.50-098.51, 098.59, 098.89, 711.00, 711.02, 711.08-711.10, 711.12, 711.18-711.20, 711.22, 711.28-711.30, 711.32, 711.38-711.40, 711.42, 711.48-711.50, 711.52, 711.58-711.60, 711.62, 711.68-711.70, 711.72, 711.78-711.80, 711.82, 711.88-711.90, 711.92, 711.98-711.99, 712.10, 712.12, 712.18-712.20, 712.22, 712.28-712.30, 712.32, 712.38-712.80, 712.82, 712.88-712.90, 712.92, 712.98-712.99, 713.0-713.8, 714.0, 715.00, 715.09-715.10, 715.12, 715.18, 715.20, 715.22, 715.28, 715.30, 715.32, 715.38-715.90, 715.92, 715.98, 716.00, 716.02, 716.08-716.10, 716.12, 716.18-716.20, 716.22, 716.28-716.30, 716.32, 716.38-716.40, 716.42, 716.48-716.50, 716.52, 716.58-716.60, 716.62, 716.68, 716.80, 716.82, 716.88-716.90, 716.92, 716.98-716.99, 718.00, 718.02, 718.08, 719.00, 719.02, 719.08-719.10, 719.12, 719.18-719.20, 719.22, 719.28-719.30, 719.32, 719.38-719.40, 719.42, 719.48-719.50, 719.52, 719.58-719.60, 719.62, 719.68-719.70, 719.78-719.80, 719.82, 719.88-719.90, 719.92, 719.98-719.99

➡ **CC Excl: For code 711.03:** 015.80-015.96, 017.90-017.96, 036.82, 056.71, 098.50-098.51, 098.59, 098.89, 711.00, 711.03, 711.08-711.10, 711.13, 711.18-711.20, 711.23, 711.28-711.30, 711.33, 711.38-711.40, 711.43, 711.48-711.50, 711.53, 711.58-711.60, 711.63, 711.68-711.70, 711.73, 711.78-711.80, 711.83, 711.88-711.90, 711.93, 711.98-711.99, 712.10, 712.13, 712.18-712.20, 712.23, 712.28-712.30, 712.33, 712.38-712.80, 712.83, 712.88-712.90, 712.93, 712.98-712.99, 713.0-713.8, 714.0, 715.00, 715.09-715.10, 715.13, 715.18, 715.20, 715.23, 715.28, 715.30, 715.33, 715.38-715.90, 715.93, 715.98, 716.00, 716.03, 716.08-716.10, 716.13, 716.18-716.20, 716.23, 716.28-716.30, 716.33, 716.38-716.40, 716.43, 716.48-716.50, 716.53, 716.58-716.60, 716.63, 716.68, 716.80, 716.83, 716.88-716.90, 716.93, 716.98-716.99, 718.00, 718.03, 718.08, 719.00, 719.03, 719.08-719.10, 719.13, 719.18-719.20, 719.23, 719.28-719.30, 719.33, 719.38-719.40, 719.43, 719.48-719.50, 719.53, 719.58-719.60, 719.63, 719.68-719.70, 719.78-719.80, 719.83, 719.88-719.90, 719.93, 719.98-719.99

➡ **CC Excl: For code 711.04:** 015.80-015.96, 017.90-017.96, 036.82, 056.71, 098.50-098.51, 098.59, 098.89, 711.00, 711.04, 711.08-711.10, 711.14, 711.18-711.20, 711.24, 711.28-711.30, 711.34, 711.38-711.40, 711.44, 711.48-711.50, 711.54, 711.58-711.60, 711.64, 711.68-711.70, 711.74, 711.78-711.80, 711.84, 711.88-711.90, 711.94, 711.98-711.99, 712.10, 712.14, 712.18-712.20, 712.24, 712.28-712.30, 712.34, 712.38-712.80, 712.84, 712.88-712.90, 712.94, 712.98-712.99, 713.0-713.8, 714.0, 715.00-715.10, 715.14, 715.18, 715.20, 715.24, 715.28, 715.30, 715.34, 715.38-715.90, 715.94, 715.98, 716.00, 716.04, 716.08-716.10, 716.14, 716.18-716.20, 716.24, 716.28-716.30, 716.34, 716.38-716.40, 716.44, 716.48-716.50, 716.54, 716.58-716.60, 716.64, 716.68, 716.80, 716.84, 716.88-716.90, 716.94, 716.98-716.99, 718.00, 718.04, 718.08, 719.00, 719.04, 719.08-719.10, 719.14, 719.18-719.20, 719.24, 719.28-719.30, 719.34, 719.38-719.40, 719.44, 719.48-719.50, 719.54, 719.58-719.60, 719.64, 719.68-719.70, 719.78-719.80, 719.84, 719.88-719.90, 719.94, 719.98-719.99

711.0 Pyogenic arthritis — *continued*

➡ **CC Excl: For code 711.05:** 015.80-015.96, 017.90-017.96, 036.82, 056.71, 098.50-098.51, 098.59, 098.89, 711.00, 711.05, 711.08-711.10, 711.15, 711.18-711.20, 711.25, 711.28-711.30, 711.35, 711.38-711.40, 711.45, 711.48-711.50, 711.55, 711.58-711.60, 711.65, 711.68-711.70, 711.75, 711.78-711.80, 711.85, 711.88-711.90, 711.95, 711.98-711.99, 712.10, 712.15, 712.18-712.20, 712.25, 712.28-712.30, 712.35, 712.38-712.80, 712.85, 712.88-712.90, 712.95, 712.98-712.99, 713.0-713.8, 714.0, 715.00, 715.09-715.10, 715.15, 715.18, 715.20, 715.25, 715.28, 715.30, 715.35, 715.38-715.90, 715.95, 715.98, 716.00, 716.05, 716.08-716.10, 716.15, 716.18-716.20, 716.25, 716.28-716.30, 716.35, 716.38-716.40, 716.45, 716.48-716.50, 716.55, 716.58-716.60, 716.65, 716.68, 716.80, 716.85, 716.88-716.90, 716.95, 716.98-716.99, 718.00, 718.05, 718.08, 719.00, 719.05, 719.08-719.10, 719.15, 719.18-719.20, 719.25, 719.28-719.30, 719.35, 719.38-719.40, 719.45, 719.48-719.50, 719.55, 719.58-719.60, 719.65, 719.68-719.70, 719.75, 719.78-719.80, 719.85, 719.88-719.90, 719.95, 719.98-719.99

➡ **CC Excl: For code 711.06:** 015.80-015.96, 017.90-017.96, 036.82, 056.71, 098.50-098.51, 098.59, 098.89, 711.00, 711.06, 711.08-711.10, 711.16, 711.18-711.20, 711.26, 711.28-711.30, 711.36, 711.38-711.40, 711.46, 711.48-711.50, 711.56, 711.58-711.60, 711.66, 711.68-711.70, 711.76, 711.78-711.80, 711.86, 711.88-711.90, 711.96, 711.98-711.99, 712.10, 712.16, 712.18-712.20, 712.26, 712.28-712.30, 712.36, 712.38-712.80, 712.86, 712.88-712.90, 712.96, 712.98-712.99, 713.0-713.8, 714.0, 715.00, 715.09-715.10, 715.16, 715.18, 715.20, 715.26, 715.28, 715.30, 715.36, 715.38-715.90, 715.96, 715.98, 716.00, 716.06, 716.08-716.10, 716.16, 716.18-716.20, 716.26, 716.28-716.30, 716.36, 716.38-716.40, 716.46, 716.48-716.50, 716.56, 716.58-716.60, 716.66, 716.68, 716.80, 716.86, 716.88-716.90, 716.96, 716.98-716.99, 718.00, 718.08, 719.00, 719.06, 719.08-719.10, 719.16, 719.18-719.20, 719.26, 719.28-719.30, 719.36, 719.38-719.40, 719.46, 719.48-719.50, 719.56, 719.58-719.60, 719.66, 719.68-719.70, 719.76, 719.78-719.80, 719.86, 719.88-719.90, 719.96, 719.98-719.99

➡ **CC Excl: For code 711.07:** 015.80-015.96, 017.90-017.96, 036.82, 056.71, 098.50-098.51, 098.59, 098.89, 711.00, 711.07-711.10, 711.17-711.20, 711.27-711.30, 711.37-711.40, 711.47-711.50, 711.57-711.60, 711.67-711.70, 711.77-711.80, 711.87-711.90, 711.97-711.99, 712.10, 712.17-712.20, 712.27-712.30, 712.37-712.80, 712.87-712.90, 712.97-712.99, 713.0-713.8, 714.0, 715.00, 715.09-715.10, 715.17-715.18, 715.20, 715.27-715.28, 715.30, 715.37-715.90, 715.97-715.98, 716.00, 716.07-716.10, 716.17-716.20, 716.27-716.30, 716.37-716.40, 716.47-716.50, 716.57-716.60, 716.67-716.68, 716.80, 716.87-716.90, 716.97-716.99, 718.00, 718.07-718.08, 719.00, 719.07-719.10, 719.17-719.20, 719.27-719.30, 719.37-719.40, 719.47-719.50, 719.57-719.60, 719.67-719.70, 719.77-719.80, 719.87-719.90, 719.97-719.99

➡ **CC Excl: For code 711.08:** 015.80-015.96, 017.90-017.96, 036.82, 056.71, 098.50-098.51, 098.59, 098.89, 711.00-711.99, 712.10-712.99, 713.0-713.8, 714.0, 715.00, 715.09-715.10, 715.18-715.98, 716.00-716.99, 718.00-718.08, 719.00-719.10, 719.18-719.99

➡ **CC Excl: For code 711.09:** see Code 711.08

➡ **AHA Coding Clinic:** 1Q, '92, 16; 1Q, '91, 15

✓5th **711.1** **Arthropathy associated with Reiter's disease and nonspecific urethritis**
[0–9]

Code first underlying disease as:
nonspecific urethritis (099.4)
Reiter's disease (099.3)

✓5th **711.2** **Arthropathy in Behçet's syndrome**
[0–9]

Code first underlying disease (136.1)

✓5th **711.3** **Postdysenteric arthropathy**
[0–9]

Code first underlying disease as:
dysentery (009.0)
enteritis, infectious (008.0-009.3)
paratyphoid fever (002.1-002.9)
typhoid fever (002.0)

Excludes: *salmonella arthritis (003.23)*

✓5th **711.4** **Arthropathy associated with other bacterial diseases**
[0–9]

Code first underlying disease as:
diseases classifiable to 010-040, 090-099, except as in 711.1, 711.3, and 713.5
leprosy (030.0-030.9)
tuberculosis (015.0-015.9)

Excludes: *gonococcal arthritis (098.50)*
meningococcal arthritis (036.82)

✓5th **711.5** **Arthropathy associated with other viral diseases**
[0–9]

Code first underlying disease as:
diseases classifiable to 045-049, 050-079, 480, 487
O'nyong nyong (066.3)

Excludes: *that due to rubella (056.71)*

✓5th **711.6** **Arthropathy associated with mycoses**
[0–9]

Code first underlying disease (110.0-118)

➡ **CC Excl: For code 711.60:** see Code 711.08

➡ **CC Excl: For code 711.61:** 015.80-015.96, 017.90-017.96, 036.82, 056.71, 098.50-098.51, 098.59, 098.89, 711.00-711.01, 711.08-711.11, 711.18-711.21, 711.28-711.31, 711.38-711.41, 711.48-711.51, 711.58-711.61, 711.68-711.71, 711.78-711.81, 711.88-711.91, 711.98-711.99, 712.10-712.11, 712.18-712.21, 712.28-712.31, 712.38-712.81, 712.88-712.91, 712.98-712.99, 713.0-713.8, 714.0, 715.00, 715.09-715.11, 715.18-715.21, 715.28, 715.30-715.31, 715.38-715.91, 715.98, 716.00-716.01, 716.08-716.11, 716.18-716.21, 716.28-716.31, 716.38-716.41, 716.48-716.51, 716.58-716.61, 716.68, 716.80-716.81, 716.88-716.91, 716.98-716.99, 718.00-718.01, 718.08, 719.00-719.01, 719.08-719.11, 719.18-719.21, 719.28-719.31, 719.38-719.41, 719.48-719.51, 719.58-719.61, 719.68-719.70, 719.78-719.81, 719.88-719.91, 719.98-719.99

➡ **CC Excl: For code 711.62:** 015.80-015.96, 017.90-017.96, 036.82, 056.71, 098.50-098.51, 098.59, 098.89, 711.00, 711.02, 711.08-711.10, 711.12, 711.18-711.20, 711.22, 711.28-711.30, 711.32, 711.38-711.40, 711.42, 711.48-711.50, 711.52, 711.58-711.60, 711.62, 711.68-711.70, 711.72, 711.78-711.80, 711.82, 711.88-711.90, 711.92, 711.98-711.99, 712.10, 712.12, 712.18-712.20, 712.22, 712.28-712.30, 712.32, 712.38-712.80, 712.82, 712.88-712.90, 712.92, 712.98-712.99, 713.0-713.8, 714.0, 715.00, 715.09-715.10, 715.12, 715.18, 715.20, 715.22, 715.28, 715.30, 715.32, 715.38-715.90, 715.92, 715.98, 716.00, 716.02, 716.08-716.10, 716.12, 716.18-716.20, 716.22, 716.28-716.30, 716.32, 716.38-716.40, 716.42, 716.48-716.50, 716.52, 716.58-716.60, 716.62, 716.68, 716.80, 716.82, 716.88-716.90, 716.92, 716.98-716.99, 718.00, 718.02, 718.08, 719.00, 719.02, 719.08-719.10, 719.12, 719.18-719.20, 719.22, 719.28-719.30, 719.32, 719.38-719.40, 719.42, 719.48-719.50, 719.52, 719.58-719.60, 719.62, 719.68-719.70, 719.78-719.80, 719.82, 719.88-719.90, 719.92, 719.98-719.99

➡ **CC Excl: For code 711.63:** 015.80-015.96, 017.90-017.96, 036.82, 056.71, 098.50-098.51, 098.59, 098.89, 711.00, 711.03, 711.08-711.10, 711.13, 711.18-711.20, 711.23, 711.28-711.30, 711.33, 711.38-711.40, 711.43, 711.48-711.50, 711.53, 711.58-711.60, 711.63, 711.68-711.70, 711.73, 711.78-711.80, 711.83, 711.88-711.90, 711.93, 711.98-711.99, 712.10, 712.13, 712.18-712.20, 712.23, 712.28-712.30, 712.33, 712.38-712.80, 712.83, 712.88-712.90, 712.93, 712.98-712.99, 713.0-713.8, 714.0, 715.00, 715.09-715.10, 715.13, 715.18, 715.20, 715.23, 715.28, 715.30, 715.33, 715.38-715.90, 715.93, 715.98, 716.00, 716.03, 716.08-716.10, 716.13, 716.18-716.20, 716.23, 716.28-716.30, 716.33, 716.38-716.40, 716.43, 716.48-716.50, 716.53, 716.58-716.60, 716.63, 716.68, 716.80, 716.83, 716.88-716.90, 716.93, 716.98-716.99, 718.00, 718.03, 718.08, 719.00, 719.03, 719.08-719.10, 719.13, 719.18-719.20, 719.23, 719.28-719.30, 719.33, 719.38-719.40, 719.43, 719.48-719.50, 719.53, 719.58-719.60, 719.63, 719.68-719.70, 719.78-719.80, 719.83, 719.88-719.90, 719.93, 719.98-719.99

➡ **CC Excl: For code 711.64:** 015.80-015.96, 017.90-017.96, 036.82, 056.71, 098.50-098.51, 098.59, 098.89, 711.00, 711.04, 711.08-711.10, 711.14, 711.18-711.20, 711.24, 711.28-711.30, 711.34, 711.38-711.40, 711.44, 711.48-711.50, 711.54, 711.58-711.60, 711.64, 711.68-711.70, 711.74, 711.78-711.80, 711.84, 711.88-711.90, 711.94, 711.98-711.99, 712.10, 712.14, 712.18-712.20, 712.24, 712.28-712.30, 712.34, 712.38-712.80, 712.84, 712.88-712.90, 712.94, 712.98-712.99, 713.0-713.8, 714.0, 715.00-715.10, 715.14, 715.18, 715.20, 715.24, 715.28, 715.30, 715.34, 715.38-715.90, 715.94, 715.98, 716.00, 716.04, 716.08-716.10, 716.14, 716.18-716.20, 716.24, 716.28-716.30, 716.34, 716.38-716.40, 716.44, 716.48-716.50, 716.54, 716.58-716.60, 716.64, 716.68, 716.80, 716.84, 716.88-716.90, 716.94, 716.98-716.99, 718.00, 718.04, 718.08, 719.00, 719.04, 719.08-719.10, 719.14, 719.18-719.20, 719.24, 719.28-719.30, 719.34, 719.38-719.40, 719.44, 719.48-719.50, 719.54, 719.58-719.60, 719.64, 719.68-719.70, 719.78-719.80, 719.84, 719.88-719.90, 719.94, 719.98-719.99

➡ **CC Excl: For code 711.65:** 015.80-015.96, 017.90-017.96, 036.82, 056.71, 098.50-098.51, 098.59, 098.89, 711.00, 711.05, 711.08-711.10, 711.15, 711.18-711.20, 711.25, 711.28-711.30, 711.35, 711.38-711.40, 711.45, 711.48-711.50, 711.55, 711.58-711.60, 711.65, 711.68-711.70, 711.75, 711.78-711.80, 711.85, 711.88-711.90, 711.95, 711.98-711.99, 712.10, 712.15, 712.18-712.20, 712.25, 712.28-712.30, 712.35, 712.38-712.80, 712.85, 712.88-712.90, 712.95, 712.98-712.99, 713.0-713.8, 714.0, 715.00, 715.09-715.10, 715.15, 715.18, 715.20, 715.25, 715.28, 715.30, 715.35, 715.38-715.90, 715.95, 715.98, 716.00, 716.05, 716.08-716.10, 716.15, 716.18-716.20, 716.25, 716.28-716.30, 716.35, 716.38-716.40, 716.45, 716.48-716.50, 716.55, 716.58-716.60, 716.65, 716.68, 716.80, 716.85, 716.88-716.90, 716.95, 716.98-716.99, 718.00, 718.05, 718.08, 719.00, 719.05, 719.08-719.10, 719.15, 719.18-719.20, 719.25, 719.28-719.30, 719.35, 719.38-719.40, 719.45, 719.48-719.50, 719.55, 719.58-719.60, 719.65, 719.68-719.70, 719.75, 719.78-719.80, 719.85, 719.88-719.90, 719.95, 719.98-719.99

➡ **CC Excl: For code 711.66:** 015.80-015.96, 017.90-017.96, 036.82, 056.71, 098.50-098.51, 098.59, 098.89, 711.00, 711.06, 711.08-711.10, 711.16, 711.18-711.20, 711.26, 711.28-711.30, 711.36, 711.38-711.40, 711.46, 711.48-711.50, 711.56, 711.58-711.60, 711.66, 711.68-711.70, 711.76, 711.78-711.80, 711.86, 711.88-711.90, 711.96, 711.98-711.99, 712.10, 712.16, 712.18-712.20, 712.26, 712.28-712.30, 712.36, 712.38-712.80, 712.86, 712.88-712.90, 712.96, 712.98-712.99, 713.0-713.8, 714.0, 715.00, 715.09-715.10, 715.16, 715.18, 715.20, 715.26, 715.28, 715.30, 715.36, 715.38-715.90, 715.96, 715.98, 716.00, 716.06, 716.08-716.10, 716.16, 716.18-716.20, 716.26, 716.28-716.30, 716.36, 716.38-716.40, 716.46, 716.48-716.50, 716.56, 716.58-716.60, 716.66, 716.68, 716.80, 716.86, 716.88-716.90, 716.96, 716.98-716.99, 718.00, 718.08, 719.00, 719.06, 719.08-719.10, 719.16, 719.18-719.20, 719.26, 719.28-719.30, 719.36, 719.38-719.40, 719.46, 719.48-719.50, 719.56, 719.58-719.60, 719.66, 719.68-719.70, 719.76, 719.78-719.80, 719.86, 719.88-719.90, 719.96, 719.98-719.99

711.6 *Arthropathy associated with mycoses — continued*

➡ **CC Excl: For code 711.67:** 015.80-015.96, 017.90-017.96, 036.82, 056.71, 098.50-098.51, 098.59, 098.89, 711.00, 711.07-711.10, 711.17-711.20, 711.27-711.30, 711.37-711.40, 711.47-711.50, 711.57-711.60, 711.67-711.70, 711.77-711.80, 711.87-711.90, 711.97-711.99, 712.10, 712.17-712.20, 712.27-712.30, 712.37-712.80, 712.87-712.90, 712.97-712.99, 713.0-713.8, 714.0, 715.00, 715.09-715.10, 715.17-715.18, 715.20, 715.27-715.28, 715.30, 715.37-715.90, 715.97-715.98, 716.00, 716.07-716.10, 716.17-716.20, 716.27-716.30, 716.37-716.40, 716.47-716.50, 716.57-716.60, 716.67-716.80, 716.87-716.90, 716.97-716.99, 718.00, 718.07-718.08, 719.00, 719.07-719.10, 719.17-719.20, 719.27-719.30, 719.37-719.40, 719.47-719.50, 719.57-719.60, 719.67-719.70, 719.77-719.80, 719.87-719.90, 719.97-719.99

➡ **CC Excl: For code 711.68:** 015.80-015.96, 017.90-017.96, 036.82, 056.71, 098.50-098.51, 098.59, 098.89, 711.00-711.99, 712.10-712.99, 713.0-713.8, 714.0, 715.00, 715.09-715.10, 715.18-715.98, 716.00-716.99, 718.00-718.08, 719.00-719.10, 719.18-719.99

➡ **CC Excl: For code 711.69:** see Code 711.68

✓5th **711.7** **Arthropathy associated with helminthiasis**
[0–9]

Code first underlying disease as:
filariasis (125.0-125.9)

✓5th **711.8** **Arthropathy associated with other infectious and parasitic diseases**
[0–9]

Code first underlying disease as:
diseases classifiable to 080-088, 100-104, 130-136

Excludes: *arthropathy associated with sarcoidosis (713.7)*

➡ **AHA Coding Clinic:** 4Q, '91, 15; 3Q, '90, 14

✓5th **711.9** **Unspecified infective arthritis**
[0–9]

Infective arthritis or polyarthritis (acute) (chronic) (subacute) NOS

712 Crystal arthropathies

Includes: crystal-induced arthritis and synovitis

Excludes: *gouty arthropathy (274.0)*

The following fifth-digit subclassification is for use with category 712; valid digits are in [brackets] under each code. See page 251 for definitions:

0 site unspecified
1 shoulder region
2 upper arm
3 forearm
4 hand
5 pelvic region and thigh
6 lower leg
7 ankle and foot
8 other specified sites
9 multiple sites

✓5th **712.1** **Chondrocalcinosis due to dicalcium phosphate crystals**
[0–9]

Chondrocalcinosis due to dicalcium phosphate crystals (with other crystals)

Code first underlying disease (275.4)

✓5th **712.2** **Chondrocalcinosis due to pyrophosphate crystals**
[0–9]

Code first underlying disease (275.4)

✓5th **712.3** **Chondrocalcinosis, unspecified**
[0–9]

Code first underlying disease (275.4)

✓5th **712.8** **Other specified crystal arthropathies**
[0–9]

✓5th **712.9** **Unspecified crystal arthropathy**
[0–9]

713 Arthropathy associated with other disorders classified elsewhere

Includes: arthritis, arthropathy, polyarthritis, polyarthropathy } associated with conditions classifiable below

713.0 **Arthropathy associated with other endocrine and metabolic disorders**

Code first underlying disease as:
acromegaly (253.0)
hemochromatosis (275.0)
hyperparathyroidism (252.0)
hypogammaglobulinemia (279.00-279.09)
hypothyroidism (243-244.9)
lipoid metabolism disorder (272.0-272.9)
ochronosis (270.2)

Excludes: *arthropathy associated with:*
amyloidosis (713.7)
crystal deposition disorders, except gout (712.1-712.9)
diabetic neuropathy (713.5)
gouty arthropathy (274.0)

713.1 **Arthropathy associated with gastrointestinal conditions other than infections**

Code first underlying disease as:
regional enteritis (555.0-555.9)
ulcerative colitis (556)

713.2 **Arthropathy associated with hematological disorders**

Code first underlying disease as:
hemoglobinopathy (282.4-282.7)
hemophilia (286.0-286.2)
leukemia (204.0-208.9)
malignant reticulosis (202.3)
multiple myelomatosis (203.0)

Excludes: *arthropathy associated with Henoch-Schönlein purpura (713.6)*

713.3 **Arthropathy associated with dermatological disorders**

Code first underlying disease as:
erythema multiforme (695.1)
erythema nodosum (695.2)

Excludes: *psoriatic arthropathy (696.0)*

713.4 **Arthropathy associated with respiratory disorders**

Code first underlying disease as:
diseases classifiable to 490-519

Excludes: *arthropathy associated with respiratory infections (711.0, 711.4-711.8)*

713.5 **Arthropathy associated with neurological disorders**

Charcot's arthropathy, Neuropathic arthritis } associated with diseases classifiable elsewhere

Code first underlying disease as:
neuropathic joint disease [Charcot's joints]:
NOS (094.0)
diabetic (250.6)
syringomyelic (336.0)
tabetic [syphilitic] (094.0)

713.6 Arthropathy associated with hypersensitivity reaction

Code first underlying disease as:
Henoch (-Schönlein) purpura (287.0)
serum sickness (999.5)

Excludes: *allergic arthritis NOS (716.2)*

713.7 Other general diseases with articular involvement

Code first underlying disease as:
amyloidosis (277.3)
familial Mediterranean fever (277.3)
sarcoidosis (135)

➡ **AHA Coding Clinic:** 2Q, '97, 12

713.8 Arthropathy associated with other conditions classifiable elsewhere

Code first underlying disease as:
conditions classifiable elsewhere except as in 711.1-711.8, 712, and 713.0-713.7

714 Rheumatoid arthritis and other inflammatory polyarthropathies

Excludes: *rheumatic fever (390)*
rheumatoid arthritis of spine NOS (720.0)

714.0 Rheumatoid arthritis

Arthritis or polyarthritis:
atrophic
rheumatic (chronic)

Use additional code to identify manifestation, as:
myopathy (359.6)
polyneuropathy (357.1)

Excludes: *juvenile rheumatoid arthritis NOS (714.30)*

714.1 Felty's syndrome

Rheumatoid arthritis with splenoadenomegaly and leukopenia

➡ **CC Excl:** 036.82, 056.71, 711.00-711.99, 712.10-712.99, 713.0-713.8, 714.0-714.4, 715.00, 715.09-715.10, 715.18-715.98, 716.00-716.99, 718.00-718.08, 719.00-719.10, 719.18-719.70, 719.75-719.99

714.2 Other rheumatoid arthritis with visceral or systemic involvement

Rheumatoid carditis

➡ **CC Excl:** see Code 714.1

✓5th **714.3 Juvenile chronic polyarthritis**

714.30 Polyarticular juvenile rheumatoid arthritis, chronic or unspecified

Juvenile rheumatoid arthritis NOS
Still's disease

➡ **CC Excl:** see Code 714.1

714.31 Polyarticular juvenile rheumatoid arthritis, acute

➡ **CC Excl:** see Code 714.1

714.32 Pauciarticular juvenile rheumatoid arthritis

➡ **CC Excl:** see Code 714.1

714.33 Monoarticular juvenile rheumatoid arthritis

➡ **CC Excl:** see Code 714.1

714.4 Chronic postrheumatic arthropathy

Chronic rheumatoid nodular fibrositis
Jaccoud's syndrome

✓5th **714.8 Other specified inflammatory polyarthropathies**

714.81 Rheumatoid lung

Caplan's syndrome
Diffuse interstitial rheumatoid disease of lung
Fibrosing alveolitis, rheumatoid

714.89 Other

714.9 Unspecified inflammatory polyarthropathy

Inflammatory polyarthropathy or polyarthritis NOS

Excludes: *polyarthropathy NOS (716.5)*

715 Osteoarthrosis and allied disorders

Note: Localized, in the subcategories below, includes bilateral involvement of the same site.

Includes: arthritis or polyarthritis:
degenerative
hypertrophic
degenerative joint disease
osteoarthritis

Excludes: *Marie-Strümpell spondylitis (720.0)*
osteoarthrosis [osteoarthritis] of spine (721.0-721.9)

The following fifth-digit subclassification is for use with category 715; valid digits are in [brackets] under each code. See page 251 for definitions:

0 site unspecified
1 shoulder region
2 upper arm
3 forearm
4 hand
5 pelvic region and thigh
6 lower leg
7 ankle and foot
8 other specified sites
9 multiple sites

✓5th **715.0 Osteoarthrosis, generalized**
[0,4,9]
Degenerative joint disease, involving multiple joints
Primary generalized hypertrophic osteoarthrosis

✓5th **715.1 Osteoarthrosis, localized, primary**
[0–8]
Localized osteoarthropathy, idiopathic

✓5th **715.2 Osteoarthrosis, localized, secondary**
[0–8]
Coxae malum senilis

✓5th **715.3 Osteoarthrosis, localized, not specified whether primary or secondary**
[0–8]
Otto's pelvis

✓5th **715.8 Osteoarthrosis involving, or with mention of more than one site, but not specified as generalized**
[0,9]

✓5th [8] **715.9 Osteoarthrosis, unspecified whether generalized or localized**
[0–8]
➡ **AHA Coding Clinic: For code 715.90:** 2Q, '97, 12

716 Other and unspecified arthropathies

Excludes: *cricoarytenoid arthropathy (478.79)*

The following fifth-digit subclassification is for use with category 716; valid digits are in [brackets] under each code. See page 251 for definitions:

0 site unspecified
1 shoulder region
2 upper arm
3 forearm
4 hand
5 pelvic region and thigh
6 lower leg
7 ankle and foot
8 other specified sites
9 multiple sites

✓5th **716.0 Kaschin-Beck disease**
[0–9]
Endemic polyarthritis

✓5th **716.1 Traumatic arthropathy**
[0–9]

✓5th **716.2 Allergic arthritis**
[0–9]
Excludes: *arthritis associated with Henoch-Schönlein purpura or serum sickness (713.6)*

✓5th **716.3 Climacteric arthritis** ♀
[0–9]
Menopausal arthritis

✓5th **716.4 Transient arthropathy**
[0–9]
Excludes: *palindromic rheumatism (719.3)*

✓5th **716.5 Unspecified polyarthropathy or polyarthritis**
[0–9]

✓5th **716.6 Unspecified monoarthritis**
[0–8]
Coxitis

✓5th **716.8 Other specified arthropathy**
[0–9]

✓5th **716.9 Arthropathy, unspecified**
[0–9]
Arthritis } (acute) (chronic) (subacute)
Arthropathy } (acute) (chronic) (subacute)
Articular rheumatism (chronic)
Inflammation of joint NOS

717 Internal derangement of knee

Includes: degeneration, rupture, old, tear, old } of articular cartilage or meniscus of knee

Excludes: *acute derangement of knee (836.0-836.6)*
ankylosis (718.5)
contracture (718.4)
current injury (836.0-836.6)
deformity (736.4-736.6)
recurrent dislocation (718.3)

717.0 Old bucket handle tear of medial meniscus
Old bucket handle tear of unspecified cartilage

717.1 Derangement of anterior horn of medial meniscus

717.2 Derangement of posterior horn of medial meniscus

717.3 Other and unspecified derangement of medial meniscus
Degeneration of internal semilunar cartilage

✓5th **717.4 Derangement of lateral meniscus**

717.40 Derangement of lateral meniscus, unspecified

717.41 Bucket handle tear of lateral meniscus

717.42 Derangement of anterior horn of lateral meniscus

717.43 Derangement of posterior horn of lateral meniscus

717.49 Other

717.5 Derangement of meniscus, not elsewhere classified
Congenital discoid meniscus
Cyst of semilunar cartilage
Derangement of semilunar cartilage NOS

717.6 Loose body in knee
Joint mice, knee
Rice bodies, knee (joint)

717.7 Chondromalacia of patella
Chondromalacia patellae
Degeneration [softening] of articular cartilage of patella

[8] Nonspecific PDX = 0

✓5th **717.8 Other internal derangement of knee**

717.81 Old disruption of lateral collateral ligament

717.82 Old disruption of medial collateral ligament

717.83 Old disruption of anterior cruciate ligament

717.84 Old disruption of posterior cruciate ligament

717.85 Old disruption of other ligaments of knee
Capsular ligament of knee

717.89 Other
Old disruption of ligaments of knee NOS

717.9 Unspecified internal derangement of knee
Derangement NOS of knee

718 Other derangement of joint

Excludes: *current injury (830.0-848.9)*
jaw (524.6)

The following fifth-digit subclassification is for use with category 718; valid digits are in [brackets] under each code. See page 251 for definitions:

- **0 site unspecified**
- **1 shoulder region**
- **2 upper arm**
- **3 forearm**
- **4 hand**
- **5 pelvic region and thigh**
- **6 lower leg**
- **7 ankle and foot**
- **8 other specified sites**
- **9 multiple sites**

✓5th **718.0 Articular cartilage disorder**
[0–5,7–9]
Meniscus:
disorder
rupture, old
tear, old
Old rupture of ligament(s) of joint NOS

Excludes: *articular cartilage disorder:*
in ochronosis (270.2)
knee (717.0-717.9)
chondrocalcinosis (275.4)
metastatic calcification (275.4)

✓5th **718.1 Loose body in joint**
[0–5,7–9]
Joint mice

Excludes: *knee (717.6)*

✓5th **718.2 Pathological dislocation**
[0–9]
Dislocation or displacement of joint, not recurrent and not current injury
Spontaneous dislocation (joint)

✓5th **718.3 Recurrent dislocation of joint**
[0–9]

➡ **AHA Coding Clinic:** N-D, '87, 7

✓5th [9] **718.4 Contracture of joint**
[0–9]

✓5th [8] **718.5 Ankylosis of joint**
[0–9]
Ankylosis of joint (fibrous) (osseous)

Excludes: *spine (724.9)*
stiffness of joint without mention of ankylosis (719.5)

✓5th **718.6 Unspecified intrapelvic protrusion of acetabulum**
[0,5]
Protrusio acetabuli, unspecified

✓5th **718.8 Other joint derangement, not elsewhere classified**
[0–9]
Flail joint (paralytic)   Instability of joint

Excludes: *deformities classifiable to 736 (736.0-736.9)*

✓5th **718.9 Unspecified derangement of joint**
[0–5,7–9]

Excludes: *knee (717.9)*

719 Other and unspecified disorders of joint

Excludes: *jaw (524.6)*

The following fifth-digit subclassification is for use with category 719; valid digits are in [brackets] under each code. See page 251 for definitions:

- **0 site unspecified**
- **1 shoulder region**
- **2 upper arm**
- **3 forearm**
- **4 hand**
- **5 pelvic region and thigh**
- **6 lower leg**
- **7 ankle and foot**
- **8 other specified sites**
- **9 multiple sites**

✓5th **719.0 Effusion of joint**
[0–9]
Hydrarthrosis
Swelling of joint, with or without pain

Excludes: *intermittent hydrarthrosis (719.3)*

✓5th **719.1 Hemarthrosis**
[0–9]

Excludes: *current injury (840.0-848.9)*

✓5th **719.2 Villonodular synovitis**
[0–9]

✓5th **719.3 Palindromic rheumatism**
[0–9]
Hench-Rosenberg syndrome
Intermittent hydrarthrosis

✓5th **719.4 Pain in joint**
[0–9]
Arthralgia

[8] Nonspecific PDX = 0
[9] Nonspecific PDX = 9

✓5th **719.5 Stiffness of joint, not elsewhere classified**
[0–9]

✓5th **719.6 Other symptoms referable to joint**
[0–9] Joint crepitus Snapping hip

✓5th **719.7 Difficulty in walking**
[0,5–9]

Excludes: *abnormality of gait (781.2)*

✓5th **719.8 Other specified disorders of joint**
[0–9] Calcification of joint Fistula of joint

Excludes: *temporomandibular joint-pain-dysfunction syndrome [Costen's syndrome] (524.6)*

✓5th **719.9 Unspecified disorder of joint**
[0–9]

DORSOPATHIES (720-724)

Excludes: *curvature of spine (737.0-737.9)*
osteochondrosis of spine (juvenile) (732.0)
adult (732.8)

720 Ankylosing spondylitis and other inflammatory spondylopathies

720.0 Ankylosing spondylitis
Rheumatoid arthritis of spine NOS
Spondylitis:
Marie-Strümpell
rheumatoid

720.1 Spinal enthesopathy
Disorder of peripheral ligamentous or muscular attachments of spine
Romanus lesion

720.2 Sacroiliitis, not elsewhere classified
Inflammation of sacroiliac joint NOS

✓5th **720.8 Other inflammatory spondylopathies**

720.81 Inflammatory spondylopathies in diseases classified elsewhere
Code first underlying disease as:
tuberculosis (015.0)

720.89 Other

720.9 Unspecified inflammatory spondylopathy
Spondylitis NOS

721 Spondylosis and allied disorders

721.0 Cervical spondylosis without myelopathy
Cervical or cervicodorsal:
arthritis
osteoarthritis
spondylarthritis

721.1 Cervical spondylosis with myelopathy
Anterior spinal artery compression syndrome
Spondylogenic compression of cervical spinal cord
Vertebral artery compression syndrome

721.2 Thoracic spondylosis without myelopathy
Thoracic:
arthritis
osteoarthritis
spondylarthritis

721.3 Lumbosacral spondylosis without myelopathy
Lumbar or lumbosacral:
arthritis
osteoarthritis
spondylarthritis

✓5th **721.4 Thoracic or lumbar spondylosis with myelopathy**

721.41 Thoracic region
Spondylogenic compression of thoracic spinal cord

721.42 Lumbar region
Spondylogenic compression of lumbar spinal cord

721.5 Kissing spine
Baastrup's syndrome

721.6 Ankylosing vertebral hyperostosis

721.7 Traumatic spondylopathy
Kümmell's disease or spondylitis

721.8 Other allied disorders of spine

✓5th **721.9 Spondylosis of unspecified site**

721.90 Without mention of myelopathy
Spinal:
arthritis (deformans) (degenerative) (hypertrophic)
osteoarthritis NOS
Spondylarthrosis NOS

721.91 With myelopathy
Spondylogenic compression of spinal cord NOS

722 Intervertebral disc disorders A: 15–124

➡ **AHA Coding Clinic:** 1Q, '88, 10

722.0 Displacement of cervical intervertebral disc without myelopathy
Neuritis (brachial) or radiculitis due to displacement or rupture of cervical intervertebral disc
Any condition classifiable to 722.2 of the cervical or cervicothoracic intervertebral disc

✓5th **722.1 Displacement of thoracic or lumbar intervertebral disc without myelopathy**

722.10 Lumbar intervertebral disc without myelopathy
Lumbago or sciatica due to displacement of intervertebral disc
Neuritis or radiculitis due to displacement or rupture of lumbar intervertebral disc
Any condition classifiable to 722.2 of the lumbar or lumbosacral intervertebral disc

722.11 Thoracic intervertebral disc without myelopathy
Any condition classifiable to 722.2 of thoracic intervertebral disc

722.2 Displacement of intervertebral disc, site unspecified, without myelopathy
Discogenic syndrome NOS
Herniation of nucleus pulposus NOS
Intervertebral disc NOS:
- extrusion
- prolapse
- protrusion
- rupture

Neuritis or radiculitis due to displacement or rupture of intervertebral disc

✓5th **722.3 Schmorl's nodes**

722.30 Unspecified region

722.31 Thoracic region

722.32 Lumbar region

722.39 Other

722.4 Degeneration of cervical intervertebral disc
Degeneration of cervicothoracic intervertebral disc

✓5th **722.5 Degeneration of thoracic or lumbar intervertebral disc**

722.51 Thoracic or thoracolumbar intervertebral disc

722.52 Lumbar or lumbosacral intervertebral disc

722.6 Degeneration of intervertebral disc, site unspecified
Degenerative disc disease NOS
Narrowing of intervertebral disc or space NOS

✓5th **722.7 Intervertebral disc disorder with myelopathy**

722.70 Unspecified region

722.71 Cervical region

722.72 Thoracic region

722.73 Lumbar region

✓5th **722.8 Postlaminectomy syndrome**
➡ **AHA Coding Clinic:** J-F, '87, 7

722.80 Unspecified region
➡ **CC Excl:** 722.51-722.93

722.81 Cervical region
➡ **CC Excl:** see Code 722.80

722.82 Thoracic region
➡ **CC Excl:** see Code 722.80

722.83 Lumbar region
➡ **CC Excl:** see Code 722.80
➡ **AHA Coding Clinic:** 2Q, '97, 15

✓5th **722.9 Other and unspecified disc disorder**
Calcification of intervertebral cartilage or disc
Discitis

722.90 Unspecified region
➡ **AHA Coding Clinic:** N-D, '84, 19

722.91 Cervical region

722.92 Thoracic region

722.93 Lumbar region

723 Other disorders of cervical region

Excludes: *conditions due to:*
intervertebral disc disorders (722.0-722.9)
spondylosis (721.0-721.9)

➡ **AHA Coding Clinic:** 2Q, '89, 14

723.0 Spinal stenosis in cervical region

723.1 Cervicalgia
Pain in neck

723.2 Cervicocranial syndrome
Barré-Liéou syndrome
Posterior cervical sympathetic syndrome

723.3 Cervicobrachial syndrome (diffuse)
➡ **AHA Coding Clinic:** N-D, '85, 12

723.4 Brachial neuritis or radiculitis NOS
Cervical radiculitis
Radicular syndrome of upper limbs
➡ **CC Excl:** 722.6-722.71, 722.80-722.81, 722.90-722.91, 723.0-723.9

723.5 **Torticollis, unspecified**
Contracture of neck

Excludes: *congenital (754.1)*
due to birth injury (767.8)
hysterical (300.11)
psychogenic (306.0)
spasmodic (333.83)
traumatic, current (847.0)

➡ **CC Excl:** 053.71, 722.6-722.71, 722.80-722.81, 722.90-722.91, 723.0-723.9

723.6 **Panniculitis specified as affecting neck**

723.7 **Ossification of posterior longitudinal ligament in cervical region**

723.8 **Other syndromes affecting cervical region**
Cervical syndrome NEC   Klippel's disease

723.9 **Unspecified musculoskeletal disorders and symptoms referable to neck**
Cervical (region) disorder NOS

724 Other and unspecified disorders of back

Excludes: *collapsed vertebra (code to cause, e.g., osteoporosis, 733.00-733.09)*
conditions due to:
intervertebral disc disorders (722.0-722.9)
spondylosis (721.0-721.9)

➡ **AHA Coding Clinic:** 2Q, '89, 14

✓5th **724.0** **Spinal stenosis, other than cervical** **A: 15–124**

724.00 **Spinal stenosis, unspecified region**

724.01 **Thoracic region**

724.02 **Lumbar region**

724.09 **Other**

724.1 **Pain in thoracic spine**

724.2 **Lumbago**
Low back pain   Lumbalgia
Low back syndrome

➡ **AHA Coding Clinic:** N-D, '85, 12

724.3 **Sciatica**
Neuralgia or neuritis of sciatic nerve

Excludes: *specified lesion of sciatic nerve (355.0)*

➡ **AHA Coding Clinic:** 2Q, '89, 12

724.4 **Thoracic or lumbosacral neuritis or radiculitis, unspecified**
Radicular syndrome of lower limbs

724.5 **Backache, unspecified**
Vertebrogenic (pain) syndrome NOS

724.6 **Disorders of sacrum**
Ankylosis } lumbosacral or sacroiliac (joint)
Instability }

✓5th **724.7** **Disorders of coccyx**

724.70 **Unspecified disorder of coccyx**

724.71 **Hypermobility of coccyx**

724.79 **Other**
Coccygodynia

724.8 **Other symptoms referable to back**
Ossification of posterior longitudinal ligament NOS
Panniculitis specified as sacral or affecting back

724.9 **Other unspecified back disorders**
Ankylosis of spine NOS
Compression of spinal nerve root NEC
Spinal disorder NOS

Excludes: *sacroiliitis (720.2)*

RHEUMATISM, EXCLUDING THE BACK (725-729)

Includes: disorders of muscles and tendons and their attachments, and of other soft tissues

725 Polymyalgia rheumatica

726 Peripheral enthesopathies and allied syndromes

Note: Enthesopathies are disorders of peripheral ligamentous or muscular attachments.

Excludes: *spinal enthesopathy (720.1)*

726.0 **Adhesive capsulitis of shoulder**

✓5th **726.1** **Rotator cuff syndrome of shoulder and allied disorders**

726.10 **Disorders of bursae and tendons in shoulder region, unspecified**
Rotator cuff syndrome NOS
Supraspinatus syndrome NOS

726.11 **Calcifying tendinitis of shoulder**

726.12 **Bicipital tenosynovitis**

726.19 **Other specified disorders**

Excludes: *complete rupture of rotator cuff, nontraumatic (727.61)*

726.2 Other affections of shoulder region, not elsewhere classified
Periarthritis of shoulder
Scapulohumeral fibrositis

✓5th **726.3 Enthesopathy of elbow region**

726.30 Enthesopathy of elbow, unspecified

726.31 Medial epicondylitis

726.32 Lateral epicondylitis
Epicondylitis NOS
Golfers' elbow
Tennis elbow

726.33 Olecranon bursitis
Bursitis of elbow

726.39 Other

726.4 Enthesopathy of wrist and carpus
Bursitis of hand or wrist
Periarthritis of wrist

726.5 Enthesopathy of hip region
Bursitis of hip
Gluteal tendinitis
Iliac crest spur
Psoas tendinitis
Trochanteric tendinitis

✓5th **726.6 Enthesopathy of knee**

726.60 Enthesopathy of knee, unspecified
Bursitis of knee NOS

726.61 Pes anserinus tendinitis or bursitis

726.62 Tibial collateral ligament bursitis
Pellegrini-Stieda syndrome

726.63 Fibular collateral ligament bursitis

726.64 Patellar tendinitis

726.65 Prepatellar bursitis

726.69 Other
Bursitis:
infrapatellar
subpatellar

✓5th **726.7 Enthesopathy of ankle and tarsus**

726.70 Enthesopathy of ankle and tarsus, unspecified
Metatarsalgia NOS

Excludes: *Morton's metatarsalgia (355.6)*

726.71 Achilles bursitis or tendinitis

726.72 Tibialis tendinitis
Tibialis (anterior) (posterior) tendinitis

726.73 Calcaneal spur

726.79 Other
Peroneal tendinitis

726.8 Other peripheral enthesopathies

✓5th **726.9 Unspecified enthesopathy**

726.90 Enthesopathy of unspecified site
Capsulitis NOS
Periarthritis NOS
Tendinitis NOS

726.91 Exostosis of unspecified site
Bone spur NOS

727 Other disorders of synovium, tendon, and bursa

✓5th **727.0 Synovitis and tenosynovitis**

727.00 Synovitis and tenosynovitis, unspecified
Synovitis NOS
Tenosynovitis NOS

727.01 *Synovitis and tenosynovitis in diseases classified elsewhere*
Code first underlying disease as:
tuberculosis (015.0-015.9)

Excludes: *crystal-induced (275.4)*
gonococcal (098.51)
gouty (274.0)
syphilitic (095.7)

727.02 Giant cell tumor of tendon sheath

727.03 Trigger finger (acquired)

727.04 Radial styloid tenosynovitis
de Quervain's disease

727.05 Other tenosynovitis of hand and wrist

727.06 Tenosynovitis of foot and ankle

727.09 Other

727.1 Bunion

727.2 Specific bursitides often of occupational origin
Beat:
elbow
hand
knee
Chronic crepitant synovitis of wrist
Miners':
elbow
knee

727.3 Other bursitis
Bursitis NOS

Excludes: *bursitis:*
gonococcal (098.52)
subacromial (726.19)
subcoracoid (726.19)
subdeltoid (726.19)
syphilitic (095.7)
"frozen shoulder" (726.0)

✓5th **727.4 Ganglion and cyst of synovium, tendon, and bursa**

727.40 Synovial cyst, unspecified

Excludes: *that of popliteal space (727.51)*
➡ **AHA Coding Clinic:** 2Q, '97, 6

727.41 Ganglion of joint

727.42 Ganglion of tendon sheath

727.43 Ganglion, unspecified

727.49 Other
Cyst of bursa

✓5th **727.5 Rupture of synovium**

727.50 Rupture of synovium, unspecified

727.51 Synovial cyst of popliteal space
Baker's cyst (knee)

727.59 Other

✓5th **727.6 Rupture of tendon, nontraumatic**

727.60 Nontraumatic rupture of unspecified tendon

727.61 Complete rupture of rotator cuff

727.62 Tendons of biceps (long head)

727.63 Extensor tendons of hand and wrist

727.64 Flexor tendons of hand and wrist

727.65 Quadriceps tendon

727.66 Patellar tendon

727.67 Achilles tendon

727.68 Other tendons of foot and ankle

727.69 Other

✓5th **727.8 Other disorders of synovium, tendon, and bursa**

727.81 Contracture of tendon (sheath)
Short Achilles tendon (acquired)

727.82 Calcium deposits in tendon and bursa
Calcification of tendon NOS
Calcific tendinitis NOS

Excludes: *peripheral ligamentous or muscular attachments (726.0-726.9)*

727.89 Other
Abscess of bursa or tendon

Excludes: *xanthomatosis localized to tendons (272.7)*
➡ **AHA Coding Clinic:** 2Q, '89, 15

727.9 Unspecified disorder of synovium, tendon, and bursa

728 Disorders of muscle, ligament, and fascia

Excludes: *enthesopathies (726.0-726.9)*
muscular dystrophies (359.0-359.1)
myoneural disorders (358.0-358.9)
myopathies (359.2-359.9)
old disruption of ligaments of knee (717.81-717.89)

728.0 Infective myositis
Myositis:
purulent
suppurative

Excludes: *myositis:*
epidemic (074.1)
interstitial (728.81)
syphilitic (095.6)
tropical (040.81)

➡ **CC Excl:** 728.0, 728.11-728.3, 728.81, 728.86
✔ **St. Anthony's Clinical Coder:** see Chapter 5

✓5th **728.1 Muscular calcification and ossification**

728.10 Calcification and ossification, unspecified
Massive calcification (paraplegic)

728.11 Progressive myositis ossificans

728.12 Traumatic myositis ossificans
Myositis ossificans (circumscripta)

728.13 Postoperative heterotopic calcification

728.19 Other
Polymyositis ossificans

728.2 Muscular wasting and disuse atrophy, not elsewhere classified
Amyotrophia NOS
Myofibrosis

Excludes: *neuralgic amyotrophy (353.5)*
progressive muscular atrophy (335.0-335.9)

728.3 Other specific muscle disorders
Arthrogryposis
Immobility syndrome (paraplegic)

Excludes: *arthrogryposis multiplex congenita (754.89)*
stiff-man syndrome (333.91)

728.4 Laxity of ligament

728.5 Hypermobility syndrome

728.6 Contracture of palmar fascia A: 15–124
Dupuytren's contracture

✓5th **728.7 Other fibromatoses**

728.71 Plantar fascial fibromatosis
Contracture of plantar fascia
Plantar fasciitis (traumatic)

728.79 Other
Garrod's or knuckle pads
Nodular fasciitis
Pseudosarcomatous fibromatosis (proliferative) (subcutaneous)

✓5th **728.8 Other disorders of muscle, ligament, and fascia**

728.81 Interstitial myositis

728.82 Foreign body granuloma of muscle
Talc granuloma of muscle

728.83 Rupture of muscle, nontraumatic

728.84 Diastasis of muscle
Diastasis recti (abdomen)

Excludes: *diastasis recti complicating pregnancy, labor, and delivery (665.8)*

728.85 Spasm of muscle

728.86 Necrotizing fasciitis
Use additional code to identify:
infectious organism (041.00-041.89)
gangrene (785.4), if applicable

➡ **CC Excl:** 728.0, 728.11-728.19, 728.2, 728.3, 728.81, 728.86

➡ **AHA Coding Clinic:** 4Q, '95, 54

728.89 Other
Eosinophilic fasciitis
Use additional E code to identify drug if drug induced

728.9 Unspecified disorder of muscle, ligament, and fascia

729 Other disorders of soft tissues

Excludes: *acroparesthesia (443.89)*
carpal tunnel syndrome (354.0)
disorders of the back (720.0-724.9)
entrapment syndromes (354.0-355.9)
palindromic rheumatism (719.3)
periarthritis (726.0-726.9)
psychogenic rheumatism (306.0)

729.0 Rheumatism, unspecified and fibrositis

729.1 Myalgia and myositis, unspecified
Fibromyositis NOS

729.2 Neuralgia, neuritis, and radiculitis, unspecified

Excludes: *brachial radiculitis (723.4)*
cervical radiculitis (723.4)
lumbosacral radiculitis (724.4)
mononeuritis (354.0-355.9)
radiculitis due to intervertebral disc involvement (722.0-722.2, 722.7)
sciatica (724.3)

✓5th **729.3 Panniculitis, unspecified**

729.30 Panniculitis, unspecified site
Weber-Christian disease

729.31 Hypertrophy of fat pad, knee
Hypertrophy of infrapatellar fat pad

729.39 Other site

Excludes: *panniculitis specified as (affecting):*
back (724.8)
neck (723.6)
sacral (724.8)

729.4 Fasciitis, unspecified

Excludes: *necrotizing fasciitis (728.86)*
nodular fasciitis (728.79)

729.5 Pain in limb

729.6 Residual foreign body in soft tissue

Excludes: *foreign body granuloma:*
muscle (728.82)
skin and subcutaneous tissue (709.4)

✓5th **729.8 Other musculoskeletal symptoms referable to limbs**

729.81 Swelling of limb
➡ **AHA Coding Clinic:** 4Q, '88, 6

729.82 Cramp

729.89 Other

Excludes: *abnormality of gait (781.2)*
tetany (781.7)
transient paralysis of limb (781.4)

➡ **AHA Coding Clinic:** 4Q, '88, 12

729.9 Other and unspecified disorders of soft tissue

Polyalgia

OSTEOPATHIES, CHONDROPATHIES, AND ACQUIRED MUSCULOSKELETAL DEFORMITIES (730-739)

730 Osteomyelitis, periostitis, and other infections involving bone

Use additional code to identify organism, such as Staphylococcus (041.1)

Excludes: *jaw (526.4-526.5)*
petrous bone (383.2)

The following fifth-digit subclassification is for use with category 730; valid digits are in [brackets] under each code. See page 251 for definitions:

- **0 site unspecified**
- **1 shoulder region**
- **2 upper arm**
- **3 forearm**
- **4 hand**
- **5 pelvic region and thigh**
- **6 lower leg**
- **7 ankle and foot**
- **8 other specified site**
- **9 multiple sites**

➡ **AHA Coding Clinic:** 4Q, '97, 43

✓5th [8] **730.0** Acute osteomyelitis

[0–9]

Abscess of any bone except accessory sinus, jaw, or mastoid

Acute or subacute osteomyelitis, with or without mention of periostitis

➡ **CC Excl: For code 730.00:** 015.50-015.56, 015.70-015.76, 015.90-015.96, 017.90-017.96, 730.00-730.39, 730.80-730.99

➡ **CC Excl: For code 730.01:** 015.50-015.56, 015.70-015.76, 015.90-015.96, 017.90-017.96, 730.00, 730.08-730.11, 730.18-730.21, 730.28-730.31, 730.38-730.39, 730.80-730.81, 730.88-730.91, 730.98-730.99

➡ **CC Excl: For code 730.02:** 015.50-015.56, 015.70-015.76, 015.90-015.96, 017.90-017.96, 730.00, 730.08-730.10, 730.12, 730.18-730.20, 730.22, 730.28-730.30, 730.32, 730.38-730.39, 730.80, 730.82, 730.88-730.90, 730.92, 730.98-730.99

➡ **CC Excl: For code 730.03:** 015.50-015.56, 015.70-015.76, 015.90-015.96, 017.90-017.96, 730.00, 730.08-730.10, 730.13, 730.18-730.20, 730.23, 730.28-730.30, 730.33, 730.38-730.39, 730.80, 730.83, 730.88-730.90, 730.93, 730.98-730.99

➡ **CC Excl: For code 730.04:** 015.50-015.56, 015.70-015.76, 015.90-015.96, 017.90-017.96, 730.00, 730.08-730.10, 730.14, 730.18-730.20, 730.24, 730.28-730.30, 730.34, 730.38-730.39, 730.80, 730.84, 730.88-730.90, 730.94, 730.98-730.99

➡ **CC Excl: For code 730.05:** 015.10-015.16, 015.50-015.56, 015.70-015.76, 015.90-015.96, 017.90-017.96, 730.00, 730.08-730.10, 730.15, 730.18-730.20, 730.25, 730.28-730.30, 730.35, 730.38-730.39, 730.80, 730.85, 730.88-730.90, 730.95, 730.98-730.99

➡ **CC Excl: For code 730.06:** 015.20-015.56, 015.70-015.76, 015.90-015.96, 017.90-017.96, 730.00, 730.08-730.10, 730.16, 730.18-730.20, 730.26, 730.28-730.30, 730.36, 730.38-730.39, 730.80, 730.86, 730.88-730.90, 730.96, 730.98-730.99

➡ **CC Excl: For code 730.07:** 015.50-015.56, 015.70-015.76, 015.90-015.96, 017.90-017.96, 730.00, 730.08-730.10, 730.17-730.20, 730.27-730.30, 730.37-730.39, 730.80, 730.87-730.90, 730.97-730.99

➡ **CC Excl: For code 730.08:** 015.00-015.06, 015.50-015.56, 015.70-015.76, 015.90-015.96, 017.90-017.96, 730.00-730.39, 730.80-730.99

➡ **CC Excl: For code 730.09:** 015.50-015.56, 015.70-015.76, 015.90-015.96, 017.90-017.96, 730.00-730.39, 730.80-730.99

✓5th [8] **730.1** Chronic osteomyelitis

[0–9]

Brodie's abscess

Chronic or old osteomyelitis, with or without mention of periostitis

Necrosis (acute) } of bone
Sequestrum } of bone

Sclerosing osteomyelitis of Garré

Excludes: *aseptic necrosis of bone (733.40-733.49)*

✓5th [8] **730.2** Unspecified osteomyelitis

[0–9]

Osteitis or osteomyelitis NOS, with or without mention of periostitis

✓5th [8] **730.3** Periostitis without mention of osteomyelitis

[0–9]

Abscess of periosteum } without mention of osteomyelitis
Periostosis } without mention of osteomyelitis

Excludes: *that in secondary syphilis (091.61)*

✓5th ***730.7*** ***Osteopathy resulting from poliomyelitis***

[0–9]

Code first underlying disease (045.0-045.9)

[8] Nonspecific PDX = 0

✓5th **730.8** ***Other infections involving bone in diseases classifiec elsewhere***
[0–9]

Code first underlying disease as:
tuberculosis (015.0-015.9)
typhoid fever (002.0)

Excludes: *syphilis of bone NOS (095.5)*

➡ **CC Excl: For code 730.80:** see Code 730.09

➡ **CC Excl: For code 730.81:** 015.50-015.56, 015.70-015.76, 015.90-015.96, 017.90-017.96, 730.00-730.01, 730.08-730.11, 730.18-730.21, 730.28-730.31, 730.38-730.39, 730.80, 730.88-730.91, 730.98-730.99

➡ **CC Excl: For code 730.82:** 015.50-015.56, 015.70-015.76, 015.90-015.96, 017.90-017.96, 730.00, 730.02, 730.08-730.10, 730.12, 730.18-730.20, 730.22, 730.28-730.30, 730.32, 730.38-730.39, 730.80, 730.88-730.90, 730.92, 730.98-730.99

➡ **CC Excl: For code 730.83:** 015.50-015.56, 015.70-015.76, 015.90-015.96, 017.90-017.96, 730.00, 730.03, 730.08-730.10, 730.13, 730.18-730.20, 730.23, 730.28-730.30, 730.33, 730.38-730.39, 730.80, 730.88-730.90, 730.93, 730.98-730.99

➡ **CC Excl: For code 730.84:** 015.50-015.56, 015.70-015.76, 015.90-015.96, 017.90-017.96, 730.00, 730.04, 730.08-730.10, 730.14, 730.18-730.20, 730.24, 730.28-730.30, 730.34, 730.38-730.39, 730.80, 730.88-730.90, 730.94, 730.98-730.99

➡ **CC Excl: For code 730.85:** 015.10-015.16, 015.50-015.56, 015.70-015.76, 015.90-015.96, 017.90-017.96, 730.00, 730.05, 730.08-730.10, 730.15, 730.18-730.20, 730.25, 730.28-730.30, 730.35, 730.38-730.39, 730.80, 730.88-730.90, 730.95, 730.98-730.99

➡ **CC Excl: For code 730.86:** 015.20-015.26, 015.50-015.56, 015.70-015.76, 015.90-015.96, 017.90-017.96, 730.00, 730.06, 730.08-730.10, 730.16, 730.18-730.20, 730.26, 730.28-730.30, 730.36, 730.38-730.39, 730.80, 730.88-730.90, 730.96, 730.98-730.99

➡ **CC Excl: For code 730.87:** 015.50-015.56, 015.70-015.76, 015.90-015.96, 017.90-017.96, 730.00, 730.07-730.10, 730.17-730.20, 730.27-730.30, 730.37-730.39, 730.80, 730.88-730.90, 730.97-730.99

➡ **CC Excl: For code 730.88:** 015.00-015.06, 015.50-015.56, 015.70-015.76, 015.90-015.96, 017.90-017.96, 730.00-730.39, 730.80-730.99

➡ **CC Excl: For code 730.89:** 015.50-015.56, 015.70-015.76, 015.90-015.96, 017.90-017.96, 730.00-730.39, 730.80-730.99

➡ **AHA Coding Clinic:** 2Q, '97, 16

✓5th **730.9** **Unspecified infection of bone**
[0–9]

➡ **CC Excl: For code 730.90:** see Code 730.89

➡ **CC Excl: For code 730.91:** 015.50-015.56, 015.70-015.76, 015.90-015.96, 017.90-017.96, 730.00-730.01, 730.08-730.11, 730.18-730.21, 730.28-730.31, 730.38-730.39, 730.80-730.81, 730.88-730.90, 730.98-730.99

➡ **CC Excl: For code 730.92:** 015.50-015.56, 015.70-015.76, 015.90-015.96, 017.90-017.96, 730.00, 730.02, 730.08-730.10, 730.12, 730.18-730.20, 730.22, 730.28-730.30, 730.32, 730.38-730.39, 730.80, 730.82, 730.88-730.90, 730.98-730.99

➡ **CC Excl: For code 730.93:** 015.50-015.56, 015.70-015.76, 015.90-015.96, 017.90-017.96, 730.00, 730.03, 730.08-730.10, 730.13, 730.18-730.20, 730.23, 730.28-730.30, 730.33, 730.38-730.39, 730.80, 730.83, 730.88-730.90, 730.98-730.99

➡ **CC Excl: For code 730.94:** 015.50-015.56, 015.70-015.76, 015.90-015.96, 017.90-017.96, 730.00, 730.04, 730.08-730.10, 730.14, 730.18-730.20, 730.24, 730.28-730.30, 730.34, 730.38-730.39, 730.80, 730.84, 730.88-730.90, 730.98-730.99

➡ **CC Excl: For code 730.95:** 015.10-015.16, 015.50-015.56, 015.70-015.76, 015.90-015.96, 017.90-017.96, 730.00, 730.05, 730.08-730.10, 730.15, 730.18-730.20, 730.25, 730.28-730.30, 730.35, 730.38-730.39, 730.80, 730.85, 730.88-730.90, 730.98-730.99

➡ **CC Excl: For code 730.96:** 015.20-015.26, 015.50-015.56, 015.70-015.76, 015.90-015.96, 017.90-017.96, 730.00, 730.06, 730.08-730.10, 730.16, 730.18-730.20, 730.26, 730.28-730.30, 730.36, 730.38-730.39, 730.80, 730.86, 730.88-730.90, 730.98-730.99

➡ **CC Excl: For code 730.97:** 015.50-015.56, 015.70-015.76, 015.90-015.96, 017.90-017.96, 730.00, 730.07-730.10, 730.17-730.20, 730.27-730.30, 730.37-730.39, 730.80, 730.87-730.90, 730.98-730.99

➡ **CC Excl: For code 730.98:** 015.00-015.06, 015.50-015.56, 015.70-015.76, 015.90-015.96, 017.90-017.96, 730.00-730.39, 730.80-730.99

➡ **CC Excl: For code 730.99:** 015.50-015.56, 015.70-015.76, 015.90-015.96, 017.90-017.96, 730.00-730.39, 730.80-730.99

731 Osteitis deformans and osteopathies associated with other disorders classified elsewhere

731.0 **Osteitis deformans without mention of bone tumor**
Paget's disease of bone

731.1 ***Osteitis deformans in diseases classified elsewhere***

Code first underlying disease as:
malignant neoplasm of bone (170.0-170.9)

731.2 **Hypertrophic pulmonary osteoarthropathy**

Bamberger-Marie disease

731.8 ***Other bone involvement in diseases classified elsewhere***

Code first underlying disease, as:
diabetes mellitus (250.8)

Use additional code to specify bone condition, such as:
acute osteomyelitis (730.00-730.09)

➡ **AHA Coding Clinic:** 4Q, '97, 43; 2Q, '97, 16

732 Osteochondropathies

732.0 **Juvenile osteochondrosis of spine**

Juvenile osteochondrosis (of):
marginal or vertebral epiphysis (of Scheuermann)
spine NOS
Vertebral epiphysitis

Excludes: *adolescent postural kyphosis (737.0)*

732.1 **Juvenile osteochondrosis of hip and pelvis**

Coxa plana
Ischiopubic synchondrosis (of van Neck)
Osteochondrosis (juvenile) of:
acetabulum
head of femur (of Legg-Calvé -Perthes)
iliac crest (of Buchanan)
symphysis pubis (of Pierson)
Pseudocoxalgia

732.2 **Nontraumatic slipped upper femoral epiphysis**

Slipped upper femoral epiphysis NOS

732.3 **Juvenile osteochondrosis of upper extremity**

Osteochondrosis (juvenile) of:
capitulum of humerus (of Panner)
carpal lunate (of Kienbock)
hand NOS
head of humerus (of Haas)
heads of metacarpals (of Mauclaire)
lower ulna (of Burns)
radial head (of Brailsford)
upper extremity NOS

732.4 **Juvenile osteochondrosis of lower extremity, excluding foot**

Osteochondrosis (juvenile) of:
lower extremity NOS
primary patellar center (of Köhler)
proximal tibia (of Blount)
secondary patellar center (of Sinding-Larsen)
tibial tubercle (of Osgood-Schlatter)
Tibia vara

732.5 **Juvenile osteochondrosis of foot**

Calcaneal apophysitis
Epiphysitis, os calcis
Osteochondrosis (juvenile) of:
astragalus (of Diaz)
calcaneum (of Sever)
foot NOS
metatarsal:
second (of Freiberg)
fifth (of Iselin)
os tibiale externum (of Haglund)
tarsal navicular (of Köhler)

732.6 **Other juvenile osteochondrosis**

Apophysitis
Epiphysitis
Osteochondritis
Osteochondrosis
} specified as juvenile, of other site, or site NOS

732.7 **Osteochondritis dissecans**

732.8 **Other specified forms of osteochondropathy**

Adult osteochondrosis of spine

732.9 **Unspecified osteochondropathy**

Apophysitis
Epiphysitis
Osteochondritis
Osteochondrosis
} NOS
not specified as adult or juvenile, of unspecified site

733 Other disorders of bone and cartilage

Excludes: *bone spur (726.91)*
cartilage of, or loose body in, joint (717.0-717.9, 718.0-718.9)
giant cell granuloma of jaw (526.3)
osteitis fibrosa cystica generalisata (252.0)
osteomalacia (268.2)
polyostotic fibrous dysplasia of bone (756.54)
prognathism, retrognathism (524.1)
xanthomatosis localized to bone (272.7)

✓5th **733.0** **Osteoporosis**

733.00 **Osteoporosis, unspecified**

Wedging of vertebra NOS

733.01 **Senile osteoporosis**

Postmenopausal osteoporosis

733.02 **Idiopathic osteoporosis**

733.03 **Disuse osteoporosis**

733.09 **Other**

Drug-induced osteoporosis

Use additional E code to identify drug

✓5th **733.1 Pathologic fracture**

Spontaneous fracture

Excludes: *traumatic fractures (800-829)*

➡ **AHA Coding Clinic:** 4Q, '93, 25; N-D, '86, 10; N-D, '85, 16

✔ **St. Anthony's Clinical Coder:** see Chapter 5

733.10 Pathologic fracture, unspecified site

➡ **CC Excl:** 733.10-733.19

733.11 Pathologic fracture of humerus

➡ **CC Excl:** see Code 733.10

733.12 Pathologic fracture of distal radius and ulna

Wrist NOS

➡ **CC Excl:** see Code 733.10

733.13 Pathologic fracture of vertebrae

Collapse of vertebra NOS

➡ **CC Excl:** see Code 733.10

DRG 239

733.14 Pathologic fracture of neck of femur

Femur NOS
Hip NOS

➡ **CC Excl:** see Code 733.10

➡ **AHA Coding Clinic:** 1Q, '96, 16

733.15 Pathologic fracture of other specified part of femur

➡ **CC Excl:** see Code 733.10

733.16 Pathologic fracture of tibia or fibula

Ankle NOS

➡ **CC Excl:** see Code 733.10

733.19 Pathologic fracture of other specified site

➡ **CC Excl:** see Code 733.10

✓5th **733.2 Cyst of bone**

733.20 Cyst of bone (localized), unspecified

733.21 Solitary bone cyst

Unicameral bone cyst

733.22 Aneurysmal bone cyst

733.29 Other

Fibrous dysplasia (monostotic)

Excludes: *cyst of jaw (526.0-526.2, 526.89)*
osteitis fibrosa cystica (252.0)
polyostotic fibrous dysplasia of bone (756.54)

733.3 Hyperostosis of skull

Hyperostosis interna frontalis
Leontiasis ossium

✓5th **733.4 Aseptic necrosis of bone**

Excludes: *necrosis of bone NOS (730.1)*
osteochondropathies (732.0-732.9)

733.40 Aseptic necrosis of bone, site unspecified

733.41 Head of humerus

733.42 Head and neck of femur

Femur NOS

Excludes: *Legg-Calvé-Perthes disease (732.1)*

733.43 Medial femoral condyle

733.44 Talus

733.49 Other

733.5 Osteitis condensans

Piriform sclerosis of ilium

733.6 Tietze's disease

Costochondral junction syndrome
Costochondritis

733.7 Algoneurodystrophy

Disuse atrophy of bone
Sudeck's atrophy

✓5th **733.8 Malunion and nonunion of fracture**

➡ **AHA Coding Clinic:** 2Q, '94, 5

733.81 Malunion of fracture

➡ **CC Excl:** 733.81-733.82

733.82 Nonunion of fracture

Pseudoarthrosis (bone)

➡ **CC Excl:** see Code 733.81

✓5th **733.9 Other and unspecified disorders of bone and cartilage**

733.90 Disorder of bone and cartilage, unspecified

733.91 Arrest of bone development or growth

Epiphyseal arrest

733.92 Chondromalacia

Chondromalacia:
- NOS
- localized, except patella
- systemic
- tibial plateau

Excludes: *chondromalacia of patella (717.7)*

733.99 Other

Diaphysitis
Hypertrophy of bone
Relapsing polychondritis

➡ **AHA Coding Clinic:** J-F, '87, 14

734 Flat foot

Pes planus (acquired)
Talipes planus (acquired)

Excludes: *congenital (754.61)*
rigid flat foot (754.61)
spastic (everted) flat foot (754.61)

735 Acquired deformities of toe

Excludes: *congenital (754.60-754.69, 755.65-755.66)*

735.0 Hallux valgus (acquired)

735.1 Hallux varus (acquired)

735.2 Hallux rigidus

735.3 Hallux malleus

735.4 Other hammer toe (acquired)

735.5 Claw toe (acquired)

735.8 Other acquired deformities of toe

735.9 Unspecified acquired deformity of toe

736 Other acquired deformities of limbs

Excludes: *congenital (754.3-755.9)*

✓5th **736.0** Acquired deformities of forearm, excluding fingers

736.00 Unspecified deformity
Deformity of elbow, forearm, hand, or wrist (acquired) NOS

736.01 Cubitus valgus (acquired)

736.02 Cubitus varus (acquired)

736.03 Valgus deformity of wrist (acquired)

736.04 Varus deformity of wrist (acquired)

736.05 Wrist drop (acquired)

736.06 Claw hand (acquired)

736.07 Club hand (acquired)

736.09 Other

736.1 Mallet finger

✓5th **736.2** Other acquired deformities of finger

736.20 Unspecified deformity
Deformity of finger (acquired) NOS

736.21 Boutonniere deformity

736.22 Swan-neck deformity

736.29 Other

Excludes: *trigger finger (727.03)*

➡ **AHA Coding Clinic:** 2Q, '89, 13

✓5th **736.3** Acquired deformities of hip

736.30 Unspecified deformity
Deformity of hip (acquired) NOS

736.31 Coxa valga (acquired)

736.32 Coxa vara (acquired)

736.39 Other

➡ **AHA Coding Clinic:** 2Q, '91, 18

✓5th **736.4** Genu valgum or varum (acquired)

736.41 Genu valgum (acquired)

736.42 Genu varum (acquired)

736.5 Genu recurvatum (acquired)

736.6 Other acquired deformities of knee
Deformity of knee (acquired) NOS

✓5th **736.7** Other acquired deformities of ankle and foot

Excludes: *deformities of toe (acquired) (735.0-735.9)*
pes planus (acquired) (734)

736.70 Unspecified deformity of ankle and foot, acquired

736.71 Acquired equinovarus deformity
Clubfoot, acquired

Excludes: *clubfoot not specified as acquired (754.5-754.7)*

736.72 Equinus deformity of foot, acquired

736.73 Cavus deformity of foot

Excludes: *that with claw foot (736.74)*

736.74 Claw foot, acquired

736.75 Cavovarus deformity of foot, acquired

736.76 Other calcaneus deformity

736.79 Other
Acquired:
pes } not elsewhere classified
talipes }

✓5th **736.8** Acquired deformities of other parts of limbs

736.81 Unequal leg length (acquired)

736.89 Other
Deformity (acquired):
arm or leg, not elsewhere classified
shoulder

736.9 Acquired deformity of limb, site unspecified

737 Curvature of spine

Excludes: *congenital (754.2)*

737.0 Adolescent postural kyphosis

Excludes: *osteochondrosis of spine (juvenile) (732.0)*
adult (732.8)

✓5th **737.1 Kyphosis (acquired)**

737.10 Kyphosis (acquired) (postural)

737.11 Kyphosis due to radiation

737.12 Kyphosis, postlaminectomy
➡ **AHA Coding Clinic:** J-F, '87, 7

737.19 Other

Excludes: *that associated with conditions classifiable elsewhere (737.41)*

✓5th **737.2 Lordosis (acquired)**

737.20 Lordosis (acquired) (postural)

737.21 Lordosis, postlaminectomy

737.22 Other postsurgical lordosis

737.29 Other

Excludes: *that associated with conditions classifiable elsewhere (737.42)*

✓5th **737.3 Kyphoscoliosis and scoliosis**

737.30 Scoliosis [and kyphoscoliosis], idiopathic

737.31 Resolving infantile idiopathic scoliosis

737.32 Progressive infantile idiopathic scoliosis

737.33 Scoliosis due to radiation

737.34 Thoracogenic scoliosis

737.39 Other

Excludes: *that associated with conditions classifiable elsewhere (737.43)*
that in kyphoscoliotic heart disease (416.1)

✓5th ***737.4 Curvature of spine associated with other conditions***
Code first associated condition, as:
Charcot-Marie-Tooth disease (356.1)
mucopolysaccharidosis (277.5)
neurofibromatosis (237.7)
osteitis deformans (731.0)
osteitis fibrosa cystica (252.0)
osteoporosis (733.00-733.09)
poliomyelitis (138)
tuberculosis [Pott's curvature] (015.0)

737.40 Curvature of spine, unspecified

737.41 Kyphosis

737.42 Lordosis

737.43 Scoliosis

737.8 Other curvatures of spine

737.9 Unspecified curvature of spine
Curvature of spine (acquired) (idiopathic) NOS
Hunchback, acquired

Excludes: *deformity of spine NOS (738.5)*

738 Other acquired deformity

Excludes: *congenital (754.0-756.9, 758.0-759.9)*
dentofacial anomalies (524.0-524.9)

738.0 Acquired deformity of nose
Deformity of nose (acquired)
Overdevelopment of nasal bones

Excludes: *deflected or deviated nasal septum (470)*

✓5th **738.1 Other acquired deformity of head**

738.10 Unspecified deformity

738.11 Zygomatic hyperplasia

738.12 Zygomatic hypoplasia

738.19 Other specified deformity

738.2 Acquired deformity of neck

738.3 Acquired deformity of chest and rib
Deformity:
chest (acquired)
rib (acquired)
Pectus:
carinatum, acquired
excavatum, acquired

738.4 Acquired spondylolisthesis

Degenerative spondylolisthesis
Spondylolysis, acquired

Excludes: *congenital (756.12)*

738.5 Other acquired deformity of back or spine

Deformity of spine NOS

Excludes: *curvature of spine (737.0-737.9)*

738.6 Acquired deformity of pelvis

Pelvic obliquity

Excludes: *intrapelvic protrusion of acetabulum (718.6)*
that in relation to labor and delivery (653.0-653.4, 653.8-653.9)

738.7 Cauliflower ear

738.8 Acquired deformity of other specified site

Deformity of clavicle

738.9 Acquired deformity of unspecified site

739 Nonallopathic lesions, not elsewhere classified

Includes: segmental dysfunction
somatic dysfunction

739.0 Head region

Occipitocervical region

739.1 Cervical region

Cervicothoracic region

739.2 Thoracic region

Thoracolumbar region

739.3 Lumbar region

Lumbosacral region

739.4 Sacral region

Sacrococcygeal region
Sacroiliac region

739.5 Pelvic region

Hip region
Pubic region

739.6 Lower extremities

739.7 Upper extremities

Acromioclavicular region
Sternoclavicular region

739.8 Rib cage

Costochondral region
Costovertebral region
Sternochondral region

739.9 Abdomen and other

➡ **AHA Coding Clinic:** 2Q, '89, 14

14. CONGENITAL ANOMALIES (740-759)

740 Anencephalus and similar anomalies

740.0 Anencephalus

Acrania
Amyelencephalus
Hemianencephaly
Hemicephaly

740.1 Craniorachischisis

740.2 Iniencephaly

741 Spina bifida

Excludes: *spina bifida occulta (756.17)*

The following fifth-digit subclassification is for use with category 741:

0 **unspecified region**
1 **cervical region**
2 **dorsal (thoracic) region**
3 **lumbar region**

➡ **AHA Coding Clinic:** 3Q, '94, 7

✓5th [8] **741.0 With hydrocephalus**

Arnold-Chiari syndrome, type II
Chiari malformation, type II
Any condition classifiable to 741.9 with any condition classifiable to 742.3

➡ **CC Excl:** 741.00-741.93, 742.59, 742.8-742.9, 759.7-759.89

➡ **AHA Coding Clinic:** 4Q, '97, 51

✓5th [8] **741.9 Without mention of hydrocephalus**

Hydromeningocele (spinal)
Hydromyelocele
Meningocele (spinal)
Meningomyelocele
Myelocele
Myelocystocele
Rachischisis
Spina bifida (aperta)
Syringomyelocele

➡ **CC Excl:** see Code 741.0

742 Other congenital anomalies of nervous system

742.0 Encephalocele

Encephalocystocele
Encephalomyelocele
Hydroencephalocele
Hydromeningocele, cranial
Meningocele, cerebral
Meningoencephalocele

➡ **AHA Coding Clinic:** 4Q, '94, 37

742.1 Microcephalus

Hydromicrocephaly
Micrencephaly

742.2 Reduction deformities of brain

Absence, Agenesis, Aplasia, Hypoplasia } of part of brain
Agyria
Arhinencephaly
Holoprosencephaly
Microgyria

➡ **AHA Coding Clinic:** 4Q, '94, 37

742.3 Congenital hydrocephalus

Aqueduct of Sylvius:
- anomaly
- obstruction, congenital
- stenosis

Atresia of foramina of Magendie and Luschka
Hydrocephalus in newborn

Excludes: *hydrocephalus:*
- *acquired (331.3-331.4)*
- *due to congenital toxoplasmosis (771.2)*
- *with any condition classifiable to 741.9 (741.0)*

742.4 Other specified anomalies of brain

Congenital cerebral cyst
Macroencephaly
Macrogyria
Megalencephaly
Multiple anomalies of brain NOS
Porencephaly
Ulegyria

✓5th **742.5 Other specified anomalies of spinal cord**

742.51 Diastematomyelia

742.53 Hydromyelia

Hydrorhachis

742.59 Other

Amyelia
Atelomyelia
Congenital anomaly of spinal meninges
Defective development of cauda equina
Hypoplasia of spinal cord
Myelatelia
Myelodysplasia

➡ **AHA Coding Clinic:** 2Q, '91, 14; 1Q, '89, 10

742.8 Other specified anomalies of nervous system

Agenesis of nerve
Displacement of brachial plexus
Familial dysautonomia
Jaw-winking syndrome
Marcus-Gunn syndrome
Riley-Day syndrome

Excludes: *neurofibromatosis (237.7)*

742.9 Unspecified anomaly of brain, spinal cord, and nervous system

Anomaly, Congenital: disease, lesion, Deformity } of { brain, nervous system, spinal cord

743 Congenital anomalies of eye

✓5th **743.0 Anophthalmos**

743.00 Clinical anophthalmos, unspecified

Agenesis, Congenital absence, Anophthalmos NOS } of eye

[8] Nonspecific PDX = 0

743.03 **Cystic eyeball, congenital**

743.06 **Cryptophthalmos**

✓5th **743.1** **Microphthalmos**

Dysplasia } of eye
Hypoplasia } of eye
Rudimentary eye

743.10 **Microphthalmos, unspecified**

743.11 **Simple microphthalmos**

743.12 **Microphthalmos associated with other anomalies of eye and adnexa**

✓5th **743.2** **Buphthalmos**

Glaucoma:
  congenital
  newborn
Hydrophthalmos

Excludes: *glaucoma of childhood (365.14)*
traumatic glaucoma due to birth injury (767.8)

743.20 **Buphthalmos, unspecified**

743.21 **Simple buphthalmos**

743.22 **Buphthalmos associated with other ocular anomalies**

Keratoglobus, congenital } associated with buphthalmos
Megalocornea } associated with buphthalmos

✓5th **743.3** **Congenital cataract and lens anomalies**

Excludes: *infantile cataract (366.00-366.09)*

743.30 **Congenital cataract, unspecified**

743.31 **Capsular and subcapsular cataract**

743.32 **Cortical and zonular cataract**

743.33 **Nuclear cataract**

743.34 **Total and subtotal cataract, congenital**

743.35 **Congenital aphakia**

Congenital absence of lens

743.36 **Anomalies of lens shape**

Microphakia
Spherophakia

743.37 **Congenital ectopic lens**

743.39 **Other**

✓5th **743.4** **Coloboma and other anomalies of anterior segment**

743.41 **Anomalies of corneal size and shape**

Microcornea

Excludes: *that associated with buphthalmos (743.22)*

743.42 **Corneal opacities, interfering with vision, congenital**

743.43 **Other corneal opacities, congenital**

743.44 **Specified anomalies of anterior chamber, chamber angle, and related structures**

Anomaly:
  Axenfeld's
  Peters'
  Rieger's

743.45 **Aniridia**

743.46 **Other specified anomalies of iris and ciliary body**

Anisocoria, congenital
Atresia of pupil
Coloboma of iris
Corectopia

743.47 **Specified anomalies of sclera**

743.48 **Multiple and combined anomalies of anterior segment**

743.49 **Other**

✓5th **743.5** **Congenital anomalies of posterior segment**

743.51 **Vitreous anomalies**

Congenital vitreous opacity

743.52 **Fundus coloboma**

743.53 **Chorioretinal degeneration, congenital**

743.54 **Congenital folds and cysts of posterior segment**

743.55 **Congenital macular changes**

743.56 **Other retinal changes, congenital**

743.57 **Specified anomalies of optic disc**

Coloboma of optic disc (congenital)

743.58 **Vascular anomalies**

Congenital retinal aneurysm

743.59 **Other**

✓5th **743.6** **Congenital anomalies of eyelids, lacrimal system, and orbit**

743.61 **Congenital ptosis**

743.62 Congenital deformities of eyelids

Ablepharon
Absence of eyelid
Accessory eyelid
Congenital:
  ectropion
  entropion

743.63 Other specified congenital anomalies of eyelid

Absence, agenesis, of cilia

743.64 Specified congenital anomalies of lacrimal gland

743.65 Specified congenital anomalies of lacrimal passages

Absence, agenesis of:
  lacrimal apparatus
  punctum lacrimale
Accessory lacrimal canal

743.66 Specified congenital anomalies of orbit

743.69 Other

Accessory eye muscles

743.8 Other specified anomalies of eye

Excludes: *congenital nystagmus (379.51)*
ocular albinism (270.2)
retinitis pigmentosa (362.74)

743.9 Unspecified anomaly of eye

Congenital:
  anomaly NOS } of eye [any part]
  deformity NOS }

744 Congenital anomalies of ear, face, and neck

Excludes: *anomaly of:*
  cervical spine (754.2, 756.10-756.19)
  larynx (748.2-748.3)
  nose (748.0-748.1)
  parathyroid gland (759.2)
  thyroid gland (759.2)
cleft lip (749.10-749.25)

✓5th **744.0 Anomalies of ear causing impairment of hearing**

Excludes: *congenital deafness without mention of cause (380.0-389.9)*

744.00 Unspecified anomaly of ear with impairment of hearing

744.01 Absence of external ear

Absence of:
  auditory canal (external)
  auricle (ear) (with stenosis or atresia of auditory canal)

744.02 Other anomalies of external ear with impairment of hearing

Atresia or stricture of auditory canal (external)

744.03 Anomaly of middle ear, except ossicles

Atresia or stricture of osseous meatus (ear)

744.04 Anomalies of ear ossicles

Fusion of ear ossicles

744.05 Anomalies of inner ear

Congenital anomaly of:
  membranous labyrinth
  organ of Corti

744.09 Other

Absence of ear, congenital

744.1 Accessory auricle

Accessory tragus
Polyotia
Preauricular appendage
Supernumerary:
  ear
  lobule

✓5th **744.2 Other specified anomalies of ear**

Excludes: *that with impairment of hearing (744.00-744.09)*

744.21 Absence of ear lobe, congenital

744.22 Macrotia

744.23 Microtia

744.24 Specified anomalies of Eustachian tube

Absence of Eustachian tube

744.29 Other

Bat ear
Darwin's tubercle
Pointed ear
Prominence of auricle
Ridge ear

Excludes: *preauricular sinus (744.46)*

744.3 Unspecified anomaly of ear

Congenital:
  anomaly NOS } of ear, NEC
  deformity NOS }

✓5th **744.4 Branchial cleft cyst or fistula; preauricular sinus**

744.41 Branchial cleft sinus or fistula

Branchial:
  sinus (external) (internal)
  vestige

744.42 Branchial cleft cyst

744.43 Cervical auricle

744.46 Preauricular sinus or fistula

744.47 Preauricular cyst

744.49 Other
Fistula (of):
auricle, congenital
cervicoaural

744.5 Webbing of neck
Pterygium colli

✓5th **744.8 Other specified anomalies of face and neck**

744.81 Macrocheilia
Hypertrophy of lip, congenital

744.82 Microcheilia

744.83 Macrostomia

744.84 Microstomia

744.89 Other

Excludes: *congenital fistula of lip (750.25)*
musculoskeletal anomalies (754.0-754.1, 756.0)

744.9 Unspecified anomalies of face and neck
Congenital:
anomaly NOS } of face [any part]
deformity NOS } or neck [any part]

745 Bulbus cordis anomalies and anomalies of cardiac septal closure

745.0 Common truncus
Absent septum } between aorta and
Communication (abnormal) } pulmonary artery
Aortic septal defect
Common aortopulmonary trunk
Persistent truncus arteriosus

➡ **CC Excl:** 429.71, 429.79, 745.0-745.9, 746.89, 746.9, 747.89, 747.9, 759.7-759.89

✓5th **745.1 Transposition of great vessels**

745.10 Complete transposition of great vessels
Transposition of great vessels:
NOS
classical

➡ **CC Excl:** see Code 745.0

745.11 Double outlet right ventricle
Dextratransposition of aorta
Incomplete transposition of great vessels
Origin of both great vessels from right ventricle
Taussig-Bing syndrome or defect

➡ **CC Excl:** see Code 745.0

745.12 Corrected transposition of great vessels
➡ **CC Excl:** see Code 745.0

745.19 Other
➡ **CC Excl:** see Code 745.0

745.2 Tetralogy of Fallot
Fallot's pentalogy
Ventricular septal defect with pulmonary stenosis or atresia, dextraposition of aorta, and hypertrophy of right ventricle

Excludes: *Fallot's triad (746.09)*

➡ **CC Excl:** see Code 745.0

745.3 Common ventricle
Cor triloculare biatriatum
Single ventricle

➡ **CC Excl:** see Code 745.0

745.4 Ventricular septal defect
Eisenmenger's defect or complex
Gerbode defect
Interventricular septal defect
Left ventricular-right atrial communication
Roger's disease

Excludes: *common atrioventricular canal type (745.69)*
single ventricle (745.3)

➡ **CC Excl:** see Code 745.0

745.5 Ostium secundum type atrial septal defect
Defect:
atrium secundum
fossa ovalis
Lutembacher's syndrome
Patent or persistent:
foramen ovale
ostium secundum

✓5th **745.6 Endocardial cushion defects**

745.60 Endocardial cushion defect, unspecified type
➡ **CC Excl:** see Code 745.0

745.61 Ostium primum defect
Persistent ostium primum

745.69 Other
Absence of atrial septum
Atrioventricular canal type ventricular septal defect
Common atrioventricular canal
Common atrium

➡ **CC Excl:** see Code 745.0

745.7 Cor biloculare
Absence of atrial and ventricular septa

➡ **CC Excl:** see Code 745.0

745.8 Other

745.9 Unspecified defect of septal closure
Septal defect NOS

746 Other congenital anomalies of heart

Excludes: *endocardial fibroelastosis (425.3)*

✓5th **746.0 Anomalies of pulmonary valve**

Excludes: *infundibular or subvalvular pulmonic stenosis (746.83)*
tetralogy of Fallot (745.2)

746.00 Pulmonary valve anomaly, unspecified type

746.01 Atresia, congenital
Congenital absence of pulmonary valve
➡ **CC Excl:** 746.00-746.09, 746.89, 746.9, 747.89, 747.9, 759.7-759.89

746.02 Stenosis, congenital
➡ **CC Excl:** see Code 746.01

746.09 Other
Congenital insufficiency of pulmonary valve
Fallot's triad or trilogy

746.1 Tricuspid atresia and stenosis, congenital
Absence of tricuspid valve
➡ **CC Excl:** 746.1-746.7, 746.89, 746.9, 747.89, 747.9, 759.7-759.89

746.2 Ebstein's anomaly
➡ **CC Excl:** see Code 746.1

746.3 Congenital stenosis of aortic valve
Congenital aortic stenosis

Excludes: *congenital:*
subaortic stenosis (746.81)
supravalvular aortic stenosis (747.22)

➡ **CC Excl:** see Code 746.1

746.4 Congenital insufficiency of aortic valve
Bicuspid aortic valve
Congenital aortic insufficiency
➡ **CC Excl:** see Code 746.1

746.5 Congenital mitral stenosis
Fused commissure } of mitral valve
Parachute deformity } of mitral valve
Supernumerary cusps } of mitral valve
➡ **CC Excl:** see Code 746.1

746.6 Congenital mitral insufficiency
➡ **CC Excl:** see Code 746.1

746.7 Hypoplastic left heart syndrome
Atresia, or marked hypoplasia, of aortic orifice or valve, with hypoplasia of ascending aorta and defective development of left ventricle (with mitral valve atresia)
➡ **CC Excl:** see Code 746.1

✓5th **746.8 Other specified anomalies of heart**

746.81 Subaortic stenosis
➡ **CC Excl:** 746.81-746.84, 746.89, 746.9, 747.89, 747.9, 759.7-759.89

746.82 Cor triatriatum
➡ **CC Excl:** see Code 746.81

746.83 Infundibular pulmonic stenosis
Subvalvular pulmonic stenosis
➡ **CC Excl:** see Code 746.81

746.84 Obstructive anomalies of heart, NEC
Uhl's disease
➡ **CC Excl:** see Code 746.81

746.85 Coronary artery anomaly
Anomalous origin or communication of coronary artery
Arteriovenous malformation of coronary artery
Coronary artery:
- absence
- arising from aorta or pulmonary trunk
- single

➡ **AHA Coding Clinic:** N-D, '85, 3

746.86 Congenital heart block
Complete or incomplete atrioventricular [AV] block
➡ **CC Excl:** 746.86, 746.89, 746.9, 747.89, 747.9, 759.7-759.89

746.87 Malposition of heart and cardiac apex
Abdominal heart
Dextrocardia
Ectopia cordis
Levocardia (isolated)
Mesocardia

Excludes: *dextrocardia with complete transposition of viscera (759.3)*

746.89 Other
Atresia } of cardiac vein
Hypoplasia } of cardiac vein
Congenital:
- cardiomegaly
- diverticulum, left ventricle
- pericardial defect

➡ **AHA Coding Clinic:** J-F, '85, 3

746.9 Unspecified anomaly of heart

Congenital:
- anomaly of heart NOS
- heart disease NOS

747 Other congenital anomalies of circulatory system

747.0 Patent ductus arteriosus

Patent ductus Botalli
Persistent ductus arteriosus

✓5th **747.1 Coarctation of aorta**

747.10 Coarctation of aorta (preductal) (postductal)

Hypoplasia of aortic arch

747.11 Interruption of aortic arch

➡ **CC Excl:** 747.10-747.22, 747.89, 747.9, 759.7-759.89

✓5th **747.2 Other anomalies of aorta**

747.20 Anomaly of aorta, unspecified

747.21 Anomalies of aortic arch

Anomalous origin, right subclavian artery
Dextraposition of aorta
Double aortic arch
Kommerell's diverticulum
Overriding aorta
Persistent:
- convolutions, aortic arch
- right aortic arch

Vascular ring

Excludes: *hypoplasia of aortic arch (747.10)*

747.22 Atresia and stenosis of aorta

Absence / Aplasia / Hypoplasia / Stricture } of aorta

Supra (valvular)-aortic stenosis

Excludes: *congenital aortic (valvular) stenosis or stricture, so stated (746.3)*
hypoplasia of aorta in hypoplastic left heart syndrome (746.7)

➡ **CC Excl:** see Code 747.11

747.29 Other

Aneurysm of sinus of Valsalva
Congenital:
- aneurysm / dilation } of aorta

747.3 Anomalies of pulmonary artery

Agenesis / Anomaly / Atresia / Coarctation / Hypoplasia / Stenosis } of pulmonary artery

Pulmonary arteriovenous aneurysm

➡ **AHA Coding Clinic:** 1Q, '94, 15

✓5th **747.4 Anomalies of great veins**

747.40 Anomaly of great veins, unspecified

Anomaly NOS of:
- pulmonary veins
- vena cava

747.41 Total anomalous pulmonary venous connection

Total anomalous pulmonary venous return [TAPVR]:
- subdiaphragmatic
- supradiaphragmatic

747.42 Partial anomalous pulmonary venous connection

Partial anomalous pulmonary venous return

747.49 Other anomalies of great veins

Absence / Congenital stenosis } of vena cava (inferior) (superior)

Persistent:
- left posterior cardinal vein
- left superior vena cava

Scimitar syndrome
Transposition of pulmonary veins NOS

747.5 Absence or hypoplasia of umbilical artery

Single umbilical artery

✓5th **747.6 Other anomalies of peripheral vascular system**

Absence / Anomaly / Atresia } of artery or vein, NEC

Arteriovenous aneurysm (peripheral)
Arteriovenous malformation of the peripheral vascular system
Congenital:
- aneurysm (peripheral)
- phlebectasia
- stricture, artery
- varix

Multiple renal arteries

Excludes: *anomalies of:*
cerebral vessels (747.81)
pulmonary artery (747.3)
congenital retinal aneurysm (743.58)
hemangioma (228.00-228.09)
lymphangioma (228.1)

747.60 Anomaly of the peripheral vascular system, unspecified site

747.61 Gastrointestinal vessel anomaly

747.62 Renal vessel anomaly

747.63 Upper limb vessel anomaly

747.64 Lower limb vessel anomaly

747.69 Anomalies of other specified sites of peripheral vascular system

✓5th **747.8 Other specified anomalies of circulatory system**

747.81 Anomalies of cerebrovascular system

Arteriovenous malformation of brain
Cerebral arteriovenous aneurysm, congenital
Congenital anomalies of cerebral vessels

Excludes: *ruptured cerebral (arteriovenous) aneurysm (430)*

747.82 Spinal vessel anomaly

Arteriovenous malformation of spinal vessel

➡ **AHA Coding Clinic:** 3Q, '95, 5

747.89 Other

Aneurysm, congenital, specified site not elsewhere classified

Excludes: *congenital aneurysm:*
coronary (746.85)
peripheral (747.6)
pulmonary (747.3)
retinal (743.58)

747.9 Unspecified anomaly of circulatory system

748 Congenital anomalies of respiratory system

Excludes: *congenital defect of diaphragm (756.6)*

748.0 Choanal atresia

Atresia } of nares (anterior) (posterior)
Congenital stenosis } of nares (anterior) (posterior)

748.1 Other anomalies of nose

Absent nose
Accessory nose
Cleft nose
Deformity of wall of nasal sinus
Congenital:
deformity of nose
notching of tip of nose
perforation of wall of nasal sinus

Excludes: *congenital deviation of nasal septum (754.0)*

748.2 Web of larynx

Web of larynx:
NOS
glottic
subglottic

748.3 Other anomalies of larynx, trachea, and bronchus

Absence or agenesis of:
bronchus
larynx
trachea
Anomaly (of):
cricoid cartilage
epiglottis
thyroid cartilage
tracheal cartilage
Atresia (of):
epiglottis
glottis
larynx
trachea
Cleft thyroid, cartilage, congenital
Congenital:
dilation, trachea
stenosis:
larynx
trachea
tracheocele
Diverticulum:
bronchus
trachea
Fissure of epiglottis
Laryngocele
Posterior cleft of cricoid cartilage (congenital)
Rudimentary tracheal bronchus
Stridor, laryngeal, congenital

748.4 Congenital cystic lung

Disease, lung:
cystic, congenital
polycystic, congenital
Honeycomb lung, congenital

Excludes: *acquired or unspecified cystic lung (518.89)*

➡ **CC Excl:** 748.4-748.9

748.5 Agenesis, hypoplasia, and dysplasia of lung

Absence of lung (fissures) (lobe)
Aplasia of lung
Hypoplasia of lung (lobe)
Sequestration of lung

➡ **CC Excl:** see Code 748.4

✓5th **748.6 Other anomalies of lung**

748.60 Anomaly of lung, unspecified

748.61 Congenital bronchiectasis

➡ **CC Excl:** 494, 496, 506.1, 506.4, 506.9, 748.61

748.69 Other

Accessory lung (lobe)
Azygos lobe (fissure), lung

748.8 Other specified anomalies of respiratory system

Abnormal communication between pericardial and pleural sacs
Anomaly, pleural folds
Atresia of nasopharynx
Congenital cyst of mediastinum

748.9 Unspecified anomaly of respiratory system

Anomaly of respiratory system NOS

749 Cleft palate and cleft lip

✓5th **749.0** Cleft palate

749.00 Cleft palate, unspecified

749.01 Unilateral, complete

749.02 Unilateral, incomplete
Cleft uvula

749.03 Bilateral, complete

749.04 Bilateral, incomplete

✓5th **749.1** Cleft lip
Cheiloschisis
Congenital fissure of lip
Harelip
Labium leporinum

749.10 Cleft lip, unspecified

749.11 Unilateral, complete

749.12 Unilateral, incomplete

749.13 Bilateral, complete

749.14 Bilateral, incomplete

✓5th **749.2** Cleft palate with cleft lip
Cheilopalatoschisis

749.20 Cleft palate with cleft lip, unspecified

749.21 Unilateral, complete

749.22 Unilateral, incomplete

749.23 Bilateral, complete
➡ **AHA Coding Clinic:** 1Q, '96, 14

749.24 Bilateral, incomplete

749.25 Other combinations

750 Other congenital anomalies of upper alimentary tract

Excludes: *dentofacial anomalies (524.0-524.9)*

750.0 Tongue tie
Ankyloglossia

✓5th **750.1** Other anomalies of tongue

750.10 Anomaly of tongue, unspecified

750.11 Aglossia

750.12 Congenital adhesions of tongue

750.13 Fissure of tongue
Bifid tongue
Double tongue

750.15 Macroglossia
Congenital hypertrophy of tongue

750.16 Microglossia
Hypoplasia of tongue

750.19 Other

✓5th **750.2** Other specified anomalies of mouth and pharynx

750.21 Absence of salivary gland

750.22 Accessory salivary gland

750.23 Atresia, salivary duct
Imperforate salivary duct

750.24 Congenital fistula of salivary gland

750.25 Congenital fistula of lip
Congenital (mucus) lip pits

750.26 Other specified anomalies of mouth
Absence of uvula

750.27 Diverticulum of pharynx
Pharyngeal pouch

750.29 Other specified anomalies of pharynx
Imperforate pharynx

750.3 Tracheoesophageal fistula, esophageal atresia and stenosis
Absent esophagus
Atresia of esophagus
Congenital:
- esophageal ring
- stenosis of esophagus
- stricture of esophagus

Congenital fistula:
- esophagobronchial
- esophagotracheal

Imperforate esophagus
Webbed esophagus

750.4 Other specified anomalies of esophagus
Dilatation, congenital (of) esophagus
Displacement, congenital (of) esophagus
Diverticulum (of) esophagus
Duplication (of) esophagus
Giant (of) esophagus
Esophageal pouch

Excludes: *congenital hiatus hernia (750.6)*

750.5 Congenital hypertrophic pyloric stenosis
Congenital or infantile:
- constriction of pylorus
- hypertrophy of pylorus
- spasm of pylorus
- stenosis of pylorus
- stricture of pylorus

750.6 Congenital hiatus hernia
Displacement of cardia through esophageal hiatus

Excludes: *congenital diaphragmatic hernia (756.6)*

750.7 Other specified anomalies of stomach

Congenital:
  cardiospasm
  hourglass stomach
Displacement of stomach
Diverticulum of stomach, congenital
Duplication of stomach
Megalogastria
Microgastria
Transposition of stomach

750.8 Other specified anomalies of upper alimentary tract

750.9 Unspecified anomaly of upper alimentary tract

Congenital:
  anomaly NOS } of upper alimentary tract [any part, except tongue]
  deformity NOS } of upper alimentary tract [any part, except tongue]

751 Other congenital anomalies of digestive system

751.0 Meckel's diverticulum

Meckel's diverticulum (displaced) (hypertrophic)
Persistent:
  omphalomesenteric duct
  vitelline duct

751.1 Atresia and stenosis of small intestine A: 0–17

Atresia of:
  duodenum
  ileum
  intestine NOS
Congenital:
  absence
  obstruction
  stenosis
  stricture
  } of small intestine or intestine NOS
Imperforate jejunum

751.2 Atresia and stenosis of large intestine, rectum, and anal canal A: 0–17

Absence:
  anus (congenital)
  appendix, congenital
  large intestine, congenital
  rectum
Atresia of:
  anus
  colon
  rectum
Congenital or infantile:
  obstruction of large intestine
  occlusion of anus
  stricture of anus
Imperforate:
  anus
  rectum
Stricture of rectum, congenital

751.3 Hirschsprung's disease and other congenital functional disorders of colon

Aganglionosis
Congenital dilation of colon
Congenital megacolon
Macrocolon

751.4 Anomalies of intestinal fixation

Congenital adhesions:
  omental, anomalous
  peritoneal
Jackson's membrane
Malrotation of colon
Rotation of cecum or colon:
  failure of
  incomplete
  insufficient
Universal mesentery

751.5 Other anomalies of intestine

Congenital diverticulum, colon
Dolichocolon
Duplication of:
  anus
  appendix
  cecum
  intestine
Ectopic anus
Megaloappendix
Megaloduodenum
Microcolon
Persistent cloaca
Transposition of:
  appendix
  colon
  intestine

✓5th **751.6 Anomalies of gallbladder, bile ducts, and liver**

751.60 Unspecified anomaly of gallbladder, bile ducts, and liver

751.61 Biliary atresia A: 0–17

Congenital:
  absence
  hypoplasia
  obstruction
  stricture
  } of bile duct (common) or passage

➡ **AHA Coding Clinic:** S-O, '87, 8

751.62 Congenital cystic disease of liver

Congenital polycystic disease of liver
Fibrocystic disease of liver

751.69 Other anomalies of gallbladder, bile ducts, and liver

Absence of:
  gallbladder, congenital
  liver (lobe)
Accessory:
  hepatic ducts
  liver
Congenital:
  choledochal cyst
  hepatomegaly
Duplication of:
  biliary duct
  cystic duct
  gallbladder
  liver
Floating:
  gallbladder
  liver
Intrahepatic gallbladder

➡ **AHA Coding Clinic:** S-O, '87, 8

751.7 Anomalies of pancreas

Absence
Agenesis
Hypoplasia
} of pancreas
Accessory pancreas
Annular pancreas
Ectopic pancreatic tissue
Pancreatic heterotopia

Excludes: *diabetes mellitus:*
  congenital (250.0-250.9)
  neonatal (775.1)
fibrocystic disease of pancreas (277.00-277.01)

751.8 Other specified anomalies of digestive system

Absence (complete) (partial) of alimentary tract NOS
Duplication } of digestive organs NOS
Malposition, congenital } of digestive organs NOS

Excludes: *congenital diaphragmatic hernia (756.6)*
congenital hiatus hernia (750.6)

751.9 Unspecified anomaly of digestive system

Congenital:
- anomaly NOS } of digestive system NOS
- deformity NOS }

752 Congenital anomalies of genital organs

Excludes: *syndromes associated with anomalies in the number and form of chromosomes (758.0-758.9)*
testicular feminization syndrome (257.8)

752.0 Anomalies of ovaries ♀

Absence, congenital } (of) ovary
Accessory }
Ectopic }
Streak }

✓5th **752.1 Anomalies of fallopian tubes and broad ligaments** ♀

752.10 Unspecified anomaly of fallopian tubes and broad ligaments

752.11 Embryonic cyst of fallopian tubes and broad ligaments

Cyst:
- epoophoron
- fimbrial

Cyst:
- Gartner's duct
- parovarian

➡ **AHA Coding Clinic:** S-O, '85, 13

752.19 Other

Absence } (of) fallopian tube or broad ligament
Accessory }
Atresia }

752.2 Doubling of uterus ♀

Didelphic uterus
Doubling of uterus [any degree] (associated with doubling of cervix and vagina)

752.3 Other anomalies of uterus ♀

Absence, congenital } of uterus
Agenesis }
Aplasia }
Bicornuate uterus
Uterus unicornis
Uterus with only one functioning horn

✓5th **752.4 Anomalies of cervix, vagina, and external female genitalia** ♀

752.40 Unspecified anomaly of cervix, vagina, and external female genitalia

752.41 Embryonic cyst of cervix, vagina, and external female genitalia

Cyst of:
- canal of Nuck, congenital
- vagina, embryonal
- vulva, congenital

752.42 Imperforate hymen

752.49 Other anomalies of cervix, vagina, and external female genitalia

Absence } of cervix, clitoris, vagina, or vulva
Agenesis }
Congenital stenosis or stricture of:
- cervical canal
- vagina

Excludes: *double vagina associated with total duplication (752.2)*

✓5th **752.5 Undescended and retractile testicle** ♂

➡ **AHA Coding Clinic:** 4Q, '96, 33

752.51 Undescended testis

Cryptorchism
Ectopic testis

752.52 Retractile testis

✓5th **752.6 Hypospadias and epispadias and other penile anomalies** ♂

➡ **AHA Coding Clinic:** 4Q, '96, 34, 35

752.61 Hypospadias

➡ **AHA Coding Clinic:** 3Q, '97, 6

752.62 Epispadias

Anaspadias

752.63 Congenital chordee

752.64 Micropenis

752.65 Hidden penis

752.69 Other penile anomalies

752.7 Indeterminate sex and pseudohermaphroditism

Gynandrism
Hermaphroditism
Ovotestis
Pseudohermaphroditism (male) (female)
Pure gonadal dysgenesis

Excludes: *pseudohermaphroditism:*
female, with adrenocortical disorder (255.2)
male, with gonadal disorder (257.8)
with specified chromosomal anomaly (758.0-758.9)
testicular feminization syndrome (257.8)

752.8 Other specified anomalies of genital organs

Absence of:
- prostate
- spermatic cord
- vas deferens

Anorchism
Aplasia (congenital) of:
- prostate
- round ligament
- testicle

Atresia of:
- ejaculatory duct
- vas deferens

Fusion of testes
Hypoplasia of testis
Monorchism
Polyorchism

Excludes: *congenital hydrocele (778.6)*
penile anomalies (752.61-752.69)
phimosis or paraphimosis (605)

752.9 Unspecified anomaly of genital organs

Congenital:
- anomaly NOS } of genital organ, NEC
- deformity NOS } of genital organ, NEC

753 Congenital anomalies of urinary system

753.0 Renal agenesis and dysgenesis

Atrophy of kidney:
- congenital
- infantile

Congenital absence of kidney(s)

Hypoplasia of kidney(s)

Code also any associated vesicoureteral reflux (593.70-593.73)

✓5th **753.1 Cystic kidney disease**

Excludes: *acquired cyst of kidney (593.2)*

➡ **AHA Coding Clinic:** 4Q, '90, 3

753.10 Cystic kidney disease, unspecified

753.11 Congenital single renal cyst

753.12 Polycystic kidney, unspecified type

753.13 Polycystic kidney, autosomal dominant

753.14 Polycystic kidney, autosomal recessive

753.15 Renal dysplasia

Code also any associated vesicoureteral reflux (593.70-593.73)

753.16 Medullary cystic kidney

Nephronopthisis

753.17 Medullary sponge kidney

753.19 Other specified cystic kidney disease

Multicystic kidney

✓5th **753.2 Obstructive defects of renal pelvis and ureter**

753.20 Unspecified obstructive defect of renal pelvis and ureter

753.21 Congenital obstruction of ureteropelvic junction

753.22 Congenital obstruction of ureterovesical junction

Adynamic ureter
Congenital hydroureter

753.23 Congenital ureterocele

753.29 Other

753.3 Other specified anomalies of kidney

Accessory kidney

Congenital:
- calculus of kidney
- displaced kidney

Discoid kidney

Double kidney with double pelvis

Ectopic kidney

Fusion of kidneys

Giant kidney

Horseshoe kidney

Hyperplasia of kidney

Lobulation of kidney

Malrotation of kidney

Trifid kidney (pelvis)

753.4 Other specified anomalies of ureter

Absent ureter

Accessory ureter

Deviation of ureter

Displaced ureteric orifice

Double ureter

Ectopic ureter

Implantation, anomalous, of ureter

753.5 Exstrophy of urinary bladder

Ectopia vesicae

Extroversion of bladder

753.6 Atresia and stenosis of urethra and bladder neck

Congenital obstruction:
- bladder neck
- urethra

Congenital stricture of:
- urethra (valvular)
- urinary meatus
- vesicourethral orifice

Imperforate urinary meatus

Impervious urethra

Urethral valve formation

753.7 Anomalies of urachus

Cyst } (of) urachus
Fistula } (of) urachus
Patent } (of) urachus

Persistent umbilical sinus

753.8 Other specified anomalies of bladder and urethra

Absence, congenital of:
- bladder
- urethra

Accessory:
- bladder
- urethra

Congenital:
- diverticulum of bladder
- hernia of bladder

Congenital urethrorectal fistula

Congenital prolapse of:
- bladder (mucosa)
- urethra

Double:
- urethra
- urinary meatus

753.9 Unspecified anomaly of urinary system

Congenital:
- anomaly NOS } of urinary system [any part, except urachus]
- deformity NOS } of urinary system [any part, except urachus]

754 Certain congenital musculoskeletal deformities

Includes: nonteratogenic deformities which are considered to be due to intrauterine malposition and pressure

754.0 Of skull, face, and jaw

Asymmetry of face

Compression facies

Depressions in skull

Deviation of nasal septum, congenital

Dolichocephaly

Plagiocephaly

Potter's facies

Squashed or bent nose, congenital

Excludes: *dentofacial anomalies (524.0-524.9)*
syphilitic saddle nose (090.5)

754.1 Of sternocleidomastoid muscle

Congenital sternomastoid torticollis
Congenital wryneck
Contracture of sternocleidomastoid (muscle)
Sternomastoid tumor

754.2 Of spine

Congenital postural:
- lordosis
- scoliosis

✓5th **754.3 Congenital dislocation of hip**

754.30 Congenital dislocation of hip, unilateral

Congenital dislocation of hip NOS

754.31 **Congenital dislocation of hip, bilateral**

754.32 **Congenital subluxation of hip, unilateral**
Congenital flexion deformity, hip or thigh
Predislocation status of hip at birth
Preluxation of hip, congenital

754.33 **Congenital subluxation of hip, bilateral**

754.35 **Congenital dislocation of one hip with subluxation of other hip**

✓5th **754.4** **Congenital genu recurvatum and bowing of long bones of leg**

754.40 **Genu recurvatum**

754.41 **Congenital dislocation of knee (with genu recurvatum)**

754.42 **Congenital bowing of femur**

754.43 **Congenital bowing of tibia and fibula**

754.44 **Congenital bowing of unspecified long bones of leg**

✓5th **754.5** **Varus deformities of feet**

Excludes: *acquired (736.71, 736.75, 736.79)*

754.50 **Talipes varus**
Congenital varus deformity of foot, unspecified
Pes varus

754.51 **Talipes equinovarus**
Equinovarus (congenital)

754.52 **Metatarsus primus varus**

754.53 **Metatarsus varus**

754.59 **Other**
Talipes calcaneovarus

✓5th **754.6** **Valgus deformities of feet**

Excludes: *valgus deformity of foot (acquired) (736.79)*

754.60 **Talipes valgus**
Congenital valgus deformity of foot, unspecified

754.61 **Congenital pes planus**
Congenital rocker bottom flat foot
Flat foot, congenital

Excludes: *pes planus (acquired) (734)*

754.62 **Talipes calcaneovalgus**

754.69 **Other**
Talipes:
equinovalgus
planovalgus

✓5th **754.7** **Other deformities of feet**

Excludes: *acquired (736.70-736.79)*

754.70 **Talipes, unspecified**
Congenital deformity of NOS

754.71 **Talipes cavus**
Cavus foot (congenital)

754.79 **Other**
Asymmetric talipes
Talipes:
calcaneus
equinus

✓5th **754.8** **Other specified nonteratogenic anomalies**

754.81 **Pectus excavatum**
Congenital funnel chest

754.82 **Pectus carinatum**
Congenital pigeon chest [breast]

754.89 **Other**
Club hand (congenital)
Congenital:
deformity of chest wall
dislocation of elbow
Generalized flexion contractures of lower limb joints, congenital
Spade-like hand (congenital)

755 Other congenital anomalies of limbs

Excludes: *those deformities classifiable to 754.0-754.8*

✓5th **755.0** **Polydactyly**

755.00 **Polydactyly, unspecified digits**
Supernumerary digits

755.01 **Of fingers**
Accessory fingers

755.02 **Of toes**
Accessory toes

✓5th **755.1** **Syndactyly**
Symphalangy
Webbing of digits

755.10 **Of multiple and unspecified sites**

755.11 **Of fingers without fusion of bone**

755.12 **Of fingers with fusion of bone**

755.13 Of toes without fusion of bone

755.14 Of toes with fusion of bone

✓5th **755.2 Reduction deformities of upper limb**

755.20 Unspecified reduction deformity of upper limb

Ectromelia NOS } of upper limb
Hemimelia NOS } of upper limb
Shortening of arm, congenital

755.21 Transverse deficiency of upper limb

Amelia of upper limb
Congenital absence of:
- fingers, all (complete or partial)
- forearm, including hand and fingers
- upper limb, complete

Congenital amputation of upper limb
Transverse hemimelia of upper limb

755.22 Longitudinal deficiency of upper limb, NEC

Phocomelia NOS of upper limb
Rudimentary arm

755.23 Longitudinal deficiency, combined, involving humerus, radius, and ulna (complete or incomplete)

Congenital absence of arm and forearm (complete or incomplete) with or without metacarpal deficiency and/or phalangeal deficiency, incomplete
Phocomelia, complete, of upper limb

755.24 Longitudinal deficiency, humeral, complete or partial (with or without distal deficiencies, incomplete)

Congenital absence of humerus (with or without absence of some [but not all] distal elements)
Proximal phocomelia of upper limb

755.25 Longitudinal deficiency, radioulnar, complete or partial (with or without distal deficiencies, incomplete)

Congenital absence of radius and ulna (with or without absence of some [but not all] distal elements)
Distal phocomelia of upper limb

755.26 Longitudinal deficiency, radial, complete or partial (with or without distal deficiencies, incomplete)

Agenesis of radius
Congenital absence of radius (with or without absence of some [but not all] distal elements)

755.27 Longitudinal deficiency, ulnar, complete or partial (with or without distal deficiencies, incomplete)

Agenesis of ulna
Congenital absence of ulna (with or without absence of some [but not all] distal elements)

755.28 Longitudinal deficiency, carpals or metacarpals, complete or partial (with or without incomplete phalangeal deficiency)

755.29 Longitudinal deficiency, phalanges, complete or partial

Absence of finger, congenital
Aphalangia of upper limb, terminal, complete or partial

Excludes: *terminal deficiency of all five digits (755.21)*
transverse deficiency of phalanges (755.21)

✓5th **755.3 Reduction deformities of lower limb**

755.30 Unspecified reduction deformity of lower limb

Ectromelia NOS } of lower limb
Hemimelia NOS } of lower limb
Shortening of leg, congenital

755.31 Transverse deficiency of lower limb

Amelia of lower limb
Congenital absence of:
- foot
- leg, including foot and toes
- lower limb, complete
- toes, all, complete

Transverse hemimelia of lower limb

755.32 Longitudinal deficiency of lower limb, NEC

Phocomelia NOS of lower limb

755.33 Longitudinal deficiency, combined, involving femur, tibia, and fibula (complete or incomplete)

Congenital absence of thigh and (lower) leg (complete or incomplete) with or without metacarpal deficiency and/or phalangeal deficiency, incomplete
Phocomelia, complete, of lower limb

755.34 Longitudinal deficiency, femoral, complete or partial (with or without distal deficiencies, incomplete)

Congenital absence of femur (with or without absence of some [but not all] distal elements)
Proximal phocomelia of lower limb

755.35 Longitudinal deficiency, tibiofibular, complete or partial (with or without distal deficiencies, incomplete)
Congenital absence of tibia and fibula (with or without absence of some [but not all] distal elements)
Distal phocomelia of lower limb

755.36 Longitudinal deficiency, tibia, complete or partial (with or without distal deficiencies, incomplete)
Agenesis of tibia
Congenital absence of tibia (with or without absence of some [but not all] distal elements)

755.37 Longitudinal deficiency, fibular, complete or partial (with or without distal deficiencies, incomplete)
Agenesis of fibula
Congenital absence of fibula (with or without absence of some [but not all] distal elements)

755.38 Longitudinal deficiency, tarsals or metatarsals, complete or partial (with or without incomplete phalangeal deficiency)

755.39 Longitudinal deficiency, phalanges, complete or partial
Absence of toe, congenital
Aphalangia of lower limb, terminal, complete or partial

Excludes: *terminal deficiency of all five digits (755.31)*
transverse deficiency of phalanges (755.31)

755.4 Reduction deformities, unspecified limb
Absence, congenital (complete or partial) of limb NOS
Amelia, Ectromelia, Hemimelia, Phocomelia } of unspecified limb

✓5th **755.5 Other anomalies of upper limb, including shoulder girdle**

755.50 Unspecified anomaly of upper limb

755.51 Congenital deformity of clavicle

755.52 Congenital elevation of scapula
Sprengel's deformity

755.53 Radioulnar synostosis

755.54 Madelung's deformity

755.55 Acrocephalosyndactyly
Apert's syndrome

755.56 Accessory carpal bones

755.57 Macrodactylia (fingers)

755.58 Cleft hand, congenital
Lobster-claw hand

755.59 Other
Cleidocranial dysostosis
Cubitus:
valgus, congenital
varus, congenital

Excludes: *club hand (congenital) (754.89)*
congenital dislocation of elbow (754.89)

✓5th **755.6 Other anomalies of lower limb, including pelvic girdle**

755.60 Unspecified anomaly of lower limb

755.61 Coxa valga, congenital

755.62 Coxa vara, congenital

755.63 Other congenital deformity of hip (joint)
Congenital anteversion of femur (neck)

Excludes: *congenital dislocation of hip (754.30-754.35)*

755.64 Congenital deformity of knee (joint)
Congenital:
absence of patella
genu valgum [knock-knee]
genu varum [bowleg]
Rudimentary patella

755.65 Macrodactylia of toes

755.66 Other anomalies of toes
Congenital:
hallux valgus
hallux varus
hammer toe

755.67 Anomalies of foot, NEC
Astragaloscaphoid synostosis
Calcaneonavicular bar
Coalition of calcaneus
Talonavicular synostosis
Tarsal coalitions

755.69 Other
Congenital:
angulation of tibia
deformity (of):
ankle (joint)
sacroiliac (joint)
fusion of sacroiliac joint

755.8 Other specified anomalies of unspecified limb

755.9 Unspecified anomaly of unspecified limb

Congenital:
anomaly NOS } of unspecified limb
deformity NOS }

Excludes: *reduction deformity of unspecified limb (755.4)*

756 Other congenital musculoskeletal anomalies

Excludes: *those deformities classifiable to 754.0-754.8*

756.0 Anomalies of skull and face bones

Absence of skull bones
Acrocephaly
Congenital deformity of forehead
Craniosynostosis
Crouzon's disease
Hypertelorism
Imperfect fusion of skull
Oxycephaly
Platybasia
Premature closure of cranial sutures
Tower skull
Trigonocephaly

Excludes: *acrocephalosyndactyly [Apert's syndrome] (755.55)*
dentofacial anomalies (524.0-524.9)
skull defects associated with brain anomalies, such as:
anencephalus (740.0)
encephalocele (742.0)
hydrocephalus (742.3)
microcephalus (742.1)

➡ **AHA Coding Clinic:** 3Q, '96, 15

✓5th **756.1 Anomalies of spine**

756.10 Anomaly of spine, unspecified

756.11 Spondylolysis, lumbosacral region

Prespondylolisthesis (lumbosacral)

756.12 Spondylolisthesis

756.13 Absence of vertebra, congenital

756.14 Hemivertebra

756.15 Fusion of spine [vertebra], congenital

756.16 Klippel-Feil syndrome

756.17 Spina bifida occulta

Excludes: *spina bifida (aperta) (741.0-741.9)*

756.19 Other

Platyspondylia
Supernumerary vertebra

756.2 Cervical rib

Supernumerary rib in the cervical region

756.3 Other anomalies of ribs and sternum

Congenital absence of:
rib
sternum
Congenital:
fissure of sternum
fusion of ribs
Sternum bifidum

Excludes: *nonteratogenic deformity of chest wall (754.81-754.89)*

756.4 Chondrodystrophy

Achondroplasia
Chondrodystrophia (fetalis)
Dyschondroplasia
Enchondromatosis
Ollier's disease

Excludes: *lipochondrodystrophy [Hurler's syndrome] (277.5)*
Morquio's disease (277.5)

➡ **AHA Coding Clinic:** S-O, '87, 10

✓5th **756.5 Osteodystrophies**

756.50 Osteodystrophy, unspecified

756.51 Osteogenesis imperfecta

Fragilitas ossium
Osteopsathyrosis

756.52 Osteopetrosis

756.53 Osteopoikilosis

756.54 Polyostotic fibrous dysplasia of bone

756.55 Chondroectodermal dysplasia

Ellis-van Creveld syndrome

756.56 Multiple epiphyseal dysplasia

756.59 Other

Albright (-McCune)-Sternberg syndrome

756.6 Anomalies of diaphragm

Absence of diaphragm
Congenital hernia:
diaphragmatic
foramen of Morgagni
Eventration of diaphragm

Excludes: *congenital hiatus hernia (750.6)*

✓5th **756.7 Anomalies of abdominal wall**

756.70 Anomaly of abdominal wall, unspecified

756.71 Prune belly syndrome

Eagle-Barrett syndrome
Prolapse of bladder mucosa

➡ **AHA Coding Clinic:** 4Q, '97, 44

756.79 Other congenital anomalies of abdominal wall

Exomphalos
Gastroschisis
Omphalocele

Excludes: *umbilical hernia (551-553 with .1)*

✓5th **756.8 Other specified anomalies of muscle, tendon, fascia, and connective tissue**

756.81 Absence of muscle and tendon

Absence of muscle (pectoral)

756.82 **Accessory muscle**

756.83 **Ehlers-Danlos syndrome**

756.89 **Other**

Amyotrophia congenita
Congenital shortening of tendon

756.9 **Other and unspecified anomalies of musculoskeletal system**

Congenital:
anomaly NOS } of musculoskeletal system, NEC
deformity NOS } of musculoskeletal system, NEC

757 Congenital anomalies of the integument

Includes: anomalies of skin, subcutaneous tissue, hair, nails, and breast

Excludes: *hemangioma (228.00-228.09)*
pigmented nevus (216.0-216.9)

757.0 **Hereditary edema of legs**

Congenital lymphedema
Hereditary trophedema
Milroy's disease

757.1 **Ichthyosis congenita**

Congenital ichthyosis
Harlequin fetus
Ichthyosiform erythroderma

757.2 **Dermatoglyphic anomalies**

Abnormal palmar creases

✓5th **757.3** **Other specified anomalies of skin**

757.31 **Congenital ectodermal dysplasia**

757.32 **Vascular hamartomas**

Birthmarks
Port-wine stain
Strawberry nevus

757.33 **Congenital pigmentary anomalies of skin**

Congenital poikiloderma
Urticaria pigmentosa
Xeroderma pigmentosum

Excludes: *albinism (270.2)*

757.39 **Other**

Accessory skin tags, congenital
Congenital scar
Epidermolysis bullosa
Keratoderma (congenital)

Excludes: *pilonidal cyst (685.0-685.1)*

757.4 **Specified anomalies of hair**

Congenital:
alopecia
atrichosis
beaded hair
Congenital:
hypertrichosis
monilethrix
Persistent lanugo

757.5 **Specified anomalies of nails**

Anonychia
Congenital:
clubnail
koilonychia
Congenital:
leukonychia
onychauxis
pachyonychia

757.6 **Specified anomalies of breast**

Absent } breast or nipple
Accessory } breast or nipple
Supernumerary } breast or nipple
Hypoplasia of breast

Excludes: *absence of pectoral muscle (756.81)*

757.8 **Other specified anomalies of the integument**

757.9 **Unspecified anomaly of the integument**

Congenital:
anomaly NOS } of integument
deformity NOS } of integument

758 Chromosomal anomalies

Includes: syndromes associated with anomalies in the number and form of chromosomes

758.0 **Down's syndrome**

Mongolism
Translocation Down's syndrome
Trisomy:
21 or 22
G

758.1 **Patau's syndrome**

Trisomy:
13
D_1

758.2 **Edwards' syndrome**

Trisomy:
18
E_3

758.3 **Autosomal deletion syndromes**

Antimongolism syndrome
Cri-du-chat syndrome

758.4 **Balanced autosomal translocation in normal individual**

758.5 **Other conditions due to autosomal anomalies**

Accessory autosomes NEC

758.6 **Gonadal dysgenesis**

Ovarian dysgenesis
Turner's syndrome
XO syndrome

Excludes: *pure gonadal dysgenesis (752.7)*

758.7 **Klinefelter's syndrome** ♂

XXY syndrome

✓5th **758.8 Other conditions due to chromosome anomalies**

758.81 Other conditions due to sex chromosome anomalies

758.89 Other

758.9 Conditions due to anomaly of unspecified chromosome

759 Other and unspecified congenital anomalies

759.0 Anomalies of spleen

Aberrant, Absent, Accessory } spleen

Congenital splenomegaly
Ectopic spleen
Lobulation of spleen

759.1 Anomalies of adrenal gland

Aberrant, Absent, Accessory } adrenal gland

Excludes: *adrenogenital disorders (255.2)*
congenital disorders of steroid metabolism (255.2)

759.2 Anomalies of other endocrine glands

Absent parathyroid gland
Accessory thyroid gland
Persistent thyroglossal or thyrolingual duct
Thyroglossal (duct) cyst

Excludes: *congenital:*
goiter (246.1)
hypothyroidism (243)

759.3 Situs inversus

Situs inversus or transversus:
abdominalis
thoracis

Transposition of viscera:
abdominal
thoracic

Excludes: *dextrocardia without mention of complete transposition (746.87)*

759.4 Conjoined twins

Craniopagus
Dicephalus
Pygopagus
Thoracopagus
Xiphopagus

759.5 Tuberous sclerosis

Bourneville's disease
Epiloia

759.6 Other hamartoses, NEC

Syndrome:
Peutz-Jeghers
Sturge-Weber (-Dimitri)
von Hippel-Lindau

Excludes: *neurofibromatosis (237.7)*

759.7 Multiple congenital anomalies, so described

Congenital:
anomaly, multiple NOS
deformity, multiple NOS

✓5th **759.8 Other specified anomalies**

➡ **AHA Coding Clinic:** S-O, '87, 9; S-O, '85, 11

759.81 Prader-Willi syndrome

759.82 Marfan syndrome

➡ **AHA Coding Clinic:** 3Q, '93, 11

759.83 Fragile X syndrome

➡ **AHA Coding Clinic:** 4Q, '94, 41

759.89 Other

Congenital malformation syndromes affecting multiple systems, NEC
Laurence-Moon-Biedl syndrome

759.9 Congenital anomaly, unspecified

15. CERTAIN CONDITIONS ORIGINATING IN THE PERINATAL PERIOD (760-779)

Use additional code(s) to further specify condition

Includes: conditions which have their origin in the perinatal period even though death or morbidity occurs later

MATERNAL CAUSES OF PERINATAL MORBIDITY AND MORTALITY (760-763)

➡ **AHA Coding Clinic:** 2Q, '89, 14; 3Q, '90, 5

760 Fetus or newborn affected by maternal conditions which may be unrelated to present pregnancy

Includes: the listed maternal conditions only when specified as a cause of mortality or morbidity of the fetus or newborn

Excludes: *maternal endocrine and metabolic disorders affecting fetus or newborn (775.0-775.9)*

➡ **AHA Coding Clinic:** 2Q, '92, 12; N-D, '84, 11

760.0 Maternal hypertensive disorders

Fetus or newborn affected by maternal conditions classifiable to 642

760.1 Maternal renal and urinary tract diseases

Fetus or newborn affected by maternal conditions classifiable to 580-599

760.2 Maternal infections

Fetus or newborn affected by maternal infectious disease classifiable to 001-136 and 487, but fetus or newborn not manifesting that disease

Excludes: *congenital infectious diseases (771.0-771.8)*
maternal genital tract and other localized infections (760.8)

760.3 Other chronic maternal circulatory and respiratory diseases

Fetus or newborn affected by chronic maternal conditions classifiable to 390-459, 490-519, 745-748

760.4 Maternal nutritional disorders

Fetus or newborn affected by:
- maternal disorders classifiable to 260-269
- maternal malnutrition NOS

Excludes: *fetal malnutrition (764.10-764.29)*

760.5 Maternal injury

Fetus or newborn affected by maternal conditions classifiable to 800-995

760.6 Surgical operation on mother

Excludes: *cesarean section for present delivery (763.4)*
damage to placenta from amniocentesis, cesarean section, or surgical induction (762.1)
previous surgery to uterus or pelvic organs (763.89)

✓5th **760.7 Noxious influences affecting fetus via placenta or breast milk**

Fetus or newborn affected by noxious substance transmitted via placenta or breast milk

Excludes: *anesthetic and analgesic drugs administered during labor and delivery (763.5)*
drug withdrawal syndrome in newborn (779.5)

➡ **AHA Coding Clinic:** 3Q, '91, 21

760.70 Unspecified noxious substance

Fetus or newborn affected by:
- Drug NEC

760.71 Alcohol

Fetal alcohol syndrome

760.72 Narcotics

760.73 Hallucinogenic agents

760.74 Anti-infectives

Antibiotics

760.75 Cocaine

➡ **AHA Coding Clinic:** 3Q, '94, 6; 2Q, '92, 12; 4Q, '91, 26

760.76 Diethylstilbestrol [DES]

➡ **AHA Coding Clinic:** 4Q, '94, 45

760.79 Other

Fetus or newborn affected by:
- immune sera } transmitted via placenta or breast milk
- medicinal agents NEC }
- toxic substance NEC }

760.8 Other specified maternal conditions affecting fetus or newborn

Maternal genital tract and other localized infection affecting fetus or newborn, but fetus or newborn not manifesting that disease

Excludes: *maternal urinary tract infection affecting fetus or newborn (760.1)*

760.9 Unspecified maternal condition affecting fetus or newborn

761 Fetus or newborn affected by maternal complications of pregnancy

Includes: the listed maternal conditions only when specified as a cause of mortality or morbidity of the fetus or newborn

761.0 Incompetent cervix

761.1 Premature rupture of membranes

761.2 Oligohydramnios

Excludes: *that due to premature rupture of membranes (761.1)*

761.3 Polyhydramnios

Hydramnios (acute) (chronic)

761.4 Ectopic pregnancy

Pregnancy:
- abdominal
- intraperitoneal
- tubal

761.5 Multiple pregnancy

Triplet (pregnancy)
Twin (pregnancy)

761.6 Maternal death

761.7 Malpresentation before labor

Breech presentation, External version, Oblique lie, Transverse lie, Unstable lie — before labor

761.8 Other specified maternal complications of pregnancy affecting fetus or newborn

Spontaneous abortion, fetus

761.9 Unspecified maternal complication of pregnancy affecting fetus or newborn

762 Fetus or newborn affected by complications of placenta, cord, and membranes A: 0

Includes: the listed maternal conditions only when specified as a cause of mortality or morbidity in the fetus or newborn

762.0 Placenta previa

762.1 Other forms of placental separation and hemorrhage

Abruptio placentae
Antepartum hemorrhage
Damage to placenta from amniocentesis, cesarean section, or surgical induction
Maternal blood loss
Premature separation of placenta
Rupture of marginal sinus

762.2 Other and unspecified morphological and functional abnormalities of placenta

Placental:
- dysfunction
- infarction
- insufficiency

762.3 Placental transfusion syndromes

Placental and cord abnormality resulting in twin-to-twin or other transplacental transfusion

Use additional code to indicate resultant condition in fetus or newborn:
- fetal blood loss (772.0)
- polycythemia neonatorum (776.4)

762.4 Prolapsed cord

Cord presentation

762.5 Other compression of umbilical cord

Cord around neck
Entanglement of cord
Knot in cord
Torsion of cord

762.6 Other and unspecified conditions of umbilical cord

Short cord, Thrombosis, Varices, Velamentous insertion — of umbilical cord
Vasa previa

Excludes: *infection of umbilical cord (771.4)*
single umbilical artery (747.5)

762.7 Chorioamnionitis

Amnionitis
Membranitis
Placentitis

762.8 Other specified abnormalities of chorion and amnion

762.9 Unspecified abnormality of chorion and amnion

763 Fetus or newborn affected by other complications of labor and delivery A: 0

Includes: the listed conditions only when specified as a cause of mortality or morbidity in the fetus or newborn

763.0 Breech delivery and extraction

763.1 Other malpresentation, malposition, and disproportion during labor and delivery

Fetus or newborn affected by:
- abnormality of bony pelvis
- contracted pelvis
- persistent occipitoposterior position
- shoulder presentation
- transverse lie
- conditions classifiable to 652, 653, and 660

763.2 Forceps delivery

Fetus or newborn affected by forceps extraction

763.3 Delivery by vacuum extractor

763.4 Cesarean delivery

Excludes: *placental separation or hemorrhage from cesarean section (762.1)*

763.5 Maternal anesthesia and analgesia

Reactions and intoxications from maternal opiates and tranquilizers during labor and delivery

Excludes: *drug withdrawal syndrome in newborn (779.5)*

763.6 Precipitate delivery

Rapid second stage

763.7 Abnormal uterine contractions

Fetus or newborn affected by:
- contraction ring
- hypertonic labor
- hypotonic uterine dysfunction
- uterine inertia or dysfunction
- conditions classifiable to 661, except 661.3

✓5th **763.8 Other specified complications of labor and delivery affecting fetus or newborn**

763.81 Abnormality in fetal heart rate or rhythm before the onset of labor

763.82 Abnormality in fetal heart rate or rhythm during labor

763.83 Abnormality in fetal heart rate or rhythm, unspecified as to time of onset

763.89 Other specified complications of labor and delivery affecting fetus and newborn

Fetus or newborn affected by:
- abnormality of maternal soft tissues
- destructive operation on live fetus to facilitate delivery
- induction of labor (medical)
- previous surgery to uterus or pelvic organs
- other conditions classifiable to 650-669
- other procedures used in labor and delivery

763.9 Unspecified complication of labor and delivery affecting fetus or newborn

OTHER CONDITIONS ORIGINATING IN THE PERINATAL PERIOD (764-779)

The following fifth-digit subclassification is for use with categories 764-765 to denote birthweight:

0	unspecified [weight]	5	1,250-1,499 grams
1	less than 500 grams	6	1,500-1,749 grams
2	500-749 grams	7	1,750-1,999 grams
3	750-999 grams	8	2,000-2,499 grams
4	1,000-1,249 grams	9	2,500 grams and over

§764 Slow fetal growth and fetal malnutrition A: 0

➡ **AHA Coding Clinic:** 2Q, '91, 19; 2Q, '89, 15

✓5th **764.0 "Light-for-dates" without mention of fetal malnutrition**

Infants underweight for gestational age
"Small-for-dates"

✓5th **764.1 "Light-for-dates" with signs of fetal malnutrition**

Infants "light-for-dates" classifiable to 764.0, who in addition show signs of fetal malnutrition, such as dry peeling skin and loss of subcutaneous tissue

✓5th **764.2 Fetal malnutrition without mention of "light-for-dates"**

Infants, not underweight for gestational age, showing signs of fetal malnutrition, such as dry peeling skin and loss of subcutaneous tissue
Intrauterine malnutrition

✓5th **764.9 Fetal growth retardation, unspecified**

Intrauterine growth retardation

➡ **AHA Coding Clinic: For code 764.97:** 1Q, '97, 6

§765 Disorders relating to short gestation and unspecified low birthweight A: 0

Includes: the listed conditions, without further specification, as causes of mortality, morbidity, or additional care, in fetus or newborn

➡ **AHA Coding Clinic:** 2Q, '91, 19; 2Q, '89, 15

✓5th [12] **765.0 Extreme immaturity**

Note: Usually implies a birthweight of less than 1000 grams and/or a gestation of less than 28 completed weeks.

➡ **CC Excl: For Codes 765.01-765.08:** 764.00-764.99, 765.00-765.19, 767.8-767.9, 779.8

✓5th **765.1 Other preterm infants**

Note: Usually implies a birthweight of 1000-2499 grams and/or a gestation of 28-37 completed weeks.

Prematurity NOS
Prematurity or small size, not classifiable to 765.0 or as "light-for-dates" in 764

➡ **AHA Coding Clinic: For code 765.10:** 1Q, '94, 14

➡ **AHA Coding Clinic: For code 765.17:** 1Q, '97, 6

766 Disorders relating to long gestation and high birthweight A: 0

Includes: the listed conditions, without further specification, as causes of mortality, morbidity, or additional care, in fetus or newborn

766.0 Exceptionally large baby

Note: Usually implies a birthweight of 4500 grams or more.

§ Requires fifth-digit. See above for codes and definitions.
[12] CC Coding = 1-8

766.1 Other "heavy-for-dates" infants

Other fetus or infant "heavy-" or "large-for-dates" regardless of period of gestation

766.2 Post-term infant, not "heavy-for-dates"

Fetus or infant with gestation period of 294 days or more [42 or more completed weeks], not "heavy-" or "large-for-dates"
Postmaturity NOS

767 Birth trauma A: 0

767.0 Subdural and cerebral hemorrhage

Subdural and cerebral hemorrhage, whether described as due to birth trauma or to intrapartum anoxia or hypoxia
Subdural hematoma (localized)
Tentorial tear

Use additional code to identify cause

Excludes: *intraventricular hemorrhage (772.1)*
subarachnoid hemorrhage (772.2)

➡ **CC Excl:** 767.0, 767.8-767.9, 779.8

767.1 Injuries to scalp

Caput succedaneum
Cephalhematoma
Chignon (from vacuum extraction)
Massive epicranial subaponeurotic hemorrhage

767.2 Fracture of clavicle

767.3 Other injuries to skeleton

Fracture of:
- long bones
- skull

Excludes: *congenital dislocation of hip (754.30-754.35)*
fracture of spine, congenital (767.4)

767.4 Injury to spine and spinal cord

Dislocation, Fracture, Laceration, Rupture } of spine or spinal cord due to birth trauma

767.5 Facial nerve injury

Facial palsy

767.6 Injury to brachial plexus

Palsy or paralysis:
- brachial
- Erb (-Duchenne)
- Klumpke (-Déjérine)

767.7 Other cranial and peripheral nerve injuries

Phrenic nerve paralysis

767.8 Other specified birth trauma

Eye damage
Hematoma of:
- liver (subcapsular)
- testes
- vulva

Rupture of:
- liver
- spleen

Scalpel wound
Traumatic glaucoma

Excludes: *hemorrhage classifiable to 772.0-772.9*

767.9 Birth trauma, unspecified

Birth injury NOS

768 Intrauterine hypoxia and birth asphyxia A: 0

Use only when associated with newborn morbidity classifiable elsewhere

➡ **AHA Coding Clinic:** 4Q, '92, 20

768.0 Fetal death from asphyxia or anoxia before onset of labor or at unspecified time

768.1 Fetal death from asphyxia or anoxia during labor

768.2 Fetal distress before onset of labor, in liveborn infant

Fetal metabolic acidemia before onset of labor, in liveborn infant

768.3 Fetal distress first noted during labor, in liveborn infant

Fetal metabolic acidemia first noted during labor, in liveborn infant

768.4 Fetal distress, unspecified as to time of onset, in liveborn infant

Fetal metabolic acidemia unspecified as to time of onset, in liveborn infant

➡ **AHA Coding Clinic:** N-D, '86, 10

768.5 Severe birth asphyxia

Birth asphyxia with neurologic involvement

➡ **CC Excl:** 768.5-768.9, 769, 770.0-770.9, 779.8

➡ **AHA Coding Clinic:** N-D, '86, 3

768.6 Mild or moderate birth asphyxia

Other specified birth asphyxia (without mention of neurologic involvement)

➡ **AHA Coding Clinic:** N-D, '86, 3

768.9 Unspecified birth asphyxia in liveborn infant

Anoxia / Asphyxia / Hypoxia } NOS, in liveborn infant

769 Respiratory distress syndrome A: 0

Cardiorespiratory distress syndrome of newborn
Hyaline membrane disease (pulmonary)
Idiopathic respiratory distress syndrome [IRDS or RDS] of newborn
Pulmonary hypoperfusion syndrome

Excludes: *transient tachypnea of newborn (770.6)*

➡ **CC Excl:** see Code 768.5

➡ **AHA Coding Clinic:** 1Q, '89, 10; N-D, '86, 6

770 Other respiratory conditions of fetus and newborn A: 0

770.0 Congenital pneumonia

Infective pneumonia acquired prenatally

Excludes: *pneumonia from infection acquired after birth (480.0-486)*

➡ **CC Excl:** see Code 768.5

770.1 Meconium aspiration syndrome

Aspiration of contents of birth canal NOS
Meconium aspiration below vocal cords
Pneumonitis:
- fetal aspiration
- meconium

➡ **CC Excl:** see Code 768.5

770.2 Interstitial emphysema and related conditions

Pneumomediastinum / Pneumopericardium / Pneumothorax } originating in the perinatal period

➡ **CC Excl:** see Code 768.5

770.3 Pulmonary hemorrhage

Hemorrhage:
- alveolar (lung)
- intra-alveolar (lung)
- massive pulmonary

} originating in the perinatal period

➡ **CC Excl:** see Code 768.5

770.4 Primary atelectasis

Pulmonary immaturity NOS

➡ **CC Excl:** see Code 768.5

770.5 Other and unspecified atelectasis

Atelectasis:
- NOS
- partial
- secondary

Pulmonary collapse

} originating in the perinatal period

➡ **CC Excl:** see Code 768.5

770.6 Transitory tachypnea of newborn

Idiopathic tachypnea of newborn
Wet lung syndrome

Excludes: *respiratory distress syndrome (769)*

➡ **AHA Coding Clinic:** 3Q, '93, 7; 1Q, '89, 10; N-D, '86, 6

770.7 Chronic respiratory disease arising in the perinatal period

Bronchopulmonary dysplasia
Interstitial pulmonary fibrosis of prematurity
Wilson-Mikity syndrome

➡ **CC Excl:** see Code 768.5

➡ **AHA Coding Clinic:** 2Q, '91, 19; N-D, '86, 11

770.8 Other respiratory problems after birth

Apneic spells NOS / Cyanotic attacks NOS / Respiratory distress NOS / Respiratory failure NOS } originating in the perinatal period

Fetal:
- acidosis
- anoxia
- asphyxia
- hypercapnia
- hypoxia

} affecting newborn

Respiratory depression of newborn

➡ **AHA Coding Clinic:** 2Q, '96, 10

770.9 Unspecified respiratory condition of fetus and newborn

771 Infections specific to the perinatal period A: 0

Includes: infections acquired before or during birth or via the umbilicus

Excludes: *congenital pneumonia (770.0)*
congenital syphilis (090.0-090.9)
maternal infectious disease as a cause of mortality or morbidity in fetus or newborn, but fetus or newborn not manifesting the disease (760.2)
ophthalmia neonatorum due to gonococcus (098.40)
other infections not specifically classified to this category

➡ **AHA Coding Clinic:** N-D, '85, 4

771.0 Congenital rubella

Congenital rubella pneumonitis

➡ **CC Excl:** 771.0-771.2, 779.8

771.1 Congenital cytomegalovirus infection

Congenital cytomegalic inclusion disease

➡ **CC Excl:** see Code 771.0

771.2 Other congenital infections

Congenital:
- herpes simplex
- listeriosis
- malaria
- toxoplasmosis
- tuberculosis

771.3 Tetanus neonatorum

Tetanus omphalitis

Excludes: *hypocalcemic tetany (775.4)*

➡ **CC Excl:** 771.3, 779.8

771.4 Omphalitis of the newborn

Infection:
- navel cord
- umbilical stump

Excludes: *tetanus omphalitis (771.3)*

771.5 Neonatal infective mastitis

Excludes: *noninfective neonatal mastitis (778.7)*

771.6 Neonatal conjunctivitis and dacryocystitis

Ophthalmia neonatorum NOS

Excludes: *ophthalmia neonatorum due to gonococcus (098.40)*

771.7 Neonatal Candida infection

Neonatal moniliasis
Thrush in newborn

771.8 Other infection specific to the perinatal period

Intra-amniotic infection of fetus:
- NOS
- clostridial
- Escherichia coli [E. coli]

Intrauterine sepsis of fetus
Neonatal urinary tract infection
Septicemia [sepsis] of newborn

➡ **CC Excl:** 771.4-771.8, 776.0-776.9, 779.8

772 Fetal and neonatal hemorrhage A: 0

Excludes: *hematological disorders of fetus and newborn (776.0-776.9)*

772.0 Fetal blood loss

Fetal blood loss from:
- cut end of co-twin's cord
- placenta
- ruptured cord
- vasa previa

Fetal exsanguination
Fetal hemorrhage into:
- co-twin
- mother's circulation

772.1 Intraventricular hemorrhage

Intraventricular hemorrhage from any perinatal cause

➡ **CC Excl:** 772.0-772.2, 772.8-772.9, 776.0-776.9, 779.8

➡ **AHA Coding Clinic:** 3Q, '92, 8; 4Q, '88, 8

772.2 Subarachnoid hemorrhage

Subarachnoid hemorrhage from any perinatal cause

Excludes: *subdural and cerebral hemorrhage (767.0)*

➡ **CC Excl:** see Code 772.1

772.3 Umbilical hemorrhage after birth

Slipped umbilical ligature

772.4 Gastrointestinal hemorrhage

Excludes: *swallowed maternal blood (777.3)*

➡ **CC Excl:** 772.0, 772.4-772.5, 772.8-772.9, 776.0-776.9, 779.8

772.5 Adrenal hemorrhage

➡ **CC Excl:** see Code 772.4

772.6 Cutaneous hemorrhage

Bruising / Ecchymoses / Petechiae / Superficial hematoma — in fetus or newborn

772.8 Other specified hemorrhage of fetus or newborn

Excludes: *hemorrhagic disease of newborn (776.0)*
pulmonary hemorrhage (770.3)

772.9 Unspecified hemorrhage of newborn

773 Hemolytic disease of fetus or newborn, due to isoimmunization A: 0

773.0 Hemolytic disease due to Rh isoimmunization

Anemia / Erythroblastosis (fetalis) / Hemolytic disease (fetus) (newborn) / Jaundice — due to Rh:
- antibodies
- isoimmunization
- maternal/fetal incompatibility

Rh hemolytic disease
Rh isoimmunization

➡ **CC Excl:** 773.0-773.5, 779.8

773.1 Hemolytic disease due to ABO isoimmunization

ABO hemolytic disease
ABO isoimmunization

Anemia / Erythroblastosis (fetalis) / Hemolytic disease (fetus) (newborn) / Jaundice — due to ABO:
- antibodies
- isoimmunization
- maternal/fetal incompatibility

➡ **CC Excl:** see Code 773.0

➡ **AHA Coding Clinic:** 3Q, '92, 8

773.2 Hemolytic disease due to other and unspecified isoimmunization

Erythroblastosis (fetalis) (neonatorum) NOS
Hemolytic disease (fetus) (newborn) NOS
Jaundice or anemia due to other and unspecified blood-group incompatibility

➡ **CC Excl:** see Code 773.0

➡ **AHA Coding Clinic:** 1Q, '94, 13

773.3 Hydrops fetalis due to isoimmunization

Use additional code to identify type of isoimmunization (773.0-773.2)

➡ **CC Excl:** see Code 773.0

773.4 Kernicterus due to isoimmunization

Use additional code to identify type of isoimmunization (773.0-773.2)

➡ **CC Excl:** see Code 773.0

773.5 Late anemia due to isoimmunization

774 Other perinatal jaundice

A: 0

774.0 *Perinatal jaundice from hereditary hemolytic anemias*

Code first underlying disease (282.0-282.9)

➡ **CC Excl:** 774.0-774.7, 779.8

774.1 Perinatal jaundice from other excessive hemolysis

Fetal or neonatal jaundice from:
- bruising
- drugs or toxins transmitted from mother
- infection
- polycythemia
- swallowed maternal blood

Use additional code to identify cause

Excludes: *jaundice due to isoimmunization (773.0-773.2)*

➡ **CC Excl:** see Code 774.0

774.2 Neonatal jaundice associated with preterm delivery

Hyperbilirubinemia of prematurity
Jaundice due to delayed conjugation associated with preterm delivery

➡ **CC Excl:** see Code 774.0

➡ **AHA Coding Clinic:** 3Q, '91, 21

✓5th **774.3 Neonatal jaundice due to delayed conjugation from other causes**

774.30 Neonatal jaundice due to delayed conjugation, cause unspecified

➡ **CC Excl:** see Code 774.0

774.31 *Neonatal jaundice due to delayed conjugation in diseases classified elsewhere*

Code first underlying diseases as:
- congenital hypothyroidism (243)
- Crigler-Najjar syndrome (277.4)
- Gilbert's syndrome (277.4)

➡ **CC Excl:** see Code 774.0

774.39 Other

Jaundice due to delayed conjugation from causes, such as:
- breast milk inhibitors
- delayed development of conjugating system

➡ **CC Excl:** see Code 774.0

774.4 Perinatal jaundice due to hepatocellular damage

Fetal or neonatal hepatitis
Giant cell hepatitis
Inspissated bile syndrome

➡ **CC Excl:** see Code 774.0

774.5 *Perinatal jaundice from other causes*

Code first underlying diseases as:
- congenital obstruction of bile duct (751.61)
- galactosemia (271.1)
- mucoviscidosis (277.00-277.01)

➡ **CC Excl:** see Code 774.0

774.6 Unspecified fetal and neonatal jaundice

Icterus neonatorum
Neonatal hyperbilirubinemia (transient)
Physiologic jaundice NOS in newborn

Excludes: *that in preterm infants (774.2)*

➡ **AHA Coding Clinic:** 1Q, '94, 13; 2Q, '89, 15

774.7 Kernicterus not due to isoimmunization

Bilirubin encephalopathy
Kernicterus of newborn NOS

Excludes: *kernicterus due to isoimmunization (773.4)*

➡ **CC Excl:** see Code 774.0

775 Endocrine and metabolic disturbances specific to the fetus and newborn A: 0

Includes: transitory endocrine and metabolic disturbances caused by the infant's response to maternal endocrine and metabolic factors, its removal from them, or its adjustment to extrauterine existence

775.0 Syndrome of "infant of a diabetic mother"

Maternal diabetes mellitus affecting fetus or newborn (with hypoglycemia)

➡ **AHA Coding Clinic:** 3Q, '91, 5

775.1 Neonatal diabetes mellitus

Diabetes mellitus syndrome in newborn infant

➡ **CC Excl:** 775.0-775.9, 779.8

➡ **AHA Coding Clinic:** 3Q, '91, 6

775.2 Neonatal myasthenia gravis

➡ **CC Excl:** see Code 775.1

775.3 Neonatal thyrotoxicosis

Neonatal hyperthyroidism (transient)

➡ **CC Excl:** see Code 775.1

775.4 Hypocalcemia and hypomagnesemia of newborn

Cow's milk hypocalcemia
Hypocalcemic tetany, neonatal
Neonatal hypoparathyroidism
Phosphate-loading hypocalcemia

➡ **CC Excl:** see Code 775.1

775.5 Other transitory neonatal electrolyte disturbances

Dehydration, neonatal

➡ **CC Excl:** see Code 775.1

775.6 Neonatal hypoglycemia

Excludes: *infant of mother with diabetes mellitus (775.0)*

➡ **CC Excl:** see Code 775.1

775.7 Late metabolic acidosis of newborn

➡ **CC Excl:** see Code 775.1

775.8 Other transitory neonatal endocrine and metabolic disturbances

Amino-acid metabolic disorders described as transitory

775.9 Unspecified endocrine and metabolic disturbances specific to the fetus and newborn

776 Hematological disorders of fetus and newborn A: 0

Includes: disorders specific to the fetus or newborn

776.0 Hemorrhagic disease of newborn

Hemorrhagic diathesis of newborn
Vitamin K deficiency of newborn

Excludes: *fetal or neonatal hemorrhage (772.0-772.9)*

➡ **CC Excl:** 776.0-776.9, 779.8

776.1 Transient neonatal thrombocytopenia

Neonatal thrombocytopenia due to:
exchange transfusion
idiopathic maternal thrombocytopenia
isoimmunization

➡ **CC Excl:** see Code 776.0

776.2 Disseminated intravascular coagulation in newborn

➡ **CC Excl:** see Code 776.0

776.3 Other transient neonatal disorders of coagulation

Transient coagulation defect, newborn

➡ **CC Excl:** see Code 776.0

776.4 Polycythemia neonatorum

Plethora of newborn
Polycythemia due to:
donor twin transfusion
maternal-fetal transfusion

776.5 Congenital anemia

Anemia following fetal blood loss

Excludes: *anemia due to isoimmunization (773.0-773.2, 773.5)*
hereditary hemolytic anemias (282.0-282.9)

776.6 Anemia of prematurity

776.7 Transient neonatal neutropenia

Isoimmune neutropenia
Maternal transfer neutropenia

Excludes: *congenital neutropenia (nontransient) (288.0)*

776.8 Other specified transient hematological disorders

776.9 Unspecified hematological disorder specific to fetus or newborn

777 Perinatal disorders of digestive system A: 0

Includes: disorders specific to the fetus and newborn

Excludes: *intestinal obstruction classifiable to 560.0-560.9*

777.1 Meconium obstruction

Congenital fecaliths
Delayed passage of meconium
Meconium ileus NOS
Meconium plug syndrome

Excludes: *meconium ileus in cystic fibrosis (277.01)*

➡ **CC Excl:** 777.1-777.9, 779.8

777.2 Intestinal obstruction due to inspissated milk

➡ **CC Excl:** see Code 777.1

777.3 Hematemesis and melena due to swallowed maternal blood
Swallowed blood syndrome in newborn

Excludes: *that not due to swallowed maternal blood (772.4)*

777.4 Transitory ileus of newborn

Excludes: *Hirschsprung's disease (751.3)*

777.5 Necrotizing enterocolitis in fetus or newborn
Pseudomembranous enterocolitis in newborn

➡ **CC Excl:** see Code 777.1

777.6 Perinatal intestinal perforation
Meconium peritonitis

➡ **CC Excl:** see Code 777.1

777.8 Other specified perinatal disorders of digestive system

777.9 Unspecified perinatal disorder of digestive system

778 Conditions involving the integument and temperature regulation of fetus and newborn

778.0 Hydrops fetalis not due to isoimmunization A: 0
Idiopathic hydrops

Excludes: *hydrops fetalis due to isoimmunization (773.3)*

➡ **CC Excl:** 778.0, 779.8

778.1 Sclerema neonatorum A: 0
Subcutaneous fat necrosis

778.2 Cold injury syndrome of newborn A: 0

778.3 Other hypothermia of newborn A: 0

778.4 Other disturbances of temperature regulation of newborn A: 0
Dehydration fever in newborn
Environmentally induced pyrexia
Hyperthermia in newborn
Transitory fever of newborn

778.5 Other and unspecified edema of newborn A: 0
Edema neonatorum

778.6 Congenital hydrocele
Congenital hydrocele of tunica vaginalis

778.7 Breast engorgement in newborn A: 0
Noninfective mastitis of newborn

Excludes: *infective mastitis of newborn (771.5)*

778.8 Other specified conditions involving the integument of fetus and newborn A: 0
Urticaria neonatorum

Excludes: *impetigo neonatorum (684)*
pemphigus neonatorum (684)

778.9 Unspecified condition involving the integument and temperature regulation of fetus and newborn A: 0

779 Other and ill-defined conditions originating in the perinatal period A: 0

779.0 Convulsions in newborn
Fits } in newborn
Seizures }

➡ **CC Excl:** 779.0-779.1, 779.8

779.1 Other and unspecified cerebral irritability in newborn

➡ **CC Excl:** see Code 779.0

779.2 Cerebral depression, coma, and other abnormal cerebral signs
CNS dysfunction in newborn NOS

779.3 Feeding problems in newborn
Regurgitation of food }
Slow feeding } in newborn
Vomiting }

➡ **CC Excl:** 779.3

➡ **AHA Coding Clinic:** 2Q, '89, 15

779.4 Drug reactions and intoxications specific to newborn
Gray syndrome from chloramphenicol administration in newborn

Excludes: *fetal alcohol syndrome (760.71)*
reactions and intoxications from maternal opiates and tranquilizers (763.5)

➡ **CC Excl:** 779.4-779.5

779.5 Drug withdrawal syndrome in newborn
Drug withdrawal syndrome in infant of dependent mother

Excludes: *fetal alcohol syndrome (760.71)*

779.6 Termination of pregnancy (fetus)
Fetal death due to:
induced abortion
termination of pregnancy

Excludes: *spontaneous abortion (fetus) (761.8)*

779.8 Other specified conditions originating in the perinatal period

➡ **AHA Coding Clinic:** 1Q, '94, 15

779.9 Unspecified condition originating in the perinatal period
Congenital debility NOS
Stillbirth NEC

16. SYMPTOMS, SIGNS, AND ILL-DEFINED CONDITIONS (780-799)

This section includes symptoms, signs, abnormal results of laboratory or other investigative procedures, and ill-defined conditions regarding which no diagnosis classifiable elsewhere is recorded.

Signs and symptoms that point rather definitely to a given diagnosis are assigned to some category in the preceding part of the classification. In general, categories 780-796 include the more ill-defined conditions and symptoms that point with perhaps equal suspicion to two or more diseases or to two or more systems of the body, and without the necessary study of the case to make a final diagnosis. Practically all categories in this group could be designated as "not otherwise specified," or as "unknown etiology," or as "transient." The Alphabetic Index should be consulted to determine which symptoms and signs are to be allocated here and which to more specific sections of the classification; the residual subcategories numbered .9 are provided for other relevant symptoms which cannot be allocated elsewhere in the classification.

The conditions and signs or symptoms included in categories 780-796 consist of: (a) cases for which no more specific diagnosis can be made even after all facts bearing on the case have been investigated; (b) signs or symptoms existing at the time of initial encounter that proved to be transient and whose causes could not be determined; (c) provisional diagnoses in a patient who failed to return for further investigation or care; (d) cases referred elsewhere for investigation or treatment before the diagnosis was made; (e) cases in which a more precise diagnosis was not available for any other reason; (f) certain symptoms which represent important problems in medical care and which it might be desired to classify in addition to a known cause.

SYMPTOMS (780-789)

➡ **AHA Coding Clinic:** 1Q, '91, 12; 2Q, '90, 3; 2Q, '90, 5; 2Q, '90, 15; M-A, '85, 3

780 General symptoms

✓5th **780.0 Alteration of consciousness**

Excludes: *coma:*
diabetic (250.2-250.3)
hepatic (572.2)
originating in the perinatal period (779.2)

➡ **AHA Coding Clinic:** 4Q, '92, 20

780.01 Coma

➡ **CC Excl:** 070.0-070.9, 250.00-250.93, 251.0-251.3, 348.8-348.9, 349.89, 349.9, 430-431, 432.0-432.9, 572.2, 780.01, 780.2, 780.3, 780.4, 780.9, 799.8, 800.00-800.99, 801.00-801.99, 803.00-803.99, 804.00-804.96, 850.0-850.9, 851.00-851.99, 852.00-852.19, 852.21-852.59, 853.00-853.19, 854.00-854.19,

➡ **AHA Coding Clinic:** 3Q, '96, 16

780.02 Transient alteration of awareness

780.03 Persistent vegetative state

➡ **CC Excl:** 070.0-070.9, 250.00-250.93, 251.0-251.3, 348.8-348.9, 349.89-349.9, 430-431, 432.0-432.9, 572.2, 780.01-780.09, 780.2, 780.4, 780.9, 799.8, 800.00-800.05, 800.10-800.19, 800.20-800.99, 801.00-801.99, 803.00-803.99, 804.00-804.55

780.09 Other

Drowsiness
Semicoma
Unconsciousness
Somnolence
Stupor

780.1 Hallucinations

Hallucinations:
NOS
auditory
gustatory
olfactory
tactile

Excludes: *those associated with mental disorders, as functional psychoses (295.0-298.9)*
organic brain syndromes (290.0-294.9, 310.0-310.9)
visual hallucinations (368.16)

➡ **CC Excl:** 780.1, 780.4, 780.9, 799.8

780.2 Syncope and collapse

Blackout
Fainting
(Near) (Pre) syncope
Vasovagal attack

Excludes: *carotid sinus syncope (337.0)*
heat syncope (992.1)
neurocirculatory asthenia (306.2)
orthostatic hypotension (458.0)
shock NOS (785.50)

➡ **AHA Coding Clinic:** 3Q, '95, 14; N-D, '85, 12

✓5th **780.3 Convulsions**

Excludes: *convulsions:*
epileptic (345.10-345.91)
in newborn (779.0)

➡ **AHA Coding Clinic:** 2Q, '97, 8; 1Q, '97, 12; 3Q, '94, 9; 1Q, '93, 24; 4Q, '92, 23; N-D, '87, 12

✓ **St. Anthony's Clinical Coder:** see Chapter 5

780.31 Febrile convulsions

Febrile seizures

➡ **CC Excl:** 345.00-345.01, 345.10-345.11, 345.2-345.3, 345.40-345.41, 345.50-345.51, 345.60-345.61, 345.70-345.71, 345.80-345.81, 345.90-345.91, 348.8-348.9, 349.89, 349.9, 779.0-779.1, 780.31, 780.39, 780.9, 799.8

➡ **AHA Coding Clinic:** 4Q, '97, 45

780.39 Other convulsions

Convulsive disorder NOS
Fit NOS
Seizure NOS

➡ **CC Excl:** see Code 780.31

780.4 Dizziness and giddiness

Light-headedness
Vertigo NOS

Excludes: *Ménière's disease and other specified vertiginous syndromes (386.0-386.9)*

➡ **AHA Coding Clinic:** 2Q, '97, 9; 2Q, '91, 17

✓5th **780.5 Sleep disturbances**

Excludes: *that of nonorganic origin (307.40-307.49)*

780.50 Sleep disturbance, unspecified

780.51 Insomnia with sleep apnea

➡ **AHA Coding Clinic:** 1Q, '93, 28; N-D, '85, 4

780.52 Other insomnia

Insomnia NOS

780.53 Hypersomnia with sleep apnea

➡ **AHA Coding Clinic:** 1Q, '93, 28; N-D, '85, 4

780.54 Other hypersomnia

Hypersomnia NOS

780.55 Disruptions of 24-hour sleep-wake cycle

Inversion of sleep rhythm
Irregular sleep-wake rhythm NOS
Non-24-hour sleep-wake rhythm

780.56 Dysfunctions associated with sleep stages or arousal from sleep

780.57 Other and unspecified sleep apnea

➡ **AHA Coding Clinic:** 1Q, '97, 5; 1Q, '93, 28

780.59 Other

780.6 Fever

Chills with fever
Fever NOS
Fever of unknown origin (FUO)
Hyperpyrexia NOS
Pyrexia NOS
Pyrexia of unknown origin

Excludes: *pyrexia of unknown origin (during):*
in newborn (778.4)
labor (659.2)
the puerperium (672)

➡ **AHA Coding Clinic:** 2Q, '91, 8

✓5th **780.7 Malaise and fatigue**

Excludes: *debility, unspecified (799.3)*
fatigue (during):
combat (308.0-308.9)
heat (992.6)
pregnancy (646.8)
neurasthenia (300.5)
senile asthenia (797)

➡ **AHA Coding Clinic:** M-A, '87, 8

780.71 Chronic fatigue syndrome

780.79 Other malaise and fatigue

Asthenia NOS
Lethargy
Postviral (asthenic) syndrome
Tiredness

780.8 Hyperhidrosis

Diaphoresis
Excessive sweating

780.9 Other general symptoms

Amnesia (retrograde)
Chill(s) NOS
Generalized pain
Hypothermia, not associated with low environmental temperature

Excludes: *hypothermia:*
NOS (accidental) (991.6)
due to anesthesia (995.89)
of newborn (778.2-778.3)
memory disturbance as part of a pattern of mental disorder

➡ **AHA Coding Clinic:** 3Q, '93, 11; N-D, '85, 12

781 Symptoms involving nervous and musculoskeletal systems

Excludes: *depression NOS (311)*
disorders specifically relating to:
back (724.0-724.9)
hearing (388.0-389.9)
joint (718.0-719.9)
limb (729.0-729.9)
neck (723.0-723.9)
vision (368.0-369.9)
pain in limb (729.5)

781.0 Abnormal involuntary movements

Abnormal head movements
Fasciculation
Spasms NOS
Tremor NOS

Excludes: *abnormal reflex (796.1)*
chorea NOS (333.5)
infantile spasms (345.60-345.61)
spastic paralysis (342.1, 343.0-344.9)
specified movement disorders classifiable to 333 (333.0-333.9)
that of nonorganic origin (307.2-307.3)

781.1 Disturbances of sensation of smell and taste

Anosmia
Parageusia
Parosmia

781.2 Abnormality of gait

Gait:
ataxic
paralytic
spastic
staggering

Excludes: *ataxia:*
NOS (781.3)
locomotor (progressive) (094.0)
difficulty in walking (719.7)

781.3 Lack of coordination

Ataxia NOS
Muscular incoordination

Excludes: *ataxic gait (781.2)*
cerebellar ataxia (334.0-334.9)
difficulty in walking (719.7)
vertigo NOS (780.4)

➡ **AHA Coding Clinic:** 3Q, '97, 12

781.4 Transient paralysis of limb
Monoplegia, transient NOS

Excludes: *paralysis (342.0-344.9)*

781.5 Clubbing of fingers

781.6 Meningismus
Dupré's syndrome
Meningism

➡ **AHA Coding Clinic:** J-F, '87, 7

781.7 Tetany
Carpopedal spasm

Excludes: *tetanus neonatorum (771.3)*
tetany:
hysterical (300.11)
newborn (hypocalcemic) (775.4)
parathyroid (252.1)
psychogenic (306.0)

➡ **CC Excl:** 037, 332.0-332.1, 333.0-333.99, 334.0-334.4, 342.10-342.12, 771.3, 780.9, 781.7, 799.8

781.8 Neurologic neglect syndrome
Asomatognosia
Hemi-akinesia
Hemi-inattention
Hemispatial neglect
Left-sided neglect
Sensory extinction
Sensory neglect
Visuospatial neglect

➡ **AHA Coding Clinic:** 4Q, '94, 37

781.9 Other symptoms involving nervous and musculoskeletal systems
Abnormal posture

782 Symptoms involving skin and other integumentary tissue

Excludes: *symptoms relating to breast (611.71-611.79)*

782.0 Disturbance of skin sensation
Anesthesia of skin
Burning or prickling sensation
Hyperesthesia
Hypoesthesia
Numbness
Paresthesia
Tingling

782.1 Rash and other nonspecific skin eruption
Exanthem

Excludes: *vesicular eruption (709.8)*

782.2 Localized superficial swelling, mass, or lump
Subcutaneous nodules

Excludes: *localized adiposity (278.1)*

782.3 Edema
Anasarca
Dropsy
Localized edema NOS

Excludes: *ascites (789.5)*
edema of:
newborn NOS (778.5)
pregnancy (642.0-642.9, 646.1)
fluid retention (276.6)
hydrops fetalis (773.3, 778.0)
hydrothorax (511.8)
nutritional edema (260, 262)

782.4 Jaundice, unspecified, not of newborn
Cholemia NOS
Icterus NOS

Excludes: *jaundice in newborn (774.0-774.7)*
due to isoimmunization (773.0-773.2, 773.4)

782.5 Cyanosis

Excludes: *newborn (770.8)*

✓5th **782.6 Pallor and flushing**

782.61 Pallor

782.62 Flushing
Excessive blushing

782.7 Spontaneous ecchymoses
Petechiae

Excludes: *ecchymosis in fetus or newborn (772.6)*
purpura (287.0-287.9)

782.8 Changes in skin texture
Induration } of skin
Thickening } of skin

782.9 Other symptoms involving skin and integumentary tissues

783 Symptoms concerning nutrition, metabolism, and development

783.0 Anorexia
Loss of appetite

Excludes: *anorexia nervosa (307.1)*
loss of appetite of nonorganic origin (307.59)

783.1 Abnormal weight gain

Excludes: *excessive weight gain in pregnancy (646.1)*
obesity (278.00)
morbid (278.01)

783.2 Abnormal loss of weight

783.3 Feeding difficulties and mismanagement
Feeding problem (elderly) (infant)

Excludes: *feeding disturbance or problems:*
in newborn (779.3)
of nonorganic origin (307.50-307.59)

➡ **AHA Coding Clinic:** 3Q, '97, 12

783.4 Lack of expected normal physiological development
Delayed milestone
Failure to gain weight
Failure to thrive
Lack of growth
Physical retardation
Short stature

Excludes: *delay in sexual development and puberty (259.0)*
specific delays in mental development (315.0-315.9)

➡ **AHA Coding Clinic:** 3Q, '97, 4

783.5 Polydipsia
Excessive thirst

783.6 Polyphagia
Excessive eating
Hyperalimentation NOS

Excludes: *disorders of eating of nonorganic origin (307.50-307.59)*

783.9 Other symptoms concerning nutrition, metabolism, and development

Hypometabolism

Excludes: *abnormal basal metabolic rate (794.7)*
dehydration (276.5)
other disorders of fluid, electrolyte, and acid-base balance (276.0-276.9)

784 Symptoms involving head and neck

Excludes: *encephalopathy NOS (348.3)*
specific symptoms involving neck classifiable to 723 (723.0-723.9)

784.0 Headache
Facial pain
Pain in head NOS

Excludes: *atypical face pain (350.2)*
migraine (346.0-346.9)
tension headache (307.81)

➡ **AHA Coding Clinic:** 3Q, '92, 14

784.1 Throat pain

Excludes: *dysphagia (787.2)*
neck pain (723.1)
sore throat (462)
chronic (472.1)

784.2 Swelling, mass, or lump in head and neck
Space-occupying lesion, intracranial NOS

784.3 Aphasia

Excludes: *developmental aphasia (315.31)*

➡ **AHA Coding Clinic:** 3Q, '97, 12

✓5th **784.4 Voice disturbance**

784.40 Voice disturbance, unspecified

784.41 Aphonia
Loss of voice

784.49 Other
Change in voice
Dysphonia
Hoarseness
Hypernasality
Hyponasality

784.5 Other speech disturbance
Dysarthria
Dysphasia
Slurred speech

Excludes: *stammering and stuttering (307.0)*
that of nonorganic origin (307.0, 307.9)

✓5th **784.6 Other symbolic dysfunction**

Excludes: *developmental learning delays (315.0-315.9)*

784.60 Symbolic dysfunction, unspecified

784.61 Alexia and dyslexia
Alexia (with agraphia)

784.69 Other
Acalculia
Agnosia
Agraphia NOS
Apraxia

784.7 Epistaxis
Hemorrhage from nose
Nosebleed

784.8 Hemorrhage from throat

Excludes: *hemoptysis (786.3)*

784.9 Other symptoms involving head and neck
Choking sensation
Halitosis
Mouth breathing
Sneezing

785 Symptoms involving cardiovascular system

Excludes: *heart failure NOS (428.9)*

785.0 Tachycardia, unspecified
Rapid heart beat

Excludes: *paroxysmal tachycardia (427.0-427.2)*

785.1 Palpitations
Awareness of heart beat

Excludes: *specified dysrhythmias (427.0-427.9)*

785.2 **Undiagnosed cardiac murmurs**
Heart murmur NOS

785.3 **Other abnormal heart sounds**
Cardiac dullness, increased or decreased
Friction fremitus, cardiac
Precordial friction

785.4 **Gangrene**
Gangrene:
NOS
spreading cutaneous
Gangrenous cellulitis
Phagedena

Code first any associated underlying condition

Use additional code for any associated condition, as:
diabetes (250.7)
Raynaud's syndrome (443.0)

Excludes: *gangrene of certain sites — see Alphabetic Index*
gangrene with atherosclerosis of the extremities (440.24)
gas gangrene (040.0)

➡ **CC Excl:** 440.24, 780.9, 785.4, 799.8

➡ **AHA Coding Clinic:** 3Q, '90, 15; M-A, '86, 12

✓5th **785.5** **Shock without mention of trauma**

785.50 **Shock, unspecified**
Failure of peripheral circulation

➡ **CC Excl:** 780.9, 785.50-785.59, 785.9, 799.8

➡ **AHA Coding Clinic:** 2Q, '96, 10

✔ **St. Anthony's Clinical Coder:** see Chapter 6

785.51 **Cardiogenic shock**

➡ **CC Excl:** see Code 785.50

✔ **St. Anthony's Clinical Coder:** see Chapters 5 & 7

785.59 **Other**
Shock:
endotoxic
gram-negative
hypovolemic
septic

Excludes: *shock (due to):*
anesthetic (995.4)
anaphylactic (995.0)
due to serum (999.4)
electric (994.8)
following abortion (639.5)
lightning (994.0)
obstetrical (669.1)
postoperative (998.0)
traumatic (958.4)

➡ **CC Excl:** see Code 785.50

✔ **St. Anthony's Clinical Coder:** see Chapters 5 & 7

785.6 **Enlargement of lymph nodes**
Lymphadenopathy
"Swollen glands"

Excludes: *lymphadenitis (chronic) (289.1-289.3)*
acute (683)

785.9 **Other symptoms involving cardiovascular system**
Bruit (arterial)
Weak pulse

786 **Symptoms involving respiratory system and other chest symptoms**

✓5th **786.0** **Dyspnea and respiratory abnormalities**

786.00 **Respiratory abnormality, unspecified**

786.01 **Hyperventilation**

Excludes: *hyperventilation, psychogenic (306.1)*

786.02 **Orthopnea**

786.03 **Apnea**

Excludes: *sleep apnea (780.51, 780.53, 780.57)*

➡ **CC Excl:** 518.81-518.89, 519.8, 519.9, 786.03, 786.04, 799.1

786.04 **Cheyne-Stokes respiration**

➡ **CC Excl:** 518.81-518.89, 519.8, 519.9, 786.03, 786.04, 799.1

786.05 **Shortness of breath**

786.06 **Tachypnea**

Excludes: *transitory tachypnea of newborn (770.6)*

786.07 **Wheezing**

Excludes: *asthma (493.00-493.91)*

786.09 **Other**
Respiratory:
distress
insufficiency

Excludes: *respiratory distress:*
following trauma and surgery (518.5)
newborn (770.8)
syndrome (newborn) (769)
adult (518.5)
respiratory failure (518.81, 518.83-518.84)
newborn (770.8)

➡ **AHA Coding Clinic:** 1Q, '97, 7

786.1 **Stridor**

Excludes: *congenital laryngeal stridor (748.3)*

786.2 **Cough**

Excludes: *cough:*
psychogenic (306.1)
smokers' (491.0)
with hemorrhage (786.3)

786.3 **Hemoptysis**
Cough with hemorrhage
Pulmonary hemorrhage NOS

Excludes: *pulmonary hemorrhage of newborn (770.3)*

➡ **CC Excl:** 780.9, 786.3-786.4, 786.9, 799.8

➡ **AHA Coding Clinic:** 4Q, '90, 26

786.4 Abnormal sputum

Abnormal: (of) sputum
- amount
- color
- odor

Excessive (of) sputum

✓5th **786.5 Chest pain**

786.50 Chest pain, unspecified

786.51 Precordial pain

786.52 Painful respiration

Pain:
- anterior chest wall
- pleuritic

Pleurodynia

Excludes: *epidemic pleurodynia (074.1)*

➡ **AHA Coding Clinic:** N-D, '84, 17

786.59 Other

Discomfort / Pressure / Tightness } in chest

Excludes: *pain in breast (611.71)*

786.6 Swelling, mass, or lump in chest

Excludes: *lump in breast (611.72)*

786.7 Abnormal chest sounds

Abnormal percussion, chest
Friction sounds, chest
Rales
Tympany, chest

Excludes: *wheezing (786.07)*

786.8 Hiccough

Excludes: *psychogenic hiccough (306.1)*

786.9 Other symptoms involving respiratory system and chest

Breath-holding spell

787 Symptoms involving digestive system

Excludes: *constipation (564.0)*
pylorospasm (537.81)
congenital (750.5)

✓5th **787.0 Nausea and vomiting**

Emesis

Excludes: *hematemesis NOS (578.0)*
vomiting:
- *bilious, following gastrointestinal surgery (564.3)*
- *cyclical (536.2)*
  - *psychogenic (306.4)*
- *excessive, in pregnancy (643.0-643.9)*
- *habit (536.2)*
- *of newborn (779.3)*
- *psychogenic NOS (307.54)*

787.01 Nausea with vomiting

787.02 Nausea alone

➡ **AHA Coding Clinic:** 2Q, '97, 9

787.03 Vomiting alone

787.1 Heartburn

Pyrosis
Waterbrash

Excludes: *dyspepsia or indigestion (536.8)*

787.2 Dysphagia

Difficulty in swallowing

787.3 Flatulence, eructation, and gas pain

Abdominal distention (gaseous)
Bloating
Tympanites (abdominal) (intestinal)

Excludes: *aerophagy (306.4)*

787.4 Visible peristalsis

Hyperperistalsis

787.5 Abnormal bowel sounds

Absent bowel sounds
Hyperactive bowel sounds

787.6 Incontinence of feces

Encopresis NOS
Incontinence of sphincter ani

Excludes: *that of nonorganic origin (307.7)*

➡ **AHA Coding Clinic:** 1Q, '97, 9

787.7 Abnormal feces

Bulky stools

Excludes: *abnormal stool content (792.1)*
melena:
- *NOS (578.1)*
- *newborn (772.4, 777.3)*

✓5th **787.9 Other symptoms involving digestive system**

Excludes: *gastrointestinal hemorrhage (578.0-578.9)*
intestinal obstruction (560.0-560.9)
specific functional digestive disorders:
esophagus (530.0-530.9)
stomach and duodenum (536.0-536.9)
those not elsewhere classified (564.0-564.9)

787.91 Diarrhea
Diarrhea NOS
➡ **AHA Coding Clinic:** 4Q, '95, 54

787.99 Other
Change in bowel habits
Tenesmus (rectal)

788 Symptoms involving urinary system

Excludes: *hematuria (599.7)*
nonspecific findings on examination of the urine (791.0-791.9)
small kidney of unknown cause (589.0-589.9)
uremia NOS (586)

788.0 Renal colic
Colic (recurrent) of:
kidney
ureter

788.1 Dysuria
Painful urination
Strangury

✓5th **788.2 Retention of urine**
✔ **St. Anthony's Clinical Coder:** see Chapter 5

788.20 Retention of urine, unspecified
➡ **CC Excl:** 274.11, 344.61, 593.3-593.5, 596.4-596.59, 596.8-596.9, 599.6, 600, 601.0-601.9, 602.0-602.9, 696.0, 753.0, 753.1, 753.20-753.23, 753.29, 753.3-753.9, 780.9, 788.20-788.29, 788.61-788.69, 788.9, 799.8
➡ **AHA Coding Clinic:** 3Q, '96, 10

788.21 Incomplete bladder emptying

788.29 Other specified retention of urine
➡ **CC Excl:** see Code 788.20

✓5th **788.3 Incontinence of urine**
Code first any underlying condition, such as:
congenital ureterocele (753.23)
genital prolapse (618.0-618.9)

Excludes: *that of nonorganic origin (307.6)*

➡ **AHA Coding Clinic:** 4Q, '92, 22

788.30 Urinary incontinence, unspecified
Enuresis NOS

788.31 Urge incontinence

788.32 Stress incontinence, male ♂

Excludes: *stress incontinence, female (625.6)*

788.33 Mixed incontinence (female) (male)
Urge and stress

788.34 Incontinence without sensory awareness

788.35 Post-void dribbling

788.36 Nocturnal enuresis

788.37 Continuous leakage

788.39 Other urinary incontinence

✓5th **788.4 Frequency of urination and polyuria**

788.41 Urinary frequency
Frequency of micturition

788.42 Polyuria

788.43 Nocturia

788.5 Oliguria and anuria
Deficient secretion of urine
Suppression of urinary secretion

Excludes: *that complicating:*
abortion (634-638 with .3, 639.3)
ectopic or molar pregnancy (639.3)
pregnancy, childbirth, or the puerperium (642.0-642.9, 646.2)

✓5th **788.6 Other abnormality of urination**

788.61 Splitting of urinary stream
Intermittent urinary stream

788.62 Slowing of urinary stream
Weak stream

788.69 Other

788.7 Urethral discharge
Penile discharge
Urethrorrhea

788.8 Extravasation of urine

788.9 Other symptoms involving urinary system
Extrarenal uremia
Vesical:
pain
tenesmus
➡ **AHA Coding Clinic:** 4Q, '88, 1

789 Other symptoms involving abdomen and pelvis

Excludes: *symptoms referable to genital organs:*
female (625.0-625.9)
male (607.0-608.9)
psychogenic (302.70-302.79)

The following fifth-digit subclassification is to be used for codes 789.0, 789.3, 789.4, 789.6

0 unspecified site
1 right upper quadrant
2 left upper quadrant
3 right lower quadrant
4 left lower quadrant
5 periumbilic
6 epigastric
7 generalized
9 other specified site
Multiple sites

✓5th [8] **789.0 Abdominal pain**
Colic:
NOS
infantile
Cramps, abdominal

Excludes: *renal colic (788.0)*

➡ **AHA Coding Clinic:** 1Q, '95, 3

789.1 Hepatomegaly
Enlargement of liver

789.2 Splenomegaly
Enlargement of spleen

✓5th [8] **789.3 Abdominal or pelvic swelling, mass, or lump**
Diffuse or generalized swelling or mass:
abdominal NOS
umbilical

Excludes: *abdominal distention (gaseous) (787.3)*
ascites (789.5)

✓5th [8] **789.4 Abdominal rigidity**

789.5 Ascites
Fluid in peritoneal cavity
➡ **CC Excl:** 780.9, 789.30-789.9, 799.8
➡ **AHA Coding Clinic:** 4Q, '89, 11
✓ **St. Anthony's Clinical Coder:** see Chapter 5

✓5th [8] **789.6 Abdominal tenderness**
Rebound tenderness

789.9 Other symptoms involving abdomen and pelvis
Umbilical:
bleeding
discharge

NONSPECIFIC ABNORMAL FINDINGS (790-796)

➡ **AHA Coding Clinic:** 2Q, '90, 16

790 Nonspecific findings on examination of blood

Excludes: *abnormality of:*
platelets (287.0-287.9)
thrombocytes (287.0-287.9)
white blood cells (288.0-288.9)

790.0 Abnormality of red blood cells
Abnormal red cell:
morphology NOS
volume NOS
Anisocytosis
Poikilocytosis

Excludes: *anemia:*
congenital (776.5)
newborn, due to isoimmunization (773.0-773.2, 773.5)
of premature infant (776.6)
other specified types (280.0-285.9)
hemoglobin disorders (282.5-282.7)
polycythemia:
familial (289.6)
neonatorum (776.4)
secondary (289.0)
vera (238.4)

790.1 Elevated sedimentation rate

790.2 Abnormal glucose tolerance test

Excludes: *that complicating pregnancy, childbirth, or the puerperium (648.8)*

➡ **AHA Coding Clinic:** 3Q, '91, 5

790.3 Excessive blood level of alcohol
Elevated blood-alcohol
➡ **AHA Coding Clinic:** S-O, '86, 3

790.4 Nonspecific elevation of levels of transaminase or lactic acid dehydrogenase [LDH]

790.5 Other nonspecific abnormal serum enzyme levels
Abnormal serum level of:
acid phosphatase
alkaline phosphatase
Abnormal serum level of:
amylase
lipase

Excludes: *deficiency of circulating enzymes (277.6)*

[8] Nonspecific PDX = 0

790.6 Other abnormal blood chemistry

Abnormal blood levels of:
- cobalt
- copper
- iron
- lithium

Abnormal blood levels of:
- magnesium
- mineral
- zinc

Excludes: *abnormality of electrolyte or acid-base balance (276.0-276.9)*
hypoglycemia NOS (251.2)
specific finding indicating abnormality of:
amino-acid transport and metabolism (270.0-270.9)
carbohydrate transport and metabolism (271.0-271.9)
lipid metabolism (272.0-272.9)
uremia NOS (586)

➡ **AHA Coding Clinic:** 4Q, '88, 1

790.7 Bacteremia

Use additional code to identify organism (041)

Excludes: *septicemia (038)*

➡ **CC Excl:** 780.9, 790.7-790.99, 799.8

✔ **St. Anthony's Clinical Coder:** see Chapter 5

790.8 Viremia, unspecified

➡ **AHA Coding Clinic:** 4Q, '88, 10

✓5th **790.9 Other nonspecific findings on examination of blood**

790.91 Abnormal arterial blood gases

790.92 Abnormal coagulation profile

Abnormal or prolonged:
- bleeding time
- coagulation time
- partial thromboplastin time [PTT]
- prothrombin time [PT]

Excludes: *coagulation (hemorrhagic) disorders (286.0-286.9)*

790.93 Elevated prostate specific antigen (PSA) A:15–124 ♂

790.94 Euthyroid sick syndrome

➡ **AHA Coding Clinic:** 4Q, '97, 45

790.99 Other

791 Nonspecific findings on examination of urine

Excludes: *hematuria NOS (599.7)*
specific findings indicating abnormality of:
amino-acid transport and metabolism (270.0-270.9)
carbohydrate transport and metabolism (271.0-271.9)

791.0 Proteinuria

Albuminuria

Bence-Jones proteinuria

Excludes: *postural proteinuria (593.6)*
that arising during pregnancy or the puerperium (642.0-642.9, 646.2)

791.1 Chyluria

Excludes: *filarial (125.0-125.9)*

➡ **CC Excl:** 780.9, 791.1, 791.9, 799.8

791.2 Hemoglobinuria

791.3 Myoglobinuria

➡ **CC Excl:** 780.9, 791.2-791.3, 791.9, 799.8

791.4 Biliuria

791.5 Glycosuria

Excludes: *renal glycosuria (271.4)*

791.6 Acetonuria

Ketonuria

791.7 Other cells and casts in urine

791.9 Other nonspecific findings on examination of urine

Crystalluria
Elevated urine levels of:
- 17-ketosteroids
- catecholamines
- indolacetic acid
- vanillylmandelic acid [VMA]

Melanuria

792 Nonspecific abnormal findings in other body substances

Excludes: *that in chromosomal analysis (795.2)*

792.0 Cerebrospinal fluid

792.1 Stool contents

Abnormal stool color
Fat in stool
Mucus in stool
Occult blood
Pus in stool

Excludes: *blood in stool [melena] (578.1)*
newborn (772.4, 777.3)

➡ **AHA Coding Clinic:** 2Q, '92, 9

792.2 Semen ♂

Abnormal spermatozoa

Excludes: *azoospermia (606.0)*
oligospermia (606.1)

792.3 Amniotic fluid ♀ A:12–55

➡ **AHA Coding Clinic:** N-D, '86, 4

792.4 Saliva

Excludes: *that in chromosomal analysis (795.2)*

792.9 Other nonspecific abnormal findings in body substances

Peritoneal fluid
Pleural fluid
Synovial fluid
Vaginal fluids

793 Nonspecific abnormal findings on radiological and other examination of body structure

Includes: nonspecific abnormal findings of:
- thermography
- ultrasound examination [echogram]
- x-ray examination

Excludes: *abnormal results of function studies and radioisotope scans (794.0-794.9)*

793.0 Skull and head

Excludes: *nonspecific abnormal echoencephalogram (794.01)*

793.1 Lung field

Coin lesion } (of) lung
Shadow } (of) lung

793.2 Other intrathoracic organ

Abnormal:
- echocardiogram
- heart shadow
- ultrasound cardiogram

Mediastinal shift

793.3 Biliary tract

Nonvisualization of gallbladder

793.4 Gastrointestinal tract

793.5 Genitourinary organs

Filling defect:
- bladder
- kidney
- ureter

793.6 Abdominal area, including retroperitoneum

793.7 Musculoskeletal system

793.8 Breast

Abnormal mammogram

793.9 Other

Abnormal:
- placental finding by x-ray or ultrasound method
- radiological findings in skin and subcutaneous tissue

Excludes: *abnormal finding by radioisotope localization of placenta (794.9)*

794 Nonspecific abnormal results of function studies

Includes: radioisotope:
- scans
- uptake studies
- scintiphotography

✓5th **794.0 Brain and central nervous system**

794.00 Abnormal function study, unspecified

794.01 Abnormal echoencephalogram

794.02 Abnormal electroencephalogram [EEG]

794.09 Other

Abnormal brain scan

✓5th **794.1 Peripheral nervous system and special senses**

794.10 Abnormal response to nerve stimulation, unspecified

794.11 Abnormal retinal function studies

Abnormal electroretinogram [ERG]

794.12 Abnormal electro-oculogram [EOG]

794.13 Abnormal visually evoked potential

794.14 Abnormal oculomotor studies

794.15 Abnormal auditory function studies

794.16 Abnormal vestibular function studies

794.17 Abnormal electromyogram [EMG]

Excludes: *that of eye (794.14)*

794.19 Other

794.2 Pulmonary

Abnormal lung scan
Reduced:
- ventilatory capacity
- vital capacity

✓5th **794.3 Cardiovascular**

794.30 Abnormal function study, unspecified

794.31 Abnormal electrocardiogram [ECG] [EKG]

794.39 Other

Abnormal:
- ballistocardiogram
- phonocardiogram
- vectorcardiogram

794.4 Kidney

Abnormal renal function test

794.5 Thyroid

Abnormal thyroid:
- scan
- uptake

794.6 Other endocrine function study

794.7 Basal metabolism

Abnormal basal metabolic rate [BMR]

794.8 Liver

Abnormal liver scan

794.9 Other

Bladder
Pancreas
Placenta
Spleen

795 Nonspecific abnormal histological and immunological findings

Excludes: *nonspecific abnormalities of red blood cells (790.0)*

795.0 Nonspecific abnormal Papanicolaou smear of cervix ♀

Dyskaryotic cervical smear

795.1 Nonspecific abnormal Papanicolaou smear of other site

795.2 Nonspecific abnormal findings on chromosomal analysis

Abnormal karyotype

795.3 Nonspecific positive culture findings

Positive culture findings in:
- nose
- sputum
- throat
- wound

Excludes: *that of:*
- *blood (790.7-790.8)*
- *urine (599.0)*

795.4 Other nonspecific abnormal histological findings

795.5 Nonspecific reaction to tuberculin skin test without active tuberculosis

Abnormal result of Mantoux test
PPD positive
Tuberculin (skin test):
- positive
- reactor

795.6 False positive serological test for syphilis

False positive Wassermann reaction

✓5th **795.7 Other nonspecific immunological findings**

Excludes: *isoimmunization, in pregnancy (656.1-656.2)*
affecting fetus or newborn (773.0-773.2)

➡ **AHA Coding Clinic:** 2Q, '93, 6

795.71 Nonspecific serologic evidence of human immunodeficiency virus [HIV]

Inconclusive human immunodeficiency virus [HIV] test (adult) (infant)

Note: This code is ONLY to be used when a test finding is reported as nonspecific. Asymptomatic positive findings are coded to V08. If any HIV infection symptom or condition is present, see code 042. Negative findings are not coded.

Excludes: *acquired immunodeficiency syndrome [AIDS] (042)*
asymptomatic human immunodeficiency virus [HIV] infection status (V08)
HIV infection, symptomatic (042)
human immunodeficiency virus [HIV] disease (042)
positive (status) NOS (V08)

➡ **AHA Coding Clinic:** 1Q, '93, 21; 1Q, '93, 22; 2Q, '92, 11; J-A, '87, 24

795.79 Other and unspecified nonspecific immunological findings

Raised antibody titer
Raised level of immunoglobulins

796 Other nonspecific abnormal findings

796.0 Nonspecific abnormal toxicological findings

Abnormal levels of heavy metals or drugs in blood, urine, or other tissue

Excludes: *excessive blood level of alcohol (790.3)*

➡ **AHA Coding Clinic:** 1Q, '97, 16

796.1 Abnormal reflex

796.2 Elevated blood pressure reading without diagnosis of hypertension

Note: This category is to be used to record an episode of elevated blood pressure in a patient in whom no formal diagnosis of hypertension has been made, or as an incidental finding.

➡ **AHA Coding Clinic:** 3Q, '90, 4; J-A, '84, 12

796.3 Nonspecific low blood pressure reading

796.4 Other abnormal clinical findings

796.5 Abnormal finding on antenatal screening

➡ **AHA Coding Clinic:** 4Q, '97, 46

796.9 Other

ILL-DEFINED AND UNKNOWN CAUSES OF MORBIDITY AND MORTALITY (797-799)

797 Senility without mention of psychosis

Old age
Senescence
Senile asthenia
Senile:
debility
exhaustion

Excludes: *senile psychoses (290.0-290.9)*

798 Sudden death, cause unknown

798.0 Sudden infant death syndrome A: 0-17

Cot death
Crib death
Sudden death of nonspecific cause in infancy

798.1 Instantaneous death

798.2 Death occurring in less than 24 hours from onset of symptoms, not otherwise explained

Death known not to be violent or instantaneous, for which no cause could be discovered
Died without sign of disease

798.9 Unattended death

Death in circumstances where the body of the deceased was found and no cause could be discovered
Found dead

799 Other ill-defined and unknown causes of morbidity and mortality

799.0 Asphyxia

Excludes: *asphyxia (due to):*
carbon monoxide (986)
inhalation of food or foreign body (932-934.9)
newborn (768.0-768.9)
traumatic (994.7)

799.1 Respiratory arrest

Cardiorespiratory failure

Excludes: *cardiac arrest (427.5)*
failure of peripheral circulation (785.50)
respiratory distress:
NOS (786.09)
acute (518.82)
following trauma or surgery (518.5)
newborn (770.8)
syndrome (newborn) (769)
adult (following trauma or surgery) (518.5)
other (518.82)
respiratory failure (518.81, 518.83-518.84)
newborn (770.8)
respiratory insufficiency (786.09)
acute (518.82)

➡ **CC Excl:** 518.81, 518.82, 780.9, 798.0, 799.0-799.1, 799.8

799.2 Nervousness

"Nerves"

799.3 Debility, unspecified

Excludes: *asthenia (780.79)*
nervous debility (300.5)
neurasthenia (300.5)
senile asthenia (797)

➡ **AHA Coding Clinic:** 3Q, '97, 11

799.4 Cachexia

Wasting disease

Excludes: *nutritional marasmus (261)*

➡ **CC Excl:** 780.9, 799.3-799.4, 799.8

➡ **AHA Coding Clinic:** 3Q, '90, 17

✔ **St. Anthony's Clinical Coder:** see Chapter 5

799.8 Other ill-defined conditions

799.9 Other unknown and unspecified cause

Undiagnosed disease, not specified as to site or system involved
Unknown cause of morbidity or mortality

➡ **AHA Coding Clinic:** 1Q, '98, 4

17. INJURY AND POISONING (800-999)

Use E code(s) to identify the cause and intent of the injury or poisoning (E800-E999)

Note:

1. The principle of multiple coding of injuries should be followed wherever possible. Combination categories for multiple injuries are provided for use when there is insufficient detail as to the nature of the individual conditions, or for primary tabulation purposes when it is more convenient to record a single code; otherwise, the component injuries should be coded separately.

   Where multiple sites of injury are specified in the titles, the word "with" indicates involvement of both sites, and the word "and" indicates involvement of either or both sites. The word "finger" includes thumb.

2. Categories for "late effect" of injuries are to be found at 905-909.

FRACTURES (800-829)

Excludes: *malunion (733.81)*
nonunion (733.82)
pathologic or spontaneous fracture (733.10-733.19)

The terms "condyle", "coronoid process", "ramus", and "symphysis" indicate the portion of the bone fractured, not the name of the bone involved

The descriptions "closed" and "open" used in the fourth-digit subdivisions include the following terms:

closed (with or without delayed healing):

comminuted	impacted
depressed	linear
elevated	march
fissured	simple
fracture NOS	slipped epiphysis
greenstick	spiral

open (with or without delayed healing):

compound	puncture
infected	with foreign body
missile	

A fracture not indicated as closed or open should be classified as closed.

➡ **AHA Coding Clinic:** 4Q, '90, 26; 3Q, '90, 5; 3Q, '90, 13; 2Q, '90, 7; 2Q, '89, 15, S-O, '85, 3

FRACTURE OF SKULL (800-804)

The following fifth-digit subclassification is for use with the appropriate codes in categories 800, 801, 803, and 804:

0 **unspecified state of consciousness**
1 **with no loss of consciousness**
2 **with brief [less than one hour] loss of consciousness**
3 **with moderate [1-24 hours] loss of consciousness**
4 **with prolonged [more than 24 hours] loss of consciousness and return to pre-existing conscious level**
5 **with prolonged [more than 24 hours] loss of consciousness, without return to pre-existing conscious level**
Use fifth-digit 5 to designate when a patient is unconscious and dies before regaining consciousness, regardless of the duration of the loss of consciousness
6 **with loss of consciousness of unspecified duration**
9 **with concussion, unspecified**

§ 800 Fracture of vault of skull

Includes: frontal bone parietal bone

✓5th **800.0** **Closed without mention of intracranial injury**
➡ **CC Excl:** 800.00-801.99, 803.00-804.99, 829.0-829.1, 850.0-852.19, 852.21-854.19, 873.8-873.9, 879.8-879.9, 905.0, 925.1-925.2, 929.0-929.9, 958.8, 959.01, 959.09, 959.8-959.9

✓5th □ **800.1** **Closed with cerebral laceration and contusion**
➡ **CC Excl:** see Code 800.0

✓5th □ **800.2** **Closed with subarachnoid, subdural, and extradural hemorrhage**
➡ **CC Excl:** see Code 800.0

✓5th □ **800.3** **Closed with other and unspecified intracranial hemorrhage**
➡ **CC Excl:** see Code 800.0

✓5th □ **800.4** **Closed with intracranial injury of other and unspecified nature**
➡ **CC Excl:** see Code 800.0

✓5th □ **800.5** **Open without mention of intracranial injury**
➡ **CC Excl:** see Code 800.0

✓5th □ **800.6** **Open with cerebral laceration and contusion**
➡ **CC Excl:** see Code 800.0

✓5th □ **800.7** **Open with subarachnoid, subdural, and extradural hemorrhage**
➡ **CC Excl:** see Code 800.0

✓5th □ **800.8** **Open with other and unspecified intracranial hemorrhage**
➡ **CC Excl:** see Code 800.0

✓5th □ **800.9** **Open with intracranial injury of other and unspecified nature**
➡ **CC Excl:** see Code 800.0

§ Requires fifth-digit. See above for codes and definitions.

§ 801 Fracture of base of skull

Includes: fossa:
- anterior
- middle
- posterior

occiput bone
orbital roof

sinus:
- ethmoid
- frontal

sphenoid bone
temporal bone

✓5th **801.0** Closed without mention of intracranial injury
➡ **CC Excl:** see Code 800.0

✓5th ☐ **801.1** Closed with cerebral laceration and contusion
➡ **CC Excl:** see Code 800.0
➡ **AHA Coding Clinic:** 4Q, '96, 36

✓5th ☐ **801.2** Closed with subarachnoid, subdural, and extradural hemorrhage
➡ **CC Excl:** see Code 800.0

✓5th ☐ **801.3** Closed with other and unspecified intracranial hemorrhage
➡ **CC Excl:** see Code 800.0

✓5th ☐ **801.4** Closed with intracranial injury of other and unspecified nature
➡ **CC Excl:** see Code 800.0

✓5th ☐ **801.5** Open without mention of intracranial injury
➡ **CC Excl:** see Code 800.0

✓5th ☐ **801.6** Open with cerebral laceration and contusion
➡ **CC Excl:** see Code 800.0

✓5th ☐ **801.7** Open with subarachnoid, subdural, and extradural hemorrhage
➡ **CC Excl:** see Code 800.0

✓5th ☐ **801.8** Open with other and unspecified intracranial hemorrhage
➡ **CC Excl:** see Code 800.0

✓5th ☐ **801.9** Open with intracranial injury of other and unspecified nature
➡ **CC Excl:** see Code 800.0

802 Fracture of face bones

802.0 Nasal bones, closed

802.1 Nasal bones, open
➡ **CC Excl:** 800.00-800.99, 801.00-801.99, 802.0-802.1, 803.00-803.99, 804.00-804.99, 829.0-829.1, 850.0-850.9, 851.00-851.99, 852.00-852.19, 852.21-852.59, 853.00-853.19, 854.00-854.19, 873.8-873.9, 879.8-879.9, 905.0, 925.1-925.2, 929.0, 929.9, 958.8, 959.01, 959.09, 959.8-959.9

✓5th **802.2** Mandible, closed
Inferior maxilla
Lower jaw (bone)

802.20 Unspecified site
➡ **CC Excl:** 800.00-800.99, 801.00-801.99, 802.20-802.5, 803.00-803.99, 804.00-804.99, 829.0-829.1, 830.0-830.1, 850.0-850.9, 851.00-851.99, 852.00-852.19, 852.21-852.59, 853.00-853.19, 854.00-854.19, 873.8-873.9, 879.8-879.9, 905.0, 925.1, 925.2, 929.0, 929.9, 958.8, 959.01, 959.09, 959.8-959.9

802.21 Condylar process
➡ **CC Excl:** see Code 802.20

802.22 Subcondylar
➡ **CC Excl:** see Code 802.20

802.23 Coronoid process
➡ **CC Excl:** see Code 802.20

802.24 Ramus, unspecified
➡ **CC Excl:** see Code 802.20

802.25 Angle of jaw
➡ **CC Excl:** see Code 802.20

802.26 Symphysis of body
➡ **CC Excl:** see Code 802.20

802.27 Alveolar border of body
➡ **CC Excl:** see Code 802.20

802.28 Body, other and unspecified
➡ **CC Excl:** see Code 802.20

802.29 Multiple sites
➡ **CC Excl:** see Code 802.20

§ Requires fifth-digit. See page 313 for codes and definitions.

✓5th **802.3** Mandible, open

802.30 Unspecified site
➡ **CC Excl:** see Code 802.20

802.31 Condylar process
➡ **CC Excl:** see Code 802.20

802.32 Subcondylar
➡ **CC Excl:** see Code 802.20

802.33 Coronoid process
➡ **CC Excl:** see Code 802.20

802.34 Ramus, unspecified
➡ **CC Excl:** see Code 802.20

802.35 Angle of jaw
➡ **CC Excl:** see Code 802.20

802.36 Symphysis of body
➡ **CC Excl:** see Code 802.20

802.37 Alveolar border of body
➡ **CC Excl:** see Code 802.20

802.38 Body, other and unspecified
➡ **CC Excl:** see Code 802.20

802.39 Multiple sites
➡ **CC Excl:** see Code 802.20

802.4 Malar and maxillary bones, closed
Superior maxilla
Upper jaw (bone)
Zygoma
Zygomatic arch
➡ **CC Excl:** see Code 802.20

802.5 Malar and maxillary bones, open
➡ **CC Excl:** see Code 802.20

802.6 Orbital floor (blow-out), closed
➡ **CC Excl:** 800.00-800.99, 801.00-801.99, 802.6-802.9, 803.00-803.99, 804.00-804.99, 829.0-829.1, 850.0-850.9, 851.00-851.99, 852.00-852.19, 852.21-852.59, 853.00-853.19, 854.00-854.19, 873.8-873.9, 879.8-879.9, 905.0, 925.1-925.2, 929.0, 929.9, 958.8, 959.01, 959.09, 959.8-959.9

802.7 Orbital floor (blow-out), open
➡ **CC Excl:** see Code 802.6

802.8 Other facial bones, closed
Alveolus
Orbit:
  NOS
  part other than roof or floor
Palate

Excludes: *orbital:*
  floor (802.6)
  roof (801.0-801.9)

➡ **CC Excl:** see Code 802.6

802.9 Other facial bones, open
➡ **CC Excl:** see Code 802.6

§ 803 Other and unqualified skull fractures

Includes: skull NOS
skull multiple NOS

✓5th **803.0** Closed without mention of intracranial injury
➡ **CC Excl:** 800.00-800.99, 801.00-801.99, 803.00-803.99, 804.00-804.99, 829.0-829.1, 850.0-850.9, 851.00-851.99, 852.00-852.19, 852.21-852.59, 853.00-853.19, 854.00-854.19, 873.8-873.9, 879.8-879.9, 905.0, 925.1-925.2, 929.0, 929.9, 958.8, 959.01, 959.09, 959.8-959.9

✓5th ☐ **803.1** Closed with cerebral laceration and contusion
➡ **CC Excl:** see Code 803.0

✓5th ☐ **803.2** Closed with subarachnoid, subdural, and extradural hemorrhage
➡ **CC Excl:** see Code 803.0

✓5th ☐ **803.3** Closed with other and unspecified intracranial hemorrhage
➡ **CC Excl:** see Code 803.0

✓5th ☐ **803.4** Closed with intracranial injury of other and unspecified nature
➡ **CC Excl:** see Code 803.0

✓5th ☐ **803.5** Open without mention of intracranial injury
➡ **CC Excl:** see Code 803.0

✓5th ☐ **803.6** Open with cerebral laceration and contusion
➡ **CC Excl:** see Code 803.0

✓5th ☐ **803.7** Open with subarachnoid, subdural, and extradural hemorrhage
➡ **CC Excl:** see Code 803.0

✓5th ☐ **803.8** Open with other and unspecified intracranial hemorrhage
➡ **CC Excl:** see Code 803.0

✓5th ☐ **803.9** Open with intracranial injury of other and unspecified nature
➡ **CC Excl:** see Code 803.0

§ Requires fifth-digit. See page 313 for codes and definitions.

§ 804 Multiple fractures involving skull or face with other bones

✓5th **804.0** Closed without mention of intracranial injury
➡ **CC Excl:** see Code 803.0

✓5th □ **804.1** Closed with cerebral laceration and contusion
➡ **CC Excl:** see Code 803.0

✓5th □ **804.2** Closed with subarachnoid, subdural, and extradural hemorrhage
➡ **CC Excl:** see Code 803.0

✓5th □ **804.3** Closed with other and unspecified intracranial hemorrhage
➡ **CC Excl:** see Code 803.0

✓5th □ **804.4** Closed with intracranial injury of other and unspecified nature
➡ **CC Excl:** see Code 803.0

✓5th □ **804.5** Open without mention of intracranial injury
➡ **CC Excl:** see Code 803.0

✓5th □ **804.6** Open with cerebral laceration and contusion
➡ **CC Excl:** see Code 803.0

✓5th □ **804.7** Open with subarachnoid, subdural, and extradural hemorrhage
➡ **CC Excl:** see Code 803.0

✓5th □ **804.8** Open with other and unspecified intracranial hemorrhage
➡ **CC Excl:** see Code 803.0

✓5th □ **804.9** Open with intracranial injury of other and unspecified nature
➡ **CC Excl:** see Code 803.0

FRACTURE OF NECK AND TRUNK (805-809)

805 Fracture of vertebral column without mention of spinal cord injury

Includes: neural arch, spine, spinous process, transverse process, vertebra

The following fifth-digit subclassification is for use with codes 805.0-805.1:

0 cervical vertebra, unspecified level
1 first cervical vertebra
2 second cervical vertebra
3 third cervical vertebra
4 fourth cervical vertebra
5 fifth cervical vertebra
6 sixth cervical vertebra
7 seventh cervical vertebra
8 multiple cervical vertebrae

✓5th **805.0** Cervical, closed
Atlas
Axis
➡ **CC Excl:** 805.00-805.18, 805.8-805.9, 806.00-806.19, 806.8-806.9, 829.0-829.1, 839.00-839.18, 839.40, 839.49-839.50, 839.59, 839.69, 839.79, 839.8-839.9, 847.0, 847.9, 848.8-848.9, 879.8-879.9, 905.1, 926.11, 929.0, 929.9, 952.00-952.09, 952.8-952.9, 958.8, 959.1, 959.8-959.9

✓5th **805.1** Cervical, open
➡ **CC Excl:** see Code 805.0

805.2 Dorsal [thoracic], closed
➡ **CC Excl:** 805.2-805.3, 805.8-805.9, 806.20-806.39, 806.8-806.9, 829.0-829.1, 839.21, 839.31, 839.40, 839.49-839.50, 839.59, 839.69, 839.79, 839.8-839.9, 847.1, 847.9, 848.8-848.9, 879.8-879.9, 905.1, 926.11, 929.0, 929.9, 952.10-952.19, 952.8-952.9, 958.8, 959.1, 959.8-959.9

805.3 Dorsal [thoracic], open
➡ **CC Excl:** see Code 805.2

805.4 Lumbar, closed
➡ **CC Excl:** 805.4-805.5, 805.8-805.9, 806.4-806.5, 806.8-806.9, 829.0-829.1, 839.20, 839.30, 839.40, 839.49-839.50, 839.59, 839.69, 839.79, 839.8-839.9, 847.2, 847.9, 848.8-848.9, 879.8-879.9, 905.1, 926.11, 929.0, 929.9, 952.2, 952.8-952.9, 958.8, 959.1, 959.8-959.9

805.5 Lumbar, open
➡ **CC Excl:** see Code 805.4

§ Requires fifth-digit. See page 313 for codes and definitions.

805.6 Sacrum and coccyx, closed

➡ **CC Excl:** 805.6-805.9, 806.60-806.9, 829.0-829.1, 839.40-839.59, 839.69, 839.79, 839.8-839.9, 846.0-846.9, 847.3-847.9, 848.5-848.9, 879.8-879.9, 905.1, 926.11, 929.0, 929.9, 952.3-952.9, 958.8, 959.1, 959.8-959.9

805.7 Sacrum and coccyx, open

➡ **CC Excl:** see Code 805.6

805.8 Unspecified, closed

➡ **CC Excl:** 733.10-733.19, 805.00-805.9, 806.00-806.9, 829.0-829.1, 839.00-839.59, 839.69, 839.79, 839.8-839.9, 846.0-846.9, 847.0-847.9, 848.5-848.9, 879.8-879.9, 905.1, 926.11, 929.0, 929.9, 952.00-952.9, 958.8, 959.1, 959.8-959.9

805.9 Unspecified, open

➡ **CC Excl:** see Code 805.8

806 Fracture of vertebral column with spinal cord injury

Includes: any condition classifiable to 805 with:
- complete or incomplete transverse lesion (of cord)
- hematomyelia
- injury to:
  - cauda equina
  - nerve
- paralysis
- paraplegia
- quadriplegia
- spinal concussion

✓5th **806.0** Cervical, closed

806.00 C_1-C_4 level with unspecified spinal cord injury

Cervical region NOS with spinal cord injury NOS

➡ **CC Excl:** 733.10-733.19, 805.00-805.18, 805.8-805.9, 806.00-806.19, 806.8-806.9, 829.0-829.1, 839.00-839.18, 839.40, 839.49-839.50, 839.59, 839.69, 839.79, 839.8-839.9, 847.9, 848.8-848.9, 879.8-879.9, 905.1, 926.11, 929.0, 929.9, 952.00-952.09, 952.8-952.9, 958.8, 959.1, 959.8-959.9

806.01 C_1-C_4 level with complete lesion of cord

➡ **CC Excl:** see Code 806.00

806.02 C_1-C_4 level with anterior cord syndrome

➡ **CC Excl:** see Code 806.00

806.03 C_1-C_4 level with central cord syndrome

➡ **CC Excl:** see Code 806.00

806.04 C_1-C_4 level with other specified spinal cord injury

C_1-C_4 level with:
- incomplete spinal cord lesion NOS
- posterior cord syndrome

➡ **CC Excl:** see Code 806.00

806.05 C_5-C_7 level with unspecified spinal cord injury

➡ **CC Excl:** see Code 806.00

806.06 C_5-C_7 level with complete lesion of cord

➡ **CC Excl:** see Code 806.00

806.07 C_5-C_7 level with anterior cord syndrome

➡ **CC Excl:** see Code 806.00

806.08 C_5-C_7 level with central cord syndrome

➡ **CC Excl:** see Code 806.00

806.09 C_5-C_7 level with other specified spinal cord injury

C_5-C_7 level with:
- incomplete spinal cord lesion NOS
- posterior cord syndrome

➡ **CC Excl:** see Code 806.00

✓5th **806.1** Cervical, open

806.10 C_1-C_4 level with unspecified spinal cord injury

➡ **CC Excl:** see Code 806.00

806.11 C_1-C_4 level with complete lesion of cord

➡ **CC Excl:** see Code 806.00

806.12 C_1-C_4 level with anterior cord syndrome

➡ **CC Excl:** see Code 806.00

806.13 C_1-C_4 level with central cord syndrome

➡ **CC Excl:** see Code 806.00

806.14 C_1-C_4 level with other specified spinal cord injury

C_1-C_4 level with:
- incomplete spinal cord lesion NOS
- posterior cord syndrome

➡ **CC Excl:** see Code 806.00

806.15 C_5-C_7 level with unspecified spinal cord injury

➡ **CC Excl:** see Code 806.00

806.16 C_5-C_7 level with complete lesion of cord

➡ **CC Excl:** see Code 806.00

806.17 C_5-C_7 level with anterior cord syndrome

➡ **CC Excl:** see Code 806.00

806.18 C_5-C_7 level with central cord syndrome

➡ **CC Excl:** see Code 806.00

806.19 C_5-C_7 level with other specified spinal cord injury

C_5-C_7 level with:
- incomplete spinal cord lesion NOS
- posterior cord syndrome

➡ **CC Excl:** see Code 806.00

✓5th **806.2** Dorsal [thoracic], closed

806.20 T_1-T_6 level with unspecified spinal cord injury

Thoracic region NOS with spinal cord injury NOS

➡ **CC Excl:** 733.10-733.19, 805.2-805.3, 805.8-805.9, 806.20-806.39, 806.8-806.9, 829.0-829.1, 839.21, 839.31, 839.40, 839.49-839.50, 839.59, 839.69, 839.79, 839.8-839.9, 847.1, 847.9, 848.8-848.9, 879.8-879.9, 905.1, 926.11, 929.0, 929.9, 952.10-952.19, 952.8-952.9, 958.8, 959.1, 959.8-959.9

806.21 T_1-T_6 level with complete lesion of cord

➡ **CC Excl:** see Code 806.20

806.22 T_1-T_6 level with anterior cord syndrome

➡ **CC Excl:** see Code 806.20

806.23 T_1-T_6 level with central cord syndrome

➡ **CC Excl:** see Code 806.20

806.24 T_1-T_6 level with other specified spinal cord injury

T_1-T_6 level with:
- incomplete spinal cord lesion NOS
- posterior cord syndrome

➡ **CC Excl:** see Code 806.20

806.25 T_7-T_{12} level with unspecified spinal cord injury

➡ **CC Excl:** see Code 806.20

806.26 T_7-T_{12} level with complete lesion of cord

➡ **CC Excl:** see Code 806.20

806.27 T_7-T_{12} level with anterior cord syndrome

➡ **CC Excl:** see Code 806.20

806.28 T_7-T_{12} level with central cord syndrome

➡ **CC Excl:** see Code 806.20

806.29 T_7-T_{12} level with other specified spinal cord injury

T_7-T_{12} level with:
- incomplete spinal cord lesion NOS
- posterior cord syndrome

➡ **CC Excl:** see Code 806.20

✓5th **806.3** Dorsal [thoracic], open

806.30 T_1-T_6 level with unspecified spinal cord injury

➡ **CC Excl:** see Code 806.20

806.31 T_1-T_6 level with complete lesion of cord

➡ **CC Excl:** see Code 806.20

806.32 T_1-T_6 level with anterior cord syndrome

➡ **CC Excl:** see Code 806.20

806.33 T_1-T_6 level with central cord syndrome

➡ **CC Excl:** see Code 806.20

806.34 T_1-T_6 level with other specified spinal cord injury

T_1-T_6 level with:
- incomplete spinal cord lesion NOS
- posterior cord syndrome

➡ **CC Excl:** see Code 806.20

806.35 T_7-T_{12} level with unspecified spinal cord injury

➡ **CC Excl:** see Code 806.20

806.36 T_7-T_{12} level with complete lesion of cord

➡ **CC Excl:** see Code 806.20

806.37 T_7-T_{12} level with anterior cord syndrome

➡ **CC Excl:** see Code 806.20

806.38 T_7-T_{12} level with central cord syndrome

➡ **CC Excl:** see Code 806.20

806.39 T_7-T_{12} level with other specified spinal cord injury

T_7-T_{12} level with:
- incomplete spinal cord lesion NOS
- posterior cord syndrome

➡ **CC Excl:** see Code 806.20

806.4 Lumbar, closed

➡ **CC Excl:** 733.10-733.19, 805.4-805.5, 805.8-805.9, 806.4-806.5, 806.8-806.9, 829.0-829.1, 839.20, 839.30, 839.40, 839.49-839.50, 839.59, 839.69, 839.79, 839.8-839.9, 847.2, 847.9, 848.8-848.9, 879.8-879.9, 905.1, 926.11, 929.0, 929.9, 952.2, 952.8-952.9, 958.8, 959.1, 959.8-959.9

806.5 Lumbar, open

➡ **CC Excl:** see Code 806.4

✓5th **806.6** Sacrum and coccyx, closed

806.60 With unspecified spinal cord injury

➡ **CC Excl:** 733.10-733.19, 805.6-805.9, 806.60-806.9, 829.0-829.1, 839.40-839.59, 839.69, 839.79, 839.8-839.9, 846.0-846.9, 847.0, 847.3-847.9, 848.5-848.9, 879.8-879.9, 905.1, 926.11, 929.0, 929.9, 952.3-952.9, 958.8, 959.1, 959.8-959.9

806.61 With complete cauda equina lesion

➡ **CC Excl:** see Code 806.60

806.62 With other cauda equina injury

➡ **CC Excl:** see Code 806.60

806.69 With other spinal cord injury

➡ **CC Excl:** see Code 806.60

✓5th **806.7** Sacrum and coccyx, open

806.70 With unspecified spinal cord injury

➡ **CC Excl:** see Code 806.60

806.71 With complete cauda equina lesion

➡ **CC Excl:** see Code 806.60

806.72 With other cauda equina injury

➡ **CC Excl:** see Code 806.60

806.79 With other spinal cord injury

➡ **CC Excl:** see Code 806.60

806.8 Unspecified, closed

➡ **CC Excl:** 733.10-733.19, 805.00-805.09, 806.00-806.9, 829.0-829.1, 839.00-839.59, 839.69, 839.79, 839.8-839.9, 846.0-846.9, 847.0-847.9, 848.5-848.9, 879.8-879.9, 905.1, 926.11, 929.0, 929.9, 952.00-952.9, 958.8, 959.1, 959.8-959.9

806.9 Unspecified, open

➡ **CC Excl:** see Code 806.8

807 Fracture of rib(s), sternum, larynx, and trachea

The following fifth-digit subclassification is for use with codes 807.0-807.1:

- **0** rib(s), unspecified
- **1** one rib
- **2** two ribs
- **3** three ribs
- **4** four ribs
- **5** five ribs
- **6** six ribs
- **7** seven ribs
- **8** eight or more ribs
- **9** multiple ribs, unspecified

✓5th [6] **807.0** Rib(s), closed

➡ **CC Excl: For codes 807.04-807.09:** 807.00-807.19, 807.4, 819.0-819.1, 828.0-828.1, 829.0-829.1, 848.8-848.9, 879.8-879.9, 929.0, 929.9, 958.8, 959.8-959.9

✓5th **807.1** Rib(s), open

➡ **CC Excl:** see Code 807.0

807.2 Sternum, closed

➡ **CC Excl:** 807.2-807.4, 829.0-829.1, 848.8-848.9, 879.8-879.9, 929.0, 929.9, 958.8, 959.8-959.9

807.3 Sternum, open

➡ **CC Excl:** see Code 807.2

807.4 Flail chest

➡ **CC Excl:** 807.00-807.4, 829.0-829.1, 848.8-848.9, 879.8-879.9, 929.0, 929.9, 958.8, 959.8-959.9

807.5 Larynx and trachea, closed

Hyoid bone
Thyroid cartilage
Trachea

➡ **CC Excl:** 807.5-807.6, 829.0-829.1, 848.8-848.9, 879.8-879.9, 929.0, 929.9, 958.8, 959.8-959.9

807.6 Larynx and trachea, open

➡ **CC Excl:** see Code 807.5

[6] CC Coding = 4-9

808 Fracture of pelvis

808.0 Acetabulum, closed

➡ **CC Excl:** 733.10-733.19, 808.0-808.1, 808.43, 808.49, 808.53, 808.59, 808.8-808.9, 809.0-809.1, 829.0-829.1, 835.00-835.13, 843.0-843.9, 846.0-846.9 848.5-848.9, 879.8-879.9, 929.0, 929.9, 958.8, 959.6, 959.8-959.9

808.1 Acetabulum, open

➡ **CC Excl:** 808.0-808.1, 808.43, 808.49, 808.53, 808.59, 808.8-808.9, 809.0-809.1, 829.0-829.1, 835.00-835.13, 843.0-843.9, 846.0-846.9, 848.5-848.9, 879.8-879.9, 929.0, 929.9, 958.8, 959.6, 959.8-959.9

808.2 Pubis, closed

➡ **CC Excl:** 733.10-733.19, 808.2-808.3, 808.43, 808.49, 808.53, 808.59, 808.8-808.9, 809.0-809.1, 829.0-829.1, 835.00-835.13, 843.0-843.9, 846.0-846.9, 848.5-848.9, 879.8-879.9, 929.0, 929.9, 958.8, 959.6, 959.8-959.9

808.3 Pubis, open

➡ **CC Excl:** see Code 808.2

✓5th **808.4** Other specified part, closed

808.41 Ilium

808.42 Ischium

808.43 Multiple pelvic fractures with disruption of pelvic circle

➡ **CC Excl:** 733.10-733.19, 808.0-808.9, 809.0-809.1, 829.0-829.1, 835.00-835.13, 843.0-843.9, 846.0-846.9, 848.5-848.9, 879.8-879.9, 929.0, 929.9, 958.8, 959.6, 959.8-959.9

808.49 Other

Innominate bone Pelvic rim

➡ **CC Excl:** see Code 808.43

✓5th **808.5** Other specified part, open

808.51 Ilium

➡ **CC Excl:** 733.10-733.19, 808.41, 808.43, 808.49, 808.51, 808.53, 808.59, 808.8-808.9, 809.0-809.1, 829.0-829.1, 835.00-835.13, 843.0-843.9, 846.0-846.9, 848.5-848.9, 879.8-879.9, 929.0, 929.9, 958.8, 959.6, 959.8-959.9

808.52 Ischium

➡ **CC Excl:** 733.10-733.19, 808.42-808.49, 808.52-808.59, 808.8-808.9, 809.0-809.1, 829.0-829.1, 835.00-835.13, 843.0-843.9, 846.0-846.9, 848.5-848.9, 879.8-879.9, 929.0, 929.9, 958.8, 959.6, 959.8-959.9

808.53 Multiple pelvic fractures with disruption of pelvic circle

➡ **CC Excl:** 733.10-733.19, 808.0-808.9 809.0-809.1, 829.0-829.1, 835.00-835.13, 843.0-843.9, 846.0-846.9, 848.5-848.9, 879.8-879.9, 929.0, 929.9, 958.8, 959.6, 959.8-959.9

808.59 Other

➡ **CC Excl:** see Code 808.53

808.8 Unspecified, closed

➡ **CC Excl:** see Code 808.53

808.9 Unspecified, open

➡ **CC Excl:** see Code 808.53

809 Ill-defined fractures of bones of trunk

Includes: bones of trunk with other bones except those of skull and face
multiple bones of trunk

Excludes: *multiple fractures of:*
pelvic bones alone (808.0-808.9)
ribs alone (807.0-807.1, 807.4)
ribs or sternum with limb bones (819.0-819.1, 828.0-828.1)
skull or face with other bones (804.0-804.9)

809.0 Fracture of bones of trunk, closed

809.1 Fracture of bones of trunk, open

FRACTURE OF UPPER LIMB (810-819)

810 Fracture of clavicle

Includes: collar bone
interligamentous part of clavicle

The following fifth-digit subclassification is for use with category 810:

0 unspecified part
Clavicle NOS
1 sternal end of clavicle
2 shaft of clavicle
3 acromial end of clavicle

✓5th **810.0** Closed

✓5th **810.1** Open

811 Fracture of scapula

Includes: shoulder blade

The following fifth-digit subclassification is for use with category 811:

0 **unspecified part**
1 **acromial process**
Acromion (process)
2 **coracoid process**
3 **glenoid cavity and neck of scapula**
9 **other**
Scapula body

✓5th **811.0 Closed**

✓5th **811.1 Open**

812 Fracture of humerus

✓5th **812.0 Upper end, closed**

812.00 Upper end, unspecified part
Proximal end
Shoulder

812.01 Surgical neck
Neck of humerus NOS

812.02 Anatomical neck

812.03 Greater tuberosity

812.09 Other
Head
Upper epiphysis

✓5th **812.1 Upper end, open**

812.10 Upper end, unspecified part

812.11 Surgical neck

812.12 Anatomical neck

812.13 Greater tuberosity

812.19 Other

✓5th **812.2 Shaft or unspecified part, closed**

812.20 Unspecified part of humerus
Humerus NOS
Upper arm NOS

812.21 Shaft of humerus

✓5th **812.3 Shaft or unspecified part, open**

812.30 Unspecified part of humerus

812.31 Shaft of humerus

✓5th **812.4 Lower end, closed**
Distal end of humerus
Elbow

812.40 Lower end, unspecified part

812.41 Supracondylar fracture of humerus

812.42 Lateral condyle
External condyle

812.43 Medial condyle
Internal epicondyle

812.44 Condyle(s), unspecified
Articular process NOS
Lower epiphysis

812.49 Other
Multiple fractures of lower end
Trochlea

✓5th **812.5 Lower end, open**

812.50 Lower end, unspecified part

812.51 Supracondylar fracture of humerus

812.52 Lateral condyle

812.53 Medial condyle

812.54 Condyle(s), unspecified

812.59 Other

813 Fracture of radius and ulna

✓5th ☐ **813.0 Upper end, closed**
Proximal end

813.00 Upper end of forearm, unspecified

813.01 Olecranon process of ulna

813.02 Coronoid process of ulna

813.03 Monteggia's fracture

813.04 Other and unspecified fractures of proximal end of ulna (alone)
Multiple fractures of ulna, upper end

813.05 Head of radius

813.06 Neck of radius

813.07 Other and unspecified fractures of proximal end of radius (alone)
Multiple fractures of radius, upper end

813.08 Radius with ulna, upper end [any part]

✓5th ☐ **813.1 Upper end, open**

813.10 Upper end of forearm, unspecified

813.11 Olecranon process of ulna

813.12 Coronoid process of ulna

813.13 Monteggia's fracture

813.14 Other and unspecified fractures of proximal end of ulna (alone)

813.15 Head of radius

813.16 Neck of radius

813.17 Other and unspecified fractures of proximal end of radius (alone)

813.18 Radius with ulna, upper end [any part]

✓5th **813.2** Shaft, closed

813.20 Shaft, unspecified

813.21 Radius (alone)

813.22 Ulna (alone)

813.23 Radius with ulna

✓5th **813.3** Shaft, open

813.30 Shaft, unspecified

813.31 Radius (alone)

813.32 Ulna (alone)

813.33 Radius with ulna

✓5th **813.4** Lower end, closed

Distal end

813.40 Lower end of forearm, unspecified

813.41 Colles' fracture

Smith's fracture

813.42 Other fractures of distal end of radius (alone)

Dupuytren's fracture, radius
Radius, lower end

813.43 Distal end of ulna (alone)

Ulna:
head
lower end

Ulna:
lower epiphysis
styloid process

813.44 Radius with ulna, lower end

✓5th **813.5** Lower end, open

813.50 Lower end of forearm, unspecified

813.51 Colles' fracture

813.52 Other fractures of distal end of radius (alone)

813.53 Distal end of ulna (alone)

813.54 Radius with ulna, lower end

✓5th □ **813.8** Unspecified part, closed

813.80 Forearm, unspecified

813.81 Radius (alone)

813.82 Ulna (alone)

813.83 Radius with ulna

✓5th □ **813.9** Unspecified part, open

813.90 Forearm, unspecified

813.91 Radius (alone)

813.92 Ulna (alone)

813.93 Radius with ulna

814 Fracture of carpal bone(s)

The following fifth-digit subclassification is for use with category 814:

0 carpal bone, unspecified
Wrist NOS
1 navicular [scaphoid] of wrist
2 lunate [semilunar] bone of wrist
3 triquetral [cuneiform] bone of wrist
4 pisiform
5 trapezium bone [larger multangular]
6 trapezoid bone [smaller multangular]
7 capitate bone [os magnum]
8 hamate [unciform] bone
9 other

✓5th **814.0** Closed

✓5th **814.1** Open

815 Fracture of metacarpal bone(s)

Includes: hand [except finger]
metacarpus

The following fifth-digit subclassification is for use with category 815:

0 metacarpal bone(s), site unspecified
1 base of thumb [first] metacarpal
Bennett's fracture
2 base of other metacarpal bone(s)
3 shaft of metacarpal bone(s)
4 neck of metacarpal bone(s)
9 multiple sites of metacarpus

✓5th **815.0** Closed

✓5th **815.1** Open

816 Fracture of one or more phalanges of hand

Includes: finger(s) thumb

The following fifth-digit subclassification is for use with category 816:

0 **phalanx or phalanges, unspecified**
1 **middle or proximal phalanx or phalanges**
2 **distal phalanx or phalanges**
3 **multiple sites**

✓5th **816.0 Closed**

✓5th **816.1 Open**

817 Multiple fractures of hand bones

Includes: metacarpal bone(s) with phalanx or phalanges of same hand

817.0 Closed

817.1 Open

818 Ill-defined fractures of upper limb

Includes: arm NOS
multiple bones of same upper limb

Excludes: *multiple fractures of:*
metacarpal bone(s) with phalanx or phalanges (817.0-817.1)
phalanges of hand alone (816.0-816.1)
radius with ulna (813.0-813.9)

818.0 Closed

818.1 Open

819 Multiple fractures involving both upper limbs, and upper limb with rib(s) and sternum

Includes: arm(s) with rib(s) or sternum
both arms [any bones]

819.0 Closed

819.1 Open

FRACTURE OF LOWER LIMB (820-829)

820 Fracture of neck of femur

✓5th **820.0 Transcervical fracture, closed**

820.00 Intracapsular section, unspecified
➡ **CC Excl:** 733.10-733.19, 820.00-820.9 821.00-821.39, 827.0-827.1, 828.0-828.1, 829.0-829.1, 843.0-843.9, 848.8-848.9, 879.8-879.9, 929.0, 929.9, 958.8, 959.6, 959.8-959.9

820.01 Epiphysis (separation) (upper)
Transepiphyseal
➡ **CC Excl:** see Code 820.00

820.02 Midcervical section
Transcervical NOS
➡ **CC Excl:** see Code 820.00

820.03 Base of neck
Cervicotrochanteric section
➡ **CC Excl:** see Code 820.00

820.09 Other
Head of femur
Subcapital
➡ **CC Excl:** see Code 820.00

✓5th **820.1 Transcervical fracture, open**

820.10 Intracapsular section, unspecified
➡ **CC Excl:** see Code 820.00

820.11 Epiphysis (separation) (upper)
➡ **CC Excl:** see Code 820.00

820.12 Midcervical section
➡ **CC Excl:** see Code 820.00

820.13 Base of neck
➡ **CC Excl:** see Code 820.00

820.19 Other
➡ **CC Excl:** see Code 820.00

✓5th **820.2 Pertrochanteric fracture, closed**

820.20 Trochanteric section, unspecified
Trochanter:
NOS
greater
lesser
➡ **CC Excl:** see Code 820.00

820.21 Intertrochanteric section
➡ **CC Excl:** see Code 820.00

820.22 Subtrochanteric section
➡ **CC Excl:** see Code 820.00

✓5th **820.3 Pertrochanteric fracture, open**

820.30 Trochanteric section, unspecified
➡ **CC Excl:** see Code 820.00

820.31 Intertrochanteric section
➡ **CC Excl:** see Code 820.00

820.32 Subtrochanteric section
➡ **CC Excl:** see Code 820.00

820.8 Unspecified part of neck of femur, closed
Hip NOS Neck of femur NOS
➡ **CC Excl:** see Code 820.00

820.9 Unspecified part of neck of femur, open
➡ **CC Excl:** see Code 820.00

821 Fracture of other and unspecified parts of femur

✓5th **821.0** **Shaft or unspecified part, closed**

821.00 **Unspecified part of femur**
Thigh
Upper leg

Excludes: *hip NOS (820.8)*

➡ **CC Excl:** see Code 820.00

821.01 **Shaft**

➡ **CC Excl:** see Code 820.00

✓5th **821.1** **Shaft or unspecified part, open**

821.10 **Unspecified part of femur**

➡ **CC Excl:** see Code 820.00

821.11 **Shaft**

➡ **CC Excl:** see Code 820.00

✓5th **821.2** **Lower end, closed**
Distal end

821.20 **Lower end, unspecified part**

821.21 **Condyle, femoral**

821.22 **Epiphysis, lower (separation)**

821.23 **Supracondylar fracture of femur**

821.29 **Other**
Multiple fractures of lower end

✓5th **821.3** **Lower end, open**

821.30 **Lower end, unspecified part**

821.31 **Condyle, femoral**

821.32 **Epiphysis, lower (separation)**

821.33 **Supracondylar fracture of femur**

821.39 **Other**

822 Fracture of patella

822.0 **Closed**

822.1 **Open**

823 Fracture of tibia and fibula

Excludes: *Dupuytren's fracture (824.4-824.5)*
ankle (824.4-824.5)
radius (813.42, 813.52)
Pott's fracture (824.4-824.5)
that involving ankle (824.0-824.9)

The following fifth-digit subclassification is for use with category 823:

0 **tibia alone**
1 **fibula alone**
2 **fibula with tibia**

✓5th □ **823.0** **Upper end, closed**
Head
Proximal end
Tibia:
condyles
tuberosity

✓5th □ **823.1** **Upper end, open**

✓5th **823.2** **Shaft, closed**

✓5th **823.3** **Shaft, open**

✓5th □ **823.8** **Unspecified part, closed**
Lower leg NOS

➡ **AHA Coding Clinic: For code 823.82:** 1Q, '97, 8

✓5th □ **823.9** **Unspecified part, open**

824 Fracture of ankle

824.0 **Medial malleolus, closed**
Tibia involving:
ankle
malleolus

824.1 **Medial malleolus, open**

824.2 **Lateral malleolus, closed**
Fibula involving:
ankle
malleolus

824.3 **Lateral malleolus, open**

824.4 **Bimalleolar, closed**
Dupuytren's fracture, fibula
Pott's fracture

824.5 **Bimalleolar, open**

824.6 **Trimalleolar, closed**
Lateral and medial malleolus with anterior or posterior lip of tibia

824.7 **Trimalleolar, open**

824.8 **Unspecified part, closed**
Ankle NOS

824.9 **Unspecified part, open**

825 Fracture of one or more tarsal and metatarsal bones

825.0 Fracture of calcaneus, closed
Heel bone   Os calcis

825.1 Fracture of calcaneus, open

✓5th **825.2** Fracture of other tarsal and metatarsal bones, closed

825.20 Unspecified bone(s) of foot [except toes]
Instep

825.21 Astragalus
Talus

825.22 Navicular [scaphoid], foot

825.23 Cuboid

825.24 Cuneiform, foot

825.25 Metatarsal bone(s)

825.29 Other
Tarsal with metatarsal bone(s) only

Excludes: *calcaneus (825.0)*

✓5th **825.3** Fracture of other tarsal and metatarsal bones, open

825.30 Unspecified bone(s) of foot [except toes]

825.31 Astragalus

825.32 Navicular [scaphoid], foot

825.33 Cuboid

825.34 Cuneiform, foot

825.35 Metatarsal bone(s)

825.39 Other

826 Fracture of one or more phalanges of foot

Includes: toe(s)

826.0 Closed

826.1 Open

827 Other, multiple, and ill-defined fractures of lower limb

Includes: leg NOS
multiple bones of same lower limb

Excludes: *multiple fractures of:*
ankle bones alone (824.4-824.9)
phalanges of foot alone (826.0-826.1)
tarsal with metatarsal bones (825.29, 825.39)
tibia with fibula (823.0-823.9 with fifth-digit 2)

827.0 Closed

827.1 Open

828 Multiple fractures involving both lower limbs, lower with upper limb, and lower limb(s) with rib(s) and sternum

Includes: arm(s) with leg(s) [any bones]
both legs [any bones]
leg(s) with rib(s) or sternum

828.0 Closed

828.1 Open

829 Fracture of unspecified bones

829.0 Unspecified bone, closed

829.1 Unspecified bone, open

DISLOCATION (830-839)

Includes: displacement   subluxation

Excludes: *congenital dislocation (754.0-755.8)*
pathological dislocation (718.2)
recurrent dislocation (718.3)

The descriptions "closed" and "open", used in the fourth-digit subdivisions, include the following terms:

closed:	open:
complete	compound
dislocation NOS	infected
partial	with foreign body
simple	
uncomplicated	

A dislocation not indicated as closed or open should be classified as closed.

➡ **AHA Coding Clinic:** 3Q, '90, 12

830 Dislocation of jaw

Includes: jaw (cartilage) (meniscus)
mandible
maxilla (inferior)
temporomandibular (joint)

830.0 Closed dislocation

830.1 Open dislocation

831 Dislocation of shoulder

Excludes: *sternoclavicular joint (839.61, 839.71)*
sternum (839.61, 839.71)

The following fifth-digit subclassification is for use with category 831:

0 **shoulder, unspecified**
Humerus NOS
1 **anterior dislocation of humerus**
2 **posterior dislocation of humerus**
3 **inferior dislocation of humerus**
4 **acromioclavicular (joint)**
Clavicle
9 **other**
Scapula

✓5th **831.0 Closed dislocation**

✓5th **831.1 Open dislocation**

832 Dislocation of elbow

The following fifth-digit subclassification is for use with category 832:

0 **elbow unspecified**
1 **anterior dislocation of elbow**
2 **posterior dislocation of elbow**
3 **medial dislocation of elbow**
4 **lateral dislocation of elbow**
9 **other**

✓5th **832.0 Closed dislocation**

✓5th **832.1 Open dislocation**

833 Dislocation of wrist

The following fifth-digit subclassification is for use with category 833:

0 **wrist, unspecified part**
Carpal (bone) Radius, distal end
1 **radioulnar (joint), distal**
2 **radiocarpal (joint)**
3 **midcarpal (joint)**
4 **carpometacarpal (joint)**
5 **metacarpal (bone), proximal end**
9 **other**
Ulna, distal end

✓5th **833.0 Closed dislocation**

✓5th **833.1 Open dislocation**

834 Dislocation of finger

Includes: finger(s)
phalanx of hand
thumb

The following fifth-digit subclassification is for use with category 834:

0 **finger, unspecified part**
1 **metacarpophalangeal (joint)**
Metacarpal (bone), distal end
2 **interphalangeal (joint), hand**

✓5th **834.0 Closed dislocation**

✓5th **834.1 Open dislocation**

835 Dislocation of hip

The following fifth-digit subclassification is for use with category 835:

0 **dislocation of hip, unspecified**
1 **posterior dislocation**
2 **obturator dislocation**
3 **other anterior dislocation**

✓5th **835.0 Closed dislocation**

✓5th **835.1 Open dislocation**

836 Dislocation of knee

Excludes: *dislocation of knee:*
old or pathological (718.2)
recurrent (718.3)
internal derangement of knee joint (717.0-717.5, 717.8-717.9)
old tear of cartilage or meniscus of knee (717.0-717.5, 717.8-717.9)

836.0 Tear of medial cartilage or meniscus of knee, current
Bucket handle tear:
NOS } current injury
medial meniscus } current injury

836.1 Tear of lateral cartilage or meniscus of knee, current

836.2 Other tear of cartilage or meniscus of knee, current
Tear of:
cartilage (semilunar) } current injury, not specified as medial or lateral
meniscus } current injury, not specified as medial or lateral

836.3 Dislocation of patella, closed

836.4 Dislocation of patella, open

✓5th **836.5** Other dislocation of knee, closed

836.50 Dislocation of knee, unspecified

836.51 Anterior dislocation of tibia, proximal end
Posterior dislocation of femur, distal end

836.52 Posterior dislocation of tibia, proximal end
Anterior dislocation of femur, distal end

836.53 Medial dislocation of tibia, proximal end

836.54 Lateral dislocation of tibia, proximal end

836.59 Other

✓5th **836.6** Other dislocation of knee, open

836.60 Dislocation of knee, unspecified

836.61 Anterior dislocation of tibia, proximal end

836.62 Posterior dislocation of tibia, proximal end

836.63 Medial dislocation of tibia, proximal end

836.64 Lateral dislocation of tibia, proximal end

836.69 Other

837 Dislocation of ankle

Includes: astragalus; fibula, distal end; navicular, foot; scaphoid, foot; tibia, distal end

837.0 Closed dislocation

837.1 Open dislocation

838 Dislocation of foot

The following fifth-digit subclassification is for use with category 838:

0 foot, unspecified
1 tarsal (bone), joint unspecified
2 midtarsal (joint)
3 tarsometatarsal (joint)
4 metatarsal (bone), joint unspecified
5 metatarsophalangeal (joint)
6 interphalangeal (joint), foot
9 other
Phalanx of foot   Toe(s)

✓5th **838.0** Closed dislocation

✓5th [7] **838.1** Open dislocation

839 Other, multiple, and ill-defined dislocations

✓5th **839.0** Cervical vertebra, closed
Cervical spine   Neck

839.00 Cervical vertebra, unspecified
➡ **CC Excl:** 805.00-805.18, 806.00-806.19, 806.8-806.9, 839.00-839.18, 847.0, 848.8-848.9, 879.8-879.9, 929.0, 929.9, 952.00-952.09, 958.8, 959.8-959.9

839.01 First cervical vertebra
➡ **CC Excl:** see Code 839.00

839.02 Second cervical vertebra
➡ **CC Excl:** see Code 839.00

839.03 Third cervical vertebra
➡ **CC Excl:** see Code 839.00

839.04 Fourth cervical vertebra
➡ **CC Excl:** see Code 839.00

839.05 Fifth cervical vertebra
➡ **CC Excl:** see Code 839.00

839.06 Sixth cervical vertebra
➡ **CC Excl:** see Code 839.00

839.07 Seventh cervical vertebra
➡ **CC Excl:** see Code 839.00

839.08 Multiple cervical vertebrae
➡ **CC Excl:**see Code 839.00

✓5th **839.1** Cervical vertebra, open

839.10 Cervical vertebra, unspecified
➡ **CC Excl:** see Code 839.00

839.11 First cervical vertebra
➡ **CC Excl:** see Code 839.00

839.12 Second cervical vertebra
➡ **CC Excl:** see Code 839.00

839.13 Third cervical vertebra
➡ **CC Excl:** see Code 839.00

839.14 Fourth cervical vertebra
➡ **CC Excl:** see Code 839.00

839.15 Fifth cervical vertebra
➡ **CC Excl:** see Code 839.00

839.16 Sixth cervical vertebra
➡ **CC Excl:** see Code 839.00

839.17 Seventh cervical vertebra
➡ **CC Excl:** see Code 839.00

839.18 Multiple cervical vertebrae
➡ **CC Excl:** see Code 839.00

[7] CC Coding = 8

✓5th **839.2 Thoracic and lumbar vertebra, closed**

839.20 Lumbar vertebra

839.21 Thoracic vertebra
Dorsal [thoracic] vertebra

✓5th **839.3 Thoracic and lumbar vertebra, open**

839.30 Lumbar vertebra

839.31 Thoracic vertebra

✓5th **839.4 Other vertebra, closed**

839.40 Vertebra, unspecified site
Spine NOS

839.41 Coccyx

839.42 Sacrum
Sacroiliac (joint)

839.49 Other

✓5th **839.5 Other vertebra, open**

839.50 Vertebra, unspecified site

839.51 Coccyx

839.52 Sacrum

839.59 Other

✓5th **839.6 Other location, closed**

839.61 Sternum
Sternoclavicular joint

839.69 Other
Pelvis

✓5th **839.7 Other location, open**

839.71 Sternum

839.79 Other

839.8 Multiple and ill-defined, closed
Arm
Back
Hand
Multiple locations, except fingers or toes alone
Other ill-defined locations
Unspecified location

839.9 Multiple and ill-defined, open

SPRAINS AND STRAINS OF JOINTS AND ADJACENT MUSCLES (840-848)

Includes: avulsion, hemarthrosis, laceration, rupture, sprain, strain, tear of: joint capsule, ligament, muscle, tendon

Excludes: *laceration of tendon in open wounds (880-884 and 890-894 with .2)*

840 Sprains and strains of shoulder and upper arm

840.0 Acromioclavicular (joint) (ligament)

840.1 Coracoclavicular (ligament)

840.2 Coracohumeral (ligament)

840.3 Infraspinatus (muscle) (tendon)

840.4 Rotator cuff (capsule)

840.5 Subscapularis (muscle)

840.6 Supraspinatus (muscle) (tendon)

840.8 Other specified sites of shoulder and upper arm

840.9 Unspecified site of shoulder and upper arm
Arm NOS
Shoulder NOS

841 Sprains and strains of elbow and forearm

841.0 Radial collateral ligament

841.1 Ulnar collateral ligament

841.2 Radiohumeral (joint)

841.3 Ulnohumeral (joint)

841.8 Other specified sites of elbow and forearm

841.9 Unspecified site of elbow and forearm
Elbow NOS

842 Sprains and strains of wrist and hand

✓5th **842.0 Wrist**

842.00 Unspecified site

842.01 Carpal (joint)

842.02 Radiocarpal (joint) (ligament)

842.09 Other
Radioulnar joint, distal

✓5th **842.1** Hand

842.10 Unspecified site

842.11 Carpometacarpal (joint)

842.12 Metacarpophalangeal (joint)

842.13 Interphalangeal (joint)

842.19 Other
Midcarpal (joint)

843 Sprains and strains of hip and thigh

843.0 Iliofemoral (ligament)

843.1 Ischiocapsular (ligament)

843.8 Other specified sites of hip and thigh

843.9 Unspecified site of hip and thigh
Hip NOS Thigh NOS

844 Sprains and strains of knee and leg

844.0 Lateral collateral ligament of knee

844.1 Medial collateral ligament of knee

844.2 Cruciate ligament of knee

844.3 Tibiofibular (joint) (ligament), superior

844.8 Other specified sites of knee and leg

844.9 Unspecified site of knee and leg
Knee NOS Leg NOS

845 Sprains and strains of ankle and foot

✓5th **845.0** Ankle

845.00 Unspecified site

845.01 Deltoid (ligament), ankle
Internal collateral (ligament), ankle

845.02 Calcaneofibular (ligament)

845.03 Tibiofibular (ligament), distal

845.09 Other
Achilles tendon

✓5th **845.1** Foot

845.10 Unspecified site

845.11 Tarsometatarsal (joint) (ligament)

845.12 Metatarsophalangeal (joint)

845.13 Interphalangeal (joint), toe

845.19 Other

846 Sprains and strains of sacroiliac region

846.0 Lumbosacral (joint) (ligament)

846.1 Sacroiliac ligament

846.2 Sacrospinatus (ligament)

846.3 Sacrotuberous (ligament)

846.8 Other specified sites of sacroiliac region

846.9 Unspecified site of sacroiliac region

847 Sprains and strains of other and unspecified parts of back

Excludes: *lumbosacral (846.0)*

847.0 Neck
Anterior longitudinal (ligament), cervical
Atlanto-axial (joints)
Atlanto-occipital (joints)
Whiplash injury

Excludes: *neck injury NOS (959.0)*
thyroid region (848.2)

847.1 Thoracic

847.2 Lumbar

847.3 Sacrum
Sacrococcygeal (ligament)

847.4 Coccyx

847.9 Unspecified site of back
Back NOS

848 Other and ill-defined sprains and strains

848.0 Septal cartilage of nose

848.1 Jaw
Temporomandibular (joint) (ligament)

848.2 Thyroid region
Cricoarytenoid (joint) (ligament)
Cricothyroid (joint) (ligament)
Thyroid cartilage

848.3 Ribs
Chondrocostal (joint) } without mention of
Costal cartilage } injury to sternum

✓5th **848.4** **Sternum**

848.40 **Unspecified site**

848.41 **Sternoclavicular (joint) (ligament)**

848.42 **Chondrosternal (joint)**

848.49 **Other**

Xiphoid cartilage

848.5 **Pelvis**

Symphysis pubis

Excludes: *that in childbirth (665.6)*

848.8 **Other specified sites of sprains and strains**

848.9 **Unspecified site of sprain and strain**

INTRACRANIAL INJURY, EXCLUDING THOSE WITH SKULL FRACTURE (850-854)

Excludes: *intracranial injury with skull fracture (800-801 and 803-804, except .0 and .5)*
open wound of head without intracranial injury (870.0-873.9)
skull fracture alone (800-801 and 803-804 with .0, .5)

The description "with open intracranial wound," used in the fourth-digit subdivisions, includes those specified as open or with mention of infection or foreign body.

The following fifth-digit subclassification is for use with categories 851-854:

0 **unspecified state of consciousness**
1 **with no loss of consciousness**
2 **with brief [less than one hour] loss of consciousness**
3 **with moderate [1-24 hours] loss of consciousness**
4 **with prolonged [more than 24 hours] loss of consciousness and return to pre-existing conscious level**
5 **with prolonged [more than 24 hours] loss of consciousness, without return to pre-existing conscious level**
Use fifth-digit 5 to designate when a patient is unconscious and dies before regaining consciousness, regardless of the duration of the loss of consciousness
6 **with loss of consciousness of unspecified duration**
9 **with concussion, unspecified**

➡ **AHA Coding Clinic:** 1Q, '93, 22

850 Concussion

Includes: commotio cerebri

Excludes: *concussion with:*
cerebral hemorrhage (852-853)
cerebral laceration or contusion (851.0-851.9)
head injury NOS (959.01)

➡ **AHA Coding Clinic:** 2Q, '92, 6; 4Q, '90, 24

850.0 **With no loss of consciousness**

Concussion with mental confusion or disorientation, without loss of consciousness

➡ **CC Excl:** 800.00-800.99, 801.00-801.99, 803.00-803.99, 804.00-804.99, 850.0-850.9, 851.00-851.99, 852.00-852.19, 852.21-852.59, 853.00-853.19, 854.00-854.19, 873.8-873.9, 879.8-879.9, 905.0, 925.1-925.2, 929.0, 929.9, 958.8, 959.01, 959.09, 959.8-959.9

850.1 **With brief loss of consciousness**

Loss of consciousness for less than one hour

➡ **CC Excl:** see Code 850.0

➡ **AHA Coding Clinic:** 2Q, '92, 5

850.2 **With moderate loss of consciousness**

Loss of consciousness for 1-24 hours

➡ **CC Excl:** see Code 850.0

850.3 **With prolonged loss of consciousness and return to pre-existing conscious level**

Loss of consciousness for more than 24 hours with complete recovery

➡ **CC Excl:** see Code 850.0

850.4 **With prolonged loss of consciousness, without return to pre-existing conscious level**

➡ **CC Excl:** see Code 850.0

850.5 **With loss of consciousness of unspecified duration**

➡ **CC Excl:** see Code 850.0

850.9 **Concussion, unspecified**

➡ **CC Excl:** see Code 850.0

§ 851 Cerebral laceration and contusion

✓5th ☐ **851.0** **Cortex (cerebral) contusion without mention of open intracranial wound**

➡ **CC Excl:** see Code 850.0

✓5th ☐ **851.1** **Cortex (cerebral) contusion with open intracranial wound**

➡ **CC Excl:** see Code 850.0

➡ **AHA Coding Clinic:** 1Q, '92, 9

✓5th ☐ **851.2** **Cortex (cerebral) laceration without mention of open intracranial wound**

➡ **CC Excl:** see Code 850.0

✓5th ☐ **851.3** **Cortex (cerebral) laceration with open intracranial wound**

➡ **CC Excl:** see Code 850.0

§ Requires fifth-digit. See above for codes and definitions.

✓5th ☐ **851.4** Cerebellar or brain stem contusion without mention of open intracranial wound
➡ **CC Excl:** see Code 850.0

✓5th ☐ **851.5** Cerebellar or brain stem contusion with open intracranial wound
➡ **CC Excl:** see Code 850.0

✓5th ☐ **851.6** Cerebellar or brain stem laceration without mention of open intracranial wound
➡ **CC Excl:** see Code 850.0

✓5th ☐ **851.7** Cerebellar or brain stem laceration with open intracranial wound
➡ **CC Excl:** see Code 850.0

✓5th ☐ **851.8** Other and unspecified cerebral laceration and contusion, without mention of open intracranial wound
Brain (membrane) NOS
➡ **CC Excl:** see Code 850.0
➡ **AHA Coding Clinic:** 4Q, '96, 37

✓5th ☐ **851.9** Other and unspecified cerebral laceration and contusion, with open intracranial wound
➡ **CC Excl:** see Code 850.0

§ 852 Subarachnoid, subdural, and extradural hemorrhage, following injury

Excludes: *cerebral contusion or laceration (with hemorrhage) (851.0-851.9)*

✓5th ☐ **852.0** Subarachnoid hemorrhage following injury without mention of open intracranial wound
Middle meningeal hemorrhage following injury
➡ **CC Excl:** see Code 850.0

✓5th ☐ **852.1** Subarachnoid hemorrhage following injury with open intracranial wound
➡ **CC Excl:** see Code 850.0

✓5th ☐ **852.2** Subdural hemorrhage following injury without mention of open intracranial wound
➡ **CC Excl: For code 852.20:** 800.00-800.99, 801.00-801.99, 803.00-803.99, 804.00-804.99, 850.0-850.9, 851.00-851.99, 852.00-852.59, 853.00-853.19, 854.00-854.19, 873.8-873.9, 879.8-879.9, 905.0, 925.1-925.2, 929.0, 929.9, 958.8, 959.01, 959.09, 959.8-959.9
➡ **CC Excl: For code 852.21:** 800.00-800.99, 801.00-801.99, 803.00-803.99, 804.00-804.99, 850.0-850.9, 851.00-851.99, 852.00-852.19, 852.21-852.59, 853.00-853.19, 854.00-854.19, 873.8-873.9, 879.8-879.9, 905.0, 925.1-925.2, 929.0, 929.9, 958.8, 959.01, 959.09, 959.8-959.9
➡ **CC Excl: For codes 852.22-852.29:** see Code 852.21
➡ **AHA Coding Clinic:** 4Q, '96, 43

✓5th ☐ **852.3** Subdural hemorrhage following injury with open intracranial wound
➡ **CC Excl:** see Code 852.21

✓5th ☐ **852.4** Extradural hemorrhage following injury without mention of open intracranial wound
Epidural hematoma following injury
➡ **CC Excl:** see Code 852.21

✓5th ☐ **852.5** Extradural hemorrhage following injury with open intracranial wound
➡ **CC Excl:** see Code 852.21

§ 853 Other and unspecified intracranial hemorrhage following injury

✓5th **853.0** Without mention of open intracranial wound
Cerebral compression due to injury
Intracranial hematoma following injury
Traumatic cerebral hemorrhage
➡ **CC Excl:** see Code 852.21
➡ **AHA Coding Clinic:** 3Q, '90, 14

✓5th **853.1** With open intracranial wound
➡ **CC Excl:** see Code 852.21

§ 854 Intracranial injury of other and unspecified nature

Includes: brain injury NOS
cavernous sinus
intracranial injury

Excludes: *any condition classifiable to 850-853*
head injury NOS (959.01)

➡ **AHA Coding Clinic:** 2Q, '92, 6

✓5th **854.0** Without mention of open intracranial wound
➡ **CC Excl:** see Code 852.21

✓5th **854.1** With open intracranial wound
➡ **CC Excl:** see Code 852.21

INTERNAL INJURY OF THORAX, ABDOMEN, AND PELVIS (860-869)

Includes: blast injuries, blunt trauma, bruise, concussion injuries (except cerebral), crushing, hematoma, laceration, puncture, tear, traumatic rupture } of internal organs

Excludes: *concussion NOS (850.0-850.9)*
flail chest (807.4)
foreign body entering through orifice (930.0-939.9)
injury to blood vessels (901.0-902.9)

The description "with open wound," used in the fourth-digit subdivisions, includes those with mention of infection or foreign body.

§ Requires fifth-digit. See page 330 for codes and definitions.

860 Traumatic pneumothorax and hemothorax

➡ **AHA Coding Clinic:** 2Q, '93, 4

860.0 Pneumothorax without mention of open wound into thorax

➡ **CC Excl:** 860.0-860.5, 861.20-861.32, 862.29, 862.39, 862.8-862.9, 875.0-875.1, 879.8-879.9, 929.0, 929.9, 958.7-958.8, 959.8-959.9

860.1 Pneumothorax with open wound into thorax

➡ **CC Excl:** see Code 860.0

860.2 Hemothorax without mention of open wound into thorax

➡ **CC Excl:** see Code 860.0

860.3 Hemothorax with open wound into thorax

➡ **CC Excl:** see Code 860.0

860.4 Pneumohemothorax without mention of open wound into thorax

➡ **CC Excl:** see Code 860.0

860.5 Pneumohemothorax with open wound into thorax

➡ **CC Excl:** see Code 860.0

861 Injury to heart and lung

Excludes: *injury to blood vessels of thorax (901.0-901.9)*

✓5th **861.0** Heart, without mention of open wound into thorax

➡ **AHA Coding Clinic:** 1Q, '92, 9

861.00 Unspecified injury

861.01 Contusion

Cardiac contusion
Myocardial contusion

➡ **CC Excl:** 861.00-861.13, 862.29, 862.39, 862.8-862.9, 875.0-875.1, 879.8-879.9, 929.0, 929.9, 958.7-958.8, 959.8-959.9

861.02 Laceration without penetration of heart chambers

➡ **CC Excl:** see Code 861.01

861.03 Laceration with penetration of heart chambers

➡ **CC Excl:** see Code 861.01

✓5th **861.1** Heart, with open wound into thorax

861.10 Unspecified injury

➡ **CC Excl:** see Code 861.01

861.11 Contusion

➡ **CC Excl:** see Code 861.01

861.12 Laceration without penetration of heart chambers

➡ **CC Excl:** see Code 861.01

861.13 Laceration with penetration of heart chambers

➡ **CC Excl:** see Code 861.01

✓5th **861.2** Lung, without mention of open wound into thorax

861.20 Unspecified injury

861.21 Contusion

861.22 Laceration

➡ **CC Excl:** 861.20-861.32, 862.29, 862.39, 862.8-862.9, 875.0-875.1, 879.8-879.9, 929.0, 929.9, 958.7-958.8, 959.8-959.9

✓5th **861.3** Lung, with open wound into thorax

861.30 Unspecified injury

➡ **CC Excl:** see Code 861.22

861.31 Contusion

➡ **CC Excl:** see Code 861.22

861.32 Laceration

➡ **CC Excl:** see Code 861.22

862 Injury to other and unspecified intrathoracic organs

Excludes: *injury to blood vessels of thorax (901.0-901.9)*

862.0 Diaphragm, without mention of open wound into cavity

862.1 Diaphragm, with open wound into cavity

➡ **CC Excl:** 862.0-862.1, 862.29, 862.39, 862.8-862.9, 875.0-875.1, 879.8-879.9, 929.0, 929.9, 958.7-958.8, 959.8-959.9

✓5th **862.2** Other specified intrathoracic organs, without mention of open wound into cavity

862.21 Bronchus

➡ **CC Excl:** 862.21, 862.29, 862.31, 862.39, 862.8-862.9, 875.0-875.1, 879.8-879.9, 929.0, 929.9, 958.7-958.8, 959.8-959.9

862.22 Esophagus

➡ **CC Excl:** 862.22, 862.29, 862.32, 862.39, 862.8-862.9, 875.0-875.1, 879.8-879.9, 929.0, 929.9, 958.7-958.8, 959.8-959.9

862.29 Other

Pleura
Thymus gland

➡ **CC Excl:** 862.29, 862.39, 862.8-862.9, 875.0-875.1, 879.8-879.9, 929.0, 929.9, 958.7-958.8, 959.8-959.9

✓5th **862.3** Other specified intrathoracic organs, with open wound into cavity

862.31 Bronchus

➡ **CC Excl:** 862.21, 862.29, 862.31, 862.39, 862.8-862.9, 875.0-875.1, 879.8-879.9, 929.0, 929.9, 958.7-958.8, 959.8-959.9

862.32 Esophagus

➡ **CC Excl:** 862.22, 862.29, 862.32, 862.39, 862.8-862.9, 875.0-875.1, 879.8-879.9, 929.0, 929.9, 958.7-958.8, 959.8-959.9

862.39 Other

➡ **CC Excl:** 862.29, 862.39, 862.8-862.9, 875.0-875.1, 879.8-879.9, 929.0, 929.9, 958.7-958.8, 959.8-959.9

862.8 Multiple and unspecified intrathoracic organs, without mention of open wound into cavity

Crushed chest
Multiple intrathoracic organs

862.9 Multiple and unspecified intrathoracic organs, with open wound into cavity

➡ **CC Excl:** see Code 862.39

863 Injury to gastrointestinal tract

Excludes: *anal sphincter laceration during delivery (664.2)*
bile duct (868.0-868.1 with fifth-digit 2)
gallbladder (868.0-868.1 with fifth-digit 2)

863.0 Stomach, without mention of open wound into cavity

863.1 Stomach, with open wound into cavity

➡ **CC Excl:** 863.0-863.1, 863.80, 863.89-863.90, 863.99, 868.00, 868.03-868.10, 868.13-868.19, 869.0-869.1, 879.2-879.9, 929.0, 929.9, 958.8, 959.8-959.9

✓5th **863.2** Small intestine, without mention of open wound into cavity

863.20 Small intestine, unspecified site

863.21 Duodenum

863.29 Other

✓5th **863.3** Small intestine, with open wound into cavity

863.30 Small intestine, unspecified site

➡ **CC Excl:** 863.20-863.39, 863.80, 863.89-863.90, 863.99, 868.00, 868.03-868.10, 868.13-868.19, 869.0-869.1, 879.2-879.9, 929.0, 929.9, 958.8, 959.8-959.9

863.31 Duodenum

➡ **CC Excl:** 863.21, 863.31, 863.39, 863.80, 863.89-863.90, 863.99, 868.00, 868.03-868.10, 868.13-868.19, 869.0-869.1, 879.2-879.9, 929.0, 929.9, 958.8, 959.8-959.9

863.39 Other

➡ **CC Excl:** 863.20-863.39, 863.80, 863.89-863.90, 863.99, 868.00, 868.03-868.10, 868.13-868.19, 869.0-869.1, 879.2-879.9, 929.0, 929.9, 958.8, 959.8-959.9

✓5th **863.4** Colon or rectum, without mention of open wound into cavity

863.40 Colon, unspecified site

863.41 Ascending [right] colon

863.42 Transverse colon

863.43 Descending [left] colon

863.44 Sigmoid colon

863.45 Rectum

863.46 Multiple sites in colon and rectum

863.49 Other

✓5th **863.5** Colon or rectum, with open wound into cavity

863.50 Colon, unspecified site

➡ **CC Excl:** 863.40-863.59, 863.80, 863.89-863.90, 863.99, 868.00, 868.03-868.10, 868.13-868.19, 869.0-869.1, 879.2-879.9, 929.0, 929.9, 958.8, 959.8-959.9

863.51 Ascending [right] colon

➡ **CC Excl:** see Code 863.50

863.52 Transverse colon

➡ **CC Excl:** see Code 863.50

863.53 Descending [left] colon

➡ **CC Excl:** see Code 863.50

863.54 Sigmoid colon

➡ **CC Excl:** see Code 863.50

863.55 Rectum

➡ **CC Excl:** see Code 863.50

863.56 Multiple sites in colon and rectum

➡ **CC Excl:** see Code 863.50

863.59 Other

➡ **CC Excl:** see Code 863.50

✓5th **863.8** **Other and unspecified gastrointestinal sites, without mention of open wound into cavity**

863.80 **Gastrointestinal tract, unspecified site**

863.81 **Pancreas, head**

863.82 **Pancreas, body**

863.83 **Pancreas, tail**

863.84 **Pancreas, multiple and unspecified sites**

863.85 **Appendix**

863.89 **Other**

Intestine NOS

✓5th **863.9** **Other and unspecified gastrointestinal sites, with open wound into cavity**

863.90 **Gastrointestinal tract, unspecified site**

➡ **CC Excl:** 863.80-863.84, 863.89-863.94, 863.99, 868.00, 868.03-868.10, 868.13-868.19, 869.0-869.1, 879.2-879.9, 929.0, 929.9, 958.8, 959.8-959.9

863.91 **Pancreas, head**

➡ **CC Excl:** 863.80-863.84, 863.91-863.94, 863.99, 868.00, 868.03-868.10, 868.13-868.19, 869.0-869.1, 879.2-879.9, 929.0, 929.9, 958.8, 959.8-959.9

863.92 **Pancreas, body**

➡ **CC Excl:** see Code 863.91

863.93 **Pancreas, tail**

➡ **CC Excl:** see Code 863.91

863.94 **Pancreas, multiple and unspecified sites**

➡ **CC Excl:** see Code 863.91

863.95 **Appendix**

➡ **CC Excl:** 863.80, 863.85, 863.95, 863.99, 868.00, 868.03-868.10, 868.13-868.19, 869.0-869.1, 879.2-879.9, 929.0, 929.9, 958.8, 959.8-959.9

863.99 **Other**

➡ **CC Excl:** 863.80, 863.99, 868.00, 868.03-868.10, 868.13-868.19, 869.0-869.1, 879.2-879.9, 929.0, 929.9, 958.8, 959.8-959.9

864 Injury to liver

The following fifth-digit subclassification is for use with category 864:

- 0 **unspecified injury**
- 1 **hematoma and contusion**
- 2 **laceration, minor**
  Laceration involving capsule only, or without significant involvement of hepatic parenchyma [i.e., less than 1 cm deep]
- 3 **laceration, moderate**
  Laceration involving parenchyma but without major disruption of parenchyma [i.e., less than 10 cm long and less than 3 cm deep]
- 4 **laceration, major**
  Laceration with significant disruption of hepatic parenchyma [i.e., 10 cm long and 3 cm deep]
  Multiple moderate lacerations, with or without hematoma
  Stellate lacerations of liver
- 5 **laceration, unspecified**
- 9 **other**

✓5th **864.0** **Without mention of open wound into cavity**

➡ **CC Excl:** 863.80, 863.99, 864.00-864.19, 868.00, 868.03-868.10, 868.13-868.19, 869.0-869.1, 879.2-879.9, 929.0, 929.9, 958.8, 959.8-959.9

✓5th **864.1** **With open wound into cavity**

➡ **CC Excl:** see Code 864.0

865 Injury to spleen

The following fifth-digit subclassification is for use with category 865:

- 0 **unspecified injury**
- 1 **hematoma without rupture of capsule**
- 2 **capsular tears, without major disruption of parenchyma**
- 3 **laceration extending into parenchyma**
- 4 **massive parenchymal disruption**
- 9 **other**

✓5th **865.0** **Without mention of open wound into cavity**

➡ **CC Excl:** 865.00-865.19, 868.00, 868.03-868.10, 868.13-868.19, 869.0-869.1, 879.2-879.9, 929.0, 929.9, 958.8, 959.8-959.9

✓5th **865.1** **With open wound into cavity**

➡ **CC Excl:** see Code 865.0

866 Injury to kidney

The following fifth-digit subclassification is for use with category 866:

0 unspecified injury
1 hematoma without rupture of capsule
2 laceration
3 complete disruption of kidney parenchyma

✓5th **866.0** Without mention of open wound into cavity

➡ **CC Excl:** 866.00-866.13, 868.00, 868.03-868.10, 868.13-868.19, 869.0-869.1, 879.2-879.9, 929.0, 929.9, 958.8, 959.8-959.9

✓5th **866.1** With open wound into cavity

➡ **CC Excl:** see Code 866.0

867 Injury to pelvic organs

Excludes: *injury during delivery (664.0-665.9)*

867.0 Bladder and urethra, without mention of open wound into cavity

➡ **CC Excl:** 867.0-867.1, 867.6-867.9, 868.00, 868.03-868.10, 868.13-868.19, 869.0-869.1, 879.2-879.9, 929.0, 929.9, 958.8, 959.8-959.9

867.1 Bladder and urethra, with open wound into cavity

➡ **CC Excl:** see Code 867.0

867.2 Ureter, without mention of open wound into cavity

➡ **CC Excl:** 867.2-867.3, 867.6-867.9, 868.00, 868.03-868.10, 868.13-868.19, 869.0-869.1, 879.2-879.9, 929.0, 929.9, 958.8, 959.8-959.9

867.3 Ureter, with open wound into cavity

➡ **CC Excl:** see Code 867.2

867.4 Uterus, without mention of open wound into cavity ♀

➡ **CC Excl:** 867.4-867.9, 868.00, 868.03-868.10, 868.13-868.19, 869.0-869.1, 879.2-879.9, 929.0, 929.9, 958.8, 959.8-959.9

867.5 Uterus, with open wound into cavity ♀

➡ **CC Excl:** see Code 867.4

867.6 Other specified pelvic organs, without mention of open wound into cavity

Fallopian tube
Ovary
Prostate
Seminal vesicle
Vas deferens

➡ **CC Excl:** 867.6-867.9, 868.00, 868.03-868.10, 868.13-868.19, 869.0-869.1, 879.2-879.9, 929.0, 929.9, 958.8, 959.8-959.9

867.7 Other specified pelvic organs, with open wound into cavity

➡ **CC Excl:** see Code 867.6

867.8 Unspecified pelvic organ, without mention of open wound into cavity

➡ **CC Excl:** see Code 867.6

867.9 Unspecified pelvic organ, with open wound into cavity

➡ **CC Excl:** see Code 867.6

868 Injury to other intra-abdominal organs

The following fifth-digit subclassification is for use with category 868:

0 unspecified intra-abdominal organ
1 adrenal gland
2 bile duct and gallbladder
3 peritoneum
4 retroperitoneum
9 other and multiple intra-abdominal organs

✓5th [8] **868.0** Without mention of open wound into cavity

➡ **CC Excl: For code 868.00:** 868.00, 868.03-868.10, 868.13-868.19, 869.0-869.1, 879.2-879.9, 929.0, 929.9, 958.8, 959.8-959.9

➡ **CC Excl: For code 868.01:** 868.00, 868.01, 868.03-868.11, 868.13-868.19, 869.0-869.1, 879.2-879.9, 929.0, 929.9, 958.8, 959.8-959.9

➡ **CC Excl: For code 868.02:** 868.00, 868.02-868.10, 868.13-868.19, 869.0-869.1, 879.2-879.9, 929.0, 929.9, 958.8, 959.8-959.9

➡ **CC Excl: For codes 868.03-868.09:** 868.00, 868.03-868.10, 868.13-868.19, 869.0-869.1, 879.2-879.9, 929.0, 929.9, 958.8, 959.8-959.9

✓5th [8] **868.1** With open wound into cavity

➡ **CC Excl: For code 868.10:** see Code 868.03

➡ **CC Excl: For code 868.11:** 868.00, 868.01, 868.03-868.11, 868.13-868.19, 869.0-869.1, 879.2-879.9, 929.0, 929.9, 958.8, 959.8-959.9

➡ **CC Excl: For code 868.12:** 868.00, 868.03-868.10, 868.12-868.19, 869.0-869.1, 879.2-879.9, 929.0, 929.9, 958.8, 959.8-959.9

➡ **CC Excl: For codes 868.13-868.19:** 868.00, 868.03-868.10, 868.13-868.14, 869.0-869.1, 879.2-879.9, 929.0, 929.9, 958.8, 959.8-959.9

[8] Nonspecific PDX = 0

869 Internal injury to unspecified or ill-defined organs

Includes: internal injury NOS
multiple internal injury NOS

869.0 Without mention of open wound into cavity

➡ **CC Excl:** see Code 868.13

869.1 With open wound into cavity

➡ **CC Excl:** see Code 868.13

➡ **AHA Coding Clinic:** 2Q, '89, 15

OPEN WOUND (870-897)

Includes: animal bite, avulsion, cut, laceration, puncture wound, traumatic amputation

Excludes: *burn (940.0-949.5)*
crushing (925-929.9)
puncture of internal organs (860.0-869.1)
superficial injury (910.0-919.9)
that incidental to:
dislocation (830.0-839.9)
fracture (800.0-829.1)
internal injury (860.0-869.1)
intracranial injury (851.0-854.1)

The description "complicated" used in the fourth-digit subdivisions includes those with mention of delayed healing, delayed treatment, foreign body, or major infection.

OPEN WOUND OF HEAD, NECK, AND TRUNK (870-879)

870 Open wound of ocular adnexa

870.0 Laceration of skin of eyelid and periocular area

870.1 Laceration of eyelid, full-thickness, not involving lacrimal passages

870.2 Laceration of eyelid involving lacrimal passages

870.3 Penetrating wound of orbit, without mention of foreign body

➡ **CC Excl:** 870.0-870.9, 871.0-871.9, 879.8-879.9, 929.0, 929.9, 958.8, 959.8-959.9

870.4 Penetrating wound of orbit with foreign body

Excludes: *retained (old) foreign body in orbit (376.6)*

➡ **CC Excl:** see Code 870.3

870.8 Other specified open wounds of ocular adnexa

➡ **CC Excl:** see Code 870.3

870.9 Unspecified open wound of ocular adnexa

➡ **CC Excl:** see Code 870.3

871 Open wound of eyeball

Excludes: *2nd cranial nerve [optic] injury (950.0-950.9)*
3rd cranial nerve [oculomotor] injury (951.0)

871.0 Ocular laceration without prolapse of intraocular tissue

➡ **CC Excl:** see Code 870.3

➡ **AHA Coding Clinic:** 3Q, '96, 7

871.1 Ocular laceration with prolapse or exposure of intraocular tissue

➡ **CC Excl:** see Code 870.3

871.2 Rupture of eye with partial loss of intraocular tissue

➡ **CC Excl:** see Code 870.3

871.3 Avulsion of eye

Traumatic enucleation

➡ **CC Excl:** see Code 870.3

871.4 Unspecified laceration of eye

➡ **CC Excl:** see Code 870.3

871.5 Penetration of eyeball with magnetic foreign body

Excludes: *retained (old) magnetic foreign body in globe (360.50-360.59)*

871.6 Penetration of eyeball with (nonmagnetic) foreign body

Excludes: *retained (old) (nonmagnetic) foreign body in globe (360.60-360.69)*

871.7 Unspecified ocular penetration

871.9 Unspecified open wound of eyeball

➡ **CC Excl:** see Code 870.3

872 Open wound of ear

✓5th **872.0 External ear, without mention of complication**

872.00 External ear, unspecified site

872.01 Auricle, ear

Pinna

872.02 Auditory canal

✓5th **872.1 External ear, complicated**

872.10 External ear, unspecified site

872.11 Auricle, ear

872.12 Auditory canal

✓5th **872.6** Other specified parts of ear, without mention of complication

872.61 Ear drum
Drumhead Tympanic membrane

872.62 Ossicles

872.63 Eustachian tube

872.64 Cochlea

872.69 Other and multiple sites

✓5th **872.7** Other specified parts of ear, complicated

872.71 Ear drum

872.72 Ossicles
➡ **CC Excl:** 872.00-872.9, 879.8-879.9, 929.0, 929.9, 958.8, 959.8-959.9

872.73 Eustachian tube
➡ **CC Excl:** see Code 872.72

872.74 Cochlea
➡ **CC Excl:** see Code 872.72

872.79 Other and multiple sites

872.8 Ear, part unspecified, without mention of complication
Ear NOS

872.9 Ear, part unspecified, complicated

873 Other open wound of head

873.0 Scalp, without mention of complication

873.1 Scalp, complicated

✓5th **873.2** Nose, without mention of complication

873.20 Nose, unspecified site

873.21 Nasal septum

873.22 Nasal cavity

873.23 Nasal sinus

873.29 Multiple sites

✓5th **873.3** Nose, complicated

873.30 Nose, unspecified site

873.31 Nasal septum

873.32 Nasal cavity

873.33 Nasal sinus
➡ **CC Excl:** 873.20-873.39, 879.8-879.9, 929.0, 929.9, 958.8, 959.8-959.9

873.39 Multiple sites

✓5th **873.4** Face, without mention of complication

873.40 Face, unspecified site

873.41 Cheek

873.42 Forehead
Eyebrow
➡ **AHA Coding Clinic:** 4Q, '96, 43

873.43 Lip

873.44 Jaw

873.49 Other and multiple sites

✓5th **873.5** Face, complicated

873.50 Face, unspecified site

873.51 Cheek

873.52 Forehead

873.53 Lip

873.54 Jaw

873.59 Other and multiple sites

✓5th **873.6** Internal structures of mouth, without mention of complication

873.60 Mouth, unspecified site

873.61 Buccal mucosa

873.62 Gum (alveolar process)

873.63 Tooth (broken)

873.64 Tongue and floor of mouth

873.65 Palate

873.69 Other and multiple sites

✓5th **873.7** Internal structures of mouth, complicated

873.70 Mouth, unspecified site

873.71 Buccal mucosa

873.72 Gum (alveolar process)

873.73 Tooth (broken)

873.74 Tongue and floor of mouth

873.75 Palate

873.79 Other and multiple sites

873.8 Other and unspecified open wound of head without mention of complication
Head NOS

873.9 Other and unspecified open wound of head, complicated
➡ **CC Excl:** 847.0, 873.40-873.79, 873.9, 874.8-874.9, 879.8-879.9, 929.0, 929.9, 958.8, 959.8-959.9

874 Open wound of neck

✓5th **874.0** Larynx and trachea, without mention of complication

874.00 Larynx with trachea
➡ **CC Excl:** 847.0, 874.00-874.12, 874.8-874.9, 879.8-879.9, 929.0, 929.9, 958.8, 959.8-959.9

874.01 Larynx
➡ **CC Excl:** see Code 874.00

874.02 Trachea
➡ **CC Excl:** see Code 874.00

✓5th **874.1** Larynx and trachea, complicated

874.10 Larynx with trachea
➡ **CC Excl:** see Code 874.00

874.11 Larynx
➡ **CC Excl:** see Code 874.00

874.12 Trachea
➡ **CC Excl:** see Code 874.00

874.2 Thyroid gland, without mention of complication

874.3 Thyroid gland, complicated
➡ **CC Excl:** 847.0, 874.2-874.3, 874.8-874.9, 879.8-879.9, 929.0, 929.9, 958.8, 959.8-959.9

874.4 Pharynx, without mention of complication
Cervical esophagus

874.5 Pharynx, complicated
➡ **CC Excl:** 847.0, 874.4-874.9, 879.8-879.9, 929.0, 929.9, 958.8, 959.8-959.9

874.8 Other and unspecified parts, without mention of complication
Nape of neck
Supraclavicular region
Throat NOS

874.9 Other and unspecified parts, complicated

875 Open wound of chest (wall)

Excludes: *open wound into thoracic cavity (860.0-862.9)*
traumatic pneumothorax and hemothorax (860.1, 860.3, 860.5)

875.0 Without mention of complication
➡ **CC Excl:** 847.1, 862.29, 862.39, 862.8-862.9, 875.0-875.1, 879.8-879.9, 929.0, 929.9, 958.7-958.8, 959.8-959.9

875.1 Complicated
➡ **CC Excl:** see Code 875.0

876 Open wound of back

Includes: loin
lumbar region

Excludes: *open wound into thoracic cavity (860.0-862.9)*
traumatic pneumothorax and hemothorax (860.1, 860.3, 860.5)

876.0 Without mention of complication

876.1 Complicated

877 Open wound of buttock

Includes: sacroiliac region

877.0 Without mention of complication

877.1 Complicated

878 Open wound of genital organs (external), including traumatic amputation

Excludes: *injury during delivery (664.0-665.9)*
internal genital organs (867.0-867.9)

878.0 Penis, without mention of complication ♂

878.1 Penis, complicated ♂

878.2 Scrotum and testes, without mention of complication ♂

878.3 Scrotum and testes, complicated ♂

878.4 Vulva, without mention of complication ♀
Labium (majus) (minus)

878.5 Vulva, complicated ♀

878.6 Vagina, without mention of complication ♀

878.7 Vagina, complicated ♀

878.8 Other and unspecified parts, without mention of complication

878.9 Other and unspecified parts, complicated

879 Open wound of other and unspecified sites, except limbs

879.0 Breast, without mention of complication

879.1 Breast, complicated

879.2 Abdominal wall, anterior, without mention of complication
Abdominal wall NOS
Epigastric region
Hypogastric region
Pubic region
Umbilical region

➡ **AHA Coding Clinic:** 2Q, '91, 22

879.3 Abdominal wall, anterior, complicated

879.4 Abdominal wall, lateral, without mention of complication
Flank
Groin
Hypochondrium
Iliac (region)
Inguinal region

879.5 Abdominal wall, lateral, complicated

879.6 Other and unspecified parts of trunk, without mention of complication
Pelvic region
Perineum
Trunk NOS

879.7 Other and unspecified parts of trunk, complicated

879.8 Open wound(s) (multiple) of unspecified site(s) without mention of complication
Multiple open wounds NOS
Open wound NOS

879.9 Open wound(s) (multiple) of unspecified site(s), complicated

OPEN WOUND OF SHOULDER AND UPPER LIMB (880-887)

➡ **AHA Coding Clinic:** N-D, '85, 5

880 Open wound of shoulder and upper arm

The following fifth-digit subclassification is for use with category 880:

0 shoulder region
1 scapular region
2 axillary region
3 upper arm
9 multiple sites

✓5th **880.0** Without mention of complication

✓5th **880.1** Complicated

✓5th **880.2** With tendon involvement

881 Open wound of elbow, forearm, and wrist

The following fifth-digit subclassification is for use with category 881:

0 forearm
1 elbow
2 wrist

✓5th **881.0** Without mention of complication

✓5th **881.1** Complicated

✓5th **881.2** With tendon involvement

882 Open wound of hand except finger(s) alone

882.0 Without mention of complication

882.1 Complicated

882.2 With tendon involvement

883 Open wound of finger(s)

Includes: fingernail
thumb (nail)

883.0 Without mention of complication

883.1 Complicated

883.2 With tendon involvement

884 Multiple and unspecified open wound of upper limb

Includes: arm NOS
multiple sites of one upper limb
upper limb NOS

884.0 Without mention of complication

884.1 Complicated

884.2 With tendon involvement

885 Traumatic amputation of thumb (complete) (partial)

Includes: thumb(s) (with finger(s) of either hand)

885.0 Without mention of complication

885.1 Complicated

886 Traumatic amputation of other finger(s) (complete) (partial)

Includes: finger(s) of one or both hands, without mention of thumb(s)

886.0 Without mention of complication

886.1 Complicated

887 Traumatic amputation of arm and hand (complete) (partial)

887.0 Unilateral, below elbow, without mention of complication
➡ **CC Excl:** 880.00-880.29, 881.00-881.22, 882.0-882.2, 883.0-883.2, 884.0-884.2, 885.0-885.1, 886.0-886.1, 887.0-887.7, 929.0, 929.9, 958.8, 959.8-959.9

887.1 Unilateral, below elbow, complicated
➡ **CC Excl:** see Code 887.0

887.2 Unilateral, at or above elbow, without mention of complication
➡ **CC Excl:** see Code 887.0

887.3 Unilateral, at or above elbow, complicated
➡ **CC Excl:** see Code 887.0

887.4 Unilateral, level not specified, without mention of complication
➡ **CC Excl:** see Code 887.0

887.5 Unilateral, level not specified, complicated
➡ **CC Excl:** see Code 887.0

887.6 Bilateral [any level], without mention of complication
One hand and other arm
➡ **CC Excl:** see Code 887.0

887.7 Bilateral [any level], complicated
➡ **CC Excl:** see Code 887.0

OPEN WOUND OF LOWER LIMB (890-897)

➡ **AHA Coding Clinic:** N-D, '85, 5

890 Open wound of hip and thigh

890.0 Without mention of complication

890.1 Complicated

890.2 With tendon involvement

891 Open wound of knee, leg [except thigh], and ankle

Includes: leg NOS
multiple sites of leg, except thigh

Excludes: *that of thigh (890.0-890.2)*
with multiple sites of lower limb (894.0-894.2)

891.0 Without mention of complication

891.1 Complicated

891.2 With tendon involvement

892 Open wound of foot except toe(s) alone

Includes: heel

892.0 Without mention of complication

892.1 Complicated

892.2 With tendon involvement

893 Open wound of toe(s)

Includes: toenail

893.0 Without mention of complication

893.1 Complicated

893.2 With tendon involvement

894 Multiple and unspecified open wound of lower limb

Includes: lower limb NOS
multiple sites of one lower limb, with thigh

894.0 Without mention of complication

894.1 Complicated

894.2 With tendon involvement

895 Traumatic amputation of toe(s) (complete) (partial)

Includes: toe(s) of one or both feet

895.0 Without mention of complication

895.1 Complicated

896 Traumatic amputation of foot (complete) (partial)

896.0 Unilateral, without mention of complication
➡ **CC Excl:** 890.0-890.2, 891.0-891.2, 892.0-892.2, 893.0-893.2, 894.0-894.2, 895.0-895.1, 896.0-896.3, 897.0-897.7, 929.0, 929.9, 958.8, 959.8-959.9

896.1 Unilateral, complicated
➡ **CC Excl:** see Code 896.0

896.2 Bilateral, without mention of complication

Excludes: *one foot and other leg (897.6-897.7)*

➡ **CC Excl:** see Code 896.0

896.3 Bilateral, complicated
➡ **CC Excl:** see Code 896.0

897 Traumatic amputation of leg(s) (complete) (partial)

897.0 Unilateral, below knee, without mention of complication
➡ **CC Excl:** see Code 896.0

897.1 Unilateral, below knee, complicated
➡ **CC Excl:** see Code 896.0

897.2 Unilateral, at or above knee, without mention of complication
➡ **CC Excl:** see Code 896.0

897.3 Unilateral, at or above knee, complicated
➡ **CC Excl:** see Code 896.0

897.4 Unilateral, level not specified, without mention of complication
➡ **CC Excl:** see Code 896.0

897.5 Unilateral, level not specified, complicated
➡ **CC Excl:** see Code 896.0

897.6 Bilateral [any level], without mention of complication
One foot and other leg
➡ **CC Excl:** see Code 896.0

897.7 Bilateral [any level], complicated
➡ **CC Excl:** see Code 896.0

INJURY TO BLOOD VESSELS (900-904)

Includes: arterial hematoma, avulsion, cut, laceration, rupture, traumatic aneurysm or fistula (arteriovenous) } of blood vessel secondary to other injuries e.g., fracture or open wound

Excludes: *accidental puncture or laceration during medical procedure (998.2)*
intracranial hemorrhage following injury (851.0-854.1)

➡ **AHA Coding Clinic:** 3Q, '90, 5

900 Injury to blood vessels of head and neck

✓5th **900.0** Carotid artery

900.00 Carotid artery, unspecified
➡ **CC Excl:** 900.00, 900.82, 900.89, 900.9, 904.9, 929.0, 929.9, 958.8, 959.8-959.9

900.01 Common carotid artery
➡ **CC Excl:** see Code 900.00

900.02 External carotid artery
➡ **CC Excl:** see Code 900.00

900.03 Internal carotid artery
➡ **CC Excl:** see Code 900.00

900.1 Internal jugular vein
➡ **CC Excl:** 900.82, 900.89, 900.9, 904.9, 929.0, 929.9, 958.8, 959.8-959.9

✓5th **900.8** Other specified blood vessels of head and neck

900.81 External jugular vein
Jugular vein NOS
➡ **CC Excl:** see Code 900.1

900.82 Multiple blood vessels of head and neck
➡ **CC Excl:** see Code 900.1

900.89 Other
➡ **CC Excl:** see Code 900.1

900.9 Unspecified blood vessel of head and neck
➡ **CC Excl:** see Code 900.1

901 Injury to blood vessels of thorax

Excludes: *traumatic hemothorax (860.2-860.5)*

901.0 Thoracic aorta
➡ **CC Excl:** 901.0, 904.9, 929.0, 929.9, 958.8, 959.8-959.9

901.1 Innominate and subclavian arteries
➡ **CC Excl:** 901.1, 904.9, 929.0, 929.9, 958.8, 959.8-959.9

901.2 Superior vena cava
➡ **CC Excl:** 901.2, 904.9, 929.0, 929.9, 958.8, 959.8-959.9

901.3 Innominate and subclavian veins
➡ **CC Excl:** 901.3, 904.9, 929.0, 929.9, 958.8, 959.8-959.9

✓5th **901.4** Pulmonary blood vessels

901.40 Pulmonary vessel(s), unspecified

901.41 Pulmonary artery
➡ **CC Excl:** 901.40, 901.41, 904.9, 929.0, 929.9, 958.8, 959.8-959.9

901.42 Pulmonary vein
➡ **CC Excl:** 901.40, 901.42, 904.9, 929.0, 929.9, 958.8, 959.8-959.9

✓5th **901.8** Other specified blood vessels of thorax

901.81 Intercostal artery or vein

901.82 Internal mammary artery or vein

901.83 Multiple blood vessels of thorax

➡ **CC Excl:** 904.9, 929.0, 929.9, 958.8, 959.8-959.9

901.89 Other

Azygos vein   Hemiazygos vein

901.9 Unspecified blood vessel of thorax

902 Injury to blood vessels of abdomen and pelvis

902.0 Abdominal aorta

➡ **CC Excl:** 902.0, 902.87, 902.89, 902.9, 904.9, 929.0, 929.9, 958.8, 959.8-959.9

✓5th **902.1** Inferior vena cava

902.10 Inferior vena cava, unspecified

➡ **CC Excl:** 902.10, 902.87, 902.89, 902.9, 904.9, 929.0, 929.9, 958.8, 959.8-959.9

902.11 Hepatic veins

➡ **CC Excl:** 902.11, 902.87, 902.89, 902.9, 904.9, 929.0, 929.9, 958.8, 959.8-959.9

902.19 Other

➡ **CC Excl:** 902.19, 902.87, 902.89, 902.9, 904.9, 929.0, 929.9, 958.8, 959.8-959.9

✓5th **902.2** Celiac and mesenteric arteries

902.20 Celiac and mesenteric arteries, unspecified

➡ **CC Excl:** 902.20, 902.87, 902.89, 902.9, 904.9, 929.0, 929.9, 958.8, 959.8-959.9

902.21 Gastric artery

902.22 Hepatic artery

➡ **CC Excl:** 902.22, 902.87, 902.89, 902.9, 904.9, 929.0, 929.9, 958.8, 959.8-959.9

902.23 Splenic artery

➡ **CC Excl:** 902.23, 902.87, 902.89, 902.9, 904.9, 929.0, 929.9, 958.8, 959.8-959.9

902.24 Other specified branches of celiac axis

➡ **CC Excl:** 902.24, 902.87, 902.89, 902.9, 904.9, 929.0, 929.9, 958.8, 959.8-959.9

902.25 Superior mesenteric artery (trunk)

➡ **CC Excl:** 902.25, 902.87, 902.89, 902.9, 904.9, 929.0, 929.9, 958.8, 959.8-959.9

902.26 Primary branches of superior mesenteric artery

Ileo-colic artery

➡ **CC Excl:** 902.26, 902.87, 902.89, 902.9, 904.9, 929.0, 929.9, 958.8, 959.8-959.9

902.27 Inferior mesenteric artery

➡ **CC Excl:** 902.27, 902.87, 902.89, 902.9, 904.9, 929.0, 929.9, 958.8, 959.8-959.9

902.29 Other

➡ **CC Excl:** 902.29, 902.87, 902.89, 902.9, 904.9, 929.0, 929.9, 958.8, 959.8-959.9

✓5th **902.3** Portal and splenic veins

902.31 Superior mesenteric vein and primary subdivisions

Ileo-colic vein

➡ **CC Excl:** 902.31, 902.87, 902.89, 902.9, 904.9, 929.0, 929.9, 958.8, 959.8-959.9

902.32 Inferior mesenteric vein

➡ **CC Excl:** 902.32, 902.87, 902.89, 902.9, 904.9, 929.0, 929.9, 958.8, 959.8-959.9

902.33 Portal vein

➡ **CC Excl:** 902.33, 902.87, 902.89, 902.9, 904.9, 929.0, 929.9, 958.8, 959.8-959.9

902.34 Splenic vein

➡ **CC Excl:** 902.34, 902.87, 902.89, 902.9, 904.9, 929.0, 929.9, 958.8, 959.8-959.9

902.39 Other

Cystic vein   Gastric vein

➡ **CC Excl:** 902.39, 902.87, 902.89, 902.9, 904.9, 929.0, 929.9, 958.8, 959.8-959.9

✓5th **902.4** Renal blood vessels

902.40 Renal vessel(s), unspecified

➡ **CC Excl:** 902.40, 902.87, 902.89, 902.9, 904.9, 929.0, 929.9, 958.8, 959.8-959.9

902.41 Renal artery

➡ **CC Excl:** 902.41, 902.87, 902.89, 902.9, 904.9, 929.0, 929.9, 958.8, 959.8-959.9

902.42 Renal vein

➡ **CC Excl:** 902.42, 902.87, 902.89, 902.9, 904.9, 929.0, 929.9, 958.8, 959.8-959.9

902.49 Other

Suprarenal arteries

➡ **CC Excl:** 902.49, 902.87, 902.89, 902.9, 904.9, 929.0, 929.9, 958.8, 959.8-959.9

✓5th **902.5** Iliac blood vessels

902.50 Iliac vessel(s), unspecified
➡ **CC Excl:** 902.50, 902.53-902.54, 902.59, 902.87, 902.89, 902.9, 904.9, 929.0, 929.9, 958.8, 959.8-959.9

902.51 Hypogastric artery
➡ **CC Excl:** 902.51, 902.87, 902.89, 902.9, 904.9, 929.0, 929.9, 958.8, 959.8-959.9

902.52 Hypogastric vein
➡ **CC Excl:** 902.52, 902.87, 902.89, 902.9, 904.9, 929.0, 929.9, 958.8, 959.8-959.9

902.53 Iliac artery
➡ **CC Excl:** 902.50, 902.53, 902.59, 902.87, 902.89, 902.9, 904.9, 929.0, 929.9, 958.8, 959.8-959.9

902.54 Iliac vein
➡ **CC Excl:** 902.50, 902.54, 902.59, 902.87, 902.89, 902.9, 904.9, 929.0, 929.9, 958.8, 959.8-959.9

902.55 Uterine artery ♀

902.56 Uterine vein ♀

902.59 Other
➡ **CC Excl:** 902.50, 902.53-902.54, 902.59, 902.87, 902.89, 902.9, 904.9, 929.0, 929.9, 958.8, 959.8-959.9

✓5th **902.8** Other specified blood vessels of abdomen and pelvis

902.81 Ovarian artery ♀

902.82 Ovarian vein ♀

902.87 Multiple blood vessels of abdomen and pelvis
➡ **CC Excl:** 902.87, 902.89, 902.9, 904.9, 929.0, 929.9, 958.8, 959.8-959.9

902.89 Other

902.9 Unspecified blood vessel of abdomen and pelvis

903 Injury to blood vessels of upper extremity

✓5th **903.0** Axillary blood vessels

903.00 Axillary vessel(s), unspecified

903.01 Axillary artery

903.02 Axillary vein

903.1 Brachial blood vessels

903.2 Radial blood vessels

903.3 Ulnar blood vessels

903.4 Palmar artery

903.5 Digital blood vessels

903.8 Other specified blood vessels of upper extremity
Multiple blood vessels of upper extremity

903.9 Unspecified blood vessel of upper extremity

904 Injury to blood vessels of lower extremity and unspecified sites

904.0 Common femoral artery
Femoral artery above profunda origin
➡ **CC Excl:** No exclusions

904.1 Superficial femoral artery

904.2 Femoral veins

904.3 Saphenous veins
Saphenous vein (greater) (lesser)

✓5th **904.4** Popliteal blood vessels

904.40 Popliteal vessel(s), unspecified

904.41 Popliteal artery

904.42 Popliteal vein

✓5th **904.5** Tibial blood vessels

904.50 Tibial vessel(s), unspecified

904.51 Anterior tibial artery

904.52 Anterior tibial vein

904.53 Posterior tibial artery

904.54 Posterior tibial vein

904.6 Deep plantar blood vessels

904.7 Other specified blood vessels of lower extremity
Multiple blood vessels of lower extremity

904.8 Unspecified blood vessel of lower extremity

904.9 Unspecified site
Injury to blood vessel NOS

LATE EFFECTS OF INJURIES, POISONINGS, TOXIC EFFECTS, AND OTHER EXTERNAL CAUSES (905-909)

Note: These categories are to be used to indicate conditions classifiable to 800-999 as the cause of late effects, which are themselves classified elsewhere. The "late effects" include those specified as such, or as sequelae, which may occur at any time after the acute injury.

905 Late effects of musculoskeletal and connective tissue injuries

905.0 Late effect of fracture of skull and face bones
Late effect of injury classifiable to 800-804
➡ AHA Coding Clinic: 3Q, '97, 12

905.1 Late effect of fracture of spine and trunk without mention of spinal cord lesion
Late effect of injury classifiable to 805, 807-809

905.2 Late effect of fracture of upper extremities
Late effect of injury classifiable to 810-819

905.3 Late effect of fracture of neck of femur
Late effect of injury classifiable to 820

905.4 Late effect of fracture of lower extremities
Late effect of injury classifiable to 821-827

905.5 Late effect of fracture of multiple and unspecified bones
Late effect of injury classifiable to 828-829

905.6 Late effect of dislocation
Late effect of injury classifiable to 830-839

905.7 Late effect of sprain and strain without mention of tendon injury
Late effect of injury classifiable to 840-848, except tendon injury

905.8 Late effect of tendon injury
Late effect of tendon injury due to:
open wound [injury classifiable to 880-884 with .2, 890-894 with .2]
sprain and strain [injury classifiable to 840-848]
➡ AHA Coding Clinic: 2Q, '89, 13; 2Q, '89, 15

905.9 Late effect of traumatic amputation
Late effect of injury classifiable to 885-887, 895-897

Excludes: *late amputation stump complication (997.60-997.69)*

906 Late effects of injuries to skin and subcutaneous tissues

906.0 Late effect of open wound of head, neck, and trunk
Late effect of injury classifiable to 870-879

906.1 Late effect of open wound of extremities without mention of tendon injury
Late effect of injury classifiable to 880-884, 890-894 except .2

906.2 Late effect of superficial injury
Late effect of injury classifiable to 910-919

906.3 Late effect of contusion
Late effect of injury classifiable to 920-924

906.4 Late effect of crushing
Late effect of injury classifiable to 925-929

906.5 Late effect of burn of eye, face, head, and neck
Late effect of injury classifiable to 940-941

906.6 Late effect of burn of wrist and hand
Late effect of injury classifiable to 944

906.7 Late effect of burn of other extremities
Late effect of injury classifiable to 943 or 945

906.8 Late effect of burns of other specified sites
Late effect of injury classifiable to 942, 946-947

906.9 Late effect of burn of unspecified site
Late effect of injury classifiable to 948-949

907 Late effects of injuries to the nervous system

907.0 Late effect intracranial injury without mention of skull fracture
Late effect of injury classifiable to 850-854

907.1 Late effect of injury to cranial nerve
Late effect of injury classifiable to 950-951

907.2 Late effect of spinal cord injury
Late effect of injury classifiable to 806, 952

907.3 Late effect of injury to nerve root(s), spinal plexus(es), and other nerves of trunk
Late effect of injury classifiable to 953-954

907.4 Late effect of injury to peripheral nerve of shoulder girdle and upper limb
Late effect of injury classifiable to 955

907.5 Late effect of injury to peripheral nerve of pelvic girdle and lower limb
Late effect of injury classifiable to 956

907.9 Late effect of injury to other and unspecified nerve
Late effect of injury classifiable to 957

908 Late effects of other and unspecified injuries

908.0 Late effect of internal injury to chest
Late effect of injury classifiable to 860-862

908.1 Late effect of internal injury to intra-abdominal organs
Late effect of injury classifiable to 863-866, 868

908.2 Late effect of internal injury to other internal organs
Late effect of injury classifiable to 867 or 869

908.3 Late effect of injury to blood vessel of head, neck, and extremities

Late effect of injury classifiable to 900, 903-904

908.4 Late effect of injury to blood vessel of thorax, abdomen, and pelvis

Late effect of injury classifiable to 901-902

908.5 Late effect of foreign body in orifice

Late effect of injury classifiable to 930-939

908.6 Late effect of certain complications of trauma

Late effect of complications classifiable to 958

908.9 Late effect of unspecified injury

Late effect of injury classifiable to 959

909 Late effects of other and unspecified external causes

909.0 Late effect of poisoning due to drug, medicinal or biological substance

Late effect of conditions classifiable to 960-979

Excludes: *late effect of adverse effect of drug, medicinal or biological substance (909.5)*

909.1 Late effect of toxic effects of nonmedical substances

Late effect of conditions classifiable to 980-989

909.2 Late effect of radiation

Late effect of conditions classifiable to 990

909.3 Late effect of complications of surgical and medical care

Late effect of conditions classifiable to 996-999

➡ **AHA Coding Clinic:** 1Q, '93, 29

909.4 Late effect of certain other external causes

Late effect of conditions classifiable to 991-994

909.5 Late effect of adverse effect of drug, medicinal or biological substance

Excludes: *late effect of poisoning due to drug, medicinal or biological substances (909.0)*

➡ **AHA Coding Clinic:** 4Q, '94, 48

909.9 Late effects of other and unspecified external causes

SUPERFICIAL INJURY (910-919)

Excludes: *burn (blisters) (940.0-949.5)*
contusion (920-924.9)
foreign body:
granuloma (728.82)
inadvertently left in operative wound (998.4)
residual, in soft tissue (729.6)
insect bite, venomous (989.5)
open wound with incidental foreign body (870.0-897.7)

➡ **AHA Coding Clinic:** 2Q, '89, 15

910 Superficial injury of face, neck, and scalp except eye

Includes: cheek, ear, gum, lip, nose, throat

Excludes: *eye and adnexa (918.0-918.9)*

910.0 Abrasion or friction burn without mention of infection

910.1 Abrasion or friction burn, infected

910.2 Blister without mention of infection

910.3 Blister, infected

910.4 Insect bite, nonvenomous, without mention of infection

910.5 Insect bite, nonvenomous, infected

910.6 Superficial foreign body (splinter) without major open wound and without mention of infection

910.7 Superficial foreign body (splinter) without major open wound, infected

910.8 Other and unspecified superficial injury of face, neck, and scalp without mention of infection

910.9 Other and unspecified superficial injury of face, neck, and scalp, infected

911 Superficial injury of trunk

Includes: abdominal wall, anus, back, breast, buttock, chest wall, flank, groin, interscapular region, labium (majus) (minus), penis, perineum, scrotum, testis, vagina, vulva

Excludes: *hip (916.0-916.9)*
scapular region (912.0-912.9)

911.0 Abrasion or friction burn without mention of infection

911.1 Abrasion or friction burn, infected

911.2 Blister without mention of infection

911.3 Blister, infected

911.4 Insect bite, nonvenomous, without mention of infection

911.5 Insect bite, nonvenomous, infected

911.6 Superficial foreign body (splinter) without major open wound and without mention of infection

911.7 Superficial foreign body (splinter) without major open wound, infected

911.8 Other and unspecified superficial injury of trunk without mention of infection

911.9 Other and unspecified superficial injury of trunk, infected

912 Superficial injury of shoulder and upper arm

Includes: axilla scapular region

912.0 Abrasion or friction burn without mention of infection

912.1 Abrasion or friction burn, infected

912.2 Blister without mention of infection

912.3 Blister, infected

912.4 Insect bite, nonvenomous, without mention of infection

912.5 Insect bite, nonvenomous, infected

912.6 Superficial foreign body (splinter) without major open wound and without mention of infection

912.7 Superficial foreign body (splinter) without major open wound, infected

912.8 Other and unspecified superficial injury of shoulder and upper arm without mention of infection

912.9 Other and unspecified superficial injury of shoulder and upper arm, infected

913 Superficial injury of elbow, forearm, and wrist

913.0 Abrasion or friction burn without mention of infection

913.1 Abrasion or friction burn, infected

913.2 Blister without mention of infection

913.3 Blister, infected

913.4 Insect bite, nonvenomous, without mention of infection

913.5 Insect bite, nonvenomous, infected

913.6 Superficial foreign body (splinter) without major open wound and without mention of infection

913.7 Superficial foreign body (splinter) without major open wound, infected

913.8 Other and unspecified superficial injury of elbow, forearm, and wrist without mention of infection

913.9 Other and unspecified superficial injury of elbow, forearm, and wrist, infected

914 Superficial injury of hand(s) except finger(s) alone

914.0 Abrasion or friction burn without mention of infection

914.1 Abrasion or friction burn, infected

914.2 Blister without mention of infection

914.3 Blister, infected

914.4 Insect bite, nonvenomous, without mention of infection

914.5 Insect bite, nonvenomous, infected

914.6 Superficial foreign body (splinter) without major open wound and without mention of infection

914.7 Superficial foreign body (splinter) without major open wound, infected

914.8 Other and unspecified superficial injury of hand without mention of infection

914.9 Other and unspecified superficial injury of hand, infected

915 Superficial injury of finger(s)

Includes: fingernail thumb (nail)

915.0 Abrasion or friction burn without mention of infection

915.1 Abrasion or friction burn, infected

915.2 Blister without mention of infection

915.3 Blister, infected

915.4 Insect bite, nonvenomous, without mention of infection

915.5 Insect bite, nonvenomous, infected

915.6 Superficial foreign body (splinter) without major open wound and without mention of infection

915.7 Superficial foreign body (splinter) without major open wound, infected

915.8 Other and unspecified superficial injury of fingers without mention of infection

915.9 Other and unspecified superficial injury of fingers, infected

916 Superficial injury of hip, thigh, leg, and ankle

916.0 Abrasion or friction burn without mention of infection

916.1 Abrasion or friction burn, infected

916.2 Blister without mention of infection

916.3 Blister, infected

916.4 Insect bite, nonvenomous, without mention of infection

916.5 Insect bite, nonvenomous, infected

916.6 Superficial foreign body (splinter) without major open wound and without mention of infection

916.7 Superficial foreign body (splinter) without major open wound, infected

916.8 Other and unspecified superficial injury of hip, thigh, leg, and ankle without mention of infection

916.9 Other and unspecified superficial injury of hip, thigh, leg, and ankle, infected

917 Superficial injury of foot and toe(s)

Includes: heel toenail

917.0 Abrasion or friction burn without mention of infection

917.1 Abrasion or friction burn, infected

917.2 Blister without mention of infection

917.3 Blister, infected

917.4 Insect bite, nonvenomous, without mention of infection

917.5 Insect bite, nonvenomous, infected

917.6 Superficial foreign body (splinter) without major open wound and without mention of infection

917.7 Superficial foreign body (splinter) without major open wound, infected

917.8 Other and unspecified superficial injury of foot and toes without mention of infection

917.9 Other and unspecified superficial injury of foot and toes, infected

918 Superficial injury of eye and adnexa

Excludes: *burn (940.0-940.9)*
foreign body on external eye (930.0-930.9)

918.0 Eyelids and periocular area

Abrasion
Insect bite
Superficial foreign body (splinter)

918.1 Cornea

Corneal abrasion
Superficial laceration

Excludes: *corneal injury due to contact lens (371.82)*

918.2 Conjunctiva

918.9 Other and unspecified superficial injuries of eye

Eye (ball) NOS

919 Superficial injury of other, multiple, and unspecified sites

Excludes: *multiple sites classifiable to the same three-digit category (910.0-918.9)*

919.0 Abrasion or friction burn without mention of infection

919.1 Abrasion or friction burn, infected

919.2 Blister without mention of infection

919.3 Blister, infected

919.4 Insect bite, nonvenomous, without mention of infection

919.5 Insect bite, nonvenomous, infected

919.6 Superficial foreign body (splinter) without major open wound and without mention of infection

919.7 Superficial foreign body (splinter) without major open wound, infected

919.8 Other and unspecified superficial injury without mention of infection

919.9 Other and unspecified superficial injury, infected

CONTUSION WITH INTACT SKIN SURFACE (920-924)

Includes: bruise, hematoma } without fracture or open wound

Excludes: *concussion (850.0-850.9)*
hemarthrosis (840.0-848.9)
internal organs (860.0-869.1)
that incidental to:
crushing injury (925-929.9)
dislocation (830.0-839.9)
fracture (800.0-829.1)
internal injury (860.0-869.1)
intracranial injury (850.0-854.1)
nerve injury (950.0-957.9)
open wound (870.0-897.7)

920 Contusion of face, scalp, and neck except eye(s)

Cheek
Ear (auricle)
Gum
Lip
Mandibular joint area
Nose
Throat

921 Contusion of eye and adnexa

921.0 Black eye, not otherwise specified

921.1 Contusion of eyelids and periocular area

921.2 Contusion of orbital tissues

921.3 Contusion of eyeball

921.9 Unspecified contusion of eye
Injury of eye NOS

922 Contusion of trunk

922.0 Breast

922.1 Chest wall

922.2 Abdominal wall
Flank
Groin

✓5th **922.3** Back

Excludes: *scapular region (923.01)*

➡ **AHA Coding Clinic:** 4Q, '96, 39

922.31 Back

Excludes: *interscapular region (922.33)*

922.32 Buttock

922.33 Interscapular region

922.4 Genital organs
Labium (majus) (minus)
Penis
Perineum
Scrotum
Testis
Vagina
Vulva

922.8 Multiple sites of trunk

922.9 Unspecified part
Trunk NOS

923 Contusion of upper limb

✓5th **923.0** Shoulder and upper arm

923.00 Shoulder region

923.01 Scapular region

923.02 Axillary region

923.03 Upper arm

923.09 Multiple sites

✓5th **923.1** Elbow and forearm

923.10 Forearm

923.11 Elbow

✓5th **923.2** Wrist and hand(s), except finger(s) alone

923.20 Hand(s)

923.21 Wrist

923.3 Finger
Fingernail
Thumb (nail)

923.8 Multiple sites of upper limb

923.9 Unspecified part of upper limb
Arm NOS

924 Contusion of lower limb and of other and unspecified sites

✓5th **924.0** Hip and thigh

924.00 Thigh

924.01 Hip

✓5th **924.1** Knee and lower leg

924.10 Lower leg

924.11 Knee

✓5th **924.2** Ankle and foot, excluding toe(s)

924.20 Foot
Heel

924.21 Ankle

924.3 Toe
Toenail

924.4 Multiple sites of lower limb

924.5 Unspecified part of lower limb
Leg NOS

924.8 Multiple sites, not elsewhere classified

924.9 Unspecified site

CRUSHING INJURY (925-929)

Excludes: *concussion (850.0-850.9)*
fractures (800-829)
internal organs (860.0-869.1)
that incidental to:
internal injury (860.0-869.1)
intracranial injury (850.0-854.1)

➡ **AHA Coding Clinic:** 2Q, '93, 7

925 Crushing injury of face, scalp, and neck
Cheek
Ear
Larynx
Pharynx
Throat

925.1 Crushing injury of face and scalp
Cheek
Ear

➡ **CC Excl:** 873.8-873.9, 905.0, 925.1-925.2, 929.0, 929.9, 958.8, 959.01, 959.09, 959.8-959.9

925.2 Crushing injury of neck
Larynx
Throat
Pharynx

➡ **CC Excl:** 873.8-873.9, 905.0, 925.1-925.2, 929.0, 929.9, 958.8, 959.01, 959.09, 959.8-959.9

926 Crushing injury of trunk

Excludes: crush injury of internal organs (860.0-869.1)

926.0 External genitalia
Labium (majus) (minus)
Penis
Scrotum
Testis
Vulva

✓5th **926.1** Other specified sites

926.11 Back

926.12 Buttock

926.19 Other
Breast

Excludes: crushing of chest (860.0-862.9)

926.8 Multiple sites of trunk

926.9 Unspecified site
Trunk NOS

927 Crushing injury of upper limb

✓5th **927.0** Shoulder and upper arm

927.00 Shoulder region

927.01 Scapular region

927.02 Axillary region

927.03 Upper arm

927.09 Multiple sites

✓5th **927.1** Elbow and forearm

927.10 Forearm

927.11 Elbow

✓5th **927.2** Wrist and hand(s), except finger(s) alone

927.20 Hand(s)

927.21 Wrist

927.3 Finger(s)

927.8 Multiple sites of upper limb

927.9 Unspecified site
Arm NOS

928 Crushing injury of lower limb

✓5th **928.0** Hip and thigh

928.00 Thigh

928.01 Hip

✓5th **928.1** Knee and lower leg

928.10 Lower leg

928.11 Knee

✓5th **928.2** Ankle and foot, excluding toe(s) alone

928.20 Foot
Heel

928.21 Ankle

928.3 Toe(s)

928.8 Multiple sites of lower limb

928.9 Unspecified site
Leg NOS

929 Crushing injury of multiple and unspecified sites

Excludes: multiple internal injury NOS (869.0-869.1)

929.0 Multiple sites, not elsewhere classified
➡ **CC Excl:** 929.0, 929.9, 958.8, 959.8-959.9

929.9 Unspecified site

EFFECTS OF FOREIGN BODY ENTERING THROUGH ORIFICE (930-939)

Excludes: foreign body:
granuloma (728.82)
inadvertently left in operative wound (998.4, 998.7)
in open wound (800-839, 851-897)
residual, in soft tissues (729.6)
superficial without major open wound (910-919 with .6 or .7)

930 Foreign body on external eye

Excludes: foreign body in penetrating wound of:
eyeball (871.5-871.6)
retained (old) (360.5-360.6)
ocular adnexa (870.4)
retained (old) (376.6)

930.0 Corneal foreign body

930.1 Foreign body in conjunctival sac

930.2 Foreign body in lacrimal punctum

930.8 Other and combined sites

930.9 Unspecified site
External eye NOS

931 Foreign body in ear

Auditory canal
Auricle

932 Foreign body in nose

Nasal sinus
Nostril

933 Foreign body in pharynx and larynx

933.0 Pharynx

Nasopharynx
Throat NOS

933.1 Larynx

Asphyxia due to foreign body
Choking due to:
food (regurgitated)
phlegm

934 Foreign body in trachea, bronchus, and lung

934.0 Trachea

934.1 Main bronchus

934.8 Other specified parts

Bronchioles
Lung

934.9 Respiratory tree, unspecified

Inhalation of liquid or vomitus, lower respiratory tract NOS

935 Foreign body in mouth, esophagus, and stomach

935.0 Mouth

935.1 Esophagus

➡ **AHA Coding Clinic:** 1Q, '88, 13

935.2 Stomach

936 Foreign body in intestine and colon

937 Foreign body in anus and rectum

Rectosigmoid (junction)

938 Foreign body in digestive system, unspecified

Alimentary tract NOS
Swallowed foreign body

939 Foreign body in genitourinary tract

939.0 Bladder and urethra

939.1 Uterus, any part ♀

Excludes: *intrauterine contraceptive device:*
complications from (996.32, 996.65)
presence of (V45.51)

939.2 Vulva and vagina ♀

939.3 Penis ♂

939.9 Unspecified site

BURNS (940-949)

Includes: burns from:
electrical heating appliance
electricity
flame
hot object
lightning
radiation
chemical burns (external) (internal)
scalds

Excludes: *friction burns (910-919 with .0, .1)*
sunburn (692.71)

➡ **AHA Coding Clinic:** 2Q, '90, 7; 4Q, '88, 3; M-A, '86, 9

940 Burn confined to eye and adnexa

940.0 Chemical burn of eyelids and periocular area

940.1 Other burns of eyelids and periocular area

940.2 Alkaline chemical burn of cornea and conjunctival sac

940.3 Acid chemical burn of cornea and conjunctival sac

940.4 Other burn of cornea and conjunctival sac

940.5 Burn with resulting rupture and destruction of eyeball

940.9 Unspecified burn of eye and adnexa

941 Burn of face, head, and neck

Excludes: *mouth (947.0)*

The following fifth-digit subclassification is for use with category 941:

0 face and head, unspecified site
1 ear [any part]
2 eye (with other parts of face, head, and neck)
3 lip(s)
4 chin
5 nose (septum)
6 scalp [any part]
Temple (region)
7 forehead and cheek
8 neck
9 multiple sites [except with eye] of face, head, and neck

✓5th **941.0 Unspecified degree**

✓5th **941.1 Erythema [first degree]**

✓5th **941.2 Blisters, epidermal loss [second degree]**

✓5th **941.3 Full-thickness skin loss [third degree NOS]**

✓5th □ **941.4 Deep necrosis of underlying tissues [deep third degree] without mention of loss of a body part**

✓5th □ **941.5 Deep necrosis of underlying tissues [deep third degree] with loss of a body part**

942 Burn of trunk

Excludes: *scapular region (943.0-943.5 with fifth-digit 6)*

The following fifth-digit subclassification is for use with category 942:

0 trunk, unspecified site
1 breast
2 chest wall, excluding breast and nipple
3 abdominal wall
  Flank — Groin
4 back [any part]
  Buttock — Interscapular region
5 genitalia
  Labium (majus) (minus) — Scrotum
  Penis — Testis
  Perineum — Vulva
9 other and multiple sites of trunk

✓5th **942.0** Unspecified degree

✓5th **942.1** Erythema [first degree]

✓5th **942.2** Blisters, epidermal loss [second degree]

✓5th **942.3** Full-thickness skin loss [third degree NOS]

✓5th □ **942.4** Deep necrosis of underlying tissues [deep third degree] without mention of loss of a body part

✓5th □ **942.5** Deep necrosis of underlying tissues [deep third degree] with loss of a body part

943 Burn of upper limb, except wrist and hand

The following fifth-digit subclassification is for use with category 943:

0 upper limb, unspecified site
1 forearm
2 elbow
3 upper arm
4 axilla
5 shoulder
6 scapular region
9 multiple sites of upper limb, except wrist and hand

✓5th **943.0** Unspecified degree

✓5th **943.1** Erythema [first degree]

✓5th **943.2** Blisters, epidermal loss [second degree]

✓5th **943.3** Full-thickness skin loss [third degree NOS]

✓5th □ **943.4** Deep necrosis of underlying tissues [deep third degree] without mention of loss of a body part

✓5th □ **943.5** Deep necrosis of underlying tissues [deep third degree] with loss of a body part

944 Burn of wrist(s) and hand(s)

The following fifth-digit subclassification is for use with category 944:

0 hand, unspecified site
1 single digit [finger (nail)] other than thumb
2 thumb (nail)
3 two or more digits, not including thumb
4 two or more digits including thumb
5 palm
6 back of hand
7 wrist
8 multiple sites of wrist(s) and hand(s)

✓5th **944.0** Unspecified degree

✓5th **944.1** Erythema [first degree]

✓5th **944.2** Blisters, epidermal loss [second degree]

✓5th **944.3** Full-thickness skin loss [third degree NOS]

✓5th □ **944.4** Deep necrosis of underlying tissues [deep third degree] without mention of loss of a body part

✓5th □ **944.5** Deep necrosis of underlying tissues [deep third degree] with loss of a body part

945 Burn of lower limb(s)

The following fifth-digit subclassification is for use with category 945:

0 lower limb [leg], unspecified site
1 toe(s) (nail)
2 foot
3 ankle
4 lower leg
5 knee
6 thigh [any part]
9 multiple sites of lower limb(s)

✓5th **945.0** Unspecified degree

✓5th **945.1** Erythema [first degree]

✓5th **945.2** Blisters, epidermal loss [second degree]

✓5th **945.3** Full-thickness skin loss [third degree NOS]

✓5th □ **945.4** Deep necrosis of underlying tissues [deep third degree] without mention of loss of a body part

✓5th □ **945.5** Deep necrosis of underlying tissues [deep third degree] with loss of a body part

946 Burns of multiple specified sites

Includes: burns of sites classifiable to more than one three-digit category in 940-945

Excludes: *multiple burns NOS (949.0-949.5)*

946.0 Unspecified degree

946.1 Erythema [first degree]

946.2 Blisters, epidermal loss [second degree]

946.3 Full-thickness skin loss [third degree NOS]

☐ **946.4** Deep necrosis of underlying tissues [deep third degree] without mention of loss of a body part

☐ **946.5** Deep necrosis of underlying tissues [deep third degree] with loss of a body part

947 Burn of internal organs

Includes: burns from chemical agents (ingested)

947.0 Mouth and pharynx
Gum
Tongue

947.1 Larynx, trachea, and lung

947.2 Esophagus

947.3 Gastrointestinal tract
Colon
Rectum
Small intestine
Stomach

947.4 Vagina and uterus ♀

947.8 Other specified sites

947.9 Unspecified site

948 Burns classified according to extent of body surface involved

Note: This category is to be used when the site of the burn is unspecified, or with categories 940-947 when the site is specified.

Excludes: *sunburn (692.71)*

The following fifth-digit subclassification is for use with category 948 to indicate the percent of *body surface* with *third degree* burn; valid digits are in [brackets] under each code:

0 less than 10 percent or unspecified
1 10-19%
2 20-29%
3 30-39%
4 40-49%
5 50-59%
6 60-69%
7 70-79%
8 80-89%
9 90% or more of body surface

✓5th **948.0** [0] Burn [any degree] involving less than 10 percent of body surface

✓5th **948.1** [0–1] 10-19 percent of body surface

✓5th **948.2** [0–2] 20-29 percent of body surface

✓5th **948.3** [0–3] 30-39 percent of body surface

✓5th **948.4** [0–4] 40-49 percent of body surface

✓5th **948.5** [0–5] 50-59 percent of body surface

✓5th **948.6** [0–6] 60-69 percent of body surface

✓5th **948.7** [0–7] 70-79 percent of body surface

✓5th **948.8** [0–8] 80-89 percent of body surface

✓5th **948.9** [0–9] 90 percent or more of body surface

949 Burn, unspecified

Includes: burn NOS
multiple burns NOS

Excludes: *burn of unspecified site but with statement of the extent of body surface involved (948.0-948.9)*

949.0 Unspecified degree

949.1 Erythema [first degree]

949.2 Blisters, epidermal loss [second degree]

949.3 Full-thickness skin loss [third degree NOS]

☐ **949.4** Deep necrosis of underlying tissues [deep third degree] without mention of loss of a body part

☐ **949.5** Deep necrosis of underlying tissues [deep third degree] with loss of a body part

INJURY TO NERVES AND SPINAL CORD (950-957)

Includes: division of nerve, lesion in continuity, traumatic neuroma, traumatic transient paralysis (with open wound)

Excludes: *accidental puncture or laceration during medical procedure (998.2)*

950 Injury to optic nerve and pathways

950.0 Optic nerve injury
Second cranial nerve

950.1 Injury to optic chiasm

950.2 Injury to optic pathways

950.3 Injury to visual cortex

950.9 Unspecified
Traumatic blindness NOS

951 Injury to other cranial nerve(s)

951.0 Injury to oculomotor nerve
Third cranial nerve

951.1 Injury to trochlear nerve
Fourth cranial nerve

951.2 Injury to trigeminal nerve
Fifth cranial nerve

951.3 Injury to abducens nerve
Sixth cranial nerve

951.4 Injury to facial nerve
Seventh cranial nerve

951.5 Injury to acoustic nerve
Auditory nerve
Eighth cranial nerve
Traumatic deafness NOS

951.6 Injury to accessory nerve
Eleventh cranial nerve

951.7 Injury to hypoglossal nerve
Twelfth cranial nerve

951.8 Injury to other specified cranial nerves
Glossopharyngeal [9th cranial] nerve
Olfactory [1st cranial] nerve
Pneumogastric [10th cranial] nerve
Traumatic anosmia NOS
Vagus [10th cranial] nerve

951.9 Injury to unspecified cranial nerve

952 Spinal cord injury without evidence of spinal bone injury

✓5th **952.0 Cervical**

952.00 C_1-C_4 level with unspecified spinal cord injury
Spinal cord injury, cervical region NOS
➡ **CC Excl:** 805.00-805.18, 805.8-805.9, 806.00-806.19, 806.8-806.9, 839.00-839.18, 839.40, 839.49-839.50, 839.59, 839.69, 839.79, 839.8-839.9, 847.9, 905.1, 926.11, 952.00-952.09, 952.8-952.9, 958.8, 959.1, 959.8-959.9

952.01 C_1-C_4 level with complete lesion of spinal cord
➡ **CC Excl:** see Code 952.00

952.02 C_1-C_4 level with anterior cord syndrome
➡ **CC Excl:** see Code 952.00

952.03 C_1-C_4 level with central cord syndrome
➡ **CC Excl:** see Code 952.00

952.04 C_1-C_4 level with other specified spinal cord injury
Incomplete spinal cord lesion at C_1-C_4 level:
NOS
with posterior cord syndrome
➡ **CC Excl:** see Code 952.00

952.05 C_5-C_7 level with unspecified spinal cord injury
➡ **CC Excl:** see Code 952.00

952.06 C_5-C_7 level with complete lesion of spinal cord
➡ **CC Excl:** see Code 952.00

952.07 C_5-C_7 level with anterior cord syndrome
➡ **CC Excl:** see Code 952.00

952.08 C_5-C_7 level with central cord syndrome
➡ **CC Excl:** see Code 952.00

952.09 C_5-C_7 level with other specified spinal cord injury
Incomplete spinal cord lesion at C_5-C_7 level:
NOS
with posterior cord syndrome
➡ **CC Excl:** see Code 952.00

✓5th **952.1** Dorsal [thoracic]

952.10 T_1-T_6 level with unspecified spinal cord injury
Spinal cord injury, thoracic region NOS
➡ **CC Excl:** 805.8-805.9, 806.20-806.39, 839.40, 839.49-839.50, 839.59, 839.69, 839.79, 839.8-839.9, 847.9, 905.1, 926.11, 952.10-952.19, 952.8-952.9, 958.8, 959.1, 959.8-959.9

952.11 T_1-T_6 level with complete lesion of spinal cord
➡ **CC Excl:** see Code 952.10

952.12 T_1-T_6 level with anterior cord syndrome
➡ **CC Excl:** see Code 952.10

952.13 T_1-T_6 level with central cord syndrome
➡ **CC Excl:** see Code 952.10

952.14 T_1-T_6 level with other specified spinal cord injury
Incomplete spinal cord lesion at T_1-T_6 level:
NOS
with posterior cord syndrome
➡ **CC Excl:** see Code 952.10

952.15 T_7-T_{12} level with unspecified spinal cord injury
➡ **CC Excl:** see Code 952.10

952.16 T_7-T_{12} level with complete lesion of spinal cord
➡ **CC Excl:** see Code 952.10

952.17 T_7-T_{12} level with anterior cord syndrome
➡ **CC Excl:** see Code 952.10

952.18 T_7-T_{12} level with central cord syndrome
➡ **CC Excl:** see Code 952.10

952.19 T_7-T_{12} level with other specified spinal cord injury
Incomplete spinal cord lesion at T_7-T_{12} level:
NOS
with posterior cord syndrome
➡ **CC Excl:** see Code 952.10

952.2 Lumbar
➡ **CC Excl:** 805.8-805.9, 806.4-806.5, 839.40, 839.49-839.50, 839.59, 839.69, 839.79, 839.8-839.9, 847.9, 905.1, 926.11, 952.2, 952.8-952.9, 958.8, 959.1, 959.8-959.9

952.3 Sacral
➡ **CC Excl:** 805.8-805.9, 806.60-806.79, 839.40, 839.49-839.50, 839.59, 839.69, 839.79, 839.8-839.9, 847.9, 905.1, 926.11, 952.3-952.4, 952.8-952.9, 958.8, 959.1, 959.8-959.9

952.4 Cauda equina
➡ **CC Excl:** see Code 952.3

952.8 Multiple sites of spinal cord
➡ **CC Excl:** 805.8-805.9, 839.40, 839.49-839.50, 839.59, 839.69, 839.79, 839.8-839.9, 847.9, 905.1, 926.11, 952.8-952.9, 958.8, 959.1, 959.8-959.9

952.9 Unspecified site of spinal cord
➡ **CC Excl:** 805.8-805.9, 839.40, 839.49-839.50, 839.59, 839.69, 839.79, 839.8-839.9, 847.9, 905.1, 926.11, 952.8, 959.1

953 Injury to nerve roots and spinal plexus

953.0 Cervical root
➡ **CC Excl:** 953.8-953.9, 958.8, 959.8-959.9

953.1 Dorsal root
➡ **CC Excl:** see Code 953.0

953.2 Lumbar root
➡ **CC Excl:** see Code 953.0

953.3 Sacral root
➡ **CC Excl:** see Code 953.0

953.4 Brachial plexus
➡ **CC Excl:** see Code 953.0

953.5 Lumbosacral plexus
➡ **CC Excl:** see Code 953.0

953.8 Multiple sites
➡ **CC Excl:** see Code 953.0

953.9 Unspecified site
➡ **CC Excl:** see Code 953.0

954 Injury to other nerve(s) of trunk, excluding shoulder and pelvic girdles

954.0 Cervical sympathetic

954.1 Other sympathetic
Celiac ganglion or plexus
Inferior mesenteric plexus
Splanchnic nerve(s)
Stellate ganglion

954.8 Other specified nerve(s) of trunk

954.9 Unspecified nerve of trunk

955 Injury to peripheral nerve(s) of shoulder girdle and upper limb

955.0 Axillary nerve

955.1 Median nerve

955.2 Ulnar nerve

955.3 Radial nerve

955.4 Musculocutaneous nerve

955.5 Cutaneous sensory nerve, upper limb

955.6 Digital nerve

955.7 Other specified nerve(s) of shoulder girdle and upper limb

955.8 Multiple nerves of shoulder girdle and upper limb

955.9 Unspecified nerve of shoulder girdle and upper limb

956 Injury to peripheral nerve(s) of pelvic girdle and lower limb

956.0 Sciatic nerve

956.1 Femoral nerve

956.2 Posterior tibial nerve

956.3 Peroneal nerve

956.4 Cutaneous sensory nerve, lower limb

956.5 Other specified nerve(s) of pelvic girdle and lower limb

956.8 Multiple nerves of pelvic girdle and lower limb

956.9 Unspecified nerve of pelvic girdle and lower limb

957 Injury to other and unspecified nerves

957.0 Superficial nerves of head and neck

957.1 Other specified nerve(s)

957.8 Multiple nerves in several parts

Multiple nerve injury NOS

957.9 Unspecified site

Nerve injury NOS

CERTAIN TRAUMATIC COMPLICATIONS AND UNSPECIFIED INJURIES (958-959)

958 Certain early complications of trauma

Excludes: *adult respiratory distress syndrome (518.5)*
flail chest (807.4)
shock lung (518.5)
that occurring during or following medical procedures (996.0-999.9)

958.0 Air embolism

Pneumathemia

Excludes: *that complicating:*
abortion (634-638 with .6, 639.6)
ectopic or molar pregnancy (639.6)
pregnancy, childbirth, or the puerperium (673.0)

➡ **CC Excl:** 958.0, 958.8, 959.8-959.9, 997.91, 997.99, 998.81-998.9, 999.1

958.1 Fat embolism

Excludes: *that complicating:*
abortion (634-638 with .6, 639.6)
pregnancy, childbirth, or the puerperium (673.8)

➡ **CC Excl:** 958.1, 958.8, 959.8-959.9, 997.91, 997.99, 998.81-998.9

958.2 Secondary and recurrent hemorrhage

➡ **CC Excl:** 958.2, 958.8, 959.8-959.9, 997.91, 997.99, 998.81-998.9

958.3 Posttraumatic wound infection, not elsewhere classified

➡ **CC Excl:** 958.3, 958.8, 959.8-959.9, 997.91, 997.99, 998.81-998.9

➡ **AHA Coding Clinic:** S-O, '85, 10

958.4 Traumatic shock

Shock (immediate) (delayed) following injury

Excludes: *shock:*
anaphylactic (995.0)
due to serum (999.4)
anesthetic (995.4)
electric (994.8)
following abortion (639.5)
lightning (994.0)
nontraumatic NOS (785.50)
obstetric (669.1)
postoperative (998.0)

➡ **CC Excl:** 958.4, 958.8, 959.8-959.9, 997.91, 997.99, 998.81-998.9

958.5 Traumatic anuria

Crush syndrome
Renal failure following crushing

Excludes: *that due to a medical procedure (997.5)*

➡ **CC Excl:** 958.5, 958.8, 959.8-959.9, 995.4, 997.91, 997.99, 998.0, 998.11-998.13, 998.81-998.9

958.6 Volkmann's ischemic contracture

Posttraumatic muscle contracture

958.7 Traumatic subcutaneous emphysema

Excludes: *subcutaneous emphysema resulting from a procedure (998.81)*

➡ **CC Excl:** 860.0-860.5, 861.20-861.32, 862.0-862.1, 862.29, 862.31-862.9, 875.0-875.1, 958.7-958.8, 959.8-959.9, 997.91, 997.99, 998.81-998.9

958.8 Other early complications of trauma

➡ **AHA Coding Clinic:** 2Q, '92, 13

959 Injury, other and unspecified

Includes: injury NOS

Excludes: *injury NOS of:*
blood vessels (900.0-904.9)
eye (921.0-921.9)
internal organs (860.0-869.1)
intracranial sites (854.0-854.1)
nerves (950.0-951.9, 953.0-957.9)
spinal cord (952.0-952.9)

✓5th **959.0 Head, face, and neck**

959.01 Head injury, unspecified

Excludes: *concussion (850.1-850.9)*
with head injury NOS (850.1-850.9)
specified intracranial injuries (850.0-854.1)

➡ **AHA Coding Clinic:** 4Q, '97, 46

959.09 Injury of face and neck

Cheek
Ear
Eyebrow
Lip
Mouth
Nose
Throat

➡ **AHA Coding Clinic:** 4Q, '97, 46

959.1 Trunk

Abdominal wall
Back
Breast
Buttock
Chest wall
External genital organs
Flank
Groin
Interscapular region
Perineum

Excludes: *scapular region (959.2)*

959.2 Shoulder and upper arm

Axilla
Scapular region

959.3 Elbow, forearm, and wrist

➡ **AHA Coding Clinic:** 1Q, '97, 8

959.4 Hand, except finger

959.5 Finger

Fingernail
Thumb (nail)

959.6 Hip and thigh

Upper leg

959.7 Knee, leg, ankle, and foot

959.8 Other specified sites, including multiple

Excludes: *multiple sites classifiable to the same four-digit category (959.0-959.7)*

959.9 Unspecified site

POISONING BY DRUGS, MEDICINAL AND BIOLOGICAL SUBSTANCES (960-979)

Use additional code to specify the effects of the poisoning

Includes: overdose of these substances
wrong substance given or taken in error

Excludes: *adverse effects ["hypersensitivity," "reaction," etc.] of correct substance properly administered. Such cases are to be classified according to the nature of the adverse effect, such as:*
adverse effect NOS (995.2)
allergic lymphadenitis (289.3)
aspirin gastritis (535.4)
blood disorders (280.0-289.9)
dermatitis:
contact (692.0-692.9)
due to ingestion (693.0-693.9)
nephropathy (583.9)
[The drug giving rise to the adverse effect may be identified by use of categories E930-E949.]
drug dependence (304.0-304.9)
drug reaction and poisoning affecting the newborn (760.0-779.9)
nondependent abuse of drugs (305.0-305.9)
pathological drug intoxication (292.2)

➡ **AHA Coding Clinic:** 2Q, '90, 11

960 Poisoning by antibiotics

Excludes: *antibiotics:*
ear, nose, and throat (976.6)
eye (976.5)
local (976.0)

960.0 Penicillins

Ampicillin
Carbenicillin
Cloxacillin
Penicillin G

960.1 Antifungal antibiotics

Amphotericin B
Griseofulvin
Nystatin
Trichomycin

Excludes: *preparations intended for topical use (976.0-976.9)*

960.2 Chloramphenicol group

Chloramphenicol
Thiamphenicol

960.3 Erythromycin and other macrolides

Oleandomycin
Spiramycin

960.4 Tetracycline group

Doxycycline
Minocycline
Oxytetracycline

960.5 Cephalosporin group

Cephalexin
Cephaloglycin
Cephaloridine
Cephalothin

960.6 Antimycobacterial antibiotics
Cycloserine
Kanamycin
Rifampin
Streptomycin

960.7 Antineoplastic antibiotics
Actinomycin such as:
Bleomycin
Cactinomycin
Dactinomycin
Daunorubicin
Mitomycin

960.8 Other specified antibiotics

960.9 Unspecified antibiotic

961 Poisoning by other anti-infectives

Excludes: *anti-infectives:*
ear, nose, and throat (976.6)
eye (976.5)
local (976.0)

961.0 Sulfonamides
Sulfadiazine
Sulfafurazole
Sulfamethoxazole

961.1 Arsenical anti-infectives

961.2 Heavy metal anti-infectives
Compounds of:
antimony
bismuth
lead
mercury

Excludes: *mercurial diuretics (974.0)*

961.3 Quinoline and hydroxyquinoline derivatives
Chiniofon
Diiodohydroxyquin

Excludes: *antimalarial drugs (961.4)*

961.4 Antimalarials and drugs acting on other blood protozoa
Chloroquine
Cycloguanil
Primaquine
Proguanil [chloroguanide]
Pyrimethamine
Quinine

961.5 Other antiprotozoal drugs
Emetine

961.6 Anthelmintics
Hexylresorcinol
Piperazine
Thiabendazole

961.7 Antiviral drugs
Methisazone

Excludes: *amantadine (966.4)*
cytarabine (963.1)
idoxuridine (976.5)

961.8 Other antimycobacterial drugs
Ethambutol
Ethionamide
Isoniazid
Para-aminosalicylic acid derivatives
Sulfones

961.9 Other and unspecified anti-infectives
Flucytosine
Nitrofuran derivatives

962 Poisoning by hormones and synthetic substitutes

Excludes: *oxytocic hormones (975.0)*

962.0 Adrenal cortical steroids
Cortisone derivatives
Desoxycorticosterone derivatives
Fluorinated corticosteroids

962.1 Androgens and anabolic congeners
Methandriol
Nandrolone
Oxymetholone
Testosterone

962.2 Ovarian hormones and synthetic substitutes
Contraceptives, oral
Estrogens
Estrogens and progestogens, combined
Progestogens

962.3 Insulins and antidiabetic agents
Acetohexamide
Biguanide derivatives, oral
Chlorpropamide
Glucagon
Insulin
Phenformin
Sulfonylurea derivatives, oral
Tolbutamide

➡ **AHA Coding Clinic:** M-A, '85, 9

962.4 Anterior pituitary hormones
Corticotropin
Gonadotropin
Somatotropin [growth hormone]

962.5 Posterior pituitary hormones
Vasopressin

Excludes: *oxytocic hormones (975.0)*

962.6 Parathyroid and parathyroid derivatives

962.7 Thyroid and thyroid derivatives
Dextrothyroxin
Levothyroxine sodium
Liothyronine
Thyroglobulin

962.8 Antithyroid agents
Iodides
Thiouracil
Thiourea

962.9 Other and unspecified hormones and synthetic substitutes

963 Poisoning by primarily systemic agents

963.0 Antiallergic and antiemetic drugs

Antihistamines
Chlorpheniramine
Diphenhydramine
Diphenylpyraline
Thonzylamine
Tripelennamine

Excludes: *phenothiazine-based tranquilizers (969.1)*

963.1 Antineoplastic and immunosuppressive drugs

Azathioprine
Busulfan
Chlorambucil
Cyclophosphamide
Cytarabine
Fluorouracil
Mercaptopurine
thio-TEPA

Excludes: *antineoplastic antibiotics (960.7)*

963.2 Acidifying agents

963.3 Alkalizing agents

963.4 Enzymes, not elsewhere classified

Penicillinase

963.5 Vitamins, not elsewhere classified

Vitamin A
Vitamin D

Excludes: *nicotinic acid (972.2)*
vitamin K (964.3)

963.8 Other specified systemic agents

Heavy metal antagonists

963.9 Unspecified systemic agent

964 Poisoning by agents primarily affecting blood constituents

964.0 Iron and its compounds

Ferric salts
Ferrous sulfate and other ferrous salts

964.1 Liver preparations and other antianemic agents

Folic acid

964.2 Anticoagulants

Coumarin
Heparin
Phenindione
Warfarin sodium

➡ **AHA Coding Clinic:** 1Q, '94, 22

964.3 Vitamin K [phytonadione]

964.4 Fibrinolysis-affecting drugs

Aminocaproic acid
Streptodornase
Streptokinase
Urokinase

964.5 Anticoagulant antagonists and other coagulants

Hexadimethrine
Protamine sulfate

964.6 Gamma globulin

964.7 Natural blood and blood products

Blood plasma
Human fibrinogen
Packed red cells
Whole blood

Excludes: *transfusion reactions (999.4-999.8)*

964.8 Other specified agents affecting blood constituents

Macromolecular blood substitutes
Plasma expanders

964.9 Unspecified agent affecting blood constituents

965 Poisoning by analgesics, antipyretics, and antirheumatics

Excludes: *drug dependence (304.0-304.9)*
nondependent abuse (305.0-305.9)

✓5th **965.0 Opiates and related narcotics**

965.00 Opium (alkaloids), unspecified

965.01 Heroin

Diacetylmorphine

965.02 Methadone

965.09 Other

Codeine [methylmorphine]
Meperidine [pethidine]
Morphine

965.1 Salicylates

Acetylsalicylic acid [aspirin]
Salicylic acid salts

965.4 Aromatic analgesics, not elsewhere classified

Acetanilid
Paracetamol [acetaminophen]
Phenacetin [acetophenetidin]

965.5 Pyrazole derivatives

Aminophenazone [aminopyrine]
Phenylbutazone

✓5th **965.6 Antirheumatics [antiphlogistics]**

Excludes: *salicylates (965.1)*
steroids (962.0-962.9)

965.61 Propionic acid derivatives

Fenoprofen
Flurbiprofen
Ibuprofen
Ketoprofen
Naproxen
Oxaprozin

965.69 Other antirheumatics

Gold salts
Indomethacin

965.7 Other non-narcotic analgesics

Pyrabital

965.8 Other specified analgesics and antipyretics

Pentazocine

965.9 Unspecified analgesic and antipyretic

966 Poisoning by anticonvulsants and anti-Parkinsonism drugs

966.0 Oxazolidine derivatives
Paramethadione
Trimethadione

966.1 Hydantoin derivatives
Phenytoin

966.2 Succinimides
Ethosuximide
Phensuximide

966.3 Other and unspecified anticonvulsants
Primidone

Excludes: *barbiturates (967.0)*
sulfonamides (961.0)

966.4 Anti-Parkinsonism drugs
Amantadine
Ethopropazine [profenamine]
Levodopa [L-dopa]

967 Poisoning by sedatives and hypnotics

Excludes: *drug dependence (304.0-304.9)*
nondependent abuse (305.0-305.9)

967.0 Barbiturates
Amobarbital [amylobarbitone]
Barbital [barbitone]
Butabarbital [butabarbitone]
Pentobarbital [pentobarbitone]
Phenobarbital [phenobarbitone]
Secobarbital [quinalbarbitone]

Excludes: *thiobarbiturate anesthetics (968.3)*

967.1 Chloral hydrate group

967.2 Paraldehyde

967.3 Bromine compounds
Bromide
Carbromal (derivatives)

967.4 Methaqualone compounds

967.5 Glutethimide group

967.6 Mixed sedatives, not elsewhere classified

967.8 Other sedatives and hypnotics

967.9 Unspecified sedative or hypnotic
Sleeping:
drug } NOS
pill } NOS
tablet } NOS

968 Poisoning by other central nervous system depressants and anesthetics

Excludes: *drug dependence (304.0-304.9)*
nondependent abuse (305.0-305.9)

968.0 Central nervous system muscle-tone depressants
Chlorphenesin (carbamate)
Methocarbamol
Mephenesin

968.1 Halothane

968.2 Other gaseous anesthetics
Ether
Halogenated hydrocarbon derivatives, except halothane
Nitrous oxide

968.3 Intravenous anesthetics
Ketamine
Methohexital [methohexitone]
Thiobarbiturates, such as thiopental sodium

968.4 Other and unspecified general anesthetics

968.5 Surface [topical] and infiltration anesthetics
Cocaine
Procaine
Lidocaine [lignocaine]
Tetracaine

➡ **AHA Coding Clinic:** 1Q, '93, 25

968.6 Peripheral nerve- and plexus-blocking anesthetics

968.7 Spinal anesthetics

968.9 Other and unspecified local anesthetics

969 Poisoning by psychotropic agents

Excludes: *drug dependence (304.0-304.9)*
nondependent abuse (305.0-305.9)

969.0 Antidepressants
Amitriptyline
Monoamine oxidase [MAO] inhibitors
Imipramine

969.1 Phenothiazine-based tranquilizers
Chlorpromazine
Prochlorperazine
Fluphenazine
Promazine

969.2 Butyrophenone-based tranquilizers
Haloperidol
Trifluperidol
Spiperone

969.3 Other antipsychotics, neuroleptics, and major tranquilizers

969.4 Benzodiazepine-based tranquilizers
Chlordiazepoxide
Lorazepam
Diazepam
Medazepam
Flurazepam
Nitrazepam

969.5 Other tranquilizers
Hydroxyzine
Meprobamate

969.6 Psychodysleptics [hallucinogens]
Cannabis (derivatives)
Mescaline
Lysergide [LSD]
Psilocin
Marihuana (derivatives)
Psilocybin

969.7 Psychostimulants
Amphetamine
Caffeine

Excludes: *central appetite depressants (977.0)*

969.8 Other specified psychotropic agents

969.9 Unspecified psychotropic agent

970 Poisoning by central nervous system stimulants

970.0 Analeptics
Lobeline
Nikethamide

970.1 Opiate antagonists
Levallorphan
Nalorphine
Naloxone

970.8 Other specified central nervous system stimulants

970.9 Unspecified central nervous system stimulant

971 Poisoning by drugs primarily affecting the autonomic nervous system

971.0 Parasympathomimetics [cholinergics]
Acetylcholine
Anticholinesterase:
organophosphorus
reversible
Pilocarpine

971.1 Parasympatholytics [anticholinergics and antimuscarinics] and spasmolytics
Atropine
Homatropine
Hyoscine [scopolamine]
Quaternary ammonium derivatives

Excludes: *papaverine (972.5)*

971.2 Sympathomimetics [adrenergics]
Epinephrine [adrenalin]
Levarterenol [noradrenalin]

971.3 Sympatholytics [antiadrenergics]
Phenoxybenzamine
Tolazoline hydrochloride

971.9 Unspecified drug primarily affecting autonomic nervous system

972 Poisoning by agents primarily affecting the cardiovascular system

972.0 Cardiac rhythm regulators
Practolol
Procainamide
Propranolol
Quinidine

Excludes: *lidocaine (968.5)*

972.1 Cardiotonic glycosides and drugs of similar action
Digitalis glycosides
Digoxin
Strophanthins

972.2 Antilipemic and antiarteriosclerotic drugs
Clofibrate
Nicotinic acid derivatives

972.3 Ganglion-blocking agents
Pentamethonium bromide

972.4 Coronary vasodilators
Dipyridamole
Nitrates [nitroglycerin]
Nitrites

972.5 Other vasodilators
Cyclandelate
Diazoxide
Papaverine

Excludes: *nicotinic acid (972.2)*

972.6 Other antihypertensive agents
Clonidine
Guanethidine
Rauwolfia alkaloids
Reserpine

972.7 Antivaricose drugs, including sclerosing agents
Sodium morrhuate
Zinc salts

972.8 Capillary-active drugs
Adrenochrome derivatives
Metaraminol

972.9 Other and unspecified agents primarily affecting the cardiovascular system

973 Poisoning by agents primarily affecting the gastrointestinal system

973.0 Antacids and antigastric secretion drugs
Aluminum hydroxide
Magnesium trisilicate

973.1 Irritant cathartics
Bisacodyl
Castor oil
Phenolphthalein

973.2 Emollient cathartics
Dioctyl sulfosuccinates

973.3 Other cathartics, including intestinal atonia drugs
Magnesium sulfate

973.4 Digestants
Pancreatin
Papain
Pepsin

973.5 Antidiarrheal drugs
Kaolin
Pectin

Excludes: *anti-infectives (960.0-961.9)*

973.6 Emetics

973.8 Other specified agents primarily affecting the gastrointestinal system

973.9 Unspecified agent primarily affecting the gastrointestinal system

974 Poisoning by water, mineral, and uric acid metabolism drugs

974.0 Mercurial diuretics
Chlormerodrin
Mercaptomerin
Mersalyl

974.1 Purine derivative diuretics
Theobromine
Theophylline

Excludes: *aminophylline [theophylline ethylenediamine] (975.7)*
caffeine (969.7)

974.2 Carbonic acid anhydrase inhibitors
Acetazolamide

974.3 Saluretics
Benzothiadiazides
Chlorothiazide group

974.4 Other diuretics
Ethacrynic acid
Furosemide

974.5 Electrolytic, caloric, and water-balance agents

974.6 Other mineral salts, not elsewhere classified

974.7 Uric acid metabolism drugs
Allopurinol
Colchicine
Probenecid

975 Poisoning by agents primarily acting on the smooth and skeletal muscles and respiratory system

975.0 Oxytocic agents
Ergot alkaloids
Oxytocin
Prostaglandins

975.1 Smooth muscle relaxants
Adiphenine
Metaproterenol [orciprenaline]

Excludes: *papaverine (972.5)*

975.2 Skeletal muscle relaxants

975.3 Other and unspecified drugs acting on muscles

975.4 Antitussives
Dextromethorphan
Pipazethate

975.5 Expectorants
Acetylcysteine
Guaifenesin
Terpin hydrate

975.6 Anti-common cold drugs

975.7 Antiasthmatics
Aminophylline [theophylline ethylenediamine]

975.8 Other and unspecified respiratory drugs

976 Poisoning by agents primarily affecting skin and mucous membrane, ophthalmological, otorhinolaryngological, and dental drugs

976.0 Local anti-infectives and anti-inflammatory drugs

976.1 Antipruritics

976.2 Local astringents and local detergents

976.3 Emollients, demulcents, and protectants

976.4 Keratolytics, keratoplastics, other hair treatment drugs and preparations

976.5 Eye anti-infectives and other eye drugs
Idoxuridine

976.6 Anti-infectives and other drugs and preparations for ear, nose, and throat

976.7 Dental drugs topically applied

Excludes: *anti-infectives (976.0)*
local anesthetics (968.5)

976.8 Other agents primarily affecting skin and mucous membrane
Spermicides [vaginal contraceptives]

976.9 Unspecified agent primarily affecting skin and mucous membrane

977 Poisoning by other and unspecified drugs and medicinal substances

977.0 Dietetics
Central appetite depressants

977.1 Lipotropic drugs

977.2 Antidotes and chelating agents, not elsewhere classified

977.3 Alcohol deterrents

977.4 Pharmaceutical excipients
Pharmaceutical adjuncts

977.8 Other specified drugs and medicinal substances
Contrast media used for diagnostic x-ray procedures
Diagnostic agents and kits

977.9 Unspecified drug or medicinal substance

978 Poisoning by bacterial vaccines

978.0 BCG

978.1 Typhoid and paratyphoid

978.2 Cholera

978.3 Plague

978.4 Tetanus

978.5 Diphtheria

978.6 Pertussis vaccine, including combinations with a pertussis component

978.8 Other and unspecified bacterial vaccines

978.9 Mixed bacterial vaccines, except combinations with a pertussis component

979 Poisoning by other vaccines and biological substances

Excludes: *gamma globulin (964.6)*

979.0 Smallpox vaccine

979.1 Rabies vaccine

979.2 Typhus vaccine

979.3 Yellow fever vaccine

979.4 Measles vaccine

979.5 Poliomyelitis vaccine

979.6 Other and unspecified viral and rickettsial vaccines
Mumps vaccine

979.7 Mixed viral-rickettsial and bacterial vaccines, except combinations with a pertussis component

Excludes: *combinations with a pertussis component (978.6)*

979.9 Other and unspecified vaccines and biological substances

TOXIC EFFECTS OF SUBSTANCES CHIEFLY NONMEDICINAL AS TO SOURCE (980-989)

Use additional code to specify the nature of the toxic effect

Excludes: *burns from chemical agents (ingested) (947.0-947.9)*
localized toxic effects indexed elsewhere (001.0-799.9)
respiratory conditions due to external agents (506.0-508.9)

980 Toxic effect of alcohol

980.0 Ethyl alcohol

Denatured alcohol
Ethanol
Grain alcohol

Use additional code to identify any associated:
acute alcohol intoxication (305.0)
in alcoholism (303.0)
drunkenness (simple) (305.0)
pathological (291.4)

➡ **AHA Coding Clinic:** 3Q, '96, 16

980.1 Methyl alcohol

Methanol
Wood alcohol

980.2 Isopropyl alcohol

Dimethyl carbinol
Isopropanol
Rubbing alcohol

980.3 Fusel oil

Alcohol:
amyl
butyl
propyl

980.8 Other specified alcohols

980.9 Unspecified alcohol

981 Toxic effect of petroleum products

Benzine
Gasoline
Kerosene
Paraffin wax
Petroleum:
ether
naphtha
spirit

982 Toxic effect of solvents other than petroleum-based

982.0 Benzene and homologues

982.1 Carbon tetrachloride

982.2 Carbon disulfide

Carbon bisulfide

982.3 Other chlorinated hydrocarbon solvents

Tetrachloroethylene
Trichloroethylene

Excludes: *chlorinated hydrocarbon preparations other than solvents (989.2)*

982.4 Nitroglycol

982.8 Other nonpetroleum-based solvents

Acetone

983 Toxic effect of corrosive aromatics, acids, and caustic alkalis

983.0 Corrosive aromatics

Carbolic acid or phenol
Cresol

983.1 Acids

Acid:
hydrochloric
nitric
sulfuric

983.2 Caustic alkalis

Lye
Potassium hydroxide
Sodium hydroxide

983.9 Caustic, unspecified

984 Toxic effect of lead and its compounds (including fumes)

Includes: that from all sources except medicinal substances

984.0 Inorganic lead compounds

Lead dioxide
Lead salts

984.1 Organic lead compounds

Lead acetate
Tetraethyl lead

984.8 Other lead compounds

984.9 Unspecified lead compound

985 Toxic effect of other metals

Includes: that from all sources except medicinal substances

985.0 Mercury and its compounds
Minamata disease

985.1 Arsenic and its compounds

985.2 Manganese and its compounds

985.3 Beryllium and its compounds

985.4 Antimony and its compounds

985.5 Cadmium and its compounds

985.6 Chromium

985.8 Other specified metals
Brass fumes; Copper salts; Iron compounds; Nickel compounds

➡ **AHA Coding Clinic:** 1Q, '88, 5

985.9 Unspecified metal

986 Toxic effect of carbon monoxide

Carbon monoxide from any source

987 Toxic effect of other gases, fumes, or vapors

987.0 Liquefied petroleum gases
Butane; Propane

987.1 Other hydrocarbon gas

987.2 Nitrogen oxides
Nitrogen dioxide; Nitrous fumes

987.3 Sulfur dioxide

987.4 Freon
Dichloromonofluoromethane

987.5 Lacrimogenic gas
Bromobenzyl cyanide; Chloroacetophenone; Ethyliodoacetate

987.6 Chlorine gas

987.7 Hydrocyanic acid gas

987.8 Other specified gases, fumes, or vapors
Phosgene; Polyester fumes

987.9 Unspecified gas, fume, or vapor

988 Toxic effect of noxious substances eaten as food

Excludes: *allergic reaction to food, such as:*
gastroenteritis (558.9)
rash (692.5, 693.1)
food poisoning (bacterial) (005.0-005.9)
toxic effects of food contaminants, such as:
aflatoxin and other mycotoxin (989.7)
mercury (985.0)

988.0 Fish and shellfish

988.1 Mushrooms

988.2 Berries and other plants

988.8 Other specified noxious substances eaten as food

988.9 Unspecified noxious substance eaten as food

989 Toxic effect of other substances, chiefly nonmedicinal as to source

989.0 Hydrocyanic acid and cyanides
Potassium cyanide; Sodium cyanide

Excludes: *gas and fumes (987.7)*

989.1 Strychnine and salts

989.2 Chlorinated hydrocarbons
Aldrin; Chlordane; DDT; Dieldrin

Excludes: *chlorinated hydrocarbon solvents (982.0-982.3)*

989.3 Organophosphate and carbamate
Carbaryl; Dichlorvos; Malathion; Parathion; Phorate; Phosdrin

989.4 Other pesticides, not elsewhere classified
Mixtures of insecticides

989.5 Venom
Bites of venomous snakes, lizards, and spiders
Tick paralysis

989.6 Soaps and detergents

989.7 Aflatoxin and other mycotoxin [food contaminants]

✓5th **989.8** Other substances, chiefly nonmedicinal as to source

➡ **AHA Coding Clinic:** 4Q, '95, 60

989.81 Asbestos

Excludes: *asbestosis (501)*
exposure to asbestos (V15.84)

989.82 Latex

989.83 Silicone

Excludes: *silicone used in medical devices, implants and grafts (996.00-996.79)*

989.84 Tobacco

989.89 Other

989.9 Unspecified substance, chiefly nonmedicinal as to source

OTHER AND UNSPECIFIED EFFECTS OF EXTERNAL CAUSES (990-995)

990 Effects of radiation, unspecified

Complication of:
phototherapy
radiation therapy

Radiation sickness

Excludes: *specified adverse effects of radiation. Such conditions are to be classified according to the nature of the adverse effect, as:*
burns (940.0-949.5)
dermatitis (692.7-692.8)
leukemia (204.0-208.9)
pneumonia (508.0)
sunburn (692.71)
[The type of radiation giving rise to the adverse effect may be identified by use of the E codes.]

991 Effects of reduced temperature

991.0 Frostbite of face

991.1 Frostbite of hand

991.2 Frostbite of foot

991.3 Frostbite of other and unspecified sites

991.4 Immersion foot
Trench foot

991.5 Chilblains
Erythema pernio
Perniosis

991.6 Hypothermia
Hypothermia (accidental)

Excludes: *hypothermia following anesthesia (995.89)*
hypothermia not associated with low environmental temperature (780.9)

991.8 Other specified effects of reduced temperature

991.9 Unspecified effect of reduced temperature
Effects of freezing or excessive cold NOS

992 Effects of heat and light

Excludes: *burns (940.0-949.5)*
diseases of sweat glands due to heat (705.0-705.9)
malignant hyperpyrexia following anesthesia (995.86)
sunburn (692.71)

992.0 Heat stroke and sunstroke
Heat apoplexy
Heat pyrexia
Ictus solaris
Siriasis
Thermoplegia

992.1 Heat syncope
Heat collapse

992.2 Heat cramps

992.3 Heat exhaustion, anhydrotic
Heat prostration due to water depletion

Excludes: *that associated with salt depletion (992.4)*

992.4 Heat exhaustion due to salt depletion
Heat prostration due to salt (and water) depletion

992.5 Heat exhaustion, unspecified
Heat prostration NOS

992.6 Heat fatigue, transient

992.7 Heat edema

992.8 Other specified heat effects

992.9 Unspecified

993 Effects of air pressure

993.0 Barotrauma, otitic
Aero-otitis media
Effects of high altitude on ears

993.1 Barotrauma, sinus
Aerosinusitis
Effects of high altitude on sinuses

993.2 Other and unspecified effects of high altitude
Alpine sickness
Andes disease
Anoxia due to high altitude
Hypobaropathy
Mountain sickness

993.3 Caisson disease
Bends
Compressed-air disease
Decompression sickness
Divers' palsy or paralysis

993.4 Effects of air pressure caused by explosion

993.8 Other specified effects of air pressure

993.9 Unspecified effect of air pressure

994 Effects of other external causes

Excludes: *certain adverse effects not elsewhere classified (995.0-995.8)*

994.0 Effects of lightning

Shock from lightning
Struck by lightning NOS

Excludes: *burns (940.0-949.5)*

994.1 Drowning and nonfatal submersion

Bathing cramp
Immersion

994.2 Effects of hunger

Deprivation of food
Starvation

994.3 Effects of thirst

Deprivation of water

994.4 Exhaustion due to exposure

994.5 Exhaustion due to excessive exertion

Overexertion

994.6 Motion sickness

Air sickness
Seasickness
Travel sickness

994.7 Asphyxiation and strangulation

Suffocation (by):
bedclothes
cave-in
constriction
mechanical

Suffocation (by):
plastic bag
pressure
strangulation

Excludes: *asphyxia from:*
carbon monoxide (986)
inhalation of food or foreign body (932-934.9)
other gases, fumes, and vapors (987.0-987.9)

994.8 Electrocution and nonfatal effects of electric current

Shock from electric current

Excludes: *electric burns (940.0-949.5)*

994.9 Other effects of external causes

Effects of:
abnormal gravitational [G] forces or states
weightlessness

995 Certain adverse effects not elsewhere classified

Excludes: *complications of surgical and medical care (996.0-999.9)*

995.0 Other anaphylactic shock

Allergic shock
Anaphylactic reaction
Anaphylaxis
} NOS or due to adverse effect of correct medicinal substance properly administered

Code first any underlying condition such as:
poisoning by drugs, medicinals and biologic substances (960-979)
toxic effects of substances chiefly nonmedical as to source (980-989)

Use additional E code to identify external cause, such as:
adverse effects of correct medicinal substance properly administered (E930-E949)

Excludes: *anaphylactic reaction to serum (999.4)*
anaphylactic shock due to adverse food reaction (995.60-995.69)

995.1 Angioneurotic edema

Giant urticaria

Excludes: *urticaria:*
due to serum (999.5)
other specified (698.2, 708.0-708.9, 757.33)

995.2 Unspecified adverse effect of drug, medicinal and biological substance

Adverse effect
Allergic reaction
Hypersensitivity
Idiosyncrasy
} (due) to correct medicinal substance properly administered

Drug:
hypersensitivity NOS
reaction NOS

Excludes: *pathological drug intoxication (292.2)*

➡ **AHA Coding Clinic:** 2Q, '97, 12; 3Q, '95, 13; 3Q, '92, 16

995.3 Allergy, unspecified

Allergic reaction NOS
Hypersensitivity NOS
Idiosyncrasy NOS

Excludes: *allergic reaction NOS to correct medicinal substance properly administered (995.2)*
specific types of allergic reaction, such as:
allergic diarrhea (558.9)
dermatitis (691.0-693.9)
hay fever (477.0-477.9)

995.4 Shock due to anesthesia

Shock due to anesthesia in which the correct substance was properly administered

Excludes: *complications of anesthesia in labor or delivery (668.0-668.9)*
overdose or wrong substance given (968.0-969.9)
postoperative shock NOS (998.0)
specified adverse effects of anesthesia classified elsewhere, such as:
anoxic brain damage (348.1)
hepatitis (070.0-070.9), etc.
unspecified adverse effect of anesthesia (995.2)

➡ **CC Excl:** 958.4, 995.4, 997.91, 997.99, 998.0, 998.11-998.13, 998.83, 998.9

✓5th **995.5 Child maltreatment syndrome** A: 0–17

Use additional code(s), if applicable, to identify any associated injuries

Use additional E code to identify:
nature of abuse (E960-E968)
perpetrator (E967.0-E967.9)

995.50 Child abuse, unspecified

995.51 Child emotional/psychological abuse

➡ **AHA Coding Clinic:** 4Q, '96, 38, 40

995.52 Child neglect (nutritional)

➡ **AHA Coding Clinic:** 4Q, '96, 38, 40

995.53 Child sexual abuse

➡ **AHA Coding Clinic:** 4Q, '96, 39, 40

995.54 Child physical abuse

Battered baby or child syndrome

Excludes: *Shaken infant syndrome (995.55)*

➡ **AHA Coding Clinic:** 4Q, '96, 39, 40

995.55 Shaken infant syndrome

Use additional code(s) to identify any associated injuries

➡ **AHA Coding Clinic:** 4Q, '96, 40, 43

995.59 Other child abuse and neglect

Multiple forms of abuse

✓5th **995.6 Anaphylactic shock due to adverse food reaction**

Anaphylactic shock due to nonpoisonous foods

995.60 Due to unspecified food

995.61 Due to peanuts

995.62 Due to crustaceans

995.63 Due to fruits and vegetables

995.64 Due to tree nuts and seeds

995.65 Due to fish

995.66 Due to food additives

995.67 Due to milk products

995.68 Due to eggs

995.69 Due to other specified food

✓5th **995.8 Other specified adverse effects, not elsewhere classified**

995.80 Adult maltreatment, unspecified A: 15–124

Abused person NOS

Use additional code to identify:
any associated injury
perpetrator (E967.0-E967.9)

➡ **AHA Coding Clinic:** 4Q, '96, 41, 43

995.81 Adult physical abuse A: 15–124

Battered:
person syndrome NEC
man
spouse
woman

Use additional code to identify:
any associated injury
nature of abuse (E960-E968)
perpetrator (E967.0-E967.9)

➡ **AHA Coding Clinic:** 4Q, '96, 42, 43

995.82 Adult emotional/psychological abuse A: 15–124

Use additional E code to identify perpetrator (E967.0-E967.9)

995.83 Adult sexual abuse A: 15–124

Use additional code to identify:
any associated injury
perpetrator (E967.0-E967.9)

995.84 Adult neglect (nutritional) A: 15–124

Use additional code to identify:
intent of neglect (E904.0-E968.4
perpetrator (E967.0, E967.9)

995.85 Other adult abuse and neglect A: 15–124

Multiple forms of abuse and neglect

Use additional code to identify any associated injury:
intent of neglect (E904.0, E968.4
nature of abuse (E960-E968)
perpetrator (E967.0-E967.9)

995.86 Malignant hyperthermia

Malignant hyperpyrexia due to anesthesia

➡ **CC Excl:** 958.4, 995.4, 995.86, 997.91, 997.99, 998.0, 998.11-998.13, 998.81-998.9

995.89 Other

Hypothermia due to anesthesia

COMPLICATIONS OF SURGICAL AND MEDICAL CARE, NOT ELSEWHERE CLASSIFIED (996-999)

Excludes: *adverse effects of medicinal agents (001.0-799.9, 995.0-995.8)*
burns from local applications and irradiation (940.0-949.5)
complications of:
conditions for which the procedure was performed
surgical procedures during abortion, labor, and delivery (630-676.9)
poisoning and toxic effects of drugs and chemicals (960.0-989.9)
postoperative conditions in which no complications are present, such as:
artificial opening status (V44.0-V44.9)
closure of external stoma (V55.0-V55.9)
fitting of prosthetic device (V52.0-V52.9)
specified complications classified elsewhere
anesthetic shock (995.4)
electrolyte imbalance (276.0-276.9)
postlaminectomy syndrome (722.80-722.83)
postmastectomy lymphedema syndrome (457.0)
postoperative psychosis (293.0-293.9)
any other condition classified elsewhere in the Alphabetic Index when described as due to a procedure

➡ **AHA Coding Clinic:** 2Q, '90, 11

996 Complications peculiar to certain specified procedures

Includes: complications, not elsewhere classified, in the use of artificial substitutes [e.g., Dacron, metal, Silastic, Teflon] or natural sources [e.g., bone] involving:
anastomosis (internal)
graft (bypass) (patch)
implant
internal device:
catheter
electronic
fixation
prosthetic
reimplant
transplant

Excludes: *accidental puncture or laceration during procedure (998.2)*
complications of internal anastomosis of:
gastrointestinal tract (997.4)
urinary tract (997.5)
other specified complications classified elsewhere, such as:
hemolytic anemia (283.1)
functional cardiac disturbances (429.4)
serum hepatitis (070.2-070.3)

✓5th **996.0 Mechanical complication of cardiac device, implant, and graft**

Breakdown (mechanical) Obstruction, mechanical
Displacement Perforation
Leakage Protrusion

996.00 Unspecified device, implant, and graft

➡ **CC Excl:** 996.00, 996.04, 996.61-996.62, 996.70-996.74, 997.91, 997.99, 998.81-998.9

996.01 Due to cardiac pacemaker (electrode)

➡ **CC Excl:** 996.01, 997.91, 997.99, 998.81-998.9

996.02 Due to heart valve prosthesis

➡ **CC Excl:** 996.02, 997.91, 997.99, 998.81-998.9

996.03 Due to coronary bypass graft

Excludes: *atherosclerosis of graft (414.02, 414.03)*
embolism [occlusion NOS] [thrombus] of graft (996.72)

➡ **CC Excl:** 996.03, 997.91, 997.99, 998.81-998.9

➡ **AHA Coding Clinic:** 2Q, '95, 17; N-D, '86, 5

996.04 Due to automatic implantable cardiac defibrillator

➡ **CC Excl:** 996.04, 997.91, 997.99, 998.81-998.9

996.09 Other

➡ **CC Excl:** 996.09, 997.91, 997.99, 998.81-998.9

➡ **AHA Coding Clinic:** 2Q, '93, 9

996.1 Mechanical complication of other vascular device, implant, and graft

Mechanical complications involving:
aortic (bifurcation) graft (replacement)
arteriovenous:
dialysis catheter, fistula, shunt } surgically created
balloon (counterpulsation) device, intra-aortic
carotid artery bypass graft
femoral-popliteal bypass graft
umbrella device, vena cava

Excludes: *atherosclerosis of biological graft (440.30-440.32)*
embolism [occlusion NOS] [thrombus] of (biological) (synthetic) graft (996.74)
peritoneal dialysis catheter (996.56)

➡ **CC Excl:** 996.1, 997.91, 997.99, 998.81-998.9

➡ **AHA Coding Clinic:** 1Q, '95, 3

996.2 Mechanical complication of nervous system device, implant, and graft

Mechanical complications involving:
- dorsal column stimulator
- electrodes implanted in brain [brain "pacemaker"]
- peripheral nerve graft
- ventricular (communicating) shunt

➡ **CC Excl:** 996.2, 996.63, 996.75, 997.91, 997.99, 998.81-998.9

➡ **AHA Coding Clinic:** S-O, '87, 10

✓5th **996.3 Mechanical complication of genitourinary device, implant, and graft**

996.30 Unspecified device, implant, and graft

➡ **CC Excl:** 996.30, 996.64-996.65, 996.76, 997.91, 997.99, 998.81-998.9

996.31 Due to urethral [indwelling] catheter

996.32 Due to intrauterine contraceptive device ♀

996.39 Other

Cystostomy catheter
Prosthetic reconstruction of vas deferens
Repair (graft) of ureter without mention of resection

Excludes: *complications due to:*
external stoma of urinary tract (997.5)
internal anastomosis of urinary tract (997.5)

➡ **CC Excl:** 996.39, 996.64-996.65, 996.76, 997.91, 997.99, 998.81-998.9

996.4 Mechanical complication of internal orthopedic device, implant, and graft

Mechanical complications involving:
- external (fixation) device utilizing internal screw(s), pin(s) or other methods of fixation
- grafts of bone, cartilage, muscle, or tendon
- internal (fixation) device such as nail, plate, rod, etc.

Excludes: *complications of external orthopedic device, such as:*
pressure ulcer due to cast (707.0)

➡ **CC Excl:** 996.4, 996.66-996.67, 996.77-996.78, 997.91, 997.99, 998.81-998.9

➡ **AHA Coding Clinic:** 2Q, '96, 11; 3Q, '95, 16; N-D, '85, 11

✓5th **996.5 Mechanical complication of other specified prosthetic device, implant, and graft**

Mechanical complications involving:
- prosthetic implant in:
  - bile duct
  - breast
  - chin
  - orbit of eye
- nonabsorbable surgical material NOS
- other graft, implant, and internal device, not elsewhere classified

➡ **AHA Coding Clinic:** 1Q, '98, 11

996.51 Due to corneal graft

➡ **CC Excl:** 996.51, 997.91, 997.99

996.52 Due to graft of other tissue, not elsewhere classified

Skin graft failure or rejection

Excludes: *failure of artificial skin graft (996.55)*
failure of decellularized allodermis (996.55)
sloughing of temporary skin allografts or xenografts (pigskin) — omit code

➡ **CC Excl:** 996.52, 996.55, 997.91, 997.99

➡ **AHA Coding Clinic:** 1Q, '96, 10

996.53 Due to ocular lens prosthesis

Excludes: *contact lenses — code to condition*

➡ **CC Excl:** 996.53, 997.91, 997.99

996.54 Due to breast prosthesis

Breast capsule (prosthesis)
Mammary implant

➡ **CC Excl:** 996.54, 997.91, 997.99

➡ **AHA Coding Clinic:** 3Q, '92, 4

996.55 Due to artificial skin graft and decellularized allodermis

Dislodgement
Displacement
Failure
Non-adherence
Poor incorporation
Shearing

➡ **CC Excl:** 996.52, 996.55-996.60, 996.68-996.69, 996.70, 996.79, 997.91, 997.99

996.56 Due to peritoneal dialysis catheter

Excludes: *mechanical complication of arteriovenous dialysis catheter (996.1)*

➡ **CC Excl:** 96.56, 996.59, 996.60, 996.68-996.70, 996.79, 997.91, 997.99

996.59 Due to other implant and internal device, not elsewhere classified

Nonabsorbable surgical material NOS
Prosthetic implant in:
- bile duct
- chin
- orbit of eye

➡ **CC Excl:** 996.59, 996.60, 996.69-996.70, 996.79, 997.91, 997.99

➡ **AHA Coding Clinic:** 3Q, '94, 7

✓5th **996.6 Infection and inflammatory reaction due to internal prosthetic device, implant, and graft**

Infection (causing obstruction), Inflammation } due to (presence of) any device, implant, and graft classifiable to 996.0-996.5

Use additional code to identify specified infections

➡ **AHA Coding Clinic:** 2Q, '89, 16; J-F, '87, 14

996.60 Due to unspecified device, implant and graft

➡ **CC Excl:** 996.00-996.30, 996.39, 996.4-996.79, 997.91, 997.99, 998.81-998.9

996.61 Due to cardiac device, implant and graft

Cardiac pacemaker or defibrillator:
- electrode(s), lead(s)
- pulse generator
- subcutaneous pocket

Coronary artery bypass graft
Heart valve prosthesis

➡ **CC Excl:** 996.00-996.1, 996.52, 996.55-996.62, 996.69-996.74, 996.79, 997.91, 997.99, 998.81-998.9

996.62 Due to vascular device, implant and graft

Arterial graft
Arteriovenous fistula or shunt
Infusion pump
Vascular catheter (arterial) (dialysis) (venous)

➡ **CC Excl:** see Code 996.61

➡ **AHA Coding Clinic:** 2Q, '94, 13

996.63 Due to nervous system device, implant and graft

Electrodes implanted in brain
Peripheral nerve graft
Spinal canal catheter
Ventricular (communicating) shunt (catheter)

➡ **CC Excl:** 996.2, 996.52, 996.55-996.60, 996.63, 996.69-996.70, 996.75, 996.79, 997.91, 997.99, 998.81-998.9

996.64 Due to indwelling urinary catheter

Use additional code to identify specified infections, such as:
- Cystitis (595.0-595.9)
- Sepsis (038.0-038.9)

➡ **CC Excl:** 599.0, 996.30, 996.39, 996.55-996.60, 996.64-996.65, 996.69-996.70, 996.76, 996.79, 997.91, 997.99, 998.81-998.9

996.65 Due to other genitourinary device, implant and graft

Intrauterine contraceptive device

➡ **CC Excl:** 996.30, 996.39, 996.52, 996.55-996.60, 996.64-996.65, 996.69-996.70, 996.76, 996.79, 997.91, 997.99, 998.81-998.9

996.66 Due to internal joint prosthesis

➡ **CC Excl:** 996.4, 996.52, 996.55-996.60, 996.66-996.70, 996.77-996.79, 997.91, 997.99, 998.81-998.9

➡ **AHA Coding Clinic:** 2Q, '91, 18

996.67 Due to other internal orthopedic device, implant and graft

Bone growth stimulator (electrode)
Internal fixation device (pin) (rod) (screw)

➡ **CC Excl:** see Code 996.66

996.68 Due to peritoneal dialysis catheter

Exit-site infection or inflammation

➡ **CC Excl:** 996.56, 996.59, 996.60, 996.68-996.70, 996.79, 997.91, 997.99

996.69 Due to other internal prosthetic device, implant and graft

Breast prosthesis
Ocular lens prosthesis
Prosthetic orbital implant

➡ **CC Excl:** 996.00-996.30, 996.39, 996.4-996.79, 997.91, 997.99, 998.81-998.9

✓5th **996.7 Other complications of internal (biological) (synthetic) prosthetic device, implant, and graft**

Complication NOS, occlusion NOS, Embolism, Fibrosis, Hemorrhage, Pain, Stenosis, Thrombus } due to (presence of) any device, implant, and graft classifiable to 996.0-996.5

Excludes: *transplant rejection (996.8)*

➡ **AHA Coding Clinic:** 1Q, '89, 9; N-D, '86, 5

996.70 Due to unspecified device, implant and graft

➡ **CC Excl:** see Code 996.69

996.71 Due to heart valve prosthesis

➡ **CC Excl:** 996.00, 996.02, 996.09, 996.1, 996.52, 996.55-996.62, 996.69-996.74, 996.79, 997.91, 997.99, 998.81-998.9

996.72 Due to other cardiac device, implant and graft

Cardiac pacemaker or defibrillator:
- electrode(s), lead(s)
- subcutaneous pocket

Coronary artery bypass (graft)

Excludes: *occlusion due to atherosclerosis (414.02-414.03)*

➡ **CC Excl:** 996.00-996.02, 996.04, 996.09, 996.1, 996.52, 996.55-996.62, 996.69-996.74, 996.79, 997.91, 997.99, 998.81-998.9

996.73 Due to renal dialysis device, implant and graft

➡ **CC Excl:** 996.1, 996.52, 996.55-996.60, 996.69-996.70, 996.73, 996.79, 997.91, 997.99, 998.81-998.9

➡ **AHA Coding Clinic:** 2Q, '91, 18

996.74 Due to vascular device, implant and graft

Excludes: *occlusion of biological graft due to atherosclerosis (440.30-440.32)*

➡ **CC Excl:** 996.00-996.1, 996.52, 996.55-996.62, 996.69-996.74, 996.79, 997.91, 997.99, 998.81-998.9

996.75 Due to nervous system device, implant and graft

➡ **CC Excl:** 996.2, 996.52, 996.55-996.60, 996.63, 996.69-996.70, 996.75, 996.79, 997.91, 997.99, 998.81-998.9

996.76 Due to genitourinary device, implant and graft

➡ **CC Excl:** 996.39, 996.52, 996.55-996.60, 996.64-996.65, 996.69-996.70, 996.76, 996.79, 997.91, 997.99, 998.81-998.9

996.77 Due to internal joint prosthesis

➡ **CC Excl:** 996.4, 996.52, 996.55-996.60, 996.66-996.67, 996.69-996.70, 996.77-996.79, 997.91, 997.99, 998.81-998.9

996.78 Due to other internal orthopedic device, implant and graft

➡ **CC Excl:** see Code 996.77

996.79 Due to other internal prosthetic device, implant and graft

➡ **CC Excl:** 996.00-996.30, 996.39, 996.4-996.79, 997.91, 997.99, 998.81-998.9

➡ **AHA Coding Clinic:** 3Q, '95, 14; 3Q, '92, 4

✓5th **996.8** Complications of transplanted organ

Transplant failure or rejection

Use additional code to identify nature of complication, such as:
Cytomegalovirus [CMV] infection (078.5)

➡ **AHA Coding Clinic:** 2Q, '93, 11; 1Q, '93, 24

996.80 Transplanted organ, unspecified

➡ **CC Excl:** 996.80, 997.91, 997.99

996.81 Kidney

➡ **CC Excl:** 996.81, 997.91, 997.99

➡ **AHA Coding Clinic:** 3Q, '94, 8; 2Q, '94, 9; 1Q, '93, 24

996.82 Liver

➡ **CC Excl:** 996.82, 997.91, 997.99

996.83 Heart

➡ **CC Excl:** 996.83, 997.91, 997.99

996.84 Lung

➡ **CC Excl:** 996.84, 997.91, 997.99

996.85 Bone marrow

Graft-versus-host disease (acute) (chronic)

➡ **CC Excl:** 996.85, 997.91, 997.99

➡ **AHA Coding Clinic:** 4Q, '90, 4

996.86 Pancreas

➡ **CC Excl:** 996.86, 997.91, 997.99

996.89 Other specified transplanted organ

Intestines

➡ **CC Excl:** 996.89, 997.91, 997.99

➡ **AHA Coding Clinic:** 3Q, '94, 5

✓5th **996.9** Complications of reattached extremity or body part

996.90 Unspecified extremity

➡ **CC Excl:** 996.90, 997.91, 997.99, 998.81-998.9

996.91 Forearm

➡ **CC Excl:** 996.91, 997.91, 997.99, 998.81-998.9

996.92 Hand

➡ **CC Excl:** 996.92, 997.91, 997.99, 998.81-998.9

996.93 Finger(s)

➡ **CC Excl:** 996.93, 997.91, 997.99, 998.81-998.9

996.94 Upper extremity, other and unspecified

➡ **CC Excl:** 996.94, 997.91, 997.99, 998.81-998.9

996.95 Foot and toe(s)

➡ **CC Excl:** 996.95, 997.91, 997.99, 998.81-998.9

996.96 Lower extremity, other and unspecified

➡ **CC Excl:** 996.96, 997.91, 997.99, 998.81-998.9

996.99 Other specified body part

➡ **CC Excl:** 996.99, 997.91, 997.99, 998.81-998.9

997 Complications affecting specified body systems, not elsewhere classified

Use additional code to identify complication

Excludes: *the listed conditions when specified as:*
causing shock (998.0)
complications of:
anesthesia:
adverse effect (001.0-799.9, 995.0-995.8)
in labor or delivery (668.0-668.9)
poisoning (968.0-969.9)
implanted device or graft (996.0-996.9)
obstetrical procedures (669.0-669.4)
reattached extremity (996.90-996.96)
transplanted organ (996.80-996.89)

➡ **AHA Coding Clinic:** 1Q, '94, 4; 1Q, '93, 26

✓5th **997.0 Nervous system complications**

➡ **CC Excl: For codes 997.00-997.09:** 997.00-997.09, 997.91, 997.99, 998.81, 998.83, 998.89, 998.9

997.00 Nervous system complication, unspecified

997.01 Central nervous system complication

Anoxic brain damage
Cerebral hypoxia

Excludes: *cerebrovascular hemorrhage or infarction (997.02)*

997.02 Iatrogenic cerebrovascular infarction or hemorrhage

Postoperative stroke

➡ **AHA Coding Clinic:** 4Q, '95, 57

997.09 Other nervous system complications

997.1 Cardiac complications

Cardiac:
arrest
insufficiency
Cardiorespiratory failure
Heart failure
} during or resulting from a procedure

Excludes: *the listed conditions as long-term effects of cardiac surgery or due to the presence of cardiac prosthetic device (429.4)*

➡ **CC Excl:** 997.1, 997.91, 997.99, 998.81-998.9

997.2 Peripheral vascular complications

Phlebitis or thrombophlebitis during or resulting from a procedure

Excludes: *the listed conditions due to:*
implant or catheter device (996.62)
infusion, perfusion, or transfusion (999.2)
complications affecting internal blood vessels, such as:
mesenteric artery (997.4)
renal artery (997.5)

➡ **CC Excl:** 997.2, 997.91, 997.99, 998.81-998.9

997.3 Respiratory complications

Mendelson's syndrome
Pneumonia (aspiration)
} resulting from a procedure

Excludes: *iatrogenic [postoperative] pneumothorax (512.1)*
iatrogenic pulmonary embolism (415.11)
Mendelson's syndrome in labor and delivery (668.0)
specified complications classified elsewhere, such as:
adult respiratory distress syndrome (518.5)
pulmonary edema, postoperative (518.4)
respiratory insufficiency, acute, postoperative (518.5)
shock lung (518.5)
tracheostomy complications (519.00-519.09)

➡ **CC Excl:** 997.3, 997.91, 997.99, 998.81-998.9

➡ **AHA Coding Clinic:** 1Q, '97, 10; 2Q, '93, 3; 2Q, '93, 9; 4Q, '90, 25

997.4 Digestive system complications

Complications of:
intestinal (internal) anastomosis and bypass, not elsewhere classified, except that involving urinary tract
Hepatic failure
Hepatorenal syndrome
Intestinal obstruction NOS
} specified as due to a procedure

Excludes: *specified gastrointestinal complications classified elsewhere, such as:*
blind loop syndrome (579.2)
colostomy or enterostomy complications (569.60-569.69)
gastrostomy complications (536.40-536.49)
gastrojejunal ulcer (534.0-534.9)
infection of external stoma (569.61)
pelvic peritoneal adhesions, female (614.6)
peritoneal adhesions (568.0)
peritoneal adhesions with obstruction (560.81)
postcholecystectomy syndrome (576.0)
postgastric surgery syndromes (564.2)

➡ **CC Excl:** 997.4, 997.91, 997.99, 998.81-998.9

➡ **AHA Coding Clinic:** 3Q, '97, 7; 1Q, '97, 11; 2Q, '95, 7; 1Q, '93, 26; 3Q, '92, 15; 2Q, '89, 15; 1Q, '88, 14

DRG 188

997.5 **Urinary complications**

Complications of:
external stoma of urinary tract
internal anastomosis and bypass of urinary tract, including that involving intestinal tract

Oliguria or anuria
Renal:
failure (acute)
insufficiency (acute)
Tubular necrosis (acute)
} specified as due to procedure

Excludes: *specified complications classified elsewhere, such as:*
postoperative stricture of:
ureter (593.3)
urethra (598.2)

➡ **CC Excl:** 997.5, 997.91, 997.99, 998.81-998.9

➡ **AHA Coding Clinic:** 3Q '96, 10, 15; 4Q, '95, 73; 1Q, '92, 13; 2Q, '89, 16; M-A, '87, 10; S-O, '85, 3

✓5th **997.6** **Amputation stump complication**

Excludes: *admission for treatment for a current traumatic amputation-code to complicated traumatic amputation*
phantom limb (syndrome) (353.6)

➡ **AHA Coding Clinic:** 4Q, '95, 82

997.60 **Unspecified complication**

997.61 **Neuroma of amputation stump**

997.62 **Infection (chronic)**

Use additional code to identify the organism

➡ **CC Excl:** 997.60, 997.62, 997.69, 997.91, 997.99, 998.81-998.9

➡ **AHA Coding Clinic:** 4Q, '96, 46

997.69 **Not elsewhere classified**

✓5th **997.9** **Complications affecting other specified body systems, not elsewhere classified**

997.91 **Hypertension**

Excludes: *essential hypertension (401.0-401.9)*

➡ **AHA Coding Clinic:** 4Q, '95, 57

997.99 **Other**

Vitreous touch syndrome

Excludes: *specified complications classified elsewhere, such as:*
broad ligament laceration syndrome (620.6)
postartificial menopause syndrome (627.4)
postoperative stricture of vagina (623.2)

➡ **CC Excl:** 997.91, 997.99, 998.81-998.9

➡ **AHA Coding Clinic:** 2Q, '94, 12; 1Q, '94, 17

998 **Other complications of procedures, NEC**

➡ **AHA Coding Clinic:** 1Q, '94, 4

998.0 **Postoperative shock**

Collapse NOS
Shock (endotoxic) (hypovolemic) (septic)
} during or resulting from a surgical procedure

Excludes: *shock:*
anaphylactic due to serum (999.4)
anesthetic (995.4)
electric (994.8)
following abortion (639.5)
obstetric (669.1)
traumatic (958.4)

➡ **CC Excl:** 958.4, 995.4, 997.91, 997.99, 998.0, 998.11-998.13, 998.81-998.9

✓5th **998.1** **Hemorrhage or hematoma or seroma complicating a procedure**

Excludes: *hemorrhage, hematoma or seroma:*
complicating cesarean section or puerperal perineal wound (674.3)

998.11 **Hemorrhage complicating a procedure**

➡ **CC Excl:** 456.0, 456.20, 530.81-530.83, 530.89, 531.00-531.01, 531.20-531.21, 531.40-531.41, 531.60-531.61, 532.00-532.01, 532.21, 532.40-532.41, 532.60-532.61, 533.00-533.01, 533.20-533.21, 533.40-533.41, 533.60-533.61, 534.00-534.01, 534.20-534.21, 534.40-534.41, 534.60-534.61, 535.01, 535.11, 535.21, 535.31, 535.41, 535.51, 535.61, 537.83, 562.02-562.03, 562.12-562.13, 569.3, 569.85, 578.0-578.1, 578.9, 772.4, 997.91, 997.99, 998.0, 998.11-998.13, 998.81, 998.89, 998.9

➡ **AHA Coding Clinic:** 4Q, '97, 52; 1Q, '97, 10

998.12 **Hematoma complicating a procedure**

➡ **CC Excl:** see code 998.11

998.13 **Seroma complicating a procedure**

➡ **CC Excl:** see Code 998.11

➡ **AHA Coding Clinic:** 4Q, '96, 46; 1Q, '93, 26; 2Q, '92, 15; S-O, '87, 8

998.2 Accidental puncture or laceration during a procedure

Accidental perforation by catheter or other instrument during a procedure on:
blood vessel
nerve
organ

Excludes: *iatrogenic [postoperative] pneumothorax (512.1)*
puncture or laceration caused by implanted device intentionally left in operation wound (996.0-996.5)
specified complications classified elsewhere, such as:
broad ligament laceration syndrome (620.6)
trauma from instruments during delivery (664.0-665.9)

➡ **CC Excl:** 997.91, 997.99, 998.2, 998.81-998.9

➡ **AHA Coding Clinic:** 3Q, '94, 6; 3Q, '90, 17; 3Q, '90, 18

998.3 Disruption of operation wound

Dehiscence } of operation wound
Rupture }

Excludes: *disruption of:*
cesarean wound (674.1)
perineal wound, puerperal (674.2)

➡ **CC Excl:** 997.91, 997.99, 998.3, 998.81-998.9

➡ **AHA Coding Clinic:** 1Q, '93, 19

998.4 Foreign body accidentally left during a procedure

Adhesions } due to foreign body accidentally left in operative wound or body cavity during a procedure
Obstruction }
Perforation }

Excludes: *obstruction or perforation caused by implanted device intentionally left in body (996.0-996.5)*

➡ **CC Excl:** 997.91, 997.99, 998.4, 998.81-998.9

➡ **AHA Coding Clinic:** 1Q, '89, 9

✓5th **998.5 Postoperative infection**

Excludes: *infection due to:*
implanted device (996.60-996.69)
infusion, perfusion, or transfusion (999.3)
postoperative obstetrical wound infection (674.3)

998.51 Infected postoperative seroma

Use additional code to identify organism

➡ **CC Excl:** 997.91, 997.99, 998.51-998.59, 998.81-998.9

➡ **AHA Coding Clinic:** 4Q, '96, 46

998.59 Other postoperative infection

Abscess: } postoperative
intra-abdominal }
stitch }
subphrenic }
wound }
Septicemia }

Use additional code to identify infection

➡ **CC Excl:** see Code 998.51

➡ **AHA Coding Clinic:** 3Q, '95, 5; 2Q, '95, 7; 3Q, '94, 6; 1Q, '93, 19; J-F, '87, 14

998.6 Persistent postoperative fistula

➡ **CC Excl:** 997.91, 997.99, 998.6, 998.81-998.9

➡ **AHA Coding Clinic:** J-F, '87, 14

998.7 Acute reaction to foreign substance accidentally left during a procedure

Peritonitis:
aseptic
chemical

➡ **CC Excl:** 997.91, 997.99, 998.7-998.9

✓5th **998.8 Other specified complications of procedures, not elsewhere classified**

➡ **AHA Coding Clinic:** 4Q, '94, 46; 1Q, '89, 9

998.81 Emphysema (subcutaneous) (surgical) resulting from a procedure

998.82 Cataract fragments in eye following cataract surgery

998.83 Non-healing surgical wound

➡ **CC Excl:** 997.91, 997.99, 998.81, 998.83, 998.89, 998.9

➡ **AHA Coding Clinic:** 4Q, '96, 47

998.89 Other specified complications

➡ **CC Excl:** 997.91, 997.99, 998.81-998.9

998.9 Unspecified complication of procedure, not elsewhere classified

Postoperative complication NOS

Excludes: *complication NOS of obstetrical surgery or procedure (669.4)*

➡ **CC Excl:** 997.91, 997.99, 998.81-998.9

999 Complications of medical care, not elsewhere classified

Includes: complications, not elsewhere classified, of:
dialysis (hemodialysis) (peritoneal) (renal)
extracorporeal circulation
hyperalimentation therapy
immunization
infusion
inhalation therapy
injection
inoculation
perfusion
transfusion
vaccination
ventilation therapy

Excludes: *specified complications classified elsewhere such as:*
complications of implanted device (996.0-996.9)
contact dermatitis due to drugs (692.3)
dementia dialysis (294.8)
transient (293.9)
dialysis disequilibrium syndrome (276.0-276.9)
poisoning and toxic effects of drugs and chemicals (960.0-989.9)
postvaccinal encephalitis (323.5)
water and electrolyte imbalance (276.0-276.9)

999.0 Generalized vaccinia

999.1 Air embolism

Air embolism to any site following infusion, perfusion, or transfusion

Excludes: *embolism specified as:*
complicating:
abortion (634-638 with .6, 639.6)
ectopic or molar pregnancy (639.6)
pregnancy, childbirth, or the puerperium (673.0)
due to implanted device (996.7)
traumatic (958.0)

➡ **CC Excl:** 958.0, 999.1

999.2 Other vascular complications

Phlebitis, Thromboembolism, Thrombophlebitis } following infusion, perfusion, or transfusion

Excludes: *the listed conditions when specified as:*
due to implanted device (996.61-996.62, 996.72-996.74)
postoperative NOS (997.2)

➡ **CC Excl:** 999.2

➡ **AHA Coding Clinic:** 2Q, '97, 5

999.3 Other infection

Infection, Sepsis, Septicemia } following infusion, injection, transfusion, or vaccination

Excludes: *the listed conditions when specified as:*
due to implanted device (996.60-996.69)
postoperative NOS (998.51-998.59)

➡ **CC Excl:** 999.3

➡ **AHA Coding Clinic:** 2Q, '97, 5; J-F, '87, 14

999.4 Anaphylactic shock due to serum

Excludes: *shock:*
allergic NOS (995.0)
anaphylactic:
NOS (995.0)
due to drugs and chemicals (995.0)

➡ **CC Excl:** 999.4

999.5 Other serum reaction

Intoxication by serum
Protein sickness
Serum rash
Serum sickness
Urticaria due to serum

Excludes: *serum hepatitis (070.2-070.3)*

➡ **CC Excl:** 999.5

999.6 ABO incompatibility reaction

Incompatible blood transfusion
Reaction to blood group incompatibility in infusion or transfusion

➡ **CC Excl:** 999.6

999.7 Rh incompatibility reaction

Reactions due to Rh factor in infusion or transfusion

➡ **CC Excl:** 999.7

999.8 Other transfusion reaction

Septic shock due to transfusion
Transfusion reaction NOS

Excludes: *postoperative shock (998.0)*

➡ **CC Excl:** 999.8

999.9 Other and unspecified complications of medical care, not elsewhere classified

Complications, not elsewhere classified, of:
electroshock, inhalation, ultrasound, ventilation } therapy
Unspecified misadventure of medical care

Excludes: *unspecified complication of:*
phototherapy (990)
radiation therapy (999)

➡ **AHA Coding Clinic:** 2Q, '97, 5

SUPPLEMENTARY CLASSIFICATION OF FACTORS INFLUENCING HEALTH STATUS AND CONTACT WITH HEALTH SERVICES (V01-V82)

This classification is provided to deal with occasions when circumstances other than a disease or injury classifiable to categories 001-999 (the main part of ICD) are recorded as "diagnoses" or "problems." This can arise mainly in three ways:

a) When a person who is not currently sick encounters the health services for some specific purpose, such as to act as a donor of an organ or tissue, to receive prophylactic vaccination, or to discuss a problem which is in itself not a disease or injury. This will be a fairly rare occurrence among hospital inpatients, but will be relatively more common among hospital outpatients and patients of family practitioners, health clinics, etc.

b) When a person with a known disease or injury, whether it is current or resolving, encounters the health care system for a specific treatment of that disease or injury (e.g., dialysis for renal disease; chemotherapy for malignancy; cast change).

c) When some circumstance or problem is present which influences the person's health status but is not in itself a current illness or injury. Such factors may be elicited during population surveys, when the person may or may not be currently sick, or be recorded as an additional factor to be borne in mind when the person is receiving care for some current illness or injury classifiable to categories 001-999.

In the latter circumstances the V code should be used only as a supplementary code and should not be the one selected for use in primary, single cause tabulations. Examples of these circumstances are a personal history of certain diseases, or a person with an artificial heart valve in situ.

PERSONS WITH POTENTIAL HEALTH HAZARDS RELATED TO COMMUNICABLE DISEASES (V01-V06)

Excludes: *family history of infectious and parasitic diseases (V18.8)*
personal history of infectious and parasitic diseases (V12.0)

➡ **AHA Coding Clinic:** J-F, '87, 8

V01 Contact with or exposure to communicable diseases

V01.0 Cholera
Conditions classifiable to 001

V01.1 Tuberculosis
Conditions classifiable to 010-018

V01.2 Poliomyelitis
Conditions classifiable to 045

V01.3 Smallpox
Conditions classifiable to 050

V01.4 Rubella
Conditions classifiable to 056

V01.5 Rabies
Conditions classifiable to 071

V01.6 Venereal diseases
Conditions classifiable to 090-099

V01.7 Other viral diseases
Conditions classifiable to 042-078 and V08, except as above
➡ **AHA Coding Clinic:** 2Q, '92, 11

V01.8 Other communicable diseases
Conditions classifiable to 001-136, except as above
➡ **AHA Coding Clinic:** J-A, '87, 24

V01.9 Unspecified communicable disease

V02 Carrier or suspected carrier of infectious diseases

V02.0 Cholera

V02.1 Typhoid

V02.2 Amebiasis

V02.3 Other gastrointestinal pathogens

V02.4 Diphtheria

✓5th **V02.5** Other specified bacterial diseases

V02.51 Group B streptococcus

V02.52 Other streptococcus

V02.59 Other specified bacterial diseases
Meningococcal
Staphylococcal

✓5th **V02.6** Viral hepatitis
Hepatitis Australian-antigen [HAA] [SH] carrier
Serum hepatitis carrier

V02.60 Viral hepatitis carrier, unspecified
➡ **AHA Coding Clinic:** 4Q, '97, 47

V02.61 Hepatitis B carrier
➡ **AHA Coding Clinic:** 4Q, '97, 47

V02.62 Viral Hepatitis C carrier
➡ **AHA Coding Clinic:** 4Q, '97, 47

V02.69 Other viral hepatitis carrier
➡ **AHA Coding Clinic:** 4Q, '97, 47

V02.7 Gonorrhea

V02.8 Other venereal diseases

V02.9 Other specified infectious organism
➡ **AHA Coding Clinic:** 3Q, '95, 18; 1Q, '93, 22; J-A, '87, 24

V03 Need for prophylactic vaccination and inoculation against bacterial diseases

Excludes: *vaccination not carried out because of contraindication (V64.0)*
vaccines against combinations of diseases (V06.0-V06.9)

V03.0 Cholera alone

V03.1 Typhoid-paratyphoid alone [TAB]

V03.2 Tuberculosis [BCG]

V03.3 Plague

V03.4 Tularemia

V Codes

V03.5 Diphtheria alone

V03.6 Pertussis alone

V03.7 Tetanus toxoid alone

✓5th **V03.8** Other specified vaccinations against single bacterial diseases

V03.81 Hemophilus influenza, type B [Hib]

V03.82 Streptococcus pneumoniae [pneumococcus]

V03.89 Other specified vaccination

V03.9 Unspecified single bacterial disease

V04 Need for prophylactic vaccination and inoculation against certain viral diseases

Excludes: *vaccines against combinations of diseases (V06.0-V06.9)*

V04.0 Poliomyelitis

V04.1 Smallpox

V04.2 Measles alone

V04.3 Rubella alone

V04.4 Yellow fever

V04.5 Rabies

V04.6 Mumps alone

V04.7 Common cold

V04.8 Influenza

V05 Need for other prophylactic vaccination and inoculation against single diseases

Excludes: *vaccines against combinations of diseases (V06.0-V06.9)*

V05.0 Arthropod-borne viral encephalitis

V05.1 Other arthropod-borne viral diseases

V05.2 Leishmaniasis

V05.3 Viral hepatitis

V05.4 Varicella

Chicken pox

V05.8 Other specified disease

➡ **AHA Coding Clinic:** 3Q, '91, 20

V05.9 Unspecified single disease

V06 Need for prophylactic vaccination and inoculation against combinations of diseases

Note: Use additional single vaccination codes from categories V03-V05 to identify any vaccinations not included in a combination code.

V06.0 Cholera with typhoid-paratyphoid [cholera + TAB]

V06.1 Diphtheria-tetanus-pertussis, combined [DTP]

V06.2 Without Diphtheria-tetanus-pertussis, with typhoid-paratyphoid [DTP + TAB]

V06.3 Diphtheria-tetanus-pertussis with poliomyelitis [DTP + polio]

V06.4 Measles-mumps-rubella [MMR]

V06.5 Tetanus-diphtheria [Td]

V06.6 Streptococcus pneumoniae [pneumococcus] and influenza

V06.8 Other combinations

Excludes: *multiple single vaccination codes (V03.0-V05.9)*

➡ **AHA Coding Clinic:** 1Q, '94, 19

V06.9 Unspecified combined vaccine

PERSONS WITH NEED FOR ISOLATION, OTHER POTENTIAL HEALTH HAZARDS AND PROPHYLACTIC MEASURES (V07-V09)

V07 Need for isolation and other prophylactic measures

Excludes: *prophylactic organ removal (V50.41-V50.49)*

[16] **V07.0** Isolation

Admission to protect the individual from his surroundings or for isolation of individual after contact with infectious diseases

V07.1 Desensitization to allergens

V07.2 Prophylactic immunotherapy

Administration of:
- antivenin
- immune sera [gamma globulin]
- RhoGAM
- tetanus antitoxin

✓5th **V07.3** Other prophylactic chemotherapy

V07.31 Prophylactic fluoride administration

[16] **V07.39** Other prophylactic chemotherapy

Excludes: *maintenance chemotherapy following disease (V58.1)*

[16] These V codes may be used as principal diagnosis on Medicare patients.

V07.4 Postmenopausal hormone replacement therapy ♀

[16] **V07.8** Other specified prophylactic measure

➡ **AHA Coding Clinic:** 1Q, '92, 11

V07.9 Unspecified prophylactic measure

V08 Asymptomatic human immunodeficiency virus [HIV] infection status

HIV positive NOS

Note: This code is ONLY to be used when NO HIV infection symptoms or conditions are present. If any HIV infection symptoms or conditions are present, see code 042.

Excludes: *AIDS (042)*
exposure to HIV (V01.7)
human immunodeficiency virus [HIV] disease (042)
nonspecific serologic evidence of HIV (795.71)
symptomatic human immunodeficiency virus [HIV] infection (042)

V09 Infection with drug-resistant microorganisms

Note: This category is intended for use as an additional code for infectious conditions classified elsewhere to indicate the presence of drug-resistance of the infectious organism.

➡ **AHA Coding Clinic:** 4Q, '93, 22

V09.0 Infection with microorganisms resistant to penicillins

V09.1 Infection with microorganisms resistant to cephalosporins and other B-lactam antibiotics

V09.2 Infection with microorganisms resistant to macrolides

V09.3 Infection with microorganisms resistant to tetracyclines

V09.4 Infection with microorganisms resistant to aminoglycosides

✓5th **V09.5** Infection with microorganisms resistant to quinolones and fluoroquinolones

V09.50 Without mention of resistance to multiple quinolones and fluoroquinoles

V09.51 With resistance to multiple quinolones and fluoroquinoles

V09.6 Infection with microorganisms resistant to sulfonamide

✓5th **V09.7** Infection with microorganisms resistant to other specified antimycobacterial agents

Excludes: *Amikacin (V09.4)*
Kanamycin (V09.4)
Streptomycin [SM] (V09.4)

V09.70 Without mention of resistance to multiple antimycobacterial agents

V09.71 With resistance to multiple antimycobacterial agents

✓5th **V09.8** Infection with microorganisms resistant to other specified drugs

V09.80 Without mention of resistance to multiple drugs

V09.81 With resistance to multiple drugs

✓5th **V09.9** Infection with drug-resistant microorganisms, unspecified

Drug resistance NOS

V09.90 Without mention of multiple drug resistance

V09.91 With multiple drug resistance

Multiple drug resistance NOS

PERSONS WITH POTENTIAL HEALTH HAZARDS RELATED TO PERSONAL AND FAMILY HISTORY (V10-V19)

Excludes: *obstetric patients where the possibility that the fetus might be affected is the reason for observation or management during pregnancy (655.0-655.9)*

➡ **AHA Coding Clinic:** J-F, '87, 1

V10 Personal history of malignant neoplasm

➡ **AHA Coding Clinic:** 2Q, '90, 9

✓5th **V10.0** Gastrointestinal tract

History of conditions classifiable to 140-159

V10.00 Gastrointestinal tract, unspecified

V10.01 Tongue

V10.02 Other and unspecified oral cavity and pharynx

V10.03 Esophagus

V10.04 Stomach

V10.05 Large intestine

➡ **AHA Coding Clinic:** 1Q, '95, 4

[16] These V codes may be used as principal diagnosis on Medicare patients.

V10.06 Rectum, rectosigmoid junction, and anus

V10.07 Liver

V10.09 Other

✓5th **V10.1** Trachea, bronchus, and lung
History of conditions classifiable to 162

V10.11 Bronchus and lung

V10.12 Trachea

✓5th **V10.2** Other respiratory and intrathoracic organs
History of conditions classifiable to 160, 161, 163-165

V10.20 Respiratory organ, unspecified

V10.21 Larynx

V10.22 Nasal cavities, middle ear, and accessory sinuses

V10.29 Other

V10.3 Breast
History of conditions classifiable to 174 and 175

➡ **AHA Coding Clinic:** 4Q, '97, 50; 1Q, '91, 16

✓5th **V10.4** Genital organs
History of conditions classifiable to 179-187

V10.40 Female genital organ, unspecified ♀

V10.41 Cervix uteri ♀

V10.42 Other parts of uterus ♀

V10.43 Ovary ♀

V10.44 Other female genital organs ♀

V10.45 Male genital organ, unspecified ♂

V10.46 Prostate ♂

V10.47 Testis ♂

V10.48 Epididymis

V10.49 Other male genital organs ♂

✓5th **V10.5** Urinary organs
History of conditions classifiable to 188 and 189

V10.50 Urinary organ, unspecified

V10.51 Bladder

V10.52 Kidney

V10.59 Other

✓5th **V10.6** Leukemia
Conditions classifiable to 204-208

Excludes: *leukemia in remission (204-208)*

➡ **AHA Coding Clinic:** 2Q, '92, 13; 4Q, '91, 26; 4Q, '90, 3

V10.60 Leukemia, unspecified

V10.61 Lymphoid leukemia

V10.62 Myeloid leukemia

V10.63 Monocytic leukemia

V10.69 Other

✓5th **V10.7** Other lymphatic and hematopoietic neoplasms
Conditions classifiable to 200-203

Excludes: *listed conditions in 200-203 in remission*

V10.71 Lymphosarcoma and reticulosarcoma

V10.72 Hodgkin's disease

V10.79 Other

✓5th **V10.8** Personal history of malignant neoplasm of other sites
History of conditions classifiable to 170-173, 190-195

V10.81 Bone

V10.82 Malignant melanoma of skin

V10.83 Other malignant neoplasm of skin

V10.84 Eye

V10.85 Brain

V10.86 Other parts of nervous system

Excludes: *peripheral, sympathetic, and parasympathetic nerves (V10.89)*

V10.87 Thyroid

V10.88 Other endocrine glands and related structures

V10.89 Other

V10.9 Unspecified personal history of malignant neoplasm

V11 Personal history of mental disorder

V11.0 Schizophrenia

Excludes: *that in remission (295.0-295.9 with fifth-digit 5)*

V11.1 Affective disorders
Personal history of manic-depressive psychosis

Excludes: *that in remission (296.0-296.6 with fifth-digit 5, 6)*

V11.2 Neurosis

V11.3 Alcoholism

V11.8 Other mental disorders

V11.9 Unspecified mental disorder

V12 Personal history of certain other diseases

✓5th **V12.0** Infectious and parasitic diseases

V12.00 Unspecified infectious and parasitic disease

V12.01 Tuberculosis

V12.02 Poliomyelitis

V12.03 Malaria

V12.09 Other

V12.1 Nutritional deficiency

V12.2 Endocrine, metabolic, and immunity disorders

Excludes: *history of allergy (V14.0-V14.9, V15.0)*

V12.3 Diseases of blood and blood-forming organs

✓5th **V12.4** Disorders of nervous system and sense organs

V12.40 Unspecified disorder of nervous system and sense organs

V12.41 Benign neoplasm of the brain

➡ **AHA Coding Clinic:** 4Q, '97, 48

V12.49 Other disorders of nervous system and sense organs

✓5th **V12.5** Diseases of circulatory system

Excludes: *old myocardial infarction (412)*
postmyocardial infarction syndrome (411.0)

➡ **AHA Coding Clinic:** 4Q, '95, 61

V12.50 Unspecified circulatory disease

V12.51 Venous thrombosis and embolism
Pulmonary embolism

V12.52 Thrombophlebitis

V12.59 Other

➡ **AHA Coding Clinic:** 4Q, '97, 37

V12.6 Diseases of respiratory system

✓5th **V12.7** Diseases of digestive system

➡ **AHA Coding Clinic:** 1Q, '95, 3; 2Q, '89, 16

V12.70 Unspecified digestive disease

V12.71 Peptic ulcer disease

V12.72 Colonic polyps

V12.79 Other

V13 Personal history of other diseases

✓5th **V13.0** Disorders of urinary system

V13.00 Unspecified urinary disorder

V13.01 Urinary calculi

V13.09 Other

V13.1 Trophoblastic disease ♀

Excludes: *supervision during a current pregnancy (V23.1)*

V13.2 Other genital system and obstetric disorders

Excludes: *supervision during a current pregnancy of a woman with poor obstetric history (V23.0-V23.9)*
habitual aborter (646.3)
without current pregnancy (629.9)

V13.3 Diseases of skin and subcutaneous tissue

V13.4 Arthritis

V13.5 Other musculoskeletal disorders

✓5th **V13.6** Congenital malformations

V13.61 Hypospadias

V13.69 Other congenital malformations

V13.7 Perinatal problems

V13.8 Other specified diseases

V13.9 Unspecified disease

V14 Personal history of allergy to medicinal agents

V14.0 Penicillin

V14.1 Other antibiotic agent

V14.2 Sulfonamides

V14.3 Other anti-infective agent

V14.4 Anesthetic agent

V14.5 Narcotic agent

V14.6 Analgesic agent

V14.7 Serum or vaccine

V14.8 Other specified medicinal agents

V14.9 Unspecified medicinal agent

V15 Other personal history presenting hazards to health

V15.0 Allergy, other than to medicinal agents

V15.1 Surgery to heart and great vessels

Excludes: *replacement by transplant or other means (V42.1-V42.2, V43.2-V43.4)*

V15.2 Surgery to other major organs

Excludes: *replacement by transplant or other means (V42.0-V43.8)*

V15.3 Irradiation

Previous exposure to therapeutic or other ionizing radiation

✓5th **V15.4** Psychological trauma

Excludes: *history of condition classifiable to 290-316 (V11.0-V11.9)*

V15.41 History of physical abuse

Rape

V15.42 History of emotional abuse

Neglect

V15.49 Other

V15.5 Injury

V15.6 Poisoning

V15.7 Contraception

Excludes: *current contraceptive management (V25.0-V25.4)*
presence of intrauterine contraceptive device as incidental finding (V45.5)

✓5th **V15.8** Other specified personal history presenting hazards to health

➡ AHA Coding Clinic: 4Q, '95, 62

V15.81 Noncompliance with medical treatment

➡ AHA Coding Clinic: 2Q, '97, 11; 1Q, '97, 12; 3Q, '96, 9

V15.82 History of tobacco use

Excludes: *tobacco dependence (305.1)*

V15.84 Exposure to asbestos

V15.85 Exposure to potentially hazardous body fluids

V15.86 Exposure to lead

V15.89 Other

V15.9 Unspecified personal history presenting hazards to health

V16 Family history of malignant neoplasm

V16.0 Gastrointestinal tract

Family history of condition classifiable to 140-159

V16.1 Trachea, bronchus, and lung

Family history of condition classifiable to 162

V16.2 Other respiratory and intrathoracic organs

Family history of condition classifiable to 160-161, 163-165

V16.3 Breast

Family history of condition classifiable to 174

➡ AHA Coding Clinic: 1Q, '92, 11

✓5th **V16.4** Genital organs

Family history of condition classifiable to 179-187

➡ AHA Coding Clinic: 4Q, '97, 48

V16.40 Genital organ, unspecified

V16.41 Ovary

V16.42 Prostate

V16.43 Testis

V16.49 Other

✓5th **V16.5** Urinary organs

Family history of condition classifiable to 189

V16.51 Kidney

V16.59 Other

V16.6 Leukemia

Family history of condition classifiable to 204-208

V16.7 Other lymphatic and hematopoietic neoplasms

Family history of condition classifiable to 200-203

V16.8 Other specified malignant neoplasm

Family history of other condition classifiable to 140-199

V16.9 Unspecified malignant neoplasm

V17 Family history of certain chronic disabling diseases

V17.0 Psychiatric condition

Excludes: *family history of mental retardation (V18.4)*

V17.1 Stroke (cerebrovascular)

V17.2 Other neurological diseases

Epilepsy
Huntington's chorea

V17.3 Ischemic heart disease

V17.4 Other cardiovascular diseases

V17.5 Asthma

V17.6 Other chronic respiratory conditions

V17.7 Arthritis

V17.8 Other musculoskeletal diseases

V18 Family history of certain other specific conditions

V18.0 Diabetes mellitus

V18.1 Other endocrine and metabolic diseases

V18.2 Anemia

V18.3 Other blood disorders

V18.4 Mental retardation

V18.5 Digestive disorders

✓5th **V18.6** Kidney diseases

V18.61 Polycystic kidney

V18.69 Other kidney diseases

V18.7 Other genitourinary diseases

V18.8 Infectious and parasitic diseases

V19 Family history of other conditions

V19.0 Blindness or visual loss

V19.1 Other eye disorders

V19.2 Deafness or hearing loss

V19.3 Other ear disorders

V19.4 Skin conditions

V19.5 Congenital anomalies

V19.6 Allergic disorders

V19.7 Consanguinity

V19.8 Other condition

PERSONS ENCOUNTERING HEALTH SERVICES IN CIRCUMSTANCES RELATED TO REPRODUCTION AND DEVELOPMENT (V20-V29)

V20 Health supervision of infant or child A: 0-17

[16] **V20.0** Foundling

V20.1 Other healthy infant or child receiving care

Medical or nursing care supervision of healthy infant in cases of:
maternal illness, physical or psychiatric
socioeconomic adverse condition at home
too many children at home preventing or interfering with normal care

➡ **AHA Coding Clinic:** 3Q, '89, 14

V20.2 Routine infant or child health check

Developmental testing of infant or child
Immunizations appropriate for age
Routine vision and hearing testing

Use additional code(s) to identify:
special screening examination(s) performed (V73.0-V82.9)

Excludes: *special screening for developmental handicaps (V79.3)*

V21 Constitutional states in development

V21.0 Period of rapid growth in childhood

V21.1 Puberty

V21.2 Other adolescence

V21.8 Other specified constitutional states in development

V21.9 Unspecified constitutional state in development

V22 Normal pregnancy ♀

Excludes: *pregnancy examination or test, pregnancy unconfirmed (V72.4)*

V22.0 Supervision of normal first pregnancy

V22.1 Supervision of other normal pregnancy

V22.2 Pregnant state, incidental

Pregnant state NOS

V23 Supervision of high-risk pregnancy ♀ A: 12-55

V23.0 Pregnancy with history of infertility

V23.1 Pregnancy with history of trophoblastic disease

Pregnancy with history of:
hydatidiform mole
vesicular mole

Excludes: *that without current pregnancy (V13.1)*

V23.2 Pregnancy with history of abortion

Pregnancy with history of conditions classifiable to 634-638

Excludes: *habitual aborter:*
care during pregnancy (646.3)
that without current pregnancy (629.9)

V23.3 Grand multiparity

Excludes: *care in relation to labor and delivery (659.4)*
that without current pregnancy (V61.5)

[16] These V codes may be used as principal diagnosis on Medicare patients.

V23.4 Pregnancy with other poor obstetric history
Pregnancy with history of other conditions classifiable to 630-676

V23.5 Pregnancy with other poor reproductive history
Pregnancy with history of stillbirth or neonatal death

V23.7 Insufficient prenatal care
History of little or no prenatal care
➡ CC Excl: V22.0-V22.2, V23.0-V23.9

✓5th **V23.8 Other high-risk pregnancy**
➡ CC Excl: see Code V23.7

V23.81 Elderly primigravida
First pregnancy in a woman who will be 35 years of age or older at expected date of delivery

Excludes: *elderly primigravida complicating pregnancy (659.5)*

V23.82 Elderly multigravida
Second or more pregnancy in a woman who will be 35 years of age or older at expected date of delivery

Excludes: *elderly multigravida complicating pregnancy (659.6)*

V23.83 Young primigravida
First pregnancy in a female less than 16 years old at expected date of delivery

Excludes: *young primigravida complicating pregnancy (659.8)*

V23.84 Young multigravida
Second or more pregnancy in a female less than 16 years old at expected date of delivery

Excludes: *young multigravida complicating pregnancy (659.8)*

V23.89 Other high-risk pregnancy

V23.9 Unspecified high-risk pregnancy
➡ CC Excl: see Code V23.7

V24 Postpartum care and examination ♀

[16] **V24.0 Immediately after delivery** A: 12-55
Care and observation in uncomplicated cases

V24.1 Lactating mother
Supervision of lactation

V24.2 Routine postpartum follow-up

V25 Encounter for contraceptive management

➡ AHA Coding Clinic: 4Q, '92, 24

✓5th **V25.0 General counseling and advice**

V25.01 Prescription of oral contraceptives ♀

V25.02 Initiation of other contraceptive measures
Fitting of diaphragm
Prescription of foams, creams, or other agents
➡ AHA Coding Clinic: 3Q, '97, 7

V25.09 Other
Family planning advice

V25.1 Insertion of intrauterine contraceptive device ♀

[16] **V25.2 Sterilization**
Admission for interruption of fallopian tubes or vas deferens

[16] **V25.3 Menstrual extraction** ♀
Menstrual regulation

✓5th **V25.4 Surveillance of previously prescribed contraceptive methods**
Checking, reinsertion, or removal of contraceptive device
Repeat prescription for contraceptive method
Routine examination in connection with contraceptive maintenance

Excludes: *presence of intrauterine contraceptive device as incidental finding (V45.5)*

V25.40 Contraceptive surveillance, unspecified

V25.41 Contraceptive pill ♀

V25.42 Intrauterine contraceptive device ♀
Checking, reinsertion, or removal of intrauterine device

V25.43 Implantable subdermal contraceptive ♀

V25.49 Other contraceptive method
➡ AHA Coding Clinic: 3Q, '97, 7

V25.5 Insertion of implantable subdermal contraceptive ♀

V25.8 Other specified contraceptive management
Postvasectomy sperm count
➡ AHA Coding Clinic: 3Q, '96, 9

V25.9 Unspecified contraceptive management

V26 Procreative management

[16] **V26.0 Tuboplasty or vasoplasty after previous sterilization**

V26.1 Artificial insemination ♀

V26.2 Investigation and testing
Fallopian insufflation Sperm counts

Excludes: *postvasectomy sperm count (V25.8)*

➡ AHA Coding Clinic: 2Q, '96, 9; N-D, '85, 15

V26.3 Genetic counseling

V26.4 General counseling and advice

[16] These V codes may be used as principal diagnosis on Medicare patients.

✓5th **V26.5** Sterilization status

V26.51 Tubal ligation status

Excludes: *infertility not due to previous tubal ligation (628.0-628.9)*

V26.52 Vasectomy status

V26.8 Other specified procreative management

V26.9 Unspecified procreative management

V27 Outcome of delivery ♀ A: 12-55

Note: This category is intended for the coding of the outcome of delivery on the mother's record.

➡ **AHA Coding Clinic:** 2Q, '91, 16

V27.0 Single liveborn

➡ **AHA Coding Clinic:** 4Q, '95, 59; 1Q, '92, 9

V27.1 Single stillborn

V27.2 Twins, both liveborn

V27.3 Twins, one liveborn and one stillborn

V27.4 Twins, both stillborn

V27.5 Other multiple birth, all liveborn

V27.6 Other multiple birth, some liveborn

V27.7 Other multiple birth, all stillborn

V27.9 Unspecified outcome of delivery

Single birth } outcome to infant unspecified
Multiple birth }

V28 Antenatal screening ♀

Excludes: *abnormal findings on screening—code to findings*
routine prenatal care (V22.0-V23.9)

V28.0 Screening for chromosomal anomalies by amniocentesis A: 12-55

V28.1 Screening for raised alpha-fetoprotein levels in amniotic fluid A: 12-55

V28.2 Other screening based on amniocentesis A: 12-55

V28.3 Screening for malformation using ultrasonics

V28.4 Screening for fetal growth retardation using ultrasonics

V28.5 Screening for isoimmunization

V28.6 Screening for Streptococcus B A: 12-55

➡ **AHA Coding Clinic:** 4Q, '97, 46

V28.8 Other specified antenatal screening

V28.9 Unspecified antenatal screening

V29 Observation and evaluation of newborns for suspected condition not found A: 0

Note: This category is to be used for newborns, within the neonatal period, (the first 28 days of life) who are suspected of having an abnormal condition resulting from exposure from the mother or the birth process, but without signs or symptoms, and which, after examination and observation, is found not to exist.

➡ **AHA Coding Clinic:** 4Q, '94, 47; 1Q, '94, 9; 4Q, '92, 21

[16] **V29.0** Observation for suspected infectious condition

[16] **V29.1** Observation for suspected neurological condition

[16] **V29.2** Observation for suspected respiratory condition

V29.3 Observation for suspected genetic or metabolic condition

[16] **V29.8** Observation for other specified suspected condition

V29.9 Observation for unspecified suspected condition

LIVEBORN INFANTS ACCORDING TO TYPE OF BIRTH (V30-V39)

Note: These categories are intended for the coding of liveborn infants who are consuming health care [e.g., crib or bassinet occupancy].

The following fourth-digit subdivisions are for use with categories V30-V39:

✓5th
.0 Born in hospital A: 0
.1 Born before admission to hospital A: 0
.2 Born outside hospital and not hospitalized

The following two fifth-digits are for use with the fourth-digit .0, Born in hospital:

0 delivered without mention of cesarean delivery
1 delivered by cesarean delivery

[18] **V30 Single liveborn**

➡ **AHA Coding Clinic:** 1Q, '94, 9

[18] **V31 Twin, mate liveborn**

➡ **AHA Coding Clinic:** 3Q, '92, 10

[18] **V32 Twin, mate stillborn**

[18] **V33 Twin, unspecified**

[18] **V34 Other multiple, mates all liveborn**

[18] **V35 Other multiple, mates all stillborn**

[18] **V36 Other multiple, mates live- and stillborn**

[18] **V37 Other multiple, unspecified**

[19] **V39 Unspecified**

PERSONS WITH A CONDITION INFLUENCING THEIR HEALTH STATUS (V40-V49)

Note: These categories are intended for use when these conditions are recorded as "diagnoses" or "problems."

V40 Mental and behavioral problems

V40.0 Problems with learning

V40.1 Problems with communication [including speech]

V40.2 Other mental problems

[16] These V codes may be used as principal diagnosis on Medicare patients.
[18] These codes, with the fourth digit of 0 or 1, may be used as a principal diagnosis for Medicare patients.
[19] These V codes are unacceptable as principal diagnosis with the fourth digit of 1 or 2.

V40.3 Other behavioral problems

V40.9 Unspecified mental or behavioral problem

V41 Problems with special senses and other special functions

V41.0 Problems with sight

V41.1 Other eye problems

V41.2 Problems with hearing

V41.3 Other ear problems

V41.4 Problems with voice production

V41.5 Problems with smell and taste

V41.6 Problems with swallowing and mastication

V41.7 Problems with sexual function

Excludes: *marital problems (V61.10)*
psychosexual disorders (302.0-302.9)

V41.8 Other problems with special functions

V41.9 Unspecified problem with special functions

V42 Organ or tissue replaced by transplant

Includes: homologous or heterologous (animal) (human) transplant organ status

V42.0 Kidney

➡ **CC Excl:** 996.80-996.81, V42.0, V42.8-V42.9

V42.1 Heart

➡ **CC Excl:** 996.80, 996.83, V42.1, V42.8-V42.9

V42.2 Heart valve

➡ **CC Excl:** 996.71, V42.2, V42.8-V42.9

V42.3 Skin

V42.4 Bone

V42.5 Cornea

V42.6 Lung

➡ **CC Excl:** 996.80, 996.84, V42.6, V42.8-V42.9

V42.7 Liver

➡ **CC Excl:** 996.80, 996.82, V42.7-V42.9

✓5th **V42.8** Other specified organ or tissue

➡ **CC Excl:** 996.80, 996.86-996.89, V42.8-V42.9

➡ **AHA Coding Clinic:** 4Q, '97, 49

V42.81 Bone marrow

V42.82 Peripheral stem cells

V42.83 Pancreas

V42.89 Other

V42.9 Unspecified organ or tissue

V43 Organ or tissue replaced by other means

Includes: replacement of organ by:
artificial device
mechanical device
prosthesis

Excludes: *cardiac pacemaker in situ (V45.01)*
fitting and adjustment of prosthetic device (V52.0-V52.9)
renal dialysis status (V45.1)

V43.0 Eye globe

V43.1 Lens

Pseudophakos

V43.2 Heart

➡ **CC Excl:** 996.80, 996.83, V42.1, V43.2

V43.3 Heart valve

V43.4 Blood vessel

V43.5 Bladder

✓5th **V43.6** Joint

V43.60 Unspecified joint

V43.61 Shoulder

V43.62 Elbow

V43.63 Wrist

V43.64 Hip

V43.65 Knee

V43.66 Ankle

V43.69 Other

V43.7 Limb

✓5th **V43.8** Other organ or tissue

V43.81 Larynx

➡ **AHA Coding Clinic:** 4Q, '95, 55

V43.82 Breast

➡ **AHA Coding Clinic:** 4Q, '95, 55

V43.83 Artificial skin

V43.89 Other

V44 Artificial opening status

Excludes: *artificial openings requiring attention or management (V55.0-V55.9)*

V44.0 Tracheostomy

V44.1 Gastrostomy

➡ **AHA Coding Clinic:** 3Q, '97, 12; 1Q, '93, 26

V44.2 Ileostomy

V44.3 Colostomy

V44.4 Other artificial opening of gastrointestinal tract

✓5th **V44.5** Cystostomy

V44.50 Cystostomy, unspecified

V44.51 Cutaneous-vesicostomy

V44.52 Appendico-vesicostomy

V44.59 Other cystostomy

V44.6 Other artificial opening of urinary tract

Nephrostomy
Urethrostomy
Ureterostomy

V44.7 Artificial vagina

V44.8 Other artificial opening status

V44.9 Unspecified artificial opening status

V45 Other postsurgical states

Excludes: *aftercare management (V51-V58.9)*
malfunction or other complication—code to condition

✓5th **V45.0** Cardiac device in situ

V45.00 Unspecified cardiac device

V45.01 Cardiac pacemaker

V45.02 Automatic implantable cardiac defibrillator

V45.09 Other specified cardiac device

Carotid sinus pacemaker in situ

V45.1 Renal dialysis status

Patient requiring intermittent renal dialysis
Presence of arterial-venous shunt (for dialysis)

Excludes: *admission for dialysis treatment or session (V56.0)*

➡ **CC Excl:** 996.73, V45.1

V45.2 Presence of cerebrospinal fluid drainage device

Cerebral ventricle (communicating) shunt, valve, or device in situ

Excludes: *malfunction (996.2)*

V45.3 Intestinal bypass or anastomosis status

V45.4 Arthrodesis status

➡ **AHA Coding Clinic:** N-D, '84, 18

✓5th **V45.5** Presence of contraceptive device

Excludes: *checking, reinsertion, or removal of device (V25.42)*
complication from device (996.32)
insertion of device (V25.1)

V45.51 Intrauterine contraceptive device ♀

V45.52 Subdermal contraceptive implant

V45.59 Other

✓5th **V45.6** States following surgery of eye and adnexa

Cataract extraction, Filtering bleb, Surgical eyelid adhesion } state following eye surgery

Excludes: *aphakia (379.31)*
artificial:
eye globe (V43.0)

➡ **AHA Coding Clinic:** 4Q, '97, 49

V45.61 Cataract extraction status

Use additional code for associated artifical lens status (V43.1)

V45.69 Other states following surgery of eye and adnexa

✓5th **V45.7** Acquired absence of organ

➡ **AHA Coding Clinic:** 4Q, '97, 50

V45.71 Acquired absence of breast

➡ **AHA Coding Clinic:** 4Q, '97, 50

V45.72 Acquired absence of intestine (large) (small)

V45.73 Acquired absence of kidney

✓5th **V45.8** Other postsurgical status

V45.81 Aortocoronary bypass status

➡ **AHA Coding Clinic:** 3Q, '97, 16

V45.82 Percutaneous transluminal coronary angioplasty status

V45.83 Breast implant removal status

➡ **AHA Coding Clinic:** 4Q, '95, 55

V45.89 Other

Presence of neuropacemaker or other electronic device

Excludes: *artificial heart valve in situ (V43.3)*
vascular prosthesis in situ (V43.4)

➡ **AHA Coding Clinic:** 1Q, '95, 11

V46 Other dependence on machines

V46.0 Aspirator

V46.1 Respirator

Iron lung

➡ **CC Excl:** V46.0-V46.1, V46.8-V46.9

➡ **AHA Coding Clinic:** J-F, '87, 7

V46.8 Other enabling machines
Hyperbaric chamber
Possum [Patient-Operated-Selector-Mechanism]

Excludes: *cardiac pacemaker (V45.01)*
kidney dialysis machine (V45.1)

V46.9 Unspecified machine dependence

V47 Other problems with internal organs

V47.0 Deficiencies of internal organs

V47.1 Mechanical and motor problems with internal organs

V47.2 Other cardiorespiratory problems
Cardiovascular exercise intolerance with pain (with):
at rest
less than ordinary activity
ordinary activity

V47.3 Other digestive problems

V47.4 Other urinary problems

V47.5 Other genital problems

V47.9 Unspecified

V48 Problems with head, neck, and trunk

V48.0 Deficiencies of head

Excludes: *deficiencies of ears, eyelids, and nose (V48.8)*

V48.1 Deficiencies of neck and trunk

V48.2 Mechanical and motor problems with head

V48.3 Mechanical and motor problems with neck and trunk

V48.4 Sensory problem with head

V48.5 Sensory problem with neck and trunk

V48.6 Disfigurements of head

V48.7 Disfigurements of neck and trunk

V48.8 Other problems with head, neck, and trunk

V48.9 Unspecified problem with head, neck, or trunk

V49 Problems with limbs and other problems

V49.0 Deficiencies of limbs

V49.1 Mechanical problems with limbs

V49.2 Motor problems with limbs

V49.3 Sensory problems with limbs

V49.4 Disfigurements of limbs

V49.5 Other problems of limbs

✓5th **V49.6** Upper limb amputation status
➡ **AHA Coding Clinic:** 4Q, '94, 39

V49.60 Unspecified level

V49.61 Thumb

V49.62 Other finger(s)

V49.63 Hand

V49.64 Wrist
Disarticulation of wrist

V49.65 Below elbow

V49.66 Above elbow
Disarticulation of elbow

V49.67 Shoulder
Disarticulation of shoulder

✓5th **V49.7** Lower limb amputation status
➡ **AHA Coding Clinic:** 4Q, '94, 39

V49.70 Unspecified level

V49.71 Great toe

V49.72 Other toe(s)

V49.73 Foot

V49.74 Ankle
Disarticulation of ankle

V49.75 Below knee

V49.76 Above knee
Disarticulation of knee

V49.77 Hip
Disarticulation of hip

V49.8 Other specified problems influencing health status

V49.9 Unspecified

PERSONS ENCOUNTERING HEALTH SERVICES FOR SPECIFIC PROCEDURES AND AFTERCARE (V50-V59)

Note: Categories V51-V58 are intended for use to indicate a reason for care in patients who may have already been treated for some disease or injury not now present, or who are receiving care to consolidate the treatment, to deal with residual states, or to prevent recurrence.

Excludes: *follow-up examination for medical surveillance following treatment (V67.0-V67.9)*

V50 Elective surgery for purposes other than remedying health states

[16] **V50.0** Hair transplant

[16] These V codes may be used as principal diagnosis on Medicare patients.

[16] **V50.1** **Other plastic surgery for unacceptable cosmetic appearance**
Breast augmentation or reduction
Face-lift

Excludes: *plastic surgery following healed injury or operation (V51)*

[16] **V50.2** **Routine or ritual circumcision** ♂
Circumcision in the absence of significant medical indication

V50.3 **Ear piercing**

✓5th **V50.4** **Prophylactic organ removal**

Excludes: *organ donations (V59.0-59.9)*
therapeutic organ removal—code to condition

➡ **AHA Coding Clinic:** 4Q, '94, 44

[16] **V50.41** **Breast**

[16] **V50.42** **Ovary** ♀

[16] **V50.49** **Other**

V50.8 **Other**

V50.9 **Unspecified**

[16] **V51** **Aftercare involving the use of plastic surgery**
Plastic surgery following healed injury or operation

Excludes: *cosmetic plastic surgery (V50.1)*
plastic surgery as treatment for current injury—code to condition
repair of scarred tissue—code to scar

V52 **Fitting and adjustment of prosthetic device and implant**
Includes: removal of device

Excludes: *malfunction or complication of prosthetic device (996.0-996.7)*
status only, without need for care (V43.0-V43.8)

➡ **AHA Coding Clinic:** 4Q, '95, 55

[16] **V52.0** **Artificial arm (complete) (partial)**

[16] **V52.1** **Artificial leg (complete) (partial)**

[16] **V52.2** **Artificial eye**

[16] **V52.3** **Dental prosthetic device**

[16] **V52.4** **Breast prosthesis and implant** ♀

Excludes: *admission for implant insertion (V50.1)*

➡ **AHA Coding Clinic:** 4Q, '95, 80, 81

[16] **V52.8** **Other specified prosthetic device**

V52.9 **Unspecified prosthetic device**

V53 **Fitting and adjustment of other device**
Includes: removal of device
replacement of device

Excludes: *status only, without need for care (V45.0-V45.8)*

✓5th **V53.0** **Devices related to nervous system and special senses**

➡ **AHA Coding Clinic:** 4Q, '97, 51

V53.01 **Fitting and adjustment of cerebral ventricular (communicating) shunt**

➡ **AHA Coding Clinic:** 4Q, '97, 51

V53.02 **Neuropacemaker (brain) (peripheral nerve) (spinal cord)**

V53.09 **Fitting and adjustment of other devices related to nervous system and special senses**
Auditory substitution device
Visual substitution device

V53.1 **Spectacles and contact lenses**

V53.2 **Hearing aid**

✓5th **V53.3** **Cardiac device**
Reprogramming

➡ **AHA Coding Clinic:** 3Q, '92, 3; M-J, '87, 8

V53.31 **Cardiac pacemaker**

Excludes: *mechanical complication of cardiac pacemaker (996.01)*

V53.32 **Automatic implantable cardiac defibrillator**

V53.39 **Other cardiac device**

V53.4 **Orthodontic devices**

V53.5 **Other intestinal appliance**

Excludes: *colostomy (V55.3)*
ileostomy (V55.2)
other artificial opening of digestive tract (V55.4)

V53.6 **Urinary devices**
Urinary catheter

Excludes: *cystostomy (V55.5)*
nephrostomy (V55.6)
ureterostomy (V55.6)
urethrostomy (V55.6)

V53.7 **Orthopedic devices**
Orthopedic:
brace
cast
Orthopedic:
corset
shoes

Excludes: *other orthopedic aftercare (V54)*

V53.8 **Wheelchair**

V53.9 **Other and unspecified device**

[16] These V codes may be used as principal diagnosis on Medicare patients.

V54 Other orthopedic aftercare

Excludes: *fitting and adjustment of orthopedic devices (V53.7)*
malfunction of internal orthopedic device (996.4)
other complication of nonmechanical nature (996.60-996.79)

➡ **AHA Coding Clinic:** 3Q, '95, 3

[16] **V54.0** **Aftercare involving removal of fracture plate or other internal fixation device**

Removal of:
pins
plates

Removal of:
rods
screws

Excludes: *removal of external fixation device (V54.8)*

V54.8 **Other orthopedic aftercare**

Change, checking, or removal of:
Kirschner wire
plaster cast
splint, external
other external fixation or traction device

V54.9 **Unspecified orthopedic aftercare**

V55 Attention to artificial openings

Includes: adjustment or repositioning of catheter
closure
passage of sounds or bougies
reforming
removal or replacement of catheter
toilet or cleansing

Excludes: *complications of external stoma (519.00-519.09, 569.60-569.69, 997.4, 997.5)*
status only, without need for care (V44.0-V44.9)

[16] **V55.0** **Tracheostomy**

[16] **V55.1** **Gastrostomy**

➡ **AHA Coding Clinic:** 3Q, '97, 7, 8; 1Q, '96, 14; 3Q, '95, 13

[16] **V55.2** **Ileostomy**

[16] **V55.3** **Colostomy**

➡ **AHA Coding Clinic:** 3Q, '97, 9

[16] **V55.4** **Other artificial opening of digestive tract**

[16] **V55.5** **Cystostomy**

[16] **V55.6** **Other artificial opening of urinary tract**

Nephrostomy
Urethrostomy
Ureterostomy

[16] **V55.7** **Artificial vagina**

[16] **V55.8** **Other specified artificial opening**

V55.9 **Unspecified artificial opening**

V56 Encounter for dialysis and dialysis catheter care

Use additional code to identify the associated condition

Excludes: *dialysis preparation—code to condition*

➡ **AHA Coding Clinic:** 1Q, '93, 29

[16] **V56.0** **Extracorporeal dialysis**

Dialysis (renal) NOS

Excludes: *dialysis status (V45.1)*

[16] **V56.1** **Fitting and adjustment of extracorporeal dialysis catheter**

Removal or replacement of catheter
Toilet or cleansing

Use additional code for any concurrent extracorporeal dialysis (V56.0)

V56.2 **Fitting and adjustment of peritoneal dialysis catheter**

Use additional code for any concurrent peritoneal dialysis (V56.8)

[16] **V56.8** **Other dialysis**

Peritoneal dialysis

V57 Care involving use of rehabilitation procedures

Use additional code to identify underlying condition

➡ **AHA Coding Clinic:** 3Q, '97, 12; S-O, '86, 3

V57.0 **Breathing exercises**

[17] **V57.1** **Other physical therapy**

Therapeutic and remedial exercises, except breathing

✓5th **V57.2** **Occupational therapy and vocational rehabilitation**

[17] **V57.21** **Encounter for occupational therapy**

[17] **V57.22** **Encounter for vocational therapy**

[17] **V57.3** **Speech therapy**

➡ **AHA Coding Clinic:** 4Q, '97, 36

V57.4 **Orthoptic training**

✓5th **V57.8** **Other specified rehabilitation procedure**

V57.81 **Orthotic training**

Gait training in the use of artificial limbs

[17] **V57.89** **Other**

Multiple training or therapy

➡ **AHA Coding Clinic:** 3Q, '97, 11, 12; S-O, '86, 4

[17] **V57.9** **Unspecified rehabilitation procedure**

[16] These V codes may be used as principal diagnosis on Medicare patients.
[17] Rehabilitation codes acceptable as a principal diagnosis when accompanied by a secondary diagnosis reflecting the condition treated.

V58 Encounter for other and unspecified procedures and aftercare

Excludes: *convalescence and palliative care (V66)*

[16] **V58.0 Radiotherapy**
Encounter or admission for radiotherapy

Excludes: *encounter for radioactive implant—code to condition*
radioactive iodine therapy-code to condition

➡ **AHA Coding Clinic:** 3Q, '92, 5; 2Q, '90, 7; J-F, '87, 13

[16] **V58.1 Chemotherapy**
Encounter or admission for chemotherapy

Excludes: *prophylactic chemotherapy against disease which has never been present (V03.0-V07.9)*

➡ **AHA Coding Clinic:** 3Q, '93, 4; 2Q, '92, 6; 2Q, '91, 17; 2Q, '90, 7; S-O, '84, 5

V58.2 Blood transfusion, without reported diagnosis

V58.3 Attention to surgical dressings and sutures
Change of dressings
Removal of sutures

✓5th **V58.4 Other aftercare following surgery**

Excludes: *attention to artificial openings (V55.0-V55.9)*
orthopedic aftercare (V54.0-V54.9)

➡ **AHA Coding Clinic:** N-D, '87, 9

[16, 20] **V58.41 Encounter for planned post-operative wound closure**

Excludes: *disruption of operative wound (998.3)*

[16, 20] **V58.49 Other specified aftercare following surgery**
➡ **AHA Coding Clinic:** 1Q, '96, 8, 9

[20] **V58.5 Orthodontics**

Excludes: *fitting and adjustment of orthodontic device (V53.4)*

✓5th **V58.6 Long-term (current) drug use**

Excludes: *drug abuse (305.00-305.93)*
drug dependence (304.00-304.93)

➡ **AHA Coding Clinic:** 4Q, '95, 61

[16, 20] **V58.61 Long-term (current) use of anticoagulants**

V58.62 Long-term (current) use of antibiotics

[16, 20] **V58.69 Long-term (current) use of other medications**
High-risk medications

➡ **AHA Coding Clinic:** 1Q, '97, 12; 2Q, '96, 7

✓5th **V58.8 Other specified procedures and aftercare**
➡ **AHA Coding Clinic:** 4Q, '94, 45; 2Q, '94, 8

[20] **V58.81 Fitting and adjustment of vascular catheter**
Removal or replacement of catheter
Toilet or cleansing

Excludes: *complication of renal dialysis catheter (996.73)*
complication of vascular catheter (996.74)
dialysis preparation—code to condition
encounter for dialysis (V56.0-V56.8)
fitting and adjustment of dialysis catheter (V56.1)

[20] **V58.82 Fitting and adjustment of nonvascular catheter NEC**
Removal or replacement of catheter
Toilet or cleansing

Excludes: *fitting and adjustment of peritoneal dialysis catheter (V56.2)*
fitting and adjustment of urinary catheter (V53.6)

[20] **V58.89 Other specified aftercare**

[20] **V58.9 Unspecified aftercare**

V59 Donors

Excludes: *examination of potential donor (V70.8)*
self-donation of organ or tissue—code to condition

➡ **AHA Coding Clinic:** 4Q, '95, 62; N-D, '84, 8

✓5th **V59.0 Blood**

V59.01 Whole blood

V59.02 Stem cells

V59.09 Other

[16] **V59.1 Skin**

[16] **V59.2 Bone**

[16] **V59.3 Bone marrow**

[16] **V59.4 Kidney**

[16] **V59.5 Cornea**

[16] **V59.6 Liver**

[16] **V59.8 Other specified organ or tissue**

V59.9 Unspecified organ or tissue

[16] These V codes may be used as principal diagnosis on Medicare patients.
[20] These V codes are acceptable as principal diagnosis when accompanied by a diagnosis of personal history of malignancy. These codes group to DRGs 465-466.

PERSONS ENCOUNTERING HEALTH SERVICES IN OTHER CIRCUMSTANCES (V60-V68)

V60 Housing, household, and economic circumstances

V60.0 Lack of housing
Hobos
Social migrants
Tramps
Transients
Vagabonds

V60.1 Inadequate housing
Lack of heating
Restriction of space
Technical defects in home preventing adequate care

V60.2 Inadequate material resources
Economic problem
Poverty NOS

V60.3 Person living alone

V60.4 No other household member able to render care
Person requiring care (has) (is):
family member too handicapped, ill, or otherwise unsuited to render care
partner temporarily away from home
temporarily away from usual place of abode

Excludes: *holiday relief care (V60.5)*

V60.5 Holiday relief care
Provision of health care facilities to a person normally cared for at home, to enable relatives to take a vacation

V60.6 Person living in residential institution
Boarding school resident

V60.8 Other specified housing or economic circumstances

V60.9 Unspecified housing or economic circumstance

V61 Other family circumstances

Includes: when these circumstances or fear of them, affecting the person directly involved or others, are mentioned as the reason, justified or not, for seeking or receiving medical advice or care

V61.0 Family disruption
Divorce
Estrangement

✓5th **V61.1 Counseling for marital and partner problems**

Excludes: *problems related to:*
psychosexual disorders (302.0-302.9)
sexual function (V41.7)

V61.10 Counseling for marital and partner problems, unspecified
Marital conflict
Partner conflict

V61.11 Counseling for victim of spousal and partner abuse

Excludes: *encounter for treatment of current injuries due to abuse (995.80-995.85)*

V61.12 Counseling for perpetrator of spousal and partner abuse

✓5th **V61.2 Parent-child problems**

V61.20 Counseling for parent-child problem, unspecified
Concern about behavior of child
Parent-child conflict

[16] **V61.21 Counseling for victim of child abuse**
Child battering
Child neglect

Excludes: *current injuries due to abuse (995.50-995.59)*

V61.22 Counseling for perpetrator of parental child abuse

Excludes: *counseling for non-parental abuser (V62.83)*

V61.29 Other
Problem concerning adopted or foster child

V61.3 Problems with aged parents or in-laws

✓5th **V61.4 Health problems within family**

V61.41 Alcoholism in family

V61.49 Other
Care of } sick or handicapped person in family or household
Presence of }

V61.5 Multiparity

V61.6 Illegitimacy or illegitimate pregnancy ♀ A: 12-55

V61.7 Other unwanted pregnancy ♀ A: 12-55

V61.8 Other specified family circumstances
Problems with family members NEC

V61.9 Unspecified family circumstance

V62 Other psychosocial circumstances

Includes: those circumstances or fear of them, affecting the person directly involved or others, mentioned as the reason, justified or not, for seeking or receiving medical advice or care

Excludes: *previous psychological trauma (V15.41-V15.49)*

V62.0 Unemployment

Excludes: *circumstances when main problem is economic inadequacy or poverty (V60.2)*

V62.1 Adverse effects of work environment

V62.2 Other occupational circumstances or maladjustment
Career choice problem
Dissatisfaction with employment

V62.3 Educational circumstances
Dissatisfaction with school environment
Educational handicap

[16] These V codes may be used as principal diagnosis on Medicare patients.

V62.4 **Social maladjustment**
Cultural deprivation
Political, religious, or sex discrimination
Social:
isolation
persecution

V62.5 **Legal circumstances**
Imprisonment
Legal investigation
Litigation
Prosecution

V62.6 **Refusal of treatment for reasons of religion or conscience**

✓5th **V62.8** **Other psychological or physical stress, not elsewhere classified**

V62.81 **Interpersonal problems, not elsewhere classified**

V62.82 **Bereavement, uncomplicated**

Excludes: *bereavement as adjustment reaction (309.0)*

V62.83 **Counseling for perpetrator of physical/sexual abuse**

Excludes: *counseling for perpetrator of parental child abuse (V61.22)*
counseling for perpetrator of spousal and partner abuse (V61.12)

V62.89 **Other**
Life circumstance problems
Phase of life problems

V62.9 **Unspecified psychosocial circumstance**

V63 **Unavailability of other medical facilities for care**

V63.0 **Residence remote from hospital or other health care facility**

V63.1 **Medical services in home not available**

Excludes: *no other household member able to render care (V60.4)*

V63.2 **Person awaiting admission to adequate facility elsewhere**

V63.8 **Other specified reasons for unavailability of medical facilities**
Person on waiting list undergoing social agency investigation

V63.9 **Unspecified reason for unavailability of medical facilities**

V64 **Persons encountering health services for specific procedures, not carried out**

V64.0 **Vaccination not carried out because of contraindication**

V64.1 **Surgical or other procedure not carried out because of contraindication**

V64.2 **Surgical or other procedure not carried out because of patient's decision**

V64.3 **Procedure not carried out for other reasons**

V64.4 **Laparoscopic surgical procedure converted to open procedure**

➡ **AHA Coding Clinic:** 4Q, '97, 52

V65 **Other persons seeking consultation without complaint or sickness**

[16] **V65.0** **Healthy person accompanying sick person**
Boarder

V65.1 **Person consulting on behalf of another person**
Advice or treatment for nonattending third party

Excludes: *concern (normal) about sick person in family (V61.41-V61.49)*

[16] **V65.2** **Person feigning illness**
Malingerer
Peregrinating patient

V65.3 **Dietary surveillance and counseling**
Dietary surveillance and counseling (in):
NOS
colitis
diabetes mellitus
food allergies or intolerance
gastritis
hypercholesterolemia
hypoglycemia
obesity

✓5th **V65.4** **Other counseling, not elsewhere classified**
Health:
advice
education
instruction

Excludes: *counseling (for):*
contraception (V25.40-V25.49)
genetic (V26.3)
on behalf of third party (V65.1)
procreative management (V26.4)

V65.40 **Counseling NOS**

V65.41 **Exercise counseling**

V65.42 **Counseling on substance use and abuse**

V65.43 **Counseling on injury prevention**

V65.44 **Human immunodeficiency virus [HIV] counseling**

V65.45 **Counseling on other sexually transmitted diseases**

V65.49 **Other specified counseling**

V65.5 **Person with feared complaint in whom no diagnosis was made**
Feared condition not demonstrated
Problem was normal state
"Worried well"

➡ **AHA Coding Clinic:** J-A, '84, 20

[16] These V codes may be used as principal diagnosis on Medicare patients.

V65.8 Other reasons for seeking consultation

Excludes: *specified symptoms*

➡ **AHA Coding Clinic:** 3Q, '92, 4

V65.9 Unspecified reason for consultation

V66 Convalescence and palliative care

V66.0 Following surgery

V66.1 Following radiotherapy

V66.2 Following chemotherapy

V66.3 Following psychotherapy and other treatment for mental disorder

V66.4 Following treatment of fracture

V66.5 Following other treatment

V66.6 Following combined treatment

V66.7 Encounter for palliative care

End-of-life care
Hospice care
Terminal care

Code first underlying disease

➡ **AHA Coding Clinic:** 1Q, '98, 11; 4Q, '96, 47, 48

V66.9 Unspecified convalescence

V67 Follow-up examination

Includes: surveillance only following completed treatment

Excludes: *surveillance of contraception (V25.40-V25.49)*

[16, 20] **V67.0** Following surgery

➡ **AHA Coding Clinic:** 4Q, '97, 50; 2Q, '95, 8; 1Q, '95, 4; 3Q, '92, 11

[16] **V67.1** Following radiotherapy

[16] **V67.2** Following chemotherapy

Cancer chemotherapy follow-up

[16] **V67.3** Following psychotherapy and other treatment for mental disorder

[16, 20] **V67.4** Following treatment of healed fracture

Excludes: *current (healing) fracture aftercare (V54.0-V54.9)*

✓5th **V67.5** Following other treatment

[16] **V67.51** Following completed treatment with high-risk medications, not elsewhere classified

Excludes: *long-term (current) drug use (V58.61-V58.69)*

➡ **AHA Coding Clinic:** 4Q, '95, 61

[16] **V67.59** Other

[16] **V67.6** Following combined treatment

V67.9 Unspecified follow-up examination

V68 Encounters for administrative purposes

V68.0 Issue of medical certificates

Issue of medical certificate of:
cause of death
fitness
incapacity

Excludes: *encounter for general medical examination (V70.0-V70.9)*

V68.1 Issue of repeat prescriptions

Issue of repeat prescription for:
appliance
glasses
medications

Excludes: *repeat prescription for contraceptives (V25.41-V25.49)*

V68.2 Request for expert evidence

✓5th **V68.8** Other specified administrative purpose

V68.81 Referral of patient without examination or treatment

V68.89 Other

V68.9 Unspecified administrative purpose

V69 Problems related to lifestyle

➡ **AHA Coding Clinic:** 4Q, '94, 48

V69.0 Lack of physical exercise

V69.1 Inappropriate diet and eating habits

Excludes: *anorexia nervosa (307.1)*
bulimia (783.6)
malnutrition and other nutritional deficiencies (260-269.9)
other and unspecified eating disorders (307.50-307.59)

V69.2 High-risk sexual behavior

V69.3 Gambling and betting

Excludes: *pathological gambling (312.31)*

V69.8 Other problems related to lifestyle

Self-damaging behavior

V69.9 Problems related to lifestyle, unspecified

[16] These V codes may be used as principal diagnosis on Medicare patients.
[20] These V codes are acceptable as principal diagnosis when accompanied by a diagnosis of personal history of malignancy. These codes group to DRGs 465-466.

PERSONS WITHOUT REPORTED DIAGNOSIS ENCOUNTERED DURING EXAMINATION AND INVESTIGATION OF INDIVIDUALS AND POPULATIONS (V70-V82)

Note: Nonspecific abnormal findings disclosed at the time of these examinations are classifiable to categories 790-796.

V70 General medical examination

Use additional code(s) to identify any special screening examination(s) performed (V73.0-V82.9)

V70.0 **Routine general medical examination at a health care facility**

Health checkup

Excludes: *health checkup of infant or child (V20.2)*

V70.1 **General psychiatric examination, requested by the authority**

V70.2 **General psychiatric examination, other and unspecified**

V70.3 **Other medical examination for administrative purposes**

General medical examination for:
- admission to old age home
- adoption
- camp
- driving license
- immigration and naturalization
- insurance certification
- marriage
- prison
- school admission
- sports competition

Excludes: *attendance for issue of medical certificates (V68.0)*
pre-employment screening (V70.5)

V70.4 **Examination for medicolegal reasons**

Blood-alcohol tests
Blood-drug tests
Paternity testing

Excludes: *examination and observation following:*
accidents (V71.3, V71.4)
assault (V71.6)
rape (V71.5)

V70.5 **Health examination of defined subpopulations**

Armed forces personnel
Inhabitants of institutions
Occupational health examinations
Pre-employment screening
Preschool children
Prisoners
Prostitutes
Refugees
School children
Students

V70.6 **Health examination in population surveys**

Excludes: *special screening (V73.0-V82.9)*

V70.7 **Examination for normal comparison or control in clinical research**

V70.8 **Other specified general medical examinations**

Examination of potential donor of organ or tissue

V70.9 **Unspecified general medical examination**

V71 Observation and evaluation for suspected conditions not found

Includes: This category is to be used when persons without a diagnosis are suspected of having an abnormal condition, without signs or symptoms, which requires study, but after examination and observation, is found not to exist. This category is also for use for administrative and legal observation status.

➡ **AHA Coding Clinic:** 4Q, '94, 47; 2Q, '90, 5; M-A, '87, 1

✓5th **V71.0** **Observation for suspected mental condition**

[16] **V71.01** **Adult antisocial behavior** **A: 15-124**

Dyssocial behavior or gang activity in adult without manifest psychiatric disorder

[16] **V71.02** **Childhood or adolescent antisocial behavior**

Dyssocial behavior or gang activity in child or adolescent without manifest psychiatric disorder

[16] **V71.09** **Other suspected mental condition**

[16] **V71.1** **Observation for suspected malignant neoplasm**

[16] **V71.2** **Observation for suspected tuberculosis**

[16] **V71.3** **Observation following accident at work**

[16] **V71.4** **Observation following other accident**

Examination of individual involved in motor vehicle traffic accident

[16] **V71.5** **Observation following alleged rape or seduction**

Examination of victim or culprit

[16] **V71.6** **Observation following other inflicted injury**

Examination of victim or culprit

[16] **V71.7** **Observation for suspected cardiovascular disease**

➡ **AHA Coding Clinic:** 3Q, '90, 10; S-O, '87, 10

[16] **V71.8** **Observation for other specified suspected conditions**

V71.9 **Observation for unspecified suspected condition**

[16] These V codes may be used as principal diagnosis on Medicare patients.

V72 Special investigations and examinations

Use additional code(s) to identify any special screening examination(s) performed (V73.0-V82.9)

Includes: routine examination of specific system

Excludes: *general medical examination (V70.0-V70.4)*
general screening examination of defined population groups (V70.5, V70.6, V70.7)
routine examination of infant or child (V20.2)

V72.0 Examination of eyes and vision

V72.1 Examination of ears and hearing

V72.2 Dental examination

V72.3 Gynecological examination ♀

Papanicolaou smear as part of general gynecological examination
Pelvic examination (annual) (periodic)

Excludes: *cervical Papanicolaou smear without general gynecological examination (V76.2)*
routine examination in contraceptive management (V25.40-V25.49)

V72.4 Pregnancy examination or test, pregnancy unconfirmed ♀

Possible pregnancy, not (yet) confirmed

Excludes: *pregnancy examination with immediate confirmation (V22.0-V22.1)*

V72.5 Radiological examination, not elsewhere classified

Routine chest x-ray

Excludes: *examination for suspected tuberculosis (V71.2)*

V72.6 Laboratory examination

Excludes: *that for suspected disorder (V71.0-V71.9)*

V72.7 Diagnostic skin and sensitization tests

Allergy tests
Skin tests for hypersensitivity

Excludes: *diagnostic skin tests for bacterial diseases (V74.0-V74.9)*

✓5th **V72.8** Other specified examinations

V72.81 Preoperative cardiovascular examination

V72.82 Preoperative respiratory examination

➡ **AHA Coding Clinic:** 3Q, '96, 14

V72.83 Other specified preoperative examination

➡ **AHA Coding Clinic:** 3Q, '96, 14

V72.84 Preoperative examination, unspecified

V72.85 Other specified examination

V72.9 Unspecified examination

V73 Special screening examination for viral and chlamydial diseases

V73.0 Poliomyelitis

V73.1 Smallpox

V73.2 Measles

V73.3 Rubella

V73.4 Yellow fever

V73.5 Other arthropod-borne viral diseases

Dengue fever
Hemorrhagic fever
Viral encephalitis:
  mosquito-borne
  tick-borne

V73.6 Trachoma

✓5th **V73.8** Other specified viral and chlamydial diseases

V73.88 Other specified chlamydial diseases

V73.89 Other specified viral diseases

✓5th **V73.9** Unspecified viral and chlamydial disease

V73.98 Unspecified chlamydial disease

V73.99 Unspecified viral disease

V74 Special screening examination for bacterial and spirochetal diseases

Includes: diagnostic skin tests for these diseases

V74.0 Cholera

V74.1 Pulmonary tuberculosis

V74.2 Leprosy [Hansen's disease]

V74.3 Diphtheria

V74.4 Bacterial conjunctivitis

V74.5 Venereal disease

V74.6 Yaws

V74.8 Other specified bacterial and spirochetal diseases
Brucellosis
Leptospirosis
Plague
Tetanus
Whooping cough

V74.9 Unspecified bacterial and spirochetal disease

V75 Special screening examination for other infectious diseases

V75.0 Rickettsial diseases

V75.1 Malaria

V75.2 Leishmaniasis

V75.3 Trypanosomiasis
Chagas' disease
Sleeping sickness

V75.4 Mycotic infections

V75.5 Schistosomiasis

V75.6 Filariasis

V75.7 Intestinal helminthiasis

V75.8 Other specified parasitic infections

V75.9 Unspecified infectious disease

V76 Special screening for malignant neoplasms

V76.0 Respiratory organs

✓5th **V76.1** Breast

V76.10 Breast screening, unspecified

V76.11 Screening mammogram for high-risk patient ♀

V76.12 Other screening mammogram

V76.19 Other screening breast examination

V76.2 Cervix ♀
Routine cervical Papanicolaou smear

Excludes: *that as part of a general gynecological examination (V72.3)*

V76.3 Bladder

✓5th **V76.4** Other sites

V76.41 Rectum

V76.42 Oral cavity

V76.43 Skin

V76.44 Prostate

V76.45 Testis

V76.49 Other

V76.8 Other neoplasm

V76.9 Unspecified

V77 Special screening for endocrine, nutritional, metabolic, and immunity disorders

V77.0 Thyroid disorders

V77.1 Diabetes mellitus

V77.2 Malnutrition

V77.3 Phenylketonuria [PKU]

V77.4 Galactosemia

V77.5 Gout

V77.6 Cystic fibrosis
Screening for mucoviscidosis

V77.7 Other inborn errors of metabolism

V77.8 Obesity

V77.9 Other and unspecified endocrine, nutritional, metabolic, and immunity disorders

V78 Special screening for disorders of blood and blood-forming organs

V78.0 Iron deficiency anemia

V78.1 Other and unspecified deficiency anemia

V78.2 Sickle-cell disease or trait

V78.3 Other hemoglobinopathies

V78.8 Other disorders of blood and blood-forming organs

V78.9 Unspecified disorder of blood and blood-forming organs

V79 Special screening for mental disorders and developmental handicaps

V79.0 Depression

V79.1 Alcoholism

V79.2 Mental retardation

V79.3 Developmental handicaps in early childhood

V79.8 Other specified mental disorders and developmental handicaps

V79.9 Unspecified mental disorder and developmental handicap

V80 Special screening for neurological, eye, and ear diseases

V80.0 Neurological conditions

V80.1 Glaucoma

V80.2 Other eye conditions

Screening for:
- cataract
- congenital anomaly of eye
- senile macular lesions

Excludes: *general vision examination (V72.0)*

V80.3 Ear disease

Excludes: *general hearing examination (V72.1)*

V81 Special screening for cardiovascular, respiratory, and genitourinary diseases

V81.0 Ischemic heart disease

V81.1 Hypertension

V81.2 Other and unspecified cardiovascular conditions

V81.3 Chronic bronchitis and emphysema

V81.4 Other and unspecified respiratory conditions

Excludes: *screening for:*
- *lung neoplasm (V76.0)*
- *pulmonary tuberculosis (V74.1)*

V81.5 Nephropathy

Screening for asymptomatic bacteriuria

V81.6 Other and unspecified genitourinary conditions

V82 Special screening for other conditions

V82.0 Skin conditions

V82.1 Rheumatoid arthritis

V82.2 Other rheumatic disorders

V82.3 Congenital dislocation of hip

V82.4 Maternal postnatal screening for chromosomal anomalies

Excludes: *antenatal screening by amniocentesis (V28.0)*

V82.5 Chemical poisoning and other contamination

Screening for:
- heavy metal poisoning
- ingestion of radioactive substance
- poisoning from contaminated water supply
- radiation exposure

V82.6 Multiphasic screening

V82.8 Other specified conditions

V82.9 Unspecified condition

SUPPLEMENTARY CLASSIFICATION OF EXTERNAL CAUSES OF INJURY AND POISONING (E800-E999)

This section is provided to permit the classification of environmental events, circumstances, and conditions as the cause of injury, poisoning, and other adverse effects. Where a code from this section is applicable, it is intended that it shall be used in addition to a code from one of the main chapters of *ICD-9-CM,* indicating the nature of the condition. Certain other conditions which may be stated to be due to external causes are classified in Chapters 1 to 16 of *ICD-9-CM.* For these, the "E" code classification should be used as an additional code for more detailed analysis.

Machinery accidents [other than those connected with transport] are classifiable to category E919, in which the fourth-digit allows a broad classification of the type of machinery involved. If a more detailed classification of type of machinery is required, it is suggested that the "Classification of Industrial Accidents according to Agency," prepared by the International Labor Office, be used in addition. This is reproduced in Appendix D, for optional use.

Categories for "late effects" of accidents and other external causes are to be found at E929, E959, E969, E977, E989, and E999.

Definitions and examples related to transport accidents

(a) A **transport accident** (E800-E848) is any accident involving a device designed primarily for, or being used at the time primarily for, conveying persons or goods from one place to another.

Includes: accidents involving:
- aircraft and spacecraft (E840-E845)
- watercraft (E830-E838)
- motor vehicle (E810-E825)
- railway (E800-E807)
- other road vehicles (E826-E829)

In classifying accidents which involve more than one kind of transport, the above order of precedence of transport accidents should be used.

Accidents involving agricultural and construction machines, such as tractors, cranes, and bulldozers, are regarded as transport accidents only when these vehicles are under their own power on a highway [otherwise the vehicles are regarded as machinery]. Vehicles which can travel on land or water, such as hovercraft and other amphibious vehicles, are regarded as watercraft when on the water, as motor vehicles when on the highway, and as off-road motor vehicles when on land, but off the highway.

Excludes: *accidents:*
- *in sports which involve the use of transport but where the transport vehicle itself was not involved in the accident*
- *involving vehicles which are part of industrial equipment used entirely on industrial premises*
- *occurring during transportation but unrelated to the hazards associated with the means of transportation [e.g., injuries received in a fight on board ship; transport vehicle involved in a cataclysm such as an earthquake]*
- *to persons engaged in the maintenance or repair of transport equipment or vehicle not in motion, unless injured by another vehicle in motion*

(b) A **railway accident** is a transport accident involving a railway train or other railway vehicle operated on rails, whether in motion or not.

Excludes: *accidents:*
- *in repair shops*
- *in roundhouse or on turntable*
- *on railway premises but not involving a train or other railway vehicle*

(c) A **railway train** or **railway vehicle** is any device with or without cars coupled to it, designed for traffic on a railway.

Includes: interurban:
- electric car, streetcar } (operated chiefly on its own right-of-way, not open to other traffic)
- railway train, any power [diesel] [electric] [steam]
  - funicular
  - monorail or two-rail
  - subterranean or elevated
- other vehicle designed to run on a railway track

Excludes: *interurban electric cars [streetcars] specified to be operating on a right-of-way that forms part of the public street or highway [definition (n)]*

(d) A **railway** or **railroad** is a right-of-way designed for traffic on rails, which is used by carriages or wagons transporting passengers or freight, and by other rolling stock, and which is not open to other public vehicular traffic

(e) A **motor vehicle accident** is a transport accident involving a motor vehicle. It is defined as a motor vehicle traffic accident or as a motor vehicle nontraffic accident according to whether the accident occurs on a public highway or elsewhere.

Excludes: *injury or damage due to cataclysm*
injury or damage while a motor vehicle, not under its own power, is being loaded on, or unloaded from, another conveyance

(f) A **motor vehicle traffic accident** is any motor vehicle accident occurring on a public highway [i.e., originating, terminating, or involving a vehicle partially on the highway]. A motor vehicle accident is assumed to have occurred on the highway unless another place is specified, except in the case of accidents involving only off-road motor vehicles which are classified as nontraffic accidents unless the contrary is stated.

(g) A **motor vehicle nontraffic accident** is any motor vehicle accident which occurs entirely in any place other than a public highway.

(h) A **public highway [trafficway]** or **street** is the entire width between property lines [or other boundary lines] of every way or place, of which any part is open to the use of the public for purposes of vehicular traffic as a matter of right or custom. A **roadway** is that part of the public highway designed, improved, and ordinarily used, for vehicular travel.

Includes: approaches (public) to:
- docks
- public building
- station

Excludes: *driveway (private)*
parking lot
ramp
roads in:
- *airfield*
- *farm*
- *industrial premises*
- *mine*
- *private grounds*
- *quarry*

E Codes

(i) A **motor vehicle** is any mechanically or electrically powered device, not operated on rails, upon which any person or property may be transported or drawn upon a highway. Any object such as a trailer, coaster, sled, or wagon being towed by a motor vehicle is considered a part of the motor vehicle.

Includes: automobile [any type]
bus
construction machinery, farm and industrial machinery, steam roller, tractor, army tank, highway grader, or similar vehicle on wheels or treads, while in transport under own power
fire engine (motorized)
motorcycle
motorized bicycle [moped] or scooter
trolley bus not operating on rails
truck
van

Excludes: *devices used solely to move persons or materials within the confines of a building and its premises, such as:*
building elevator
coal car in mine
electric baggage or mail truck used solely within a railroad station
electric truck used solely within an industrial plant
moving overhead crane

(j) A **motorcycle** is a two-wheeled motor vehicle having one or two riding saddles and sometimes having a third wheel for the support of a sidecar. The sidecar is considered part of the motorcycle.

Includes: motorized:
bicycle [moped]
scooter
tricycle

(k) An **off-road motor vehicle** is a motor vehicle of special design, to enable it to negotiate rough or soft terrain or snow. Examples of special design are high construction, special wheels and tires, driven by treads, or support on a cushion of air.

Includes: all terrain vehicle [ATV]
army tank
hovercraft, on land or swamp
snowmobile

(l) A **driver** of a motor vehicle is the occupant of the motor vehicle operating it or intending to operate it. A **motorcyclist** is the driver of a motorcycle. Other authorized occupants of a motor vehicle are **passengers**.

(m) An **other road vehicle** is any device, except a motor vehicle, in, on, or by which any person or property may be transported on a highway.

Includes: animal carrying a person or goods
animal-drawn vehicle
animal harnessed to conveyance
bicycle [pedal cycle]
streetcar
tricycle (pedal)

Excludes: *pedestrian conveyance [definition (q)]*

(n) A **streetcar** is a device designed and used primarily for transporting persons within a municipality, running on rails, usually subject to normal traffic control signals, and operated principally on a right-of-way that forms part of the traffic way. A trailer being towed by a streetcar is considered a part of the streetcar.

Includes: interurban or intraurban electric or streetcar, when specified to be operating on a street or public highway
tram (car)
trolley (car)

(o) A **pedal cycle** is any road transport vehicle operated solely by pedals.

Includes: bicycle
pedal cycle
tricycle

Excludes: *motorized bicycle [definition (i)]*

(p) A **pedal cyclist** is any person riding on a pedal cycle or in a sidecar attached to such a vehicle.

(q) A **pedestrian conveyance** is any human powered device by which a pedestrian may move other than by walking or by which a walking person may move another pedestrian.

Includes: baby carriage
coaster wagon
ice skates
perambulator
pushcart
pushchair
roller skates
scooter
skateboard
skis
sled
wheelchair

(r) A **pedestrian** is any person involved in an accident who was not at the time of the accident riding in or on a motor vehicle, railroad train, streetcar, animal-drawn or other vehicle, or on a bicycle or animal.

Includes: person:
changing tire of vehicle
in or operating a pedestrian conveyance
making adjustment to motor of vehicle
on foot

(s) A **watercraft** is any device for transporting passengers or goods on the water.

(t) A **small boat** is any watercraft propelled by paddle, oars, or small motor, with a passenger capacity of less than ten.

Includes: boat NOS
canoe
coble
dinghy
punt
raft
rowboat
rowing shell
scull
skiff
small motorboat

Excludes: *barge*
lifeboat (used after abandoning ship)
raft (anchored) being used as a diving platform
yacht

(u) An **aircraft** is any device for transporting passengers or goods in the air.

Includes: airplane [any type]
balloon
bomber
dirigible
glider (hang)
military aircraft
parachute

(v) A **commercial transport aircraft** is any device for collective passenger or freight transportation by air, whether run on commercial lines for profit or by government authorities, with the exception of military craft.

RAILWAY ACCIDENTS (E800-E807)

Note: For definitions of railway accident and related terms see definitions (a) to (d).

Excludes: *accidents involving railway train and:*
aircraft (E840.0-E845.9)
motor vehicle (E810.0-E825.9)
watercraft (E830.0-E838.9)

The following fourth-digit subdivisions are for use with categories E800-E807 to identify the injured person:

.0 Railway employee
Any person who by virtue of his employment in connection with a railway, whether by the railway company or not, is at increased risk of involvement in a railway accident, such as:
catering staff of train
driver
guard
porter
postal staff on train
railway fireman
shunter
sleeping car attendant

.1 Passenger on railway
Any authorized person traveling on a train, except a railway employee.

Excludes: *intending passenger waiting at station (.8)*
unauthorized rider on railway vehicle (.8)

.2 Pedestrian
See definition (r)

.3 Pedal cyclist
See definition (p)

.8 Other specified person
Intending passenger or bystander waiting at station
Unauthorized rider on railway vehicle

.9 Unspecified person

§ E800 Railway accident involving collision with rolling stock

Includes: collision between railway trains or railway vehicles, any kind
collision NOS on railway
derailment with antecedent collision with rolling stock or NOS

§ E801 Railway accident involving collision with other object

Includes: collision of railway train with:
buffers
fallen tree on railway
gates
platform
rock on railway
streetcar
other nonmotor vehicle
other object

Excludes: *collision with:*
aircraft (E840.0-E842.9)
motor vehicle (E810.0-E810.9, E820.0-E822.9)

§ Requires fourth-digit. See above for codes and definitions.

§ E802 Railway accident involving derailment without antecedent collision

§ E803 Railway accident involving explosion, fire, or burning

Excludes: *explosion or fire, with antecedent derailment (E802.0-E802.9)*
explosion or fire, with mention of antecedent collision (E800.0-E801.9)

§ E804 Fall in, on, or from railway train

Includes: fall while alighting from or boarding railway train

Excludes: *fall related to collision, derailment, or explosion of railway train (E800.0-E803.9)*

§ E805 Hit by rolling stock

Includes: crushed, injured, killed, knocked down, run over } by railway train or part

Excludes: *pedestrian hit by object set in motion by railway train (E806.0-E806.9)*

§ E806 Other specified railway accident

Includes: hit by object falling in railway train
injured by door or window on railway train
nonmotor road vehicle or pedestrian hit by object set in motion by railway train
railway train hit by falling:
earth NOS
rock
tree
other object

Excludes: *railway accident due to cataclysm (E908-E909)*

§ E807 Railway accident of unspecified nature

Includes: found dead, injured } on railway right-of-way NOS
railway accident NOS

MOTOR VEHICLE TRAFFIC ACCIDENTS (E810-E819)

Note: For definitions of motor vehicle traffic accident, and related terms, see definitions (e) to (k).

Excludes: *accidents involving motor vehicle and aircraft (E840.0-E845.9)*

The following fourth-digit subdivisions are for use with categories E810-E819 to identify the injured person:

.0 Driver of motor vehicle other than motorcycle
See definition (l)

.1 Passenger in motor vehicle other than motorcycle
See definition (l)

.2 Motorcyclist
See definition (l)

.3 Passenger on motorcycle
See definition (l)

.4 Occupant of streetcar

.5 Rider of animal; occupant of animal-drawn vehicle

.6 Pedal cyclist
See definition (p)

.7 Pedestrian
See definition (r)

.8 Other specified person
Occupant of vehicle other than above
Person in railway train involved in accident
Unauthorized rider of motor vehicle

.9 Unspecified person

§ E810 Motor vehicle traffic accident involving collision with train

Excludes: *motor vehicle collision with object set in motion by railway train (E815.0-E815.9)*
railway train hit by object set in motion by motor vehicle (E818.0-E818.9)

§ E811 Motor vehicle traffic accident involving re-entrant collision with another motor vehicle

Includes: collision between motor vehicle which accidentally leaves the roadway then re-enters the same roadway, or the opposite roadway on a divided highway, and another motor vehicle

Excludes: *collision on the same roadway when none of the motor vehicles involved have left and re-entered the roadway (E812.0-E812.9)*

§ E812 Other motor vehicle traffic accident involving collision with motor vehicle

Includes: collision with another motor vehicle parked, stopped, stalled, disabled, or abandoned on the highway
motor vehicle collision NOS

Excludes: *collision with object set in motion by another motor vehicle (E815.0-E815.9)*
re-entrant collision with another motor vehicle (E811.0-E811.9)

§ Requires fourth-digit. See above for codes and definitions.

§ E813 Motor vehicle traffic accident involving collision with other vehicle

Includes: collision between motor vehicle, any kind, and:
other road (nonmotor transport) vehicle, such as:
animal carrying a person
animal-drawn vehicle
pedal cycle
streetcar

Excludes: *collision with:*
object set in motion by nonmotor road vehicle (E815.0-E815.9)
pedestrian (E814.0-E814.9)
nonmotor road vehicle hit by object set in motion by motor vehicle (E818.0-E818.9)

§ E814 Motor vehicle traffic accident involving collision with pedestrian

Includes: collision between motor vehicle, any kind, and pedestrian
pedestrian dragged, hit, or run over by motor vehicle, any kind

Excludes: *pedestrian hit by object set in motion by motor vehicle (E818.0-E818.9)*

§ E815 Other motor vehicle traffic accident involving collision on the highway

Includes: collision (due to loss of control) (on highway) between motor vehicle, any kind, and:
abutment (bridge) (overpass)
animal (herded) (unattended)
fallen stone, traffic sign, tree, utility pole
guard rail or boundary fence
interhighway divider
landslide (not moving)
object set in motion by railway train or road vehicle (motor) (nonmotor)
object thrown in front of motor vehicle
safety island
temporary traffic sign or marker
wall of cut made for road
other object, fixed, movable, or moving

Excludes: *collision with:*
any object off the highway (resulting from loss of control) (E816.0-E816.9)
any object which normally would have been off the highway and is not stated to have been on it (E816.0-E816.9)
motor vehicle parked, stopped, stalled, disabled, or abandoned on highway (E812.0-E812.9)
moving landslide (E909)
motor vehicle hit by object:
set in motion by railway train or road vehicle (motor) (nonmotor) (E818.0-E818.9)
thrown into or on vehicle (E818.0-E818.9)

§ E816 Motor vehicle traffic accident due to loss of control, without collision on the highway

Includes: motor vehicle:
- failing to make curve
- going out of control (due to):
  - blowout
  - burst tire
  - driver falling asleep
  - driver inattention
  - excessive speed
  - failure of mechanical part

and:
- colliding with object off the highway
- overturning
- stopping abruptly off the highway

Excludes: *collision on highway following loss of control (E810.0-E815.9)*
loss of control of motor vehicle following collision on the highway (E810.0-E815.9)

§ E817 Noncollision motor vehicle traffic accident while boarding or alighting

Includes: while boarding or alighting:
- fall down stairs of motor bus
- fall from car in street
- injured by moving part of the vehicle
- trapped by door of motor bus

§ E818 Other noncollision motor vehicle traffic accident

Includes: motor vehicle while in motion:
- accidental poisoning from exhaust gas generated by
- breakage of any part of
- explosion of any part of
- fall, jump, or being accidentally pushed from
- fire starting in
- hit by object thrown into or on
- injured by being thrown against some part of, or object in
- injury from moving part of
- object falling in or on
- object thrown on

collision of railway train or road vehicle except motor vehicle, with object set in motion by motor vehicle
motor vehicle hit by object set in motion by railway train or road vehicle (motor) (nonmotor)
pedestrian, railway train, or road vehicle (motor) (nonmotor) hit by object set in motion by motor vehicle

Excludes: *collision between motor vehicle and:*
object set in motion by railway train or road vehicle (motor) (nonmotor) (E815.0-E815.9)
object thrown towards the motor vehicle (E815.0-E815.9)
person overcome by carbon monoxide generated by stationary motor vehicle off the roadway with motor running (E868.2)

§ E819 Motor vehicle traffic accident of unspecified nature

Includes: motor vehicle traffic accident NOS
traffic accident NOS

MOTOR VEHICLE NONTRAFFIC ACCIDENTS (E820-E825)

Note: For definitions of motor vehicle nontraffic accident and related terms see definition (a) to (k).

Includes: accidents involving motor vehicles being used in recreational or sporting activities off the highway
collision and noncollision motor vehicle accidents occurring entirely off the highway

Excludes: *accidents involving motor vehicle and:*
aircraft (E840.0-E845.9)
watercraft (E830.0-E838.9)
accidents, not on the public highway, involving agricultural and construction machinery but not involving another motor vehicle (E919.0, E919.2, E919.7)

§ Requires fourth-digit. See page E-4 for codes and definitions.

The following fourth-digit subdivisions are for use with categories E820-E825 to identify the injured person:

.0 Driver of motor vehicle other than motorcycle
See definition (l)

.1 Passenger in motor vehicle other than motorcycle
See definition (l)

.2 Motorcyclist
See definition (l)

.3 Passenger on motorcycle
See definition (l)

.4 Occupant of streetcar

.5 Rider of animal; occupant of animal-drawn vehicle

.6 Pedal cyclist
See definition (p)

.7 Pedestrian
See definition (r)

.8 Other specified person
Occupant of vehicle other than above
Person on railway train involved in accident
Unauthorized rider of motor vehicle

.9 Unspecified person

§ E820 Nontraffic accident involving motor-driven snow vehicle

Includes: breakage of part of / fall from / hit by / overturning of / run over or dragged by } motor-driven snow vehicle (not on public highway)
collision of motor-driven snow vehicle with:
animal (being ridden) (-drawn vehicle)
another off-road motor vehicle
other motor vehicle, not on public highway
railway train
other object, fixed or movable
injury caused by rough landing of motor-driven snow vehicle (after leaving ground on rough terrain)

Excludes: *accident on the public highway involving motor driven snow vehicle (E810.0-E819.9)*

§ E821 Nontraffic accident involving other off-road motor vehicle

Includes: breakage of part of / fall from / hit by / overturning of / run over or dragged by / thrown against some part of or object in } off-road motor vehicle, except snow vehicle (not on public highway)
collision with:
animal (being ridden) (-drawn vehicle)
another off-road motor vehicle, except snow vehicle
other motor vehicle, not on public highway
other object, fixed or movable

Excludes: *accident on public highway involving off-road motor vehicle (E810.0-E819.9)*
collision between motor driven snow vehicle and other off-road motor vehicle (E820.0-E820.9)
hovercraft accident on water (E830.0-E838.9)

§ E822 Other motor vehicle nontraffic accident involving collision with moving object

Includes: collision, not on public highway, between motor vehicle, except off-road motor vehicle and:
animal
nonmotor vehicle
other motor vehicle, except off-road motor vehicle
pedestrian
railway train
other moving object

Excludes: *collision with:*
motor-driven snow vehicle (E820.0-E820.9)
other off-road motor vehicle (E821.0-E821.9)

§ E823 Other motor vehicle nontraffic accident involving collision with stationary object

Includes: collision, not on public highway, between motor vehicle, except off-road motor vehicle, and any object, fixed or movable, but not in motion

§ Requires fourth-digit. See above for codes and definitions.

§ E824 Other motor vehicle nontraffic accident while boarding and alighting

Includes: fall, injury from moving part of motor vehicle, trapped by door of motor vehicle } while boarding or alighting from motor vehicle, except off-road motor vehicle, not on public highway

§ E825 Other motor vehicle nontraffic accident of other and unspecified nature

Includes: accidental poisoning from carbon monoxide generated by; breakage of any part of; explosion of any part of; fall, jump, or being accidentally pushed from; fire starting in; hit by object thrown into, towards, or on; injured by being thrown against some part of, or object in; injury from moving part of; object falling in or on } motor vehicle while in motion, not on public highway

motor vehicle nontraffic accident NOS

Excludes: *fall from or in stationary motor vehicle (E884.9, E885)*
overcome by carbon monoxide or exhaust gas generated by stationary motor vehicle off the roadway with motor running (E868.2)
struck by falling object from or in stationary motor vehicle (E916)

OTHER ROAD VEHICLE ACCIDENTS (E826-E829)

Note: Other road vehicle accidents are transport accidents involving road vehicles other than motor vehicles. For definitions of other road vehicle and related terms see definitions (m) to (o).

Includes: accidents involving other road vehicles being used in recreational or sporting activities

Excludes: *collision of other road vehicle [any] with:*
aircraft (E840.0-E845.9)
motor vehicle (E813.0-E813.9, E820.0-E822.9)
railway train (E801.0-E801.9)

The following fourth-digit subdivisions are for use with categories E826-E829 to identify the injured person:

.0 Pedestrian
See definition (r)

.1 Pedal cyclist
See definition (p)

.2 Rider of animal

.3 Occupant of animal-drawn vehicle

.4 Occupant of streetcar

.8 Other specified person

.9 Unspecified person

§§ E826 Pedal cycle accident
[0–9]

Includes: breakage of any part of pedal cycle
collision between pedal cycle and:
animal (being ridden) (herded) (unattended)
another pedal cycle
nonmotor road vehicle, any
pedestrian
other object, fixed, movable, or moving, not set in motion by motor vehicle, railway train, or aircraft
entanglement in wheel of pedal cycle
fall from pedal cycle
hit by object falling or thrown on the pedal cycle
pedal cycle accident NOS
pedal cycle overturned

§§ E827 Animal-drawn vehicle accident
[0,2–4,8,9]

Includes: breakage of any part of vehicle
collision between animal-drawn vehicle and:
animal (being ridden) (herded) (unattended)
nonmotor road vehicle, except pedal cycle
pedestrian, pedestrian conveyance, or pedestrian vehicle
other object, fixed, movable, or moving, not set in motion by motor vehicle, railway train, or aircraft
fall from; knocked down by; overturning of; run over by; thrown from } animal-drawn vehicle

Excludes: *collision of animal-drawn vehicle with pedal cycle (E826.0-E826.9)*

§ Requires fourth-digit. See page E-6 for codes and definitions.
§§ Requires fourth-digit. See above for codes and definitions.

§ E828 Accident involving animal being ridden

[0,2,4,8,9]

Includes: collision between animal being ridden and:
another animal
nonmotor road vehicle, except pedal cycle, and animal-drawn vehicle
pedestrian, pedestrian conveyance, or pedestrian vehicle
other object, fixed, movable, or moving, not set in motion by motor vehicle, railway train, or aircraft
fall from / knocked down by / thrown from / trampled by } animal being ridden
ridden animal stumbled and fell

Excludes: *collision of animal being ridden with:*
animal-drawn vehicle (E827.0-E827.9)
pedal cycle (E826.0-E826.9)

§ E829 Other road vehicle accidents

[0,4,8,9]

Includes: accident while boarding or alighting from / blow from object in / breakage of any part of / caught in door of / derailment of / fall in, on, or from / fire in } streetcar, nonmotor road vehicle not classifiable to E826-E828
collision between streetcar or nonmotor road vehicle, except as in E826-E828, and:
animal (not being ridden)
another nonmotor road vehicle not classifiable to E826-E828
pedestrian
other object, fixed, movable, or moving, not set in motion by motor vehicle, railway train, or aircraft
nonmotor road vehicle accident NOS
streetcar accident NOS

Excludes: *collision with:*
animal being ridden (E828.0-E828.9)
animal-drawn vehicle (E827.0-E827.9)
pedal cycle (E826.0-E826.9)

WATER TRANSPORT ACCIDENTS (E830-E838)

Note: For definitions of water transport accident and related terms see definitions (a), (s), and (t).

Includes: watercraft accidents in the course of recreational activities

Excludes: *accidents involving both aircraft, including objects set in motion by aircraft, and watercraft (E840.0-E845.9)*

§ Requires fourth-digit. See page E-7 for codes and definitions.
§§ Requires fourth-digit. See above for codes and definitions.

The following fourth-digit subdivisions are for use with categories E830-E838 to identify the injured person:

.0 Occupant of small boat, unpowered

.1 Occupant of small boat, powered
See definition (t)

Excludes: *water skier (.4)*

.2 Occupant of other watercraft — crew
Persons:
engaged in operation of watercraft
providing passenger services [cabin attendants, ship's physician, catering personnel]
working on ship during voyage in other capacity [musician in band, operators of shops and beauty parlors]

.3 Occupant of other watercraft — other than crew
Passenger
Occupant of lifeboat, other than crew, after abandoning ship

.4 Water skier

.5 Swimmer

.6 Dockers, stevedores
Longshoreman employed on the dock in loading and unloading ships

.8 Other specified person
Immigration and custom officials on board ship
Person:
accompanying passenger or member of crew visiting boat
Pilot (guiding ship into port)

.9 Unspecified person

§§ E830 Accident to watercraft causing submersion

Includes: submersion and drowning due to:
boat overturning
boat submerging
falling or jumping from burning ship
falling or jumping from crushed watercraft
ship sinking
other accident to watercraft

§ E831 Accident to watercraft causing other injury

Includes: any injury, except submersion and drowning, as a result of an accident to watercraft
burned while ship on fire
crushed between ships in collision
crushed by lifeboat after abandoning ship
fall due to collision or other accident to watercraft
hit by falling object due to accident to watercraft
injured in watercraft accident involving collision
struck by boat or part thereof after fall or jump from damaged boat

Excludes: *burns from localized fire or explosion on board ship (E837.0-E837.9)*

§ E832 Other accidental submersion or drowning in water transport accident

Includes: submersion or drowning as a result of an accident other than accident to the watercraft, such as:
fall:
from gangplank
from ship
overboard
thrown overboard by motion of ship
washed overboard

Excludes: *submersion or drowning of swimmer or diver who voluntarily jumps from boat not involved in an accident (E910.0-E910.9)*

§ E833 Fall on stairs or ladders in water transport

Excludes: *fall due to accident to watercraft (E831.0-E831.9)*

§ E834 Other fall from one level to another in water transport

Excludes: *fall due to accident to watercraft (E831.0-E831.9)*

§ E835 Other and unspecified fall in water transport

Excludes: *fall due to accident to watercraft (E831.0-E831.9)*

§ E836 Machinery accident in water transport

Includes: injuries in water transport caused by:
deck, engine room, galley, laundry, loading } machinery

§ E837 Explosion, fire, or burning in watercraft

Includes: explosion of boiler on steamship
localized fire on ship

Excludes: *burning ship (due to collision or explosion) resulting in:*
submersion or drowning (E830.0-E830.9)
other injury (E831.0-E831.9)

§ E838 Other and unspecified water transport accident

Includes: accidental poisoning by gases or fumes on ship
atomic power plant malfunction in watercraft
crushed between ship and stationary object [wharf]
crushed between ships without accident to watercraft
crushed by falling object on ship or while loading or unloading
hit by boat while water skiing
struck by boat or part thereof (after fall from boat)
watercraft accident NOS

§ Requires fourth-digit. See page E-8 for codes and definitions.

AIR AND SPACE TRANSPORT ACCIDENTS (E840-E845)

Note: For definition of aircraft and related terms see definitions (u) and (v).

The following fourth-digit subdivisions are for use with categories E840-E845 to identify the injured person:

.0 Occupant of spacecraft

.1 Occupant of military aircraft, any

Crew
Passenger
(civilian)
(military)
Troops
} in military aircraft [air force] [army] [national guard] [navy]

Excludes: *occupants of aircraft operated under jurisdiction of police departments (.5)*
parachutist (.7)

.2 Crew of commercial aircraft (powered) in surface to surface transport

.3 Other occupant of commercial aircraft (powered) in surface to surface transport

Flight personnel:
not part of crew
on familiarization flight
Passenger on aircraft (powered) NOS

.4 Occupant of commercial aircraft (powered) in surface to air transport

Occupant [crew] [passenger] of aircraft (powered) engaged in activities, such as:
aerial spraying (crops) (fire retardants)
air drops of emergency supplies
air drops of parachutists, except from military craft
crop dusting
lowering of construction material [bridge or telephone pole]
sky writing

.5 Occupant of other powered aircraft

Occupant [crew] [passenger] of aircraft [powered] engaged in activities, such as:
aerobatic flying
aircraft racing
rescue operation
storm surveillance
traffic surveillance
Occupant of private plane NOS

.6 Occupant of unpowered aircraft, except parachutist

Occupant of aircraft classifiable to E842

.7 Parachutist (military) (other)

Person making voluntary descent

Excludes: *person making descent after accident to aircraft (.1-.6)*

.8 Ground crew, airline employee

Persons employed at airfields (civil) (military) or launching pads, not occupants of aircraft

.9 Other person

§ Requires fourth-digit. See above for codes and definitions.

§ E840 Accident to powered aircraft at takeoff or landing

Includes:
collision of aircraft with any object, fixed, movable, or moving
crash
explosion on aircraft
fire on aircraft
} while taking off or landing
forced landing

§ E841 Accident to powered aircraft, other and unspecified

Includes:
aircraft accident NOS
aircraft crash or wreck NOS
any accident to powered aircraft while in transit or when not specified whether in transit, taking off, or landing
collision of aircraft with another aircraft, bird, or any object, while in transit
explosion on aircraft while in transit
fire on aircraft while in transit

§ E842 Accident to unpowered aircraft

[6–9]

Includes:
any accident, except collision with powered aircraft, to:
balloon
glider
hang glider
kite carrying a person
hit by object falling from unpowered aircraft

§ E843 Fall in, on, or from aircraft

[0–9]

Includes:
accident in boarding or alighting from aircraft, any kind
fall in, on, or from aircraft [any kind], while in transit, taking off, or landing, except when as a result of an accident to aircraft

§ E844 Other specified air transport accidents

[0–9]

Includes: hit by:
- aircraft
- object falling from aircraft

injury by or from:
- machinery on aircraft
- rotating propeller
- voluntary parachute descent

poisoning by carbon monoxide from aircraft while in transit

sucked into jet

(all of the above: without accident to aircraft)

any accident involving other transport vehicle (motor) (nonmotor) due to being hit by object set in motion by aircraft (powered)

Excludes: *air sickness (E903)*
effects of:
high altitude (E902.0-E902.1)
pressure change (E902.0-E902.1)
injury in parachute descent due to accident to aircraft (E840.0-E842.9)

§ E845 Accident involving spacecraft

[0,8,9]

Includes: launching pad accident

Excludes: *effects of weightlessness in spacecraft (E928.0)*

VEHICLE ACCIDENTS NOT ELSEWHERE CLASSIFIABLE (E846-E848)

E846 Accidents involving powered vehicles used solely within the buildings and premises of industrial or commercial establishment

Accident to, on, or involving:
- battery powered airport passenger vehicle
- battery powered trucks (baggage) (mail)
- coal car in mine
- logging car
- self propelled truck, industrial
- station baggage truck (powered)
- tram, truck, or tub (powered) in mine or quarry

Breakage of any part of vehicle

Collision with:
- pedestrian
- other vehicle or object within premises

Explosion of / Fall from / Overturning of / Struck by — powered vehicle, industrial or commercial

Excludes: *accidental poisoning by exhaust gas from vehicle not elsewhere classifiable (E868.2)*
injury by crane, lift (fork), or elevator (E919.2)

§ Requires fourth-digit. See page E-10 for codes and definitions.

E847 Accidents involving cable cars not running on rails

Accident to, on, or involving:
- cable car, not on rails
- ski chair-lift
- ski-lift with gondola
- téléférique

Breakage of cable

Caught or dragged by / Fall or jump from / Object thrown from or in — cable car, not on rails

E848 Accidents involving other vehicles, not elsewhere classifiable

Accident to, on, or involving:
- ice yacht
- land yacht
- nonmotor, nonroad vehicle NOS

□ **E849 *Place of occurrence***

The following category is for use to denote the place where the injury or poisoning occurred.

□ ***E849.0 Home***

Apartment
Boarding house
Farm house
Home premises
House (residential)
Noninstitutional place of residence
Private:
- *driveway*
- *garage*
- *garden*
- *home*
- *walk*

Swimming pool in private house or garden
Yard of home

Excludes: *home under construction but not yet occupied (E849.3)*
institutional place of residence (E849.7)

□ ***E849.1 Farm***

Farm:
- *buildings*
- *land under cultivation*

Excludes: *farm house and home premises of farm (E849.0)*

□ ***E849.2 Mine and quarry***

Gravel pit
Sand pit
Tunnel under construction

□ ***E849.3 Industrial place and premises***

Building under construction
Dockyard
Dry dock
Factory:
- *building*
- *premises*

Garage (place of work)
Industrial yard
Loading platform (factory) (store)
Plant, industrial
Railway yard
Shop (place of work)
Warehouse
Workhouse

☐ ***E849.4*** ***Place for recreation and sport***

Amusement park
Baseball field
Basketball court
Beach resort
Cricket ground
Fives court
Football field
Golf course
Gymnasium
Hockey field
Holiday camp
Ice palace
Lake resort
Mountain resort
Playground, including school playground
Public park
Racecourse
Resort NOS
Riding school
Rifle range
Seashore resort
Skating rink
Sports ground
Sports palace
Stadium
Swimming pool, public
Tennis court
Vacation resort

Excludes: *that in private house or garden (E849.0)*

☐ ***E849.5*** ***Street and highway***

☐ ***E849.6*** ***Public building***

Building (including adjacent grounds) used by the general public or by a particular group of the public, such as:

airport
bank
café
casino
church
cinema
clubhouse
courthouse
dance hall
garage building (for car storage)
hotel
market (grocery or other commodity)
movie house
music hall
nightclub
office
office building
opera house
post office
public hall
radio broadcasting station
restaurant
school (state) (public) (private)
shop, commercial
station (bus) (railway)
store
theater

Excludes: *home garage (E849.0)*
industrial building or workplace (E849.3)

☐ ***E849.7*** ***Residential institution***

Children's home
Dormitory
Hospital
Jail
Old people's home
Orphanage
Prison
Reform school

☐ ***E849.8*** ***Other specified places***

Beach NOS
Canal
Caravan site NOS
Derelict house
Desert
Dock
Forest
Harbor
Hill
Lake NOS
Mountain
Parking lot
Parking place
Pond or pool (natural)
Prairie
Public place NOS
Railway line
Reservoir
River
Sea
Seashore NOS
Stream
Swamp
Trailer court
Woods

☐ ***E849.9*** ***Unspecified place***

ACCIDENTAL POISONING BY DRUGS, MEDICINAL SUBSTANCES, AND BIOLOGICALS (E850-E858)

Includes: accidental overdose of drug, wrong drug given or taken in error, and drug taken inadvertently
accidents in the use of drugs and biologicals in medical and surgical procedures

Excludes: *administration with suicidal or homicidal intent or intent to harm, or in circumstances classifiable to E980-E989 (E950.0-E950.5, E962.0, E980.0-E980.5)*
correct drug properly administered in therapeutic or prophylactic dosage, as the cause of adverse effect (E930.0-E949.9)

See Alphabetic Index for more complete list of specific drugs to be classified under the fourth-digit subdivisions. The American Hospital Formulary numbers can be used to classify new drugs listed by the American Hospital Formulary Service (AHFS). See appendix C.

E850 Accidental poisoning by analgesics, antipyretics, and antirheumatics

☐ **E850.0** **Heroin**

Diacetylmorphine

☐ **E850.1** **Methadone**

☐ **E850.2** **Other opiates and related narcotics**

Codeine [methylmorphine]
Meperidine [pethidine]
Morphine
Opium (alkaloids)

☐ **E850.3** **Salicylates**

Acetylsalicylic acid [aspirin]
Amino derivatives of salicylic acid
Salicylic acid salts

☐ **E850.4** **Aromatic analgesics, not elsewhere classified**

Acetanilid
Paracetamol [acetaminophen]
Phenacetin [acetophenetidin]

☐ **E850.5** **Pyrazole derivatives**

Aminophenazone [amidopyrine]
Phenylbutazone

☐ **E850.6** **Antirheumatics [antiphlogistics]**

Gold salts
Indomethacin

Excludes: *salicylates (E850.3)*
steroids (E858.0)

☐ **E850.7** **Other non-narcotic analgesics**

Pyrabital

E850.8 **Other specified analgesics and antipyretics**

Pentazocine

E850.9 **Unspecified analgesic or antipyretic**

E851 Accidental poisoning by barbiturates

Amobarbital [amylobarbitone]
Barbital [barbitone]
Butabarbital [butabarbitone]
Pentobarbital [pentobarbitone]
Phenobarbital [phenobarbitone]
Secobarbital [quinalbarbitone]

Excludes: *thiobarbiturates (E855.1)*

E852 Accidental poisoning by other sedatives and hypnotics

E852.0 Chloral hydrate group

E852.1 Paraldehyde

E852.2 Bromine compounds
Bromides
Carbromal (derivatives)

E852.3 Methaqualone compounds

E852.4 Glutethimide group

E852.5 Mixed sedatives, not elsewhere classified

E852.8 Other specified sedatives and hypnotics

E852.9 Unspecified sedative or hypnotic
Sleeping:
drug NOS
pill NOS
tablet NOS

E853 Accidental poisoning by tranquilizers

E853.0 Phenothiazine-based tranquilizers
Chlorpromazine
Fluphenazine
Prochlorperazine
Promazine

E853.1 Butyrophenone-based tranquilizers
Haloperidol
Spiperone
Trifluperidol

E853.2 Benzodiazepine-based tranquilizers
Chlordiazepoxide
Diazepam
Flurazepam
Lorazepam
Medazepam
Nitrazepam

E853.8 Other specified tranquilizers
Hydroxyzine
Meprobamate

E853.9 Unspecified tranquilizer

E854 Accidental poisoning by other psychotropic agents

E854.0 Antidepressants
Amitriptyline
Imipramine
Monoamine oxidase [MAO] inhibitors

E854.1 Psychodysleptics [hallucinogens]
Cannabis derivatives
Lysergide [LSD]
Marihuana (derivatives)
Mescaline
Psilocin
Psilocybin

E854.2 Psychostimulants
Amphetamine
Caffeine

Excludes: *central appetite depressants (E858.8)*

E854.3 Central nervous system stimulants
Analeptics
Opiate antagonists

E854.8 Other psychotropic agents

E855 Accidental poisoning by other drugs acting on central and autonomic nervous system

E855.0 Anticonvulsant and anti-Parkinsonism drugs
Amantadine
Hydantoin derivatives
Levodopa [L-dopa]
Oxazolidine derivatives [paramethadione] [trimethadione]
Succinimides

E855.1 Other central nervous system depressants
Ether
Gaseous anesthetics
Halogenated hydrocarbon derivatives
Intravenous anesthetics
Thiobarbiturates, such as thiopental sodium

E855.2 Local anesthetics
Cocaine
Lidocaine [lignocaine]
Procaine
Tetracaine

E855.3 Parasympathomimetics [cholinergics]
Acetylcholine
Anticholinesterase:
organophosphorus
reversible
Pilocarpine

E855.4 Parasympatholytics [anticholinergics and antimuscarinics] and spasmolytics
Atropine
Homatropine
Hyoscine [scopolamine]
Quaternary ammonium derivatives

E855.5 Sympathomimetics [adrenergics]
Epinephrine [adrenalin]
Levarterenol [noradrenalin]

E855.6 Sympatholytics [antiadrenergics]
Phenoxybenzamine
Tolazoline hydrochloride

E855.8 Other specified drugs acting on central and autonomic nervous systems

E855.9 Unspecified drug acting on central and autonomic nervous systems

E856 Accidental poisoning by antibiotics

E857 Accidental poisoning by other anti-infectives

E858 Accidental poisoning by other drugs

E858.0 Hormones and synthetic substitutes

E858.1 **Primarily systemic agents**

E858.2 **Agents primarily affecting blood constituents**

E858.3 **Agents primarily affecting cardiovascular system**

E858.4 **Agents primarily affecting gastrointestinal system**

E858.5 **Water, mineral, and uric acid metabolism drugs**

E858.6 **Agents primarily acting on the smooth and skeletal muscles and respiratory system**

E858.7 **Agents primarily affecting skin and mucous membrane, ophthalmological,otorhinolaryngological, and dental drugs**

E858.8 **Other specified drugs**
Central appetite depressants

E858.9 **Unspecified drug**

ACCIDENTAL POISONING BY OTHER SOLID AND LIQUID SUBSTANCES, GASES, AND VAPORS (E860-E869)

Note: Categories in this section are intended primarily to indicate the external cause of poisoning states classifiable to 980-989. They may also be used to indicate external causes of localized effects classifiable to 001-799.

E860 Accidental poisoning by alcohol, not elsewhere classified

E860.0 **Alcoholic beverages**
Alcohol in preparations intended for consumption

E860.1 **Other and unspecified ethyl alcohol and its products**
Denatured alcohol
Ethanol NOS
Grain alcohol NOS
Methylated spirit

E860.2 **Methyl alcohol**
Methanol
Wood alcohol

E860.3 **Isopropyl alcohol**
Dimethyl carbinol
Isopropanol
Rubbing alcohol substitute
Secondary propyl alcohol

E860.4 **Fusel oil**
Alcohol:
amyl
butyl
propyl

E860.8 **Other specified alcohols**

E860.9 **Unspecified alcohol**

E861 Accidental poisoning by cleansing and polishing agents, disinfectants, paints, and varnishes

E861.0 **Synthetic detergents and shampoos**

E861.1 **Soap products**

E861.2 **Polishes**

E861.3 **Other cleansing and polishing agents**
Scouring powders

E861.4 **Disinfectants**
Household and other disinfectants not ordinarily used on the person

Excludes: *carbolic acid or phenol (E864.0)*

E861.5 **Lead paints**

E861.6 **Other paints and varnishes**
Lacquers
Oil colors
Paints, other than lead
White washes

E861.9 **Unspecified**

E862 Accidental poisoning by petroleum products, other solvents and their vapors, not elsewhere classified

E862.0 **Petroleum solvents**
Petroleum:
ether
benzine
naphtha

E862.1 **Petroleum fuels and cleaners**
Antiknock additives to petroleum fuels
Gas oils
Gasoline or petrol
Kerosene

Excludes: *kerosene insecticides (E863.4)*

E862.2 **Lubricating oils**

E862.3 **Petroleum solids**
Paraffin wax

E862.4 **Other specified solvents**
Benzene

E862.9 **Unspecified solvent**

E863 Accidental poisoning by agricultural and horticultural chemical and pharmaceutical preparations other than plant foods and fertilizers

Excludes: *plant foods and fertilizers (E866.5)*

E863.0 Insecticides of organochlorine compounds

Benzene hexachloride
Chlordane
DDT
Dieldrin
Endrine
Toxaphene

E863.1 Insecticides of organophosphorus compounds

Demeton
Diazinon
Dichlorvos
Malathion
Methyl parathion
Parathion
Phenylsulphthion
Phorate
Phosdrin

E863.2 Carbamates

Aldicarb
Carbaryl
Propoxur

E863.3 Mixtures of insecticides

E863.4 Other and unspecified insecticides

Kerosene insecticides

E863.5 Herbicides

2, 4-Dichlorophenoxyacetic acid [2, 4-D]
2, 4, 5-Trichlorophenoxyacetic acid [2, 4, 5-T]
Chlorates
Diquat
Mixtures of plant foods and fertilizers with herbicides
Paraquat

E863.6 Fungicides

Organic mercurials (used in seed dressing)
Pentachlorophenols

E863.7 Rodenticides

Fluoroacetates
Squill and derivatives
Thallium
Warfarin
Zinc phosphide

E863.8 Fumigants

Cyanides
Methyl bromide
Phosphine

E863.9 Other and unspecified

E864 Accidental poisoning by corrosives and caustics, not elsewhere classified

Excludes: *those as components of disinfectants (E861.4)*

E864.0 Corrosive aromatics

Carbolic acid or phenol

E864.1 Acids

Acid:
- hydrochloric
- nitric
- sulfuric

E864.2 Caustic alkalis

Lye

E864.3 Other specified corrosives and caustics

E864.4 Unspecified corrosives and caustics

E865 Accidental poisoning from poisonous foodstuffs and poisonous plants

Includes: any meat, fish, or shellfish
plants, berries, and fungi eaten as, or in mistake for food, or by a child

Excludes: *anaphylactic shock due to adverse food reaction (995.6)*
food poisoning (bacterial) (005.0-005.9)
poisoning and toxic reactions to venomous plants (E905.6-E905.7)

E865.0 Meat

E865.1 Shellfish

E865.2 Other fish

E865.3 Berries and seeds

E865.4 Other specified plants

E865.5 Mushrooms and other fungi

E865.8 Other specified foods

E865.9 Unspecified foodstuff or poisonous plant

E866 Accidental poisoning by other and unspecified solid and liquid substances

Excludes: *these substances as a component of:*
medicines (E850.0-E858.9)
paints (E861.5-E861.6)
pesticides (E863.0-E863.9)
petroleum fuels (E862.1)

E866.0 Lead and its compounds and fumes

E866.1 Mercury and its compounds and fumes

E866.2 Antimony and its compounds and fumes

E866.3 Arsenic and its compounds and fumes

E866.4 Other metals and their compounds and fumes

Beryllium (compounds)
Brass fumes
Cadmium (compounds)
Copper salts
Iron (compounds)
Manganese (compounds)
Nickel (compounds)
Thallium (compounds)

E866.5 Plant foods and fertilizers

Excludes: *mixtures with herbicides (E863.5)*

E866.6 Glues and adhesives

E866.7 Cosmetics

E866.8 Other specified solid or liquid substances

E866.9 Unspecified solid or liquid substance

E867 Accidental poisoning by gas distributed by pipeline

Carbon monoxide from incomplete combustion of piped gas
Coal gas NOS
Liquefied petroleum gas distributed through pipes (pure or mixed with air)
Piped gas (natural) (manufactured)

E868 Accidental poisoning by other utility gas and other carbon monoxide

E868.0 Liquefied petroleum gas distributed in mobile containers

Butane, Liquefied hydrocarbon gas NOS, Propane } or carbon monoxide from incomplete combustion of these gases

E868.1 Other and unspecified utility gas

Acetylene, Gas NOS used for lighting, heating, or cooking, Water gas } or carbon monoxide from incomplete combustion of these gases

E868.2 Motor vehicle exhaust gas

Exhaust gas from:
- farm tractor, not in transit
- gas engine
- motor pump
- motor vehicle, not in transit
- any type of combustion engine not in watercraft

Excludes: *poisoning by carbon monoxide from:*
aircraft while in transit (E844.0-E844.9)
motor vehicle while in transit (E818.0-E818.9)
watercraft whether or not in transit (E838.0-E838.9)

E868.3 Carbon monoxide from incomplete combustion of other domestic fuel

Carbon monoxide from incomplete combustion of:
coal, coke, kerosene, wood } in domestic stove or fireplace

Excludes: *carbon monoxide from smoke and fumes due to conflagration (E890.0-E893.9)*

E868.8 Carbon monoxide from other sources

Carbon monoxide from:
- blast furnace gas
- incomplete combustion of fuels in industrial use
- kiln vapor

E868.9 Unspecified carbon monoxide

E869 Accidental poisoning by other gases and vapors

Excludes: *effects of gases used as anesthetics (E855.1, E938.2)*
fumes from heavy metals (E866.0-E866.4)
smoke and fumes due to conflagration or explosion (E890.0-E899)

E869.0 Nitrogen oxides

E869.1 Sulfur dioxide

E869.2 Freon

E869.3 Lacrimogenic gas [tear gas]

Bromobenzyl cyanide
Chloroacetophenone
Ethyliodoacetate

E869.4 Second-hand tobacco smoke

E869.8 Other specified gases and vapors

Chlorine
Hydrocyanic acid gas

E869.9 Unspecified gases and vapors

MISADVENTURES TO PATIENTS DURING SURGICAL AND MEDICAL CARE (E870-E876)

Excludes: *accidental overdose of drug and wrong drug given in error (E850.0-E858.9)*
surgical and medical procedures as the cause of abnormal reaction by the patient, without mention of misadventure at the time of procedure (E878.0-E879.9)

E870 Accidental cut, puncture, perforation, or hemorrhage during medical care

E870.0 Surgical operation

E870.1 Infusion or transfusion

E870.2 Kidney dialysis or other perfusion

E870.3 Injection or vaccination

E870.4 Endoscopic examination

E870.5 Aspiration of fluid or tissue, puncture, and catheterization

Abdominal paracentesis
Aspirating needle biopsy
Blood sampling
Lumbar puncture
Thoracentesis

Excludes: *heart catheterization (E870.6)*

E870.6 Heart catheterization

E870.7 Administration of enema

E870.8 Other specified medical care

E870.9 Unspecified medical care

E871 Foreign object left in body during procedure

E871.0 Surgical operation

E871.1 Infusion or transfusion

E871.2 Kidney dialysis or other perfusion

E871.3 Injection or vaccination

E871.4 Endoscopic examination

E871.5 Aspiration of fluid or tissue, puncture, and catheterization

Abdominal paracentesis
Aspiration needle biopsy
Blood sampling
Lumbar puncture
Thoracentesis

Excludes: *heart catheterization (E871.6)*

E871.6 Heart catheterization

E871.7 Removal of catheter or packing

E871.8 Other specified procedures

E871.9 Unspecified procedure

E872 Failure of sterile precautions during procedure

E872.0 Surgical operation

E872.1 Infusion or transfusion

E872.2 Kidney dialysis or other perfusion

E872.3 Injection or vaccination

E872.4 Endoscopic examination

E872.5 Aspiration of fluid or tissue, puncture, and catheterization

Abdominal paracentesis
Aspirating needle biopsy
Blood sampling
Lumbar puncture
Thoracentesis

Excludes: *heart catheterization (E872.6)*

E872.6 Heart catheterization

E872.8 Other specified procedures

E872.9 Unspecified procedure

E873 Failure in dosage

Excludes: *accidental overdose of drug, medicinal or biological substance (E850.0-E858.9)*

E873.0 Excessive amount of blood or other fluid during transfusion or infusion

E873.1 Incorrect dilution of fluid during infusion

E873.2 Overdose of radiation in therapy

E873.3 Inadvertent exposure of patient to radiation during medical care

E873.4 Failure in dosage in electroshock or insulin-shock therapy

E873.5 Inappropriate [too hot or too cold] temperature in local application and packing

E873.6 Nonadministration of necessary drug or medicinal substance

E873.8 Other specified failure in dosage

E873.9 Unspecified failure in dosage

E874 Mechanical failure of instrument or apparatus during procedure

E874.0 Surgical operation

E874.1 Infusion or transfusion

Air in system

E874.2 Kidney dialysis or other perfusion

E874.3 Endoscopic examination

E874.4 Aspiration of fluid or tissue, puncture, and catheterization

Abdominal paracentesis
Aspirating needle biopsy
Blood sampling
Lumbar puncture
Thoracentesis

Excludes: *heart catheterization (E874.5)*

E874.5 Heart catheterization

E874.8 Other specified procedures

E874.9 Unspecified procedure

E875 Contaminated or infected blood, other fluid, drug, or biological substance

Includes: presence of:
bacterial pyrogens
endotoxin-producing bacteria
serum hepatitis-producing agent

E875.0 Contaminated substance transfused or infused

E875.1 Contaminated substance injected or used for vaccination

E875.2 Contaminated drug or biological substance administered by other means

E875.8 Other

E875.9 Unspecified

E876 Other and unspecified misadventures during medical care

E876.0 Mismatched blood in transfusion

E876.1 Wrong fluid in infusion

E876.2 Failure in suture and ligature during surgical operation

E876.3 Endotracheal tube wrongly placed during anesthetic procedure

E876.4 Failure to introduce or to remove other tube or instrument

Excludes: *foreign object left in body during procedure (E871.0-E871.9)*

E876.5 Performance of inappropriate operation

E876.8 Other specified misadventures during medical care

Performance of inappropriate treatment NEC

E876.9 Unspecified misadventure during medical care

SURGICAL AND MEDICAL PROCEDURES AS THE CAUSE OF ABNORMAL REACTION OF PATIENT OR LATER COMPLICATION, WITHOUT MENTION OF MISADVENTURE AT THE TIME OF PROCEDURE (E878-E879)

Includes: procedures as the cause of abnormal reaction, such as:
displacement or malfunction of prosthetic device
hepatorenal failure, postoperative
malfunction of external stoma
postoperative intestinal obstruction
rejection of transplanted organ

Excludes: *anesthetic management properly carried out as the cause of adverse effect (E937.0-E938.9)*
infusion and transfusion, without mention of misadventure in the technique of procedure (E930.0-E949.9)

E878 Surgical operation and other surgical procedures as the cause of abnormal reaction of patient, or of later complication, without mention of misadventure at the time of operation

E878.0 Surgical operation with transplant of whole organ

Transplantation of:
heart
kidney
liver

E878.1 Surgical operation with implant of artificial internal device

Cardiac pacemaker
Electrodes implanted in brain
Heart valve prosthesis
Internal orthopedic device

E878.2 Surgical operation with anastomosis, bypass, or graft, with natural or artificial tissues used as implant

Anastomosis:
arteriovenous
gastrojejunal
Graft of blood vessel, tendon, or skin

Excludes: *external stoma (E878.3)*

E878.3 Surgical operation with formation of external stoma

Colostomy
Cystostomy
Duodenostomy
Gastrostomy
Ureterostomy

E878.4 Other restorative surgery

E878.5 Amputation of limb(s)

E878.6 Removal of other organ (partial) (total)

E878.8 Other specified surgical operations and procedures

E878.9 Unspecified surgical operations and procedures

E879 Other procedures, without mention of misadventure at the time of procedure, as the cause of abnormal reaction of patient, or of later complication

E879.0 Cardiac catheterization

E879.1 Kidney dialysis

E879.2 Radiological procedure and radiotherapy

Excludes: *radio-opaque dyes for diagnostic x-ray procedures (E947.8)*

E879.3 Shock therapy

Electroshock therapy
Insulin-shock therapy

E879.4 Aspiration of fluid

Lumbar puncture
Thoracentesis

E879.5 Insertion of gastric or duodenal sound

E879.6 Urinary catheterization

E879.7 Blood sampling

E879.8 Other specified procedures

Blood transfusion

E879.9 Unspecified procedure

ACCIDENTAL FALLS (E880-E888)

Excludes: *falls (in or from):*
burning building (E890.8, E891.8)
into fire (E890.0-E899)
into water (with submersion or drowning) (E910.0-E910.9)
machinery (in operation) (E919.0-E919.9)
on edged, pointed, or sharp object (E920.0-E920.9)
transport vehicle (E800.0-E845.9)
vehicle not elsewhere classifiable (E846-E848)

E880 Fall on or from stairs or steps

E880.0 Escalator

E880.1 Fall on or from sidewalk curb

Excludes: *fall from moving sidewalk (E885)*

E880.9 Other stairs or steps

E881 Fall on or from ladders or scaffolding

E881.0 Fall from ladder

E881.1 Fall from scaffolding

E882 Fall from or out of building or other structure

Fall from:
balcony
bridge
building
flagpole
tower

Fall from:
turret
viaduct
wall
window

Fall through roof

Excludes: *collapse of a building or structure (E916)*
fall or jump from burning building (E890.8, E891.8)

E883 Fall into hole or other opening in surface

Includes: fall into:
cavity
dock
hole
pit
quarry

fall into:
shaft
swimming pool
tank
well

Excludes: *fall into water NOS (E910.9)*
that resulting in drowning or submersion without mention of injury (E910.0-E910.9)

E883.0 Accident from diving or jumping into water [swimming pool]

Strike or hit:
against bottom when jumping or diving into water
wall or board of swimming pool
water surface

Excludes: *diving with insufficient air supply (E913.2)*
effects of air pressure from diving (E902.2)

E883.1 Accidental fall into well

E883.2 Accidental fall into storm drain or manhole

E883.9 Fall into other hole or other opening in surface

E884 Other fall from one level to another

E884.0 Fall from playground equipment

Excludes: *recreational machinery (E919.8)*

E884.1 Fall from cliff

E884.2 Fall from chair

E884.3 Fall from wheelchair

E884.4 Fall from bed

E884.5 Fall from other furniture

E884.6 Fall from commode

Toilet

E884.9 Other fall from one level to another

Fall from:
embankment
haystack

Fall from:
stationary vehicle
tree

E885 Fall on same level from slipping, tripping, or stumbling

Fall on moving sidewalk

E886 Fall on same level from collision, pushing, or shoving, by or with other person

Excludes: *crushed or pushed by a crowd or human stampede (E917.1)*

E886.0 In sports

Tackles in sports

Excludes: *kicked, stepped on, struck by object, in sports (E917.0)*

E886.9 Other and unspecified

Fall from collision of pedestrian (conveyance) with another pedestrian (conveyance)

E887 Fracture, cause unspecified

E888 Other and unspecified fall

Accidental fall NOS
Fall from bumping against object
Fall on same level NOS

ACCIDENTS CAUSED BY FIRE AND FLAMES (E890-E899)

Includes: asphyxia or poisoning due to conflagration or ignition
burning by fire
secondary fires resulting from explosion

Excludes: *arson (E968.0)*
fire in or on:
machinery (in operation) (E919.0-E919.9)
transport vehicle other than stationary vehicle (E800.0-E845.9)
vehicle not elsewhere classifiable (E846-E848)

E890 Conflagration in private dwelling

Includes: conflagration in:
apartment
boarding house
camping place
caravan
farmhouse
house
lodging house
mobile home
private garage
rooming house
tenement
conflagration originating from sources classifiable to E893-E898 in the above buildings

E890.0 Explosion caused by conflagration

E890.1 Fumes from combustion of polyvinylchloride [PVC] and similar material in conflagration

E890.2 Other smoke and fumes from conflagration

Carbon monoxide, Fumes NOS, Smoke NOS } from conflagration in private building

E890.3 Burning caused by conflagration

E890.8 Other accident resulting from conflagration

Collapse of, Fall from, Hit by object falling from, Jump from } burning private building

E890.9 Unspecified accident resulting from conflagration in private dwelling

E891 Conflagration in other and unspecified building or structure

Conflagration in:
barn
church
convalescent and other residential home
dormitory of educational institution
factory

Conflagration in:
farm outbuildings
hospital
hotel
school
store
theater

Conflagration originating from sources classifiable to E893-E898, in the above buildings

E891.0 Explosion caused by conflagration

E891.1 Fumes from combustion of polyvinylchloride [PVC] and similar material in conflagration

E891.2 Other smoke and fumes from conflagration

Carbon monoxide, Fumes NOS, Smoke NOS } from conflagration in building or structure

E891.3 Burning caused by conflagration

E891.8 Other accident resulting from conflagration

Collapse of, Fall from, Hit by object falling from, Jump from } burning building or structure

E891.9 Unspecified accident resulting from conflagration of other and unspecified building or structure

E892 Conflagration not in building or structure

Fire (uncontrolled) (in) (of):
forest
grass
hay
lumber
mine
prairie
transport vehicle [any], except while in transit
tunnel

E893 Accident caused by ignition of clothing

Excludes: *ignition of clothing:*
from highly inflammable material (E894)
with conflagration (E890.0-E892)

E893.0 From controlled fire in private dwelling

Ignition of clothing from:
normal fire (charcoal) (coal) (electric) (gas) (wood) in:
brazier
fireplace
furnace
stove
} in private dwelling (as listed in E890)

E893.1 From controlled fire in other building or structure

Ignition of clothing from:
normal fire (charcoal) (coal) (electric) (gas) (wood) in:
brazier
fireplace
furnace
stove
} in other building or structure (as listed in E891)

E893.2 From controlled fire not in building or structure

Ignition of clothing from:
bonfire (controlled)
brazier fire (controlled), not in building or structure
trash fire (controlled)

Excludes: *conflagration not in building (E892)*
trash fire out of control (E892)

E893.8 From other specified sources

Ignition of clothing from:
- blowlamp
- blowtorch
- burning bedspread
- candle
- cigar

Ignition of clothing from:
- cigarette
- lighter
- matches
- pipe
- welding torch

E893.9 Unspecified source

Ignition of clothing (from controlled fire NOS) (in building NOS) NOS

E894 Ignition of highly inflammable material

Ignition of:
- benzine
- gasoline
- fat
- kerosene
- paraffin
- petrol

(with ignition of clothing)

Excludes: *ignition of highly inflammable material with:*
conflagration (E890.0-E892)
explosion (E923.0-E923.9)

E895 Accident caused by controlled fire in private dwelling

Burning by (flame of) normal fire (charcoal) (coal) (electric) (gas) (wood) in:
- brazier
- fireplace
- furnace
- stove

in private dwelling (as listed in E890)

Excludes: *burning by hot objects not producing fire or flames (E924.0-E924.9)*
ignition of clothing from these sources (E893.0)
poisoning by carbon monoxide from incomplete combustion of fuel (E867-E868.9)
that with conflagration (E890.0-E890.9)

E896 Accident caused by controlled fire in other and unspecified building or structure

Burning by (flame of) normal fire (charcoal) (coal) (electric) (gas) (wood) in:
- brazier
- fireplace
- furnace
- stove

in other building or structure (as listed in E891)

Excludes: *burning by hot objects not producing fire or flames (E924.0-E924.9)*
ignition of clothing from these sources (E893.1)
poisoning by carbon monoxide from incomplete combustion of fuel (E867-E868.9)
that with conflagration (E891.0-E891.9)

E897 Accident caused by controlled fire not in building or structure

Burns from flame of:
- bonfire (controlled)
- brazier fire (controlled), not in building or structure
- trash fire (controlled)

Excludes: *ignition of clothing from these sources (E893.2)*
trash fire out of control (E892)
that with conflagration (E892)

E898 Accident caused by other specified fire and flames

Excludes: *conflagration (E890.0-E892)*
that with ignition of:
clothing (E893.0-E893.9)
highly inflammable material (E894)

E898.0 Burning bedclothes

Bed set on fire NOS

E898.1 Other

Burning by:
- blowlamp
- blowtorch
- candle
- cigar
- cigarette
- fire in room NOS

Burning by:
- lamp
- lighter
- matches
- pipe
- welding torch

E899 Accident caused by unspecified fire

Burning NOS

ACCIDENTS DUE TO NATURAL AND ENVIRONMENTAL FACTORS (E900-E909)

E900 Excessive heat

E900.0 Due to weather conditions

Excessive heat as the external cause of:
- ictus solaris
- siriasis
- sunstroke

E900.1 Of man-made origin

Heat (in):
- boiler room
- drying room
- factory
- furnace room

Heat (in):
- generated in transport vehicle
- kitchen

E900.9 Of unspecified origin

E901 Excessive cold

E901.0 Due to weather conditions

Excessive cold as the cause of:
- chilblains NOS
- immersion foot

E901.1 Of man-made origin

Contact with or inhalation of:
- dry ice
- liquid air
- liquid hydrogen
- liquid nitrogen

Prolonged exposure in:
- deep freeze unit
- refrigerator

E901.8 **Other specified origin**

E901.9 **Of unspecified origin**

E902 High and low air pressure and changes in air pressure

E902.0 **Residence or prolonged visit at high altitude**

Residence or prolonged visit at high altitude as the cause of:
- Acosta syndrome
- Alpine sickness
- altitude sickness
- Andes disease
- anoxia, hypoxia
- barotitis, barodontalgia, barosinusitis, otitic barotrauma
- hypobarism, hypobaropathy
- mountain sickness
- range disease

E902.1 **In aircraft**

Sudden change in air pressure in aircraft during ascent or descent as the cause of:
- aeroneurosis
- aviators' disease

E902.2 **Due to diving**

High air pressure from rapid descent in water / Reduction in atmospheric pressure while surfacing from deep water diving } as the cause of:
- caisson disease
- divers' disease
- divers' palsy or paralysis

E902.8 **Due to other specified causes**

Reduction in atmospheric pressure while surfacing from underground

E902.9 **Unspecified cause**

E903 Travel and motion

E904 Hunger, thirst, exposure, and neglect

Excludes: *any condition resulting from homicidal intent (E968.0-E968.9)*
hunger, thirst, and exposure resulting from accidents connected with transport (E800.0-E848)

E904.0 **Abandonment or neglect of infants and helpless persons**

Exposure to weather conditions / Hunger or thirst } resulting from abandonment or neglect

Desertion of newborn
Inattention at or after birth
Lack of care (helpless person) (infant)

Excludes: *criminal [purposeful] neglect (E968.4)*

E904.1 **Lack of food**

Lack of food as the cause of:
- inanition
- insufficient nourishment
- starvation

Excludes: *hunger resulting from abandonment or neglect (E904.0)*

E904.2 **Lack of water**

Lack of water as the cause of:
- dehydration
- inanition

Excludes: *dehydration due to acute fluid loss (276.5)*

E904.3 **Exposure (to weather conditions), not elsewhere classifiable**

Exposure NOS
Humidity
Struck by hailstones

Excludes: *struck by lightning (E907)*

E904.9 **Privation, unqualified**

Destitution

E905 Venomous animals and plants as the cause of poisoning and toxic reactions

Includes: chemical released by animal
insects
release of venom through fangs, hairs, spines, tentacles, and other venom apparatus

Excludes: *eating of poisonous animals or plants (E865.0-E865.9)*

E905.0 **Venomous snakes and lizards**

Cobra
Copperhead snake
Coral snake
Fer de lance
Gila monster
Krait
Mamba
Rattlesnake
Sea snake
Snake (venomous)
Viper
Water moccasin

Excludes: *bites of snakes and lizards known to be nonvenomous (E906.2)*

E905.1 **Venomous spiders**

Black widow spider
Brown spider
Tarantula (venomous)

E905.2 **Scorpion**

E905.3 **Hornets, wasps, and bees**

Yellow jacket

E905.4 **Centipede and venomous millipede (tropical)**

E905.5 **Other venomous arthropods**

Sting of:
- ant
- caterpillar

E905.6 Venomous marine animals and plants

Puncture by sea urchin spine
Sting of:
coral
jelly fish
Sting of:
nematocysts
sea anemone
sea cucumber
other marine animal or plant

Excludes: *bites and other injuries caused by nonvenomous marine animal (E906.2-E906.8)*
bite of sea snake (venomous) (E905.0)

E905.7 Poisoning and toxic reactions caused by other plants

Injection of poisons or toxins into or through skin by plant thorns, spines, or other mechanisms

Excludes: *puncture wound NOS by plant thorns or spines (E920.8)*

E905.8 Other specified

E905.9 Unspecified

Sting NOS
Venomous bite NOS

E906 Other injury caused by animals

Excludes: *poisoning and toxic reactions caused by venomous animals and insects (E905.0-E905.9)*
road vehicle accident involving animals (E827.0-E828.9)
tripping or falling over an animal (E885)

E906.0 Dog bite

E906.1 Rat bite

E906.2 Bite of nonvenomous snakes and lizards

E906.3 Bite of other animal except arthropod

Cats
Moray eel
Rodents, except rats
Shark

E906.4 Bite of nonvenomous arthropod

Insect bite NOS

E906.5 Bite by unspecified animal

Animal bite NOS

E906.8 Other specified injury caused by animal

Butted by animal
Fallen on by horse or other animal, not being ridden
Gored by animal
Implantation of quills of porcupine
Pecked by bird
Run over by animal, not being ridden
Stepped on by animal, not being ridden

Excludes: *injury by animal being ridden (E828.0-E828.9)*

E906.9 Unspecified injury caused by animal

E907 Lightning

Excludes: *injury from:*
fall of tree or other object caused by lightning (E916)
fire caused by lightning (E890.0-E892)

E908 Cataclysmic storms, and floods resulting from storms

Excludes: *collapse of dam or man-made structure causing flood (E909.3)*

E908.0 Hurricane

Storm surge
"Tidal wave" caused by storm action
Typhoon

E908.1 Tornado

Cyclone
Twisters

E908.2 Floods

Flash flood
Torrential rainfall

Excludes: *collapse of dam or man-made structure causing flood (E909.3)*

E908.3 Blizzard (snow) (ice)

E908.4 Dust storm

E908.8 Other cataclysmic storms

E908.9 Unspecified cataclysmic storms, and floods resulting from storms

Storm NOS

E909 Cataclysmic earth surface movements and eruptions

Excludes: *"tidal wave" caused by storm action (E908.0)*
transport accident involving collision with avalanche or landslide not in motion (E800.0-E848)

E909.0 Earthquakes

E909.1 Volcanic eruptions

Ash inhalation
Burns from lava

E909.2 Avalanche, landslide, or mudslide

E909.3 Collapse of dam or man-made structure

E909.4 Tidal wave caused by earthquake

Tidal wave NOS
Tsunami

Excludes: *tidal wave caused by tropical storm (E908.0)*

E909.8 Other cataclysmic earth surface movements and eruptions

E909.9 Unspecified cataclysmic earth surface movements and eruptions

ACCIDENTS CAUSED BY SUBMERSION, SUFFOCATION, AND FOREIGN BODIES (E910-E915)

E910 Accidental drowning and submersion

Includes: immersion
swimmers' cramp

Excludes: *diving accident (NOS) (resulting in injury except drowning) (E883.0)*
diving with insufficient air supply (E913.2)
drowning and submersion due to:
cataclysm (E908-E909)
machinery accident (E919.0-E919.9)
transport accident (E800.0-E845.9)
effect of high and low air pressure (E902.2)
injury from striking against objects while in running water (E917.2)

E910.0 While water-skiing

Fall from water skis with submersion or drowning

Excludes: *accident to water-skier involving a watercraft and resulting in submersion or other injury (E830.4, E831.4)*

E910.1 While engaged in other sport or recreational activity with diving equipment

Scuba diving NOS
Skin diving NOS
Underwater spear fishing NOS

E910.2 While engaged in other sport or recreational activity without diving equipment

Fishing or hunting, except from boat or with diving equipment
Ice skating
Playing in water
Surfboarding
Swimming NOS
Voluntarily jumping from boat, not involved in accident, for swim NOS
Wading in water

Excludes: *jumping into water to rescue another person (E910.3)*

E910.3 While swimming or diving for purposes other than recreation or sport

Marine salvage
Pearl diving
Placement of fishing nets
Rescue (attempt) of another person
Underwater construction or repairs
} (with diving equipment)

E910.4 In bathtub

E910.8 Other accidental drowning or submersion

Drowning in:
quenching tank
swimming pool

E910.9 Unspecified accidental drowning or submersion

Accidental fall into water NOS
Drowning NOS

E911 Inhalation and ingestion of food causing obstruction of respiratory tract or suffocation

Aspiration and inhalation of food [any] (into respiratory tract) NOS
Asphyxia by
Choked on
Suffocation by
} food [including bone, seed in food, regurgitated food]
Compression of trachea
Interruption of respiration
Obstruction of respiration
} by food lodged in esophagus
Obstruction of pharynx by food (bolus)

Excludes: *injury, except asphyxia and obstruction of respiratory passage, caused by food (E915)*
obstruction of esophagus by food without mention of asphyxia or obstruction of respiratory passage (E915)

E912 Inhalation and ingestion of other object causing obstruction of respiratory tract or suffocation

Aspiration and inhalation of foreign body except food (into respiratory tract) NOS
Foreign object [bean] [marble] in nose
Obstruction of pharynx by foreign body
Compression
Interruption of respiration
Obstruction of respiration
} by foreign body in esophagus

Excludes: *injury, except asphyxia and obstruction of respiratory passage, caused by foreign body (E915)*
obstruction of esophagus by foreign body without mention of asphyxia or obstruction in respiratory passage (E915)

E913 Accidental mechanical suffocation

Excludes: *mechanical suffocation from or by:*
accidental inhalation or ingestion of:
food (E911)
foreign object (E912)
cataclysm (E908-E909)
explosion (E921.0-E921.9, E923.0-E923.9)
machinery accident (E919.0-E919.9)

E913.0 In bed or cradle

Excludes: *suffocation by plastic bag (E913.1)*

E913.1 By plastic bag

E913.2 Due to lack of air (in closed place)

Accidentally closed up in refrigerator or other airtight enclosed space
Diving with insufficient air supply

Excludes: *suffocation by plastic bag (E913.1)*

E913.3 By falling earth or other substance

Cave-in NOS

Excludes: *cave-in caused by cataclysmic earth surface movements and eruptions (E909)*
struck by cave-in without asphyxiation or suffocation (E916)

E913.8 Other specified means

Accidental hanging, except in bed or cradle

E913.9 Unspecified means

Asphyxia, mechanical NOS
Strangulation NOS
Suffocation NOS

E914 Foreign body accidentally entering eye and adnexa

Excludes: *corrosive liquid (E924.1)*

E915 Foreign body accidentally entering other orifice

Excludes: *aspiration and inhalation of foreign body, any, (into respiratory tract) NOS (E911-E912)*

OTHER ACCIDENTS (E916-E928)

E916 Struck accidentally by falling object

Collapse of building, except on fire
Falling:
- rock
- snowslide NOS
- stone
- tree

Object falling from:
- machine, not in operation
- stationary vehicle

Code first:
- collapse of building on fire (E890.0-E891.9)
- falling object in:
  - cataclysm (E908-E909)
  - machinery accidents (E919.0-E919.9)
  - transport accidents (E800.0-E845.9)
  - vehicle accidents not elsewhere classifiable (E846-E848)
- object set in motion by:
  - explosion (E921.0-E921.9, E923.0-E923.9)
  - firearm (E922.0-E922.9)
- projected object (E917.0-E917.9)

E917 Striking against or struck accidentally by objects or persons

Includes: bumping into or against, colliding with, kicking against, stepping on, struck by — object (moving) (projected) (stationary), pedestrian conveyance, person

Excludes: *fall from:*
- *bumping into or against object (E888)*
- *collision with another person, except when caused by a crowd (E886.0-E886.9)*
- *stumbling over object (E885)*

injury caused by:
- *assault (E960.0-E960.1, E967.0-E967.9)*
- *cutting or piercing instrument (E920.0-E920.9)*
- *explosion (E921.0-E921.9, E923.0-E923.9)*
- *firearm (E922.0-E922.9)*
- *machinery (E919.0-E919.9)*
- *transport vehicle (E800.0-E845.9)*
- *vehicle not elsewhere classifiable (E846-E848)*

E917.0 In sports

Kicked or stepped on during game (football) (rugby)
Knocked down while boxing
Struck by hit or thrown ball
Struck by hockey stick or puck

E917.1 Caused by a crowd, by collective fear or panic

Crushed, Pushed, Stepped on — by crowd or human stampede

E917.2 In running water

Excludes: *drowning or submersion (E910.0-E910.9)*
that in sports (E917.0)

E917.9 Other

E918 Caught accidentally in or between objects

Caught, crushed, jammed, or pinched in or between moving or stationary objects, such as:
- escalator
- folding object
- hand tools, appliances, or implements
- sliding door and door frame
- under packing crate
- washing machine wringer

Excludes: *injury caused by:*
- *cutting or piercing instrument (E920.0-E920.9)*
- *machinery (E919.0-E919.9)*
- *transport vehicle (E800.0-E845.9)*
- *vehicle not elsewhere classifiable (E846-E848)*

struck accidentally by:
- *falling object (E916)*
- *object (moving) (projected) (E917.0-E917.9)*

E919 Accidents caused by machinery

Includes: burned by
caught in (moving parts of)
collapse of
crushed by
cut or pierced by
drowning or submersion caused by
explosion of, on, in
fall from or into moving part of
fire starting in or on
mechanical suffocation caused by
object falling from, on, in motion by
overturning of
pinned under
run over by
struck by
thrown from
} machinery (accident)

caught between machinery and other object
machinery accident NOS

Excludes: *accidents involving machinery, not in operation (E884.9, E916-E918)*
injury caused by:
electric current in connection with machinery (E925.0-E925.9)
escalator (E880.0, E918)
explosion of pressure vessel in connection with machinery (E921.0-E921.9)
moving sidewalk (E885)
powered hand tools, appliances, and implements (E916-E918, E920.0-E921.9, E923.0-E926.9)
transport vehicle accidents involving machinery (E800.0-E848.9)
poisoning by carbon monoxide generated by machine (E868.8)

E919.0 Agricultural machines

Animal-powered agricultural machine
Combine
Derrick, hay
Farm machinery NOS
Farm tractor
Harvester
Hay mower or rake
Reaper
Thresher

Excludes: *that in transport under own power on the highway (E810.0-E819.9)*
that being towed by another vehicle on the highway (E810.0-E819.9, E827.0-E827.9, E829.0-E829.9)
that involved in accident classifiable to E820-E829 (E820.0-E829.9)

E919.1 Mining and earth-drilling machinery

Bore or drill (land) (seabed)
Shaft hoist
Shaft lift
Under-cutter

Excludes: *coal car, tram, truck, and tub in mine (E846)*

E919.2 Lifting machines and appliances

Chain hoist
Crane
Derrick
Elevator (building) (grain)
Forklift truck
Lift
Pulley block
Winch
} except in agricultural or mining operations

Excludes: *that being towed by another vehicle on the highway (E810.0-E819.9, E827.0-E827.9, E829.0-E829.9)*
that in transport under own power on the highway (E810.0-E819.9)
that involved in accident classifiable to E820-E829 (E820.0-E829.9)

E919.3 Metalworking machines

Abrasive wheel
Forging machine
Lathe
Mechanical shears
Metal:
drilling machine
milling machine
power press
rolling-mill
sawing machine

E919.4 Woodworking and forming machines

Band saw
Bench saw
Circular saw
Molding machine
Overhead plane
Powered saw
Radial saw
Sander

Excludes: *hand saw (E920.1)*

E919.5 Prime movers, except electrical motors

Gas turbine
Internal combustion engine
Steam engine
Water driven turbine

Excludes: *that being towed by other vehicle on the highway (E810.0-E819.9, E827.0-E827.9, E829.0-E829.9)*
that in transport under own power on the highway (E810.0-E819.9)

E919.6 Transmission machinery

Transmission:
belt
cable
chain
gear
Transmission:
pinion
pulley
shaft

E919.7 Earth moving, scraping, and other excavating machines

Bulldozer
Road scraper
Steam shovel

Excludes: *that being towed by other vehicle on the highway (E810.0-E819.9, E827.0-E827.9, E829.0-E829.9)*
that in transport under own power on the highway (E810.0-E819.9)

E919.8 Other specified machinery

Machines for manufacture of:
- clothing
- foodstuffs and beverages
- paper

Printing machine
Recreational machinery
Spinning, weaving, and textile machines

E919.9 Unspecified machinery

E920 Accidents caused by cutting and piercing instruments or objects

Includes: accidental injury by / fall on } object:
- edged
- pointed
- sharp

E920.0 Powered lawn mower

E920.1 Other powered hand tools

Any powered hand tool [compressed air] [electric] [explosive cartridge] [hydraulic power], such as:
- drill
- hand saw
- hedge clipper
- rivet gun
- snow blower
- staple gun

Excludes: *band saw (E919.4)*
bench saw (E919.4)

E920.2 Powered household appliances and implements

Blender
Electric:
- beater or mixer
- can opener
- fan

Electric:
- knife
- sewing machine

Garbage disposal appliance

E920.3 Knives, swords, and daggers

E920.4 Other hand tools and implements

Axe
Can opener NOS
Chisel
Fork
Hand saw
Hoe
Ice pick
Needle (sewing)
Paper cutter
Pitchfork
Rake
Scissors
Screwdriver
Sewing machine, not powered
Shovel

E920.5 Hypodermic needle

Contaminated needle
Needle stick

E920.8 Other specified cutting and piercing instruments or objects

Arrow
Broken glass
Dart
Edge of stiff paper
Lathe turnings
Nail
Plant thorn
Splinter
Tin can lid

Excludes: *animal spines or quills (E906.8)*
flying glass due to explosion (E921.0-E923.9)

E920.9 Unspecified cutting and piercing instrument or object

E921 Accident caused by explosion of pressure vessel

Includes: accidental explosion of pressure vessels, whether or not part of machinery

Excludes: *explosion of pressure vessel on transport vehicle (E800.0-E845.9)*

E921.0 Boilers

E921.1 Gas cylinders

Air tank
Pressure gas tank

E921.8 Other specified pressure vessels

Aerosol can
Automobile tire
Pressure cooker

E921.9 Unspecified pressure vessel

E922 Accident caused by firearm, and air gun missile

E922.0 Handgun

Pistol
Revolver

Excludes: *Verey pistol (E922.8)*

E922.1 Shotgun (automatic)

E922.2 Hunting rifle

E922.3 Military firearms

Army rifle
Machine gun

E922.4 Air gun

BB gun
Pellet gun

E922.8 Other specified firearm missile

Verey pistol [flare]

E922.9 Unspecified firearm missile

Gunshot wound NOS
Shot NOS

E923 Accident caused by explosive material

Includes: flash burns and other injuries resulting from explosion of explosive material
ignition of highly explosive material with explosion

Excludes: *explosion:*
in or on machinery (E919.0-E919.9)
on any transport vehicle, except stationary motor vehicle (E800.0-E848)
with conflagration (E890.0, E891.0, E892)
secondary fires resulting from explosion (E890.0-E899)

E923.0 Fireworks

E923.1 Blasting materials

Blasting cap
Detonator
Dynamite
Explosive [any] used in blasting operations

E923.2 Explosive gases

Acetylene
Butane
Coal gas
Explosion in mine NOS
Fire damp
Gasoline fumes
Methane
Propane

E923.8 Other explosive materials

Bomb
Explosive missile
Grenade
Mine
Shell
Torpedo
Explosion in munitions:
dump
factory

E923.9 Unspecified explosive material

Explosion NOS

E924 Accident caused by hot substance or object, caustic or corrosive material, and steam

Excludes: *burning NOS (E899)*
chemical burn resulting from swallowing a corrosive substance (E860.0-E864.4)
fire caused by these substances and objects (E890.0-E894)
radiation burns (E926.0-E926.9)
therapeutic misadventures (E870.0-E876.9)

E924.0 Hot liquids and vapors, including steam

Burning or scalding by:
boiling water
hot or boiling liquids not primarily caustic or corrosive
liquid metal
steam
other hot vapor

Excludes: *hot (boiling) tap water (E924.2)*

E924.1 Caustic and corrosive substances

Burning by:
acid [any kind]
ammonia
caustic oven cleaner or other substance
corrosive substance
lye
vitriol

E924.2 Hot (boiling) tap water

E924.8 Other

Burning by:
heat from electric heating appliance
hot object NOS
light bulb
steam pipe

E924.9 Unspecified

E925 Accident caused by electric current

Includes: electric current from exposed wire, faulty appliance, high voltage cable, live rail, or open electric socket as the cause of:
burn
cardiac fibrillation
convulsion
electric shock
electrocution
puncture wound
respiratory paralysis

Excludes: *burn by heat from electrical appliance (E924.8)*
lightning (E907)

E925.0 Domestic wiring and appliances

E925.1 Electric power generating plants, distribution stations, transmission lines

Broken power line

E925.2 Industrial wiring, appliances, and electrical machinery

Conductors
Control apparatus
Electrical equipment and machinery
Transformers

E925.8 Other electric current

Wiring and appliances in or on:
farm [not farmhouse]
outdoors
public building
Wiring and appliances in or on:
residential institutions
schools

E925.9 Unspecified electric current

Burns or other injury from electric current NOS
Electric shock NOS
Electrocution NOS

E926 Exposure to radiation

Excludes: *abnormal reaction to or complication of treatment without mention of misadventure (E879.2)*
atomic power plant malfunction in water transport (E838.0-E838.9)
misadventure to patient in surgical and medical procedures (E873.2-E873.3)
use of radiation in war operations (E996-E997.9)

E926.0 Radiofrequency radiation

Overexposure to: microwave radiation, radar radiation, radiofrequency, radiofrequency radiation [any] } from:
- high-powered radio and television transmitters
- industrial radiofrequency induction heaters
- radar installations

E926.1 Infra-red heaters and lamps

Exposure to infra-red radiation from heaters and lamps as the cause of:
- blistering
- burning
- charring
- inflammatory change

Excludes: *physical contact with heater or lamp (E924.8)*

E926.2 Visible and ultraviolet light sources

Arc lamps
Black light sources
Electrical welding arc
Oxygas welding torch
Sun rays

Excludes: *excessive heat from these sources (E900.1-E900.9)*

E926.3 X-rays and other electromagnetic ionizing radiation

Gamma rays
X-rays (hard) (soft)

E926.4 Lasers

E926.5 Radioactive isotopes

Radiobiologicals
Radiopharmaceuticals

E926.8 Other specified radiation

Artificially accelerated beams of ionized particles generated by:
- betatrons
- synchrotrons

E926.9 Unspecified radiation

Radiation NOS

E927 Overexertion and strenuous movements

Excessive physical exercise
Overexertion (from):
- lifting
- pulling
- pushing

Strenuous movements in:
- recreational activities
- other activities

E928 Other and unspecified environmental and accidental causes

E928.0 Prolonged stay in weightless environment

Weightlessness in spacecraft (simulator)

E928.1 Exposure to noise

Noise (pollution)
Sound waves
Supersonic waves

E928.2 Vibration

E928.8 Other

E928.9 Unspecified accident

Accident NOS
Blow NOS
Casualty (not due to war), Decapitation, Injury [any part of body, or unspecified], Killed, Knocked down, Mangled, Wound } stated as accidentally inflicted, but not otherwise specified

Excludes: *fracture, cause unspecified (E887)*
injuries undetermined whether accidentally or purposely inflicted (E980.0-E989)

LATE EFFECTS OF ACCIDENTAL INJURY (E929)

Note: This category is to be used to indicate accidental injury as the cause of death or disability from late effects, which are themselves classifiable elsewhere. The "late effects" include conditions reported as such, or as sequelae, which may occur at any time after the acute injury.

E929 Late effects of accidental injury

Excludes: *late effects of:*
surgical and medical procedures (E870.0-E879.9)
therapeutic use of drugs and medicines (E930.0-E949.9)

E929.0 Late effects of motor vehicle accident

Late effects of accidents classifiable to E810-E825

E929.1 Late effects of other transport accident

Late effects of accidents classifiable to E800-E807, E826-E838, E840-E848

E929.2 Late effects of accidental poisoning

Late effects of accidents classifiable to E850-E858, E860-E869

E929.3 Late effects of accidental fall

Late effects of accidents classifiable to E880-E888

E929.4 Late effects of accident caused by fire

Late effects of accidents classifiable to E890-E899

E929.5 Late effects of accident due to natural and environmental factors

Late effects of accidents classifiable to E900-E909

E929.8 Late effects of other accidents
Late effects of accidents classifiable to E910-E928.8

E929.9 Late effects of unspecified accident
Late effects of accidents classifiable to E928.9

DRUGS, MEDICINAL AND BIOLOGICAL SUBSTANCES CAUSING ADVERSE EFFECTS IN THERAPEUTIC USE (E930-E949)

Includes: correct drug properly administered in therapeutic or prophylactic dosage, as the cause of any adverse effect including allergic or hypersensitivity reactions

Excludes: *accidental overdose of drug and wrong drug given or taken in error (E850.0-E858.9)*
accidents in the technique of administration of drug or biological substance such as accidental puncture during injection, or contamination of drug (E870.0-E876.9)
administration with suicidal or homicidal intent or intent to harm, or in circumstances classifiable to E980-E989 (E950.0-E950.5, E962.0, E980.0-E980.5)

See Alphabetic Index for more complete list of specific drugs to be classified under the fourth-digit subdivisions. The American Hospital Formulary numbers can be used to classify new drugs listed by the American Hospital Formulary Service (AHFS). See Appendix C.

E930 Antibiotics

Excludes: *that used as eye, ear, nose, and throat [ENT], and local anti-infectives (E946.0-E946.9)*

E930.0 Penicillins
Natural
Synthetic
Semisynthetic, such as:
ampicillin
cloxacillin
nafcillin
oxacillin

E930.1 Antifungal antibiotics
Amphotericin B
Griseofulvin
Hachimycin [trichomycin]
Nystatin

E930.2 Chloramphenicol group
Chloramphenicol
Thiamphenicol

E930.3 Erythromycin and other macrolides
Oleandomycin
Spiramycin

E930.4 Tetracycline group
Doxycycline
Minocycline
Oxytetracycline

E930.5 Cephalosporin group
Cephalexin
Cephaloglycin
Cephaloridine
Cephalothin

E930.6 Antimycobacterial antibiotics
Cycloserine
Kanamycin
Rifampin
Streptomycin

E930.7 Antineoplastic antibiotics
Actinomycins, such as:
Bleomycin
Cactinomycin
Dactinomycin
Daunorubicin
Mitomycin

Excludes: *other antineoplastic drugs (E933.1)*

E930.8 Other specified antibiotics

E930.9 Unspecified antibiotic

E931 Other anti-infectives

Excludes: *ENT, and local anti-infectives (E946.0-E946.9)*

E931.0 Sulfonamides
Sulfadiazine
Sulfafurazole
Sulfamethoxazole

E931.1 Arsenical anti-infectives

E931.2 Heavy metal anti-infectives
Compounds of:
antimony
bismuth
Compounds of:
lead
mercury

Excludes: *mercurial diuretics (E944.0)*

E931.3 Quinoline and hydroxyquinoline derivatives
Chiniofon
Diiodohydroxyquin

Excludes: *antimalarial drugs (E931.4)*

E931.4 Antimalarials and drugs acting on other blood protozoa
Chloroquine phosphate
Cycloguanil
Primaquine
Proguanil [chloroguanide]
Pyrimethamine
Quinine (sulphate)

E931.5 Other antiprotozoal drugs
Emetine

E931.6 Anthelmintics
Hexylresorcinol
Male fern oleoresin
Piperazine
Thiabendazole

E931.7 Antiviral drugs
Methisazone

Excludes: *amantadine (E936.4)*
cytarabine (E933.1)
idoxuridine (E946.5)

E931.8 Other antimycobacterial drugs
Ethambutol
Ethionamide
Isoniazid
Para-aminosalicylic acid derivatives
Sulfones

E931.9 Other and unspecified anti-infectives
Flucytosine
Nitrofuran derivatives

E932 Hormones and synthetic substitutes

E932.0 Adrenal cortical steroids
Cortisone derivatives
Desoxycorticosterone derivatives
Fluorinated corticosteroids

E932.1 Androgens and anabolic congeners
Nandrolone phenpropionate
Oxymetholone
Testosterone and preparations

E932.2 Ovarian hormones and synthetic substitutes
Contraceptives, oral
Estrogens
Estrogens and progestogens combined
Progestogens

E932.3 Insulins and antidiabetic agents
Acetohexamide
Biguanide derivatives, oral
Chlorpropamide
Glucagon
Insulin
Phenformin
Sulfonylurea derivatives, oral
Tolbutamide

Excludes: *adverse effect of insulin administered for shock therapy (E879.3)*

E932.4 Anterior pituitary hormones
Corticotropin
Gonadotropin
Somatotropin [growth hormone]

E932.5 Posterior pituitary hormones
Vasopressin

Excludes: *oxytocic agents (E945.0)*

E932.6 Parathyroid and parathyroid derivatives

E932.7 Thyroid and thyroid derivatives
Dextrothyroxine
Levothyroxine sodium
Liothyronine
Thyroglobulin

E932.8 Antithyroid agents
Iodides
Thiouracil
Thiourea

E932.9 Other and unspecified hormones and synthetic substitutes

E933 Primarily systemic agents

E933.0 Antiallergic and antiemetic drugs
Antihistamines
Chlorpheniramine
Diphenhydramine
Diphenylpyraline
Thonzylamine
Tripelennamine

Excludes: *phenothiazine-based tranquilizers (E939.1)*

E933.1 Antineoplastic and immunosuppressive drugs
Azathioprine
Busulfan
Chlorambucil
Cyclophosphamide
Cytarabine
Fluorouracil
Mechlorethamine hydrochloride
Mercaptopurine
Triethylenethiophosphoramide [thio-TEPA]

Excludes: *antineoplastic antibiotics (E930.7)*

E933.2 Acidifying agents

E933.3 Alkalizing agents

E933.4 Enzymes, not elsewhere classified
Penicillinase

E933.5 Vitamins, not elsewhere classified
Vitamin A
Vitamin D

Excludes: *nicotinic acid (E942.2)*
vitamin K (E934.3)

E933.8 Other systemic agents, not elsewhere classified
Heavy metal antagonists

E933.9 Unspecified systemic agent

E934 Agents primarily affecting blood constituents

E934.0 Iron and its compounds
Ferric salts
Ferrous sulphate and other ferrous salts

E934.1 Liver preparations and other antianemic agents
Folic acid

E934.2 Anticoagulants
Coumarin
Heparin
Phenindione
Prothrombin synthesis inhibitor
Warfarin sodium

E934.3 Vitamin K [phytonadione]

E934.4 Fibrinolysis-affecting drugs
Aminocaproic acid
Streptodornase
Streptokinase
Urokinase

E934.5 Anticoagulant antagonists and other coagulants
Hexadimethrine bromide
Protamine sulfate

E934.6 Gamma globulin

E934.7 Natural blood and blood products
Blood plasma
Human fibrinogen
Packed red cells
Whole blood

E934.8 Other agents affecting blood constituents
Macromolecular blood substitutes

E934.9 Unspecified agent affecting blood constituents

E935 Analgesics, antipyretics, and antirheumatics

E935.0 Heroin
Diacetylmorphine

☐ **E935.1 Methadone**

☐ **E935.2 Other opiates and related narcotics**
Codeine [methylmorphine]
Morphine
Opium (alkaloids)
Meperidine [pethidine]

☐ **E935.3 Salicylates**
Acetylsalicylic acid [aspirin]
Amino derivatives of salicylic acid
Salicylic acid salts

☐ **E935.4 Aromatic analgesics, not elsewhere classified**
Acetanilid
Paracetamol [acetaminophen]
Phenacetin [acetophenetidin]

☐ **E935.5 Pyrazole derivatives**
Aminophenazone [aminopyrine]
Phenylbutazone

☐ **E935.6 Antirheumatics [antiphlogistics]**
Gold salts
Indomethacin

Excludes: *salicylates (E935.3)*
steroids (E932.0)

☐ **E935.7 Other non-narcotic analgesics**
Pyrabital

E935.8 Other specified analgesics and antipyretics
Pentazocine

E935.9 Unspecified analgesic and antipyretic

E936 Anticonvulsants and anti-Parkinsonism drugs

E936.0 Oxazolidine derivatives
Paramethadione
Trimethadione

E936.1 Hydantoin derivatives
Phenytoin

E936.2 Succinimides
Ethosuximide
Phensuximide

E936.3 Other and unspecified anticonvulsants
Beclamide
Primidone

E936.4 Anti-Parkinsonism drugs
Amantadine
Ethopropazine [profenamine]
Levodopa [L-dopa]

E937 Sedatives and hypnotics

E937.0 Barbiturates
Amobarbital [amylobarbitone]
Barbital [barbitone]
Butabarbital [butabarbitone]
Pentobarbital [pentobarbitone]
Phenobarbital [phenobarbitone]
Secobarbital [quinalbarbitone]

Excludes: *thiobarbiturates (E938.3)*

E937.1 Chloral hydrate group

E937.2 Paraldehyde

E937.3 Bromine compounds
Bromide
Carbromal (derivatives)

E937.4 Methaqualone compounds

E937.5 Glutethimide group

E937.6 Mixed sedatives, not elsewhere classified

E937.8 Other sedatives and hypnotics

E937.9 Unspecified
Sleeping:
drug } NOS
pill } NOS
tablet } NOS

E938 Other central nervous system depressants and anesthetics

E938.0 Central nervous system muscle-tone depressants
Chlorphenesin (carbamate)
Mephenesin
Methocarbamol

E938.1 Halothane

E938.2 Other gaseous anesthetics
Ether
Halogenated hydrocarbon derivatives, except halothane
Nitrous oxide

E938.3 Intravenous anesthetics
Ketamine
Methohexital [methohexitone]
Thiobarbiturates, such as thiopental sodium

E938.4 Other and unspecified general anesthetics

E938.5 Surface and infiltration anesthetics
Cocaine
Lidocaine [lignocaine]
Procaine
Tetracaine

E938.6 Peripheral nerve- and plexus-blocking anesthetics

E938.7 Spinal anesthetics

E938.9 Other and unspecified local anesthetics

E939 Psychotropic agents

E939.0 Antidepressants
Amitriptyline
Imipramine
Monoamine oxidase [MAO] inhibitors

E939.1 Phenothiazine-based tranquilizers
Chlorpromazine
Fluphenazine
Phenothiazine
Prochlorperazine
Promazine

E939.2 Butyrophenone-based tranquilizers
Haloperidol
Spiperone
Trifluperidol

E939.3 Other antipsychotics, neuroleptics, and major tranquilizers

E939.4 Benzodiazepine-based tranquilizers
Chlordiazepoxide
Diazepam
Flurazepam
Lorazepam
Medazepam
Nitrazepam

E939.5 Other tranquilizers
Hydroxyzine
Meprobamate

E939.6 Psychodysleptics [hallucinogens]
Cannabis (derivatives)
Lysergide [LSD]
Marihuana (derivatives)
Mescaline
Psilocin
Psilocybin

E939.7 Psychostimulants
Amphetamine
Caffeine

Excludes: *central appetite depressants (E947.0)*

E939.8 Other psychotropic agents

E939.9 Unspecified psychotropic agent

E940 Central nervous system stimulants

E940.0 Analeptics
Lobeline
Nikethamide

E940.1 Opiate antagonists
Levallorphan
Nalorphine
Naloxone

E940.8 Other specified central nervous system stimulants

E940.9 Unspecified central nervous system stimulant

E941 Drugs primarily affecting the autonomic nervous system

E941.0 Parasympathomimetics [cholinergics]
Acetylcholine
Anticholinesterase:
organophosphorus
reversible
Pilocarpine

E941.1 Parasympatholytics [anticholinergics and antimuscarinics] and spasmolytics
Atropine
Homatropine
Hyoscine [scopolamine]
Quaternary ammonium derivatives

Excludes: *papaverine (E942.5)*

E941.2 Sympathomimetics [adrenergics]
Epinephrine [adrenalin]
Levarterenol [noradrenalin]

E941.3 Sympatholytics [antiadrenergics]
Phenoxybenzamine
Tolazoline hydrochloride

E941.9 Unspecified drug primarily affecting the autonomic nervous system

E942 Agents primarily affecting the cardiovascular system

E942.0 Cardiac rhythm regulators
Practolol
Procainamide
Propranolol
Quinidine

E942.1 Cardiotonic glycosides and drugs of similar action
Digitalis glycosides
Digoxin
Strophanthins

E942.2 Antilipemic and antiarteriosclerotic drugs
Cholestyramine
Clofibrate
Nicotinic acid derivatives
Sitosterols

Excludes: *dextrothyroxine (E932.7)*

E942.3 Ganglion-blocking agents
Pentamethonium bromide

E942.4 Coronary vasodilators
Dipyridamole
Nitrates [nitroglycerin]
Nitrites
Prenylamine

E942.5 Other vasodilators
Cyclandelate
Diazoxide
Hydralazine
Papaverine

E942.6 Other antihypertensive agents
Clonidine
Guanethidine
Rauwolfia alkaloids
Reserpine

E942.7 Antivaricose drugs, including sclerosing agents
Monoethanolamine
Zinc salts

E942.8 Capillary-active drugs
Adrenochrome derivatives
Bioflavonoids
Metaraminol

E942.9 Other and unspecified agents primarily affecting the cardiovascular system

E943 Agents primarily affecting gastrointestinal system

E943.0 Antacids and antigastric secretion drugs
Aluminum hydroxide
Magnesium trisilicate

E943.1 Irritant cathartics
Bisacodyl
Castor oil
Phenolphthalein

E943.2 Emollient cathartics
Sodium dioctyl sulfosuccinate

E943.3 Other cathartics, including intestinal atonia drugs
Magnesium sulfate

E943.4 Digestants
Pancreatin
Papain
Pepsin

E943.5 Antidiarrheal drugs
Bismuth subcarbonate
Kaolin
Pectin

Excludes: *anti-infectives (E930.0-E931.9)*

E943.6 Emetics

E943.8 Other specified agents primarily affecting the gastrointestinal system

E943.9 Unspecified agent primarily affecting the gastrointestinal system

E944 Water, mineral, and uric acid metabolism drugs

E944.0 Mercurial diuretics
Chlormerodrin
Mercaptomerin
Mercurophylline
Mersalyl

E944.1 Purine derivative diuretics
Theobromine
Theophylline

Excludes: *aminophylline [theophylline ethylenediamine] (E945.7)*

E944.2 Carbonic acid anhydrase inhibitors
Acetazolamide

E944.3 Saluretics
Benzothiadiazides
Chlorothiazide group

E944.4 Other diuretics
Ethacrynic acid
Furosemide

E944.5 Electrolytic, caloric, and water-balance agents

E944.6 Other mineral salts, not elsewhere classified

E944.7 Uric acid metabolism drugs
Cinchophen and congeners
Colchicine
Phenoquin
Probenecid

E945 Agents primarily acting on the smooth and skeletal muscles and respiratory system

E945.0 Oxytocic agents
Ergot alkaloids
Prostaglandins

E945.1 Smooth muscle relaxants
Adiphenine
Metaproterenol [orciprenaline]

Excludes: *papaverine (E942.5)*

E945.2 Skeletal muscle relaxants
Alcuronium chloride
Suxamethonium chloride

E945.3 Other and unspecified drugs acting on muscles

E945.4 Antitussives
Dextromethorphan
Pipazethate hydrochloride

E945.5 Expectorants
Acetylcysteine
Cocillana
Guaifenesin [glyceryl guaiacolate]
Ipecacuanha
Terpin hydrate

E945.6 Anti-common cold drugs

E945.7 Antiasthmatics
Aminophylline [theophylline ethylenediamine]

E945.8 Other and unspecified respiratory drugs

E946 Agents primarily affecting skin and mucous membrane, ophthalmological, otorhinolaryngological, and dental drugs

E946.0 Local anti-infectives and anti-inflammatory drugs

E946.1 Antipruritics

E946.2 Local astringents and local detergents

E946.3 Emollients, demulcents, and protectants

E946.4 Keratolytics, keratoplastics, other hair treatment drugs and preparations

E946.5 Eye anti-infectives and other eye drugs
Idoxuridine

E946.6 Anti-infectives and other drugs and preparations for ear, nose, and throat

E946.7 Dental drugs topically applied

E946.8 Other agents primarily affecting skin and mucous membrane
Spermicides

E946.9 Unspecified agent primarily affecting skin and mucous membrane

E947 Other and unspecified drugs and medicinal substances

E947.0 Dietetics

E947.1 Lipotropic drugs

E947.2 Antidotes and chelating agents, not elsewhere classified

E947.3 Alcohol deterrents

E947.4 Pharmaceutical excipients

E947.8 Other drugs and medicinal substances
Contrast media used for diagnostic x-ray procedures
Diagnostic agents and kits

E947.9 Unspecified drug or medicinal substance

E948 Bacterial vaccines

E948.0 BCG vaccine

E948.1 Typhoid and paratyphoid

E948.2 Cholera

E948.3 Plague

E948.4 Tetanus

E948.5 Diphtheria

E948.6 Pertussis vaccine, including combinations with a pertussis component

E948.8 Other and unspecified bacterial vaccines

E948.9 Mixed bacterial vaccines, except combinations with a pertussis component

E949 Other vaccines and biological substances

Excludes: *gamma globulin (E934.6)*

E949.0 Smallpox vaccine

E949.1 Rabies vaccine

E949.2 Typhus vaccine

E949.3 Yellow fever vaccine

E949.4 Measles vaccine

E949.5 Poliomyelitis vaccine

E949.6 Other and unspecified viral and rickettsial vaccines
Mumps vaccine

E949.7 Mixed viral-rickettsial and bacterial vaccines, except combinations with a pertussis component

Excludes: *combinations with a pertussis component (E948.6)*

E949.9 Other and unspecified vaccines and biological substances

SUICIDE AND SELF-INFLICTED INJURY (E950-E959)

Includes: injuries in suicide and attempted suicide
self-inflicted injuries specified as intentional

E950 Suicide and self-inflicted poisoning by solid or liquid substances

E950.0 Analgesics, antipyretics, and antirheumatics

E950.1 Barbiturates

E950.2 Other sedatives and hypnotics

E950.3 Tranquilizers and other psychotropic agents

E950.4 Other specified drugs and medicinal substances

E950.5 Unspecified drug or medicinal substance

E950.6 Agricultural and horticultural chemical and pharmaceutical preparations other than plant foods and fertilizers

E950.7 Corrosive and caustic substances
Suicide and self-inflicted poisoning by substances classifiable to E864

E950.8 Arsenic and its compounds

E950.9 Other and unspecified solid and liquid substances

E951 Suicide and self-inflicted poisoning by gases in domestic use

E951.0 Gas distributed by pipeline

E951.1 Liquefied petroleum gas distributed in mobile containers

E951.8 Other utility gas

E952 Suicide and self-inflicted poisoning by other gases and vapors

E952.0 Motor vehicle exhaust gas

E952.1 Other carbon monoxide

E952.8 Other specified gases and vapors

E952.9 Unspecified gases and vapors

E953 Suicide and self-inflicted injury by hanging, strangulation, and suffocation

E953.0 Hanging

E953.1 Suffocation by plastic bag

E953.8 Other specified means

E953.9 Unspecified means

E954 Suicide and self-inflicted injury by submersion [drowning]

E955 Suicide and self-inflicted injury by firearms, air guns and explosives

E955.0 Handgun

E955.1 Shotgun

E955.2 Hunting rifle

E955.3 Military firearms

E955.4 Other and unspecified firearm
Gunshot NOS   Shot NOS

E955.5 Explosives

E955.6 Air gun
BB gun   Pellet gun

E955.9 Unspecified

E956 Suicide and self-inflicted injury by cutting and piercing instrument

E957 Suicide and self-inflicted injuries by jumping from high place

E957.0 Residential premises

E957.1 Other man-made structures

E957.2 Natural sites

E957.9 Unspecified

E958 Suicide and self-inflicted injury by other and unspecified means

E958.0 Jumping or lying before moving object

E958.1 Burns, fire

E958.2 Scald

E958.3 Extremes of cold

E958.4 Electrocution

E958.5 Crashing of motor vehicle

E958.6 Crashing of aircraft

E958.7 Caustic substances, except poisoning

Excludes: *poisoning by caustic substance (E950.7)*

E958.8 Other specified means

E958.9 Unspecified means

E959 Late effects of self-inflicted injury

Note: This category is to be used to indicate circumstances classifiable to E950-E958 as the cause of death or disability from late effects, which are themselves classifiable elsewhere. The "late effects" include conditions reported as such, or as sequelae, which may occur at any time after the attempted suicide or self-inflicted injury.

HOMICIDE AND INJURY PURPOSELY INFLICTED BY OTHER PERSONS (E960-E969)

Includes: injuries inflicted by another person with intent to injure or kill, by any means

Excludes: *injuries due to:*
legal intervention (E970-E978)
operations of war (E990-E999)

E960 Fight, brawl, rape

E960.0 Unarmed fight or brawl

Beatings NOS
Brawl or fight with hands, fists, feet
Injured or killed in fight NOS

Excludes: *homicidal:*
injury by weapons (E965.0-E966, E969)
strangulation (E963)
submersion (E964)

E960.1 Rape

E961 Assault by corrosive or caustic substance, except poisoning

Injury or death purposely caused by corrosive or caustic substance, such as:
acid [any]
corrosive substance
vitriol

Excludes: *burns from hot liquid (E968.3)*
chemical burns from swallowing a corrosive substance (E962.0-E962.9)

E962 Assault by poisoning

E962.0 Drugs and medicinal substances

Homicidal poisoning by any drug or medicinal substance

E962.1 Other solid and liquid substances

E962.2 Other gases and vapors

E962.9 Unspecified poisoning

E963 Assault by hanging and strangulation

Homicidal (attempt):
garrotting or ligature
hanging
strangulation
suffocation

E964 Assault by submersion [drowning]

E965 Assault by firearms and explosives

E965.0 Handgun

Pistol
Revolver

E965.1 Shotgun

E965.2 Hunting rifle

E965.3 Military firearms

E965.4 Other and unspecified firearm

E965.5 Antipersonnel bomb

E965.6 Gasoline bomb

E965.7 Letter bomb

E965.8 Other specified explosive

Bomb NOS (placed in):
car
house
Dynamite

E965.9 Unspecified explosive

E966 Assault by cutting and piercing instrument

Assassination (attempt), homicide (attempt) by any instrument classifiable under E920
Homicidal:
cut, puncture, stab } any part of body
Stabbed

E967 Child and adult battering and other maltreatment

E967.0 By father or stepfather

E967.1 By other specified person

E967.2 By mother or stepmother

E967.3 By spouse or partner

Ex-spouse
Ex-partner

E967.4 By child

E967.5 By sibling

E967.6 By grandparent

E967.7 By other relative

E967.8 By non-related caregiver

E967.9 By unspecified person

E968 Assault by other and unspecified means

E968.0 Fire

Arson
Homicidal burns NOS

Excludes: *burns from hot liquid (E968.3)*

E968.1 Pushing from a high place

E968.2 Striking by blunt or thrown object

E968.3 Hot liquid

Homicidal burns by scalding

E968.4 Criminal neglect

Abandonment of child, infant, or other helpless person with intent to injure or kill

E968.5 Transport vehicle

Being struck by other vehicle or run down with intent to injure
Pushed in front of, thrown from, or dragged by moving vehicle with intent to injure

E968.6 Air gun

BB gun
Pellet gun

E968.8 Other specified means

Bite of human being

E968.9 Unspecified means

Assassination (attempt) NOS
Homicidal (attempt):
  injury NOS
  wound NOS
Manslaughter (nonaccidental)
Murder (attempt) NOS
Violence, non-accidental

E969 Late effects of injury purposely inflicted by other person

Note: This category is to be used to indicate circumstances classifiable to E960-E968 as the cause of death or disability from late effects, which are themselves classifiable elsewhere. The "late effects" include conditions reported as such, or as sequelae, which may occur at any time after the acute injury.

LEGAL INTERVENTION (E970-E978)

Includes: injuries inflicted by the police or other law-enforcing agents, including military on duty, in the course of arresting or attempting to arrest lawbreakers, suppressing disturbances, maintaining order, and other legal action
legal execution

Excludes: *injuries caused by civil insurrections (E990.0-E999)*

E970 Injury due to legal intervention by firearms

Gunshot wound
Injury by:
  machine gun
  revolver
Injury by:
  rifle pellet or rubber bullet
  shot NOS

E971 Injury due to legal intervention by explosives

Injury by:
  dynamite
  explosive shell
Injury by:
  grenade
  mortar bomb

E972 Injury due to legal intervention by gas

Asphyxiation by gas
Injury by tear gas
Poisoning by gas

E973 Injury due to legal intervention by blunt object

Hit, struck by:
  baton (nightstick)
  blunt object
  stave

E974 Injury due to legal intervention by cutting and piercing instrument

Cut
Incised wound
Injured by bayonet
Stab wound

E975 Injury due to legal intervention by other specified means

Blow
Manhandling

E976 Injury due to legal intervention by unspecified means

E977 Late effects of injuries due to legal intervention

Note: This category is to be used to indicate circumstances classifiable to E970-E976 as the cause of death or disability from late effects, which are themselves classifiable elsewhere. The "late effects" include conditions reported as such, or as sequelae, which may occur at any time after the acute injury due to legal intervention.

E978 Legal execution

All executions performed at the behest of the judiciary or ruling authority [whether permanent or temporary] as:
asphyxiation by gas
beheading, decapitation (by guillotine)
capital punishment
electrocution
hanging
poisoning
shooting
other specified means

INJURY UNDETERMINED WHETHER ACCIDENTALLY OR PURPOSELY INFLICTED (E980-E989)

Note: Categories E980-E989 are for use when it is unspecified or it cannot be determined whether the injuries are accidental (unintentional), suicide (attempted), or assault.

E980 Poisoning by solid or liquid substances, undetermined whether accidentally or purposely inflicted

E980.0 Analgesics, antipyretics, and antirheumatics

E980.1 Barbiturates

E980.2 Other sedatives and hypnotics

E980.3 Tranquilizers and other psychotropic agents

E980.4 Other specified drugs and medicinal substances

E980.5 Unspecified drug or medicinal substance

E980.6 Corrosive and caustic substances

Poisoning, undetermined whether accidental or purposeful, by substances classifiable to E864

E980.7 Agricultural and horticultural chemical and pharmaceutical preparations other than plant foods and fertilizers

E980.8 Arsenic and its compounds

E980.9 Other and unspecified solid and liquid substances

E981 Poisoning by gases in domestic use, undetermined whether accidentally or purposely inflicted

E981.0 Gas distributed by pipeline

E981.1 Liquefied petroleum gas distributed in mobile containers

E981.8 Other utility gas

E982 Poisoning by other gases, undetermined whether accidentally or purposely inflicted

E982.0 Motor vehicle exhaust gas

E982.1 Other carbon monoxide

E982.8 Other specified gases and vapors

E982.9 Unspecified gases and vapors

E983 Hanging, strangulation, or suffocation, undetermined whether accidentally, or purposely inflicted

E983.0 Hanging

E983.1 Suffocation by plastic bag

E983.8 Other specified means

E983.9 Unspecified means

E984 Submersion [drowning], undetermined whether accidentally or purposely inflicted

E985 Injury by firearms, air guns and explosives, undetermined whether accidentally, or purposely inflicted

E985.0 Handgun

E985.1 Shotgun

E985.2 Hunting rifle

E985.3 Military firearms

E985.4 Other and unspecified firearm

E985.5 Explosives

E985.6 Air gun
BB gun
Pellet gun

E986 Injury by cutting and piercing instruments, undetermined whether accidentally or purposely inflicted

E987 Falling from high place, undetermined whether accidentally or purposely inflicted

E987.0 Residential premises

E987.1 Other man-made structures

E987.2 Natural sites

E987.9 Unspecified site

E988 Injury by other and unspecified means, undetermined whether accidentally or purposely inflicted

E988.0 Jumping or lying before moving object

E988.1 Burns, fire

E988.2 Scald

E988.3 Extremes of cold

E988.4 Electrocution

E988.5 Crashing of motor vehicle

E988.6 Crashing of aircraft

E988.7 Caustic substances, except poisoning

E988.8 Other specified means

E988.9 Unspecified means

E989 Late effects of injury, undetermined whether accidentally or purposely inflicted

Note: This category is to be used to indicate circumstances classifiable to E980-E988 as the cause of death or disability from late effects, which are themselves classifiable elsewhere. The "late effects" include conditions reported as such, or as sequelae, which may occur at any time after the acute injury, undetermined whether accidentally or purposely inflicted.

INJURY RESULTING FROM OPERATIONS OF WAR (E990-E999)

Includes: injuries to military personnel and civilians caused by war and civil insurrections and occurring during the time of war and insurrection

Excludes: *accidents during training of military personnel, manufacture of war material and transport, unless attributable to enemy action*

E990 Injury due to war operations by fires and conflagrations

Includes: asphyxia, burns, or other injury originating from fire caused by a fire-producing device or indirectly by any conventional weapon

E990.0 From gasoline bomb

E990.9 From other and unspecified source

E991 Injury due to war operations by bullets and fragments

E991.0 Rubber bullets (rifle)

E991.1 Pellets (rifle)

E991.2 Other bullets

Bullet [any, except rubber bullets and pellets]
- carbine
- machine gun
- pistol
- rifle
- shotgun

E991.3 Antipersonnel bomb (fragments)

E991.9 Other and unspecified fragments

Fragments from:
- artillery shell
- bombs, except antipersonnel
- grenade
- guided missile

Fragments from:
- land mine
- rockets
- shell

Shrapnel

E992 Injury due to war operations by explosion of marine weapons

Depth charge
Marine mines
Mine NOS, at sea or in harbor
Sea-based artillery shell
Torpedo
Underwater blast

E993 Injury due to war operations by other explosion

Accidental explosion of munitions being used in war
Accidental explosion of own weapons
Air blast NOS
Blast NOS
Explosion NOS

Explosion of:
- artillery shell
- breech block
- cannon block
- mortar bomb

Injury by weapon burst

E994 Injury due to war operations by destruction of aircraft

Airplane:
- burned
- exploded
- shot down

Crushed by falling airplane

E995 Injury due to war operations by other and unspecified forms of conventional warfare

Battle wounds
Bayonet injury
Drowned in war operations

E996 Injury due to war operations by nuclear weapons

Blast effects
Exposure to ionizing radiation from nuclear weapons
Fireball effects
Heat
Other direct and secondary effects of nuclear weapons

E997 Injury due to war operations by other forms of unconventional warfare

E997.0 Lasers

E997.1 Biological warfare

E997.2 Gases, fumes, and chemicals

E997.8 Other specified forms of unconventional warfare

E997.9 Unspecified form of unconventional warfare

E998 Injury due to war operations but occurring after cessation of hostilities

Injuries due to operations of war but occurring after cessation of hostilities by any means classifiable under E990-E997
Injuries by explosion of bombs or mines placed in the course of operations of war, if the explosion occurred after cessation of hostilities

E999 Late effect of injury due to war operations

Note: This category is to be used to indicate circumstances classifiable to E990-E998 as the cause of death or disability from late effects, which are themselves classifiable elsewhere. The "late effects" include conditions reported as such, or as sequelae, which may occur at any time after the acute injury, resulting from operations of war.

MORPHOLOGY OF NEOPLASMS

The World Health Organization has published an adaptation of the International Classification of Diseases for oncology (ICD-O). It contains a coded nomenclature for the morphology of neoplasms, which is reproduced here for those who wish to use it in conjunction with Chapter 2 of the International Classification of Diseases, 9th Revision, Clinical Modification.

The morphology code numbers consist of five digits; the first four identify the histological type of the neoplasm and the fifth indicates its behavior. The one-digit behavior code is as follows:

/0 Benign

/1 Uncertain whether benign or malignant
Borderline malignancy

/2 Carcinoma in situ
Intraepithelial
Noninfiltrating
Noninvasive

/3 Malignant, primary site

/6 Malignant, metastatic site
Secondary site

/9 Malignant, uncertain whether primary or metastatic site

In the nomenclature below, the morphology code numbers include the behavior code appropriate to the histological type of neoplasm, but this behavior code should be changed if other reported information makes this necessary. For example, "chordoma (M9370/3)" is assumed to be malignant; the term "benign chordoma" should be coded M9370/0. Similarly, "superficial spreading adenocarcinoma (M8143/3)" described as "noninvasive" should be coded M8143/2 and "melanoma (M8720/3)" described as "secondary" should be coded M8720/6.

The following table shows the correspondence between the morphology code and the different sections of Chapter 2:

Morphology Code Histology/Behavior			ICD-9-CM Chapter 2
Any	0	210-229	Benign neoplasms
M8000-M8004	1	239	Neoplasms of unspecified nature
M8010+	1	235-238	Neoplasms of uncertain behavior
Any	2	230-234	Carcinoma in situ
Any	3	140-195 200-208	Malignant neoplasms, stated or presumed to be primary
Any	6	196-198	Malignant neoplasms, stated or presumed to be secondary

The ICD-O behavior digit /9 is inapplicable in an ICD context, since all malignant neoplasms are presumed to be primary (/3) or secondary (/6) according to other information on the medical record.

Only the first-listed term of the full ICD-O morphology nomenclature appears against each code number in the list below. The ICD-9-CM Alphabetical Index (Volume 2), however, includes all the ICD-O synonyms as well as a number of other morphological names still likely to be encountered on medical records but omitted from ICD-O as outdated or otherwise undesirable.

A coding difficulty sometimes arises where a morphological diagnosis contains two qualifying adjectives that have different code numbers. An example is "transitional cell epidermoid carcinoma." "Transitional cell carcinoma NOS" is M8120/3 and "epidermoid carcinoma NOS" is M8070/3. In such circumstances, the higher number (M8120/3 in this example) should be used, as it is usually more specific.

CODED NOMENCLATURE FOR MORPHOLOGY OF NEOPLASMS

M800 Neoplasms NOS

M8000/0 *Neoplasm, benign*
M8000/1 *Neoplasm, uncertain whether benign or malignant*
M8000/3 *Neoplasm, malignant*
M8000/6 *Neoplasm, metastatic*
M8000/9 *Neoplasm, malignant, uncertain whether primary or metastatic*
M8001/0 *Tumor cells, benign*
M8001/1 *Tumor cells, uncertain whether benign or malignant*
M8001/3 *Tumor cells, malignant*
M8002/3 *Malignant tumor, small cell type*
M8003/3 *Malignant tumor, giant cell type*
M8004/3 *Malignant tumor, fusiform cell type*

M801-M804 Epithelial neoplasms NOS

M8010/0 *Epithelial tumor, benign*
M8010/2 *Carcinoma in situ NOS*
M8010/3 *Carcinoma NOS*
M8010/6 *Carcinoma, metastatic NOS*
M8010/9 *Carcinomatosis*
M8011/0 *Epithelioma, benign*
M8011/3 *Epithelioma, malignant*
M8012/3 *Large cell carcinoma NOS*
M8020/3 *Carcinoma, undifferentiated type NOS*
M8021/3 *Carcinoma, anaplastic type NOS*
M8022/3 *Pleomorphic carcinoma*
M8030/3 *Giant cell and spindle cell carcinoma*
M8031/3 *Giant cell carcinoma*
M8032/3 *Spindle cell carcinoma*
M8033/3 *Pseudosarcomatous carcinoma*
M8034/3 *Polygonal cell carcinoma*
M8035/3 *Spheroidal cell carcinoma*
M8040/1 *Tumorlet*
M8041/3 *Small cell carcinoma NOS*
M8042/3 *Oat cell carcinoma*
M8043/3 *Small cell carcinoma, fusiform cell type*

M805-M808 Papillary and squamous cell neoplasms

M8050/0 *Papilloma NOS (except Papilloma of urinary bladder M8120/1)*
M8050/2 *Papillary carcinoma in situ*
M8050/3 *Papillary carcinoma NOS*
M8051/0 *Verrucous papilloma*
M8051/3 *Verrucous carcinoma NOS*
M8052/0 *Squamous cell papilloma*
M8052/3 *Papillary squamous cell carcinoma*
M8053/0 *Inverted papilloma*
M8060/0 *Papillomatosis NOS*
M8070/2 *Squamous cell carcinoma in situ NOS*
M8070/3 *Squamous cell carcinoma NOS*
M8070/6 *Squamous cell carcinoma, metastatic NOS*
M8071/3 *Squamous cell carcinoma, keratinizing type NOS*
M8072/3 *Squamous cell carcinoma, large cell, nonkeratinizing type*
M8073/3 *Squamous cell carcinoma, small cell, nonkeratinizing type*
M8074/3 *Squamous cell carcinoma, spindle cell type*
M8075/3 *Adenoid squamous cell carcinoma*
M8076/2 *Squamous cell carcinoma in situ with questionable stromal invasion*
M8076/3 *Squamous cell carcinoma, microinvasive*
M8080/2 *Queyrat's erythroplasia*
M8081/2 *Bowen's disease*
M8082/3 *Lymphoepithelial carcinoma*

M809-M811 Basal cell neoplasms

M8090/1 *Basal cell tumor*
M8090/3 *Basal cell carcinoma NOS*
M8091/3 *Multicentric basal cell carcinoma*
M8092/3 *Basal cell carcinoma, morphea type*
M8093/3 *Basal cell carcinoma, fibroepithelial type*
M8094/3 *Basosquamous carcinoma*
M8095/3 *Metatypical carcinoma*
M8096/0 *Intraepidermal epithelioma of Jadassohn*
M8100/0 *Trichoepithelioma*
M8101/0 *Trichofolliculoma*
M8102/0 *Tricholemmoma*
M8110/0 *Pilomatrixoma*

M812-M813 Transitional cell papillomas and carcinomas

M8120/0 *Transitional cell papilloma NOS*
M8120/1 *Urothelial papilloma*
M8120/2 *Transitional cell carcinoma in situ*
M8120/3 *Transitional cell carcinoma NOS*
M8121/0 *Schneiderian papilloma*
M8121/1 *Transitional cell papilloma, inverted type*
M8121/3 *Schneiderian carcinoma*
M8122/3 *Transitional cell carcinoma, spindle cell type*
M8123/3 *Basaloid carcinoma*
M8124/3 *Cloacogenic carcinoma*
M8130/3 *Papillary transitional cell carcinoma*

M814-M838 Adenomas and adenocarcinomas

M8140/0 *Adenoma NOS*
M8140/1 *Bronchial adenoma NOS*
M8140/2 *Adenocarcinoma in situ*

M8140/3	*Adenocarcinoma NOS*
M8140/6	*Adenocarcinoma, metastatic NOS*
M8141/3	*Scirrhous adenocarcinoma*
M8142/3	*Linitis plastica*
M8143/3	*Superficial spreading adenocarcinoma*
M8144/3	*Adenocarcinoma, intestinal type*
M8145/3	*Carcinoma, diffuse type*
M8146/0	*Monomorphic adenoma*
M8147/0	*Basal cell adenoma*
M8150/0	*Islet cell adenoma*
M8150/3	*Islet cell carcinoma*
M8151/0	*Insulinoma NOS*
M8151/3	*Insulinoma, malignant*
M8152/0	*Glucagonoma NOS*
M8152/3	*Glucagonoma, malignant*
M8153/1	*Gastrinoma NOS*
M8153/3	*Gastrinoma, malignant*
M8154/3	*Mixed islet cell and exocrine adenocarcinoma*
M8160/0	*Bile duct adenoma*
M8160/3	*Cholangiocarcinoma*
M8161/0	*Bile duct cystadenoma*
M8161/3	*Bile duct cystadenocarcinoma*
M8170/0	*Liver cell adenoma*
M8170/3	*Hepatocellular carcinoma NOS*
M8180/0	*Hepatocholangioma, benign*
M8180/3	*Combined hepatocellular carcinoma and cholangiocarcinoma*
M8190/0	*Trabecular adenoma*
M8190/3	*Trabecular adenocarcinoma*
M8191/0	*Embryonal adenoma*
M8200/0	*Eccrine dermal cylindroma*
M8200/3	*Adenoid cystic carcinoma*
M8201/3	*Cribriform carcinoma*
M8210/0	*Adenomatous polyp NOS*
M8210/3	*Adenocarcinoma in adenomatous polyp*
M8211/0	*Tubular adenoma NOS*
M8211/3	*Tubular adenocarcinoma*
M8220/0	*Adenomatous polyposis coli*
M8220/3	*Adenocarcinoma in adenomatous polyposis coli*
M8221/0	*Multiple adenomatous polyps*
M8230/3	*Solid carcinoma NOS*
M8231/3	*Carcinoma simplex*
M8240/1	*Carcinoid tumor NOS*
M8240/3	*Carcinoid tumor, malignant*
M8241/1	*Carcinoid tumor, argentaffin NOS*
M8241/3	*Carcinoid tumor, argentaffin, malignant*
M8242/1	*Carcinoid tumor, nonargentaffin NOS*
M8242/3	*Carcinoid tumor, nonargentaffin, malignant*
M8243/3	*Mucocarcinoid tumor, malignant*
M8244/3	*Composite carcinoid*
M8250/1	*Pulmonary adenomatosis*
M8250/3	*Bronchiolo-alveolar adenocarcinoma*
M8251/0	*Alveolar adenoma*
M8251/3	*Alveolar adenocarcinoma*
M8260/0	*Papillary adenoma NOS*
M8260/3	*Papillary adenocarcinoma NOS*
M8261/1	*Villous adenoma NOS*
M8261/3	*Adenocarcinoma in villous adenoma*
M8262/3	*Villous adenocarcinoma*
M8263/0	*Tubulovillous adenoma*
M8270/0	*Chromophobe adenoma*
M8270/3	*Chromophobe carcinoma*
M8280/0	*Acidophil adenoma*
M8280/3	*Acidophil carcinoma*
M8281/0	*Mixed acidophil-basophil adenoma*
M8281/3	*Mixed acidophil-basophil carcinoma*
M8290/0	*Oxyphilic adenoma*
M8290/3	*Oxyphilic adenocarcinoma*
M8300/0	*Basophil adenoma*
M8300/3	*Basophil carcinoma*
M8310/0	*Clear cell adenoma*
M8310/3	*Clear cell adenocarcinoma NOS*
M8311/1	*Hypernephroid tumor*
M8312/3	*Renal cell carcinoma*
M8313/0	*Clear cell adenofibroma*
M8320/3	*Granular cell carcinoma*
M8321/0	*Chief cell adenoma*
M8322/0	*Water-clear cell adenoma*
M8322/3	*Water-clear cell adenocarcinoma*
M8323/0	*Mixed cell adenoma*
M8323/3	*Mixed cell adenocarcinoma*
M8324/0	*Lipoadenoma*
M8330/0	*Follicular adenoma*
M8330/3	*Follicular adenocarcinoma NOS*
M8331/3	*Follicular adenocarcinoma, well-differentiated type*
M8332/3	*Follicular adenocarcinoma, trabecular type*
M8333/0	*Microfollicular adenoma*
M8334/0	*Macrofollicular adenoma*
M8340/3	*Papillary and follicular adenocarcinoma*
M8350/3	*Nonencapsulated sclerosing carcinoma*
M8360/1	*Multiple endocrine adenomas*
M8361/1	*Juxtaglomerular tumor*
M8370/0	*Adrenal cortical adenoma NOS*
M8370/3	*Adrenal cortical carcinoma*
M8371/0	*Adrenal cortical adenoma, compact cell type*
M8372/0	*Adrenal cortical adenoma, heavily pigmented variant*
M8373/0	*Adrenal cortical adenoma, clear cell type*
M8374/0	*Adrenal cortical adenoma, glomerulosa cell type*
M8375/0	*Adrenal cortical adenoma, mixed cell type*
M8380/0	*Endometrioid adenoma NOS*
M8380/1	*Endometrioid adenoma, borderline malignancy*
M8380/3	*Endometrioid carcinoma*
M8381/0	*Endometrioid adenofibroma NOS*
M8381/1	*Endometrioid adenofibroma, borderline malignancy*
M8381/3	*Endometrioid adenofibroma, malignant*

M839-M842 Adnexal and skin appendage neoplasms

M8390/0	*Skin appendage adenoma*
M8390/3	*Skin appendage carcinoma*
M8400/0	*Sweat gland adenoma*
M8400/1	*Sweat gland tumor NOS*
M8400/3	*Sweat gland adenocarcinoma*
M8401/0	*Apocrine adenoma*
M8401/3	*Apocrine adenocarcinoma*
M8402/0	*Eccrine acrospiroma*
M8403/0	*Eccrine spiradenoma*
M8404/0	*Hidrocystoma*
M8405/0	*Papillary hydradenoma*
M8406/0	*Papillary syringadenoma*
M8407/0	*Syringoma NOS*
M8410/0	*Sebaceous adenoma*
M8410/3	*Sebaceous adenocarcinoma*
M8420/0	*Ceruminous adenoma*
M8420/3	*Ceruminous adenocarcinoma*

M843 Mucoepidermoid neoplasms

M8430/1	*Mucoepidermoid tumor*
M8430/3	*Mucoepidermoid carcinoma*

M844-M849 Cystic, mucinous, and serous neoplasms

M8440/0	*Cystadenoma NOS*
M8440/3	*Cystadenocarcinoma NOS*
M8441/0	*Serous cystadenoma NOS*
M8441/1	*Serous cystadenoma, borderline malignancy*
M8441/3	*Serous cystadenocarcinoma NOS*
M8450/0	*Papillary cystadenoma NOS*
M8450/1	*Papillary cystadenoma, borderline malignancy*
M8450/3	*Papillary cystadenocarcinoma NOS*
M8460/0	*Papillary serous cystadenoma NOS*
M8460/1	*Papillary serous cystadenoma, borderline malignancy*
M8460/3	*Papillary serous cystadenocarcinoma*
M8461/0	*Serous surface papilloma NOS*
M8461/1	*Serous surface papilloma, borderline malignancy*
M8461/3	*Serous surface papillary carcinoma*
M8470/0	*Mucinous cystadenoma NOS*
M8470/1	*Mucinous cystadenoma, borderline malignancy*
M8470/3	*Mucinous cystadenocarcinoma NOS*
M8471/0	*Papillary mucinous cystadenoma NOS*
M8471/1	*Papillary mucinous cystadenoma, borderline malignancy*
M8471/3	*Papillary mucinous cystadenocarcinoma*
M8480/0	*Mucinous adenoma*
M8480/3	*Mucinous adenocarcinoma*
M8480/6	*Pseudomyxoma peritonei*
M8481/3	*Mucin-producing adenocarcinoma*
M8490/3	*Signet ring cell carcinoma*
M8490/6	*Metastatic signet ring cell carcinoma*

M850-M854 Ductal, lobular, and medullary neoplasms

M8500/2	*Intraductal carcinoma, noninfiltrating NOS*
M8500/3	*Infiltrating duct carcinoma*
M8501/2	*Comedocarcinoma, noninfiltrating*
M8501/3	*Comedocarcinoma NOS*

M8502/3 *Juvenile carcinoma of the breast*
M8503/0 *Intraductal papilloma*
M8503/2 *Noninfiltrating intraductal papillary adenocarcinoma*
M8504/0 *Intracystic papillary adenoma*
M8504/2 *Noninfiltrating intracystic carcinoma*
M8505/0 *Intraductal papillomatosis NOS*
M8506/0 *Subareolar duct papillomatosis*
M8510/3 *Medullary carcinoma NOS*
M8511/3 *Medullary carcinoma with amyloid stroma*
M8512/3 *Medullary carcinoma with lymphoid stroma*
M8520/2 *Lobular carcinoma in situ*
M8520/3 *Lobular carcinoma NOS*
M8521/3 *Infiltrating ductular carcinoma*
M8530/3 *Inflammatory carcinoma*
M8540/3 *Paget's disease, mammary*
M8541/3 *Paget's disease and infiltrating duct carcinoma of breast*
M8542/3 *Paget's disease, extramammary (except Paget's disease of bone)*

M855 Acinar cell neoplasms

M8550/0 *Acinar cell adenoma*
M8550/1 *Acinar cell tumor*
M8550/3 *Acinar cell carcinoma*

M856-M858 Complex epithelial neoplasms

M8560/3 *Adenosquamous carcinoma*
M8561/0 *Adenolymphoma*
M8570/3 *Adenocarcinoma with squamous metaplasia*
M8571/3 *Adenocarcinoma with cartilaginous and osseous metaplasia*
M8572/3 *Adenocarcinoma with spindle cell metaplasia*
M8573/3 *Adenocarcinoma with apocrine metaplasia*
M8580/0 *Thymoma, benign*
M8580/3 *Thymoma, malignant*

M859-M867 Specialized gonadal neoplasms

M8590/1 *Sex cord-stromal tumor*
M8600/0 *Thecoma NOS*
M8600/3 *Theca cell carcinoma*
M8610/0 *Luteoma NOS*
M8620/1 *Granulosa cell tumor NOS*
M8620/3 *Granulosa cell tumor, malignant*
M8621/1 *Granulosa cell-theca cell tumor*
M8630/0 *Androblastoma, benign*
M8630/1 *Androblastoma NOS*
M8630/3 *Androblastoma, malignant*
M8631/0 *Sertoli-Leydig cell tumor*
M8632/1 *Gynandroblastoma*
M8640/0 *Tubular androblastoma NOS*
M8640/3 *Sertoli cell carcinoma*
M8641/0 *Tubular androblastoma with lipid storage*
M8650/0 *Leydig cell tumor, benign*
M8650/1 *Leydig cell tumor NOS*
M8650/3 *Leydig cell tumor, malignant*
M8660/0 *Hilar cell tumor*
M8670/0 *Lipid cell tumor of ovary*
M8671/ *Adrenal rest tumor*

M868-M871 Paragangliomas and glomus tumors

M8680/1 *Paraganglioma NOS*
M8680/3 *Paraganglioma, malignant*
M8681/1 *Sympathetic paraganglioma*
M8682/1 *Parasympathetic paraganglioma*
M8690/1 *Glomus jugulare tumor*
M8691/1 *Aortic body tumor*
M8692/1 *Carotid body tumor*
M8693/1 *Extra-adrenal paraganglioma NOS*
M8693/3 *Extra-adrenal paraganglioma, malignant*
M8700/0 *Pheochromocytoma NOS*
M8700/3 *Pheochromocytoma, malignant*
M8710/3 *Glomangiosarcoma*
M8711/0 *Glomus tumor*
M8712/0 *Glomangioma*

M872-M879 Nevi and melanomas

M8720/0 *Pigmented nevus NOS*
M8720/3 *Malignant melanoma NOS*
M8721/3 *Nodular melanoma*
M8722/0 *Balloon cell nevus*
M8722/3 *Balloon cell melanoma*
M8723/0 *Halo nevus*
M8724/0 *Fibrous papule of the nose*
M8725/0 *Neuronevus*
M8726/0 *Magnocellular nevus*
M8730/0 *Nonpigmented nevus*
M8730/3 *Amelanotic melanoma*
M8740/0 *Junctional nevus*
M8740/3 *Malignant melanoma in junctional nevus*
M8741/2 *Precancerous melanosis NOS*
M8741/3 *Malignant melanoma in precancerous melanosis*
M8742/2 *Hutchinson's melanotic freckle*
M8742/3 *Malignant melanoma in Hutchinson's melanotic freckle*
M8743/3 *Superficial spreading melanoma*
M8750/0 *Intradermal nevus*
M8760/0 *Compound nevus*
M8761/1 *Giant pigmented nevus*
M8761/3 *Malignant melanoma in giant pigmented nevus*
M8770/0 *Epithelioid and spindle cell nevus*
M8771/3 *Epithelioid cell melanoma*
M8772/3 *Spindle cell melanoma NOS*
M8773/3 *Spindle cell melanoma, type A*
M8774/3 *Spindle cell melanoma, type B*
M8775/3 *Mixed epithelioid and spindle cell melanoma*
M8780/0 *Blue nevus NOS*
M8780/3 *Blue nevus, malignant*
M8790/0 *Cellular blue nevus*

M880 Soft tissue tumors and sarcomas NOS

M8800/0 *Soft tissue tumor, benign*
M8800/3 *Sarcoma NOS*
M8800/9 *Sarcomatosis NOS*
M8801/3 *Spindle cell sarcoma*
M8802/3 *Giant cell sarcoma (except of bone M9250/3)*
M8803/3 *Small cell sarcoma*
M8804/3 *Epithelioid cell sarcoma*

M881-M883 Fibromatous neoplasms

M8810/0 *Fibroma NOS*
M8810/3 *Fibrosarcoma NOS*
M8811/0 *Fibromyxoma*
M8811/3 *Fibromyxosarcoma*
M8812/0 *Periosteal fibroma*
M8812/3 *Periosteal fibrosarcoma*
M8813/0 *Fascial fibroma*
M8813/3 *Fascial fibrosarcoma*
M8814/3 *Infantile fibrosarcoma*
M8820/0 *Elastofibroma*
M8821/1 *Aggressive fibromatosis*
M8822/1 *Abdominal fibromatosis*
M8823/1 *Desmoplastic fibroma*
M8830/0 *Fibrous histiocytoma NOS*
M8830/1 *Atypical fibrous histiocytoma*
M8830/3 *Fibrous histiocytoma, malignant*
M8831/0 *Fibroxanthoma NOS*
M8831/1 *Atypical fibroxanthoma*
M8831/3 *Fibroxanthoma, malignant*
M8832/0 *Dermatofibroma NOS*
M8832/1 *Dermatofibroma protuberans*
M8832/3 *Dermatofibrosarcoma NOS*

M884 Myxomatous neoplasms

M8840/0 *Myxoma NOS*
M8840/3 *Myxosarcoma*

M885-M888 Lipomatous neoplasms

M8850/0 *Lipoma NOS*
M8850/3 *Liposarcoma NOS*
M8851/0 *Fibrolipoma*
M8851/3 *Liposarcoma, well-differentiated type*
M8852/0 *Fibromyxolipoma*
M8852/3 *Myxoid liposarcoma*
M8853/3 *Round cell liposarcoma*
M8854/3 *Pleomorphic liposarcoma*
M8855/3 *Mixed type liposarcoma*
M8856/0 *Intramuscular lipoma*
M8857/0 *Spindle cell lipoma*
M8860/0 *Angiomyolipoma*
M8860/3 *Angiomyoliposarcoma*
M8861/0 *Angiolipoma NOS*
M8861/1 *Angiolipoma, infiltrating*
M8870/0 *Myelolipoma*

M8880/0 *Hibernoma*
M8881/0 *Lipoblastomatosis*

M889-M892 Myomatous neoplasms

M8890/0 *Leiomyoma NOS*
M8890/1 *Intravascular leiomyomatosis*
M8890/3 *Leiomyosarcoma NOS*
M8891/1 *Epithelioid leiomyoma*
M8891/3 *Epithelioid leiomyosarcoma*
M8892/1 *Cellular leiomyoma*
M8893/0 *Bizarre leiomyoma*
M8894/0 *Angiomyoma*
M8894/3 *Angiomyosarcoma*
M8895/0 *Myoma*
M8895/3 *Myosarcoma*
M8900/0 *Rhabdomyoma NOS*
M8900/3 *Rhabdomyosarcoma NOS*
M8901/3 *Pleomorphic rhabdomyosarcoma*
M8902/3 *Mixed type rhabdomyosarcoma*
M8903/0 *Fetal rhabdomyoma*
M8904/0 *Adult rhabdomyoma*
M8910/3 *Embryonal rhabdomyosarcoma*
M8920/3 *Alveolar rhabdomyosarcoma*

M893-M899 Complex mixed and stromal neoplasms

M8930/3 *Endometrial stromal sarcoma*
M8931/1 *Endolymphatic stromal myosis*
M8932/0 *Adenomyoma*
M8940/0 *Pleomorphic adenoma*
M8940/3 *Mixed tumor, malignant NOS*
M8950/3 *Mullerian mixed tumor*
M8951/3 *Mesodermal mixed tumor*
M8960/1 *Mesoblastic nephroma*
M8960/3 *Nephroblastoma NOS*
M8961/3 *Epithelial nephroblastoma*
M8962/3 *Mesenchymal nephroblastoma*
M8970/3 *Hepatoblastoma*
M8980/3 *Carcinosarcoma NOS*
M8981/3 *Carcinosarcoma, embryonal type*
M8982/0 *Myoepithelioma*
M8990/0 *Mesenchymoma, benign*
M8990/1 *Mesenchymoma NOS*
M8990/3 *Mesenchymoma, malignant*
M8991/3 *Embryonal sarcoma*

M900-M903 Fibroepithelial neoplasms

M9000/0 *Brenner tumor NOS*
M9000/1 *Brenner tumor, borderline malignancy*
M9000/3 *Brenner tumor, malignant*
M9010/0 *Fibroadenoma NOS*
M9011/0 *Intracanalicular fibroadenoma NOS*
M9012/0 *Pericanalicular fibroadenoma*
M9013/0 *Adenofibroma NOS*
M9014/0 *Serous adenofibroma*
M9015/0 *Mucinous adenofibroma*
M9020/0 *Cellular intracanalicular fibroadenoma*
M9020/1 *Cystosarcoma phyllodes NOS*
M9020/3 *Cystosarcoma phyllodes, malignant*
M9030/0 *Juvenile fibroadenoma*

M904 Synovial neoplasms

M9040/0 *Synovioma, benign*
M9040/3 *Synovial sarcoma NOS*
M9041/3 *Synovial sarcoma, spindle cell type*
M9042/3 *Synovial sarcoma, epithelioid cell type*
M9043/3 *Synovial sarcoma, biphasic type*
M9044/3 *Clear cell sarcoma of tendons and aponeuroses*

M905 Mesothelial neoplasms

M9050/0 *Mesothelioma, benign*
M9050/3 *Mesothelioma, malignant*
M9051/0 *Fibrous mesothelioma, benign*
M9051/3 *Fibrous mesothelioma, malignant*
M9052/0 *Epithelioid mesothelioma, benign*
M9052/3 *Epithelioid mesothelioma, malignant*
M9053/0 *Mesothelioma, biphasic type, benign*
M9053/3 *Mesothelioma, biphasic type, malignant*
M9054/0 *Adenomatoid tumor NOS*

M906-M909 Germ cell neoplasms

M9060/3 *Dysgerminoma*
M9061/3 *Seminoma NOS*
M9062/3 *Seminoma, anaplastic type*
M9063/3 *Spermatocytic seminoma*
M9064/3 *Germinoma*
M9070/3 *Embryonal carcinoma NOS*
M9071/3 *Endodermal sinus tumor*
M9072/3 *Polyembryoma*
M9073/1 *Gonadoblastoma*
M9080/0 *Teratoma, benign*
M9080/1 *Teratoma NOS*
M9080/3 *Teratoma, malignant NOS*
M9081/3 *Teratocarcinoma*
M9082/3 *Malignant teratoma, undifferentiated type*
M9083/3 *Malignant teratoma, intermediate type*
M9084/0 *Dermoid cyst*
M9084/3 *Dermoid cyst with malignant transformation*
M9090/0 *Struma ovarii NOS*
M9090/3 *Struma ovarii, malignant*
M9091/1 *Strumal carcinoid*

M910 Trophoblastic neoplasms

M9100/0 *Hydatidiform mole NOS*
M9100/1 *Invasive hydatidiform mole*
M9100/3 *Choriocarcinoma*
M9101/3 *Choriocarcinoma combined with teratoma*
M9102/3 *Malignant teratoma, trophoblastic*

M911 Mesonephromas

M9110/0 *Mesonephroma, benign*
M9110/1 *Mesonephric tumor*
M9110/3 *Mesonephroma, malignant*
M9111/1 *Endosalpingioma*

M912-M916 Blood vessel tumors

M9120/0 *Hemangioma NOS*
M9120/3 *Hemangiosarcoma*
M9121/0 *Cavernous hemangioma*
M9122/0 *Venous hemangioma*
M9123/0 *Racemose hemangioma*
M9124/3 *Kupffer cell sarcoma*
M9130/0 *Hemangioendothelioma, benign*
M9130/1 *Hemangioendothelioma NOS*
M9130/3 *Hemangioendothelioma, malignant*
M9131/0 *Capillary hemangioma*
M9132/0 *Intramuscular hemangioma*
M9140/3 *Kaposi's sarcoma*
M9141/0 *Angiokeratoma*
M9142/0 *Verrucous keratotic hemangioma*
M9150/0 *Hemangiopericytoma, benign*
M9150/1 *Hemangiopericytoma NOS*
M9150/3 *Hemangiopericytoma, malignant*
M9160/0 *Angiofibroma NOS*
M9161/1 *Hemangioblastoma*

M917 Lymphatic vessel tumors

M9170/0 *Lymphangioma NOS*
M9170/3 *Lymphangiosarcoma*
M9171/0 *Capillary lymphangioma*
M9172/0 *Cavernous lymphangioma*
M9173/0 *Cystic lymphangioma*
M9174/0 *Lymphangiomyoma*
M9174/1 *Lymphangiomyomatosis*
M9175/0 *Hemolymphangioma*

M918-M920 Osteomas and osteosarcomas

M9180/0 *Osteoma NOS*
M9180/3 *Osteosarcoma NOS*
M9181/3 *Chondroblastic osteosarcoma*
M9182/3 *Fibroblastic osteosarcoma*
M9183/3 *Telangiectatic osteosarcoma*
M9184/3 *Osteosarcoma in Paget's disease of bone*
M9190/3 *Juxtacortical osteosarcoma*
M9191/0 *Osteoid osteoma NOS*
M9200/0 *Osteoblastoma*

M921-M924 Chondromatous neoplasms

M9210/0 *Osteochondroma*
M9210/1 *Osteochondromatosis NOS*

M9220/0 *Chondroma NOS*
M9220/1 *Chondromatosis NOS*
M9220/3 *Chondrosarcoma NOS*
M9221/0 *Juxtacortical chondroma*
M9221/3 *Juxtacortical chondrosarcoma*
M9230/0 *Chondroblastoma NOS*
M9230/3 *Chondroblastoma, malignant*
M9240/3 *Mesenchymal chondrosarcoma*
M9241/0 *Chondromyxoid fibroma*

M925 Giant cell tumors

M9250/1 *Giant cell tumor of bone NOS*
M9250/3 *Giant cell tumor of bone, malignant*
M9251/1 *Giant cell tumor of soft parts NOS*
M9251/3 *Malignant giant cell tumor of soft parts*

M926 Miscellaneous bone tumors

M9260/3 *Ewing's sarcoma*
M9261/3 *Adamantinoma of long bones*
M9262/0 *Ossifying fibroma*

M927-M934 Odontogenic tumors

M9270/0 *Odontogenic tumor, benign*
M9270/1 *Odontogenic tumor NOS*
M9270/3 *Odontogenic tumor, malignant*
M9271/0 *Dentinoma*
M9272/0 *Cementoma NOS*
M9273/0 *Cementoblastoma, benign*
M9274/0 *Cementifying fibroma*
M9275/0 *Gigantiform cementoma*
M9280/0 *Odontoma NOS*
M9281/0 *Compound odontoma*
M9282/0 *Complex odontoma*
M9290/0 *Ameloblastic fibro-odontoma*
M9290/3 *Ameloblastic odontosarcoma*
M9300/0 *Adenomatoid odontogenic tumor*
M9301/0 *Calcifying odontogenic cyst*
M9310/0 *Ameloblastoma NOS*
M9310/3 *Ameloblastoma, malignant*
M9311/0 *Odontoameloblastoma*
M9312/0 *Squamous odontogenic tumor*
M9320/0 *Odontogenic myxoma*
M9321/0 *Odontogenic fibroma NOS*
M9330/0 *Ameloblastic fibroma*
M9330/3 *Ameloblastic fibrosarcoma*
M9340/0 *Calcifying epithelial odontogenic tumor*

M935-M937 Miscellaneous tumors

M9350/1 *Craniopharyngioma*
M9360/1 *Pinealoma*
M9361/1 *Pineocytoma*
M9362/3 *Pineoblastoma*
M9363/0 *Melanotic neuroectodermal tumor*
M9370/3 *Chordoma*

M938-M948 Gliomas

M9380/3 *Glioma, malignant*
M9381/3 *Gliomatosis cerebri*
M9382/3 *Mixed glioma*
M9383/1 *Subependymal glioma*
M9384/1 *Subependymal giant cell astrocytoma*
M9390/0 *Choroid plexus papilloma NOS*
M9390/3 *Choroid plexus papilloma, malignant*
M9391/3 *Ependymoma NOS*
M9392/3 *Ependymoma, anaplastic type*
M9393/1 *Papillary ependymoma*
M9394/1 *Myxopapillary ependymoma*
M9400/3 *Astrocytoma NOS*
M9401/3 *Astrocytoma, anaplastic type*
M9410/3 *Protoplasmic astrocytoma*
M9411/3 *Gemistocytic astrocytoma*
M9420/3 *Fibrillary astrocytoma*
M9421/3 *Pilocytic astrocytoma*
M9422/3 *Spongioblastoma NOS*
M9423/3 *Spongioblastoma polare*
M9430/3 *Astroblastoma*
M9440/3 *Glioblastoma NOS*
M9441/3 *Giant cell glioblastoma*
M9442/3 *Glioblastoma with sarcomatous component*
M9443/3 *Primitive polar spongioblastoma*
M9450/3 *Oligodendroglioma NOS*
M9451/3 *Oligodendroglioma, anaplastic type*
M9460/3 *Oligodendroblastoma*
M9470/3 *Medulloblastoma NOS*
M9471/3 *Desmoplastic medulloblastoma*
M9472/3 *Medullomyoblastoma*
M9480/3 *Cerebellar sarcoma NOS*
M9481/3 *Monstrocellular sarcoma*

M949-M952 Neuroepitheliomatous neoplasms

M9490/0 *Ganglioneuroma*
M9490/3 *Ganglioneuroblastoma*
M9491/0 *Ganglioneuromatosis*
M9500/3 *Neuroblastoma NOS*
M9501/3 *Medulloepithelioma NOS*
M9502/3 *Teratoid medulloepithelioma*
M9503/3 *Neuroepithelioma NOS*
M9504/3 *Spongioneuroblastoma*
M9505/1 *Ganglioglioma*
M9506/0 *Neurocytoma*
M9507/0 *Pacinian tumor*
M9510/3 *Retinoblastoma NOS*
M9511/3 *Retinoblastoma, differentiated type*
M9512/3 *Retinoblastoma, undifferentiated type*
M9520/3 *Olfactory neurogenic tumor*
M9521/3 *Esthesioneurocytoma*
M9522/3 *Esthesioneuroblastoma*
M9523/3 *Esthesioneuroepithelioma*

M953 Meningiomas

M9530/0 *Meningioma NOS*
M9530/1 *Meningiomatosis NOS*
M9530/3 *Meningioma, malignant*
M9531/0 *Meningotheliomatous meningioma*
M9532/0 *Fibrous meningioma*
M9533/0 *Psammomatous meningioma*
M9534/0 *Angiomatous meningioma*
M9535/0 *Hemangioblastic meningioma*
M9536/0 *Hemangiopericytic meningioma*
M9537/0 *Transitional meningioma*
M9538/1 *Papillary meningioma*
M9539/3 *Meningeal sarcomatosis*

M954-M957 Nerve sheath tumor

M9540/0 *Neurofibroma NOS*
M9540/1 *Neurofibromatosis NOS*
M9540/3 *Neurofibrosarcoma*
M9541/0 *Melanotic neurofibroma*
M9550/0 *Plexiform neurofibroma*
M9560/0 *Neurilemmoma NOS*
M9560/1 *Neurinomatosis*
M9560/3 *Neurilemmoma, malignant*
M9570/0 *Neuroma NOS*

M958 Granular cell tumors and alveolar soft part sarcoma

M9580/0 *Granular cell tumor NOS*
M9580/3 *Granular cell tumor, malignant*
M9581/3 *Alveolar soft part sarcoma*

M959-M963 Lymphomas, NOS or diffuse

M9590/0 *Lymphomatous tumor, benign*
M9590/3 *Malignant lymphoma NOS*
M9591/3 *Malignant lymphoma, non Hodgkin's type*
M9600/3 *Malignant lymphoma, undifferentiated cell type NOS*
M9601/3 *Malignant lymphoma, stem cell type*
M9602/3 *Malignant lymphoma, convoluted cell type NOS*
M9610/3 *Lymphosarcoma NOS*
M9611/3 *Malignant lymphoma, lymphoplasmacytoid type*
M9612/3 *Malignant lymphoma, immunoblastic type*
M9613/3 *Malignant lymphoma, mixed lymphocytic-histiocytic NOS*
M9614/3 *Malignant lymphoma, centroblastic-centrocytic, diffuse*
M9615/3 *Malignant lymphoma, follicular center cell NOS*
M9620/3 *Malignant lymphoma, lymphocytic, well-differentiated NOS*
M9621/3 *Malignant lymphoma, lymphocytic, intermediate differentiation NOS*
M9622/3 *Malignant lymphoma, centrocytic*
M9623/3 *Malignant lymphoma, follicular center cell, cleaved NOS*
M9630/3 *Malignant lymphoma, lymphocytic, poorly differentiated NOS*
M9631/3 *Prolymphocytic lymphosarcoma*

M9632/3 *Malignant lymphoma, centroblastic type NOS*
M9633/3 *Malignant lymphoma, follicular center cell, noncleaved NOS*

M964 Reticulosarcomas

M9640/3 *Reticulosarcoma NOS*
M9641/3 *Reticulosarcoma, pleomorphic cell type*
M9642/3 *Reticulosarcoma, nodular*

M965-M966 Hodgkin's disease

M9650/3 *Hodgkin's disease NOS*
M9651/3 *Hodgkin's disease, lymphocytic predominance*
M9652/3 *Hodgkin's disease, mixed cellularity*
M9653/3 *Hodgkin's disease, lymphocytic depletion NOS*
M9654/3 *Hodgkin's disease, lymphocytic depletion, diffuse fibrosis*
M9655/3 *Hodgkin's disease, lymphocytic depletion, reticular type*
M9656/3 *Hodgkin's disease, nodular sclerosis NOS*
M9657/3 *Hodgkin's disease, nodular sclerosis, cellular phase*
M9660/3 *Hodgkin's paragranuloma*
M9661/3 *Hodgkin's granuloma*
M9662/3 *Hodgkin's sarcoma*

M969 Lymphomas, nodular or follicular

M9690/3 *Malignant lymphoma, nodular NOS*
M9691/3 *Malignant lymphoma, mixed lymphocytic-histiocytic, nodular*
M9692/3 *Malignant lymphoma, centroblastic-centrocytic, follicular*
M9693/3 *Malignant lymphoma, lymphocytic, well differentiated, nodular*
M9694/3 *Malignant lymphoma, lymphocytic, intermediate differentiation, nodular*
M9695/3 *Malignant lymphoma, follicular center cell, cleaved, follicular*
M9696/3 *Malignant lymphoma, lymphocytic, poorly differentiated, nodular*
M9697/3 *Malignant lymphoma, centroblastic type, follicular*
M9698/3 *Malignant lymphoma, follicular center cell, noncleaved, follicular*

M970 Mycosis fungoides

M9700/3 *Mycosis fungoides*
M9701/3 *Sezary's disease*

M971-M972 Miscellaneous reticuloendothelial neoplasms

M9710/3 *Microglioma*
M9720/3 *Malignant histiocytosis*
M9721/3 *Histiocytic medullary reticulosis*
M9722/3 *Letterer-Siwe's disease*

M973 Plasma cell tumors

M9730/3 *Plasma cell myeloma*
M9731/0 *Plasma cell tumor, benign*
M9731/1 *Plasmacytoma NOS*
M9731/3 *Plasma cell tumor, malignant*

M974 Mast cell tumors

M9740/1 *Mastocytoma NOS*
M9740/3 *Mast cell sarcoma*
M9741/3 *Malignant mastocytosis*

M975 Burkitt's tumor

M9750/3 *Burkitt's tumor*

M980-M994 Leukemias

M980 Leukemias NOS

M9800/3 *Leukemia NOS*
M9801/3 *Acute leukemia NOS*
M9802/3 *Subacute leukemia NOS*
M9803/3 *Chronic leukemia NOS*
M9804/3 *Aleukemic leukemia NOS*

M981 Compound leukemias

M9810/3 *Compound leukemia*

M982 Lymphoid leukemias

M9820/3 *Lymphoid leukemia NOS*
M9821/3 *Acute lymphoid leukemia*
M9822/3 *Subacute lymphoid leukemia*
M9823/3 *Chronic lymphoid leukemia*
M9824/3 *Aleukemic lymphoid leukemia*
M9825/3 *Prolymphocytic leukemia*

M983 Plasma cell leukemias

M9830/3 *Plasma cell leukemia*

M984 Erythroleukemias

M9840/3 *Erythroleukemia*
M9841/3 *Acute erythremia*
M9842/3 *Chronic erythremia*

M985 Lymphosarcoma cell leukemias

M9850/3 *Lymphosarcoma cell leukemia*

M986 Myeloid leukemias

M9860/3 *Myeloid leukemia NOS*
M9861/3 *Acute myeloid leukemia*
M9862/3 *Subacute myeloid leukemia*
M9863/3 *Chronic myeloid leukemia*
M9864/3 *Aleukemic myeloid leukemia*
M9865/3 *Neutrophilic leukemia*
M9866/3 *Acute promyelocytic leukemia*

M987 Basophilic leukemias

M9870/3 *Basophilic leukemia*

M988 Eosinophilic leukemias

M9880/3 *Eosinophilic leukemia*

M989 Monocytic leukemias

M9890/3 *Monocytic leukemia NOS*
M9891/3 *Acute monocytic leukemia*
M9892/3 *Subacute monocytic leukemia*
M9893/3 *Chronic monocytic leukemia*
M9894/3 *Aleukemic monocytic leukemia*

M990-M994 Miscellaneous leukemias

M9900/3 *Mast cell leukemia*
M9910/3 *Megakaryocytic leukemia*
M9920/3 *Megakaryocytic myelosis*
M9930/3 *Myeloid sarcoma*
M9940/3 *Hairy cell leukemia*

M995-M997 Miscellaneous myeloproliferative and lymphoproliferative disorders

M9950/1 *Polycythemia vera*
M9951/1 *Acute panmyelosis*
M9960/1 *Chronic myeloproliferative disease*
M9961/1 *Myelosclerosis with myeloid metaplasia*
M9962/1 *Idiopathic thrombocythemia*
M9970/1 *Chronic lymphoproliferative disease*

GLOSSARY OF MENTAL DISORDERS

The psychiatric terms which appear in Chapter 5, "Mental Disorders," are listed here in alphabetic sequence. Many of the glossary descriptions originally appeared in the section on Mental Disorders in the *International Classification of Diseases, 9th Revision*,[1] and others are included to define the psychiatric conditions added to *ICD-9-CM*. The additional definitions are based on material furnished by the American Psychiatric Association's Task Force on Nomenclature and Statistics[2] and from *A Psychiatric Glossary*.[3] In a few instances definitions were obtained from *Dorland's Illustrated Medical Dictionary*[4] and from *Stedman's Medical Dictionary, Illustrated*.[5]

1. Manual of the *International Classification of Diseases, Injuries, and Causes of Death*, 9th Revision. World Health Organization, Geneva, Switzerland, 1975.
2. American Psychiatric Association, Task Force on Nomenclature and Statistics, Robert L. Spitzer, Chairman.
3. *A Psychiatric Glossary*, Fourth Edition, American Psychiatric Association, Washington, D.C., 1975.
4. *Dorland's Illustrated Medical Dictionary*, Twenty-fifth Edition, W.B. Saunders Company, Philadelphia, 1974.
5. *Stedman's Medical Dictionary, Illustrated*, Twenty-third Edition, the Williams and Wilkins Company, Baltimore, 1976.

Academic underachievement disorder: Failure to achieve in most school tasks despite adequate intellectual capacity, a supportive and encouraging social environment, and apparent effort. The failure occurs in the absence of a demonstrable specific learning disability and is caused by emotional conflict not clearly associated with any other mental disorder.[2]

Adaptation reaction—*see* Adjustment reaction

Adjustment reaction or disorder: Mild or transient disorders lasting longer than acute stress reactions which occur in individuals of any age without any apparent pre-existing mental disorder. Such disorders are often relatively circumscribed or situation-specific, are generally reversible, and usually last only a few months. They are usually closely related in time and content to stresses such as bereavement, migration, or other experiences. Reactions to major stress that last longer than a few days are also included. In children such disorders are associated with no significant distortion of development.[1]

conduct disturbance: Mild or transient disorders in which the main disturbance predominantly involves a disturbance of conduct (e.g., an adolescent grief reaction resulting in aggressive or antisocial disorder).[1]

depressive reaction: States of depression, not specifiable as manic-depressive, psychotic, or neurotic.[1]

brief: Generally transient, in which the depressive symptoms are usually closely related in time and content to some stressful event.[1]

prolonged: Generally long-lasting, usually developing in association with prolonged exposure to a stressful situation.[1]

emotional disturbance: An adjustment disorder in which the main symptoms are emotional in type (e.g., anxiety, fear, worry) but not specifically depressive.[1]

mixed conduct and emotional disturbance: An adjustment reaction in which both emotional disturbance and disturbance of conduct are prominent features.[1]

Affective psychoses: Mental disorders, usually recurrent, in which there is a severe disturbance of mood (mostly compounded of depression and anxiety but also manifested as elation, and excitement) which is accompanied by one or more of the following: delusions, perplexity, disturbed attitude to self, disorder of perception and behavior; these are all in keeping with the individual's prevailing mood (as are hallucinations when they occur). There is a strong tendency to suicide. For practical reasons, mild disorders of mood may also be included here if the symptoms match closely the descriptions given; this applies particularly to mild hypomania.[1]

bipolar: A manic-depressive psychosis which has appeared in both the depressive and manic form, either alternating or separated by an interval of normality.[1]

atypical: An episode of affective psychosis with some, but not all, of the features of the one form of the disorder in individuals who have had a previous episode of the other form of the disorder.[2]

depressed: A manic-depressive psychosis, circular type, in which the depressive form is currently present.[1]

manic: A manic-depressive psychosis, circular type, in which the manic form is currently present.[1]

mixed: A manic-depressive psychosis, circular type, in which both manic and depressive symptoms are present at the same time.[1]

depressed type: A manic-depressive psychosis in which there is a widespread depressed mood of gloom and wretchedness with some degree of anxiety. There is often reduced activity but there may be restlessness and agitation. There is marked tendency to recurrence; in a few cases this may be at regular intervals.[1]

atypical: An affective depressive disorder that cannot be classified as a manic-depressive psychosis, depressed type, or chronic depressive personality psychosis, or as an adjustment disorder.[2]

manic type: A manic-depressive psychosis characterized by states of elation or excitement out of keeping with the individual's circumstances and varying from enhanced liveliness (hypomania) to violent, almost uncontrollable, excitement. Aggression and anger, flight of ideas, distractibility, impaired judgment, and grandiose ideas are common.[1]

mixed type: Manic-depressive psychosis syndromes corresponding to both the manic and depressed types, but which for other reasons cannot be classified more specifically.[1]

Aggressive personality—*see* Personality disorder, explosive type

Agoraphobia—*see* agoraphobia under Phobia

Alcohol dependence syndrome: A state, psychic and usually also physical, resulting from taking alcohol, characterized by behavioral and other responses that always include a compulsion to take alcohol on a continuous or periodic basis in order to experience its psychic effects, and sometimes to avoid the discomfort of its absence; tolerance may or may not be present. A person may be dependent on alcohol and other drugs; if so, also record the diagnosis of drug dependence to identify the agent. If alcohol dependence is associated with alcoholic psychosis or with physical complications, *both* diagnoses should be recorded.[1]

Alcohol intoxication

acute: A psychic and physical state resulting from alcohol ingestion characterized by slurred speech, unsteady gait, poor coordination, flushed facies, nystagmus, sluggish reflexes, fetor alcoholica, loud speech, emotional instability (e.g., jollity followed by lugubriousness), excessive conviviality, loquacity, and poorly inhibited sexual and agressive behavior.[2]

idiosyncratic: Acute psychotic episodes induced by relatively small amounts of alcohol. These are regarded as individual idiosyncratic reactions to alcohol, not due to excessive consumption and without conspicuous neurological signs of intoxication.[1]

pathological—*see* Alcohol intoxication, idiosyncratic

Alcoholic psychoses: Organic psychotic states due mainly to excessive consumption of alcohol; defects of nutrition are thought to play an important role.[1]

alcohol abstinence syndrome—*see* alcohol withdrawal syndrome below

alcohol amnestic syndrome: A syndrome of prominent and lasting reduction of memory span, including striking loss of recent memory, disordered time appreciation and confabulation, occurring in alcoholics as the sequel to an acute alcoholic psychosis (especially delirium tremens) or, more rarely, in the course of chronic alcoholism. It is usually accompanied by peripheral neuritis and may be associated with Wernicke's encephalopathy.[1]

alcohol withdrawal delirium [delirium tremens]: Acute or subacute organic psychotic states in alcoholics, characterized by clouded consciousness, disorientation, fear, illusions, delusions, hallucinations of any kind, notably visual and tactile, and restlessness, tremor and sometimes fever.[1]

alcohol withdrawal hallucinosis: A psychosis usually of less than six months' duration, with slight or no clouding of consciousness and much anxious restlessness in which auditory hallucinations, mostly of voices uttering insults and threats, predominate.[1]

alcohol withdrawal syndrome: Tremor of hands, tongue, and eyelids following cessation of prolonged heavy drinking of alcohol. Nausea and vomiting, dry mouth, headache, heavy perspiration, fitful sleep, acute anxiety attacks, mood depression, feelings of guilt and remorse, and irritability are associated features.[2]

alcohol delirium—*see* alcohol withdrawal delirium above

alcoholic dementia: Nonhallucinatory dementias occurring in association with alcoholism, but not characterized by the features of either alcohol withdrawal delirium [delirium tremens] or alcohol amnestic syndrome [Korsakoff's alcoholic psychosis].[1]

alcoholic hallucinosis—*see* alcohol withdrawal hallucinosis above

alcoholic jealousy: Chronic paranoid psychosis characterized by delusional jealousy and associated with alcoholism.[1]

alcoholic paranoia—*see* Alcoholic jealousy

alcoholic polyneuritic psychosis—*see* alcohol amnestic syndrome above

Alcoholism

acute—*see* Alcohol intoxication, acute

chronic—*see* Alcohol dependence syndrome

Alexia: Loss of a previously possessed reading facility that cannot be explained by defective visual acuity.[3]

Amnesia, psychogenic: A form of dissociative hysteria in which there is a temporary disturbance in the ability to recall important personal information which has already been registered and stored in memory. The sudden onset of this disturbance in the absence of an underlying organic mental disorder, and the extent of the disturbance being too great to be explained by ordinary forgetfulness, are the essential features.[2]

Amnestic syndrome: A syndrome of prominent and lasting reduction of memory span, including striking loss of recent memory, disordered time appreciation, and confabulation. The commonest causes are chronic alcoholism [alcohol amnestic syndrome; Korsakoff's alcoholic psychosis], chronic barbiturate dependence, and malnutrition. An amnestic syndrome may be the predominating disturbance in the early states of presenile and senile dementia, arteriosclerotic dementia, and in encephalitis and other inflammatory and degenerative diseases in which there is particular bilateral involvement of the temporal lobes, and certain temporal lobe tumors.[2]

alcoholic—*see* alcohol amnestic syndrome under Alcoholic psychoses

Amoral personality—*see* Personality disorder, antisocial type

Anancastic [anankastic] neurosis—*see* Neurotic disorder, obsessive-compulsive

Anancastic [anankastic] personality—*see* Personality disorder, compulsive type

Anorexia nervosa: A disorder in which the main features are persistent active refusal to eat and marked loss of weight. The level of activity and alertness is characteristically high in relation to the degree of emaciation. Typically the disorder begins in teenage girls but it may sometimes begin before puberty and rarely it occurs in males. Amenorrhea is usual and there may be a variety of other physiological changes including slow pulse and respiration, low body temperature, and dependent edema. Unusual eating habits and attitudes toward food are typical and sometimes starvation follows or alternates with periods of overeating. The accompanying psychiatric symptoms are diverse.[1]

Anxiety hysteria—*see* phobia under Neurotic disorders

Anxiety state (neurotic): Apprehension, tension, or uneasiness that stems from the anticipation of danger, the source of which is largely unknown or unrecognized.[3]

atypical: An anxiety disorder that does not fulfill the criteria of generalized or panic attack anxiety. An example might be an individual with a single morbid fear.[2]

generalized: A disorder of at least six months' duration in which the predominant feature is limited to diffuse and persistent anxiety without the specific symptoms that characterize phobic disorders, panic disorder, or obsessive-compulsive disorder.[2]

panic attack: An episodic and often chronic, recurrent disorder in which the predominant features are anxiety attacks and nervousness. The anxiety attacks are manifested by discrete periods of sudden onset of intense apprehension, fearfulness, or terror often associated with feelings of impending doom.[2]

Aphasia, developmental: A delay in the production of spoken language. Rarely, there is also a developmental delay in the comprehension of speech sounds.[1]

Arteriosclerotic dementia: Dementia attributable, because of physical signs (on examination of the central nervous system), to degenerative arterial disease of the brain. Symptoms suggesting a focal lesion in the brain are common. There may be a fluctuating or patchy intellectual defect with insight, and an intermittent course is common. Clinical differentiation from senile or presenile dementia, which may coexist with it, may be very difficult or impossible. The diagnosis of cerebral atherosclerosis should also be recorded.[1]

Asocial personality—*see* Personality disorder, antisocial type

Astasia-abasia, hysterical: A form of conversion hysteria in which the individual is unable to stand or walk although the legs are otherwise under control.[4]

Asthenia, psychogenic—*see* neurasthenia under Neurotic disorders

Asthenic personality—*see* Personality disorder, dependent type

Attention deficit disorder—*see* attention deficit disorder under Hyperkinetic syndrome of childhood.

Autism, infantile: A syndrome present from birth or beginning almost invariably in the first 30 months. Responses to auditory and sometimes to visual stimuli are abnormal, and there are usually severe problems in the understanding of spoken language. Speech is delayed and, if it develops, is characterized by echolalia, the reversal of pronouns, immature grammatical structure, and inability to use abstract terms. There is generally an impairment in the social use of both verbal and gestural language. Problems in social relationships are most severe before the age of five years and include an impairment in the development of eye-to-eye gaze, social attachments, and cooperative play. Ritualistic behavior is usual and may include abnormal routines, resistance to change, attachment to odd objects, and stereotyped patterns of play. The capacity for abstract or symbolic thought and for imaginative play is diminished. Intelligence ranges from severely subnormal to normal or above. Performance is usually better on tasks involving rote memory or visuospatial skills than on those requiring symbolic or linguistic skills.[1]

Avoidant personality—*see* Personality disorder, avoidant type

"Bad trips": Acute intoxication from hallucinogen abuse, manifested by hallucinatory states lasting only a few days or less.[1]

Barbiturate abuse: Cases where an individual has taken the drug to the detriment of his health or social functioning, in doses above or for periods beyond those normally regarded as therapeutic.[1]

Bestiality—*see* Zoophilia

Bipolar disorder—*see* Affective psychosis, bipolar

atypical—*see* Affective psychosis, bipolar, atypical

Body-rocking—*see* Stereotyped repetitive movements

Borderline personality—*see* Personality disorder, borderline type

Borderline psychosis of childhood—*see* Psychosis, atypical childhood

Borderline schizophrenia—*see* Schizophrenia, latent

Bouffée délirante—*see* Paranoid reaction, acute

Briquet's disorder—*see* somatization disorder under Neurotic disorders

Bulimia: An episodic pattern of overeating [binge eating] accompanied by an awareness of the disordered eating pattern with a fear of not being able to stop eating voluntarily. Depressive moods and self-deprecating thoughts follow the episodes of binge eating.[2]

Catalepsy schizophrenia—*see* Schizophrenia, catatonic type

Catastrophic stres—*see* Gross stress reaction

Catatonia (schizophrenic)—*see* Schizophrenia, catatonic type

Character neurosis—*see* Personality disorders

Childhood autism—*see* Autism, infantile

Childhood type schizophrenia—*see* Psychosis, child

Chronic alcoholic brain syndrome—*see* alcoholic dementia under Alcoholic psychoses

Clay-eating—*see* Pica

Clumsiness syndrome—*see* coordination disorder under Developmental delay disorders, specific

Combat fatigue—*see* Posttraumatic disorder, acute

Compensation neurosis—*see* compensation neurosis under Neurotic disorders

Compulsive conduct disorder—*see* impulse control disorders under Conduct disorders

Compulsive neurosis—*see* Neurotic disorder, obsessive-compulsive

Compulsive personality—*see* Personality disorder, compulsive type

Concentration camp syndrome—*see* Posttraumatic stress disorder, prolonged

Conduct disorders: Disorders mainly involving aggressive and destructive behavior and disorders involving delinquency. It should be used for abnormal behavior, in individuals of any age, which gives rise to social disapproval but which is not part of any other psychiatric condition. Minor emotional disturbances may also be present. To be included, the behavior, as judged by its frequency, severity, and type of associations with other symptoms, must be abnormal in its context. Disturbances of conduct are distinguished from an adjustment reaction by a longer duration and by a lack of close relationship in time and content to some stress. They differ from a personality disorder by the absence of deeply ingrained maladaptive patterns of behavior present from adolescence or earlier.[1]

impulse control disorders: A failure to resist an impulse, drive, or temptation to perform some action which is harmful to the individual or to others. The impulse may or may not be consciously resisted, and the act may or may not be premeditated or planned. Prior to committing the act, there is an increasing sense of tension, and at the time of committing the act, there is an experience of either pleasure, gratification, or release. Immediately following the act, there may or may not be genuine regret, self-reproach, or guilt.[2] *See also* Intermittent explosive disorder, Isolated explosive disorder, Kleptomania, Pathological gambling, and Pyromania.

mixed disturbance of conduct and emotions: A disorder characterized by features of undersocialized and socialized disturbance of conduct, but in which there is also considerable emotional disturbance as shown, for example, by anxiety, misery, or obsessive manifestations.[1]

socialized conduct disorder: Conduct disorders in individuals who have acquired the values or behavior of a delinquent peer group to whom they are loyal and with whom they characteristically steal, play truant, and stay out late at night. There may also be sexual promiscuity.[1]

undersocialized conduct disturbance

aggressive type: A disorder characterized by a persistent pattern of disrespect for the feelings and well-being of others (bullying, physical aggression, cruel behavior, hostility, verbal abusiveness, impudence, defiance, negativism), aggressive antisocial behavior (destructiveness, stealing, persistent lying, frequent truancy, and vandalism), and failure to develop close and stable relationships with others.[2]

unaggressive type: A disorder in which there is a lack of concern for the rights and feelings of others to a degree which indicates a failure to establish a normal degree of affection, empathy, or bond with others. There are two patterns of behavior found. In one, the child is fearful and timid, lacking self-assertiveness, resorts to self-protective and manipulative lying, indulges in whining demandingness and temper tantrums, feels rejected and unfairly treated, and is mistrustful of others. In the other pattern of the disorder, the child approaches others strictly for his own gains and acts exclusively because of exploitative and extractive goals. The child lies brazenly and steals, appearing to feel no guilt, and forms no social bonds to other individuals.[2]

Confusion, psychogenic—*see* Psychosis, reactive confusion

Confusion, reactive—*see* Psychosis, reactive confusion

Confusional state

acute—*see* Delirium, acute

epileptic—*see* Delirium, acute

subacute—*see* Delirium, subacute

Conversion hysteria—*see* hysteria, conversion type under Neurotic disorders

Coordination disorder—*see* coordination disorder under Developmental delay disorders, specific

Culture shock: A form of stress reaction associated with an individual's assimilation into a new culture which is vastly different from that in which he was raised.[5]

Cyclic schizophrenia—*see* Schizophrenia, schizo-affective type

Cyclothymic personality or disorder—*see* Personality disorder, cyclothymic type

Delirium: Transient organic psychotic conditions with a short course in which there is a rapidly developing onset of disorganization of higher mental processes manifested by some degree of impairment of information processing, impaired or abnormal attention, perception, memory, and thinking. Clouded consciousness, confusion, disorientation, delusions, illusions, and often vivid hallucinations predominate in the clinical picture.[1,2]

acute: short-lived states, lasting hours or days, of the above type.[1]

subacute: states of the above type in which the symptoms, usually less florid, last for several weeks or longer, during which they may show marked fluctuations in intensity.[1]

Delirium tremens—*see* alcohol withdrawal delirium under Alcoholic psychoses

Delusions, systematized—*see* Paranoia

Dementia: A decrement in intellectual functioning of sufficient severity to interfere with occupational or social performance, or both. There is impairment of memory and abstract thinking, the ability to learn new skills, problem solving, and judgment. There is often also personality change or impairment in impulse control. Dementia in organic psychoses may be of a chronic or progressive nature, which if untreated are usually irreversible and terminal.[1,2]

alcoholic—*see* alcoholic dementia under Alcoholic psychoses

arteriosclerotic—*see* Arteriosclerotic dementia

multi-infarct—*see* Arteriosclerotic dementia

presenile—*see* Presenile dementia

repeated infarct—*see* Arteriosclerotic dementia

senile—*see* Senile dementia

Depersonalization syndrome—*see* depersonalization syndrome under Neurotic disorders

Depression: States of depression, usually of moderate but occasionally of marked intensity, which have no specifically manic-depressive or other psychotic depressive features, and which do not appear to be associated with stressful events or other features specified under neurotic depression.[1]

anxiety—*see* depression under Neurotic disorders

endogenous—*see* Affective psychosis, depressed type

monopolar—*see* Affective psychosis, depressed type

neurotic—*see* depression under Neurotic disorders

psychotic—*see* Affective psychosis, depressed type

psychotic reactive—*see* Psychosis, depressive

reactive—*see* depression under Neurotic disorders

reactive psychotic—*see* Psychosis, depressive

Depressive personality or character—*see* Personality disorder, chronic depressive type

Depressive reaction—*see* depressive reaction under Adjustment reaction

Depressive psychosis—*see* Affective psychosis, depressed type

Derealization (neurotic)—*see* depersonalization syndrome under Neurotic disorders

Developmental delay disorders, specific: A group of disorders in which a specific delay in development is the main feature. For many the delay is not explicable in terms of general intellectual retardation or of inadequate schooling. In each case development is related to biological maturation, but it is also influenced by nonbiological factors. A diagnosis of a specific developmental delay carries no etiological implications. A diagnosis of specific delay in development should not be made if it is due to a known neurological disorder.[1]

arithmetical disorder: Disorders in which the main feature is a serious impairment in the development of arithmetical skills.[1]

articulation disorder: A delay in the development of normal word-sound production resulting in defects of articulation. Omissions or substitutions of consonants are most frequent.[1]

coordination disorder: Disorders in which the main feature is a serious impairment in the development of motor coordination which is not explicable in terms of general intellectual retardation. The clumsiness is commonly associated with perceptual difficulties.[1]

mixed development disorder: A delay in the development of one specific skill (e.g., reading, arithmetic, speech, or coordination) is frequently associated with lesser delays in other skills. When this occurs the diagnosis should be made according to the skill most seriously impaired. The mixed category should be used only where the mixture of delayed skills is such that no one skill is preponderantly affected.[1]

motor retardation—*see* coordination disorder above

reading disorder or retardation: Disorders in which the main feature is a serious impairment in the development of reading or spelling skills which is not explicable in terms of general intellectual retardation or of inadequate schooling. Speech or language difficulties, impaired right-left differentiation, perceptuo-motor problems, and coding difficulties are frequently associated. Similar problems are often present in other members of the family. Adverse psychosocial factors may be present.[1]

speech or language disorder: Disorders in which the main feature is a serious impairment in the development of speech or language (syntax or semantic) which is not explicable in terms of general intellectual retardation. Most commonly there is a delay in the development of normal word-sound production resulting in defects of articulation. Omissions or substitutions of consonants are most frequent. There may also be a delay in the production of spoken language. Rarely, there is also a developmental delay in the comprehension of sounds. Includes cases in which delay is largely due to environmental privation.[1]

Dipsomania—*see* Alcohol dependence syndrome

Disorganized schizophrenia—*see* Schizophrenia, disorganized type

Dissociative hysteria—*see* hysteria, dissociative type under Neurotic disorders

Drug abuse: Includes cases where an individual, for whom no other diagnosis is possible, has come under medical care because of the maladaptive effect of a drug on which he is not dependent (*see* Drug dependence) and that he has taken on his own initiative to the detriment of his health or social functioning. When drug abuse is secondary to a psychiatric disorder, record the disorder as an additional diagnosis.[1]

Drug dependence: A state, psychic and sometimes also physical, resulting from taking a drug, characterized by behavioral and other responses that always include a compulsion to take a drug on a continuous or periodic basis in order to experience its psychic effects, and sometimes to avoid the discomfort of its absence. Tolerance may or may not be present. A person may be dependent on more than one drug.[1]

Drug psychoses: Organic mental syndromes which are due to consumption of drugs (notably amphetamines, barbiturates, and opiate and LSD groups) and solvents. Some of the syndromes in this group are not as severe as most conditions labeled "psychotic," but they are included here for practical reasons. The drug should be identified, and also a diagnosis of drug dependence should be recorded, if present.[1]

drug-induced hallucinosis: Hallucinatory states of more than a few days, but not more than a few months' duration, associated with large or prolonged intake of drugs, notably of the amphetamine and LSD groups. Auditory hallucinations usually predominate and there may be anxiety or restlessness. States following LSD or other hallucinogens lasting only a few days or less ["bad trips"] are not included.[1]

drug-induced organic delusional syndrome: Paranoid states of more than a few days, but not more than a few months' duration, associated with large or prolonged intake of drugs, notably of the amphetamine and LSD groups.[1]

drug withdrawal syndrome: States associated with drug withdrawal ranging from severe, as specified for alcohol withdrawal delirium [delirium tremens], to less severe states characterized by one or more symptoms such as convulsions, tremor, anxiety, restlessness, gastrointestinal and muscular complaints, and mild disorientation and memory disturbance.[1]

Drunkenness:

acute—*see* Alcohol intoxication, acute

pathologic—*see* Alcohol intoxication, idiosyncratic

simple: A state of inebriation due to alcohol consumption without conspicuous neurological signs of intoxication.[2]

sleep: An inability to fully arouse from the sleep state characterized by failure to attain full consciousness after arousal.[2]

Dyscalculia—*see* arithmetical disorder under Developmental delay disorders, specific

Dyslalia—*see* articulation disorder under Developmental delay disorders, specific

Dyslexia, developmental: A disorder in which the main feature is a serious impairment of reading skills which is not explicable in terms of general intellectual retardation or of inadequate schooling. Word-blindness and strephosymbolia (tendency to reverse letters and words in reading) are included.[1,3]

Dysmenorrhea, psychogenic: Painful menstruation due to disturbance of psychic control.[4]

Dyspareunia, functional—*see* functional dyspareunia under Psychosexual dysfunctions

Dyspraxia syndrome—*see* coordination disorder under Developmental delay disorders, specific

Dyssocial personality—*see* Personality disorder, antisocial type

Dysuria, psychogenic: Difficulty in passing urine due to psychic factors.[4]

Eating disorders: A group of disorders characterized by a conspicuous disturbance in eating behavior.[2] *See also* Bulimia, Pica, and Rumination, psychogenic.

Eccentric personality—*see* Personality disorder, eccentric type

Elective mutism: A pervasive and persistent refusal to speak in situations not attributable to a mental disorder. In some cases the behavior may manifest a form of withdrawal reaction to a specific stressful situation, or as a predominant feature in children exhibiting shyness or social withdrawal disorders.[2]

Emancipation disorder: An adjustment reaction in adolescents or young adults in which there is symptomatic expression (e.g., difficulty in making independent decisions, increased dependence on parental advice, adoption of values deliberately oppositional to parents) of a conflict over independence following the recent assumption of a status in which the individual is more independent of parental control or supervision.[2]

Emotional disturbances specific to childhood and adolescence: Less well-differentiated emotional disorders characteristic of the childhood period. When the emotional disorder takes the form of a neurosis, the appropriate diagnosis should be made. These disorders differ from adjustment reactions in terms of longer duration and by the lack of close relationship in time and content to some stress.[1] *See also* Academic underachievement disorder, Elective mutism, Identity disorder, Introverted disorder of childhood, Misery and unhappiness disorder, Oppositional disorder, Overanxious disorder, and Shyness disorder of childhood.

Encopresis: A disorder in which the main manifestation is the persistent voluntary or involuntary passage of formed stools of normal or near-normal consistency into places not intended for that purpose in the individual's own sociocultural setting. Sometimes the child has failed to gain bowel control, and sometimes he has gained control but then later again became encopretic. There may be a variety of associated psychiatric symptoms and there may be smearing of feces. The condition would not usually be diagnosed under the age of four years.[1]

Endogenous depression—*see* Affective psychosis, depressed type

Enuresis: A disorder in which the main manifestation is a persistent involuntary voiding of urine by day or night which is considered abnormal for the age of the individual. Sometimes the child will have failed to gain bladder control and in other cases he will have gained control and then lost it. Episodic or fluctuating enuresis should be included. The disorder would not usually be diagnosed under the age of four years.[1]

Epileptic confusional or twilight state—*see* Delirium, acute

Excitation

catatonic—*see* Schizophrenia, catatonic type

psychogenic—*see* Psychosis, excitative type

reactive—*see* Psychosis, excitative type

Exhaustion delirium—*see* Stress reaction, acute

Exhibitionism: Sexual deviation in which the main sexual pleasure and gratification is derived from exposure of the genitals to a person of the opposite sex.[1]

Explosive personality disorder—*see* Personality disorder, explosive type

Factitious illness: A form of hysterical neurosis in which there are physical or psychological symptoms that are not real, genuine, or natural, which are produced by the individual and are under his voluntary control.[2]

physical symptom type: The presentation of physical symptoms that may be total fabrication, self-inflicted, an exaggeration or exacerbation of a pre-existing physical condition, or any combination or variation of these.[2]

psychological symptom type: The voluntary production of symptoms suggestive of a mental disorder. Behavior may mimic psychosis or, rather, the individual's idea of psychosis.[2]

Fanatic personality—*see* Personality disorder, paranoid type

Fatigue neurosis—*see* neurasthenia under Neurotic disorders

Feeble-minded—*see* Mental retardation, mild

Fetishism: A sexual deviation in which nonliving objects are utilized as a preferred or exclusive method of stimulating erotic arousal.[2]

Finger-flicking—*see* Stereotyped repetitive movements

Folie à deux—*see* Shared paranoid disorder

Frigidity: A psychosexual dysfunction in which there is partial or complete failure to attain or maintain the lubrication-swelling response of sexual excitement until completion of the sexual act.[2]

Frontal lobe syndrome: Changes in behavior following damage to the frontal areas of the brain or following interference with the connections of those areas. There is a general diminution of self-control, foresight, creativity, and spontaneity, which may be manifest as increased irritability, selfishness, restlessness and lack of concern for others. Conscientiousness and powers of concentration are often diminished, but measurable deterioration of intellect or memory is not necessarily present. The overall picture is often one of emotional dullness, lack of drive, and slowness; but, particularly in persons previously with energetic, restless, or aggressive characteristics, there may be a change towards impulsiveness, boastfulness, temper outbursts, silly fatuous humor, and the development of unrealistic ambitions; the direction of change usually depends upon the previous personality. A considerable degree of recovery is possible and may continue over the course of several years.[1]

Fugue, psychogenic: A form of dissociative hysteria characterized by an episode of wandering with inability to recall one's prior identity. Both onset and recovery are rapid. Following recovery there is no recollection of events which took place during the fugue state.[2]

Ganser's syndrome (hysterical): A form of factitious illness in which the patient voluntarily produces symptoms suggestive of a mental disorder.[2]

Gender identity disorder—*see* gender identity disorder under Psychosexual identity disorders

Gilles de la Tourette's disorder or syndrome—*see* Gilles de la Tourette's disorder under Tics

Grief reaction—*see* depressive reaction, brief under Adjustment reaction

Gross stress reaction—*see* Stress reaction, acute

Group delinquency—*see* socialized conduct disorder under Conduct disorders

Habit spasm—*see* chronic motor tic disorder under Tics

Hangover (alcohol)—*see* Drunkenness, simple

Head-banging—*see* Stereotyped repetitive movements

Hebephrenia—*see* Schizophrenia, disorganized type

Heller's syndrome—*see* Psychosis, disintegrative

High grade defect—*see* Mental retardation, mild

Homosexuality: Exclusive or predominant sexual attraction for persons of the same sex with or without physical relationship. Record homosexuality as a diagnosis whether or not it is considered as a mental disorder.[1]

Hospital addiction syndrome—*see* Munchausen syndrome

Hospital hoboes—*see* Munchausen syndrome

Hospitalism: A mild or transient adjustment reaction characterized by withdrawal seen in hospitalized patients. In young children this may be manifested by elective mutism.[1]

Hyperkinetic syndrome of childhood: Disorders in which the essential features are short attention-span and distractibility. In early childhood the most striking symptom is disinhibited, poorly organized and poorly regulated extreme overactivity but in adolescence this may be replaced by underactivity. Impulsiveness, marked mood fluctuations, and aggression are also common symptoms. Delays in the development of specific skills are often present and disturbed, poor relationships are common. If the hyperkinesis is symptomatic of an underlying disorder, the diagnosis of the underlying disorder is recorded instead.[1]

attention deficit disorder: Cases of hyperkinetic syndrome in which short attention span, distractibility, and overactivity are the main manifestations without significant disturbance of conduct or delay in specific skills.[1]

hyperkinesis with developmental delay: Cases in which the hyperkinetic syndrome is associated with speech delay, clumsiness, reading difficulties, or other delays of specific skills.[1]

hyperkinetic conduct disorder: Cases in which the hyperkinetic syndrome is associated with marked conduct disturbance but not developmental delay.[1]

Hypersomnia: A disorder of initiating arousal from sleep or maintaining wakefulness.[2]

persistent: Chronic difficulty in initiating arousal from sleep or maintaining wakefulness associated with major or minor depressive mental disorders.[2]

transient: Episodes of difficulty in arousal from sleep or maintaining wakefulness associated with acute or intermittent emotional reactions or conflicts.[2]

Hypochondriasis—*see* hypochondriasis under Neurotic disorders

Hypomania—*see* Affective psychosis, manic type

Hypomanic personality—*see* Personality disorder, chronic hypomanic type

Hyposomnia—*see* Insomnia

Hysteria—*see* hysteria under Neurotic disorders

anxiety—*see* phobia under Neurotic disorders

psychosis—*see* Psychosis, reactive

acute—*see* Psychosis, excitative type

Hysterical personality—*see* Personality disorder, histrionic type

Identity disorder: An emotional disorder caused by distress over the inability to reconcile aspects of the self into a relatively coherent and acceptable sense of self, not secondary to another mental disorder. The disturbance is manifested by intense subjective distress regarding uncertainty about a variety of issues relating to identity, including long-term goals, career choice, friendship patterns, values, and loyalties.[2]

Idiocy—*see* Mental retardation, profound

Imbecile—*see* Mental retardation, moderate

Impotence: A psychosexual dysfunction in which there is partial or complete failure to attain or maintain erection until completion of the sexual act.[2]

Impulse control disorder—*see* impulse control disorders under Conduct disorders

Inadequate personality—*see* Personality disorder, dependent type

Induced paranoid disorder—*see* Shared paranoid disorder

Inebriety—*see* Drunkenness, simple

Infantile autism—*see* Autism, infantile

Insomnia: A disorder of initiating or maintaining sleep.[2]

persistent: A chronic state of sleeplessness associated with chronic anxiety, major or minor depressive disorders, or psychoses.[2]

transient: Episodes of sleeplessness associated with acute or intermit tent emotional reactions or conflicts.[2]

Intermittent explosive disorder: Recurrent episodes of sudden and significant loss of control of aggressive impulses, not accounted for by any other mental disorder, which results in serious assault or destruction of property. The magnitude of the behavior during an episode is grossly out of proportion to any psychosocial stressors which may have played a role in eliciting the episode of lack of control. Following each episode there is genuine regret or self-reproach at the consequences of the actionand the inability to control the aggressive impulse.[2]

Introverted disorder of childhood: An emotional disturbance in children chiefly manifested by a lack of interest in social relationships and indifference to social praise or criticism.[2]

Introverted personality—*see* Personality disorder, introverted type

Involutional melancholia—*see* Affective psychosis, depressed type

Involutional paranoid state—*see* Paraphrenia

Isolated explosive disorder: A disorder of impulse control in which there is a single discrete episode characterized by failure to resist an impulse which leads to a single, violent externally-directed act, which has a catastrophic impact on others, and for which the available information does not justify the diagnosis of another mental disorder.[2]

Isolated phobia—*see* simple phobia under Phobia

Jet lag syndrome: A phase-shift disruption of the 24-hour sleep-wake cycle due to rapid time-zone changes experienced in long-distance travel.[2]

Kanner's syndrome—*see* Autism, infantile

Kleptomania: A disorder of impulse control characterized by a recurrent failure to resist impulses to steal objects not for immediate use or their monetary value. An increasing sense of tension is experienced prior to committing the act, with an intense experience of gratification at the time of committing the theft.[2]

Korsakoff's psychosis:

alcoholic—*see* alcohol amnestic syndrome under Alcoholic psychoses

nonalcoholic—*see* Amnestic syndrome

Latent schizophrenia—*see* Schizophrenia, latent

Lesbianism—*see* Homosexuality

Lobotomy syndrome—*see* Frontal lobe syndrome

LSD reaction: Acute intoxication from hallucinogen abuse, manifested by hallucinatory states lasting only a few days or less.[1]

Major depressive disorder—*see* Affective psychosis, depressed type

Malingering: A clinical picture in which the predominant feature is the presentation of fake or grossly exaggerated physical or psychiatric illness apparently under voluntary control. In contrast to factitious illness, the symptoms produced in malingering are in pursuit of a goal which, when known, is recognizable and obviously understandable in light of knowledge of the individual's circumstances. Examples of understandable goals include, but are not limited to, becoming a "patient" in order to avoid conscription or military duty, avoid work, obtain financial compensation, evade criminal prosecution, and obtain drugs.[2]

Mania (monopolar)—*see* Affective psychosis, manic type

Manic-depressive psychosis

circular type—*see* Affective psychosis, bipolar

depressed type—*see* Affective psychosis, depressed type

manic type—*see* Affective psychosis, manic type

mixed type—*see* Affective psychosis, mixed type

Manic disorder—*see* Affective psychosis, manic type

atypical—*see* Affective psychosis, manic type, atypical

Masochistic personality—*see* Personality disorder, masochistic type

Melancholia—*see* Affective psychoses

involutional—*see* Affective psychosis, depressed type

Mental retardation: A condition of arrested or incomplete development of mind which is especially characterized by subnormality of intelligence. The coding should be made on the individual's *current* level of functioning *without regard to its nature* or causation, such as psychosis, cultural deprivation, Down's syndrome, etc. Where there is a specific cognitive handicap—such as in speech—the diagnosis of mental retardation should be based on assessments of cognition *outside the area of specific handicap.* The assessment of intellectual level should be based on whatever information is available, including clinical evidence, adaptive behavior, and psychometric findings. The IQ levels given are based on a test with a mean of 100 and a standard deviation of 15, such as the Wechsler scales. They are provided only as a guide and should not be applied rigidly. Mental retardation often involves psychiatric disturbances and may often develop as a result of some physical disease or injury. In these cases, an additional diagnosis should be recorded to identify any associated condition, psychiatric or physical.[1]

mild mental retardation: IQ criteria 50-70. Individuals with this level of retardation are usually educable. During the pre-school period they can develop social and communication skills, have minimal retardation in sensorimotor areas, and often are not distinguished from normal children until a later age. During the school age period they can learn academic skills up to approximately the sixth-grade level. During the adult years, they can usually achieve social and vocational skills adequate for minimum self-support, but may need guidance and assistance when under social or economic stress.[2]

moderate mental retardation: IQ criteria 35-49. Individuals with this level of retardation are usually trainable. During the pre-school period they can talk or learn to communicate. They have poor social awareness and fair motor development. During the school age period they can profit from training in social and occupational skills, but they are unlikely to progress beyond the second-grade level in academic subjects. During their adult years they may achieve self-maintenance in unskilledor semi-skilled work under sheltered conditions. They need supervision and guidance when under mild social or economic stress.[2]

severe mental retardation: IQ criteria 20-34. Individuals with this level of retardation evidence poor motor development, minimal speech, and are generally unable to profit from training and self-help during the pre-school period. During the school age period they can talk or learn to communicate, can be trained in elementary health habits, and may profit from systematic habit training. During the adult years they may contribute partially to self-maintenance under complete supervision.[2]

profound mental retardation: IQ criteria under 20. Individuals with this level of retardation evidence minimal capacity for sensorimotor functioning and need nursing care during the pre-school period. During the school age period some further motor development may occur, and they may respond to minimal or limited training in self-help. During the adult years some motor and speech development may occur, and they may achieve very limited self-care and need nursing care.[2]

Merycism—*see* Rumination, psychogenic

Minimal brain dysfunction [MBD]—*see* Hyperkinetic syndrome of childhood

Misery and unhappiness disorder: An emotional disorder characteristic of childhood in which the main symptoms involve misery and unhappiness. There may also be eating and sleep disturbances.[1]

Mood swings (brief compensatory) (rebound): Mild disorders of mood (depression and anxiety or elation and excitement, occurring alternatingly or episodically) seen in affective psychosis.[1]

Motor tic disorders—*see* Tics

Motor-verbal tic disorder—*see* Gilles de la Tourette's disorder under Tics

Multi-infarct dementia or psychosis—*see* Arteriosclerotic dementia

Multiple operations syndrome—*see* Munchausen syndrome

Multiple personality: A form of dissociative hysteria in which there is the domination of the individual at any one time by one of two or more distinct personalities. Each personality is a fully-integrated and complex unit with memories, behavior patterns, and social friendships which determine the nature of the individual's acts when uppermost in consciousness.[2]

Munchausen syndrome: A chronic form of factitious illness in which the individual demonstrates a plausible presentation of voluntarily produced physical symptomatology of such a degree that he is able to obtain and sustain multiple hospitalizations.[2]

Narcissistic personality—*see* Personality disorder, narcissistic type

Nervous debility—*see* neurasthenia under Neurotic disorders

Neurasthenia—*see* neurasthenia under Neurotic disorders

Neurotic delinquency—*see* mixed disturbance of conduct and emotions under Conduct disorders

Neurotic disorders: Neurotic disorders are mental disorders without any demonstrable organic basis in which the individual may have considerable insight and has unimpaired reality testing, in that he usually does not confuse his morbid subjective experiences and fantasies with external reality. Behavior may be greatly affected although usually remaining within socially acceptable limits, but personality is not disorganized. The principal manifestations include excessive anxiety, hysterical symptoms, phobias, obsessional and compulsive symptoms, and depression.[1]

anxiety states: Various combinations of physical and mental manifestations of anxiety, not attributable to real danger and occurring either in attacks [*see* Anxiety state, panic attacks] or as a persisting state [*see* Anxiety state, generalized]. The anxiety is usually diffuse and may extend to panic. Other neurotic features such as obsessional or hysterical symptoms may be present but do not dominate the clinical picture.[1]

compensation neurosis: Certain unconscious neurotic reactions in which features of secondary gain, such as a situational or financial advantage, are prominent.[3]

depersonalization: A neurotic disorder with an unpleasant state of disturbed perception in which external objects or parts of one's own body are experienced as changed in their quality, unreal, remote, or automatized. The patient is aware of the subjective nature of the change he experiences. If depersonalization occurs as a feature of anxiety, schizophrenia, or other mental disorder, the condition is classified according to the major psychiatric disorder.[1]

depression: A neurotic disorder characterized by disproportionate depression which has usually recognizably ensued on a distressing experience; it does not include among its features delusions or hallucinations, and there is often preoccupation with the psychic trauma which preceded the illness, e.g., loss of a cherished person or possession. Anxiety is also frequently present and mixed states of anxiety and depression should be included here. The distinction between depressive neurosis and psychosis should be made not only upon the degree of depression but also on the presence or absence of other neurotic and psychotic characteristics, and upon the degree of disturbance of the individual's behavior.[1]

hypochondriasis: A neurotic disorder in which the conspicuous features are excessive concern with one's health in general or the integrity and functioning of some part of one's body, or less frequently, one's mind. It is usually associated with anxiety and depression. It may occur as a feature of some other severe mental disorder (e.g., manic-depressive psychosis, depressed type, schizophrenia, hysteria) and in that case should be classified according to the corresponding major disorder.[1]

hysteria: A neurotic mental disorder in which motives, of which the patient seems unaware, produce either a restriction of the field of consciousness or disturbances of motor or sensory function which may seem to have psychological advantage or symbolic value.[1] There are three subtypes:

conversion type: The chief or only symptoms of the hysterical neurosis consist of psychogenic disturbance of function in some part of the body, e.g., paralysis, tremor, blindness, deafness, seizures.[1]

dissociative type: The most prominent feature of the hysterical neurosis is a narrowing of the field of consciousness which seems to serve an unconscious purpose and is commonly accompanied or followed by a selective amnesia. There may be dramatic but essentially superficial changes of personality [multiple personality], or sometimes the patient enters into a wandering state [fugue].[1]

factitious illness: Physical or psychological symptoms that are not real, genuine, or natural, which are produced by the individual and are under his voluntary control.[2]

neurasthenia: A neurotic disorder characterized by fatigue, irritability, headache, depression, insomnia, difficulty in concentration, and lack of capacity for enjoyment [anhedonia]. It may follow or accompany an infection or exhaustion, or arise from continued emotional stress. If neurasthenia is associated with a physical disorder, the latter should also be recorded as a diagnosis.[1]

obsessive-compulsive: States in which the outstanding symptom is a feeling of subjective compulsion, which must be resisted, to carry out some action, to dwell on an idea, to recall an experience, or to ruminate on an abstract topic. Unwanted thoughts which intrude, the insistency of words or ideas, ruminations or trains of thought are perceived by the individual to be inappropriate or nonsensical. The obsessional urge or idea is recognized as alien to the personality but as coming from within the self. Obsessional actions may be quasi-ritual performances designed to relieve anxiety, e.g., washing the hands to cope with contamination. Attempts to dispel the unwelcome thoughts or urges may lead to a severe inner struggle, with intense anxiety.[1]

occupational: A neurosis characterized by a functional disorder of a group of muscles used chiefly in one's occupation, marked by the occurrence of spasm, paresis, or incoordination on attempt to repeat the habitual movements (e.g., writers' cramp).[5]

phobic disorders: Neurotic states with abnormally intense dread of certain objects or specific situations which would not normally have that effect. If the anxiety tends to spread from a specified situation or object to a wider range of circumstances, it becomes akin to or identical with anxiety state and should be classified as such.[1] *See also* Phobia.

somatization disorder: A chronic, but fluctuating, neurotic disorder which begins early in life and is characterized by recurrent and multiple somatic complaints for which medical attention is sought but which are not apparently due to any physical illness. Complaints are presented in a dramatic, vague, or exaggerated way, or are part of a complicated medical history in which often many specific diagnoses have allegedly been made by other physicians. Complaints invariably refer to many organ systems (headache, fatigue, palpitations, fainting, nausea and vomiting, abdominal pains, bowel trouble, allergies, menstrual and sexual difficulties), and the individual frequently receives medical care from a number of physicians, sometimes simultaneously.[2]

Neurosis—*see* Neurotic disorders

Nightmares: Anxiety attacks occurring in dreams during REM sleep.[2]

Night terrors: A pathology of arousal from stage 4 sleep in which the individual experiences excessive terror and extreme panic (screaming, verbalizations), symptoms of autonomic activity, confusion, and poor recall for event.[2]

Nymphomania: Abnormal and excessive need or desire in the woman for sexual intercourse.[3]

Obsessional personality—*see* Personality disorder, compulsive type

Occupational neurosis—*see* Neurotic disorder, occupational

Oneirophrenia—*see* Schizophrenia, acute episode

Oppositional disorder of childhood or adolescence: A disorder characterized by pervasive opposition to all in authority regardless ofself-interest, a continuous argumentativeness, and an unwillingness to respond to reasonable persuasion, not accounted for by a conduct disorder, adjustment disorder, or a psychosis of childhood. The oppositional behavior in this disorder is evoked by any demand, rule, suggestion, request, or admonishment placed on the individual.[2]

Organic affective syndrome: A clinical picture in which the predominating symptoms closely resemble those seen in either the depressive or manic affective disorders, occurring in the presence of evidence or history of a specific organic factor which is etiologically related to the disturbance, such as head trauma, endocranial tumors, and exocranial tumors secreting neurotoxic diatheses (e.g., pancreatic carcinoma). Excessive use of steroids, Cushing's syndrome, and other endocrine disorders may lead to an organic affective syndrome.[2]

Organic personality syndrome: Chronic, mild states of memory disturbance and intellectual deterioration, of nonpsychotic nature, often accompanied by increased irritability, querulousness, lassitude, and complaints of physical weakness. These states are often associated with old age, and may precede more severe states due to brain damage classifiable under senile or presenile dementia, dementia associated with other chronic organic psychotic brain syndromes, or delirium, delusions, hallucinosis, and depression in transient organic psychotic conditions.[1]

Organic psychosyndrome, focal (partial): A nonpsychotic organic mental disorder resembling the postconcussion syndrome associated with localized diseases of the brain or surrounding tissues.[1]

Organic psychotic conditions: Syndromes in which there is impairment of orientation, memory, comprehension, calculation, learning capacity, and judgment. These are the essential features but there may also be shallowness or lability of affect, or a more persistent disturbance of mood, lowering of ethical standards and exaggeration or emergence of personality traits, and diminished capacity for independent decision.[1] *See also* Alcohol psychoses, Arteriosclerotic dementia, Drug psychoses, Presenile dementia, and Senile dementia.

acute delirium: Short-lived states, lasting hours or days, of the above type.[1]

mixed paranoid and affective: Organic psychosis in which depressive and paranoid symptoms are the main features.[1]

subacute delirium: States of the above type in which the symptoms, usually less florid, last for several weeks or longer during which they may show marked fluctuations in intensity.[1]

transient: States characterized by clouded consciousness, confusion, disorientation, illusions, and often vivid hallucinations. They are usually due to some intra- or extracerebral toxic, infectious, metabolic or other systemic disturbance and are generally reversible. Depressive and paranoid symptoms may also be present but are not the main feature. The diagnosis of the associated physical or neurological condition should also be recorded.[1]

Organic reaction—*see* Organic psychotic conditions, transient

Overanxious disorder: An ill-defined emotional disorder characteristic of childhood in which the main symptoms involve anxiety and fearfulness.[1]

Panic disorder—*see* panic attack under Anxiety state

Paranoia: A rare chronic psychosis in which logically constructed systematized delusions have developed gradually without concomitant hallucinations or the schizophrenic type of disordered thinking. The delusions are mostly of grandeur (the paranoiac prophet or inventor), persecution, or somatic abnormality.[1]

alcoholic—*see* alcoholic jealousy under Alcoholic psychoses

querulans: A paranoid state which, though in many ways akin to schizophrenic or affective states, differs from other paranoid states and psychogenic paranoid psychosis.[1]

senile—*see* Paraphrenia

Paranoid personality—*see* Personality disorder, paranoid type

Paranoid reaction, acute: Paranoid states apparently provoked by some emotional stress. The stress is often misconstrued as an attack or threat. Such states are particularly prone to occur in prisoners or as acute reactions to a strange and threatening environment, e.g., in immigrants.[1]

Paranoid schizophrenia—*see* Schizophrenia, paranoid type

Paranoid state

involutional—*see* Paraphrenia

senile—*see* Paraphrenia

simple: A psychosis, acute or chronic, not classifiable as schizophrenia or affective psychosis, in which delusions, especially of being influenced, persecuted, or treated in some special way, are the main symptoms. The delusions are of a fairly fixed, elaborate, and systematized kind.[1]

Paranoid traits—*see* Personality disorder, paranoid type

Paraphilia—*see* Sexual deviations

Paraphrenia: Paranoid psychosis in which there are conspicuous hallucinations, often in several modalities. Affective symptoms and disordered thinking, if present, do not dominate the clinical picture, and the personality is well preserved.[1]

Paraphrenic schizophrenia—*see* Schizophrenia, paranoid type

Passive-aggressive personality—*see* Personality disorder, passive-aggressive type

Passive personality—*see* Personality disorder, dependent type

Pathological

alcohol intoxication—*see* Alcohol intoxication, idiosyncratic

drug intoxication: Individual idiosyncratic reactions to comparatively small quantities of a drug, which take the form of acute, brief psychotic states of any type.[1]

drunkenness—*see* Alcohol intoxication, idiosyncratic

gambling: A disorder of impulse control characterized by a chronic and progressive preoccupation with gambling and urge to gamble, with subsequent gambling behavior that compromises, disrupts, or damages personal, family, and vocational pursuits.[2]

personality—*see* Personality disorder

Pedophilia: Sexual deviations in which an adult engages in sexual activity with a child of the same or opposite sex.[1]

Peregrinating patient—*see* Malingering

Personality disorders: Deeply ingrained maladaptive patterns of behavior generally recognizable by the time of adolescence or earlier and continuing throughout most of adult life, although often becoming less obvious in middle or old age. The personality is abnormal either in the balance of its components, their quality and expression, or in its total aspect. Because of this deviation or psychopathy the patient suffers or others have to suffer, and there is an adverse effect upon the individual or on society. It includes what is sometimes called psychopathic personality, but if this is determined primarily by malfunctioning of the brain, it should be classified as one of the nonpsychotic organic brain syndromes. When the patient exhibits an anomaly of personality directly related to his neurosis or psychosis, e.g., schizoid personality and schizophrenia or anancastic personality and obsessive compulsive neurosis, the relevant neurosis or psychosis which is in evidence should be diagnosed in addition.[1]

affective type: A chronic personality disorder characterized by lifelong predominance of a pronounced mood. The illness does not have a clear onset, and there may be intermittent periods of disturbed mood separated by periods of normal mood.[1]

anancastic [anankastic] type—*see* Personality disorder, compulsive type

antisocial type: A personality disorder characterized by disregard for social obligations, lack of feeling for others, and impetuous violence or callous unconcern. There is a gross disparity between behavior and the prevailing social norms. Behavior is not readily modifiable by experience, including punishment. People with this personality are often affectively cold, and may be abnormally aggressive or irresponsible. Their tolerance to frustration is low; they blame others or offer plausible rationalizations for the behavior which brings them into conflict with society.[1]

asthenic type—*see* Personality disorder, dependent type

avoidant type: Individuals with this disorder exhibit excessive social inhibitions and shyness, a tendency to withdraw from opportunities for developing close relationships, and a fearful expectation that they will be belittled and humiliated. Desires for affection and acceptance are strong, but they are unwilling to enter relationships unless given unusually strong guarantees that they will be uncritically accepted. Therefore, they have few close relationships and suffer from feelings of loneliness and isolation.[2]

borderline type: Individuals with this disorder are characterized by instability in a variety of areas, including interpersonal relationships, behavior, mood, and self image. Interpersonal relationships are often intense and unstable with marked shifts of attitude over time. Frequently there is impulsive and unpredictable behavior which is potentially physically self-damaging. There may be problems tolerating being alone, and chronic feelings of emptiness or boredom.[2]

chronic depressive type: An affective personality disorder characterized by lifelong predominance of a chronic nonpsychotic disturbance involving either intermittent or sustained periods of depressed mood (marked by worry, pessimism, low output of energy, and a sense of futility).[2]

chronic hypomanic type: An affective personality disorder characterized by lifelong predominance of a chronic nonpsychotic disturbance involving either intermittent or sustained periods of abnormally elevated mood (unshakable optimism and an enhanced zest for life and activity).[2]

compulsive type: A personality disorder characterized by feelings of personal insecurity, doubt, and incompleteness leading to excessive conscientiousness, checking, stubbornness, and caution. There may be insistent and unwelcome thoughts or impulses which do not attain the severity of an obsessional neurosis. There is perfectionism and meticulous accuracy and a need to check repeatedly in an attempt to ensure this. Rigidity and excessive doubt may be conspicuous.[1]

cyclothymic type: A chronic nonpsychotic disturbance involving depressed and elevated mood, lasting at least two years, separated by periods of normal mood.[2]

dependent type: A personality disorder characterized by passive compliance with the wishes of elders and others and a weak inadequate response to the demands of daily life. Lack of vigor may show itself in the intellectual or emotional spheres; there is little capacity for enjoyment.[1]

eccentric type: A personality disorder characterized by oddities of behavior which do not conform to the clinical syndromes of personality disorders described elsewhere.[2]

explosive type: A personality disorder characterized by instability of mood with liability to intemperate outbursts of anger, hate, violence, or affection. Aggression may be expressed in words or in physical violence. The outbursts cannot readily be controlled by the affected persons, who are not otherwise prone to antisocial behavior.[1]

histrionic type: A personality disorder characterized by shallow, labile affectivity, dependence on others, craving for appreciation and attention, suggestibility, and theatricality. There is often sexual immaturity, e.g., frigidity and over-responsiveness to stimuli. Under stress hysterical symptoms [neurosis] may develop.[1]

hysterical type—*see* Personality disorder, histrionic type

inadequate type—*see* Personality disorder, dependent type

introverted type: A form of schizoid personality in which the essential features are a profound defect in the ability to form social relationships and to respond to the usual forms of social reinforcements. Such patients are characteristically "loners" who do not appear distressed by their social distance and are not interested in greater social involvement.[2]

masochistic type: A personality disorder in which the individual appears to arrange life situations so as to be defeated and humiliated.[2]

narcissistic type: A personality disorder in which interpersonal difficulties are caused by an inflated sense of self-worth, and indifference to the welfare of others. Achievement deficits and social irresponsibilities are justified and sustained by a boastful arrogance, expansive fantasies, facile rationalization, and frank prevarication.[2]

paranoid type: A personality disorder in which there is excessive sensitiveness to setbacks or to what are taken to be humiliations and rebuffs, a tendency to distort experience by misconstruing the neutral or friendly actions of others as hostile or contemptuous, and a combative and tenacious sense of personal rights. There may be a proneness to jealousy or excessive self-importance. Such persons may feel helplessly humiliated and put upon; others, likewise excessively sensitive, are aggressive and insistent. In all cases there is excessive self-reference.[1]

passive-aggressive type: A personality disorder characterized by aggressive behavior manifested in passive ways, such as obstructionism, pouting, procrastination, intentional inefficiency, or stubbornness. The *aggression* often arises from resentment at failing to find gratification in a relationship with an individual or institution upon which the individual is overdependent.[3]

passive type—*see* Personality disorder, dependent type

schizoid type: A personality disorder in which there is withdrawal from affectional, social, and other contacts with autistic preference for fantasy and introspective reserve. Behavior may be slightly eccentric or indicate avoidance of competitive situations. Apparent coolness and detachment may mask an incapacity to express feeling.[1]

schizotypal type: A form of schizoid personality in which individuals with this disorder manifest various oddities of thinking, perception, communication, and behavior. The disturbance in thinking may be expressed as magical thinking, ideas of reference, or paranoid ideation. Perceptual disturbances may include recurrent illusions and derealization [depersonalization]. Frequently, but not invariably, the behavioral manifestations include social isolation and constricted or inappropriate affect which interferes with rapport in face-to-face interaction without any of the frank psychotic features which characterize schizophrenia.[2]

Phobia: Neurotic states with abnormally intense dread of certain objects or specific situations which would not normally have that effect. If the anxiety tends to spread from a specified situation or object to a wider range of circumstances, it becomes akin to or identical with anxiety state, and should be classified as such.[1]

acrophobia: Fear of heights[3]

agoraphobia: Fear of leaving the familiar setting of the home, and is almost always preceded by a phase during which there are recurrent panic attacks. Because of the anticipatory fear of helplessness when having a panic attack, the patient is reluctant or refuses to be alone, travel or walk alone, or to be in situations where there is no ready access to help, such as in crowds, closed or open spaces, or crowded stores.[2]

ailurophobia: Fear of cats[3]

algophobia: Fear of pain[3]

claustrophobia: Fear of closed spaces[3]

isolated phobia—*see* simple phobia below

mysophobia: Fear of dirt or germs[3]

obsessional—*see* Neurotic disorder, obsessive-compulsive

panphobia: Fear of everything[3]

simple phobia: Fear of a discrete object or situation which is neither fear of leaving the familiar setting of the home [agoraphobia], or of being observed by others in certain situations [social phobia]. Examples of simple phobia are fear of animals, acrophobia, and claustrophobia.[2]

social phobia: Fear of situations in which the subject is exposed to possible scrutiny by others, and the possibility exists that he may act in a fashion that will be considered shameful. The most common social phobias are fears of public speaking, blushing, eating in public, writing in front of others, or using public lavatories.[2]

xenophobia: Fear of strangers[3]

Pica: Perverted appetite of nonorganic origin in which there is persistent eating of non-nutritional substances. Typically, infants ingest paint, plaster, string, hair, or cloth. Older children may have access to animal droppings, sand, bugs, leaves, or pebbles. In the adult, eating of starch or clay-earth has been observed.[2]

Postconcussion syndrome: States occurring after generalized contusion of the brain, in which the symptom picture may resemble that of the frontal lobe syndrome or that of any of the neurotic disorders, but in which in addition, headache, giddiness, fatigue, insomnia, and a subjective feeling of impaired intellectual ability are usually prominent. Mood may fluctuate, and quite ordinary stress may produce exaggerated fear and apprehension. There may be marked intolerance of mental and physical exertion, undue sensitivity to noise, and hypochondriacal preoccupation. The symptoms are more common in persons who have previously suffered from neurotic or personality disorders, or when there is a possibility of compensation. This syndrome is particularly associated with the closed type of head injury when signs of localized brain damage are slight or absent, but it may also occur in other conditions.[1]

Postcontusion syndrome or encephalopathy—*see* Postconcussion syndrome

Postencephalitic syndrome: A nonpsychotic organic mental disorder resembling the postconcussion syndrome associated with central nervous system infections.[1]

Postleucotomy syndrome—*see* Frontal lobe syndrome

Posttraumatic brain syndrome, nonpsychotic—*see* Postconcussion syndrome

Posttraumatic organic psychosis—*see* Organic psychotic conditions, transient

Posttraumatic stress disorder: The development of characteristic symptoms (re-experiencing the traumatic event, numbing of responsiveness to or involvement with the external world, and a variety of other autonomic, dysphoric, or cognitive symptoms) after experiencing a psychologically traumatic event or events outside the normal range of human experience (e.g., rape or assault, military combat, natural catastrophes such as flood or earthquake, or other disaster, such as airplane crash, fires, bombings).[2]

acute: Brief, episodic, or recurrent disorders lasting less than six months' duration after the onset of trauma.[2]

prolonged: Chronic disorders of the above type lasting six months or more following the trauma.[2]

Premature ejaculation—*see* premature ejaculation under Psychosexual dysfunctions

Prepsychotic schizophrenia—*see* Schizophrenia, latent

Presbyophrenia—*see* Organic personality syndrome

Presenile dementia: Dementia occurring usually before the age of 65 in patients with the relatively rare forms of diffuse or lobar cerebral atrophy. The associated neurological condition (e.g., Alzheimer's disease, Pick's disease, Jakob-Creutzfeldt disease) should also be recorded as a diagnosis.[1]

Prodromal schizophrenia—*see* Schizophrenia, latent

Pseudoneurotic schizophrenia—*see* Schizophrenia, latent

Psychalgia: Pains of mental origin, e.g., headache or backache, for which a more precise medical or psychiatric diagnosis cannot be made.[1]

Psychasthenia: A functional neurosis marked by stages of pathological fear or anxiety, obsessions, fixed ideas, tics, feelings of inadequacy, self-accusation, and peculiar feelings of strangeness, unreality, and depersonalization.[4]

Psychic shock: A sudden disturbance of mental equilibrium produced by strong emotion in response to physical or mental stress.[4]

Psychic factors associated with physical disease: Mental disturbances or psychic factors of any type thought to have played a major part in the etiology of physical conditions, usually involving tissue damage, classified elsewhere. The mental disturbance is usually mild and nonspecific, and the psychic factors (worry, fear, conflict, etc.) may be present without any overt psychiatric disorder. Examples of these conditions are asthma, dermatitis, eczema, duodenal ulcer, ulcerative colitis, and urticaria, specified as due to psychogenic factors.

Use an additional diagnosis to identify the physical condition. In the rare instance that an overt psychiatric disorder is thought to have caused the physical condition, the psychiatric diagnosis should be recorded in addition.[1]

Psychoneurosis—*see* Neurotic disorders

Psycho-organic syndrome—*see* Organic psychotic conditions, transient

Psychopathic constitutional state—*see* Personality disorders

Psychopathic personality—*see* Personality disorders

Psychophysiological disorders: A variety of physical symptoms or types of physiological malfunctions of mental origin, not involving tissue damage, and usually mediated through the autonomic nervous system. The disorders are classified according to the body system involved. If the physical symptom is secondary to a psychiatric disorder classifiable elsewhere, the physical symptom is not classified as a psychophysiological disorder. If tissue damage is involved, then the diagnosis is classified as a *Psychic factor associated with diseases classified elsewhere.*[1]

Psychosexual dysfunctions: A group of disorders in which there is recurrent and persistent dysfunction encountered during sexual activity. The dysfunction may be lifelong or acquired, generalized or situational, and total or partial.[2]

functional dyspareunia: Recurrent and persistent genital pain associated with coitus.[2]

functional vaginismus: A history of recurrent and persistent involuntary spasm of the musculature of the outer one-third of the vagina that interferes with sexual activity.[2]

inhibited female orgasm: Recurrent and persistent inhibition of the female orgasm as manifested by a delay or absence of orgasm following a normal sexual excitement phase during sexual activity.[2]

inhibited male orgasm: Recurrent and persistent inhibition of the male orgasm as manifested by a delay or absence of either the emission or ejaculation phases, or more usually, both following an adequate phase of sexual excitement.[2]

inhibited sexual desire: Persistent inhibition of desire for engaging in a particular form of sexual activity.[2]

inhibited sexual excitement: Recurrent and persistent inhibition of sexual excitement during sexual activity, manifested either by partial or complete failure to attain or maintain erection until completion of the sexual act [impotence], or partial or complete failure to attain or maintain the lubrication-swelling response of sexual excitement until completion of the sexual act [frigidity].[2]

premature ejaculation: Ejaculation occurs before the individual wishes it, because of recurrent and persistent absence of reasonable voluntary control of ejaculation and orgasm during sexual activity.[2]

Psychosexual gender identity disorders: Behavior occurring in preadolescents of immature psychosexuality, or in adults, in which there is an incongruence between the individual's anatomic sex and gender identity.[2]

gender identity disorder: In children or in adults a condition in which the individual would prefer to be of the other sex, and strongly prefers the clothes, toys, activities, and companionship of the other sex. Cross-dressing is intermittent, although it may be frequent. In children the commonest form is feminism in boys.[2]

trans-sexualism: A psychosexual identity disorder centered around fixed beliefs that the overt bodily sex is wrong. The resulting behavior is directed towards either changing the sexual organs by operation, or completely concealing the bodily sex by adopting both the dress and behavior of the opposite sex.[1]

Psychosomatic disorders—*see* Psychophysiological disorders

Psychosis: Mental disorders in which impairment of mental function has developed to a degree that interferes grossly with insight, ability to meet some ordinary demands of life or to maintain adequate contact with reality. It is not an exact or well defined term. Mental retardation is excluded.[2]

affective—*see* Affective psychoses

alcoholic—*see* Alcoholic psychoses

atypical childhood: A variety of atypical infantile psychoses which may show some, but not all, of the features of infantile autism. Symptoms may include stereotyped repetitive movements, hyperkinesis, self-injury, retarded speech development, echolalia, and impaired social relationships. Such disorders may occur in children of any level of intelligence but are particularly common in those with mental retardation.[1]

borderline, of childhood—see Psychosis, atypical childhood

child: A group of disorders in children, characterized by distortions in the timing, rate, and sequence of many psychological functions involving language development and social relations in which the severe qualitative abnormalities are not normal for any stage of development.[2] *See also* Autism, infantile, Psychosis, disintegrative, Psychosis, atypical childhood.

depressive—*see* Affective psychosis, depressed type

depressive type: A depressive psychosis which can be similar in its symptoms to manic-depressive psychosis, depressed type but is apparently provoked by saddening stress such as a bereavement, or a severe disappointment or frustration. There may be less diurnal variation of symptoms than in manic-depressive psychosis, depressed type, and the delusions are more often understandable in the context of the life experiences. There is usually a serious disturbance of behavior, e.g., major suicidal attempt.[1]

disintegrative: A disorder in which normal or near-normal development for the first few years is followed by a loss of social skills and of speech, together with a severe disorder of emotions, behavior, and relationships. Usually this loss of speech and of social competence takes place over a period of a few months and is accompanied by the emergence of overactivity and of stereotypies. In most cases there is intellectual impairment, but this is not a necessary part of the disorder. The condition may follow overt brain disease, such as measles encephalitis, but it may also occur in the absence of any known organic brain disease or damage. Any associated neurological disorder should also be recorded.[1]

epileptic: An organic psychotic condition associated with epilepsy.[1]

excitative type: An affective psychosis similar in its symptoms to manic-depressive psychosis, manic type, but apparently provoked by emotional stress.[1]

hypomanic—*see* Affective psychosis, manic type

hysterical—*see* Psychosis, reactive

acute—*see* Psychosis, excitative type

induced—*see* Shared paranoid disorder

infantile—*see* Autism, infantile

infective—*see* Organic psychotic conditions, transient

Korsakoff's:

alcoholic—*see* alcohol amnestic syndrome under Alcoholic psychoses

nonalcoholic—*see* Amnestic syndrome

manic-depressive—*see* Affective psychoses

multi-infarct—*see* Arteriosclerotic dementia

paranoid

chronic—*see* Paranoia

protracted reactive—*see* Psychosis, paranoid, psychogenic

psychogenic: Psychogenic or reactive paranoid psychosis of anytype which is more protracted than the reactions described under Paranoid reaction, acute.[1]

acute—*see* Paranoid reaction, acute

postpartum—*see* Psychosis, puerperal

psychogenic—*see* Psychosis, reactive

depressive—*see* Psychosis, depressive type

puerperal: Any psychosis occurring within a fixed period (approximately 90 days) after childbirth.[3] The diagnosis should be classified according to the predominant symptoms or characteristics, such as schizophrenia, affective psychosis, paranoid states, or other specified psychosis.

reactive: A psychotic condition which is largely or entirely attributable to a recent life experience. This diagnosis is not used for the wider range of psychoses in which environmental factors play some, but not the major, part in etiology.[1]

brief: A florid psychosis of at least a few hours' duration but lasting no more than two weeks, with sudden onset immediately following a severe environmental stress and eventually terminating in complete recovery to the pre-psychotic state.[2]

confusion: Mental disorders with clouded consciousness, disorientation (though less marked than in organic confusion), and diminished accessibility often accompanied by excessive activity and apparently provoked by emotional stress.[1]

depressive—*see* Psychosis, depressive type

schizo-affective—*see* Schizophrenia, schizo-affective type

schizophrenic—*see* Schizophrenia

schizophreniform—*see* Schizophrenia

affective type—*see* Schizophrenia, schizo-affective type

confusional type—*see* Schizophrenia, acute episode

senile—*see* Senile dementia, delusional type

Pyromania: A disorder of impulse control characterized by a recurrent failure to resist impulses to set fires without regard for the consequences, or with deliberate destructive intent. Invariably there is intense fascination with the setting of fires, seeing fires burn, and a satisfaction with the resultant destruction.[2]

Relationship problems of childhood: Emotional disorders characteristic of childhood in which the main symptoms involve relationship problems.[1]

Repeated infarct dementia—*see* Arteriosclerotic dementia

Residual schizophrenia—*see* Schizophrenia, residual type

Restzustand (schizophrenia)—*see* Schizophrenia, residual type

Rumination:

obsessional: The constant preoccupation with certain thoughts, with inability to dismiss them from the mind.[4] *See* Neurotic disorder, obsessive-compulsive.

psychogenic: In children the regurgitation of food, with failure to thrive or weight loss developing after a period of normal functioning. Food is brought up without nausea, retching, or disgust. The food is then ejected from the mouth, or chewed and reswallowed.[2]

Sander's disease—*see* Paranoia

Satyriasis: Pathologic or exaggerated sexual desire or excitement in the man.[3]

Schizoid personality disorder—*see* Personality disorder, schizoid type

Schizophrenia: A group of psychoses in which there is a fundamental disturbance of personality, a characteristic distortion of thinking, often a sense of being controlled by alien forces, delusions which may be bizarre, disturbed perception, abnormal affect out of keeping with the real situation, and autism. Nevertheless, clear consciousness and intellectual capacity are usually maintained. The disturbance of personality involves its most basic functions which give the normal person his feeling of individuality, uniqueness, and self-direction. The most intimate thoughts, feelings, and acts are often felt to be known to or shared by others and explanatory delusions may develop, to the effect that natural or supernatural forces are at work to influence the schizophrenic person's thoughts and actions in ways that are often bizarre. He may see himself as the pivot of all that happens. Hallucinations, especially of hearing, are common and may comment on the patient or address him. Perception is frequently disturbed in other ways; there may be perplexity, irrelevant features may become all-important and accompanied by passivity feelings, may lead the patient to believe that everyday objects and situations possess a special, usually sinister, meaning intended for him. In the characteristic schizophrenic disturbance of thinking, peripheral and irrelevant features of a total concept, which are inhibited in normal directed mental activity, are brought to the forefront and utilized in place of the elements relevant and appropriate to the situation. Thus, thinking becomes vague, elliptical and obscure, and its expression in speech sometimes incomprehensible. Breaks and interpolations in the flow of consecutive thought are frequent, and the patient may be convinced that his thoughts are being withdrawn by some outside agency. Mood may be shallow, capricious, or incongruous. Ambivalence and disturbance of volition may appear as inertia, negativism, or stupor. Catatonia may be present. The diagnosis "schizophrenia" should not be made unless there is, or has been evident during the same illness, characteristic disturbance of thought, perception, mood, conduct, or personality—preferably in at least two of these areas. The diagnosis should not be restricted to conditions running a protracted, deteriorating, or chronic course. In addition to making the diagnosis on the criteria just given, effort should be made to specify one of the following subtypes of schizophrenia, according to the predominant symptoms.[1]

acute (undifferentiated): Schizophrenia of florid nature which cannot be classified as simple, catatonic, hebephrenic, paranoid, or any other types.[1]

acute episode: Schizophrenic disorders, other than simple, hebephrenic, catatonic, and paranoid, in which there is a dream-like state with slight clouding of consciousness and perplexity. External things, people, and events may become charged with personal significance for the patient. There may be ideas of reference and emotional turmoil. In many such cases remission occurs within a few weeks or months, even without treatment.[1]

atypical—*see* Schizophrenia, acute (undifferentiated)

borderline—*see* Schizophrenia, latent

catatonic type: Includes as an essential feature prominent psychomotor disturbances often alternating between extremes such as hyperkinesis and stupor, or automatic obedience and negativism. Constrained attitudes may be maintained for long periods: if the patient's limbs are put in some unnatural position they may be held there for some time after the external force has been removed. Severe excitement may be a striking feature of the condition. Depressive or hypomanic concomitants may be present.[1]

cenesthopathic—*see* Schizophrenia, acute (undifferentiated)

childhood type—*see* Psychosis, child

chronic undifferentiated—*see* Schizophrenia, residual

cyclic—*see* Schizophrenia, schizo-affective type

disorganized type: A form of schizophrenia in which affective changes are prominent, delusions and hallucinations fleeting and fragmentary, behavior irresponsible and unpredictable, and mannerisms common. The mood is shallow and inappropiate, accompanied by giggling or self-satisfied, self-absorbed smiling, or by a lofty manner, grimaces, mannerisms, pranks, hypochondriacal complaints, and reiterated phrases. Thought is disorganized. There is a tendency to remain solitary, and behavior seems empty of purpose and feeling. This form of schizophrenia usually starts between the ages of 15 and 25 years.[1]

hebephrenic type—*see* Schizophrenia, disorganized type

latent: It has not been possible to produce a generally acceptable description for this condition. It is not recommended for general use, but a description is provided for those who believe it to be useful: a condition of eccentric or inconsequent behavior and anomalies of affect which give the impression of schizophrenia though no definite and characteristic schizophrenic anomalies, present or past, have been manifest.[1]

paranoid type: The form of schizophrenia in which relatively stable delusions, which may be accompanied by hallucinations, dominate the clinical picture. The delusions are frequently of persecution, but may take other forms (for example, of jealousy, exalted birth, Messianic mission, or bodily change). Hallucinations and erratic behavior may occur; in some cases conduct is seriously disturbed from the outset, thought disorder may be gross, and affective flattening with fragmentary delusions and hallucinations may develop.[1]

prepsychotic—*see* Schizophrenia, latent

prodromal—*see* Schizophrenia, latent

pseudoneurotic—*see* Schizophrenia, latent

pseudopsychopathic—*see* Schizophrenia, latent

residual: A chronic form of schizophrenia in which the symptoms that persist from the acute phase have mostly lost their sharpness. Emotional response is blunted and thought disorder, even when gross, does not prevent the accomplishment of routine work.[1]

schizo-affective type: A psychosis in which pronounced manic or depressive features are intermingled with schizophrenic features and which tends towards remission without permanent defect, but which is prone to recur. The diagnosis should be made only when both the affective and schizophrenic symptoms are pronounced.[1]

simple type: A psychosis in which there is insidious development of oddities of conduct, inability to meet the demands of society, and decline in total performance. Delusions and hallucinations are not in evidence and the condition is less obviously psychotic than are the hebephrenic, catatonic, and paranoid types of schizophrenia. With increasing social impoverishment vagrancy may ensue and the patient becomes self-absorbed, idle, and aimless. Because the schizophrenic symptoms are not clear-cut, diagnosis of this form should be made sparingly, if at all.[1]

simplex—*see* Schizophrenia, simple type

Schizophrenic syndrome of childhood—*see* Psychosis, child

Schizophreniform

attack—*see* Schizophrenia, acute episode

disorder—*see* Schizophrenia, acute episode

psychosis—*see* Schizophrenia

affective type—*see* Schizophrenia, schizo-affective type

confusional type—*see* Schizophrenia, acute episode

Schizotypal personality—*see* Personality disorder, schizotypal type

Senile dementia: Dementia occurring usually after the age of 65 in which any cerebral pathology other than that of senile atrophic change can be reasonably excluded.[1]

delirium: Senile dementia with a superimposed reversible episode of acute confusional state.[1]

delusional type: A type of senile dementia characterized by development in advanced old age, progressive in nature, in which delusions, varying from simple poorly formed paranoid delusions to highly formed paranoid delusional states, and hallucinations are also present.[1,2]

depressed type: A type of senile dementia characterized by development in advanced old age, progressive in nature, in which depressive features, ranging from mild to severe forms of manic-depressive affective psychosis, are also present. Disturbance of the sleep-waking cycle and preoccupation with dead people are often particularly prominent.[1,2]

paranoid type—*see* Senile dementia, delusional type

simple type—*see* Senile dementia

Sensitiver Beziehungswahn: A paranoid state which, though in many ways akin to schizophrenic or affective states, differs from paranoia, simple paranoid state, shared paranoid disorder, or psychogenic psychosis.[1]

Sensitivity reaction of childhood or adolescence—*see* Shyness disorder of childhood

Separation anxiety disorder: A clinical disorder in children in which the predominant disturbance is
exaggerated distress at separation from parents, home, or other familial surroundings. When separation is instituted, the child may experience anxiety to the point of panic. In adults a similar disorder is seen in agoraphobic reactions.[2]

Sexual deviations: Abnormal sexual inclinations or behavior which are part of a referral problem. The limits and features of normal sexual behavior have not been stated absolutely in different societies and cultures, but are broadly such as serve approved social and biological purposes. The sexual activity of affected persons is directed primarily either towards people not of the opposite sex, or towards sexual acts not associated with coitus normally, or towards coitus performed under abnormal circumstances. If the anomalous behavior becomes manifest only during psychosis or other mental illness the condition should be classified under the major illness. It is common for more than one anomaly to occur together in the same individual; in that case the predominant deviation is classified. It is preferablenot to diagnose sexual deviation in individuals who perform deviantsexual acts when normal sexual outlets are not available to them.[1] *See also* Exhibitionism, Fetishism, Homosexuality, Nymphomania, Pedophilia, Satyriasis, Sexual masochism, Sexual sadism, Transvestism, Voyeurism, and Zoophilia.

Gender identity disorder and trans-sexualism are considered to be psychosexual gender identity disorders and are not included here.

Sexual masochism: A sexual deviation in which sexual arousal and pleasure is produced in an individual by his own physical or psychological suffering, and in which there are insistent and persistent fantasies wherein sexual excitement is produced as a result of suffering.[2]

Sexual sadism: A sexual deviation in which physical or psychological suffering inflicted on another person is utilized as a method of stimulating erotic excitement and orgasm, and in which there are insistent and persistent fantasies wherein sexual excitement is produced as a result of suffering inflicted on the partner.[2]

Shared paranoid disorder: Mainly delusional psychosis, usually chronic and often without florid features, which appears to have developed as a result of a close, if not dependent, relationship with another person who already has an established similar psychosis. The delusions are at least partly shared. The rare cases in which several persons are affected should also be included here.[1]

Shifting sleep-work schedule: A sleep disorder in which the phase-shift disruption of the 24-hour sleep-wake cycle occurs due to rapid changes in the individual's work schedule.[2]

Short sleeper: Individuals who typically need only 4-6 hours of sleep within the 24-hour cycle.[2]

Shyness disorder of childhood: A persistent and excessive shrinking from familiarity or contact with all strangers of sufficient severity as to interfere with peer functioning, yet there are warm and satisfying relationships with family members. A critical feature of this disorder is that the avoidant behavior with strangers persists even after prolonged exposure or contact.[2]

Sibling jealousy or rivalry: An emotional disorder related to competition between siblings for the love of a parent or for other recognition or gain.[3]

Simple phobia—*see* simple phobia under Phobia

Situational disturbance, acute—*see* Stress reaction, acute

Social phobia—*see* social phobia under Phobia

Social withdrawal of childhood—*see* Introverted disorder of childhood

Socialized conduct disorder—*see* socialized conduct disorder under Conduct disorders

Somatization disorder—*see* somatization disorder under Neurotic disorders

Somatoform disorder, atypical—*see* hypochondriasis under Neurotic disorders

Spasmus nutans—*see* Stereotyped repetitive movements

Specific academic or work inhibition: An adjustment reaction in which a specific academic or work inhibition occurs in an individual whose intellectual capacity, skills, and previous academic or work performance have been at least adequate, and in which the inhibition occurs despite apparent effort and is not due to any other mental disorder.[2]

Stammering—*see* Stuttering

Starch-eating—*see* Pica

Status postcommotio cerebri—*see* Postconcussion syndrome

Stereotyped repetitive movements: Disorders in which voluntary repetitive stereotyped movements, which are not due to any psychiatric or neurological condition, constitute the main feature. Includes head-banging, spasmus nutans, rocking, twirling, finger-flicking mannerisms, and eye poking. Such movements are particularly common in cases of mental retardation with sensory impairment or with environmental monotony.[1]

Stereotypies—*see* Stereotyped repetitive movements

Stress reaction

acute: Acute transient disorders of any severity and nature of emotions, consciousness, and psychomotor states (singly or in combination) which occur in individuals, without any apparent pre-existing mental disorder, in response to exceptional physical or mental stress, such as natural catastrophe or battle, and which usually subside within hours or days.[1]

chronic—*see* Adjustment reaction

Stupor

catatonic—*see* Schizophrenia, catatonic type

psychogenic—*see* Psychosis, reactive

Stuttering: Disorders in the rhythm of speech, in which the individual knows precisely what he wishes to say, but at the time is unable to say it because of an involuntary, repetitive prolongation or cessation of a sound.[1]

Subjective insomnia complaint: A complaint of insomnia made by the individual, which has not been investigated or proven.[2]

Tension headache: Headache of mental origin for which a more precise medical or psychiatric diagnosis cannot be made.[1]

Systematized delusions—*see* Paranoia

Tics: Disorders of no known organic origin in which the outstanding feature consists of quick, involuntary, apparently purposeless, and frequently repeated movements which are not due to any neurological condition. Any part of the body may be involved but the face is most frequently affected. Only one form of tic may be present, or there may be a combination of tics which are carried out simultaneously, alternatively, or consecutively.[1]

chronic motor tic disorder: A tic disorder starting in childhood and persisting into adult life. The tic is limited to no more than three motor areas, and rarely has a verbal component.[2]

Gilles de la Tourette's disorder [motor-verbal tic disorder]: A rare disorder occurring in individuals of any level of intelligence in which facial tics and tic-like throat noises become more marked and more generalized, and in which later whole words or short sentences (often with obscene content) are ejaculated spasmodically and involuntarily. There is some overlap with other varieties of tic.[1]

transient tic disorder of childhood: Facial or other tics beginning in childhood, but limited to one year in duration.[2]

Tobacco use disorder: Cases in which tobacco is used to the detriment of a person's health or social functioning or in which there is tobacco dependence. Dependence is included here rather than under drug dependence because tobacco differs from other drugs of dependence in its psychotoxic effects.[1]

Tranquilizer abuse: Cases where an individual has taken the drug to the detriment of his health or social functioning, in doses above or for periods beyond those normally regarded as therapeutic.[1]

Transient organic psychotic condition—*see* Organic psychotic conditions, transient

Trans-sexualism—see trans-sexualism under Psychosexual identity disorders

Transvestism: Sexual deviation in which there is recurrent and persistent dressing in clothes of the opposite sex, and initially in the early stage of the illness, for the purpose of sexual arousal.[2]

Twilight state

confusional—*see* Delirium, acute

psychogenic—*see* Psychosis, reactive confusion

Undersocialized conduct disorder—*see* undersocialized conduct disorder under Conduct disorders

Unsocialized aggressive disorder—*see* undersocialized conduct disorder, aggressive type under Conduct disorders

Vaginismus, functional—*see* functional vaginismus under Psychosexual dysfunctions

Vorbeireden: The symptom of the approximate answer or talking past the point, seen in the Ganser syndrome, a form of factitious illness.[2]

Voyeurism: A sexual deviation in which the individual repetitively seeks out situations in which he engages in looking at unsuspecting women who are either naked, in the act of disrobing, or engaging in sexual activity. The act of looking is accompanied by sexual excitement, frequently with orgasm. In its severe form, the act of peeping constitutes the preferred or exclusive sexual activity of the individual.[2]

Wernicke-Korsakoff syndrome—*see* alcohol amnestic syndrome under Alcoholic psychoses

Withdrawal reaction of childhood or adolescence—*see* Introverted disorder of childhood

Word-deafness: A developmental delay in the comprehension of speech sounds.[1]

Zoophillia: Sexual or anal intercourse with animals.[1]

1. Manual of the *International Classification of Diseases, Injuries, and Causes of Death,* 9th Revision, World Health Organization, Geneva, Switzerland, 1975.
2. American Psychiatric Association, Task Force on Nomenclature and Statistics, Robert L. Spitzer, Chairman.
3. *A Psychiatiric Glossary*, Fourth Edition, American Psychiatric Association, Washington, D.C., 1975
4. *Dorland's Illustrated Medical Dictionary*, Twenty-fifth Edition, W.B. Saunders Company, Philadelphia, 1974.
5. *Stedman's Medical Dictionary, Illustrated*, Twenty-third Edition, the Williams and Wilkins Company, Baltimore, 1976.

CLASSIFICATION OF DRUGS BY AMERICAN HOSPITAL FORMULARY SERVICE LIST NUMBER AND THEIR ICD-9-CM EQUIVALENTS

The coding of adverse effects of drugs is keyed to the continually revised Hospital Formulary of the American Hospital Formulary Service (AHFS) published under the direction of the American Society of Hospital Pharmacists. The following section gives the ICD-9-CM diagnosis code for each AHFS list.

	AHFS* List	ICD-9-CM Diagnosis Code
4:00	ANTIHISTAMINE DRUGS	963.0
8:00	ANTI-INFECTIVE AGENTS	
8:04	Amebacides	961.5
	hydroxyquinoline derivatives	961.3
	arsenical anti-infectives	961.1
8:08	Anthelmintics	961.6
	quinoline derivatives	961.3
8:12.04	Antifungal Antibiotics	960.1
	nonantibiotics	961.9
8:12.06	Cephalosporins	960.5
8:12.08	Chloramphenicol	960.2
8:12.12	The Erythromycins	960.3
8:12.16	The Penicillins	960.0
8:12.20	The Streptomycins	960.6
8:12.24	The Tetracyclines	960.4
8:12.28	Other Antibiotics	960.8
	antimycobacterial antibiotics	960.6
	macrolides	960.3
8:16	Antituberculars	961.8
	antibiotics	960.6
8:18	Antivirals	961.7
8:20	Plasmodicides (antimalarials)	961.4
8:24	Sulfonamides	961.0
8:26	The Sulfones	961.8
8:28	Treponemicides	961.2
8:32	Trichomonacides	961.5
	hydroxyquinoline derivatives	961.3
	nitrofuran derivatives	961.9
8:36	Urinary Germicides	961.9
	quinoline derivatives	961.3
8:40	Other Anti-Infectives	961.9
10:00	ANTINEOPLASTIC AGENTS	963.1
	antibiotics	960.7
	progestogens	962.2
12:00	AUTONOMIC DRUGS	
12:04	Parasympathomimetic (Cholinergic) Agents	971.0
12:08	Parasympatholytic (Cholinergic Blocking) Agents	971.1
12:12	Sympathomimetic (Adrenergic) Agents	971.2
12:16	Sympatholytic (Adrenergic Blocking) Agents	971.3
12:20	Skeletal Muscle Relaxants	975.2
	central nervous system muscle-tone depressants	968.0
16:00	BLOOD DERIVATIVES	964.7
20:00	BLOOD FORMATION AND COAGULATION	
20:04	Antianemia Drugs	964.1
20:04.04	Iron Preparations	964.0
20:04.08	Liver and Stomach Preparations	964.1
20:12.04	Anticoagulants	964.2
20:12.08	Antiheparin agents	964.5
20:12.12	Coagulants	964.5
20:12.16	Hemostatics	964.5
	capillary-active drugs	972.8
	fibrinolysis-affecting agents	964.4
	natural products	964.7

*American Hospital Formulary Service

	AHFS* List	ICD-9-CM Diagnosis Code
24:00	CARDIOVASCULAR DRUGS	
24:04	Cardiac Drugs	972.9
	cardiotonic agents	972.1
	rhythm regulators	972.0
24:06	Antilipemic Agents	972.2
	thyroid derivatives	962.7
24:08	Hypotensive Agents	972.6
	adrenergic blocking agents	971.3
	ganglion-blocking agents	972.3
	vasodilators	972.5
24:12	Vasodilating Agents	972.5
	coronary	972.4
	nicotinic acid derivatives	972.2
24:16	Sclerosing Agents	972.7
28:00	CENTRAL NERVOUS SYSTEM DRUG	
28.04	General Anesthetics	968.4
	gaseous anesthetics	968.2
	halothane	968.1
	intravenous anesthetics	968.3
28:08	Analgesics and Antipyretics	965.9
	antirheumatics	965.6
	aromatic analgesics	965.4
	non-narcotics NEC	965.7
	opium alkaloids	965.00
	heroin	965.01
	methadone	965.02
	specified type NEC	965.09
	pyrazole derivatives	965.5
	salicylates	965.1
	specified type NEC	965.8
28:10	Narcotic Antagonists	970.1
28:12	Anticonvulsants	966.3
	barbiturates	967.0
	benzodiazepine-based tranquilizers	969.4
	bromides	967.3
	hydantoin derivatives	966.1
	oxazolidine derivative	966.0
	succinimides	966.2
28:16.04	Antidepressants	969.0
28:16.08	Tranquilizers	969.5
	benzodiazepine-based	969.4
	butyrophenone-based	969.2
	major NEC	969.3
	phenothiazine-based	969.1
28:16.12	Other Psychotherapeutic Agents	969.8
28:20	Respiratory and Cerebral Stimulants	970.9
	analeptics	970.0
	anorexigenic agents	977.0
	psychostimulants	969.7
	specified type NEC	970.8
28:24	Sedatives and Hypnotics	967.9
	barbiturates	967.0
	benzodiazepine-based tranquilizers	969.4
	chloral hydrate group	967.1
	glutethamide group	967.5
	intravenous anesthetics	968.3
	methaqualone	967.4
	paraldehyde	967.2
	phenothiazine-based tranquilizers	969.1
	specified type NEC	967.8
	thiobarbiturates	968.3
	tranquilizer NEC	969.5
36:00	DIAGNOSTIC AGENTS	977.8
40:00	ELECTROLYTE, CALORIC, AND WATER BALANCE AGENTS NEC	974.5
40:04	Acidifying Agents	963.2
40:08	Alkalinizing Agents	963.3
40:10	Ammonia Detoxicants	974.5
40:12	Replacement Solutions NEC	974.5
	plasma volume expanders	964.8
40:16	Sodium-Removing Resins	974.5
40:18	Potassium-Removing Resins	974.5

	AHFS* List	ICD-9-CM Diagnosis Code
40:20	Caloric Agents	974.5
40:24	Salt and Sugar Substitutes	974.5
40:28	Diuretics NEC	974.4
	carbonic acid anhydrase inhibitors	974.2
	mercurials	974.0
	purine derivatives	974.1
	saluretics	974.3
40:36	Irrigating Solutions	974.5
40:40	Uricosuric Agents	974.7
44:00	ENZYMES NEC	963.4
	fibrinolysis-affecting agents	964.4
	gastric agents	973.4
48:00	EXPECTORANTS AND COUGH PREPARATIONS	
	antihistamine agents	963.0
	antitussives	975.4
	codeine derivatives	965.09
	expectorants	975.5
	narcotic agents NEC	965.09
52:00	EYE, EAR, NOSE, AND THROAT PREPARATIONS	
52:04	Anti-Infectives	
	ENT	976.6
	ophthalmic	976.5
52:04.06	Antibiotics	
	ENT	976.6
	ophthalmic	976.5
52:04.04	Antivirals	
	ENT	976.6
	ophthalmic	976.5
52:04.08	Sulfonamides	
	ENT	976.6
	ophthalmic	976.5
52:04.12	Miscellaneous Anti-Infectives	
	ENT	976.6
	ophthalmic	976.5
52:08	Anti-Inflammatory Agents	
	ENT	976.6
	ophthalmic	976.5
52:10	Carbonic Anhydrase Inhibitors	974.2
52:12	Contact Lens Solutions	976.5
52:16	Local Anesthetics	968.5
52:20	Miotics	971.0
52:24	Mydriatics	
	adrenergics	971.2
	anticholinergics	971.1
	antimuscarinics	971.1
	parasympatholytics	971.1
	spasmolytics	971.1
	sympathomimetics	971.2
52:28	Mouth Washes and Gargles	976.6
52:32	Vasoconstrictors	971.2
52:36	Unclassified Agents	
	ENT	976.6
	ophthalmic	976.5
56:00	GASTROINTESTINAL DRUGS	
56:04	Antacids and Absorbents	973.0
56:08	Anti-Diarrhea Agents	973.5
56:10	Antiflatulents	973.8
56:12	Cathartics NEC	973.3
	emollients	973.2
	irritants	973.1
56:16	Digestants	973.4
56:20	Emetics and Antiemetics	
	antiemetics	963.0
	emetics	973.6
56:24	Lipotropic Agents	977.1
60:00	GOLD COMPOUNDS	965.6

*American Hospital Formulary Service

	AHFS* List	ICD-9-CM Diagnosis Code
64:00	HEAVY METAL ANTAGONISTS	963.8
68:00	HORMONES AND SYNTHETIC SUBSTITUTES	
68:04	Adrenals	962.0
68:08	Androgens	962.1
68:12	Contraceptives	962.2
68:16	Estrogens	962.2
68:18	Gonadotropins	962.4
68:20	Insulins and Antidiabetic Agents	962.3
68:20.08	Insulins	962.3
68:24	Parathyroid	962.6
68:28	Pituitary	
	anterior	962.4
	posterior	962.5
68:32	Progestogens	962.2
68:34	Other Corpus Luteum Hormones	962.2
68:36	Thyroid and Antithyroid	
	antithyroid	962.8
	thyroid	962.7
72:00	LOCAL ANESTHETICS NEC	968.9
	topical (surface) agents	968.5
	infiltrating agents (intradermal) (subcutaneous) (submucosal)	968.5
	nerve blocking agents (peripheral) (plexus) (regional)	968.6
	spinal	968.7
76:00	OXYTOCICS	975.0
78:00	RADIOACTIVE AGENTS	990
80:00	SERUMS, TOXOIDS, AND VACCINES	
80:04	Serums	979.9
	immune globulin (gamma) (human)	964.6
80:08	Toxoids NEC	978.8
	diphtheria	978.5
	and tetanus	978.9
	with pertussis component	978.6
	tetanus	978.4
	and diphtheria	978.9
	with pertussis component	978.6
80:12	Vaccines NEC	979.9
	bacterial NEC	978.8
	with	
	other bacterial component	978.9
	pertussis component	978.6
	viral and rickettsial component	979.7
	rickettsial NEC	979.6
	with	
	bacterial component	979.7
	pertussis component	978.6
	viral component	979.7
	viral NEC	979.6
	with	
	bacterial component	979.7
	pertussis component	978.6
	rickettsial component	979.7
84:00	SKIN AND MUCOUS MEMBRANE PREPARATIONS	
84:04	Anti-Infectives	976.0
84:04.04	Antibiotics	976.0
84:04.08	Fungicides	976.0
84:04.12	Scabicides and Pediculicides	976.0
84:04.16	Miscellaneous Local Anti-Infectives	976.0
84:06	Anti-Inflammatory Agents	976.0
84:08	Antipruritics and Local Anesthetics	
	antipruritics	976.1
	local anesthetics	968.5
84:12	Astringents	976.2
84:16	Cell Stimulants and Proliferants	976.8
84:20	Detergents	976.2
84:24	Emollients, Demulcents, and Protectants	976.3

	AHFS* List	ICD-9-CM Diagnosis Code
84:28	Keratolytic Agents	976.4
84:32	Keratoplastic Agents	976.4
84:36	Miscellaneous Agents	976.8
86:00	SPASMOLYTIC AGENTS	975.1
	antiasthmatics	975.7
	papaverine	972.5
	theophyllin	974.1
88:00	VITAMINS	
88:04	Vitamin A	963.5
88:08	Vitamin B Complex	963.5
	hematopoietic vitamin	964.1
	nicotinic acid derivatives	972.2
88:12	Vitamin C	963.5
88:16	Vitamin D	963.5
88:20	Vitamin E	963.5
88:24	Vitamin K Activity	964.3
88:28	Multivitamin Preparations	963.5
92:00	UNCLASSIFIED THERAPEUTIC AGENTS	977.8

*American Hospital Formulary Service

CLASSIFICATION OF INDUSTRIAL ACCIDENTS ACCORDING TO AGENCY

Annex B to the Resolution concering Statistics of Employment Injuries adopted by the Tenth International Conference of Labor Statistician on 12 October 1962

1 MACHINES

11 Prime-Movers, except Electrical Motors

111 *Steam engines*
112 *Internal combustion engines*
119 *Others*

12 Transmission Machinery

121 *Transmission shafts*
122 *Transmission belts, cables, pulleys, pinions, chains, gears*
129 *Others*

13 Metalworking Machines

131 *Power presses*
132 *Lathes*
133 *Milling machines*
134 *Abrasive wheels*
135 *Mechanical shears*
136 *Forging machines*
137 *Rolling-mills*
139 *Others*

14 Wood and Assimilated Machines

141 *Circular saws*
142 *Other saws*
143 *Molding machines*
144 *Overhand planes*
149 *Others*

15 Agricultural Machines

151 *Reapers (including combine reapers)*
152 *Threshers*
159 *Others*

16 Mining Machinery

161 *Under-cutters*
169 *Others*

19 Other Machines Not Elsewhere Classified

191 *Earth-moving machines, excavating and scraping machines, except means of transport*
192 *Spinning, weaving and other textile machines*
193 *Machines for the manufacture of foodstuffs and beverages*
194 *Machines for the manufacture of paper*
195 *Printing machines*
199 *Others*

2 MEANS OF TRANSPORT AND LIFTING EQUIPMENT

21 Lifting Machines and Appliances

211 *Cranes*
212 *Lifts and elevators*
213 *Winches*
214 *Pulley blocks*
219 *Others*

22 Means of Rail Transport

221 *Inter-urban railways*
222 *Rail transport in mines, tunnels, quarries, industrial establishments, docks, etc.*
229 *Others*

23 Other Wheeled Means of Transport, Excluding Rail Transport

231 *Tractors*
232 *Lorries*
233 *Trucks*
234 *Motor vehicles, not elsewhere classified*
235 *Animal-drawn vehicles*
236 *Hand-drawn vehicles*
239 *Others*

24 Means of Air Transport

25 Means of Water Transport

251 *Motorized means of water transport*
252 *Non-motorized means of water transport*

26 Other Means of Transport

261 *Cable-cars*
262 *Mechanical conveyors, except cable-cars*
269 *Others*

3 OTHER EQUIPMENT

31 Pressure Vessels

311 *Boilers*
312 *Pressurized containers*
313 *Pressurized piping and accessories*
314 *Gas cylinders*
315 *Caissons, diving equipment*
319 *Others*

32 Furnaces, Ovens, Kilns

321 *Blast furnaces*
322 *Refining furnaces*
323 *Other furnaces*
324 *Kilns*
325 *Ovens*

33 Refrigerating Plants

34 Electrical Installations, Including Electric Motors, but Excluding Electric Hand Tools

341 *Rotating Machines*
342 *Conductors*
343 *Transformers*
344 *Control apparatus*
349 *Others*

35 Electric Hand Tools

36 Tools, Implements, and Appliances, Except Electric Hand Tools

361 *Power-driven hand tools, except electric hand tools*
362 *Hand tools, not power-driven*
369 *Others*

37 Ladders, Mobile Ramps

38 Scaffolding

39 Other Equipment, Not Elsewhere Classified

4 MATERIALS, SUBSTANCES AND RADIATIONS

41 Explosives

42 Dusts, Gases, Liquids and Chemicals, Excluding Explosives

421 *Dusts*
422 *Gases, vapors, fumes*
423 *Liquids, not elsewhere classified*
424 *Chemicals, not elsewhere classified*

43 Flying Fragments

44 Radiations

441 *Ionizing radiations*
449 *Others*

49 Other Materials and Substances Not Elsewhere Classified

5 WORKING ENVIRONMENT

51 Outdoor

511 *Weather*
512 *Traffic and working surfaces*
513 *Water*
519 *Others*

52 Indoor

521 *Floors*
522 *Confined quarters*
523 *Stairs*
524 *Other traffic and working surfaces*
525 *Floor openings and wall openings*
526 *Environmental factors (lighting, ventilation, temperature, noise, etc.)*
529 *Others*

53 Underground

531 *Roofs and faces of mine roads and tunnels, etc.*
532 *Floors of mine roads and tunnels, etc.*
533 *Working-faces of mines, tunnels, etc.*
534 *Mine shafts*
535 *Fire*
536 *Water*
539 *Others*

6 OTHER AGENCIES, NOT ELSEWHERE CLASSIFIED

61 Animals

611 *Live animals*
612 *Animals products*

69 Other Agencies, Not Elsewhere Classified

7 AGENCIES NOT CLASSIFIED FOR LACK OF SUFFFICIENT DATA

LIST OF THREE-DIGIT CATEGORIES

1. INFECTIOUS AND PARASITIC DISEASES

Intestinal infectious diseases (001-009)

001 Cholera
002 Typhoid and paratyphoid fevers
003 Other salmonella infections
004 Shigellosis
005 Other food poisoning (bacterial)
006 Amebiasis
007 Other protozoal intestinal diseases
008 Intestinal infections due to other organisms
009 Ill-defined intestinal infections

Tuberculosis (010-018)

010 Primary tuberculous infection
011 Pulmonary tuberculosis
012 Other respiratory tuberculosis
013 Tuberculosis of meninges and central nervous system
014 Tuberculosis of intestines, peritoneum, and mesenteric glands
015 Tuberculosis of bones and joints
016 Tuberculosis of genitourinary system
017 Tuberculosis of other organs
018 Miliary tuberculosis

Zoonotic bacterial diseases (020-027)

020 Plague
021 Tularemia
022 Anthrax
023 Brucellosis
024 Glanders
025 Melioidosis
026 Rat-bite fever
027 Other zoonotic bacterial diseases

Other bacterial diseases (030-041)

030 Leprosy
031 Diseases due to other mycobacteria
032 Diphtheria
033 Whooping cough
034 Streptococcal sore throat and scarlet fever
035 Erysipelas
036 Meningococcal infection
037 Tetanus
038 Septicemia
039 Actinomycotic infections
040 Other bacterial diseases
041 Bacterial infection in conditions classified elsewhere and of unspecified site

Human immunodeficiency virus (042)

042 Human immunodeficiency virus [HIV] disease

Poliomyelitis and other non-arthropod-borne viral diseases of central nervous system (045-049)

045 Acute poliomyelitis
046 Slow virus infection of central nervous system
047 Meningitis due to enterovirus
048 Other enterovirus diseases of central nervous system
049 Other non-arthropod-borne viral diseases of central nervous system

Viral diseases accompanied by exanthem (050-057)

050 Smallpox
051 Cowpox and paravaccinia
052 Chickenpox
053 Herpes zoster
054 Herpes simplex
055 Measles
056 Rubella
057 Other viral exanthemata

Arthropod-borne viral diseases (060-066)

060 Yellow fever
061 Dengue
062 Mosquito-borne viral encephalitis
063 Tick-borne viral encephalitis
064 Viral encephalitis transmitted by other and unspecified arthropods
065 Arthropod-borne hemorrhagic fever
066 Other arthropod-borne viral diseases

Other diseases due to viruses and Chlamydiae (070-079)

070 Viral hepatitis
071 Rabies
072 Mumps
073 Ornithosis
074 Specific diseases due to Coxsackie virus
075 Infectious mononucleosis
076 Trachoma
077 Other diseases of conjunctiva due to viruses and Chlamydiae
078 Other diseases due to viruses and Chlamydiae
079 Viral and chlamydial infection in conditions classified elsewhere and of unspecified site

Rickettsioses and other arthropod-borne diseases (080-088)

080 Louse-borne [epidemic] typhus
081 Other typhus
082 Tick-borne rickettsioses
083 Other rickettsioses
084 Malaria
085 Leishmaniasis
086 Trypanosomiasis
087 Relapsing fever
088 Other arthropod-borne diseases

Syphilis and other venereal diseases (090-099)

090 Congenital syphilis
091 Early syphilis, symptomatic
092 Early syphilis, latent
093 Cardiovascular syphilis
094 Neurosyphilis
095 Other forms of late syphilis, with symptoms
096 Late syphilis, latent
097 Other and unspecified syphilis
098 Gonococcal infections
099 Other venereal diseases

Other spirochetal diseases (100-104)

100 Leptospirosis
101 Vincent's angina
102 Yaws
103 Pinta
104 Other spirochetal infection

Mycoses (110-118)

110 Dermatophytosis
111 Dermatomycosis, other and unspecified
112 Candidiasis
114 Coccidioidomycosis
115 Histoplasmosis
116 Blastomycotic infection
117 Other mycoses
118 Opportunistic mycoses

Helminthiases (120-129)

120 Schistosomiasis [bilharziasis]
121 Other trematode infections
122 Echinococcosis
123 Other cestode infection
124 Trichinosis
125 Filarial infection and dracontiasis
126 Ancylostomiasis and necatoriasis
127 Other intestinal helminthiases
128 Other and unspecified helminthiases
129 Intestinal parasitism, unspecified

Other infectious and parasitic diseases (130-136)

130 Toxoplasmosis
131 Trichomoniasis
132 Pediculosis and phthirus infestation
133 Acariasis
134 Other infestation
135 Sarcoidosis
136 Other and unspecified infectious and parasitic diseases

Late effects of infectious and parasitic diseases (137-139)

137 Late effects of tuberculosis
138 Late effects of acute poliomyelitis
139 Late effects of other infectious and parasitic diseases

2. NEOPLASMS (140-239)

Malignant neoplasm of lip, oral cavity, and pharynx (140-149)

140 Malignant neoplasm of lip
141 Malignant neoplasm of tongue
142 Malignant neoplasm of major salivary glands
143 Malignant neoplasm of gum
144 Malignant neoplasm of floor of mouth
145 Malignant neoplasm of other and unspecified parts of mouth
146 Malignant neoplasm of oropharynx
147 Malignant neoplasm of nasopharynx
148 Malignant neoplasm of hypopharynx
149 Malignant neoplasm of other and ill-defined sites within the lip, oral cavity, and pharynx

Malignant neoplasm of digestive organs and peritoneum (150-159)

150 Malignant neoplasm of esophagus
151 Malignant neoplasm of stomach
152 Malignant neoplasm of small intestine, including duodenum
153 Malignant neoplasm of colon
154 Malignant neoplasm of rectum, rectosigmoid junction, and anus
155 Malignant neoplasm of liver and intrahepatic bile ducts
156 Malignant neoplasm of gallbladder and extrahepatic bile ducts
157 Malignant neoplasm of pancreas
158 Malignant neoplasm of retroperitoneum and peritoneum
159 Malignant neoplasm of other and ill-defined sites within the digestive organs and peritoneum

Malignant neoplasm of respiratory and intrathoracic organs (160-165)

160 Malignant neoplasm of nasal cavities, middle ear, and accessory sinuses
161 Malignant neoplasm of larynx
162 Malignant neoplasm of trachea, bronchus, and lung
163 Malignant neoplasm of pleura
164 Malignant neoplasm of thymus, heart, and mediastinum
165 Malignant neoplasm of other and ill-defined sites within the respiratory system and intrathoracic organs

Malignant neoplasm of bone, connective tissue, skin, and breast (170-176)

170 Malignant neoplasm of bone and articular cartilage
171 Malignant neoplasm of connective and other soft tissue
172 Malignant melanoma of skin
173 Other malignant neoplasm of skin
174 Malignant neoplasm of female breast
175 Malignant neoplasm of male breast
176 Kaposi's sarcoma

Malignant neoplasm of genitourinary organs (179-189)

179 Malignant neoplasm of uterus, part unspecified
180 Malignant neoplasm of cervix uteri
181 Malignant neoplasm of placenta
182 Malignant neoplasm of body of uterus
183 Malignant neoplasm of ovary and other uterine adnexa
184 Malignant neoplasm of other and unspecified female genital organs
185 Malignant neoplasm of prostate
186 Malignant neoplasm of testis
187 Malignant neoplasm of penis and other male genital organs
188 Malignant neoplasm of bladder
189 Malignant neoplasm of kidney and other and unspecified urinary organs

Malignant neoplasm of other and unspecified sites (190-199)

190 Malignant neoplasm of eye
191 Malignant neoplasm of brain
192 Malignant neoplasm of other and unspecified parts of nervous system
193 Malignant neoplasm of thyroid gland
194 Malignant neoplasm of other endocrine glands and related structures
195 Malignant neoplasm of other and ill-defined sites
196 Secondary and unspecified malignant neoplasm of lymph nodes
197 Secondary malignant neoplasm of respiratory and digestive systems
198 Secondary malignant neoplasm of other specified sites
199 Malignant neoplasm without specification of site

Malignant neoplasm of lymphatic and hematopoietic tissue (200-208)

200 Lymphosarcoma and reticulosarcoma
201 Hodgkin's disease
202 Other malignant neoplasm of lymphoid and histiocytic tissue
203 Multiple myeloma and immunoproliferative neoplasms
204 Lymphoid leukemia
205 Myeloid leukemia
206 Monocytic leukemia
207 Other specified leukemia
208 Leukemia of unspecified cell type

Benign neoplasms (210-229)

210 Benign neoplasm of lip, oral cavity, and pharynx
211 Benign neoplasm of other parts of digestive system
212 Benign neoplasm of respiratory and intrathoracic organs
213 Benign neoplasm of bone and articular cartilage
214 Lipoma
215 Other benign neoplasm of connective and other soft tissue
216 Benign neoplasm of skin
217 Benign neoplasm of breast
218 Uterine leiomyoma
219 Other benign neoplasm of uterus
220 Benign neoplasm of ovary
221 Benign neoplasm of other female genital organs
222 Benign neoplasm of male genital organs
223 Benign neoplasm of kidney and other urinary organs
224 Benign neoplasm of eye
225 Benign neoplasm of brain and other parts of nervous system
226 Benign neoplasm of thyroid gland
227 Benign neoplasm of other endocrine glands and related structures
228 Hemangioma and lymphangioma, any site
229 Benign neoplasm of other and unspecified sites

Carcinoma in situ (230-234)

230 Carcinoma in situ of digestive organs
231 Carcinoma in situ of respiratory system
232 Carcinoma in situ of skin
233 Carcinoma in situ of breast and genitourinary system
234 Carcinoma in situ of other and unspecified sites

Neoplasms of uncertain behavior (235-238)

235 Neoplasm of uncertain behavior of digestive and respiratory systems
236 Neoplasm of uncertain behavior of genitourinary organs
237 Neoplasm of uncertain behavior of endocrine glands and nervous system
238 Neoplasm of uncertain behavior of other and unspecified sites and tissues

Neoplasms of unspecified nature (239)

239 Neoplasm of unspecified nature

3. ENDOCRINE, NUTRITIONAL AND METABOLIC DISEASES, AND IMMUNITY DISORDERS (240-279)

Disorders of thyroid gland (240-246)

240 Simple and unspecified goiter
241 Nontoxic nodular goiter
242 Thyrotoxicosis with or without goiter
243 Congenital hypothyroidism
244 Acquired hypothyroidism
245 Thyroiditis
246 Other disorders of thyroid

Diseases of other endocrine glands (250-259)

250 Diabetes mellitus
251 Other disorders of pancreatic internal secretion
252 Disorders of parathyroid gland
253 Disorders of the pituitary gland and its hypothalamic control
254 Diseases of thymus gland
255 Disorders of adrenal glands
256 Ovarian dysfunction
257 Testicular dysfunction
258 Polyglandular dysfunction and related disorders
259 Other endocrine disorders

Nutritional deficiencies (260-269)

260 Kwashiorkor
261 Nutritional marasmus
262 Other severe protein-calorie malnutrition
263 Other and unspecified protein-calorie malnutrition
264 Vitamin A deficiency
265 Thiamine and niacin deficiency states

266 Deficiency of B-complex components
267 Ascorbic acid deficiency
268 Vitamin D deficiency
269 Other nutritional deficiencies

Other metabolic and immunity disorders (270-279)

270 Disorders of amino-acid transport and metabolism
271 Disorders of carbohydrate transport and metabolism
272 Disorders of lipoid metabolism
273 Disorders of plasma protein metabolism
274 Gout
275 Disorders of mineral metabolism
276 Disorders of fluid, electrolyte, and acid-base balance
277 Other and unspecified disorders of metabolism
278 Obesity and other hyperalimentation
279 Disorders involving the immune mechanism

4. DISEASES OF BLOOD AND BLOOD-FORMING ORGANS (280-289)

Diseases of blood and blood-forming organs (280-289)

280 Iron deficiency anemias
281 Other deficiency anemias
282 Hereditary hemolytic anemias
283 Acquired hemolytic anemias
284 Aplastic anemia
285 Other and unspecified anemias
286 Coagulation defects
287 Purpura and other hemorrhagic conditions
288 Diseases of white blood cells
289 Other diseases of blood and blood-forming organs

5. MENTAL DISORDERS (290-319)

Organic psychotic conditions (290-294)

290 Senile and presenile organic psychotic conditions
291 Alcoholic psychoses
292 Drug psychoses
293 Transient organic psychotic conditions
294 Other organic psychotic conditions (chronic)

Other psychoses (295-299)

295 Schizophrenic disorders
296 Affective psychoses
297 Paranoid states
298 Other nonorganic psychoses
299 Psychoses with origin specific to childhood

Neurotic disorders, personality disorders, and other nonpsychotic mental disorders (300-316)

300 Neurotic disorders
301 Personality disorders
302 Sexual deviations and disorders
303 Alcohol dependence syndrome
304 Drug dependence
305 Nondependent abuse of drugs
306 Physiological malfunction arising from mental factors
307 Special symptoms or syndromes, not elsewhere classified
308 Acute reaction to stress
309 Adjustment reaction
310 Specific nonpsychotic mental disorders due to organic brain damage
311 Depressive disorder, not elsewhere classified
312 Disturbance of conduct, not elsewhere classified
313 Disturbance of emotions specific to childhood and adolescence
314 Hyperkinetic syndrome of childhood
315 Specific delays in development
316 Psychic factors associated with diseases classified elsewhere

Mental retardation (317-319)

317 Mild mental retardation
318 Other specified mental retardation
319 Unspecified mental retardation

6. DISEASES OF THE NERVOUS SYSTEM AND SENSE ORGANS (320-389)

Inflammatory diseases of the central nervous system (320-326)

320 Bacterial meningitis
321 Meningitis due to other organisms
322 Meningitis of unspecified cause
323 Encephalitis, myelitis, and encephalomyelitis
324 Intracranial and intraspinal abscess
325 Phlebitis and thrombophlebitis of intracranial venous sinuses
326 Late effects of intracranial abscess or pyogenic infection

Hereditary and degenerative diseases of the central nervous system (330-337)

330 Cerebral degenerations usually manifest in childhood
331 Other cerebral degenerations
332 Parkinson's disease
333 Other extrapyramidal disease and abnormal movement disorders
334 Spinocerebellar disease
335 Anterior horn cell disease
336 Other diseases of spinal cord
337 Disorders of the autonomic nervous system

Other disorders of the central nervous system (340-349)

340 Multiple sclerosis
341 Other demyelinating diseases of central nervous system
342 Hemiplegia and hemiparesis
343 Infantile cerebral palsy
344 Other paralytic syndromes
345 Epilepsy
346 Migraine
347 Cataplexy and narcolepsy
348 Other conditions of brain
349 Other and unspecified disorders of the nervous system

Disorders of the peripheral nervous system (350-359)

350 Trigeminal nerve disorders
351 Facial nerve disorders
352 Disorders of other cranial nerves
353 Nerve root and plexus disorders
354 Mononeuritis of upper limb and mononeuritis multiplex
355 Mononeuritis of lower limb and unspecified sites
356 Hereditary and idiopathic peripheral neuropathy
357 Inflammatory and toxic neuropathy
358 Myoneural disorders
359 Muscular dystrophies and other myopathies

Disorders of the eye and adnexa (360-379)

360 Disorders of the globe
361 Retinal detachments and defects
362 Other retinal disorders
363 Chorioretinal inflammations and scars and other disorders of choroid
364 Disorders of iris and ciliary body
365 Glaucoma
366 Cataract
367 Disorders of refraction and accommodation
368 Visual disturbances
369 Blindness and low vision
370 Keratitis
371 Corneal opacity and other disorders of cornea
372 Disorders of conjunctiva
373 Inflammation of eyelids
374 Other disorders of eyelids
375 Disorders of lacrimal system
376 Disorders of the orbit
377 Disorders of optic nerve and visual pathways
378 Strabismus and other disorders of binocular eye movements
379 Other disorders of eye

Diseases of the ear and mastoid process (380-389)

380 Disorders of external ear
381 Nonsuppurative otitis media and Eustachian tube disorders
382 Suppurative and unspecified otitis media
383 Mastoiditis and related conditions
384 Other disorders of tympanic membrane
385 Other disorders of middle ear and mastoid
386 Vertiginous syndromes and other disorders of vestibular system
387 Otosclerosis
388 Other disorders of ear
389 Hearing loss

7. DISEASES OF THE CIRCULATORY SYSTEM (390-459)

Acute rheumatic fever (390-392)

390 Rheumatic fever without mention of heart involvement
391 Rheumatic fever with heart involvement
392 Rheumatic chorea

Chronic rheumatic heart disease (393-398)

393 Chronic rheumatic pericarditis
394 Diseases of mitral valve
395 Diseases of aortic valve
396 Diseases of mitral and aortic valves
397 Diseases of other endocardial structures
398 Other rheumatic heart disease

Hypertensive disease (401-405)

401 Essential hypertension
402 Hypertensive heart disease
403 Hypertensive renal disease
404 Hypertensive heart and renal disease
405 Secondary hypertension

Ischemic heart disease (410-414)

410 Acute myocardial infarction
411 Other acute and subacute form of ischemic heart disease
412 Old myocardial infarction
413 Angina pectoris
414 Other forms of chronic ischemic heart disease

Diseases of pulmonary circulation (415-417)

415 Acute pulmonary heart disease
416 Chronic pulmonary heart disease
417 Other diseases of pulmonary circulation

Other forms of heart disease (420-429)

420 Acute pericarditis
421 Acute and subacute endocarditis
422 Acute myocarditis
423 Other diseases of pericardium
424 Other diseases of endocardium
425 Cardiomyopathy
426 Conduction disorders
427 Cardiac dysrhythmias
428 Heart failure
429 Ill-defined descriptions and complications of heart disease

Cerebrovascular disease (430-438)

430 Subarachnoid hemorrhage
431 Intracerebral hemorrhage
432 Other and unspecified intracranial hemorrhage
433 Occlusion and stenosis of precerebral arteries
434 Occlusion of cerebral arteries
435 Transient cerebral ischemia
436 Acute but ill-defined cerebrovascular disease
437 Other and ill-defined cerebrovascular disease
438 Late effects of cerebrovascular disease

Diseases of arteries, arterioles, and capillaries (440-448)

440 Atherosclerosis
441 Aortic aneurysm and dissection
442 Other aneurysm
443 Other peripheral vascular disease
444 Arterial embolism and thrombosis
446 Polyarteritis nodosa and allied conditions
447 Other disorders of arteries and arterioles
448 Diseases of capillaries

Diseases of veins and lymphatics, and other diseases of circulatory system (451-459)

451 Phlebitis and thrombophlebitis
452 Portal vein thrombosis
453 Other venous embolism and thrombosis
454 Varicose veins of lower extremities
455 Hemorrhoids
456 Varicose veins of other sites
457 Noninfective disorders of lymphatic channels
458 Hypotension
459 Other disorders of circulatory system

8. DISEASES OF THE RESPIRATORY SYSTEM (460-519)

Acute respiratory infections (460-466)

460 Acute nasopharyngitis [common cold]
461 Acute sinusitis
462 Acute pharyngitis
463 Acute tonsillitis
464 Acute laryngitis and tracheitis
465 Acute upper respiratory infections of multiple or unspecified sites
466 Acute bronchitis and bronchiolitis

Other diseases of upper respiratory tract (470-478)

470 Deviated nasal septum
471 Nasal polyps
472 Chronic pharyngitis and nasopharyngitis
473 Chronic sinusitis
474 Chronic disease of tonsils and adenoids
475 Peritonsillar abscess
476 Chronic laryngitis and laryngotracheitis
477 Allergic rhinitis
478 Other diseases of upper respiratory tract

Pneumonia and influenza (480-487)

480 Viral pneumonia
481 Pneumococcal pneumonia [Streptococcus pneumoniae pneumonia]
482 Other bacterial pneumonia
483 Pneumonia due to other specified organism
484 Pneumonia in infectious diseases classified elsewhere
485 Bronchopneumonia, organism unspecified
486 Pneumonia, organism unspecified
487 Influenza

Chronic obstructive pulmonary disease and allied conditions (490-496)

490 Bronchitis, not specified as acute or chronic
491 Chronic bronchitis
492 Emphysema
493 Asthma
494 Bronchiectasis
495 Extrinsic allergic alveolitis
496 Chronic airways obstruction, not elsewhere classified

Pneumoconioses and other lung diseases due to external agents (500-508)

500 Coalworkers' pneumoconiosis
501 Asbestosis
502 Pneumoconiosis due to other silica or silicates
503 Pneumoconiosis due to other inorganic dust
504 Pneumopathy due to inhalation of other dust
505 Pneumoconiosis, unspecified
506 Respiratory conditions due to chemical fumes and vapors
507 Pneumonitis due to solids and liquids
508 Respiratory conditions due to other and unspecified external agents

Other diseases of respiratory system (510-519)

510 Empyema
511 Pleurisy
512 Pneumothorax
513 Abscess of lung and mediastinum
514 Pulmonary congestion and hypostasis
515 Postinflammatory pulmonary fibrosis
516 Other alveolar and parietoalveolar pneumopathy
517 Lung involvement in conditions classified elsewhere
518 Other diseases of lung
519 Other diseases of respiratory system

9. DISEASES OF THE DIGESTIVE SYSTEM (520-579)

Diseases of oral cavity, salivary glands, and jaws (520-529)

520 Disorders of tooth development and eruption
521 Diseases of hard tissues of teeth
522 Diseases of pulp and periapical tissues
523 Gingival and periodontal diseases
524 Dentofacial anomalies, including malocclusion
525 Other diseases and conditions of the teeth and supporting structures
526 Diseases of the jaws
527 Diseases of the salivary glands
528 Diseases of the oral soft tissues, excluding lesions specific for gingiva and tongue
529 Diseases and other conditions of the tongue

Diseases of esophagus, stomach, and duodenum (530-537)

530 Diseases of esophagus
531 Gastric ulcer
532 Duodenal ulcer
533 Peptic ulcer, site unspecified
534 Gastrojejunal ulcer

535 Gastritis and duodenitis
536 Disorders of function of stomach
537 Other disorders of stomach and duodenum

Appendicitis (540-543)

540 Acute appendicitis
541 Appendicitis, unqualified
542 Other appendicitis
543 Other diseases of appendix

Hernia of abdominal cavity (550-553)

550 Inguinal hernia
551 Other hernia of abdominal cavity, with gangrene
552 Other hernia of abdominal cavity, with obstruction, but without mention of gangrene
553 Other hernia of abdominal cavity without mention of obstruction or gangrene

Noninfective enteritis and colitis (555-558)

555 Regional enteritis
556 Ulcerative colitis
557 Vascular insufficiency of intestine
558 Other noninfective gastroenteritis and colitis

Other diseases of intestines and peritoneum (560-569)

560 Intestinal obstruction without mention of hernia
562 Diverticula of intestine
564 Functional digestive disorders, not elsewhere classified
565 Anal fissure and fistula
566 Abscess of anal and rectal regions
567 Peritonitis
568 Other disorders of peritoneum
569 Other disorders of intestine

Other diseases of digestive system (570-579)

570 Acute and subacute necrosis of liver
571 Chronic liver disease and cirrhosis
572 Liver abscess and sequelae of chronic liver disease
573 Other disorders of liver
574 Cholelithiasis
575 Other disorders of gallbladder
576 Other disorders of biliary tract
577 Diseases of pancreas
578 Gastrointestinal hemorrhage
579 Intestinal malabsorption

10. DISEASES OF THE GENITOURINARY SYSTEM (580-629)

Nephritis, nephrotic syndrome, and nephrosis (580-589)

580 Acute glomerulonephritis
581 Nephrotic syndrome
582 Chronic glomerulonephritis
583 Nephritis and nephropathy, not specified as acute or chronic
584 Acute renal failure
585 Chronic renal failure
586 Renal failure, unspecified
587 Renal sclerosis, unspecified
588 Disorders resulting from impaired renal function
589 Small kidney of unknown cause

Other diseases of urinary system (590-599)

590 Infections of kidney
591 Hydronephrosis
592 Calculus of kidney and ureter
593 Other disorders of kidney and ureter
594 Calculus of lower urinary tract
595 Cystitis
596 Other disorders of bladder
597 Urethritis, not sexually transmitted, and urethral syndrome
598 Urethral stricture
599 Other disorders of urethra and urinary tract

Diseases of male genital organs (600-608)

600 Hyperplasia of prostate
601 Inflammatory diseases of prostate
602 Other disorders of prostate
603 Hydrocele
604 Orchitis and epididymitis
605 Redundant prepuce and phimosis
606 Infertility, male
607 Disorders of penis
608 Other disorders of male genital organs

Disorders of breast (610-611)

610 Benign mammary dysplasias
611 Other disorders of breast

Inflammatory disease of female pelvic organs (614-616)

614 Inflammatory disease of ovary, fallopian tube, pelvic cellular tissue, and peritoneum
615 Inflammatory diseases of uterus, except cervix
616 Inflammatory disease of cervix, vagina, and vulva

Other disorders of female genital tract (617-629)

617 Endometriosis
618 Genital prolapse
619 Fistula involving female genital tract
620 Noninflammatory disorders of ovary, fallopian tube, and broad ligament
621 Disorders of uterus, not elsewhere classified
622 Noninflammatory disorders of cervix
623 Noninflammatory disorders of vagina
624 Noninflammatory disorders of vulva and perineum
625 Pain and other symptoms associated with female genital organs
626 Disorders of menstruation and other abnormal bleeding from female genital tract
627 Menopausal and postmenopausal disorders
628 Infertility, female
629 Other disorders of female genital organs

11. COMPLICATIONS OF PREGNANCY, CHILDBIRTH, AND THE PUERPERIUM (630-679)

Ectopic and molar pregnancy and other pregnancy with abortive outcome (630-633)

630 Hydatidiform mole
631 Other abnormal product of conception
632 Missed abortion
633 Ectopic pregnancy

Other pregnancy with abortive outcome (634-639)

634 Spontaneous abortion
635 Legally induced abortion
636 Illegally induced abortion
637 Unspecified abortion
638 Failed attempted abortion
639 Complications following abortion and ectopic and molar pregnancies

Complications mainly related to pregnancy (640-648)

640 Hemorrhage in early pregnancy
641 Antepartum hemorrhage, abruptio placentae, and placenta previa
642 Hypertension complicating pregnancy, childbirth, and the puerperium
643 Excessive vomiting in pregnancy
644 Early or threatened labor
645 Prolonged pregnancy
646 Other complications of pregnancy, not elsewhere classified
647 Infective and parasitic conditions in the mother classifiable elsewhere but complicating pregnancy, childbirth, or the puerperium
648 Other current conditions in the mother classifiable elsewhere but complicating pregnancy, childbirth, or the puerperium

Normal delivery, and other indications for care in pregnancy, labor, and delivery (650-659)

650 Normal delivery
651 Multiple gestation
652 Malposition and malpresentation of fetus
653 Disproportion
654 Abnormality of organs and soft tissues of pelvis
655 Known or suspected fetal abnormality affecting management of mother
656 Other fetal and placental problems affecting management of mother
657 Polyhydramnios
658 Other problems associated with amniotic cavity and membranes
659 Other indications for care or intervention related to labor and delivery, not elsewhere classified

Complications occurring mainly in the course of labor and delivery (660-669)

660 Obstructed labor
661 Abnormality of forces of labor
662 Long labor
663 Umbilical cord complications
664 Trauma to perineum and vulva during delivery
665 Other obstetrical trauma
666 Postpartum hemorrhage
667 Retained placenta or membranes, without hemorrhage
668 Complications of the administration of anesthetic or other sedation in labor and delivery
669 Other complications of labor and delivery, not elsewhere classified

Complications of the puerperium (670-677)

670 Major puerperal infection
671 Venous complications in pregnancy and the puerperium
672 Pyrexia of unknown origin during the puerperium
673 Obstetrical pulmonary embolism
674 Other and unspecified complications of the puerperium, not elsewhere classified
675 Infections of the breast and nipple associated with childbirth
676 Other disorders of the breast associated with childbirth, and disorders of lactation
677 Late effect of complication of pregnancy, childbirth, and the puerperium

12. DISEASES OF THE SKIN AND SUBCUTANEOUS TISSUE (680-709)

Infections of skin and subcutaneous tissue (680-686)

680 Carbuncle and furuncle
681 Cellulitis and abscess of finger and toe
682 Other cellulitis and abscess
683 Acute lymphadenitis
684 Impetigo
685 Pilonidal cyst
686 Other local infections of skin and subcutaneous tissue

Other inflammatory conditions of skin and subcutaneous tissue (690-698)

690 Erythematosquamous dermatosis
691 Atopic dermatitis and related conditions
692 Contact dermatitis and other eczema
693 Dermatitis due to substances taken internally
694 Bullous dermatoses
695 Erythematous conditions
696 Psoriasis and similar disorders
697 Lichen
698 Pruritus and related conditions

Other diseases of skin and subcutaneous tissue (700-709)

700 Corns and callosities
701 Other hypertrophic and atrophic conditions of skin
702 Other dermatoses
703 Diseases of nail
704 Diseases of hair and hair follicles
705 Disorders of sweat glands
706 Diseases of sebaceous glands
707 Chronic ulcer of skin
708 Urticaria
709 Other disorders of skin and subcutaneous tissue

13. DISEASES OF THE MUSCULOSKELETAL SYSTEM AND CONNECTIVE TISSUE (710-739)

Arthropathies and related disorders (710-719)

710 Diffuse diseases of connective tissue
711 Arthropathy associated with infections
712 Crystal arthropathies
713 Arthropathy associated with other disorders classified elsewhere
714 Rheumatoid arthritis and other inflammatory polyarthropathies
715 Osteoarthrosis and allied disorders
716 Other and unspecified arthropathies
717 Internal derangement of knee
718 Other derangement of joint
719 Other and unspecified disorder of joint

Dorsopathies (720-724)

720 Ankylosing spondylitis and other inflammatory spondylopathies
721 Spondylosis and allied disorders
722 Intervertebral disc disorders
723 Other disorders of cervical region
724 Other and unspecified disorders of back

Rheumatism, excluding the back (725-729)

725 Polymyalgia rheumatica
726 Peripheral enthesopathies and allied syndromes
727 Other disorders of synovium, tendon, and bursa
728 Disorders of muscle, ligament, and fascia
729 Other disorders of soft tissues

Osteopathies, chondropathies, and acquired musculoskeletal deformities (730-739)

730 Osteomyelitis, periostitis, and other infections involving bone
731 Osteitis deformans and osteopathies associated with other disorders classified elsewhere
732 Osteochondropathies
733 Other disorders of bone and cartilage
734 Flat foot
735 Acquired deformities of toe
736 Other acquired deformities of limbs
737 Curvature of spine
738 Other acquired deformity
739 Nonallopathic lesions, not elsewhere classified

14. CONGENITAL ANOMALIES (740-759)

740 Anencephalus and similar anomalies
741 Spina bifida
742 Other congenital anomalies of nervous system
743 Congenital anomalies of eye
744 Congenital anomalies of ear, face, and neck
745 Bulbus cordis anomalies and anomalies of cardiac septal closure
746 Other congenital anomalies of heart
747 Other congenital anomalies of circulatory system
748 Congenital anomalies of respiratory system
749 Cleft palate and cleft lip
750 Other congenital anomalies of upper alimentary tract
751 Other congenital anomalies of digestive system
752 Congenital anomalies of genital organs
753 Congenital anomalies of urinary system
754 Certain congenital musculoskeletal deformities
755 Other congenital anomalies of limbs
756 Other congenital musculoskeletal anomalies
757 Congenital anomalies of the integument
758 Chromosomal anomalies
759 Other and unspecified congenital anomalies

15. CERTAIN CONDITIONS ORIGINATING IN THE PERINATAL PERIOD (760-779)

Maternal causes of perinatal morbidity and mortality (760-763)

760 Fetus or newborn affected by maternal conditions which may be unrelated to present pregnancy
761 Fetus or newborn affected by maternal complications of pregnancy
762 Fetus or newborn affected by complications of placenta, cord, and membranes
763 Fetus or newborn affected by other complications of labor and delivery

Other conditions originating in the perinatal period (764-779)

764 Slow fetal growth and fetal malnutrition
765 Disorders relating to short gestation and unspecified low birthweight
766 Disorders relating to long gestation and high birthweight
767 Birth trauma
768 Intrauterine hypoxia and birth asphyxia
769 Respiratory distress syndrome
770 Other respiratory conditions of fetus and newborn
771 Infections specific to the perinatal period
772 Fetal and neonatal hemorrhage
773 Hemolytic disease of fetus or newborn, due to isoimmunization
774 Other perinatal jaundice
775 Endocrine and metabolic disturbances specific to the fetus and newborn
776 Hematological disorders of fetus and newborn
777 Perinatal disorders of digestive system
778 Conditions involving the integument and temperature regulation of fetus and newborn
779 Other and ill-defined conditions originating in the perinatal period

16. SYMPTOMS, SIGNS, AND ILL-DEFINED CONDITIONS (780-799)

Symptoms (780-789)

780 General symptoms
781 Symptoms involving nervous and musculoskeletal systems
782 Symptoms involving skin and other integumentary tissue
783 Symptoms concerning nutrition, metabolism, and development
784 Symptoms involving head and neck
785 Symptoms involving cardiovascular system
786 Symptoms involving respiratory system and other chest symptoms
787 Symptoms involving digestive system
788 Symptoms involving urinary system
789 Other symptoms involving abdomen and pelvis

Nonspecific abnormal findings (790-796)

790 Nonspecific findings on examination of blood
791 Nonspecific findings on examination of urine
792 Nonspecific abnormal findings in other body substances
793 Nonspecific abnormal findings on radiological and other examination of body structure
794 Nonspecific abnormal results of function studies
795 Nonspecific abnormal histological and immunological findings
796 Other nonspecific abnormal findings

Ill-defined and unknown causes of morbidity and mortality (797-799)

797 Senility without mention of psychosis
798 Sudden death, cause unknown
799 Other ill-defined and unknown causes of morbidity and mortality

17. INJURY AND POISONING (800-899)

Fracture of skull (800-804)

800 Fracture of vault of skull
801 Fracture of base of skull
802 Fracture of face bones
803 Other and unqualified skull fractures
804 Multiple fractures involving skull or face with other bones

Fracture of neck and trunk (805-809)

805 Fracture of vertebral column without mention of spinal cord injury
806 Fracture of vertebral column with spinal cord injury
807 Fracture of rib(s), sternum, larynx, and trachea
808 Fracture of pelvis
809 Ill-defined fractures of bones of trunk

Fracture of upper limb (810-819)

810 Fracture of clavicle
811 Fracture of scapula
812 Fracture of humerus
813 Fracture of radius and ulna
814 Fracture of carpal bone(s)
815 Fracture of metacarpal bone(s)
816 Fracture of one or more phalanges of hand
817 Multiple fractures of hand bones
818 Ill-defined fractures of upper limb
819 Multiple fractures involving both upper limbs, and upper limb with rib(s) and sternum

Fracture of lower limb (820-829)

820 Fracture of neck of femur
821 Fracture of other and unspecified parts of femur
822 Fracture of patella
823 Fracture of tibia and fibula
824 Fracture of ankle
825 Fracture of one or more tarsal and metatarsal bones
826 Fracture of one or more phalanges of foot
827 Other, multiple, and ill-defined fractures of lower limb
828 Multiple fractures involving both lower limbs, lower with upper limb, and lower limb(s) with rib(s) and sternum
829 Fracture of unspecified bones

Dislocation (830-839)

830 Dislocation of jaw
831 Dislocation of shoulder
832 Dislocation of elbow
833 Dislocation of wrist
834 Dislocation of finger
835 Dislocation of hip
836 Dislocation of knee
837 Dislocation of ankle
838 Dislocation of foot
839 Other, multiple, and ill-defined dislocations

Sprains and strains of joints and adjacent muscles (840-848)

840 Sprains and strains of shoulder and upper arm
841 Sprains and strains of elbow and forearm
842 Sprains and strains of wrist and hand
843 Sprains and strains of hip and thigh
844 Sprains and strains of knee and leg
845 Sprains and strains of ankle and foot
846 Sprains and strains of sacroiliac region
847 Sprains and strains of other and unspecified parts of back
848 Other and ill-defined sprains and strains

Intracranial injury, excluding those with skull fracture (850-854)

850 Concussion
851 Cerebral laceration and contusion
852 Subarachnoid, subdural, and extradural hemorrhage, following injury
853 Other and unspecified intracranial hemorrhage following injury
854 Intracranial injury of other and unspecified nature

Internal injury of thorax, abdomen, and pelvis (860-869)

860 Traumatic pneumothorax and hemothorax
861 Injury to heart and lung
862 Injury to other and unspecified intrathoracic organs
863 Injury to gastrointestinal tract
864 Injury to liver
865 Injury to spleen
866 Injury to kidney
867 Injury to pelvic organs
868 Injury to other intra-abdominal organs
869 Internal injury to unspecified or ill-defined organs

Open wound of head, neck, and trunk (870-879)

870 Open wound of ocular adnexa
871 Open wound of eyeball
872 Open wound of ear
873 Other open wound of head
874 Open wound of neck
875 Open wound of chest (wall)
876 Open wound of back
877 Open wound of buttock
878 Open wound of genital organs (external), including traumatic amputation
879 Open wound of other and unspecified sites, except limbs

Open wound of upper limb (880-887)

880 Open wound of shoulder and upper arm
881 Open wound of elbow, forearm, and wrist
882 Open wound of hand except finger(s) alone
883 Open wound of finger(s)
884 Multiple and unspecified open wound of upper limb
885 Traumatic amputation of thumb (complete) (partial)
886 Traumatic amputation of other finger(s) (complete) (partial)
887 Traumatic amputation of arm and hand (complete) (partial)

Open wound of lower limb (890-897)

890 Open wound of hip and thigh
891 Open wound of knee, leg [except thigh], and ankle
892 Open wound of foot except toe(s) alone
893 Open wound of toe(s)
894 Multiple and unspecified open wound of lower limb
895 Traumatic amputation of toe(s) (complete) (partial)
896 Traumatic amputation of foot (complete) (partial)
897 Traumatic amputation of leg(s) (complete) (partial)

Injury to blood vessels (900-904)

900 Injury to blood vessels of head and neck
901 Injury to blood vessels of thorax
902 Injury to blood vessels of abdomen and pelvis
903 Injury to blood vessels of upper extremity
904 Injury to blood vessels of lower extremity and unspecified sites

Late effects of injuries, poisonings, toxic effects, and other externalcauses (905-909)

905 Late effects of musculoskeletal and connective tissue injuries

906 Late effects of injuries to skin and subcutaneous tissues
907 Late effects of injuries to the nervous system
908 Late effects of other and unspecified injuries
909 Late effects of other and unspecified external causes

Superficial injury (910-919)

910 Superficial injury of face, neck, and scalp except eye
911 Superficial injury of trunk
912 Superficial injury of shoulder and upper arm
913 Superficial injury of elbow, forearm, and wrist
914 Superficial injury of hand(s) except finger(s) alone
915 Superficial injury of finger(s)
916 Superficial injury of hip, thigh, leg, and ankle
917 Superficial injury of foot and toe(s)
918 Superficial injury of eye and adnexa
919 Superficial injury of other, multiple, and unspecified sites

Contusion with intact skin surface (920-924)

920 Contusion of face, scalp, and neck except eye(s)
921 Contusion of eye and adnexa
922 Contusion of trunk
923 Contusion of upper limb
924 Contusion of lower limb and of other and unspecified sites

Crushing injury (925-929)

925 Crushing injury of face, scalp, and neck
926 Crushing injury of trunk
927 Crushing injury of upper limb
928 Crushing injury of lower limb
929 Crushing injury of multiple and unspecified sites

Effects of foreign body entering through orifice (930-939)

930 Foreign body on external eye
931 Foreign body in ear
932 Foreign body in nose
933 Foreign body in pharynx and larynx
934 Foreign body in trachea, bronchus, and lung
935 Foreign body in mouth, esophagus, and stomach
936 Foreign body in intestine and colon
937 Foreign body in anus and rectum
938 Foreign body in digestive system, unspecified
939 Foreign body in genitourinary tract

Burns (940-949)

940 Burn confined to eye and adnexa
941 Burn of face, head, and neck
942 Burn of trunk
943 Burn of upper limb, except wrist and hand
944 Burn of wrist(s) and hand(s)
945 Burn of lower limb(s)
946 Burns of multiple specified sites
947 Burn of internal organs
948 Burns classified according to extent of body surface involved
949 Burn, unspecified

Injury to nerves and spinal cord (950-957)

950 Injury to optic nerve and pathways
951 Injury to other cranial nerve(s)
952 Spinal cord injury without evidence of spinal bone injury
953 Injury to nerve roots and spinal plexus
954 Injury to other nerve(s) of trunk excluding shoulder and pelvic girdles
955 Injury to peripheral nerve(s) of shoulder girdle and upper limb
956 Injury to peripheral nerve(s) of pelvic girdle and lower limb
957 Injury to other and unspecified nerves

Certain traumatic complications and unspecified injuries (958-959)

958 Certain early complications of trauma
959 Injury, other and unspecified

Poisoning by drugs, medicinal and biological substances (960-979)

960 Poisoning by antibiotics
961 Poisoning by other anti-infectives
962 Poisoning by hormones and synthetic substitutes
963 Poisoning by primarily systemic agents
964 Poisoning by agents primarily affecting blood constituents
965 Poisoning by analgesics, antipyretics, and antirheumatics
966 Poisoning by anticonvulsants and anti-Parkinsonism drugs
967 Poisoning by sedatives and hypnotics
968 Poisoning by other central nervous system depressants and anesthetics
969 Poisoning by psychotropic agents
970 Poisoning by central nervous system stimulants
971 Poisoning by drugs primarily affecting the autonomic nervous system
972 Poisoning by agents primarily affecting the cardiovascular system
973 Poisoning by agents primarily affecting the gastrointestinal system
974 Poisoning by water, mineral, and uric acid metabolism drugs
975 Poisoning by agents primarily acting on the smooth and skeletal muscles and respiratory system
976 Poisoning by agents primarily affecting skin and mucous membrane, ophthalmological, otorhinolaryngological, and dental drugs
977 Poisoning by other and unspecified drugs and medicinals
978 Poisoning by bacterial vaccines
979 Poisoning by other vaccines and biological substances

Toxic effects of substances chiefly nonmedicinal as to source (980-989)

980 Toxic effect of alcohol
981 Toxic effect of petroleum products
982 Toxic effect of solvents other than petroleum-based
983 Toxic effect of corrosive aromatics, acids, and caustic alkalis
984 Toxic effect of lead and its compounds (including fumes)
985 Toxic effect of other metals
986 Toxic effect of carbon monoxide
987 Toxic effect of other gases, fumes, or vapors
988 Toxic effect of noxious substances eaten as food
989 Toxic effect of other substances, chiefly nonmedicinal as to source

Other and unspecified effects of external causes (990-995)

990 Effects of radiation, unspecified
991 Effects of reduced temperature
992 Effects of heat and light
993 Effects of air pressure
994 Effects of other external causes
995 Certain adverse effects, not elsewhere classified

Complications of surgical and medical care, not elsewhere classified (996-999)

996 Complications peculiar to certain specified procedures
997 Complications affecting specified body systems, not elsewhere classified
998 Other complications of procedures, not elsewhere classified
999 Complications of medical care, not elsewhere classified

SUPPLEMENTARY CLASSIFICATION OF FACTORS INFLUENCING HEALTH STATUS AND CONTACT WITH HEALTH SERVICES

Persons with potential health hazards related to communicable diseases (V01-V09)

V01 Contact with or exposure to communicable diseases
V02 Carrier or suspected carrier of infectious diseases
V03 Need for prophylactic vaccination and inoculation against bacterial diseases
V04 Need for prophylactic vaccination and inoculation against certain viral diseases
V05 Need for other prophylactic vaccination and inoculation against single diseases
V06 Need for prophylactic vaccination and inoculation against combinations of diseases
V07 Need for isolation and other prophylactic measures
V08 Asymptomatic human immunodeficiency virus [HIV] infection status
V09 Infection with drug-resistant microorganisms

Persons with potential health hazards related to personal and family history (V10-V19)

V10 Personal history of malignant neoplasm
V11 Personal history of mental disorder
V12 Personal history of certain other diseases
V13 Personal history of other diseases
V14 Personal history of allergy to medicinal agents
V15 Other personal history presenting hazards to health
V16 Family history of malignant neoplasm
V17 Family history of certain chronic disabling diseases
V18 Family history of certain other specific conditions
V19 Family history of other conditions

Persons encountering health services in circumstances related to reproduction and development (V20-V29)

V20 Health supervision of infant or child

V21 Constitutional states in development
V22 Normal pregnancy
V23 Supervision of high-risk pregnancy
V24 Postpartum care and examination
V25 Encounter for contraceptive management
V26 Procreative management
V27 Outcome of delivery
V28 Antenatal screening
V29 Observation and evaluation of newborns and infants for suspected condition not found

Liveborn infants according to type of birth (V30-V39)

V30 Single liveborn
V31 Twin, mate liveborn
V32 Twin, mate stillborn
V33 Twin, unspecified
V34 Other multiple, mates all liveborn
V35 Other multiple, mates all stillborn
V36 Other multiple, mates live- and stillborn
V37 Other multiple, unspecified
V39 Unspecified

Persons with a condition influencing their health status (V40-V49)

V40 Mental and behavioral problems
V41 Problems with special senses and other special functions
V42 Organ or tissue replaced by transplant
V43 Organ or tissue replaced by other means
V44 Artificial opening status
V45 Other postsurgical states
V46 Other dependence on machines
V47 Other problems with internal organs
V48 Problems with head, neck, and trunk
V49 Problems with limbs and other problems

Persons encountering health services for specific procedures and aftercare (V50-V59)

V50 Elective surgery for purposes other than remedying health states
V51 Aftercare involving the use of plastic surgery
V52 Fitting and adjustment of prosthetic device
V53 Fitting and adjustment of other device
V54 Other orthopedic aftercare
V55 Attention to artificial openings
V56 Encounter for dialysis and dialysis catheter care
V57 Care involving use of rehabilitation procedures
V58 Encounter for other and unspecified procedures and aftercare
V59 Donors

Persons encountering health services in other circumstances (V60-V69)

V60 Housing, household, and economic circumstances
V61 Other family circumstances
V62 Other psychosocial circumstances
V63 Unavailability of other medical facilities for care
V64 Persons encountering health services for specific procedures, not carried out
V65 Other persons seeking consultation without complaint or sickness
V66 Convalescence and palliative care
V67 Follow-up examination
V68 Encounters for administrative purposes
V69 Problems related to lifestyle

Persons without reported diagnosis encountered during examination and investigation of individuals and populations (V70-V82)

V70 General medical examination
V71 Observation and evaluation for suspected conditions
V72 Special investigations and examinations
V73 Special screening examination for viral and chlamydial diseases
V74 Special screening examination for bacterial and spirochetal diseases
V75 Special screening examination for other infectious diseases
V76 Special screening for malignant neoplasms
V77 Special screening for endocrine, nutritional, metabolic, and immunity disorders
V78 Special screening for disorders of blood and blood-forming organs
V79 Special screening for mental disorders and developmental handicaps
V80 Special screening for neurological, eye, and ear diseases
V81 Special screening for cardiovascular, respiratory, and genitourinary diseases
V82 Special screening for other conditions

SUPPLEMENTARY CLASSIFICATION OF EXTERNAL CAUSES OF INJURY AND POISONING

Railway accidents (E800-E807)

E800 Railway accident involving collision with rolling stock
E801 Railway accident involving collision with other object
E802 Railway accident involving derailment without antecedent collision
E803 Railway accident involving explosion, fire, or burning
E804 Fall in, on, or from railway train
E805 Hit by rolling stock
E806 Other specified railway accident
E807 Railway accident of unspecified nature

Motor vehicle traffic accidents (E810-E819)

E810 Motor vehicle traffic accident involving collision with train
E811 Motor vehicle traffic accident involving re-entrant collision with another motor vehicle
E812 Other motor vehicle traffic accident involving collision with another motor vehicle
E813 Motor vehicle traffic accident involving collision with other vehicle
E814 Motor vehicle traffic accident involving collision with pedestrian
E815 Other motor vehicle traffic accident involving collision on the highway
E816 Motor vehicle traffic accident due to loss of control, withoutcollision on the highway
E817 Noncollision motor vehicle traffic accident while boarding oralighting
E818 Other noncollision motor vehicle traffic accident
E819 Motor vehicle traffic accident of unspecified nature

Motor vehicle nontraffic accidents (E820-E825)

E820 Nontraffic accident involving motor-driven snow vehicle
E821 Nontraffic accident involving other off-road motor vehicle
E822 Other motor vehicle nontraffic accident involving collision with moving object
E823 Other motor vehicle nontraffic accident involving collision with stationary object
E824 Other motor vehicle nontraffic accident while boarding and alighting
E825 Other motor vehicle nontraffic accident of other and unspecified nature

Other road vehicle accidents (E826-E829)

E826 Pedal cycle accident
E827 Animal-drawn vehicle accident
E828 Accident involving animal being ridden
E829 Other road vehicle accidents

Water transport accidents (E830-E838)

E830 Accident to watercraft causing submersion
E831 Accident to watercraft causing other injury
E832 Other accidental submersion or drowning in water transport accident
E833 Fall on stairs or ladders in water transport
E834 Other fall from one level to another in water transport
E835 Other and unspecified fall in water transport
E836 Machinery accident in water transport
E837 Explosion, fire, or burning in watercraft
E838 Other and unspecified water transport accident

Air and space transport accidents (E840-E845)

E840 Accident to powered aircraft at takeoff or landing
E841 Accident to powered aircraft, other and unspecified
E842 Accident to unpowered aircraft
E843 Fall in, on, or from aircraft
E844 Other specified air transport accidents
E845 Accident involving spacecraft

Vehicle accidents, not elsewhere classifiable (E846-E849)

E846 Accidents involving powered vehicles used solely within the buildings and premises of an industrial or commercial establishment
E847 Accidents involving cable cars not running on rails
E848 Accidents involving other vehicles, not elsewhere classifiable
E849 Place of occurrence

Accidental poisoning by drugs, medicinal substances, and biologicals (E850-E858)

E850 Accidental poisoning by analgesics, antipyretics, and antirheumatics
E851 Accidental poisoning by barbiturates
E852 Accidental poisoning by other sedatives and hypnotics

E853 Accidental poisoning by tranquilizers
E854 Accidental poisoning by other psychotropic agents
E855 Accidental poisoning by other drugs acting on central and autonomic nervous systems
E856 Accidental poisoning by antibiotics
E857 Accidental poisoning by anti-infectives
E858 Accidental poisoning by other drugs

Accidental poisoning by other solid and liquid substances, gases, and vapors (E860-E869)

E860 Accidental poisoning by alcohol, not elsewhere classified
E861 Accidental poisoning by cleansing and polishing agents, disinfectants, paints, and varnishes
E862 Accidental poisoning by petroleum products, other solvents and their vapors, not elsewhere classified
E863 Accidental poisoning by agricultural and horticultural chemical and pharmaceutical preparations other than plant foods and fertilizers
E864 Accidental poisoning by corrosives and caustics, not elsewhere classified
E865 Accidental poisoning from poisonous foodstuffs and poisonous plants
E866 Accidental poisoning by other and unspecified solid and liquid substances
E867 Accidental poisoning by gas distributed by pipeline
E868 Accidental poisoning by other utility gas and other carbon monoxide
E869 Accidental poisoning by other gases and vapors

Misadventures to patients during surgical and medical care (E870-E876)

E870 Accidental cut, puncture, perforation, or hemorrhage during medical care
E871 Foreign object left in body during procedure
E872 Failure of sterile precautions during procedure
E873 Failure in dosage
E874 Mechanical failure of instrument or apparatus during procedure
E875 Contaminated or infected blood, other fluid, drug, or biological substance
E876 Other and unspecified misadventures during medical care

Surgical and medical procedures as the cause of abnormal reaction of patient or later complication, without mention of misadventure at the time of procedure (E878-E879)

E878 Surgical operation and other surgical procedures as the cause of abnormal reaction of patient, or of later complication, without mention of misadventure at the time of operation
E879 Other procedures, without mention of misadventure at the time of procedure, as the cause of abnormal reaction of patient, or of later complication

Accidental falls (E880-E888)

E880 Fall on or from stairs or steps
E881 Fall on or from ladders or scaffolding
E882 Fall from or out of building or other structure
E883 Fall into hole or other opening in surface
E884 Other fall from one level to another
E885 Fall on same level from slipping, tripping, or stumbling
E886 Fall on same level from collision, pushing or shoving, by or with other person
E887 Fracture, cause unspecified
E888 Other and unspecified fall

Accidents caused by fire and flames (E890-E899)

E890 Conflagration in private dwelling
E891 Conflagration in other and unspecified building or structure
E892 Conflagration not in building or structure
E893 Accident caused by ignition of clothing
E894 Ignition of highly inflammable material
E895 Accident caused by controlled fire in private dwelling
E896 Accident caused by controlled fire in other and unspecified building or structure
E897 Accident caused by controlled fire not in building or structure
E898 Accident caused by other specified fire and flames
E899 Accident caused by unspecified fire

Accidents due to natural and environmental factors (E900-E909)

E900 Excessive heat
E901 Excessive cold
E902 High and low air pressure and changes in air pressure
E903 Travel and motion
E904 Hunger, thirst, exposure, and neglect
E905 Venomous animals and plants as the cause of poisoning and toxic reactions
E906 Other injury caused by animals
E907 Lightning
E908 Cataclysmic storms, and floods resulting from storms
E909 Cataclysmic earth surface movements and eruptions

Accidents caused by submersion, suffocation, and foreign bodies (E910-E915)

E910 Accidental drowning and submersion
E911 Inhalation and ingestion of food causing obstruction of respiratory tract or suffocation
E912 Inhalation and ingestion of other object causing obstruction of respiratory tract or suffocation
E913 Accidental mechanical suffocation
E914 Foreign body accidentally entering eye and adnexa
E915 Foreign body accidentally entering other orifice

Other accidents (E916-E928)

E916 Struck accidentally by falling object
E917 Striking against or struck accidentally by objects or persons
E918 Caught accidentally in or between objects
E919 Accidents caused by machinery
E920 Accidents caused by cutting and piercing instruments or objects
E921 Accident caused by explosion of pressure vessel
E922 Accident caused by firearm missile
E923 Accident caused by explosive material
E924 Accident caused by hot substance or object, caustic or corrosive material, and steam
E925 Accident caused by electric current
E926 Exposure to radiation
E927 Overexertion and strenuous movements
E928 Other and unspecified environmental and accidental causes

Late effects of accidental injury (E929)

E929 Late effects of accidental injury

Drugs, medicinal and biological substances causing adverse effects in therapeutic use (E930-E949)

E930 Antibiotics
E931 Other anti-infectives
E932 Hormones and synthetic substitutes
E933 Primarily systemic agents
E934 Agents primarily affecting blood constituents
E935 Analgesics, antipyretics, and antirheumatics
E936 Anticonvulsants and anti-Parkinsonism drugs
E937 Sedatives and hypnotics
E938 Other central nervous system depressants and anesthetics
E939 Psychotropic agents
E940 Central nervous system stimulants
E941 Drugs primarily affecting the autonomic nervous system
E942 Agents primarily affecting the cardiovascular system
E943 Agents primarily affecting gastrointestinal system
E944 Water, mineral, and uric acid metabolism drugs
E945 Agents primarily acting on the smooth and skeletal muscles and respiratory system
E946 Agents primarily affecting skin and mucous membrane, ophthalmological, otorhinolaryngological, and dental drugs
E947 Other and unspecified drugs and medicinal substances
E948 Bacterial vaccines
E949 Other vaccines and biological substances

Suicide and self-inflicted injury (E950-E959)

E950 Suicide and self-inflicted poisoning by solid or liquid substances
E951 Suicide and self-inflicted poisoning by gases in domestic use
E952 Suicide and self-inflicted poisoning by other gases and vapors
E953 Suicide and self-inflicted injury by hanging, strangulation, and suffocation
E954 Suicide and self-inflicted injury by submersion [drowning]
E955 Suicide and self-inflicted injury by firearms and explosives
E956 Suicide and self-inflicted injury by cutting and piercing instruments
E957 Suicide and self-inflicted injuries by jumping from high place
E958 Suicide and self-inflicted injury by other and unspecified means
E959 Late effects of self-inflicted injury

Homicide and injury purposely inflicted by other persons (E960-E969)

E960 Fight, brawl, and rape
E961 Assault by corrosive or caustic substance, except poisoning
E962 Assault by poisoning
E963 Assault by hanging and strangulation
E964 Assault by submersion [drowning]

E965 Assault by firearms and explosives
E966 Assault by cutting and piercing instrument
E967 Child and adult battering and other maltreatment
E968 Assault by other and unspecified means
E969 Late effects of injury purposely inflicted by other person

Legal intervention (E970-E978)

E970 Injury due to legal intervention by firearms
E971 Injury due to legal intervention by explosives
E972 Injury due to legal intervention by gas
E973 Injury due to legal intervention by blunt object
E974 Injury due to legal intervention by cutting and piercing instrument
E975 Injury due to legal intervention by other specified means
E976 Injury due to legal intervention by unspecified means
E977 Late effects of injuries due to legal intervention
E978 Legal execution

Injury undetermined whether accidentally or purposely inflicted (E980-E989)

E980 Poisoning by solid or liquid substances, undetermined whether accidentally or purposely inflicted
E981 Poisoning by gases in domestic use, undetermined whether accidentally or purposely inflicted
E982 Poisoning by other gases, undetermined whether accidentally or purposely inflicted
E983 Hanging, strangulation, or suffocation, undetermined whether accidentally or purposely inflicted
E984 Submersion [drowning], undetermined whether accidentally or purposely inflicted
E985 Injury by firearms and explosives, undetermined whether accidentally or purposely inflicted
E986 Injury by cutting and piercing instruments, undetermined whether accidentally or purposely inflicted
E987 Falling from high place, undetermined whether accidentally or purposely inflicted
E988 Injury by other and unspecified means, undetermined whether accidentally or purposely inflicted
E989 Late effects of injury, undetermined whether accidentally or purposely inflicted

Injury resulting from operations of war (E990-E999)

E990 Injury due to war operations by fires and conflagrations
E991 Injury due to war operations by bullets and fragments
E992 Injury due to war operations by explosion of marine weapons
E993 Injury due to war operations by other explosion
E994 Injury due to war operations by destruction of aircraft
E995 Injury due to war operations by other and unspecified forms of conventional warfare
E996 Injury due to war operations by nuclear weapons
E997 Injury due to war operations by other forms of unconventional warfare
E998 Injury due to war operations but occurring after cessation of hostilities
E999 Late effects of injury due to war operations

NOTES

NOTES

NOTES

NOTES

NOTES

NOTES

A

- **Abbe operation**
  - construction of vagina 70.61
  - intestinal anastomosis — *see* Anastomosis intestine
- **Abciximab, infusion** 99.20
- **Abdominocentesis** 54.91
- **Abdominohysterectomy** 68.4
- **Abdominoplasty** 86.83
- **Abdominoscopy** 54.21
- **Abdominouterotomy** 68.0
  - obstetrical 74.99
- **Abduction, arytenoid** 31.69
- **Ablation**
  - biliary ducts (lesion) by ERCP 51.64
  - endometrial (hysteroscopic) 68.23
  - inner ear (cryosurgery) (ultrasound) 20.79
    - by injection 20.72
  - lesion
    - esophagus 42.39
      - endoscopic 42.33
    - heart (ventricular) 37.33
      - by cardiac catheter 37.34
    - intestine
      - large 45.49
        - endoscopic 45.43
    - large intestine 45.49
      - endoscopic 45.43
    - pituitary 07.69
      - by
        - Cobalt-60 92.32
        - implantation (strontium-yttrium) (Y) NEC 07.68
          - transfrontal approach 07.64
          - transphenoidal approach 07.65
        - proton beam (Bragg peak) 92.33
    - prostate
      - by
        - cryoablation 60.62
        - radical cryosurgical ablation (RCSA) 60.62
- **Abortion, therapeutic** 69.51
  - by
    - aspiration curettage 69.51
    - dilation and curettage 69.01
    - hysterectomy — *see* Hysterectomy
    - hysterotomy 74.91
    - insertion
      - laminaria 69.93
      - prostaglandin suppository 96.49
    - intra-amniotic injection (saline) 75.0
- **Abrasion**
  - corneal epithelium 11.41
    - for smear or culture 11.21
  - epicardial surface 36.39
  - pleural 34.6
  - skin 86.25
- **Abscission, cornea** 11.49
- **Absorptiometry**
  - photon (dual) (single) 88.98
- **Aburel operation** (intra-amniotic injection for abortion) 75.0
- **Accouchement forcé** 73.99
- **Acetabulectomy** 77.85
- **Acetabuloplasty** NEC 81.40
  - with prosthetic implant 81.52
- **Achillorrhaphy** 83.64
  - delayed 83.62
- **Achillotenotomy** 83.11
  - plastic 83.85
- **Achillotomy** 83.11
  - plastic 83.85
- **Acid peel, skin** 86.24
- **Acromionectomy** 77.81
- **Acromioplasty** 81.83
  - for recurrent dislocation of shoulder 81.82
  - partial replacement 81.81
  - total replacement 81.80
- **Actinotherapy** 99.82
- **Activities of daily living** (ADL)
  - therapy 93.83
  - training for the blind 93.78
- **Acupuncture** 99.92
  - with smouldering moxa 93.35
  - for anesthesia 99.91
- **Adams operation**
  - advancement of round ligament 69.22
  - crushing of nasal septum 21.88
  - excision of palmar fascia 82.35
- **Adenectomy** — *see also* Excision, by site
  - prostate NEC 60.69
    - retropubic 60.4
- **Adenoidectomy** (without tonsillectomy) 28.6
  - with tonsillectomy 28.3
- **Adhesiolysis** — *see also* Lysis, adhesions
  - for collapse of lung 33.39
  - middle ear 20.23
- **Adipectomy** 86.83
- **Adjustment**
  - cardiac pacemaker program (reprogramming)—*omit code*
  - cochlear prosthetic device (external components) 95.49
  - dental 99.97
  - occlusal 24.8
  - spectacles 95.31
- **Administration** (of) — *see also* Injection
  - antitoxins NEC 99.58
    - botulism 99.57
    - diphtheria 99.58
    - gas gangrene 99.58
    - scarlet fever 99.58
    - tetanus 99.56
  - Bender Visual-Motor Gestalt test 94.02
  - Benton Visual Retention test 94.02
  - intelligence test or scale (Stanford-Binet) (Wechsler) (adult) (children) 94.01
  - Minnesota Multiphasic Personality Inventory (MMPI) 94.02
  - MMPI (Minnesota Multiphasic Personality Inventory) 94.02
  - psychologic test 94.02
  - Stanford-Binet test 94.01
  - toxoid
    - diphtheria 99.36
      - with tetanus and pertussis, combined (DTP) 99.39
    - tetanus 99.38
      - with diphtheria and pertussis, combined (DTP) 99.39
  - vaccine — *see also* Vaccination
    - BCG 99.33
    - measles-mumps-rubella (MMR) 99.48
    - poliomyelitis 99.41
    - TAB 99.32
  - Wechsler
    - Intelligence Scale (adult) (children) 94.01
    - Memory Scale 94.02
- **Adrenalectomy** (unilateral) 07.22
  - with partial removal of remaining gland 07.29
- **Adrenalectomy** (unilateral) — *continued*
  - bilateral 07.3
    - partial 07.29
    - subtotal 07.29
  - complete 07.3
  - partial NEC 07.29
  - remaining gland 07.3
  - subtotal NEC 07.29
  - total 07.3
- **Adrenalorrhaphy** 07.44
- **Adrenalotomy** (with drainage) 07.41
- **Advancement**
  - extraocular muscle 15.12
    - multiple (with resection or recession) 15.3
  - eyelid muscle 08.59
  - eye muscle 15.12
    - multiple (with resection or recession) 15.3
  - graft — *see* Graft
  - leaflet (heart) 35.10
  - pedicle (flap) 86.72
  - profundus tendon (Wagner) 82.51
  - round ligament 69.22
  - tendon 83.71
    - hand 82.51
    - profundus (Wagner) 82.51
  - Wagner (profundus tendon) 82.51
- **Albee operation**
  - bone peg, femoral neck 78.05
  - graft for slipping patella 78.06
  - sliding inlay graft, tibia 78.07
- **Albert operation** (arthrodesis of knee) 81.22
- **Aldridge** (-Studdiford) operation (urethral sling) 59.5
- **Alexander operation**
  - prostatectomy
    - perineal 60.62
    - suprapubic 60.3
  - shortening of round ligaments 69.22
- **Alexander-Adams operation** (shortening of round ligaments) 69.22
- **Alimentation, parenteral** 99.29
- **Allograft** — *see* Graft
- **Almoor operation** (extrapetrosal drainage) 20.22
- **Altemeier operation** (perineal rectal pull-through) 48.49
- **Alveolectomy** (interradicular) (intraseptal) (radical) (simple) (with graft) (with implant) 24.5
- **Alveoloplasty** (with graft or implant) 24.5
- **Alveolotomy** (apical) 24.0
- **Ambulatory cardiac monitoring** (ACM) 89.50
- **Ammon operation** (dacryocystotomy) 09.53
- **Amniocentesis** (transuterine) (diagnostic) 75.1
  - with intra-amniotic injection of saline 75.0
- **Amniography** 87.81
- **Amnioinfusion** 75.37
- **Amnioscopy, internal** 75.31
- **Amniotomy** 73.09
  - to induce labor 73.01
- **Amputation** (cineplastic) (closed flap) (guillotine) (kineplastic) (open) 84.91
  - abdominopelvic 84.19
  - above-elbow 84.07
  - above-knee (AK) 84.17
  - ankle (disarticulation) 84.13
    - through malleoli of tibia and fibula 84.14

B

C

D

E

Note — Use the following fourth-digit subclassification with categories 90-91 to identify type of examination:
1 bacterial smear
2 culture
3 culture and sensitivity
4 parasitology
5 toxicology
6 cell block and Papanicolaou smear
9 other microscopic examination

F

G

H

I

J

K

L

M

N

O

P

Q

R

S

T

U

V

W

X

Y

Z

NOTES

NOTES

NOTES

NOTES

NOTES

NOTES

NOTES

NOTES

1. OPERATIONS ON THE NERVOUS SYSTEM (01-05)

01 Incision and excision of skull, brain, and cerebral meninges

01.0 Cranial puncture

01.01 Cisternal puncture
Cisternal tap

Excludes: *pneumocisternogram (87.02)*

01.02 Ventriculopuncture through previously implanted catheter
Puncture of ventricular shunt tubing

01.09 Other cranial puncture
Aspiration of:
 subarachnoid space
 subdural space
Cranial aspiration NOS
Puncture of anterior fontanel
Subdural tap (through fontanel)

01.1 Diagnostic procedures on skull, brain, and cerebral meninges

[22] **01.11 Closed [percutaneous] [needle] biopsy of cerebral meninges**
Burr hole approach

[21] **01.12 Open biopsy of cerebral meninges**

[22] **01.13 Closed [percutaneous] [needle] biopsy of brain**
Burr hole approach
Stereotactic method

➡ **AHA Coding Clinic:** M-A, '87, 9

[21] **01.14 Open biopsy of brain**

01.15 Biopsy of skull

01.18 Other diagnostic procedures on brain and cerebral meninges

Excludes: *cerebral:*
 arteriography (88.41)
 thermography (88.81)
contrast radiogram of brain (87.01-87.02)
echoencephalogram (88.71)
electroencephalogram (89.14)
microscopic examination of specimen from nervous system and of spinal fluid (90.01-90.09)
neurologic examination (89.13)
phlebography of head and neck (88.61)
pneumoencephalogram (87.01)
radioisotope scan:
 cerebral (92.11)
 head NEC (92.12)
tomography of head:
 C.A.T. scan (87.03)
 other (87.04)

01.19 Other diagnostic procedures on skull

Excludes: *transillumination of skull (89.16)*
x-ray of skull (87.17)

01.2 Craniotomy and craniectomy

Excludes: *decompression of skull fracture (02.02)*
exploration of orbit (16.01-16.09)
that as operative approach — omit code

01.21 Incision and drainage of cranial sinus

01.22 Removal of intracranial neurostimulator

Excludes: *removal with synchronous replacement (02.93)*

01.23 Reopening of craniotomy site

01.24 Other craniotomy
Cranial:
 decompression
 exploration
 trephination
Craniotomy NOS
Craniotomy with removal of:
 epidural abscess
 extradural hematoma
 foreign body of skull

Excludes: *removal of foreign body with incision into brain (01.39)*

➡ **AHA Coding Clinic:** 2Q, '91, 14

01.25 Other craniectomy
Debridement of skull NOS
Sequestrectomy of skull

Excludes: *debridement of compound fracture of skull (02.02)*
strip craniectomy (02.01)

[21] Open biopsy
[22] Closed biopsy

01.3 Incision of brain and cerebral meninges

01.31 Incision of cerebral meninges
Drainage of:
intracranial hygroma
subarachnoid abscess (cerebral)
subdural empyema

01.32 Lobotomy and tractotomy
Division of:
brain tissue
cerebral tracts
Percutaneous (radiofrequency) cingulotomy

01.39 Other incision of brain
Amygdalohippocampotomy
Drainage of intracerebral hematoma
Incision of brain NOS

Excludes: *division of cortical adhesions (02.91)*

01.4 Operations on thalamus and globus pallidus

01.41 Operations on thalamus
Chemothalamectomy
Thalamotomy

01.42 Operations on globus pallidus
Pallidoansectomy
Pallidotomy

01.5 Other excision or destruction of brain and meninges

01.51 Excision of lesion or tissue of cerebral meninges
Decortication, Resection, Stripping of subdural membrane } of (cerebral) meninges

Excludes: *biopsy of cerebral meninges (01.11-01.12)*

01.52 Hemispherectomy

01.53 Lobectomy of brain

01.59 Other excision or destruction of lesion or tissue of brain
Curettage of brain
Debridement of brain
Marsupialization of brain cyst
Transtemporal (mastoid) excision of brain tumor

Excludes: *biopsy of brain (01.13-01.14)*
that by stereotactic radiosurgery (92.3)

➡ **AHA Coding Clinic:** 1Q, '98, 6

01.6 Excision of lesion of skull
Removal of granulation tissue of cranium

Excludes: *biopsy of skull (01.15)*
sequestrectomy (01.25)

02 Other operations on skull, brain, and cerebral meninges

02.0 Cranioplasty

Excludes: *that with synchronous repair of encephalocele (02.12)*

02.01 Opening of cranial suture
Linear craniectomy
Strip craniectomy

02.02 Elevation of skull fracture fragments
Debridement of compound fracture of skull
Decompression of skull fracture
Reduction of skull fracture

Code also any synchronous debridement of brain (01.59)

Excludes: *debridement of skull NOS (01.25)*
removal of granulation tissue of cranium (01.6)

02.03 Formation of cranial bone flap
Repair of skull with flap

02.04 Bone graft to skull
Pericranial graft (autogenous) (heterogenous)

02.05 Insertion of skull plate
Replacement of skull plate

02.06 Other cranial osteoplasty
Repair of skull NOS
Revision of bone flap of skull

02.07 Removal of skull plate

Excludes: *removal with synchronous replacement (02.05)*

02.1 Repair of cerebral meninges

Excludes: *marsupialization of cerebral lesion (01.59)*

02.11 Simple suture of dura mater of brain

02.12 Other repair of cerebral meninges
Closure of fistula of cerebrospinal fluid
Dural graft
Repair of encephalocele including synchronous cranioplasty
Repair of meninges NOS
Subdural patch

02.13 Ligation of meningeal vessel
Ligation of:
longitudinal sinus
middle meningeal artery

02.14 Choroid plexectomy
Cauterization of choroid plexus

02.2 Ventriculostomy
Anastomosis of ventricle to:
cervical subarachnoid space
cisterna magna
Insertion of Holter valve
Ventriculocisternal intubation

02.3 Extracranial ventricular shunt
Includes: that with insertion of valve

02.31 Ventricular shunt to structure in head and neck
Ventricle to nasopharynx shunt
Ventriculomastoid anastomosis

02.32 Ventricular shunt to circulatory system
Ventriculoatrial anastomosis
Ventriculocaval shunt

02.33 Ventricular shunt to thoracic cavity
Ventriculopleural anastomosis

02.34 Ventricular shunt to abdominal cavity and organs
Ventriculocholecystostomy
Ventriculoperitoneostomy

02.35 Ventricular shunt to urinary system
Ventricle to ureter shunt

02.39 Other operations to establish drainage of ventricle
Ventricle to bone marrow shunt
Ventricular shunt to extracranial site NEC

02.4 Revision, removal, and irrigation of ventricular shunt

Excludes: *revision of distal catheter of ventricular shunt (54.95)*

02.41 Irrigation of ventricular shunt

02.42 Replacement of ventricular shunt
Reinsertion of Holter valve
Replacement of ventricular catheter
Revision of ventriculoperitoneal shunt at ventricular site

➡ **AHA Coding Clinic:** N-D, '86, 8

02.43 Removal of ventricular shunt

➡ **AHA Coding Clinic:** N-D, '86, 8

02.9 Other operations on skull, brain, and cerebral meninges

Excludes: *operations on:*
pineal gland (07.17, 07.51-07.59)
pituitary gland [hypophysis] (07.13-07.15, 07.61-07.79)

02.91 Lysis of cortical adhesions

02.92 Repair of brain

02.93 Implantation of intracranial neurostimulator
Implantation, insertion, placement, or replacement of intracranial:
brain pacemaker [neuropacemaker]
depth electrodes
electroencephalographic receiver
epidural pegs
foramen ovale electrodes
intracranial electrostimulator
subdural grids
subdural strips

➡ **AHA Coding Clinic:** 4Q, '97, 57; 4Q, '92, 28

02.94 Insertion or replacement of skull tongs or halo traction device

➡ **AHA Coding Clinic:** 3Q, '96, 14

02.95 Removal of skull tongs or halo traction device

02.96 Insertion of sphenoidal electrodes

➡ **AHA Coding Clinic:** 4Q, '92, 28

02.99 Other

Excludes: *chemical shock therapy (94.24)*
electroshock therapy:
subconvulsive (94.26)
other (94.27)

03 Operations on spinal cord and spinal canal structures

03.0 Exploration and decompression of spinal canal structures

03.01 Removal of foreign body from spinal canal

03.02 Reopening of laminectomy site

03.09 Other exploration and decompression of spinal canal
Decompression:
laminectomy
laminotomy
Exploration of spinal nerve root
Foraminotomy

Excludes: *drainage of spinal fluid by anastomosis (03.71-03.79)*
laminectomy with excision of intervertebral disc (80.51)
spinal tap (03.31)
that as operative approach — omit code

➡ **AHA Coding Clinic:** 2Q, '97, 6; 2Q, '95, 9; 2Q, '95, 10; 2Q, '90, 22

03.1 Division of intraspinal nerve root
Rhizotomy

03.2 Chordotomy

03.21 Percutaneous chordotomy
Stereotactic chordotomy

03.29 Other chordotomy
Chordotomy NOS
Tractotomy (one-stage) (two-stage) of spinal cord
Transection of spinal cord tracts

03.3 Diagnostic procedures on spinal cord and spinal canal structures

03.31 Spinal tap
Lumbar puncture for removal of dye

Excludes: *lumbar puncture for injection of dye [myelogram] (87.21)*

➡ **AHA Coding Clinic:** 2Q, '90, 22

03.32 Biopsy of spinal cord or spinal meninges

03.39 Other diagnostic procedures on spinal cord and spinal canal structures

Excludes: *microscopic examination of specimen from nervous system or of spinal fluid (90.01-90.09)*
x-ray of spine (87.21-87.29)

03.4 Excision or destruction of lesion of spinal cord or spinal meninges
Curettage, Debridement, Marsupialization of cyst, Resection — of spinal cord or spinal meninges

Excludes: *biopsy of spinal cord or meninges (03.32)*

➡ **AHA Coding Clinic:** 3Q, '95, 5

03.5 Plastic operations on spinal cord structures

03.51 Repair of spinal meningocele
Repair of meningocele NOS

03.52 Repair of spinal myelomeningocele

03.53 Repair of vertebral fracture
Elevation of spinal bone fragments
Reduction of fracture of vertebrae
Removal of bony spicules from spinal canal

➡ **AHA Coding Clinic:** 3Q, '96, 14

03.59 Other repair and plastic operations on spinal cord structures
Repair of:
diastematomyelia
spina bifida NOS
spinal cord NOS
spinal meninges NOS
vertebral arch defect

03.6 Lysis of adhesions of spinal cord and nerve roots

03.7 Shunt of spinal theca
Includes: that with valve

03.71 Spinal subarachnoid-peritoneal shunt

03.72 Spinal subarachnoid-ureteral shunt

03.79 Other shunt of spinal theca
Lumbar-subarachnoid shunt NOS
Pleurothecal anastomosis
Salpingothecal anastomosis

➡ **AHA Coding Clinic:** 1Q, '97, 7

03.8 Injection of destructive agent into spinal canal

03.9 Other operations on spinal cord and spinal canal structures

03.90 Insertion of catheter into spinal canal for infusion of therapeutic or palliative substances
Insertion of catheter into epidural, subarachnoid, or subdural space of spine with intermittent or continuous infusion of drug (with creation of any reservoir)

Code also any implantation of infusion pump (86.06)

03.91 Injection of anesthetic into spinal canal for analgesia

Excludes: *that for operative anesthesia — omit code*

03.92 **Injection of other agent into spinal canal**
Intrathecal injection of steroid
Subarachnoid perfusion of refrigerated saline

Excludes: *injection of:*
contrast material for myelogram (87.21)
destructive agent into spinal canal (03.8)

03.93 **Insertion or replacement of spinal neurostimulator**

03.94 **Removal of spinal neurostimulator**

03.95 **Spinal blood patch**

03.96 **Percutaneous denervation of facet**

03.97 **Revision of spinal thecal shunt**

03.98 **Removal of spinal thecal shunt**

03.99 **Other**

04 Operations on cranial and peripheral nerves

04.0 **Incision, division, and excision of cranial and peripheral nerves**

Excludes: *opticociliary neurectomy (12.79)*
sympathetic ganglionectomy (05.21-05.29)

04.01 **Excision of acoustic neuroma**

Excludes: *that by stereotactic radiosurgery (92.3)*

➡ **AHA Coding Clinic:** 4Q, '92, 26

04.02 **Division of trigeminal nerve**
Retrogasserian neurotomy

04.03 **Division or crushing of other cranial and peripheral nerves**

Excludes: *that of:*
glossopharyngeal nerve (29.92)
laryngeal nerve (31.91)
nerves to adrenal glands (07.42)
phrenic nerve for collapse of lung (33.31)
vagus nerve (44.00-44.03)

04.04 **Other incision of cranial and peripheral nerves**

04.05 **Gasserian ganglionectomy**

04.06 **Other cranial or peripheral ganglionectomy**

Excludes: *sympathetic ganglionectomy (05.21-05.29)*

04.07 **Other excision or avulsion of cranial and peripheral nerves**
Curettage, Debridement, Resection } of peripheral nerve
Excision of peripheral neuroma [Morton's]

Excludes: *biopsy of cranial or peripheral nerve (04.11-04.12)*

➡ **AHA Coding Clinic:** 4Q, '92, 26

04.1 **Diagnostic procedures on peripheral nervous system**

[22] **04.11** **Closed [percutaneous] [needle] biopsy of cranial or peripheral nerve or ganglion**

[21] **04.12** **Open biopsy of cranial or peripheral nerve or ganglion**

04.19 **Other diagnostic procedures on cranial and peripheral nerves and ganglia**

Excludes: *microscopic examination of specimen from nervous system (90.01-90.09)*
neurologic examination (89.13)

04.2 **Destruction of cranial and peripheral nerves**
Destruction of cranial or peripheral nerves by:
cryoanalgesia
injection of neurolytic agent
radiofrequency

➡ **AHA Coding Clinic:** 4Q, '95, 74

04.3 **Suture of cranial and peripheral nerves**

04.4 **Lysis of adhesions and decompression of cranial and peripheral nerves**

04.41 **Decompression of trigeminal nerve root**

04.42 **Other cranial nerve decompression**

04.43 **Release of carpal tunnel**

04.44 **Release of tarsal tunnel**

04.49 **Other peripheral nerve or ganglion decompression or lysis of adhesions**
Peripheral nerve neurolysis NOS

04.5 **Cranial or peripheral nerve graft**

04.6 **Transposition of cranial and peripheral nerves**
Nerve transplantation

04.7 **Other cranial or peripheral neuroplasty**

04.71 **Hypoglossal-facial anastomosis**

04.72 **Accessory-facial anastomosis**

04.73 **Accessory-hypoglossal anastomosis**

04.74 **Other anastomosis of cranial or peripheral nerve**

[21] Open biopsy
[22] Closed biopsy

04.75 Revision of previous repair of cranial and peripheral nerves

04.76 Repair of old traumatic injury of cranial and peripheral nerves

04.79 Other neuroplasty

04.8 Injection into peripheral nerve

Excludes: *destruction of nerve (by injection of neurolytic agent) (04.2)*

04.80 Peripheral nerve injection, not otherwise specified

04.81 Injection of anesthetic into peripheral nerve for analgesia

Excludes: *that for operative anesthesia — omit code*

04.89 Injection of other agent, except neurolytic

Excludes: *injection of neurolytic agent (04.2)*

04.9 Other operations on cranial and peripheral nerves

04.91 Neurectasis

04.92 Implantation or replacement of peripheral neurostimulator

➡ **AHA Coding Clinic:** 3Q, '96, 12

04.93 Removal of peripheral neurostimulator

04.99 Other

05 Operations on sympathetic nerves or ganglia

Excludes: *paracervical uterine denervation (69.3)*

05.0 Division of sympathetic nerve or ganglion

Excludes: *that of nerves to adrenal glands (07.42)*

05.1 Diagnostic procedures on sympathetic nerves or ganglia

05.11 Biopsy of sympathetic nerve or ganglion

05.19 Other diagnostic procedures on sympathetic nerves or ganglia

05.2 Sympathectomy

05.21 Sphenopalatine ganglionectomy

05.22 Cervical sympathectomy

05.23 Lumbar sympathectomy

05.24 Presacral sympathectomy

05.25 Periarterial sympathectomy

05.29 Other sympathectomy and ganglionectomy

Excision or avulsion of sympathetic nerve NOS
Sympathetic ganglionectomy NOS

Excludes: *biopsy of sympathetic nerve or ganglion (05.11)*
opticociliary neurectomy (12.79)
periarterial sympathectomy (05.25)
tympanosympathectomy (20.91)

05.3 Injection into sympathetic nerve or ganglion

Excludes: *injection of ciliary sympathetic ganglion (12.79)*

05.31 Injection of anesthetic into sympathetic nerve for analgesia

05.32 Injection of neurolytic agent into sympathetic nerve

05.39 Other injection into sympathetic nerve or ganglion

05.8 Other operations on sympathetic nerves or ganglia

05.81 Repair of sympathetic nerve or ganglion

05.89 Other

05.9 Other operations on nervous system

2. OPERATIONS ON THE ENDOCRINE SYSTEM (06-07)

06 Operations on thyroid and parathyroid glands

Includes: incidental resection of hyoid bone

06.0 Incision of thyroid field

Excludes: *division of isthmus (06.91)*

06.01 Aspiration of thyroid field

Percutaneous or needle drainage of thyroid field

Excludes: *aspiration biopsy of thyroid (06.11)*
drainage by incision (06.09)
postoperative aspiration of field (06.02)

06.02 Reopening of wound of thyroid field

Reopening of wound of thyroid field for:
- control of (postoperative) hemorrhage
- examination
- exploration
- removal of hematoma

06.09 Other incision of thyroid field

Drainage of hematoma } by incision
Drainage of thyroglossal tract } by incision
Exploration: } by incision
- neck
- thyroid (field)

Removal of foreign body
Thyroidotomy NOS

Excludes: *postoperative exploration (06.02)*
removal of hematoma by aspiration (06.01)

06.1 Diagnostic procedures on thyroid and parathyroid glands

[22] **06.11 Closed [percutaneous] [needle] biopsy of thyroid gland**

Aspiration biopsy of thyroid

[21] **06.12 Open biopsy of thyroid gland**

06.13 Biopsy of parathyroid gland

06.19 Other diagnostic procedures on thyroid and parathyroid glands

Excludes: *radioisotope scan of:*
parathyroid (92.13)
thyroid (92.01)
soft tissue x-ray of thyroid field (87.09)

06.2 Unilateral thyroid lobectomy

Complete removal of one lobe of thyroid (with removal of isthmus or portion of other lobe)
Hemithyroidectomy

Excludes: *partial substernal thyroidectomy (06.51)*

06.3 Other partial thyroidectomy

06.31 Excision of lesion of thyroid

Excludes: *biopsy of thyroid (06.11-06.12)*

06.39 Other

Isthmectomy
Partial thyroidectomy NOS

Excludes: *partial substernal thyroidectomy (06.51)*

06.4 Complete thyroidectomy

Excludes: *complete substernal thyroidectomy (06.52)*
that with laryngectomy (30.3-30.4)

06.5 Substernal thyroidectomy

06.50 Substernal thyroidectomy, not otherwise specified

06.51 Partial substernal thyroidectomy

06.52 Complete substernal thyroidectomy

06.6 Excision of lingual thyroid

Excision of thyroid by:
- submental route
- transoral route

06.7 Excision of thyroglossal duct or tract

06.8 Parathyroidectomy

06.81 Complete parathyroidectomy

06.89 Other parathyroidectomy

Parathyroidectomy NOS
Partial parathyroidectomy

Excludes: *biopsy of parathyroid (06.13)*

06.9 Other operations on thyroid (region) and parathyroid

06.91 Division of thyroid isthmus

Transection of thyroid isthmus

06.92 Ligation of thyroid vessels

06.93 Suture of thyroid gland

06.94 Thyroid tissue reimplantation

Autotransplantation of thyroid tissue

06.95 Parathyroid tissue reimplantation

Autotransplantation of parathyroid tissue

06.98 Other operations on thyroid glands

06.99 Other operations on parathyroid glands

[21] Open biopsy
[22] Closed biopsy

07 Operations on other endocrine glands

Includes: operations on:
adrenal glands
pituitary gland
pineal gland
thymus

Excludes: *operations on:*
aortic and carotid bodies (39.8)
ovaries (65.0-65.99)
pancreas (52.01-52.99)
testes (62.0-62.99)

07.0 Exploration of adrenal field

Excludes: *incision of adrenal (gland) (07.41)*

07.00 Exploration of adrenal field, not otherwise specified

07.01 Unilateral exploration of adrenal field

07.02 Bilateral exploration of adrenal field

07.1 Diagnostic procedures on adrenal glands, pituitary gland, pineal gland, and thymus

[22] **07.11 Closed [percutaneous] [needle] biopsy of adrenal gland**

[21] **07.12 Open biopsy of adrenal gland**

07.13 Biopsy of pituitary gland, transfrontal approach

07.14 Biopsy of pituitary gland, transsphenoidal approach

07.15 Biopsy of pituitary gland, unspecified approach

07.16 Biopsy of thymus

07.17 Biopsy of pineal gland

07.19 Other diagnostic procedures on adrenal glands, pituitary gland, pineal gland, and thymus

Excludes: *microscopic examination of specimen from endocrine gland (90.11-90.19)*
radioisotope scan of pituitary gland (92.11)

07.2 Partial adrenalectomy

07.21 Excision of lesion of adrenal gland

Excludes: *biopsy of adrenal gland (07.11-07.12)*

07.22 Unilateral adrenalectomy
Adrenalectomy NOS

Excludes: *excision of remaining adrenal gland (07.3)*

07.29 Other partial adrenalectomy
Partial adrenalectomy NOS

07.3 Bilateral adrenalectomy
Excision of remaining adrenal gland

Excludes: *bilateral partial adrenalectomy (07.29)*

07.4 Other operations on adrenal glands, nerves, and vessels

07.41 Incision of adrenal gland
Adrenalotomy (with drainage)

07.42 Division of nerves to adrenal glands

07.43 Ligation of adrenal vessels

07.44 Repair of adrenal gland

07.45 Reimplantation of adrenal tissue
Autotransplantation of adrenal tissue

07.49 Other

07.5 Operations on pineal gland

07.51 Exploration of pineal field

Excludes: *that with incision of pineal gland (07.52)*

07.52 Incision of pineal gland

07.53 Partial excision of pineal gland

Excludes: *biopsy of pineal gland (07.17)*

07.54 Total excision of pineal gland
Pinealectomy (complete) (total)

07.59 Other operations on pineal gland

07.6 Hypophysectomy

07.61 Partial excision of pituitary gland, transfrontal approach

Cryohypophysectomy, partial
Division of hypophyseal stalk
Excision of lesion of pituitary [hypophysis]
Hypophysectomy, subtotal
Infundibulectomy, hypophyseal
} transfrontal approach

Excludes: *biopsy of pituitary gland, transfrontal approach (07.13)*

[21] Open biopsy
[22] Closed biopsy

07.62 **Partial excision of pituitary gland, transsphenoidal approach**

Excludes: *biopsy of pituitary gland, transsphenoidal approach (07.14)*

07.63 **Partial excision of pituitary gland, unspecified approach**

Excludes: *biopsy of pituitary gland NOS (07.15)*

07.64 **Total excision of pituitary gland, transfrontal approach**

Ablation of pituitary by implantation (strontium-yttrium) (Y) } transfrontal approach
Cryohypophysectomy, complete } transfrontal approach

07.65 **Total excision of pituitary gland, transsphenoidal approach**

07.68 **Total excision of pituitary gland, other specified approach**

07.69 **Total excision of pituitary gland, unspecified approach**

Hypophysectomy NOS
Pituitectomy NOS

07.7 **Other operations on hypophysis**

07.71 **Exploration of pituitary fossa**

Excludes: *exploration with incision of pituitary gland (07.72)*

07.72 **Incision of pituitary gland**

Aspiration of:
- craniobuccal pouch
- craniopharyngioma
- hypophysis
- pituitary gland
- Rathke's pouch

07.79 **Other**

Insertion of pack into sella turcica

07.8 **Thymectomy**

07.80 **Thymectomy, not otherwise specified**

07.81 **Partial excision of thymus**

Excludes: *biopsy of thymus (07.16)*

07.82 **Total excision of thymus**

07.9 **Other operations on thymus**

07.91 **Exploration of thymus field**

Excludes: *exploration with incision of thymus (07.92)*

07.92 **Incision of thymus**

07.93 **Repair of thymus**

07.94 **Transplantation of thymus**

07.99 **Other**

Thymopexy

3. OPERATIONS ON THE EYE (08-16)

08 Operations on eyelids

Includes: operations on the eyebrow

08.0 Incision of eyelid

08.01 Incision of lid margin

08.02 Severing of blepharorrhaphy

08.09 Other incision of eyelid

08.1 Diagnostic procedures on eyelid

08.11 Biopsy of eyelid

08.19 Other diagnostic procedures on eyelid

08.2 Excision or destruction of lesion or tissue of eyelid

Code also any synchronous reconstruction (08.61-08.74)

Excludes: *biopsy of eyelid (08.11)*

08.20 Removal of lesion of eyelid, not otherwise specified
Removal of meibomian gland NOS

08.21 Excision of chalazion

08.22 Excision of other minor lesion of eyelid
Excision of:
verruca
wart

08.23 Excision of major lesion of eyelid, partial-thickness
Excision involving one-fourth or more of lid margin, partial-thickness

08.24 Excision of major lesion of eyelid, full-thickness
Excision involving one-fourth or more of lid margin, full-thickness
Wedge resection of eyelid

08.25 Destruction of lesion of eyelid

08.3 Repair of blepharoptosis and lid retraction

08.31 Repair of blepharoptosis by frontalis muscle technique with suture

08.32 Repair of blepharoptosis by frontalis muscle technique with fascial sling

08.33 Repair of blepharoptosis by resection or advancement of levator muscle or aponeurosis

08.34 Repair of blepharoptosis by other levator muscle techniques

08.35 Repair of blepharoptosis by tarsal technique

08.36 Repair of blepharoptosis by other techniques
Correction of eyelid ptosis NOS
Orbicularis oculi muscle sling for correction of blepharoptosis

08.37 Reduction of overcorrection of ptosis

08.38 Correction of lid retraction

08.4 Repair of entropion or ectropion

08.41 Repair of entropion or ectropion by thermocauterization

08.42 Repair of entropion or ectropion by suture technique

08.43 Repair of entropion or ectropion with wedge resection

08.44 Repair of entropion or ectropion with lid reconstruction

08.49 Other repair of entropion or ectropion

08.5 Other adjustment of lid position

08.51 Canthotomy
Enlargement of palpebral fissure

08.52 Blepharorrhaphy
Canthorrhaphy
Tarsorrhaphy

08.59 Other
Canthoplasty NOS
Repair of epicanthal fold

08.6 Reconstruction of eyelid with flaps or grafts

Excludes: *that associated with repair of entropion and ectropion (08.44)*

08.61 Reconstruction of eyelid with skin flap or graft

08.62 Reconstruction of eyelid with mucous membrane flap or graft

08.63 Reconstruction of eyelid with hair follicle graft

08.64 Reconstruction of eyelid with tarsoconjunctival flap
Transfer of tarsoconjunctival flap from opposing lid

08.69 Other reconstruction of eyelid with flaps or grafts

08.7 Other reconstruction of eyelid

Excludes: *that associated with repair of entropion and ectropion (08.44)*

08.70 Reconstruction of eyelid, not otherwise specified
➡ **AHA Coding Clinic:** 2Q, '96, 11

08.71 Reconstruction of eyelid involving lid margin, partial-thickness

08.72 Other reconstruction of eyelid, partial-thickness

08.73 Reconstruction of eyelid involving lid margin, full-thickness

08.74 Other reconstruction of eyelid, full-thickness

08.8 Other repair of eyelid

08.81 Linear repair of laceration of eyelid or eyebrow

08.82 Repair of laceration involving lid margin, partial-thickness

08.83 Other repair of laceration of eyelid, partial thickness

08.84 Repair of laceration involving lid margin, full-thickness

08.85 Other repair of laceration of eyelid, full-thickness

08.86 Lower eyelid rhytidectomy

08.87 Upper eyelid rhytidectomy
➡ **AHA Coding Clinic:** 2Q, '96, 11

08.89 Other eyelid repair

08.9 Other operations on eyelids

08.91 Electrosurgical epilation of eyelid

08.92 Cryosurgical epilation of eyelid

08.93 Other epilation of eyelid

08.99 Other

09 Operations on lacrimal system

09.0 Incision of lacrimal gland
Incision of lacrimal cyst (with drainage)

09.1 Diagnostic procedures on lacrimal system

09.11 Biopsy of lacrimal gland

09.12 Biopsy of lacrimal sac

09.19 Other diagnostic procedures on lacrimal system

Excludes: *contrast dacryocystogram (87.05)*
soft tissue x-ray of nasolacrimal duct (87.09)

09.2 Excision of lesion or tissue of lacrimal gland

09.20 Excision of lacrimal gland, not otherwise specified

09.21 Excision of lesion of lacrimal gland

Excludes: *biopsy of lacrimal gland (09.11)*

09.22 Other partial dacryoadenectomy

Excludes: *biopsy of lacrimal gland (09.11)*

09.23 Total dacryoadenectomy

09.3 Other operations on lacrimal gland

09.4 Manipulation of lacrimal passage
Includes: removal of calculus
that with dilation

Excludes: *contrast dacryocystogram (87.05)*

09.41 Probing of lacrimal punctum

09.42 Probing of lacrimal canaliculi

09.43 Probing of nasolacrimal duct

Excludes: *that with insertion of tube or stent (09.44)*

09.44 Intubation of nasolacrimal duct
Insertion of stent into nasolacrimal duct

09.49 Other manipulation of lacrimal passage

09.5 Incision of lacrimal sac and passages

09.51 Incision of lacrimal punctum

09.52 Incision of lacrimal canaliculi

09.53 Incision of lacrimal sac

09.59 Other incision of lacrimal passages
Incision (and drainage) of nasolacrimal duct NOS

09.6 Excision of lacrimal sac and passage

Excludes: *biopsy of lacrimal sac (09.12)*

09.7 Repair of canaliculus and punctum

Excludes: *repair of eyelid (08.81-08.89)*

09.71 Correction of everted punctum

09.72 Other repair of punctum

09.73 Repair of canaliculus

09.8 Fistulization of lacrimal tract to nasal cavity

09.81 Dacryocystorhinostomy [DCR]

09.82 Conjunctivocystorhinostomy

Conjunctivodacryocystorhinostomy [CDCR]

Excludes: *that with insertion of tube or stent (09.83)*

09.83 Conjunctivorhinostomy with insertion of tube or stent

09.9 Other operations on lacrimal system

09.91 Obliteration of lacrimal punctum

09.99 Other

➡ **AHA Coding Clinic:** 2Q, '94, 11

10 Operations on conjunctiva

10.0 Removal of embedded foreign body from conjunctiva by incision

Excludes: *removal of:*
embedded foreign body without incision (98.22)
superficial foreign body (98.21)

10.1 Other incision of conjunctiva

10.2 Diagnostic procedures on conjunctiva

10.21 Biopsy of conjunctiva

10.29 Other diagnostic procedures on conjunctiva

10.3 Excision or destruction of lesion or tissue of conjunctiva

10.31 Excision of lesion or tissue of conjunctiva

Excision of ring of conjunctiva around cornea

Excludes: *biopsy of conjunctiva (10.21)*

➡ **AHA Coding Clinic:** 3Q, '96, 7

10.32 Destruction of lesion of conjunctiva

Excludes: *excision of lesion (10.31)*
thermocauterization for entropion (08.41)

10.33 Other destructive procedures on conjunctiva

Removal of trachoma follicles

10.4 Conjunctivoplasty

10.41 Repair of symblepharon with free graft

➡ **AHA Coding Clinic:** 3Q, '96, 7

10.42 Reconstruction of conjunctival cul-de-sac with free graft

Excludes: *revision of enucleation socket with graft (16.63)*

10.43 Other reconstruction of conjunctival cul-de-sac

Excludes: *revision of enucleation socket (16.64)*

10.44 Other free graft to conjunctiva

10.49 Other conjunctivoplasty

Excludes: *repair of cornea with conjunctival flap (11.53)*

10.5 Lysis of adhesions of conjunctiva and eyelid

Division of symblepharon (with insertion of conformer)

10.6 Repair of laceration of conjunctiva

Excludes: *that with repair of sclera (12.81)*

10.9 Other operations on conjunctiva

10.91 Subconjunctival injection

➡ **AHA Coding Clinic:** 3Q, '96, 7

10.99 Other

11 Operations on cornea

11.0 Magnetic removal of embedded foreign body from cornea

Excludes: *that with incision (11.1)*

11.1 Incision of cornea

Incision of cornea for removal of foreign body

11.2 Diagnostic procedures on cornea

11.21 Scraping of cornea for smear or culture

11.22 Biopsy of cornea

11.29 Other diagnostic procedures on cornea

11.3 Excision of pterygium

11.31 Transposition of pterygium

11.32 Excision of pterygium with corneal graft

11.39 Other excision of pterygium

11.4 Excision or destruction of tissue or other lesion of cornea

11.41 Mechanical removal of corneal epithelium

That by chemocauterization

Excludes: *that for smear or culture (11.21)*

11.42 Thermocauterization of corneal lesion

11.43 Cryotherapy of corneal lesion

11.49 Other removal or destruction of corneal lesion
Excision of cornea NOS

Excludes: *biopsy of cornea (11.22)*

11.5 Repair of cornea

11.51 Suture of corneal laceration
➡ **AHA Coding Clinic:** 3Q, '96, 7

11.52 Repair of postoperative wound dehiscence of cornea

11.53 Repair of corneal laceration or wound with conjunctival flap

11.59 Other repair of cornea

11.6 Corneal transplant

Excludes: *excision of pterygium with corneal graft (11.32)*

11.60 Corneal transplant, not otherwise specified
Keratoplasty NOS

11.61 Lamellar keratoplasty with autograft

11.62 Other lamellar keratoplasty
➡ **AHA Coding Clinic:** S-O, '85, 6

11.63 Penetrating keratoplasty with autograft
Perforating keratoplasty with autograft

11.64 Other penetrating keratoplasty
Perforating keratoplasty (with homograft)

11.69 Other corneal transplant

11.7 Other reconstructive and refractive surgery on cornea

11.71 Keratomileusis

11.72 Keratophakia

11.73 Keratoprosthesis

11.74 Thermokeratoplasty

11.75 Radial keratotomy

11.76 Epikeratophakia

11.79 Other

11.9 Other operations on cornea

11.91 Tattooing of cornea

11.92 Removal of artificial implant from cornea

11.99 Other

12 Operations on iris, ciliary body, sclera, and anterior chamber

Excludes: *operations on cornea (11.0-11.99)*

12.0 Removal of intraocular foreign body from anterior segment of eye

12.00 Removal of intraocular foreign body from anterior segment of eye, not otherwise specified

12.01 Removal of intraocular foreign body from anterior segment of eye with use of magnet

12.02 Removal of intraocular foreign body from anterior segment of eye without use of magnet

12.1 Iridotomy and simple iridectomy

Excludes: *iridectomy associated with:*
cataract extraction (13.11-13.69)
removal of lesion (12.41-12.42)
scleral fistulization (12.61-12.69)

12.11 Iridotomy with transfixion

12.12 Other iridotomy
Corectomy
Discission of iris
Iridotomy NOS

12.13 Excision of prolapsed iris

12.14 Other iridectomy
Iridectomy (basal) (peripheral) (total)

12.2 Diagnostic procedures on iris, ciliary body, sclera, and anterior chamber

12.21 Diagnostic aspiration of anterior chamber of eye

12.22 Biopsy of iris

12.29 Other diagnostic procedures on iris, ciliary body, sclera, and anterior chamber

12.3 Iridoplasty and coreoplasty

12.31 Lysis of goniosynechiae
Lysis of goniosynechiae by injection of air or liquid

12.32 Lysis of other anterior synechiae
Lysis of anterior synechiae:
NOS
by injection of air or liquid

12.33 Lysis of posterior synechiae
Lysis of iris adhesions NOS

12.34 Lysis of corneovitreal adhesions

12.35 Coreoplasty
Needling of pupillary membrane

12.39 Other iridoplasty

12.4 Excision or destruction of lesion of iris and ciliary body

12.40 Removal of lesion of anterior segment of eye, not otherwise specified

12.41 Destruction of lesion of iris, nonexcisional
Destruction of lesion of iris by:
cauterization
cryotherapy
photocoagulation

12.42 Excision of lesion of iris

Excludes: *biopsy of iris (12.22)*

12.43 Destruction of lesion of ciliary body, nonexcisional

12.44 Excision of lesion of ciliary body

12.5 Facilitation of intraocular circulation

12.51 Goniopuncture without goniotomy

12.52 Goniotomy without goniopuncture

12.53 Goniotomy with goniopuncture

12.54 Trabeculotomy ab externo

12.55 Cyclodialysis

12.59 Other facilitation of intraocular circulation

12.6 Scleral fistulization

Excludes: *exploratory sclerotomy (12.89)*

12.61 Trephination of sclera with iridectomy

12.62 Thermocauterization of sclera with iridectomy

12.63 Iridencleisis and iridotasis

12.64 Trabeculectomy ab externo

12.65 Other scleral fistulization with iridectomy

12.66 Postoperative revision of scleral fistulization procedure
Revision of filtering bleb

Excludes: *repair of fistula (12.82)*

12.69 Other fistulizing procedure
➡ **AHA Coding Clinic:** 3Q, '96, 4

12.7 Other procedures for relief of elevated intraocular pressure

12.71 Cyclodiathermy

12.72 Cyclocryotherapy

12.73 Cyclophotocoagulation

12.74 Diminution of ciliary body, not otherwise specified

12.79 Other glaucoma procedures

12.8 Operations on sclera

Excludes: *those associated with:*
retinal reattachment (14.41-14.59)
scleral fistulization (12.61-12.69)

12.81 Suture of laceration of sclera
Suture of sclera with synchronous repair of conjunctiva

12.82 Repair of scleral fistula

Excludes: *postoperative revision of scleral fistulization procedure (12.66)*

12.83 Revision of operative wound of anterior segment, not elsewhere classified

Excludes: *postoperative revision of scleral fistulization procedure (12.66)*

12.84 Excision or destruction of lesion of sclera

12.85 Repair of scleral staphyloma with graft

12.86 Other repair of scleral staphyloma

12.87 Scleral reinforcement with graft

12.88 Other scleral reinforcement

12.89 Other operations on sclera
Exploratory sclerotomy

12.9 Other operations on iris, ciliary body, and anterior chamber

12.91 Therapeutic evacuation of anterior chamber
Paracentesis of anterior chamber

Excludes: *diagnostic aspiration (12.21)*

12.92 Injection into anterior chamber
Injection of:
air } into anterior chamber
liquid } into anterior chamber
medication } into anterior chamber
➡ **AHA Coding Clinic:** J-A, '84, 1

12.93 Removal or destruction of epithelial downgrowth from anterior chamber

Excludes: *that with iridectomy (12.41-12.42)*

12.97 Other operations on iris

12.98 Other operations on ciliary body

12.99 Other operations on anterior chamber

13 Operations on lens

13.0 Removal of foreign body from lens

Excludes: *removal of pseudophakos (13.8)*

13.00 Removal of foreign body from lens, not otherwise specified

13.01 Removal of foreign body from lens with use of magnet

13.02 Removal of foreign body from lens without use of magnet

13.1 Intracapsular extraction of lens

Code also any synchronous insertion of pseudophakos (13.71)

➡ **AHA Coding Clinic:** S-O, '85, 6

13.11 Intracapsular extraction of lens by temporal inferior route

13.19 Other intracapsular extraction of lens

Cataract extraction NOS
Cryoextraction of lens
Erysiphake extraction of cataract
Extraction of lens NOS

13.2 Extracapsular extraction of lens by linear extraction technique

➡ **AHA Coding Clinic:** S-O, '85, 6

13.3 Extracapsular extraction of lens by simple aspiration (and irrigation) technique

Irrigation of traumatic cataract

➡ **AHA Coding Clinic:** S-O, '85, 6

13.4 Extracapsular extraction of lens by fragmentation and aspiration technique

➡ **AHA Coding Clinic:** S-O, '85, 6

13.41 Phacoemulsification and aspiration of cataract

➡ **AHA Coding Clinic:** 3Q, '96, 4; 1Q, '94, 16

13.42 Mechanical phacofragmentation and aspiration of cataract by posterior route

Code also any synchronous vitrectomy (14.74)

13.43 Mechanical phacofragmentation and other aspiration of cataract

13.5 Other extracapsular extraction of lens

Code also any synchronous insertion of pseudophakos (13.71)

➡ **AHA Coding Clinic:** S-O, '85, 6

13.51 Extracapsular extraction of lens by temporal inferior route

13.59 Other extracapsular extraction of lens

13.6 Other cataract extraction

Code also any synchronous insertion of pseudophakos (13.71)

➡ **AHA Coding Clinic:** S-O, '85, 6

13.64 Discission of secondary membrane [after cataract]

13.65 Excision of secondary membrane [after cataract]

Capsulectomy

13.66 Mechanical fragmentation of secondary membrane [after cataract]

13.69 Other cataract extraction

13.7 Insertion of prosthetic lens [pseudophakos]

➡ **AHA Coding Clinic:** J-A, '84, 1

13.70 Insertion of pseudophakos, not otherwise specified

13.71 Insertion of intraocular lens prosthesis at time of cataract extraction, one-stage

Code also synchronous extraction of cataract (13.11-13.69)

➡ **AHA Coding Clinic:** 3Q, '96, 4

13.72 Secondary insertion of intraocular lens prosthesis

13.8 Removal of implanted lens

Removal of pseudophakos

13.9 Other operations on lens

14 Operations on retina, choroid, vitreous, and posterior chamber

14.0 Removal of foreign body from posterior segment of eye

Excludes: *removal of surgically implanted material (14.6)*

14.00 Removal of foreign body from posterior segment of eye, not otherwise specified

14.01 Removal of foreign body from posterior segment of eye with use of magnet

14.02 Removal of foreign body from posterior segment of eye without use of magnet

14.1 Diagnostic procedures on retina, choroid, vitreous, and posterior chamber

14.11 Diagnostic aspiration of vitreous

14.19 Other diagnostic procedures on retina, choroid, vitreous, and posterior chamber

14.2 Destruction of lesion of retina and choroid

Includes: destruction of chorioretinopathy or isolated chorioretinal lesion

Excludes: that for repair of retina (14.31-14.59)

14.21 Destruction of chorioretinal lesion by diathermy

14.22 Destruction of chorioretinal lesion by cryotherapy

14.23 Destruction of chorioretinal lesion by xenon arc photocoagulation

14.24 Destruction of chorioretinal lesion by laser photocoagulation

14.25 Destruction of chorioretinal lesion by photocoagulation of unspecified type

14.26 Destruction of chorioretinal lesion by radiation therapy

14.27 Destruction of chorioretinal lesion by implantation of radiation source

14.29 Other destruction of chorioretinal lesion

Destruction of lesion of retina and choroid NOS

14.3 Repair of retinal tear

Includes: repair of retinal defect

Excludes: repair of retinal detachment (14.41-14.59)

14.31 Repair of retinal tear by diathermy

14.32 Repair of retinal tear by cryotherapy

14.33 Repair of retinal tear by xenon arc photocoagulation

14.34 Repair of retinal tear by laser photocoagulation

14.35 Repair of retinal tear by photocoagulation of unspecified type

14.39 Other repair of retinal tear

14.4 Repair of retinal detachment with scleral buckling and implant

14.41 Scleral buckling with implant

➡ **AHA Coding Clinic:** 3Q, '96, 6

14.49 Other scleral buckling

Scleral buckling with:
- air tamponade
- resection of sclera
- vitrectomy

➡ **AHA Coding Clinic:** 1Q, '94, 16

14.5 Other repair of retinal detachment

Includes: that with drainage

14.51 Repair of retinal detachment with diathermy

14.52 Repair of retinal detachment with cryotherapy

14.53 Repair of retinal detachment with xenon arc photocoagulation

14.54 Repair of retinal detachment with laser photocoagulation

➡ **AHA Coding Clinic:** N-D, '87, 10

14.55 Repair of retinal detachment with photocoagulation of unspecified type

14.59 Other

14.6 Removal of surgically implanted material from posterior segment of eye

14.7 Operations on vitreous

14.71 Removal of vitreous, anterior approach

Open sky technique
Removal of vitreous, anterior approach (with replacement)

14.72 Other removal of vitreous

Aspiration of vitreous by posterior sclerotomy

14.73 Mechanical vitrectomy by anterior approach

➡ **AHA Coding Clinic:** 3Q, '96, 4, 5

14.74 Other mechanical vitrectomy

➡ **AHA Coding Clinic:** 3Q, '96, 4, 5

14.75 Injection of vitreous substitute

Excludes: that associated with removal (14.71-14.72)

➡ **AHA Coding Clinic:** 1Q, '98, 6; 3Q, '96, 4, 5

14.79 Other operations on vitreous

➡ **AHA Coding Clinic:** 1Q, '98, 6

14.9 Other operations on retina, choroid, and posterior chamber

➡ **AHA Coding Clinic:** 3Q, '96, 5

15 Operations on extraocular muscles

15.0 Diagnostic procedures on extraocular muscles or tendons

15.01 Biopsy of extraocular muscle or tendon

15.09 Other diagnostic procedures on extraocular muscles and tendons

15.1 **Operations on one extraocular muscle involving temporary detachment from globe**

15.11 **Recession of one extraocular muscle**
➡ **AHA Coding Clinic:** 3Q, '96, 3

15.12 **Advancement of one extraocular muscle**

15.13 **Resection of one extraocular muscle**

15.19 **Other operations on one extraocular muscle involving temporary detachment from globe**

Excludes: *transposition of muscle (15.5)*

15.2 **Other operations on one extraocular muscle**

15.21 **Lengthening procedure on one extraocular muscle**

15.22 **Shortening procedure on one extraocular muscle**

15.29 **Other**

15.3 **Operations on two or more extraocular muscles involving temporary detachment from globe, one or both eyes**
➡ **AHA Coding Clinic:** 3Q, '96, 3

15.4 **Other operations on two or more extraocular muscles, one or both eyes**

15.5 **Transposition of extraocular muscles**

Excludes: *that for correction of ptosis (08.31-08.36)*

15.6 **Revision of extraocular muscle surgery**

15.7 **Repair of injury of extraocular muscle**
Freeing of entrapped extraocular muscle
Lysis of adhesions of extraocular muscle
Repair of laceration of extraocular muscle, tendon, or Tenon's capsule

15.9 **Other operations on extraocular muscles and tendons**

16 Operations on orbit and eyeball

Excludes: *reduction of fracture of orbit (76.78-76.79)*

16.0 **Orbitotomy**

16.01 **Orbitotomy with bone flap**
Orbitotomy with lateral approach

16.02 **Orbitotomy with insertion of orbital implant**

Excludes: *that with bone flap (16.01)*

16.09 **Other orbitotomy**

16.1 **Removal of penetrating foreign body from eye, not otherwise specified**

Excludes: *removal of nonpenetrating foreign body (98.21)*

16.2 **Diagnostic procedures on orbit and eyeball**

16.21 **Ophthalmoscopy**

16.22 **Diagnostic aspiration of orbit**

16.23 **Biopsy of eyeball and orbit**

16.29 **Other diagnostic procedures on orbit and eyeball**

Excludes: *examination of form and structure of eye (95.11-95.16)*
general and subjective eye examination (95.01-95.09)
microscopic examination of specimen from eye (90.21-90.29)
objective functional tests of eye (95.21-95.26)
ocular thermography (88.82)
tonometry (89.11)
x-ray of orbit (87.14, 87.16)

16.3 **Evisceration of eyeball**

16.31 **Removal of ocular contents with synchronous implant into scleral shell**

16.39 **Other evisceration of eyeball**

16.4 **Enucleation of eyeball**

16.41 **Enucleation of eyeball with synchronous implant into Tenon's capsule with attachment of muscles**
Integrated implant of eyeball

16.42 **Enucleation of eyeball with other synchronous implant**

16.49 **Other enucleation of eyeball**
Removal of eyeball NOS

16.5 **Exenteration of orbital contents**

16.51 **Exenteration of orbit with removal of adjacent structures**
Radical orbitomaxillectomy

16.52 **Exenteration of orbit with therapeutic removal of orbital bone**

16.59 **Other exenteration of orbit**
Evisceration of orbit NOS
Exenteration of orbit with temporalis muscle transplant

16.6 Secondary procedures after removal of eyeball

Excludes: *that with synchronous:*
enucleation of eyeball (16.41-16.42)
evisceration of eyeball (16.31)

16.61 Secondary insertion of ocular implant

16.62 Revision and reinsertion of ocular implant

16.63 Revision of enucleation socket with graft

16.64 Other revision of enucleation socket

16.65 Secondary graft to exenteration cavity

16.66 Other revision of exenteration cavity

16.69 Other secondary procedures after removal of eyeball

16.7 Removal of ocular or orbital implant

16.71 Removal of ocular implant

16.72 Removal of orbital implant

16.8 Repair of injury of eyeball and orbit

16.81 Repair of wound of orbit

Excludes: *reduction of orbital fracture (76.78-76.79)*
repair of extraocular muscles (15.7)

16.82 Repair of rupture of eyeball
Repair of multiple structures of eye

Excludes: *repair of laceration of:*
cornea (11.51-11.59)
sclera (12.81)

16.89 Other repair of injury of eyeball or orbit

16.9 Other operations on orbit and eyeball

Excludes: *irrigation of eye (96.51)*
prescription and fitting of low vision aids (95.31-95.33)
removal of:
eye prosthesis NEC (97.31)
nonpenetrating foreign body from eye without incision (98.21)

16.91 Retrobulbar injection of therapeutic agent

Excludes: *injection of radiographic contrast material (87.14)*
opticociliary injection (12.79)

16.92 Excision of lesion of orbit

Excludes: *biopsy of orbit (16.23)*

16.93 Excision of lesion of eye, unspecified structure

Excludes: *biopsy of eye NOS (16.23)*

16.98 Other operations on orbit

16.99 Other operations on eyeball

4. OPERATIONS ON THE EAR (18-20)

18 Operations on external ear

Includes: operations on:
- external auditory canal
- skin and cartilage of:
  - auricle
  - meatus

18.0 Incision of external ear

Excludes: *removal of intraluminal foreign body (98.11)*

18.01 Piercing of ear lobe
Piercing of pinna

18.02 Incision of external auditory canal

18.09 Other incision of external ear

18.1 Diagnostic procedures on external ear

18.11 Otoscopy

18.12 Biopsy of external ear

18.19 Other diagnostic procedures on external ear

Excludes: *microscopic examination of specimen from ear (90.31-90.39)*

18.2 Excision or destruction of lesion of external ear

18.21 Excision of preauricular sinus
Radical excision of preauricular sinus or cyst

Excludes: *excision of preauricular remnant [appendage] (18.29)*

18.29 Excision or destruction of other lesion of external ear

Cauterization, Coagulation, Cryosurgery, Curettage, Electrocoagulation, Enucleation } of external ear

Excision of:
- exostosis of external auditory canal
- preauricular remnant [appendage]

Partial excision of ear

Excludes:
- *biopsy of external ear (18.12)*
- *radical excision of lesion (18.31)*
- *removal of cerumen (96.52)*

18.3 Other excision of external ear

Excludes: *biopsy of external ear (18.12)*

18.31 Radical excision of lesion of external ear

Excludes: *radical excision of preauricular sinus (18.21)*

18.39 Other
Amputation of external ear

Excludes: *excision of lesion (18.21-18.29, 18.31)*

18.4 Suture of laceration of external ear

18.5 Surgical correction of prominent ear
Ear:
- pinning
- setback

18.6 Reconstruction of external auditory canal
Canaloplasty of external auditory meatus
Construction [reconstruction] of external meatus of ear:
- osseous portion
- skin-lined portion (with skin graft)

18.7 Other plastic repair of external ear

18.71 Construction of auricle of ear
Prosthetic appliance for absent ear
Reconstruction:
- auricle
- ear

18.72 Reattachment of amputated ear

18.79 Other plastic repair of external ear

18.9 Other operations on external ear

Excludes:
- *irrigation of ear (96.52)*
- *packing of external auditory canal (96.11)*
- *removal of:*
  - *cerumen (96.52)*
  - *foreign body (without incision) (98.11)*

19 Reconstructive operations on middle ear

19.0 Stapes mobilization
Division, otosclerotic:
- material
- process

Remobilization of stapes
Stapediolysis
Transcrural stapes mobilization

Excludes: *that with synchronous stapedectomy (19.11-19.19)*

19.1 Stapedectomy

Excludes: *revision of previous stapedectomy (19.21-19.29)*
stapes mobilization only (19.0)

19.11 Stapedectomy with incus replacement
Stapedectomy with incus:
homograft
prosthesis

19.19 Other stapedectomy

19.2 Revision of stapedectomy

19.21 Revision of stapedectomy with incus replacement

19.29 Other revision of stapedectomy

19.3 Other operations on ossicular chain

19.4 Myringoplasty
Epitympanic, type I
Myringoplasty by:
cauterization
graft
Tympanoplasty (type I)

19.5 Other tympanoplasty

19.52 Type II tympanoplasty
Closure of perforation with graft against incus or malleus

19.53 Type III tympanoplasty
Graft placed in contact with mobile and intact stapes

➡ **AHA Coding Clinic:** M-A, '85, 15

19.54 Type IV tympanoplasty
Mobile footplate left exposed with air pocket between round window and graft

19.55 Type V tympanoplasty
Fenestra in horizontal semicircular canal covered by graft

19.6 Revision of tympanoplasty

19.9 Other repair of middle ear
Closure of mastoid fistula
Mastoid myoplasty
Obliteration of tympanomastoid cavity

20 Other operations on middle and inner ear

20.0 Myringotomy

20.01 Myringotomy with insertion of tube
Myringotomy

20.09 Other myringotomy
Aspiration of middle ear NOS

20.1 Removal of tympanostomy tube

20.2 Incision of mastoid and middle ear

20.21 Incision of mastoid

20.22 Incision of petrous pyramid air cells

20.23 Incision of middle ear
Atticotomy
Division of tympanum
Lysis of adhesions of middle ear

Excludes: *division of otosclerotic process (19.0)*
stapediolysis (19.0)
that with stapedectomy (19.11-19.19)

20.3 Diagnostic procedures on middle and inner ear

20.31 Electrocochleography

20.32 Biopsy of middle and inner ear

20.39 Other diagnostic procedures on middle and inner ear

Excludes: *auditory and vestibular function tests (89.13, 95.41-95.49)*
microscopic examination of specimen from ear (90.31-90.39)

20.4 Mastoidectomy
Code also any:
skin graft (18.79)
tympanoplasty (19.4-19.55)

Excludes: *that with implantation of cochlear prosthetic device (20.96-20.98)*

20.41 Simple mastoidectomy

20.42 Radical mastoidectomy

20.49 Other mastoidectomy
Atticoantrostomy
Mastoidectomy:
NOS
modified radical

20.5 Other excision of middle ear

Excludes: *that with synchronous mastoidectomy (20.41-20.49)*

20.51 Excision of lesion of middle ear

Excludes: *biopsy of middle ear (20.32)*

20.59 Other
Apicectomy of petrous pyramid
Tympanectomy

20.6 Fenestration of inner ear

20.61 Fenestration of inner ear (initial)

Fenestration of:
- labyrinth, semicircular canals, vestibule } with graft (skin) (vein)

Excludes: *that with tympanoplasty, type V (19.55)*

20.62 Revision of fenestration of inner ear

20.7 Incision, excision, and destruction of inner ear

20.71 Endolymphatic shunt

20.72 Injection into inner ear

Destruction by injection (alcohol):
- inner ear
- semicircular canals
- vestibule

20.79 Other incision, excision, and destruction of inner ear

Decompression of labyrinth
Drainage of inner ear
Fistulization:
- endolymphatic sac
- labyrinth

Incision of endolymphatic sac
Labyrinthectomy (transtympanic)
Opening of bony labyrinth
Perilymphatic tap

Excludes: *biopsy of inner ear (20.32)*

20.8 Operations on Eustachian tube

Catheterization, Inflation, Injection (Teflon paste), Insufflation (boric acid-salicylic acid), Intubation, Politzerization } of Eustachian tube

20.9 Other operations on inner and middle ear

20.91 Tympanosympathectomy

20.92 Revision of mastoidectomy

20.93 Repair of oval and round windows

Closure of fistula:
- oval window
- perilymph
- round window

20.94 Injection of tympanum

20.95 Implantation of electromagnetic hearing device

Bone conduction hearing device

Excludes: *cochlear prosthetic device (20.96-20.98)*

➡ **AHA Coding Clinic:** 4Q, '89, 5

20.96 Implantation or replacement of cochlear prosthetic device, not otherwise specified

Implantation of receiver (within skull) and insertion of electrode(s) in the cochlea
Mastoidectomy

Excludes: *electromagnetic hearing device (20.95)*

➡ **AHA Coding Clinic:** 4Q, '89, 5

20.97 Implantation or replacement of cochlear prosthetic device, single channel

Implantation of receiver (within skull) and insertion of electrode in the cochlea
Mastoidectomy

Excludes: *electromagnetic hearing device (20.95)*

➡ **AHA Coding Clinic:** 4Q, '89, 5

20.98 Implantation or replacement of cochlear prosthetic device, multiple channel

Implantation of receiver (within skull) and insertion of electrode in the cochlea
Mastoidectomy

Excludes: *electromagnetic hearing device (20.95)*

➡ **AHA Coding Clinic:** 4Q, '89, 5

20.99 Other operations on middle and inner ear

Repair or removal of cochlear prosthetic device (receiver) (electrode)

Excludes: *adjustment (external components) of cochlear prosthetic device (95.49)*
fitting of hearing aid (95.48)

➡ **AHA Coding Clinic:** 4Q, '89, 7

5. OPERATIONS ON THE NOSE, MOUTH, AND PHARYNX (21-29)

21 Operations on nose

Includes: operations on:
bone } of nose
skin }

21.0 Control of epistaxis

21.00 Control of epistaxis, not otherwise specified

21.01 Control of epistaxis by anterior nasal packing

21.02 Control of epistaxis by posterior (and anterior) packing

21.03 Control of epistaxis by cauterization (and packing)

21.04 Control of epistaxis by ligation of ethmoidal arteries

21.05 Control of epistaxis by (transantral) ligation of the maxillary artery

21.06 Control of epistaxis by ligation of the external carotid artery

21.07 Control of epistaxis by excision of nasal mucosa and skin grafting of septum and lateral nasal wall

21.09 Control of epistaxis by other means

21.1 Incision of nose

Chondrotomy
Incision of skin of nose
Nasal septotomy

21.2 Diagnostic procedures on nose

21.21 Rhinoscopy

21.22 Biopsy of nose

21.29 Other diagnostic procedures on nose

Excludes: *microscopic examination of specimen from nose (90.31-90.39)*
nasal:
function study (89.12)
rhinomanometry (89.12)
x-ray (87.16)

21.3 Local excision or destruction of lesion of nose

Excludes: *biopsy of nose (21.22)*
nasal fistulectomy (21.82)

21.30 Excision or destruction of lesion of nose, not otherwise specified

21.31 Local excision or destruction of intranasal lesion

Nasal polypectomy

21.32 Local excision or destruction of other lesion of nose

➡ **AHA Coding Clinic:** 2Q, '89, 16

21.4 Resection of nose

Amputation of nose

21.5 Submucous resection of nasal septum

21.6 Turbinectomy

21.61 Turbinectomy by diathermy or cryosurgery

21.62 Fracture of the turbinates

21.69 Other turbinectomy

Excludes: *turbinectomy associated with sinusectomy (22.31-22.39, 22.42, 22.60-22.64)*

21.7 Reduction of nasal fracture

21.71 Closed reduction of nasal fracture

21.72 Open reduction of nasal fracture

21.8 Repair and plastic operations on the nose

21.81 Suture of laceration of nose

21.82 Closure of nasal fistula

Nasolabial }
Nasopharyngeal } fistulectomy
Oronasal }

21.83 Total nasal reconstruction

Reconstruction of nose with:
arm flap
forehead flap

21.84 Revision rhinoplasty

Rhinoseptoplasty
Twisted nose rhinoplasty

21.85 Augmentation rhinoplasty

Augmentation rhinoplasty with:
graft
synthetic implant

21.86 Limited rhinoplasty

Plastic repair of nasolabial flaps
Tip rhinoplasty

21.87 Other rhinoplasty

Rhinoplasty NOS

21.88 Other septoplasty

Crushing of nasal septum
Repair of septal perforation

Excludes: *septoplasty associated with submucous resection of septum (21.5)*

21.89 Other repair and plastic operations on nose

Reattachment of amputated nose

21.9 **Other operations on nose**

21.91 **Lysis of adhesions of nose**
Posterior nasal scrub

21.99 **Other**

Excludes: *dilation of frontonasal duct (96.21)*
irrigation of nasal passages (96.53)
removal of:
intraluminal foreign body without incision (98.12)
nasal packing (97.32)
replacement of nasal packing (97.21)

22 Operations on nasal sinuses

22.0 **Aspiration and lavage of nasal sinus**

22.00 **Aspiration and lavage of nasal sinus, not otherwise specified**

22.01 **Puncture of nasal sinus for aspiration or lavage**

22.02 **Aspiration or lavage of nasal sinus through natural ostium**

22.1 **Diagnostic procedures on nasal sinus**

[22] **22.11** **Closed [endoscopic] [needle] biopsy of nasal sinus**

[21] **22.12** **Open biopsy of nasal sinus**

22.19 **Other diagnostic procedures on nasal sinuses**
Endoscopy without biopsy

Excludes: *transillumination of sinus (89.35)*
x-ray of sinus (87.15-87.16)

22.2 **Intranasal antrotomy**

Excludes: *antrotomy with external approach (22.31-22.39)*

22.3 **External maxillary antrotomy**

22.31 **Radical maxillary antrotomy**
Removal of lining membrane of maxillary sinus using Caldwell-Luc approach

22.39 **Other external maxillary antrotomy**
Exploration of maxillary antrum with Caldwell-Luc approach

22.4 **Frontal sinusotomy and sinusectomy**

22.41 **Frontal sinusotomy**

22.42 **Frontal sinusectomy**
Excision of lesion of frontal sinus
Obliteration of frontal sinus (with fat)

Excludes: *biopsy of nasal sinus (22.11-22.12)*

22.5 **Other nasal sinusotomy**

22.50 **Sinusotomy, not otherwise specified**

22.51 **Ethmoidotomy**

22.52 **Sphenoidotomy**

22.53 **Incision of multiple nasal sinuses**

22.6 **Other nasal sinusectomy**
Includes: that with incidental turbinectomy

Excludes: *biopsy of nasal sinus (22.11-22.12)*

22.60 **Sinusectomy, not otherwise specified**

22.61 **Excision of lesion of maxillary sinus with Caldwell-Luc approach**

22.62 **Excision of lesion of maxillary sinus with other approach**

22.63 **Ethmoidectomy**

22.64 **Sphenoidectomy**

22.7 **Repair of nasal sinus**

22.71 **Closure of nasal sinus fistula**
Repair of oro-antral fistula

22.79 **Other repair of nasal sinus**
Reconstruction of frontonasal duct
Repair of bone of accessory sinus

22.9 **Other operations on nasal sinuses**
Exteriorization of maxillary sinus
Fistulization of sinus

Excludes: *dilation of frontonasal duct (96.21)*

[21] Open biopsy
[22] Closed biopsy

23 Removal and restoration of teeth

23.0 Forceps extraction of tooth

23.01 Extraction of deciduous tooth

23.09 Extraction of other tooth

Extraction of tooth NOS

23.1 Surgical removal of tooth

23.11 Removal of residual root

23.19 Other surgical extraction of tooth

Odontectomy NOS
Removal of impacted tooth
Tooth extraction with elevation of mucoperiosteal flap

23.2 Restoration of tooth by filling

23.3 Restoration of tooth by inlay

23.4 Other dental restoration

23.41 Application of crown

23.42 Insertion of fixed bridge

23.43 Insertion of removable bridge

23.49 Other

23.5 Implantation of tooth

23.6 Prosthetic dental implant

Endosseous dental implant

23.7 Apicoectomy and root canal therapy

23.70 Root canal, not otherwise specified

23.71 Root canal therapy with irrigation

23.72 Root canal therapy with apicoectomy

23.73 Apicoectomy

24 Other operations on teeth, gums, and alveoli

24.0 Incision of gum or alveolar bone

Apical alveolotomy

24.1 Diagnostic procedures on teeth, gums, and alveoli

24.11 Biopsy of gum

24.12 Biopsy of alveolus

24.19 Other diagnostic procedures on teeth, gums, and alveoli

Excludes: *dental:*
examination (89.31)
x-ray:
full-mouth (87.11)
other (87.12)
microscopic examination of dental specimen (90.81-90.89)

24.2 Gingivoplasty

Gingivoplasty with bone or soft tissue graft

24.3 Other operations on gum

24.31 Excision of lesion or tissue of gum

Excludes: *biopsy of gum (24.11)*
excision of odontogenic lesion (24.4)

24.32 Suture of laceration of gum

24.39 Other

24.4 Excision of dental lesion of jaw

Excision of odontogenic lesion

24.5 Alveoloplasty

Alveolectomy (interradicular) (intraseptal) (radical) (simple) (with graft or implant)

Excludes: *biopsy of alveolus (24.12)*
en bloc resection of alveolar process and palate (27.32)

24.6 Exposure of tooth

24.7 Application of orthodontic appliance

Application, insertion, or fitting of:
arch bars
orthodontic obturator
orthodontic wiring
periodontal splint

Excludes: *nonorthodontic dental wiring (93.55)*

24.8 Other orthodontic operation

Closure of diastema (alveolar) (dental)
Occlusal adjustment
Removal of arch bars
Repair of dental arch

Excludes: *removal of nonorthodontic wiring (97.33)*

24.9 Other dental operations

24.91 Extension or deepening of buccolabial or lingual sulcus

24.99 Other

Excludes: *dental:*
debridement (96.54)
examination (89.31)
prophylaxis (96.54)
scaling and polishing (96.54)
wiring (93.55)
fitting of dental appliance [denture] (99.97)
microscopic examination of dental specimen (90.81-90.89)
removal of dental:
packing (97.34)
prosthesis (97.35)
wiring (97.33)
replacement of dental packing (97.22)

25 Operations on tongue

25.0 Diagnostic procedures on tongue

[22] **25.01 Closed [needle] biopsy of tongue**

[21] **25.02 Open biopsy of tongue**
Wedge biopsy

25.09 Other diagnostic procedures on tongue

25.1 Excision or destruction of lesion or tissue of tongue

Excludes: *biopsy of tongue (25.01-25.02)*
frenumectomy:
labial (27.41)
lingual (25.92)

25.2 Partial glossectomy

25.3 Complete glossectomy
Glossectomy NOS

Code also any neck dissection (40.40-40.42)

25.4 Radical glossectomy
Code also any:
neck dissection (40.40-40.42)
tracheostomy (31.1-31.29)

25.5 Repair of tongue and glossoplasty

25.51 Suture of laceration of tongue

25.59 Other repair and plastic operations on tongue
Fascial sling of tongue
Fusion of tongue (to lip)
Graft of mucosa or skin to tongue

Excludes: *lysis of adhesions of tongue (25.93)*

➡ **AHA Coding Clinic:** 1Q, '97, 5

25.9 Other operations on tongue

25.91 Lingual frenotomy

Excludes: *labial frenotomy (27.91)*

25.92 Lingual frenectomy

Excludes: *labial frenectomy (27.41)*

25.93 Lysis of adhesions of tongue

25.94 Other glossotomy

25.99 Other

26 Operations on salivary glands and ducts

Includes: operations on:
lesser salivary, parotid, sublingual, submaxillary } gland and duct

Code also any neck dissection (40.40-40.42)

26.0 Incision of salivary gland or duct

26.1 Diagnostic procedures on salivary glands and ducts

[22] **26.11 Closed [needle] biopsy of salivary gland or duct**

[21] **26.12 Open biopsy of salivary gland or duct**

26.19 Other diagnostic procedures on salivary glands and ducts

Excludes: *x-ray of salivary gland (87.09)*

26.2 Excision of lesion of salivary gland

26.21 Marsupialization of salivary gland cyst

26.29 Other excision of salivary gland lesion

Excludes: *biopsy of salivary gland (26.11-26.12)*
salivary fistulectomy (26.42)

26.3 Sialoadenectomy

26.30 Sialoadenectomy, not otherwise specified

26.31 Partial sialoadenectomy

26.32 Complete sialoadenectomy
En bloc excision of salivary gland lesion
Radical sialoadenectomy

26.4 Repair of salivary gland or duct

26.41 Suture of laceration of salivary gland

26.42 Closure of salivary fistula

26.49 Other repair and plastic operations on salivary gland or duct
Fistulization of salivary gland
Plastic repair of salivary gland or duct NOS
Transplantation of salivary duct opening

[21] Open biopsy
[22] Closed biopsy

26.9 Other operations on salivary gland or duct

26.91 Probing of salivary duct

26.99 Other

27 Other operations on mouth and face

Includes: operations on:
lips
palate
soft tissue of face and mouth, except tongue and gingiva

Excludes: *operations on:*
gingiva (24.0-24.99)
tongue (25.01-25.99)

27.0 Drainage of face and floor of mouth

Drainage of:
facial region (abscess)
fascial compartment of face
Ludwig's angina

Excludes: *drainage of thyroglossal tract (06.09)*

27.1 Incision of palate

27.2 Diagnostic procedures on oral cavity

27.21 Biopsy of bony palate

27.22 Biopsy of uvula and soft palate

27.23 Biopsy of lip

27.24 Biopsy of mouth, unspecified structure

27.29 Other diagnostic procedures on oral cavity

Excludes: *soft tissue x-ray (87.09)*

27.3 Excision of lesion or tissue of bony palate

27.31 Local excision or destruction of lesion or tissue of bony palate

Local excision or destruction of palate by:
cautery
chemotherapy
cryotherapy

Excludes: *biopsy of bony palate (27.21)*

27.32 Wide excision or destruction of lesion or tissue of bony palate

En bloc resection of alveolar process and palate

27.4 Excision of other parts of mouth

27.41 Labial frenectomy

Excludes: *division of labial frenum (27.91)*

27.42 Wide excision of lesion of lip

27.43 Other excision of lesion or tissue of lip

27.49 Other excision of mouth

Excludes: *biopsy of mouth NOS (27.24)*
excision of lesion of:
palate (27.31-27.32)
tongue (25.1)
uvula (27.72)
fistulectomy of mouth (27.53)
frenectomy of:
lip (27.41)
tongue (25.92)

27.5 Plastic repair of mouth

Excludes: *palatoplasty (27.61-27.69)*

27.51 Suture of laceration of lip

27.52 Suture of laceration of other part of mouth

27.53 Closure of fistula of mouth

Excludes: *fistulectomy:*
nasolabial (21.82)
oro-antral (22.71)
oronasal (21.82)

27.54 Repair of cleft lip

27.55 Full-thickness skin graft to lip and mouth

27.56 Other skin graft to lip and mouth

27.57 Attachment of pedicle or flap graft to lip and mouth

27.59 Other plastic repair of mouth

27.6 Palatoplasty

27.61 Suture of laceration of palate

27.62 Correction of cleft palate

Correction of cleft palate by push-back operation

Excludes: *revision of cleft palate repair (27.63)*

27.63 Revision of cleft palate repair

Secondary:
attachment of pharyngeal flap
lengthening of palate

➡ **AHA Coding Clinic:** 1Q, '96, 14

27.69 Other plastic repair of palate

Excludes: *fistulectomy of mouth (27.53)*

➡ **AHA Coding Clinic:** 1Q, '97, 14

27.7 Operations on uvula

27.71 Incision of uvula

27.72 Excision of uvula

Excludes: *biopsy of uvula (27.22)*

27.73 Repair of uvula

Excludes: *that with synchronous cleft palate repair (27.62)*
uranostaphylorrhaphy (27.62)

27.79 Other operations on uvula

27.9 Other operations on mouth and face

27.91 Labial frenotomy

Division of labial frenum

Excludes: *lingual frenotomy (25.91)*

27.92 Incision of mouth, unspecified structure

Excludes: *incision of:*
gum (24.0)
palate (27.1)
salivary gland or duct (26.0)
tongue (25.94)
uvula (27.71)

27.99 Other operations on oral cavity

Graft of buccal sulcus

Excludes: *removal of:*
intraluminal foreign body (98.01)
penetrating foreign body from mouth without incision (98.22)

28 Operations on tonsils and adenoids

28.0 Incision and drainage of tonsil and peritonsillar structures

Drainage (oral) (transcervical) of:
parapharyngeal, peritonsillar, retropharyngeal, tonsillar } abscess

28.1 Diagnostic procedures on tonsils and adenoids

28.11 Biopsy of tonsils and adenoids

28.19 Other diagnostic procedures on tonsils and adenoids

Excludes: *soft tissue x-ray (87.09)*

28.2 Tonsillectomy without adenoidectomy

➡ **AHA Coding Clinic:** 1Q, '97, 5; 2Q, '90, 23

28.3 Tonsillectomy with adenoidectomy

28.4 Excision of tonsil tag

28.5 Excision of lingual tonsil

28.6 Adenoidectomy without tonsillectomy

Excision of adenoid tag

28.7 Control of hemorrhage after tonsillectomy and adenoidectomy

28.9 Other operations on tonsils and adenoids

28.91 Removal of foreign body from tonsil and adenoid by incision

Excludes: *that without incision (98.13)*

28.92 Excision of lesion of tonsil and adenoid

Excludes: *biopsy of tonsil and adenoid (28.11)*

28.99 Other

29 Operations on pharynx

Includes: operations on:
hypopharynx
nasopharynx
oropharynx
pharyngeal pouch
pyriform sinus

29.0 Pharyngotomy

Drainage of pharyngeal bursa

Excludes: *incision and drainage of retropharyngeal abscess (28.0)*
removal of foreign body (without incision) (98.13)

29.1 Diagnostic procedures on pharynx

29.11 Pharyngoscopy

29.12 Pharyngeal biopsy

Biopsy of supraglottic mass

29.19 Other diagnostic procedures on pharynx

Excludes: *x-ray of nasopharynx:*
contrast (87.06)
other (87.09)

29.2 Excision of branchial cleft cyst or vestige

Excludes: *branchial cleft fistulectomy (29.52)*

29.3 Excision or destruction of lesion or tissue of pharynx

➡ **AHA Coding Clinic:** 2Q, '89, 18

29.31 Cricopharyngeal myotomy

Excludes: *that with pharyngeal diverticulectomy (29.32)*

29.32 Pharyngeal diverticulectomy

29.33 Pharyngectomy (partial)

Excludes: *laryngopharyngectomy (30.3)*

29.39 Other excision or destruction of lesion or tissue of pharynx

29.4 Plastic operation on pharynx

Correction of nasopharyngeal atresia

Excludes: *pharyngoplasty associated with cleft palate repair (27.62-27.63)*

➡ **AHA Coding Clinic:** 1Q, '97, 5

29.5 Other repair of pharynx

29.51 Suture of laceration of pharynx

29.52 Closure of branchial cleft fistula

29.53 Closure of other fistula of pharynx

Pharyngoesophageal fistulectomy

29.54 Lysis of pharyngeal adhesions

29.59 Other

➡ **AHA Coding Clinic:** 2Q, '89, 18

29.9 Other operations on pharynx

29.91 Dilation of pharynx

Dilation of nasopharynx

29.92 Division of glossopharyngeal nerve

29.99 Other

Excludes: *insertion of radium into pharynx and nasopharynx (92.27)*
removal of intraluminal foreign body (98.13)

6. OPERATIONS ON THE RESPIRATORY SYSTEM (30-34)

30 Excision of larynx

30.0 Excision or destruction of lesion or tissue of larynx

30.01 Marsupialization of laryngeal cyst

30.09 Other excision or destruction of lesion or tissue of larynx
Stripping of vocal cords

Excludes: *biopsy of larynx (31.43)*
laryngeal fistulectomy (31.62)
laryngotracheal fistulectomy (31.62)

30.1 Hemilaryngectomy

30.2 Other partial laryngectomy

30.21 Epiglottidectomy

30.22 Vocal cordectomy
Excision of vocal cords

30.29 Other partial laryngectomy
Excision of laryngeal cartilage

30.3 Complete laryngectomy
Block dissection of larynx (with thyroidectomy) (with synchronous tracheostomy)
Laryngopharyngectomy

Excludes: *that with radical neck dissection (30.4)*

30.4 Radical laryngectomy
Complete [total] laryngectomy with radical neck dissection (with thyroidectomy) (with synchronous tracheostomy)

31 Other operations on larynx and trachea

31.0 Injection of larynx
Injection of inert material into larynx or vocal cords

31.1 Temporary tracheostomy
Tracheotomy for assistance in breathing
➡ **AHA Coding Clinic:** 1Q, '97, 6

31.2 Permanent tracheostomy

31.21 Mediastinal tracheostomy

31.29 Other permanent tracheostomy

Excludes: *that with laryngectomy (30.3-30.4)*

31.3 Other incision of larynx or trachea

Excludes: *that for assistance in breathing (31.1-31.29)*

31.4 Diagnostic procedures on larynx and trachea

31.41 Tracheoscopy through artificial stoma

Excludes: *that with biopsy (31.43-31.44)*

31.42 Laryngoscopy and other tracheoscopy

Excludes: *that with biopsy (31.43-31.44)*

[22] **31.43** Closed [endoscopic] biopsy of larynx

[22] **31.44** Closed [endoscopic] biopsy of trachea

[21] **31.45** Open biopsy of larynx or trachea

31.48 Other diagnostic procedures on larynx

Excludes: *contrast laryngogram (87.07)*
microscopic examination of specimen from larynx (90.31-90.39)
soft tissue x-ray of larynx NEC (87.09)

31.49 Other diagnostic procedures on trachea

Excludes: *microscopic examination of specimen from trachea (90.41-90.49)*
x-ray of trachea (87.49)

31.5 Local excision or destruction of lesion or tissue of trachea

Excludes: *biopsy of trachea (31.44-31.45)*
laryngotracheal fistulectomy (31.62)
tracheoesophageal fistulectomy (31.73)

31.6 Repair of larynx

31.61 Suture of laceration of larynx

31.62 Closure of fistula of larynx
Laryngotracheal fistulectomy
Take-down of laryngostomy

31.63 Revision of laryngostomy

31.64 Repair of laryngeal fracture

31.69 Other repair of larynx
Arytenoidopexy
Graft of larynx
Transposition of vocal cords

Excludes: *construction of artificial larynx (31.75)*

31.7 Repair and plastic operations on trachea

31.71 Suture of laceration of trachea

31.72 Closure of external fistula of trachea
Closure of tracheotomy

[21] Open biopsy
[22] Closed biopsy

31.73 **Closure of other fistula of trachea**
Tracheoesophageal fistulectomy

Excludes: *laryngotracheal fistulectomy (31.62)*

31.74 **Revision of tracheostomy**

31.75 **Reconstruction of trachea and construction of artificial larynx**
Tracheoplasty with artificial larynx

31.79 **Other repair and plastic operations on trachea**

31.9 **Other operations on larynx and trachea**

31.91 **Division of laryngeal nerve**

31.92 **Lysis of adhesions of trachea or larynx**

31.93 **Replacement of laryngeal or tracheal stent**

31.94 **Injection of locally-acting therapeutic substance into trachea**

31.95 **Tracheoesophageal fistulization**

31.98 **Other operations on larynx**
Dilation, Division of congenital web, Removal of keel or stent } of larynx

Excludes: *removal of intraluminal foreign body from larynx without incision (98.14)*

31.99 **Other operations on trachea**

Excludes: *removal of:*
intraluminal foreign body from trachea without incision (98.15)
tracheostomy tube (97.37)
replacement of tracheostomy tube (97.23)
tracheostomy toilette (96.55)

➡ **AHA Coding Clinic:** 1Q, '97, 14

32 Excision of lung and bronchus

Includes: rib resection, sternotomy, sternum-splitting incision, thoracotomy } as operative approach

Code also any synchronous bronchoplasty (33.48)

32.0 **Local excision or destruction of lesion or tissue of bronchus**

Excludes: *biopsy of bronchus (33.24-33.25)*
bronchial fistulectomy (33.42)

➡ **AHA Coding Clinic:** 4Q, '88, 11

32.01 **Endoscopic excision or destruction of lesion or tissue of bronchus**

32.09 **Other local excision or destruction of lesion or tissue of bronchus**

Excludes: *that by endoscopic approach (32.01)*

32.1 **Other excision of bronchus**
Resection (wide sleeve) of bronchus

Excludes: *radical dissection [excision] of bronchus (32.6)*

32.2 **Local excision or destruction of lesion or tissue of lung**

32.21 **Plication of emphysematous bleb**

➡ **Def:** Stitching of a swollen vesicle/blister into a tuck.

32.22 **Lung volume reduction surgery**

➡ **AHA Coding Clinic:** 1Q, '97, 6; 3Q, '96, 20; 4Q, '95, 64

32.28 **Endoscopic excision or destruction of lesion or tissue of lung**

Excludes: *biopsy of lung (33.26-33.27)*

32.29 **Other local excision or destruction of lesion or tissue of lung**
Resection of lung:
NOS
wedge

Excludes: *biopsy of lung (33.26-33.27)*
that by endoscopic approach (32.28)
wide excision of lesion of lung (32.3)

32.3 **Segmental resection of lung**
Partial lobectomy

32.4 **Lobectomy of lung**
Lobectomy with segmental resection of adjacent lobes of lung

Excludes: *that with radical dissection [excision] of thoracic structures (32.6)*

32.5 **Complete pneumonectomy**
Excision of lung NOS
Pneumonectomy (with mediastinal dissection)

32.6 **Radical dissection of thoracic structures**
Block [en bloc] dissection of bronchus, lobe of lung, brachial plexus, intercostal structure, ribs (transverse process), and sympathetic nerves

32.9 **Other excision of lung**

Excludes: *biopsy of lung and bronchus (33.24-33.27)*
pulmonary decortication (34.51)

33 Other operations on lung and bronchus

Includes: rib resection, sternotomy, sternum-splitting incision, thoracotomy } as operative approach

33.0 Incision of bronchus

33.1 Incision of lung

Excludes: *puncture of lung (33.93)*

33.2 Diagnostic procedures on lung and bronchus

33.21 Bronchoscopy through artificial stoma

Excludes: *that with biopsy (33.24, 33.27)*

33.22 Fiber-optic bronchoscopy

Excludes: *that with biopsy (33.24, 33.27)*

33.23 Other bronchoscopy

Excludes: *that for:*
aspiration (96.05)
biopsy (33.24, 33.27)

[22] **33.24 Closed [endoscopic] biopsy of bronchus**

Bronchoscopy (fiberoptic) (rigid) with:
brush biopsy of "lung"
brushing or washing for specimen collection
excision (bite) biopsy

Excludes: *closed biopsy of lung, other than brush biopsy of "lung" (33.26, 33.27)*

➡ **AHA Coding Clinic:** 4Q, '92, 27; 3Q, '91, 15

[21] **33.25 Open biopsy of bronchus**

Excludes: *open biopsy of lung (33.28)*

[22] **33.26 Closed [percutaneous] [needle] biopsy of lung**

Excludes: *endoscopic biopsy of lung (33.27)*

➡ **AHA Coding Clinic:** 3Q, '92, 12

33.27 Closed endoscopic biopsy of lung

Fiber-optic (flexible) bronchoscopy with fluoroscopic guidance with biopsy
Transbronchial lung biopsy

Excludes: *brush biopsy of "lung" (33.24)*
percutaneous biopsy of lung (33.26)

➡ **AHA Coding Clinic:** 4Q, '92, 27; 3Q, '91, 15

[21] **33.28 Open biopsy of lung**

➡ **AHA Coding Clinic:** 3Q, '92, 12

33.29 Other diagnostic procedures on lung and bronchus

Excludes: *contrast bronchogram:*
endotracheal (87.31)
other (87.32)
lung scan (92.15)
magnetic resonance imaging (88.92)
microscopic examination of specimen from bronchus or lung (90.41-90.49)
routine chest x-ray (87.44)
ultrasonography of lung (88.73)
vital capacity determination (89.37)
x-ray of bronchus or lung NOS (87.49)

33.3 Surgical collapse of lung

33.31 Destruction of phrenic nerve for collapse of lung

33.32 Artificial pneumothorax for collapse of lung

Thoracotomy for collapse of lung

33.33 Pneumoperitoneum for collapse of lung

33.34 Thoracoplasty

33.39 Other surgical collapse of lung

Collapse of lung NOS

33.4 Repair and plastic operation on lung and bronchus

33.41 Suture of laceration of bronchus

33.42 Closure of bronchial fistula

Closure of bronchostomy
Fistulectomy:
bronchocutaneous
bronchoesophageal
bronchovisceral

Excludes: *closure of fistula:*
bronchomediastinal (34.73)
bronchopleural (34.73)
bronchopleuromediastinal (34.73)

33.43 Closure of laceration of lung

33.48 Other repair and plastic operations on bronchus

33.49 Other repair and plastic operations on lung

Excludes: *closure of pleural fistula (34.73)*

33.5 Lung transplant

Code also cardiopulmonary bypass [extracorporeal circulation] [heart-lung machine] 39.61

Excludes: *combined heart-lung transplantation (33.6)*

➡ **AHA Coding Clinic:** 4Q, '95, 75

33.50 Lung transplantation, not otherwise specified

33.51 Unilateral lung transplantation

33.52 Bilateral lung transplantation

Double-lung transplantation
En bloc transplantation

[21] Open biopsy
[22] Closed biopsy

33.6 **Combined heart-lung transplantation**

Code also cardiopulmonary bypass [extracorporeal circulation] [heart-lung machine] (39.61)

33.9 **Other operations on lung and bronchus**

33.91 **Bronchial dilation**

➡ **AHA Coding Clinic:** 1Q, '97, 14

33.92 **Ligation of bronchus**

33.93 **Puncture of lung**

Excludes: *needle biopsy (33.26)*

33.98 **Other operations on bronchus**

Excludes: *bronchial lavage (96.56)*
removal of intraluminal foreign body from bronchus without incision (98.15)

33.99 **Other operations on lung**

Excludes: *other continuous mechanical ventilation (96.70-96.72)*
respiratory therapy (93.90-93.99)

34 Operations on chest wall, pleura, mediastinum, and diaphragm

Excludes: *operations on breast (85.0-85.99)*

34.0 **Incision of chest wall and pleura**

Excludes: *that as operative approach — omit code*

34.01 **Incision of chest wall**

Extrapleural drainage

Excludes: *incision of pleura (34.09)*

➡ **AHA Coding Clinic:** 1Q, '92, 13

34.02 **Exploratory thoracotomy**

34.03 **Reopening of recent thoracotomy site**

34.04 **Insertion of intercostal catheter for drainage**

Chest tube
Closed chest drainage
Revision of intercostal catheter (chest tube) (with lysis of adhesions)

➡ **AHA Coding Clinic:** 1Q, '95, 5; 1Q, '92, 12

34.05 **Creation of pleuroperitoneal shunt**

➡ **AHA Coding Clinic:** 4Q, '94, 50

34.09 **Other incision of pleura**

Creation of pleural window for drainage
Intercostal stab
Open chest drainage

Excludes: *thoracoscopy (34.21)*
thoracotomy for collapse of lung (33.32)

➡ **AHA Coding Clinic:** 1Q, '94, 7

34.1 **Incision of mediastinum**

Excludes: *mediastinoscopy (34.22)*
mediastinotomy associated with pneumonectomy (32.5)

34.2 **Diagnostic procedures on chest wall, pleura, mediastinum, and diaphragm**

34.21 **Transpleural thoracoscopy**

34.22 **Mediastinoscopy**

Code also any lymph node biopsy (40.11)

34.23 **Biopsy of chest wall**

34.24 **Pleural biopsy**

➡ **AHA Coding Clinic:** 1Q, '92, 14

[22] **34.25** **Closed [percutaneous] [needle] biopsy of mediastinum**

[21] **34.26** **Open biopsy of mediastinum**

34.27 **Biopsy of diaphragm**

[21] Open biopsy
[22] Closed biopsy

34.28 Other diagnostic procedures on chest wall, pleura, and diaphragm

Excludes: *angiocardiography (88.50-88.58)*
aortography (88.42)
arteriography of:
intrathoracic vessels NEC (88.44)
pulmonary arteries (88.43)
microscopic examination of specimen from chest wall, pleura, and diaphragm (90.41-90.49)
phlebography of:
intrathoracic vessels NEC (88.63)
pulmonary veins (88.62)
radiological examinations of thorax:
C.A.T. scan (87.41)
diaphragmatic x-ray (87.49)
intrathoracic lymphangiogram (87.34)
routine chest x-ray (87.44)
sinogram of chest wall (87.38)
soft tissue x-ray of chest wall NEC (87.39)
tomogram of thorax NEC (87.42)
ultrasonography of thorax (88.73)

34.29 Other diagnostic procedures on mediastinum

Excludes: *mediastinal:*
pneumogram (87.33)
x-ray NEC (87.49)

34.3 Excision or destruction of lesion or tissue of mediastinum

Excludes: *biopsy of mediastinum (34.25-34.26)*
mediastinal fistulectomy (34.73)

34.4 Excision or destruction of lesion of chest wall

Excision of lesion of chest wall NOS (with excision of ribs)

Excludes: *biopsy of chest wall (34.23)*
costectomy not incidental to thoracic procedure (77.91)
excision of lesion of:
breast (85.20-85.25)
cartilage (80.89)
skin (86.2-86.3)
fistulectomy (34.73)

34.5 Pleurectomy

34.51 Decortication of lung

34.59 Other excision of pleura

Excision of pleural lesion

Excludes: *biopsy of pleura (34.24)*
pleural fistulectomy (34.73)

34.6 Scarification of pleura

Pleurosclerosis

Excludes: *injection of sclerosing agent (34.92)*

➡ **AHA Coding Clinic:** 1Q, '92, 12

34.7 Repair of chest wall

34.71 Suture of laceration of chest wall

Excludes: *suture of skin and subcutaneous tissue alone (86.59)*

34.72 Closure of thoracostomy

34.73 Closure of other fistula of thorax

Closure of:
bronchopleural } fistula
bronchopleurocutaneous } fistula
bronchopleuromediastinal } fistula

34.74 Repair of pectus deformity

Repair of:
pectus carinatum } (with implant)
pectus excavatum } (with implant)

34.79 Other repair of chest wall

Repair of chest wall NOS

➡ **AHA Coding Clinic:** J-F, '87, 13

34.8 Operations on diaphragm

34.81 Excision of lesion or tissue of diaphragm

Excludes: *biopsy of diaphragm (34.27)*

34.82 Suture of laceration of diaphragm

34.83 Closure of fistula of diaphragm

Thoracicoabdominal } fistulectomy
Thoracicogastric } fistulectomy
Thoracicointestinal } fistulectomy

34.84 Other repair of diaphragm

Excludes: *repair of diaphragmatic hernia (53.7-53.82)*

34.85 Implantation of diaphragmatic pacemaker

34.89 Other operations on diaphragm

34.9 Other operations on thorax

34.91 Thoracentesis

➡ **AHA Coding Clinic:** S-O, '85, 6

34.92 Injection into thoracic cavity

Chemical pleurodesis
Injection of cytotoxic agent or tetracycline
Requires additional code for any cancer chemotherapeutic substance (99.25)

Excludes: *that for collapse of lung (33.32)*

➡ **AHA Coding Clinic:** 1Q, '92, 12; 2Q, '89, 17

34.93 Repair of pleura

34.99 Other

Excludes: *removal of:*
mediastinal drain (97.42)
sutures (97.43)
thoracotomy tube (97.41)

➡ **AHA Coding Clinic:** 1Q, '88, 9

7. OPERATIONS ON THE CARDIOVASCULAR SYSTEM (35-39)

35 Operations on valves and septa of heart

Includes: sternotomy (median) (transverse) thoracotomy } as operative approach

Code also cardiopulmonary bypass [extracorporeal circulation] [heart-lung machine] (39.61)

35.0 Closed heart valvotomy

Excludes: *percutaneous (balloon) valvuloplasty (35.96)*

35.00 Closed heart valvotomy, unspecified valve

35.01 Closed heart valvotomy, aortic valve

35.02 Closed heart valvotomy, mitral valve

35.03 Closed heart valvotomy, pulmonary valve

35.04 Closed heart valvotomy, tricuspid valve

35.1 Open heart valvuloplasty without replacement

Includes: open heart valvotomy

Code also cardiopulmonary bypass, if performed [extracorporeal circulation] [heart-lung machine] (39.61)

Excludes: *that associated with repair of:*
endocardial cushion defect (35.54,35.63, 35.73)
percutaneous (balloon) valvuloplasty (35.96)
valvular defect associated with atrial and ventricular septal defects (35.54, 35.63, 35.73)

35.10 Open heart valvuloplasty without replacement, unspecified valve

35.11 Open heart valvuloplasty of aortic valve without replacement

35.12 Open heart valvuloplasty of mitral valve without replacement

➡ **AHA Coding Clinic:** 1Q, '97, 13

35.13 Open heart valvuloplasty of pulmonary valve without replacement

35.14 Open heart valvuloplasty of tricuspid valve without replacement

35.2 Replacement of heart valve

Includes: excision of heart valve with replacement

Code also cardiopulmonary bypass [extracorporeal circulation] [heart-lung machine] (39.61)

Excludes: *that associated with repair of:*
endocardial cushion defect (35.54,35.63, 35.73)
valvular defect associated with atrial and ventricular septal defects (35.54, 35.63, 35.73)

35.20 Replacement of unspecified heart valve

Repair of unspecified heart valve with tissue graft or prosthetic implant

35.21 Replacement of aortic valve with tissue graft

Repair of aortic valve with tissue graft (autograft) (heterograft) (homograft)

➡ **AHA Coding Clinic:** 2Q, '97, 8

35.22 Other replacement of aortic valve

Repair of aortic valve with replacement:
NOS
prosthetic (partial) (synthetic) (total)

➡ **AHA Coding Clinic:** 1Q, '96, 11

35.23 Replacement of mitral valve with tissue graft

Repair of mitral valve with tissue graft (autograft) (heterograft) (homograft)

35.24 Other replacement of mitral valve

Repair of mitral valve with replacement:
NOS
prosthetic (partial) (synthetic) (total)

➡ **AHA Coding Clinic:** 4Q, '97, 55

35.25 Replacement of pulmonary valve with tissue graft

Repair of pulmonary valve with tissue graft (autograft) (heterograft) (homograft)

➡ **AHA Coding Clinic:** 2Q, '97, 8

35.26 Other replacement of pulmonary valve

Repair of pulmonary valve with replacement:
NOS
prosthetic (partial) (synthetic) (total)

35.27 Replacement of tricuspid valve with tissue graft

Repair of tricuspid valve with tissue graft (autograft) (heterograft) (homograft)

35.28 Other replacement of tricuspid valve

Repair of tricuspid valve with replacement:
NOS
prosthetic (partial) (synthetic) (total)

35.3 Operations on structures adjacent to heart valves

Code also cardiopulmonary bypass [extracorporeal circulation] [heart-lung machine] (39.61)

35.31 Operations on papillary muscle

Division
Reattachment } of papillary muscle
Repair

35.32 Operations on chordae tendineae
Division } of chordae tendineae
Repair }

35.33 Annuloplasty
Plication of annulus
➡ **AHA Coding Clinic:** 1Q, '97, 13; 1Q, '88, 10

35.34 Infundibulectomy
Right ventricular infundibulectomy

35.35 Operations on trabeculae carneae cordis
Division } of trabeculae carneae cordis
Excision }
Excision of aortic subvalvular ring

35.39 Operations on other structures adjacent to valves of heart
Repair of sinus of Valsalva (aneurysm)

35.4 Production of septal defect in heart

35.41 Enlargement of existing atrial septal defect
Rashkind procedure
Septostomy (atrial) (balloon)

35.42 Creation of septal defect in heart
Blalock-Hanlon operation

35.5 Repair of atrial and ventricular septa with prosthesis
Includes: repair of septa with synthetic implant or patch
Code also cardiopulmonary bypass [extracorporeal circulation] [heart-lung machine] (39.61)

35.50 Repair of unspecified septal defect of heart with prosthesis
Excludes: *that associated with repair of:*
endocardial cushion defect (35.54)
septal defect associated with valvular defect (35.54)

35.51 Repair of atrial septal defect with prosthesis, open technique
Atrioseptoplasty } with prosthesis
Correction of atrial septal defect }
Repair: }
foramen ovale (patent) }
ostium secundum defect }
Excludes: *that associated with repair of:*
atrial septal defect associated with val vular and ventricular septal defects (35.54)
endocardial cushion defect (35.54)

35.52 Repair of atrial septal defect with prosthesis, closed technique
Insertion of atrial septal umbrella [King-Mills]

35.53 Repair of ventricular septal defect with prosthesis
Correction of ventricular septal defect } with prosthesis
Repair of supracristal defect }
Excludes: *that associated with repair of:*
endocardial cushion defect (35.54)
ventricular defect associated with valvular and atrial septal defects (35.54)

35.54 Repair of endocardial cushion defect with prosthesis
Repair: } with prosthesis (grafted to septa)
atrioventricular canal }
ostium primum defect }
valvular defect associated with atrial and ventricular septal defects }
Excludes: *repair of isolated:*
atrial septal defect (35.51-35.52)
valvular defect (35.20, 35.22, 35.24, 35.26, 35.28)
ventricular septal defect (35.53)

35.6 Repair of atrial and ventricular septa with tissue graft
Code also cardiopulmonary bypass [extracorporeal circulation] [heart-lung machine] (39.61)

35.60 Repair of unspecified septal defect of heart with tissue graft
Excludes: *that associated with repair of:*
endocardial cushion defect (35.63)
septal defect associated with valvular defect (35.63)

35.61 Repair of atrial septal defect with tissue graft
Atrioseptoplasty } with tissue graft
Correction of atrial septal defect }
Repair: }
foramen ovale (patent) }
ostium secundum defect }
Excludes: *that associated with repair of:*
atrial septal defect associated with valvular and ventricular septal defects (35.63)
endocardial cushion defect (35.63)

35.62 Repair of ventricular septal defect with tissue graft

Correction of ventricular septal defect } with tissue graft
Repair of supracristal defect } with tissue graft

Excludes: *that associated with repair of:*
endocardial cushion defect (35.63)
ventricular defect associated with valvular and atrial septal defects (35.63)

35.63 Repair of endocardial cushion defect with tissue graft

Repair:
- atrioventricular canal } with tissue graft
- ostium primum defect } with tissue graft
- valvular defect associated with atrial and ventricular septal defects } with tissue graft

Excludes: *repair of isolated:*
atrial septal defect (35.61)
valvular defect (35.20-35.21, 35.23, 35.25, 35.27)
ventricular septal defect (35.62)

35.7 Other and unspecified repair of atrial and ventricular septa

Code also cardiopulmonary bypass [extracorporeal circulation] [heart-lung machine] (39.61)

35.70 Other and unspecified repair of unspecified septal defect of heart

Repair of septal defect NOS

Excludes: *that associated with repair of:*
endocardial cushion defect (35.73)
septal defect associated with valvular defect (35.73)

35.71 Other and unspecified repair of atrial septal defect

Repair NOS:
- atrial septum
- foramen ovale (patent)
- ostium secundum defect

Excludes: *that associated with repair of:*
atrial septal defect associated with valvular and ventricular septal defects (35.73)
endocardial cushion defect (35.73)

35.72 Other and unspecified repair of ventricular septal defect

Repair NOS:
- supracristal defect
- ventricular septum

Excludes: *that associated with repair of:*
endocardial cushion defect (35.73)
ventricular septal defect associated with valvular and atrial septal defects (35.73)

35.73 Other and unspecified repair of endocardial cushion defect

Repair NOS:
- atrioventricular canal
- ostium primum defect
- valvular defect associated with atrial and ventricular septal defects

Excludes: *repair of isolated:*
atrial septal defect (35.71)
valvular defect (35.20, 35.22, 35.24, 35.26, 35.28)
ventricular septal defect (35.72)

35.8 Total repair of certain congenital cardiac anomalies

Note: For partial repair of defect [e.g. repair of atrial septal defect in tetralogy of Fallot] — code to specific procedure

35.81 Total repair of tetralogy of Fallot

One-stage total correction of tetralogy of Fallot with or without:
- commissurotomy of pulmonary valve
- infundibulectomy
- outflow tract prosthesis
- patch graft of outflow tract
- prosthetic tube for pulmonary artery
- repair of ventricular septal defect (with prosthesis)
- take-down of previous systemic-pulmonary artery anastomosis

35.82 Total repair of total anomalous pulmonary venous connection

One-stage total correction of total anomalous pulmonary venous connection with or without:
- anastomosis between (horizontal) common pulmonary trunk and posterior wall of left atrium (side-to-side)
- enlargement of foramen ovale
- incision [excision] of common wall between posterior left atrium and coronary sinus and roofing of resultant defect with patch graft (synthetic)
- ligation of venous connection (descending anomalous vein) (to left innominate vein) (to superior vena cava)
- repair of atrial septal defect (with prosthesis)

35.83 Total repair of truncus arteriosus

One-stage total correction of truncus arteriosus with or without:
- construction (with aortic homograft) (with prosthesis) of a pulmonary artery placed from right ventricle to arteries supplying the lung
- ligation of connections between aorta and pulmonary artery
- repair of ventricular septal defect (with prosthesis)

35.84 Total correction of transposition of great vessels, not elsewhere classified

Arterial switch operation [Jatene]
Total correction of transposition of great arteries at the arterial level by switching the great arteries, including the left or both coronary arteries, implanted in the wall of the pulmonary artery

Excludes: *baffle operation [Mustard] [Senning] (35.91)*
creation of shunt between right ventricle and pulmonary artery [Rastelli] (35.92)

35.9 Other operations on valves and septa of heart

Code also cardiopulmonary bypass, if performed [extracorporeal circulation] [heart-lung machine] (39.61)

35.91 Interatrial transposition of venous return

Baffle:
- atrial
- interatrial

Mustard's operation
Resection of atrial septum and insertion of patch to direct systemic venous return to tricuspid valve and pulmonary venous return to mitral valve

35.92 Creation of conduit between right ventricle and pulmonary artery

Creation of shunt between right ventricle and (distal) pulmonary artery

Excludes: *that associated with total repair of truncus arteriosus (35.83)*

35.93 Creation of conduit between left ventricle and aorta

Creation of apicoaortic shunt
Shunt between apex of left ventricle and aorta

35.94 Creation of conduit between atrium and pulmonary artery

Fontan procedure

35.95 Revision of corrective procedure on heart

Replacement of prosthetic heart valve poppet
Resuture of prosthesis of:
- septum
- valve

Excludes: *complete revision — code to specific procedure*
replacement of prosthesis or graft of:
septum (35.50-35.63)
valve (35.20-35.28)

35.96 Percutaneous valvuloplasty

Percutaneous balloon valvuloplasty

35.98 Other operations on septa of heart

35.99 Other operations on valves of heart

36 Operations on vessels of heart

Includes: sternotomy (median) (transverse) } as operative approach
thoracotomy } as operative approach

Code also cardiopulmonary bypass, if performed [extracorporeal circulation] [heart-lung machine] (39.61)

Code also any injection or infusion of platelet inhibitor (99.20)

36.0 Removal of coronary artery obstruction and insertion of stent(s)

➡ **AHA Coding Clinic:** 4Q, '95, 66; 2Q, '94, 13; 1Q, '94, 3; 2Q, '90, 23; N-D, '86, 8

36.01 Single vessel percutaneous transluminal coronary angioplasty [PTCA] or coronary atherectomy without mention of thrombolytic agent

Balloon angioplasty of coronary artery
Coronary atherectomy
Percutaneous coronary angioplasty NOS
PTCA NOS

Code also any insertion of coronary stent(s) (36.06)

Excludes: *multiple vessel percutaneous transluminal coronary angioplasty [PTCA] or coronary atherectomy performed during the same operation (36.05)*

➡ **AHA Coding Clinic:** 3Q, '91, 24

36.02 Single vessel percutaneous transluminal coronary angioplasty [PTCA] or coronary atherectomy with mention of thrombolytic agent

Balloon angioplasty of coronary artery with infusion of thrombolytic agent [streptokinase]
Coronary atherectomy

Code also any insertion of coronary stent(s) (36.06)

Excludes: *multiple vessel percutaneous transluminal coronary angioplasty [PTCA] or coronary atherectomy performed during the same operation (36.05)*
single vessel PTCA or coronary atherectomy without mention of thrombolytic agent (36.01)

➡ **AHA Coding Clinic:** 1Q, '97, 3

36.03 Open chest coronary artery angioplasty

Coronary (artery):
endarterectomy (with patch graft)
thromboendarterectomy (with patch graft)
Open surgery for direct relief of coronary artery obstruction

Code also any insertion of coronary stent(s) (36.06)

Excludes: *that with coronary artery bypass graft (36.10-36.19)*

36.04 Intracoronary artery thrombolytic infusion

Enzyme infusion
Platelet inhibitor
That by direct coronary artery injection, infusion, or catheterization

Excludes: *infusion of platelet inhibitor (99.20)*
infusion of thrombolytic agent (99.10)
that administered intravenously [IV infusion] (99.29)
that associated with any procedure in 36.02, 36.03

➡ **AHA Coding Clinic:** 1Q, '97, 3; 4Q, '95, 67

36.05 Multiple vessel percutaneous transluminal coronary angioplasty [PTCA] or coronary atherectomy performed during the same operation, with or without mention of thrombolytic agent

Balloon angioplasty of multiple coronary arteries
Coronary atherectomy

Code also any:
insertion of coronary artery stent(s) (36.06)
intracoronary artery thrombolytic infusion (36.04)

Excludes: *single vessel [PTCA] or coronary atherectomy without mention of thrombolytic agent (36.01)*
with mention of thrombolytic agent (36.02)

➡ **AHA Coding Clinic:** 1Q, '94, 3

36.06 Insertion of coronary artery stent(s)

Stent graft

Code also any:
open chest coronary artery angioplasty (36.03)
percutaneous transluminal coronary angioplasty [PTCA] or coronary atherectomy (36.01, 36.02, 36.05)

36.09 Other removal of coronary artery obstruction

Coronary angioplasty NOS

Excludes: *that by open angioplasty (36.03)*
that by percutaneous transluminal coronary angioplasty [PTCA] or coronary atherectomy (36.01-36.02, 36.05)

36.1 Bypass anastomosis for heart revascularization

Code also cardiopulmonary bypass [extracorporeal circulation] [heart-lung machine] (39.61)

➡ **AHA Coding Clinic:** 2Q, '96, 7; 3Q, '95, 7; 3Q, '93, 8; 1Q, '91, 7; 2Q, '90, 24; 4Q, '89, 3

36.10 Aortocoronary bypass for heart revascularization, not otherwise specified

Direct revascularization:
cardiac, coronary, heart muscle, myocardial } with catheter stent, prosthesis, or vein graft
Heart revascularization NOS

36.11 Aortocoronary bypass of one coronary artery

36.12 Aortocoronary bypass of two coronary arteries

36.13 Aortocoronary bypass of three coronary arteries

36.14 Aortocoronary bypass of four or more coronary arteries

36.15 Single internal mammary-coronary artery bypass
Anastomosis (single):
mammary artery to coronary artery
thoracic artery to coronary artery

36.16 Double internal mammary-coronary artery bypass
Anastomosis, double:
mammary artery to coronary artery
thoracic artery to coronary artery

36.17 Abdominal-coronary artery bypass
Anastomosis:
gastroepiploic artery to coronary artery
➡ **AHA Coding Clinic:** 3Q, '97, 14; 4Q, '96, 64

36.19 Other bypass anastomosis for heart revascularization

36.2 Heart revascularization by arterial implant
Implantation of:
aortic branches [ascending aortic branches] into heart muscle
blood vessels into myocardium
internal mammary artery [internal thoracic artery] into:
heart muscle
myocardium
ventricle
ventricular wall
Indirect heart revascularization NOS

36.3 Other heart revascularization

36.31 Open chest transmyocardial revascularization

36.32 Other transmyocardial revascularization
Percutaneous transmyocardial revascularization
Thoracoscopic transmyocardial revascularization

36.39 Other heart revascularization
Abrasion of epicardium
Cardio-omentopexy
Intrapericardial poudrage
Myocardial graft:
mediastinal fat
omentum
pectoral muscles

36.9 Other operations on vessels of heart
Code also cardiopulmonary bypass [extracorporeal circulation] [heart-lung machine] (39.61)

36.91 Repair of aneurysm of coronary vessel

36.99 Other operations on vessels of heart
Exploration, Incision, Ligation } of coronary artery
Repair of arteriovenous fistula

37 Other operations on heart and pericardium
Code also any injection or infusion of platelet inhibitor (99.20)

37.0 Pericardiocentesis

37.1 Cardiotomy and pericardiotomy
Code also cardiopulmonary bypass [extracorporeal circulation] [heart-lung machine] (39.61)

37.10 Incision of heart, not otherwise specified
Cardiolysis NOS

37.11 Cardiotomy
Incision of:
atrium
endocardium
myocardium
ventricle

37.12 Pericardiotomy
Pericardial window operation
Pericardiolysis
Pericardiotomy

37.2 Diagnostic procedures on heart and pericardium

37.21 Right heart cardiac catheterization
Cardiac catheterization NOS
Excludes: *that with catheterization of left heart (37.23)*
➡ **AHA Coding Clinic:** 2Q, '90, 23; M-J, '87, 11

37.22 Left heart cardiac catheterization
Excludes: *that with catheterization of right heart (37.23)*
➡ **AHA Coding Clinic:** 2Q, '90, 23; 4Q, '88, 4; M-J, '87, 11

37.23 Combined right and left heart cardiac catheterization
➡ **AHA Coding Clinic:** 2Q, '90, 23; M-J, '87, 11

37.24 Biopsy of pericardium

37.25 Biopsy of heart
➡ **AHA Coding Clinic:** 3Q, '94, 8

37.26 Cardiac electrophysiologic stimulation and recording studies
Electrophysiologic studies [EPS]
Programmed electrical stimulation
Code also any concomitant procedure
Excludes: *His bundle recording (37.29)*
➡ **AHA Coding Clinic:** 2Q, '97, 10

37.27 Cardiac mapping
Code also any concomitant procedure
Excludes: *electrocardiogram (89.52)*
His bundle recording (37.29)

37.29 Other diagnostic procedures on heart and pericardium
Excludes: *angiocardiography (88.50-88.58)*
cardiac function tests (89.41-89.69)
cardiovascular radioisotopic scan and function study (92.05)
coronary arteriography (88.55-88.57)
diagnostic pericardiocentesis (37.0)
diagnostic ultrasound of heart (88.72)
x-ray of heart (87.49)
➡ **AHA Coding Clinic:** S-O, '87, 3

37.3 Pericardiectomy and excision of lesion of heart

Code also cardiopulmonary bypass [extracorporeal circulation] [heart-lung machine] (39.61)

37.31 Pericardiectomy

Excision of:
- adhesions of pericardium
- constricting scar of:
  - epicardium
  - pericardium

37.32 Excision of aneurysm of heart

Repair of aneurysm of heart

37.33 Excision or destruction of other lesion or tissue of heart

Excludes: *catheter ablation of lesion or tissues of heart (37.34)*

➡ **AHA Coding Clinic:** 2Q, '94, 12

37.34 Catheter ablation of lesion or tissues of heart

Cryoablation, Electrocurrent, Resection } of lesion or tissues of heart

37.35 Partial ventriculectomy

Ventricular reduction surgery
Ventricular remodeling

Code also any synchronous:
- mitral valve repair (35.02, 35.12)
- mitral valve replacement (35.23-35.24)

➡ **AHA Coding Clinic:** 4Q, '97, 54, 55

37.4 Repair of heart and pericardium

➡ **AHA Coding Clinic:** 2Q, '90, 24

37.5 Heart transplantation

Excludes: *combined heart-lung transplantation (33.6)*

37.6 Implantation of heart assist system

➡ **AHA Coding Clinic:** 4Q, '95, 68

37.61 Implant of pulsation balloon

37.62 Implant of other heart assist system

Insertion of
- centrifugal pump
- heart assist system, not specified as pulsatile

Insertion of heart assist system, NOS

➡ **AHA Coding Clinic:** 2Q, '90, 25

37.63 Replacement and repair of heart assist system

37.64 Removal of heart assist system

Excludes: *that with replacement of implant (37.63)*

37.65 Implant of an external, pulsatile heart assist system

Note: Device not implantable (outside the body but connected to heart) with external circulation and pump

Excludes: *implant of pulsation balloon (37.61)*

37.66 Implant of an implantable, pulsatile heart assist system

Note: Device directly connected to the heart and implanted in the upper left quadrant of peritoneal cavity

Transportable, implantable heart assist system

Excludes: *implant of pulsation balloon (37.61)*

37.67 Implantation of cardiomyostimulation system

Note: Two-step open procedure consisting of transfer of one end of the latissimus dorsi muscle; wrapping it around the heart; rib resection; implantation of epicardial cardiac pacing leads into right ventricle, tunneling and pocket creation for the cardiomyostimulator.

➡ **AHA Coding Clinic:** 1Q, '98, 8

37.7 Insertion, revision, replacement, and removal of pacemaker leads; insertion of temporary pacemaker system; or revision of pocket

Code also any insertion and replacement of pacemaker device (37.80-37.87)

➡ **AHA Coding Clinic:** M-J, '87, 1

[23] **37.70 Initial insertion of lead [electrode], not otherwise specified**

Excludes: *insertion of temporary transvenous pacemaker system (37.78)*
replacement of atrial and/or ventricular lead(s) (37.76)

[23] **37.71 Initial insertion of transvenous lead [electrode] into ventricle**

Excludes: *insertion of temporary transvenous pacemaker system (37.78)*
replacement of atrial and/or ventricular lead(s) (37.76)

[24] **37.72 Initial insertion of transvenous leads [electrodes] into atrium and ventricle**

Excludes: *insertion of temporary transvenous pacemaker system (37.78)*
replacement of atrial and/or ventricular lead(s) (37.76)

➡ **AHA Coding Clinic:** 2Q, '97, 4

[23] Valid OR procedure code if accompanied by one of the following codes: 37.80, 37.81, 37.82, 37.85, 37.86, 37.87
[24] Valid OR procedure code if accompanied by one of the following codes: 37.80, 37.83

[23] **37.73 Initial insertion of transvenous lead [electrode] into atrium**

Excludes: *insertion of temporary transvenous pacemaker system (37.78)*
replacement of atrial and/or ventricular lead(s) (37.76)

[26] **37.74 Insertion or replacement of epicardial lead [electrode] into epicardium**

Insertion or replacement of epicardial lead by:
sternotomy
thoracotomy

Excludes: *replacement of atrial and/or ventricular lead(s) (37.76)*

37.75 Revision of lead [electrode]

Repair of electrode [removal with re-insertion]
Repositioning of lead [electrode]
Revision of lead NOS

Excludes: *repositioning of temporary transvenous pacemaker system — omit code*

[25] **37.76 Replacement of transvenous atrial and/or ventricular lead(s) [electrode]**

Removal or abandonment of existing transvenous or epicardial lead(s) with transvenous lead(s) replacement

Excludes: *replacement of epicardial lead [electrode] (37.74)*

37.77 Removal of lead(s) [electrode] without replacement

Removal:
epicardial lead (transthoracic approach)
transvenous lead(s)

Excludes: *removal of temporary transvenous pacemaker system — omit code*
that with replacement of:
atrial and/or ventricular lead(s) [electrode] (37.76)
epicardial lead [electrode] (37.74)

37.78 Insertion of temporary transvenous pacemaker system

Excludes: *intraoperative cardiac pacemaker (39.64)*

➡ **AHA Coding Clinic:** 3Q, '93, 12; 1Q, '89, 2

37.79 Revision or relocation of pacemaker pocket

Debridement and reforming pocket (skin and subcutaneous tissue)
Relocation of pocket [creation of new pocket]

37.8 Insertion, replacement, removal, and revision of pacemaker device

Code also any lead insertion, lead replacement, lead removal and/or lead revision (37.70-37.77)

➡ **AHA Coding Clinic:** M-J, '87, 1

37.80 Insertion of permanent pacemaker, initial or replacement, type of device not specified

[27] **37.81 Initial insertion of single-chamber device, not specified as rate responsive**

Excludes: *replacement of existing pacemaker device (37.85-37.87)*

[27] **37.82 Initial insertion of a single-chamber device, rate responsive**

Rate responsive to physiologic stimuli other than atrial rate

Excludes: *replacement of existing pacemaker device (37.85-37.87)*

[28] **37.83 Initial insertion of dual-chamber device**

Atrial ventricular sequential device

Excludes: *replacement of existing pacemaker device (37.85-37.87)*

➡ **AHA Coding Clinic:** 2Q, '97, 4

37.85 Replacement of any type pacemaker device with single-chamber device, not specified as rate responsive

37.86 Replacement of any type pacemaker device with single-chamber device, rate responsive

Rate responsive to physiologic stimuli other than atrial rate

37.87 Replacement of any type pacemaker device with dual-chamber device

Atrial ventricular sequential device

37.89 Revision or removal of pacemaker device

Repair of pacemaker device

Excludes: *removal of temporary transvenous pacemaker system — omit code*
replacement of existing pacemaker device (37.85-37.87)

➡ **AHA Coding Clinic:** N-D, '86, 1

37.9 Other operations on heart and pericardium

➡ **AHA Coding Clinic:** 3Q, '90, 11

37.91 Open chest cardiac massage

Excludes: *closed chest cardiac massage (99.63)*

➡ **AHA Coding Clinic:** 4Q, '88, 12

[23] Valid OR procedure code if accompanied by one of the following codes: 37.80, 37.81, 37.82, 37.85, 37.86, 37.87
[25] Valid OR procedure code if accompanied by any one of the following codes: 37.80, 37.85. 37.86, 37.87
[26] Valid OR procedure code if accompanied by any one of the following codes: 37.80, 37.81. 37.82, 37.83, 37.85, 37.86, 37.87
[27] Valid OR procedure code if accompanied by any other pacemaker procedure except 37.72, 37.74
[28] Valid OR procedure code if accompanied by any other pacemaker procedure except 37.70, 37.71, 37.73, 37.74

37.92 Injection of therapeutic substance into heart

37.93 Injection of therapeutic substance into pericardium

37.94 Implantation or replacement of automatic cardioverter/defibrillator, total system [AICD]

Implantation of defibrillator with leads (epicardial patches), formation of pocket (abdominal fascia) (subcutaneous), any transvenous leads, intraoperative procedures for evaluation of lead signals, and obtaining defibrillator threshold measurements

Techniques: lateral thoracotomy
medial sternotomy
subxiphoid procedure

Code also extracorporeal circulation, if performed (39.61)

Code also any concomitant procedure [e.g., coronary bypass] (36.00-36.19)

➡ **AHA Coding Clinic:** S-O, '87, 5

37.95 Implantation of automatic cardioverter/defibrillator lead(s) only

37.96 Implantation of automatic cardioverter/defibrillator pulse generator only

37.97 Replacement of automatic cardioverter/defibrillator lead(s) only

37.98 Replacement of automatic cardioverter/defibrillator pulse generator only

37.99 Other

Removal of cardioverter/defibrillator pulse generator only without replacement
Repositioning of lead(s) (sensing) (pacing) [electrode]
Repositioning of pulse generator
Revision of cardioverter/defibrillator (automatic) pocket

Excludes: *cardiac retraining (93.36)*
conversion of cardiac rhythm (99.60-99.69)

➡ **AHA Coding Clinic:** 1Q, '97, 12; 1Q, '94, 19; 1Q, '89, 11

38 Incision, excision, and occlusion of vessels

Code also cardiopulmonary bypass [extracorporeal circulation] [heart-lung machine] (39.61)

Excludes: *that of coronary vessels (36.01-36.99)*

The following fourth-digit subclassification is for use with appropriate categories in sections 38.0, 38.1, 38.3, 38.5, 38.6 and 38.8 according to site.

0 **unspecified site**

1 **intracranial vessels**
Cerebral (anterior) (middle)
Circle of Willis
Posterior communicating artery

2 **other vessels of head and neck**
Carotid artery (common) (external) (internal)
Jugular vein (external) (internal)

3 **upper limb vessels**
Axillary
Brachial
Radial
Ulnar

4 **aorta**

5 **other thoracic vessels**
Inniminate
Pulmonary (artery) (vein)
Subclavian
Vena cava, superior

6 **abdominal arteries**
Celiac
Gastric
Hepatic
Iliac
Mesenteric
Renal
Splenic
Umbilical

Excludes: *abdominal aorta (4)*

7 **abdominal veins**
Iliac
Portal
Renal
Splenic
Vena cava (inferior)

8 **lower limb arteries**
Femoral (common) (superficial)
Popliteal
Tibial

9 **lower limb veins**
Femoral
Popliteal
Saphenous
Tibial

[29] § **38.0 Incision of vessel**
[0-9]
Embolectomy
Thrombectomy

Excludes: *puncture or catheterization of any:*
artery (38.91, 38.98)
vein (38.92-38.95, 38.99)

[29] § **38.1 Endarterectomy**
[0-6, 8]
Endarterectomy with:
embolectomy
patch graft
temporary bypass during procedure
thrombectomy

§ Requires fourth-digit; valid digits are in [brackets] under each code. See above, this page for definitions.
[29] Non-specific OR procedure equals fourth digit 0

38.2 Diagnostic procedures on blood vessels

38.21 Biopsy of blood vessel

38.22 Percutaneous angioscopy

Excludes: *angioscopy of eye (95.12)*

38.29 Other diagnostic procedures on blood vessels

Excludes: *blood vessel thermography (88.86)*
circulatory monitoring (89.61-89.69)
contrast:
angiocardiography (88.50-88.58)
arteriography (88.40-88.49)
phlebography (88.60-88.67)
impedance phlebography (88.68)
peripheral vascular ultrasonography (88.77)
plethysmogram (89.58)

[29] §§ **38.3 Resection of vessel with anastomosis**
[0-9]

Angiectomy
Excision of:
aneurysm (arteriovenous)
blood vessel (lesion)
} with anastomosis

[29] § **38.4 Resection of vessel with replacement**
[0-9]

Angiectomy
Excision of:
aneurysm (arteriovenous) or
blood vessel (lesion)
} with replacement

Requires the use of one of the following fourth-digit subclassifications to identify site:

0 unspecified site
1 intracranial vessels
Cerebral (anterior) (middle)
Circle of Willis
Posterior communicating artery
2 other vessels of head and neck
Carotid artery (common) (external) (internal)
Jugular vein (external) (internal)
3 upper limb vessels
Axillary
Brachial
Radial
Ulnar
4 aorta, abdominal
Code also any thoracic vessel involvement (thoracoabdominal procedure) (38.45)
5 other thoracic vessels
Aorta (thoracic)
Innominate
Pulmonary (artery) (vein)
Subclavian
Vena cava, superior

Code also any abdominal aorta involvement (thoracoabdominal procedure) (38.44)

6 abdominal arteries
Celiac
Gastric
Hepatic
Iliac
Mesenteric
Renal
Splenic
Umbilical

Excludes: *abdominal aorta (4)*

7 abdominal veins
Iliac
Portal
Renal
Splenic
Vena cava (inferior)
8 lower limb arteries
Femoral (common) (superficial)
Tibial
9 lower limb veins
Femoral
Popliteal
Saphenous
Tibial

[29] §§ **38.5 Ligation and stripping of varicose veins**
[0-3,5,7,9]

Excludes: *ligation of varices:*
esophageal (42.91)
gastric (44.91)

➡ **AHA Coding Clinic: For code 38.59:** 2Q, '97, 7

§§ Requires fourth-digit; valid digits are in [brackets] under each code. See page P-47 for definitions.
§ Requires fourth-digit; valid digits are in [brackets] under each code. See above, this page for definitions.
[29] Non-specific OR procedure equals fourth digit 0

[29] § **38.6** **Other excision of vessels**
[0-9] Excision of blood vessel (lesion) NOS

Excludes: *excision of vessel for aortocoronary bypass (36.10-36.14)*
excision with:
anastomosis (38.30-38.39)
graft replacement (38.40-38.49)
implant (38.40-38.49)

➡ **AHA Coding Clinic:** 3Q, '90, 17

38.7 **Interruption of the vena cava**
Insertion of implant or sieve in vena cava
Ligation of vena cava (inferior) (superior)
Plication of vena cava

➡ **AHA Coding Clinic:** 2Q, '94, 9; S-O, '85, 5

[29] § **38.8** **Other surgical occlusion of vessels**
[0-9] Clamping, Divison, Ligation, Occlusion } of blood vessel

Excludes: *adrenal vessels (07.43)*
esophageal varices (42.91)
gastric or duodenal vessel for ulcer (44.40-44.49)
gastric varices (44.91)
meningeal vessel (02.13)
spermatic vein for varicocele (63.1)
surgical occlusion of vena cava (38.7)
that for chemoembolization (99.25)
that for control of (postoperative) hemorrhage:
anus (49.95)
bladder (57.93)
following vascular procedure (39.41)
nose (21.00-21.09)
prostate (60.94)
thyroid vessel (06.92)
tonsil (28.7)

➡ **AHA Coding Clinic:** M-A, '87, 9

➡ **AHA Coding Clinic: For code 38.86:** N-D, '87, 4

38.9 **Puncture of vessel**

Excludes: *that for circulatory monitoring (89.61-89.69)*

38.91 **Arterial catheterization**

➡ **AHA Coding Clinic:** 1Q, '97, 3; 1Q, '95, 3; 2Q, '91, 15; 2Q, '90, 23

38.92 **Umbilical vein catheterization**

38.93 **Venous catheterization, not elsewhere classified**

Excludes: *that for cardiac catheterization (37.21-37.23)*
that for renal dialysis (38.95)

➡ **AHA Coding Clinic:** 1Q, '96, 3; 2Q, '96, 15; 3Q, '91, 13; 4Q, '90, 14; 2Q, '90, 24; 3Q, '88, 13

38.94 **Venous cutdown**

38.95 **Venous catheterization for renal dialysis**

Excludes: *insertion of totally implantable vascular access device [VAD] (86.07)*

38.98 **Other puncture of artery**

Excludes: *that for:*
arteriography (88.40-88.49)
coronary arteriography (88.55-88.57)

38.99 **Other puncture of vein**
Phlebotomy

Excludes: *that for:*
angiography (88.60-88.69)
extracorporeal circulation (39.61, 50.92)
injection or infusion of:
sclerosing solution (39.92)
therapeutic or prophylactic substance (99.11-99.29)
perfusion (39.96, 39.97)
phlebography (88.60-88.69)
transfusion (99.01-99.09)

➡ **AHA Coding Clinic:** 4Q, '94, 50; 1Q, '88, 11

39 Other operations on vessels

Excludes: *those on coronary vessels (36.0-36.99)*

39.0 **Systemic to pulmonary artery shunt**
Descending aorta-pulmonary artery, Left to right, Subclavian-pulmonary } anastomosis (graft)

Code also cardiopulmonary bypass [extracorporeal circulation] [heart-lung machine] (39.61)

39.1 **Intra-abdominal venous shunt**
Anastomosis:
mesocaval
portacaval
portal vein to inferior vena cava
splenic and renal veins
transjugular intrahepatic portosystemic shunt [TIPS]

Excludes: *peritoneovenous shunt (54.94)*

➡ **AHA Coding Clinic:** 4Q, '94, 50; 4Q, '93, 31; 2Q, '93, 8

39.2 **Other shunt or vascular bypass**

39.21 **Caval-pulmonary artery anastomosis**
Code also cardiopulmonary bypass (39.61)

§ Requires fourth-digit; valid digits are in [brackets] under each code. See page P-47 for definitions.
[29] Non-specific OR procedure equals fourth digit 0

39.22 Aorta-subclavian-carotid bypass

Bypass (arterial):
- aorta to carotid and brachial
- aorta to subclavian and carotid
- carotid to subclavian

39.23 Other intrathoracic vascular shunt or bypass

Intrathoracic (arterial) bypass graft NOS

Excludes: *coronary artery bypass (36.10-36.19)*

39.24 Aorta-renal bypass

39.25 Aorta-iliac-femoral bypass

Bypass:
- aortofemoral
- aortoiliac
- aortoiliac to popliteal
- aortopopliteal
- iliofemoral [iliac-femoral]

➡ **AHA Coding Clinic:** 4Q, '90, 27; 1Q, '88, 10

39.26 Other intra-abdominal vascular shunt or bypass

Bypass:
- aortoceliac
- aortic-superior mesenteric
- common hepatic-common iliac-renal
- Intra-abdominal arterial bypass graft NOS

Excludes: *peritoneovenous shunt (54.94)*

39.27 Arteriovenostomy for renal dialysis

Anastomosis for renal dialysis
Formation of (peripheral) arteriovenous fistula for renal [kidney] dialysis

Code also any renal dialysis (39.95)

39.28 Extracranial-intracranial (EC-IC) vascular bypass

➡ **AHA Coding Clinic:** 2Q, '92, 7; 4Q, '91, 22

39.29 Other (peripheral) vascular shunt or bypass

Bypass (graft):
- axillary-brachial
- axillary-femoral [axillofemoral] (superficial)
- brachial
- femoral-femoral
- femoroperoneal
- femoropopliteal (arteries)
- femorotibial (anterior) (posterior)
- popliteal
- vascular NOS

Excludes: *peritoneovenous shunt (54.94)*

➡ **AHA Coding Clinic:** S-O, '85, 13

39.3 Suture of vessel

Repair of laceration of blood vessel

Excludes: *any other vascular puncture closure device — omit code*
suture of aneurysm (39.52)
that for control of hemorrhage (postoperative):
- *anus (49.95)*
- *bladder (57.93)*
- *following vascular procedure (39.41)*
- *nose (21.00-21.09)*
- *prostate (60.94)*
- *tonsil (28.7)*

39.30 Suture of unspecified blood vessel

39.31 Suture of artery

39.32 Suture of vein

39.4 Revision of vascular procedure

39.41 Control of hemorrhage following vascular surgery

Excludes: *that for control of hemorrhage (postoperative):*
- *anus (49.95)*
- *bladder (57.93)*
- *nose (21.00-21.09)*
- *prostate (60.94)*
- *tonsil (28.7)*

39.42 Revision of arteriovenous shunt for renal dialysis

Conversion of renal dialysis:
- end-to-end anastomosis to end-to-side
- end-to-side anastomosis to end-to-end
- vessel-to-vessel cannula to arteriovenous shunt

Removal of old arteriovenous shunt and creation of new shunt

Excludes: *replacement of vessel-to-vessel cannula (39.94)*

39.43 Removal of arteriovenous shunt for renal dialysis

Excludes: *that with replacement [revision] of shunt (39.42)*

39.49 Other revision of vascular procedure

Declotting (graft)
Revision of:
- anastomosis of blood vessel
- vascular procedure (previous)

➡ **AHA Coding Clinic:** 1Q, '97, 3; 2Q, '94, 15

39.5 Other repair of vessels

39.50 Angioplasty or artherectomy of non-coronary vessel

Percutaneous transluminal angioplasty (PTA) of non-coronary vessels:
head and neck arteries:
basilar
carotid
vertebral
lower extremity vessels
mesenteric artery
renal artery
upper extremity vessels

Code also any:
Injection or infusion of thrombolytic agent (99.10)
Insertion of noncoronary stent(s) or stent graft(s) (39.90)

➡ **AHA Coding Clinic:** 1Q, '97, 3; 4Q, '96, 63; 4Q, '95, 66

39.51 Clipping of aneurysm

Excludes: *clipping of arteriovenous fistula (39.53)*

39.52 Other repair of aneurysm

Repair of aneurysm by:
coagulation
electrocoagulation
filipuncture
methyl methacrylate
suture
wiring
wrapping

Excludes: *re-entry operation (aorta) (39.54)*
that with:
graft replacement (38.40-38.49)
resection (38.30-38.49, 38.60-38.69)

➡ **AHA Coding Clinic:** 1Q, '88, 10

39.53 Repair of arteriovenous fistula

Embolization of carotid cavernous fistula
Repair of arteriovenous fistula by:
clipping
coagulation
ligation and division

Excludes: *repair of arteriovenous shunt for renal dialysis (39.42)*
that with:
graft replacement (38.40-38.49)
resection (38.30-38.49, 38.60-38.69)

39.54 Re-entry operation (aorta)

Fenestration of dissecting aneurysm of thoracic aorta

Code also cardiopulmonary bypass [extracorporeal circulation] [heart-lung machine] (39.61)

39.55 Reimplantation of aberrant renal vessel

39.56 Repair of blood vessel with tissue patch graft

Excludes: *that with resection (38.40-38.49)*

39.57 Repair of blood vessel with synthetic patch graft

Excludes: *that with resection (38.40-38.49)*

39.58 Repair of blood vessel with unspecified type of patch graft

Excludes: *that with resection (38.40-38.49)*

39.59 Other repair of vessel

Aorticopulmonary window operation
Arterioplasty NOS
Construction of venous valves (peripheral)
Plication of vein (peripheral)
Reimplantation of artery

Code also cardiopulmonary bypass [extracorporeal circulation] [heart-lung machine] (39.61)

Excludes: *interruption of the vena cava (38.7)*
reimplantation of renal artery (39.55)
that with:
graft (39.56-39.58)
resection (38.30-38.49, 38.60-38.69)

➡ **AHA Coding Clinic:** 2Q, '89, 17; N-D, '86, 8; S-O, '85, 5; M-A, '85, 15

39.6 Extracorporeal circulation and procedures auxiliary to heart surgery

➡ **AHA Coding Clinic:** 1Q, '95, 5

39.61 Extracorporeal circulation auxiliary to open heart surgery

Artificial heart and lung
Cardiopulmonary bypass
Pump oxygenator

Excludes: *extracorporeal hepatic assistance (50.92)*
extracorporeal membrane oxygenation [ECMO] (39.65)
hemodialysis (39.95)
percutaneous cardiopulmonary bypass (39.66)

➡ **AHA Coding Clinic:** 4Q, '97, 55; 3Q, '97, 14; 2Q, '97, 8; 2Q, '90, 24

39.62 Hypothermia (systemic) incidental to open heart surgery

39.63 Cardioplegia

Arrest:
anoxic
circulatory

39.64 Intraoperative cardiac pacemaker
Temporary pacemaker used during and immediately following cardiac surgery

➡ **AHA Coding Clinic:** 1Q, '89, 2; M-J, '87, 3

39.65 Extracorporeal membrane oxygenation [ECMO]

Excludes: *extracorporeal circulation auxiliary to open heart surgery (39.61)*
percutaneous cardiopulmonary bypass (39.66)

➡ **AHA Coding Clinic:** 2Q, '90, 23; 2Q, '89, 17

39.66 Percutaneous cardiopulmonary bypass
Closed chest

Excludes: *extracorporeal circulation auxiliary to open heart surgery (39.61)*
extracorporeal hepatic assistance (50.92)
extracorporeal membrane oxygenation [ECMO] (39.65)
hemodialysis (39.95)

➡ **AHA Coding Clinic:** 3Q, '96, 11

39.8 Operations on carotid body and other vascular bodies
Chemodectomy
Denervation of:
  aortic body
  carotid body
Glomectomy, carotid
Implantation into carotid body:
  electronic stimulator
  pacemaker

Excludes: *excision of glomus jugulare (20.51)*

39.9 Other operations on vessels

39.90 Insertion of non-coronary artery stent or stents
Endovascular recanalization techniques
Stent graft(s)

Code also any noncoronary angioplasty or atherectomy (39.50)

➡ **AHA Coding Clinic:** 4Q, '96, 63

39.91 Freeing of vessel
Dissection and freeing of adherent tissue:
  artery-vein-nerve bundle
  vascular bundle

39.92 Injection of sclerosing agent into vein

Excludes: *injection:*
  esophageal varices (42.33
  hemorrhoids (49.42)

➡ **AHA Coding Clinic:** 2Q, '92, 17

39.93 Insertion of vessel-to-vessel cannula
Formation of:
  arteriovenous:
    fistula } by external cannula
    shunt }

Code also any renal dialysis (39.95)

➡ **AHA Coding Clinic:** S-O, '85, 5 & 12

39.94 Replacement of vessel-to-vessel cannula
Revision of vessel-to-vessel cannula

39.95 Hemodialysis
Artificial kidney
Hemodiafiltration
Hemofiltration
Renal dialysis

Excludes: *peritoneal dialysis (54.98)*

➡ **AHA Coding Clinic:** S-O, '86, 11

39.96 Total body perfusion
Code also substance perfused (99.21-99.29)

39.97 Other perfusion
Perfusion NOS
Perfusion, local [regional] of:
  carotid artery
  coronary artery
  head
  lower limb
  neck
  upper limb

Code also substance perfused (99.21-99.29)

Excludes: *perfusion of:*
  kidney (55.95)
  large intestine (46.96)
  liver (50.93)
  small intestine (46.95)

➡ **AHA Coding Clinic:** 3Q, '96, 11

39.98 Control of hemorrhage, not otherwise specified
Angiotripsy
Control of postoperative hemorrhage NOS
Venotripsy

Excludes: *control of hemorrhage (postoperative):*
  anus (49.95)
  bladder (57.93)
  following vascular procedure (39.41)
  nose (21.00-21.09)
  prostate (60.94)
  tonsil (28.7)
that by:
  ligation (38.80-38.89)
  suture (39.30-39.32)

39.99 Other operations on vessels

Excludes: *injection or infusion of therapeutic or prophylactic substance (99.11-99.29)*
transfusion of blood and blood components (99.01-99.09)

➡ **AHA Coding Clinic:** 1Q, '89, 11

8. OPERATIONS ON THE HEMIC AND LYMPHATIC SYSTEM (40-41)

40 Operations on lymphatic system

40.0 **Incision of lymphatic structures**

40.1 **Diagnostic procedures on lymphatic structures**

40.11 **Biopsy of lymphatic structure**

40.19 **Other diagnostic procedures on lymphatic structures**

Excludes: *lymphangiogram:*
abdominal (88.04)
cervical (87.08)
intrathoracic (87.34)
lower limb (88.36)
upper limb (88.34)
microscopic examination of specimen (90.71-90.79)
radioisotope scan (92.16)
thermography (88.89)

40.2 **Simple excision of lymphatic structure**

Excludes: *biopsy of lymphatic structure (40.11)*

40.21 **Excision of deep cervical lymph node**

40.22 **Excision of internal mammary lymph node**

40.23 **Excision of axillary lymph node**

40.24 **Excision of inguinal lymph node**

40.29 **Simple excision of other lymphatic structure**

Excision of:
cystic hygroma
lymphangioma
Simple lymphadenectomy

40.3 **Regional lymph node excision**

Extended regional lymph node excision
Regional lymph node excision with excision of lymphatic drainage area including skin, subcutaneous tissue, and fat

➡ **AHA Coding Clinic:** 2Q, '92, 7

40.4 **Radical excision of cervical lymph nodes**

Resection of cervical lymph nodes down to muscle and deep fascia

Excludes: *that associated with radical laryngectomy (30.4)*

40.40 **Radical neck dissection, not otherwise specified**

40.41 **Radical neck dissection, unilateral**

40.42 **Radical neck dissection, bilateral**

40.5 **Radical excision of other lymph nodes**

Excludes: *that associated with radical mastectomy (85.45-85.48)*

40.50 **Radical excision of lymph nodes, not otherwise specified**

Radical (lymph) node dissection NOS

40.51 **Radical excision of axillary lymph nodes**

40.52 **Radical excision of periaortic lymph nodes**

40.53 **Radical excision of iliac lymph nodes**

40.54 **Radical groin dissection**

40.59 **Radical excision of other lymph nodes**

Excludes: *radical neck dissection (40.40-40.42)*

40.6 **Operations on thoracic duct**

40.61 **Cannulation of thoracic duct**

40.62 **Fistulization of thoracic duct**

40.63 **Closure of fistula of thoracic duct**

40.64 **Ligation of thoracic duct**

40.69 **Other operations on thoracic duct**

40.9 **Other operations on lymphatic structures**

Anastomosis, Dilation, Ligation, Obliteration, Reconstruction, Repair, Transplantation } of peripheral lymphatics
Correction of lymphedema of limb, NOS

Excludes: *reduction of elephantiasis of scrotum (61.3)*

41 Operations on bone marrow and spleen

41.0 Bone marrow or hematopoietic stem cell transplant

Excludes: *aspiration of bone marrow from donor (41.91)*

➡ **AHA Coding Clinic:** 1Q, '91, 3

41.00 Bone marrow transplant, not otherwise specified

[30] **41.01 Autologous bone marrow transplant**
Autograft of bone marrow NOS
With extracorporeal purging of malignant cells from marrow
Autograft of bone marrow NOS

[31] **41.02 Allogeneic bone marrow transplant with purging**
Allograft of bone marrow with in vitro removal (purging) of T-cells

[31] **41.03 Allogeneic bone marrow transplant without purging**
Allograft of bone marrow NOS

[30] **41.04 Autologous hematopoietic stem cell transplant**
➡ **AHA Coding Clinic:** 4Q, '94, 52

[30] **41.05 Allogeneic hematopoietic stem cell transplant**
➡ **AHA Coding Clinic:** 4Q, '97, 55

[30] **41.06 Cord blood stem cell transplant**
➡ **AHA Coding Clinic:** 4Q, '97, 56

41.1 Puncture of spleen

Excludes: *aspiration biopsy of spleen (41.32)*

41.2 Splenotomy

41.3 Diagnostic procedures on bone marrow and spleen

41.31 Biopsy of bone marrow

[22] **41.32 Closed [aspiration] [percutaneous] biopsy of spleen**
Needle biopsy of spleen

[21] **41.33 Open biopsy of spleen**

41.38 Other diagnostic procedures on bone marrow

Excludes: *microscopic examination of specimen from bone marrow (90.61-90.69)*
radioisotope scan (92.05)

41.39 Other diagnostic procedures on spleen

Excludes: *microscopic examination of specimen from spleen (90.61-90.69)*
radioisotope scan (92.05)

41.4 Excision or destruction of lesion or tissue of spleen

Excludes: *excision of accessory spleen (41.93)*

41.41 Marsupialization of splenic cyst

41.42 Excision of lesion or tissue of spleen

Excludes: *biopsy of spleen (41.32-41.33)*

41.43 Partial splenectomy

41.5 Total splenectomy
Splenectomy NOS

41.9 Other operations on spleen and bone marrow

41.91 Aspiration of bone marrow from donor for transplant

Excludes: *biopsy of bone marrow (41.31)*

➡ **AHA Coding Clinic:** 1Q, '91, 3

41.92 Injection into bone marrow

Excludes: *bone marrow transplant (41.00-41.03)*

➡ **AHA Coding Clinic:** 3Q, '96, 17

41.93 Excision of accessory spleen

41.94 Transplantation of spleen

41.95 Repair and plastic operations on spleen

41.98 Other operations on bone marrow

41.99 Other operations on spleen

[21] Open biopsy
[22] Closed biopsy
[30] Noncovered procedure only if none of the following codes are present as either a principle or secondary diagnosis: 200.00-202.08, 202.80-202.98, 204.01, 205.01, 206.01, 207.01, 208.01.
[31] Noncovered procedure only if none of the following codes are present as either a principle or secondary diagnosis: 204.00-208.91, 279.12, 279.2, 284.0-284.9.

9. OPERATIONS ON THE DIGESTIVE SYSTEM (42-54)

42 Operations on esophagus

42.0 Esophagotomy

42.01 Incision of esophageal web

42.09 Other incision of esophagus
Esophagotomy NOS

Excludes: *esophagomyotomy (42.7)*
esophagostomy (42.10-42.19)

42.1 Esophagostomy

42.10 Esophagostomy, not otherwise specified

42.11 Cervical esophagostomy

42.12 Exteriorization of esophageal pouch

42.19 Other external fistulization of esophagus
Thoracic esophagostomy
Code also any resection (42.40-42.42)

42.2 Diagnostic procedures on esophagus

42.21 Operative esophagoscopy by incision

42.22 Esophagoscopy through artificial stoma

Excludes: *that with biopsy (42.24)*

42.23 Other esophagoscopy

Excludes: *that with biopsy (42.24)*

[22] **42.24** Closed [endoscopic] biopsy of esophagus

Esophagoscopy with biopsy
Suction biopsy of the esophagus

Excludes: *esophagogastroduodenoscopy [EGD] with closed biopsy (45.16)*

[21] **42.25** Open biopsy of esophagus

42.29 Other diagnostic procedures on esophagus

Excludes: *barium swallow (87.61)*
esophageal manometry (89.32)
microscopic examination of specimen from esophagus (90.81-90.89)

42.3 Local excision or destruction of lesion or tissue of esophagus

42.31 Local excision of esophageal diverticulum

42.32 Local excision of other lesion or tissue of esophagus

Excludes: *biopsy of esophagus (42.24-42.25)*
esophageal fistulectomy (42.84)

42.33 Endoscopic excision or destruction of lesion or tissue of esophagus

Ablation of esophageal neoplasm
Control of esophageal bleeding
Esophageal polypectomy
Esophageal varices
Injection of esophageal varices
} by endoscopic approach

Excludes: *biopsy of esophagus (42.24-42.25)*
fistulectomy (42.84)
open ligation of esophageal varices (42.91)

42.39 Other destruction of lesion or tissue of esophagus

Excludes: *that by endoscopic approach (42.33)*

42.4 Excision of esophagus

Excludes: *esophagogastrectomy NOS (43.99)*

42.40 Esophagectomy, not otherwise specified

42.41 Partial esophagectomy
Code also any synchronous:
anastomosis other than end-to-end (42.51-42.69)
esophagostomy (42.10-42.19)
gastrostomy (43.11-43.19)

42.42 Total esophagectomy
Code also any synchronous:
gastrostomy (43.11-43.19)
interposition or anastomosis other than end-to-end (42.51-42.69)

Excludes: *esophagogastrectomy (43.99)*

➡ **AHA Coding Clinic:** 4Q, '88, 11

[21] Open biopsy
[22] Closed biopsy

42.5 Intrathoracic anastomosis of esophagus

Code also any synchronous:
esophagectomy (42.40-42.42)
gastrostomy (43.1)

42.51 Intrathoracic esophagoesophagostomy

42.52 Intrathoracic esophagogastrostomy

42.53 Intrathoracic esophageal anastomosis with interposition of small bowel

42.54 Other intrathoracic esophagoenterostomy

Anastomosis of esophagus to intestinal segment NOS

42.55 Intrathoracic esophageal anastomosis with interposition of colon

42.56 Other intrathoracic esophagocolostomy

Esophagocolostomy NOS

42.58 Intrathoracic esophageal anastomosis with other interposition

Construction of artificial esophagus
Retrosternal formation of reversed gastric tube

42.59 Other intrathoracic anastomosis of esophagus

➡ **AHA Coding Clinic:** 4Q, '88, 11

42.6 Antesternal anastomosis of esophagus

Code also any synchronous:
esophagectomy (42.40-42.42)
gastrostomy (43.1)

42.61 Antesternal esophagoesophagostomy

42.62 Antesternal esophagogastrostomy

42.63 Antesternal esophageal anastomosis with interposition of small bowel

42.64 Other antesternal esophagoenterostomy

Antethoracic:
esophagoenterostomy
esophagoileostomy
esophagojejunostomy

42.65 Antesternal esophageal anastomosis with interposition of colon

42.66 Other antesternal esophagocolostomy

Antethoracic esophagocolostomy

42.68 Other antesternal esophageal anastomosis with interposition

42.69 Other antesternal anastomosis of esophagus

42.7 Esophagomyotomy

42.8 Other repair of esophagus

42.81 Insertion of permanent tube into esophagus

➡ **AHA Coding Clinic:** 1Q, '97, 15

42.82 Suture of laceration of esophagus

42.83 Closure of esophagostomy

42.84 Repair of esophageal fistula, not elsewhere classified

Excludes: *repair of fistula:*
bronchoesophageal (33.42)
esophagopleurocutaneous (34.73)
pharyngoesophageal (29.53)
tracheoesophageal (31.73)

42.85 Repair of esophageal stricture

42.86 Production of subcutaneous tunnel without esophageal anastomosis

42.87 Other graft of esophagus

Excludes: *antesternal esophageal anastomosis with interposition of:*
colon (42.65)
small bowel (42.63)
antesternal esophageal anastomosis with other interposition (42.68)
intrathoracic esophageal anastomosis with interposition of:
colon (42.55)
small bowel (42.53)
intrathoracic esophageal anastomosis with other interposition (42.58)

42.89 Other repair of esophagus

42.9 Other operations on esophagus

42.91 Ligation of esophageal varices

Excludes: *that by endoscopic approach (42.33)*

42.92 Dilation of esophagus

Dilation of cardiac sphincter

Excludes: *intubation of esophagus (96.03, 96.06-96.08)*

42.99 Other

Excludes: *insertion of Sengstaken tube (96.06)*
intubation of esophagus (96.03, 96.06-96.08)
removal of intraluminal foreign body from esophagus without incision (98.02)
tamponade of esophagus (96.06)

43 Incision and excision of stomach

43.0 Gastrotomy

Excludes: *gastrostomy (43.11-43.19) that for control of hemorrhage (44.49)*

➡ **AHA Coding Clinic:** 3Q, '89, 14

43.1 Gastrostomy

➡ **AHA Coding Clinic:** S-O, '85, 5

43.11 Percutaneous [endoscopic] gastrostomy [PEG]
Percutaneous transabdominal gastrostomy

43.19 Other gastrostomy

Excludes: *percutaneous [endoscopic] gastrostomy [PEG] (43.11)*

➡ **AHA Coding Clinic:** 1Q, '92, 14; 3Q, '89, 14

43.3 Pyloromyotomy

43.4 Local excision or destruction of lesion or tissue of stomach

43.41 Endoscopic excision or destruction of lesion or tissue of stomach
Gastric polypectomy by endoscopic approach
Gastric varices by endoscopic approach

Excludes: *biopsy of stomach (44.14-44.15)*
control of hemorrhage (44.43)
open ligation of gastric varices (44.91)

➡ **AHA Coding Clinic:** 3Q, '96, 10

43.42 Local excision of other lesion or tissue of stomach

Excludes: *biopsy of stomach (44.14-44.15)*
gastric fistulectomy (44.62-44.63)
partial gastrectomy (43.5-43.89)

43.49 Other destruction of lesion or tissue of stomach

Excludes: *that by endoscopic approach (43.41)*

➡ **AHA Coding Clinic:** N-D, '87, 5; S-O, '85, 6

43.5 Partial gastrectomy with anastomosis to esophagus
Proximal gastrectomy

43.6 Partial gastrectomy with anastomosis to duodenum
Billroth I operation
Gastropylorectomy
Distal gastrectomy

43.7 Partial gastrectomy with anastomosis to jejunum
Billroth II operation

43.8 Other partial gastrectomy

43.81 Partial gastrectomy with jejunal transposition
Henley jejunal transposition operation

Code also any synchronous intestinal resection (45.51)

43.89 Other
Partial gastrectomy with bypass gastrogastrostomy
Sleeve resection of stomach

43.9 Total gastrectomy

43.91 Total gastrectomy with intestinal interposition

43.99 Other total gastrectomy
Complete gastroduodenectomy
Esophagoduodenostomy with complete gastrectomy
Esophagogastrectomy NOS
Esophagojejunostomy with complete gastrectomy
Radical gastrectomy

44 Other operations on stomach

44.0 Vagotomy

44.00 Vagotomy, not otherwise specified
Division of vagus nerve NOS

44.01 Truncal vagotomy

44.02 Highly selective vagotomy
Parietal cell vagotomy
Selective proximal vagotomy

44.03 Other selective vagotomy

44.1 Diagnostic procedures on stomach

44.11 Transabdominal gastroscopy
Intraoperative gastroscopy

Excludes: *that with biopsy (44.14)*

44.12 Gastroscopy through artificial stoma

Excludes: *that with biopsy (44.14)*

44.13 Other gastroscopy

Excludes: *that with biopsy (44.14)*

[22] **44.14** Closed [endoscopic] biopsy of stomach
Brushing or washing for specimen collection

Excludes: *esophagogastroduodenoscopy [EGD] with closed biopsy (45.16)*

➡ **AHA Coding Clinic:** N-D, '87, 5

[21] **44.15** Open biopsy of stomach

44.19 Other diagnostic procedures on stomach

Excludes: *gastric lavage (96.33)*
microscopic examination of specimen from stomach (90.81-90.89)
upper GI series (87.62)

[21] Open biopsy
[22] Closed biopsy

44.2 Pyloroplasty

44.21 Dilation of pylorus by incision

44.22 Endoscopic dilation of pylorus
Dilation with balloon endoscope
Endoscopic dilation of gastrojejunostomy site

44.29 Other pyloroplasty
Pyloroplasty NOS
Revision of pylorus

44.3 Gastroenterostomy without gastrectomy

44.31 High gastric bypass
Printen and Mason gastric bypass

44.39 Other gastroenterostomy
Bypass:
gastroduodenostomy
gastroenterostomy
gastrogastrostomy
Gastrojejunostomy without gastrectomy NOS

44.4 Control of hemorrhage and suture of ulcer of stomach or duodenum

44.40 Suture of peptic ulcer, not otherwise specified

44.41 Suture of gastric ulcer site

Excludes: *ligation of gastric varices (44.91)*

44.42 Suture of duodenal ulcer site
➡ **AHA Coding Clinic:** J-F, '87, 11

44.43 Endoscopic control of gastric or duodenal bleeding
➡ **AHA Coding Clinic:** 2Q, '92, 17

44.44 Transcatheter embolization for gastric or duodenal bleeding

Excludes: *surgical occlusion of abdominal vessels (38.86-38.87)*

44.49 Other control of hemorrhage of stomach or duodenum
That with gastrotomy

44.5 Revision of gastric anastomosis
Closure of:
gastric anastomosis
gastroduodenostomy
gastrojejunostomy
Pantaloon operation

44.6 Other repair of stomach

44.61 Suture of laceration of stomach

Excludes: *that of ulcer site (44.41)*

44.62 Closure of gastrostomy

44.63 Closure of other gastric fistula
Closure of:
gastrocolic fistula
gastrojejunocolic fistula

44.64 Gastropexy

44.65 Esophagogastroplasty
Belsey operation
Esophagus and stomach cardioplasty

44.66 Other procedures for creation of esophagogastric sphincteric competence
Fundoplication
Gastric cardioplasty
Nissen's fundoplication
Restoration of cardio-esophageal angle

44.69 Other
Inversion of gastric diverticulum
Repair of stomach NOS
➡ **AHA Coding Clinic:** N-D, '84, 13

44.9 Other operations on stomach

44.91 Ligation of gastric varices

Excludes: *that by endoscopic approach (43.41)*

44.92 Intraoperative manipulation of stomach
Reduction of gastric volvulus

44.93 Insertion of gastric bubble (balloon)

44.94 Removal of gastric bubble (balloon)

44.99 Other

Excludes: *change of gastrostomy tube (97.02)*
dilation of cardiac sphincter (42.92)
gastric:
cooling (96.31)
freezing (96.32)
gavage (96.35)
hypothermia (96.31)
lavage (96.33)
insertion of nasogastric tube (96.07)
irrigation of gastrostomy (96.36)
irrigation of nasogastric tube (96.34)
removal of:
gastrostomy tube (97.51)
intraluminal foreign body from stomach without incision (98.03)
replacement of:
gastrostomy tube (97.02)
(naso-)gastric tube (97.01)

45 Incision, excision, and anastomosis of intestine

45.0 Enterotomy

Excludes: *duodenocholedochotomy (51.41-51.42, 51.51)*
that for destruction of lesion (45.30-45.34)
that of exteriorized intestine (46.14, 46.24, 46.31)

45.00 Incision of intestine, not otherwise specified

45.01 Incision of duodenum

45.02 Other incision of small intestine

45.03 Incision of large intestine

Excludes: *proctotomy (48.0)*

45.1 Diagnostic procedures on small intestine

Code also any laparotomy (54.11-54.19)

45.11 Transabdominal endoscopy of small intestine
Intraoperative endoscopy of small intestine

Excludes: *that with biopsy (45.14)*

45.12 Endoscopy of small intestine through artificial stoma

Excludes: *that with biopsy (45.14)*

45.13 Other endoscopy of small intestine
Esophagogastroduodenoscopy [EGD]

Excludes: *that with biopsy (45.14, 45.16)*

➡ **AHA Coding Clinic:** N-D, '87, 5

[22] **45.14 Closed [endoscopic] biopsy of small intestine**
Brushing or washing for specimen collection

Excludes: *esophagogastroduodenoscopy [EGD] with closed biopsy (45.16)*

[21] **45.15 Open biopsy of small intestine**

45.16 Esophagogastroduodenoscopy [EGD] with closed biopsy
Biopsy of one or more sites involving esophagus, stomach, and/or duodenum

45.19 Other diagnostic procedures on small intestine

Excludes: *microscopic examination of specimen from small intestine (90.91-90.99)*
radioisotope scan (92.04)
ultrasonography (88.74)
x-ray (87.61-87.69)

45.2 Diagnostic procedures on large intestine

Code also any laparotomy (54.11-54.19)

45.21 Transabdominal endoscopy of large intestine
Intraoperative endoscopy of large intestine

Excludes: *that with biopsy (45.25)*

45.22 Endoscopy of large intestine through artificial stoma

Excludes: *that with biopsy (45.25)*

45.23 Colonoscopy
Flexible fiberoptic colonoscopy

Excludes: *endoscopy of large intestine through artificial stoma (45.22)*
flexible sigmoidoscopy (45.24)
rigid proctosigmoidoscopy (48.23)
transabdominal endoscopy of large intestine (45.21)

➡ **AHA Coding Clinic:** S-O, '85, 5

45.24 Flexible sigmoidoscopy
Endoscopy of descending colon

Excludes: *rigid proctosigmoidoscopy (48.23)*

[22] **45.25 Closed [endoscopic] biopsy of large intestine**
Biopsy, closed, of unspecified intestinal site
Brushing or washing for specimen collection
Colonoscopy with biopsy

Excludes: *proctosigmoidoscopy with biopsy (48.24)*

[21] **45.26 Open biopsy of large intestine**

45.27 Intestinal biopsy, site unspecified

45.28 Other diagnostic procedures on large intestine

45.29 Other diagnostic procedures on intestine, site unspecified

Excludes: *microscopic examination of specimen (90.91-90.99)*
scan and radioisotope function study (92.04)
ultrasonography (88.74)
x-ray (87.61-87.69)

[21] Open biopsy
[22] Closed biopsy

45.3 Local excision or destruction of lesion or tissue of small intestine

45.30 Endoscopic excision or destruction of lesion of duodenum

Excludes: *biopsy of duodenum (45.14-45.15)*
control of hemorrhage (44.43)
fistulectomy (46.72)

45.31 Other local excision of lesion of duodenum

Excludes: *biopsy of duodenum (45.14-45.15)*
fistulectomy (46.72)
multiple segmental resection (45.61)
that by endoscopic approach (45.30)

45.32 Other destruction of lesion of duodenum

Excludes: *that by endoscopic approach (45.30)*

➡ **AHA Coding Clinic:** N-D, '87, 5; S-O, '85, 6

45.33 Local excision of lesion or tissue of small intestine, except duodenum

Excision of redundant mucosa of ileostomy

Excludes: *biopsy of small intestine (45.14-45.15)*
fistulectomy (46.74)
multiple segmental resection (45.61)

45.34 Other destruction of lesion of small intestine, except duodenum

45.4 Local excision or destruction of lesion or tissue of large intestine

➡ **AHA Coding Clinic:** N-D, '87, 11

45.41 Excision of lesion or tissue of large intestine

Excision of redundant mucosa of colostomy

Excludes: *biopsy of large intestine (45.25-45.27)*
endoscopic polypectomy of large intestine (45.42)
fistulectomy (46.76)
multiple segmental resection (45.71)
that by endoscopic approach (45.42-45.43)

45.42 Endoscopic polypectomy of large intestine

Excludes: *that by open approach (45.41)*

➡ **AHA Coding Clinic:** 2Q, '90, 25

45.43 Endoscopic destruction of other lesion or tissue of large intestine

Endoscopic ablation of tumor of large intestine
Endoscopic control of colonic bleeding

Excludes: *endoscopic polypectomy of large intestine (45.42)*

45.49 Other destruction of lesion of large intestine

Excludes: *that by endoscopic approach (45.43)*

45.5 Isolation of intestinal segment

Code also any synchronous:
anastomosis other than end-to-end (45.90-45.94)
enterostomy (46.10-46.39)

45.50 Isolation of intestinal segment, not otherwise specified

Isolation of intestinal pedicle flap
Reversal of intestinal segment

45.51 Isolation of segment of small intestine

Isolation of ileal loop
Resection of small intestine for interposition

45.52 Isolation of segment of large intestine

Resection of colon for interposition

45.6 Other excision of small intestine

Code also any synchronous:
anastomosis other than end-to-end (45.90-45.93, 45.95)
colostomy (46.10-46.13)
enterostomy (46.10-46.39)

Excludes: *cecectomy (45.72)*
enterocolectomy (45.79)
gastroduodenectomy (43.6-43.99)
ileocolectomy (45.73)
pancreatoduodenectomy (52.51-52.7)

45.61 Multiple segmental resection of small intestine
Segmental resection for multiple traumatic lesions of small intestine

45.62 Other partial resection of small intestine
Duodenectomy
Ileectomy
Jejunectomy

Excludes: *duodenectomy with synchronous pancreatectomy (52.51-52.7)*
resection of cecum and terminal ileum (45.72)

45.63 Total removal of small intestine

45.7 Partial excision of large intestine

Code also any synchronous:
anastomosis other than end-to-end (45.92-45.94)
enterostomy (46.10-46.39)

➡ **AHA Coding Clinic:** 4Q, '92, 27

45.71 Multiple segmental resection of large intestine
Segmental resection for multiple traumatic lesions of large intestine

45.72 Cecectomy
Resection of cecum and terminal ileum

45.73 Right hemicolectomy
Ileocolectomy
Right radical colectomy

45.74 Resection of transverse colon

45.75 Left hemicolectomy

Excludes: *proctosigmoidectomy (48.41-48.69)*
second stage Mikulicz operation (46.04)

45.76 Sigmoidectomy
➡ **AHA Coding Clinic:** 3Q, '89, 15

45.79 Other partial excision of large intestine
Enterocolectomy NEC
➡ **AHA Coding Clinic:** 3Q, '97, 9; 2Q, '91, 16

45.8 Total intra-abdominal colectomy
Excision of cecum, colon, and sigmoid

Excludes: *coloproctectomy (48.41-48.69)*

45.9 Intestinal anastomosis

Code also any synchronous resection (45.31-45.8, 48.41-48.69)

Excludes: *end-to-end anastomosis — omit code*

45.90 Intestinal anastomosis, not otherwise specified

45.91 Small-to-small intestinal anastomosis

45.92 Anastomosis of small intestine to rectal stump
Hampton procedure

45.93 Other small-to-large intestinal anastomosis
➡ **AHA Coding Clinic:** N-D, '86, 11

45.94 Large-to-large intestinal anastomosis

Excludes: *rectorectostomy (48.74)*

➡ **AHA Coding Clinic:** 3Q, '89, 15

45.95 Anastomosis to anus
Formation of endorectal ileal pouch (J-pouch) (H-pouch) (S-pouch) with anastomosis of small intestine to anus

46 Other operations on intestine

46.0 Exteriorization of intestine

Includes: loop enterostomy
multiple stage resection of intestine

46.01 Exteriorization of small intestine
Loop ileostomy

46.02 Resection of exteriorized segment of small intestine

46.03 Exteriorization of large intestine
Exteriorization of intestine NOS
First stage Mikulicz exteriorization of intestine
Loop colostomy

46.04 Resection of exteriorized segment of large intestine
Resection of exteriorized segment of intestine NOS
Second stage Mikulicz operation

46.1 Colostomy

Code also any synchronous resection (45.49, 45.71-45.79, 45.8)

Excludes: *loop colostomy (46.03)*
that with abdominoperineal resection of rectum (48.5)
that with synchronous anterior rectal resection (48.62)

46.10 Colostomy, not otherwise specified

46.11 Temporary colostomy

46.13 Permanent colostomy

46.14 Delayed opening of colostomy

46.2 Ileostomy

Code also any synchronous resection (45.34, 45.61-45.63)

Excludes: *loop ileostomy (46.01)*

46.20 Ileostomy, not otherwise specified

46.21 Temporary ileostomy

46.22 Continent ileostomy

Kock pouch for gastriontestinal diversion

46.23 Other permanent ileostomy

46.24 Delayed opening of ileostomy

46.3 Other enterostomy

Code also any synchronous resection (45.61-45.8)

46.31 Delayed opening of other enterostomy

46.32 Percutaneous (endoscopic) jejunostomy [PEJ]

Endoscopic conversion of gastrostomy to jejunostomy

46.39 Other

Duodenostomy
Feeding enterostomy

➡ **AHA Coding Clinic:** 3Q, '89, 15

46.4 Revision of intestinal stoma

46.40 Revision of intestinal stoma, not otherwise specified

Plastic enlargement of intestinal stoma
Reconstruction of stoma of intestine
Release of scar tissue of intestinal stoma

Excludes: *excision of redundant mucosa (45.41)*

46.41 Revision of stoma of small intestine

Excludes: *excision of redundant mucosa (45.33)*

46.42 Repair of pericolostomy hernia

46.43 Other revision of stoma of large intestine

Excludes: *excision of redundant mucosa (45.41)*

46.5 Closure of intestinal stoma

Code also any synchronous resection (45.34, 45.49, 45.61-45.8)

46.50 Closure of intestinal stoma, not otherwise specified

46.51 Closure of stoma of small intestine

46.52 Closure of stoma of large intestine

Closure or take-down of:
cecostomy
colostomy
sigmoidostomy

➡ **AHA Coding Clinic:** 3Q, '97, 9; 2Q, '91, 16; N-D, '87, 8

46.6 Fixation of intestine

46.60 Fixation of intestine, not otherwise specified

Fixation of intestine to abdominal wall

46.61 Fixation of small intestine to abdominal wall

Ileopexy

46.62 Other fixation of small intestine

Noble plication of small intestine
Plication of jejunum

46.63 Fixation of large intestine to abdominal wall

Cecocoloplicopexy
Sigmoidopexy (Moschowitz)

46.64 Other fixation of large intestine

Cecofixation
Colofixation

46.7 **Other repair of intestine**

Excludes: *closure of:*
ulcer of duodenum (44.42)
vesicoenteric fistula (57.83)

46.71 **Suture of laceration of duodenum**

46.72 **Closure of fistula of duodenum**

46.73 **Suture of laceration of small intestine, except duodenum**

46.74 **Closure of fistula of small intestine, except duodenum**

Excludes: *closure of:*
artificial stoma (46.51)
vaginal fistula (70.74)
repair of gastrojejunocolic fistula (44.63)

46.75 **Suture of laceration of large intestine**

46.76 **Closure of fistula of large intestine**

Excludes: *closure of:*
gastrocolic fistula (44.63)
rectal fistula (48.73)
sigmoidovesical fistula (57.83)
stoma (46.52)
vaginal fistula (70.72-70.73)
vesicocolic fistula (57.83)
vesicosigmoidovaginal fistula (57.83)

46.79 **Other repair of intestine**

46.8 **Dilation and manipulation of intestine**

46.80 **Intra-abdominal manipulation of intestine, not otherwise specified**

Correction of intestinal malrotation
Reduction of:
intestinal torsion
intestinal volvulus
intussusception

Excludes: *reduction of intussusception with:*
fluoroscopy
ionizing radiation enema
ultrasonography guidance
} *96.29*

46.81 **Intra-abdominal manipulation of small intestine**

46.82 **Intra-abdominal manipulation of large intestine**

46.85 **Dilation of intestine**

Dilation (balloon) of duodenum
Dilation (balloon) of jejunum
Endoscopic dilation (balloon) of large intestine
That through rectum or colostomy

➡ **AHA Coding Clinic:** 3Q, '89, 15

46.9 **Other operations on intestines**

46.91 **Myotomy of sigmoid colon**

46.92 **Myotomy of other parts of colon**

46.93 **Revision of anastomosis of small intestine**

46.94 **Revision of anastomosis of large intestine**

46.95 **Local perfusion of small intestine**

Code also substance perfused (99.21-99.29)

46.96 **Local perfusion of large intestine**

Code also substance perfused (99.21-99.29)

46.99 **Other**

Ileoentectropy

Excludes: *diagnostic procedures on intestine (45.11-45.29)*
dilation of enterostomy stoma (96.24)
intestinal intubation (96.08)
removal of:
intraluminal foreign body from large intestine without incision (98.04)
intraluminal foreign body from small intestine without incision (98.03)
tube from large intestine (97.53)
tube from small intestine (97.52)
replacement of:
large intestine tube or enterostomy device (97.04)
small intestine tube or enterostomy device (97.03)

➡ **AHA Coding Clinic:** 1Q, '89, 11

47 Operations on appendix

Includes: appendiceal stump

47.0 **Appendectomy**

Excludes: *incidental appendectomy, so described (47.11, 47.19)*

➡ **AHA Coding Clinic:** 4Q, '96, 64; 3Q, '92, 12

47.01 **Laparoscopic appendectomy**

➡ **AHA Coding Clinic:** 4Q, '96, 64

47.09 **Other appendectomy**

➡ **AHA Coding Clinic:** 4Q, '97, 52

47.1 **Incidental appendectomy**

47.11 **Laparoscopic incidental appendectomy**

47.19 **Other incidental appendectomy**

➡ **AHA Coding Clinic:** 4Q, '96, 65

47.2 **Drainage of appendiceal abscess**

Excludes: *that with appendectomy (47.0)*

47.9 **Other operations on appendix**

47.91 **Appendicostomy**

47.92 **Closure of appendiceal fistula**

47.99 **Other**

Anastomosis of appendix

Excludes: *diagnostic procedures on appendix (45.21-45.29)*

48 Operations on rectum, rectosigmoid, and perirectal tissue

48.0 Proctotomy

Decompression of imperforate anus
Panas' operation [linear proctotomy]

Excludes: *incision of perirectal tissue (48.81)*

48.1 Proctostomy

48.2 Diagnostic procedures on rectum, rectosigmoid, and perirectal tissue

48.21 Transabdominal proctosigmoidoscopy

Intraoperative proctosigmoidoscopy

Excludes: *that with biopsy (48.24)*

48.22 Proctosigmoidoscopy through artificial stoma

Excludes: *that with biopsy (48.24)*

48.23 Rigid proctosigmoidoscopy

Excludes: *flexible sigmoidoscopy (45.24)*

[22] **48.24 Closed [endoscopic] biopsy of rectum**

Brushing or washing for specimen collection
Proctosigmoidoscopy with biopsy

[21] **48.25 Open biopsy of rectum**

48.26 Biopsy of perirectal tissue

48.29 Other diagnostic procedures on rectum, rectosigmoid, and perirectal tissue

Excludes: *digital examination of rectum (89.34)*
lower GI series (87.64)
microscopic examination of specimen from rectum (90.91-90.99)

48.3 Local excision or destruction of lesion or tissue of rectum

48.31 Radical electrocoagulation of rectal lesion or tissue

48.32 Other electrocoagulation of rectal lesion or tissue

48.33 Destruction of rectal lesion or tissue by laser

48.34 Destruction of rectal lesion or tissue by cryosurgery

48.35 Local excision of rectal lesion or tissue

Excludes: *biopsy of rectum (48.24-48.25)*
[endoscopic] polypectomy of rectum (48.36)
excision of perirectal tissue (48.82)
hemorrhoidectomy (49.46)
rectal fistulectomy (48.73)

48.36 [Endoscopic] polypectomy of rectum

➡ **AHA Coding Clinic:** 4Q, '95, 65

48.4 Pull-through resection of rectum

Code also any synchronous anastomosis other than end-to-end (45.90, 45.92-45.95)

48.41 Soave submucosal resection of rectum

Endorectal pull-through operation

48.49 Other pull-through resection of rectum

Abdominoperineal pull-through
Altemeier operation
Swenson proctectomy

Excludes: *Duhamel abdominoperineal pull-through (48.65)*

48.5 Abdominoperineal resection of rectum

Combined abdominoendorectal resection
Complete proctectomy
With synchronous colostomy

Code also any synchronous anastomosis other than end-to-end (45.90, 45.92-45.95)

Excludes: *Duhamel abdominoperineal pull-through (48.65)*
that as part of pelvic exenteration (68.8)

➡ **AHA Coding Clinic:** 2Q, '97, 5

48.6 Other resection of rectum

Code also any synchronous anastomosis other than end-to-end (45.90, 45.92-45.95)

48.61 Transsacral rectosigmoidectomy

48.62 Anterior resection of rectum with synchronous colostomy

48.63 Other anterior resection of rectum

Excludes: *that with synchronous colostomy (48.62)*

➡ **AHA Coding Clinic:** 1Q, '96, 9

48.64 Posterior resection of rectum

48.65 Duhamel resection of rectum

Duhamel abdominoperineal pull-through

48.69 Other

Partial proctectomy
Rectal resection NOS

➡ **AHA Coding Clinic:** J-F, '87, 11; N-D, '86, 11

[21] Open biopsy
[22] Closed biopsy

48.7 Repair of rectum

Excludes: *repair of:*
current obstetric laceration (75.62)
vaginal rectocele (70.50, 70.52)

48.71 Suture of laceration of rectum

48.72 Closure of proctostomy

48.73 Closure of other rectal fistula

Excludes: *fistulectomy:*
perirectal (48.93)
rectourethral (58.43)
rectovaginal (70.73)
rectovesical (57.83)
rectovesicovaginal (57.83)

48.74 Rectorectostomy
Rectal anastomosis NOS

48.75 Abdominal proctopexy
Frickman procedure
Ripstein repair of rectal prolapse

48.76 Other proctopexy
Delorme repair of prolapsed rectum
Proctosigmoidopexy
Puborectalis sling operation

Excludes: *manual reduction of rectal prolapse (96.26)*

48.79 Other repair of rectum
Repair of old obstetric laceration of rectum

Excludes: *anastomosis to:*
large intestine (45.94)
small intestine (45.92-45.93)
repair of:
current obstetrical laceration (75.62)
vaginal rectocele (70.50, 70.52)

48.8 Incision or excision of perirectal tissue or lesion

Includes: pelvirectal tissue
rectovaginal septum

48.81 Incision of perirectal tissue
Incision of rectovaginal septum

48.82 Excision of perirectal tissue

Excludes: *perirectal biopsy (48.26)*
perirectofistulectomy (48.93)
rectal fistulectomy (48.73)

48.9 Other operations on rectum and perirectal tissue

48.91 Incision of rectal stricture

48.92 Anorectal myectomy

48.93 Repair of perirectal fistula

Excludes: *that opening into rectum (48.73)*

48.99 Other

Excludes: *digital examination of rectum (89.34)*
dilation of rectum (96.22)
insertion of rectal tube (96.09)
irrigation of rectum (96.38-96.39)
manual reduction of rectal prolapse (96.26)
proctoclysis (96.37)
rectal massage (99.93)
rectal packing (96.19)
removal of:
impacted feces (96.38)
intraluminal foreign body from rectum without incision (98.05)
rectal packing (97.59)
transanal enema (96.39)

49 Operations on anus

49.0 Incision or excision of perianal tissue

49.01 Incision of perianal abscess

49.02 Other incision of perianal tissue
Undercutting of perianal tissue

Excludes: *anal fistulotomy (49.11)*

49.03 Excision of perianal skin tags

49.04 Other excision of perianal tissue

Excludes: *anal fistulectomy (49.12)*
biopsy of perianal tissue (49.22)

49.1 Incision or excision of anal fistula

Excludes: *closure of anal fistula (49.73)*

49.11 Anal fistulotomy

49.12 Anal fistulectomy

49.2 Diagnostic procedures on anus and perianal tissue

49.21 Anoscopy

49.22 Biopsy of perianal tissue

49.23 Biopsy of anus

49.29 Other diagnostic procedures on anus and perianal tissue

Excludes: *microscopic examination of specimen from anus (90.91-90.99)*

49.3 **Local excision or destruction of other lesion or tissue of anus**
Anal cryptotomy
Cauterization of lesion of anus

Excludes: *biopsy of anus (49.23)*
control of (postoperative) hemorrhage of anus (49.95)
hemorrhoidectomy (49.46)

49.31 **Endoscopic excision or destruction of lesion or tissue of anus**

49.39 **Other local excision or destruction of lesion or tissue of anus**

Excludes: *that by endoscopic approach (49.31)*

49.4 **Procedures on hemorrhoids**

49.41 **Reduction of hemorrhoids**

49.42 **Injection of hemorrhoids**

49.43 **Cauterization of hemorrhoids**
Clamp and cautery of hemorrhoids

49.44 **Destruction of hemorrhoids by cryotherapy**

49.45 **Ligation of hemorrhoids**

49.46 **Excision of hemorrhoids**
Hemorrhoidectomy NOS

49.47 **Evacuation of thrombosed hemorrhoids**

49.49 **Other procedures on hemorrhoids**
Lord procedure

49.5 **Division of anal sphincter**

49.51 **Left lateral anal sphincterotomy**

49.52 **Posterior anal sphincterotomy**

49.59 **Other anal sphincterotomy**
Division of sphincter NOS

49.6 **Excision of anus**

49.7 **Repair of anus**

Excludes: *repair of current obstetric laceration (75.62)*

49.71 **Suture of laceration of anus**

49.72 **Anal cerclage**

49.73 **Closure of anal fistula**

Excludes: *excision of anal fistula (49.12)*

49.74 **Gracilis muscle transplant for anal incontinence**

49.79 **Other repair of anal sphincter**
Repair of old obstetric laceration of anus

Excludes: *anoplasty with synchronous hemorrhoidectomy (49.46)*
repair of current obstetric laceration (75.62)

➡ **AHA Coding Clinic:** 1Q, '97, 9

49.9 **Other operations on anus**

Excludes: *dilation of anus (sphincter) (96.23)*

49.91 **Incision of anal septum**

49.92 **Insertion of subcutaneous electrical anal stimulator**

49.93 **Other incision of anus**
Removal of:
foreign body from anus with incision
seton from anus

Excludes: *anal fistulotomy (49.11)*
removal of intraluminal foreign body without incision (98.05)

49.94 **Reduction of anal prolapse**

Excludes: *manual reduction of rectal prolapse (96.26)*

49.95 **Control of (postoperative) hemorrhage of anus**

49.99 **Other**

50 Operations on liver

50.0 **Hepatotomy**
Incision of abscess of liver
Removal of gallstones from liver
Stromeyer-Little operation

50.1 **Diagnostic procedures on liver**

[22] **50.11** **Closed (percutaneous) [needle] biopsy of liver**
Diagnostic aspiration of liver

[21] **50.12** **Open biopsy of liver**
Wedge biopsy

50.19 **Other diagnostic procedures on liver**

Excludes: *liver scan and radioisotope function study (92.02)*
microscopic examination of specimen from liver (91.01-91.09)

[21] Open biopsy
[22] Closed biopsy

50.2 Local excision or destruction of liver tissue or lesion

50.21 Marsupialization of lesion of liver

50.22 Partial hepatectomy
Wedge resection of liver

Excludes: *biopsy of liver (50.11-50.12)*
hepatic lobectomy (50.3)

50.29 Other destruction of lesion of liver
Cauterization, Enucleation, Evacuation } of heptic lesion

Excludes: *percutaneous aspiration of lesion (50.91)*

50.3 Lobectomy of liver
Total hepatic lobectomy with partial excision of other lobe

50.4 Total hepatectomy

50.5 Liver transplant

50.51 Auxiliary liver transplant
Auxiliary hepatic transplantation leaving patient's own liver in situ

50.59 Other transplant of liver

50.6 Repair of liver

50.61 Closure of laceration of liver

50.69 Other repair of liver
Hepatopexy

50.9 Other operations on liver

Excludes: *lysis of adhesions (54.5)*

50.91 Percutaneous aspiration of liver

Excludes: *percutaneous biopsy (50.11)*

50.92 Extracorporeal hepatic assistance

50.93 Localized perfusion of liver

50.94 Other injection of therapeutic substance into liver

50.99 Other

51 Operations on gallbladder and biliary tract

Includes: operations on:
ampulla of Vater
common bile duct
cystic duct
hepatic duct
intrahepatic bile duct
sphincter of Oddi

51.0 Cholecystotomy and cholecystostomy

51.01 Percutaneous aspiration of gallbladder

Excludes: *needle biopsy (51.12)*

51.02 Trocar cholecystostomy
➡ **AHA Coding Clinic:** 3Q, '89, 18

51.03 Other cholecystostomy

51.04 Other cholecystotomy
Cholelithotomy NOS

51.1 Diagnostic procedures on biliary tract

Excludes: *that for endoscopic procedures classifiable to 51.64, 51.84-51.88, 52.14, 52.21, 52.93 -52.94, 52.97-52.98*

➡ **AHA Coding Clinic:** 2Q, '97, 7

51.10 Endoscopic retrograde cholangiopancreatography [ERCP]

Excludes: *endoscopic retrograde:*
cholangiography [ERC] (51.11)
pancreatography [ERP] (52.13)

51.11 Endoscopic retrograde cholangiography [ERC]

Excludes: *endoscopic retrograde:*
cholangiopancreatography [ERCP] (51.10)
pancreatography [ERP] (52.13)

➡ **AHA Coding Clinic:** 1Q, '96, 12; 4Q, '88, 7

[22] **51.12 Percutaneous biopsy of gallbladder or bile ducts**
Needle biopsy of gallbladder

[21] **51.13 Open biopsy of gallbladder or bile ducts**

51.14 Other closed [endoscopic] biopsy of biliary duct or sphincter of Oddi
Brushing or washing for specimen collection
Closed biopsy of biliary duct or sphincter of Oddi by procedures classifiable to 51.10-51.11, 52.13

51.15 Pressure measurement of sphincter of Oddi
Pressure measurement of sphincter by procedures classifiable to 51.10-51.11, 52.13

51.19 Other diagnostic procedures on biliary tract

Excludes: *biliary tract x-ray (87.51-87.59)*
microscopic examination of specimen from biliary tract (91.01-91.09)

[21] Open biopsy
[22] Closed biopsy

51.2 Cholecystectomy

➡ **AHA Coding Clinic:** 1Q, '93, 17; 4Q, '91, 26; 3Q, '89, 18

51.21 Other partial cholecystectomy

Revision of prior cholecystectomy

Excludes: *that by laparoscope (51.24)*

➡ **AHA Coding Clinic:** 4Q, '96, 69

51.22 Cholecystectomy

Excludes: *laparoscopic cholecystectomy (51.23)*

➡ **AHA Coding Clinic:** 4Q, '97, 52; 2Q, '91, 16

51.23 Laparoscopic cholecystectomy

That by laser

➡ **AHA Coding Clinic:** 4Q, '97, 52; 1Q, '96, 12

51.24 Laparoscopic partial cholecystectomy

➡ **AHA Coding Clinic:** 4Q, '96, 69

51.3 Anastomosis of gallbladder or bile duct

Excludes: *resection with end-to-end anastomosis (51.61-51.69)*

51.31 Anastomosis of gallbladder to hepatic ducts

51.32 Anastomosis of gallbladder to intestine

51.33 Anastomosis of gallbladder to pancreas

51.34 Anastomosis of gallbladder to stomach

51.35 Other gallbladder anastomosis

Gallbladder anastomosis NOS

51.36 Choledochoenterostomy

51.37 Anastomosis of hepatic duct to gastrointestinal tract

51.39 Other bile duct anastomosis

Anastomosis of bile duct NOS
Anastomosis of unspecified bile duct to:
- intestine
- liver
- pancreas
- stomach

51.4 Incision of bile duct for relief of obstruction

51.41 Common duct exploration for removal of calculus

Excludes: *percutaneous extraction (51.96)*

➡ **AHA Coding Clinic:** 1Q, '96, 12; 4Q, '88, 7

51.42 Common duct exploration for relief of other obstruction

51.43 Insertion of choledochohepatic tube for decompression

Hepatocholedochostomy

➡ **AHA Coding Clinic:** 3Q, '89, 18; 4Q, '88, 7

51.49 Incision of other bile ducts for relief of obstruction

51.5 Other incision of bile duct

Excludes: *that for relief of obstruction (51.41-51.49)*

51.51 Exploration of common duct

Incision of common bile duct

➡ **AHA Coding Clinic:** 2Q, '97, 16; 1Q, '96, 12

51.59 Incision of other bile duct

➡ **AHA Coding Clinic:** 2Q, '97, 16

51.6 Local excision or destruction of lesion or tissue of biliary ducts and sphincter of Oddi

Code also anastomosis other than end-to-end (51.31, 51.36-51.39)

Excludes: *biopsy of bile duct (51.12-51.13)*

51.61 Excision of cystic duct remnant

51.62 Excision of ampulla of Vater (with reimplantation of common duct)

51.63 Other excision of common duct

Choledochectomy

Excludes: *fistulectomy (51.72)*

51.64 Endoscopic excision or destruction of lesion of biliary ducts or sphincter of Oddi

Excision or destruction of lesion of biliary duct by procedures classifiable to 51.10-51.11, 52.13

51.69 Excision of other bile duct

Excision of lesion of bile duct NOS

Excludes: *fistulectomy (51.79)*

51.7 Repair of bile ducts

51.71 Simple suture of common bile duct

51.72 Choledochoplasty

Repair of fistula of common bile duct

51.79 Repair of other bile ducts

Closure of artificial opening of bile duct NOS
Suture of bile duct NOS

Excludes: *operative removal of prosthetic device (51.95)*

51.8 Other operations on biliary ducts and sphincter of Oddi

51.81 Dilation of sphincter of Oddi
Dilation of ampulla of Vater

Excludes: that by endoscopic approach (51.84)

51.82 Pancreatic sphincterotomy
Incision of pancreatic sphincter
Transduodenal ampullary sphincterotomy

Excludes: that by endoscopic approach (51.85)

51.83 Pancreatic sphincteroplasty

51.84 Endoscopic dilation of ampulla and biliary duct
Dilation of ampulla and biliary duct by procedures classifiable to 51.10-51.11, 52.13

51.85 Endoscopic sphincterotomy and papillotomy
Sphincterotomy and papillotomy by procedures classifiable to 51.10-51.11, 52.13

➡ **AHA Coding Clinic:** 2Q, '97, 7

51.86 Endoscopic insertion of nasobiliary drainage tube
Insertion of nasobiliary tube by procedures classifiable to 51.10-51.11, 52.13

51.87 Endoscopic insertion of stent (tube) into bile duct
Endoprosthesis of bile duct
Insertion of stent into bile duct by procedures classifiable to 51.10-51.11, 52.13

Excludes: nasobiliary drainage tube (51.86)
replacement of stent (tube) (97.05)

51.88 Endoscopic removal of stone(s) from biliary tract
Laparoscopic removal of stone(s) from biliary tract
Removal of biliary tract stone(s) by procedures classifiable to 51.10-51.11, 52.13

Excludes: percutaneous extraction of common duct stones (51.96)

➡ **AHA Coding Clinic:** 2Q, '97, 7

51.89 Other operations on sphincter of Oddi

51.9 Other operations on biliary tract

51.91 Repair of laceration of gallbladder

51.92 Closure of cholecystostomy

51.93 Closure of other biliary fistula
Cholecystogastroenteric fistulectomy

51.94 Revision of anastomosis of biliary tract

51.95 Removal of prosthetic device from bile duct

Excludes: nonoperative removal (97.55)

51.96 Percutaneous extraction of common duct stones

➡ **AHA Coding Clinic:** 4Q, '88, 7

51.98 Other percutaneous procedures on biliary tract
Percutaneous biliary endoscopy via existing T-tube or other tract for:
- dilation of biliary duct stricture
- exploration (postoperative)
- removal of stone(s) except common duct stone

Percutaneous transhepatic biliary drainage

Excludes: percutaneous aspiration of gallbladder (51.01)
percutaneous biopsy and/or collection of specimen by brushing or washing (51.12)
percutaneous removal of common duct stone(s) (51.96)

➡ **AHA Coding Clinic:** 1Q, '97, 14; 3Q, '89, 18; N-D, '87, 1

51.99 Other
Insertion or replacement of biliary tract prosthesis

Excludes: biopsy of gallbladder (51.12-51.13)
irrigation of cholecystostomy and other biliary tube (96.41)
lysis of peritoneal adhesions (54.5)
nonoperative removal of:
cholecystostomy tube (97.54)
tube from biliary tract or liver (97.55)

52 Operations on pancreas

Includes: operations on pancreatic duct

52.0 Pancreatotomy

52.01 Drainage of pancreatic cyst by catheter

52.09 Other pancreatotomy
Pancreatolithotomy

Excludes: drainage by anastomosis (52.4, 52.96)
incision of pancreatic sphincter (51.82)
marsupialization of cyst (52.3)

52.1 Diagnostic procedures on pancreas

[22] **52.11 Closed [aspiration] [needle] [percutaneous] biopsy of pancreas**

[21] **52.12 Open biopsy of pancreas**

52.13 Endoscopic retrograde pancreatography [ERP]

Excludes: *endoscopic retrograde:*
cholangiography [ERC] (51.11)
cholangiopancreatography [ERCP] (51.10)
that for procedures classifiable to 51.14-51.15, 51.64, 51.84-51.88, 52.14, 52.21, 52.92-52.94, 52.97-52.98

52.14 Closed [endoscopic] biopsy of pancreatic duct

Closed biopsy of pancreatic duct by procedures classifiable to 51.10-51.11, 52.13

52.19 Other diagnostic procedures on pancreas

Excludes: *contrast pancreatogram (87.66)*
endoscopic retrograde pancreatography [ERP] (52.13)
microscopic examination of specimen from pancreas (91.01-91.09)

52.2 Local excision or destruction of pancreas and pancreatic duct

Excludes: *biopsy of pancreas (52.11-52.12, 52.14)*
pancreatic fistulectomy (52.95)

52.21 Endoscopic excision or destruction of lesion or tissue of pancreatic duct

Excision or destruction of lesion or tissue of pancreatic duct by procedures classifiable to 51.10-51.11, 52.13

52.22 Other excision or destruction of lesion or tissue of pancreas or pancreatic duct

52.3 Marsupialization of pancreatic cyst

Excludes: *drainage of cyst by catheter (52.01)*

52.4 Internal drainage of pancreatic cyst

Pancreaticocystoduodenostomy
Pancreaticocystogastrostomy
Pancreaticocystojejunostomy

52.5 Partial pancreatectomy

Excludes: *pancreatic fistulectomy (52.95)*

52.51 Proximal pancreatectomy

Excision of head of pancreas (with part of body)
Proximal pancreatectomy with synchronous duodenectomy

52.52 Distal pancreatectomy

Excision of tail of pancreas (with part of body)

52.53 Radical subtotal pancreatectomy

52.59 Other partial pancreatectomy

52.6 Total pancreatectomy

Pancreatectomy with synchronous duodenectomy

➡ **AHA Coding Clinic:** 4Q, '96, 71

52.7 Radical pancreaticoduodenectomy

One-stage pancreaticoduodenal resection with choledochojejunal anastomosis, pancreaticojejunal anastomosis, and gastrojejunostomy
Two-stage pancreaticoduodenal resection (first stage) (second stage)
Radical resection of the pancreas
Whipple procedure

Excludes: *radical subtotal pancreatectomy (52.53)*

52.8 Transplant of pancreas

52.80 Pancreatic transplant, not otherwise specified

52.81 Reimplantation of pancreatic tissue

52.82 Homotransplant of pancreas

52.83 Heterotransplant of pancreas

52.84 Autotransplantation of cells of islets of Langerhans

Homotransplantation of islet cells of pancreas

➡ **AHA Coding Clinic:** 4Q, '96, 70, 71

52.85 Allotransplantation of cells of islets of Langerhans

Heterotransplantation of islet cells of pancreas

➡ **AHA Coding Clinic:** 4Q, '96, 70, 71

52.86 Transplantation of cells of islets of Langerhans, not otherwise specified

➡ **AHA Coding Clinic:** 4Q, '96, 70

52.9 Other operations on pancreas

52.92 Cannulation of pancreatic duct

Excludes: *that by endoscopic approach (52.93)*

52.93 Endoscopic insertion of stent (tube) into pancreatic duct

Insertion of cannula or stent into pancreatic duct by procedures classifiable to 51.10-51.11, 52.13

Excludes: *endoscopic insertion of nasopancreatic drainage tube (52.97)*
replacement of stent (tube) (97.05)

➡ **AHA Coding Clinic:** 2Q, '97, 7

52.94 Endoscopic removal of stone(s) from pancreatic duct

Removal of stone(s) from pancreatic duct by procedures classifiable to 51.10-51.11, 52.13

52.95 Other repair of pancreas

Fistulectomy } of pancreas
Simple suture } of pancreas

[21] Open biopsy
[22] Closed biopsy

52.96 **Anastomosis of pancreas**

Anastomosis of pancreas (duct) to:
intestine
jejunum
stomach

Excludes: *anastomosis to:*
bile duct (51.39)
gallbladder (51.33)

52.97 **Endoscopic insertion of nasopancreatic drainage tube**

Insertion of nasopancreatic drainage tube by procedures classifiable to 51.10-51.11, 52.13

Excludes: *drainage of pancreatic cyst by catheter (52.01)*
replacement of stent (tube) (97.05)

52.98 **Endoscopic dilation of pancreatic duct**

Dilation of Wirsung's duct by procedures classifiable to 51.10-51.11, 52.13

52.99 **Other**

Dilation of pancreatic [Wirsung's] duct } by open approach
Repair of pancreatic [Wirsung's] duct } by open approach

Excludes: *irrigation of pancreatic tube (96.42)*
removal of pancreatic tube (97.56)

53 Repair of Hernia

Includes: herniopplasty
herniorrhaphy
herniotomy

Excludes: *manual reduction of hernia (96.27)*

➡ **AHA Coding Clinic:** 3Q, '94, 8

53.0 Unilateral repair of inguinal hernia

53.00 **Unilateral repair of inguinal hernia, not otherwise specified**

Inguinal herniorrhaphy NOS

53.01 **Repair of direct inguinal hernia**

➡ **AHA Coding Clinic:** 4Q, '96, 66

53.02 **Repair of indirect inguinal hernia**

53.03 **Repair of direct inguinal hernia with graft or prosthesis**

53.04 **Repair of indirect inguinal hernia with graft or prosthesis**

53.05 **Repair of inguinal hernia with graft or prosthesis, not otherwise specified**

53.1 Bilateral repair of inguinal hernia

53.10 **Bilateral repair of inguinal hernia, not otherwise specified**

53.11 **Bilateral repair of direct inguinal hernia**

53.12 **Bilateral repair of indirect inguinal hernia**

53.13 **Bilateral repair of inguinal hernia, one direct and one indirect**

53.14 **Bilateral repair of direct inguinal hernia with graft or prosthesis**

53.15 **Bilateral repair of indirect inguinal hernia with graft or prosthesis**

53.16 **Bilateral repair of inguinal hernia, one direct and one indirect, with graft or prosthesis**

53.17 **Bilateral inguinal hernia repair with graft or prosthesis, not otherwise specified**

53.2 Unilateral repair of femoral hernia

53.21 **Unilateral repair of femoral hernia with graft or prosthesis**

53.29 **Other unilateral femoral herniorrhaphy**

53.3 Bilateral repair of femoral hernia

53.31 **Bilateral repair of femoral hernia with graft or prosthesis**

53.39 **Other bilateral femoral herniorrhaphy**

53.4 Repair of umbilical hernia

Excludes: *repair of gastroschisis (54.71)*

53.41 **Repair of umbilical hernia with prosthesis**

53.49 **Other umbilical herniorrhaphy**

53.5 Repair of other hernia of anterior abdominal wall (without graft or prosthesis)

53.51 **Incisional hernia repair**

53.59 **Repair of other hernia of anterior abdominal wall**

Repair of hernia:
epigastric
hypogastric
spigelian
ventral

➡ **AHA Coding Clinic:** 3Q, '96, 15

53.6 Repair of other hernia of anterior abdominal wall with graft or prosthesis

53.61 **Incisional hernia repair with prosthesis**

53.69 **Repair of other hernia of anterior abdominal wall with prosthesis**

53.7 Repair of diaphragmatic hernia, abdominal approach

53.8 Repair of diaphragmatic hernia, thoracic approach

53.80 Repair of diaphragmatic hernia with thoracic approach, not otherwise specified
Thoracoabdominal repair of diaphragmatic hernia

53.81 Plication of the diaphragm

53.82 Repair of parasternal hernia

53.9 Other hernia repair
Repair of hernia:
ischiatic
ischiorectal
lumbar
obturator
Repair of hernia:
omental
retroperitoneal
sciatic

Excludes: *relief of strangulated hernia with exteriorization of intestine (46.01, 46.03)*
repair of pericolostomy hernia (46.42)
repair of vaginal enterocele (70.92)

54 Other operations on abdominal region

Includes: operations on:
epigastric region
flank
groin region
hypochondrium
inguinal region
loin region
male pelvic cavity
mesentery
omentum
peritoneum
retroperitoneal
tissue space

Excludes: *female pelvic cavity (69.01-70.92)*
hernia repair (53.00-53.9)
obliteration of cul-de-sac (70.92)
retroperitoneal tissue dissection (59.00-59.09)
skin and subcutaneous tissue of abdominal wall (86.01-86.99)

54.0 Incision of abdominal wall
Drainage of:
abdominal wall
extraperitoneal abscess
retroperitoneal abscess

Excludes: *incision of peritoneum (54.95) laparotomy (54.11-54.19)*

➡ **AHA Coding Clinic:** 1Q, '97, 11; N-D, '87, 12

54.1 Laparotomy

54.11 Exploratory laparotomy

Excludes: *exploration incidental to intra-abdominal surgery — omit code*

➡ **AHA Coding Clinic:** 3Q, '89, 14; 4Q, '88, 12

54.12 Reopening of recent laparotomy site
Reopening of recent laparotomy site for:
control of hemorrhage
exploration
incision of hematoma

54.19 Other laparotomy
Drainage of intraperitoneal abscess or hematoma

Excludes: *culdocentesis (70.0)*
drainage of appendiceal abscess (47.2)
exploration incidental to intra-abdominal surgery — omit code
Ladd operation (54.95)
removal of foreign body (54.92)

54.2 Diagnostic procedures of abdominal region

54.21 Laparoscopy
Peritoneoscopy

Excludes: *laparoscopic cholecystectomy (51.23)*
that incidental to destruction of fallopian tubes (66.21-66.29)

54.22 Biopsy of abdominal wall or umbilicus

54.23 Biopsy of peritoneum
Biopsy of:
mesentery
omentum
peritoneal implant

Excludes: *closed biopsy of:*
omentum (54.24)
peritoneum (54.24)

54.24 Closed [percutaneous] [needle] biopsy of intra-abdominal mass
Closed biopsy of:
omentum
peritoneum

Excludes: *that of:*
fallopian tube (66.11)
ovary (65.11)
peritoneum (54.23)
uterine ligaments (68.15)
uterus (68.16)

➡ **AHA Coding Clinic:** 4Q, '97, 57

54.25 Peritoneal lavage
Diagnostic peritoneal lavage

Excludes: *peritoneal dialysis (54.98)*

➡ **AHA Coding Clinic:** 4Q, '93, 28

54.29 Other diagnostic procedures on abdominal region

Excludes: *abdominal lymphangiogram (88.04)*
abdominal x-ray NEC (88.19)
angiocardiography of venae cavae (88.51)
C.A.T. scan of abdomen (88.01)
contrast x-ray of abdominal cavity (88.11-88.15)
intra-abdominal arteriography NEC (88.47)
microscopic examination of peritoneal and retroperitoneal specimen (91.11-91.19)
phlebography of:
intra-abdominal vessels NEC (88.65)
portal venous system (88.64)
sinogram of abdominal wall (88.03)
soft tissue x-ray of abdominal wall NEC (88.09)
tomography of abdomen NEC (88.02)
ultrasonography of abdomen and retroperitoneum (88.76)

54.3 Excision or destruction of lesion or tissue of abdominal wall or umbilicus

Debridement of abdominal wall
Omphalectomy

Excludes: *biopsy of abdominal wall or umbilicus (54.22)*
size reduction operation (86.83)
that of skin of abdominal wall (86.22, 86.26, 86.3)

➡ **AHA Coding Clinic:** 1Q, '89, 11

54.4 Excision or destruction of peritoneal tissue

Excision of:
appendices epiploicae
falciform ligament
gastrocolic ligament
lesion of:
mesentery
omentum
peritoneum
presacral lesion NOS
retroperitoneal lesion NOS

Excludes: *biopsy of peritoneum (54.23)*
endometrectomy of cul-de-sac (70.32)

54.5 Lysis of peritoneal adhesions

Freeing of adhesions of:
biliary tract
intestines
liver
pelvic peritoneum
peritoneum
spleen
uterus

Excludes: *lysis of adhesions of:*
bladder (59.11)
fallopian tube and ovary (65.81, 65.89)
kidney (59.02)
ureter (59.01-59.02)

➡ **AHA Coding Clinic:** 3Q, '94, 8; 4Q, '90, 18

54.51 Laparoscopic lysis of peritoneal adhesions

➡ **AHA Coding Clinic:** 4Q, '96, 65

54.59 Other lysis of peritoneal adhesions

➡ **AHA Coding Clinic:** 4Q, '96, 66

54.6 Suture of abdominal wall and peritoneum

54.61 Reclosure of postoperative disruption of abdominal wall

54.62 Delayed closure of granulating abdominal wound

Tertiary subcutaneous wound closure

54.63 Other suture of abdominal wall

Suture of laceration of abdominal wall

Excludes: *closure of operative wound — omit code*

54.64 Suture of peritoneum

Secondary suture of peritoneum

Excludes: *closure of operative wound — omit code*

54.7 Other repair of abdominal wall and peritoneum

54.71 Repair of gastroschisis

54.72 Other repair of abdominal wall

54.73 Other repair of peritoneum

Suture of gastrocolic ligament

54.74 Other repair of omentum

Epiplorrhaphy
Graft of omentum
Omentopexy
Reduction of torsion of omentum

Excludes: *cardio-omentopexy (36.39)*

➡ **AHA Coding Clinic:** J-F, '87, 11

54.75 Other repair of mesentery

Mesenteric plication
Mesenteropexy

54.9 Other operations of abdominal region

Excludes: *removal of ectopic pregnancy (74.3)*

54.91 Percutaneous abdominal drainage

Paracentesis

Excludes: *creation of cutaneoperitoneal fistula (54.93)*

➡ **AHA Coding Clinic:** 1Q, '92, 14; 2Q, '90, 25

54.92 Removal of foreign body from peritoneal cavity

➡ **AHA Coding Clinic:** 1Q, '89, 11

54.93 Creation of cutaneoperitoneal fistula

➡ **AHA Coding Clinic:** 2Q, '95, 10; N-D, '84, 6

54.94 Creation of peritoneovascular shunt

Peritoneovenous shunt

➡ **AHA Coding Clinic:** 1Q, '94, 7; 1Q, '88, 9; S-O, '85, 6

54.95 Incision of peritoneum

Ladd operation
Revision of distal catheter of ventricular shunt
Revision of ventriculoperitoneal shunt at peritoneal site

Excludes: *that incidental to laparotomy (54.11-54.19)*

➡ **AHA Coding Clinic:** 4Q, '95, 65

54.96 Injection of air into peritoneal cavity

Pneumoperitoneum

Excludes: *that for:*
collapse of lung (33.33)
radiography (88.12-88.13, 88.15)

54.97 Injection of locally-acting therapeutic substance into peritoneal cavity

Excludes: *peritoneal dialysis (54.98)*

54.98 Peritoneal dialysis

Excludes: *peritoneal lavage (diagnostic) (54.25)*

➡ **AHA Coding Clinic:** N-D, '84, 6

54.99 Other

Excludes: *removal of:*
abdominal wall sutures (97.83)
peritoneal drainage device (97.82)
retroperitoneal drainage device (97.81)

10. OPERATIONS ON THE URINARY SYSTEM (55-59)

55 Operations on kidney

Includes: operations on renal pelvis

Excludes: *perirenal tissue (59.00-59.09, 59.21-59.29, 59.91-59.92)*

55.0 Nephrotomy and nephrostomy

Excludes: *drainage by:*
anastomosis (55.86)
aspiration (55.92)
incision of kidney pelvis (55.11-55.12)

55.01 Nephrotomy
Evacuation of renal cyst
Exploration of kidney
Nephrolithotomy

55.02 Nephrostomy
➡ **AHA Coding Clinic:** 2Q, '97, 4

55.03 Percutaneous nephrostomy without fragmentation
Nephrostolithotomy, percutaneous (nephroscopic)
Percutaneous removal of kidney stone(s) by:
basket extraction
forceps extraction (nephroscopic)
Pyelostolithotomy, percutaneous (nephroscopic)

Excludes: *percutaneous removal by fragmentation (55.04)*
repeat nephroscopic removal during current episode (55.92)

➡ **AHA Coding Clinic:** 2Q, '96, 5

55.04 Percutaneous nephrostomy with fragmentation
Percutaneous nephrostomy with disruption of kidney stone by ultrasonic energy and extraction (suction) through endoscope
With placement of catheter down ureter
With fluoroscopic guidance

Excludes: *repeat fragmentation during current episode (59.95)*

➡ **AHA Coding Clinic:** 1Q, '89, 1; S-O, '86, 11

55.1 Pyelotomy and pyelostomy

Excludes: *drainage by anastomosis (55.86)*
percutaneous pyelostolithotomy (55.03)
removal of calculus without incision (56.0)

55.11 Pyelotomy
Exploration of renal pelvis
Pyelolithotomy

55.12 Pyelostomy
Insertion of drainage tube into renal pelvis

55.2 Diagnostic procedures on kidney

55.21 Nephroscopy

55.22 Pyeloscopy

[22] **55.23 Closed [percutaneous] [needle] biopsy of kidney**
Endoscopic biopsy via existing nephrostomy, nephrotomy, pyelostomy, or pyelotomy

[21] **55.24 Open biopsy of kidney**

55.29 Other diagnostic procedures on kidney

Excludes: *microscopic examination of specimen from kidney (91.21-91.29)*
pyelogram:
intravenous (87.73)
percutaneous (87.75)
retrograde (87.74)
radioisotope scan (92.03)
renal arteriography (88.45)
tomography:
C.A.T scan (87.71)
other (87.72)

55.3 Local excision or destruction of lesion or tissue of kidney

55.31 Marsupialization of kidney lesion

55.39 Other local destruction or excision of renal lesion or tissue
Obliteration of calyceal diverticulum

Excludes: *biopsy of kidney (55.23-55.24)*
partial nephrectomy (55.4)
percutaneous aspiration of kidney (55.92)
wedge resection of kidney (55.4)

55.4 Partial nephrectomy
Calycectomy
Wedge resection of kidney

Code also any synchronous resection of ureter (56.40-56.42)

55.5 Complete nephrectomy

Code also any synchronous excision of:
bladder segment (57.6)
lymph nodes (40.3, 40.52-40.59)

55.51 Nephroureterectomy
Nephroureterectomy with bladder cuff
Total nephrectomy (unilateral)

Excludes: *removal of transplanted kidney (55.53)*

[21] Open biopsy
[22] Closed biopsy

55.52 **Nephrectomy of remaining kidney**
Removal of solitary kidney

Excludes: *removal of transplanted kidney (55.53)*

55.53 **Removal of transplanted or rejected kidney**

55.54 **Bilateral nephrectomy**

Excludes: *complete nephrectomy NOS (55.51)*

55.6 **Transplant of kidney**

55.61 **Renal autotransplantation**

55.69 **Other kidney transplantation**
➡ **AHA Coding Clinic:** 4Q, '96, 71

55.7 **Nephropexy**
Fixation or suspension of movable [floating] kidney

55.8 **Other repair of kidney**

55.81 **Suture of laceration of kidney**

55.82 **Closure of nephrostomy and pyelostomy**

55.83 **Closure of other fistula of kidney**

55.84 **Reduction of torsion of renal pedicle**
➡ **Def:** Restoration of a twisted renal pedicle into its normal position.

55.85 **Symphysiotomy for horseshoe kidney**

55.86 **Anastomosis of kidney**
Nephropyeloureterostomy
Pyeloureterovesical anastomosis
Ureterocalyceal anastomosis

Excludes: *nephrocystanastomosis NOS (56.73)*

55.87 **Correction of ureteropelvic junction**

55.89 **Other**

55.9 **Other operations on kidney**

Excludes: *lysis of perirenal adhesions (59.02)*

55.91 **Decapsulation of kidney**
Capsulectomy } of kidney
Decortication } of kidney

55.92 **Percutaneous aspiration of kidney (pelvis)**
Aspiration of renal cyst
Renipuncture

Excludes: *percutaneous biopsy of kidney (55.23)*

➡ **AHA Coding Clinic:** N-D, '84, 20

55.93 **Replacement of nephrostomy tube**

55.94 **Replacement of pyelostomy tube**

55.95 **Local perfusion of kidney**

55.96 **Other injection of therapeutic substance into kidney**
Injection into renal cyst

55.97 **Implantation or replacement of mechanical kidney**

55.98 **Removal of mechanical kidney**

55.99 **Other**

Excludes: *removal of pyelostomy or nephrostomy tube (97.61)*

56 Operations on ureter

56.0 **Transurethral removal of obstruction from ureter and renal pelvis**
Removal of:
blood clot } from ureter or renal pelvis without incision
calculus } from ureter or renal pelvis without incision
foreign body } from ureter or renal pelvis without incision

Excludes: *manipulation without removal of obstruction (59.8)*
that by incision (55.11,56.2)
transurethral insertion of ureteral stent for passage of calculus (59.8)

➡ **AHA Coding Clinic:** 1Q, '89, 1; S-O, '86, 12

56.1 **Ureteral meatotomy**

56.2 **Ureterotomy**
Incision of ureter for:
drainage
exploration
removal of calculus

Excludes: *cutting of ureterovesical orifice (56.1)*
removal of calculus without incision (56.0)
transurethral insertion of ureteral stent for passage of calculus (59.8)
urinary diversion (56.51-56.79)

➡ **AHA Coding Clinic:** S-O, '86, 10

56.3 **Diagnostic procedures on ureter**

56.31 **Ureteroscopy**

[22] **56.32** **Closed percutaneous biopsy of ureter**

Excludes: *endoscopic biopsy of ureter (56.33)*

[22] Closed biopsy

56.33 Closed endoscopic biopsy of ureter
Cystourethroscopy with ureteral biopsy
Transurethral biopsy of ureter
Ureteral endoscopy with biopsy through ureterotomy
Ureteroscopy with biopsy

Excludes: *percutaneous biopsy of ureter (56.32)*

[21] **55.34 Open biopsy of ureter**

56.35 Endoscopy (cystoscopy) (looposcopy) of ileal conduit

56.39 Other diagnostic procedures on ureter

Excludes: *microscopic examination of specimen from ureter (91.21-91.29)*

56.4 Ureterectomy

Code also anastomosis other than end-to-end (56.51-56.79)

Excludes: *fistulectomy (56.84)*
nephroureterectomy (55.51-55.54)

56.40 Ureterectomy, not otherwise specified

56.41 Partial ureterotomy
Excision of lesion of ureter
Shortening of ureter with reimplantation

Excludes: *biopsy of ureter (56.32-56.34)*

56.42 Total ureterectomy

56.5 Cutaneous uretero-ileostomy

56.51 Formation of cutaneous uretero-ileostomy
Construction of ileal conduit
External ureteral ileostomy
Formation of open ileal bladder
Ileal loop operation
Ileoureterostomy (Bricker's) (ileal bladder)
Kock pouch for urinary diversion
Transplantation of ureter into ileum with external diversion

Excludes: *closed ileal bladder (57.87)*
replacement of ureteral defect by ileal segment (56.89)

56.52 Revision of cutaneous uretero-ileostomy
➡ **AHA Coding Clinic:** 3Q, '96, 15; 4Q, '88, 7

56.6 Other external urinary diversion

56.61 Formation of other cutaneous ureterostomy
Anastomosis of ureter to skin
Ureterostomy NOS

56.62 Revision of other cutaneous ureterostomy
Revision of ureterostomy stoma

Excludes: *nonoperative removal of ureterostomy tube (97.62)*

56.7 Other anastomosis or bypass of ureter

Excludes: *ureteropyelostomy (55.86)*

56.71 Urinary diversion to intestine
Anastomosis of ureter to intestine
Internal urinary diversion NOS

Code also any synchronous colostomy (46.10-46.13)

Excludes: *external ureteral ileostomy (56.51)*

56.72 Revision of ureterointestinal anastomosis

Excludes: *revision of external ureteral ileostomy (56.52)*

56.73 Nephrocystanastomosis, not otherwise specified

56.74 Ureteroneocystostomy
Replacement of ureter with bladder flap
Ureterovesical anastomosis

56.75 Transureteroureterostomy

Excludes: *ureteroureterostomy associated with partial resection (56.41)*

56.79 Other

56.8 Repair of ureter

56.81 Lysis of intraluminal adhesions of ureter

Excludes: *lysis of periureteral adhesions (59.01-59.02)*
ureterolysis (59.01-59.02)

56.82 Suture of laceration of ureter

56.83 Closure of ureterostomy

56.84 Closure of other fistula of ureter

56.85 Ureteropexy

56.86 Removal of ligature from ureter

[21] Open biopsy

56.89 Other repair of ureter
Graft of ureter
Replacement of ureter with ileal segment implanted into bladder
Ureteroplication

56.9 Other operations on ureter

56.91 Dilation of ureteral meatus

56.92 Implantation of electronic ureteral stimulator

56.93 Replacement of electronic ureteral stimulator

56.94 Removal of electronic ureteral stimulator

Excludes: *that with synchronous replacement (56.93)*

56.95 Ligation of ureter

56.99 Other

Excludes: *removal of ureterostomy tube and ureteral catheter (97.62)*
ureteral catheterization (59.8)

57 Operations on urinary bladder

Excludes: *perivesical tissue (59.11-59.29, 59.91-59.92)*
ureterovesical orifice (56.0-56.99)

57.0 Transurethral clearance of bladder
Drainage of bladder without incision
Removal of:
blood clots, calculus, foreign body } from bladder without incision

Excludes: *that by incision (57.19)*

➡ **AHA Coding Clinic:** S-O, '86, 11

57.1 Cystotomy and cystostomy

Excludes: *cystotomy and cystostomy as operative approach — omit code*

57.11 Percutaneous aspiration of bladder

57.12 Lysis of intraluminal adhesions with incision into bladder

Excludes: *transurethral lysis of intraluminal adhesions (57.41)*

57.17 Percutaneous cystostomy
Closed cystostomy
Percutaneous suprapubic cystostomy

Excludes: *removal of cystostomy tube (97.63)*
replacement of cystostomy tube (59.94)

57.18 Other suprapubic cystostomy

Excludes: *percutaneous cystostomy (57.17)*
removal of cystostomy tube (97.63)
replacement of cystostomy tube (59.94)

57.19 Other cystotomy
Cystolithotomy

Excludes: *percutaneous cystostomy (57.17)*
suprapubic cystostomy (57.18)

➡ **AHA Coding Clinic:** 4Q, '95, 73; S-O, '86, 11

57.2 Vesicostomy

Excludes: *percutaneous cystostomy (57.17)*
suprapubic cystostomy (57.18)

57.21 Vesicostomy
Creation of permanent opening from bladder to skin using a bladder flap

57.22 Revision or closure of vesicostomy

Excludes: *closure of cystostomy (57.82)*

57.3 Diagnostic procedures on bladder

57.31 Cystoscopy through artificial stoma

57.32 Other cystoscopy
Transurethral cystoscopy

Excludes: *cystourethroscopy with ureteral biopsy (56.33)*
retrograde pyelogram (87.74)
that for control of hemorrhage (postoperative):
bladder (57.93)
prostate (60.94)

[22] **57.33 Closed [transurethral] biopsy of bladder**

[21] **57.34 Open biopsy of bladder**

57.39 Other diagnostic procedures on bladder

Excludes: *cystogram NEC (87.77)*
microscopic examination of specimen from bladder (91.31-91.39)
retrograde cystourethrogram (87.76)

[21] Open biopsy
[22] Closed biopsy

57.4 Transurethral excision or destruction of bladder tissue

57.41 Transurethral lysis of intraluminal adhesions

57.49 Other transurethral excision or destruction of lesion or tissue of bladder

Endoscopic resection of bladder lesion

Excludes: *transurethral biopsy of bladder (57.33)*
transurethral fistulectomy (57.83-57.84)

57.5 Other excision or destruction of bladder tissue

Excludes: *that with transurethral approach (57.41-57.49)*

57.51 Excision of urachus

Excision of urachal sinus of bladder

Excludes: *excision of urachal cyst of abdominal wall (54.3)*

57.59 Open excision or destruction of other lesion or tissue of bladder

Endometrectomy of bladder
Suprapubic excision of bladder lesion

Excludes: *biopsy of bladder (57.33-57.34)*
fistulectomy of bladder (57.83-57.84)

57.6 Partial cystectomy

Excision of bladder dome
Trigonectomy
Wedge resection of bladder

57.7 Total cystectomy

Includes: total cystectomy with urethrectomy

57.71 Radical cystectomy

Pelvic exenteration in male
Removal of bladder, prostate, seminal vesicles and fat
Removal of bladder, urethra, and fat in a female

Code also any:
lymph node dissection (40.3, 40.5)
urinary diversion (56.51-56.79)

Excludes: *that as part of pelvic exenteration in female (68.8)*

57.79 Other total cystectomy

57.8 Other repair of urinary bladder

Excludes: *repair of:*
current obstetric laceration (75.61)
cystocele (70.50-70.51)
that for stress incontinence (59.3-59.79)

57.81 Suture of laceration of bladder

57.82 Closure of cystostomy

57.83 Repair of fistula involving bladder and intestine

Rectovesicovaginal } fistulectomy
Vesicosigmoidovaginal }

57.84 Repair of other fistula of bladder

Cervicovesical }
Urethroperineovesical } fistulectomy
Uterovesical }
Vaginovesical }

Excludes: *vesicoureterovaginal fistulectomy (56.84)*

57.85 Cystourethroplasty and plastic repair of bladder neck

Plication of sphincter of urinary bladder
V-Y plasty of bladder neck

57.86 Repair of bladder exstrophy

57.87 Reconstruction of urinary bladder

Anastomosis of bladder with isolated segment of ileum
Augmentation of bladder
Replacement of bladder with ileum or sigmoid [closed ileal bladder]

Code also resection of intestine (45.50-45.52)

57.88 Other anastomosis of bladder

Anastomosis of bladder to intestine NOS
Cystocolic anastomosis

Excludes: *formation of closed ileal bladder (57.87)*

57.89 Other repair of bladder

Bladder suspension, not elsewhere classified
Cystopexy NOS
Repair of old obstetric laceration of bladder

Excludes: *repair of current obstetric laceration (75.61)*

57.9 Other operations on bladder

57.91 Sphincterotomy of bladder

Division of bladder neck

➡ **AHA Coding Clinic:** 2Q, '90, 26

57.92 Dilation of bladder neck

57.93 Control of (postoperative) hemorrhage of bladder

57.94 Insertion of indwelling urinary catheter

57.95 Replacement of indwelling urinary catheter

57.96 Implantation of electronic bladder stimulator

57.97 Replacement of electronic bladder stimulator

57.98 Removal of electronic bladder stimulator

Excludes: *that with synchronous replacement (57.97)*

57.99 Other

Excludes: *irrigation of:*
cystostomy (96.47)
other indwelling urinary catheter (96.48)
lysis of external adhesions (59.11)
removal of:
cystostomy tube (97.63)
other urinary drainage device (97.64)
therapeutic distention of bladder (96.25)

58 Operations on urethra

Includes: operations on:
bulbourethral gland [Cowper's gland]
periurethral tissue

58.0 Urethrotomy

Excision of urethral septum
Formation of urethrovaginal fistula
Perineal urethrostomy
Removal of calculus from urethra by incision

Excludes: *drainage of bulbourethral gland or periurethral tissue (58.91)*
internal urethral meatotomy (58.5)
removal of urethral calculus without incision (58.6)

58.1 Urethral meatotomy

Excludes: *internal urethral meatotomy (58.5)*

58.2 Diagnostic procedures on urethra

58.21 Perineal urethroscopy

58.22 Other urethroscopy

58.23 Biopsy of urethra

58.24 Biopsy of periurethral tissue

58.29 Other diagnostic procedures on urethra and periurethral tissue

Excludes: *microscopic examination of specimen from urethra (91.31-91.39)*
retrograde cystourethrogram (87.76)
urethral pressure profile (89.25)
urethral sphincter electromyogram (89.23)

58.3 Excision or destruction of lesion or tissue of urethra

Excludes: *biopsy of urethra (58.23)*
excision of bulbourethral gland (58.92)
fistulectomy (58.43)
urethrectomy as part of:
complete cystectomy (57.79)
pelvic evisceration (68.8)
radical cystectomy (57.71)

58.31 Endoscopic excision or destruction of lesion or tissue of urethra

Fulguration of urethral lesion

58.39 Other local excision or destruction of lesion or tissue of urethra

Excision of:
congenital valve, lesion, stricture } of urethra
Urethrectomy

Excludes: *that by endoscopic appoach (58.31)*

58.4 Repair of urethra

Excludes: *repair of current obstetric laceration (75.61)*

58.41 Suture of laceration of urethra

58.42 Closure of urethrostomy

58.43 Closure of other fistula of urethra

Excludes: *repair of urethroperineovesical fistula (57.84)*

58.44 Reanastomosis of urethra

Anastomosis of urethra

58.45 Repair of hypospadias or epispadias

➡ **AHA Coding Clinic:** 3Q, '97, 6; 4Q, '96, 35

58.46 Other reconstruction of urethra

Urethral construction

58.47 Urethral meatoplasty

58.49 Other repair of urethra

Benenenti rotation of bulbous urethra
Repair of old obstetric laceration of urethra
Urethral plication

Excludes: *repair of:*
current obstetric laceration (75.61)
urethrocele (70.50-70.51)

58.5 Release of urethral stricture
Cutting of urethral sphincter
Internal urethral meatotomy
Urethrolysis
➡ **AHA Coding Clinic:** 1Q, '97, 13

58.6 Dilation of urethra
Dilation of urethrovesical junction
Passage of sounds through urethra
Removal of calculus from urethra without incision

Excludes: *urethral calibration (89.29)*
➡ **AHA Coding Clinic:** 1Q, '97, 13

58.9 Other operations on urethra and periurethral tissue

58.91 Incision of periurethral tissue

58.92 Excision of periurethral tissue

Excludes: *biopsy of periurethral tissue (58.24)*
lysis of periurethral adhesions (59.11-59.12)

58.93 Implantation of artificial urinary sphincter [AUS]
Placement of inflatable:
urethral sphincter
bladder sphincter
Removal with replacement of sphincter device [AUS]
With pump and/or reservoir

58.99 Other
Repair of inflatable sphincter pump and/or reservoir
Surgical correction of hydraulic pressure of inflatable sphincter device
Removal of inflatable urinary sphincter without replacement

Excludes: *removal of:*
intraluminal foreign body from urethra without incision (98.19)
urethral stent (97.65)

59 Other operations on urinary tract

59.0 Dissection of retroperitoneal tissue

59.00 Retroperitoneal dissection, not otherwise specified

59.02 Other lysis of perirenal or periureteral adhesions

Excludes: *that by laparoscope (59.03)*

59.03 Laparoscopic lysis of perirenal or periureteral adhesions

59.09 Other incision of perirenal or periureteral tissue
Exploration of perinephric area
Incision of perirenal abscess

59.1 Incision of perivesical tissue

59.11 Other lysis of perivesical adhesions

59.12 Laparoscopic lysis of perivesical adhesions

59.19 Other incision of perivesical tissue
Exploration of perivesical tissue
Incision of hematoma of space of Retzius
Retropubic exploration

59.2 Diagnostic procedures on perirenal and perivesical tissue

59.21 Biopsy of perirenal or perivesical tissue

59.29 Other diagnostic procedures on perirenal tissue, perivesical tissue, and retroperitoneum

Excludes: *microscopic examination of specimen from:*
perirenal tissue (91.21-91.29)
perivesical tissue (91.31-91.39)
retroperitoneum NEC (91.11-91.19)
retroperitoneal x-ray (88.14-88.16)

59.3 Plication of urethrovesical junction
Kelly-Kennedy operation on urethra
Kelly-Stoeckel urethral plication

59.4 Suprapubic sling operation
Goebel-Frangenheim-Stoeckel urethrovesical suspension
Millin-Read urethrovesical suspension
Oxford operation for urinary incontinence
Urethrocystopexy by suprapubic suspension

59.5 Retropubic urethral suspension
Burch procedure
Marshall-Marchetti-Krantz operation
Suture of periurethral tissue to symphysis pubis
Urethral suspension NOS
➡ **AHA Coding Clinic:** 1Q, '97, 11

59.6 Paraurethral suspension
Pereyra paraurethral suspension
Periurethral suspension

59.7 Other repair of urinary stress incontinence

59.71 Levator muscle operation for urethrovesical suspension

Cystourethropexy with levator muscle sling
Gracilis muscle transplant for urethrovesical suspension
Pubococcygeal sling

59.72 Injection of implant into urethra and/or bladder neck

Collagen implant
Endoscopic injection of implant
Fat implant
Polytef implant

➡ **AHA Coding Clinic:** 4Q, '95, 72, 73

59.79 Other

Anterior urethropexy
Augmentation urethroplasty
Repair of stress incontinence NOS
Tudor "rabbit ear" urethropexy

59.8 Ureteral catheterization

Drainage of kidney by catheter
Insertion of ureteral stent
Ureterovesical orifice dilation

Code also any ureterotomy (56.2)

Excludes: *that for:*
retrograde pyelogram (87.74)
transurethral removal of calculus or clot from ureter and renal pelvis (56.0)

➡ **AHA Coding Clinic:** 1Q, '89, 1; S-O, '86, 10

59.9 Other operations on urinary system

Excludes: *nonoperative removal of therapeutic device (97.61-97.69)*

59.91 Excision of perirenal or perivesical tissue

Excludes: *biopsy of perirenal or perivesical tissue (59.21)*

59.92 Other operations on perirenal or perivesical tissue

59.93 Replacement of ureterostomy tube

Change of ureterostomy tube
Reinsertion of ureterostomy tube

Excludes: *nonoperative removal of ureterostomy tube (97.62)*

59.94 Replacement of cystostomy tube

Excludes: *nonoperative removal of cystostomy tube (97.63)*

59.95 Ultrasonic fragmentation of urinary stones

Shattered urinary stones

Excludes: *percutaneous nephrostomy with fragmentation (55.04)*
shockwave disintegration (98.51)

➡ **AHA Coding Clinic:** 1Q, '89, 1; S-O, '86, 11

59.99 Other

Excludes: *instillation of medication into urinary tract (96.49)*
irrigation of urinary tract (96.45-96.48)

11. OPERATIONS ON THE MALE GENITAL ORGANS (60-64)

60 Operations on prostate and seminal vesicles ♂

Includes: operations on periprostatic tissue

Excludes: *that associated with radical cystectomy (57.71)*

60.0 Incision of prostate

Drainage of prostatic abscess
Prostatolithotomy

Excludes: *drainage of periprostatic tissue only (60.81)*

60.1 Diagnostic procedures on prostate and seminal vesicles

[22] **60.11 Closed [percutaneous] [needle] biopsy of prostate**

Approach:
transrectal
transurethral
Punch biopsy

[21] **60.12 Open biopsy of prostate**

[22] **60.13 Closed [percutaneous] biopsy of seminal vesicles**

Needle biopsy of seminal vesicles

[21] **60.14 Open biopsy of seminal vesicles**

60.15 Biopsy of periprostatic tissue

60.18 Other diagnostic procedures on prostate and periprostatic tissue

Excludes: *microscopic examination of specimen from prostate (91.31-91.39)*
x-ray of prostate (87.92)

60.19 Other diagnostic procedures on seminal vesicles

Excludes: *microscopic examination of specimen from seminal vesicles (91.31-91.39)*
x-ray:
contrast seminal vesiculogram (87.91)
other (87.92)

60.2 Transurethral prostatectomy

Excludes: *ocal excision of lesion of prostate (60.61)*

➡ **AHA Coding Clinic:** 2Q, '94, 9; 3Q, '92, 13

60.21 Transurethral (ultrasound) guided laser induced prostatectomy (TULIP)

Ablation (contact) (noncontact) by laser

➡ **AHA Coding Clinic:** 4Q, '95, 71

60.29 Other transurethral prostatectomy

Excision of median bar by transurethral approach
Transurethral electrovaporization of prostate (TEVAP)
Transurethral enucleative procedure
Transurethral prostatectomy NOS
Transurethral resection of prostate (TURP)

➡ **AHA Coding Clinic:** 3Q, '97, 3

60.3 Suprapubic prostatectomy

Transvesical prostatectomy

Excludes: *local excision of lesion of prostate (60.61)*
radical prostatectomy (60.5)

60.4 Retropubic prostatectomy

Excludes: *local excision of lesion of prostate (60.61)*
radical prostatectomy (60.5)

60.5 Radical prostatectomy

Prostatovesiculectomy
Radical prostatectomy by any approach

Excludes: *cystoprostatectomy (57.71)*

➡ **AHA Coding Clinic:** 3Q, '93, 12

60.6 Other prostatectomy

60.61 Local excision of lesion of prostate

Excision of prostatic lesion by any approach

Excludes: *biopsy of prostate (60.11-60.12)*

60.62 Perineal prostatectomy

Cryoablation of prostate
Cryoprostatectomy
Cryosurgery of prostate
Radical cryosurcial ablation of prostate (RCSA)

Excludes: *local excision of lesion of prostate (60.61)*

➡ **AHA Coding Clinic:** 4Q, '95, 71

60.69 Other

60.7 Operations on seminal vesicles

60.71 Percutaneous aspiration of seminal vesicle

Excludes: *needle biopsy of seminal vesicle (60.13)*

60.72 Incision of seminal vesicle

60.73 Excision of seminal vesicle

Excision of Müllerian duct cyst
Spermatocystectomy

Excludes: *biopsy of seminal vesicle (60.13-60.14)*
prostatovesiculectomy (60.5)

60.79 Other operations on seminal vesicles

[21] Open biopsy
[22] Closed biopsy

60.8 **Incision or excision of periprostatic tissue**

60.81 **Incision of periprostatic tissue**
Drainage of periprostatic abscess

60.82 **Excision of periprostatic tissue**
Excision of lesion of periprostatic tissue

Excludes: *biopsy of periprostatic tissue (60.15)*

60.9 **Other operations on prostate**

60.91 **Percutaneous aspiration of prostate**

Excludes: *needle biopsy of prostate (60.11)*

60.92 **Injection into prostate**

60.93 **Repair of prostate**

60.94 **Control of (postoperative) hemorrhage of prostate**
Coagulation of prostatic bed
Cystoscopy for control of prostatic hemorrhage

60.95 **Transurethral balloon dilation of the prostatic urethra**
➡ **AHA Coding Clinic:** 4Q, '91, 23

60.99 **Other**

Excludes: *prostatic massage (99.94)*
➡ **AHA Coding Clinic:** 3Q, '90, 12

61 Operations on scrotum and tunica vaginalis ♂

61.0 **Incision and drainage of scrotum and tunica vaginalis**

Excludes: *percutaneous aspiration of hydrocele (61.91)*

61.1 **Diagnostic procedures on scrotum and tunica vaginalis**

61.11 **Biopsy of scrotum or tunica vaginalis**

61.19 **Other diagnostic procedures on scrotum and tunica vaginalis**

61.2 **Excision of hydrocele (of tunica vaginalis)**
Bottle repair of hydrocele of tunica vaginalis

Excludes: *percutaneous aspiration of hydrocele (61.91)*

61.3 **Excision or destruction of lesion or tissue of scrotum**
Fulguration of lesion } of scrotum
Reduction of elephantiasis } of scrotum
Partial scrotectomy

Excludes: *biopsy of scrotum (61.11)*
scrotal fistulectomy (61.42)

61.4 **Repair of scrotum and tunica vaginalis**

61.41 **Suture of laceration of scrotum and tunica vaginalis**

61.42 **Repair of scrotal fistula**

61.49 **Other repair of scrotum and tunica vaginalis**
Reconstruction with rotational or pedicle flaps

61.9 **Other operations on scrotum and tunica vaginalis**

61.91 **Percutaneous aspiration of tunica vaginalis**
Aspiration of hydrocele of tunica vaginalis

61.92 **Excision of lesion of tunica vaginalis other than hydrocele**
Excision of hematocele of tunica vaginalis

61.99 **Other**

Excludes: *removal of foreign body from scrotum without incision (98.24)*

62 Operations on testes ♂

62.0 **Incision of testis**

62.1 **Diagnostic procedures on testes**

[22] **62.11** **Closed [percutaneous] [needle] biopsy of testis**

[21] **62.12** **Open biopsy of testis**

62.19 **Other diagnostic procedures on testes**

62.2 **Excision or destruction of testicular lesion**
Excision of appendix testis
Excision of cyst of Morgagni in the male

Excludes: *biopsy of testis (62.11-62.12)*

62.3 **Unilateral orchiectomy**
Orchidectomy (with epididymectomy) NOS

62.4 **Bilateral orchiectomy**
Male castration
Radical bilateral orchiectomy (with epididymectomy)

Code also any synchronous lymph node dissection (40.3, 40.5)

62.41 **Removal of both testes at same operative episode**
Bilateral orchidectomy NOS

62.42 **Removal of remaining testis**
Removal of solitary testis

62.5 **Orchiopexy**
Mobilization and replacement of testis in scrotum
Orchiopexy with detorsion of testis
Torek (-Bevan) operation (orchidopexy) (first stage) (second stage)
Transplantation to and fixation of testis in scrotum

62.6 **Repair of testes**

Excludes: *reduction of torsion (63.52)*

62.61 **Suture of laceration of testis**

62.69 **Other repair of testis**
Testicular graft

[21] Open biopsy
[22] Closed biopsy

62.7 Insertion of testicular prosthesis

62.9 Other operations on testes

62.91 Aspiration of testis

Excludes: *percutaneous biopsy of testis (62.11)*

62.92 Injection of therapeutic substance into testis

62.99 Other

63 Operations on spermatic cord, epididymis, and vas deferens ♂

63.0 Diagnostic procedures on spermatic cord, epididymis, and vas deferens

63.01 Biopsy of spermatic cord, epididymis, or vas deferens

63.09 Other diagnostic procedures on spermatic cord, epididymis, and vas deferens

Excludes: *contrast epididymogram (87.93)*
contrast vasogram (87.94)
other x-ray of epididymis and vas deferens (87.95)

63.1 Excision of varicocele and hydrocele of spermatic cord

High ligation of spermatic vein
Hydrocelectomy of canal of Nuck

63.2 Excision of cyst of epididymis

Spermatocelectomy

63.3 Excision of other lesion or tissue of spermatic cord and epididymis

Excision of appendix epididymis

Excludes: *biopsy of spermatic cord or epididymis (63.01)*

63.4 Epididymectomy

Excludes: *that synchronous with orchiectomy (62.3-62.42)*

63.5 Repair of spermatic cord and epididymis

63.51 Suture of laceration of spermatic cord and epididymis

63.52 Reduction of torsion of testis or spermatic cord

Excludes: *that associated with orchiopexy (62.5)*

63.53 Transplantation of spermatic cord

63.59 Other repair of spermatic cord and epididymis

63.6 Vasotomy

Vasostomy

63.7 Vasectomy and ligation of vas deferens

63.70 Male sterilization procedure, not otherwise specified

63.71 Ligation of vas deferens

Crushing of vas deferens
Division of vas deferens

63.72 Ligation of spermatic cord

63.73 Vasectomy

63.8 Repair of vas deferens and epididymis

63.81 Suture of laceration of vas deferens and epididymis

63.82 Reconstruction of surgically divided vas deferens

63.83 Epididymovasostomy

63.84 Removal of ligature from vas deferens

63.85 Removal of valve from vas deferens

63.89 Other repair of vas deferens and epididymis

63.9 Other operations on spermatic cord, epididymis, and vas deferens

63.91 Aspiration of spermatocele

63.92 Epididymotomy

63.93 Incision of spermatic cord

63.94 Lysis of adhesions of spermatic cord

63.95 Insertion of valve in vas deferens

63.99 Other

64 Operations on penis ♂

Includes: operations on:
corpora cavernosa
glans penis
prepuce

64.0 Circumcision

64.1 Diagnostic procedures on the penis

64.11 Biopsy of penis

64.19 Other diagnostic procedures on penis

64.2 **Local excision or destruction of lesion of penis**

Excludes: *biopsy of penis (64.11)*

64.3 **Amputation of penis**

64.4 **Repair and plastic operation on penis**

64.41 **Suture of laceration of penis**

64.42 **Release of chordee**

➡ **AHA Coding Clinic:** 4Q, '96, 34

64.43 **Construction of penis**

64.44 **Reconstruction of penis**

64.45 **Replantation of penis**

Reattachment of amputated penis

64.49 **Other repair of penis**

Excludes: *repair of epispadias and hypospadias (58.45)*

64.5 **Operations for sex transformation, not elsewhere classified**

64.9 **Other operations on male genital organs**

64.91 **Dorsal or lateral slit of prepuce**

64.92 **Incision of penis**

64.93 **Division of penile adhesions**

64.94 **Fitting of external prosthesis of penis**

Penile prosthesis NOS

64.95 **Insertion or replacement of non-inflatable penile prosthesis**

Insertion of semi-rigid rod prosthesis into shaft of penis

Excludes: *external penile prosthesis (64.94)*
inflatable penile prosthesis (64.97)
plastic repair, penis (64.43-64.49)
that associated with:
construction (64.43)
reconstruction (64.44)

64.96 **Removal of internal prosthesis of penis**

Removal without replacement of non-inflatable or inflatable penile prosthesis

64.97 **Insertion or replacement of inflatable penile prosthesis**

Insertion of cylinders into shaft of penis and placement of pump and reservoir

Excludes: *external penile prosthesis (64.94)*
non-inflatable penile prosthesis (64.95)
that associated with plastic repair, of penis (64.43-64.49)

64.98 **Other operations on penis**

Corpora cavernosa-corpus spongiosum shunt
Corpora-saphenous shunt
Irrigation of corpus cavernosum

Excludes: *removal of foreign body:*
intraluminal (98.19)
without incision (98.24)
stretching of foreskin (99.95)

➡ **AHA Coding Clinic:** 3Q, '92, 9

64.99 **Other**

Excludes: *collection of sperm for artificial insemination (99.96)*

12. OPERATIONS ON THE FEMALE GENITAL ORGANS (65-71)

65 Operations on ovary ♀

65.0 Oophorotomy
Salpingo-oophorotomy

65.01 Laparoscopic oophorotomy

65.09 Other oophorectomy

65.1 Diagnostic procedures on ovaries

65.11 Aspiration biopsy of ovary

65.12 Other biopsy of ovary

65.13 Laparoscopic biopsy of ovary
➡ **AHA Coding Clinic:** 4Q, '96, 67

65.14 Other laparoscopic diagnostic procedures on ovaries

65.19 Other diagnostic procedures on ovaries

Excludes: *microscopic examination of specimen from ovary (91.41-91.49)*

65.2 Local excision or destruction of ovarian lesion or tissue

65.21 Marsupialization of ovarian cyst

Excludes: *that by laparoscope (65.23)*

65.22 Wedge resection of ovary

Excludes: *that by laparoscope (65.24)*

65.23 Laparoscopic marsupialization of ovarian cyst

65.24 Laparoscopic wedge resection of ovary

65.25 Other laparoscopic local excision or destruction of ovary

65.29 Other local excision or destruction of ovary
Bisection } of ovary
Cauterization } of ovary
Partial excision } of ovary

Excludes: *biopsy of ovary (65.11-65.13)*
that by laparoscope (65.25)

65.3 Unilateral oophorectomy
➡ **AHA Coding Clinic:** 4Q, '96, 66

65.31 Laparoscopic unilateral oophorectomy

65.39 Other unilateral oophorectomy

Excludes: *that by laparoscope (65.31)*

65.4 Unilateral salpingo-oophorectomy

65.41 Laparoscopic unilateral salpingo-oophorectomy
➡ **AHA Coding Clinic:** 4Q, '96, 67

65.49 Other unilateral salpingo-oophorectomy

65.5 Bilateral oophorectomy

65.51 Other removal of both ovaries at same operative episode
Female castration

Excludes: *that by laparoscope (65.53)*

65.52 Other removal of remaining ovary
Removal of solitary ovary

Excludes: *that by laparoscope (65.54)*

65.53 Laparoscopic removal of both ovaries at same operative eisode

65.54 Laparoscopic removal of remaining ovary

65.6 Bilateral salpingo-oophorectomy

65.61 Other removal of both ovaries and tubes at same operative episode

Excludes: *that by laparoscope (65.53)*
➡ **AHA Coding Clinic:** 4Q, '96, 65

65.62 Other removal of remaining ovary and tube
Removal of solitary ovary and tube

Excludes: *that by laparoscope (65.54)*

65.63 Laparoscopic removal of both ovaries and tubes at the same operative episode
➡ **AHA Coding Clinic:** 4Q, '96, 68

65.64 Laparoscopic removal of remaining ovary and tube

65.7 Repair of ovary

Excludes: *salpingo-oophorostomy (66.72)*

65.71 Other simple suture of ovary

Excludes: *that by laparoscope (65.74)*

65.72 Other reimplantation of ovary

Excludes: *that by laparoscope (65.75)*

65.73 Other salpingo-oophoroplasty

Excludes: *that by laparoscope (65.76)*

65.74 Laparoscopic simple suture of ovary

65.75 Laparoscopic reimplantation of ovary

65.76 Laparoscopic salpingo-oophoroplasty

65.79 Other repair of ovary
Oophoropexy

65.8 **Lysis of adhesions of ovary and fallopian tube**

65.81 **Laparoscopic lysis of adhesions of ovary and fallopian tube**

➡ **AHA Coding Clinic:** 4Q, '96, 67

65.89 **Other lysis of adhesions of ovary and fallopian tube**

Excludes: *that by laparoscope (65.81)*

65.9 **Other operations on ovary**

65.91 **Aspiration of ovary**

Excludes: *aspiration biopsy of ovary (65.11)*

65.92 **Transplantation of ovary**

Excludes: *reimplantation of ovary (65.72, 65.75)*

65.93 **Manual rupture of ovarian cyst**

65.94 **Ovarian denervation**

65.95 **Release of torsion of ovary**

65.99 **Other**

66 Operations on fallopian tubes ♀

66.0 **Salpingotomy and salpingostomy**

66.01 **Salpingotomy**

66.02 **Salpingostomy**

66.1 **Diagnostic procedures on fallopian tubes**

66.11 **Biopsy of fallopian tube**

66.19 **Other diagnostic procedures on fallopian tubes**

Excludes: *microscopic examination of specimen from fallopian tubes (91.41-91.49)*
radiography of fallopian tubes (87.82-87.83, 87.85)
Rubin's test (66.8)

66.2 **Bilateral endoscopic destruction or occlusion of fallopian tubes**

Includes: bilateral endoscopic destruction or occlusion of fallopian tubes by:
- culdoscopy
- endoscopy
- hysteroscopy
- laparoscopy
- peritoneoscopy

endoscopic destruction of solitary fallopian tube

66.21 **Bilateral endoscopic ligation and crushing of fallopian tubes**

66.22 **Bilateral endoscopic ligation and division of fallopian tubes**

66.29 **Other bilateral endoscopic destruction or occlusion of fallopian tubes**

66.3 **Other bilateral destruction or occlusion of fallopian tubes**

Includes: destruction of solitary fallopian tube

Excludes: *endoscopic destruction or occlusion of fallopian tubes (66.21-66.29)*

66.31 **Other bilateral ligation and crushing of fallopian tubes**

66.32 **Other bilateral ligation and division of fallopian tubes**

Pomeroy operation

66.39 **Other bilateral destruction or occlusion of fallopian tubes**

Female sterilization operation NOS

66.4 **Total unilateral salpingectomy**

66.5 **Total bilateral salpingectomy**

Excludes: *bilateral partial salpingectomy for sterilization (66.39)*
that with oophorectomy (65.61-65.64)

66.51 **Removal of both fallopian tubes at same operative episode**

66.52 **Removal of remaining fallopian tube**

Removal of solitary fallopian tube

66.6 **Other salpingectomy**

Includes: salpingectomy by:
- cauterization
- coagulation
- electrocoagulation
- excision

Excludes: *fistulectomy (66.73)*

66.61 **Excision or destruction of lesion of fallopian tube**

Excludes: *biopsy of fallopian tube (66.11)*

66.62 **Salpingectomy with removal of tubal pregnancy**

Code also any synchronous oophorectomy (65.31, 65.39)

➡ **AHA Coding Clinic:** 3Q, '95, 15

66.63 **Bilateral partial salpingectomy, not otherwise specified**

66.69 **Other partial salpingectomy**

66.7 **Repair of fallopian tube**

66.71 **Simple suture of fallopian tube**

66.72 **Salpingo-oophorostomy**

66.73 **Salpingo-salpingostomy**

66.74 **Salpingo-uterostomy**

66.79 **Other repair of fallopian tube**
Graft of fallopian tube
Reopening of divided fallopian tube
Salpingoplasty

66.8 **Insufflation of fallopian tube**
Insufflation of fallopian tube with:
air
dye
gas
saline
Rubin's test

Excludes: *insufflation of therapeutic agent (66.95)*
that for hysterosalpingography (87.82-87.83)

66.9 **Other operations on fallopian tubes**

66.91 **Aspiration of fallopian tube**

66.92 **Unilateral destruction or occlusion of fallopian tube**

Excludes: *that of solitary tube (66.21-66.39)*

66.93 **Implantation or replacement of prosthesis of fallopian tube**

66.94 **Removal of prosthesis of fallopian tube**

66.95 **Insufflation of therapeutic agent into fallopian tubes**

66.96 **Dilation of fallopian tube**

66.97 **Burying of fimbriae in uterine wall**

66.99 **Other**

Excludes: *lysis of adhesions of ovary and tube (65.81, 65.89)*

➡ **AHA Coding Clinic:** 2Q, '94, 11

67 Operations on cervix ♀

67.0 **Dilation of cervical canal**

Excludes: *dilation and curettage (69.01-69.09)*
that for induction of labor (73.1)

67.1 **Diagnostic procedures on cervix**

67.11 **Endocervical biopsy**

Excludes: *conization of cervix (67.2)*

67.12 **Other cervical biopsy**
Punch biopsy of cervix NOS

Excludes: *conization of cervix (67.2)*

67.19 **Other diagnostic procedures on cervix**

Excludes: *microscopic examination of specimen from cervix (91.41-91.49)*

67.2 **Conization of cervix**

Excludes: *that by:*
cryosurgery (67.33)
electrosurgery (67.32)

67.3 **Other excision or destruction of lesion or tissue of cervix**

67.31 **Marsupialization of cervical cyst**

67.32 **Destruction of lesion of cervix by cauterization**
Electroconization of cervix
LEEP (loop electrosurgical excision procedure)
LLETZ (large loop excision of the transformation zone)

➡ **AHA Coding Clinic:** 1Q, '98, 3

67.33 **Destruction of lesion of cervix by cryosurgery**
Cryoconization of cervix

67.39 **Other excision or destruction of lesion or tissue of cervix**

Excludes: *biopsy of cervix (67.11-67.12)*
cervical fistulectomy (67.62)
conization of cervix (67.2)

67.4 **Amputation of cervix**
Cervicectomy with synchronous colporrhaphy

67.5 **Repair of internal cervical os**
Cerclage of isthmus uteri
Shirodkar operation

67.6 **Other repair of cervix**

Excludes: *repair of current obstetric laceration (75.51)*

67.61 **Suture of laceration of cervix**

67.62 **Repair of fistula of cervix**
Cervicosigmoidal fistulectomy

Excludes: *fistulectomy:*
cervicovesical (57.84)
ureterocervical (56.84)
vesicocervicovaginal (57.84)

67.69 **Other repair of cervix**
Repair of old obstetric laceration of cervix

68 Other incision and excision of uterus ♀

68.0 Hysterotomy
Hysterotomy with removal of hydatidiform mole

Excludes: *hysterotomy for termination of pregnancy (74.91)*

68.1 Diagnostic procedures on uterus and supporting structures

68.11 Digital examination of uterus

Excludes: *pelvic examination, so described (89.26)*
postpartal manual exploration of uterine cavity (75.7)

68.12 Hysteroscopy

Excludes: *that with biopsy (68.16)*

[21] **68.13 Open biopsy of uterus**

Excludes: *closed biopsy of uterus (68.16)*

[21] **68.14 Open biopsy of uterine ligaments**

Excludes: *closed biopsy of uterine ligaments (68.15)*

[22] **68.15 Closed biopsy of uterine ligaments**
Endoscopic (laparoscopy) biopsy of uterine adnexa, except ovary and fallopian tube

[22] **68.16 Closed biopsy of uterus**
Endoscopic (laparoscopy) (hysteroscopy) biopsy of uterus

Excludes: *open biopsy of uterus (68.13)*

68.19 Other diagnostic procedures on uterus and supporting structures

Excludes: *diagnostic:*
aspiration curettage (69.59)
dilation and curettage (69.09)
microscopic examination of specimen from uterus (91.41-91.49)
pelvic examination (89.26)
radioisotope scan of:
placenta (92.17)
uterus (92.19)
ultrasonography of uterus (88.78-88.79)
x-ray of uterus (87.81-87.89)

68.2 Excision or destruction of lesion or tissue of uterus

68.21 Division of endometrial synechiae
Lysis of intraluminal uterine adhesions

68.22 Incision or excision of congenital septum of uterus

68.23 Endometrial ablation
Dilation and curettage
Hysteroscopic endometrial ablation
➡ **AHA Coding Clinic:** 4Q, '96, 68

68.29 Other excision or destruction of lesion of uterus
Uterine myomectomy

Excludes: *biopsy of uterus (68.13)*
uterine fistulectomy (69.42)

➡ **AHA Coding Clinic:** 1Q, '96, 14

68.3 Subtotal abdominal hysterectomy
Supracervical hysterectomy

68.4 Total abdominal hysterectomy
Hysterectomy:
extended

Code also any synchronous removal of tubes and ovaries (65.3-65.6)

➡ **AHA Coding Clinic:** 4Q, '96, 65

68.5 Vaginal hysterectomy
Code also any synchronous:
removal of tubes and ovaries (65.31-65.64)
repair of cystocele or rectocele (70.50-70.52)
repair of pelvic floor (70.79)

68.51 Laparoscopically assisted vaginal hysterectomy (LAVH)
➡ **AHA Coding Clinic:** 4Q, '96, 68

68.59 Other vaginal hysterectomy

Excludes: *laparoscopically assisted vaginal hysterectomy (68.51)*
radical vaginal hysterectomy (68.7)

68.6 Radical abdominal hysterectomy
Modified radical hysterectomy
Wertheim's operation

Code also any synchronous:
lymph gland dissection (40.3, 40.5)
removal of tubes and ovaries (65.61-65.64)

Excludes: *pelvic evisceration (68.8)*

68.7 Radical vaginal hysterectomy
Schauta operation

Code also any synchronous:
lymph gland dissection (40.3, 40.5)
removal of tubes and ovaries (65.61-65.64)

68.8 Pelvic evisceration
Removal of ovaries, tubes, uterus, vagina, bladder, and urethra (with removal of sigmoid colon and rectum)

Code also any synchronous:
colostomy (46.12-46.13)
lymph gland dissection (40.3, 40.5)
urinary diversion (56.51-56.79)

[21] Open biopsy
[22] Closed biopsy

68.9 Other and unspecified hysterectomy
Hysterectomy NOS

Excludes: *abdominal hysterectomy, any approach (68.3, 68.4, 68.6)*
vaginal hysterectomy, any approach (68.51, 68.59, 68.7)

69 Other operations on uterus and supporting structures ♀

69.0 Dilation and curettage of uterus

Excludes: *aspiration curettage of uterus (69.51-69.59)*

69.01 Dilation and curettage for termination of pregnancy
➡ **AHA Coding Clinic:** 1Q, '98, 4

69.02 Dilation and curettage following delivery or abortion

69.09 Other dilation and curettage
Diagnostic D and C
➡ **AHA Coding Clinic:** 1Q, '98, 4

69.1 Excision or destruction of lesion or tissue of uterus and supporting structures

69.19 Other excision or destruction of uterus and supporting structures

Excludes: *biopsy of uterine ligament (68.14)*

69.2 Repair of uterine supporting structures

69.21 Interposition operation
Watkins procedure

69.22 Other uterine suspension
Hysteropexy
Manchester operation
Plication of uterine ligament

69.23 Vaginal repair of chronic inversion of uterus

69.29 Other repair of uterus and supporting structures

69.3 Paracervical uterine denervation

69.4 Uterine repair

Excludes: *repair of current obstetric laceration (75.50-75.52)*

69.41 Suture of laceration of uterus

69.42 Closure of fistula of uterus

Excludes: *uterovesical fistulectomy (57.84)*

69.49 Other repair of uterus
Repair of old obstetric laceration of uterus

69.5 Aspiration curettage of uterus

Excludes: *menstrual extraction (69.6)*

69.51 Aspiration curettage of uterus for termination of pregnancy
Therapeutic abortion NOS

69.52 Aspiration curettage following delivery or abortion

69.59 Other aspiration curettage of uterus
➡ **AHA Coding Clinic:** 1Q, '98, 7

69.6 Menstrual extraction or regulation

69.7 Insertion of intrauterine contraceptive device

69.9 Other operations on uterus, cervix, and supporting structures

Excludes: *obstetric dilation or incision of cervix (73.1, 73.93)*

69.91 Insertion of therapeutic device into uterus

Excludes: *insertion of:*
intrauterine contraceptive device (69.7)
laminaria (69.93)
obstetric insertion of bag, bougie, or pack (73.1)

69.92 Artificial insemination

69.93 Insertion of laminaria

69.94 Manual replacement of inverted uterus

Excludes: *that in immediate postpartal period (75.94)*

69.95 Incision of cervix

Excludes: *that to assist delivery (73.93)*

69.96 Removal of cerclage material from cervix

69.97 Removal of other penetrating foreign body from cervix

Excludes: *removal of intraluminal foreign body from cervix (98.16)*

69.98 Other operations on supporting structures of uterus

Excludes: *biopsy of uterine ligament (68.14)*

69.99 **Other operations on cervix and uterus**

Excludes: *removal of:*
foreign body (98.16)
intrauterine contraceptive device (97.71)
obstetric bag, bougie, or pack (97.72)
packing (97.72)

70 Operations on vagina and cul-de-sac ♀

70.0 **Culdocentesis**

➡ **AHA Coding Clinic:** 2Q, '90, 26

70.1 **Incision of vagina and cul-de-sac**

70.11 **Hymenotomy**

70.12 **Culdotomy**

70.13 **Lysis of intraluminal adhesions of vagina**

70.14 **Other vaginotomy**
Division of vaginal septum
Drainage of hematoma of vaginal cuff

70.2 **Diagnostic procedures on vagina and cul-de-sac**

70.21 **Vaginoscopy**

70.22 **Culdoscopy**

70.23 **Biopsy of cul-de-sac**

70.24 **Vaginal biopsy**

70.29 **Other diagnostic procedures on vagina and cul-de-sac**

70.3 **Local excision or destruction of vagina and cul-de-sac**

70.31 **Hymenectomy**

70.32 **Excision or destruction of lesion of cul-de-sac**
Endometrectomy of cul-de-sac

Excludes: *biopsy of cul-de-sac (70.23)*

70.33 **Excision or destruction of lesion of vagina**

Excludes: *biopsy of vagina (70.24)*
vaginal fistulectomy (70.72-70.75)

70.4 **Obliteration and total excision of vagina**
Vaginectomy

Excludes: *obliteration of vaginal vault (70.8)*

70.5 **Repair of cystocele and rectocele**

70.50 **Repair of cystocele and rectocele**

70.51 **Repair of cystocele**
Anterior colporrhaphy (with urethrocele repair)

➡ **AHA Coding Clinic:** N-D, '84, 20

70.52 **Repair of rectocele**
Posterior colporrhaphy

70.6 **Vaginal construction and reconstruction**

70.61 **Vaginal construction**

70.62 **Vaginal reconstruction**

➡ **AHA Coding Clinic:** N-D, '84, 20

70.7 **Other repair of vagina**

Excludes: *lysis of intraluminal adhesions (70.13)*
repair of current obstetric laceration (75.69)
that associated with cervical amputation (67.4)

70.71 **Suture of laceration of vagina**

➡ **AHA Coding Clinic:** N-D, '84, 20

70.72 **Repair of colovaginal fistula**

70.73 **Repair of rectovaginal fistula**

70.74 **Repair of other vaginoenteric fistula**

70.75 **Repair of other fistula of vagina**

Excludes: *repair of fistula:*
rectovesicovaginal (57.83)
ureterovaginal (56.84)
urethrovaginal (58.43)
uterovaginal (69.42)
vesicocervicovaginal (57.84)
vesicosigmoidovaginal (57.83)
vesicoureterovaginal (56.84)
vesicovaginal (57.84)

70.76 **Hymenorrhaphy**

70.77 **Vaginal suspension and fixation**

70.79 **Other repair of vagina**
Colpoperineoplasty
Repair of old obstetric laceration of vagina

70.8 **Obliteration of vaginal vault**
LeFort operation

70.9 **Other operations on vagina and cul-de-sac**

70.91 Other operations on vagina

Excludes: *insertion of:*
diaphragm (96.17)
mold (96.15)
pack (96.14)
pessary (96.18)
suppository (96.49)
removal of:
diaphragm (97.73)
foreign body (98.17)
pack (97.75)
pessary (97.74)
replacement of:
diaphragm (97.24)
pack (97.26)
pessary (97.25)
vaginal dilation (96.16)
vaginal douche (96.44)

70.92 Other operations on cul-de-sac
Obliteration of cul-de-sac
Repair of vaginal enterocele

➡ **AHA Coding Clinic:** 4Q, '94, 54

71 Operations on vulva and perineum ♀

71.0 Incision of vulva and perineum

71.01 Lysis of vulvar adhesions

71.09 Other incision of vulva and perineum
Enlargement of introitus NOS

Excludes: *removal of foreign body without incision (98.23)*

71.1 Diagnostic procedures on vulva

71.11 Biopsy of vulva

71.19 Other diagnostic procedures on vulva

71.2 Operations on Bartholin's gland

71.21 Percutaneous aspiration of Bartholin's gland (cyst)

71.22 Incision of Bartholin's gland (cyst)

71.23 Marsupialization of Bartholin's gland (cyst)

71.24 Excision or other destruction of Bartholin's gland (cyst)

71.29 Other operations on Bartholin's gland

71.3 Other local excision or destruction of vulva and perineum
Division of Skene's gland

Excludes: *biopsy of vulva (71.11)*
vulvar fistulectomy (71.72)

71.4 Operations on clitoris
Amputation of clitoris
Clitoridotomy
Female circumcision

71.5 Radical vulvectomy
Code also any synchronous lymph gland dissection (40.3, 40.5)

71.6 Other vulvectomy

71.61 Unilateral vulvectomy

71.62 Bilateral vulvectomy
Vulvectomy NOS

71.7 Repair of vulva and perineum

Excludes: *repair of current obstetric laceration (75.69)*

71.71 Suture of laceration of vulva or perineum

71.72 Repair of fistula of vulva or perineum

Excludes: *repair of fistula:*
urethroperineal (58.43)
urethroperineovesical (57.84)
vaginoperineal (70.75)

71.79 Other repair of vulva and perineum
Repair of old obstetric laceration of vulva or perineum

➡ **AHA Coding Clinic:** 1Q, '97, 9

71.8 Other operations on vulva

Excludes: *removal of:*
foreign body without incision (98.23)
packing (97.75)
replacement of packing (97.26)

71.9 Other operations on female genital organs

13. OBSTETRICAL PROCEDURES (72-75)

72 Forceps, vacuum, and breech delivery ♀

72.0 Low forceps operation
Outlet forceps operation

72.1 Low forceps operation with episiotomy
Outlet forceps operation with episiotomy

72.2 Mid forceps operation

72.21 Mid forceps operation with episiotomy

72.29 Other mid forceps operation

72.3 High forceps operation

72.31 High forceps operation with episiotomy

72.39 Other high forceps operation

72.4 Forceps rotation of fetal head
DeLee maneuver
Key-in-lock rotation
Kielland rotation
Scanzoni's maneuver

Code also any associated forceps extraction (72.0-72.39)

72.5 Breech extraction

72.51 Partial breech extraction with forceps to aftercoming head

72.52 Other partial breech extraction

72.53 Total breech extraction with forceps to aftercoming head

72.54 Other total breech extraction

72.6 Forceps application to aftercoming head
Piper forceps operation

Excludes: *partial breech extraction with forceps to aftercoming head (72.51)*
total breech extraction with forceps to aftercoming head (72.53)

72.7 Vacuum extraction
Includes: Malstöm's extraction

72.71 Vacuum extraction with episiotomy

72.79 Other vacuum extraction

72.8 Other specified instrumental delivery

72.9 Unspecified instrumental delivery

73 Other procedures inducing or assisting delivery ♀

73.0 Artificial rupture of membranes

73.01 Induction of labor by artificial rupture of membranes
Surgical induction NOS

Excludes: *artificial rupture of membranes after onset of labor (73.09)*

73.09 Other artificial rupture of membranes
Artificial rupture of membranes at time of delivery

73.1 Other surgical induction of labor
Induction by cervical dilation

Excludes: *injection for abortion (75.0)*
insertion of suppository for abortion (96.49)

73.2 Internal and combined version and extraction

73.21 Internal and combined version without extraction
Version NOS

73.22 Internal and combined version with extraction

73.3 Failed forceps
Application of forceps without delivery
Trial forceps

73.4 Medical induction of labor

Excludes: *medication to augment active labor — omit code*

73.5 Manually assisted delivery

73.51 Manual rotation of fetal head

73.59 Other manually assisted delivery
Assisted spontaneous delivery
Credé maneuver

73.6 Episiotomy
Episioproctotomy
Episiotomy with subsequent episiorrhaphy

Excludes: *that with:*
high forceps (72.31)
low forceps (72.1)
mid forceps (72.21)
outlet forceps (72.1)
vacuum extraction (72.71)

➡ **AHA Coding Clinic:** 1Q, '92, 10

73.8 Operations on fetus to facilitate delivery
Clavicotomy on fetus
Destruction of fetus
Needling of hydrocephalic head

73.9 Other operations assisting delivery

73.91 External version

73.92 Replacement of prolapsed umbilical cord

73.93 Incision of cervix to assist delivery
Dührssen's incisions

73.94 Pubiotomy to assist delivery
Obstetrical symphysiotomy

73.99 Other

Excludes: *dilation of cervix, obstetrical, to induce labor (73.1)*
insertion of bag or bougie to induce labor (73.1)
removal of cerclage material (69.96)

74 Cesarean section and removal of fetus ♀

Code also any synchronous:
hysterectomy (68.3-68.4, 68.6, 68.8)
myomectomy (68.29)
sterilization (66.31-66.39, 66.63)

74.0 Classical cesarean section
Transperitoneal classical cesarean section

74.1 Low cervical cesarean section
Lower uterine segment cesarean section

74.2 Extraperitoneal cesarean section
Supravesical cesarean section

74.3 Removal of extratubal ectopic pregnancy
Removal of:
ectopic abdominal pregnancy
fetus from peritoneal or extraperitoneal cavity following uterine or tubal rupture

Excludes: *that by salpingostomy (66.02)*
that by salpingotomy (66.01)
that with synchronous salpingectomy (66.62)

➡ **AHA Coding Clinic:** 4Q, '92, 25; 2Q, '90, 25; 2Q, '90, 27; 1Q, '89, 11

74.4 Cesarean section of other specified type
Peritoneal exclusion cesareansection
Transperitoneal cesarean section NOS
Vaginal cesarean section

74.9 Cesarean section of unspecified type

74.91 Hysterotomy to terminate pregnancy
Therapeutic abortion by hysterotomy

74.99 Other cesarean section of unspecified type
Cesarean section NOS
Obstetrical abdominouterotomy
Obstetrical hysterotomy

75 Other obstetric operations ♀

75.0 Intra-amniotic injection for abortion
Injection of:
prostaglandin } for induction of abortion
saline }
Termination of pregnancy by intrauterine injection

Excludes: *insertion of prostaglandin suppository for abortion (96.49)*

75.1 Diagnostic amniocentesis

75.2 Intrauterine transfusion
Exchange transfusion in utero
Insertion of catheter into abdomen of fetus for transfusion

Code also any hysterotomy approach (68.0)

75.3 Other intrauterine operations on fetus and amnion

Code also any hysterotomy approach (68.0)

75.31 Amnioscopy
Fetoscopy
Laparoamnioscopy

75.32 Fetal EKG (scalp)

75.33 Fetal blood sampling and biopsy

75.34 Fetal monitoring, not otherwise specified

75.35 Other diagnostic procedures on fetus and amnion
Intrauterine pressure determination

Excludes: *amniocentesis (75.1)*
diagnostic procedures on gravid uterus and placenta (87.81, 88.46, 88.78, 92.17)

75.36 Correction of fetal defect

75.37 Amnioinfusion
Code also injection of antibiotic (99.21)

75.4 Manual removal of retained placent

Excludes: *aspiration curettage (69.52)*
dilation and curettage (69.02)

75.5 Repair of current obstetric laceration of uterus

75.50 Repair of current obstetric laceration of uterus, not otherwise specified

75.51 Repair of current obstetric laceration of cervix

75.52 Repair of current obstetric laceration of corpus uteri

75.6 Repair of other current obstetric laceration

➡ **AHA Coding Clinic:** 1Q, '92, 11

75.61 Repair of current obstetric laceration of bladder and urethra

75.62 Repair of current obstetric laceration of rectum and sphincter ani

75.69 Repair of other current obstetric laceration

Episioperineorrhaphy
Repair of:
  pelvic floor
  perineum
  vagina
  vulva
Secondary repair of episiotomy

Excludes: *repair of routine episiotomy (73.6)*

75.7 Manual exploration of uterine cavity, postpartum

75.8 Obstetric tamponade of uterus or vagina

Excludes: *antepartum tamponade (73.1)*

75.9 Other obstetric operations

75.91 Evacuation of obstetrical incisional hematoma of perineum

Evacuation of hematoma of:
  episiotomy
  perineorrhaphy

75.92 Evacuation of other hematoma of vulva or vagina

75.93 Surgical correction of inverted uterus

Spintelli operation

Excludes: *vaginal repair of chronic inversion of uterus (69.23)*

75.94 Manual replacement of inverted uterus

75.99 Other

14. OPERATIONS ON THE MUSCULOSKELETAL SYSTEM (76-84)

76 Operations on facial bones and joints

Excludes: *accessory sinuses (22.00-22.9)*
nasal bones (21.00-21.99)
skull (01.01-02.99)

76.0 Incision of facial bone without division

76.01 Sequestrectomy of facial bone
Removal of necrotic bone chip from facial bone

76.09 Other incision of facial bone
Reopening of osteotomy site of facial bone

Excludes: *osteotomy associated with orthognathic surgery (76.61-76.69)*
removal of internal fixation device (76.97)

76.1 Diagnostic procedures on facial bones and joints

76.11 Biopsy of facial bone

76.19 Other diagnostic procedures on facial bones and joints

Excludes: *contrast arthrogram of temporomandibular joint (87.13)*
other x-ray (87.11-87.12, 87.14-87.16)

➡ **AHA Coding Clinic:** N-D, '87, 12

76.2 Local excision or destruction of lesion of facial bone

Excludes: *biopsy of facial bone (76.11)*
excision of odontogenic lesion (24.4)

76.3 Partial ostectomy of facial bone

76.31 Partial mandibulectomy
Hemimandibulectomy

Excludes: *that associated with temporomandibular arthroplasty (76.5)*

76.39 Partial ostectomy of other facial bone
Hemimaxillectomy (with bonegraft or prosthesis)

➡ **AHA Coding Clinic:** J-F, '87, 14

76.4 Excision and reconstruction of facial bones

76.41 Total mandibulectomy with synchronous reconstruction

76.42 Other total mandibulectomy

76.43 Other reconstruction of mandible

Excludes: *genioplasty (76.67-76.68)*
that with synchronous total mandibulectomy (76.41)

76.44 Total ostectomy of other facial bone with synchronous reconstruction

76.45 Other total ostectomy of other facial bone

76.46 Other reconstruction of other facial bone

Excludes: *that with synchronous total ostectomy (76.44)*

76.5 Temporomandibular arthroplasty

76.6 Other facial bone repair and orthognathic surgery

Code also any synchronous:
- bone graft (76.91)
- synthetic implant (76.92)

Excludes: *reconstruction of facial bones (76.41-76.46)*

76.61 Closed osteoplasty [osteotomy] of mandibular ramus
Gigli saw osteotomy

76.62 Open osteoplasty [osteotomy] of mandibular ramus

76.63 Osteoplasty [osteotomy] of body of mandible

76.64 Other orthognathic surgery on mandible
Mandibular osteoplasty NOS
Segmental or subapical osteotomy

76.65 Segmental osteoplasty [osteotomy] of maxilla
Maxillary osteoplasty NOS

76.66 Total osteoplasty [osteotomy] of maxilla

76.67 Reduction genioplasty
Reduction mentoplasty

76.68 Augmentation genioplasty
Mentoplasty:
- NOS
- with graft or implant

76.69 Other facial bone repair
Osteoplasty of facial bone NOS

76.7 Reduction of facial fracture

Includes: internal fixation

Code also any synchronous:
bone graft (76.91)
synthetic implant (76.92)

Excludes: *that of nasal bones (21.71-21.72)*

76.70 Reduction of facial fracture, not otherwise specified

76.71 Closed reduction of malar and zygomatic fracture

76.72 Open reduction of malar and zygomatic fracture

76.73 Closed reduction of maxillary fracture

76.74 Open reduction of maxillary fracture

76.75 Closed reduction of mandibular fracture

76.76 Open reduction of mandibular fracture

76.77 Open reduction of alveolar fracture

Reduction of alveolar fracture with stabilization of teeth

76.78 Other closed reduction of facial fracture

Closed reduction of orbital fracture

Excludes: *nasal bone (21.71)*

76.79 Other open reduction of facial fracture

Open reduction of orbit rim or wall

Excludes: *nasal bone (21.72)*

76.9 Other operations on facial bones and joints

76.91 Bone graft to facial bone

Autogenous, Bone bank, Heterogenous } graft to facial bone

76.92 Insertion of synthetic implant in facial bone

Alloplastic implant to facial bone

76.93 Closed reduction of temporomandibular dislocation

76.94 Open reduction of temporomandibular dislocation

76.95 Other manipulation of temporomandibular joint

76.96 Injection of therapeutic substance into temporomandibular joint

76.97 Removal of internal fixation device from facial bone

Excludes: *removal of:*
dental wiring (97.33)
external mandibular fixation device NEC (97.36)

76.99 Other

77 Incision, excision, and division of other bones

Excludes: *laminectomy for decompression (03.09)*
operations on:
accessory sinuses (22.00-22.9)
ear ossicles (19.0-19.55)
facial bones (76.01-76.99)
joint structures (80.00-81.99)
mastoid (19.9-20.99)
nasal bones (21.00-21.99)
skull (01.01-02.99)

The following fourth-digit subclassification is for use with the appropriate codes in section 77, marked with a symbol (§), to identify the site:

0 unspecified site
1 scapula, clavicle, and thorax [ribs and sternum]
2 humerus
3 radius and ulna
4 carpals and metacarpals
5 femur
6 patella
7 tibia and fibula
8 tarsals and metatarsals
9 other
Pelvic bones
Phalanges (of foot) (of hand)
Vertebrae

[29] § **77.0 Sequestrectomy**
[0-9]

[29] § **77.1 Other incision of bone without division**
[0-9]

Reopening of osteotomy site

Excludes: *aspiration of bone marrow, (41.31, 41.91)*
removal of internal fixation device (78.60-78.69)

[29] § **77.2 Wedge osteotomy**
[0-9]

Excludes: *that for hallux valgus (77.51)*

§ **77.3 Other division of bone**
[0-9]

Osteoarthrotomy

Excludes: *clavicotomy of fetus (73.8)*
laminotomy or incision of vertebra (03.01-03.09)
pubiotomy to assist delivery (73.94)
sternotomy incidental to thoracic operation — omit code

§ **77.4 Biopsy of bone**
[0-9]

§ Requires fourth-digit; valid digits are in [brackets] under each code. See above, this page for definitions.
[29] Non-specific OR procedure equals fourth digit of 0

77.5 **Excision and repair of bunion and other toe deformities**

77.51 **Bunionectomy with soft tissue correction and osteotomy of the first metatarsal**

77.52 **Bunionectomy with soft tissue correction and arthrodesis**

77.53 **Other bunionectomy with soft tissue correction**

77.54 **Excision or correction of bunionette**
That with osteotomy

77.56 **Repair of hammer toe**
Fusion } of hammer toe
Phalangectomy (partial) } of hammer toe
Filleting } of hammer toe

77.57 **Repair of claw toe**
Fusion } of claw toe
Phalangectomy (partial) } of claw toe
Capsulotomy } of claw toe
Tendon lengthening } of claw toe

77.58 **Other excision, fusion, and repair of toes**
Cockup toe repair
Overlapping toe repair
That with use of prosthetic materials

77.59 **Other bunionectomy**
Resection of hallux valgus joint with insertion of prosthesis

[29]§§ **77.6** **Local excision of lesion or tissue of bone**
[0-9]
Excludes: *biopsy of bone (77.40-77.49)*
debridement of compound fracture (79.60-79.69)

➡ **AHA Coding Clinic: For code 77.65:** S-O, '85, 4

[29]§§ **77.7** **Excision of bone for graft**
[0-9]

[29]§§ **77.8** **Other partial ostectomy**
[0-9]
Condylectomy

Excludes: *amputation (84.00-84.19, 84.91)*
arthrectomy (80.90-80.99)
excision of bone ends associated with:
arthrodesis (81.00-81.29)
arthroplasty (81.51-81.89, 81.71-81.81, 81.84)
excision of cartilage (80.5-80.6, 80.80-80.99)
excision of head of femur with synchronous replacement (81.51-81.53)
hemilaminectomy (03.01-03.09)
laminectomy (03.01-03.09)
ostectomy for hallux valgus (77.51-77.59)
partial amputation:
finger (84.01)
thumb (84.02)
toe (84.11)
resection of ribs incidental to thoracic operation — omit code
that incidental to other operation — omit code

[29]§§ **77.9** **Total ostectomy**
[0-9]
Excludes: *amputation of limb (84.00-84.19, 84.91)*
that incidental to other operation — omit code

78 Other operations on bones, except facial bones

Excludes: *operations on:*
accessory sinuses (22.00-22.9)
facial bones (76.01-76.99)
joint structures (80.00-81.99)
nasal bones (21.00-21.99)
skull (01.01-02.99)

The following fourth-digit subclassification is for use with categories in section 78 to identify the site:

0 **unspecified site**
1 **scapula, clavicle, and thorax [ribs and sternum]**
2 **humerus**
3 **radius and ulna**
4 **carpals and metacarpals**
5 **femur**
6 **patella**
7 **tibia and fibula**
8 **tarsals and metatarsals**
9 **other**
Pelvic bones
Phalanges (of foot) (of hand)
Vertebrae

[29] § **78.0** **Bone graft**
[0-9]
Bone:
bank graft
graft (autogenous) (heterogenous)
That with debridement of bone graft site (removal of sclerosed, fibrous, or necrotic bone or tissue)
Transplantation of bone

Code also any excision of bone for graft (77.70-77.79)

Excludes: *that for bone lengthening (78.30-78.39)*

[29] § **78.1** **Application of external fixation device**
[0-9]
Minifixator with insertion of pins/wires/screws into bone

Excludes: *other immobilization, pressure, and attention to wound (93.51-93.59)*

➡ **AHA Coding Clinic:** 2Q, '94, 4

[29] § **78.2** **Limb shortening procedures**
[0,2-5,7-9]
Epiphyseal stapling
Open epiphysiodesis
Percutaneous epiphysiodesis
Resection/osteotomy

§§ Requires fourth-digit; valid digits are in [brackets] under each code. See page P-100 for definitions.
§ Requires fourth-digit; valid digits are in [brackets] under each code. See above, this page for definitions.
[29] Non-specific OR procedure equals fourth digit of 0

[29]§§ **78.3** **Limb lengthening procedures**
[0,2-5,7-9]
Bone graft with or without internal fixation devices or osteotomy
Distraction technique with or without corticotomy/osteotomy

Code also any application of an external fixation device (78.10-78.19)

[29]§§ **78.4** **Other repair or plastic operations on bone**
[0-9]
Other operation on bone NEC
Repair of malunion or nonunion fracture NEC

Excludes: *application of external fixation device (78.10-78.19)*
limb lengthening procedures (78.30-78.39)
limb shortening procedures (78.20-78.29)
osteotomy (77.3)
reconstruction of thumb (82.61-82.69)
repair of pectus deformity (34.74)
repair with bone graft (78.00-78.09)

➡ **AHA Coding Clinic: For code 78.47:** 3Q, '91, 20

➡ **AHA Coding Clinic: For code 78.49:** 1Q, '97, 5

[29]§§ **78.5** **Internal fixation of bone without fracture reduction**
[0-9]
Internal fixation of bone (prophylactic)
Reinsertion of internal fixation device
Revision of displaced or broken fixation device

Excludes: *arthroplasty and arthrodesis (81.00-81.87)*
bone graft (78.00-78.09)
limb shortening procedures (78.20-78.29)
that for fracture reduction (79.10-79.19, 79.30-79.59)

➡ **AHA Coding Clinic:** 2Q, '94, 4

§§ **78.6** **Removal of implanted devices from bone**
[0-9]
External fixator device (invasive)
Internal fixation device
Removal of bone growth stimulator (invasive)

Excludes: *removal of cast, splint, and traction device (Kirschner wire) (Steinmann pin) (97.88)*
removal of skull tongs or halo traction device (02.95)

[29]§§ **78.7** **Osteoclasis**
[0-9]

§§ **78.8** **Diagnostic procedures on bone, not elsewhere classified**
[0-9]

Excludes: *biopsy of bone (77.40-77.49)*
magnetic resonance imaging (88.94)
microscopic examination of specimen from bone (91.51-91.59)
radioisotope scan (92.14)
skeletal x-ray (87.21-87.29, 87.43, 88.21-88.33)
thermography (88.83)

[29]§§ **78.9** **Insertion of bone growth stimulator**
[0-9]
Insertion of:
bone stimulator (electrical) to aid bone healing
osteogenic electrodes for bone growth stimulation
totally implanted device (invasive)

Excludes: *non-invasive (transcutaneous) (surface) stimulator (99.86)*

79 Reduction of fracture and dislocation

Includes: application of cast or splint
reduction with insertion of traction device (Kirschner wire) (Steinmann pin)

Code also any application of external fixation device (78.10-78.19)

Excludes: *external fixation alone for immobilization of fracture (93.51-93.56, 93.59)*
internal fixation without reduction of fracture (78.50-78.59)
operations on:
facial bones (76.70-76.79)
nasal bones (21.71-21.72)
orbit (76.78-76.79)
skull (02.02)
vertebrae (03.53)
removal of cast or splint (97.88)
replacement of cast or splint (97.11-97.14)
traction alone for reduction of fracture (93.41-93.46)

The following fourth-digit subclassification is for use with appropriate categories in section 79, marked with a symbol (§), to identify the site:

0 **unspecified site**
1 **humerus**
2 **radius and ulna**
Arm NOS
3 **carpals and metacarpals**
Hand NOS
4 **phalanges of hand**
5 **femur**
6 **tibia and fibula**
Leg NOS
7 **tarsals and metatarsals**
Foot NOS
8 **phalanges of foot**
9 **other specified bone**

§ **79.0** **Closed reduction of fracture without internal fixation**
[0-9]

Excludes: *that for separation of epiphysis (79.40-79.49)*

➡ **AHA Coding Clinic:** 2Q, '94, 3

➡ **AHA Coding Clinic: For code 79.05:** 3Q, '89, 16

§§ Requires fourth-digit; valid digits are in [brackets] under each code. See page P-101 for definitions.
§ Requires fourth-digit; valid digits are in [brackets] under each code. See above, this page for definitions.
[29] Non-specific OR procedure equals fourth digit of 0

[29] § **79.1** **Closed reduction of fracture with internal fixation**
[0-9]

Excludes: *that for separation of epiphysis (79.40-79.49)*

➡ **AHA Coding Clinic:** 2Q, '94, 4; 4Q, '93, 35; 1Q, '93, 27

[29] § **79.2** **Open reduction of fracture without internal fixation**
[0-9]

Excludes: *that for separation of epiphysis (79.50-79.59)*

➡ **AHA Coding Clinic:** 2Q, '94, 3

[29] § **79.3** **Open reduction of fracture with internal fixation**
[0-9]

Excludes: *that for separation of epiphysis (79.50-79.59)*

➡ **AHA Coding Clinic:** 3Q, '94, 10; 2Q, '94, 3

[29] § **79.4** **Closed reduction of separated epiphysis**
[0-2,5-6,9]

Reduction with or without internal fixation

[29] § **79.5** **Open reduction of separated epiphysis**
[0-2,5-6,9]

Reduction with or without internal fixation

[29] § **79.6** **Debridement of open fracture site**
[0-9]

➡ **AHA Coding Clinic:** 3Q, '95, 12; 3Q, '89, 16

79.7 **Closed reduction of dislocation**

Includes: closed reduction (with external traction device)

Excludes: *closed reduction of dislocation of temporomandibular joint (76.93)*

79.70 **Closed reduction of dislocation of unspecified site**

79.71 **Closed reduction of dislocation of shoulder**

79.72 **Closed reduction of dislocation of elbow**

79.73 **Closed reduction of dislocation of wrist**

79.74 **Closed reduction of dislocation of hand and finger**

79.75 **Closed reduction of dislocation of hip**

79.76 **Closed reduction of dislocation of knee**

➡ **AHA Coding Clinic:** N-D, '86, 7

79.77 **Closed reduction of dislocation of ankle**

79.78 **Closed reduction of dislocation of foot and toe**

79.79 **Closed reduction of dislocation of other specified sites**

79.8 **Open reduction of dislocation**

Includes: open reduction (with internal and external fixation devices)

Excludes: *open reduction of dislocation of temporomandibular joint (76.94)*

79.80 **Open reduction of dislocation of unspecified site**

79.81 **Open reduction of dislocation of shoulder**

79.82 **Open reduction of dislocation of elbow**

79.83 **Open reduction of dislocation of wrist**

79.84 **Open reduction of dislocation of hand and finger**

79.85 **Open reduction of dislocation of hip**

79.86 **Open reduction of dislocation of knee**

79.87 **Open reduction of dislocation of ankle**

79.88 **Open reduction of dislocation of foot and toe**

79.89 **Open reduction of dislocation of other specified sites**

[29] § **79.9** **Unspecified operation on bone injury**
[0-9]

§ Requires fourth-digit; valid digits are in [brackets] under each code. See page P-102 for definitions.
[29] Non-specific OR procedure equals fourth digit of 0

80 Incision and excision of joint structures

Includes: operations on:
capsule of joint
cartilage
condyle
ligament
meniscus
synovial membrane

Excludes: *cartilage of:*
ear (18.01-18.9)
nose (21.00-21.99)
temporomandibular joint (76.01-76.99)

The following fourth-digit subclassification is for use with appropriate categories in section 80, marked with a symbol (§§), to identify the site:

0 unspecified site
1 shoulder
2 elbow
3 wrist
4 hand and finger
5 hip
6 knee
7 ankle
8 foot and toe
9 other specified sites
Spine

[29] § **80.0 Arthrotomy for removal of prosthesis**

Includes: cement spacer

➡ **AHA Coding Clinic:** 2Q, '91, 18

➡ **AHA Coding Clinic: For code 80.06:** 2Q, '97, 10

[29] § **80.1 Other arthrotomy**

Excludes: *that for:*
arthrography (88.32)
arthroscopy (80.20-80.29)
injection of drug (81.92)
operative approach — omit code

[29] § **80.2 Arthroscopy**

§ **80.3 Biopsy of joint structure**

Aspiration biopsy

[29] § **80.4 Division of joint capsule, ligament, or cartilage**

Goldner clubfoot release
Heyman-Herndon(-Strong) correction of metatarsus varus
Release of:
adherent or constrictive joint capsule
joint
ligament

Excludes: *symphysiotomy to assist delivery (73.94)*
that for:
carpal tunnel syndrome (04.43)
tarsal tunnel syndrome (04.44)

80.5 Excision or destruction of intervertebral disc

80.50 Excision or destruction of intervertebral disc, unspecified

Unspecified asto excision or destruction

80.51 Excision of intervertebral disc

Diskectomy
Level: cervical
thoracic
lumbar (lumbosacral)
Removal of herniated nucleus
That by laminotomy or hemilaminectomy
That with decompression of spinal nerve root at same level

Code also any:
concomitant decompression of spinal nerve root at different level from excision site
concurrent spinal fusion (81.00-81.09)

Excludes: *intervertebral chemonucleolysis (80.52)*
laminectomy for exploration of intraspinal canal (03.09)
laminotomy for decompression of spinal nerve root only (03.09)

➡ **AHA Coding Clinic:** 1Q, '96, 7; 2Q, '90, 27; S-O, '86, 12

80.52 Intervertebral chemonucleolysis

With aspiration of disc fragments
With diskography
Injection of proteolytic enzyme into intervertebral space (chymopapain)

Excludes: *injection of:*
anesthetic substance (03.91)
injection of other substances (03.92)

80.59 Other destruction of intervertebral disc

Destruction NEC
That by laser

➡ **AHA Coding Clinic:** 1Q, '89, 11; 4Q, '88, 11

80.6 Excision of semilunar cartilage of knee

Excision of meniscus of knee

➡ **AHA Coding Clinic:** 2Q, '96, 3; 1Q, '93, 23

[29] § **80.7 Synovectomy**

Complete or partial resection of synovial membrane

Excludes: *excision of Baker's cyst (83.39)*

[29] § **80.8 Other local excision or destruction of lesion of joint**

[29] § **80.9 Other excision of joint**

Excludes: *cheilectomy of joint (77.80-77.89)*
excision of bone ends (77.80-77.89)

81 Repair and plastic operations on joint structures

81.0 Spinal fusion

Includes: arthrodesis of spine with:
bone graft
internal fixation

81.00 Spinal fusion, not otherwise specified

81.01 Atlas-axis spinal fusion

Craniocervical fusion, C1-C2 fusion, Occiput-C2 fusion } by anterior transoral or posterior technique

Excludes: *that for pseudarthrosis (81.09)*

§ Requires fourth-digit: See above, this page for definitions.
[29] Non-specific OR procedure equals fourth digit of 0

81.02 **Other cervical fusion, anterior technique**
Arthrodesis of C2 level or below:
anterior (interbody) technique
anterolateral technique

Excludes: *that for pseudarthrosis (81.09)*

➡ **AHA Coding Clinic:** 1Q, '96, 7

81.03 **Other cervical fusion, posterior technique**
Arthrodesis of C2 level or below:
posterior (interbody) technique
posterolateral technique

Excludes: *that for pseudarthrosis (81.09)*

81.04 **Dorsal and dorsolumbar fusion, anterior technique**
Arthrodesis of thoracic or thoracolumbar region:
anterior (interbody) technique
anterolateral technique

Excludes: *that for pseudarthrosis (81.09)*

81.05 **Dorsal and dorsolumbar fusion, posterior technique**
Arthrodesis of thoracic or thoracolumbar region:
posterior (interbody) technique
posterolateral technique

Excludes: *that for pseudarthrosis (81.09)*

81.06 **Lumbar and lumbosacral fusion, anterior technique**
Arthrodesis of lumbar or lumbosacral region:
anterior (interbody) technique
anterolateral technique

Excludes: *that for pseudarthrosis (81.09)*

81.07 **Lumbar and lumbosacral fusion, lateral transverse process technique**

Excludes: *that for pseudarthrosis (81.09)*

81.08 **Lumbar and lumbosacral fusion, posterior technique**
Arthrodesis of lumbar or lumbosacral region:
posterior (interbody) technique
posterolateral technique

81.09 **Refusion of spine, any level or technique**
Correction of pseudarthrosis of spine

81.1 **Arthrodesis of foot and ankle**
Includes: arthrodesis of foot and ankle with:
bone graft
external fixation device

81.11 **Ankle fusion**
Tibiotalar fusion

81.12 **Triple arthrodesis**
Talus to calcaneus and calcaneus to cuboid and navicular

81.13 **Subtalar fusion**

81.14 **Midtarsal fusion**

81.15 **Tarsometatarsal fusion**

81.16 **Metatarsophalangeal fusion**

81.17 **Other fusion of foot**

81.2 **Arthrodesis of other joint**
Includes: arthrodesis with:
bone graft
external fixation device
excision of bone ends and compression

81.20 **Arthrodesis of unspecified joint**

81.21 **Arthrodesis of hip**

81.22 **Arthrodesis of knee**

81.23 **Arthrodesis of shoulder**

81.24 **Arthrodesis of elbow**

81.25 **Carporadial fusion**

81.26 **Metacarpocarpal fusion**

81.27 **Metacarpophalangeal fusion**

81.28 **Interphalangeal fusion**

81.29 **Arthrodesis of other specified joints**

81.4 **Other repair of joint of lower extremity**
Includes: arthroplasty of lower extremity with:
external traction or fixation
graft of bone (chips) or cartilage
internal fixation device

➡ **AHA Coding Clinic:** S-O, '85, 4

81.40 **Repair of hip, not elsewhere classified**

81.42 **Five-in-one repair of knee**
Medial meniscectomy, medial collateral ligament repair, vastus medialis advancement, semitendinosus advancement, and pes anserinus transfer

81.43 **Triad knee repair**
Medial meniscectomy with repair of the anterior cruciate ligament and the medial collateral ligament
O'Donoghue procedure

81.44 **Patellar stabilization**
Roux-Goldthwait operation for recurrent dislocation of patella

81.45 **Other repair of the cruciate ligaments**
➡ **AHA Coding Clinic:** M-A, '87, 12

81.46 **Other repair of the collateral ligaments**

81.47 **Other repair of knee**
➡ **AHA Coding Clinic:** 1Q, '96, 3; 3Q, '93, 5

81.49 **Other repair of ankle**

81.5 Joint replacement of lower extremity

Includes: arthroplasty of lower extremity with:
external traction or fixation
graft of bone (chips) or cartilage
internal fixation device or prosthesis
removal of cement spacer

➡ **AHA Coding Clinic:** S-O, '85, 4

81.51 Total hip replacement

Replacement of both femoral head and acetabulum by prosthesis
Total reconstruction of hip

➡ **AHA Coding Clinic:** 2Q, '91, 18

81.52 Partial hip replacement

Bipolar endoprosthesis

➡ **AHA Coding Clinic:** 2Q, '91, 18

81.53 Revision of hip replacement

Partial
Total

➡ **AHA Coding Clinic:** 3Q, '97, 12

81.54 Total knee replacement

Bicompartmental
Tricompartmental
Unicompartmental (hemijoint)

81.55 Revision of knee replacement

Excludes: *arthrodesis of knee (81.22)*

➡ **AHA Coding Clinic:** 2Q, '97, 10

81.56 Total ankle replacement

81.57 Replacement of joint of foot and toe

81.59 Revision of joint replacement of lower extremity, not elsewhere classified

81.7 Arthroplasty and repair of hand, fingers, and wrist

Includes: arthroplasty of hand and finger with:
external traction or fixation
graft of bone (chips) or cartilage
internal fixation device or prosthesis

Excludes: *operations on muscle, tendon, and fascia of hand (82.01-82.99)*

81.71 Arthroplasty of metacarpophalangeal and interphalangeal joint with implant

81.72 Arthroplasty of metacarpophalangeal and interphalangeal joint without implant

➡ **AHA Coding Clinic:** 1Q, '93, 28

81.73 Total wrist replacement

81.74 Arthroplasty of carpocarpal or carpometacarpal joint with implant

81.75 Arthroplasty of carpocarpal or carpometacarpal joint without implant

81.79 Other repair of hand, fingers, and wrist

81.8 Arthroplasty and repair of shoulder and elbow

Includes: arthroplasty of upper limb NEC with:
external traction or fixation
graft of bone (chips) or cartilage
internal fixation device or prosthesis

81.80 Total shoulder replacement

81.81 Partial shoulder replacement

81.82 Repair of recurrent dislocation of shoulder

➡ **AHA Coding Clinic:** 3Q, '95, 15

81.83 Other repair of shoulder

Revision of arthroplasty of shoulder

➡ **AHA Coding Clinic:** 3Q, '93, 5

81.84 Total elbow replacement

81.85 Other repair of elbow

81.9 Other operations on joint structures

81.91 Arthrocentesis

Joint aspiration

Excludes: *that for:*
arthrography (88.32)
biopsy of joint structure (80.30-80.39)
injection of drug (81.92)

81.92 Injection of therapeutic substance into joint or ligament

➡ **AHA Coding Clinic:** 3Q, '89, 16

81.93 Suture of capsule or ligament of upper extremity

Excludes: *that associated with arthroplasty (81.71-81.75, 81.80-81.81, 81.84)*

81.94 Suture of capsule or ligament of ankle and foot

Excludes: *that associated with arthroplasty (81.56-81.59)*

81.95 Suture of capsule or ligament of other lower extremity

Excludes: *that associated with arthroplasty (81.51-81.55, 81.59)*

81.96 Other repair of joint

81.97 Revision of joint replacement of upper extremity

Partial
Total
Removal of cement spacer

81.98 Other diagnostic procedures on joint structures

Excludes: *arthroscopy (80.20-80.29)*
biopsy of joint structure (80.30-80.39)
microscopic examination of specimen from joint (91.51-91.59)
thermography (88.83)
x-ray (87.21-87.29, 88.21-88.33)

81.99 Other

82 Operations on muscle, tendon, and fascia of hand

Includes: operations on:
aponeurosis
synovial membrane (tendon sheath)
tendon sheath

82.0 Incision of muscle, tendon, fascia, and bursa of hand

82.01 Exploration of tendon sheath of hand

Incision of } tendon sheath of hand
Removal of rice bodies in } tendon sheath of hand

Excludes: *division of tendon (82.11)*

82.02 Myotomy of hand

Excludes: *myotomy for division (82.19)*

82.03 Bursotomy of hand

82.04 Incision and drainage of palmar or thenar space

82.09 Other incision of soft tissue of hand

Excludes: *incision of skin and subcutaneous tissue alone (86.01-86.09)*

➡ **AHA Coding Clinic:** N-D, '87, 10

82.1 Division of muscle, tendon, and fascia of hand

82.11 Tenotomy of hand

Division of tendon of hand

82.12 Fasciotomy of hand

Division of fascia of hand

82.19 Other division of soft tissue of hand

Division of muscle of hand

82.2 Excision of lesion of muscle, tendon, and fascia of hand

82.21 Excision or lesion of tendon sheath of hand

Ganglionectomy of tendon sheath (wrist)

82.22 Excision of lesion of muscle of hand

82.29 Excision of other lesion of soft tissue of hand

Excludes: *excision of lesion of skin and subcutaneous tissue (86.21-86.3)*

82.3 Other excision of soft tissue of hand

Code also any skin graft (86.61-86.62, 86.73)

Excludes: *excision of skin and subcutaneous tissue (86.21-86.3)*

82.31 Bursectomy of hand

82.32 Excision of tendon of hand for graft

82.33 Other tenonectomy of hand

Tenosynovectomy of hand

Excludes: *excision of lesion of:*
tendon (82.29)
sheath (82.21)

82.34 Excision of muscle or fascia of hand for graft

82.35 Other fasciectomy of hand

Release of Dupuytren's contracture

Excludes: *excision of lesion of fascia (82.29)*

82.36 Other myectomy of hand

Excludes: *excision of lesion of muscle (82.22)*

82.39 Other excision of soft tissue of hand

Excludes: *excision of skin (86.21-86.3)*
excision of soft tissue lesion (82.29)

82.4 Suture of muscle, tendon, and fascia of hand

82.41 Suture of tendon sheath of hand

82.42 Delayed suture of flexor tendon of hand

82.43 Delayed suture of other tendon of hand

82.44 Other suture of flexor tendon of hand

Excludes: *delayed suture of flexor tendon of hand (82.42)*

82.45 Other suture of other tendon of hand

Excludes: *delayed suture of other tendon of hand (82.43)*

82.46 Suture of muscle or fascia of hand

82.5 Transplantation of muscle and tendon of hand

82.51 Advancement of tendon of hand

82.52 Recession of tendon of hand

82.53 Reattachment of tendon of hand

82.54 Reattachment of muscle of hand

82.55 Other change in hand muscle or tendon length

82.56 Other hand tendon transfer or transplantation

Excludes: *pollicization of thumb (82.61)*
transfer of finger, except thumb (82.81)

82.57 Other hand tendon transposition

➡ **AHA Coding Clinic:** 1Q, '93, 28

82.58 Other hand muscle transfer or transplantation

82.59 Other hand muscle transposition

82.6 Reconstruction of thumb

Includes: digital transfer to act as thumb

Code also any amputation for digital transfer (84.01, 84.11)

82.61 Pollicization operation carrying over nerves and blood supply

82.69 Other reconstruction of thumb

"Cocked-hat" procedure [skin flap and bone]
Grafts:
bone } to thumb
skin (pedicle) } to thumb

82.7 Plastic operation on hand with graft or implant

82.71 Tendon pulley reconstruction

Reconstruction for opponensplasty

82.72 Plastic operation on hand with graft of muscle or fascia

82.79 Plastic operation on hand with other graft or implant

Tendon graft to hand

➡ **AHA Coding Clinic:** J-F, '87, 6

82.8 Other plastic operations on hand

82.81 Transfer of finger, except thumb

Excludes: *pollicization of thumb (82.61)*

82.82 Repair of cleft hand

82.83 Repair of macrodactyly

82.84 Repair of mallet finger

82.85 Other tenodesis of hand

Tendon fixation of hand NOS

82.86 Other tenoplasty of hand

Myotenoplasty of hand

82.89 Other plastic operations on hand

Plication of fascia
Repair of fascial hernia

Excludes: *that with graft or implant (82.71-82.79)*

82.9 Other operations on muscle, tendon, and fascia of hand

Excludes: *diagnostic procedures on soft tissue of hand (83.21-83.29)*

82.91 Lysis of adhesions of hand

Freeing of adhesions of fascia, muscle, and tendon of hand

Excludes: *decompression of carpal tunnel (04.43)*
that by stretching or manipulation only (93.26)

82.92 Aspiration of bursa of hand

82.93 Aspiration of other soft tissue of hand

Excludes: *skin and subcutaneous tissue (86.01)*

82.94 Injection of therapeutic substance into bursa of hand

82.95 Injection of therapeutic substance into tendon of hand

82.96 Other injection of locally-acting therapeutic substance into soft tissue of hand

Excludes: *subcutaneous or intramuscular injection (99.11-99.29)*

82.99 Other operations on muscle, tendon, and fascia of hand

83 Operations on muscle, tendon, fascia, and bursa, except hand

Includes: operations on:
aponeurosis
synovial membrane of bursa and tendon sheaths
tendon sheaths

Excludes: *diaphragm (34.81-34.89)*
hand (82.01-82.99)
muscles of eye (15.01-15.9)

83.0 Incision of muscle, tendon, fascia, and bursa

83.01 Exploration of tendon sheath
Incision of tendon sheath
Removal of rice bodies from tendon sheath

83.02 Myotomy

Excludes: *cricopharyngeal myotomy (29.31)*

➡ **AHA Coding Clinic:** 2Q, '89, 18

83.03 Bursotomy
Removal of calcareous deposit of bursa

Excludes: *aspiration of bursa (percutaneous) (83.94)*

83.09 Other incision of soft tissue
Incision of fascia

Excludes: *incision of skin and subcutaneous tissue alone (86.01-86.09)*

83.1 Division of muscle, tendon, and fascia

83.11 Achillotenotomy

83.12 Adductor tenotomy of hip

83.13 Other tenotomy
Aponeurotomy
Division of tendon
Tendon release
Tendon transection
Tenotomy for thoracic outlet decompression

83.14 Fasciotomy
Division of fascia
Division of iliotibial band
Fascia stripping
Release of Volkmann's contracture by fasciotomy

83.19 Other division of soft tissue
Division of muscle
Muscle release
Myotomy for thoracic outlet decompression
Myotomy with division
Scalenotomy
Transection of muscle

83.2 Diagnostic procedures on muscle, tendon, fascia, and bursa, including that of hand

83.21 Biopsy of soft tissue

Excludes: *biopsy of chest wall (34.23)*
biopsy of skin and subcutaneous tissue (86.11)

83.29 Other diagnostic procedures on muscle, tendon, fascia, and bursa, including that of hand

Excludes: *microscopic examination of specimen (91.51-91.-59)*
soft tissue x-ray (87.09, 87.38-87.39, 88.09, 88.35, 88.37)
thermography of muscle (88.84)

83.3 Excision of lesion of muscle, tendon, fascia, and bursa

Excludes: *biopsy of soft tissue (83.21)*

83.31 Excision of lesion of tendon sheath
Excision of ganglion of tendon sheath, except of hand

83.32 Excision of lesion of muscle
Excision of:
heterotopic bone
muscle scar for release of Volkmann's contracture
myositis ossificans

83.39 Excision of lesion of other soft tissue
Excision of Baker's cyst

Excludes: *bursectomy (83.5)*
excision of lesion of skin and subcutaneous tissue (86.3)
synovectomy (80.70-80.79)

➡ **AHA Coding Clinic:** 2Q, '97, 6

83.4 Other excision of muscle, tendon, and fascia

83.41 Excision of tendon for graft

83.42 Other tenonectomy
Excision of:
aponeurosis
tendon sheath
Tenosynovectomy

83.43 Excision of muscle or fascia for graft

83.44 Other fasciectomy

83.45 Other myectomy
Debridement of muscle NOS
Scalenectomy

83.49 Other excision of soft tissue

83.5 Bursectomy

83.6 Suture of muscle, tendon, and fascia

83.61 Suture of tendon sheath

83.62 Delayed suture of tendon

83.63 Rotator cuff repair

➡ **AHA Coding Clinic:** 2Q, '93, 8

83.64 Other suture of tendon

Achillorrhaphy
Aponeurorrhaphy

Excludes: *delayed suture of tendon (83.62)*

83.65 Other suture of muscle or fascia

Repair of diastasis recti

83.7 Reconstruction of muscle and tendon

Excludes: *reconstruction of muscle and tendon associated with arthroplasty*

83.71 Advancement of tendon

83.72 Recession of tendon

83.73 Reattachment of tendon

83.74 Reattachment of muscle

83.75 Tendon transfer or transplantation

83.76 Other tendon transposition

83.77 Muscle transfer or transplantation

Release of Volkmann's contracture by muscle transplantation

83.79 Other muscle transposition

83.8 Other plastic operations on muscle, tendon, and fascia

Excludes: *plastic operations on muscle, tendon, and fascia associated with arthroplasty*

83.81 Tendon graft

83.82 Graft of muscle or fascia

83.83 Tendon pulley reconstruction

83.84 Release of clubfoot, not elsewhere classified

Evans operation on clubfoot

83.85 Other change in muscle or tendon length

Hamstring lengthening
Heel cord shortening
Plastic achillotenotomy
Tendon plication

83.86 Quadricepsplasty

83.87 Other plastic operations on muscle

Musculoplasty
Myoplasty

➡ **AHA Coding Clinic:** 1Q, '97, 9

83.88 Other plastic operations on tendon

Myotenoplasty
Tendon fixation
Tenodesis
Tenoplasty

83.89 Other plastic operations on fascia

Fascia lengthening
Fascioplasty
Plication of fascia

83.9 Other operations on muscle, tendon, fascia, and bursa

Excludes: *nonoperative:*
manipulation (93.25-93.29)
stretching (93.27-93.29)

83.91 Lysis of adhesions of muscle, tendon, fascia, and bursa

Excludes: *that for tarsal tunnel syndrome (04.44)*

83.92 Insertion or replacement of skeletal muscle stimulator

83.93 Removal of skeletal muscle stimulator

83.94 Aspiration of bursa

83.95 Aspiration of other soft tissue

Excludes: *that of skin and subcutaneous tissue (86.01)*

83.96 Injection of therapeutic substance into bursa

83.97 Injection of therapeutic substance into tendon

83.98 Injection of locally-acting therapeutic substance into other soft tissue

Excludes: *subcutaneous or intramuscular injection (99.11-99.29)*

83.99 Other operations on muscle, tendon, fascia, and bursa

Suture of bursa

84 Other procedures on musculoskeletal system

84.0 Amputation of upper limb

Excludes: *revision of amputation stump (84.3)*

84.00 Upper limb amputation, not otherwise specified

Closed flap amputation, Kineplastic amputation, Open or guillotine amputation, Revision of current traumatic amputation } of upper limb NOS

84.01 Amputation and disarticulation of finger

Excludes: *ligation of supernumerary finger (86.26)*

84.02 Amputation and disarticulation of thumb

84.03 Amputation through hand

Amputation through carpals

84.04 Disarticulation of wrist

84.05 Amputation through forearm

Forearm amputation

84.06 Disarticulation of elbow

84.07 Amputation through humerus

Upper arm amputation

84.08 Disarticulation of shoulder

84.09 Interthoracoscapular amputation

Forequarter amputation

84.1 Amputation of lower limb

Excludes: *revision of amputation stump (84.3)*

84.10 Lower limb amputation, not otherwise specified

Closed flap amputation, Kineplastic amputation, Open or guillotine amputation, Revision of current traumatic amputation } of lower limb NOS

84.11 Amputation of toe

Amputation through metatarsophalangeal joint
Disarticulation of toe

Excludes: *ligation of supernumerary toe (86.26)*

84.12 Amputation through foot

Amputation of forefoot
Amputation through middle of foot
Chopart's amputation
Midtarsal amputation
Transmetatarsal amputation

84.13 Disarticulation of ankle

84.14 Amputation of ankle through malleoli of tibia and fibula

84.15 Other amputation below knee

Amputation of leg through tibia and fibula NOS

84.16 Disarticulation of knee/

Batch, Spitler, and McFaddin amputation
Mazet amputation
S.P. Roger's amputation

84.17 Amputation above knee

Amputation of leg through femur
Amputation of thigh
Conversion of below-knee amputation into above-knee amputation
Supracondylar above-knee amputation

84.18 Disarticulation of hip

84.19 Abdominopelvic amputation

Hemipelvectomy
Hindquarter amputation

84.2 Reattachment of extremity

84.21 Thumb reattachment

84.22 Finger reattachment

84.23 Forearm, wrist, or hand reattachment

84.24 Upper arm reattachment

Reattachment of arm NOS

84.25 Toe reattachment

84.26 Foot reattachment

84.27 Lower leg or ankle reattachment

Reattachment of leg NOS

84.28 Thigh reattachment

84.29 Other reattachment

84.3 Revision of amputation stump

Reamputation, Secondary closure, Trimming } of stump

Excludes: *revision of current traumatic amputation [revision by further amputation of current injury] (84.00-84.19, 84.91)*

➡ **AHA Coding Clinic:** 4Q, '88, 12

84.4 Implantation or fitting of prosthetic limb device

84.40 Implantation or fitting of prosthetic limb device, not otherwise specified

84.41 Fitting of prosthesis of upper arm and shoulder

84.42 Fitting of prosthesis of lower arm and hand

84.43 Fitting of prosthesis of arm, not otherwise specified

84.44 Implantation of prosthetic device of arm

84.45 Fitting of prosthesis above knee

84.46 Fitting of prosthesis below knee

84.47 Fitting of prosthesis of leg, not otherwise specified

84.48 Implantation of prosthetic device of leg

84.9 Other operations on musculoskeletal system

Excludes: *nonoperative manipulation (93.25-93.29)*

84.91 Amputation, not otherwise specified

84.92 Separation of equal conjoined twins

84.93 Separation of unequal conjoined twins
Separation of conjoined twins NOS

84.99 Other

15. OPERATIONS ON THE INTEGUMENTARY SYSTEM (85-86)

85 Operations on the breast

Includes: operations on the skin and subcutaneous tissue of:
- breast } female or male
- previous mastectomy site } female or male
- revision or previous mastectomy site

85.0 Mastotomy

Incision of breast (skin)
Mammotomy

Excludes: *aspiration of breast (85.91)*
removal of implant (85.94)

➡ **AHA Coding Clinic:** 2Q, '90, 27

85.1 Diagnostic procedures on breast

[22] **85.11 Closed [percutaneous] [needle] biopsy of breast**

➡ **AHA Coding Clinic:** 3Q, '89, 17

[21] **85.12 Open biopsy of breast**

➡ **AHA Coding Clinic:** 3Q, '89, 17; M-A, '86, 11

85.19 Other diagnostic procedures on breast

Excludes: *mammary ductogram (87.35)*
mammography NEC (87.37)
manual examination (89.36)
microscopic examination of specimen (91.61-91.69)
thermography (88.85)
ultrasonography (88.73)
xerography (87.36)

85.2 Excision or destruction of breast tissue

Excludes: *mastectomy (85.41-85.48)*
reduction mammoplasty (85.31-85.32)

85.20 Excision or destruction of breast tissue, not otherwise specified

85.21 Local excision of lesion of breast

Lumpectomy
Removal of area of fibrosis from breast

Excludes: *biopsy of breast (85.11-85.12)*

➡ **AHA Coding Clinic:** 2Q, '90, 27; 3Q, '89, 17; M-A, '86, 11

85.22 Resection of quadrant of breast

85.23 Subtotal mastectomy

Excludes: *quadrant resection (85.22)*

➡ **AHA Coding Clinic:** 2Q, '92, 7

85.24 Excision of ectopic breast tissue

Excision of accessory nipple

85.25 Excision of nipple

Excludes: *excision of accessory nipple (85.24)*

85.3 Reduction mammoplasty and subcutaneous mammectomy

➡ **AHA Coding Clinic:** 4Q, '95, 79, 80

85.31 Unilateral reduction mammoplasty

Unilateral:
- amputative mammoplasty
- size reduction mammoplasty

85.32 Bilateral reduction mammoplasty

Amputative mammoplasty
Reduction mammoplasty (for gynecomastia)

85.33 Unilateral subcutaneous mammectomy with synchronous implant

Excludes: *that without synchronous implant (85.34)*

85.34 Other unilateral subcutaneous mammectomy

Removal of breast tissue with preservation of skin and nipple
Subcutaneous mammectomy NOS

85.35 Bilateral subcutaneous mammectomy with synchronous implant

Excludes: *that without synchronous implant (85.36)*

85.36 Other bilateral subcutaneous mammectomy

85.4 Mastectomy

85.41 Unilateral simple mastectomy

Mastectomy:
- NOS
- complete

85.42 Bilateral simple mastectomy

Bilateral complete mastectomy

85.43 Unilateral extended simple mastectomy

Extended simple mastectomy NOS
Modified radical mastectomy
Simple mastectomy with excision of regional lymph nodes

➡ **AHA Coding Clinic:** 3Q, '91, 24; 2Q, '91, 21

85.44 Bilateral extended simple mastectomy

➡ **AHA Coding Clinic:** 3Q, '91, 24; 2Q, '91, 21

[21] Open biopsy
[22] Closed biopsy

85.45 **Unilateral radical mastectomy**
Excision of breast, pectoral muscles, and regional lymph nodes [axillary, clavicular, supraclavicular]
Radical mastectomy NOS
➡ **AHA Coding Clinic:** 2Q, '91, 21

85.46 **Bilateral radical mastectomy**
➡ **AHA Coding Clinic:** 2Q, '91, 21

85.47 **Unilateral extended radical mastectomy**
Excision of breast, muscles, and lymph nodes [axillary, clavicular, supraclavicular, internal mammary, and mediastinal]
Extended radical mastectomy NOS

85.48 **Bilateral extended radical mastectomy**

85.5 **Augmentation mammoplasty**

Excludes: *that associated with subcutaneous mammectomy (85.33, 85.35)*

➡ **AHA Coding Clinic:** 3Q, '97, 12; 4Q, '95, 76, 80

85.50 **Augmentation mammoplasty, not otherwise specified**

85.51 **Unilateral injection into breast for augmentation**

85.52 **Bilateral injection into breast for augmentation**
Injection into breast for augmentation NOS

85.53 **Unilateral breast implant**

85.54 **Bilateral breast implant**
Breast implant NOS

85.6 **Mastopexy**

85.7 **Total reconstruction of breast**
➡ **AHA Coding Clinic:** 4Q, '95, 77; 1Q, '93, 27

85.8 **Other repair and plastic operations on breast**

Excludes: *that for:*
augmentation (85.50-85.54)
reconstruction (85.7)
reduction (85.31-85.32)

➡ **AHA Coding Clinic:** 4Q, '95, 77

85.81 **Suture of laceration of breast**

85.82 **Split-thickness graft to breast**

85.83 **Full-thickness graft to breast**
➡ **AHA Coding Clinic:** 4Q, '95, 77

85.84 **Pedicle graft to breast**
➡ **AHA Coding Clinic:** 4Q, '95, 77

85.85 **Muscle flap graft to breast**
➡ **AHA Coding Clinic:** 4Q, '95, 77

85.86 **Transposition of nipple**
➡ **AHA Coding Clinic:** 4Q, '95, 78

85.87 **Other repair or reconstruction of nipple**
➡ **AHA Coding Clinic:** 4Q, '95, 78

85.89 **Other mammoplasty**

85.9 **Other operations on the breast**

85.91 **Aspiration of breast**

Excludes: *percutaneous biopsy of breast (85.11)*

85.92 **Injection of therapeutic agent into breast**

Excludes: *that for augmentation of breast (85.51-85.52)*

85.93 **Revision of implant of breast**
➡ **AHA Coding Clinic:** 4Q, '95, 76

85.94 **Removal of implant of breast**
➡ **AHA Coding Clinic:** 3Q, '92, 4

85.95 **Insertion of breast tissue expander**
Insertion (soft tissue) of tissue expander (one or more) under muscle or platysma to develop skin flaps for donor use

85.96 **Removal of breast tissue expander(s)**
➡ **AHA Coding Clinic:** 4Q, '95, 77

85.99 **Other**

86 Operations on skin and subcutaneous tissue

Includes: operations on:
hair follicles
male perineum
nails
sebaceous glands
subcutaneous fat pads
sudoriferous glands
superficial fossae

Excludes: *those on skin of:*
anus (49.01-49.99)
breast (mastectomy site) (85.0-85.99)
ear (18.01-18.9)
eyebrow (08.01-08.99)
eyelid (08.01-08.99)
female perineum (71.01-71.9)
lips (27.0-27.99)
nose (21.00-21.99)
penis (64.0-64.99)
scrotum (61.0-61.99)
vulva (71.01-71.9)

86.0 **Incision of skin and subcutaneous tissue**

86.01 **Aspiration of skin and subcutaneous tissue**
Aspiration of:
abscess } of nail, skin, or subcutaneous tissue
hematoma }
seroma }

➡ **AHA Coding Clinic:** 3Q, '89, 16

86.02 Injection or tattooing of skin lesion or defect

Injection } of filling material
Insertion }
Pigmenting of skin

86.03 Incision of pilonidal sinus or cyst

Excludes: *marsupialization (86.21)*

86.04 Other incision with drainage of skin and subcutaneous tissue

Excludes: *drainage of:*
fascial compartments of face and mouth (27.0)
palmar or thenar space (82.04)
pilonidal sinus or cyst (86.03)

86.05 Incision with removal of foreign body from skin and subcutaneous tissue

Removal of tissue expander(s) from skin or soft tissue other than breast tissue

Excludes: *removal of foreign body without incision (98.20-98.29)*

➡ **AHA Coding Clinic:** 2Q, '96, 15; N-D, '87, 10; N-D, '86, 9

86.06 Insertion of totally implantable infusion pump

Code also any associated catheterization

Excludes: *insertion of totally implantable vascular access device (86.07)*

➡ **AHA Coding Clinic:** 4Q, '90, 14

86.07 Insertion of totally implantable vascular access device [VAD]

Totally implanted port

Excludes: *insertion of totally implantable infusion pump (86.06)*

➡ **AHA Coding Clinic:** 1Q, '96, 3; 2Q, '94, 11; 3Q, '91, 13; 4Q, '90, 15

86.09 Other incision of skin and subcutaneous tissue

Creation of thalamic stimulator pulse generator pocket, new site
Exploration:
sinus tract, skin
superficial fossa
Undercutting of hair follicle

Excludes: *that of:*
cardiac pacemaker pocket, new site (37.79)
fascial compartments of face and mouth (27.0)

➡ **AHA Coding Clinic:** 4Q, '97, 57; 3Q, '89, 17; N-D, '86, 1; N-D, '84, 6

86.1 Diagnostic procedures on skin and subcutaneous tissue

86.11 Biopsy of skin and subcutaneous tissue

86.19 Other diagnostic procedures on skin and subcutaneous tissue

Excludes: *microscopic examination of specimen from skin and subcutaneous tissue (91.61-91.79)*

86.2 Excision or destruction of lesion or tissue of skin and subcutaneous tissue

86.21 Excision of pilonidal cyst or sinus

Marsupialization of cyst

Excludes: *incision of pilonidal cyst or sinus (86.03)*

86.22 Excisional debridement of wound, infection, or burn

Removal by excision of:
devitalized tissue
necrosis
slough

Excludes: *debridement of:*
abdominal wall (wound) (54.3)
bone (77.60-77.69)
muscle (83.45)
of hand (82.36)
nail (bed) (fold) (86.27)
nonexcisional debridement of wound, infection, or burn (86.28)
open fracture site (79.60-79.69)
pedicle or flap graft (86.75)

➡ **AHA Coding Clinic:** 2Q, '92, 17; 3Q, '91, 18; 3Q, '89, 16; 4Q, '88, 5; N-D, '86, 1

86.23 Removal of nail, nailbed, or nail fold

86.24 Chemosurgery of skin

Chemical peel of skin

86.25 Dermabrasion

That with laser

Excludes: *dermabrasion of wound to remove embedded debris (86.28)*

86.26 Ligation of dermal appendage

Excludes: *excision of preauricular appendage (18.29)*

86.27 Debridement of nail, nail bed, or nail fold

Removal of:
necrosis
slough

Excludes: *removal of nail, nail bed, or nail fold (86.23)*

86.28 Nonexcisional debridement of wound, infection, or burn
Debridement NOS
Removal of devitalized tissue, necrosis, and slough by such methods as:
brushing
irrigation (under pressure)
scrubbing
washing

➡ **AHA Coding Clinic:** 3Q, '91, 18; 4Q, '88, 5

86.3 Other local excision or destruction of lesion or tissue of skin and subcutaneous tissue
Destruction of skin by:
cauterization
cryosurgery
fulguration
laser beam
That with Z-plasty

Excludes: *adipectomy (86.83)*
biopsy of skin (86.11)
wide or radical excision of skin (86.4)
Z-plasty without excision (86.84)

➡ **AHA Coding Clinic:** 1Q, '96, 15; 2Q, '90, 27; 1Q, '89, 12

86.4 Radical excision of skin lesion
Wide excision of skin lesion involving underlying or adjacent structure

Code also any lymph node dissection (40.3-40.5)

86.5 Suture of skin and subcutaneous tissue

86.51 Replantation of scalp

86.59 Suture of skin and subcutaneous tissue of other sites

86.6 Free skin graft
Includes: excision of skin for autogenous graft

Excludes: *construction or reconstruction of:*
penis (64.43-64.44)
trachea (31.75)
vagina (70.61-70.62)

86.60 Free skin graft, not otherwise specified

86.61 Full-thickness skin graft to hand

Excludes: *heterograft (86.65)*
homograft (86.66)

86.62 Other skin graft to hand

Excludes: *heterograft (86.65)*
homograft (86.66)

86.63 Full-thickness skin graft to other sites

Excludes: *heterograft (86.65)*
homograft (86.66)

86.64 Hair transplant

Excludes: *hair follicle transplant to eyebrow or eyelash (08.63)*

86.65 Heterograft to skin
Pigskin graft
Porcine graft

86.66 Homograft to skin
Graft to skin of:
amnionic membrane } from donor
skin } from donor

86.67 Dermal regenerative graft
Artificial skin NOS
Creation of "neodermis"
Decellularized allodermis
Integumentary matrix implants
Prosthetic implant of dermal layer of skin
Regenerate dermal layer of skin

Excludes: *heterograft to skin (86.65)*
homograft to skin (86.66)

86.69 Other skin graft to other sites

Excludes: *heterograft (86.65)*
homograft (86.66)

86.7 Pedicle grafts or flaps

Excludes: *construction or reconstruction of:*
penis (64.43-64.44)
trachea (31.75)
vagina (70.61-70.62)

86.70 Pedicle or flap graft, not otherwise specified

86.71 Cutting and preparation of pedicle grafts or flaps
Elevation of pedicle from its bed
Flap design and raising
Partial cutting of pedicle or tube
Pedicle delay

Excludes: *pollicization or digital transfer (82.61,82.81)*
revision of pedicle (86.75)

86.72 Advancement of pedicle graft

86.73 Attachment of pedicle or flap graft to hand

Excludes: *pollicization or digital transfer (82.61, 82.81)*

86.74 Attachment of pedicle or flap graft to other sites
Attachment by:
advanced flap
double pedicled flap
pedicle graft
rotating flap
sliding flap
tube graft

➡ **AHA Coding Clinic:** 1Q, '96, 15

86.75 Revision of pedicle or flap graft
Debridement } of pedicle or flap graft
Defatting } of pedicle or flap graft

86.8 Other repair and reconstruction of skin and subcutaneous tissue

86.81 Repair for facial weakness

86.82 Facial rhytidectomy
Face lift

Excludes: *rhytidectomy of eyelid (08.86-08.87)*

86.83 Size reduction plastic operation
Liposuction
Reduction of adipose tissue of:
abdominal wall (pendulous)
arms (batwing)
buttock
thighs (trochanteric lipomatosis)

Excludes: *breast (85.31-85.32)*

86.84 Relaxation of scar or web contracture of skin
Z-plasty of skin

Excludes: *Z-plasty with excision of lesion (86.3)*

86.85 Correction of syndactyly

86.86 Onychoplasty

86.89 Other repair and reconstruction of skin and subcutaneous tissue

Excludes: *mentoplasty (76.67-76.68)*

➡ **AHA Coding Clinic:** 2Q, '93, 11; 2Q, '92, 17

86.9 Other operations on skin and subcutaneous tissue

86.91 Excision of skin for graft
Excision of skin with closure of donor site

Excludes: *that with graft at same operative episode (86.60-86.69)*

86.92 Electrolysis and other epilation of skin

Excludes: *epilation of eyelid (08.91-08.93)*

86.93 Insertion of tissue expander
Insertion (subcutaneous) (soft tissue) of expander (one or more) in scalp (subgaleal space), face, neck, trunk except breast, and upper and lower extremities for development of skin flaps for donor use

Excludes: *flap graft preparation (86.71)*
tissue expander, breast (85.95)

86.99 Other

Excludes: *removal of sutures from:*
abdomen (97.83)
head and neck (97.38)
thorax (97.43)
trunk NEC (97.84)
wound catheter:
irrigation (96.58)
replacement (97.15)

➡ **AHA Coding Clinic:** 4Q, '97, 57; N-D, '86, 1

16. MISCELLANEOUS DIAGNOSTIC AND THERAPEUTIC PROCEDURES (87-99)

87 Diagnostic radiology

87.0 Soft tissue x-ray of face, head, and neck

Excludes: *angiography (88.40-88.68)*

87.01 Pneumoencephalogram

87.02 Other contrast radiogram of brain and skull
Pneumocisternogram
Pneumoventriculogram
Posterior fossa myelogram

87.03 Computerized axial tomography of head
C.A.T. scan of head

87.04 Other tomography of head

87.05 Contrast dacryocystogram

87.06 Contrast radiogram of nasopharynx

87.07 Contrast laryngogram

87.08 Cervical lymphangiogram

87.09 Other soft tissue x-ray of face, head, and neck
Noncontrast x-ray of:
- adenoid
- larynx
- nasolacrimal duct
- nasopharynx
- salivary gland
- thyroid region
- uvula

Excludes: *x-ray study of eye (95.14)*

87.1 Other x-ray of face, head, and neck

Excludes: *angiography (88.40-88.68)*

87.11 Full-mouth x-ray of teeth

87.12 Other dental x-ray
Orthodontic cephalogram or cephalometrics
Panorex examination of mandible
Root canal x-ray

87.13 Temporomandibular contrast arthrogram

87.14 Contrast radiogram of orbit

87.15 Contrast radiogram of sinus

87.16 Other x-ray of facial bones
X-ray of:
- frontal area
- mandible
- maxilla
- nasal sinuses
- nose
- orbit
- supraorbital area
- symphysis menti
- zygomaticomaxillary complex

87.17 Other x-ray of skull
Lateral projection, Sagittal projection, Tangenital projection } of skull

87.2 X-ray of spine

87.21 Contrast myelogram

87.22 Other x-ray of cervical spine

87.23 Other x-ray of thoracic spine

87.24 Other x-ray of lumbosacral spine
Sacrococcygeal x-ray

87.29 Other x-ray of spine
Spinal x-ray NOS

87.3 Soft tissue x-ray of thorax

Excludes: *angiocardiography (88.50-88.58)*
angiography (88.40-88.68)

87.31 Endotracheal bronchogram

87.32 Other contrast bronchogram
Transcricoid bronchogram

87.33 Mediastinal pneumogram

87.34 Intrathoracic lymphangiogram

87.35 Contrast radiogram of mammary ducts

87.36 Xerography of breast

87.37 Other mammography
➡ **AHA Coding Clinic:** 3Q, '89, 17

87.38 Sinogram of chest wall
Fistulogram of chest wall

87.39 Other soft tissue x-ray of chest wall

87.4 Other x-ray of thorax

Excludes: *angiocardiography (88.50-88.58)*
angiography (88.40-88.68)

87.41 Computerized axial tomography of thorax
C.A.T. scan
Crystal linea scan of x-ray beam
Electronic subtraction
Photoelectric response
Tomography with use of computer, x-rays, and camera
} of thorax

87.42 Other tomography of thorax
Cardiac tomogram

87.43 X-ray of ribs, sternum, and clavicle
Examination for:
cervical rib
fracture

87.44 Routine chest x-ray, so described
X-ray of chest NOS

87.49 Other chest x-ray
X-ray of:
bronchus NOS
diaphragm NOS
heart NOS
lung NOS
mediastinum NOS
trachea NOS

87.5 Biliary tract x-ray

87.51 Percutaneous hepatic cholangiogram
➡ **AHA Coding Clinic:** 2Q, '90, 28; N-D, '87, 1

87.52 Intravenous cholangiogram

87.53 Intraoperative cholangiogram
➡ **AHA Coding Clinic:** 1Q, '96, 12; 2Q, '90, 28; 3Q, '89, 18; 4Q, '88, 7

87.54 Other cholangiogram

87.59 Other biliary tract x-ray
Cholecystogram

87.6 Other x-ray of digestive system

87.61 Barium swallow

87.62 Upper GI series

87.63 Small bowel series

87.64 Lower GI series

87.65 Other x-ray of intestine

87.66 Contrast pancreatogram

87.69 Other digestive tract x-ray

87.7 X-ray of urinary system

Excludes: *angiography of renal vessels (88.45, 88.65)*

87.71 Computerized axial tomography of kidney
C.A.T scan of kidney

87.72 Other nephrotomogram

87.73 Intravenous pyelogram
Diuretic infusion pyelogram

87.74 Retrograde pyelogram

87.75 Percutaneous pyelogram

87.76 Retrograde cystourethrogram

87.77 Other cystogram

87.78 Ileal conduitogram

87.79 Other x-ray of the urinary system
KUB x-ray

87.8 X-ray of female genital organs ♀

87.81 X-ray of gravid uterus
Intrauterine cephalometry by x-ray

87.82 Gas contrast hysterosalpingogram

87.83 Opaque dye contrast hysterosalpingogram

87.84 Percutaneous hysterogram

87.85 Other x-ray of fallopian tubes and uterus

87.89 Other x-ray of female genital organs

87.9 X-ray of male genital organs ♂

87.91 Contrast seminal vesiculogram

87.92 Other x-ray of prostate and seminal vesicles

87.93 Contrast epididymogram

87.94 Contrast vasogram

87.95 Other x-ray of epididymis and vas deferens

87.99 Other x-ray of male genital organs

88 Other diagnostic radiology and related techniques

88.0 Soft tissue x-ray of abdomen

Excludes: *angiography (88.40-88.68)*

88.01 **Computerized axial tomography of abdomen**
C.A.T. scan of abdomen

Excludes: *CA.T. scan of kidney (87.71)*

88.02 **Other abdomen tomography**

Excludes: *nephrotomogram (87.72)*

88.03 **Sinogram of abdominal wall**
Fistulogram of abdominal wall

88.04 **Abdominal lymphangiogram**

88.09 **Other soft tissue x-ray of abdominal wall**

88.1 **Other x-ray of abdomen**

88.11 **Pelvic opaque dye contrast radiography**

88.12 **Pelvic gas contrast radiography**
Pelvic pneumoperitoneum

88.13 **Other peritoneal pneumogram**

88.14 **Retroperitoneal fistulogram**

88.15 **Retroperitoneal pneumogram**

88.16 **Other retroperitoneal x-ray**

88.19 **Other x-ray of abdomen**
Flat plate of abdomen

88.2 **Skeletal x-ray of extremities and pelvis**

Excludes: *contrast radiogram of joint (88.32)*

88.21 **Skeletal x-ray of shoulder and upper arm**

88.22 **Skeletal x-ray of elbow and forearm**

88.23 **Skeletal x-ray of wrist and hand**

88.24 **Skeletal x-ray of upper limb, not otherwise specified**

88.25 **Pelvimetry**

88.26 **Other skeletal x-ray of pelvis and hip**

88.27 **Skeletal x-ray of thigh, knee, and lower leg**

88.28 **Skeletal x-ray of ankle and foot**

88.29 **Skeletal x-ray of lower limb, not otherwise specified**

88.3 **Other x-ray**

88.31 **Skeletal series**
X-ray of whole skeleton

88.32 **Contrast arthrogram**

Excludes: *that of temporomandibular joint (87.13)*

88.33 **Other skeletal x-ray**

Excludes: *skeletal x-ray of:*
extremities and pelvis (88.21-88.29)
face, head, and neck (87.11-87.17)
spine (87.21-87.29)
thorax (87.43)

88.34 **Lymphangiogram of upper limb**

88.35 **Other soft tissue x-ray of upper limb**

88.36 **Lymphangiogram of lower limb**

88.37 **Other soft tissue x-ray of lower limb**

Excludes: *femoral angiography (88.48, 88.66)*

88.38 **Other computerized axial tomography**
C.A.T. scan NOS

Excludes: *C.A.T. scan of:*
abdomen (88.01)
head (87.03)
kidney (87.71)
thorax (87.41)

88.39 **X-ray, other and unspecified**

88.4 **Arteriography using contrast material**

Includes: angiography of arteries
arterial puncture for injection of contrast material
radiography of arteries (by fluoroscopy)
retrograde arteriography

Note: The fourth-digit subclassification identifies the site to be viewed, not the site of injection.

Excludes: *arteriography using:*
radioisotopes or radionuclides (92.01-92.19)
ultrasound (88.71-88.79)
fluorescein angiography of eye (95.12)

➡ **AHA Coding Clinic:** N-D, '85, 14

88.40 **Arteriography using contrast material, unspecified site**

88.41 Arteriography of cerebral arteries

Angiography of:
basilar artery
carotid (internal)
posterior cerebral circulation
vertebral artery

➡ **AHA Coding Clinic:** 1Q, '97, 3

88.42 Aortography

Arteriography of aorta and aortic arch

88.43 Arteriography of pulmonary arteries

88.44 Arteriography of other intrathoracic vessels

Excludes: *angiocardiography (88.50-88.58)*
arteriography of coronary arteries (88.55-88.57)

88.45 Arteriography of renal arteries

88.46 Arteriography of placenta ♀

Placentogram using contrast material

88.47 Arteriography of other intra-abdominal arteries

➡ **AHA Coding Clinic:** N-D, '87, 4

88.48 Arteriography of femoral and other lower extremity arteries

➡ **AHA Coding Clinic:** 2Q, '96, 6; 2Q, '89, 17

88.49 Arteriography of other specified sites

88.5 Angiocardiography using contrast material

Includes: arterial puncture and insertion of arterial catheter for injection of contrast material
cineangiocardiography
selective angiocardiography

Code also synchronous cardiac catheterization (37.21-37.23)

Excludes: *angiography of pulmonary vessels (88.43, 88.62)*

➡ **AHA Coding Clinic:** 3Q, '92, 10

88.50 Angiocardiography, not otherwise specified

88.51 Angiocardiography of venae cavae

Inferior vena cavography
Phlebography of vena cava (inferior) (superior)

88.52 Angiocardiography of right heart structures

Angiocardiography of:
pulmonary valve
right atrium
right ventricle (outflow tract)

Excludes: *that combined with left heart angiocardiography (88.54)*

88.53 Angiocardiography of left heart structures

Angiocardiography of:
aortic valve
left atrium
left ventricle (outflow tract)

Excludes: *that combined with right heart angiocardiography (88.54)*

➡ **AHA Coding Clinic:** 4Q, '88, 4

88.54 Combined right and left heart angiocardiography

88.55 Coronary arteriography using a single catheter

Coronary arteriography by Sones technique
Direct selective coronary arteriography using a single catheter

88.56 Coronary arteriography using two catheters

Coronary arteriography by:
Judkins technique
Ricketts and Abrams technique
Direct selective coronary arteriography using two catheters

➡ **AHA Coding Clinic:** 4Q, '88, 4

88.57 Other and unspecified coronary arteriography

Coronary arteriography NOS

88.58 Negative-contrast cardiac roentgenography

Cardiac roentgenography with injection of carbon dioxide

88.6 Phlebography

Includes: angiography of veins
radiography of veins (by fluoroscopy)
retrograde phlebography
venipuncture for injection of contrast material
venography using contrast material

Note: The fourth-digit subclassification (88.60-88.67) identifies the site to be viewed, not the site of injection.

Excludes: *angiography using:*
radioisotopes or radionuclides (92.01-92.19)
ultrasound (88.71-88.79)
fluorescein angiography of eye (95.12)

88.60 Phlebography using contrast material, unspecified site

88.61 Phlebography of veins of head and neck using contrast material

88.62 Phlebography of pulmonary veins using contrast material

88.63 Phlebography of other intrathoracic veins using contrast material

88.64 **Phlebography of the portal venous system using contrast material**
Splenoportogram (by splenic arteriography)

88.65 **Phlebography of other intra-abdominal veins using contrast material**

88.66 **Phlebography of femoral and other lower extremity veins using contrast material**

88.67 **Phlebography of other specified sites using contrast material**

88.68 **Impedance phlebography**

88.7 **Diagnostic ultrasound**

Includes: echography
ultrasonic angiography
ultrasonography

88.71 **Diagnostic ultrasound of head and neck**
Determination of midline shift of brain
Echoencephalography

Excludes: *eye (95.13)*

➡ **AHA Coding Clinic:** 1Q, '92, 11

88.72 **Diagnostic ultrasound of heart**
Echocardiography

88.73 **Diagnostic ultrasound of other sites of thorax**
Aortic arch, Breast, Lung } ultrasonography

88.74 **Diagnostic ultrasound of digestive system**

88.75 **Diagnostic ultrasound of urinary system**

88.76 **Diagnostic ultrasound of abdomen and retroperitoneum**

88.77 **Diagnostic ultrasound of peripheral vascular system**
Deep vein thrombosis ultrasonic scanning

➡ **AHA Coding Clinic:** 1Q, '92, 11

88.78 **Diagnostic ultrasound of gravid uterus** ♀
Intrauterine cephalometry:
echo
ultrasonic
Placental localization by ultrasound

88.79 **Other diagnostic ultrasound**
Ultrasonography of:
multiple sites
nongravid uterus
total body

88.8 **Thermography**

88.81 **Cerebral thermography**

88.82 **Ocular thermography**

88.83 **Bone thermography**
Osteoarticular thermography

88.84 **Muscle thermography**

88.85 **Breast thermography**

88.86 **Blood vessel thermography**
Deep vein thermography

88.89 **Thermography of other sites**
Lymph gland thermography
Thermography NOS

88.9 **Other diagnostic imaging**

88.90 **Diagnostic imaging, not elsewhere classified**

88.91 **Magnetic resonance imaging of brain and brain stem**

88.92 **Magnetic resonance imaging of chest and myocardium**
For evaluation of hilar and mediastinal lymphadenopathy

88.93 **Magnetic resonance imaging of spinal canal**
Spinal cord levels:
cervical
thoracic
lumbar (lumbosacral)
Spinal cord
Spine

88.94 **Magnetic resonance imaging of musculoskeletal**
Bone marrow blood supply
Extremities (upper) (lower)

88.95 **Magnetic resonance imaging of pelvis, prostate, and bladder**

88.97 **Magnetic resonance imaging of other and unspecified sites**
Abdomen
Face
Neck
Eye orbit

88.98 **Bone mineral density studies**
Dual photon absorptiometry
Quantitative computed tomography (CT) studies
Radiographic densitometry
Single photon absorptiometry

89 Interview, evaluation, consultation, and examination

89.0 **Diagnostic interview, consultation, and evaluation**

Excludes: *psychiatric diagnostic interview (94.11-94.19)*

89.01 Interview and evaluation, described as brief
Abbreviated history and evaluation

89.02 Interview and evaluation, described as limited
Interval history and evaluation

89.03 Interview and evaluation, described as comprehensive
History and evaluation of new problem

89.04 Other interview and evaluation

89.05 Diagnostic interview and evaluation, not otherwise specified

89.06 Consultation, described as limited
Consultation on a single organ system

89.07 Consultation, described as comprehensive

89.08 Other consultation

89.09 Consultation, not otherwise specified

89.1 Anatomic and physiologic measurements and manual examinations — nervous system and sense organs

Excludes: *ear examination (95.41-95.49)*
eye examination (95.01-95.26)
the listed procedures when done as part of a general physical examination (89.7)

89.10 Intracarotid amobarbital test
Wada test

89.11 Tonometry

89.12 Nasal function study
Rhinomanometry

89.13 Neurologic examination

89.14 Electroencephalogram

Excludes: *that with polysomnogram (89.17)*

89.15 Other nonoperative neurologic function tests
➡ **AHA Coding Clinic:** 2Q, '91, 14; J-F, '87, 16; N-D, '84, 6

89.16 Transillumination of newborn skull

89.17 Polysomnogram
Sleep recording

89.18 Other sleep disorder function tests
Multiple sleep latency test [MSLT]

89.19 Video and radio-telemetered electroencephalographic monitoring
Radiographic } EEG monitoring
Video }
➡ **AHA Coding Clinic:** 1Q, '92, 17

89.2 Anatomic and physiologic measurements and manual examinations — genitourinary system

Excludes: *the listed procedures when done as part of a general physical examination (89.7)*

➡ **AHA Coding Clinic:** 1Q, '90, 27

89.21 Urinary manometry
Manometry through:
indwelling ureteral catheter
nephrostomy
pyelostomy
ureterostomy

89.22 Cystometrogram

89.23 Urethral sphincter electromyogram

89.24 Uroflowmetry [UFR]

89.25 Urethral pressure profile [UPP]

89.26 Gynecological examination ♀
Pelvic examination

89.29 Other nonoperative genitourinary system measurements
Bioassay of urine
Renal clearance
Urine chemistry
➡ **AHA Coding Clinic:** N-D, '84, 6

89.3 Other anatomic and physiologic measurements and manual examinations

Excludes: *the listed procedures when done as part of a general physical examination (89.7)*

89.31 Dental examination
Oral mucosal survey
Periodontal survey

89.32 Esophageal manometry
➡ **AHA Coding Clinic:** 3Q, '96, 13

89.33 Digital examination of enterostomy stoma
Digital examination of colostomy stoma

89.34 Digital examination of rectum

89.35 Transillumination of nasal sinuses

89.36 Manual examination of breast

89.37 Vital capacity determination

89.38 Other nonoperative respiratory measurements
Plethysmography for measurement of respiratory function
Thoracic impedance plethysmography

➡ **AHA Coding Clinic:** S-O, '87, 6

89.39 Other nonoperative measurements and examinations
^{14}C-Urea breath test
Basal metabolic rate [BMR]
Gastric:
analysis
function NEC

Excludes: *body measurement (93.07)*
cardiac tests (89.41-89.69)
fundus photography (95.11)
limb length measurement (93.06)

➡ **AHA Coding Clinic:** 3Q, '96, 12; 1Q, '94, 18; N-D, '84, 6

89.4 Cardiac stress tests and pacemaker checks

89.41 Cardiovascular stress test using treadmill
➡ **AHA Coding Clinic:** 1Q, '88, 11

89.42 Masters' two-step stress test
➡ **AHA Coding Clinic:** 1Q, '88, 11

89.43 Cardiovascular stress test using bicycle ergometer
➡ **AHA Coding Clinic:** 1Q, '88, 11

89.44 Other cardiovascular stress test
Thallium stress test with or without transesophageal pacing

89.45 Artificial pacemaker rate check
Artificial pacemaker function check NOS

89.46 Artificial pacemaker artifact wave form check

89.47 Artificial pacemaker electrode impedance check

89.48 Artificial pacemaker voltage or amperage threshold check

89.5 Other nonoperative cardiac and vascular diagnostic procedures

Excludes: *fetal EKG (75.32)*

89.50 Ambulatory cardiac monitoring
Analog devices [Holter-type]
➡ **AHA Coding Clinic:** 4Q, '91, 23

89.51 Rhythm electrocardiogram
Rhythm EKG (with one to three leads)

89.52 Electrocardiogram
ECG NOS
EKG (with 12 or more leads)
➡ **AHA Coding Clinic:** 1Q, '88, 11; S-O, '87, 6

89.53 Vectorcardiogram (with ECG)

89.54 Electrographic monitoring
Telemetry

Excludes: *ambulatory cardiac monitoring (89.50)*
electrographic monitoring during surgery — omit code

➡ **AHA Coding Clinic:** 4Q, '91, 23; 1Q, '88, 11

89.55 Phonocardiogram with ECG lead

89.56 Carotid pulse tracing with ECG lead

Excludes: *oculoplethysmography (89.58)*

89.57 Apexcardiogram (with ECG lead)
➡ **AHA Coding Clinic:** J-F, '87, 16

89.58 Plethysmogram

Excludes: *plethysmography (for):*
measurement of respiratory function (89.38)
thoracic impedance (89.38)

➡ **AHA Coding Clinic:** S-O, '87, 7

89.59 Other nonoperative cardiac and vascular measurements
➡ **AHA Coding Clinic:** 2Q, '92, 12

89.6 Circulatory monitoring

Excludes: *electrocardiographic monitoring during surgery — omit code*

➡ **AHA Coding Clinic:** M-J, '87, 11

89.61 Systemic arterial pressure monitoring

89.62 Central venous pressure monitoring

89.63 Pulmonary artery pressure monitoring

Excludes: *pulmonary artery wedge monitoring (89.64)*

89.64 Pulmonary artery wedge monitoring
Pulmonary capillary wedge [PCW] monitoring
Swan-Ganz catheterization

89.65 Measurement of systemic arterial blood gases

89.66 Measurement of mixed venous blood gases

89.67 Monitoring of cardiac output by oxygen consumption technique
Fick method

89.68 Monitoring of cardiac output by other technique
Cardiac output monitor by thermodilution indicator

89.69 Monitoring of coronary blood flow
Coronary blood flow monitoring by coincidence counting technique

89.7 General physical examination

89.8 Autopsy

90 Microscopic examination - I

The following fourth-digit subclassification is for use with categories in section 90 to identify type of examination:

1 **bacterial smear**
2 **culture**
3 **culture and sensitivity**
4 **parasitology**
5 **toxicology**
6 **cell block and Papanicolaou smear**
9 **other microscopic examination**

90.0 Microscopic examination of specimen from nervous system and of spinal fluid

90.1 Microscopic examination of specimen from endocrine gland, not elsewhere classified

90.2 Microscopic examination of specimen from eye

90.3 Microscopic examination of specimen from ear, nose, throat, and larynx

90.4 Microscopic examination of specimen from trachea, bronchus, pleura, lung, and other thoracic specimen, and of sputum

90.5 Microscopic examination of blood

90.6 Microscopic examination of specimen from spleen and of bone marrow

90.7 Microscopic examination of specimen from lymph node and of lymph

90.8 Microscopic examination of specimen from upper gastrointestinal tract and of vomitus

90.9 Microscopic examination of specimen from lower gastrointestinal tract and of stool

91 Microscopic examination - II

The following fourth-digit subclassification is for use with categories in section 91 to identify type of examination:

1 **bacterial smear**
2 **culture**
3 **culture and sensitivity**
4 **parasitology**
5 **toxicology**
6 **cell block and Papanicolaou smear**
9 **other microscopic examination**

91.0 Microscopic examination of specimen from liver, biliary tract, and pancreas

91.1 Microscopic examination of peritoneal and retroperitoneal specimen

91.2 Microscopic examination of specimen from kidney, ureter, perirenal and periureteral tissue

91.3 Microscopic examination of specimen from bladder, urethra, prostate, seminal vesicle, perivesical tissue, and of urine and semen

91.4 Microscopic examination of specimen from female genital tract ♀
Amnionic sac
Fetus

91.5 Microscopic examination of specimen from musculoskeletal system and of joint fluid
Microscopic examination of:
bone
bursa
cartilage
fascia
ligament
muscle
synovial membrane
tendon

91.6 Microscopic examination of specimen from skin and other integument
Microscopic examination of:
hair
nails
skin

Excludes: *mucous membrane — code to organ site that of operative wound (91.70-91.79)*

91.7 Microscopic examination of specimen from operative wound

91.8 Microscopic examination of specimen from other site

91.9 Microscopic examination of specimen from unspecified site

92 Nuclear medicine

92.0 Radioisotope scan and function study

92.01 **Thyroid scan and radioisotope function studies**
Iodine-131 uptake
Protein-bound iodine
Radio-iodine uptake

92.02 **Liver scan and radioisotope function study**

92.03 **Renal scan and radioisotope function study**
Renal clearance study

92.04 **Gastrointestinal scan and radioisotope function study**
Radio-cobalt B12 Schilling test
Radio-iodinated triolein study

92.05 **Cardiovascular and hematopoietic scan and radioisotope function study**
Bone marrow, Cardiac output, Circulation time, Radionuclide cardiac ventriculogram, Spleen } scan or function study
➡ **AHA Coding Clinic:** 2Q, '92, 7; 1Q, '88, 11

92.09 **Other radioisotope function studies**

92.1 **Other radioisotope scan**

92.11 **Cerebral scan**
Pituitary

92.12 **Scan of other sites of head**
Excludes: *eye (95.16)*

92.13 **Parathyroid scan**

92.14 **Bone scan**

92.15 **Pulmonary scan**

92.16 **Scan of lymphatic system**

92.17 **Placental scan** ♀

92.18 **Total body scan**

92.19 **Scan of other sites**

92.2 **Therapeutic radiology and nuclear medicine**
Excludes: *that for:*
ablation of pituitary gland (07.64-07.69)
destruction of chorioretinal lesion (14.26-14.27)
➡ **AHA Coding Clinic:** 3Q, '92, 5

92.21 **Superficial radiation**
Contact radiation [up to 150 KVP]

92.22 **Orthovoltage radiation**
Deep radiation [200-300 KVP]

92.23 **Radioisotopic teleradiotherapy**
Teleradiotherapy using:
cobalt-60
iodine-125
radioactive cesium

92.24 **Teleradiotherapy using photons**
Megavoltage NOS
Supervoltage NOS
Use of:
Betatron
linear accelerator

92.25 **Teleradiotherapy using electrons**
Beta particles

92.26 **Teleradiotherapy of other particulate radiation**
Neutrons
Protons NOS

92.27 **Implantation or insertion of radioactive elements**
Code also incision of site
➡ **AHA Coding Clinic:** 3Q, '94, 11; 1Q, '88, 4

92.28 **Injection or instillation of radioisotopes**
Intracavitary, Intravenous } injection or instillation

92.29 **Other radiotherapeutic procedure**

92.3 **Stereotactic radiosurgery**
Code also stereotactic head frame application (93.59)
Excludes: *stereotactic biopsy*
➡ **AHA Coding Clinic:** 4Q, '95, 70

92.30 **Stereotactic radiosurgery, not otherwise specified**

92.31 **Single source photon radiosurgery**
High energy x-rays
Linear accelerator (LINAC)

92.32 **Multi-source photon radiosurgery**
Cobalt 60 radiation
Gamma irradiation

92.33 **Particulate radiosurgery**
Particle beam radiation (cyclotron)
Proton accelerator

92.39 **Stereotactic radiosurgery, not elsewhere classified**

93 Physical therapy, respiratory therapy, rehabilitation, and related procedures

93.0 **Diagnostic physical therapy**
➡ **AHA Coding Clinic:** N-D, '86, 7

93.01 **Functional evaluation**

93.02 **Orthotic evaluation**

93.03 **Prosthetic evaluation**

93.04 **Manual testing of muscle function**
➡ **AHA Coding Clinic:** J-F, '87, 16

93.05 **Range of motion testing**
➡ **AHA Coding Clinic:** J-F, '87, 16

93.06 **Measurement of limb length**

93.07 **Body measurement**
Girth measurement
Measurement of skull circumference

93.08 **Electromyography**

Excludes: *eye EMG (95.25)*
that with polysomnogram (89.17)
urethral sphincter EMG (89.23)

➡ **AHA Coding Clinic:** J-F, '87, 16

93.09 **Other diagnostic physical therapy procedure**

93.1 **Physical therapy exercises**
➡ **AHA Coding Clinic:** J-F, '87, 16; N-D, '86, 7

93.11 **Assisting exercise**

Excludes: *assisted exercise in pool (93.31)*

93.12 **Other active musculoskeletal exercise**

93.13 **Resistive exercise**

93.14 **Training in joint movements**

93.15 **Mobilization of spine**

93.16 **Mobilization of other joints**

Excludes: *manipulation of temporomandibular joint (76.95)*

93.17 **Other passive musculoskeletal exercise**

93.18 **Breathing exercise**

93.19 **Exercise, not elsewhere classified**

93.2 **Other physical therapy musculoskeletal manipulation**
➡ **AHA Coding Clinic:** N-D, '86, 7

93.21 **Manual and mechanical traction**

Excludes: *skeletal traction (93.43-93.44)*
skin traction (93.45-93.46)
spinal traction (93.41-93.42)

93.22 **Ambulation and gait training**

93.23 **Fitting of orthotic device**

93.24 **Training in use of prosthetic or orthotic device**
Training in crutch walking

93.25 **Forced extension of limb**

93.26 **Manual rupture of joint adhesions**

93.27 **Stretching of muscle or tendon**

93.28 **Stretching of fascia**

93.29 **Other forcible correction of deformity**
➡ **AHA Coding Clinic:** N-D, ;85, 11

93.3 **Other physical therapy therapeutic procedures**

93.31 **Assisted exercise in pool**

93.32 **Whirlpool treatment**

93.33 **Other hydrotherapy**

93.34 **Diathermy**

93.35 **Other heat therapy**
Acupuncture with smouldering moxa
Hot packs
Hyperthermia NEC
Infrared irradiation
Moxibustion
Paraffin bath

Excludes: *hyperthermia for treatment of cancer (99.85)*

93.36 **Cardiac retraining**

93.37 **Prenatal training**
Training for natural childbirth

93.38 **Combined physical therapy without mention of the components**

93.39 **Other physical therapy**
➡ **AHA Coding Clinic:** 3Q, '97, 12; 3Q, '91, 15

93.4 **Skeletal traction and other traction**

93.41 **Spinal traction using skull device**
Traction using:
caliper tongs
Crutchfield tongs
halo device
Vinke tongs

Excludes: *insertion of tongs or halo traction device (02.94)*

➡ **AHA Coding Clinic:** 3Q, '96, 14

93.42 **Other spinal traction**
Cotrel's traction

Excludes: *cervical collar (93.52)*

93.43 **Intermittent skeletal traction**

93.44 Other skeletal traction
Bryant's traction
Dunlop's traction
Lyman Smith traction
Russell's traction

93.45 Thomas' splint traction

93.46 Other skin traction of limbs
Adhesive tape traction
Boot traction
Buck's traction
Gallows traction

93.5 Other immobilization, pressure, and attention to wound

Excludes: *wound cleansing (96.58-96.59)*

93.51 Application of plaster jacket

Excludes: *Minerva jacket (93.52)*

93.52 Application of neck support
Application of:
cervical collar
Minerva jacket
molded neck support

93.53 Application of other cast

93.54 Application of splint
Plaster splint
Tray splint

Excludes: *periodontal splint (24.7)*

93.55 Dental wiring

Excludes: *that for orthodontia (24.7)*

93.56 Application of pressure dressing
Application of:
Gibney bandage
Robert Jones' bandage
Shanz dressing

93.57 Application of other wound dressing

93.58 Application of pressure trousers
Application of:
anti-shock trousers
MAST trousers
vasopneumatic device

➡ **AHA Coding Clinic:** 3Q, '96, 13

93.59 Other immobilization, pressure, and attention to wound
Elastic stockings
Electronic gaiter
Intermittent pressure device
Oxygenation of wound (hyperbaric)
Stereotactic head frame application
Velpeau dressing

➡ **AHA Coding Clinic:** 1Q, '91, 11; 1Q, '89, 12

93.6 Osteopathic manipulative treatment

93.61 Osteopathic manipulative treatment for general mobilization
General articulatory treatment

93.62 Osteopathic manipulative treatment using high-velocity, low-amplitude forces
Thrusting forces

93.63 Osteopathic manipulative treatment using low-velocity, high-amplitude forces
Springing forces

93.64 Osteopathic manipulative treatment using isotonic, isometric forces

93.65 Osteopathic manipulative treatment using indirect forces

93.66 Osteopathic manipulative treatment to move tissue fluids
Lymphatic pump

93.67 Other specified osteopathic manipulative treatment

93.7 Speech and reading rehabilitation and rehabilitation of the blind

93.71 Dyslexia training

93.72 Dysphasia training

➡ **Def:** Training patients with speech impairments to coordinate and arrange words in the proper order.

93.73 Esophageal speech training

➡ **Def:** Speech training after removal of the voice box; sound is produced by the vibration of an air column in the esophagus against the contracting ringlike musculature closing of the windpipe.

93.74 Speech defect training

93.75 Other speech training and therapy

➡ **AHA Coding Clinic:** 4Q, '97, 36; 3Q, '97, 12

93.76 Training in use of lead dog for the blind

93.77 Training in braille or Moon

93.78 Other rehabilitation for the blind

93.8 Other rehabilitation therapy

93.81 Recreational therapy
Diversional therapy
Play therapy

Excludes: *play psychotherapy (94.36)*

93.82 Educational therapy
Education of bed-bound children
Special schooling for the handicapped

93.83 Occupational therapy
Daily living activities therapy

Excludes: *training in activities of daily living for the blind (93.78)*

➡ **AHA Coding Clinic:** 3Q, '97, 12

93.84 Music therapy

93.85 Vocational rehabilitation
Sheltered employment
Vocational:
  assessment
  retraining
  training

93.89 Rehabilitation, not elsewhere classified

93.9 Respiratory therapy

Excludes: *insertion of airway (96.01-96.05)*
other continuous mechanical ventilation (96.70-96.72)

93.90 Continuous positive airway pressure [CPAP]
➡ **AHA Coding Clinic:** 4Q, '91, 21

93.91 Intermittent positive pressure breathing [IPPB]
➡ **AHA Coding Clinic:** 4Q, '91, 21

93.93 Nonmechanical methods of resuscitation
Artificial respiration
Manual resuscitation
Mouth-to-mouth resuscitition

93.94 Respiratory medication administered by nebulizer
Mist therapy

93.95 Hyperbaric oxygenation

Excludes: *oxygenation of wound (93.59)*

93.96 Other oxygen enrichment
Catalytic oxygen therapy
Cytoreductive effect
Oxygenators
Oxygen therapy

Excludes: *oxygenation of wound (93.59)*

93.97 Decompression chamber

93.98 Other control of atmospheric pressure and composition
Antigen-free air conditioning
Helium therapy

93.99 Other respiratory procedures
Continuous negative pressure ventilation [CNP]
Postural drainage
➡ **AHA Coding Clinic:** 4Q, '91, 22

94 Procedures related to the psyche

94.0 Psychologic evaluation and testing

94.01 Administration of intelligence test
Administration of:
  Stanford-Binet
  Wechsler Adult Intelligence Scale
  Wechsler Intelligence Scale for Children

94.02 Administration of psychologic test
Administration of:
  Bender Visual-Motor Gestalt Test
  Benton Visual Retention Test
  Minnesota Multiphasic Personality Inventory
  Wechsler Memory Scale

94.03 Character analysis

94.08 Other psychologic evaluation and testing

94.09 Psychologic mental status determination, not otherwise specified

94.1 Psychiatric interviews, consultations, and evaluations

94.11 Psychiatric mental status determination
Clinical psychiatric mental status determination
Evaluation for criminal responsibility
Evaluation for testimentary capacity
Medicolegal mental status determination
Mental status determination NOS

94.12 Routine psychiatric visit, not otherwise specified

94.13 Psychiatric commitment evaluation
Pre-commitment interview

94.19 Other psychiatric interview and evaluation
Follow-up psychiatric interview NOS

94.2 Psychiatric somatotherapy

94.21 Narcoanalysis
Narcosynthesis

94.22 Lithium therapy

94.23 Neuroleptic therapy

94.24 Chemical shock therapy

94.25 Other psychiatric drug therapy
➡ **AHA Coding Clinic:** S-O, '86, 4

94.26 Subconvulsive electroshock therapy

94.27 Other electroshock therapy
Electroconvulsive therapy (ECT)
EST

94.29 Other psychiatric somatotherapy

94.3 Individual psychotherapy

94.31 Psychoanalysis

94.32 Hypnotherapy
Hypnodrome
Hypnosis

94.33 Behavior therapy
Aversion therapy
Behavior modification
Desensitization therapy
Extinction therapy
Relaxation training
Token economy

94.34 Individual therapy for psychosexual dysfunction

Excludes: *that performed in group setting (94.41)*

94.35 Crisis intervention

94.36 Play psychotherapy

94.37 Exploratory verbal psychotherapy

94.38 Supportive verbal psychotherapy

94.39 Other individual psychotherapy
Biofeedback

94.4 Other psychotherapy and counseling

94.41 Group therapy for psychosexual dysfunction

94.42 Family therapy

94.43 Psychodrama

94.44 Other group therapy

94.45 Drug addiction counseling

94.46 Alcoholism counseling

94.49 Other counseling

94.5 Referral for psychologic rehabilitation

94.51 Referral for psychotherapy

94.52 Referral for psychiatric aftercare
That in:
halfway house
outpatient (clinic) facility

94.53 Referral for alcoholism rehabilitation

94.54 Referral for drug addiction rehabilitation

94.55 Referral for vocational rehabilitation

94.59 Referral for other psychologic rehabilitation

94.6 Alcohol and drug rehabilitation and detoxification
➡ **AHA Coding Clinic:** 2Q, '91, 12

94.61 Alcohol rehabilitation

94.62 Alcohol detoxification

94.63 Alcohol rehabilitation and detoxification

94.64 Drug rehabilitation

94.65 Drug detoxification

94.66 Drug rehabilitation and detoxification

94.67 Combined alcohol and drug rehabilitation

94.68 Combined alcohol and drug detoxification

94.69 Combined alcohol and drug rehabilitation and detoxification

95 Ophthalmologic and otologic diagnosis and treatment

95.0 General and subjective eye examination

95.01 Limited eye examination
Eye examination with prescription of spectacles

95.02 Comprehensive eye examination
Eye examination covering all aspects of the visual system

95.03 Extended ophthalmologic work-up
Examination (for):
glaucoma
neuro-ophthalmology
retinal disease

95.04 Eye examination under anesthesia
Code also type of examination

95.05 Visual field study

95.06 Color vision study

95.07 Dark adaptation study

95.09 Eye examination, not otherwise specified
Vision check NOS

95.1 Examinations of form and structure of eye

95.11 Fundus photography

95.12 Fluorescein angiography or angioscopy of eye

95.13 Ultrasound study of eye

95.14 X-ray study of eye

95.15 Ocular motility study

95.16 P^{32} and other tracer studies of eye

95.2 Objective functional tests of eye

Excludes: *that with polysomnogram (89.17)*

95.21 Electroretinogram [ERG]

95.22 Electro-oculogram [EOG]

95.23 Visual evoked potential [VEP]

95.24 Electronystagmogram [ENG]

95.25 Electromyogram of eye [EMG]

95.26 Tonography, provocative tests, and other glaucoma testing

95.3 Special vision services

95.31 Fitting and dispensing of spectacles

95.32 Prescription, fitting, and dispensing of contact lens

95.33 Dispensing of other low vision aids

95.34 Ocular prosthetics

95.35 Orthoptic training

95.36 Ophthalmologic counselling and instruction
Counselling in:
adaptation to visual loss
use of low vision aids

95.4 Nonoperative procedures related to hearing

95.41 Audiometry
Békésy 5-tone audiometry
Impedance audiometry
Stapedial reflex response
Subjective audiometry
Tympanogram

95.42 Clinical test of hearing
Tuning fork test
Whispered speech test

95.43 Audiological evaluation
Audiological evaluation by:
Bárány noise machine
blindfold test
delayed feedback
masking
Weber lateralization

95.44 Clinical vestibular function tests
Thermal test of vestibular function

95.45 Rotation tests
Bárány chair

95.46 Other auditory and vestibular function tests

95.47 Hearing examination, not otherwise specified

95.48 Fitting of hearing aid

Excludes: *implantation of electromagnetic hearing device (20.95)*

➡ **AHA Coding Clinic:** 4Q, '89, 5

95.49 Other nonoperative procedures related to hearing
Adjustment (external components) of cochlear prosthetic device

96 Nonoperative intubation and irrigation

96.0 Nonoperative intubation of gastrointestinal and respiratory tracts

96.01 Insertion of nasopharyngeal airway

96.02 Insertion of oropharyngeal airway

96.03 Insertion of esophageal obturator airway

96.04 Insertion of endotracheal tube

96.05 Other intubation of respiratory tract

➡ **AHA Coding Clinic:** 1Q, '97, 14

96.06 Insertion of Sengstaken tube
Esophageal tamponade

96.07 Insertion of other (naso-)gastric tube
Intubation for decompression

Excludes: *that for enteral infusion of nutritional substance (96.6)*

96.08 Insertion of (naso-)intestinal tube
Miller-Abbott tube (for decompression)

96.09 Insertion of rectal tube
Replacement of rectal tube

96.1 **Other nonoperative insertion**

Excludes: *nasolacrimal intubation (09.44)*

96.11 **Packing of external auditory canal**

96.14 **Vaginal packing** ♀

96.15 **Insertion of vaginal mold** ♀

96.16 **Other vaginal dilation** ♀

96.17 **Insertion of vaginal diaphragm** ♀

96.18 **Insertion of other vaginal pessary** ♀

96.19 **Rectal packing**

96.2 **Nonoperative dilation and manipulation**

96.21 **Dilation of frontonasal duct**

96.22 **Dilation of rectum**

96.23 **Dilation of anal sphincter**

96.24 **Dilation and manipulation of enterostomy stoma**

96.25 **Therapeutic distention of bladder**
Intermittent distention of bladder

96.26 **Manual reduction of rectal prolapse**

96.27 **Manual reduction of hernia**

96.28 **Manual reduction of enterostomy prolapse**
➡ **AHA Coding Clinic:** N-D, '87, 11

96.29 **Reduction of intussusception of alimentary tract**
With:
Fluoroscopy
Ionizing radiation enema
Ultrasonography guidance
Hydrostatic reduction
Pneumatic reduction

Excludes: *intra-abdominal manipulation of intestine, not otherwise specified (46.80)*

96.3 **Nonoperative alimentary tract irrigation, cleaning, and local instillation**

96.31 **Gastric cooling**
Gastric hypothermia

96.32 **Gastric freezing**

96.33 **Gastric lavage**

96.34 **Other irrigation of (naso-)gastric tube**

96.35 **Gastric gavage**

96.36 **Irrigation of gastrostomy or enterostomy**

96.37 **Proctoclysis**

96.38 **Removal of impacted feces**
Removal of impaction:
by flushing
manually

96.39 **Other transanal enema**
Rectal irrigation

Excludes: *reduction of intussusception of alimentary tract by ionizing radiation enema (96.29)*

96.4 **Nonoperative irrigation, cleaning, and local instillation of other digestive and genitourinary organs**

96.41 **Irrigation of cholecystostomy and other biliary tube**

96.42 **Irrigation of pancreatic tube**

96.43 **Digestive tract instillation, except gastric gavage**

96.44 **Vaginal douche** ♀

96.45 **Irrigation of nephrostomy and pyelostomy**

96.46 **Irrigation of ureterostomy and ureteral catheter**

96.47 **Irrigation of cystostomy**

96.48 **Irrigation of other indwelling urinary catheter**

96.49 **Other genitourinary instillation**
Insertion of prostaglandin suppository

96.5 **Other nonoperative irrigation and cleaning**

96.51 **Irrigation of eye**
Irrigation of cornea

Excludes: *irrigation with removal of foreign body (98.21)*

96.52 **Irrigation of ear**
Irrigation with removal of cerumen

96.53 **Irrigation of nasal passages**

96.54 **Dental scaling, polishing, and debridement**
Dental prophylaxis
Plaque removal

96.55 **Tracheostomy toilette**

96.56 **Other lavage of bronchus and trachea**

96.57 **Irrigation of vascular catheter**
➡ **AHA Coding Clinic:** 3Q, '93, 5

96.58 **Irrigation of wound catheter**

96.59 **Other irrigation of wound**
Wound cleaning NOS

Excludes: *debridement (86.22, 86.27-86.28)*
➡ **AHA Coding Clinic:** S-O, '85, 7

96.6 **Enteral infusion of concentrated-nutritional substances**

96.7 Other continuous mechanical ventilation

Includes: Endotracheal respiratory assistance
Intermittent mandatory ventilation [IMV]
Positive end expiratory pressure [PEEP]
Pressure support ventilation [PSV]
That by tracheostomy
Weaning of an intubated (endotracheal tube) patient

Code also any associated:
endotracheal tube insertion (96.04)
tracheostomy (31.1-31.29)

Excludes: *bi-level airway pressure (93.90)*
continuous negative pressure ventilation [CNP] (iron lung) (cuirass) (93.99)
continuous positive airway pressure [CPAP] (93.90)
intermittent positive pressure breathing [IPPB] (93.91)
that by face mask (93.90-93.99)
that by nasal cannula (93.90-93.99)
that by nasal catheter (93.90-93.99)

➡ **AHA Coding Clinic:** 4Q, '91, 16

Note: Endotracheal intubation

To calculate the number of hours (duration) of continuous mechanical ventilation during a hospitalization, begin the count from the start of the (endotracheal) intubation. The duration ends with (endotracheal) extubation.

If a patient is intubated prior to admission, begin counting the duration from the time of the admission. If a patient is transferred (discharged) while intubated, the duration would end at the time of transfer (discharge).

For patients who begin on (endotracheal) intubation and subsequently have a tracheostomy performed for mechanical ventilation, the duration begins with the (endotracheal) intubation and ends when the mechanical ventilation is turned off (after the weaning period).

Tracheostomy

To calculate the number of hours of continuous mechanical ventilation during a hospitalization, begin counting the duration when mechanical ventilation is started. The duration ends when the mechanical ventilator is turned off (after the weaning period).

If a patient has received a tracheostomy prior to admission and is on mechanical ventilation at the time of admission, begin counting the duration from the time of admission. If a patient is transferred (discharged) while still on mechanical ventilation via tracheostomy, the duration would end at the time of the transfer (discharge).

➡ **AHA Coding Clinic:** 2Q, '92, 13; 4Q, '91, 16; 4Q, '91, 18; 4Q, '91, 21

96.70 Continuous mechanical ventilation of unspecified duration

Mechanical ventilation NOS

96.71 Continuous mechanical ventilation for less than 96 consecutive hours

96.72 Continuous mechanical ventilation for 96 consecutive hours or more

97 Replacement and removal of therapeutic appliances

97.0 Nonoperative replacement of gastrointestinal appliance

97.01 Replacement of (naso-)gastric or esophagostomy tube

97.02 Replacement of gastrostomy tube

➡ **AHA Coding Clinic:** 1Q, '97, 11

97.03 Replacement of tube or enterostomy device of small intestine

97.04 Replacement of tube or enterostomy device of large intestine

97.05 Replacement of stent (tube) in biliary or pancreatic duct

97.1 Nonoperative replacement of musculoskeletal and integumentary system appliance

97.11 Replacement of cast on upper limb

97.12 Replacement of cast on lower limb

97.13 Replacement of other cast

97.14 Replacement of other device for musculoskeletal immobilization

97.15 Replacement of wound catheter

97.16 Replacement of wound packing or drain

Excludes: *repacking of:*
dental wound (97.22)
vulvar wound (97.26)

97.2 Other nonoperative replacement

97.21 Replacement of nasal packing

97.22 Replacement of dental packing

97.23 Replacement of tracheostomy tube

➡ **AHA Coding Clinic:** N-D, '87, 11

97.24 Replacement and refitting of vaginal diaphragm ♀

97.25 Replacement of other vaginal pessary ♀

97.26 Replacement of vaginal or vulvar packing or drain ♀

97.29 Other nonoperative replacements

97.3 Nonoperative removal of therapeutic device from head and neck

97.31 Removal of eye prosthesis

Excludes: *removal of ocular implant (16.71)*
removal of orbital implant (16.72)

97.32 Removal of nasal packing

97.33 Removal of dental wiring

97.34 Removal of dental packing

97.35 Removal of dental prosthesis

97.36 Removal of other external mandibular fixation device

97.37 Removal of tracheostomy tube

97.38 Removal of sutures from head and neck

97.39 Removal of other therapeutic device from head and neck

Excludes: *removal of skull tongs (02.94)*

97.4 Nonoperative removal of therapeutic device from thorax

97.41 Removal of thoracotomy tube or pleural cavity drain

97.42 Removal of mediastinal drain

97.43 Removal of sutures from thorax

97.49 Removal of other device from thorax
➡ **AHA Coding Clinic:** N-D, '86, 9

97.5 Nonoperative removal of therapeutic device from digestive system

97.51 Removal of gastrostomy tube

97.52 Removal of tube from small intestine

97.53 Removal of tube from large intestine or appendix

97.54 Removal of cholecystostomy tube

97.55 Removal of T-tube, other bile duct tube, or liver tube

97.56 Removal of pancreatic tube or drain

97.59 Removal of other device from digestive system
Removal of rectal packing

97.6 Nonoperative removal of therapeutic device from urinary system

97.61 Removal of pyelostomy and nephrostomy tube

97.62 Removal of ureterostomy tube and ureteral catheter

97.63 Removal of cystostomy tube

97.64 Removal of other urinary drainage device
Removal of indwelling urinary catheter

97.65 Removal of urethral stent

97.69 Removal of other device from urinary system

97.7 Nonoperative removal of therapeutic device from genital system

97.71 Removal of intrauterine contraceptive device ♀

97.72 Removal of intrauterine pack ♀

97.73 Removal of vaginal diaphragm ♀

97.74 Removal of other vaginal pessary ♀

97.75 Removal of vaginal or vulvar packing ♀

97.79 Removal of other device from genital tract
Removal of sutures

97.8 Other nonoperative removal of therapeutic device

97.81 Removal of retroperitoneal drainage device

97.82 Removal of peritoneal drainage device
➡ **AHA Coding Clinic:** 2Q, '90, 28; S-O, '86, 12

97.83 Removal of abdominal wall sutures

97.84 Removal of sutures from trunk, not elsewhere classified

97.85 Removal of packing from trunk, not elsewhere classified

97.86 Removal of other device from abdomen

97.87 Removal of other device from trunk

97.88 Removal of external immobilization device
Removal of:
- brace
- cast
- splint

97.89 Removal of other therapeutic device

98 Nonoperative removal of foreign body or calculus

98.0 **Removal of intraluminal foreign body from digestive system without incision**

Excludes: *removal of therapeutic device (97.51-97.59)*

98.01 **Removal of intraluminal foreign body from mouth without incision**

98.02 **Removal of intraluminal foreign body from esophagus without incision**

98.03 **Removal of intraluminal foreign body from stomach and small intestine without incision**

98.04 **Removal of intraluminal foreign body from large intestine without incision**

98.05 **Removal of intraluminal foreign body from rectum and anus without incision**

98.1 **Removal of intraluminal foreign body from other sites without incision**

Excludes: *removal of therapeutic device (97.31-97.49, 97.61-97.89)*

98.11 **Removal of intraluminal foreign body from ear without incision**

98.12 **Removal of intraluminal foreign body from nose without incision**

98.13 **Removal of intraluminal foreign body from pharynx without incision**

98.14 **Removal of intraluminal foreign body from larynx without incision**

98.15 **Removal of intraluminal foreign body from trachea and bronchus without incision**

98.16 **Removal of intraluminal foreign body from uterus without incision** ♀

Excludes: *removal of intrauterine contraceptive device (97.71)*

98.17 **Removal of intraluminal foreign body from vagina without incision** ♀

98.18 **Removal of intraluminal foreign body from artificial stoma without incision**

98.19 **Removal of intraluminal foreign body from urethra without incision**

98.2 **Removal of other foreign body without incision**

Excludes: *removal of intraluminal foreign body (98.01-98.19)*

98.20 **Removal of foreign body, not otherwise specified**

98.21 **Removal of superficial foreign body from eye without incision**

98.22 **Removal of other foreign body without incision from head and neck**

Removal of embedded foreign body from eyelid or conjunctiva without incision

98.23 **Removal of foreign body from vulva without incision** ♀

98.24 **Removal of foreign body from scrotum or penis without incision** ♂

98.25 **Removal of other foreign body without incision from trunk except scrotum, penis, or vulva**

98.26 **Removal of foreign body from hand without incision**

➡ **AHA Coding Clinic:** N-D, '87, 10

98.27 **Removal of foreign body without incision from upper limb, except hand**

98.28 **Removal of foreign body from foot without incision**

98.29 **Removal of foreign body without incision from lower limb, except foot**

98.5 **Extracorporeal shockwave lithotripsy [ESWL]**

Lithotriptor tank procedure
Disintegration of stones by extracorporeal induced shockwaves
That with insertion of stent

98.51 **Extracorporeal shockwave lithotripsy [ESWL] of the kidney, ureter and/or bladder**

➡ **AHA Coding Clinic:** 4Q, '95, 73; 1Q, '89, 2

98.52 **Extracorporeal shockwave lithotripsy [ESWL] of the gallbladder and/or bile duct**

98.59 **Extracorporeal shockwave lithotripsy of other sites**

99 Other nonoperative procedures

99.0 **Transfusion of blood and blood components**

Use additional code for that done via catheter or cutdown (38.92-38.94)

99.00 Perioperative autologous transfusion of whole blood or blood components
Intraoperative blood collection
Postoperative blood collection
Salvage
➡ **AHA Coding Clinic:** 4Q, '95, 69

99.01 Exchange transfusion
Transfusion:
exsanguination
replacement
➡ **AHA Coding Clinic:** 2Q, '89, 15

99.02 Transfusion of previously collected autologous blood
Blood component
➡ **AHA Coding Clinic:** 4Q, '95, 69; J-A, '85, 16

99.03 Other transfusion of whole blood
Transfusion:
NOS
blood NOS
hemodilution

99.04 Transfusion of packed cells

99.05 Transfusion of platelets
Transfusion of thrombocytes

99.06 Transfusion of coagulation factors
Transfusion of antihemophilic factor

99.07 Transfusion of other serum
Transfusion of plasma

Excludes: *injection [transfusion] of:*
antivenin (99.16)
gamma globulin (99.14)

99.08 Transfusion of blood expander
Transfusion of Dextran

99.09 Transfusion of other substance
Transfusion of:
blood surrogate
granulocytes

Excludes: *transplantation [transfusion] of bone marrow (41.0)*

99.1 Injection or infusion of therapeutic or prophylactic substance

Includes: injection or infusion given:
hypodermically
intramuscularly
intravenously
} acting locally or systemically

99.10 Injection or infusion of thrombolytic agent
Streptokinase
Tissue plasminogen activator (TPA)
Urokinase

Excludes: *aspirin — omit code*
GP IIb/IIIa platelet inhibitors (99.20)
heparin (99.29)
single vessel percutaneous transluminal coronary angioplasty [PTCA] or coronary atherectomy with mention of thrombolytic agent (36.02)
warfarin— omit code

99.11 Injection of Rh immune globulin
Injection of:
Anti-D (Rhesus) globulin
RhoGAM

99.12 Immunization for allergy
Desensitization

99.13 Immunization for autoimmune disease

99.14 Injection of gamma globulin
Injection of immune sera

99.15 Parenteral infusion of concentrated nutritional substances
Hyperalimentation
Total parenteral nutrition [TPN]
Peripheral parenteral nutrition [PPN]

99.16 Injection of antidote
Injection of:
antivenin
heavy metal antagonist

99.17 Injection of insulin

99.18 Injection or infusion of electrolytes

99.19 Injection of anticoagulant

99.2 Injection or infusion of other therapeutic or prophylactic substance

Includes: injection or infusion given:
hypodermically
intramuscularly
intravenously
} acting locally or systemically

Use additional code for:
injection (into):
breast (85.92)
bursa (82.94, 83.96)
intraperitoneal (cavity) (54.97)
intrathecal (03.92)
joint (76.96, 81.92)
kidney (55.96)
liver (50.94)
orbit (16.91)
other sites — see Alphabetic Index
perfusion:
NOS (39.97)
intestine (46.95, 46.96)
kidney (55.95)
liver (50.93)
total body (39.96)

99.20 Injection or infusion of platelet inhibitor
Glycoprotein IIb/IIIa inhibitor
GP IIb/IIIa inhibitor
GP IIb-IIIa inhibitor

Excludes: *infusion of heparin (99.29)*
injection or infusion of thrombolytic agent (99.10)

99.21 Injection of antibiotic
➡ **AHA Coding Clinic:** 2Q, '90, 24; M-A, '87, 9

99.22 Injection of other anti-infective

99.23 Injection of steroid
Injection of cortisone
Subdermal implantation of progesterone
➡ **AHA Coding Clinic:** 3Q, 96, 7; 3Q, '92, 9; S-O, '85, 7

99.24 **Injection of other hormone**

99.25 **Injection or infusion of cancer chemotherapeutic substance**
Chemoembolization
Injection or infusion of antineoplastic agent

Excludes: *immunotherapy, antineoplastic (99.28)*
injection or infusion of biological response modifier [BRM] as an antineoplastic agent (99.28)
injection of radioisotope (92.28)

➡ **AHA Coding Clinic:** 1Q, '98, 6; 3Q, '96, 11; 4Q, '95, 67; 2Q, '92, 7; 1Q, '92, 12; 1Q, '88, 8; N-D, '86, 11

99.26 **Injection of tranquilizer**

99.27 **Iontophoresis**

99.28 **Injection or infusion of biological response modifier [BRM] as an antineoplastic agent**
Immunotherapy, antineoplastic
Tumor vaccine

➡ **AHA Coding Clinic:** 4Q, '94, 51

99.29 **Injection or infusion of other therapeutic or prophylactic substance.**

Excludes: *immunization (99.31-99.59)*
injection of sclerosing agent into:
esophageal varices (42.33)
hemorrhoids (49.42)
veins (39.92)
injection or infusion of platelet inhibitor (99.20)
injection or infusion of thrombolytic agent (99.10)

➡ **AHA Coding Clinic:** 1Q, '98, 6; 2Q, '97, 11; 1Q, '97, 3; 4Q, '95, 67; 2Q, '95, 12; 4Q, '90, 14; 2Q, '90, 23; 2Q, '89, 17; 1Q, '88, 9; N-D, '87, 4; S-O, '87, 11

99.3 **Prophylactic vaccination and inoculation against certain bacterial diseases**

99.31 **Vaccination against cholera**

99.32 **Vaccination against typhoid and paratyphoid fever**
Administration of TAB vaccine

99.33 **Vaccination against tuberculosis**
Administration of BCG vaccine

99.34 **Vaccination against plague**

99.35 **Vaccination against tularemia**

99.36 **Administration of diphtheria toxoid**

Excludes: *administration of:*
diphtheria antitoxin (99.58)
diphtheria-tetanus-pertussis, combined (99.39)

99.37 **Vaccination against pertussis**

Excludes: *administration of:*
diphtheria-tetanus-pertussis, combined (99.39)

99.38 **Administration of tetanus toxoid**

Excludes: *administration of:*
diphtheria-tetanus-pertussis, combined (99.39)
tetanus antitoxin (99.56)

99.39 **Administration of diphtheria-tetanus-pertussis, combined**

99.4 **Prophylactic vaccination and inoculation against certain viral diseases**

99.41 **Administration of poliomyelitis vaccine**

99.42 **Vaccination against smallpox**

99.43 **Vaccination against yellow fever**

99.44 **Vaccination against rabies**

99.45 **Vaccination against measles**

Excludes: *administration of measles-mumps-rubella vaccine (99.48)*

99.46 **Vaccination against mumps**

Excludes: *administration of measles-mumps-rubella vaccine (99.48)*

99.47 **Vaccination against rubella**

Excludes: *administration of measles-mumps-rubella vaccine (99.48)*

99.48 **Administration of measles-mumps-rubella vaccine**

99.5 **Other vaccination and inoculation**

99.51 **Prophylactic vaccination against the common cold**

99.52 **Prophylactic vaccination against influenza**

99.53 **Prophylactic vaccination against arthropod-borne viral encephalitis**

99.54 **Prophylactic vaccination against other arthropod-borne viral diseases**

99.55 Prophylactic administration of vaccine against other diseases

Vaccination against:
- anthrax
- brucellosis
- Rocky Mountain spotted fever
- Staphylococcus
- Streptococcus
- typhus

99.56 Administration of tetanus antitoxin

99.57 Administration of botulism antitoxin

99.58 Administration of other antitoxins

Administration of:
- diphtheria antitoxin
- gas gangrene antitoxin
- scarlet fever antitoxin

99.59 Other vaccination and inoculation

Vaccination NOS

Excludes: *injection of:*
gamma globulin (99.14)
Rh immune globulin (99.11)
immunization for:
allergy (99.12)
autoimmune disease (99.13)

99.6 Conversion of cardiac rhythm

Excludes: *open chest cardiac:*
electric stimulation (37.91)
massage (37.91)

99.60 Cardiopulmonary resuscitation, not otherwise specified

99.61 Atrial cardioversion

99.62 Other electric countershock of heart

Cardioversion:
- NOS
- external

Conversion to sinus rhythm
Defibrillation
External electrode stimulation

99.63 Closed chest cardiac massage

Cardiac massage NOS
Manual external cardiac massage

99.64 Carotid sinus stimulation

99.69 Other conversion of cardiac rhythm

➡ **AHA Coding Clinic:** 4Q, '88, 11

99.7 Therapeutic apheresis

99.71 Therapeutic plasmapheresis

99.72 Therapeutic leukopheresis

Therapeutic leukocytapheresis

99.73 Therapeutic erythrocytapheresis

Therapeutic erythropheresis

99.74 Therapeutic plateletpheresis

99.79 Other

Apheresis (harvest) of stem cells

➡ **AHA Coding Clinic:** 4Q, '97, 55

99.8 Miscellaneous physical procedures

99.81 Hypothermia (central) (local)

Excludes: *gastric cooling (96.31)*
gastric freezing (96.32)
that incidental to open heart surgery (39.62)

99.82 Utraviolet light therapy

Actinotherapy

99.83 Other phototherapy

Phototherapy of the newborn

Excludes: *extracorporeal photochemotherapy (99.88)*
photocoagulation of retinal lesion (14.23-14.25, 14.33-14.35, 14.53-14.55)

➡ **AHA Coding Clinic:** 2Q, '89, 15

99.84 Isolation

Isolation after contact with infectious disease
Protection of individual from his surroundings
Protection of surroundings from individual

99.85 Hyperthermia for treatment of cancer

Hyperthermia (adjunct therapy) induced by microwave, ultrasound, low energy radio frequency, probes (interstitial), or other means in the treatment of cancer

Code also any concurrent chemotherapy or radiation therapy

➡ **AHA Coding Clinic:** 3Q, '96, 11; 3Q, '89, 17

99.86 Non-invasive placement of bone growth stimulator

Transcutaneous (surface) placement of pads or patches for stimulation to aid bone healing

Excludes: *insertion of invasive or semi-invasive bone growth stimulators (device) (percutaneous electrodes) (78.90-78.99)*

99.88 Therapeutic photopheresis

Extracorporeal photochemotherapy
Extracorporeal photopheresis

Excludes: *other phototherapy (99.83)*
ultraviolet light therapy (99.82)

99.9 **Other miscellaneous procedures**

99.91 **Acupuncture for anesthesia**

99.92 **Other acupuncture**

Excludes: *that with smouldering moxa (93.35)*

99.93 **Rectal massage (for levator spasm)**

99.94 **Prostatic massage** ♂

99.95 **Stretching of foreskin** ♂

99.96 **Collection of sperm for artificial insemination** ♂

99.97 **Fitting of denture**

99.98 **Extraction of milk from lactating breast** ♀

99.99 **Other**

RENEWAL ORDER FORM

Fill out the card below to receive next year's codes at this year's price!

To lock in this year's low price when you renew your ICD-9-CM code book(s), just send in this early Renewal Order Form today!

By ordering now you guarantee earliest possible delivery of your code books and avoid annual price increases.

Furthermore, you'll continue to benefit from these ICD-9-CM code book features, including:

- New codes and code changes
- Updated AHA *Coding Clinic* References
- Updated official coding guidelines
- Plus much more!

In this ever-changing world of health care reimbursement, it's more important than ever to have the most up-to-date coding information available!

Take a moment to ensure you're getting the most out of your St. Anthony publication by filling out this convenient Renewal Order Form and dropping it in the mail, or call toll-free

1-800-632-0123

This Renewal Order Form is an EASY and convenient way to renew anytime during your subscription! Plus, you'll lock in this year's low price by renewing TODAY!

---

source code: 16843-1-A

RENEWAL ORDER FORM

❑ Yes, please place my order for the year 2001 edition of *Professional ICD-9-CM Code Book* early for $69.95 each.(CCS)

❑ Yes, please renew my *Professional ICD-9-CM Code Book*, Updatable (Binder) for $99.95 each. (ICD)

VA RESIDENTS, PLEASE ADD 4.5% SALES TAX	$______
OH RESIDENTS, PLEASE ADD 5% SALES TAX	$______
ADD SHIPPING AND HANDLING:	$ **8.95**
TOTAL ENCLOSED:	$______

Payment Options

❑ Check enclosed, payable to: **St. Anthony Publishing, Inc.**

❑ Bill me ❑ Visa ❑ MC ❑ AE ❑ Disc

Acct #______________________ Exp. Date ________

Signature______________________________

Customer #______________________________

Ship to:

Organization______________________________

Mailing Address______________________________

City/State/Zip______________________________

Phone (_______) ________________ Ext. ______ FAX (_______) ________________

Name______________________________ Title______________________________

Email______________________________

THREE EASY WAYS TO RENEW!

1. CALL toll-free 1-800-632-0123.
2. FAX this Renewal Form to 703/707-5700.
3. MAIL this Renewal Form with payment to:

St. Anthony Publishing, Inc.
PO Box 96561
Washington, DC 20090

NOTES

NOTES